ST/ESA/STAT/SER.G/64 (Vol. I)

Department of Economic and Social Affairs
Statistics Division

2015
International Trade Statistics Yearbook

Volume I
Trade by Country

United Nations
New York, 2016

DEPARTMENT OF ECONOMIC AND SOCIAL AFFAIRS

The Department of Economic and Social Affairs of the United Nations Secretariat is a vital interface between global policies in the economic, social and environmental spheres and national action. The Department works in three main interlinked areas: (i) it compiles, generates and analyses a wide range of economic, social and environmental data and information on which Member States of the United Nations draw to review common problems and to take stock of policy options; (ii) it facilitates the negotiations of Member States in many intergovernmental bodies on joint courses of action to address ongoing or emerging global challenges; and (iii) it advises interested Governments on the ways and means of translating policy frameworks developed in United Nations conferences and summits into programmes at the country level and, through technical assistance, helps build national capacities.

NOTE

Symbols of United Nations documents are composed of capital letters combined with figures.

The designations employed and the presentation of material in this publication do not imply the expression of any opinion whatsoever on the part of the Secretariat of the United Nations concerning the legal status of any country, territory, city or area, or of its authorities, or concerning the delimitation of its frontiers or boundaries.

Where the designation "country or area" appears in this publication, it covers countries, territories, cities or areas. In previous issues of this publication, where the designation "country" appears in the headings of tables, it should be interpreted to cover countries, territories, cities or areas.

In some tables, the designation "developed" economies is intended for statistical convenience and does not necessarily express a judgement about the stage reached by a particular country or area in the development process.

ST/ESA/STAT/SER.G/64 Vol. I

UNITED NATIONS PUBLICATION
Sales No. E.16.XVII.2 H

ISBN 978-92-1-161611-8
eISBN 978-92-1-058149-3
ISSN 1010-447X

Enquiries should be directed to
Sales and Marketing Section
Outreach Division
Department of Public Information
United Nations
New York 10017
USA

E-mail: publications@un.org
Internet: http://unp.un.org

PREFACE

The *2015 International Trade Statistics Yearbook* (2015 ITSY) is the sixty-fourth edition of this yearbook. Its objective is to inform about the detailed merchandise and services imports and exports of individual countries (areas) by commodity and service category and by partner country (volume I), the world trade in individual commodities (3-digit SITC groups and 11 main EBOPS categories) (volume II) and total world merchandise trade up to the year 2015. The two volumes are prepared at different points in time during 2016: *Volume I - Trade by Country* is made electronically available in June, and *Volume II - Trade by Commodity,* in December, as the preparation of the tables in Volume II requires additional country data which, normally, become available later in the year.

Beginning with 2013 edition, trade in services data was introduced to the *International Trade Statistics Yearbook: Volume I - Trade by Country*. Therefore, the content and format of the yearbook were redesigned to take into account new additions of graphs, tables and analytical text. The data used in the tables and graphs in both volumes of the yearbook are taken at a specific time (June 2016) from the publicly available UN Comtrade (http://comtrade.un.org) database. Users are advised to visit the database for additional and more current information as it is continuously updated.

The *International Trade Statistics Yearbook* is prepared by the Trade Statistics Branch of the Statistics Division, Department of Economic and Social Affairs of the United Nations Secretariat. Under the general supervision of the Chief of Branch, Ronald Jansen, the programme manager is Markie Muryawan and the chief editor is Habibur Rahman Khan, assisted by Marjorie Imperial-Damaso. Bekuretsion Amdemariam and Htu Aung have the leading role in the processing of merchandise data and of services data, respectively. Habibur Rahman Khan, Kenneth Iversen, Nancy Snyder, Karoly Kovacs, Salomon Cameo and Markie Muryawan provided valuable contribution to the inclusion of trade in services data and the improvement of production processes. However, all staff of the branch are involved in the generation of the data and the review/validation of the yearbook. Markie Muryawan, Salomon Cameo and Luis Gonzalez Morales developed the original software which is maintained by Melissa Paca and Salomon Cameo.

Comments and feedback on the yearbook are welcome. They may be sent to comtrade@un.org / tradeserv@un.org or to United Nations Statistics Division, Trade Statistics Branch, New York, New York 10017, USA.

TABLE OF CONTENTS

Page

Introduction ... vii

Concepts and definitions of International Merchandise Trade Statistics ... viii

Concepts and definitions of Statistics of International Trade in Services ... x

Description of world trade tables of part 1 (Tables A and D) ... xiv

Description of tables and graphs of Country profiles in part 2 ... xv

Sources ... xvii

Method of Estimation ... xvii

Conversion of classification ... xviii

Currency conversion and Period ... xix

Country Nomenclature and Country Grouping ... xix

Abbreviations and Explanation of symbols ... xxiii

Disclaimer ... xxiv

Contact ... xxiv

Part 1: World Trade Tables ... 1

Total merchandise trade by regions and countries or areas (Table A) ... 2

World merchandise exports by provenance and destination (Table D) ... 20

Part 2: Country Trade Profiles ... 57

Countries (or areas) ... 58

European Union ... 398

Part 2: COUNTRY TRADE PROFILES

	Page
Afghanistan	58
Albania	60
Algeria	62
Andorra	64
Antigua and Barbuda	66
Argentina	68
Armenia	70
Aruba	72
Australia	74
Austria	76
Azerbaijan	78
Bahamas	80
Bahrain	82
Bangladesh	84
Barbados	86
Belarus	88
Belgium	90
Belize	92
Benin	94
Bermuda	96
Bhutan	98
Bolivia (Plurinational State of)	100
Bosnia and Herzegovina	102
Botswana	104
Brazil	106
Brunei Darussalam	108
Bulgaria	110
Burkina Faso	112
Burundi	114
Cabo Verde	116
Cambodia	118
Cameroon	120
Canada	122

	Page
Central African Republic	124
Chile	126
China	132
China, Hong Kong Special Administrative Region	128
China, Macao Special Administrative Region	130
Colombia	134
Comoros	136
Congo	138
Cook Islands	140
Costa Rica	142
Côte d'Ivoire	144
Croatia	146
Cyprus	148
Czech Republic	150
Denmark	152
Dominica	154
Dominican Republic	156
Ecuador	158
Egypt	160
El Salvador	162
Estonia	164
Ethiopia	166
Fiji	168
Finland	170
France including Monaco	172
French Polynesia	174
Gambia	176
Georgia	178
Germany	180
Ghana	182

	Page
Greece	184
Greenland	186
Guatemala	188
Guinea	190
Guyana	192
Honduras	194
Hungary	196
Iceland	198
India	200
Indonesia	202
Iran (Islamic Republic of)	204
Ireland	206
Israel	208
Italy	210
Jamaica	212
Japan	214
Jordan	216
Kazakhstan	218
Kenya	220
Kiribati	222
Korea, Republic of	224
Kuwait	226
Kyrgyzstan	228
Latvia	230
Lebanon	232
Lesotho	234
Lithuania	236
Luxembourg	238
Madagascar	240
Malawi	242
Malaysia	244
Maldives	246
Mali	248
Malta	250
Mauritania	252

	Page
Mauritius	254
Mexico	256
Micronesia (Federated Staes of)	258
Mongolia	260
Montenegro	262
Montserrat	264
Morocco	266
Mozambique	268
Namibia	270
Nepal	272
Netherlands	274
New Caledonia	276
New Zealand	278
Nicaragua	280
Niger	282
Nigeria	284
Norway, including Svalbard and Jan Mayen Islands	286
Oman	288
Pakistan	290
Panama	292
Papua New Guinea	294
Paraguay	296
Peru	298
Philippines	300
Poland	302
Portugal	304
Qatar	306
Republic of Moldova	308
Romania	310
Russian Federation	312
Rwanda	314
Saint Kitts and Nevis	316
Saint Lucia	318
Saint Vincent and the Grenadines	320

	Page
Samoa	322
Sao Tome and Principe	324
Saudi Arabia	326
Senegal	328
Serbia	330
Sierra Leone	332
Singapore	334
Slovakia	336
Slovenia	338
Solomon Islands	340
South Africa	342
Spain	344
Sri Lanka	346
State of Palestine	348
Sudan	350
Suriname	352
Sweden	354
Switzerland-Liechtenstein	356
Thailand	358
The former Yugoslav Republic of Macedonia	360
Togo	362
Tonga	364
Tunisia	366
Turkey	368
Turks and Caicos Islands	370
Uganda	372
Ukraine	374
United Arab Emirates	376
United Kingdom	378
United Republic of Tanzania	380
United States of America, including Puerto Rico and US Virgin Islands	382

	Page
Uruguay	384
Vanuatu	386
Venezuela (Bolivarian Republic of)	388
Viet Nam	390
Yemen	392
Zambia	394
Zimbabwe	396
European Union (28 member states)	398

INTRODUCTION

1. The *International Trade Statistics Yearbook: Volume I - Trade by Country*, provides an overview of the latest trends of trade in goods and services of most countries and areas in the world. The publication is aimed at both specialist trade data users and common audience at large. The presented data, charts and analyses will benefit policy makers, government agencies, non-government organizations, civil society organizations, journalists, academics, researchers, students, businesses and anyone who is interested in trade issues.

2. The main content of the yearbook is divided into two parts. Part 1 consists of two detailed world data tables on merchandise trade. One presents total merchandise imports and exports by countries, areas and regions in a time series up to the latest year, the other shows world merchandise exports by group of commodity and by provenance and destination in many smaller time series sub-tables. Part 2 contains the country trade profiles for most countries and areas in the world. The profiles offer an insight into the merchandise and services trade performance of individual countries and areas by means of brief descriptive text, concise data tables and charts using latest available data. For further information on data availability, please see the sources section of this Introduction.

3. The yearbook is also made available online at the publications repository of the UN Statistics Division (http://unstats.un.org/unsd/pubs). For more detailed and latest available data, please consult UN Comtrade (http://comtrade.un.org), which is the source of the information presented in the yearbook, and which is continuously updated.

Concepts and definitions of International Merchandise Trade Statistics

4. The merchandise trade data in this Yearbook have been compiled by national statistical authorities largely complying with the United Nations recommended *International Merchandise Trade Statistics, Concepts and Definitions 2010* (IMTS 2010).[1] The main elements of the concepts and definitions are:

i. Coverage: As a general guideline, it is recommended that international merchandise trade statistics record all goods which add to or subtract from the stock of material resources of a country by entering (imports) or leaving (exports) its economic territory. The general guideline is subject to the clarifications provided in IMTS 2010, in particular, to the specific guidelines in chapter 1 concerning the inclusion or exclusion of certain categories of goods.

ii. Time of recording: As a general guideline, it is recommended that goods be recorded at the time when they enter or leave the economic territory of a country.

iii. Statistical territory: The statistical territory of a country is the territory with respect to which trade data are being compiled. The definition of the statistical territory may or may not coincide with the economic territory of a country or its customs territory, depending on the availability of data sources and other considerations. It follows that when the statistical territory of a country and its economic territory differ, international merchandise trade statistics do not provide a complete record of inward and outward flows of goods.

iv. Trade systems: Depending on what parts of the economic territory are included in the statistical territory, the trade data-compilation system adopted by a country (its trade system) may be referred to as general or special.

a) The general trade system is in use when the statistical territory coincides with the economic territory. Consequently, it is recommended that the statistical territory of a country applying the general trade system comprises all applicable territorial elements. In this case, imports include goods entering the free circulation area, premises for inward processing, industrial free zones, premises for customs warehousing or commercial free zones and exports include goods leaving those territorial elements;

b) The special trade system is in use when the statistical territory comprises only a particular part of the economic territory, so that certain flows of goods which are in the scope of IMTS 2010 are not included in either import or export statistics of the compiling country. The strict definition of the special trade system is in use when the statistical territory comprises only the free circulation area, that is, the part within which goods "may be

---

[1] At its forty-first session, held from 23 to 26 February 2010, the Statistical Commission adopted the revised recommendations "International merchandise trade statistics: concepts and definitions 2010" (IMTS 2010) which provide very important amendments while retaining the existing conceptual framework contained in the previous recommendations. The publication is available under Statistical Papers, Series M No. 52, Rev.3 (United Nations publication, Sales No. E.10.XVII.13) and electronically at: http://unstats.un.org/unsd/pubs/gesgrid.asp?id=449.

disposed of without customs restriction". Consequently, in such a case, imports include only goods entering the free circulation area of a compiling country and exports include only goods leaving the free circulation area of a compiling country.

c) The relaxed definition of the special trade system is in use when (a) goods that enter a country for, or leave it after, inward processing, as well as (b) goods that enter or leave an industrial free zone, are also recorded and included in international merchandise trade statistics

v. Classification: It is recommended that countries use the *Harmonized Commodity Description and Coding System* (HS) for the collection, compilation and dissemination of international merchandise trade statistics as suggested by the Statistical Commission at its twenty-seventh session (22 February to 3 March 1993).[2] The Harmonized System was adopted by the Customs Co-operation Council in June 1983, and the International Convention on the Harmonized System (HS Convention) entered into force on 1 January 1988 (HS 1988).[3] In accordance with the preamble to the HS Convention, which recognized the importance of ensuring that the HS be kept up to date in the light of changes in technology or in patterns of international trade, the HS is regularly reviewed and revised. The fifth edition, HS 2012, came into effect 1 January 2012.[4] The *Standard International Trade Classification (SITC)*[5] which was in the past used by countries in data compilation and reporting has been recognized for its continued use in analysis.[6]

vi. Valuation: At its fifteenth session, in 1953, the Economic and Social Council, taking the view that trade statistics must reflect economic realities, recommended that the Governments of Member States of the United Nations, wherever possible, use transaction values in the compilation of their national statistics of external trade or, when national practices are based on other values, endeavour to provide supplementary statistical data based on transaction values (Economic and Social Council resolution 469 B (XV)). To promote the comparability of international merchandise trade statistics and taking into account the commercial and data reporting practices of the majority of countries, it is recommended that: (a) The statistical value of imported goods be a CIF-type value; (b) The statistical value of exported goods be an FOB-type value; however, countries are encouraged to compile FOB-type value of imported goods as supplementary information. FOB-type values include the transaction value of the goods and the value of services performed to deliver goods to the border of the exporting country. CIF-type values include the transaction value of the goods, the value of services performed to deliver goods to the border of the exporting country and the value of the

---

[2] See Official Records of the Economic and Social Council, 1993, Supplement No. 6 (E/1993/26), para. 162 (d).

[3] See Customs Co-operation Council, The Harmonized Commodity Description and Coding System, Brussels, 1989.

[4] See World Customs Organization, Harmonized Commodity Description and Coding System, Fifth Edition (2012), Brussels 2010.

[5] Standard International Trade Classification, Original, Statistical Papers, Series M No.10, Second Edition, 1951 (United Nations publication, Sales No. E.51.XVII.1); subsequent editions are published as United Nations publications under Series M No.34.

[6] See Official Records of the Economic and Social Council, 1999, Supplement No. 4 (E/1993/24), para. 24 (c).

services performed to deliver the goods from the border of the exporting country to the border of the importing country.

vii. Partner country: It is recommended that in the case of imports, the country of origin be recorded; and that in the case of exports, the country of last known destination be recorded. The country of origin of a good (for imports) is determined by rules of origin established by each country. The country of last known destination is the last country - as far as it is known at the time of exportation - to which goods are to be delivered, irrespective of where they have been initially dispatched to and whether or not, on their way to that last country, they are subject to any commercial transactions or other operations which change their legal status. Further, it is recommended that country of consignment be recorded for imports as the second partner country attribution, alongside country of origin; the compilation of export statistics on the country of consignment basis is only encouraged, depending on a country's needs and circumstances.

5. The pages containing the country profiles (Part 2 of this publication) indicate the trade system, valuation and partner attribution each country is following. For more detailed information on national practices in the compilation and dissemination of international merchandise trade data please go to http://unstats.un.org/unsd/tradereport/introduction_MM.asp.

Concepts and definitions of Statistics of International Trade in Services

6. The trade in services data in this Yearbook have been compiled by national statistical authorities or central banks largely complying with the *Manual on Statistics of International Trade in Services 2010* (MSITS 2010).[7]

7. The main elements of the concepts and definitions of MSITS 2010 are:

i. Definitions: In general, MSITS 2010 respects the 2008 SNA use of the term services, which is defined as follows (2008 SNA, para. 6.17):

a) Services are the result of a production activity that changes the conditions of the consuming units, or facilitates the exchange of products or financial assets. These types of service may be described as change-effecting services and margin services, respectively. Change-effecting services are outputs produced to order and typically consist of changes in the conditions of the consuming units realized by the activities of producers at the demand of the consumers. They can also be referred to as "transformation services". Change-effecting services are not separate entities over which ownership rights can be established. They cannot be traded separately from their

[7] At its forty-first session, held from 23 to 26 February 2010, the Statistical Commission adopted the revised "Manual on Statistics of International Trade in Services" (MSITS 2010) , which sets out an internationally agreed framework for the compilation and reporting of statistics of international trade in services and align with the revisions of well-established revised international statistical standards. The publication is available under Statistical Papers, Series M No. 86, Rev.1 (United Nations publication, Sales No.E.10.XVII.14) and electronically at http://unstats.un.org/unsd/tradeserv/TFSITS/msits2010.htm.

production. By the time their production is completed, they must have been provided to the consumers.

b) MSITS 2010 defines "international trade in services" as trade in services between residents and non-residents of an economy, as well as the supply of services through foreign affiliates established abroad and the supply of services through the presence of foreign individuals, either as foreign service suppliers themselves or as employees of a foreign service supplier.

Importantly, the services data included in this Yearbook only reflect trade in services between residents and non-residents.

ii. Concept and definition of residence: The residence of an institutional unit is the economic territory with which it has the strongest connection, constituting its centre of predominant economic interest. Each institutional unit is a resident of one and only one economic territory, as determined by its centre of predominant economic interest. An institutional unit is resident in an economic territory when there exists, within the economic territory, some location, dwelling, place of production, or other premises on which or from which the unit engages and intends to continue engaging, either indefinitely or over a finite but long period of time, in economic activities and transactions on a significant scale. The location need not be fixed as long as it remains within the economic territory. Actual or intended location for one year or more is used as an operational criterion. While the choice of one year as a specific period is somewhat arbitrary, it is adopted to eliminate uncertainty and facilitate international consistency. More specific criteria for determining residence are given in the MSITS 2010.

iii. Valuation: The market price is used as the basis for valuation of transactions in international trade in services. Market prices for transactions are defined as amounts of money that willing buyers pay to acquire something from willing sellers. The exchanges are made between independent parties and based on commercial considerations only and are sometimes called "at arm's length" transactions. These transactions will generally be valued at the actual price agreed between the supplier and the consumer.

iv. Time of recording of transactions: The appropriate time for recording transactions in services is when they are delivered or received (the "accruals basis"). Some services, such as certain transport or hotel services are provided within a discrete period, in which case there is no problem in determining the time of recording. Other services are supplied or take place on a continuous basis, for example, construction, operating leasing and insurance services. When construction takes place with a prior contract of sale, the ownership of the structure is effectively transferred progressively as the work proceeds. When services are provided over a period of time (such as freight, insurance and construction), there may be advance payments or settlements at later dates for such services. The provision of services should be recorded on an accrual basis in each accounting period, that is to say it should be recorded when the service is rendered and not when the payment occurs.

v. Framework and scope: MSITS 2010 recommends that the Sixth Edition of the Balance of Payments and International Investment Position Manual (BPM6)[8] recommendations on the principles of recording (regarding residence, valuation, time of recording, currency of recording and conversion) should be followed. The Extended Balance of Payments Services Classification (EBOPS) is a more detailed classification than that of BPM5 for international trade in services between residents and non-residents, by breaking down a number of the BPM5 service items. The main components of the EBOPS classification are presented in paragraph 7.vii below.

vi. Partner country: It is recommended that the breakdown by partner economy for services transactions between residents and non-residents be recorded, the aim being to report partner detail, first, at the level of services trade as a whole and, second, for each of the main types of services in EBOPS and (as a longer-term goal) for the more detailed EBOPS items. Partner country data for trade in services are not included in this publication, as most countries do not currently compile these data by partner country.

vii. Classification: In 1996, OECD and Eurostat, in consultation with IMF, developed for use by their members a more detailed classification than that presented in the IMF's Balance of Payments Manual (BPM5) for international trade in services between residents and non-residents, by breaking down a number of the BPM5 service items. This more detailed classification is termed the Extended Balance of Payments Services Classification (EBOPS). The EBOPS classification was published in 2002 in the MSITS 2002 and was subsequently revised to the EBOPS 2010 classification, as published in the MSITS 2010. The services data in this Yearbook follow the EBOPS 2002 classification (which corresponds to the BPM5 recommendations) due to the fact that many countries have not yet transitioned to the EBOPS 2010 classification (which corresponds to the BPM6 recommendations).

The 11 main EBOPS 2002 standard services components (as presented in the MSITS 2002) are:[9]

a) Transportation: covers all transportation services that are performed by residents of one economy for those of another and that involve the carriage of passengers, the movement of goods (freight), rentals (charters) of carriers with crew, and related supporting and auxiliary services. Some related items that are excluded from transportation services are freight insurance (included in insurance services); goods procured in ports by non-resident carriers and repairs of transportation equipment (both are treated as goods, not services); repairs of railway facilities, harbours and airfield facilities (included in

[8] International Monetary Fund. *Sixth Edition of the Balance of Payments Manual (BPM6)*. 2009. http://www.imf.org/external/pubs/ft/bop/2007/pdf/bpm6.pdf. The previous edition of this manual was the *Fifth Edition of the Balance of Payments Manual (BPM5)*, which was published in 1992. https://www.imf.org/external/pubs/ft/bopman/bopman.pdf.

[9] The full detailed EBOPS 2002 classification is available as an on-line annex to the MSITS 2002. http://unstats.un.org/unsd/tradekb/Attachment358.aspx.

construction services); and rentals or charters of carriers without crew (included in operational leasing services).

b) Travel: covers primarily the goods and services acquired from an economy by travelers during visits of less than one year to that economy. Includes business and personal travel, which includes health-related expenditure (total expenditure by those travelling for medical reasons), education-related expenditure (i.e., total expenditure by students), and all other personal travel expenditure.

c) Communications services: covers postal and courier services (which cover the pick-up, transport and delivery of letters, newspapers, periodicals, brochures, other printed matter, parcels and packages, including post office counter and mailbox rental services) and telecommunications services (which cover the transmission of sound, images or other information by telephone, telex, telegram, radio and television cable and broadcasting, satellite, electronic mail, facsimile services etc., including business network services, teleconferencing and support services). It does not include the value of the information transported. Also included are cellular telephone services, Internet backbone services and on-line access services, including provision of access to the Internet.

d) Construction services: covers work performed on construction projects and installation by employees of an enterprise in locations outside the territory of an enterprise.

e) Insurance services: covers the provision of various types of insurance to non-residents by resident insurance enterprises, and vice versa. These services are estimated or valued by the service charges included in total premiums rather than by the total value of the premiums.

f) Financial services: covers financial intermediation and auxiliary services, except those of life insurance enterprises and pension funds (which are included in life insurance and pension funding) and other insurance services that are conducted between residents and non-residents. Such services may be provided by banks, stock exchanges, factoring enterprises, credit card enterprises and other enterprises.

g) Computer and information services: covers hardware and software-related services and data-processing services; news agency services include the provision of news, photographs, and feature articles to the media; and database services and web search portals (search engine services that find internet addresses for clients who input keyword queries).

h) Royalties and license fees: covers international payments and receipts of franchising fees and the royalties paid for the use of registered trademarks and international payments and receipts for the authorised use of intangible, non-produced, non-financial assets and proprietary rights (such as patents, copyrights and industrial processes and designs) and with the use, through licensing agreements, of produced originals or prototypes (such as manuscripts, computer programs, and cinematographic works and sound recordings).

i) Other business services: covers merchanting, other trade-related services, operational leasing services, legal services, accounting, auditing, bookkeeping and tax consulting services, business and management consulting and public relations services, advertising, market research and public opinion polling, research and development, architectural, engineering and other technical services, waste treatment and de-pollution, agricultural, mining, and other on-site processing services, other business services, and services between related enterprises, not included elsewhere (n.i.e.).

j) Personal, cultural, and recreational services: covers services and associated fees related to the production of motion pictures (on film or videotape), radio and television programmes (live or on tape) and musical recordings services, as well as those services associated with museums, libraries, archives and other cultural, sporting and recreational activities.

k) Government services, not included elsewhere (n.i.e.): covers government transactions (including those of international organizations) not contained in the other components of EBOPS as defined above. Included are all transactions (in both goods and services) by embassies, consulates, military units and defence agencies with residents of economies in which the embassies, consulates, military units and defence agencies are located and all transactions with other economies. Excluded are transactions with residents of the home economies represented by the embassies, consulates, military units and defence agencies, and transactions in the commissaries, post exchanges and these embassies and consulates.

Description of world trade tables of part 1 (Tables A and D)

8. Table A: Total merchandise trade by regions and countries or areas in U.S. dollars: It provides a breakdown of merchandise imports, exports and trade balance for world, regional groupings, selected economic and/or trade groupings and individual countries or areas.

9. Table D: World merchandise exports by provenance and destination in U.S. dollars: In addition to total, table D also provides details by SITC sections or groupings of sections by regions and countries or areas (brief description of SITC sections can be found in the country profiles in Part 2).

10. The totals of imports and exports presented in table A on the one hand and table D and the country profiles on the other hand are not necessarily identical as IFS and UN Comtrade are based on different data collection systems with different aims, procedures, timetable and sources for update and maintenance. Nevertheless, discrepancies are in general minor and usually do not affect the overall comparability of information provided in these tables. A systematic comparison of the figures from both sources (which includes the description of known and relevant conceptual differences) is available at http://unstats.un.org/unsd/trade/imts/annual%20totals.htm. Overall, the discrepancy in the world total or world aggregate of exports in table A and table D is around 0.5 percent or less in average, which is minor, given the differences between the two sources.

11. A slightly different version of Table A containing quarterly and monthly data is published on a monthly basis as table 34 in the *United Nations Monthly Bulletin of Statistics*

(MBS). Updated, although different versions of Table D, are published as table 40, 41 and 42 in the July, September and November editions of the MBS. An updated version of these tables will be published in Volume II of the 20154 ITSY which will be produced later this year.

Description of tables and graphs of Country profiles in part 2

12. Part 2 contains detailed data for individual countries or areas. In addition, given the economic importance of the European Union (EU), separate pages have been included for the external trade of the EU (with its 28 members) as a whole.

13. Not all countries have data up to 2015 and not all countries have data for imports and exports for all years. The inclusion of a country (or area) in part 2 requires that at least some data are available for any year from 2011 onwards. Depending on the availability of data the following tables and graphs usually appear for each country or area:

14. Graph 1: Total merchandise trade, by value: This graph presents the trend of merchandise imports, exports and trade balance over the last 14 years.

15. Graph 2: Total services trade, by value: This graph presents the trend of services imports, exports and trade balance over the last 14 years.

16. Graph 3: Exports of services by EBOPS category: This graph presents the shares of total exports of services accounted for by each service category for the latest year such data are available.

17. Graph 4: Merchandise trade balance by MDG Regions: This graph presents, in the most recent year for which information on exports and imports are available, the trade balance by regions. The regional groupings were created for the purpose of this publication and are presented in paragraph 38.

18. Graph 5: Partner concentration of merchandise trade: This graph shows the partner concentration of imports and exports for the latest available year. Graph presents the top 25 partners which usually account for a very large share of exports or imports for most countries. On the horizontal axis from the center to the right are the cumulative percent of exports and from the center to the left the cumulative percent of imports. On the vertical axis is the cumulative number of partners ranked by total value of exports and imports in a decreasing order. So, on each side, the first bar represents share accounted for by the largest partner; second bar represents share accounted for by the largest two partners and so on.

19. Graph 5 also presents the Herfindahl-Hirschman (HH) Index for imports and exports which is a measure of concentration. In the case of exports (imports), the HH index is the sum of squares of the partner's share of total exports (imports):

$$HH\ Index = \sum_{i=1}^{n} \left(\frac{X_i}{X} \right)^2$$

20. n is the number of trading partners for exports (imports) and X_i is the value of exports (imports) to partner country i and X is the total value of exports (imports). The lower the HH index, the lower the partner concentration, and vice versa. If there is only one trading partner the HH index would equal 1. [10]

21. It should be noted that the HH index for a given country's exports (imports) depends on the distribution of share of exports (imports) among its partners. Hence a country with few major partners might have a lower HH index value, indicating low concentration, than a country with more partners if the former has its trade more evenly distributed among its partners than the latter.

22. Graph 6: Imports of services by EBOPS category: This graph presents the shares of total imports of services accounted for by each service category for the latest year such data are available.

23. Table 1 and table 4: Top 10 export and import commodities: These tables present the top 10 commodities in terms of 4-digit HS headings for exports and imports, respectively, using the aggregate of trade values for the last three reporting years as available. It should be noted that exports contain re-exports and imports contain re-imports. So one or more top exports of a country may be commodities which the country does not actually produce. Data on re-exports and re-imports can be found in UN Comtrade (http://comtrade.un.org). For countries which reported the last three years of data in HS 2007 the data in these tables follow HS 2007. For most other countries the data in these tables are presented in HS 2002 with data for some years converted from HS 2007 into HS 2002 as required (see paragraph 33). For a few countries the table contains data according to the HS 1996 or even HS 1992. For the convenience of users the last column shows the SITC group (3 digits) that corresponds to the HS heading. The SITC group is identified based on the correlation and conversion tables between HS and SITC, Rev 3.[11]

24. In addition to trade values, the table 1 and table 4 also present unit values. Unit values are expressed in U.S. dollars (US$) per unit (kg, unit, Megawatt-hours (Mwh), pair, litre, carat etc.). The calculation of unit values on the heading level requires the availability of value and quantity information for all of the underlying detailed data (6-digit subheadings). In some cases the quantity information for some sub-headings was estimated (see paragraph 32) and thus the unit value for the heading appears in italics. If quantity information appears incorrect it is not shown.

25. Table 2 and table 3: Merchandise Exports and Imports by SITC sections: These tables show the structure of exports and imports in the latest available year by SITC sections in terms of value, share of the total, growth in comparison with the previous year and annual average growth for the last four years which is calculated as the geometric mean.

[10] For the application of HH index to measure partner concentration in merchandise trade, no thresholds are known to be established. Users might wish to define a specific limit of the HH index to indicate low concentration and a limit to indicate high concentration. However, based on the analyses of the data presented in the yearbook, following thresholds were applied to determine level of concentration of merchandise trade, both exports and imports: HH < 0.15 → Diversified; 0.15 < HH < 0.25 → Moderately concentrated; HH > 0.25 → Highly concentrated.

[11] The conversion tables are available on the website of UNSD at http://unstats.un.org/unsd/trade/methodology%20imts.htm.

Sources

26. Data on the total merchandise imports and exports of countries (or areas) presented in world table A are mainly taken from *International Financial Statistics* (IFS) published monthly by the International Monetary Fund (IMF). They are supplemented with data from other sources such as national publications and websites and the *United Nations Monthly Bulletin of Statistics Questionnaire* for the following countries: Andorra, Bermuda, Cayman Islands, Cuba, Gibraltar, Montenegro (beginning 2006), Niue, Russian Federation (beginning 1994), Serbia and Montenegro (before 2006), State of Palestine, Turkmenistan, Turks and Caicos, Tuvalu and Uzbekistan. Data on world merchandise exports by provenance and destination presented in world table D are derived from UN Comtrade data supplemented by estimated data for non-available countries and areas.

27. The data in the country profiles in part 2 of the publication (country trade profiles) are obtained from data directly submitted by countries to the United Nations Statistics Division (UNSD). All data published in the country profiles is available in UN Comtrade (http://comtrade.un.org).

28. In some cases, original country data are received via international and regional partner organizations, such as the Organization for Economic Co-operation and Development (OECD), the Food and Agriculture Organization of the United Nations (FAO), the International Monetary Fund (IMF), the International Trade Centre (ITC), the Caribbean Community (CARICOM) Secretariat, the Common Market of Eastern and Southern Africa (COMESA), the Economic Community of West African States (ECOWAS) and the UN regional commissions such as the Economic Commission for Latin America and the Caribbean (ECLAC) and the Economic and Social Commission for Western Asia (ESCWA). Data for the European Union (EU-28) is received from the Statistical Office of the European Union (Eurostat).

29. Table A shows data as available by end of May 2016 and table D uses data as available on UN Comtrade by early June 2016. The country tables and graphs contain data available in UN Comtrade by early June 2016.

Method of Estimation

30. Estimates for missing data in Table A are made in order to arrive at regional totals, but estimated data are not shown. The estimation process is automated using quarterly year-on-year growth rates for the extrapolation of missing quarterly data, unless quarterly data can be estimated using available monthly data within the quarter. Regional totals containing estimated data are printed in bold. Estimates are reviewed and adjusted where necessary.

31. Data for missing reporters in Table D are estimated either through the extrapolation of the data of the two adjacent years, or, if this is not possible, through the use of the data reported by the trading partners, that is, through mirror data. Mirror statistics are also used in case the partner distribution or confidential data make it necessary to adjust the reported data. All estimates are reviewed and adjusted where necessary.

32. For part 2, the country trade profiles, modifications to the received data are only made in cases where the provided data are obviously incomplete, in particular in the case of unreported petroleum oils exports in merchandise data. Quantity information that is missing or does not comply with the World Customs Organization's recommendations are estimated and flagged in UN Comtrade accordingly. For data processed before June 2009 some quantity information that were identified as 'extreme' – meaning far outside a pre-defined 'normal' range – were replaced in UN Comtrade with estimates. The estimation of quantities is either based on the country's own data or uses standard unit values (SUVs) which are derived from the available information for all countries in the previous year.

Conversion of classification

33. Conversion of classification for merchandise data: All countries follow recommendation to report their detailed merchandise trade data according to the Harmonized Commodity Description and Coding System (HS) (see paragraph 4.C.v). In order to provide comparable time series data in UN Comtrade for all countries, the data reported in the latest HS classification is converted into earlier versions of the HS, and to corresponding or earlier versions of the Standard International Trade Classification (SITC).[12] The latest edition of the HS classification was its fifth and was released in 2012. The commodities in this publication are mostly presented according to the one-digit sections of SITC, Rev.3 as the SITC sections provide a limited set of economically meaningful main categories.[13] In addition, data according to SITC, Rev.3 is available for long time series. In two tables, commodities are presented in terms of four-digit headings of the HS, often according to the 2007 version of HS but in many cases also in earlier HS versions.[14] The HS headings provide a meaningful description of traded commodities at a relatively detailed level and also allow the presentation of quantity information.

34. Conversion of classification for trade in services data: For services data, many countries are still compiling data according to the EBOPS 2002 classification and, therefore, all services data presented in this Yearbook are presented according to this classification. For the cases in which a country has transitioned to the EBOPS 2010 classification (as presented in MSTIS 2010) and did not provide UNSD with data based on EBOPS 2002, and for those countries for which the IMF is the only data source,[15] the data were converted to the EBOPS 2002 classification in order to maintain consistency across countries. The conversion was based on the IMF's BPM5-

---

[12] Detailed information on the data conversions used for UN Comtrade can be found on the website of the United Nations Statistics Division at:
http://unstats.un.org/unsd/trade/conversions/HS%20Correlation%20and%20Conversion%20tables.htm.

[13] Standard International Trade Classification, Revision 3, Statistical Papers, Series M No.34/Rev.3, (United Nations publication, Sales No. E.86.XVII.12). SITC, Revision 4 was accepted by the United Nations Statistical Commission at its thirty-seventh session in March 2006 (see Official Records of the Economic and Social Council, 2006, Supplement No. 4, (E/CN.3/2006/32), chapter III, para. 26 (b)). Yet, it will require several years until a time series of data according to SITC, Revision 4 will be sufficiently long for publication.

[14] World Customs Organization, Harmonized Commodity Description and Coding System, Third Edition (2002) (HS 2002); World Customs Organization, Harmonized Commodity Description and Coding System, Second Edition (1996) (HS 1996); World Customs Organization, Harmonized Commodity Description and Coding System (1992) (HS 1992).

[15] The IMF is only presenting data on a BPM6 basis (which corresponds to the EBOPS 2010 classification) for data from 2009 onwards.

to-BPM6 Conversion Matrix (available at http://www.imf.org/external/pubs/ft/bop/2008/08-10b.pdf).

Currency conversion and Period

35. Currency conversion: For both merchandise and trade in services data in this publication, conversion of values from national currencies into United States dollars is done by means of currency conversion factors based on official exchange rates. Values in currencies subject to fluctuation are converted into United States dollars using weighted average exchange rates specially calculated for this purpose. The weighted average exchange rate for a given currency for a given year is the component monthly factors, furnished by the International Monetary Fund in its IFS publication, weighted by the value of the relevant trade in each month; a monthly factor is the exchange rate (or the simple average rate) in effect during that month. These factors are applied to total imports and exports and to the trade in individual commodities with individual countries. The conversion factors applied to the data presented in table A are published quarterly in the *UN Monthly Bulletin of Statistics* at http://unstats.un.org/unsd/mbs/default.aspx and are also available at http://unstats.un.org/unsd/trade/data/tables.asp. For data published on UN Comtrade the applied conversion factors are available in a country's metadata on UN Comtrade.

36. Period: Generally, data refer to calendar years; however, for those countries which report according to some other reference year, the data are presented in the calendar year which covers the majority of the reference year used by the country.

Country Nomenclature and Country Grouping

37. Country nomenclature: The naming of countries (or areas) in this publication follows in general the *United Nations Standard Country or Area Codes for Statistical Use.*[16] The names and composition of countries as reporter are changing over time. Also, countries rarely follow the identical nomenclature in the recording of partner information. For example when former geographical entities commonly referred to in national statistics have changed, countries may introduce the corresponding changes in their statistics at different times. In this publication, wherever possible, areas of the world have been designated the names they currently bear.

It should be noted that, in this publication:

i. Data published for China exclude those for Taiwan Province of China. Data representing the trade with Taiwan Province, which may have been reported by any reporting country or area, are included in the grouping Asia, nes. For statistical purposes, data for China also do not include those for Hong Kong Special Administrative Region and Macao Special Administrative Region.

ii. Beginning 1 January 2000, Botswana, Lesotho, Namibia, South Africa and Swaziland provide their international trade statistics separately.

---

[16] Standard Country or Area Codes for Statistical Use, Series M No. 49, Rev.4, (United Nations publication, Sales No. M.98.XVII.9). The latest information is available online at: http://unstats.un.org/unsd/methods/m49/m49.htm.

iii. On 4 February 2003, the official name of the Federal Republic of Yugoslavia has been changed to Serbia and Montenegro.

iv. On 3 June 2006, Serbia and Montenegro formally dissolved into two independent countries: Montenegro and Serbia.

v. On 10 October 2010 the federation of the Netherlands Antilles was formally dissolved. The former Dutch Caribbean dependency ceased to exist with a change of the five islands' constitutional status. Under the new political structure, Curaçao and Sint Maarten (Dutch part) have become autonomous countries within the Kingdom of the Netherlands, joining Aruba, which gained the status in 1986. The islands of the remaining territorial grouping, alternately known as Bonaire, Sint Eustatius and Saba or the BES islands, are special municipalities and part of the country of the Netherlands and overseas territories of the European Union. For statistical purposes, the data for the Netherlands do not include the BES islands. Data referring to Netherlands Antilles (as a partner) prior to 2011 refer to the former territory which included Curaçao, Sint Maarten (Dutch part), Bonaire, Sint Eustatius and Saba.

vi. On 9 July 2011, Sudan formally dissolved into two independent countries: Sudan and South Sudan. Data provided for Sudan prior to 1 January 2012 refer to the former Sudan (including South Sudan). Data referring to Sudan (as a partner) for 2012 are attributed to Sudan excluding South Sudan.

vii. From January 2013 onwards, Saint Barthélemy is no longer part of the customs territory of France. Therefore, it is recognised as a separate statistical area both as reporter and partner. Whereas from January 2014 onwards, Mayotte became part of statistical area of France and it is no longer shown as a reporter or a partner.

38. Regional groupings: This publication uses the earlier version of regional groupings of the Millennium Development Goal (MDG) Indicator Database which are shown below (for their composition, see table A and http://comtrade.un.org/pb/groupings.aspx). The category 'Other' applies only to the presentation of data by trading partner and consists of Antarctica, Bunkers, Free Zones, 'Special Categories' (confidential partner) and Areas nes.:

World
Developed Countries
- Asia-Pacific
- Europe
- North America

South-eastern Europe
Commonwealth of Independent States
- CIS Europe
- CIS Asia

Northern Africa
Sub-Saharan Africa
Latin America & the Caribbean
- Caribbean
- Latin America

Eastern Asia
Southern Asia
South-eastern Asia
Western Asia
Oceania
Other

39. Aggregations: All regional aggregations are calculated as the sum of their components. This also includes the regional and world totals presented in table A (in bold) which, up to the 2007 edition of this yearbook and in the tables currently published in the *United Nations Monthly Bulletin of Statistics,* are calculated by subtracting re-exports from the imports and exports.

40. Additional country groupings: The composition of the additional country groupings which are used in world table A is as follows:

ANCOM-Andean Common Market
Bolivia (Plurinational State of), Colombia, Ecuador and Peru

APEC-Asian-Pacific Economic Co-operation
Australia, Brunei Darussalam, Canada, Chile, China, Hong Kong Special Administrative Region of China, Indonesia, Japan, Malaysia, Mexico, New Zealand, Papua New Guinea, Peru, Philippines, Republic of Korea, Russian Federation, Singapore, Taiwan Province of China, Thailand, United States of America and Viet Nam

ASEAN-Association of South-East Asian Nations
Brunei Darussalam, Cambodia, Indonesia, Lao People's Democratic Republic, Malaysia, Myanmar, Philippines, Singapore, Thailand and Viet Nam

CACM-Central American Common Market
Costa Rica, El Salvador, Guatemala, Honduras and Nicaragua

CARICOM-Caribbean Community and Common Market
Antigua and Barbuda, Bahamas (member of the Community only), Barbados, Belize, Dominica, Grenada, Guyana, Haiti, Jamaica, Montserrat, Saint Kitts and Nevis, Saint Lucia, Saint Vincent and the Grenadines, Suriname, Trinidad and Tobago

COMESA-Common Market for Eastern and Southern Africa
Burundi, Comoros, Democratic Republic of the Congo, Djibouti, Egypt, Eritrea, Ethiopia, Kenya, Libya, Madagascar, Malawi, Mauritius, Rwanda, Seychelles, Sudan, Swaziland, Uganda, Zambia and Zimbabwe

ECOWAS - Economic Community of West African States
Benin, Burkina Faso, Cape Verde, Cote d'Ivoire, Gambia, Ghana, Guinea, Guinea-Bissau, Liberia, Mali, Niger, Nigeria, Senegal, Sierra Leone and Togo

EMCCA – Economic and Monetary Community of Central Africa
Cameroon, Central African Republic, Chad, Congo, Equatorial Guinea and Gabon

EU-28 - European Union 28
Austria, Belgium, Bulgaria, Croatia, Cyprus, Czech Republic, Denmark, Estonia, Finland, France, Germany, Greece, Hungary, Ireland, Italy, Latvia, Lithuania, Luxembourg, Malta, Netherlands, Poland, Portugal, Romania, Spain, Slovakia, Slovenia, Sweden and United Kingdom.

EU-27 - European Union 27
Austria, Belgium, Bulgaria, Cyprus, Czech Republic, Denmark, Estonia, Finland, France, Germany, Greece, Hungary, Ireland, Italy, Latvia, Lithuania, Luxembourg, Malta, Netherlands, Poland, Portugal, Romania, Spain, Slovakia, Slovenia, Sweden and United Kingdom.

EU-25 - European Union 25
Austria, Belgium, Denmark, Finland, France, Germany, Greece, Ireland, Italy, Luxembourg, Netherlands, Portugal, Spain, Sweden and United Kingdom (EU15) plus Czech Republic, Estonia, Hungary, Latvia, Lithuania, Malta, Poland, Slovakia, Slovenia, and Cyprus

EU-15 – European Union 15
Austria, Belgium, Denmark, Finland, France, Germany, Greece, Ireland, Italy, Luxembourg, Netherlands, Portugal, Spain, Sweden, United Kingdom.

LAIA - Latin American Integration Association (formerly Latin American Free Trade Association)
Argentina, Bolivia (Plurinational State of), Brazil, Chile, Colombia, Cuba, Ecuador, Mexico, Panama, Paraguay, Peru, Uruguay and Venezuela (Bolivarian Republic of)

LDC - Least developed countries
Afghanistan, Angola, Bangladesh, Benin, Bhutan, Burkina Faso, Burundi, Cambodia, Central African Republic, Chad, Comoros, Democratic Republic of the Congo, Djibouti, Equatorial Guinea, Eritrea, Ethiopia, Gambia, Guinea, Guinea-Bissau, Haiti, Kiribati, Lao People's Democratic Republic, Lesotho, Liberia, Madagascar, Malawi, Mali, Mauritania, Mozambique, Myanmar, Nepal, Niger, Rwanda, Sao Tome and Principe, Senegal, Sierra Leone, Solomon Islands, Somalia, South Sudan, Sudan, Timor-Leste, Togo, Tuvalu, Uganda, United Republic of Tanzania, Vanuatu, Yemen and Zambia

MERCOSUR-Mercado Comun Sud-Americano
Argentina, Bolivia, Brazil, Paraguay, Uruguay and Venezuela

NAFTA-Northern American Free Trade Area
Canada, Mexico and United States of America

OECD-Organization for Economic Cooperation and Development
Australia, Austria, Belgium, Canada, Chile, Czech Republic, Denmark, Estonia, Finland, France, Germany, Greece, Hungary, Iceland, Ireland, Israel, Italy, Japan, Luxembourg, Mexico, Netherlands, New Zealand, Norway, Poland, Portugal, Republic of Korea, Slovakia, Slovenia, Spain, Sweden, Switzerland, Turkey, United Kingdom and United States of America

OPEC-Organization of Petroleum Exporting Countries
Algeria, Angola, Ecuador, Indonesia, Iran (Islamic Republic of), Iraq, Kuwait, Libya, Nigeria, Qatar, Saudi Arabia, United Arab Emirates and Venezuela (Bolivarian Republic of).

Abbreviations and Explanation of symbols

Names of some countries (or areas) or groups of countries (or areas) and of some commodities or groups of commodities have been abbreviated. Exact titles of countries or commodities can be found in various editions of the following publications:

(i) Standard Country or Area Codes for Statistical Use
(ii) Standard International Trade Classification (SITC)
(iii) Harmonized Commodity Description and Coding System (HS)

In addition, the following abbreviations and symbols are used in this publication:

Not available	(na)
Not available	blank
Not available	...
Not applicable	–
Not applicable	.
Magnitude of less than half the unit used	0 or 0.0
More than 100,000 percent	>
Thousand	thsd
Million	mln
Billion	bln
Weight (kilograms)	kg
Megawatt-hours	Mwh
Average	Avg.
Not elsewhere specified	nes
U.S. dollar	US$
Imports	Imp
Exports	Exp
Balance	Bal
General trade system	G
Special trade system	S
Cost, insurance and freight	CIF
Free on board	FOB
Not included elsewhere	n.i.e.
(Royalties and) license (fees)	lic.

Disclaimer

The tables, graphs and text contained in Part 2 of this publication are provided only for illustration and despite all efforts might contain errors. When using this data users are advised to verify the latest information on UN Comtrade which is the source of this data.

Contact

This yearbook has been produced by the Trade Statistics Branch of the United Nations Statistics Division/ Department of Economic and Social Affairs. For questions or comments please contact us at:

Trade Statistics Branch
United Nations Statistics Division
2 United Nations Plaza, DC2-1540
New York, New York 10017
e-mail (merchandise): comtrade@un.org
e-mail (services): tradeserv@un.org

http://unstats.un.org/unsd/trade

2015
INTERNATIONAL TRADE
STATISTICS YEARBOOK

VOLUME I
TRADE BY COUNTRY

PART 1 – WORLD TRADE TABLES

Total merchandise trade by regions and countries or areas in U.S. dollars (Table A)

World merchandise exports by provenance and destination in U.S. dollars (Table D)

Total merchandise trade by regions and countries or areas (Table A)

Imports CIF, exports FOB and balance: million U.S. dollars

Commerce total de marchandises par régions et pays ou zones (Tableau A)

Importations CIF, exportations FOB, et balance : en millions de dollars E.-U.

Country or Area - Pays ou Zone	IMP EXP BAL	G/S	2000	2007	2008	2009	2010	2011	2012	2013	2014	2015
World	IMP		**6517591**	**14038778**	**16229126**	**12490178**	**15157516**	**18084002**	**18128884**	**18422338**	**18593360**	**1643714**
Monde	EXP		**6356764**	**13797305**	**16005638**	**12408938**	**15106213**	**18031287**	**18080788**	**18466353**	**18648959**	**1650029**
	BAL		**-160827**	**-241474**	**-223488**	**-81240**	**-51303**	**-52715**	**-48096**	**44015**	**55598**	**6315**
Developed Countries[1,2]	IMP		**4494086**	**8807945**	**9838808**	**7405620**	**8629159**	**10095387**	**9855373**	**9872690**	**10018397**	**886494**
Pays Developpés[1,2]	EXP		**4131926**	**7952499**	**8872659**	**6880040**	**7996035**	**9292855**	**9071029**	**9199385**	**9327952**	**822665**
	BAL		**-362160**	**-855446**	**-966149**	**-525581**	**-633124**	**-802531**	**-784343**	**-673305**	**-690445**	**-63829**
Asia-Pacific	IMP		461429	808813	987974	734728	917455	1125802	1173988	1105373	1082073	88491
Asie-Pacifique	EXP		557030	883403	1000104	759544	1014394	1131781	1092678	1008667	972098	84750
	BAL		95601	74590	12129	24816	96939	5980	-81309	-96706	-109975	-3740
Australia[3]	IMP	G	67704	157687	191312	158919	193201	234357	250560	232596	227648	20004
Australie[3]	EXP	G	63878	141091	187150	153966	212337	271733	256675	252981	241238	18836
	BAL		-3827	-16596	-4162	-4953	19136	37376	6115	20385	13590	-1167
Japan	IMP	G	379490	619662	762626	550550	692435	854098	885610	832424	811882	64831
Japon	EXP	G	479274	714211	782049	580719	769772	822564	798621	714613	690202	62478
	BAL		99783	94549	19422	30169	77337	-31534	-86989	-117811	-121681	-2352
New Zealand	IMP	G	14235	31463	34036	25259	31819	37346	37818	40354	42542	3655
Nouvelle-Zélande	EXP	G	13879	28102	30905	24859	32285	37484	37383	41074	40658	3436
	BAL		-356	-3362	-3131	-401	466	138	-435	720	-1884	-219
Europe	IMP		2533380	5595812	6269975	4741968	5347880	6249719	5879532	5973037	6054193	**524453**
Europe	EXP		2515992	5500085	6128101	4749960	5315137	6227981	5977073	6152439	6261488	**546466**
	BAL		-17388	-95727	-141874	7991	-32742	-21738	97541	179402	207295	**22013**
Andorra	IMP	S	1021	1917	1931	1589	1518	1596	1396	1455	1556	129
Andorre	EXP	S	45	127	96	63	54	77	68	99	98	8
	BAL		-975	-1790	-1835	-1526	-1464	-1519	-1327	-1356	-1458	-120
Austria	IMP	S	68986	156760	176172	136081	150601	182340	169657	172596	171388	14743
Autriche	EXP	S	64167	157317	173397	130791	144889	169519	158821	166546	169186	14585
	BAL		-4819	557	-2775	-5290	-5712	-12821	-10836	-6050	-2202	-158
Belgium	IMP	S	176992	413074	466437	354666	391333	466833	439492	451921	455390	38022
Belgique	EXP	S	187876	431850	471932	371397	407055	475981	446637	467831	474090	40117
	BAL		10884	18776	5494	16731	15721	9148	7145	15910	18700	2094
Croatia	IMP	G	7887	25830	30728	21203	20051	22708	20762	20961	22523	2058
Croatie	EXP	G	4432	12364	14112	10474	11806	13375	12347	11928	13686	1284
	BAL		-3455	-13465	-16617	-10729	-8244	-9333	-8415	-9033	-8837	-773
Czech Republic	IMP	S	33934	118467	142172	105256	126600	152122	141515	144320	154233	14131
République tchèque	EXP	S	29057	122760	146406	113175	133020	162897	157167	162302	175017	15864
	BAL		-4877	4293	4234	7920	6420	10775	15652	17983	20784	1732
Denmark	IMP	S	44364	97366	109158	80372	83170	96431	92295	98374	99127	8452
Danemark	EXP	S	50390	101599	115929	91817	95758	111900	106125	111349	110494	9423
	BAL		6025	4233	6772	11445	12589	15469	13830	12975	11367	970
Estonia	IMP	S	4236	15064	16058	10151	12282	17757	17797	18142	17992	1450
Estonie	EXP	S	3166	10960	12468	9058	11607	16724	16083	16291	15931	1292
	BAL		-1070	-4105	-3590	-1094	-675	-1033	-1714	-1851	-2061	-157
Faeroe Islands	IMP	G	532	1016	988	783	780	986	1144	1110	1045	..
Iles Féroé	EXP	G	472	746	852	762	839	1007	945	1080	1110	..
	BAL		-60	-270	-136	-22	59	20	-199	-29	65	..
Finland	IMP	G	33900	81756	92160	60866	68773	84235	76558	77590	76767	6033
Finlande	EXP	G	45482	90092	96890	62872	69492	79126	73114	74446	74335	5971
	BAL		11582	8336	4730	2005	719	-5108	-3444	-3144	-2432	-61

Total merchandise trade by regions and countries or areas (Table A)

Imports CIF, exports FOB and balance: million U.S. dollars

Commerce total de marchandises par régions et pays ou zones (Tableau A)

Importations CIF, exportations FOB, et balance : en millions de dollars E.-U.

Country or Area - Pays ou Zone	IMP EXP BAL	G/S	2000	2007	2008	2009	2010	2011	2012	2013	2014	2015
France	IMP	S	310831	631447	715783	560484	608657	712906	667251	673329	668661	562685
France	EXP	S	298765	550458	608942	476098	516955	585319	558597	568500	568031	493845
	BAL		-12066	-80989	-106840	-84386	-91703	-127586	-108654	-104829	-100630	-68840
Germany	IMP	S	495450	1055997	1186681	926154	1056170	1256168	1164626	1192751	1209307	1051844
Allemagne	EXP	S	550223	1323818	1451390	1120666	1261577	1476955	1408370	1451631	1492545	1326359
	BAL		54773	267822	264709	194512	205408	220787	243744	258880	283238	274515
Gibraltar	IMP		480	796	769	679	627	703	605	748	705	...
Gibraltar	EXP		126	304	281	266	259	246	253	279	267	...
	BAL		-354	-492	-488	-413	-368	-457	-353	-469	-438	...
Greece	IMP	S	28323	84853	96711	74072	69199	68071	63713	62419	64190	48306
Grèce	EXP	S	10965	26557	31298	25133	28203	33948	35452	36236	36007	28705
	BAL		-17359	-58295	-65413	-48939	-40996	-34124	-28261	-26183	-28183	-19601
Hungary	IMP	S	31955	94397	106380	78034	87612	100989	94282	99091	103942	91361
Hongrie	EXP	S	28016	93985	107465	84586	94759	110897	103047	108426	112438	100324
	BAL		-3939	-412	1085	6552	7147	9908	8765	9335	8496	8963
Iceland	IMP	G	2591	6097	5614	3604	3920	4833	4772	4787	5240	5307
Islande	EXP	G	1891	4342	5191	4057	4604	5344	5064	4990	4980	4740
	BAL		-700	-1755	-423	453	685	510	292	204	-260	-567
Ireland	IMP	G	51437	87047	84925	62595	60692	67173	63230	65996	70769	71465
Irlande	EXP	G	77093	122252	127052	119264	118951	127011	117771	115333	118637	122093
	BAL		25656	35205	42127	56669	58260	59838	54541	49337	47867	50628
Italy	IMP	S	238021	511870	563436	414725	486968	558813	489096	477292	470392	407924
Italie	EXP	S	239902	500239	544962	406685	446852	523283	501534	517628	528041	458478
	BAL		1881	-11631	-18474	-8040	-40116	-35530	12438	40336	57648	50554
Latvia	IMP	S	3187	15182	15775	9346	11143	15442	16078	16781	16790	13894
Lettonie	EXP	S	1867	7892	9278	7174	8850	11995	12683	13317	13600	11522
	BAL		-1320	-7290	-6497	-2173	-2292	-3446	-3395	-3464	-3190	-2372
Lithuania	IMP	G	5219	24445	31295	18341	23385	31811	31988	34814	35243	28151
Lituanie	EXP	G	3548	17162	23770	16496	20726	28077	29625	32604	32399	25481
	BAL		-1671	-7283	-7525	-1845	-2658	-3733	-2363	-2210	-2844	-2670
Luxembourg	IMP	S	10707	22572	25828	19246	21738	26312	24180	23912	23545	19308
Luxembourg	EXP	S	7833	16359	17734	12905	14293	16798	13989	14086	15069	13099
	BAL		-2875	-6213	-8094	-6342	-7444	-9515	-10190	-9826	-8476	-6209
Malta	IMP	G	3400	4508	5744	4845	5735	7415	7923	7479	8122	6442
Malte	EXP	G	2443	2985	3609	2921	3721	5284	5697	5182	4836	3851
	BAL		-957	-1523	-2135	-1924	-2014	-2131	-2226	-2297	-3286	-2591
Netherlands	IMP	S	198926	421092	495056	382278	440024	507759	500643	513108	508207	419168
Pays-Bas	EXP	S	213425	472660	545897	431695	492742	569513	554707	567658	574233	471087
	BAL		14499	51568	50840	49418	52718	61754	54064	54550	66027	51919
Norway	IMP	G	34395	80378	90293	68970	77326	90787	87316	89988	88053	75677
Norvège	EXP	G	60064	136371	171764	116778	130669	160305	161026	153188	142301	103413
	BAL		25669	55992	81471	47808	53344	69518	73710	63201	54247	27736
Poland	IMP	S	48970	162437	204873	149723	178149	206844	196198	205174	219859	194134
Pologne	EXP	S	31684	138756	168674	136786	159829	187151	183523	202107	216666	198232
	BAL		-17285	-23680	-36200	-12938	-18320	-19693	-12675	-3067	-3193	4098
Portugal	IMP	S	38196	76376	94726	71742	75576	82481	72307	75068	77742	66458
Portugal	EXP	S	23280	50246	57558	44350	48738	59608	58256	62840	64061	55402
	BAL		-14916	-26129	-37168	-27393	-26838	-22872	-14051	-12227	-13681	-11057

Total merchandise trade by regions and countries or areas (Table A)

Imports CIF, exports FOB and balance: million U.S. dollars

Commerce total de marchandises par régions et pays ou zones (Tableau A)

Importations CIF, exportations FOB, et balance : en millions de dollars E.-U.

Country or Area - Pays ou Zone	IMP EXP BAL	G/S	2000	2007	2008	2009	2010	2011	2012	2013	2014	2015
Slovakia	IMP	S	13413	62102	74034	56898	66110	81505	79077	83632	83500	74862
Slovaquie	EXP	S	11889	57765	70982	55553	64012	79011	79882	85244	85923	75406
	BAL		-1524	-4337	-3052	-1345	-2098	-2494	805	1612	2423	544
Slovenia	IMP	S	10116	29499	33991	24085	26305	31405	28392	29380	30052	25769
Slovénie	EXP	S	8732	26857	29600	22646	24717	29242	27080	28629	30522	26616
	BAL		-1384	-2642	-4391	-1439	-1588	-2163	-1312	-751	471	847
Spain	IMP	S	152901	384956	417049	290744	315548	362835	325836	333932	351452	304314
Espagne	EXP	S	113348	248917	277695	220848	246274	298458	286219	310996	318860	277423
	BAL		-39553	-136038	-139353	-69897	-69274	-64377	-39618	-22936	-32592	-26892
Sweden	IMP	G	73328	153463	168993	120262	148474	174730	164113	159665	159535	136297
Suède	EXP	G	87737	168979	183907	131042	158090	187243	172725	167620	162588	139459
	BAL		14409	15516	14914	10780	9616	12513	8612	7955	3053	3163
Switzerland	IMP	S	76104	153181	173686	147894	166924	196790	188618	191705	195148	172770
Suisse	EXP	S	74867	164809	191813	166847	185790	223225	213982	217079	227605	210864
	BAL		-1237	11627	18127	18953	18866	26435	25364	25374	32457	38094
United Kingdom	IMP	G	333579	621869	642529	486279	562493	638940	648671	645516	663718	...
Royaume-Uni	EXP	G	283206	440556	467157	356758	410006	478460	476284	476991	477934	...
	BAL		-50373	-181312	-175372	-129521	-152487	-160480	-172387	-168525	-185785	...
North America	IMP		**1499277**	**2403320**	**2580859**	**1928924**	**2363824**	**2719866**	**2801853**	**2794280**	**2882132**	**2735497**
Amérique du Nord	EXP		**1058904**	**1569011**	**1744454**	**1370536**	**1666503**	**1933093**	**2001278**	**2038279**	**2094366**	**1914477**
	BAL		**-440373**	**-834309**	**-836404**	**-558388**	**-697321**	**-786773**	**-800575**	**-756001**	**-787766**	**-821020**
Bermuda	IMP	G	720	1151	1145	1034	970	869	885	1005	962	929
Bermudes	EXP	G	...	25	24	29	15	13	17	22	12	9
	BAL		...	-1125	-1122	-1005	-955	-855	-868	-983	-950	-920
Canada[3]	IMP	G	238811	380701	408827	321247	392119	451246	462423	461925	465958	423779
Canada[3]	EXP	G	276641	420293	456419	314002	387481	452132	454833	458397	469981	409002
	BAL		37830	39593	47593	-7245	-4638	886	-7590	-3528	4023	-14777
Greenland	IMP	G	363	678	895	742	808	915	850	780	762	580
Groenland	EXP	G	272	431	487	360	380	475	480	490	537	353
	BAL		-92	-247	-407	-382	-428	-441	-370	-290	-225	-227
United States[4]	IMP	G	1259300	2020400	2169490	1605300	1969180	2265890	2336520	2329060	2412550	2307950
Etats-Unis[4]	EXP	G	781918	1148200	1287440	1056040	1278490	1480290	1545710	1579050	1623410	1504580
	BAL		-477382	-872200	-882050	-549260	-690690	-785600	-790810	-750010	-789140	-803370
South-Eastern Europe	IMP		29538	140118	170987	116942	125499	154705	145630	152532	159084	**138594**
Europe du Sud-est	EXP		19546	76657	93954	76983	89833	115572	107537	122799	129370	**110371**
	BAL		-9992	-63462	-77033	-39959	-35666	-39133	-38093	-29733	-29714	**-28222**
Albania	IMP	G	1090	4188	5251	4526	4592	5396	4882	4902	5230	4320
Albanie	EXP	G	258	1078	1355	1104	1550	1951	1968	2332	2431	1930
	BAL		-832	-3110	-3896	-3422	-3042	-3445	-2914	-2571	-2799	-2390
Bosnia and Herzegovina	IMP	S	3083	9772	12282	8794	9204	11047	10018	10303	10988	8983
Bosnie-Herzégovine	EXP	S	1067	4166	5066	3939	4802	5850	5160	5688	5893	5096
	BAL		-2017	-5606	-7217	-4856	-4402	-5196	-4858	-4615	-5095	-3887
Bulgaria	IMP	S	6505	30086	37018	23552	25473	32579	32712	34350	34730	...
Bulgarie	EXP	S	4809	18575	22485	16378	20571	28222	26670	29492	30930	...
	BAL		-1696	-11511	-14532	-7175	-4902	-4357	-6042	-4858	-3799	...
Montenegro	IMP	S	.	2855	3748	2313	2186	2544	2309	2354	2369	2039
Monténégro	EXP	S	.	624	617	388	437	632	471	498	447	352
	BAL		.	-2231	-3131	-1926	-1749	-1912	-1838	-1856	-1921	-1687

Total merchandise trade by regions and countries or areas (Table A)

Imports CIF, exports FOB and balance: million U.S. dollars

Commerce total de marchandises par régions et pays ou zones (Tableau A)

Importations CIF, exportations FOB, et balance : en millions de dollars E.-U.

Country or Area - Pays ou Zone	IMP EXP BAL	G/S	2000	2007	2008	2009	2010	2011	2012	2013	2014	2015
Romania	IMP	S	13055	69602	82965	54256	61885	76251	70260	73452	77882	69855
Roumanie	EXP	S	10367	40042	49539	40621	49357	62659	57904	65881	69891	60604
	BAL		-2688	-29560	-33426	-13635	-12528	-13592	-12355	-7571	-7991	-9252
Serbia	IMP	S	.	18400	22880	18462	16686	19862	18927	20551	20608	18172
Serbie	EXP	S	.	8817	10971	11862	9766	11779	11348	14609	14844	13355
	BAL		.	-9584	-11908	-6599	-6920	-8082	-7579	-5942	-5765	-4817
Serbia and Montenegro[5]	IMP	S	3711	.	.	.	.	.	.	.	.	.
Serbie et Monténégro[5]	EXP	S	1723	.	.	.	.	.	.	.	.	.
	BAL		-1988	.	.	.	.	.	.	.	.	.
TFYR Macedonia	IMP	S	2094	5216	6843	5038	5474	7027	6522	6620	7277	6400
L'ex-Ry de Macédoine	EXP	S	1323	3356	3920	2692	3351	4478	4015	4299	4934	4490
	BAL		-771	-1860	-2923	-2346	-2123	-2549	-2507	-2321	-2343	-1910
CIS	IMP		**70777**	**352324**	**470015**	**304022**	**385468**	**510023**	**530798**	**536057**	**479860**	**335865**
CEI	EXP		**143257**	**497686**	**707851**	**440378**	**575087**	**762078**	**777787**	**762333**	**720560**	**499930**
	BAL		**72480**	**145362**	**237837**	**136356**	**189620**	**252054**	**246989**	**226276**	**240701**	**164065**
Asia	IMP		**13519**	**59569**	**73098**	**59331**	**56330**	**70849**	**80313**	**95612**	**92943**	**81345**
Asie	EXP		**17794**	**70845**	**139142**	**76439**	**99189**	**133567**	**135352**	**132114**	**130330**	**89599**
	BAL		**4275**	**11275**	**66043**	**17108**	**42859**	**62718**	**55039**	**36503**	**37387**	**8254**
Armenia	IMP	S	882	3282	4427	3303	3783	4196	4267	4386	4402	3254
Arménie	EXP	S	294	1219	1057	698	1011	1316	1428	1479	1519	1487
	BAL		-588	-2063	-3370	-2605	-2771	-2881	-2839	-2907	-2882	-1767
Azerbaijan	IMP	G	1172	5714	7170	6123	6601	9756	9653	10713	9188	9221
Azerbaïdjan	EXP	G	1745	6058	47756	14701	21360	26571	23908	23975	21829	11425
	BAL		573	345	40586	8578	14760	16815	14255	13263	12641	2203
Georgia	IMP	G	710	5212	6302	4500	5257	7038	8037	8012	8593	7707
Géorgie	EXP	G	324	1232	1495	1134	1677	2187	2376	2910	2861	2204
	BAL		-386	-3980	-4806	-3367	-3580	-4852	-5661	-5102	-5732	-5503
Kazakhstan	IMP	G	5040	33260	38452	28409	24024	30000	35307	45966	41202	...
Kazakhstan	EXP	G	8812	48351	71971	43196	57244	83316	88575	81912	79117	...
	BAL		3772	15091	33519	14787	33220	53316	53268	35945	37915	...
Kyrgyzstan	IMP	S	558	2417	4072	3040	3223	4261	5576	6070	5732	4070
Kirghizistan	EXP	S	511	1338	1874	1694	1779	2267	1955	2058	1897	1441
	BAL		-47	-1079	-2198	-1347	-1444	-1994	-3622	-4012	-3836	-2628
Tajikistan	IMP	G	675	2547	3273	2570	2657	3206	3778	4151	4297	3435
Tadjikistan	EXP	G	784	1468	1409	1010	1195	1257	1360	1162	977	891
	BAL		109	-1079	-1864	-1560	-1462	-1949	-2418	-2989	-3320	-2544
Uzbekistan	IMP	G	2697	4848	7076	9023	8386	9953	...	13799	...	...
Ouzbékistan	EXP	G	2817	8029	10369	10735	11587	13254	...	15087	...	...
	BAL		120	3181	3293	1712	3201	3301	...	1288	...	...
Europe	IMP		57259	292755	396916	244691	329137	439175	450485	440445	386917	254519
Europe	EXP		125463	426842	568710	363939	475898	628511	642436	630218	590230	410331
	BAL		68205	134087	171794	119248	146761	189336	191951	189773	203313	155812
Belarus	IMP	G	8646	28693	39381	28569	34884	45771	46404	42999	40502	30312
Bélarus	EXP	G	7326	24275	32571	21304	25284	41419	46060	37232	36081	26686
	BAL		-1320	-4418	-6811	-7265	-9601	-4352	-345	-5766	-4422	-3626
Republic of Moldova	IMP	G	776	3690	4899	3278	3855	5191	5213	5493	5317	3986
République de Moldova	EXP	G	472	1340	1591	1283	1542	2217	2162	2399	2340	1968
	BAL		-305	-2350	-3308	-1995	-2314	-2975	-3051	-3094	-2978	-2019

Total merchandise trade by regions and countries or areas (Table A)

Imports CIF, exports FOB and balance: million U.S. dollars

Commerce total de marchandises par régions et pays ou zones (Tableau A)

Importations CIF, exportations FOB, et balance : en millions de dollars E.-U.

Country or Area - Pays ou Zone	IMP EXP BAL	G/S	2000	2007	2008	2009	2010	2011	2012	2013	2014	2015
Russian Federation	IMP	G	33880	199754	267101	167411	229655	305605	314150	314967	286669	182719
Fédération de Russie	EXP	G	103093	351930	467581	301656	397668	516481	525383	527266	497909	343543
	BAL		69213	152176	200480	134245	168013	210877	211233	212299	211240	160824
Ukraine	IMP	G	13956	60618	85535	45433	60742	82608	84718	76987	54429	37502
Ukraine	EXP	G	14573	49296	66967	39696	51405	68394	68831	63321	53902	38135
	BAL		617	-11322	-18568	-5737	-9337	-14214	-15887	-13666	-527	633
Northern Africa	IMP		**46956**	**112469**	**164473**	**146452**	**161273**	**182419**	**208466**	**211607**	**209267**	**184225**
Afrique du nord	EXP		**49865**	**153521**	**207537**	**134078**	**164438**	**161707**	**199678**	**177149**	**147739**	**102065**
	BAL		**2909**	**41051**	**43064**	**-12374**	**3165**	**-20712**	**-8787**	**-34458**	**-61527**	**-82160**
Algeria	IMP	S	9172	27525	39578	39333	40228	47279	50352	54965	58367	51763
Algérie	EXP	S	22019	59761	79587	45240	57786	73661	72857	65555	61413	35278
	BAL		12848	32236	40010	5907	17558	26383	22505	10590	3046	-16485
Egypt[6,7]	IMP	G	13963	27063	48775	44946	52923	58903	65774	59662	61010	...
Egypte[6,7]	EXP	G	4675	16200	26246	23062	26438	30528	29409	28493	24736	...
	BAL		-9288	-10863	-22528	-21884	-26485	-28376	-36365	-31169	-36275	...
Libya	IMP	G	3703	6753	9116	10037	10506	7999	22996	27011	18994	...
Libye	EXP	G	10137	47048	62031	37265	46016	18015	58954	43986	20994	...
	BAL		6434	40295	52915	27228	35510	10016	35959	16976	2000	...
Morocco	IMP	S	11534	32010	42366	32881	35385	44267	44885	45641	46057	...
Maroc	EXP	S	7175	15340	20345	14054	17765	21650	21444	22049	23836	...
	BAL		-4359	-16670	-22021	-18827	-17620	-22617	-23441	-23592	-22221	...
Tunisia	IMP	G	8567	19101	24622	19241	22218	23958	24447	24317	24828	20221
Tunisie	EXP	G	5850	15163	19319	14449	16427	17847	17008	17061	16756	14073
	BAL		-2717	-3938	-5303	-4791	-5791	-6111	-7439	-7256	-8072	-6148
Sub-Saharan Africa	IMP		**78694**	**245445**	**301987**	**253559**	**290980**	**362954**	**354078**	**379648**	**398810**	**388432**
Afrique subsaharienne	EXP		**93704**	**279964**	**357213**	**260698**	**341766**	**431211**	**420738**	**423889**	**420053**	**369720**
	BAL		**15011**	**34519**	**55226**	**7139**	**50786**	**68257**	**66660**	**44241**	**21243**	**-18712**
Angola[3]	IMP	S	3040	13662	20982	22660	16667	22938	23717	26344	28587	20095
Angola[3]	EXP	S	7703	44396	63914	40828	50595	67310	71093	68247	59170	33168
	BAL		4663	30735	42932	18168	33928	44373	47376	41903	30583	13073
Benin	IMP	S	567	2037	2290	1553	1494	2701	2202	2148	...	...
Bénin	EXP	S	392	1052	1285	423	437	1397	1402	1154	...	...
	BAL		-174	-984	-1005	-1130	-1057	-1304	-800	-995	...	...
Botswana	IMP	G	2079	4077	5232	4771	5666	7300	8114	8424	8077	7237
Botswana	EXP	G	2661	5170	5077	3514	4692	5893	5971	7774	8509	6309
	BAL		581	1093	-155	-1257	-975	-1407	-2143	-649	431	-928
Burkina Faso	IMP	G	608	1685	2009	2084	2157	2574	3420	4163	3351	...
Burkina Faso	EXP	G	213	623	693	868	1319	2353	2183	2356	2487	...
	BAL		-395	-1062	-1315	-1216	-837	-221	-1237	-1807	-864	...
Burundi	IMP	S	148	319	402	402	509	752	751	811	769	724
Burundi	EXP	S	50	62	54	62	100	122	132	99	124	113
	BAL		-98	-257	-348	-340	-409	-630	-619	-712	-645	-611
Cabo Verde	IMP	G	237	753	819	709	743	947	766	727	653	...
Cabo Verde	EXP	G	11	19	32	35	45	69	53	69	115	...
	BAL		-227	-734	-788	-674	-698	-878	-713	-658	-538	...
Cameroon	IMP	S	1483	4671	5699	4442	5051	6802	6515	6657	7553	...
Cameroun	EXP	S	1823	4230	5241	3552	3881	4523	4585	4521	5153	...
	BAL		341	-441	-458	-890	-1170	-2280	-1930	-2136	-2400	...

Total merchandise trade by regions and countries or areas (Table A)

Imports CIF, exports FOB and balance: million U.S. dollars

Commerce total de marchandises par régions et pays ou zones (Tableau A)

Importations CIF, exportations FOB, et balance : en millions de dollars E.-U.

Country or Area - Pays ou Zone	IMP EXP BAL	G/S	2000	2007	2008	2009	2010	2011	2012	2013	2014	2015
Cent. Afr. Rep.	IMP	S	118	251	298	273	244	276	276	250	...	...
Rép. centrafricaine	EXP	S	163	181	150	81	91	116	112	140	...	...
	BAL		45	-70	-149	-192	-153	-161	-163	-111	...	...
Chad	IMP	S	483	1794	1906	2289	2507	2700	2600	2997	3496	...
Tchad	EXP	S	236	3653	4345	2636	3411	4599	3901	4496	4194	...
	BAL		-248	1859	2439	347	903	1899	1301	1498	698	...
Comoros	IMP	S	43	139	174	171	190	277	300	285	...	...
Comores	EXP	S	14	14	9	16	18	25	25	25	...	...
	BAL		-29	-125	-165	-155	-172	-251	-275	-260	...	...
Congo	IMP	S	479	2606	3142	2987	2987	5200	5200	5500	6200	...
Congo	EXP	S	2489	5635	8300	6100	8200	11500	11000	9800	8614	...
	BAL		2010	3029	5159	3113	5213	6300	5800	4300	2414	...
Cote d'Ivoire	IMP	S	2485	6694	7863	7023	7863	6714	9774	12628	10722	...
Côte d'Ivoire	EXP	S	3611	8692	10301	10326	10285	10928	10861	13687	12634	...
	BAL		1127	1998	2438	3303	2423	4214	1087	1060	1911	...
Dem. Rep. of the Congo	IMP	S	697	2950	4300	3900	4500	5500	6100	6300	6500	...
Rép. dém. du Congo	EXP	S	824	2600	4400	3500	5300	6600	6300	6300	6600	...
	BAL		126	-350	100	-400	800	1100	200	0	100	...
Djibouti	IMP	G	207	473	574	451	420	511	580	560	...	...
Djibouti	EXP	G	32	58	69	77	100	93	95	120	...	...
	BAL		-175	-415	-505	-373	-320	-418	-485	-440	...	...
Equatorial Guinea	IMP	G	451	2369	3934	5205	5680	6014	5987	6990	6492	...
Guinée équatoriale	EXP	G	1097	10205	15996	9108	9964	13532	15467	13981	11587	...
	BAL		646	7836	12062	3903	4285	7518	9480	6990	5094	...
Ethiopia	IMP	G	1261	5797	8268	7644	8535	8897	11914	11510	16244	...
Ethiopie	EXP	G	482	1282	1561	1522	2270	2974	3186	3005	3495	...
	BAL		-779	-4516	-6708	-6123	-6265	-5922	-8728	-8505	-12750	...
Gabon	IMP	S	996	2155	2607	2514	2984	3666	3630	3886	3105	...
Gabon	EXP	S	2605	6302	9566	5451	8691	9768	7704	9514	8949	...
	BAL		1610	4147	6959	2937	5706	6102	4075	5628	5844	...
Gambia	IMP	G	187	323	325	304	300	336	380	348	...	...
Gambie	EXP	G	15	13	14	15	15	11	18	8	...	...
	BAL		-172	-310	-311	-289	-285	-325	-362	-340	...	...
Ghana	IMP	G	2974	8057	10243	8069	11032	12606	13626	12793	...	...
Ghana	EXP	G	1317	4322	5625	5840	7960	12784	11976	13691	...	...
	BAL		-1657	-3735	-4618	-2229	-3072	179	-1649	898	...	...
Guinea	IMP	S	612	1218	1366	1060	1405	2106	2300	2150	2115	...
Guinée	EXP	S	666	1203	1342	1050	1471	1433	1400	1300	1428	...
	BAL		54	-15	-24	-10	66	-673	-900	-850	-687	...
Guinea-Bissau	IMP	G	60	110	199	202	197	260	250	240	...	...
Guinée-Bissau	EXP	G	62	107	128	120	120	230	130	210	...	...
	BAL		3	-3	-71	-82	-77	-30	-120	-30	...	...
Kenya	IMP	G	3105	8989	11080	10207	12074	14783	16288	16358	18397	16021
Kenya	EXP	G	1734	4080	4975	4463	5149	5756	6126	5856	6046	5880
	BAL		-1371	-4910	-6105	-5743	-6925	-9027	-10162	-10503	-12351	-10141
Lesotho	IMP	G	809	1741	1995	1973	2206	1454	1598	2284	2207	...
Lesotho	EXP	G	221	770	883	723	801	775	676	934	924	...
	BAL		-589	-971	-1113	-1250	-1404	-678	-922	-1350	-1283	...

Total merchandise trade by regions and countries or areas (Table A)

Imports CIF, exports FOB and balance: million U.S. dollars

Commerce total de marchandises par régions et pays ou zones (Tableau A)

Importations CIF, exportations FOB, et balance : en millions de dollars E.-U.

Country or Area - Pays ou Zone	IMP EXP BAL	G/S	2000	2007	2008	2009	2010	2011	2012	2013	2014	2015
Liberia	IMP	S	...	499	813	551	710	814	1076	1210	1046	...
Libéria	EXP	S	...	200	242	149	222	367	459	540	583	...
	BAL		...	-299	-571	-402	-488	-447	-617	-670	-463	...
Madagascar	IMP	S	999	2449	3843	3160	2546	2628	2486	3201	3254	...
Madagascar	EXP	S	828	1371	1670	1095	1082	1249	1236	1951	2142	...
	BAL		-171	-1078	-2173	-2065	-1464	-1379	-1250	-1250	-1112	...
Malawi	IMP	G	533	1380	1700	2096	2162	2426	2334	2831	2960	...
Malawi	EXP	G	379	709	860	1080	1130	1398	1183	1196	1370	...
	BAL		-153	-671	-840	-1015	-1032	-1027	-1151	-1636	-1590	...
Mali	IMP	S	807	2183	3343	2487	3430	3391	2940	3699	3951	...
Mali	EXP	S	552	1567	2082	1783	1996	2392	2163	2601	2097	...
	BAL		-255	-616	-1261	-704	-1434	-999	-776	-1098	-1854	...
Mauritania	IMP	S	354	1428	1669	1337	1708	2453	2971	3975	3612	3702
Mauritanie	EXP	S	343	1356	1651	1407	1799	2458	2624	2685	2289	1656
	BAL		-11	-72	-18	70	91	6	-347	-1290	-1323	-2046
Mauritius	IMP	G	2206	3894	4655	3734	4387	5149	5355	5399	5610	...
Maurice	EXP	G	1803	2238	2386	1939	2262	2565	2649	2872	3083	...
	BAL		-403	-1656	-2269	-1795	-2125	-2584	-2706	-2527	-2527	...
Mozambique	IMP	S	1162	3050	4008	3764	3864	6312	8688	10099	8717	7908
Mozambique	EXP	S	364	2412	2653	2147	2333	3604	3856	4024	4725	3198
	BAL		-798	-638	-1355	-1617	-1530	-2708	-4832	-6075	-3991	-4710
Namibia	IMP	G	1539	4544	5260	6465	6510	6625	7321	7568	...	...
Namibie	EXP	G	1317	4466	5373	5122	5290	5362	5481	5740	...	...
	BAL		-222	-78	114	-1343	-1219	-1263	-1840	-1828	...	...
Niger	IMP	S	390	1163	1659	1502	2179	1814	1799	1909	2247	...
Niger	EXP	S	284	664	902	593	642	903	1503	1613	1498	...
	BAL		-107	-499	-757	-909	-1537	-910	-296	-295	-749	...
Nigeria	IMP	G	8721	37576	42378	33906	44235	64410	35703	44598	...	...
Nigéria	EXP	G	20975	65133	80615	56742	84000	114500	114000	...	...	...
	BAL		12254	27557	38237	22836	39765	50090	78297	...	...	...
Rwanda	IMP	G	211	736	1131	1227	1401	1775	1999	2480	2457	...
Rwanda	EXP	G	52	176	267	193	255	464	470	689	736	...
	BAL		-159	-559	-865	-1035	-1146	-1311	-1529	-1792	-1721	...
Saint Helena[8]	IMP	G	10	16	16	16	...	...	...	...	...	...
Sainte-Hélèna[8]	EXP	G	0	0	0	1	...	...	...	...	...	...
	BAL		-10	-15	-16	-16	...	...	...	...	...	...
Sao Tome and Principe	IMP	S	30	79	114	103	112	132	140	140	172	...
Sao Tomé-et-Principe	EXP	S	3	7	11	8	11	11	11	12	17	...
	BAL		-27	-72	-103	-95	-101	-121	-129	-128	-155	...
Senegal	IMP	G	1513	4271	5700	4550	4442	5390	5883	6067	6047	...
Sénégal	EXP	G	921	1652	1995	1834	2059	2432	2382	2440	2617	...
	BAL		-592	-2618	-3705	-2716	-2383	-2958	-3501	-3627	-3430	...
Seychelles	IMP	G	343	861	1106	807	989	1049	1074	1098	1144	...
Seychelles	EXP	G	193	356	437	402	400	483	497	578	539	...
	BAL		-150	-506	-668	-405	-589	-566	-577	-520	-605	...
Sierra Leone	IMP	S	149	446	534	522	776	1714	1603	1617	1568	...
Sierra Leone	EXP	S	13	244	216	233	319	350	1122	1910	1552	...
	BAL		-136	-202	-318	-288	-458	-1365	-482	292	-16	...

Total merchandise trade by regions and countries or areas (Table A)

Imports CIF, exports FOB and balance: million U.S. dollars

Commerce total de marchandises par régions et pays ou zones (Tableau A)

Importations CIF, exportations FOB, et balance : en millions de dollars E.-U.

Country or Area - Pays ou Zone	IMP EXP BAL	G/ S	2000	2007	2008	2009	2010	2011	2012	2013	2014	2015
South Africa[3,9]	IMP	G	26795	79873	94901	64439	80132	99713	101415	101262	99924	85715
Afrique du Sud[3,9]	EXP	G	29987	69787	84488	62627	81826	96930	87372	83542	91194	81646
	BAL		3192	-10086	-10413	-1812	1695	-2783	-14043	-17719	-8730	-4069
Sudan	IMP	G	1553	8450	9352	9691	10045	9236	9230	9918	9211	...
Soudan	EXP	G	1807	8866	11671	8257	11404	10193	4067	4790	4350	...
	BAL		254	416	2319	-1434	1360	957	-5164	-5128	-4861	...
Swaziland	IMP	G	1039	1853	1665	1617	1710	1940	1946	1525	...	...
Swaziland	EXP	G	903	1885	1681	1479	1557	1901	1897	1894	...	...
	BAL		-137	33	16	-138	-153	-39	-49	370	...	...
Togo	IMP	S	562	1243	1499	1951	996	1800	1793	2108	...	...
Togo	EXP	S	362	700	901	811	641	1100	997	1048	...	...
	BAL		-200	-543	-598	-1140	-356	-700	-796	-1059	...	...
Uganda	IMP	G	1511	3497	4559	4265	4709	4565	5230	4927	5086	4761
Ouganda	EXP	G	469	2003	2717	3004	3115	2399	2861	2847	2667	2698
	BAL		-1043	-1494	-1841	-1261	-1594	-2166	-2369	-2080	-2420	-2063
United Rep. of Tanzania	IMP	G	1523	5337	7081	6296	7708	10702	11266	12235	...	...
Rép.-Unie de Tanzanie	EXP	G	663	2022	2674	2367	3522	4392	5075	5043	...	...
	BAL		-860	-3315	-4407	-3929	-4186	-6310	-6191	-7191	...	...
Zambia	IMP	S	888	4010	5017	3791	5319	7276	8810	10177	9545	8451
Zambie	EXP	S	893	4621	5067	4310	7206	8824	9375	10600	9696	6983
	BAL		4	611	50	519	1888	1549	565	423	151	-1468
Zimbabwe	IMP	G	1861	2550	2950	2900	3800	4400	4400	4300	4200	...
Zimbabwe	EXP	G	1923	2400	2200	2269	3199	3512	3800	3552	3438	...
	BAL		62	-150	-750	-631	-601	-888	-600	-748	-762	...
Latin America & The Caribbean	IMP		**376134**	**733270**	**896727**	**673750**	**855961**	**1048707**	**1077809**	**1117303**	**1116665**	**1003677**
Amérique latine et les Caraïbes	EXP		**355954**	**759828**	**888668**	**680162**	**861934**	**1074338**	**1086815**	**1091081**	**1067452**	**949030**
	BAL		**-20181**	**26557**	**-8059**	**6412**	**5974**	**25631**	**9006**	**-26222**	**-49213**	**-54646**
The Caribbean	IMP		**26914**	**50405**	**61394**	**48541**	**50664**	**57124**	**56514**	**53650**	**52897**	**53758**
Les Caraïbes	EXP		**11431**	**24776**	**30405**	**19530**	**22196**	**29573**	**29999**	**31452**	**32616**	**33547**
	BAL		**-15483**	**-25628**	**-30990**	**-29011**	**-28468**	**-27550**	**-26516**	**-22198**	**-20281**	**-20210**
Anguilla	IMP	S	99	248	272	169	157	153	150	145	152	158
Anguilla	EXP	S	4	9	11	23	12	16	8	4	2	2
	BAL		-95	-239	-260	-146	-145	-137	-142	-141	-150	-157
Antigua and Barbuda	IMP	G	338	727	806	699	501	471	535	515	553	488
Antigua-et-Barbuda	EXP	G	42	174	92	206	35	29	29	32	25	26
	BAL		-296	-553	-713	-493	-466	-442	-506	-483	-528	-462
Aruba	IMP	S	835	1114	1134	1147	1069	1283	1258	1303	1265	...
Aruba	EXP	S	173	98	100	136	125	151	173	167	116	...
	BAL		-662	-1016	-1034	-1012	-945	-1132	-1085	-1136	-1150	...
Bahamas[10]	IMP	G	2074	2449	2354	2699	2863	3411	3658	3276	...	...
Bahamas[10]	EXP	G	576	485	560	585	621	727	829	715	...	...
	BAL		-1498	-1965	-1794	-2114	-2241	-2684	-2829	-2561	...	...
Barbados	IMP	G	1156	1709	1879	1471	1562	1805	1806	1759	1739	1618
Barbade	EXP	G	272	419	445	369	429	465	570	463	474	483
	BAL		-884	-1291	-1433	-1102	-1133	-1340	-1236	-1296	-1265	-1135
Cayman Islands	IMP	G	693	1029	1078	893	828	911	910	929	976	...
Îles Caïmanes	EXP	G	4	21	15	19	13	22	20	30	26	...
	BAL		-689	-1008	-1064	-874	-815	-890	-890	-899	-950	...

Total merchandise trade by regions and countries or areas (Table A)

Imports CIF, exports FOB and balance: million U.S. dollars

Commerce total de marchandises par régions et pays ou zones (Tableau A)

Importations CIF, exportations FOB, et balance : en millions de dollars E.-U.

Country or Area - Pays ou Zone	IMP EXP BAL	G/S	2000	2007	2008	2009	2010	2011	2012	2013	2014	2015
Cuba	IMP	S	3363	10889	14249	...	...	...	...	...	...	...
Cuba	EXP	S	1219	3998	3680	...	...	...	...	...	...	...
	BAL		-2144	-6892	-10570	...	...	...	...	...	...	...
Dominica	IMP	S	148	196	247	225	224	226	208	203	230	218
Dominique	EXP	S	54	38	40	34	37	31	34	35	36	30
	BAL		-95	-158	-207	-191	-187	-195	-174	-168	-194	-188
Dominican Republic[3,11]	IMP	G	6416	11289	14020	10057	12885	14522	14939	13876	13838	...
République dominicaine[3,11]	EXP	G	966	2635	2394	1690	2711	3678	4129	4474	4677	...
	BAL		-5450	-8654	-11626	-8367	-10174	-10845	-10810	-9401	-9162	...
Grenada	IMP	S	246	365	377	293	317	329	336	368	336	353
Grenade	EXP	S	78	33	30	29	24	28	35	33	40	34
	BAL		-168	-332	-347	-264	-293	-302	-301	-336	-296	-319
Haiti	IMP	G	1040	1681	2310	2121	3147	3018	3170	3400	3734	...
Haïti	EXP	G	313	522	475	576	579	767	814	885	950	...
	BAL		-727	-1159	-1835	-1546	-2568	-2251	-2356	-2516	-2785	...
Jamaica	IMP	G	3302	6394	7734	4860	5201	6489	6485	6200	5840	...
Jamaïque	EXP	G	1295	2070	2542	1319	1331	1603	1709	1574	1444	...
	BAL		-2007	-4324	-5192	-3540	-3870	-4886	-4776	-4626	-4396	...
Montserrat	IMP	S	22	30	38	30	29	33	37	42	41	39
Montserrat	EXP	S	1	3	4	3	1	2	2	6	3	3
	BAL		-21	-27	-34	-26	-28	-31	-35	-36	-38	-36
Neth. Antilles[12]	IMP	S	2862	2549	3079	2607	2687	...	...	...	...	...
Antilles néer.[12]	EXP	S	2009	676	1088	810	811	...	...	...	...	...
	BAL		-853	-1872	-1991	-1797	-1876	...	...	...	...	...
Saint Kitts-Nevis	IMP	S	196	272	325	302	228	248	226	249	268	374
Saint-Kitts-et-Nevis	EXP	S	29	32	43	43	45	34	50	50	53	58
	BAL		-167	-241	-282	-260	-183	-214	-176	-199	-215	-315
Saint Lucia	IMP	S	355	635	657	539	601	670	683	598	556	570
Sainte-Lucie	EXP	S	47	107	145	163	228	256	156	171	168	180
	BAL		-308	-528	-512	-376	-373	-414	-527	-427	-388	-390
Saint Vincent-Grenadines	IMP	S	148	327	373	334	345	332	357	378	362	334
St.Vincent-Grenadines	EXP	S	50	48	52	50	44	39	44	48	48	46
	BAL		-97	-279	-321	-284	-301	-293	-314	-330	-314	-288
Trinidad and Tobago	IMP	S	3308	7662	9596	6953	6483	9976	9400	8799	8750	...
Trinité-et-Tobago	EXP	S	4274	13393	18663	9140	10188	14842	13100	12700	11600	...
	BAL		966	5731	9067	2187	3705	4866	3700	3902	2850	...
Turks and Caicos Islands	IMP	G	149	581	591	375	302	318	347	345	414	...
Îles Turques et Caïques	EXP	G	9	16	25	21	16	15	15	6	6	...
	BAL		-140	-564	-566	-355	-286	-303	-332	-339	-408	...
Latin America	IMP		**349220**	**682866**	**835333**	**625209**	**805297**	**991584**	**1021295**	**1063653**	**1063768**	**949919**
Amérique latine	EXP		**344523**	**735051**	**858264**	**660632**	**839739**	**1044765**	**1056816**	**1059629**	**1034836**	**915483**
	BAL		**-4698**	**52185**	**22931**	**35423**	**34442**	**53182**	**35521**	**-4023**	**-28932**	**-34436**
Argentina	IMP	S	25154	44707	57413	39105	48048	74319	68505	74002	65323	59789
Argentine	EXP	S	26341	55779	70588	56065	64722	84269	75219	83026	71936	59706
	BAL		1187	11072	13175	16961	16674	9950	6713	9024	6613	-83
Belize	IMP	G	524	684	837	669	709	831	882	930	1005	...
Belize	EXP	G	218	254	290	224	280	340	340	315	303	...
	BAL		-306	-430	-547	-445	-430	-491	-541	-616	-701	...

Total merchandise trade by regions and countries or areas (Table A)

Imports CIF, exports FOB and balance: million U.S. dollars

Commerce total de marchandises par régions et pays ou zones (Tableau A)

Importations CIF, exportations FOB, et balance : en millions de dollars E.-U.

Country or Area - Pays ou Zone	IMP EXP BAL	G/S	2000	2007	2008	2009	2010	2011	2012	2013	2014	2015
Bolivia (Plurinational State	IMP	G	1830	3457	5081	4545	5590	7927	8578	9338	10421	9480
Bolivie (État plurinational de)	EXP	G	1230	4458	7058	4918	6179	8107	10312	11189	12266	8261
	BAL		-600	1001	1977	373	589	179	1733	1851	1845	-1219
Brazil	IMP	G	58643	126645	182377	133673	191537	236946	228377	244677	239156	178832
Brésil	EXP	G	55119	160649	197942	152995	201915	256040	242580	242179	225101	191134
	BAL		-3524	34004	15565	19322	10378	19094	14203	-2498	-14055	12302
Chile	IMP	S	18507	47164	61903	41364	57928	73545	79080	80443	72433	62797
Chili	EXP	S	19210	67666	66456	51963	68996	80027	79712	77877	74547	64087
	BAL		703	20502	4553	10599	11068	6482	632	-2566	2113	1290
Colombia	IMP	G	11539	33164	39320	32898	40683	54675	58633	59397	64060	54058
Colombie	EXP	G	13043	29786	38265	32784	39710	56507	59573	58657	54788	35606
	BAL		1505	-3378	-1055	-114	-973	1832	941	-740	-9272	-18451
Costa Rica	IMP	S	6389	12957	15366	11460	13557	16218	17513	17923	17229	15425
Costa Rica	EXP	S	5850	9376	9575	8711	9343	10238	11151	11542	11217	9525
	BAL		-539	-3582	-5791	-2750	-4214	-5980	-6362	-6381	-6012	-5900
Ecuador	IMP	G	3721	13565	18852	15090	20591	24286	25304	27146	27740	...
Equateur	EXP	G	4927	13852	18818	13863	17415	22345	23765	24848	25732	18366
	BAL		1206	287	-34	-1227	-3176	-1941	-1539	-2298	-2007	...
El Salvador	IMP	S	4948	8677	9754	7255	8548	10118	10270	10772	10513	10416
El Salvador	EXP	S	2941	3977	4579	3797	4472	4979	5340	5491	5273	5485
	BAL		-2006	-4700	-5175	-3457	-4077	-5139	-4929	-5281	-5240	-4931
Guatemala	IMP	S	5171	11861	12835	10066	12051	14518	14873	14368	14921	14998
Guatemala	EXP	S	2711	4489	5412	3835	5907	7201	7139	6975	7366	7176
	BAL		-2460	-7371	-7423	-6232	-6145	-7317	-7734	-7392	-7555	-7822
Guyana	IMP	S	582	1059	1312	1161	1397	1763	1997	1750	1780	...
Guyana	EXP	S	502	679	795	763	880	1116	1415	1380	1160	...
	BAL		-80	-381	-518	-398	-517	-647	-581	-370	-620	...
Honduras	IMP	S	2980	6762	8831	6133	7079	8953	9464	9169	9311	9424
Honduras	EXP	S	1297	2120	2883	2304	2712	3892	4427	3923	4063	3911
	BAL		-1682	-4642	-5948	-3829	-4367	-5060	-5037	-5246	-5247	-5513
Mexico[3,13]	IMP	G	174500	283264	310561	234385	301482	350856	370746	381202	399977	395232
Mexique[3,13]	EXP	G	166368	272055	291827	229683	298138	349569	370889	380107	397658	380763
	BAL		-8132	-11209	-18734	-4702	-3344	-1287	143	-1095	-2319	-14469
Nicaragua	IMP	G	1805	3579	4300	3438	4229	5180	5847	5647	5874	5899
Nicaragua	EXP	G	643	1194	1473	1393	1845	2294	2644	2408	2626	2423
	BAL		-1163	-2385	-2827	-2045	-2384	-2886	-3204	-3239	-3248	-3476
Panama	IMP	S	3379	6872	9050	7801	9145	11340	12494	13024	13705	12136
Panama	EXP	S	859	1164	1247	948	832	785	822	844	818	696
	BAL		-2519	-5709	-7803	-6853	-8313	-10554	-11672	-12180	-12887	-11440
Paraguay	IMP	S	2193	5859	9033	6940	10040	12317	11502	12142	12169	10215
Paraguay	EXP	S	2200	4724	6407	5080	6517	7776	7283	9456	9636	8357
	BAL		7	-1136	-2626	-1860	-3524	-4540	-4219	-2686	-2533	-1858
Peru[3]	IMP	S	7407	19580	28373	21006	28818	37112	41089	42199	40766	...
Pérou[3]	EXP	S	6955	27882	31529	26885	35565	46118	45600	41484	37870	33970
	BAL		-452	8301	3157	5879	6747	9005	4510	-715	-2897	...
Suriname	IMP	G	243	1111	1518	1356	1380	1667	1963	2141	1982	1949
Suriname	EXP	G	395	1287	1668	1393	1851	2345	2659	2380	2113	1585
	BAL		152	177	149	37	471	677	696	239	131	-364

Total merchandise trade by regions and countries or areas (Table A)

Imports CIF, exports FOB and balance: million U.S. dollars

Commerce total de marchandises par régions et pays ou zones (Tableau A)

Importations CIF, exportations FOB, et balance : en millions de dollars E.-U.

Country or Area - Pays ou Zone	IMP EXP BAL	G/ S	2000	2007	2008	2009	2010	2011	2012	2013	2014	2015
Uruguay	IMP	G	3466	5726	8943	6209	8619	10623	10642	10990	10901	9095
Uruguay	EXP	G	2295	4485	6421	5417	6707	7997	8601	8844	9475	7742
	BAL		-1171	-1241	-2523	-792	-1912	-2626	-2041	-2146	-1425	-1354
Venezuela (Bolivarian Rep.	IMP	G	16213	46097	49602	40597	33815	38346	43501	46363	44478	...
Venezuela (Rép.	EXP	G	31413	69165	95021	57603	65745	92811	97340	86700	...	...
	BAL		15200	23068	45419	17006	31930	54465	53840	40337	...	...
Eastern Asia	IMP		**742209**	**1909513**	**2206817**	**1857749**	**2521545**	**3055326**	**3137294**	**3285271**	**3333544**	**2893496**
Asie Orientale	EXP		**774892**	**2185425**	**2473784**	**2091251**	**2717456**	**3202603**	**3352356**	**3546624**	**3717587**	**3568653**
	BAL		**32683**	**275912**	**266968**	**233502**	**195911**	**147278**	**215061**	**261352**	**384043**	**675156**
China	IMP	S	225024	956233	1131620	1004170	1396200	1742850	1818170	1949300	1963110	1680790
Chine	EXP	S	249203	1217790	1428660	1201790	1578270	1899180	2048940	2210250	2343190	2284480
	BAL		24179	261557	297040	197620	182070	156330	230770	260950	380080	603690
China, Hong Kong SAR	IMP	G	212805	367647	388505	347311	433111	483633	504405	523558	544112	521984
Chine, Hong Kong RAS	EXP	G	201860	344509	362675	318510	390143	428732	442799	458959	473659	465077
	BAL		-10945	-23138	-25830	-28801	-42968	-54901	-61606	-64599	-70453	-56907
China, Macao SAR	IMP	G	2255	5366	5365	4622	5513	7769	8877	10141	11262	10603
Chine, Macao RAS	EXP	G	2539	2543	1997	961	870	869	1021	1138	1241	1339
	BAL		284	-2823	-3368	-3661	-4643	-6899	-7856	-9002	-10021	-9264
Korea, Republic of	IMP	G	160479	356852	435275	323085	425212	524413	519585	515585	525514	436499
Corée, République de	EXP	G	172272	371492	422007	363534	466384	555216	547879	559632	572665	526756
	BAL		11793	14640	-13268	40449	41172	30803	28294	44047	47151	90257
Mongolia	IMP	G	615	2117	3616	2131	3278	6527	6739	6355	5237	3797
Mongolie	EXP	G	536	1889	2539	1903	2899	4780	4385	4273	5775	4670
	BAL		-79	-228	-1077	-229	-379	-1747	-2354	-2082	538	872
Southern Asia	IMP		94740	343079	465659	379515	505555	639137	658774	625092	**630824**	**571873**
Asie Méridionale	EXP		91012	271120	350844	282590	373614	491233	453797	461490	**470545**	**436788**
	BAL		-3728	-71959	-114815	-96925	-131941	-147904	-204976	-163602	**-160279**	**-135085**
Afghanistan	IMP	G	1176	2819	3020	3336	5154	6390	6200	5400	...	...
Afghanistan	EXP	G	137	497	540	403	388	376	350	500	...	...
	BAL		-1039	-2322	-2480	-2933	-4766	-6014	-5850	-4900	...	...
Bangladesh	IMP	G	8358	17263	22473	20631	26071	33978	34133	33576	35249	...
Bangladesh	EXP	G	4787	10233	11777	12443	14195	19807	25113	27033	21058	...
	BAL		-3572	-7030	-10695	-8188	-11877	-14171	-9020	-6543	-14191	...
Bhutan	IMP	G	235	526	543	529	854	1052	992	911	810	...
Bhoutan	EXP	G	127	675	520	495	641	678	535	544	555	...
	BAL		-108	148	-23	-34	-213	-374	-457	-367	-255	...
India[14]	IMP	G	51563	229349	321025	257200	350192	464507	489689	465424	462909	392043
Inde[14]	EXP	G	42378	150160	194816	164912	226334	302892	296827	314802	322513	267414
	BAL		-9185	-79189	-126210	-92288	-123858	-161615	-192863	-150622	-140396	-124629
Iran (Islamic Rep. of)[15,16]	IMP	S	14347	45000	57401	50768	65404	61760	56500	49000	52000	...
Iran (Rép. islamique d')[15,16]	EXP	S	28345	83000	113668	78830	101316	130500	95500	82000	88800	...
	BAL		13998	38000	56267	28062	35912	68740	39000	33000	36800	...
Maldives	IMP	G	389	1092	1382	963	1091	1465	1554	1733	1993	...
Maldives	EXP	G	76	108	126	76	74	127	162	167	145	...
	BAL		-313	-984	-1256	-886	-1017	-1338	-1393	-1567	-1848	...
Nepal	IMP	G	1526	3139	3562	4392	5495	5762	6499	6428	...	...
Népal	EXP	G	700	870	937	823	950	917	960	926	...	...
	BAL		-826	-2269	-2625	-3569	-4545	-4845	-5539	-5502	...	...

Total merchandise trade by regions and countries or areas (Table A)

Imports CIF, exports FOB and balance: million U.S. dollars

Commerce total de marchandises par régions et pays ou zones (Tableau A)

Importations CIF, exportations FOB, et balance : en millions de dollars E.-U.

Country or Area - Pays ou Zone	IMP EXP BAL	G/S	2000	2007	2008	2009	2010	2011	2012	2013	2014	2015
Pakistan	IMP	G	10864	32590	42300	31647	37783	43955	44105	44647	47434	43795
Pakistan	EXP	G	9028	17838	20323	17523	21410	25383	24567	25121	24706	22089
	BAL		-1836	-14752	-21977	-14124	-16373	-18572	-19537	-19526	-22729	-21706
Sri Lanka	IMP	G	6281	11301	13953	10049	13512	20268	19102	17973	19652	...
Sri Lanka	EXP	G	5433	7740	8137	7085	8307	10553	9784	10397	11199	...
	BAL		-848	-3560	-5816	-2965	-5205	-9715	-9318	-7576	-8452	...
South-eastern Asia	IMP		379470	774039	939039	728238	954566	1152044	1226074	1244020	**1236379**	**1087985**
Asie du Sud-est	EXP		429596	865146	988287	813295	1049619	1232120	1252135	1269326	**1288107**	**1162454**
	BAL		50126	91106	49248	85057	95053	80076	26061	25305	**51728**	**74469**
Brunei Darussalam	IMP	S	1107	2101	2572	2449	2539	3602	3563	3612	3597	...
Brunéi Darussalam	EXP	S	3907	7693	10322	7200	8908	12458	12982	11447	10588	...
	BAL		2801	5592	7750	4751	6369	8855	9418	7835	6990	...
Cambodia	IMP	S	1424	5300	6508	5830	6791	9300	11000	13000	13500	...
Cambodge	EXP	S	1123	4400	4708	4196	5143	6950	8200	9100	10800	...
	BAL		-302	-900	-1800	-1634	-1648	-2350	-2800	-3900	-2700	...
Indonesia	IMP	S	43075	93101	127538	93786	135323	176881	190992	186351	178182	142691
Indonésie	EXP	S	65404	118014	139606	119646	158074	200587	188516	182659	176341	150358
	BAL		22329	24913	12068	25860	22751	23706	-2476	-3692	-1841	7667
Lao P.Dem.R.	IMP	S	535	1067	1405	1461	2060	2404	3055	3020	3300	...
Rép. dém. populaire lao	EXP	S	330	842	1085	1053	1746	2190	2271	2264	2650	...
	BAL		-205	-225	-320	-408	-314	-215	-784	-756	-650	...
Malaysia	IMP	G	81963	146171	156348	123757	164622	187473	196393	205898	208874	175962
Malaisie	EXP	G	98229	175966	199414	157244	198612	228086	227538	228331	234139	199876
	BAL		16266	29795	43066	33487	33990	40613	31145	22434	25265	23915
Myanmar	IMP	G	2371	3247	4256	4348	4760	9019	9151	12043	16227	...
Myanmar	EXP	G	1620	6253	6882	6662	8661	9238	8877	11233	11299	...
	BAL		-751	3006	2626	2314	3901	219	-274	-810	-4928	...
Philippines	IMP	G	36887	57708	60491	45856	58533	64097	65845	65645	68700	70086
Philippines	EXP	G	37767	50518	49462	38421	51541	48316	52072	56647	62148	58653
	BAL		880	-7190	-11030	-7436	-6992	-15781	-13772	-8999	-6552	-11433
Singapore	IMP	G	134546	263155	319781	245785	310791	365770	379723	373016	366247	296745
Singapour	EXP	G	137806	299270	338176	269832	351867	409503	408393	410250	405295	346638
	BAL		3259	36115	18396	24048	41076	43733	28670	37234	39048	49893
Thailand	IMP	S	61923	141294	179168	134734	185121	229137	250587	249652	227997	201901
Thaïlande	EXP	S	68963	153858	175897	151910	193366	220221	227752	224863	225190	211033
	BAL		7039	12563	-3270	17176	8245	-8916	-22835	-24789	-2807	9132
Timor-Leste	IMP	S	.	199	258	283	246	319	664	523	...	...
Timor-Leste	EXP	S	.	19	49	35	42	53	77	53	...	...
	BAL		.	-180	-209	-248	-205	-266	-587	-470	...	...
Viet Nam	IMP	G	15638	60697	80714	69949	83779	104041	115101	131260	148770	162825
Viet Nam	EXP	G	14447	48313	62685	57096	71658	94518	115458	132478	149565	162061
	BAL		-1191	-12384	-18029	-12853	-12121	-9523	357	1218	795	-764
Western Asia	IMP		**198063**	**606001**	757727	609870	710884	864312	915188	976582	**988166**	**946039**
Asie Occidentale	EXP		**261901**	**745446**	1054195	740948	925948	1255255	1347118	1401162	**1345041**	**1061328**
	BAL		**63838**	**139444**	296468	131078	215064	390943	431929	424581	**356874**	**115289**
Bahrain	IMP	G	4633	11488	10800	7300	9800	12730	14900	13000	...	...
Bahreïn	EXP	G	6194	13634	17316	11874	15400	19650	20500	17500	...	...
	BAL		1561	2146	6516	4574	5600	6920	5600	4500	...	...

Total merchandise trade by regions and countries or areas (Table A)

Imports CIF, exports FOB and balance: million U.S. dollars

Commerce total de marchandises par régions et pays ou zones (Tableau A)

Importations CIF, exportations FOB, et balance : en millions de dollars E.-U.

Country or Area - Pays ou Zone	IMP EXP BAL	G/S	2000	2007	2008	2009	2010	2011	2012	2013	2014	2015
Cyprus	IMP	G	3846	8687	10873	7937	8647	8791	7379	6419	6828	5667
Chypre	EXP	G	951	2539	1755	1352	1507	1956	1828	2136	1924	1931
	BAL		-2895	-6148	-9118	-6585	-7139	-6835	-5551	-4283	-4904	-3736
Iraq	IMP		...	...	33000	37000	43915	49000	57000	61000	59000	...
Iraq	EXP		...	...	61273	41929	52483	83300	94400	89550	88968	...
	BAL		...	...	28273	4929	8567	34300	37400	28550	29968	...
Israel[17]	IMP	S	31404	59039	67656	49278	61209	75830	75392	74861	75483	64955
Israël[17]	EXP	S	31404	54065	60825	47934	58392	67648	63191	66607	68553	63594
	BAL		0	-4973	-6831	-1344	-2817	-8182	-12201	-8254	-6931	-1361
Jordan	IMP	G	4597	13511	16764	14534	15085	18463	20691	21701	22952	20016
Jordanie	EXP	G	1899	5725	7788	6531	7023	7964	7926	7896	8376	7849
	BAL		-2698	-7786	-8976	-8002	-8062	-10499	-12765	-13804	-14576	-12166
Kuwait	IMP	S	7157	21353	24840	19891	22691	25144	27259	29299	31020	31903
Koweït	EXP	S	19434	62703	87538	54012	66619	102078	114513	114115	100810	55151
	BAL		12278	41350	62699	34121	43927	76934	87254	84816	69791	23248
Lebanon	IMP	G	6230	12251	16754	16574	18460	20165	21287	21236	21138	...
Liban	EXP	G	715	3574	4454	4187	5021	4267	4485	4059	4548	...
	BAL		-5515	-8677	-12300	-12387	-13439	-15898	-16802	-17176	-16589	...
Oman	IMP	G	5040	15978	22925	17865	19775	23620	29447	34333	29432	29007
Oman	EXP	G	11319	24136	37719	28053	36601	47092	53174	56429	52834	34734
	BAL		6279	8158	14795	10188	16827	23472	23727	22096	23402	5727
Qatar	IMP	S	3252	23430	27900	24922	23240	22333	25223	27038	30471	32609
Qatar	EXP	S	11594	44456	67307	48007	74800	114448	132985	136855	131261	77893
	BAL		8342	21027	39407	23085	51560	92115	107761	109817	100789	45283
Saudi Arabia	IMP	S	30197	90215	115133	95544	106864	131587	155592	168155	173908	169968
Arabie saoudite	EXP	S	77480	233300	313427	192296	251147	364699	388371	375872	342481	202238
	BAL		47283	143086	198294	96752	144283	233112	232779	207718	168573	32269
State of Palestine	IMP	S	2383	3284	3466	3601	3959	4374	4697	4580	5055	4942
État de Palestine	EXP	S	401	513	558	518	576	746	782	839	865	912
	BAL		-1982	-2771	-2908	-3082	-3383	-3628	-3915	-3740	-4190	-4030
Syrian Arab Rep.	IMP	S	4055	14655	18105	15291	16950	16400	7800	5800	...	...
République arabe syrienne	EXP	S	4674	11546	15410	10855	14000	10700	4000	3000	...	...
	BAL		620	-3109	-2695	-4436	-2950	-5700	-3800	-2800	...	...
Turkey	IMP	S	54503	170063	201964	140928	185544	240842	236545	251661	242177	207191
Turquie	EXP	S	27775	107272	132027	102143	113883	134907	152462	151803	157614	144047
	BAL		-26728	-62791	-69937	-38785	-71661	-105935	-84083	-99858	-84563	-63144
United Arab Emirates	IMP	G	35009	132500	177000	150000	165000	205000	220000	245000	262000	...
Emirats arabes unis	EXP	G	49835	154000	239213	185000	220000	285000	300000	365000	359000	...
	BAL		14827	21500	62213	35000	55000	80000	80000	120000	97000	...
Yemen	IMP	S	2327	8513	10548	9206	9746	10034	11975	12500	...	...
Yémen	EXP	S	3795	6299	7584	6256	8497	10801	8500	9500	...	...
	BAL		1469	-2215	-2964	-2949	-1249	766	-3475	-3000	...	...
Oceania	IMP		**6924**	**14574**	**16887**	**14460**	**16625**	**18988**	**19400**	**21536**	**22364**	**22014**
Océanie	EXP		**5111**	**10015**	**10645**	**8515**	**10481**	**12314**	**11797**	**11116**	**14552**	**13307**
	BAL		**-1813**	**-4559**	**-6242**	**-5945**	**-6144**	**-6673**	**-7603**	**-10421**	**-7812**	**-8707**
American Samoa[18]	IMP	S	506	527	655	547	434	463	514	479	...	...
Samoa américaines[18]	EXP	S	346	464	592	491	316	278	419	386	...	...
	BAL		-160	-64	-63	-56	-118	-185	-96	-92	...	...

Total merchandise trade by regions and countries or areas (Table A)

Imports CIF, exports FOB and balance: million U.S. dollars

Commerce total de marchandises par régions et pays ou zones (Tableau A)

Importations CIF, exportations FOB, et balance : en millions de dollars E.-U.

Country or Area - Pays ou Zone	IMP EXP BAL	G/S	2000	2007	2008	2009	2010	2011	2012	2013	2014	2015
Cook Islands	IMP	G	50	106	105	82	91	110	112	116	121	110
Iles Cook	EXP	G	9	5	4	3	5	3	5	11	18	14
	BAL		-41	-101	-101	-79	-85	-107	-106	-105	-103	-96
Fiji	IMP	G	857	1801	2265	1441	1817	2182	2254	2827	2655	...
Fidji	EXP	G	539	755	922	631	842	1070	1224	1108	1220	...
	BAL		-318	-1046	-1343	-811	-975	-1112	-1030	-1718	-1435	...
French Polynesia	IMP	S	905	1863	2187	1732	1740	1796	1706	1801	1762	1527
Polynésie française	EXP	S	200	197	195	148	153	168	139	152	170	130
	BAL		-705	-1667	-1991	-1584	-1587	-1628	-1567	-1649	-1592	-1397
Guam	IMP	G	...	688	649	635	698	708	693	687	707	...
Guam	EXP	G	...	91	105	51	46	55	46	45	41	40
	BAL		...	-596	-544	-584	-652	-653	-647	-642	-666	...
Kiribati	IMP	G	39	70	75	67	73	92	100	112	...	...
Kiribati	EXP	G	4	10	8	6	4	9	6	8	...	...
	BAL		-36	-60	-68	-61	-69	-83	-94	-105	...	...
Marshall Islands	IMP	G	55	...	...	...	...	...	...	...	...	...
Iles Marshall	EXP	G	9	...	...	...	...	...	...	...	...	...
	BAL		-46	...	...	...	...	...	...	...	...	...
Micronesia[3]	IMP	S	...	146	160	171	168	188	194	188	...	...
Micronésie[3]	EXP	S	...	16	21	18	23	43	52	35	...	...
	BAL		...	-130	-139	-153	-145	-145	-142	-153	...	...
New Caledonia	IMP	S	922	2809	3233	2574	3312	3698	3245	3240	3323	2717
Nouvelle-Calédonie	EXP	S	606	2104	1300	993	1493	1661	1321	1196	1565	1288
	BAL		-317	-705	-1933	-1581	-1820	-2037	-1923	-2044	-1758	-1429
Niue	IMP	G	2	7	8	6	...	...	...	...	...	...
Nioué	EXP	G	0	3	0	...	...	...	...	...	...	...
	BAL		-2	-4	-8	...	...	...	...	...	...	...
Palau	IMP	S	123	108	130	94	103	125	136	145	162	...
Palaos	EXP	S	...	...	...	...	...	...	...	...	...	...
	BAL		...	...	...	...	...	...	...	...	...	...
Papua New Guinea	IMP	G	1151	2945	3547	3198	3950	4887	5500	...	...	...
Papouasie-Nouvelle-Guinée	EXP	G	2068	4684	5714	4404	5742	6908	6328	5951	8852	...
	BAL		917	1738	2167	1206	1792	2021	828	...	...	...
Samoa	IMP	S	90	227	249	204	278	319	308	326	...	...
Samoa	EXP	S	14	15	11	12	13	17	34	24	...	...
	BAL		-76	-212	-238	-193	-264	-302	-274	-302	...	...
Solomon Islands	IMP	S	92	287	329	270	300	474	446	465	460	...
Iles Salomon	EXP	S	69	165	210	163	221	411	502	448	455	...
	BAL		-23	-123	-119	-107	-79	-64	56	-16	-5	...
Tonga	IMP	G	69	143	168	145	159	193	199	198	218	...
Tonga	EXP	G	9	9	10	8	8	17	17	22	23	...
	BAL		-60	-134	-158	-137	-151	-176	-182	-176	-196	...
Tuvalu	IMP	G	5	16	...	...	...	...	...	...	...	...
Tuvalu	EXP	G	0	0	...	...	...	...	...	...	...	...
	BAL		-5	-16	...	...	...	...	...	...	...	...
Vanuatu	IMP	G	87	231	314	294	285	305	296	313	313	367
Vanuatu	EXP	G	26	50	57	57	49	67	55	39	63	39
	BAL		-61	-180	-257	-237	-237	-238	-241	-275	-250	-328

Total merchandise trade by regions and countries or areas (Table A)

Imports CIF, exports FOB and balance: million U.S. dollars

Commerce total de marchandises par régions et pays ou zones (Tableau A)

Importations CIF, exportations FOB, et balance : en millions de dollars E.-U.

Country or Area - Pays ou Zone	IMP EXP BAL	G/S	2000	2007	2008	2009	2010	2011	2012	2013	2014	2015
Additional Country Groupings												
ANCOM	IMP		24496	69767	91626	73539	95681	124001	133604	138080	142987	**121811**
ANCOM	EXP		26154	75978	95671	78449	98869	133077	139249	136177	130656	96203
	BAL		1658	6212	4045	4911	3188	9076	5645	-1903	-12331	**-25608**
APEC	IMP		3308360	6427228	7360477	5694102	7352092	8784903	9105185	**9203730**	**9284723**	**8231802**
CEAP	EXP		3110918	6209913	7051036	5633051	7233306	8473047	8699870	8865744	9055196	**8288448**
	BAL		-197442	-217315	-309441	-61051	-118787	-311856	-405314	**-337986**	**-229527**	**56645**
ASEAN	IMP		379470	773840	938781	727955	954320	1151725	1225410	1243497	1235395	**1087557**
ANASE	EXP		429596	865127	988238	813260	1049577	1232067	1252058	1269272	1288015	**1162289**
	BAL		50126	91287	49457	85305	95258	80342	26648	25776	52620	**74731**
CACM	IMP		21293	43836	51085	38353	45464	54987	57967	57879	57847	56162
MCAC	EXP		13442	21156	23921	20040	24279	28604	30701	30340	30545	28520
	BAL		-7850	-22680	-27164	-18313	-21186	-26383	-27266	-27539	-27302	-27642
CARICOM	IMP		13681	25302	30362	23710	24987	31270	31742	30608	**30344**	**28598**
CARICOM	EXP		8146	19543	25844	14895	16573	22624	21785	20786	**19090**	**17047**
	BAL		-5535	-5760	-4519	-8815	-8414	-8646	-9957	-9822	**-11254**	**-11550**
COMESA	IMP		**34644**	**82873**	**119508**	**112045**	**127911**	**139475**	**169244**	**170341**	**169739**	**157811**
COMESA	EXP		**27212**	**95981**	**128312**	**94008**	**117014**	**97116**	**132277**	**118867**	**92097**	**72818**
	BAL		**-7431**	**13107**	**8803**	**-18037**	**-10897**	**-42359**	**-36967**	**-51474**	**-77642**	**-84993**
ECOWAS	IMP		**20021**	68257	81039	66473	81958	107576	83516	96405	**107830**	**123198**
CEDEAO	EXP		**29437**	86192	106373	80821	111531	151248	150650	**154063**	**151934**	**148904**
	BAL		**9416**	17935	25334	14348	29574	43672	67134	**57658**	**44104**	**25706**
EMCCA	IMP		4010	13845	17587	17709	19453	24659	24208	26281	**27066**	**28621**
CEMAC	EXP		8414	30206	43598	26928	34237	44037	42770	42451	**38666**	**35901**
	BAL		4404	16361	26011	9219	14784	19379	18562	16170	**11600**	**7280**
LAIA	IMP		329913	646990	794758	**596085**	**767217**	**941853**	**966821**	**1008250**	**1007543**	**894612**
ALAI	EXP		331178	715662	835258	**642519**	**817386**	**1018486**	**1029302**	**1034645**	**1012412**	**898657**
	BAL		1265	68672	40500	**46433**	**50169**	**76633**	**62480**	**26395**	**4869**	**4045**
LDCs	IMP		**41558**	**120633**	**157988**	**151734**	**165794**	**203792**	**220623**	**238603**	**250968**	**251240**
PMA	EXP		**33384**	**126081**	**165747**	**124003**	**155445**	**197000**	**203023**	**211893**	**200861**	**185393**
	BAL		**-8175**	**5448**	**7759**	**-27731**	**-10350**	**-6792**	**-17600**	**-26709**	**-50107**	**-65846**
MERCOSUR	IMP		107498	232491	312450	231068	297650	380478	371105	397511	382447	**306501**
MERCOSUR	EXP		118597	299260	383437	282077	351785	457001	441334	441393	**409296**	**350654**
	BAL		11099	66769	70987	51010	54135	76522	70229	43882	**26849**	**44153**
NAFTA	IMP		1672611	2684365	2888878	2160932	2662781	3067992	3169689	3172187	3278485	3126961
ALENA	EXP		1224927	1840548	2035686	1599725	1964109	2281991	2371432	2417554	2491049	2294345
	BAL		-447684	-843816	-853191	-561207	-698672	-786001	-798257	-754633	-787436	-832616
OECD	IMP		4910588	9648414	10826394	8135497	9594770	11277483	11053915	11089800	11244373	**9955832**
OCDE	EXP		4535677	8782950	9793207	7636646	8955040	10419490	10222810	10370090	10532016	**9349611**
	BAL		-374911	-865463	-1033187	-498851	-639730	-857993	-831105	-719710	-712357	**-606221**
OPEC	IMP		**181037**	**571811**	743320	633533	728480	876962	934139	992270	**1022908**	**993104**
OPEP	EXP		**363696**	**1016513**	1422020	971261	1245995	1669255	1752295	**1746823**	**1644782**	**1304234**
	BAL		**182659**	**444702**	678699	337727	517515	792293	818156	**754553**	**621874**	**311130**
EU28	IMP		2441663	5460802	6127549	4604194	5192789	6071644	5706031	5797465	5881886	**5092177**
UE28	EXP		2394652	5254542	5831883	4519538	5064357	5930614	5682138	5873232	5987873	**5231036**
	BAL		-47011	-206260	-295666	-84656	-128432	-141030	-23893	75766	105987	**138859**

Total merchandise trade by regions and countries or areas (Table A)

Imports CIF, exports FOB and balance: million U.S. dollars

Commerce total de marchandises par régions et pays ou zones (Tableau A)

Importations CIF, exportations FOB, et balance : en millions de dollars E.-U.

Country or Area - Pays ou Zone	IMP EXP BAL	G/S	2000	2007	2008	2009	2010	2011	2012	2013	2014	2015
Extra-EU28[19,20]	IMP		913310	1985545	2336609	1721874	2029009	2405295	2311903	2234492	2233120	1914903
Extra-UE28[19,20]	EXP		781270	1694259	1928718	1527320	1791433	2161865	2162563	2305992	2259963	1985139
	BAL		-132040	-291287	-407891	-194554	-237576	-243430	-149340	71500	26843	70235
Memorandum Items												
World excluding intra-EU28 trade	IMP		**4989238**	**10563522**	**12438185**	**9607857**	**11993737**	**14417653**	**14734756**	**14859364**	**14944595**	**13259870**
Monde excl. le intra-UE28 com.	EXP		**4743381**	**10237022**	**12102472**	**9416720**	**11833289**	**14262538**	**14561213**	**14899113**	**14921049**	**13254400**
	BAL		**-245856**	**-326500**	**-335713**	**-191137**	**-160448**	**-155115**	**-173543**	**39749**	**-23546**	**-5470**
World excluding intra-EU28 trade as percent of World	IMP		**77**	**75**	**77**	**77**	**79**	**80**	**81**	**81**	**80**	**81**
Monde excl. le intra-UE28 com.comme pour cent du Monde	EXP		**75**	**74**	**76**	**76**	**78**	**79**	**81**	**81**	**80**	**80**

Total merchandise trade by regions and countries or areas (Table A)

Imports CIF, exports FOB and balance: million U.S. dollars

Commerce total de marchandises par régions et pays ou zones (Tableau A)

Importations CIF, exportations FOB, et balance: en millions de dollars E.-U.

General notes:

For further information on Sources, Method of Estimation, Currency Conversion, Period, Country Nomenclature and Country Grouping of this table, as well as for a brief table description, please see the Introduction.

1 This classification is intended for statistical convenience and does not, necessarily, express a judgement about the stage reached by a particular country in the development process.

2 Developed Economies of America, Europe, and the Asia-Pacific region.

3 Imports FOB.

4 Including the trade of the U.S. Virgin Islands and Puerto Rico but excluding shipments of merchandise between the United States and its other possessions (Guam and American Samoa). Data include imports and exports of non-monetary gold.

5 Beginning 2006, data for Serbia and Montenegro is reported separately.

6 Prior to 2008, special trade.

7 Imports exclude petroleum imported without stated value. Exports cover domestic exports.

8 Year ending 31 March of the following year.

9 Exports include gold.

10 Trade statistics exclude certain oil and chemical products.

11 Export and import values exclude trade in the processing zone.

12 The Netherlands Antilles was dissolved on October 10, 2010. Beginning 2011, data are reported separately for Curaçao, Sint Maarten (Dutch part), Bonaire, Saint Eustatius and Saba.

13 Trade data include maquiladoras and exclude goods from customs-bonded warehouses. Total exports include revaluation and exports of silver.

14 Excluding military goods, fissionable materials, bunkers, ships, and aircraft.

15 Data include oil and gas.The value of oil exports and total exports are rough estimates based on information published in various petroleum industry journals.

16 Year ending 20 March of the year stated.

17 Imports and exports net of returned goods. The figures also exclude Judea and Samaria and the Gaza area.

18 Year ending 30 September of the years stated.

19 Excluding intra-EU trade.

20 In the year 2000, the trade values refer to EU-27.

Remarque générale:

Pour plus d'information en ce qui concerne les sources, la méthode d'estimation, taux d'exchange, période, nomenclature des pays et groupement de pays, ainsi que pour une brève description de ce tableau, veuillez voir l'introduction.

1 Cette classification est utilisée pour plus de commodité dans la présentation des statistiques et n'implique pas nécessairement un jugement quant au stade de développement auquel est parvenu un pays donné.

2 Économies développées de l'Amérique, de l'Europe, et de la région Asie-Pacifique.

3 Importations FOB.

4 Y compris le commerce des Iles Vierges américaines et de Porto Rico mais non compris les échanges de marchandise, entre les Etats-Unis et leurs autres possessions (Guam et Samoa américaines). Les données comprennent les importations et exportations d'or non-monétaire.

5 Depuis début 2006, les données relatives à la Serbie et au Monténégro sont déclarées séparément.

6 Avant 2008, commerce special.

7 Non compris le pétrole brute dont la valeur des importations ne sont pas stipulée. Les exportations sont les exportations d'intérieur.

8 Année finissant le 31 mars de l'année suivante.

9 Les exportations comprennent l'or.

10 Les statistiques commerciales font exclusion de certains produits pétroliers et chimiques.

11 Les valeurs à l'exportation et à l'importation excluent le commerce de la zone de transformation.

12 Les Antilles néerlandaises ont été dissoutes le 10 Octobre 2010. A partir de 2011, les données sont présentées séparément pour Curaçao, Saint-Martin (partie néerlandaise), Bonaire, Saint-Eustache et Saba.

13 Les statistiques du commerce extérieur comprennent maquiladoras et ne comprennent pas les marchandises provenant des entrepôts en douane. Les exportations comprennent la réévaluation et les données sur les exportations d'argent.

14 À l'exclusion des marchandises militaires, des matières fissibles, des soutes, des bateaux, et de l'avion.

15 Les données comprennent le pétrole et le gaz. La valeur des exportations de pétrole et des exportations totales sont des évaluations grossières basées sur l'information publiée à divers journaux d'industrie de pétrole.

16 Année finissant le 20 mars de l'année indiquée.

17 Importations et exportations nets, ne comprennant pas les marchandises retournées. Sont également exclues les données de la Judée et de Samaria et ainsi que la zone de Gaza.

18 Année finissant le 30 septembre de l'année indiquée.

19 Non compris le commerce d'intra-UE.

20 En l'année 2000, les valeurs du commerce se réfèrent à extra-UE27.

World merchandise exports by provenance and destination (Table D)

In million U.S. dollars f.o.b.

Exports to ⟶			Developed economies 2/ Économies développées 2/							Commonwealth of Independent States Communauté d'Etats Indépendants	
				Asia-Pacific Asie-Pacifique		Europe		North America Amérique du Nord			
↓ Exports from	Year	World 1/ Monde 1/	Total	Total	Japan Japon	Total	Germany Allemagne	Total	U.S.A. É.-U.	Total	Europe
					Total trade (SITC, Rev. 3, 0-9)						
World 1/	2000	6352822	4381437	405282	329102	2562449	476021	1413706	1162427	77194	65057
	2012	18307815	9717732	970262	710752	6103167	1092825	2644303	2113036	563806	457030
	2013	18822606	9849618	942773	693241	6244528	1124131	2662317	2121129	574091	457061
	2014	18829254	9947300	931739	681796	6267689	1146876	2747872	2215907	509708	397023
	2015	16696668	8751166	787480	559494	5400218	992806	2563468	2098688	340281	255548
Developed Economies -	2000	556339	283778	30765	14422	93424	21063	159589	150831	1004	824
Asia-Pacific 2/	2012	1092168	364316	88355	52281	108421	23072	167539	155029	15874	14309
	2013	1006696	328635	80526	47092	91811	21049	156298	146034	14226	12588
	2014	972298	321560	76593	45578	90725	20833	154242	144629	12123	10415
	2015	846984	291496	58940	31890	82723	17833	149833	140386	6817	5947
Japan	2000	479276	243818	9835	.	83786	19997	150197	142480	793	624
	2012	798620	259334	20385	.	86581	20796	152368	142085	14587	13203
	2013	715097	238107	19161	.	75694	18959	143252	134540	13036	11583
	2014	690217	230734	16545	.	75397	19055	138792	130773	11161	9622
	2015	625025	218324	14966	.	69154	16237	134204	126393	6106	5342
Developed Economies -	2000	2526900	2122788	63492	46070	1802309	345340	256988	232390	31182	28101
Europe 2/	2012	6075609	4529563	131635	80280	3935540	784496	462389	415736	224075	203627
	2013	6414413	4722857	130825	79674	4119430	819665	472603	423588	230801	207727
	2014	6380891	4771279	127111	78899	4146086	834936	498083	450355	195398	173666
	2015	5659352	4210289	115700	71766	3594291	707790	500297	454402	127899	110589
France	2000	295345	239365	6445	4983	204528	44461	28392	25937	2392	1952
	2012	558461	398133	13801	9507	346411	92317	37922	34123	14719	13361
	2013	567988	406238	13292	9026	353231	93525	39714	35765	13666	11799
	2014	566656	408722	13132	9056	355259	93804	40331	36382	12084	10293
	2015	573056	382928	12768	8592	317332	79574	52829	47959	10488	8637
Germany	2000	549607	458641	15684	12137	382583	.	60374	56393	8923	8069
	2012	1410130	1015963	35612	22237	856484	.	123866	112269	67004	61471
	2013	1450951	1045764	35759	22873	879257	.	130748	118864	65874	59901
	2014	1498158	1090773	34610	22778	916753	.	139409	127771	53090	47763
	2015	1331194	985479	29594	19004	817511	.	138375	126751	33749	30015
Developed Economies -	2000	1058097	699432	86744	71383	194041	31365	418647	241762	3505	2716
North America 2/	2012	1999759	1091379	117024	80323	342718	51773	631637	338266	17395	14578
	2013	2035018	1088477	106858	75539	334120	50053	647500	346045	18050	14770
	2014	2094325	1129693	109247	76532	343606	51716	676840	363524	17041	13409
	2015	1911947	1026638	100589	70098	332957	52324	593092	312166	10454	8650
United States	2000	780332	436300	79685	65252	179776	29242	176839	.	3325	2563
	2012	1544932	697842	104242	69972	300394	48372	293206	.	15329	12771
	2013	1577587	693458	94545	65214	297671	46863	301242	.	16210	13210
	2014	1619743	715439	97575	66826	304833	49028	313031	.	15533	12121
	2015	1503870	672423	91125	62470	300697	49617	280601	.	9661	8022
South-Eastern Europe	2000	19514	13492	50	37	12585	2634	857	764	813	674
	2012	107446	69938	405	314	67472	16854	2062	1761	6667	5617
	2013	122815	80861	451	359	78056	20172	2353	2072	8107	7070
	2014	126593	84885	449	334	82039	21296	2397	2107	7467	6446
	2015	111621	76527	452	329	73983	19718	2091	1921	4698	4004
Commonwealth of	2000	143026	80581	2953	2937	70362	11064	7266	5777	28980	24076
Independent States	2012	780388	417115	21839	21532	374885	30611	20391	16618	158395	118377
	2013	764752	418064	25794	25281	375029	28440	17240	13858	150028	106557
	2014	720731	394382	27805	27180	352840	31254	13737	11942	124807	86045
	2015	500361	227270	15599	15043	200547	19797	11125	9901	78446	50238
Russian Federation 4/	2000	103093	65496	2771	2764	57875	9232	4850	4648	13824	10807
	2012	524766	311421	19915	19799	278139	24039	13368	13022	85499	60058
	2013	527266	319303	24351	23948	283303	22962	11649	11177	82694	53358
	2014	497834	298000	26678	26128	261106	25071	10216	9611	66100	41063
	2015	343908	160929	14932	14426	137152	15906	8845	8393	38258	19900

For general note and footnotes see end of table

Les exportations de marchandises du monde par provenance et destination (Tableau D)

En millions de dollars E.-U. f.o.b.

← Exportations vers

South-Eastern Europe Europe du Sud-Est	Northern Africa Afrique septentrionale	Sub-Saharan Africa Afrique subsaharienne	Latin America and the Caribbean Amérique latine et Caraïbes	Eastern Asia Asie orientale	Southern Asia Asie méridionale	South-eastern Asia Asie du Sud-Est	Western Asia Asie occidentale	Oceania Océanie	Other 3/ Autres 3/	Année	Exportations en provenance de ↓
			Commerce total (CTCI, Rev. 3, 0-9)								
27386	53310	74884	362944	708919	81835	355905	188600	6997	33413	2000	Monde 1/
140365	221803	400714	1142902	3269769	577752	1190532	857406	31506	193531	2012	
144013	227083	421367	1124806	3495583	554667	1248869	931679	32323	218507	2013	
153324	229171	429268	1108684	3378686	582183	1264767	969889	33063	223211	2014	
132484	194940	376257	992916	2894385	508917	1139888	883598	32104	449732	2015	
153	1694	4909	22054	140231	6988	78409	13637	2260	1223	2000	Économies développées - Asie-Pacifique 2/
631	4358	13622	45255	408941	30358	159487	38983	7788	2555	2012	
546	3659	12465	37490	401064	23127	138235	37565	6139	3545	2013	
670	3881	11124	34842	375972	22751	135524	40364	6013	7474	2014	
556	3147	9149	30330	315890	22930	117875	36450	5606	6737	2015	
108	1196	3721	20779	124536	4751	68494	10619	460	0	2000	Japon
470	3013	9884	41088	293380	14536	129394	30310	2624	...	2012	
411	2418	8968	34412	265544	11749	110974	27839	1638	...	2013	
465	2319	8097	31727	256625	12158	104638	30346	1948	0	2014	
431	1935	6605	27241	225936	12720	95026	28316	2382	0	2015	
19337	29952	31466	57254	78361	22286	40575	83737	1259	8704	2000	Économies développées - Europe 2/
90436	92242	105313	164873	335238	101674	122321	265747	3367	40762	2012	
97751	98558	111042	166286	402563	93518	135297	305329	3788	46622	2013	
104269	99114	107618	157331	396954	88497	122386	291177	4215	42654	2014	
92117	86162	95002	148771	359687	83449	109503	277812	4007	64655	2015	
1282	9180	7741	7237	9366	2416	4752	10136	822	658	2000	France
5392	20927	15593	16084	34443	6210	18081	25935	1617	1325	2012	
5975	20739	16237	17563	33997	5160	19032	26597	2077	706	2013	
6199	20113	16373	15468	36237	5427	17704	25903	1779	646	2014	
5361	21966	19714	22837	36152	7166	16678	35179	2305	12282	2015	
4185	4001	5607	13858	21330	4087	9799	17506	132	1537	2000	Allemagne
19396	10722	17808	42462	118655	19161	29397	63942	452	5168	2012	
20644	11179	18360	43204	124265	17064	29456	69800	361	4982	2013	
23412	12171	18116	41175	137348	17483	29891	69086	916	4697	2014	
21872	10657	16451	36982	114537	15765	25661	66332	796	2913	2015	
562	5659	6351	174585	88893	5619	48919	23871	393	307	2000	Économies développées - Amérique du Nord 2/
1687	11728	24840	411302	242708	29856	80395	87133	1149	187	2012	
1638	12736	26408	421401	261421	30042	84248	89619	769	207	2013	
1893	13903	28331	435408	262999	29873	83922	90438	802	22	2014	
1476	10176	20186	399303	246588	30520	80091	85673	812	29	2015	
509	5028	5928	170376	83248	4635	47368	22928	378	307	2000	Etats-Unis
1333	10196	22523	397316	215595	26210	75394	81963	1055	175	2012	
1400	11243	23993	408200	231836	26259	78930	85191	689	180	2013	
1637	12555	25497	422568	236263	25630	78554	85345	721	0	2014	
1290	9011	17844	387749	223363	25544	75041	81257	687	...	2015	
2212	358	156	160	218	139	76	1700	1	188	2000	Europe du Sud-Est
13023	2270	1207	839	2451	890	391	9255	87	425	2012	
13256	3103	1182	1319	2795	866	921	10081	46	277	2013	
13475	3392	1076	1126	2489	896	1244	10075	15	454	2014	
12067	2899	839	825	2281	823	817	8439	308	1096	2015	
2633	1375	555	5983	9128	2991	1714	9063	4	19	2000	Communauté d'Etats Indépendants
17616	12960	3235	9923	83752	19501	11817	44591	100	1385	2012	
12896	9967	3301	10258	86356	16431	15427	40918	19	1089	2013	
12834	11303	3427	8412	87143	13864	16396	47074	17	1074	2014	
8122	8787	2897	6195	64361	11535	8126	30529	37	54056	2015	
1822	746	344	4307	6980	1896	1120	6556	2	0	2000	Fédération de Russie 4/
11230	8053	1611	6987	57350	11039	7306	23997	90	184	2012	
7804	5559	1664	8216	60125	9571	8491	23771	16	50	2013	
7082	6464	2019	6690	63718	6644	11864	29200	13	39	2014	
4084	5450	1904	4904	46130	6399	5352	17365	34	53097	2015	

Voir la fin du tableau pour la remarque générale et les notes.

World merchandise exports by provenance and destination (Table D)

In million U.S. dollars f.o.b.

Exports from ↓ / Exports to →	Year	World 1/ Monde 1/	Developed economies 2/ Économies développées 2/ — Total	Asia-Pacific Asie-Pacifique — Total	Asia-Pacific — Japan Japon	Europe — Total	Europe — Germany Allemagne	North America Amérique du Nord — Total	North America — U.S.A. É.-U.	Commonwealth of Independent States Communauté d'Etats Indépendants — Total	CIS — Europe
			Total trade (SITC, Rev. 3, 0-9) ***[cont.]***								
Northern Africa	2000	50201	41077	490	424	35543	3933	5043	4216	101	81
	2012	198662	142341	3734	2402	116691	10010	21916	16590	816	659
	2013	177790	127695	3196	2258	110187	9182	14311	10543	847	697
	2014	151606	105213	2122	1953	93377	5481	9714	7456	794	745
	2015	104246	68833	1277	1110	60769	3794	6788	5245	724	670
Sub-Saharan Africa	2000	94707	59346	2659	2086	34051	3102	22637	21663	238	190
	2012	458786	206535	18486	12876	130074	9189	57975	51569	1066	881
	2013	410516	173550	17212	12172	119248	8887	37090	32346	1187	1034
	2014	411472	165378	17184	12464	120373	8400	27821	24634	1072	937
	2015	355428	146536	13716	9566	111098	8464	21722	19479	949	800
South Africa	2000	26298	15863	1874	1362	10979	1902	3011	2790	79	33
	2012	98872	35544	6718	5734	20476	4067	8350	7833	508	460
	2013	95112	33845	6525	5611	20064	3841	7256	6888	526	460
	2014	90612	34364	5826	4869	21276	4234	7263	6550	499	461
	2015	69631	26128	4313	3644	16145	4237	5670	5248	391	350
Latin America and the Caribbean	2000	353079	266101	8563	7720	43769	6931	213769	207456	1330	1280
	2012	1097380	623871	29013	24846	143499	19646	451359	407217	8947	8264
	2013	1095015	627442	27406	23527	135852	17513	464185	410447	9253	8307
	2014	1077103	632517	25205	21178	129136	17162	478177	426299	9946	9044
	2015	953056	574786	20312	16876	112599	14531	441875	393988	7137	6442
Brazil	2000	55119	33697	2853	2481	16230	2520	14614	14048	522	487
	2012	242580	93136	8555	7990	52776	7503	31806	28723	4283	3851
	2013	242178	88583	8496	7973	50893	6822	29194	26487	4119	3504
	2014	225098	83960	7230	6741	45003	6937	31728	29375	4538	4106
	2015	191127	68402	5309	4845	36512	5172	26580	24216	2831	2563
Eastern Asia	2000	776206	410964	101774	90096	125359	27229	183831	173168	4995	3848
	2012	3396494	1280549	290196	227960	462088	92423	528266	487973	96059	69061
	2013	3613890	1296680	283874	221402	464466	90393	548340	506633	104292	74913
	2014	3761025	1374589	283683	218679	501588	95806	589318	546795	104595	74652
	2015	3594184	1337458	265010	200013	478181	91030	594268	553052	74490	51874
China	2000	249203	142806	45499	41654	41976	9278	55331	52156	3183	2411
	2012	2048782	911389	193226	151627	337391	69213	380772	352438	75653	52425
	2013	2209007	931031	191818	150133	340740	67343	398473	369064	83517	58425
	2014	2342343	992282	193296	149410	371686	72703	427300	397105	85740	60007
	2015	2281856	979974	181198	135897	358170	69217	440607	410805	58058	39174
Southern Asia	2000	91623	55028	8441	7705	29131	3854	17456	16377	1848	1204
	2012	446154	155486	11481	7792	91789	12846	52216	48741	5731	3804
	2013	482859	170887	12304	8722	99497	14360	59085	55233	5986	4081
	2014	465586	152569	18594	14897	78250	13024	55724	52451	6109	4258
	2015	432165	154481	18198	13503	79813	14306	56469	52819	5624	3671
South-Eastern Asia	2000	426829	219020	69565	58132	65516	12052	83939	80928	606	556
	2012	1254006	430613	179815	128377	134565	24483	116233	109321	7014	6369
	2013	1272620	427990	173883	123499	130777	25874	123330	115707	7683	6827
	2014	1294771	442907	172315	120418	138716	26760	131876	124089	7460	6372
	2015	1162634	409985	148560	105529	131817	26420	129608	122350	6508	5428
Western Asia	2000	251304	126781	27996	27198	55353	7270	43432	26846	2577	1496
	2012	1391554	401106	75228	70900	193900	17100	131979	63886	21759	11479
	2013	1415502	380688	76781	72742	184290	18121	119617	58265	23622	12482
	2014	1358534	364342	66295	62257	188580	19579	109468	61156	22881	11022
	2015	1051788	220412	24158	21133	140270	16528	55983	32668	16529	7228
Oceania	2000	4996	3047	1789	892	1006	185	252	249	14	10
	2012	9411	4919	3052	869	1525	322	342	329	8	6
	2013	10720	5793	3663	973	1766	424	364	359	10	8
	2014	14319	7986	5138	1426	2373	629	475	466	15	12
	2015	12902	6456	4969	2638	1170	272	317	309	5	5

For general note and footnotes see end of table

Les exportations de marchandises du monde par provenance et destination (Tableau D)

En millions de dollars E.-U. f.o.b.

South-Eastern Europe Europe du Sud-Est	Northern Africa Afrique septentrionale	Sub-Saharan Africa Afrique subsaharienne	Latin America and the Caribbean Amérique latine et Caraïbes	Eastern Asia Asie orientale	Southern Asia Asie méridionale	South-eastern Asia Asie du Sud-Est	Western Asia Asie occidentale	Oceania Océanie	Other 3/ Autres 3/	Année	← Exportations vers / Exportations en provenance de ↓
			Commerce total (CTCI, Rev. 3, 0-9) ***[suite]***								
92	1179	336	2058	315	793	277	3122	1	849	2000	Afrique septentrionale
435	8031	4079	6315	11981	6613	2701	13164	4	2182	2012	
651	8832	3911	5323	7422	5571	2091	13503	3	1942	2013	
680	8173	3951	4943	5774	4355	2241	13559	4	1918	2014	
615	5582	3816	3380	4052	2894	1642	11153	3	1552	2015	
66	417	12384	2549	9498	5265	1960	2134	40	809	2000	Afrique subsaharienne
655	2871	83000	20550	79527	35656	11022	14391	544	2968	2012	
482	1372	84060	13834	75283	29020	11637	17015	731	2347	2013	
529	1271	80947	14873	73362	33371	15531	20897	536	3705	2014	
560	2844	72039	13313	47650	31298	13186	18432	628	7994	2015	
30	91	4123	576	2662	531	739	1013	6	587	2000	Afrique du sud
93	558	27071	2052	17451	7118	3997	3552	58	871	2012	
84	535	26829	1700	18905	4981	3548	3628	32	500	2013	
68	401	27209	1370	14383	4898	2792	4024	48	556	2014	
38	591	21149	1046	8740	3670	1840	2439	44	3553	2015	
324	1359	1674	61584	8835	2276	2799	2808	17	3972	2000	Amérique latine et Caraïbes
2058	10110	12088	232867	139263	19524	26901	20217	52	1483	2012	
2155	9871	9747	217428	151669	19136	24353	19976	41	3944	2013	
1971	9806	9022	200699	141693	20546	26290	19756	45	4812	2014	
1652	7762	7698	162354	121571	16902	20206	17188	60	15740	2015	
129	506	888	13886	2603	621	926	1338	4	...	2000	Brésil
817	5553	7041	51001	50333	8797	10573	11019	25	4	2012	
766	5020	6488	54642	56920	6079	9216	10318	19	9	2013	
637	4830	5329	47148	49457	7443	11455	10282	17	0	2014	
470	3995	4204	39145	42417	6866	10710	9636	26	2427	2015	
688	3066	8359	25181	220125	13063	68296	18700	1258	1511	2000	Asie orientale
6060	27012	78186	183955	1082672	121929	371270	136350	8710	3741	2012	
6244	27541	86818	182688	1198807	127288	419757	147808	11886	4081	2013	
7369	31412	96253	184599	1177417	151601	451805	164704	12898	3785	2014	
6919	32244	97133	177757	1094988	149628	447047	159194	14509	2815	2015	
356	1410	3602	7125	62121	4510	17341	6683	65	2	2000	Chine
4890	20558	64612	134484	456791	82048	204337	90746	3275	...	2012	
4937	21765	70897	133232	525547	89284	244087	101780	2929	...	2013	
5722	24223	81627	135094	519029	110175	272116	113647	2688	...	2014	
5360	25608	82910	131495	489955	112164	279021	111964	5281	65	2015	
48	2664	2171	1903	13210	3396	3785	7528	32	8	2000	Asie méridionale
622	8332	24594	16396	88398	27008	36395	75076	165	7952	2012	
737	8250	31310	16979	85281	32282	41302	77613	164	12067	2013	
1017	5519	31794	16707	81755	47671	33387	86239	146	2674	2014	
810	4345	23733	12403	78992	43797	28710	76752	241	2277	2015	
156	1009	4130	6783	75960	11331	97875	8579	996	386	2000	Asie du Sud-est
760	5884	25124	36007	314313	60992	325303	38302	7720	1974	2012	
809	6004	25629	36946	324905	61160	330360	41987	7345	1802	2013	
901	6123	26423	35085	330947	62479	328529	44214	7362	2341	2014	
887	5239	22205	29887	299038	55267	285720	39782	5043	3071	2015	
1113	4579	2355	2574	63644	7672	10937	13718	654	14700	2000	Asie occidentale
6381	36002	25358	14479	479267	123511	41828	114192	1413	126258	2012	
6846	37188	25404	14690	496616	115916	44399	130256	977	138900	2013	
7715	35275	29214	14416	440058	105848	46311	141372	510	150593	2014	
6702	25750	21501	8377	255983	59676	26154	122181	503	288022	2015	
2	0	37	277	502	15	286	2	80	736	2000	Océanie
1	3	69	142	1257	239	701	6	405	1660	2012	
1	2	90	164	1401	310	843	9	413	1684	2013	
2	2	88	246	2123	430	1200	20	501	1707	2014	
0	1	59	21	3304	199	811	14	346	1687	2015	

Voir la fin du tableau pour la remarque générale et les notes.

World merchandise exports by provenance and destination (Table D)

In million U.S. dollars f.o.b.

Exports to ⟶ / ↓ Exports from	Year	World 1/ Monde 1/	Developed economies 2/ Économies développées 2/ Total	Asia-Pacific Asie-Pacifique Total	Japan Japon	Europe Total	Germany Allemagne	North America Amérique du Nord Total	U.S.A. É.-U.	Commonwealth of Independent States Communauté d'Etats Indépendants Total	Europe
					Food, beverages and tobacco (SITC, Rev. 3, 0 and 1)						
World 1/	2000	386930	271500	40652	36978	175516	32547	55332	43857	9839	8637
	2012	1179838	681886	75117	60268	472505	80540	134265	101356	54877	44549
	2013	1259959	726138	73236	57145	511790	86994	141112	106939	59091	47631
	2014	1299261	746891	74329	56800	520728	89239	151833	116274	54346	42345
	2015	1173487	674175	66353	50632	458296	77708	149526	115313	37661	28295
Developed Economies - Asia-Pacific 2/	2000	19827	9707	4295	3298	2445	277	2967	2615	52	44
	2012	52653	18479	8972	5281	3981	473	5526	4821	697	558
	2013	54669	17947	8455	4667	4121	505	5371	4695	744	613
	2014	58666	20123	8439	4580	4315	458	7369	6572	552	413
	2015	53232	18936	7286	3958	4012	436	7638	6794	254	173
Japan	2000	2088	612	72	.	107	14	432	395	9	9
	2012	4432	1035	106	.	186	35	744	695	31	31
	2013	4447	1025	104	.	199	42	722	671	37	36
	2014	4530	1097	106	.	218	32	773	715	45	41
	2015	4934	1146	116	.	244	37	786	728	30	26
Developed Economies - Europe 2/	2000	178437	151894	5172	4319	136289	26443	10433	8969	3784	3519
	2012	491511	398498	10286	6965	365640	65056	22572	18754	19192	17954
	2013	537335	435478	10766	7116	400623	71667	24090	20069	21056	19673
	2014	545670	441530	11563	7664	404615	71871	25352	21295	16855	15311
	2015	476520	386131	9967	6396	351204	62007	24961	21204	9566	8378
France	2000	31410	26548	981	902	23387	4572	2180	1853	351	335
	2012	66853	50771	1752	1423	44928	7288	4091	3318	1056	971
	2013	71698	54041	1798	1404	47933	7682	4310	3498	1128	1031
	2014	69131	52259	1813	1403	46031	7417	4415	3668	926	813
	2015	61725	45587	1629	1228	39417	6309	4542	3859	515	431
Germany	2000	21712	18446	290	250	17384	.	772	696	643	595
	2012	74353	62122	946	555	58947	.	2229	1882	3119	2815
	2013	80143	67110	903	515	63885	.	2323	1955	2915	2630
	2014	81732	68275	1122	699	64839	.	2314	1967	2226	1949
	2015	68766	56482	816	434	53651	.	2015	1718	1470	1250
Developed Economies - North America 2/	2000	63461	38882	13374	12837	6728	914	18779	10626	987	887
	2012	142075	71830	17539	15493	11106	1430	43185	20389	2898	2517
	2013	151832	75222	16218	14122	12885	1715	46120	22061	2237	1888
	2014	160276	79744	17281	14985	14196	1837	48267	23483	1582	1305
	2015	147627	74866	14917	12815	13231	1705	46718	22812	504	323
United States	2000	47084	25762	11994	11534	5619	835	8149	.	955	858
	2012	106959	46582	14966	13184	8925	1296	22691	.	2149	1816
	2013	114236	48372	13812	11962	10651	1590	23909	.	1697	1410
	2014	119839	50588	14848	12800	11169	1683	24571	.	1096	862
	2015	109146	47301	12870	11005	10798	1575	23633	.	425	270
South-Eastern Europe	2000	1232	651	17	12	588	125	45	39	75	57
	2012	10843	5568	89	66	5343	595	136	113	470	443
	2013	12941	6190	69	44	5944	639	177	147	575	532
	2014	13237	6362	71	40	6117	661	174	143	779	718
	2015	11938	5812	112	76	5510	565	189	160	579	539
Commonwealth of Independent States	2000	3263	709	150	145	524	90	35	32	2117	1721
	2012	36896	5696	501	486	5064	360	131	113	15933	9494
	2013	37067	5642	575	547	4928	447	139	120	17976	10799
	2014	39784	6259	349	324	5762	543	149	131	17209	9623
	2015	31204	4874	350	344	4388	403	136	119	13043	7170
Russian Federation 4/	2000	1016	394	140	137	231	34	23	21	379	91
	2012	14132	1872	268	265	1550	141	54	45	4053	1353
	2013	13709	1774	224	218	1485	138	65	52	4732	1656
	2014	16338	2265	251	246	1957	167	57	49	4983	1593
	2015	13891	1899	291	287	1557	98	51	42	4026	1258

For general note and footnotes see end of table

Les exportations de marchandises du monde par provenance et destination (Tableau D)

En millions de dollars E.-U. f.o.b.

← Exportations vers

South-Eastern Europe / Europe du Sud-Est	Northern Africa / Afrique septentrionale	Sub-Saharan Africa / Afrique subsaharienne	Latin America and the Caribbean / Amérique latine et Caraïbes	Eastern Asia / Asie orientale	Southern Asia / Asie méridionale	South-eastern Asia / Asie du Sud-Est	Western Asia / Asie occidentale	Oceania / Océanie	Other 3/ / Autres 3/	Année	Exportations en provenance de ↓
Produits alimentaires, boisson et tabac (CTCI, Rev. 3, 0 et 1)											
2494	7285	8336	22176	23739	5234	16062	17736	783	1746	2000	Monde 1/
13187	29798	46694	73876	97292	26505	75830	73076	2611	4206	2012	
13988	29148	49114	74883	108664	28421	83508	79642	2571	4790	2013	
14493	31781	48163	76849	116173	30102	90015	83749	2637	4064	2014	
13259	25637	41658	67924	112920	28939	85729	77584	2292	5707	2015	
5	396	398	490	3385	864	3024	963	445	98	2000	Économies développées - Asie-Pacifique 2/
7	1158	1253	1111	12433	2083	9444	4160	1210	619	2012	
6	990	1504	1080	14981	1551	9379	4513	1170	804	2013	
6	1357	1311	882	16191	1645	10552	4810	1135	100	2014	
6	1086	956	928	14643	1908	9049	3400	838	1228	2015	
0	0	18	23	1135	6	205	26	56	0	2000	Japon
0	7	56	23	2360	20	787	72	41	...	2012	
0	31	45	24	2338	14	825	76	33	...	2013	
1	27	44	16	2367	15	797	88	33	...	2014	
1	35	52	15	2696	13	817	98	29	...	2015	
1688	2963	3064	3113	2851	484	2053	5467	136	941	2000	Économies développées - Europe 2/
8216	8054	11034	6553	13391	2181	7011	16310	368	704	2012	
9182	8850	12142	7034	14822	1923	7786	17775	390	897	2013	
9468	10197	12396	7352	17708	2588	8202	18113	409	851	2014	
8604	8385	10499	6748	17544	1854	7510	18020	349	1309	2015	
79	984	883	429	542	106	406	968	112	2	2000	France
391	3122	2648	774	3311	209	1880	2374	279	38	2012	
389	3537	2921	896	3458	156	2038	2794	296	43	2013	
394	3699	2764	749	3425	167	2086	2309	312	39	2014	
324	2773	2361	746	3996	287	2046	2222	261	606	2015	
193	367	112	203	255	126	188	974	1	204	2000	Allemagne
1272	652	739	388	1662	611	725	2927	3	133	2012	
1455	737	942	463	1770	477	801	3280	4	189	2013	
1554	848	888	531	2239	939	917	3108	4	204	2014	
1350	892	1067	523	2276	452	747	3331	4	173	2015	
73	1936	802	9306	5481	818	2248	2777	78	74	2000	Économies développées - Amérique du Nord 2/
162	2370	3061	27646	19580	2225	7121	5020	161	1	2012	
166	2733	3201	29848	21841	2618	8187	5598	166	17	2013	
136	2664	2998	32520	22726	2896	8822	5994	178	16	2014	
117	1898	2294	28946	22023	3540	7878	5347	192	22	2015	
71	1499	658	8266	4943	268	1952	2558	77	74	2000	États-Unis
144	1590	2455	25220	17334	1083	6189	4065	149	...	2012	
133	1982	2438	27075	19384	1215	7052	4725	155	7	2013	
116	1882	2158	29562	20347	1282	7818	4826	164	...	2014	
99	1153	1626	26417	19436	1512	6654	4344	178	...	2015	
284	44	6	3	4	34	5	114	1	13	2000	Europe du Sud-Est
2874	455	58	18	129	115	34	1100	0	23	2012	
2662	1176	66	16	360	109	100	1671	0	16	2013	
2811	1137	123	22	228	70	137	1544	0	24	2014	
2545	760	115	23	211	166	117	1588	0	21	2015	
27	17	15	7	160	30	2	163	...	14	2000	Communauté d'Etats Indépendants
217	4241	695	142	2646	1592	115	5521	0	97	2012	
209	2456	1018	234	3001	1466	422	4551	0	93	2013	
233	3219	1398	238	3369	1945	377	5424	3	112	2014	
210	2395	1068	112	3207	1558	297	4351	2	88	2015	
6	6	0	1	155	7	1	67	...	0	2000	Fédération de Russie 4/
127	1920	327	105	2212	631	26	2840	0	18	2012	
105	877	621	197	2514	472	141	2262	0	14	2013	
110	1401	1060	195	2415	677	94	3127	0	11	2014	
96	1106	830	83	2475	739	84	2545	0	8	2015	

Voir la fin du tableau pour la remarque générale et les notes.

World merchandise exports by provenance and destination (Table D)

In million U.S. dollars f.o.b.

Exports to → / ↓ Exports from	Year	World 1/ Monde 1/	Developed economies 2/ Économies développées 2/: Total	Asia-Pacific Asie-Pacifique: Total	Asia-Pacific Asie-Pacifique: Japan Japon	Europe: Total	Europe: Germany Allemagne	North America Amérique du Nord: Total	North America Amérique du Nord: U.S.A. É.-U.	Commonwealth of Independent States Communauté d'Etats Indépendants: Total	Commonwealth of Independent States Communauté d'Etats Indépendants: Europe
					Food, beverages and tobacco (SITC, Rev. 3, 0 and 1) *[cont.]*						
Northern Africa	2000	2277	1661	281	279	1299	71	81	58	63	63
	2012	8542	3821	158	149	3437	254	225	174	487	476
	2013	9723	4258	174	162	3813	214	271	209	584	574
	2014	9892	4374	188	178	3936	272	250	199	570	559
	2015	9476	4161	179	169	3724	253	258	205	529	520
Sub-Saharan Africa	2000	10612	6482	527	454	5341	620	613	538	113	112
	2012	40243	18103	951	780	14278	1303	2875	2604	501	421
	2013	37820	16504	992	785	13808	1193	1704	1423	517	449
	2014	39374	16568	849	676	13656	1294	2063	1759	518	445
	2015	37171	15552	663	500	12899	1279	1989	1702	499	423
South Africa	2000	2168	1261	176	144	923	69	161	110	8	7
	2012	8293	2701	274	169	2086	216	341	214	182	176
	2013	9003	3247	482	349	2412	248	353	216	209	205
	2014	9172	3082	314	208	2392	232	376	236	190	184
	2015	7718	2720	172	85	2213	251	334	201	189	178
Latin America and the Caribbean	2000	46823	31100	2604	2313	13571	2246	14925	14245	1095	1082
	2012	169745	82071	7734	6786	37108	5874	37229	34642	6919	6519
	2013	175180	84998	8008	7008	37206	5177	39784	37440	6871	6350
	2014	175767	86824	7041	5844	37521	6175	42261	39714	7525	6976
	2015	161553	82848	6463	5331	33823	5242	42562	40140	5243	4825
Brazil	2000	10142	6609	710	514	4599	667	1300	1179	471	460
	2012	57354	21630	2886	2748	14964	2486	3780	3044	3537	3246
	2013	57396	21110	2822	2693	14609	2106	3679	3036	3402	3038
	2014	53971	19611	2265	2121	13724	2701	3622	3019	3789	3436
	2015	48285	17454	2137	1990	11702	2171	3614	3102	2278	2049
Eastern Asia	2000	21064	11180	7893	7699	1446	308	1841	1605	297	254
	2012	71870	29943	15052	13750	6329	1468	8562	7454	2786	2298
	2013	75457	29137	13895	12564	6743	1458	8499	7441	2977	2435
	2014	80817	29810	13923	12494	7009	1551	8878	7742	3160	2571
	2015	80396	28464	12905	11558	6864	1523	8695	7643	2544	1990
China	2000	13027	7217	4960	4877	1214	296	1044	910	189	162
	2012	54667	25005	11801	10847	5938	1416	7267	6357	2449	2011
	2013	58335	24830	11208	10172	6351	1423	7272	6393	2657	2171
	2014	61797	25090	11097	10030	6562	1504	7431	6515	2828	2287
	2015	61527	24050	10268	9259	6443	1481	7339	6481	2260	1752
Southern Asia	2000	8344	3486	828	754	1715	288	944	857	581	432
	2012	39148	8189	1247	950	4694	542	2247	1983	1592	1099
	2013	46695	9715	1311	1000	5446	615	2958	2619	1661	1131
	2014	44579	10089	1125	784	5674	732	3289	2910	1690	1258
	2015	40337	9806	1084	760	5390	746	3332	2954	1667	1278
South-Eastern Asia	2000	23691	12540	5244	4705	3056	465	4240	3874	168	159
	2012	82778	31577	11919	9200	9351	1701	10307	9248	1120	989
	2013	83728	32467	12114	8791	9654	1721	10699	9608	1182	1058
	2014	91088	35352	12683	8800	10487	1957	12181	10962	1169	1050
	2015	87070	33424	11787	8396	10108	1843	11529	10351	1037	947
Western Asia	2000	7421	2826	153	106	2317	625	356	327	508	307
	2012	32149	7250	410	228	5787	1315	1052	854	2275	1777
	2013	36098	7681	418	227	6185	1423	1077	889	2701	2122
	2014	38162	8601	488	263	6821	1560	1291	1060	2721	2103
	2015	35897	8704	476	244	6893	1628	1335	1052	2192	1725
Oceania	2000	478	383	114	58	197	76	73	72	0	0
	2012	1388	862	258	135	386	169	217	206	7	6
	2013	1412	898	241	111	434	222	222	219	10	8
	2014	1950	1256	328	167	618	329	310	304	14	11
	2015	1068	597	164	84	249	81	184	179	5	5

For general note and footnotes see end of table

Les exportations de marchandises du monde par provenance et destination (Tableau D)

En millions de dollars E.-U. f.o.b.

South-Eastern Europe Europe du Sud-Est	Northern Africa Afrique septentrionale	Sub-Saharan Africa Afrique subsaharienne	Latin America and the Caribbean Amérique latine et Caraïbes	Eastern Asia Asie orientale	Southern Asia Asie méridionale	South-eastern Asia Asie du Sud-Est	Western Asia Asie occidentale	Oceania Océanie	Other 3/ Autres 3/	Année	← Exportations vers / Exportations en provence de ↓
			Produits alimentaires, boisson et tabac (CTCI, Rev. 3, 0 et 1) *[suite]*								
10	169	84	5	11	2	10	238	1	24	2000	Afrique septentrionale
36	892	904	56	51	94	106	2008	1	86	2012	
50	1014	1048	56	77	82	116	2326	2	110	2013	
58	1072	1014	43	89	109	128	2319	2	115	2014	
47	763	1036	45	89	80	111	2458	2	155	2015	
23	203	2073	82	236	458	190	714	6	32	2000	Afrique subsaharienne
142	619	11446	2158	933	2146	1720	2395	11	68	2012	
148	579	12196	349	1029	1908	1563	2949	18	60	2013	
262	615	11972	340	1356	2749	1978	2937	9	69	2014	
312	585	10689	281	1134	3308	1904	2852	7	48	2015	
4	8	536	11	103	65	36	130	0	7	2000	Afrique du sud
3	27	3866	357	392	63	236	442	7	16	2012	
2	24	4078	137	479	56	280	476	5	11	2013	
8	29	4096	53	698	85	352	553	5	21	2014	
7	41	3321	30	476	63	333	526	5	8	2015	
167	810	562	8676	1541	396	736	1499	11	229	2000	Amérique latine et Caraïbes
729	7681	5846	32581	12128	3847	7883	9740	23	296	2012	
735	7010	4773	32327	14308	3477	9367	10836	20	458	2013	
672	7112	3986	31327	13523	4035	10343	9977	25	418	2014	
663	5770	3502	26900	13244	3798	10067	9005	24	489	2015	
85	185	264	1061	372	139	250	705	0	...	2000	Brésil
419	4421	3547	5564	5803	3180	3131	6110	8	4	2012	
436	3603	3180	5851	6935	2751	3667	6455	7	0	2013	
376	3268	2629	5885	5608	2892	4200	5706	6	...	2014	
280	2994	2141	4991	5422	3024	4339	5354	7	...	2015	
26	145	346	185	6265	195	2052	310	34	28	2000	Asie orientale
102	634	1826	1922	18154	1108	13276	1825	281	13	2012	
97	687	2083	2192	19507	1046	15642	1820	256	11	2013	
94	671	2189	2039	22272	1203	17085	2029	256	9	2014	
83	674	2056	1968	22386	1411	18534	1982	285	8	2015	
26	142	295	145	3365	152	1242	247	5	...	2000	Chine
97	571	1653	1775	11645	907	9113	1350	101	...	2012	
93	645	1880	2076	12956	954	10712	1428	104	...	2013	
87	623	1984	1849	14650	1074	11971	1506	134	...	2014	
77	630	1851	1785	14695	1289	13259	1481	149	0	2015	
11	216	182	102	413	819	622	1907	2	1	2000	Asie méridionale
60	1026	4184	325	1984	6194	6215	9355	9	15	2012	
66	1078	4466	340	1946	8853	8095	10431	13	31	2013	
55	1167	3817	384	2172	7411	7627	10098	12	55	2014	
80	903	3470	341	2298	5804	6315	9609	10	32	2015	
36	127	650	150	3275	655	4999	975	46	70	2000	Asie du Sud-est
133	1164	4315	1159	13804	2485	21861	3760	369	1030	2012	
156	1023	4171	1181	14506	2515	21726	3721	377	703	2013	
136	1102	4602	1419	16007	2507	23391	3716	457	1231	2014	
141	986	3634	1378	15669	2736	22836	3435	474	1319	2015	
143	258	146	58	96	479	86	2609	0	213	2000	Asie occidentale
509	1504	2071	202	1981	2433	800	11881	5	1239	2012	
510	1552	2444	225	2213	2868	869	13450	5	1581	2013	
560	1465	2353	281	402	2939	990	16786	7	1056	2014	
450	1430	2338	253	389	2775	851	15533	5	975	2015	
0	...	7	0	21	0	33	0	22	10	2000	Océanie
1	0	2	4	77	3	243	1	171	16	2012	
1	0	2	2	75	3	257	1	153	10	2013	
2	1	3	2	130	5	382	2	145	8	2014	
0	0	1	1	81	2	260	4	104	14	2015	

Voir la fin du tableau pour la remarque générale et les notes.

World merchandise exports by provenance and destination (Table D)

In million U.S. dollars f.o.b.

Exports to ⟶ / ↓ Exports from	Year	World 1/ Monde 1/	Developed economies 2/ Économies développées 2/ Total	Asia-Pacific Asie-Pacifique Total	Asia-Pacific Japan Japon	Europe Total	Europe Germany Allemagne	North America Amérique du Nord Total	North America U.S.A. É.-U.	Commonwealth of Independent States Communauté d'Etats Indépendants Total	CIS Europe
		Crude materials (excluding fuels), oils, fats (SITC, Rev. 3, 2 and 4)									
World 1/	2000	213012	135143	21294	19748	83978	15235	29871	23136	3273	2922
	2012	843117	341419	54570	50735	229640	44130	57209	43701	16871	13513
	2013	840410	331870	53247	49783	224501	43301	54122	41383	17144	13993
	2014	803973	325576	50657	46824	219082	40480	55837	42621	15703	12262
	2015	659652	265885	37775	34443	180660	33632	47450	35920	11474	8847
Developed Economies - Asia-Pacific 2/	2000	17277	6994	3049	2577	2422	328	1523	1155	175	174
	2012	105350	19828	13304	12646	4429	1004	2095	1420	587	569
	2013	114849	18065	12596	11980	3656	775	1812	1377	415	387
	2014	104439	15931	11026	10376	3308	755	1597	1348	381	369
	2015	73912	10775	6793	6362	2677	563	1305	1044	129	117
Japan	2000	3369	747	30	.	437	96	280	268	5	4
	2012	13453	1950	35	.	1050	308	865	847	87	80
	2013	12528	1635	34	.	898	238	703	686	76	67
	2014	11444	1521	29	.	731	220	761	739	84	73
	2015	9555	1331	25	.	640	170	667	636	106	95
Developed Economies - Europe 2/	2000	61182	51586	1529	1332	47688	9926	2369	2050	811	783
	2012	186578	139367	2373	1918	132203	28791	4791	4067	4052	3811
	2013	186642	139949	2623	2140	132138	29319	5188	4316	4162	3888
	2014	182492	139082	2450	1911	130920	27927	5712	4683	3287	2987
	2015	150143	114023	2142	1688	106748	22693	5132	4187	2353	2118
France	2000	6036	5195	62	54	4960	957	173	159	43	39
	2012	15292	12518	92	70	12037	2681	390	353	221	212
	2013	14614	11859	84	64	11420	2313	355	324	271	257
	2014	14339	11768	96	71	11299	2128	373	335	171	161
	2015	12248	9838	132	93	9232	1857	475	449	123	115
Germany	2000	9272	7481	98	75	7114	.	269	236	175	169
	2012	29907	23874	178	116	22681	.	1014	922	755	717
	2013	28377	22684	208	150	21456	.	1020	941	638	608
	2014	28058	22873	189	132	21635	.	1049	957	491	447
	2015	22324	18392	160	110	17341	.	891	812	333	294
Developed Economies - North America 2/	2000	53044	35072	6996	6675	10362	1672	17714	12780	61	49
	2012	140939	49309	8792	8240	18013	3410	22504	14153	416	329
	2013	134151	49107	9086	8567	17418	3000	22603	14769	568	512
	2014	134365	51537	9027	8453	18094	2617	24415	16059	507	466
	2015	114288	44832	7608	7112	16410	2594	20815	13740	378	369
United States	2000	30471	15489	4053	3903	6505	965	4931	.	55	43
	2012	96250	23572	4093	3773	11129	2593	8350	.	388	303
	2013	90192	23164	4293	3992	11040	2340	7831	.	547	493
	2014	90214	24484	4611	4272	11519	2042	8354	.	477	437
	2015	76335	21669	3953	3664	10646	2020	7070	.	368	359
South-Eastern Europe	2000	1742	850	9	8	826	121	15	5	105	105
	2012	7939	3754	183	182	3463	415	109	21	74	71
	2013	8901	4558	227	227	4235	520	97	30	66	62
	2014	7923	4072	159	156	3857	678	56	40	75	70
	2015	6269	3439	94	89	3284	643	61	56	61	58
Commonwealth of Independent States	2000	9234	4892	597	597	4206	457	88	79	1628	1361
	2012	40434	11407	451	433	10771	685	186	180	7840	5234
	2013	38353	11390	658	642	10520	736	212	196	7744	5398
	2014	37260	10598	654	645	9683	746	261	209	7423	4886
	2015	28140	7691	527	523	6974	575	190	158	4980	3176
Russian Federation 4/	2000	4752	2850	588	587	2214	173	48	40	338	229
	2012	18783	6072	404	404	5512	405	156	151	2858	1052
	2013	18172	6158	552	551	5411	348	194	180	2973	1208
	2014	17990	5562	555	551	4788	352	220	170	2999	1164
	2015	13916	3964	451	450	3346	291	166	136	2062	752

For general note and footnotes see end of table

Les exportations de marchandises du monde par provenance et destination (Tableau D)

En millions de dollars E.-U. f.o.b.

← Exportations vers

South-Eastern Europe Europe du Sud-Est	Northern Africa Afrique septentrionale	Sub-Saharan Africa Afrique subsaharienne	Latin America and the Caribbean Amérique latine et Caraïbes	Eastern Asia Asie orientale	Southern Asia Asie méridionale	South-eastern Asia Asie du Sud-Est	Western Asia Asie occidentale	Oceania Océanie	Other 3/ Autres 3/	Année	Exportations en provenance de ↓
Matières brutes (sauf combustibles), huiles et graisses (CTCI, Rev. 3, 2 et 4)											
1140	2714	3052	10267	32703	6996	9138	6352	83	2151	2000	Monde 1/
7648	12821	14125	33289	291772	45983	41024	36300	290	1577	2012	
7930	12033	14013	31045	308207	41453	38834	35169	274	2437	2013	
7567	12136	14110	31197	278230	43261	39317	35127	302	1447	2014	
6142	10723	12828	26503	219073	38553	33973	26839	270	7388	2015	
56	116	351	117	6159	678	1505	377	29	721	2000	Economies développées - Asie-Pacifique 2/
124	57	695	318	73912	3324	4488	1781	111	127	2012	
110	72	809	271	85088	2769	4859	2168	99	125	2013	
163	99	756	214	76186	2583	5445	2483	99	98	2014	
82	85	483	213	50684	1922	3653	391	82	5413	2015	
1	3	41	33	1879	111	525	22	1	...	2000	Japon
11	8	199	97	9119	245	1642	89	4	...	2012	
19	7	210	111	8509	222	1635	101	2	...	2013	
16	4	222	100	7386	248	1737	124	2	...	2014	
14	3	209	93	5796	266	1623	113	2	...	2015	
397	1141	627	613	2814	636	651	1535	11	360	2000	Economies développées - Europe 2/
3402	4418	1928	2002	16738	4117	2432	7897	23	202	2012	
3712	4120	1865	2090	17475	3189	2314	7500	29	237	2013	
3649	4358	1679	1910	15068	3644	2086	7533	22	173	2014	
2950	3386	1456	1670	13569	3097	1982	5399	16	244	2015	
16	118	62	61	280	115	29	109	7	0	2000	France
93	354	123	126	1047	174	217	397	16	6	2012	
110	318	117	179	1085	133	203	315	13	9	2013	
106	302	123	123	1096	138	226	264	12	10	2014	
95	286	115	136	995	170	223	244	9	14	2015	
95	91	101	110	601	125	140	206	1	146	2000	Allemagne
353	521	376	341	1995	555	338	798	0	1	2012	
337	438	267	335	2166	407	353	749	0	1	2013	
352	509	228	324	1755	453	329	737	0	5	2014	
292	430	192	271	1270	369	267	505	1	3	2015	
26	190	315	5415	8290	523	1923	975	21	232	2000	Economies développées - Amérique du Nord 2/
223	2267	740	14397	57632	2980	6531	6241	29	175	2012	
97	1771	647	13624	53986	2602	6699	4837	40	172	2013	
112	1716	591	14483	50441	3184	7140	4598	56	0	2014	
109	1166	509	13496	40196	3571	6368	3604	58	...	2015	
21	165	250	5057	6440	360	1472	911	19	232	2000	Etats-Unis
46	1972	557	12593	43651	2315	5739	5221	19	175	2012	
36	1511	523	12229	39797	2085	5800	4294	33	172	2013	
44	1530	461	13113	37601	2320	6022	4108	54	0	2014	
62	1101	413	12354	29241	2528	5495	3069	37	...	2015	
231	122	2	8	102	6	3	310	0	3	2000	Europe du Sud-Est
1224	187	274	17	538	46	12	1782	0	31	2012	
1175	186	252	14	702	110	32	1769	0	36	2013	
1086	197	208	8	532	178	29	1500	0	37	2014	
960	186	176	16	386	35	9	968	1	32	2015	
127	270	6	47	1256	178	63	768	0	0	2000	Communauté d'Etats Indépendants
673	1853	123	275	11682	2729	258	3593	0	0	2012	
807	1369	72	190	10758	2334	358	3330	0	0	2013	
748	1566	136	229	10002	2632	274	3652	0	0	2014	
671	1112	127	227	8392	1930	283	2726	0	0	2015	
23	190	1	12	973	45	21	300	0	0	2000	Fédération de Russie 4/
197	945	71	160	5827	598	184	1872	0	0	2012	
213	748	21	117	5671	497	183	1591	0	0	2013	
185	1103	48	153	5269	630	136	1904	0	0	2014	
149	799	65	179	4609	496	156	1436	0	0	2015	

Voir la fin du tableau pour la remarque générale et les notes.

World merchandise exports by provenance and destination (Table D)

In million U.S. dollars f.o.b.

Exports to ⟶			Developed economies 2/ Économies développées 2/							Commonwealth of Independent States Communauté d'Etats Indépendants	
				Asia-Pacific Asie-Pacifique		Europe		North America Amérique du Nord			
↓ Exports from	Year	World 1/ Monde 1/	Total	Total	Japan Japon	Total	Germany Allemagne	Total	U.S.A. É.-U.	Total	Europe
			Crude materials (excluding fuels), oils, fats (SITC, Rev. 3, 2 and 4) *[cont.]*								
Northern Africa	2000	1414	946	61	24	773	42	111	102	12	12
	2012	5375	2366	116	22	1629	123	622	599	75	70
	2013	4666	2343	92	26	1682	116	568	537	33	29
	2014	4327	2166	93	23	1620	119	454	356	40	30
	2015	4004	1958	88	21	1444	111	426	331	32	22
Sub-Saharan Africa	2000	7465	4484	522	506	3429	537	533	472	14	14
	2012	46045	17288	1863	1728	13453	1544	1972	1473	268	196
	2013	41600	14485	1706	1620	10695	1231	2084	1587	369	344
	2014	36077	12269	1818	1749	8597	1068	1853	1329	248	211
	2015	31887	10537	1138	1074	7862	1209	1538	1267	246	199
South Africa	2000	2693	1932	411	400	1205	338	315	306	8	8
	2012	16943	5134	1338	1292	3034	308	762	735	84	74
	2013	17538	4975	1237	1198	3041	284	697	678	86	78
	2014	15297	4609	1251	1211	2559	364	799	574	114	99
	2015	9607	2964	494	478	1917	464	553	543	87	75
Latin America and the Caribbean	2000	25139	15210	2677	2602	7713	1255	4819	3999	149	149
	2012	142095	48982	13434	12814	25482	4827	10065	7904	933	857
	2013	147808	47893	12462	11997	25166	4430	10265	8085	1217	1080
	2014	140424	45622	11349	10810	23283	3657	10989	8849	1611	1411
	2015	117419	36375	7967	7329	18674	2757	9734	7553	1435	1227
Brazil	2000	9140	6169	900	881	4222	771	1047	980	12	12
	2012	65790	20170	3666	3627	13786	1796	2718	1945	206	181
	2013	71528	20962	3813	3778	14234	2146	2915	2195	127	100
	2014	65951	19141	3104	3073	12445	1758	3592	2802	374	373
	2015	52067	14322	1706	1675	9584	1078	3032	2169	402	376
Eastern Asia	2000	11347	4318	1979	1894	1471	229	869	814	91	88
	2012	32189	10862	3840	3549	3996	893	3025	2660	450	412
	2013	31576	10448	3538	3257	4021	955	2889	2588	411	367
	2014	33608	10884	3571	3285	4242	998	3070	2783	402	362
	2015	29259	9508	3149	2842	3611	813	2748	2478	351	309
China	2000	4575	2767	1241	1205	1051	169	475	454	56	53
	2012	14925	7173	2226	2061	2792	681	2155	1927	288	256
	2013	15192	6975	2102	1931	2811	695	2062	1891	244	213
	2014	16504	7359	2143	1965	3038	729	2178	2011	268	235
	2015	14627	6515	1934	1728	2626	603	1956	1786	222	186
Southern Asia	2000	2589	1252	296	277	664	105	292	279	92	72
	2012	23729	8933	704	547	2212	444	6016	5853	236	182
	2013	20467	5528	710	615	1915	385	2903	2784	217	156
	2014	19530	5126	675	575	1976	419	2475	2327	199	163
	2015	16351	3750	477	383	1913	400	1360	1228	183	130
South-Eastern Asia	2000	18170	7767	3106	2833	3213	376	1448	1324	71	69
	2012	94320	25349	8773	8079	10997	1578	5579	5156	1553	1480
	2013	91612	23762	8702	8038	9927	1408	5132	4789	1575	1506
	2014	83860	23111	8518	7770	9945	970	4648	4360	1205	1082
	2015	72406	19624	7211	6565	8570	829	3844	3614	1057	939
Western Asia	2000	2643	1085	120	114	882	115	83	72	61	47
	2012	15384	2531	156	125	2142	293	232	202	387	303
	2013	16454	2647	161	122	2137	265	349	307	367	264
	2014	15308	2771	280	199	2208	287	283	256	324	225
	2015	13246	2372	229	170	1858	256	284	251	269	184
Oceania	2000	1765	687	353	308	328	71	7	6	3	0
	2012	2740	1445	580	452	852	122	13	13	0	0
	2013	3333	1696	686	551	991	161	20	20	0	0
	2014	4361	2406	1037	874	1347	239	22	22	0	0
	2015	2327	1000	353	284	635	189	12	12	0	0

For general note and footnotes see end of table

Les exportations de marchandises du monde par provenance et destination (Tableau D)

En millions de dollars E.-U. f.o.b.

South-Eastern Europe Europe du Sud-Est	Northern Africa Afrique septentrio-nale	Sub-Saharan Africa Afrique subsahari-enne	Latin America and the Caribbean Amérique latine et Caraïbes	Eastern Asia Asie orientale	Southern Asia Asie méridionale	South-eastern Asia Asie du Sud-Est	Western Asia Asie occidentale	Oceania Océanie	Other 3/ Autres 3/	Année	← Exportations vers Exportations en provence de ↓
Matières brutes (sauf combustibles), huiles et graisses (CTCI, Rev. 3, 2 et 4) *[suite]*											
35	45	13	89	63	63	32	106	0	9	2000	Afrique septentrionale
97	371	204	309	415	669	188	605	0	77	2012	
61	224	197	209	359	430	215	576	0	19	2013	
68	284	175	237	321	430	108	477	0	19	2014	
74	206	189	229	300	434	112	449	0	21	2015	
18	109	1008	116	757	328	374	227	1	27	2000	Afrique subsaharienne
311	140	4857	1794	14280	2668	2619	1473	3	345	2012	
130	173	4949	267	14857	1878	2728	1680	9	74	2013	
37	155	4456	256	12795	2361	2008	1414	13	66	2014	
34	1547	4440	175	10228	1577	1639	1461	2	3	2015	
10	6	112	23	358	62	154	29	0	0	2000	Afrique du sud
15	16	739	112	8504	1231	901	202	1	5	2012	
8	28	680	89	9718	837	884	228	1	3	2013	
4	30	708	128	7598	1346	496	250	12	1	2014	
3	12	661	57	4815	567	299	140	2	1	2015	
145	361	222	3372	3244	1370	669	389	1	7	2000	Amérique latine et Caraïbes
1008	1519	807	11212	62919	6391	4213	3839	3	270	2012	
1234	2121	556	11472	68745	5667	4148	3566	3	1187	2013	
1048	1620	632	11006	63671	6571	4369	3816	2	458	2014	
791	1220	628	8123	53222	7002	4373	3108	4	1138	2015	
41	196	50	682	1211	328	210	241	1	...	2000	Brésil
235	781	220	2307	34428	1407	3068	2967	1	...	2012	
274	956	184	2458	40350	941	2692	2584	1	...	2013	
196	827	205	2369	35874	1174	2936	2854	1	...	2014	
146	571	192	1423	27787	1672	3181	2370	1	...	2015	
7	33	46	98	5248	440	948	116	1	1	2000	Asie orientale
94	221	400	840	11362	1979	4926	1049	5	0	2012	
119	224	407	825	11362	1967	4779	1029	5	0	2013	
121	192	490	870	12160	2054	5240	1188	6	0	2014	
107	213	537	830	9840	1929	4805	1133	6	0	2015	
6	18	23	42	1000	251	360	52	0	...	2000	Chine
84	179	192	478	2962	990	1891	686	2	...	2012	
106	189	200	486	3394	984	1950	664	1	...	2013	
104	158	288	563	3487	1128	2306	842	2	...	2014	
90	183	358	572	2696	1113	2054	821	2	...	2015	
6	31	39	56	495	215	223	179	0	0	2000	Asie méridionale
29	120	190	229	8767	2263	1807	1150	2	4	2012	
27	145	217	220	8233	2508	1708	1644	3	18	2013	
31	155	230	188	7836	2335	1662	1738	5	26	2014	
25	120	212	160	6233	2455	1473	1734	4	1	2015	
41	202	375	281	4015	2228	2375	794	15	4	2000	Asie du Sud-est
171	1424	3594	1626	29176	15910	12821	2587	83	26	2012	
144	1338	3672	1590	31061	15451	10334	2584	73	27	2013	
148	1469	4326	1450	25275	14189	10074	2505	81	25	2014	
131	1156	3623	1205	22398	11970	8786	2366	74	16	2015	
49	93	39	55	150	319	142	577	0	72	2000	Asie occidentale
294	241	313	154	3724	2697	410	4304	10	320	2012	
313	288	368	124	4761	2279	276	4486	2	542	2013	
355	325	432	128	3151	2701	354	4223	0	544	2014	
209	326	449	154	2590	2496	350	3501	11	519	2015	
1	...	7	1	110	10	229	...	4	714	2000	Océanie
0	3	0	117	627	210	319	0	19	0	2012	
0	2	0	149	820	270	384	0	11	0	2013	
0	1	0	218	791	399	528	0	16	0	2014	
0	1	0	5	1034	135	142	0	10	0	2015	

Voir la fin du tableau pour la remarque générale et les notes.

World merchandise exports by provenance and destination (Table D)

In million U.S. dollars f.o.b.

Exports to → / ↓ Exports from	Year	World 1/ Monde 1/	Developed economies 2/ Économies développées 2/ Total	Asia-Pacific Asie-Pacifique Total	Asia-Pacific Asie-Pacifique Japan Japon	Europe Total	Europe Germany Allemagne	North America Amérique du Nord Total	North America Amérique du Nord U.S.A. É.-U.	Commonwealth of Independent States Communauté d'Etats Indépendants Total	Commonwealth of Independent States Communauté d'Etats Indépendants Europe
						Mineral fuels and related materials (SITC. Rev. 3, 3)					
World 1/	2000	656806	433226	62968	57982	221568	28416	148690	122471	11138	9697
	2012	3304504	1682447	223400	186509	1016173	99961	442874	322018	68909	58876
	2013	3245874	1659335	218799	182948	1028693	117311	411843	283556	61220	50070
	2014	3016033	1495755	207962	173238	906847	103051	380946	265131	47485	39350
	2015	2063752	876254	116510	90565	543710	67115	216035	141583	22036	16402
Developed Economies - Asia-Pacific 2/	2000	15224	7843	5798	5119	901	85	1144	1143	7	7
	2012	88097	38156	34040	30389	3255	158	862	853	68	65
	2013	83321	36401	32427	27684	3174	108	799	750	70	65
	2014	81097	33817	31044	27154	2241	94	532	529	142	140
	2015	59524	15278	12493	9492	2059	123	727	726	151	148
Japan	2000	1520	518	83	.	40	4	395	394	7	7
	2012	13434	2434	1706	.	113	9	614	606	68	65
	2013	16682	4809	3385	.	660	10	764	715	67	64
	2014	15824	3212	2562	.	180	11	470	467	68	66
	2015	11403	3011	2360	.	125	8	526	526	52	50
Developed Economies - Europe 2/	2000	131109	119060	136	102	101983	20560	16941	13150	384	367
	2012	526990	427971	1212	1067	392414	65614	34345	31108	4175	3664
	2013	550180	447827	1118	1001	414804	84517	31905	27643	4862	4292
	2014	489319	397373	1581	1483	368054	74041	27738	24453	4786	4346
	2015	329870	257239	564	486	239203	49915	17472	14761	2381	2125
France	2000	8183	7258	28	13	6660	1009	570	561	16	15
	2012	24831	18718	77	73	16920	1729	1721	1592	86	84
	2013	22236	17650	107	71	16091	1420	1452	1389	30	26
	2014	21984	17477	20	16	16209	1453	1248	1193	37	30
	2015	19760	13543	50	46	12656	1004	837	781	26	20
Germany	2000	7757	5384	13	9	4961	.	410	406	35	33
	2012	34322	32298	45	25	32018	.	235	181	561	490
	2013	35042	33105	45	22	32875	.	186	149	694	617
	2014	33726	31135	40	19	30880	.	216	143	1459	1388
	2015	28276	17844	32	16	17687	.	125	94	253	202
Developed Economies - North America 2/	2000	49930	41758	1513	1356	2025	104	38220	35442	8	8
	2012	253499	162733	5012	4564	32446	1195	125275	106342	589	577
	2013	269090	173704	4660	4226	31682	876	137362	112367	509	497
	2014	284043	186961	4162	3717	29331	745	153468	120628	445	431
	2015	183352	117208	2826	2539	19581	585	94801	73520	426	417
United States	2000	13340	5570	1001	845	1793	80	2776	.	8	7
	2012	137139	51475	3101	2658	29441	1074	18933	.	557	546
	2013	148724	57405	3138	2708	29277	795	24991	.	459	448
	2014	155416	61820	3143	2703	25849	667	32828	.	408	396
	2015	106008	41738	2038	1753	18426	496	21274	.	311	304
South-Eastern Europe	2000	1442	243	...	...	231	6	12	12	225	152
	2012	9230	3141	0	0	3021	145	121	121	1598	1018
	2013	10104	3297	0	0	3264	242	33	33	2031	1482
	2014	9178	2218	0	0	2216	189	2	2	1483	1008
	2015	6453	1740	0	0	1719	82	21	21	790	482
Commonwealth of Independent States	2000	62917	41875	302	302	40039	3736	1534	215	10329	9053
	2012	479966	318963	16991	16947	291341	20952	10631	7719	61301	52769
	2013	479776	329612	21758	21429	300177	19995	7678	5162	52561	43049
	2014	447874	306009	24143	23667	276332	21385	5535	4559	39253	32643
	2015	276714	154419	12463	12033	137916	12491	4040	3465	17018	12574
Russian Federation 4/	2000	52166	36681	302	302	36076	3554	303	189	6979	6287
	2012	368853	249657	16959	16947	226629	18304	6070	6052	49373	42798
	2013	372036	261566	21626	21298	235749	17369	4191	4135	42715	34922
	2014	346119	240786	23933	23458	212876	18238	3978	3811	29754	24918
	2015	216101	116155	12343	11913	100636	10865	3176	3056	11583	8402

For general note and footnotes see end of table

Les exportations de marchandises du monde par provenance et destination (Tableau D)

En millions de dollars E.-U. f.o.b.

South-Eastern Europe Europe du Sud-Est	Northern Africa Afrique septentrio-nale	Sub-Saharan Africa Afrique subsahari-enne	Latin America and the Caribbean Amérique latine et Caraïbes	Eastern Asia Asie orientale	Southern Asia Asie méridionale	South-eastern Asia Asie du Sud-Est	Western Asia Asie occidentale	Oceania Océanie	Other 3/ Autres 3/	← Exportations vers Année	Exportations en provenance de ↓
					Combustibles minéraux et produits assimiles (CTCI, Rev. 3, 3)						
3229	6265	5870	33590	98455	11365	25377	9836	1760	16696	2000	Monde 1/
22754	44368	61981	191104	754957	125915	208305	80485	6202	57079	2012	
17258	43974	64560	166204	749672	120111	213810	80381	4969	64382	2013	
16553	36202	67941	168954	708131	128261	209456	81078	4885	51332	2014	
10553	19789	45304	115722	451381	70216	133068	49918	3343	266168	2015	
0	8	65	320	3610	499	1633	112	421	706	2000	Économies développées - Asie-Pacifique 2/
0	1	265	1917	28115	6408	10050	326	842	1950	2012	
1	1	246	872	28438	5072	9281	160	706	2073	2013	
1	1	158	1455	29223	5044	10008	168	705	375	2014	
13	1	102	1522	16039	4201	5640	294	385	15898	2015	
...	0	2	42	701	27	220	4	0	...	2000	Japon
0	1	23	622	6042	429	3752	28	37	...	2012	
0	1	84	103	7351	231	3961	62	13	...	2013	
0	1	51	351	7969	210	3695	78	189	...	2014	
0	1	6	431	4906	66	2651	86	193	...	2015	
784	1350	1171	767	506	436	286	1985	6	4375	2000	Économies développées - Europe 2/
6145	14122	17024	9628	9609	1006	4676	17061	77	15497	2012	
5681	13750	17555	10018	7857	532	4615	16313	18	21152	2013	
5286	11703	17253	7159	7842	551	4198	15979	12	17177	2014	
3764	7847	11684	4348	5982	561	3902	9986	48	22131	2015	
8	212	257	130	23	21	19	204	3	34	2000	France
29	1555	1464	366	86	263	66	1689	4	505	2012	
32	742	1397	265	153	26	121	1642	5	172	2013	
26	643	1939	224	254	27	108	1210	4	36	2014	
18	686	1214	68	56	21	57	630	4	3436	2015	
22	10	35	117	35	12	13	38	0	2056	2000	Allemagne
81	33	212	282	220	59	75	353	60	89	2012	
94	45	198	121	259	50	78	257	0	140	2013	
129	37	101	189	290	44	73	178	0	89	2014	
109	36	78	108	214	40	52	154	0	9388	2015	
73	105	134	6228	821	95	419	287	2	0	2000	Économies développées - Amérique du Nord 2/
312	1414	1906	68708	8028	1815	4984	2931	78	1	2012	
177	2411	3463	70139	8322	1471	5138	3730	28	...	2013	
302	2562	3885	74959	6304	1493	4328	2797	8	0	2014	
134	1218	1247	52544	4897	1302	2663	1684	29	0	2015	
61	96	125	6142	582	85	418	251	2	...	2000	États-Unis
271	1337	1903	67527	4594	1642	4978	2777	78	...	2012	
154	2409	3460	69436	5406	1249	5071	3648	28	...	2013	
256	2555	3883	74025	4404	1251	4232	2574	8	...	2014	
104	1199	1245	52283	3686	1155	2651	1608	29	...	2015	
661	13	65	17	0	1	12	186	...	19	2000	Europe du Sud-Est
2019	324	325	5	1	60	71	1657	1	27	2012	
1864	326	342	2	2	40	431	1722	1	45	2013	
1846	463	153	2	1	31	737	2182	1	61	2014	
1459	567	18	1	4	14	347	1472	0	41	2015	
1626	28	22	4633	697	251	464	2989	1	2	2000	Communauté d'Etats Indépendants
14058	2483	185	1426	53181	3580	6703	17523	80	483	2012	
9314	2282	212	2290	55889	2452	9596	15345	0	222	2013	
8884	2945	176	1176	59337	2718	13083	14116	0	175	2014	
4982	1175	319	853	40083	1661	4904	9024	17	42260	2015	
1407	24	15	3416	590	15	428	2611	0	0	2000	Fédération de Russie 4/
9784	1997	175	831	40255	837	3943	11771	80	149	2012	
6386	1669	189	1748	41732	621	4665	10726	...	19	2013	
5330	2283	159	1003	47731	555	9977	8529	0	11	2014	
2790	807	309	732	31976	399	3263	5884	17	42186	2015	

Voir la fin du tableau pour la remarque générale et les notes.

World merchandise exports by provenance and destination (Table D)

In million U.S. dollars f.o.b.

Exports to → / ↓ Exports from	Year	World 1/ Monde 1/	Developed economies 2/ Économies développées 2/ Total	Asia-Pacific Asie-Pacifique Total	Asia-Pacific Asie-Pacifique Japan Japon	Europe Total	Europe Germany Allemagne	North America Amérique du Nord Total	North America Amérique du Nord U.S.A. É.-U.	Commonwealth of Independent States Communauté d'Etats Indépendants Total	Commonwealth of Independent States Communauté d'Etats Indépendants Europe
					Mineral fuels and related materials (SITC. Rev. 3, 3) *[cont.]*						
Northern Africa	2000	34262	28468	95	95	24088	2706	4285	3508	10	0
	2012	141267	110381	3296	2118	87947	7444	19138	14056	99	1
	2013	119360	94261	2815	1984	80187	6476	11258	8132	115	1
	2014	91136	69818	1672	1672	61434	2662	6712	5158	50	49
	2015	50144	37258	842	842	32631	1347	3785	2918	70	48
Sub-Saharan Africa	2000	45320	27722	229	193	9449	279	18045	17389	3	3
	2012	243808	119373	10349	5929	65176	2460	43849	38745	1	1
	2013	202181	93627	9398	5456	59312	2693	24918	21404	1	1
	2014	205623	83848	9467	6241	59197	2069	15184	13690	93	93
	2015	173712	75553	7541	4553	57360	2061	10652	9641	88	88
South Africa	2000	2664	1005	72	36	902	32	31	29	0	0
	2012	11296	1468	72	58	1272	59	124	124	1	1
	2013	10108	1425	63	54	1237	53	126	123	0	0
	2014	9507	1798	29	21	1517	72	251	239	42	42
	2015	8161	882	24	15	740	84	118	95	36	36
Latin America and the Caribbean	2000	62277	44109	434	371	3996	406	39679	38840	2	1
	2012	256032	128396	1272	1272	24193	182	102931	81745	5	5
	2013	236214	125980	1160	1150	24190	612	100630	69140	9	9
	2014	219250	110215	798	798	22225	468	87191	58294	10	10
	2015	154406	68615	1217	1216	13223	117	54175	28161	14	12
Brazil	2000	908	600	0	0	66	6	533	529	...	...
	2012	26469	11098	31	31	4601	66	6466	5736	0	0
	2013	17822	7720	11	1	3425	111	4284	3704	0	0
	2014	20650	6571	0	0	2816	72	3755	3608	0	...
	2015	13748	3450	0	0	1141	13	2309	2196	0	0
Eastern Asia	2000	19505	7958	5952	5704	452	46	1553	1477	97	78
	2012	113233	25724	15886	11514	5122	551	4716	4517	568	460
	2013	113941	26581	16067	10621	5456	426	5059	4853	615	433
	2014	109829	24732	14868	8368	5072	382	4792	4602	602	368
	2015	89962	22484	14081	7739	4251	248	4152	3998	491	354
China	2000	7855	3226	2080	1973	436	46	711	689	70	51
	2012	31013	6185	2823	2472	1915	549	1447	1308	382	295
	2013	33786	5479	2105	1829	1879	423	1496	1307	443	286
	2014	34446	5139	2175	1446	1520	374	1444	1294	429	221
	2015	27944	5097	2653	1531	1367	241	1078	960	332	218
Southern Asia	2000	26842	16073	5332	5317	10595	184	147	146	11	3
	2012	122537	30429	3423	3164	25783	10	1224	1222	75	11
	2013	128429	32445	3595	3504	25040	39	3810	3747	67	12
	2014	121106	20913	10508	10141	5886	30	4518	4517	215	12
	2015	87867	15288	9549	8428	3596	7	2143	2142	359	8
South-Eastern Asia	2000	45382	18836	16791	13818	423	19	1622	1616	2	2
	2012	229305	66901	61134	40562	3394	63	2374	2146	49	44
	2013	221348	59266	53720	35161	2296	39	3250	3069	67	64
	2014	206984	54199	49344	30762	2360	74	2494	2326	63	50
	2015	149899	37549	33515	22570	1862	63	2172	2073	68	53
Western Asia	2000	161896	78684	25789	25604	27385	284	25510	9532	58	22
	2012	840061	250233	70742	68941	82082	1188	97410	33443	381	260
	2013	831415	236276	72025	70675	79110	1288	85141	27256	311	166
	2014	749983	205569	60291	59154	72500	910	72778	26372	343	200
	2015	497457	71226	19021	18514	30309	76	21895	157	179	92
Oceania	2000	699	597	597	0	0	...	0	0	...	...
	2012	481	44	44	42	0	0	0	0	...	...
	2013	515	57	57	55	0	0	0	0	...	...
	2014	611	84	84	82	0	0	0	0	...	...
	2015	4391	2399	2399	2154	0	0	0	0	...	...

For general note and footnotes see end of table

Les exportations de marchandises du monde par provenance et destination (Tableau D)

En millions de dollars E.-U. f.o.b.

← Exportations vers

South-Eastern Europe / Europe du Sud-Est	Northern Africa / Afrique septentrionale	Sub-Saharan Africa / Afrique subsaharienne	Latin America and the Caribbean / Amérique latine et Caraïbes	Eastern Asia / Asie orientale	Southern Asia / Asie méridionale	South-eastern Asia / Asie du Sud-Est	Western Asia / Asie occidentale	Oceania / Océanie	Other 3/ / Autres 3/	Année	Exportations en provenance de ↓
			Combustibles minéraux et produits assimiles (CTCI, Rev. 3, 3) *[suite]*								
35	472	59	1830	167	173	173	2219	...	656	2000	Afrique septentrionale
5	3354	425	4462	11016	4044	1899	4027	...	1554	2012	
96	4166	297	3493	6648	3627	1366	3962	0	1330	2013	
119	3673	450	3457	5017	2207	1555	3497	0	1292	2014	
87	2164	319	2046	3376	909	936	2024	0	956	2015	
9	37	3583	1794	6330	4023	787	293	28	711	2000	Afrique subsaharienne
30	948	22696	14981	52166	25844	4198	1566	460	1543	2012	
34	49	20108	11865	47617	21372	4773	1505	231	998	2013	
52	145	21762	12724	48341	24032	8204	4025	42	2354	2014	
64	465	19930	11650	27907	22722	6936	3270	41	5087	2015	
2	35	580	45	129	83	42	168	1	573	2000	Afrique du sud
22	38	3171	256	1695	2059	840	1012	17	717	2012	
27	23	3435	300	1437	1815	505	716	2	422	2013	
6	110	3290	187	350	2168	404	663	22	468	2014	
3	413	2416	139	191	2456	163	322	27	1116	2015	
3	1	92	15534	438	209	179	105	0	1602	2000	Amérique latine et Caraïbes
0	84	812	71254	37237	7588	8768	1461	1	425	2012	
0	21	152	52298	41385	7923	5982	1056	0	1407	2013	
0	103	844	53155	38303	7863	5557	1486	2	1712	2014	
5	50	656	37176	32438	3158	992	1049	2	10250	2015	
...	...	25	238	36	1	8	0	...	...	2000	Brésil
0	...	67	5625	4848	3432	1261	137	1	0	2012	
...	0	54	3638	4051	1587	736	35	0	...	2013	
...	0	60	7075	3485	2348	1062	49	1	...	2014	
0	0	47	4464	4147	1109	491	40	...	...	2015	
10	7	77	364	6606	489	2581	66	133	1116	2000	Asie orientale
6	21	1683	5943	33182	1926	38582	1554	948	3096	2012	
0	145	2388	4020	31436	2080	40870	1712	971	3123	2013	
8	259	1578	3143	28747	2875	41403	1763	1473	3245	2014	
12	96	1083	2321	24498	2348	32055	1299	1212	2063	2015	
10	6	59	209	2528	334	1360	53	0	...	2000	Chine
6	18	713	4251	10539	409	7461	797	252	...	2012	
0	11	763	3230	11246	1000	10465	856	293	...	2013	
8	4	952	2734	11000	1806	11197	916	262	...	2014	
12	33	590	1883	9428	1489	7966	872	244	0	2015	
0	2008	8	679	7173	177	501	212	0	0	2000	Asie méridionale
16	3450	6089	5433	38462	2821	12057	16519	1	7184	2012	
14	3194	9451	3846	33460	2704	12639	19660	5	10944	2013	
3	662	10871	4446	38232	16046	7574	21154	2	987	2014	
2	117	5272	807	36194	13011	4280	11339	17	1180	2015	
3	9	28	78	13205	1669	10915	110	523	3	2000	Asie du Sud-est
13	43	2147	244	56474	12230	86524	1188	2877	615	2012	
0	223	2855	533	52381	12800	88345	1637	2525	717	2013	
2	2	3101	518	45663	13902	85948	830	2248	509	2014	
2	15	3029	155	35733	10008	61296	377	1148	519	2015	
25	2228	564	1346	58802	3344	7426	1270	645	7506	2000	Asie occidentale
149	18123	8422	7087	427423	58593	29766	14674	743	24469	2012	
77	17408	7489	6825	436155	60038	30738	13579	368	22150	2013	
52	13684	7707	6753	401000	51498	26800	13081	253	23241	2014	
30	6075	1645	2295	222825	10296	8783	8099	354	165649	2015	
0	...	0	...	99	...	2	...	1	0	2000	Océanie
...	...	2	17	61	0	28	0	94	235	2012	
...	...	0	3	82	1	37	0	115	221	2013	
...	...	1	7	120	0	60	...	136	204	2014	
...	...	1	3	1405	25	334	0	90	134	2015	

Voir la fin du tableau pour la remarque générale et les notes.

World merchandise exports by provenance and destination (Table D)

In million U.S. dollars f.o.b.

Exports to ⟶ / ↓ Exports from	Year	World 1/ Monde 1/	Developed economies 2/ Économies développées 2/ Total	Asia-Pacific Asie-Pacifique Total	Japan Japon	Europe Total	Germany Allemagne	North America Amérique du Nord Total	U.S.A. É.-U.	Commonwealth of Independent States Communauté d'Etats Indépendants Total	Europe
Chemicals (SITC, Rev. 3, 5)											
World 1/	2000	565715	375859	29409	21467	260891	42879	85560	66201	7295	6110
	2012	1907429	1105183	87787	61490	785643	137088	231754	184873	59450	50376
	2013	1963003	1130706	82686	57674	815590	142667	232430	183818	63842	53745
	2014	1998253	1156737	81872	56947	833020	144369	241845	193851	59421	49381
	2015	1830020	1066771	76688	53301	745160	130101	244922	200387	45015	36685
Developed Economies - Asia-Pacific 2/	2000	39061	14664	1393	353	6096	976	7176	6972	23	19
	2012	89464	21631	2579	584	9065	1848	9987	9703	191	179
	2013	85259	20662	2354	549	8202	1748	10107	9764	200	192
	2014	80828	20113	2237	567	7871	1707	10006	9738	201	191
	2015	70289	18132	1986	475	7267	1486	8879	8569	146	139
Japan	2000	35160	12405	386	.	5500	899	6520	6354	22	18
	2012	78940	17200	490	.	7949	1573	8761	8589	179	169
	2013	75823	16498	424	.	7236	1522	8838	8610	180	173
	2014	72120	16090	364	.	6989	1511	8737	8557	180	171
	2015	62862	14386	377	.	6383	1304	7626	7409	134	128
Developed Economies - Europe 2/	2000	317313	260846	11710	8572	212447	36797	36689	33954	4360	4031
	2012	970490	760083	31352	21641	624831	117639	103900	94443	36282	33241
	2013	1023751	797191	30910	21025	661812	122864	104469	93711	39551	36008
	2014	1039812	811239	28184	18759	673004	123843	110050	99852	36156	32719
	2015	947528	738281	28025	19222	590919	110516	119337	109732	26320	23474
France	2000	40440	32870	1270	908	27982	5990	3618	3362	530	469
	2012	97808	70990	3493	2691	60749	13141	6749	5951	3219	2936
	2013	101349	72277	3209	2400	62603	13895	6465	5633	3698	3350
	2014	100776	71878	2785	2015	62524	13746	6569	5844	3418	3051
	2015	94298	66455	2511	1865	56822	12858	7122	6443	2447	2153
Germany	2000	69666	53574	3003	2398	43607	.	6964	6328	1211	1124
	2012	207554	157248	6443	4761	131407	.	19398	17946	9818	9095
	2013	217212	163425	6543	4809	135933	.	20948	19298	10417	9643
	2014	225383	171076	6711	4926	140798	.	23567	21829	9460	8736
	2015	198979	151264	6102	4426	121272	.	23890	22265	6715	6131
Developed Economies - North America 2/	2000	94873	61284	8502	6582	24816	2845	27966	12116	312	267
	2012	243965	137714	17140	13017	60875	7911	59699	27212	1432	1311
	2013	246579	137651	15429	11383	61165	7617	61056	27828	1548	1337
	2014	249795	141285	16017	12089	62995	7820	62273	28210	1264	1085
	2015	242980	140609	15178	11194	66732	8027	58699	27348	1178	1067
United States	2000	80057	48161	8179	6371	24133	2719	15849	.	302	260
	2012	206918	106558	16601	12727	57476	7517	32481	.	1375	1257
	2013	208859	105871	14935	11128	57714	7199	33222	.	1478	1274
	2014	211822	108977	15014	11323	59906	7559	34057	.	1205	1033
	2015	206459	109954	14574	10815	64035	7782	31346	.	1140	1037
South-Eastern Europe	2000	1338	541	2	2	513	46	26	26	148	138
	2012	7825	3917	20	13	3625	1174	272	263	1081	980
	2013	8402	4392	25	15	4190	1420	177	173	1219	1097
	2014	8531	4480	21	13	4270	1344	188	180	1195	1061
	2015	7838	4361	24	11	4208	1494	129	116	836	732
Commonwealth of Independent States	2000	8542	4566	35	33	3214	282	1318	1286	1361	839
	2012	43599	16074	185	60	13883	725	2005	1631	10519	7640
	2013	36854	11997	157	70	9978	842	1862	1504	10663	7623
	2014	36540	12395	148	76	10766	722	1482	1237	10095	7015
	2015	31604	10381	131	71	8620	547	1629	1457	8389	5833
Russian Federation 4/	2000	6181	3740	23	21	2535	218	1183	1165	607	189
	2012	24610	8517	103	34	7272	486	1142	1054	5858	3958
	2013	23533	8703	75	27	7508	569	1120	1004	6383	4272
	2014	23517	9009	70	31	7906	441	1033	959	6078	3971
	2015	19950	7328	60	34	5936	336	1331	1244	5199	3471

For general note and footnotes see end of table

Les exportations de marchandises du monde par provenance et destination (Tableau D)

En millions de dollars E.-U. f.o.b.

← Exportations vers

South-Eastern Europe Europe du Sud-Est	Northern Africa Afrique septentrio-nale	Sub-Saharan Africa Afrique subsahari-enne	Latin America and the Caribbean Amérique latine et Caraïbes	Eastern Asia Asie orientale	Southern Asia Asie méridionale	South-eastern Asia Asie du Sud-Est	Western Asia Asie occidentale	Oceania Océanie	Other 3/ Autres 3/	Année	Exportations en provenance de ↓
				Produits chimiques (CTCI, Rev. 3, 5)							
2698	4621	7730	38936	67250	9464	27959	16789	324	6790	2000	Monde 1/
17404	20293	35935	143750	274141	58359	106590	74213	1630	10481	2012	
19094	21897	39275	146756	280340	56707	110579	80354	1558	11894	2013	
19477	23202	41759	147627	271231	65524	120270	88001	1136	3870	2014	
17434	21050	38604	134644	243811	65013	109339	79352	969	8019	2015	
2	52	161	1390	16114	491	5662	301	95	107	2000	Économies développées - Asie-Pacifique 2/
33	82	385	1482	51412	1626	11287	1035	278	22	2012	
31	81	310	1352	49480	1403	10571	885	273	11	2013	
37	89	293	1399	45433	1533	10572	890	251	16	2014	
34	86	225	1266	38304	1700	9250	894	221	32	2015	
2	45	105	1298	15458	446	5143	230	6	...	2000	Japon
26	69	229	1150	48442	1174	9650	813	8	...	2012	
26	67	220	1029	46953	1084	9041	719	6	...	2013	
30	70	216	1095	43388	1203	9133	711	6	...	2014	
31	76	162	1026	36815	1382	8154	691	4	...	2015	
2196	3328	3858	9213	8702	2805	4847	10663	146	6351	2000	Économies développées - Europe 2/
13642	11882	12306	31411	39297	9778	15497	37413	380	2519	2012	
14964	13053	13193	33565	42462	9941	16453	40456	382	2540	2013	
15178	13442	13505	34024	45374	10414	16704	40948	435	2395	2014	
13481	12023	12813	31454	43318	9686	15605	37932	320	6296	2015	
193	1065	1052	1207	1065	286	690	1358	122	2	2000	France
907	3114	3168	3779	4076	966	2762	4487	298	43	2012	
1058	3367	3530	4282	4435	991	2699	4676	312	24	2013	
1098	3398	3154	4534	4598	1045	2662	4664	308	18	2014	
1064	3031	3644	4188	4527	1217	2559	4580	264	322	2015	
423	372	616	2378	2718	681	1316	2344	6	4026	2000	Allemagne
2500	1513	2011	7454	12669	2758	3528	7877	6	172	2012	
2723	1618	2059	7829	13591	2779	3740	8855	7	170	2013	
2930	1644	2334	7772	14353	2918	3986	8755	6	148	2014	
2659	1442	2106	7147	13396	2561	3510	8028	6	144	2015	
19	215	666	17202	9187	676	3844	1453	13	0	2000	Économies développées - Amérique du Nord 2/
69	916	2130	53460	28820	4110	10147	5130	36	0	2012	
91	959	2106	55199	29113	3853	10608	5417	35	0	2013	
112	963	2093	55304	29479	3749	9980	5533	32	0	2014	
103	871	1950	51047	28163	4034	9801	5181	43	0	2015	
17	207	648	16767	8305	619	3605	1413	12	...	2000	États-Unis
64	897	1950	51483	27047	3765	8804	4951	23	...	2012	
87	940	1964	53283	27082	3445	9445	5235	29	...	2013	
103	949	1933	53588	27451	3326	8949	5318	23	...	2014	
97	848	1840	49042	26096	3601	8864	4956	21	...	2015	
223	21	21	18	9	19	19	262	0	57	2000	Europe du Sud-Est
1584	125	63	148	90	84	40	687	1	4	2012	
1714	120	70	55	93	82	43	610	0	5	2013	
1730	85	57	64	107	132	57	611	0	13	2014	
1597	76	46	45	93	106	48	398	0	233	2015	
65	78	40	548	1031	245	118	488	1	1	2000	Communauté d'Etats Indépendants
424	223	823	4347	5509	2454	1301	1878	0	49	2012	
444	276	783	3462	4798	1294	981	2106	0	51	2013	
438	206	563	3728	4829	1173	1150	1905	10	48	2014	
416	162	450	2952	4555	1706	1123	1434	1	36	2015	
38	48	16	378	889	159	62	243	1	0	2000	Fédération de Russie 4/
267	76	468	2887	3021	1580	784	1145	0	6	2012	
335	111	449	2595	2280	682	577	1410	...	8	2013	
338	142	341	2812	2152	757	614	1257	9	8	2014	
318	112	252	2244	1822	1030	638	1001	0	6	2015	

Voir la fin du tableau pour la remarque générale et les notes.

World merchandise exports by provenance and destination (Table D)

In million U.S. dollars f.o.b.

Exports to ⟶ / ↓ Exports from	Year	World 1/ Monde 1/	Developed economies 2/ Économies développées 2/ Total	Asia-Pacific Asie-Pacifique Total	Japan Japon	Europe Total	Germany Allemagne	North America Amérique du Nord Total	U.S.A. É.-U.	Commonwealth of Independent States Communauté d'Etats Indépendants Total	Europe
						Chemicals (SITC, Rev. 3, 5) *[cont.]*					
Northern Africa	2000	2349	1095	25	2	1015	49	55	54	3	3
	2012	10870	4093	34	6	3620	68	439	410	47	35
	2013	10658	3938	18	10	3636	42	284	274	25	18
	2014	11150	4677	71	5	4212	99	393	373	32	23
	2015	9075	3328	71	4	2882	66	374	354	24	19
Sub-Saharan Africa	2000	2847	948	141	79	446	64	361	331	38	38
	2012	12034	2969	597	473	1380	109	992	960	40	40
	2013	11954	2549	284	103	1406	152	858	811	46	45
	2014	12092	2851	224	89	1682	330	946	923	39	37
	2015	10082	2241	169	66	1263	220	809	790	19	17
South Africa	2000	2055	874	137	79	382	57	355	324	1	0
	2012	7349	2312	590	467	933	78	788	772	5	5
	2013	6857	1757	281	103	795	87	681	660	7	6
	2014	7042	2074	217	84	1100	281	757	735	6	5
	2015	5564	1495	162	60	761	169	572	555	18	17
Latin America and the Caribbean	2000	16493	7456	325	259	2074	315	5056	4937	12	11
	2012	56780	24315	930	686	8341	721	15044	14437	74	64
	2013	55150	22787	860	564	7130	743	14796	14128	79	73
	2014	54178	22503	848	580	7523	798	14132	13492	92	83
	2015	48932	20844	766	529	6358	721	13719	13064	71	63
Brazil	2000	3565	1471	157	141	649	152	665	641	3	3
	2012	15004	6816	434	373	2980	323	3401	3315	23	21
	2013	14268	6148	328	281	2835	313	2984	2898	26	24
	2014	13221	5290	327	278	2587	304	2376	2287	43	41
	2015	11440	4530	287	232	2310	261	1934	1859	26	23
Eastern Asia	2000	45641	11728	4104	3441	4184	868	3439	3221	444	369
	2012	232344	63041	21103	16074	22041	4118	19897	18565	5364	4162
	2013	243655	62881	19570	15133	23236	4201	20075	18696	5794	4414
	2014	259062	69033	20194	15465	26093	4703	22746	21228	5812	4501
	2015	238493	64933	18796	14155	24563	4364	21574	20161	4645	3502
China	2000	12098	6060	1714	1493	2570	645	1775	1661	131	93
	2012	113522	43570	12106	8894	17083	3251	14381	13432	3836	2942
	2013	119566	43841	11424	8422	17573	3319	14844	13836	4278	3238
	2014	134486	47728	12338	8918	19127	3538	16263	15160	4474	3474
	2015	129617	46108	11957	8421	18429	3336	15722	14689	3445	2580
Southern Asia	2000	5011	1852	170	101	1149	223	533	481	233	152
	2012	42498	14909	1063	636	7132	1312	6714	6261	1312	916
	2013	46689	16982	1172	711	8408	1541	7401	6943	1414	1018
	2014	47395	16178	1083	641	7743	1380	7351	6977	1217	881
	2015	52171	16717	1120	646	7543	1301	8054	7664	1104	702
South-Eastern Asia	2000	21083	6188	2395	1681	2424	199	1369	1309	43	41
	2012	108668	31940	11346	7866	15655	558	4939	4673	333	283
	2013	106897	26844	11030	7773	10728	560	5086	4892	334	292
	2014	111749	28664	11088	7827	11406	613	6170	5725	367	336
	2015	98255	26237	9162	6391	11504	568	5571	5180	285	258
Western Asia	2000	11146	4687	606	361	2511	215	1570	1514	316	201
	2012	88534	24324	1295	351	15166	881	7863	6313	2775	1524
	2013	86696	22584	673	225	15656	906	6256	5091	2969	1626
	2014	86486	22981	1477	674	15399	964	6106	5913	2952	1448
	2015	72596	20606	1165	536	13294	790	6146	5951	1997	880
Oceania	2000	17	3	1	0	2	0	0	0	...	...
	2012	360	174	142	82	30	24	2	2	0	0
	2013	458	249	203	113	43	32	2	2	0	0
	2014	634	338	280	162	55	47	2	2	0	0
	2015	178	101	93	1	7	0	1	1	0	0

For general note and footnotes see end of table

Les exportations de marchandises du monde par provenance et destination (Tableau D)

En millions de dollars E.-U. f.o.b.

South-Eastern Europe / Europe du Sud-Est	Northern Africa / Afrique septentrionale	Sub-Saharan Africa / Afrique subsaharienne	Latin America and the Caribbean / Amérique latine et Caraïbes	Eastern Asia / Asie orientale	Southern Asia / Asie méridionale	South-eastern Asia / Asie du Sud-Est	Western Asia / Asie occidentale	Oceania / Océanie	Other 3/ / Autres 3/	Année	⟵ Exportations vers / Exportations en provenance de ↓
			Produits chimiques (CTCI, Rev. 3, 5)*[suite]*								
9	172	44	118	32	545	42	255	...	34	2000	Afrique septentrionale
125	792	768	1365	186	1651	147	1583	0	111	2012	
237	813	760	1414	87	1274	69	1931	0	109	2013	
181	753	875	1078	78	1388	104	1861	0	123	2014	
182	617	835	952	75	1311	103	1542	0	107	2015	
5	9	1247	105	116	233	72	66	0	6	2000	Afrique subsaharienne
20	65	6351	425	546	667	511	404	4	31	2012	
18	50	7084	391	430	573	381	411	2	21	2013	
21	38	6851	342	532	504	441	455	3	17	2014	
19	29	6340	166	333	293	360	260	2	20	2015	
5	9	658	101	114	160	70	62	0	1	2000	Afrique du sud
1	31	3316	365	399	240	352	303	3	21	2012	
1	22	3489	366	352	289	316	247	1	11	2013	
2	21	3442	277	378	214	363	258	2	7	2014	
1	19	2978	150	283	149	286	172	2	10	2015	
2	19	147	8159	362	66	163	83	0	24	2000	Amérique latine et Caraïbes
30	119	545	27846	2143	342	591	482	1	292	2012	
27	114	492	27599	2056	403	609	618	0	367	2013	
22	131	521	27103	2126	416	549	458	0	256	2014	
29	121	423	24091	1754	433	521	387	1	258	2015	
1	10	88	1693	156	21	80	40	0	...	2000	Brésil
2	59	334	6345	868	115	196	246	1	0	2012	
3	46	310	6202	821	176	261	270	0	5	2013	
2	50	260	6021	894	204	219	237	0	...	2014	
7	50	229	5115	810	258	193	222	0	...	2015	
42	205	629	1317	23684	1635	5179	759	17	3	2000	Asie orientale
432	1883	5470	13259	86326	19563	28811	8065	125	5	2012	
451	1985	6278	14764	90164	20253	31636	9306	137	5	2013	
480	2265	6966	15993	88850	23366	35135	10992	156	14	2014	
454	2138	6526	15183	77995	23091	33466	9870	176	15	2015	
23	91	219	511	2632	779	1356	290	6	...	2000	Chine
304	1113	3965	9461	17086	13636	15511	4959	82	...	2012	
295	1200	4625	10708	17610	14005	17493	5424	87	...	2013	
325	1386	5395	11947	19272	17018	20391	6438	112	...	2014	
299	1346	5106	11621	18146	17424	20270	5711	140	0	2015	
8	65	352	280	647	492	517	560	4	0	2000	Asie méridionale
137	617	3532	2818	5864	4118	4296	4817	23	56	2012	
205	702	4475	2794	5920	4597	4541	4854	28	178	2013	
211	648	4410	2806	8107	5056	3915	4809	27	13	2014	
211	776	4362	2681	10883	6979	3322	5070	25	40	2015	
14	55	275	232	6051	1229	6583	369	43	1	2000	Asie du Sud-est
39	285	1605	4720	30034	6955	30382	2094	243	39	2012	
41	294	1655	4051	31612	7475	32238	2088	232	32	2013	
55	325	1731	3376	33402	8164	33129	2315	180	42	2014	
49	341	1587	2840	28252	7075	29341	2062	149	37	2015	
113	403	284	354	1315	1028	911	1529	0	206	2000	Asie occidentale
870	3304	1944	2468	23801	7010	3548	10624	514	7351	2012	
872	3450	2052	2111	24005	5560	2407	11672	441	8574	2013	
1012	4255	3884	2409	12728	9628	8470	17224	9	933	2014	
859	3812	3045	1967	10063	8598	6375	14321	9	944	2015	
0	0	7	0	0	0	3	...	4	0	2000	Océanie
0	...	13	0	113	1	33	0	25	0	2012	
0	...	19	0	119	1	43	0	27	0	2013	
0	...	10	2	186	0	63	0	34	1	2014	
0	0	3	1	25	0	24	0	23	1	2015	

Voir la fin du tableau pour la remarque générale et les notes.

World merchandise exports by provenance and destination (Table D)

In million U.S. dollars f.o.b.

Exports to ⟶ / ↓ Exports from	Year	World 1/ Monde 1/	Developed economies 2/ Économies développées 2/ Total	Asia-Pacific Asie-Pacifique Total	Asia-Pacific Asie-Pacifique Japan Japon	Europe Total	Europe Germany Allemagne	North America Amérique du Nord Total	North America Amérique du Nord U.S.A. É.-U.	Commonwealth of Independent States Communauté d'Etats Indépendants Total	Commonwealth of Independent States Communauté d'Etats Indépendants Europe
Manufactured goods classified chiefly by material (SITC, Rev. 3, 6)											
World 1/	2000	864756	568529	40345	31005	366131	71067	162053	130376	10944	8876
	2012	2227966	1187427	97037	65667	801071	155728	289319	231929	80028	58699
	2013	2273259	1192331	94967	62681	806849	157872	290515	234694	82912	59543
	2014	2323844	1230003	97751	64025	823119	161158	309133	252161	74280	52636
	2015	2058516	1086506	85326	56558	709940	138707	291241	239985	52374	34817
Developed Economies - Asia-Pacific 2/	2000	56349	18597	3849	1803	5456	1114	9292	8625	158	116
	2012	123177	27405	5947	2058	8622	1418	12837	11844	1468	1280
	2013	111365	24183	5331	1738	7665	1265	11187	10400	1609	1358
	2014	106747	24479	5669	2388	7069	1264	11742	10977	1345	1117
	2015	90860	21129	4155	1459	6418	1116	10556	9859	863	713
Japan	2000	46676	13690	850	.	4552	1022	8288	7686	157	115
	2012	105772	20610	1735	.	7206	1349	11669	10737	1452	1268
	2013	94294	17683	1580	.	5891	1181	10212	9478	1594	1346
	2014	89889	17525	1347	.	5693	1203	10485	9792	1332	1107
	2015	77204	15636	1100	.	5036	1068	9501	8841	857	708
Developed Economies - Europe 2/	2000	389015	325036	7269	4783	285846	59601	31921	29032	4806	4377
	2012	815973	626109	10679	5966	571384	122304	44045	39224	24409	22322
	2013	832412	632292	10505	5574	579159	125066	42628	38141	25174	22977
	2014	835212	643851	10148	5658	586135	127546	47568	42954	21980	19701
	2015	710443	551638	8795	4854	499824	108017	43020	38738	15398	12900
France	2000	41170	35053	654	444	31193	7735	3206	2793	205	180
	2012	62636	48366	1009	636	43774	11673	3582	3201	809	728
	2013	61940	47455	869	477	43004	11705	3581	3206	778	691
	2014	62090	48176	797	473	43406	11792	3973	3570	625	542
	2015	56698	43462	801	499	38458	10204	4203	3836	1055	408
Germany	2000	76521	63845	1352	846	56559	.	5935	5391	1276	1198
	2012	181058	141075	2387	1279	127266	.	11422	10425	6259	5810
	2013	182614	141620	2427	1223	127822	.	11370	10341	5998	5537
	2014	185402	145491	2270	1289	131261	.	11961	10909	5327	4881
	2015	156167	123969	1955	1080	111021	.	10993	10012	3401	3098
Developed Economies - North America 2/	2000	111271	77888	5107	4208	13229	1973	59552	35016	124	99
	2012	194111	114123	6671	4187	25694	3861	81758	41676	674	558
	2013	196400	112562	6453	4135	25147	3529	80963	41870	742	617
	2014	202869	114858	6313	4046	26911	3896	81633	42702	778	652
	2015	185804	104899	6021	4001	24193	3892	74685	40200	578	449
United States	2000	71990	40258	4380	3549	11348	1845	24529	.	112	89
	2012	141915	67078	5943	3712	21062	3692	40073	.	566	462
	2013	144933	66177	5824	3658	21274	3355	39079	.	626	518
	2014	150544	67724	5707	3590	23096	3692	38921	.	686	568
	2015	137729	61376	5505	3627	21395	3690	34475	.	532	407
South-Eastern Europe	2000	4672	3293	9	7	2958	442	327	279	107	89
	2012	21808	13889	29	11	13311	2683	548	440	1036	976
	2013	23028	15014	37	21	14464	3439	513	405	1244	1163
	2014	23108	15638	85	66	14878	2980	675	519	1043	960
	2015	20693	13932	106	88	13359	2704	466	425	643	596
Commonwealth of Independent States	2000	27530	14483	1243	1239	10727	1615	2513	2426	4232	3251
	2012	101751	43128	2991	2932	35259	5098	4878	4731	26049	17639
	2013	92257	38029	2024	1994	31363	4064	4642	4435	25856	16267
	2014	88110	35952	2088	2059	28803	3598	5061	4736	21965	13601
	2015	70223	29443	1574	1532	23967	2728	3902	3667	15825	9495
Russian Federation 4/	2000	18349	11959	1176	1174	8853	1330	1930	1887	1126	399
	2012	57214	32063	1731	1719	26511	3476	3821	3722	10899	5338
	2013	53831	28754	1466	1453	23568	3146	3720	3554	11691	5112
	2014	52753	26997	1531	1508	21442	2624	4025	3760	10055	4168
	2015	43494	22949	1244	1207	18512	2004	3193	3010	7398	2756

For general note and footnotes see end of table

Les exportations de marchandises du monde par provenance et destination (Tableau D)

En millions de dollars E.-U. f.o.b.

← Exportations vers

South-Eastern Europe Europe du Sud-Est	Northern Africa Afrique septentrio-nale	Sub-Saharan Africa Afrique subsahari-enne	Latin America and the Caribbean Amérique latine et Caraïbes	Eastern Asia Asie orientale	Southern Asia Asie méridionale	South-eastern Asia Asie du Sud-Est	Western Asia Asie occidentale	Oceania Océanie	Other 3/ Autres 3/	Année	Exportations en provence de ↓
Articles manufacturés classés principalement d'après la matière première (CTCI, Rev. 3, 6)											
6497	9130	11601	47741	109823	18164	42179	36373	1018	2756	2000	Monde 1/
26512	35397	59215	137190	281025	93158	166715	152537	2377	6384	2012	
28052	36855	63975	136381	285797	100667	177706	159490	1914	7181	2013	
30729	39179	66684	138298	285232	106570	185537	159650	1821	5859	2014	
26750	35033	60369	126299	247431	98235	174847	144059	1758	4855	2015	
6	153	545	1540	21930	1109	10186	1524	317	285	2000	Economies développées - Asie-Pacifique 2/
81	425	1323	4192	48794	3644	29622	5495	672	56	2012	
42	427	1477	4173	44258	3291	26733	4532	594	46	2013	
50	487	1180	4222	41173	3411	25038	4799	507	55	2014	
52	423	1031	3882	35153	3552	20514	3770	450	40	2015	
6	150	429	1446	19458	961	8894	1421	64	...	2000	Japon
77	359	1035	3966	44551	3279	25073	5259	111	...	2012	
39	386	1275	4017	39040	2959	22914	4296	91	...	2013	
46	417	1039	4061	36755	3027	21062	4566	59	0	2014	
49	409	901	3718	30903	3129	17965	3582	55	...	2015	
4904	5803	3785	6690	10369	6568	4383	14766	158	1746	2000	Economies développées - Europe 2/
18142	16776	12347	18147	32532	19180	11476	33877	323	2654	2012	
19345	17248	12552	18488	34392	20305	12492	37222	283	2619	2013	
21155	17469	12005	17474	33199	18212	11137	35778	283	2668	2014	
18512	14591	9987	14918	27665	14995	9279	31290	231	1936	2015	
247	1711	670	619	814	243	357	1144	103	4	2000	France
887	2783	1502	1378	2420	949	733	2619	170	19	2012	
962	2697	1426	1571	2543	639	741	2934	172	22	2013	
1006	2684	1576	1370	2474	625	656	2687	173	38	2014	
896	2363	1379	1182	2465	545	674	2487	148	42	2015	
1158	761	652	1783	2199	610	950	2114	10	1163	2000	Allemagne
3712	1419	1777	4878	9004	2609	3028	6743	23	532	2012	
3892	1300	1805	4851	9370	1963	3410	7736	20	649	2013	
4514	1367	1888	4402	9856	1835	2657	7531	24	510	2014	
3914	1118	1578	3691	8049	1663	2156	6317	19	293	2015	
24	187	594	21582	5486	517	2135	2709	25	0	2000	Economies développées - Amérique du Nord 2/
83	417	1584	42877	15948	4595	3834	9908	67	0	2012	
95	432	1901	44004	16354	5790	3983	10475	60	0	2013	
122	462	2414	45771	17474	5658	4023	11276	33	0	2014	
96	391	1886	43807	15169	5841	3603	9492	42	0	2015	
20	139	569	20958	4946	431	1954	2581	24	...	2000	Etats-Unis
67	358	1462	40921	14347	3998	3571	9486	60	...	2012	
81	355	1516	42218	14976	5170	3711	10047	55	...	2013	
105	372	1763	43994	16080	5088	3817	10887	29	...	2014	
85	342	1337	42222	13858	5244	3426	9272	37	...	2015	
462	83	27	82	64	29	16	492	0	16	2000	Europe du Sud-Est
3045	326	57	176	963	122	55	2134	0	5	2012	
3047	374	77	192	853	101	95	2007	0	24	2013	
2846	410	86	207	701	83	65	2023	0	6	2014	
2736	357	83	184	782	62	81	1827	0	5	2015	
549	670	232	540	3148	826	845	2005	1	0	2000	Communauté d'Etats Indépendants
1208	1482	839	1109	7698	3927	1924	14373	10	5	2012	
1135	1857	800	1161	6497	2899	1309	12704	6	3	2013	
1579	2612	759	1964	6287	3143	820	13026	0	3	2014	
1001	2270	558	1455	5095	2539	591	11350	0	97	2015	
160	310	122	368	2218	603	455	1027	...	0	2000	Fédération de Russie 4/
386	559	175	723	3293	2835	1043	5226	8	4	2012	
334	549	173	896	3141	2031	671	5584	6	2	2013	
735	940	214	1692	3319	2181	483	6133	0	2	2014	
383	1070	180	1236	2558	1890	364	5370	0	96	2015	

Voir la fin du tableau pour la remarque générale et les notes.

World merchandise exports by provenance and destination (Table D)

In million U.S. dollars f.o.b.

Exports from ↓ / Exports to →	Year	World 1/ Monde 1/	Developed economies 2/ Économies développées 2/ Total	Asia-Pacific Asie-Pacifique Total	Japan Japon	Europe Total	Germany Allemagne	North America Amérique du Nord Total	U.S.A. É.-U.	Commonwealth of Independent States Communauté d'Etats Indépendants Total	Europe
Manufactured goods classified chiefly by material (SITC, Rev. 3, 6) *[cont.]*											
Northern Africa	2000	1898	1326	21	18	1193	68	112	104	8	1
	2012	8796	3623	31	20	3197	250	396	367	68	59
	2013	8805	3594	30	19	3191	225	372	346	42	35
	2014	8164	3603	32	19	3197	234	374	334	41	36
	2015	6993	3090	31	17	2681	186	379	341	25	23
Sub-Saharan Africa	2000	14280	9998	787	671	8133	262	1079	980	7	7
	2012	51384	26925	3605	3431	19925	1230	3395	3307	35	34
	2013	53012	27048	3730	3600	20182	1187	3136	3055	46	41
	2014	54870	25850	3546	3064	18684	1146	3620	3205	41	38
	2015	45997	21105	3180	2813	14535	1139	3391	3019	31	28
South Africa	2000	7487	4495	649	539	2888	176	958	862	2	2
	2012	23585	12985	3466	3309	6571	1064	2947	2864	33	31
	2013	23644	12913	3444	3322	6745	984	2724	2675	41	38
	2014	22679	11779	2856	2729	6269	1013	2654	2582	37	36
	2015	18016	9639	2571	2462	4699	1035	2369	2313	27	26
Latin America and the Caribbean	2000	41952	27454	1553	1438	6816	560	19085	18487	15	13
	2012	107721	54746	2955	1698	14182	1386	37609	36175	165	111
	2013	102812	51814	2221	1445	12254	944	37339	35948	173	130
	2014	102993	53909	2484	1598	13244	1210	38182	36714	169	93
	2015	90144	47247	1534	1190	10890	1084	34823	33395	123	83
Brazil	2000	11043	6548	666	612	2768	273	3114	2909	5	5
	2012	26626	12969	1057	958	5238	842	6674	6416	40	38
	2013	24903	12045	988	920	4603	460	6455	6275	78	73
	2014	26579	13898	1024	947	5548	680	7325	7112	63	38
	2015	24877	12526	791	721	5414	618	6321	6089	63	61
Eastern Asia	2000	132034	46467	12333	10253	13552	2451	20582	18744	644	460
	2012	502331	173731	42296	31169	62527	10325	68908	61413	18645	11691
	2013	524944	173483	40186	28613	62127	10577	71170	63695	20515	12839
	2014	572050	189855	41572	29576	68786	11561	79498	71371	19652	12832
	2015	543492	183845	38216	26289	64367	10974	81262	73322	13610	8305
China	2000	42546	19264	5932	5145	6238	1178	7093	6500	332	189
	2012	334162	122405	27203	18747	46115	8275	49088	43273	16726	10167
	2013	361782	125175	26382	17859	46924	8448	51870	45989	18452	11265
	2014	401765	135926	27267	18566	52417	9257	56242	49869	17609	11306
	2015	393490	136280	25593	16636	50873	8969	59814	53520	11815	6980
Southern Asia	2000	24537	13671	1221	881	6258	1141	6192	5799	248	135
	2012	86340	31723	2197	1081	15195	2451	14330	13507	1022	598
	2013	102507	37253	2311	1202	17655	2692	17287	16376	1087	697
	2014	94260	36691	2119	1106	17885	2569	16688	15830	991	644
	2015	87717	34965	2011	972	16391	2387	16562	15805	817	392
South-Eastern Asia	2000	34735	14653	6032	4932	4461	660	4161	3876	30	22
	2012	105266	33291	16809	12381	8361	1413	8121	7567	375	316
	2013	110722	35287	18686	13629	8232	1471	8369	7840	396	315
	2014	117358	37597	19011	13310	9409	1436	9177	8570	446	336
	2015	104848	34986	17893	12350	8172	1293	8921	8343	314	266
Western Asia	2000	25804	15276	739	616	7349	1174	7188	6956	564	305
	2012	106961	36847	1197	579	23220	3309	12430	11613	6082	3115
	2013	112257	39433	1381	574	25207	3414	12845	12118	6026	3104
	2014	114072	44368	1683	1001	27860	3716	14825	14158	5830	2626
	2015	100277	39729	1509	888	25019	3186	13201	12796	4147	1567
Oceania	2000	679	387	183	155	153	7	51	50	0	0
	2012	2346	1888	1631	153	194	0	63	63	...	...
	2013	2738	2338	2069	136	203	0	65	65	0	0
	2014	4031	3351	3002	136	258	0	91	91	0	0
	2015	1026	498	302	107	123	0	74	73	0	0

For general note and footnotes see end of table

Les exportations de marchandises du monde par provenance et destination (Tableau D)

En millions de dollars E.-U. f.o.b.

South-Eastern Europe Europe du Sud-Est	Northern Africa Afrique septentrio-nale	Sub-Saharan Africa Afrique subsahari-enne	Latin America and the Caribbean Amérique latine et Caraïbes	Eastern Asia Asie orientale	Southern Asia Asie méridionale	South-eastern Asia Asie du Sud-Est	Western Asia Asie occidentale	Oceania Océanie	Other 3/ Autres 3/	Année	⟵ Exportations vers Exportations en provence de ↓
Articles manufacturés classés principalement d'après la matière première (CTCI, Rev. 3, 6)*[suite]*											
2	208	62	15	40	5	18	167	0	47	2000	Afrique septentrionale
38	1578	726	82	232	125	61	2174	1	87	2012	
36	1556	729	108	191	97	22	2330	0	101	2013	
32	1409	674	86	204	120	40	1855	1	99	2014	
36	1091	648	68	151	116	69	1617	0	83	2015	
4	23	1744	338	1023	157	390	582	1	14	2000	Afrique subsaharienne
62	126	10458	573	7596	838	742	3722	28	279	2012	
68	79	11116	405	7419	969	1043	4508	21	290	2013	
76	72	12107	324	7303	1969	1737	5068	4	320	2014	
67	75	9562	288	7149	1891	1358	4279	7	185	2015	
3	10	819	295	947	114	317	483	1	2	2000	Afrique du sud
3	20	5380	495	2735	341	556	988	24	26	2012	
8	19	5242	362	3213	282	612	913	19	17	2013	
16	20	5439	304	3231	279	508	1041	2	24	2014	
9	13	4010	238	2670	281	406	709	5	9	2015	
2	110	254	10516	2518	113	462	461	2	45	2000	Amérique latine et Caraïbes
35	223	692	29222	18802	418	2169	1174	8	67	2012	
61	204	950	27999	17781	378	1844	1336	4	270	2013	
72	184	858	26104	17579	453	2173	1439	6	48	2014	
38	329	805	22696	15467	419	1777	1177	9	56	2015	
1	69	138	3135	666	47	255	179	1	...	2000	Brésil
12	69	446	8766	2604	224	1182	309	4	0	2012	
18	78	520	7882	2875	122	952	330	3	0	2013	
16	97	555	7239	2685	219	1200	604	4	...	2014	
16	165	546	6877	2684	254	1000	743	3	...	2015	
153	769	2159	5196	52188	5025	13626	5344	374	90	2000	Asie orientale
1313	6874	20836	33430	99635	34382	77214	35719	539	14	2012	
1444	7269	23367	32235	100988	37810	88931	38357	535	9	2013	
1684	8286	25933	33922	103736	45912	100804	41663	589	14	2014	
1517	8579	26502	32198	91813	43241	101097	40377	697	17	2015	
68	375	1160	1430	13538	1247	3224	1881	28	...	2000	Chine
1081	6083	19353	27177	46295	21753	47582	25295	412	...	2012	
1218	6572	21833	26266	49032	24877	59667	28291	398	...	2013	
1360	7463	24191	27998	53299	31514	71078	30877	450	...	2014	
1226	7827	24956	26841	48022	31896	73641	30429	558	1	2015	
12	251	1016	435	3964	991	1173	2763	10	3	2000	Asie méridionale
190	1280	4318	3097	17408	7146	4644	15098	36	379	2012	
219	1307	5069	3442	21491	7859	6360	17952	30	438	2013	
339	1372	4782	3828	19031	7982	5236	13860	38	110	2014	
206	1119	4009	3053	17003	7403	5318	13650	23	153	2015	
11	247	670	605	6881	1588	8241	1690	115	1	2000	Asie du Sud-est
71	932	2045	2481	20961	5997	32585	5828	616	86	2012	
87	837	2253	2478	23844	6585	32776	5767	308	103	2013	
107	826	2125	2666	27162	7239	32165	6608	293	124	2014	
101	767	1817	2415	22253	6910	29021	5845	250	169	2015	
365	626	499	193	1968	1231	702	3870	0	508	2000	Asie occidentale
2247	4959	3952	1805	10113	12762	2374	23033	35	2751	2012	
2473	5265	3630	1692	11480	14550	2100	22299	31	3278	2013	
2667	5589	3719	1727	10854	12370	2277	22249	11	2411	2014	
2387	5042	3446	1333	9305	11246	2135	19380	12	2114	2015	
1	0	14	9	245	5	2	0	14	1	2000	Océanie
0	0	39	0	343	20	14	1	41	0	2012	
0	...	54	2	250	33	16	2	42	0	2013	
0	0	43	3	528	19	23	6	57	1	2014	
0	0	34	2	425	21	4	4	36	1	2015	

Voir la fin du tableau pour la remarque générale et les notes.

World merchandise exports by provenance and destination (Table D)

In million U.S. dollars f.o.b.

Exports to ⟶ / ↓ Exports from	Year	World 1/ Monde 1/	Developed economies 2/ Économies développées 2/ Total	Asia-Pacific Asie-Pacifique Total	Asia-Pacific Japan Japon	Europe Total	Europe Germany Allemagne	North America Amérique du Nord Total	North America U.S.A. É.-U.	Commonwealth of Independent States Communauté d'Etats Indépendants Total	Commonwealth of Independent States Europe
Machinery and transport equipment (SITC, Rev. 3, 7)											
World 1/	2000	2619162	1799360	137031	102485	985974	188838	676356	554574	19729	15833
	2012	5863018	3011108	276212	172532	1700256	375962	1034639	854271	208029	173692
	2013	6073452	3089009	269179	173966	1759098	383484	1060732	880837	204432	167372
	2014	6263080	3264528	270986	178464	1866139	411833	1127404	944664	176379	140148
	2015	5941076	3102078	254887	166329	1730075	377405	1117116	945507	115780	88941
Developed Economies - Asia-Pacific 2/	2000	338298	189906	9501	291	63126	14800	117279	110881	536	422
	2012	492813	188957	18499	225	54595	13523	115864	107338	12423	11279
	2013	430090	172130	15489	204	47968	12058	108673	101536	10662	9553
	2014	415926	167670	14257	193	48809	12144	104605	97944	9074	7848
	2015	381324	159031	12568	209	45073	10363	101390	95050	4705	4133
Japan	2000	329680	185109	7675	.	61931	14533	115503	109214	526	414
	2012	476231	181269	15212	.	53111	13249	112945	104736	12354	11228
	2013	414378	164643	12381	.	46456	11812	105806	98909	10583	9501
	2014	400127	159755	11059	.	47084	11900	101612	95220	9011	7806
	2015	366811	151816	9721	.	43649	10123	98446	92309	4661	4109
Developed Economies - Europe 2/	2000	1019028	835584	24276	16826	697327	127649	113981	104692	11248	9772
	2012	2059897	1422775	51130	25924	1194016	257306	177628	160563	103961	94816
	2013	2148745	1486378	51516	27015	1247515	267731	187347	169904	101903	91590
	2014	2233922	1576744	50160	27638	1322136	287871	204448	185776	84319	74540
	2015	2054719	1462072	44219	23821	1207067	258575	210786	191535	52250	45069
France	2000	132952	103387	1699	1089	86545	19223	15143	14101	962	653
	2012	214196	137648	4646	2308	117354	45484	15648	14624	7748	7052
	2013	216670	142086	4757	2583	120385	45840	16944	15750	6247	5113
	2014	217572	145586	5133	3043	123041	46581	17412	16134	5484	4488
	2015	239121	142665	4378	2030	115369	40260	22918	20615	4859	4191
Germany	2000	272345	223326	8768	6855	175308	.	39250	37072	4105	3664
	2012	669188	440127	20933	12240	343644	.	75550	68039	36844	33770
	2013	685121	451478	20960	12898	350066	.	80452	72889	35772	32333
	2014	711427	476324	19523	12376	372205	.	84596	77505	26929	24038
	2015	639034	440262	16226	10001	338117	.	85919	78458	15808	13966
Developed Economies - North America 2/	2000	523642	335335	36797	28252	99424	18364	199113	101673	1535	1086
	2012	651948	336488	34155	15699	78588	19928	223745	97842	8094	6672
	2013	649387	326321	28689	14735	76668	18351	220964	95424	8201	6623
	2014	671070	337566	29186	15124	82831	19076	225549	98359	7588	5990
	2015	643672	326497	29164	15206	82781	19736	214552	97939	4123	3247
United States	2000	412200	227821	35994	27866	94397	17580	97431	.	1458	1018
	2012	532526	229646	32613	15149	71152	18592	125881	.	7138	5884
	2013	533880	222984	27345	14238	70117	17235	125522	.	7306	5897
	2014	552090	230615	27865	14610	75582	18105	127168	.	6890	5435
	2015	526393	220381	27894	14693	75884	18705	116603	.	3685	2913
South-Eastern Europe	2000	2785	2115	3	0	2009	521	103	93	83	72
	2012	31144	23552	55	20	22900	8188	596	550	1846	1604
	2013	38264	29053	60	29	28002	9704	991	944	2278	2086
	2014	40805	31779	70	32	30796	11192	912	861	2286	2082
	2015	37616	29743	73	36	28841	10398	829	781	1419	1273
Commonwealth of Independent States	2000	10405	3201	38	34	2870	479	293	271	4444	3311
	2012	43083	7056	353	313	6121	1190	582	540	28425	19954
	2013	42250	7296	267	247	6525	1229	505	481	26750	17827
	2014	37043	8586	92	82	8010	3337	484	448	20955	12483
	2015	29859	8296	415	405	7082	2398	799	775	14029	8385
Russian Federation 4/	2000	6422	2634	35	34	2410	387	189	179	1573	749
	2012	18478	3576	324	308	2878	515	374	349	9528	4566
	2013	21365	4413	249	246	3787	709	376	360	11096	5168
	2014	20107	5607	84	81	5153	2769	370	344	9082	3465
	2015	18509	6176	408	404	5035	1995	733	716	6351	2610

For general note and footnotes see end of table

Les exportations de marchandises du monde par provenance et destination (Tableau D)

En millions de dollars E.-U. f.o.b.

← Exportations vers

South-Eastern Europe Europe du Sud-Est	Northern Africa Afrique septentrionale	Sub-Saharan Africa Afrique subsaharienne	Latin America and the Caribbean Amérique latine et Caraïbes	Eastern Asia Asie orientale	Southern Asia Asie méridionale	South-eastern Asia Asie du Sud-Est	Western Asia Asie occidentale	Oceania Océanie	Other 3/ Autres 3/	Année	Exportations en provenence de ↓
			Machines et matériel de transport (CTCI, Rev. 3, 7)								
7389	17519	28905	158680	287505	22810	198726	71362	2013	5163	2000	Monde 1/
37984	60047	124139	414009	1122953	123698	451077	286922	13687	9365	2012	
41689	61975	133818	426815	1208126	119149	453437	306956	16170	11875	2013	
46198	66388	129368	406299	1227674	129882	458941	326586	17239	13597	2014	
42365	61979	118245	387822	1172193	131987	444457	324648	19534	19990	2015	
76	919	3093	17123	67403	2899	46357	8977	622	389	2000	Economies développées - Asie-Pacifique 2/
348	2499	8697	32937	135948	8372	73948	24659	3998	26	2012	
319	1710	7391	27500	118547	6092	59601	23284	2822	36	2013	
378	1727	6641	24552	115595	6565	55462	25431	2762	69	2014	
332	1351	5354	20634	104668	6906	50635	24530	3043	136	2015	
74	909	2942	16949	66606	2790	45359	8114	304	0	2000	Japon
321	2457	7984	32414	134182	8139	71889	22832	2391	...	2012	
293	1667	6830	27085	116889	5913	57656	21356	1462	...	2013	
338	1688	6197	24121	113966	6403	53474	23543	1630	...	2014	
303	1313	4959	20344	103280	6733	48692	22639	2073	0	2015	
6113	11744	15238	29109	38549	8198	22947	36131	553	3614	2000	Economies développées - Europe 2/
29776	30058	39972	73124	161971	27397	56402	109251	1795	3415	2012	
32945	33196	41737	76737	170048	24750	56409	119743	2232	2668	2013	
36242	33655	40661	71288	185157	25233	55194	120175	2617	2637	2014	
33244	32386	37123	71646	154814	25657	48692	127201	2637	6997	2015	
536	4200	4160	4149	5250	1384	2817	5172	337	600	2000	France
2537	8201	5240	8126	18303	2937	10984	11466	558	449	2012	
2817	8173	5428	8814	16874	2528	11573	11029	977	124	2013	
2935	7430	5399	6985	18600	2669	10244	11410	647	182	2014	
2530	10458	6562	14994	19019	4043	9240	20566	1325	2860	2015	
1738	1857	3307	7626	12322	1917	5981	9509	102	555	2000	Allemagne
8968	5425	10476	24003	78725	9693	17680	36872	340	34	2012	
9232	5842	10790	24217	81504	8924	17118	39737	304	203	2013	
10701	6321	10645	22635	91845	8660	17362	39079	854	72	2014	
10266	5578	9646	20101	74211	8060	14953	39341	734	73	2015	
266	2440	3057	84855	48797	2259	32401	12524	171	1	2000	Economies développées - Amérique du Nord 2/
574	3202	10749	150453	67191	6552	31754	36363	520	8	2012	
698	3449	10635	153823	74177	6961	29817	35070	234	1	2013	
791	4686	10482	155240	80898	6783	30427	36394	215	1	2014	
649	3458	7922	152123	77684	5900	29266	35803	248	1	2015	
244	2348	2934	83422	47397	2166	32085	12159	164	1	2000	Etats-Unis
494	2938	9664	146566	64611	5960	30359	34667	484	...	2012	
613	3120	9786	149945	71269	6539	28479	33642	197	...	2013	
715	4470	9559	151985	77818	6416	29007	34434	181	...	2014	
592	3261	7129	148894	74851	5438	27924	34027	211	...	2015	
193	70	20	25	35	42	17	154	0	30	2000	Europe du Sud-Est
1346	797	403	430	651	409	136	1490	83	2	2012	
1649	823	321	983	709	352	187	1864	42	3	2013	
1753	940	368	757	776	301	177	1657	11	2	2014	
1658	841	318	470	676	363	168	1654	305	1	2015	
197	155	103	138	841	677	146	496	1	6	2000	Communauté d'Etats Indépendants
869	566	231	864	1673	2206	595	589	7	2	2012	
800	496	223	982	2283	1870	881	657	11	1	2013	
690	690	258	641	2535	1668	340	676	3	1	2014	
695	930	208	507	2491	1342	629	715	16	1	2015	
165	100	84	117	765	568	115	294	1	6	2000	Fédération de Russie 4/
453	460	113	549	1441	1618	508	231	2	1	2012	
394	389	92	747	1720	1448	717	338	10	0	2013	
305	543	118	425	2103	1296	239	388	2	0	2014	
331	823	147	365	2189	1073	572	466	16	0	2015	

Voir la fin du tableau pour la remarque générale et les notes.

World merchandise exports by provenance and destination (Table D)

In million U.S. dollars f.o.b.

Exports to → / ↓ Exports from	Year	World 1/ Monde 1/	Developed economies 2/ Économies développées 2/ Total	Asia-Pacific Asie-Pacifique Total	Asia-Pacific Asie-Pacifique Japan Japon	Europe Total	Europe Germany Allemagne	North America Amérique du Nord Total	North America Amérique du Nord U.S.A. É.-U.	Commonwealth of Independent States Communauté d'Etats Indépendants Total	Commonwealth of Independent States Communauté d'Etats Indépendants Europe
			Machinery and transport equipment (SITC, Rev. 3, 7)*cont.*								
Northern Africa	2000	1754	1566	1	1	1559	277	6	5	1	1
	2012	11153	8632	86	79	8316	1016	230	224	27	9
	2013	12560	9746	52	49	9441	1183	253	251	33	28
	2014	14624	10969	53	48	10649	1267	267	256	47	36
	2015	13285	10108	46	45	9815	1100	246	235	32	27
Sub-Saharan Africa	2000	5313	3395	404	155	2349	969	642	609	15	14
	2012	28923	10660	934	412	6381	2183	3346	3135	201	171
	2013	31198	9307	998	553	5567	2068	2741	2631	178	147
	2014	29923	11990	1133	626	8531	2169	2327	2123	118	105
	2015	27572	11935	869	545	9211	2196	1854	1667	53	41
South Africa	2000	4570	3150	390	143	2156	950	604	577	14	14
	2012	19088	8360	892	395	4473	2106	2995	2823	188	160
	2013	17873	7690	940	539	4362	1999	2387	2311	159	129
	2014	18693	8368	1106	610	5170	2122	2093	1904	100	90
	2015	15598	7917	851	540	5476	2151	1591	1419	26	17
Latin America and the Caribbean	2000	122218	108761	764	615	6613	1779	101384	98502	19	18
	2012	264067	201072	2177	1203	16685	5780	182211	175164	782	645
	2013	281720	213910	2284	1085	16818	4519	194808	188015	819	585
	2014	287504	232120	2312	1301	13418	3809	216390	208850	480	422
	2015	283585	237235	1946	991	13374	3911	221916	213771	213	198
Brazil	2000	15416	8675	358	290	3065	497	5252	5157	3	3
	2012	38251	12475	319	135	6599	1514	5557	5289	435	327
	2013	44217	14272	435	249	8053	1173	5784	5527	441	226
	2014	33089	12818	403	262	5130	880	7286	7031	237	191
	2015	31266	12155	315	198	4053	829	7787	7499	39	33
Eastern Asia	2000	347610	188128	37113	32789	64660	14462	86355	82182	1052	698
	2012	1671067	615849	118498	93313	226120	46842	271230	252965	42156	32627
	2013	1784500	623865	118253	94235	223738	45126	281874	262763	42454	32497
	2014	1856480	667359	120386	96306	239780	48147	307194	287579	40671	30838
	2015	1820938	642032	114171	89880	228876	46277	298986	280717	30475	22348
China	2000	82600	46255	10601	9716	16464	3921	19191	18323	325	217
	2012	965289	426072	79268	62662	159779	33007	187026	176118	27721	20981
	2013	1039527	431489	81346	65041	155907	30957	194236	183018	27873	21045
	2014	1071841	463617	83312	66585	168765	33904	211540	199913	27514	20702
	2015	1067094	444432	77339	60447	159706	32303	207387	196562	18813	13337
Southern Asia	2000	3620	1639	150	103	956	203	532	511	71	33
	2012	42021	14328	988	481	8653	1604	4687	4492	973	728
	2013	48153	15402	1122	614	9292	1685	4988	4769	881	704
	2014	50104	15225	1066	588	8743	1559	5416	5211	763	616
	2015	45034	15225	1252	885	8490	1542	5483	5200	559	417
South-Eastern Asia	2000	225601	118448	27613	23210	38204	7472	52631	51246	145	131
	2012	449603	144968	48242	34475	49891	12607	46835	44775	2685	2429
	2013	470298	154513	49401	34811	55432	13731	49680	46965	3081	2620
	2014	482703	160651	51242	36199	57477	14107	51932	49722	3147	2524
	2015	465486	157830	49299	33963	55751	14408	52780	50698	2888	2167
Western Asia	2000	18734	11177	342	205	6817	1835	4018	3892	570	265
	2012	116997	36584	967	387	27967	5796	7650	6651	6457	2758
	2013	135930	40877	897	387	32106	6098	7875	7124	7193	3112
	2014	142445	43628	837	326	34942	7152	7850	7507	6932	2662
	2015	137744	41969	812	343	33678	6499	7480	7125	5034	1634
Oceania	2000	154	106	30	4	59	28	18	17	10	10
	2012	302	187	128	1	26	0	34	33	0	0
	2013	357	210	152	1	25	1	33	32	0	0
	2014	531	241	192	1	19	0	30	27	0	0
	2015	244	105	52	0	36	0	17	16	0	0

For general note and footnotes see end of table

Les exportations de marchandises du monde par provenance et destination (Tableau D)

En millions de dollars E.-U. f.o.b.

South-Eastern Europe / Europe du Sud-Est	Northern Africa / Afrique septentrionale	Sub-Saharan Africa / Afrique subsaharienne	Latin America and the Caribbean / Amérique latine et Caraïbes	Eastern Asia / Asie orientale	Southern Asia / Asie méridionale	South-eastern Asia / Asie du Sud-Est	Western Asia / Asie occidentale	Oceania / Océanie	Other 3/ / Autres 3/	Année	← Exportations vers / Exportations en provenance de ↓
				Machines et matériel de transport (CTCI, Rev. 3, 7)*[suite]*							
0	62	28	0	1	3	1	65	0	26	2000	Afrique septentrionale
126	696	334	20	41	15	296	778	1	187	2012	
160	710	357	23	24	27	294	998	1	186	2013	
189	683	446	22	33	65	299	1689	1	182	2014	
172	507	438	21	31	31	305	1487	1	153	2015	
4	25	1374	92	140	40	118	98	3	8	2000	Afrique subsaharienne
47	954	14726	524	518	288	340	531	37	98	2012	
42	425	18282	500	646	239	433	626	443	78	2013	
44	232	12952	818	1103	222	901	1040	463	40	2014	
36	124	11253	706	635	343	950	937	565	35	2015	
4	21	967	88	136	25	96	65	2	2	2000	Afrique du sud
27	417	8451	445	400	211	247	261	5	78	2012	
21	408	7809	417	523	164	277	376	3	25	2013	
19	187	8066	385	366	186	428	560	3	25	2014	
12	83	5970	411	217	140	338	463	2	18	2015	
3	47	290	11636	632	99	526	174	1	30	2000	Amérique latine et Caraïbes
236	229	1983	49545	5242	692	2621	1607	14	45	2012	
76	220	1878	55227	5596	612	1889	1333	10	150	2013	
110	452	1566	41785	5835	565	2855	1676	8	52	2014	
96	251	1427	35230	4805	565	2251	1383	18	111	2015	
1	41	254	6013	131	70	97	130	1	...	2000	Brésil
137	148	1544	19694	1510	372	1283	646	8	0	2012	
22	182	1477	25658	988	233	588	346	6	3	2013	
17	392	1101	15466	676	247	1580	552	3	...	2014	
13	198	889	14504	1417	234	1411	393	12	0	2015	
234	1157	3450	11495	92408	4161	37353	7456	528	188	2000	Asie orientale
2795	11765	31072	89714	604304	49229	158080	59726	6360	16	2012	
2948	11301	35158	91472	682508	48023	174525	62643	9567	35	2013	
3676	13426	37161	92359	678235	55163	188150	70221	10015	43	2014	
3478	13393	37245	88043	676161	59279	191766	67323	11650	94	2015	
39	283	1034	2120	21483	1303	7934	1814	10	...	2000	Chine
2097	7307	22619	58353	266916	34676	84396	32947	2185	...	2012	
2155	7574	25174	59245	317400	34170	96227	36382	1838	...	2013	
2654	8734	27596	59661	294623	39931	104657	41345	1509	...	2014	
2513	8856	27524	56929	308619	43175	112235	40094	3846	59	2015	
3	69	318	125	154	336	455	448	1	1	2000	Asie méridionale
144	1660	4741	2600	1585	3039	5934	6893	23	101	2012	
131	1563	5394	3332	2032	4309	6324	8499	28	257	2013	
275	1309	5669	3455	2169	6250	5793	9162	33	2	2014	
126	1078	4515	3563	1775	5211	5406	7401	129	44	2015	
31	254	1347	3706	37740	3156	57969	2659	114	32	2000	Asie du Sud-est
285	1694	4787	11568	134569	14347	117581	16261	737	124	2012	
326	1938	5459	13427	139872	13433	118739	18749	641	121	2013	
380	2067	4769	13006	149007	13468	115114	20038	830	226	2014	
404	1659	4461	13289	141842	13644	109211	19249	780	229	2015	
268	575	587	375	803	941	422	2180	7	829	2000	Asie occidentale
1437	5927	6432	2229	9248	11150	3334	28774	84	5342	2012	
1595	6145	6975	2802	11666	12479	4265	33487	108	8338	2013	
1670	6522	8368	2364	6282	13593	4110	38425	209	10341	2014	
1476	6001	7962	1582	6592	12733	5153	36962	92	12187	2015	
0	...	1	1	2	0	13	0	13	10	2000	Océanie
0	0	11	4	12	1	57	1	28	0	2012	
0	0	10	7	20	1	73	2	32	1	2013	
0	0	27	12	52	6	117	3	72	1	2014	
0	0	19	7	20	15	25	2	50	1	2015	

Voir la fin du tableau pour la remarque générale et les notes.

World merchandise exports by provenance and destination (Table D)

In million U.S. dollars f.o.b.

Exports to → / ↓ Exports from	Year	World 1/ Monde 1/	Developed economies 2/ Économies développées 2/ Total	Asia-Pacific Asie-Pacifique Total	Asia-Pacific Japan Japon	Europe Total	Europe Germany Allemagne	North America Amérique du Nord Total	North America U.S.A. É.-U.	Commonwealth of Independent States Communauté d'Etats Indépendants Total	CIS Europe
Miscellaneous manufactured articles (SITC, Rev. 3, 8)											
World 1/	2000	777143	591603	64445	53830	316465	67232	210692	183886	9403	8001
	2012	1982372	1218836	132218	99900	720288	140181	366330	314144	65020	49566
	2013	2079421	1276831	130049	96842	763013	147412	383769	330648	73535	56708
	2014	2186949	1339103	127920	93699	811632	155324	399550	346575	72822	54329
	2015	2083734	1315241	121475	87671	770543	144837	423224	371992	49389	36033
Developed Economies - Asia-Pacific 2/	2000	46250	23611	1476	127	8212	2530	13923	13423	60	51
	2012	70374	25012	2734	204	10234	3213	12044	11431	323	296
	2013	62263	23042	2594	174	9165	2932	11283	10791	348	333
	2014	62176	23138	2558	183	9635	2874	10945	10474	303	283
	2015	55903	21585	2548	178	8353	2416	10684	10200	195	183
Japan	2000	43292	21705	525	.	7829	2456	13351	12873	58	49
	2012	63824	20268	684	.	8841	2942	10742	10227	305	280
	2013	55894	18425	625	.	7872	2701	9927	9533	323	309
	2014	55789	18481	539	.	8378	2686	9564	9197	290	275
	2015	49769	17237	727	.	7237	2238	9273	8884	183	175
Developed Economies - Europe 2/	2000	288632	246097	10521	8421	201318	41326	34258	31916	4596	4268
	2012	658662	510051	20510	14380	433139	79193	56402	51999	26424	23413
	2013	705048	544793	20248	14040	464256	85780	60289	55836	27995	25036
	2014	741140	576608	20716	14365	491461	92493	64431	59744	24530	21767
	2015	698303	543315	20095	14198	451858	83878	71362	66793	16504	13945
France	2000	28497	23630	1558	1416	19052	3940	3020	2668	226	204
	2012	60025	45858	2229	1880	38760	7356	4869	4299	1281	1093
	2013	63882	48785	2143	1780	40918	7729	5724	5175	1253	1083
	2014	65520	50060	2192	1810	42554	7914	5313	4721	1171	966
	2015	83080	60229	3243	2816	44380	6985	12607	11878	1459	1317
Germany	2000	51366	43807	1667	1311	37120	.	5020	4704	988	898
	2012	142204	108704	3863	2703	93562	.	11279	10427	7107	6527
	2013	149119	114133	3917	2744	98344	.	11872	10981	7013	6377
	2014	154704	119739	3932	2753	103637	.	12170	11291	5852	5242
	2015	136422	105984	3548	2404	91066	.	11370	10551	3694	3221
Developed Economies - North America 2/	2000	111719	73198	11745	9882	26291	4281	35162	16857	271	219
	2012	171706	103560	14953	10790	42143	6775	46463	15443	1096	918
	2013	176013	104460	14582	10534	43619	7038	46259	15248	1242	1071
	2014	181704	107538	14076	9967	46690	7412	46772	15687	1234	1029
	2015	180578	105444	13319	9533	46342	7366	45783	17253	993	791
United States	2000	93184	55116	11494	9680	25322	4102	18299	.	237	190
	2012	151590	85882	14495	10567	40381	6505	31006	.	969	814
	2013	156292	86963	14143	10309	41826	6795	30995	.	1104	953
	2014	161371	89602	13647	9742	44886	7166	31070	.	1138	949
	2015	159067	86070	12926	9322	44625	7153	28518	.	939	754
South-Eastern Europe	2000	5919	5677	9	6	5347	1365	322	303	70	60
	2012	16069	14269	26	20	14000	3336	244	219	544	508
	2013	17751	15630	30	20	15301	3642	298	275	669	628
	2014	19042	16873	39	25	16534	3724	300	274	588	533
	2015	16990	15068	39	25	14714	3389	314	283	360	317
Commonwealth of Independent States	2000	3707	1869	6	6	1486	462	377	366	874	707
	2012	11152	3450	100	96	2914	1362	436	416	5873	4269
	2013	12138	3115	162	158	2520	788	432	416	6427	4551
	2014	12357	3619	242	238	2805	781	572	549	6206	4198
	2015	10364	2680	138	134	2281	639	261	250	4551	3069
Russian Federation 4/	2000	2063	973	5	5	735	130	233	228	223	87
	2012	4855	1522	85	84	1038	517	398	382	1860	864
	2013	5830	1507	157	155	961	371	389	379	2126	955
	2014	6238	1886	237	235	1174	359	475	461	2247	918
	2015	5737	1302	135	132	974	319	194	188	1638	651

For general note and footnotes see end of table

Les exportations de marchandises du monde par provenance et destination (Tableau D)

En millions de dollars E.-U. f.o.b.

← Exportations vers

South-Eastern Europe / Europe du Sud-Est	Northern Africa / Afrique septentrionale	Sub-Saharan Africa / Afrique subsaharienne	Latin America and the Caribbean / Amérique latine et Caraïbes	Eastern Asia / Asie orientale	Southern Asia / Asie méridionale	South-eastern Asia / Asie du Sud-Est	Western Asia / Asie occidentale	Oceania / Océanie	Other 3/ / Autres 3/	Année	Exportations en provenance de ↓
Articles manifacturés divers (CTCI, Rev. 3, 8)											
3356	4479	6415	39226	70778	4456	24515	20227	620	2065	2000	Monde 1/
11563	14318	34250	97897	301496	36746	94426	103391	1493	2936	2012	
12537	15527	35280	95943	313874	35680	107370	107784	1448	3612	2013	
14113	16445	41162	96721	329283	39313	114019	118181	1399	4389	2014	
13003	17931	43693	95584	282736	37624	108762	114541	1330	3900	2015	
14	52	174	802	15385	388	4933	577	118	133	2000	Economies développées - Asie-Pacifique 2/
20	90	291	2416	30955	1021	9083	838	314	10	2012	
16	79	242	1621	27279	840	7659	780	341	17	2013	
20	87	228	1602	27424	752	7506	812	283	20	2014	
22	69	201	1234	24214	752	6654	703	252	22	2015	
12	51	135	765	14980	343	4673	551	20	...	2000	Japon
18	85	184	2305	30404	903	8589	751	14	...	2012	
14	72	152	1519	26801	716	7188	671	13	...	2013	
18	81	153	1490	26909	666	6994	694	11	0	2014	
19	64	135	1120	23573	677	6158	591	10	...	2015	
2800	2669	2338	5393	9423	1359	3371	8797	208	1581	2000	Economies développées - Europe 2/
8195	5472	6872	13077	42438	6066	10297	28880	344	545	2012	
9013	6143	7279	13577	45867	5496	11341	32192	348	1003	2013	
10011	6233	7446	13694	49912	5449	11885	34079	380	912	2014	
9064	6382	9777	13226	47438	5425	12118	33497	347	1211	2015	
184	765	524	431	1157	181	296	967	132	4	2000	France
456	1513	1109	1097	4428	481	1097	2382	259	65	2012	
505	1604	1100	1137	4742	482	1306	2603	266	100	2013	
536	1646	1097	1045	5013	499	1384	2686	289	93	2014	
431	2345	4293	1489	5062	873	1848	4388	267	395	2015	
366	283	418	1004	1617	294	717	1320	6	546	2000	Allemagne
1593	780	1303	3074	10367	1649	2185	5368	12	61	2012	
1761	774	1298	3391	11224	1521	2233	5677	16	79	2013	
2031	827	1304	3233	11887	1550	2434	5820	11	16	2014	
1799	695	1192	2937	10995	1512	2365	5220	10	17	2015	
35	510	453	21696	8327	463	4596	2133	38	0	2000	Economies développées - Amérique du Nord 2/
148	524	1291	28080	20564	2413	6481	7480	71	0	2012	
172	475	1334	28944	21553	2651	6895	8223	63	0	2013	
184	538	1375	30309	23452	2286	6797	7919	72	0	2014	
160	581	1154	30015	25278	2364	6803	7735	49	0	2015	
33	502	434	21555	8197	450	4561	2062	37	...	2000	Etats-Unis
133	496	1195	27518	19925	2330	6282	6796	64	...	2012	
156	435	1236	28418	20863	2563	6661	7836	58	...	2013	
168	502	1295	29706	22676	2214	6579	7422	68	...	2014	
145	533	1077	29462	24562	2282	6594	7357	45	...	2015	
125	2	4	2	2	1	0	31	0	3	2000	Europe du Sud-Est
756	52	15	41	78	45	27	240	1	3	2012	
874	90	24	50	76	35	23	278	0	2	2013	
906	97	28	59	115	44	29	298	0	4	2014	
859	79	30	79	126	36	30	320	0	4	2015	
19	18	30	20	503	223	31	118	0	0	2000	Communauté d'Etats Indépendants
164	66	43	109	548	475	144	267	0	13	2012	
177	37	92	89	607	470	369	740	1	14	2013	
195	59	56	53	658	561	178	756	0	15	2014	
145	737	132	69	473	776	245	546	0	10	2015	
11	9	23	12	492	213	29	76	0	0	2000	Fédération de Russie 4/
15	61	32	98	514	427	134	186	0	6	2012	
30	30	78	78	553	429	357	636	0	7	2013	
21	53	41	43	611	536	167	625	0	7	2014	
17	733	115	64	442	755	236	430	0	4	2015	

Voir la fin du tableau pour la remarque générale et les notes.

World merchandise exports by provenance and destination (Table D)

In million U.S. dollars f.o.b.

Exports to → / ↓ Exports from	Year	World 1/ Monde 1/	Developed economies 2/ Économies développées 2/ Total	Asia-Pacific Asie-Pacifique Total	Asia-Pacific Japan Japon	Europe Total	Europe Germany Allemagne	North America Amérique du Nord Total	North America U.S.A. É.-U.	Commonwealth of Independent States Communauté d'Etats Indépendants Total	CIS Europe
Miscellaneous manufactured articles (SITC, Rev. 3, 8)*[cont.]*											
Northern Africa	2000	6113	5902	6	5	5598	719	297	290	0	0
	2012	10149	8920	13	7	8128	852	779	758	11	9
	2013	10354	8934	14	9	8114	924	806	788	14	12
	2014	10420	9050	12	7	8246	822	792	772	13	11
	2015	9695	8395	17	12	7506	723	872	853	11	10
Sub-Saharan Africa	2000	3655	2664	41	19	1667	357	956	939	1	1
	2012	7661	3012	63	11	1710	318	1240	1209	17	15
	2013	8117	3350	59	12	1899	319	1393	1357	10	7
	2014	10033	4822	63	14	3300	303	1459	1385	14	6
	2015	9370	4686	65	12	3301	277	1320	1237	14	4
South Africa	2000	1101	790	29	14	556	276	204	200	0	0
	2012	3175	827	40	4	492	209	294	285	15	13
	2013	3038	728	36	6	464	169	228	219	5	2
	2014	3033	596	38	7	402	144	156	148	9	4
	2015	2455	476	37	6	306	81	133	121	8	3
Latin America and the Caribbean	2000	31659	27813	183	101	1145	310	26485	26284	6	6
	2012	53780	42482	325	212	2811	539	39346	38517	65	58
	2013	55951	45491	314	188	2834	596	42343	41498	75	68
	2014	60090	49789	327	204	3040	600	46422	45558	56	49
	2015	64766	55480	394	268	7359	509	47727	46864	36	31
Brazil	2000	3455	2315	52	34	590	135	1673	1624	3	3
	2012	4770	1847	90	47	899	240	858	823	41	38
	2013	4523	1842	87	39	858	228	897	858	45	42
	2014	4500	1782	82	35	875	224	825	776	31	27
	2015	4102	1730	71	28	746	182	913	871	21	19
Eastern Asia	2000	195615	139896	31957	28207	38835	8850	69104	65047	2369	1902
	2012	714517	358856	72879	58213	134583	28167	151394	140036	26076	17403
	2013	754532	367288	71341	56248	138137	27534	157811	145816	31476	21892
	2014	791742	380359	68532	52734	149123	28392	162704	151085	34277	23170
	2015	739517	383879	63256	47193	144177	26762	176446	164347	22364	15060
China	2000	85989	57952	18935	17210	13990	3023	25027	23605	2080	1646
	2012	533788	280936	57792	45938	103749	22028	119395	110009	24249	15773
	2013	579090	293211	57250	44878	109282	22073	126680	116614	29561	20208
	2014	619237	307389	54961	41899	120241	23393	132187	122329	32610	21781
	2015	585526	317471	51451	37872	118716	22280	147304	136800	21167	14121
Southern Asia	2000	19583	16334	407	249	7486	1660	8442	7944	597	371
	2012	75827	45688	1823	906	27392	6400	16474	14904	517	268
	2013	72721	50959	1976	975	30785	7146	18199	16472	657	361
	2014	72675	47955	1896	943	30167	6300	15891	14583	1026	677
	2015	82011	57990	2587	1312	36049	7801	19354	17649	930	742
South-Eastern Asia	2000	49644	37171	7497	6364	11949	2503	17725	16987	118	106
	2012	136531	81637	18321	14821	26075	5897	37241	35222	841	797
	2013	145575	86453	18227	14224	28040	6278	40186	37980	963	913
	2014	160687	93652	18911	14736	30272	7034	44469	41957	1044	980
	2015	156159	93220	18515	14524	30351	7149	44353	41796	831	784
Western Asia	2000	13531	10559	123	88	6868	2865	3568	3457	442	309
	2012	54718	21812	405	240	17144	4126	4263	3985	3233	1611
	2013	57699	23225	426	259	18334	4435	4465	4166	3658	1834
	2014	63554	25608	471	283	20349	4588	4788	4501	3530	1625
	2015	58762	23440	459	279	18245	3926	4736	4457	2600	1096
Oceania	2000	1117	811	474	355	264	3	73	73	0	0
	2012	1226	86	65	0	15	0	6	6	0	0
	2013	1258	92	76	0	11	0	5	5	0	0
	2014	1329	93	77	0	11	1	5	5	0	0
	2015	1318	59	41	0	8	1	10	10	0	0

For general note and footnotes see end of table

Les exportations de marchandises du monde par provenance et destination (Tableau D)

En millions de dollars E.-U. f.o.b.

South-Eastern Europe Europe du Sud-Est	Northern Africa Afrique septentrionale	Sub-Saharan Africa Afrique subsaharienne	Latin America and the Caribbean Amérique latine et Caraïbes	Eastern Asia Asie orientale	Southern Asia Asie méridionale	South-eastern Asia Asie du Sud-Est	Western Asia Asie occidentale	Oceania Océanie	Other 3/ Autres 3/	Année	← Exportations vers Exportations en provence de ↓
			Articles manifacturés divers (CTCI, Rev. 3, 8) *[suite]*								
0	52	46	3	1	1	1	53	0	54	2000	Afrique septentrionale
8	310	234	20	38	11	4	517	0	76	2012	
11	315	234	19	35	8	5	694	0	86	2013	
14	271	242	17	31	12	5	677	0	87	2014	
15	208	265	19	30	6	6	665	0	75	2015	
0	4	827	18	16	8	17	91	1	7	2000	Afrique subsaharienne
43	13	4246	89	53	52	51	68	1	16	2012	
40	12	4306	53	78	31	38	180	2	17	2013	
32	10	4233	66	141	40	51	536	3	85	2014	
24	15	3795	45	137	38	36	476	2	103	2015	
0	3	231	10	10	6	15	33	1	1	2000	Afrique du sud
22	10	2142	22	24	30	32	44	1	7	2012	
17	10	2093	28	18	9	14	104	1	10	2013	
12	6	2166	36	30	20	32	113	2	11	2014	
4	11	1783	19	22	14	14	96	2	6	2015	
2	10	26	3566	98	18	41	48	1	29	2000	Amérique latine et Caraïbes
15	23	387	9876	390	61	220	179	1	79	2012	
17	21	235	9129	385	70	204	228	2	94	2013	
17	31	257	8926	385	63	278	252	2	33	2014	
13	16	198	7881	455	57	197	380	1	52	2015	
1	4	17	1022	30	13	20	30	0	...	2000	Brésil
9	14	365	2167	79	36	94	118	1	...	2012	
10	16	209	2008	90	47	92	163	1	...	2013	
10	24	210	1981	98	34	155	174	1	0	2014	
7	11	150	1701	96	33	91	262	1	0	2015	
215	740	1632	6514	32754	949	6154	4211	168	14	2000	Asie orientale
1313	5608	16877	38787	179129	12586	46699	28134	447	5	2012	
1168	5903	17087	36887	188885	15614	57321	32489	404	10	2013	
1301	6308	21914	36220	193091	20100	61293	36463	398	16	2014	
1258	7146	23102	37158	149786	18143	59637	36542	483	19	2015	
184	486	801	2665	17527	283	1857	2137	16	...	2000	Chine
1221	5286	16117	32988	100530	9676	37833	24710	241	...	2012	
1071	5574	16423	31220	112500	13294	47297	28734	207	...	2013	
1185	5854	21221	30340	120620	17704	50372	31721	221	...	2014	
1142	6730	22454	31860	86538	15778	49490	32553	342	2	2015	
7	23	241	213	345	182	255	1371	14	2	2000	Asie méridionale
43	171	1393	1442	3518	1032	1273	20599	27	124	2012	
59	172	1843	1627	2825	1012	1417	12011	37	102	2013	
100	197	2004	1581	4166	999	1516	12167	30	934	2014	
156	214	1880	1759	4515	1244	1530	11633	32	128	2015	
15	102	478	676	3729	624	5001	1660	60	7	2000	Asie du Sud-est
46	291	1396	3570	21365	2520	19464	5098	249	55	2012	
51	278	1197	3559	23365	2243	21267	5890	212	97	2013	
58	285	1625	3795	27423	2327	23469	6628	199	184	2014	
58	279	1450	3685	27866	2331	20563	5544	141	190	2015	
123	297	164	58	171	238	110	1136	0	233	2000	Asie occidentale
811	1698	1206	391	2405	10461	676	11088	14	922	2012	
940	2003	1402	387	2913	7209	824	14077	12	1050	2013	
1273	2328	1750	398	2451	6681	1003	17585	4	943	2014	
1229	2203	1709	415	2377	6452	939	16497	4	897	2015	
0	0	2	266	23	0	3	1	10	1	2000	Océanie
0	0	1	1	14	3	6	3	23	1089	2012	
0	0	4	0	6	0	7	2	24	1121	2013	
0	0	3	1	33	0	7	8	28	1156	2014	
0	0	0	0	41	0	5	3	18	1191	2015	

Voir la fin du tableau pour la remarque générale et les notes.

World merchandise exports by provenance and destination (Table D)

In million U.S. dollars f.o.b.

Exports to → / ↓ Exports from	Year	World 1/ Monde 1/	Developed economies 2/ Économies développées 2/ Total	Asia-Pacific Asie-Pacifique Total	Asia-Pacific Asie-Pacifique Japan Japon	Europe Total	Europe Germany Allemagne	North America Amérique du Nord Total	North America Amérique du Nord U.S.A. É.-U.	Commonwealth of Independent States Communauté d'Etats Indépendants Total	Commonwealth of Independent States Communauté d'Etats Indépendants Europe
Commodities and transactions not classified elsewhere in the SITC (SITC, Rev. 3, 9)											
World 1/	2000	269300	189728	7686	4557	137698	42898	44344	37483	6249	1948
	2012	999571	489377	22823	13187	367214	64505	99340	72846	10455	7626
	2013	1087227	444526	20579	12188	335206	49931	88741	60272	12221	8312
	2014	937861	390223	20034	11822	288187	46552	82001	55383	10131	7516
	2015	886431	338956	18529	10306	247792	22756	72635	46903	6039	5130
Developed Economies - Asia-Pacific 2/	2000	24052	12469	639	317	5868	977	5962	5827	13	10
	2012	70240	23811	1177	152	15711	1506	6923	6533	112	84
	2013	64879	16206	1281	95	7859	1658	7066	6720	177	88
	2014	62418	15586	1136	154	7338	1613	7112	6789	151	83
	2015	61939	15554	1290	115	6547	1324	7717	7394	84	52
Japan	2000	17490	9032	214	.	3389	974	5429	5296	10	9
	2012	42534	14570	418	.	8125	1331	6028	5647	110	83
	2013	41051	13389	626	.	6482	1453	6281	5938	176	86
	2014	40494	13052	541	.	6123	1493	6389	6085	151	83
	2015	42487	13761	541	.	5841	1290	7379	7060	83	51
Developed Economies - Europe 2/	2000	142183	119326	2654	1660	105919	39503	10753	9217	897	489
	2012	365508	245729	4102	2699	210069	53792	31557	28783	5421	4271
	2013	430300	240077	3106	1747	219335	37560	17636	14987	6401	4575
	2014	313323	187081	2309	1429	170971	34399	13800	12612	4318	3207
	2015	291827	143369	1776	1052	133746	11650	7848	7105	2904	2470
France	2000	6657	5424	194	157	4748	1034	482	440	59	57
	2012	16819	13263	502	425	11890	2967	872	785	299	285
	2013	15599	12085	325	246	10877	2941	883	790	261	248
	2014	15245	11519	296	225	10195	2774	1027	916	252	242
	2015	6125	1149	25	14	999	97	126	98	4	2
Germany	2000	40968	32604	131	106	31812	.	661	578	272	195
	2012	71544	46456	791	552	43256	.	2408	2174	2412	2118
	2013	73323	48620	745	503	45393	.	2483	2290	2429	2157
	2014	77727	53762	823	584	49403	.	3536	3169	2285	2024
	2015	81226	60863	754	533	56942	.	3167	2841	2060	1837
Developed Economies - North America 2/	2000	50157	36014	2709	1591	11165	1213	22141	17252	208	103
	2012	201516	115622	12763	8332	73853	7262	29007	15209	2195	1696
	2013	211565	109450	11740	7836	65535	7926	32174	16478	3001	2224
	2014	210203	110205	13186	8152	62558	8313	34462	18397	3644	2450
	2015	213647	112282	11555	7699	63688	8419	37039	19354	2274	1988
United States	2000	32007	18124	2589	1504	10659	1116	4876	.	197	98
	2012	171634	87050	12430	8204	60827	7103	13793	.	2187	1689
	2013	180473	82521	11055	7218	55772	7554	15694	.	2993	2217
	2014	178447	81629	12741	7787	52826	8113	16062	.	3634	2441
	2015	182733	83934	11365	7591	54888	8197	17681	.	2262	1977
South-Eastern Europe	2000	385	121	1	0	113	8	8	8	1	0
	2012	2589	1848	3	3	1809	320	36	35	19	16
	2013	3424	2726	2	2	2657	568	67	65	26	19
	2014	4769	3463	3	3	3370	528	90	88	17	13
	2015	3824	2432	4	4	2347	445	81	80	9	7
Commonwealth of Independent States	2000	17427	5846	121	120	5460	545	265	258	4947	1277
	2012	23506	11340	266	266	9533	239	1541	1289	2456	1377
	2013	26058	10982	194	193	9018	340	1771	1544	2050	1042
	2014	21764	10963	89	89	10680	141	194	73	1700	1596
	2015	22254	9486	0	0	9318	16	168	10	612	535
Russian Federation 4/	2000	12145	3124	43	43	2983	9	98	95	3551	221
	2012	17841	8143	40	39	6750	194	1353	1266	1069	129
	2013	18790	6428	1	0	4834	312	1594	1513	977	65
	2014	14772	5886	18	18	5810	121	58	57	900	865
	2015	12309	1156	...	...	1155	0	1	...	1	0

For general note and footnotes see end of table

Les exportations de marchandises du monde par provenance et destination (Tableau D)

En millions de dollars E.-U. f.o.b.

South-Eastern Europe Europe du Sud-Est	Northern Africa Afrique septentrio-nale	Sub-Saharan Africa Afrique subsahari-enne	Latin America and the Caribbean Amérique latine et Caraïbes	Eastern Asia Asie orientale	Southern Asia Asie méridionale	South-eastern Asia Asie du Sud-Est	Western Asia Asie occidentale	Oceania Océanie	Other 3/ Autres 3/	⟵ Exportations vers Année	Exportations en provence de ↓
Articles et transactions non classés ailleurs dans la CTCI (CTCI, Rev. 3, 9)											
3045	964	2616	11749	16612	2889	11605	9343	192	14308	2000	Monde 1/
4594	4616	24082	50479	147670	67105	46279	49973	2958	101983	2012	
4158	5582	21091	46592	240643	52505	63580	80329	3421	112581	2013	
5449	3356	19919	42742	169538	39176	47771	76946	3467	129145	2014	
2828	2634	14679	37510	158222	37406	48225	64411	2480	173041	2015	
14	38	56	223	5818	98	4875	414	33	1	2000	Économies développées - Asie-Pacifique 2/
18	30	389	517	29689	3727	10499	927	104	418	2012	
20	300	486	622	32994	2110	10152	1244	134	434	2013	
17	31	400	548	31699	1158	11490	844	93	402	2014	
15	35	197	506	25862	1259	11156	612	207	6451	2015	
14	38	50	223	4319	68	3474	251	11	0	2000	Japon
17	26	174	512	18281	347	8012	467	18	...	2012	
19	186	153	525	17662	611	7755	558	19	...	2013	
15	31	175	493	17885	386	7746	542	17	...	2014	
15	34	182	493	17966	454	8967	516	17	...	2015	
396	639	1175	1824	3863	1580	1911	3780	17	6775	2000	Économies développées - Europe 2/
4197	1330	3864	9992	18685	31818	15338	14314	60	14760	2012	
3603	2105	4479	4589	69380	27410	23843	32553	108	15751	2013	
4530	1577	2667	4401	42657	22370	12987	18127	57	12551	2014	
2347	1010	1387	3998	49153	21962	10253	14095	58	41290	2015	
19	125	133	210	235	80	139	214	7	11	2000	France
92	286	341	437	772	231	342	521	34	201	2012	
102	301	317	419	706	205	351	604	36	212	2013	
98	311	319	437	778	257	338	672	34	231	2014	
2	23	148	33	31	8	30	61	26	4609	2015	
92	190	245	317	1089	210	238	502	6	5201	2000	Allemagne
915	360	897	1984	3825	1172	1670	2792	6	9054	2012	
1149	400	802	1942	4165	914	1604	2681	9	8608	2013	
1199	617	729	2079	5122	1084	2133	3880	17	4820	2014	
1483	466	589	2193	4125	1108	1611	3435	21	3271	2015	
45	77	330	8301	2504	268	1350	1015	44	0	2000	Économies développées - Amérique du Nord 2/
116	618	3380	25683	24945	5166	9542	14060	186	3	2012	
142	507	3121	25821	36076	4095	12921	16269	145	17	2013	
133	312	4493	26821	32225	3825	12405	15928	207	4	2014	
108	593	3224	27327	33177	3968	13710	16826	151	6	2015	
42	72	311	8210	2437	257	1321	994	43	...	2000	États-Unis
114	607	3338	25486	24086	5116	9471	13999	179	...	2012	
140	491	3069	25595	33059	3994	12712	15766	134	...	2013	
130	296	4444	26594	29886	3733	12129	15777	195	...	2014	
106	575	3177	27076	31633	3783	13433	16625	129	...	2015	
32	3	10	5	3	8	4	150	0	48	2000	Europe du Sud-Est
175	5	12	6	1	9	17	166	1	331	2012	
271	9	30	7	1	37	10	160	2	146	2013	
496	61	53	7	29	59	13	260	2	308	2014	
254	34	54	6	3	41	17	213	2	759	2015	
2523	78	24	50	1150	287	61	2461	0	1	2000	Communauté d'Etats Indépendants
4	2046	297	1651	814	2537	777	847	1	735	2012	
10	1193	102	1851	2523	3645	1510	1486	0	706	2013	
67	7	81	383	126	23	174	7518	0	720	2014	
2	5	35	21	64	24	55	384	0	11565	2015	
2513	...	0	2	556	12	23	2363	...	...	2000	Fédération de Russie 4/
1	2034	250	1634	787	2513	682	727	0	0	2012	
8	1186	42	1838	2515	3392	1180	1224	...	...	2013	
59	0	38	369	117	13	152	7237	0	...	2014	
...	...	6	...	59	17	40	234	...	10797	2015	

Voir la fin du tableau pour la remarque générale et les notes.

World merchandise exports by provenance and destination (Table D)

In million U.S. dollars f.o.b.

Exports to ⟶ / ↓ Exports from	Year	World 1/ Monde 1/	Developed economies 2/ Économies développées 2/ Total	Asia-Pacific Asie-Pacifique Total	Asia-Pacific Japan Japon	Europe Total	Europe Germany Allemagne	North America Amérique du Nord Total	North America U.S.A. É.-U.	Commonwealth of Independent States Communauté d'Etats Indépendants Total	CIS Europe
Commodities and transactions not classified elsewhere in the SITC (SITC, Rev. 3, 9) *[cont.]*											
Northern Africa	2000	135	114	1	1	17	0	95	95	2	0
	2012	2511	505	0	0	417	2	88	2	0	0
	2013	1663	622	0	0	123	4	499	6	0	0
	2014	1893	556	1	0	84	6	471	9	1	1
	2015	1573	535	1	0	85	7	448	9	1	1
Sub-Saharan Africa	2000	5215	3653	10	9	3236	14	407	405	46	1
	2012	28688	8205	124	111	7773	42	307	135	2	2
	2013	24633	6680	45	41	6379	44	256	79	19	0
	2014	23480	7181	84	7	6726	21	370	220	1	1
	2015	19638	4927	91	3	4667	82	170	158	0	0
South Africa	2000	3561	2358	8	8	1967	3	383	381	46	0
	2012	9142	1758	46	38	1614	26	99	16	0	0
	2013	7051	1110	42	39	1007	16	60	5	19	0
	2014	5190	2058	14	0	1867	5	177	132	1	1
	2015	2512	35	1	0	32	2	1	1	...	...
Latin America and the Caribbean	2000	6518	4198	22	22	1840	60	2336	2160	31	0
	2012	47161	41806	185	176	14697	336	26925	18634	6	5
	2013	40180	34569	97	90	10253	492	24220	16193	12	12
	2014	36896	31536	45	42	8882	444	22609	14828	2	1
	2015	32251	26143	26	23	8898	190	17218	11041	3	2
Brazil	2000	1449	1310	9	9	270	19	1031	1030	25	0
	2012	8315	6131	72	72	3708	236	2350	2153	0	0
	2013	7521	4484	10	10	2277	284	2196	1995	1	1
	2014	7137	4849	24	24	1876	317	2948	2741	2	0
	2015	5342	2236	3	2	1562	20	671	430	2	2
Eastern Asia	2000	3390	1290	442	110	759	15	88	79	1	1
	2012	58943	2514	636	376	1367	58	510	345	13	9
	2013	85285	2996	1024	730	1008	117	963	780	49	37
	2014	57437	2545	636	451	1479	70	431	400	19	10
	2015	52129	2310	436	357	1470	67	404	384	10	5
China	2000	514	64	37	36	13	0	15	14	0	...
	2012	1417	42	7	6	21	6	14	14	2	0
	2013	1729	32	1	1	15	5	15	15	9	0
	2014	2267	33	3	2	15	4	14	14	6	0
	2015	2031	21	3	3	10	4	8	8	4	0
Southern Asia	2000	1096	720	37	23	307	50	375	359	16	4
	2012	14055	1288	35	28	728	83	524	520	4	3
	2013	17197	2602	107	102	957	257	1538	1524	2	1
	2014	15937	392	122	119	175	35	95	95	8	8
	2015	20678	739	118	117	440	122	181	177	4	3
South-Eastern Asia	2000	8523	3416	887	589	1786	358	743	696	27	25
	2012	47534	14951	3271	994	10842	667	838	532	58	31
	2013	42440	9398	2003	1072	6467	666	927	565	85	58
	2014	40343	9681	1518	1015	7359	569	804	468	20	13
	2015	28511	7115	1178	769	5499	266	438	296	27	14
Western Asia	2000	10130	2488	124	104	1224	156	1140	1096	58	38
	2012	136750	21526	56	49	20393	193	1077	825	169	131
	2013	138953	7965	800	274	5557	293	1608	1314	397	255
	2014	148525	10816	769	357	8500	401	1547	1389	249	133
	2015	135809	12366	487	160	10974	168	905	878	111	50
Oceania	2000	88	72	39	11	3	0	31	31	1	...
	2012	569	233	204	2	22	6	6	6	0	0
	2013	649	253	179	6	58	8	17	16	0	0
	2014	873	218	138	4	65	11	16	15	0	...
	2015	2352	1698	1566	7	113	1	19	18	0	...

For general note and footnotes see end of table

Les exportations de marchandises du monde par provenance et destination (Tableau D)

En millions de dollars E.-U. f.o.b.

South-Eastern Europe / Europe du Sud-Est	Northern Africa / Afrique septentrionale	Sub-Saharan Africa / Afrique subsaharienne	Latin America and the Caribbean / Amérique latine et Caraïbes	Eastern Asia / Asie orientale	Southern Asia / Asie méridionale	South-eastern Asia / Asie du Sud-Est	Western Asia / Asie occidentale	Oceania / Océanie	Other 3/ / Autres 3/	Année	← Exportations vers / Exportations en provence de ↓
Articles et transactions non classés ailleurs dans la CTCI (CTCI, Rev. 3, 9) [suite]											
0	0	0	0	0	0	0	18	0	0	2000	Afrique septentrionale
0	39	484	0	2	4	0	1472	...	4	2012	
0	34	289	1	2	26	2	686	...	1	2013	
20	27	75	3	1	25	1	1184	0	0	2014	
3	26	86	1	0	8	1	911	...	2	2015	
2	5	528	4	880	18	11	62	0	4	2000	Afrique subsaharienne
2	5	8219	6	3433	3154	841	4234	0	588	2012	
2	4	6018	4	3207	2050	678	5156	5	809	2013	
6	4	6614	3	1791	1494	211	5423	0	753	2014	
4	5	6031	2	127	1129	2	4897	0	2513	2015	
2	...	220	4	865	17	8	42	0	...	2000	Afrique du sud
0	...	6	0	3302	2942	833	300	0	0	2012	
0	0	3	0	3165	1528	659	567	0	0	2013	
0	0	3	0	1733	600	209	587	0	0	2014	
...	0	11	0	67	0	1	12	0	2386	2015	
0	0	80	125	3	4	22	49	0	2006	2000	Amérique latine et Caraïbes
6	231	1015	1332	400	184	436	1734	1	9	2012	
5	161	711	1376	1413	606	311	1004	1	11	2013	
29	173	359	1293	271	580	166	653	0	1835	2014	
17	5	59	257	186	1469	27	698	2	3384	2015	
0	...	54	41	0	1	6	12	0	...	2000	Brésil
4	61	517	533	193	32	358	485	1	...	2012	
3	138	554	945	811	222	228	135	1	...	2013	
20	173	309	1111	138	326	103	106	0	...	2014	
0	4	10	69	55	282	4	251	2	2427	2015	
1	10	20	14	971	171	402	437	2	71	2000	Asie orientale
5	6	21	56	50378	1156	3652	277	4	861	2012	
18	27	49	292	73956	494	6053	452	11	887	2013	
6	4	20	51	50216	926	2695	386	4	564	2014	
10	5	82	57	42417	186	5686	667	1	696	2015	
0	9	11	1	47	161	8	209	0	2	2000	Chine
...	1	1	1	818	2	549	2	...	...	2012	
0	0	1	0	1409	1	276	1	0	...	2013	
...	0	1	2	2079	1	143	2	...	...	2014	
0	3	71	4	1812	2	107	3	...	4	2015	
0	2	15	14	18	183	38	88	0	1	2000	Asie méridionale
4	9	146	453	10811	396	169	643	44	90	2012	
16	91	393	1378	9374	440	218	2562	21	100	2013	
3	8	11	19	42	1591	64	13251	0	548	2014	
5	18	12	38	91	1689	1066	16316	0	699	2015	
4	12	307	1054	1062	182	1791	321	80	268	2000	Asie du Sud-est
2	51	5235	10639	7930	549	4086	1487	2547	0	2012	
5	73	4368	10128	8264	657	4935	1551	2977	1	2013	
17	45	4144	8856	7009	685	5239	1572	3074	1	2014	
1	35	2604	4920	5024	593	4666	905	2026	593	2015	
26	99	72	134	340	92	1139	547	1	5133	2000	Asie occidentale
65	247	1019	144	571	18405	920	9813	8	83864	2012	
66	1078	1044	522	3424	10934	2920	17206	10	93388	2013	
125	1105	1001	356	3190	6438	2307	11799	16	111123	2014	
61	861	907	377	1842	5079	1568	7887	16	104735	2015	
...	...	0	0	1	0	1	0	13	0	2000	Océanie
...	0	1	0	10	1	2	0	3	320	2012	
...	0	1	0	30	1	26	0	8	330	2013	
0	0	1	0	283	1	20	0	14	336	2014	
0	0	0	0	273	1	18	0	15	346	2015	

Voir la fin du tableau pour la remarque générale et les notes.

World merchandise exports by provenance and destination (Table D)
Les exportations de marchandises du monde par provenance et destination (Tableau D)

General note:

For further information on Sources, Method of Estimation, Currency Conversion, Period, Country Nomenclature and Country Grouping of this table, as well as for a brief table description, please see the Introduction

Footnotes:

1 Exports for which country of destination is not available are included in the totals for the 'World' and in region "Others" (see footnote number 3 for further explanation)

2 This classification is intended for statistical convenience and does not, necessarily, express a judgment about the stage reached by a particular country in the development process.

3 The region "Others" as destination for exports contains the following trading partners: Antarctica, bunkers, free zones, confidential and not elsewhere specified countries

Remarque générale:

Pour plus d'information en ce qui concerne les sources, la méthode d'estimation, taux d'exchange, période, nomenclature des pays et groupement de pays, ainsi que pour une brève description de ce tableau, veuillez voir l'Introduction

1 Exportations dont les pays de destination n'est pas disponible sont incluses dansles totaux pour le 'Monde ' et dans la région "les autres " (voir note n ° 3 pour plus d'explications)

2 Cette classification est utilisée pour plus de commodité dans la présentation des statistiques et n'implique pas nécessairement un jugement quant au stade de développement auquel est parvenuun pays donné.

3 La région "Autres" comme destination des exportations comprend les partenaires commerciaux suivants: Antarctique, combustibles de soute, zones franches, partenaires confidentiels ou non specifiés ailleurs

2015 INTERNATIONAL TRADE STATISTICS YEARBOOK

VOLUME I TRADE BY COUNTRY

PART 2 – COUNTRY TRADE PROFILES

170 Countries (or areas)

European Union

Afghanistan

Goods Imports: CIF, by origin | **Goods Exports: FOB, by last known destination** | **Trade System: General**

Overview:

In 2014, the value of merchandise exports of Afghanistan increased substantially by 10.8 percent to reach 570.5 mln US$, while its merchandise imports decreased moderately by 10.0 percent to reach 7.7 bln US$ (see graph 1, table 2 and table 3). The merchandise trade balance recorded a large deficit of 7.1 bln US$ (see graph 1). The largest merchandise trade balance was with MDG Southern Asia at -2.6 bln US$ (see graph 4). Merchandise exports in Afghanistan were highly concentrated amongst partners; imports were also highly concentrated. The top 3 partners accounted for 80 percent or more of exports and 3 partners accounted for 80 percent or more of imports (see graph 5). In 2014, the value of exports of services of Afghanistan increased substantially by 32.9 percent, reaching 1.2 bln US$, while its imports of services decreased substantially by 19.1 percent and reached 1.7 bln US$ (see graph 2). There was a moderate trade in services deficit of 517.3 mln US$.

Graph 1: Total merchandise trade, by value

(Bln US$ by year)

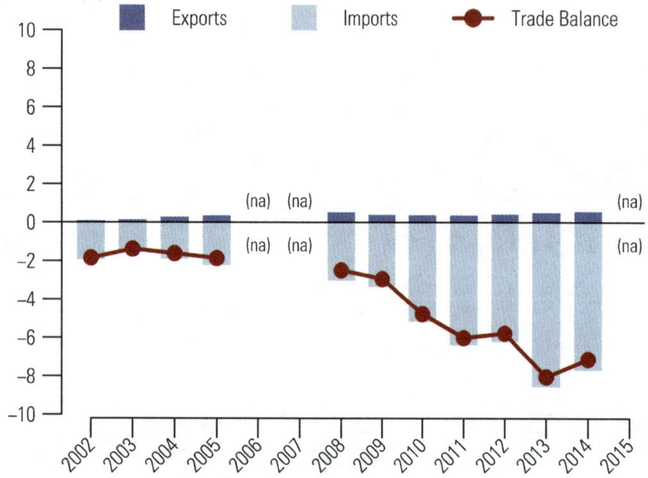

Graph 2: Total services trade, by value

(Bln US$ by year)

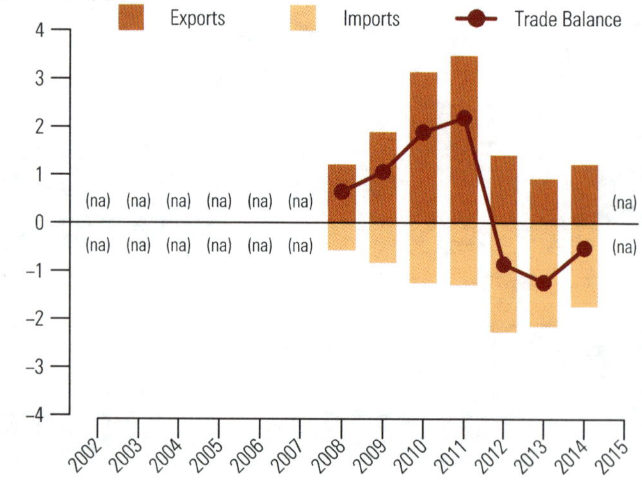

Exports Profile:

"Not classified elsewhere in the SITC" (SITC section 9), "Goods classified chiefly by material" (SITC section 6) and "Food, animals + beverages, tobacco" (SITC section 0+1) were the largest commodity groups for exports in 2014, representing respectively 70.7, 14.7 and 12.4 percent of exported goods (see table 2). From 2012 to 2014, the largest export commodity was "Commodities not specified according to kind" (HS code 9999) (see table 1). The top three destinations for merchandise exports were Pakistan, Areas nes and India, accounting for respectively 38.8, 27.7 and 22.0 percent of total exports. "Construction services" (EBOPS code 249) accounted for the largest share of exports of services in 2014 at 473.9 mln US$, followed by "Other business services" (EBOPS code 268) at 187.2 mln US$ and "Financial services" (EBOPS code 260) at 172.9 mln US$ (see graph 3).

Graph 3: Exports of services by EBOPS category

(% share in 2014)

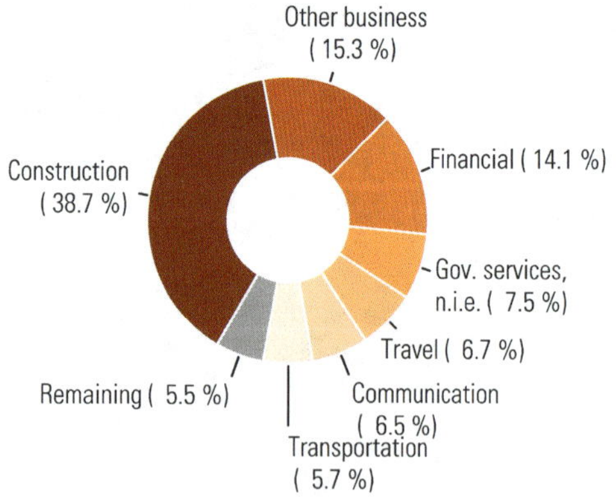

Table 1: Top 10 export commodities 2012 to 2014

HS code	4-digit heading of Harmonized System 2002	Value (million US$) 2012	2013	2014	Unit value 2012	2013	2014	Unit	SITC code
	All Commodities	428.9	515.0	570.5					
9999	Commodities not specified according to kind	280.3	371.3	403.6					931
5701	Carpets and other textile floor coverings, knotted	72.8	73.2	84.0	*107.9*	*103.2*	*103.5*	US$/m²	659
0909	Seeds of anise, badian, fennel, coriander, cumin or caraway	54.1	61.1	70.8	3.3	4.0	3.4	US$/kg	075
1207	Other oil seeds and oleaginous fruits	20.6	9.1	11.9	1.6	1.1	1.5	US$/kg	222
0504	Guts, bladders and stomachs of animals (other than fish)	1.0	0.2	0.3	*3.4*	*3.3*	*3.9*	US$/kg	291

Services Imports and Exports: EBOPS 2002 categories

Table 2: Merchandise exports by SITC

(Value in million US$, growth and shares in percentage)

SITC	2014	Avg. Growth rates 2010-2014	Avg. Growth rates 2013-2014	2014 share
Total	570.5	10.1	10.8	100.0
0+1	70.8	-14.2	15.9	12.4
2+4	12.1	-34.9	30.4	2.1
6	84.0	2.5	14.7	14.7
9	403.6	37.2	8.7	70.7

Table 3: Merchandise imports by SITC

(Value in million US$, growth and shares in percentage)

SITC	2014	Avg. Growth rates 2010-2014	Avg. Growth rates 2013-2014	2014 share
Total	7 697.2	10.5	-10.0	100.0
0+1	732.3	5.7	13.4	9.5
3	1 488.6	8.5	2.5	19.3
5	91.8	2.7	-47.0	1.2
6	511.5	4.2	31.3	6.6
7	6.6	-62.6	2230.9	0.1
8	37.3	-28.0	3.4	0.5
9	4 829.1	19.4	-17.6	62.7

SITC Legend

SITC Code	Description
Total	All commodities
0+1	Food, animals + beverages, tobacco
2+4	Crude materials + anim. & veg. oils
3	Mineral fuels, lubricants
5	Chemicals
6	Goods classified chiefly by material
7	Machinery and transport equipment
8	Miscellaneous manufactured articles
9	Not classified elsewhere in the SITC

Graph 4: Merchandise trade balance

(Bln US$ by MDG Regions in 2014)

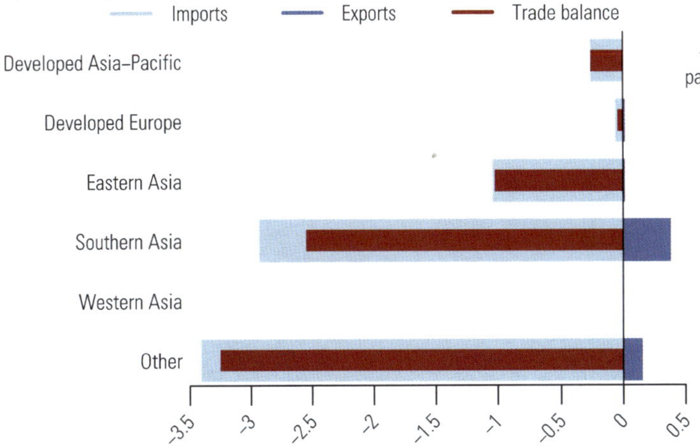

Graph 5: Partner concentration of merchandise trade

(Cumulative share by ranked partners in 2014)

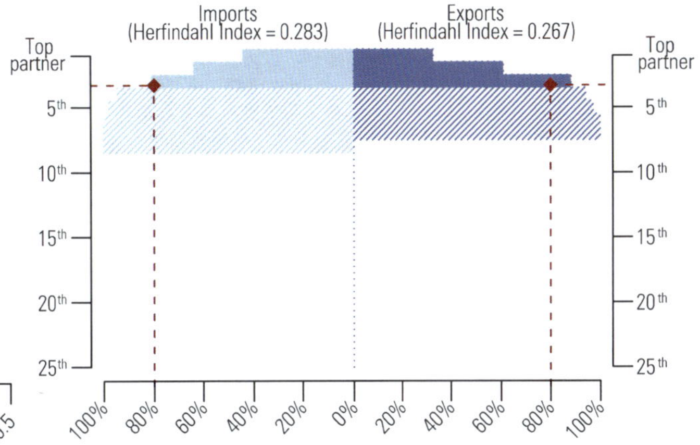

Graph 6: Imports of services by EBOPS category

(% share in 2014)

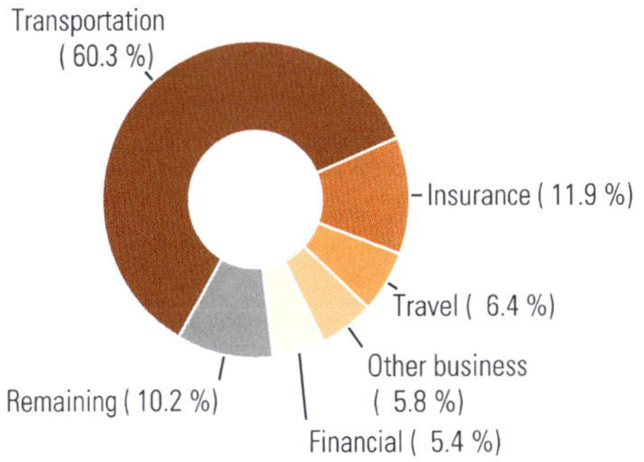

Imports Profile:

"Not classified elsewhere in the SITC" (SITC section 9), "Mineral fuels, lubricants" (SITC section 3) and "Food, animals + beverages, tobacco" (SITC section 0+1) were the largest commodity groups for imports in 2014, representing respectively 62.7, 19.3 and 9.5 percent of imported goods (see table 3). From 2012 to 2014, the largest import commodity was "Commodities not specified according to kind" (HS code 9999) (see table 4). The top three partners for merchandise imports were Areas nes, Pakistan and the Islamic Republic of Iran, accounting for respectively 58.3, 13.8 and 12.1 percent of total imports. "Transportation" (EBOPS code 205) accounted for the largest share of imports of services in 2014 at 1.1 bln US$, followed by "Insurance services" (EBOPS code 253) at 207.5 mln US$ and "Travel" (EBOPS code 236) at 110.9 mln US$ (see graph 6).

Table 4: Top 10 import commodities 2012 to 2014

HS code	4-digit heading of Harmonized System 2002	Value (million US$) 2012	Value (million US$) 2013	Value (million US$) 2014	Unit value 2012	Unit value 2013	Unit value 2014	Unit	SITC code
	All Commodities	6 205.0	8 554.4	7 697.2					
9999	Commodities not specified according to kind	4 014.2	5 857.5	4 829.1					931
2703	Peat (including peat litter)	1 517.5	1 452.5	1 488.6	0.8	0.5	1.6	US$/kg	322
1101	Wheat or meslin flour	175.5	429.1	498.9	0.3	0.3	0.3	US$/kg	046
5808	Braids in the piece; ornamental trimmings	110.2	151.4	295.9	*22.0*	*24.1*	*24.2*	US$/kg	656
6801	Setts, curbstones and flagstones, of natural stone (except slate)	163.3	219.7	160.3	0.1	0.1	0.1	US$/kg	661
0902	Tea, whether or not flavoured	69.1	151.1	111.7	1.3	1.5	1.1	US$/kg	074
3006	Pharmaceutical goods specified in Note 4 to this Chapter	36.0	139.6	68.4					541
1701	Cane or beet sugar and pure sucrose, in solid form	6.9	61.6	117.6	0.4	0.5	0.5	US$/kg	061
6206	Women's or girls' blouses, shirts and shirt-blouses	20.9	27.8	23.5	*9.7*	*10.1*	*10.8*	US$/unit	842
4012	Retreaded or used pneumatic tyres of rubber	31.1	10.2	29.2	*40.4*	*39.3*	*35.5*	US$/unit	625

Source: UN Comtrade

Albania

Goods Imports: CIF, by origin **Goods Exports: FOB, by last known destination** **Trade System: Special**

Overview:

In 2015, the value of merchandise exports of Albania decreased substantially by 20.6 percent to reach 1.9 bln US$, while its merchandise imports decreased substantially by 17.4 percent to reach 4.3 bln US$ (see graph 1, table 2 and table 3). The merchandise trade balance recorded a large deficit of 2.4 bln US$ (see graph 1). The largest merchandise trade balance was with MDG Developed Europe at -1.2 bln US$ (see graph 4). Merchandise exports in Albania were highly concentrated amongst partners; imports were diversified. The top 7 partners accounted for 80 percent or more of exports and 15 partners accounted for 80 percent or more of imports (see graph 5). In 2014, the value of exports of services of Albania increased slightly by 0.7 percent, reaching 2.2 bln US$, while its imports of services decreased moderately by 5.6 percent and reached 2.1 bln US$ (see graph 2). There was a relatively small trade in services surplus of 151.0 mln US$. See footnote*.

Graph 1: Total merchandise trade, by value

(Bln US$ by year)

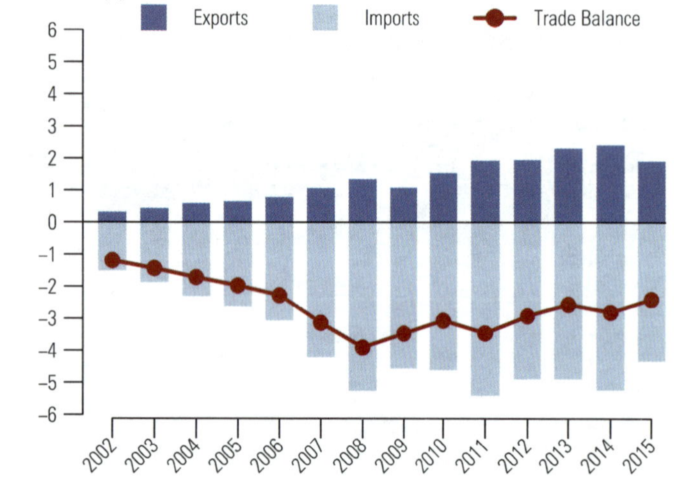

Graph 2: Total services trade, by value

(Bln US$ by year)

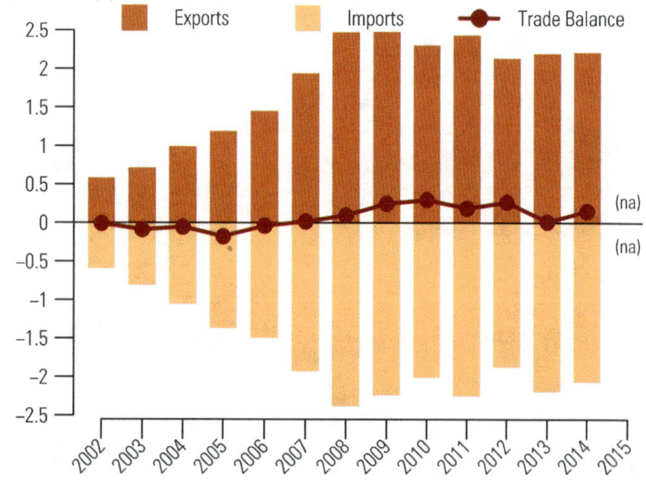

Exports Profile:

"Miscellaneous manufactured articles" (SITC section 8), "Not classified elsewhere in the SITC" (SITC section 9) and "Goods classified chiefly by material" (SITC section 6) were the largest commodity groups for exports in 2015, representing respectively 36.0, 23.0 and 14.9 percent of exported goods (see table 2). From 2013 to 2015, the largest export commodity was "Commodities not specified according to kind" (HS code 9999) (see table 1). The top three destinations for merchandise exports were Italy, Serbia and Spain, accounting for respectively 49.7, 8.4 and 7.3 percent of total exports. "Travel" (EBOPS code 236) accounted for the largest share of exports of services in 2014 at 1.7 bln US$, followed by "Transportation" (EBOPS code 205) at 188.8 mln US$ and "Communications services" (EBOPS code 245) at 155.4 mln US$ (see graph 3).

Graph 3: Exports of services by EBOPS category

(% share in 2014)

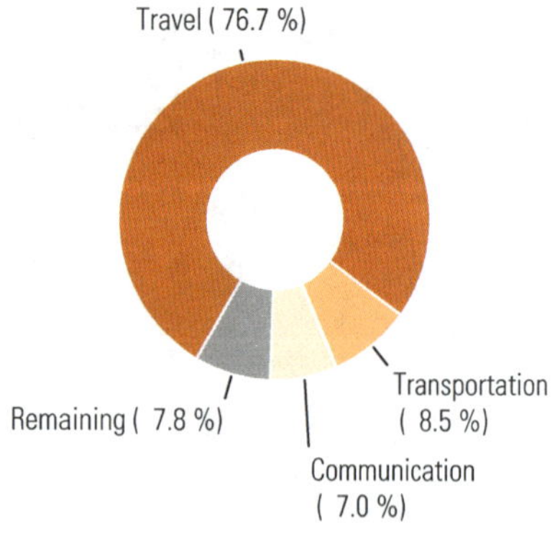

Table 1: Top 10 export commodities 2013 to 2015

HS code	4-digit heading of Harmonized System 2012	Value (million US$) 2013	2014	2015	Unit value 2013	2014	2015	Unit	SITC code
	All Commodities	2331.5	2430.7	1929.7					
9999	Commodities not specified according to kind	1.5	1415.0	444.5					931
2709	Petroleum oils and oils obtained from bituminous minerals, crude	658.0	...	91.8	0.5		0.2	US$/kg	333
6403	Footwear with outer soles of rubber, plastics, leather	156.8	151.9	151.2	18.2	17.8	15.0	US$/pair	851
6406	Parts of footwear	132.8	151.2	137.5	22.0	24.1	21.5	US$/kg	851
6203	Men's or boys'suits, ensembles, jackets, blazers, trousers	89.9	77.3	90.7	11.5	10.2	10.2	US$/unit	841
2610	Chromium ores and concentrates	91.1	74.0	71.4	0.1	0.2	0.1	US$/kg	287
7214	Other bars and rods of iron or non-alloy steel	123.0	...	65.7	0.6		0.4	US$/kg	676
6205	Men's or boys'shirts	41.6	52.3	45.8	10.2	10.8	*9.3*	US$/unit	841
4819	Cartons, boxes, cases, bags and other packing containers, of paper	41.6	54.7	40.3	3.7	4.8	3.0	US$/kg	642
2523	Portland cement, aluminous cement, slag cement	67.7	1.5	39.5	0.1	0.1	0.1	US$/kg	661

*In 2014, the reported share of non-standard HS codes increased significantly.

Services Imports and Exports: EBOPS 2002 categories

Table 2: Merchandise exports by SITC

(Value in million US$, growth and shares in percentage)

SITC	2015	Avg. Growth rates 2011-2015	Avg. Growth rates 2014-2015	2015 share
Total	1 929.7	-0.2	-20.6	100.0
0+1	108.9	8.5	49.2	5.6
2+4	160.6	-11.2	17.5	8.3
3	169.9	-19.9	346.0	8.8
5	10.8	-12.9	66.8	0.6
6	287.7	-9.5	201.2	14.9
7	53.2	-8.5	177.0	2.8
8	694.0	0.8	7.3	36.0
9	444.5	261.2	-68.6	23.0

Table 3: Merchandise imports by SITC

(Value in million US$, growth and shares in percentage)

SITC	2015	Avg. Growth rates 2011-2015	Avg. Growth rates 2014-2015	2015 share
Total	4320.2	-5.4	-17.4	100.0
0+1	589.5	-8.2	17.0	13.6
2+4	124.4	-18.4	59.6	2.9
3	414.6	-18.7	-2.6	9.6
5	421.8	-5.2	30.1	9.8
6	859.4	-7.5	28.4	19.9
7	767.0	-7.9	42.9	17.8
8	512.9	-2.6	16.1	11.9
9	630.6	266.3	-72.0	14.6

SITC Legend

SITC Code	Description
Total	All commodities
0+1	Food, animals + beverages, tobacco
2+4	Crude materials + anim. & veg. oils
3	Mineral fuels, lubricants
5	Chemicals
6	Goods classified chiefly by material
7	Machinery and transport equipment
8	Miscellaneous manufactured articles
9	Not classified elsewhere in the SITC

Graph 4: Merchandise trade balance

(Bln US$ by MDG Regions in 2015)

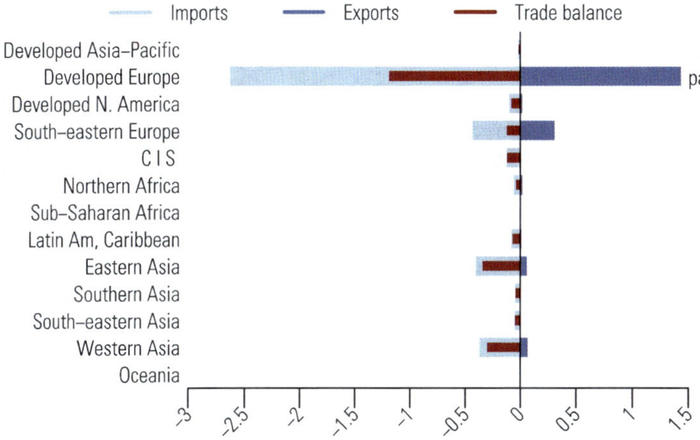

Graph 5: Partner concentration of merchandise trade

(Cumulative share by ranked partners in 2015)

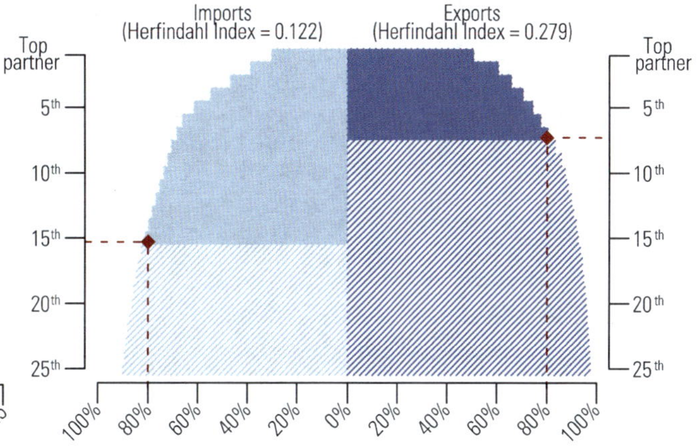

Graph 6: Imports of services by EBOPS category

(% share in 2014)

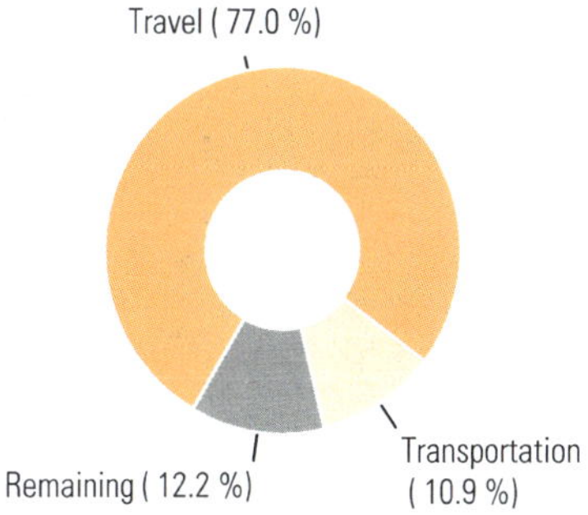

Imports Profile:

"Goods classified chiefly by material" (SITC section 6), "Machinery and transport equipment" (SITC section 7) and "Not classified elsewhere in the SITC" (SITC section 9) were the largest commodity groups for imports in 2015, representing respectively 19.9, 17.8 and 14.6 percent of imported goods (see table 3). From 2013 to 2015, the largest import commodity was "Commodities not specified according to kind" (HS code 9999) (see table 4). The top three partners for merchandise imports were Italy, Greece and China, accounting for respectively 31.0, 8.8 and 7.5 percent of total imports. "Travel" (EBOPS code 236) accounted for the largest share of imports of services in 2014 at 1.6 bln US$, followed by "Transportation" (EBOPS code 205) at 224.7 mln US$ (see graph 6).

Table 4: Top 10 import commodities 2013 to 2015

HS code	4-digit heading of Harmonized System 2012	Value (million US$) 2013	Value (million US$) 2014	Value (million US$) 2015	Unit value 2013	Unit value 2014	Unit value 2015	Unit	SITC code
	All Commodities	4880.6	5230.0	4320.2					
9999	Commodities not specified according to kind	2.3	2250.6	630.6					931
2710	Petroleum oils, other than crude	628.6	395.3	270.2	1.0	0.9	0.6	US$/kg	334
8703	Motor cars and other motor vehicles principally designed for the transport	191.9	183.4	168.3	3.2	2.3		thsd US$/unit	781
3004	Medicaments (excluding goods of heading 30.02, 30.05 or 30.06)	136.5	108.4	127.5	41.5	46.2	39.5	US$/kg	542
4107	Leather further prepared after tanning or crusting	82.5	88.9	81.6	18.8	19.4	19.0	US$/kg	611
6406	Parts of footwear	73.3	76.2	72.5	8.8	8.4	7.6	US$/kg	851
2716	Electrical energy	107.2	...	101.0	64.0		52.2	US$/MWh	351
1001	Wheat and meslin	81.0	41.3	55.7	0.3	0.3	0.2	US$/kg	041
2402	Cigars, cheroots, cigarillos and cigarettes	84.8	20.3	23.8	22.9	18.3	16.8	US$/kg	122
8517	Electrical apparatus for line telephony or line telegraphy	39.5	22.1	67.1					764

Algeria

Goods Imports: CIF, by origin | **Goods Exports: FOB, by last known destination** | **Trade System: Special**

Overview:

In 2014, the value of merchandise exports of Algeria decreased slightly by 4.2 percent to reach 63.2 bln US$, while its merchandise imports increased moderately by 6.8 percent to reach 58.6 bln US$ (see graph 1, table 2 and table 3). The merchandise trade balance recorded a relatively small surplus of 4.6 bln US$ (see graph 1). The largest merchandise trade balance was with MDG Developed Europe at 10.6 bln US$ (see graph 4). Merchandise exports in Algeria were diversified amongst partners; imports were also diversified. The top 11 partners accounted for 80 percent or more of exports and 19 partners accounted for 80 percent or more of imports (see graph 5). In 2014, the value of exports of services of Algeria decreased moderately by 6.2 percent, reaching 3.5 bln US$, while its imports of services increased moderately by 9.0 percent and reached 11.7 bln US$ (see graph 2). There was a large trade in services deficit of 8.1 bln US$.

Graph 1: Total merchandise trade, by value

(Bln US$ by year)

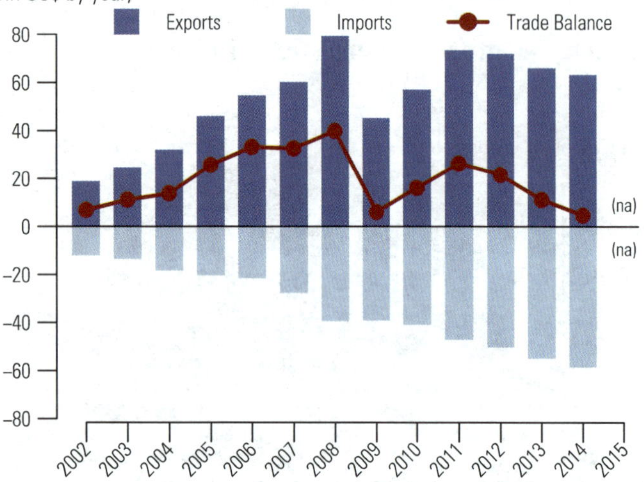

Graph 2: Total services trade, by value

(Bln US$ by year)

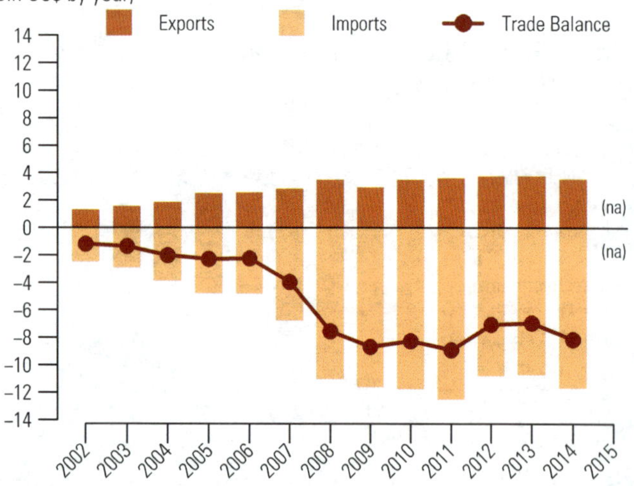

Exports Profile:

"Mineral fuels, lubricants" (SITC section 3) accounted for majority of exported goods (97.4 percent) in 2014 (see table 2). From 2012 to 2014, the largest export commodity was "Petroleum oils and oils obtained from bituminous minerals, crude" (HS code 2709) (see table 1). The top three destinations for merchandise exports were Italy, Spain and the United States, accounting for respectively 14.4, 13.8 and 10.4 percent of total exports. "Other business services" (EBOPS code 268) accounted for the largest share of exports of services in 2014 at 1.6 bln US$, followed by "Transportation" (EBOPS code 205) at 835.1 mln US$ and "Construction services" (EBOPS code 249) at 277.5 mln US$ (see graph 3).

Graph 3: Exports of services by EBOPS category

(% share in 2014)

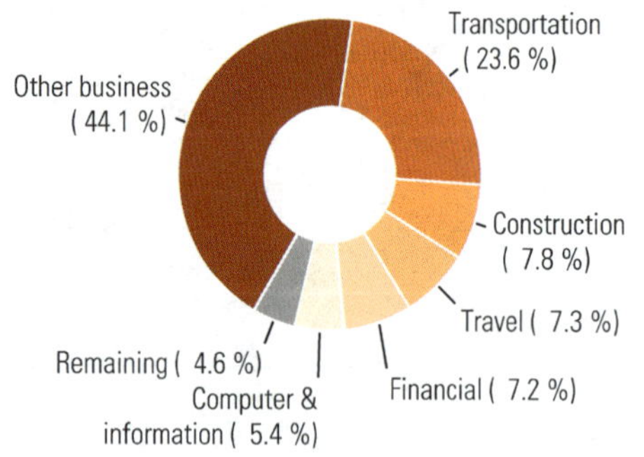

Table 1: Top 10 export commodities 2012 to 2014

HS code	4-digit heading of Harmonized System 2012	Value (million US$) 2012	2013	2014	Unit value 2012	2013	2014	Unit	SITC code
	All Commodities	71 865.7	65 998.1	63 227.8					
2709	Petroleum oils and oils obtained from bituminous minerals, crude	32 879.4	30 380.1	24 376.9	0.9	0.8	0.8	US$/kg	333
2711	Petroleum gases and other gaseous hydrocarbons	27 001.3	25 676.5	24 144.3		*0.5*	*0.7*	US$/kg	343
2710	Petroleum oils, other than crude	9 921.6	7 769.5	12 091.1	0.9	0.8	0.8	US$/kg	334
2707	Oils and other products of high temperature coal tar	909.0	1 067.7	943.7	1.4	1.3	1.4	US$/kg	335
2814	Ammonia, anhydrous or in aqueous solution	420.8	303.9	570.9	0.6	0.5	0.5	US$/kg	522
1701	Cane or beet sugar and chemically pure sucrose, in solid form	208.0	272.5	229.4	0.7	0.6	0.5	US$/kg	061
2510	Natural calcium phosphates	152.9	96.7	96.5	0.1	0.1	0.1	US$/kg	272
3102	Mineral or chemical fertilisers, nitrogenous	9.3	38.4	294.0	0.2	0.3	0.3	US$/kg	562
2905	Acyclic alcohols and their derivatives	34.0	45.2	47.6					512
2902	Cyclic hydrocarbons	...	...	124.4			1.1	US$/kg	511

Table 2: Merchandise exports by SITC

(Value in million US$, growth and shares in percentage)

SITC	2014	Avg. Growth rates 2010-2014	Avg. Growth rates 2013-2014	2014 share
Total	63 227.8	2.6	-4.2	100.0
0+1	325.5	1.2	-19.0	0.5
2+4	112.2	1.9	-0.6	0.2
3	61 581.0	2.4	-5.1	97.4
5	1 098.5	37.0	147.4	1.7
6	90.8	-18.5	-21.3	0.1
7	14.2	0.1	-0.2	0.0
8	5.6	-12.7	-26.4	0.0

Table 3: Merchandise imports by SITC

(Value in million US$, growth and shares in percentage)

SITC	2014	Avg. Growth rates 2010-2014	Avg. Growth rates 2013-2014	2014 share
Total	58 618.1	9.3	6.8	100.0
0+1	10 877.6	16.1	15.4	18.6
2+4	1 961.2	6.0	-1.4	3.3
3	2 843.0	34.6	-33.7	4.9
5	6 832.9	11.3	9.6	11.7
6	10 976.4	2.8	15.8	18.7
7	22 245.9	7.4	9.9	38.0
8	2 879.9	16.0	-11.2	4.9
9	1.2	...	-62.6	0.0

SITC Legend

SITC Code	Description
Total	All commodities
0+1	Food, animals + beverages, tobacco
2+4	Crude materials + anim. & veg. oils
3	Mineral fuels, lubricants
5	Chemicals
6	Goods classified chiefly by material
7	Machinery and transport equipment
8	Miscellaneous manufactured articles
9	Not classified elsewhere in the SITC

Graph 4: Merchandise trade balance

(Bln US$ by MDG Regions in 2014)

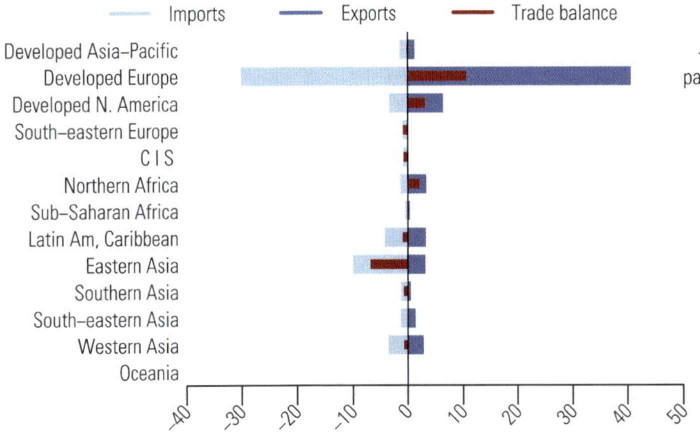

Graph 5: Partner concentration of merchandise trade

(Cumulative share by ranked partners in 2014)

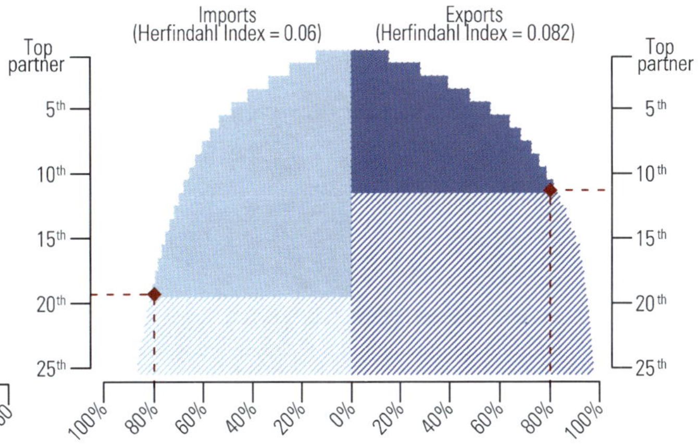

Graph 6: Imports of services by EBOPS category

(% share in 2014)

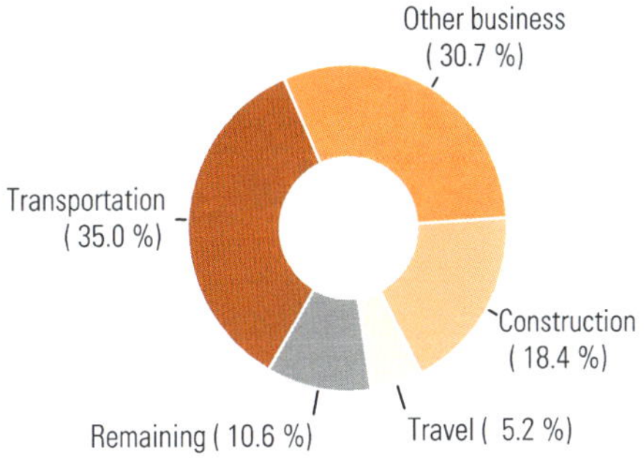

Imports Profile:

"Machinery and transport equipment" (SITC section 7), "Goods classified chiefly by material" (SITC section 6) and "Food, animals + beverages, tobacco" (SITC section 0+1) were the largest commodity groups for imports in 2014, representing respectively 38.0, 18.7 and 18.6 percent of imported goods (see table 3). From 2012 to 2014, the largest import commodity was "Motor cars and other motor vehicles principally designed for the transport" (HS code 8703) (see table 4). The top three partners for merchandise imports were China, France and Italy, accounting for respectively 12.8, 11.6 and 9.7 percent of total imports. "Transportation" (EBOPS code 205) accounted for the largest share of imports of services in 2014 at 4.1 bln US$, followed by "Other business services" (EBOPS code 268) at 3.6 bln US$ and "Construction services" (EBOPS code 249) at 2.2 bln US$ (see graph 6).

Table 4: Top 10 import commodities 2012 to 2014

HS code	4-digit heading of Harmonized System 2012	Value (million US$) 2012	Value (million US$) 2013	Value (million US$) 2014	Unit value 2012	Unit value 2013	Unit value 2014	Unit	SITC code
	All Commodities	50 369.4	54 910.0	58 618.1					
8703	Motor cars and other motor vehicles principally designed for the transport	3 908.7	3 728.7	2 965.5	9.9	10.5	*14.0*	thsd US$/unit	781
2710	Petroleum oils, other than crude	4 435.9	3 770.5	2 191.4	*0.8*	*1.0*	0.9	US$/kg	334
1001	Wheat and meslin	2 129.0	2 123.4	2 372.5	0.3	0.3	0.3	US$/kg	041
8704	Motor vehicles for the transport of goods	2 205.5	2 225.3	2 110.3					782
7214	Other bars and rods of iron or non-alloy steel	2 098.4	1 862.5	1 884.3	0.7	*0.6*	0.6	US$/kg	676
3004	Medicaments (excluding goods of heading 30.02, 30.05 or 30.06)	1 754.8	1 807.7	1 949.4	*54.9*	*64.6*	68.0	US$/kg	542
0402	Milk and cream, concentrated or containing added sugar	1 093.4	1 076.7	1 800.3	3.6	4.1	4.8	US$/kg	022
8411	Turbo-jets, turbo-propellers and other gas turbines	526.0	1 274.8	1 700.8					714
1005	Maize (corn)	941.9	892.6	977.3	0.3	0.3	0.2	US$/kg	044
1701	Cane or beet sugar and chemically pure sucrose, in solid form	960.9	881.8	840.9	*0.6*	0.5	0.4	US$/kg	061

Andorra

Goods Imports: CIF, by origin | **Goods Exports: FOB, by last known destination** | **Trade System: General**

Overview:

In 2014, the value of merchandise exports of Andorra decreased slightly by 4.2 percent to reach 94.8 mln US$, while its merchandise imports increased slightly by 4.6 percent to reach 1.6 bln US$ (see graph 1, table 2 and table 3). The merchandise trade balance recorded a large deficit of 1.5 bln US$ (see graph 1). The largest merchandise trade balance was with MDG Developed Europe at -1.3 bln US$ (see graph 4). Merchandise exports in Andorra were highly concentrated amongst partners; imports were also highly concentrated. The top 3 partners accounted for 80 percent or more of exports and the same number of partners accounted for 80 percent or more of imports (see graph 5). No trade in services data is available.

Graph 1: Total merchandise trade, by value

(Bln US$ by year)

Graph 2: No Data Available

Exports Profile:

"Machinery and transport equipment" (SITC section 7), "Miscellaneous manufactured articles" (SITC section 8) and "Goods classified chiefly by material" (SITC section 6) were the largest commodity groups for exports in 2014, representing respectively 42.0, 41.7 and 6.7 percent of exported goods (see table 2). From 2012 to 2014, the largest export commodity was "Prepared unrecorded media for sound recording" (HS code 8523) (see table 1). The top three destinations for merchandise exports were Spain, France and Norway, accounting for respectively 57.6, 17.8 and 4.6 percent of total exports. Services data by detailed EBOPS category is not available for exports.

Graph 3: No Data Available

Table 1: Top 10 export commodities 2012 to 2014

HS code	4-digit heading of Harmonized System 2012	Value (million US$) 2012	2013	2014	Unit value 2012	2013	2014	Unit	SITC code
	All Commodities	105.9	99.0	94.8					
8523	Prepared unrecorded media for sound recording	15.3	17.3	13.7					898
8703	Motor cars and other motor vehicles principally designed for the transport	11.0	13.0	14.1	*22.4*	*22.3*	*20.4*	thsd US$/unit	781
9021	Orthopaedic appliances, including crutches, surgical belts and trusses	7.9	8.7	11.4					899
7113	Articles of jewellery and parts thereof, of precious metal	6.1	5.1	2.6	1.2	5.5	5.2	thsd US$/kg	897
9102	Wrist-watches, pocket-watches and other watches, of base metal	3.8	4.1	4.7					885
8542	Electronic integrated circuits	4.5	1.4	1.9					776
7204	Ferrous waste and scrap; remelting scrap ingots of iron or steel	2.1	1.8	2.2	0.3	0.3	0.3	US$/kg	282
7326	Other articles of iron or steel	2.2	2.2	1.3	3.6	5.7	0.4	US$/kg	699
6211	Track suits, ski suits and swimwear; other garments	2.4	1.0	2.1					845
7108	Gold (including gold plated with platinum)	2.7	1.6	0.9	39.6	39.2	34.2	thsd US$/kg	971

Services Imports and Exports: EBOPS 2002 categories

Table 2: Merchandise exports by SITC

(Value in million US$, growth and shares in percentage)

SITC	2014	Avg. Growth rates 2010-2014	Avg. Growth rates 2013-2014	2014 share
Total	94.8	0.7	-4.2	100.0
0+1	0.8	2.7	146.5	0.9
2+4	5.2	-1.4	8.7	5.5
3	0.1	187.6	-13.4	0.1
5	1.5	-15.4	-31.7	1.6
6	6.3	-15.7	-4.0	6.7
7	39.9	0.9	-2.6	42.0
8	39.5	8.1	-5.7	41.7
9	1.5	-18.0	-30.9	1.6

Table 3: Merchandise imports by SITC

(Value in million US$, growth and shares in percentage)

SITC	2014	Avg. Growth rates 2010-2014	Avg. Growth rates 2013-2014	2014 share
Total	1 556.0	0.3	4.6	100.0
0+1	355.8	1.6	2.4	22.9
2+4	18.2	1.4	10.4	1.2
3	167.3	1.9	-11.7	10.8
5	183.2	-0.2	6.3	11.8
6	113.2	-5.5	2.4	7.3
7	313.5	1.0	8.7	20.1
8	380.3	-1.6	5.2	24.4
9	24.6	128.9	2012.4	1.6

SITC Legend

SITC Code	Description
Total	All commodities
0+1	Food, animals + beverages, tobacco
2+4	Crude materials + anim. & veg. oils
3	Mineral fuels, lubricants
5	Chemicals
6	Goods classified chiefly by material
7	Machinery and transport equipment
8	Miscellaneous manufactured articles
9	Not classified elsewhere in the SITC

Graph 4: Merchandise trade balance

(Bln US$ by MDG Regions in 2014)

Graph 5: Partner concentration of merchandise trade

(Cumulative share by ranked partners in 2014)

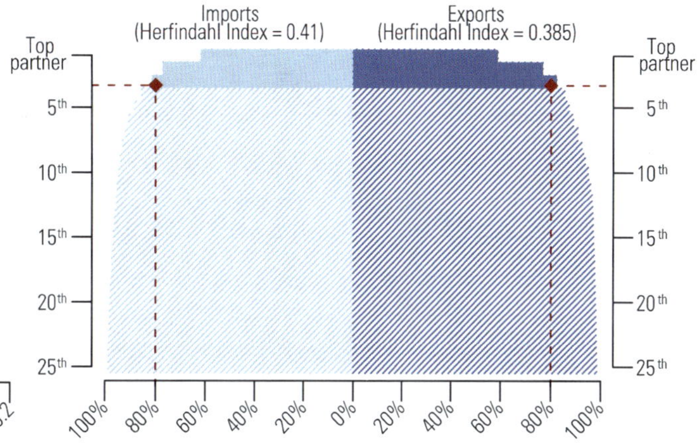

Graph 6: No Data Available

Imports Profile:

"Miscellaneous manufactured articles" (SITC section 8), "Food, animals + beverages, tobacco" (SITC section 0+1) and "Machinery and transport equipment" (SITC section 7) were the largest commodity groups for imports in 2014, representing respectively 24.4, 22.9 and 20.1 percent of imported goods (see table 3). From 2012 to 2014, the largest import commodity was "Petroleum oils, other than crude" (HS code 2710) (see table 4). The top three partners for merchandise imports were Spain, France and China, accounting for respectively 61.8, 16.6 and 3.9 percent of total imports. Services data by detailed EBOPS category is not available for imports.

Table 4: Top 10 import commodities 2012 to 2014

HS code	4-digit heading of Harmonized System 2012	Value (million US$) 2012	2013	2014	Unit value 2012	2013	2014	Unit	SITC code
	All Commodities	1 417.7	1 487.2	1 556.0					
2710	Petroleum oils, other than crude	154.3	147.0	133.0	0.8	0.8	0.9	US$/kg	334
8703	Motor cars and other motor vehicles principally designed for the transport	57.0	73.2	102.4	*22.7*	*23.1*	*23.1*	thsd US$/unit	781
6211	Track suits, ski suits and swimwear; other garments	46.9	39.2	36.6					845
2208	Alcohol of a strength by volume of less than 80 % vol	37.1	40.2	44.6	*5.9*	*6.6*	*6.8*	US$/litre	112
2716	Electrical energy	42.8	39.9	32.1	*66.1*	*66.1*	*60.6*	US$/MWh	351
3307	Pre-shave, shaving or after-shave preparations	33.6	38.2	32.9	31.0	26.6	24.0	US$/kg	553
2403	Other manufactured tobacco and tobacco substitutes	32.5	34.5	33.4	18.2	19.3	20.9	US$/kg	122
3004	Medicaments (excluding goods of heading 30.02, 30.05 or 30.06)	33.1	32.8	34.1	51.9	56.0	65.0	US$/kg	542
3303	Perfumes and toilet waters	24.0	31.4	40.7	48.1	65.6	75.2	US$/kg	553
8517	Electrical apparatus for line telephony or line telegraphy	24.4	28.1	30.7					764

Antigua and Barbuda

Goods Imports: CIF, by origin | **Goods Exports: CIF, by last known destination** | **Trade System: General**

Overview:

In 2015, the value of merchandise exports of Antigua and Barbuda increased substantially by 12.8 percent to reach 26.0 mln US$, while its merchandise imports decreased substantially by 15.7 percent to reach 465.1 mln US$ (see graph 1, table 2 and table 3). The merchandise trade balance recorded a large deficit of 439.1 mln US$ (see graph 1). The largest merchandise trade balance was with MDG Developed North America at -193.5 mln US$ (see graph 4). Merchandise exports in Antigua and Barbuda were moderately concentrated amongst partners; imports were also moderately concentrated. The top 7 partners accounted for 80 percent or more of exports and 11 partners accounted for 80 percent or more of imports (see graph 5). In 2013, the value of exports of services of Antigua and Barbuda decreased slightly by 3.6 percent, reaching 465.0 mln US$, while its imports of services increased moderately by 7.6 percent and reached 219.5 mln US$ (see graph 2). There was a large trade in services surplus of 245.5 mln US$.

Graph 1: Total merchandise trade, by value

(Mln US$ by year)

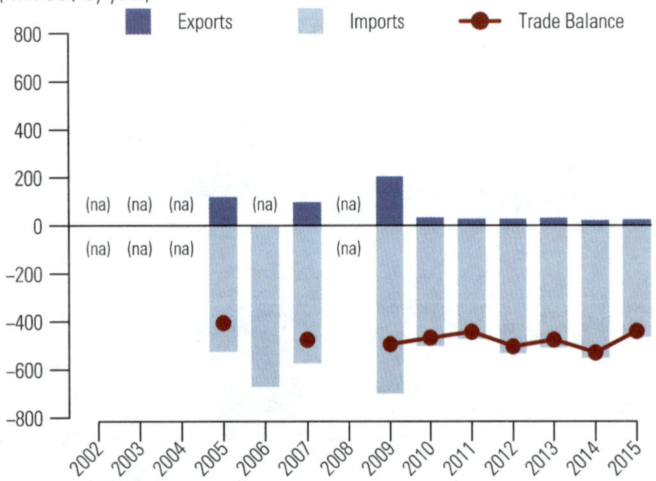

Graph 2: Total services trade, by value

(Mln US$ by year)

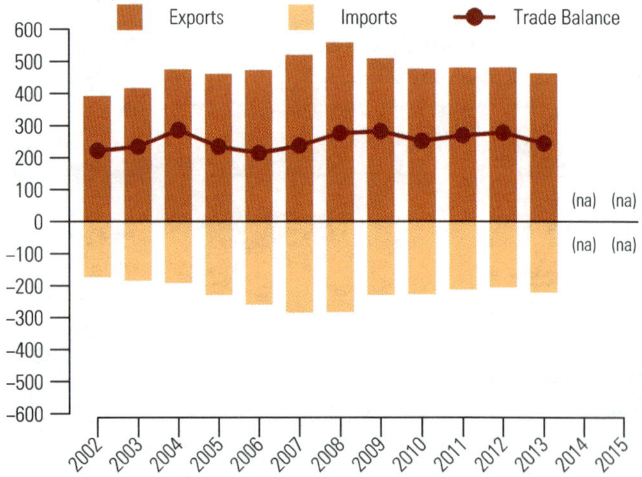

Exports Profile:

"Goods classified chiefly by material" (SITC section 6), "Machinery and transport equipment" (SITC section 7) and "Miscellaneous manufactured articles" (SITC section 8) were the largest commodity groups for exports in 2015, representing respectively 42.7, 33.3 and 14.3 percent of exported goods (see table 2). From 2013 to 2015, the largest export commodity was "Tarpaulins, awnings and sunblinds; tents; sails for boats, sailboards" (HS code 6306) (see table 1). The top three destinations for merchandise exports were the United States, the United Kingdom and Areas nes, accounting for respectively 25.9, 24.1 and 5.1 percent of total exports. "Travel" (EBOPS code 236) accounted for the largest share of exports of services in 2013 at 298.6 mln US$, followed by "Transportation" (EBOPS code 205) at 108.0 mln US$ (see graph 3).

Graph 3: Exports of services by EBOPS category

(% share in 2013)

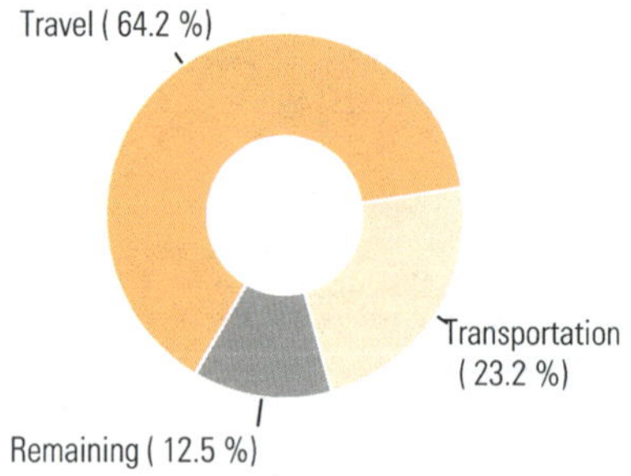

Table 1: Top 10 export commodities 2013 to 2015

HS code	4-digit heading of Harmonized System 2007	Value (million US$) 2013	2014	2015	Unit value 2013	2014	2015	Unit	SITC code
	All Commodities	32.9	23.1	26.0					
6306	Tarpaulins, awnings and sunblinds; tents; sails for boats, sailboards	9.4	5.1	7.2	97.5	45.9	23.8	US$/kg	658
2710	Petroleum oils, other than crude	4.1	1.0	0.3			1.6	US$/kg	334
8903	Yachts and other vessels for pleasure or sports; rowing boats and canoes	2.3	1.1	1.0	31.7	32.6		thsd US$/unit	793
2208	Alcohol of a strength by volume of less than 80 % vol.	1.0	0.9	0.9	23.8	8.6	*2.3*	US$/litre	112
7326	Other articles of iron or steel	1.3	0.4	1.0	10.7	26.2	15.6	US$/kg	699
8803	Parts of goods of heading 88.01 or 88.02	0.1	2.4	0.1	975.2	459.7	187.1	US$/kg	792
7204	Ferrous waste and scrap; remelting scrap ingots of iron or steel	1.3	0.9	0.3	0.4	0.2	0.2	US$/kg	282
9999	Commodities not specified according to kind	0.0	2.1	...					931
7010	Carboys, bottles, flasks, jars, pots, phials, ampoules	0.5	0.5	0.7					665
8525	Transmission apparatus for radio-telephony, radio-broadcasting	0.8	0.1	0.7					764

Services Imports and Exports: EBOPS 2002 categories

Table 2: Merchandise exports by SITC

(Value in million US$, growth and shares in percentage)

SITC	2015	Avg. Growth rates 2011-2015	Avg. Growth rates 2014-2015	2015 share
Total	26.0	-2.7	12.8	100.0
0+1	1.4	-21.0	-19.9	5.5
2+4	0.5	28.9	-52.0	1.8
3	0.3	-20.1	-71.9	1.1
5	0.3	-19.1	-37.4	1.3
6	11.1	3.3	42.4	42.7
7	8.7	-5.8	22.3	33.3
8	3.7	6.1	107.9	14.3

Table 3: Merchandise imports by SITC

(Value in million US$, growth and shares in percentage)

SITC	2015	Avg. Growth rates 2011-2015	Avg. Growth rates 2014-2015	2015 share
Total	465.1	-0.3	-15.7	100.0
0+1	124.3	2.8	1.2	26.7
2+4	11.8	5.6	4.5	2.5
3	77.1	126.9	-53.0	16.6
5	34.3	3.4	7.8	7.4
6	60.2	7.7	-5.4	12.9
7	93.3	13.4	-3.5	20.1
8	64.0	6.1	4.6	13.8
9	0.0	-90.1	2.3	0.0

SITC Legend

SITC Code	Description
Total	All commodities
0+1	Food, animals + beverages, tobacco
2+4	Crude materials + anim. & veg. oils
3	Mineral fuels, lubricants
5	Chemicals
6	Goods classified chiefly by material
7	Machinery and transport equipment
8	Miscellaneous manufactured articles
9	Not classified elsewhere in the SITC

Graph 4: Merchandise trade balance

(Mln US$ by MDG Regions in 2015)

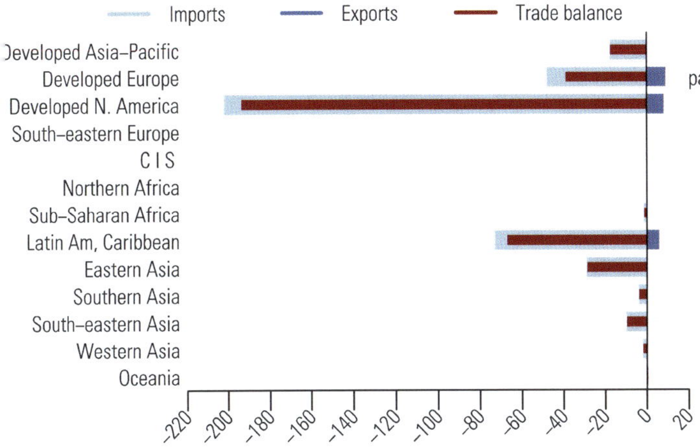

Graph 5: Partner concentration of merchandise trade

(Cumulative share by ranked partners in 2015)

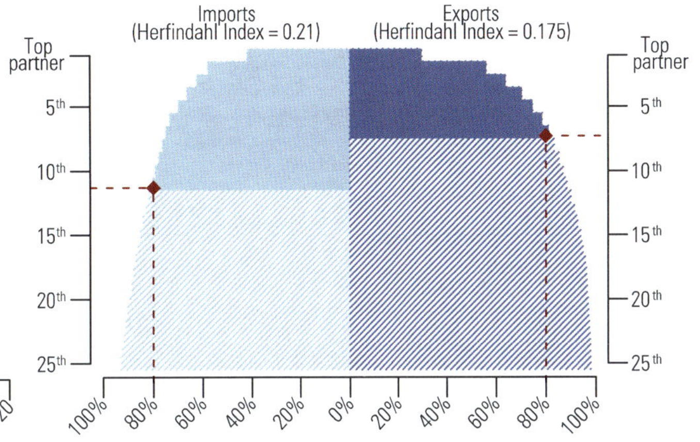

Graph 6: Imports of services by EBOPS category

(% share in 2013)

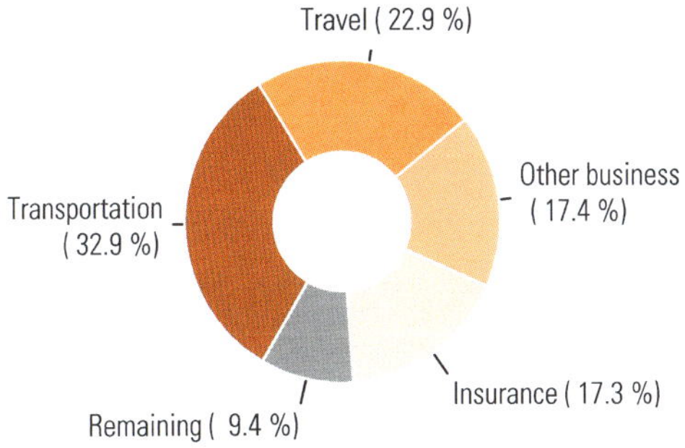

Imports Profile:

"Food, animals + beverages, tobacco" (SITC section 0+1), "Machinery and transport equipment" (SITC section 7) and "Mineral fuels, lubricants" (SITC section 3) were the largest commodity groups for imports in 2015, representing respectively 26.7, 20.1 and 16.6 percent of imported goods (see table 3). From 2013 to 2015, the largest import commodity was "Petroleum oils, other than crude" (HS code 2710) (see table 4). The top three partners for merchandise imports were the United States, Areas nes and Special Categories, accounting for respectively 37.1, 21.7 and 14.5 percent of total imports. "Transportation" (EBOPS code 205) accounted for the largest share of imports of services in 2013 at 72.2 mln US$, followed by "Travel" (EBOPS code 236) at 50.4 mln US$ and "Other business services" (EBOPS code 268) at 38.3 mln US$ (see graph 6).

Table 4: Top 10 import commodities 2013 to 2015

HS code	4-digit heading of Harmonized System 2007	Value (million US$) 2013	2014	2015	Unit value 2013	2014	2015	Unit	SITC code
	All Commodities	507.9	551.8	465.1					
2710	Petroleum oils, other than crude	168.3	164.2	77.0	*1.3*		*1.1*	US$/kg	334
8703	Motor cars and other motor vehicles principally designed for the transport	15.7	25.0	25.0	*13.9*	*15.1*	*18.1*	thsd US$/unit	781
0207	Meat and edible offal, of the poultry of heading 01.05	12.4	12.1	10.9	2.1	2.1	1.7	US$/kg	012
2202	Waters with added sugar	9.1	9.5	8.3	*1.1*	*1.1*	*1.0*	US$/litre	111
7113	Articles of jewellery and parts thereof, of precious metal	7.8	8.9	7.9	2.3	2.8	2.9	thsd US$/kg	897
2106	Food preparations not elsewhere specified or included	6.6	6.9	7.0	2.0	2.2	1.6	US$/kg	098
3004	Medicaments (excluding goods of heading 30.02, 30.05 or 30.06)	6.3	5.8	7.4	33.2	26.6	29.6	US$/kg	542
6306	Tarpaulins, awnings and sunblinds; tents; sails for boats, sailboards	7.3	5.0	5.4	64.2	21.5	48.5	US$/kg	658
9403	Other furniture and parts thereof	4.4	6.4	6.4					821
8704	Motor vehicles for the transport of goods	2.5	5.0	8.8					782

Argentina

Goods Imports: CIF, by origin | **Goods Exports: FOB, by last known destination** | **Trade System: Special**

Overview:

In 2015, the value of merchandise exports of Argentina decreased substantially by 16.9 percent to reach 56.8 bln US$, while its merchandise imports decreased moderately by 8.5 percent to reach 59.8 bln US$ (see graph 1, table 2 and table 3). The merchandise trade balance recorded a relatively small deficit of 3.0 bln US$ (see graph 1). The largest merchandise trade balance was with MDG Eastern Asia at -7.3 bln US$ (see graph 4). Merchandise exports in Argentina were diversified amongst partners; imports were also diversified. The top 27 partners accounted for 80 percent or more of exports and 15 partners accounted for 80 percent or more of imports (see graph 5). In 2014, the value of exports of services of Argentina decreased slightly by 3.4 percent, reaching 13.8 bln US$, while its imports of services decreased moderately by 8.9 percent and reached 17.0 bln US$ (see graph 2). There was a moderate trade in services deficit of 3.2 bln US$.

Graph 1: Total merchandise trade, by value

(Bln US$ by year)

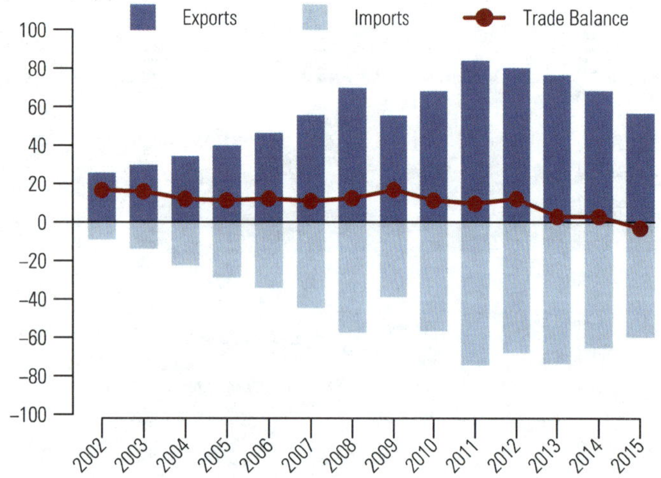

Graph 2: Total services trade, by value

(Bln US$ by year)

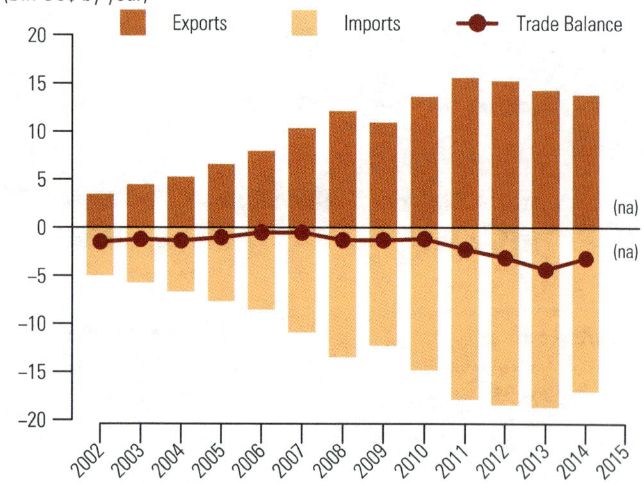

Exports Profile:

"Food, animals + beverages, tobacco" (SITC section 0+1), "Crude materials + anim. & veg. oils" (SITC section 2+4) and "Machinery and transport equipment" (SITC section 7) were the largest commodity groups for exports in 2015, representing respectively 43.5, 18.8 and 13.5 percent of exported goods (see table 2). From 2013 to 2015, the largest export commodity was "Oil-cake and other solid residues" (HS code 2304) (see table 1). The top three destinations for merchandise exports were Brazil, China and the United States, accounting for respectively 19.9, 7.5 and 5.8 percent of total exports. "Travel" (EBOPS code 236) accounted for the largest share of exports of services in 2014 at 4.6 bln US$, followed by "Other business services" (EBOPS code 268) at 4.4 bln US$ and "Transportation" (EBOPS code 205) at 2.5 bln US$ (see graph 3).

Graph 3: Exports of services by EBOPS category

(% share in 2014)

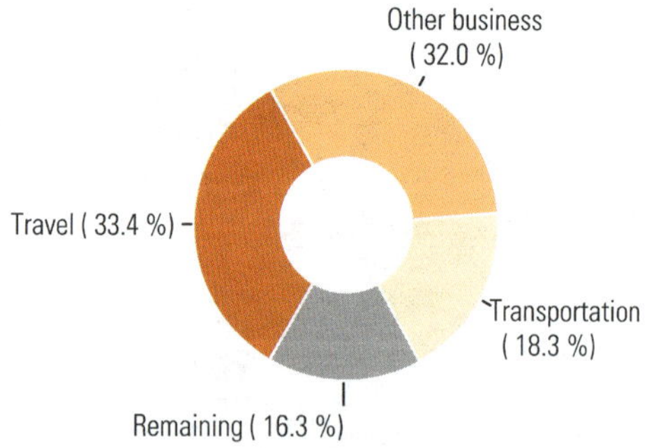

Table 1: Top 10 export commodities 2013 to 2015

HS code	4-digit heading of Harmonized System 2012	Value (million US$) 2013	2014	2015	Unit value 2013	2014	2015	Unit	SITC code
	All Commodities	76633.9	68335.1	56752.4					
2304	Oil-cake and other solid residues	10660.6	11840.7	9674.7	0.5	0.5	0.4	US$/kg	081
1005	Maize (corn)	5848.0	3524.7	3131.4	0.3	0.2		US$/kg	044
1201	Soya beans, whether or not broken	4089.4	3776.8	4270.5	0.5	0.5	0.4	US$/kg	222
1507	Soya-bean oil and its fractions	4089.3	3467.7	3815.4	1.0	0.9	0.7	US$/kg	421
8704	Motor vehicles for the transport of goods	4116.8	3856.5	3001.2	26.9	26.6		thsd US$/unit	782
8703	Motor cars and other motor vehicles principally designed for the transport	4123.4	3085.4	1914.4	14.7	14.8	*14.3*	thsd US$/unit	781
7108	Gold (including gold plated with platinum)	1846.6	1827.6	2274.4	5.8			thsd US$/kg	971
9999	Commodities not specified according to kind	2119.9	1837.5	956.4					931
2709	Petroleum oils and oils obtained from bituminous minerals, crude	1736.8	1618.4	672.6	0.7	0.7	0.3	US$/kg	333
8708	Parts and accessories of the motor vehicles of headings 87.01 to 87.05	1417.1	1097.1	873.5	*10.4*	*11.1*	11.6	US$/kg	784

Services Imports and Exports: EBOPS 2002 categories

Table 2: Merchandise exports by SITC

(Value in million US$, growth and shares in percentage)

SITC	2015	Avg. Growth rates 2011-2015	Avg. Growth rates 2014-2015	2015 share
Total	56 752.4	-9.4	-16.9	100.0
0+1	24 689.5	-5.9	-14.3	43.5
2+4	10 658.4	-9.4	2.2	18.8
3	1 428.3	-26.7	-55.3	2.5
5	5 289.1	-8.2	-18.1	9.3
6	3 287.0	-13.9	-29.4	5.8
7	7 641.0	-13.0	-27.1	13.5
8	524.2	-14.2	-18.5	0.9
9	3 234.9	-5.9	-11.7	5.7

Table 3: Merchandise imports by SITC

(Value in million US$, growth and shares in percentage)

SITC	2015	Avg. Growth rates 2011-2015	Avg. Growth rates 2014-2015	2015 share
Total	59 786.8	-5.3	-8.5	100.0
0+1	1 511.0	-2.9	0.0	2.5
2+4	1 660.2	-11.2	-19.4	2.8
3	6 571.0	-8.6	-40.4	11.0
5	11 276.6	-2.4	-3.1	18.9
6	7 232.1	-4.7	2.0	12.1
7	26 691.8	-5.6	-2.1	44.6
8	4 302.3	-4.3	6.7	7.2
9	541.7	-3.4	-23.4	0.9

SITC Legend

SITC Code	Description
Total	All commodities
0+1	Food, animals + beverages, tobacco
2+4	Crude materials + anim. & veg. oils
3	Mineral fuels, lubricants
5	Chemicals
6	Goods classified chiefly by material
7	Machinery and transport equipment
8	Miscellaneous manufactured articles
9	Not classified elsewhere in the SITC

Graph 4: Merchandise trade balance

(Bln US$ by MDG Regions in 2015)

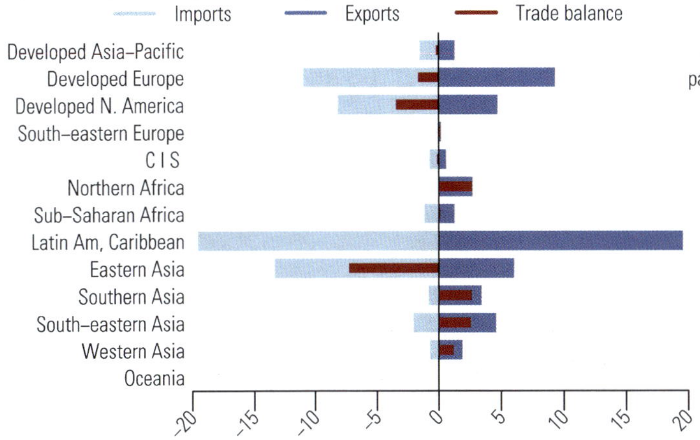

Graph 5: Partner concentration of merchandise trade

(Cumulative share by ranked partners in 2015)

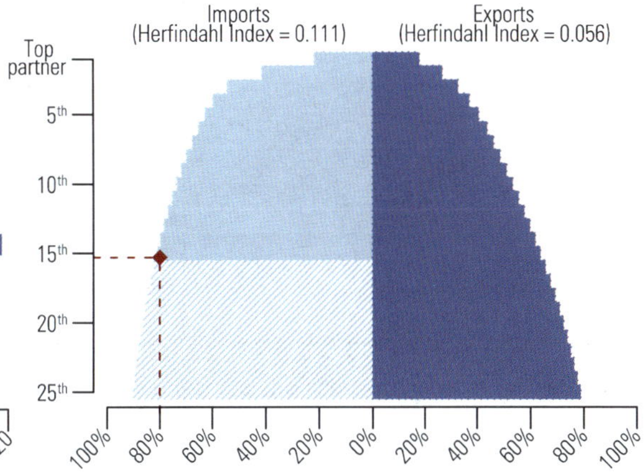

Graph 6: Imports of services by EBOPS category

(% share in 2014)

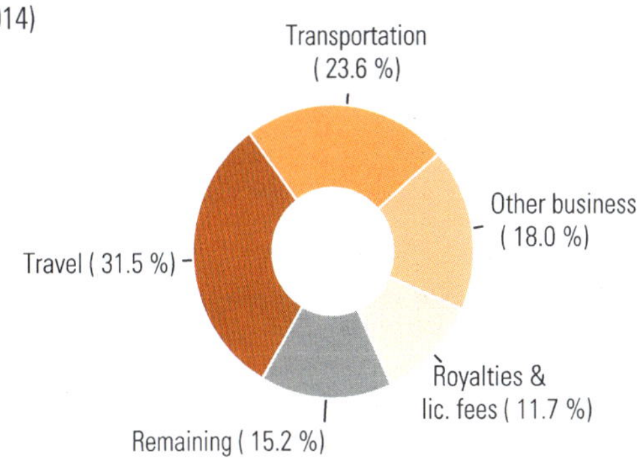

Imports Profile:

"Machinery and transport equipment" (SITC section 7), "Chemicals" (SITC section 5) and "Goods classified chiefly by material" (SITC section 6) were the largest commodity groups for imports in 2015, representing respectively 44.6, 18.9 and 12.1 percent of imported goods (see table 3). From 2013 to 2015, the largest import commodity was "Petroleum gases and other gaseous hydrocarbons" (HS code 2711) (see table 4). The top three partners for merchandise imports were Brazil, China and the United States, accounting for respectively 23.3, 17.0 and 12.4 percent of total imports. "Travel" (EBOPS code 236) accounted for the largest share of imports of services in 2014 at 5.4 bln US$, followed by "Transportation" (EBOPS code 205) at 4.0 bln US$ and "Other business services" (EBOPS code 268) at 3.1 bln US$ (see graph 6).

Table 4: Top 10 import commodities 2013 to 2015

HS code	4-digit heading of Harmonized System 2012	Value (million US$) 2013	2014	2015	Unit value 2013	2014	2015	Unit	SITC code
	All Commodities	73 655.5	65 323.4	59 786.8					
2711	Petroleum gases and other gaseous hydrocarbons	5 023.7	5 911.1	3 553.0	*0.7*	*0.7*	0.4	US$/kg	343
8703	Motor cars and other motor vehicles principally designed for the transport	7 064.4	3 567.8	3 345.0	12.5	12.2	*16.3*	thsd US$/unit	781
2710	Petroleum oils, other than crude	5 010.4	4 080.7	2 121.0	*1.0*	*0.9*	0.6	US$/kg	334
8708	Parts and accessories of the motor vehicles of headings 87.01 to 87.05	4 054.3	3 163.5	2 820.6	*8.9*	*8.9*	8.1	US$/kg	784
8517	Electrical apparatus for line telephony or line telegraphy	2 615.9	2 034.4	2 778.5					764
3004	Medicaments (excluding goods of heading 30.02, 30.05 or 30.06)	1 126.0	1 081.3	1 227.3	*60.2*	*55.7*	72.2	US$/kg	542
8704	Motor vehicles for the transport of goods	1 410.8	941.4	941.2	22.5	23.1		thsd US$/unit	782
3002	Human blood; animal blood prepared for therapeutic uses	843.5	855.9	965.1	*593.0*	*776.4*	759.0	US$/kg	541
8471	Automatic data processing machines and units thereof	817.1	659.2	701.4	48.7	*52.8*		US$/unit	752
8529	Parts suitable for use with the apparatus of headings 85.25 to 85.28	857.6	626.7	658.5	*28.4*	*27.4*	29.1	US$/kg	764

Source: UN Comtrade

Armenia

Goods Imports: CIF, by origin | **Goods Exports: FOB, by last known destination** | **Trade System: General**

Overview:

In 2015, the value of merchandise exports of Armenia decreased slightly by 0.5 percent to reach 1.5 bln US$, while its merchandise imports decreased substantially by 21.7 percent to reach 3.3 bln US$ (see graph 1, table 2 and table 3). The merchandise trade balance recorded a large deficit of 1.8 bln US$ (see graph 1). The largest merchandise trade balance was with MDG CIS at -840.0 mln US$ (see graph 4). Merchandise exports in Armenia were diversified amongst partners; imports were also diversified. The top 11 partners accounted for 80 percent or more of exports and 16 partners accounted for 80 percent or more of imports (see graph 5). In 2014, the value of exports of services of Armenia increased substantially by 48.3 percent, reaching 1.6 bln US$, while its imports of services increased substantially by 41.8 percent and reached 1.7 bln US$ (see graph 2). There was a relatively small trade in services deficit of 92.2 mln US$.

Graph 1: Total merchandise trade, by value

(Bln US$ by year)

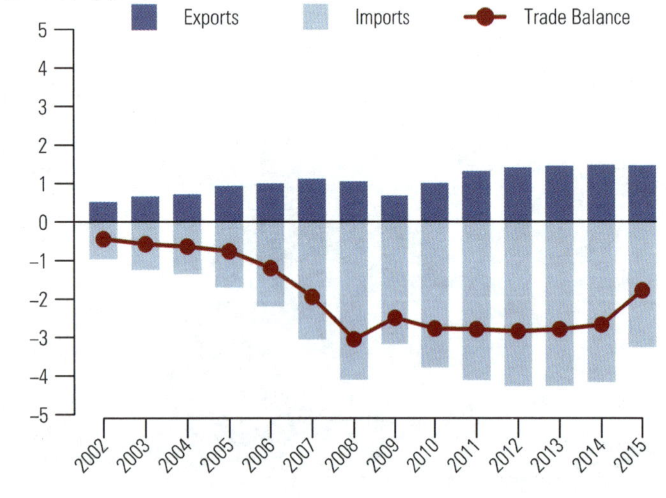

Graph 2: Total services trade, by value

(Bln US$ by year)

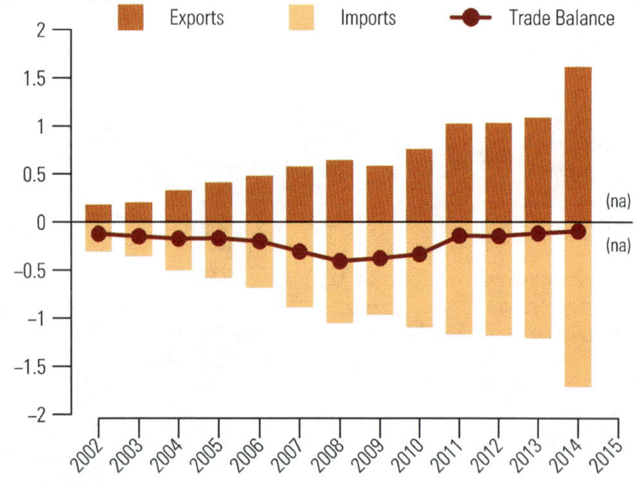

Exports Profile:

"Crude materials + anim. & veg. oils" (SITC section 2+4), "Food, animals + beverages, tobacco" (SITC section 0+1) and "Goods classified chiefly by material" (SITC section 6) were the largest commodity groups for exports in 2015, representing respectively 26.2, 25.6 and 22.2 percent of exported goods (see table 2). From 2013 to 2015, the largest export commodity was "Copper ores and concentrates" (HS code 2603) (see table 1). The top three destinations for merchandise exports were the Russian Federation, China and Germany, accounting for respectively 19.4, 9.1 and 8.8 percent of total exports. "Travel" (EBOPS code 236) accounted for the largest share of exports of services in 2014 at 965.8 mln US$, followed by "Construction services" (EBOPS code 249) at 211.4 mln US$ and "Transportation" (EBOPS code 205) at 181.5 mln US$ (see graph 3).

Graph 3: Exports of services by EBOPS category

(% share in 2014)

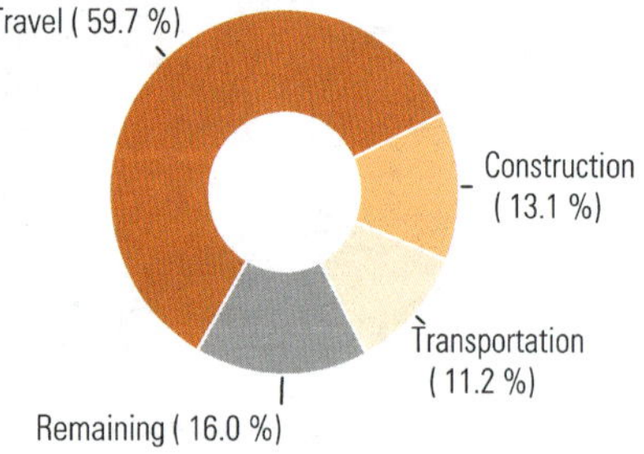

Table 1: Top 10 export commodities 2013 to 2015

HS code	4-digit heading of Harmonized System 2012	Value (million US$) 2013	2014	2015	Unit value 2013	2014	2015	Unit	SITC code
	All Commodities	1 467.8	1 490.2	1 482.7					
2603	Copper ores and concentrates	279.9	235.9	316.6	1.6	1.3	1.0	US$/kg	283
2208	Alcohol of a strength by volume of less than 80 % vol	186.2	163.7	92.5	13.2	12.5	8.7	US$/litre	112
2402	Cigars, cheroots, cigarillos and cigarettes	68.0	115.9	170.5	10.2	11.0	10.3	US$/kg	122
7102	Diamonds, whether or not worked, but not mounted or set	88.1	118.0	77.3					667
7202	Ferro-alloys	102.4	109.7	55.5	15.4	16.9	9.9	US$/kg	671
7108	Gold (including gold plated with platinum)	73.6	81.9	98.9	26.8	22.6	34.0	thsd US$/kg	971
7607	Aluminium foil (whether or not printed or backed with paper, paperboard	80.4	88.5	82.9	3.0	2.9	2.8	US$/kg	684
2716	Electrical energy	78.0	81.3	77.5	59.4	61.9	55.1	US$/MWh	351
7402	Unrefined copper; copper anodes for electrolytic refining	90.2	71.8	65.5	8.3	7.3	5.6	US$/kg	682
2616	Precious metal ores and concentrates	0.0	32.7	31.6	4.5	5.6	4.9	US$/kg	289

Services Imports and Exports: EBOPS 2002 categories

Table 2: Merchandise exports by SITC

(Value in million US$, growth and shares in percentage)

SITC	2015	Avg. Growth rates 2011-2015	2014-2015	2015 share
Total	1482.7	2.9	-0.5	100.0
0+1	379.7	14.2	-7.2	25.6
2+4	387.7	5.3	27.2	26.2
3	92.4	-2.3	2.3	6.2
5	22.4	10.5	11.2	1.5
6	329.1	-9.2	-26.3	22.2
7	26.3	-17.7	1.5	1.8
8	132.2	33.3	23.1	8.9
9	112.8	8.5	31.7	7.6

Table 3: Merchandise imports by SITC

(Value in million US$, growth and shares in percentage)

SITC	2015	Avg. Growth rates 2011-2015	2014-2015	2015 share
Total	3257.0	-5.6	-21.7	100.0
0+1	608.0	-4.0	-18.2	18.7
2+4	108.6	-1.3	-11.6	3.3
3	673.7	-4.4	-17.2	20.7
5	370.4	-1.6	-17.2	11.4
6	608.7	-5.9	-26.5	18.7
7	589.8	-6.7	-15.2	18.1
8	273.5	-3.3	-20.1	8.4
9	24.2	-41.7	-85.4	0.7

SITC Legend

SITC Code	Description
Total	All commodities
0+1	Food, animals + beverages, tobacco
2+4	Crude materials + anim. & veg. oils
3	Mineral fuels, lubricants
5	Chemicals
6	Goods classified chiefly by material
7	Machinery and transport equipment
8	Miscellaneous manufactured articles
9	Not classified elsewhere in the SITC

Graph 4: Merchandise trade balance

(Bln US$ by MDG Regions in 2015)

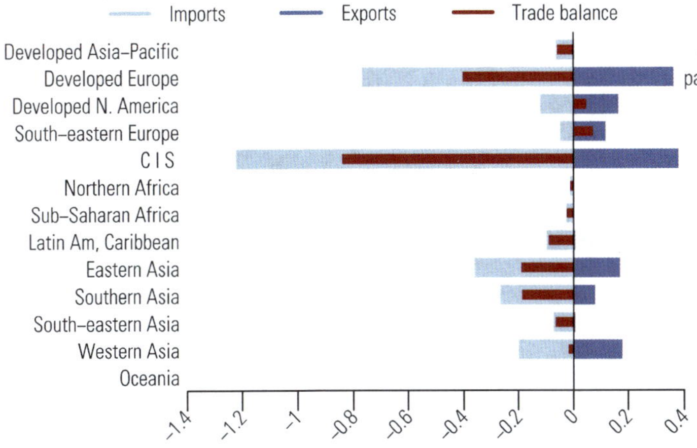

Graph 5: Partner concentration of merchandise trade

(Cumulative share by ranked partners in 2015)

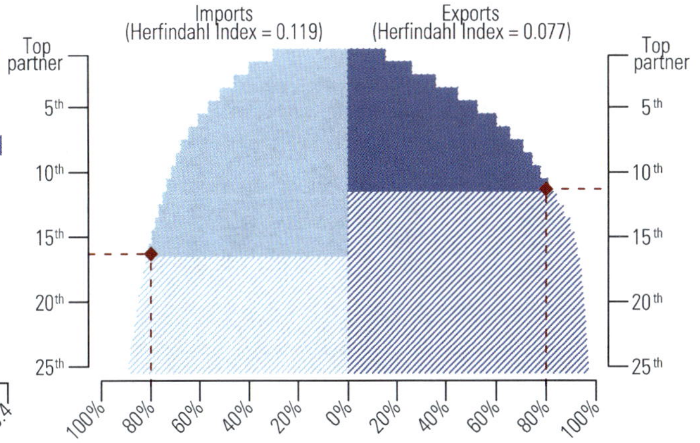

Graph 6: Imports of services by EBOPS category

(% share in 2014)

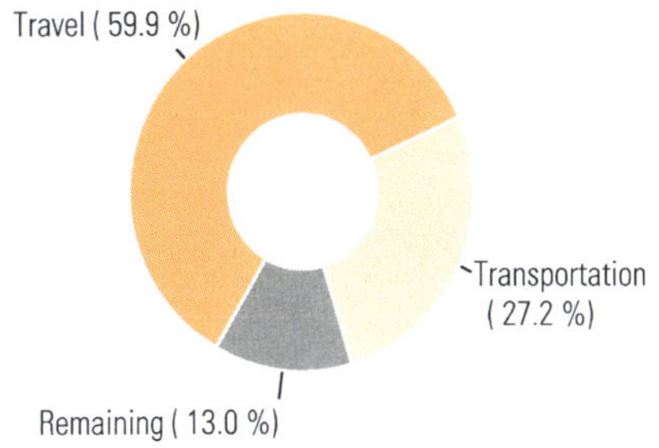

Imports Profile:

"Mineral fuels, lubricants" (SITC section 3), "Goods classified chiefly by material" (SITC section 6) and "Food, animals + beverages, tobacco" (SITC section 0+1) were the largest commodity groups for imports in 2015, representing respectively 20.7, 18.7 and 18.7 percent of imported goods (see table 3). From 2013 to 2015, the largest import commodity was "Petroleum gases and other gaseous hydrocarbons" (HS code 2711) (see table 4). The top three partners for merchandise imports were the Russian Federation, China and the Islamic Republic of Iran, accounting for respectively 27.1, 9.5 and 5.1 percent of total imports. "Travel" (EBOPS code 236) accounted for the largest share of imports of services in 2014 at 1.0 bln US$, followed by "Transportation" (EBOPS code 205) at 465.1 mln US$ (see graph 6).

Table 4: Top 10 import commodities 2013 to 2015

HS code	4-digit heading of Harmonized System 2012	Value (million US$) 2013	2014	2015	Unit value 2013	2014	2015	Unit	SITC code
	All Commodities	4256.2	4159.5	3257.0					
2711	Petroleum gases and other gaseous hydrocarbons	575.6	467.3	432.9	0.3	0.3	0.3	US$/kg	343
2710	Petroleum oils, other than crude	341.6	321.2	217.4	1.0	1.0	0.8	US$/kg	334
7102	Diamonds, whether or not worked, but not mounted or set	116.4	148.3	87.4					667
7108	Gold (including gold plated with platinum)	168.6	145.1	23.3	43.9	40.8	36.6	thsd US$/kg	971
3004	Medicaments (excluding goods of heading 30.02, 30.05 or 30.06)	109.6	101.0	93.9	80.8	75.8	*25.3*	US$/kg	542
1001	Wheat and meslin	108.7	100.8	70.6	0.3	0.3	0.2	US$/kg	041
8703	Motor cars and other motor vehicles principally designed for the transport	61.6	60.8	87.9	17.3	19.5	4.9	thsd US$/unit	781
7601	Unwrought aluminium	53.3	57.7	59.5	2.1	2.1	2.1	US$/kg	684
8517	Electrical apparatus for line telephony or line telegraphy	48.9	59.2	46.1					764
2402	Cigars, cheroots, cigarillos and cigarettes	60.0	43.7	43.3	20.2	18.7	15.5	US$/kg	122

Aruba

Goods Imports: CIF, by origin | **Goods Exports: FOB, by last known destination** | **Trade System: General**

Overview:

In 2014, the value of merchandise exports of Aruba decreased substantially by 30.7 percent to reach 116.2 mln US$, while its merchandise imports decreased slightly by 1.5 percent to reach 1.3 bln US$ (see graph 1, table 2 and table 3). The merchandise trade balance recorded a large deficit of 1.2 bln US$ (see graph 1). The largest merchandise trade balance was with MDG Developed North America at -699.9 mln US$ (see graph 4). Merchandise exports in Aruba were moderately concentrated amongst partners; imports were highly concentrated. The top 4 partners accounted for 80 percent or more of exports and 5 partners accounted for 80 percent or more of imports (see graph 5). In 2014, the value of exports of services of Aruba increased moderately by 8.4 percent, reaching 2.0 bln US$, while its imports of services increased slightly by 2.9 percent and reached 917.3 mln US$ (see graph 2). There was a large trade in services surplus of 1.1 bln US$.

Graph 1: Total merchandise trade, by value

(Bln US$ by year)

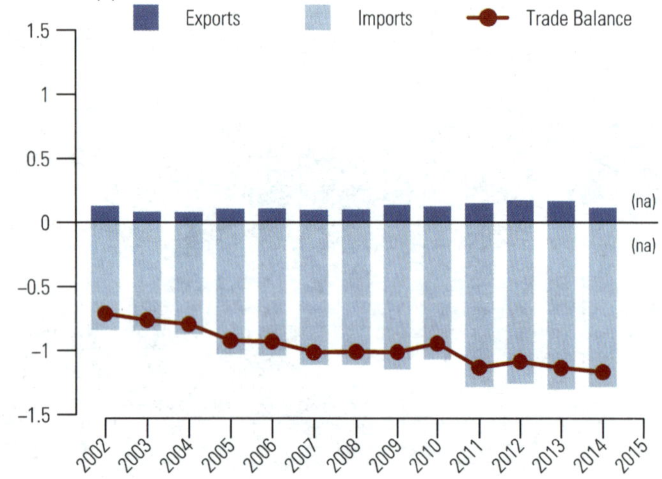

Graph 2: Total services trade, by value

(Bln US$ by year)

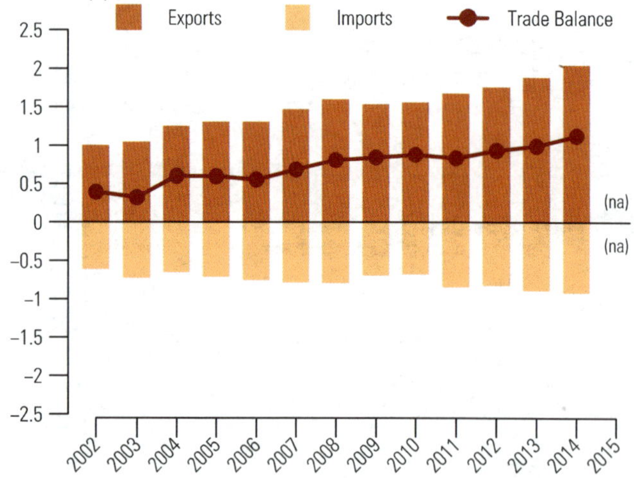

Exports Profile:

"Food, animals + beverages, tobacco" (SITC section 0+1), "Miscellaneous manufactured articles" (SITC section 8) and "Machinery and transport equipment" (SITC section 7) were the largest commodity groups for exports in 2014, representing respectively 68.1, 9.2 and 9.1 percent of exported goods (see table 2). From 2012 to 2014, the largest export commodity was "Alcohol of a strength by volume of less than 80 % vol" (HS code 2208) (see table 1). The top three destinations for merchandise exports were Colombia, the Bolivarian Republic of Venezuela and Curaçao, accounting for respectively 36.3, 18.8 and 14.0 percent of total exports. "Travel" (EBOPS code 236) accounted for the largest share of exports of services in 2014 at 1.6 bln US$, followed by "Other business services" (EBOPS code 268) at 248.0 mln US$ and "Transportation" (EBOPS code 205) at 112.8 mln US$ (see graph 3).

Graph 3: Exports of services by EBOPS category

(% share in 2014)

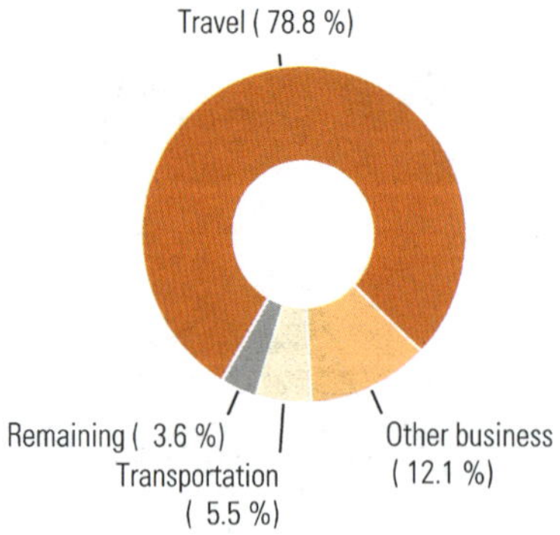

Table 1: Top 10 export commodities 2012 to 2014

HS code	4-digit heading of Harmonized System 2007	Value (million US$) 2012	2013	2014	Unit value 2012	2013	2014	Unit	SITC code
	All Commodities	173.1	167.8	116.2					
2208	Alcohol of a strength by volume of less than 80 % vol	70.0	78.4	61.2	*11.5*	*12.6*	*14.3*	US$/litre	112
2402	Cigars, cheroots, cigarillos and cigarettes	56.0	44.8	15.7	10.9	11.5	10.0	US$/kg	122
7113	Articles of jewellery and parts thereof, of precious metal	4.4	8.4	3.8	1.9	5.3	5.0	thsd US$/kg	897
9999	Commodities not specified according to kind	3.9	3.9	2.9					931
7204	Ferrous waste and scrap; remelting scrap ingots of iron or steel	2.2	2.7	2.8	0.2	0.2	0.3	US$/kg	282
7108	Gold (including gold plated with platinum)	3.4	2.3	0.0		12.0		thsd US$/kg	971
3303	Perfumes and toilet waters	1.9	1.6	1.3	40.8	52.6	34.7	US$/kg	553
7305	Other tubes and pipes (for example, welded, riveted or similarly closed)	2.9	0.5	0.0	2.5	1.9	2.3	US$/kg	679
2204	Wine of fresh grapes, including fortified wines	1.7	1.0	0.7	*3.6*	*2.9*	*3.5*	US$/litre	112
4202	Trunks, suit-cases, vanity-cases, executive-cases, brief-cases	0.4	0.7	1.7					831

Services Imports and Exports: EBOPS 2002 categories

Table 2: Merchandise exports by SITC

(Value in million US$, growth and shares in percentage)

SITC	2014	Avg. Growth rates 2010-2014	Avg. Growth rates 2013-2014	2014 share
Total	116.2	-1.7	-30.7	100.0
0+1	79.2	-6.2	-36.7	68.1
2+4	3.2	63.0	-1.0	2.7
3	0.3	20.9	4884.3	0.2
5	5.3	17.1	-6.4	4.6
6	4.0	6.4	-21.5	3.5
7	10.6	21.9	12.3	9.1
8	10.7	14.4	-17.8	9.2
9	3.0	-10.0	-52.6	2.5

Table 3: Merchandise imports by SITC

(Value in million US$, growth and shares in percentage)

SITC	2014	Avg. Growth rates 2010-2014	Avg. Growth rates 2013-2014	2014 share
Total	1 284.1	4.6	-1.5	100.0
0+1	351.8	1.2	-13.5	27.4
2+4	22.6	4.2	4.9	1.8
3	93.0	7.4	-1.0	7.2
5	114.7	3.5	11.2	8.9
6	133.9	5.1	-4.8	10.4
7	261.0	7.0	8.1	20.3
8	286.4	5.7	2.0	22.3
9	20.7	30.4	34.9	1.6

SITC Legend

SITC Code	Description
Total	All commodities
0+1	Food, animals + beverages, tobacco
2+4	Crude materials + anim. & veg. oils
3	Mineral fuels, lubricants
5	Chemicals
6	Goods classified chiefly by material
7	Machinery and transport equipment
8	Miscellaneous manufactured articles
9	Not classified elsewhere in the SITC

Graph 4: Merchandise trade balance

(Mln US$ by MDG Regions in 2014)

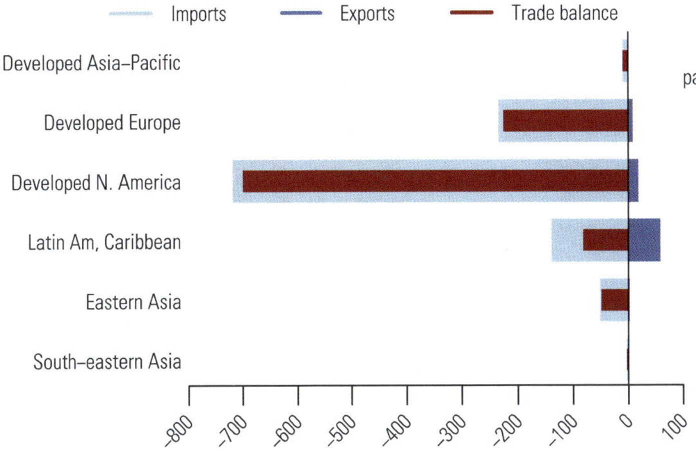

Graph 5: Partner concentration of merchandise trade

(Cumulative share by ranked partners in 2014)

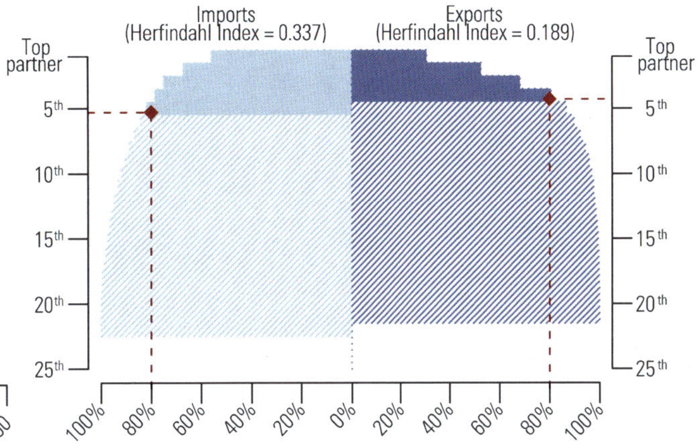

Graph 6: Imports of services by EBOPS category

(% share in 2014)

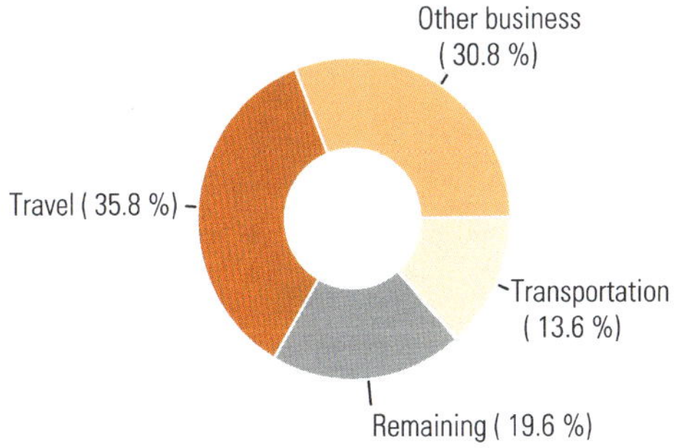

Imports Profile:

"Food, animals + beverages, tobacco" (SITC section 0+1), "Miscellaneous manufactured articles" (SITC section 8) and "Machinery and transport equipment" (SITC section 7) were the largest commodity groups for imports in 2014, representing respectively 27.4, 22.3 and 20.3 percent of imported goods (see table 3). From 2012 to 2014, the largest import commodity was "Petroleum oils, other than crude" (HS code 2710) (see table 4). The top three partners for merchandise imports were the United States, the Netherlands and Areas nes, accounting for respectively 50.7, 11.3 and 10.0 percent of total imports. "Travel" (EBOPS code 236) accounted for the largest share of imports of services in 2014 at 328.5 mln US$, followed by "Other business services" (EBOPS code 268) at 282.7 mln US$ and "Transportation" (EBOPS code 205) at 125.1 mln US$ (see graph 6).

Table 4: Top 10 import commodities 2012 to 2014

HS code	4-digit heading of Harmonized System 2007	Value (million US$) 2012	2013	2014	Unit value 2012	2013	2014	Unit	SITC code
	All Commodities	1 259.8	1 303.3	1 284.1					
2710	Petroleum oils, other than crude	94.8	86.2	91.2	1.0	1.0	1.0	US$/kg	334
2208	Alcohol of a strength by volume of less than 80 % vol	77.9	97.6	61.0	*9.2*	*12.6*	*12.5*	US$/litre	112
8703	Motor cars and other motor vehicles principally designed for the transport	47.8	51.4	51.1	*15.9*	*15.5*	*14.7*	thsd US$/unit	781
7113	Articles of jewellery and parts thereof, of precious metal	38.0	46.6	44.4	2.2	3.0	1.0	thsd US$/kg	897
2402	Cigars, cheroots, cigarillos and cigarettes	61.8	43.5	16.4	11.9	11.6	10.3	US$/kg	122
8517	Electrical apparatus for line telephony or line telegraphy	21.1	29.5	28.0					764
9102	Wrist-watches, pocket-watches and other watches, of base metal	20.2	15.7	18.3					885
3004	Medicaments (excluding goods of heading 30.02, 30.05 or 30.06)	19.0	15.2	18.7	51.2	49.1	39.8	US$/kg	542
9403	Other furniture and parts thereof	13.1	18.6	20.5					821
9101	Wrist-watches, pocket-watches and other watches, precious metal	14.8	18.6	17.0					885

Source: UN Comtrade

Australia

Goods Imports: FOB, by origin **Goods Exports: FOB, by last known destination** **Trade System: General**

Overview:

In 2015, the value of merchandise exports of Australia decreased substantially by 21.9 percent to reach 187.8 bln US$, while its merchandise imports decreased substantially by 12.1 percent to reach 200.1 bln US$ (see graph 1, table 2 and table 3). The merchandise trade balance recorded a relatively small deficit of 12.3 bln US$ (see graph 1). The largest merchandise trade balance was with MDG Developed Europe at -27.3 bln US$ (see graph 4). Merchandise exports in Australia were diversified amongst partners; imports were also diversified. The top 11 partners accounted for 80 percent or more of exports and 15 partners accounted for 80 percent or more of imports (see graph 5). In 2014, the value of exports of services of Australia increased slightly by 1.3 percent, reaching 54.5 bln US$, while its imports of services decreased moderately by 6.6 percent and reached 63.0 bln US$ (see graph 2). There was a relatively small trade in services deficit of 8.5 bln US$.

Graph 1: Total merchandise trade, by value

(Bln US$ by year)

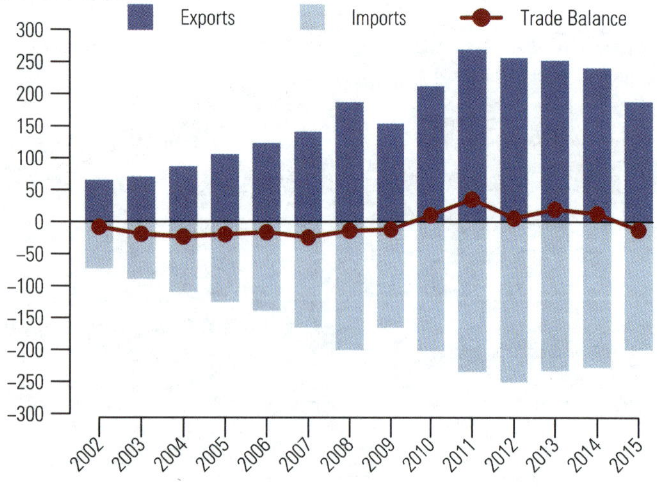

Graph 2: Total services trade, by value

(Bln US$ by year)

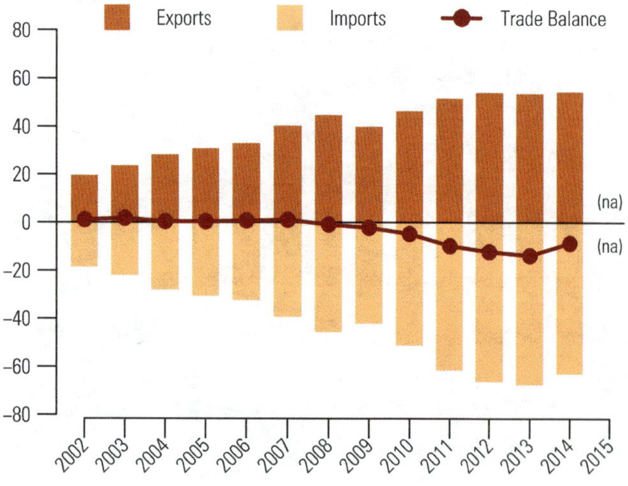

Exports Profile:

"Crude materials + anim. & veg. oils" (SITC section 2+4), "Mineral fuels, lubricants" (SITC section 3) and "Food, animals + beverages, tobacco" (SITC section 0+1) were the largest commodity groups for exports in 2015, representing respectively 32.0, 25.3 and 15.3 percent of exported goods (see table 2). From 2013 to 2015, the largest export commodity was "Iron ores and concentrates, including roasted iron pyrites" (HS code 2601) (see table 1). The top three destinations for merchandise exports were China, Japan and the Republic of Korea, accounting for respectively 33.8, 15.3 and 7.2 percent of total exports. "Travel" (EBOPS code 236) accounted for the largest share of exports of services in 2014 at 32.0 bln US$, followed by "Other business services" (EBOPS code 268) at 8.2 bln US$ and "Transportation" (EBOPS code 205) at 4.7 bln US$ (see graph 3).

Graph 3: Exports of services by EBOPS category

(% share in 2014)

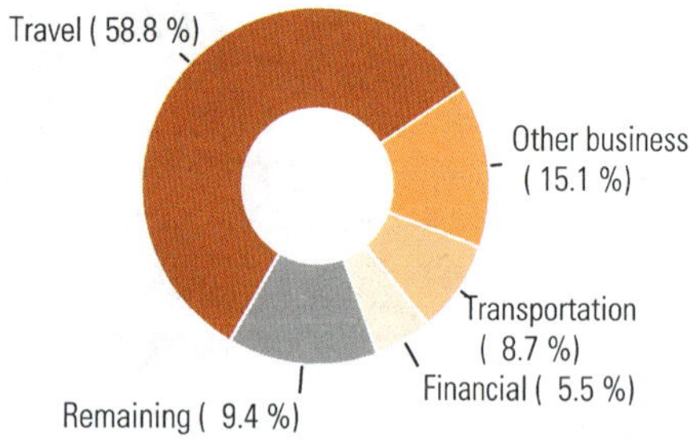

Table 1: Top 10 export commodities 2013 to 2015

HS code	4-digit heading of Harmonized System 2012	Value (million US$) 2013	2014	2015	Unit value 2013	2014	2015	Unit	SITC code
	All Commodities	252155.1	240444.7	187792.2					
2601	Iron ores and concentrates, including roasted iron pyrites	67209.0	60174.4	36735.5	0.1	0.1	0.0	US$/kg	281
2701	Coal; briquettes, ovoids and similar solid fuels manufactured from coal	38423.5	34430.8	28418.5	0.1	0.1	0.1	US$/kg	321
2711	Petroleum gases and other gaseous hydrocarbons	15255.0	17154.0	12884.8	*0.6*	*0.7*	*0.4*	US$/kg	343
7108	Gold (including gold plated with platinum)	13385.9	12031.1	10683.1	42.4	38.2	35.3	thsd US$/kg	971
9999	Commodities not specified according to kind	8648.1	7947.9	7095.4					931
2709	Petroleum oils and oils obtained from bituminous minerals, crude	8675.4	9633.2	4570.3	0.9	0.8	0.4	US$/kg	333
2818	Artificial corundum, whether or not chemically defined	5338.2	5270.6	4990.8	0.3	0.3	0.3	US$/kg	522
1001	Wheat and meslin	5875.6	5343.4	4371.5	0.3	0.3	0.3	US$/kg	041
2603	Copper ores and concentrates	4968.5	4911.3	3659.5	2.3	2.2	1.9	US$/kg	283
0202	Meat of bovine animals, frozen	3566.5	4676.6	4506.2	4.0	4.5	4.4	US$/kg	011

Services Imports and Exports: EBOPS 2002 categories

Table 2: Merchandise exports by SITC

(Value in million US$, growth and shares in percentage)

SITC	2015	Avg. Growth rates 2011-2015	Avg. Growth rates 2014-2015	2015 share
Total	187 792.2	-8.6	-21.9	100.0
0+1	28 706.4	1.3	-4.1	15.3
2+4	60 149.3	-11.3	-31.6	32.0
3	47 494.2	-11.0	-25.7	25.3
5	5 513.3	-9.1	-16.7	2.9
6	11 101.3	-9.4	-19.7	5.9
7	12 050.7	-1.9	-9.0	6.4
8	4 741.4	-3.0	-2.5	2.5
9	18 035.5	-9.0	-10.2	9.6

Table 3: Merchandise imports by SITC

(Value in million US$, growth and shares in percentage)

SITC	2015	Avg. Growth rates 2011-2015	Avg. Growth rates 2014-2015	2015 share
Total	200 113.8	-3.9	-12.1	100.0
0+1	12 543.2	2.4	-6.5	6.3
2+4	2 913.4	-4.0	-8.8	1.5
3	21 747.5	-13.9	-40.0	10.9
5	20 188.3	-4.9	-9.9	10.1
6	24 414.8	-1.2	-5.9	12.2
7	79 237.9	-2.3	-6.8	39.6
8	30 263.4	1.1	-3.4	15.1
9	8 805.2	-10.7	-11.9	4.4

SITC Legend

SITC Code	Description
Total	All commodities
0+1	Food, animals + beverages, tobacco
2+4	Crude materials + anim. & veg. oils
3	Mineral fuels, lubricants
5	Chemicals
6	Goods classified chiefly by material
7	Machinery and transport equipment
8	Miscellaneous manufactured articles
9	Not classified elsewhere in the SITC

Graph 4: Merchandise trade balance

(Bln US$ by MDG Regions in 2015)

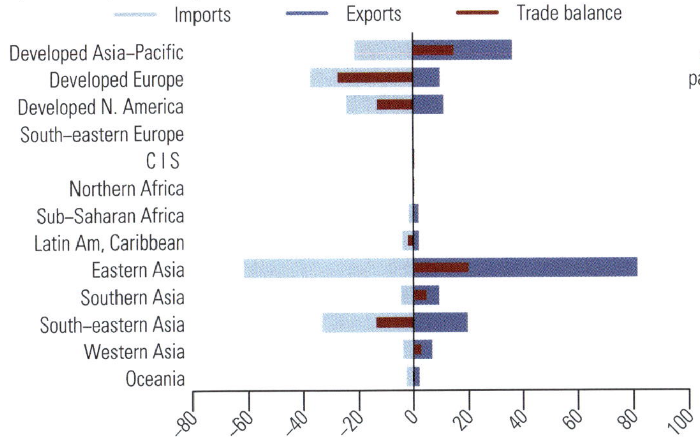

Graph 5: Partner concentration of merchandise trade

(Cumulative share by ranked partners in 2015)

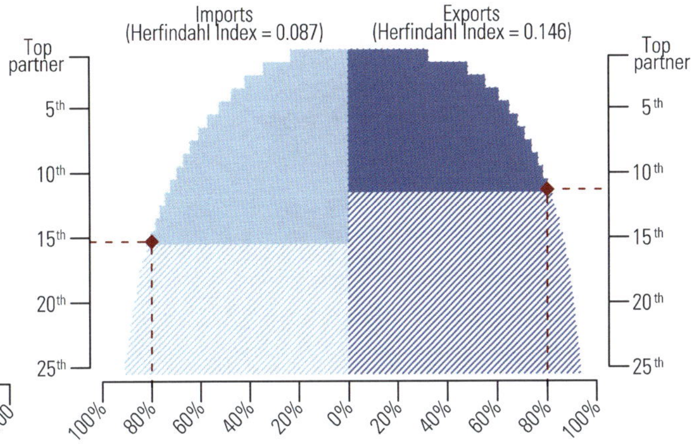

Graph 6: Imports of services by EBOPS category

(% share in 2014)

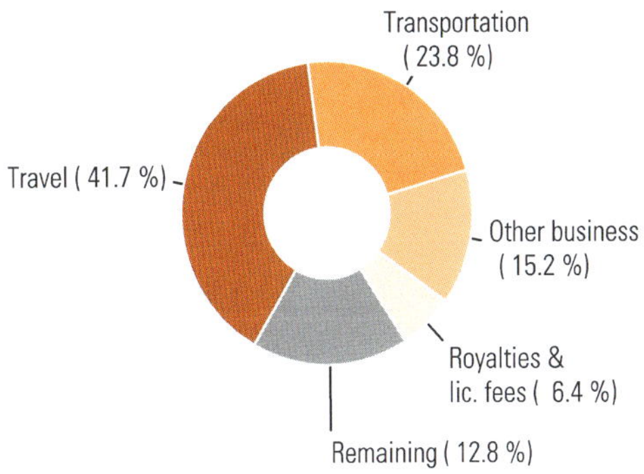

Imports Profile:

"Machinery and transport equipment" (SITC section 7), "Miscellaneous manufactured articles" (SITC section 8) and "Goods classified chiefly by material" (SITC section 6) were the largest commodity groups for imports in 2015, representing respectively 39.6, 15.1 and 12.2 percent of imported goods (see table 3). From 2013 to 2015, the largest import commodity was "Motor cars and other motor vehicles principally designed for the transport" (HS code 8703) (see table 4). The top three partners for merchandise imports were China, the United States and Japan, accounting for respectively 20.9, 10.7 and 7.3 percent of total imports. "Travel" (EBOPS code 236) accounted for the largest share of imports of services in 2014 at 26.3 bln US$, followed by "Transportation" (EBOPS code 205) at 15.0 bln US$ and "Other business services" (EBOPS code 268) at 9.6 bln US$ (see graph 6).

Table 4: Top 10 import commodities 2013 to 2015

HS code	4-digit heading of Harmonized System 2012	Value (million US$) 2013	2014	2015	Unit value 2013	2014	2015	Unit	SITC code
	All Commodities	232 481.3	227 544.2	200 113.8					
8703	Motor cars and other motor vehicles principally designed for the transport	17 646.8	15 849.9	15 298.5	19.4	19.2	16.8	thsd US$/unit	781
2710	Petroleum oils, other than crude	17 592.8	16 866.4	13 867.0	*0.9*	*0.9*	*0.6*	US$/kg	334
2709	Petroleum oils and oils obtained from bituminous minerals, crude	19 494.4	18 305.8	7 103.2	0.9	0.8	0.4	US$/kg	333
8517	Electrical apparatus for line telephony or line telegraphy	6 898.3	7 064.8	7 003.9					764
3004	Medicaments (excluding goods of heading 30.02, 30.05 or 30.06)	7 488.5	6 707.5	5 451.2	*131.1*	*116.6*		US$/kg	542
8471	Automatic data processing machines and units thereof	6 657.9	6 549.6	6 301.6	284.1	273.5	311.5	US$/unit	752
9999	Commodities not specified according to kind	4 782.3	6 375.6	5 453.3					931
8704	Motor vehicles for the transport of goods	6 037.3	5 260.9	4 929.3	*27.3*	*25.8*	*20.5*	thsd US$/unit	782
7108	Gold (including gold plated with platinum)	4 389.0	3 439.5	2 925.3	*32.0*	*29.4*	*27.7*	thsd US$/kg	971
8708	Parts and accessories of the motor vehicles of headings 87.01 to 87.05	2 552.3	2 343.4	2 177.5	*8.1*	*9.1*	*7.6*	US$/kg	784

Source: UN Comtrade

Austria

Goods Imports: CIF, by origin | **Goods Exports: FOB, by last known destination** | **Trade System: Special**

Overview:

In 2014, the value of merchandise exports of Austria increased slightly by 2.1 percent to reach 169.7 bln US$, while its merchandise imports decreased slightly by 0.5 percent to reach 172.4 bln US$ (see graph 1, table 2 and table 3). The merchandise trade balance recorded a relatively small deficit of 2.7 bln US$ (see graph 1). The largest merchandise trade balance was with MDG Developed Europe at -7.4 bln US$ (see graph 4). Merchandise exports in Austria were diversified amongst partners; imports were moderately concentrated. The top 17 partners accounted for 80 percent or more of exports and 15 partners accounted for 80 percent or more of imports (see graph 5). In 2014, the value of exports of services of Austria increased slightly by 3.8 percent, reaching 67.0 bln US$, while its imports of services increased slightly by 4.6 percent and reached 49.4 bln US$ (see graph 2). There was a moderate trade in services surplus of 17.6 bln US$.

Graph 1: Total merchandise trade, by value

(Bln US$ by year)

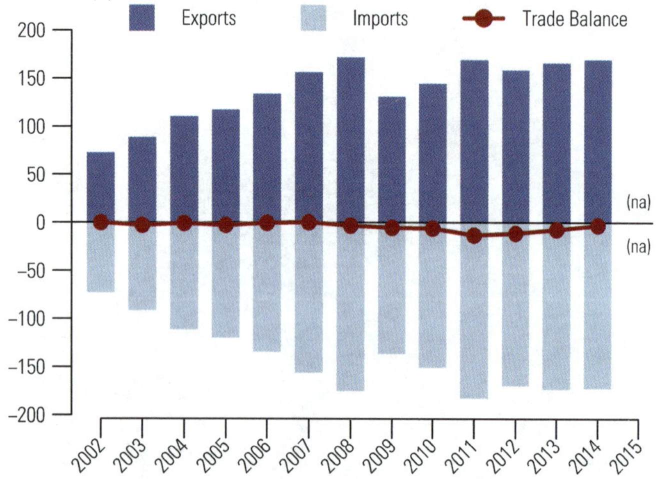

Graph 2: Total services trade, by value

(Bln US$ by year)

Exports Profile:

"Machinery and transport equipment" (SITC section 7), "Goods classified chiefly by material" (SITC section 6) and "Chemicals" (SITC section 5) were the largest commodity groups for exports in 2014, representing respectively 39.2, 21.2 and 12.5 percent of exported goods (see table 2). From 2012 to 2014, the largest export commodity was "Commodities not specified according to kind" (HS code 9999) (see table 1). The top three destinations for merchandise exports were Germany, Italy and the United States, accounting for respectively 29.5, 6.3 and 5.5 percent of total exports. "Travel" (EBOPS code 236) accounted for the largest share of exports of services in 2014 at 20.8 bln US$, followed by "Other business services" (EBOPS code 268) at 18.1 bln US$ and "Transportation" (EBOPS code 205) at 15.7 bln US$ (see graph 3).

Graph 3: Exports of services by EBOPS category

(% share in 2014)

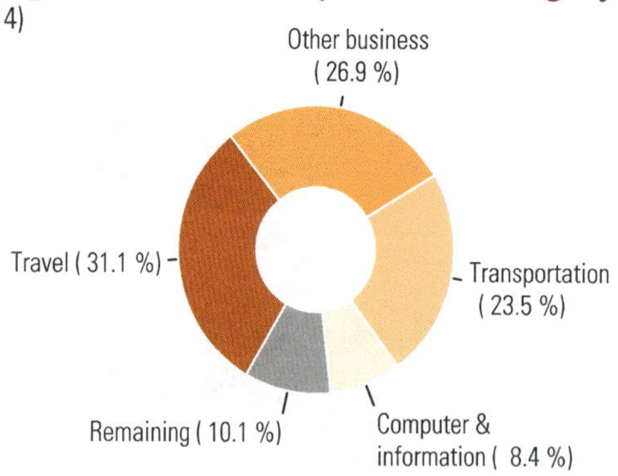

Table 1: Top 10 export commodities 2012 to 2014

HS code	4-digit heading of Harmonized System 2012	Value (million US$) 2012	2013	2014	Unit value 2012	2013	2014	Unit	SITC code
	All Commodities	158821.0	166271.4	169715.0					
9999	Commodities not specified according to kind	6228.7	6388.2	5651.0					931
3004	Medicaments (excluding goods of heading 30.02, 30.05 or 30.06)	5320.4	5510.0	5879.8	*69.6*	*54.9*	*76.6*	US$/kg	542
8703	Motor cars and other motor vehicles principally designed for the transport	4921.6	5734.1	5625.5		*20.6*	*20.9*	thsd US$/unit	781
8708	Parts and accessories of the motor vehicles of headings 87.01 to 87.05	4556.3	4728.7	4826.7	*9.4*	*10.2*	*10.5*	US$/kg	784
8408	Compression-ignition internal combustion piston engines	2518.7	2763.5	2893.6					713
3002	Human blood; animal blood prepared for therapeutic uses	2400.5	2650.7	2659.1	*379.9*	*384.8*	*272.9*	US$/kg	541
2710	Petroleum oils, other than crude	2342.4	2267.3	2133.8	*1.1*			US$/kg	334
8407	Spark-ignition reciprocating or rotary internal combustion piston engines	2378.8	2123.8	2179.4					713
8517	Electrical apparatus for line telephony or line telegraphy	1736.9	2059.3	2314.9					764
2202	Waters with added sugar	1955.6	1819.4	1811.6		*1.5*	*1.5*	US$/litre	111

Source: UN Comtrade

Services Imports and Exports: EBOPS 2002 categories

Table 2: Merchandise exports by SITC

(Value in million US$, growth and shares in percentage)

SITC	2014	Avg. Growth rates 2010-2014	Avg. Growth rates 2013-2014	2014 share
Total	169715.0	4.0	2.1	100.0
0+1	11932.2	5.7	3.6	7.0
2+4	4447.1	1.1	-3.4	2.6
3	4062.9	-3.3	-9.5	2.4
5	21271.0	6.2	7.3	12.5
6	35900.0	3.1	3.0	21.2
7	66507.2	5.0	1.7	39.2
8	19082.9	3.9	4.7	11.2
9	6511.8	-1.0	-11.5	3.8

Table 3: Merchandise imports by SITC

(Value in million US$, growth and shares in percentage)

SITC	2014	Avg. Growth rates 2010-2014	Avg. Growth rates 2013-2014	2014 share
Total	172447.5	3.4	-0.5	100.0
0+1	12611.6	6.0	3.3	7.3
2+4	8091.2	0.3	-2.0	4.7
3	17290.3	1.8	-11.8	10.0
5	23212.0	5.3	4.3	13.5
6	26677.3	2.8	1.4	15.5
7	57137.5	3.9	-0.6	33.1
8	25109.4	3.8	4.7	14.6
9	2318.2	-6.4	-28.6	1.3

SITC Legend

SITC Code	Description
Total	All commodities
0+1	Food, animals + beverages, tobacco
2+4	Crude materials + anim. & veg. oils
3	Mineral fuels, lubricants
5	Chemicals
6	Goods classified chiefly by material
7	Machinery and transport equipment
8	Miscellaneous manufactured articles
9	Not classified elsewhere in the SITC

Graph 4: Merchandise trade balance

(Bln US$ by MDG Regions in 2014)

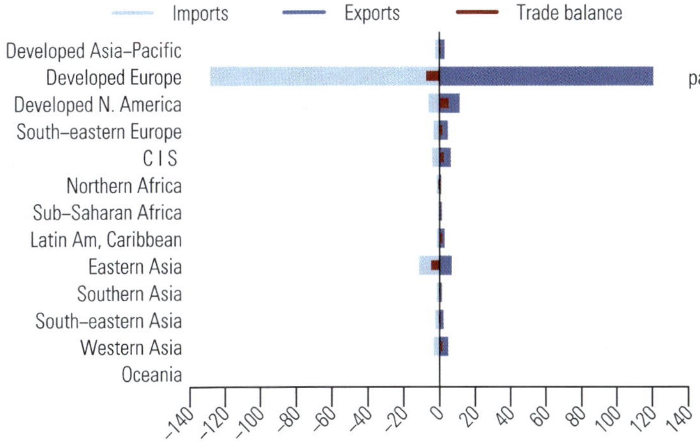

Graph 5: Partner concentration of merchandise trade

(Cumulative share by ranked partners in 2014)

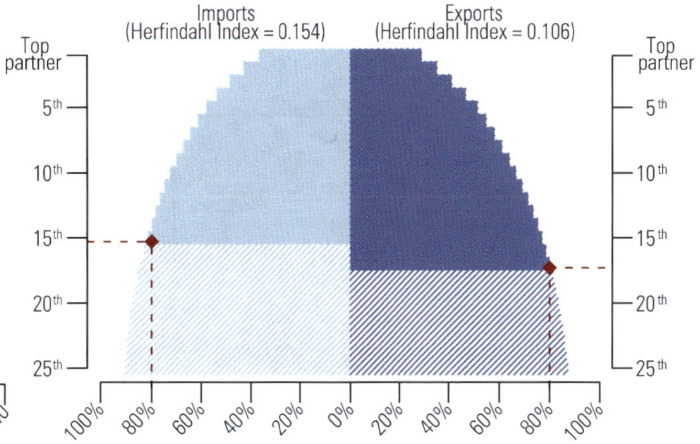

Graph 6: Imports of services by EBOPS category

(% share in 2014)

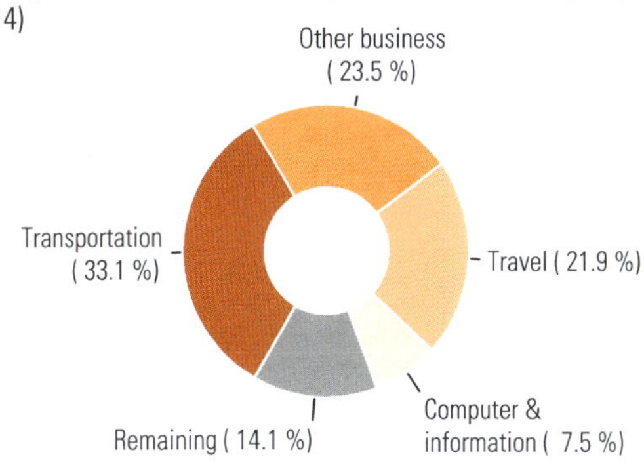

Imports Profile:

"Machinery and transport equipment" (SITC section 7), "Goods classified chiefly by material" (SITC section 6) and "Miscellaneous manufactured articles" (SITC section 8) were the largest commodity groups for imports in 2014, representing respectively 33.1, 15.5 and 14.6 percent of imported goods (see table 3). From 2012 to 2014, the largest import commodity was "Motor cars and other motor vehicles principally designed for the transport" (HS code 8703) (see table 4). The top three partners for merchandise imports were Germany, Italy and Switzerland, accounting for respectively 36.8, 6.1 and 5.3 percent of total imports. "Transportation" (EBOPS code 205) accounted for the largest share of imports of services in 2014 at 16.3 bln US$, followed by "Other business services" (EBOPS code 268) at 11.6 bln US$ and "Travel" (EBOPS code 236) at 10.8 bln US$ (see graph 6).

Table 4: Top 10 import commodities 2012 to 2014

HS code	4-digit heading of Harmonized System 2012	Value (million US$) 2012	2013	2014	Unit value 2012	2013	2014	Unit	SITC code
	All Commodities	169663.2	173357.5	172447.5					
8703	Motor cars and other motor vehicles principally designed for the transport	8632.3	8762.6	8831.0		*18.9*	*19.0*	thsd US$/unit	781
2709	Petroleum oils and oils obtained from bituminous minerals, crude	6357.4	6534.0	5971.0	0.9	0.8	*0.8*	US$/kg	333
2710	Petroleum oils, other than crude	7330.6	6015.7	5413.6	*1.1*			US$/kg	334
8708	Parts and accessories of the motor vehicles of headings 87.01 to 87.05	4488.5	4644.3	4480.1	*9.1*	*9.6*	*10.4*	US$/kg	784
2711	Petroleum gases and other gaseous hydrocarbons	5655.5	4311.7	3513.2	*0.6*	*0.6*	*0.5*	US$/kg	343
3004	Medicaments (excluding goods of heading 30.02, 30.05 or 30.06)	3283.0	3495.7	3736.8	*56.5*	*68.1*	*67.0*	US$/kg	542
2937	Hormones, prostaglandins, thromboxanes and leukotrienes	2635.2	3104.0	3260.6					541
8517	Electrical apparatus for line telephony or line telegraphy	2486.3	2610.2	2721.9					764
7108	Gold (including gold plated with platinum)	2577.6	2468.9	1849.9		*44.6*		thsd US$/kg	971
8409	Parts suitable for use with the engines of heading 84	2098.0	2180.4	2292.8	*12.4*	*12.4*	*12.3*	US$/kg	713

Azerbaijan

Goods Imports: CIF, by origin | **Goods Exports: FOB, by last known destination** | **Trade System: General**

Overview:

In 2014, the value of merchandise exports of Azerbaijan decreased moderately by 9.0 percent to reach 21.8 bln US$, while its merchandise imports decreased substantially by 14.7 percent to reach 9.2 bln US$ (see graph 1, table 2 and table 3). The merchandise trade balance recorded a large surplus of 12.6 bln US$ (see graph 1). The largest merchandise trade balance was with MDG Developed Europe at 8.5 bln US$ (see graph 4). Merchandise exports in Azerbaijan were diversified amongst partners; imports were also diversified. The top 13 partners accounted for 80 percent or more of exports and 14 partners accounted for 80 percent or more of imports (see graph 5). In 2014, the value of exports of services of Azerbaijan increased slightly by 3.3 percent, reaching 4.2 bln US$, while its imports of services increased substantially by 24.8 percent and reached 10.3 bln US$ (see graph 2). There was a large trade in services deficit of 6.1 bln US$.

Graph 1: Total merchandise trade, by value
(Bln US$ by year)

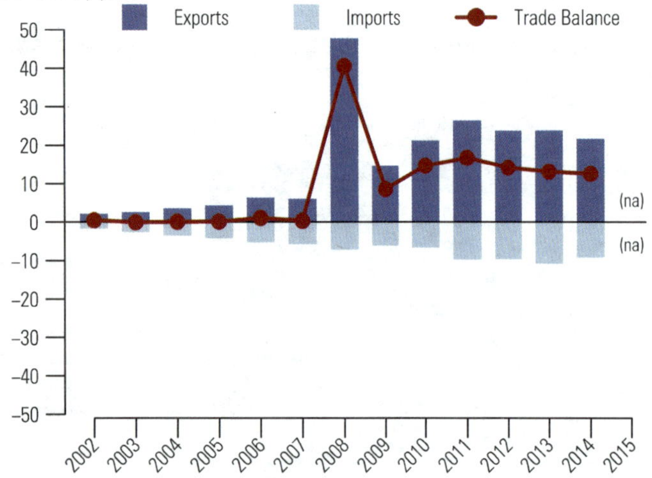

Graph 2: Total services trade, by value
(Bln US$ by year)

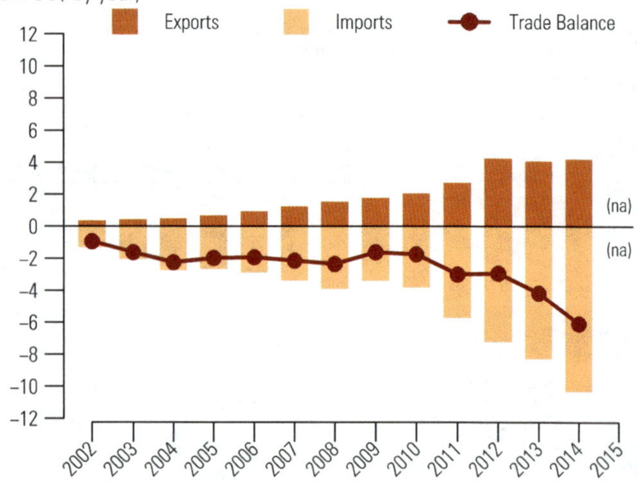

Exports Profile:

"Mineral fuels, lubricants" (SITC section 3), "Food, animals + beverages, tobacco" (SITC section 0+1) and "Chemicals" (SITC section 5) were the largest commodity groups for exports in 2014, representing respectively 92.8, 3.2 and 1.1 percent of exported goods (see table 2). From 2012 to 2014, the largest export commodity was "Petroleum oils and oils obtained from bituminous minerals, crude" (HS code 2709) (see table 1). The top three destinations for merchandise exports were Italy, Indonesia and Israel, accounting for respectively 23.5, 9.4 and 6.8 percent of total exports. "Travel" (EBOPS code 236) accounted for the largest share of exports of services in 2014 at 2.4 bln US$, followed by "Transportation" (EBOPS code 205) at 1.1 bln US$ and "Other business services" (EBOPS code 268) at 427.8 mln US$ (see graph 3).

Graph 3: Exports of services by EBOPS category
(% share in 2014)

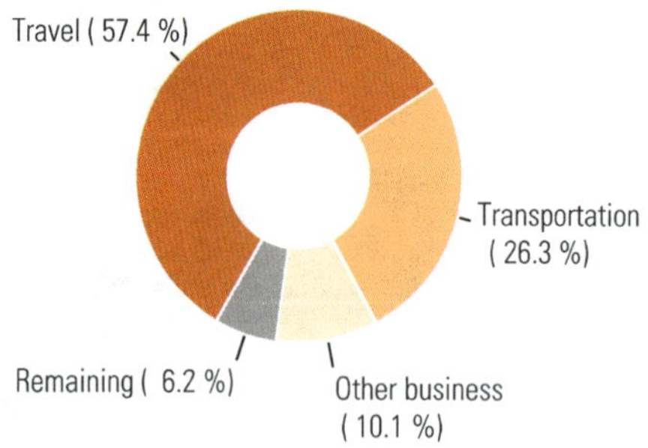

Table 1: Top 10 export commodities 2012 to 2014

HS code	4-digit heading of Harmonized System 2012	Value (million US$) 2012	2013	2014	Unit value 2012	2013	2014	Unit	SITC code
	All Commodities	23827.2	23904.1	21751.7					
2709	Petroleum oils and oils obtained from bituminous minerals, crude	20232.6	20244.1	18404.9	0.8	0.8	0.8	US$/kg	333
2710	Petroleum oils, other than crude	1321.2	1208.5	1365.0	0.8	0.7	0.6	US$/kg	334
2711	Petroleum gases and other gaseous hydrocarbons	661.6	732.6	325.0	0.3	0.3	0.2	US$/kg	343
1701	Cane or beet sugar and chemically pure sucrose, in solid form	214.2	243.6	221.2	1.0	1.0	1.0	US$/kg	061
9999	Commodities not specified according to kind	21.8	131.5	175.3					931
0810	Other fruit, fresh	103.5	87.8	72.2	0.8	0.8	1.0	US$/kg	057
7601	Unwrought aluminium	94.5	81.9	80.3	1.6	1.5	1.5	US$/kg	684
3901	Polymers of ethylene, in primary forms	61.6	75.8	104.6	1.1	1.2	1.2	US$/kg	571
1516	Animal or vegetable fats and oils	74.7	72.8	59.5	2.5	2.5	2.3	US$/kg	431
0802	Other nuts, fresh or dried, whether or not shelled or peeled	45.9	45.2	68.8	4.4	4.3	5.7	US$/kg	057

Services Imports and Exports: EBOPS 2002 categories

Table 2: Merchandise exports by SITC

(Value in million US$, growth and shares in percentage)

SITC	2014	Avg. Growth rates 2010-2014	Avg. Growth rates 2013-2014	2014 share
Total	21 751.7	0.6	-9.0	100.0
0+1	692.9	12.2	0.5	3.2
2+4	172.4	-0.8	-25.0	0.8
3	20 177.2	0.1	-9.2	92.8
5	231.1	15.4	31.7	1.1
6	200.9	4.1	-24.6	0.9
7	87.2	-20.5	-46.7	0.4
8	14.8	-9.5	-18.1	0.1
9	175.3	92.9	33.3	0.8

Table 3: Merchandise imports by SITC

(Value in million US$, growth and shares in percentage)

SITC	2014	Avg. Growth rates 2010-2014	Avg. Growth rates 2013-2014	2014 share
Total	9 178.6	8.6	-14.7	100.0
0+1	1 451.6	6.5	-1.5	15.8
2+4	220.6	-4.4	-46.6	2.4
3	297.1	41.7	109.8	3.2
5	865.7	10.3	-6.8	9.4
6	1 807.7	6.1	-9.1	19.7
7	3 462.1	6.5	-17.4	37.7
8	615.7	12.1	-8.9	6.7
9	458.0	80.2	-51.9	5.0

SITC Legend

SITC Code	Description
Total	All commodities
0+1	Food, animals + beverages, tobacco
2+4	Crude materials + anim. & veg. oils
3	Mineral fuels, lubricants
5	Chemicals
6	Goods classified chiefly by material
7	Machinery and transport equipment
8	Miscellaneous manufactured articles
9	Not classified elsewhere in the SITC

Graph 4: Merchandise trade balance

(Bln US$ by MDG Regions in 2014)

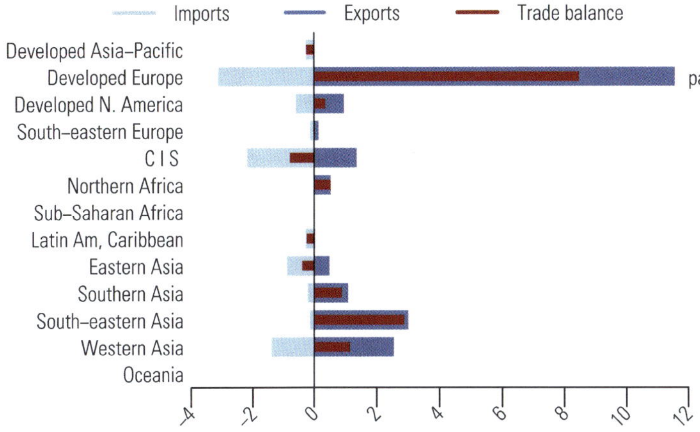

Graph 5: Partner concentration of merchandise trade

(Cumulative share by ranked partners in 2014)

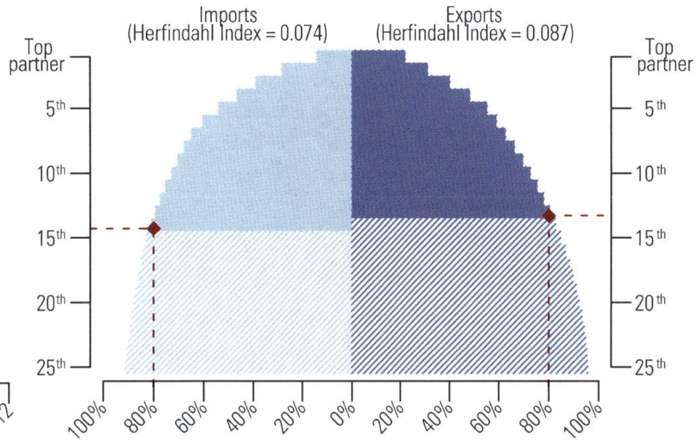

Graph 6: Imports of services by EBOPS category

(% share in 2014)

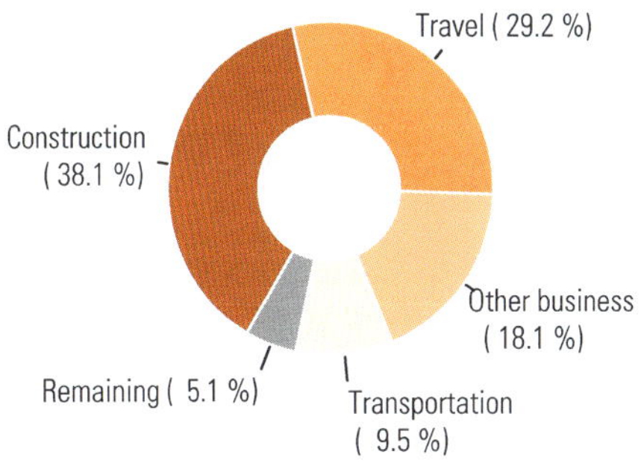

Imports Profile:

"Machinery and transport equipment" (SITC section 7), "Goods classified chiefly by material" (SITC section 6) and "Food, animals + beverages, tobacco" (SITC section 0+1) were the largest commodity groups for imports in 2014, representing respectively 37.7, 19.7 and 15.8 percent of imported goods (see table 3). From 2012 to 2014, the largest import commodity was "Motor cars and other motor vehicles principally designed for the transport" (HS code 8703) (see table 4). The top three partners for merchandise imports were Turkey, the Russian Federation and the United Kingdom, accounting for respectively 14.5, 14.2 and 9.5 percent of total imports. "Construction services" (EBOPS code 249) accounted for the largest share of imports of services in 2014 at 3.9 bln US$, followed by "Travel" (EBOPS code 236) at 3.0 bln US$ and "Other business services" (EBOPS code 268) at 1.9 bln US$ (see graph 6).

Table 4: Top 10 import commodities 2012 to 2014

HS code	4-digit heading of Harmonized System 2012	Value (million US$) 2012	2013	2014	Unit value 2012	2013	2014	Unit	SITC code
	All Commodities	9641.7	10763.4	9178.6					
8703	Motor cars and other motor vehicles principally designed for the transport	547.2	556.3	472.6	10.5	8.2	12.3	thsd US$/unit	781
7108	Gold (including gold plated with platinum)	0.0	896.0	410.1		44.8	40.4	thsd US$/kg	971
2402	Cigars, cheroots, cigarillos and cigarettes	298.5	333.0	390.2	22.9	27.7	32.7	US$/kg	122
1001	Wheat and meslin	330.0	395.3	293.9	0.2	0.3	0.2	US$/kg	041
8802	Other aircraft (for example, helicopters, aeroplanes); spacecraft	341.0	420.3	15.0	11.0	22.1	5.0	mln US$/unit	792
8431	Parts suitable for use principally with the machinery of headings 84.25	189.3	222.9	243.2	18.5	16.2	25.8	US$/kg	723
3004	Medicaments (excluding goods of heading 30.02, 30.05 or 30.06)	209.5	214.2	195.9	16.5	14.4	12.6	US$/kg	542
7304	Tubes, pipes and hollow profiles, seamless, of iron (other than cast iron)	198.7	240.7	176.2	3.0	2.4	3.0	US$/kg	679
1701	Cane or beet sugar and chemically pure sucrose, in solid form	175.6	201.5	205.3	0.5	0.5	0.5	US$/kg	061
8481	Taps, cocks, valves and similar appliances for pipes, boiler shells	136.6	193.1	166.5	27.5	29.5	32.2	US$/kg	747

Bahamas

Goods Imports: CIF, by origin | **Goods Exports: FOB, by last known destination** | **Trade System: General**

Overview:

In 2014, the value of merchandise exports of the Bahamas decreased substantially by 15.1 percent to reach 689.2 mln US$, while its merchandise imports increased substantially by 12.6 percent to reach 3.8 bln US$ (see graph 1, table 2 and table 3). The merchandise trade balance recorded a large deficit of 3.1 bln US$ (see graph 1). The largest merchandise trade balance was with MDG Developed North America at -2.7 bln US$ (see graph 4). Merchandise exports in the Bahamas were highly concentrated amongst partners; imports were also highly concentrated. The top 1 partner accounted for 80 percent or more of exports and the same number of partners accounted for 80 percent or more of imports (see graph 5). In 2014, the value of exports of services of the Bahamas increased slightly by 1.7 percent, reaching 2.7 bln US$, while its imports of services increased moderately by 5.6 percent and reached 1.7 bln US$ (see graph 2). There was a moderate trade in services surplus of 996.6 mln US$.

Graph 1: Total merchandise trade, by value

(Bln US$ by year)

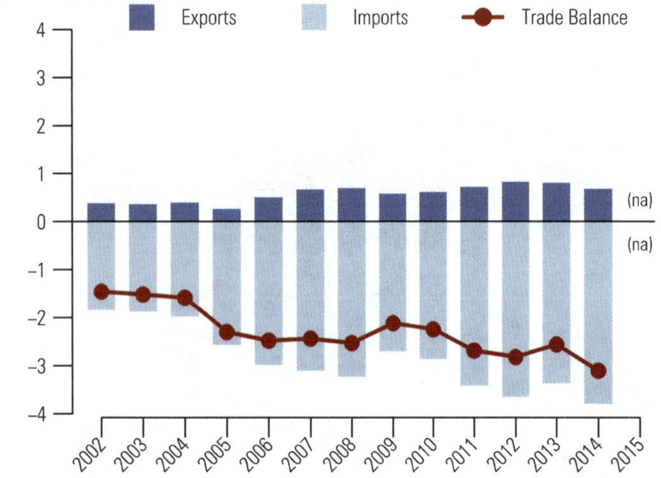

Graph 2: Total services trade, by value

(Bln US$ by year)

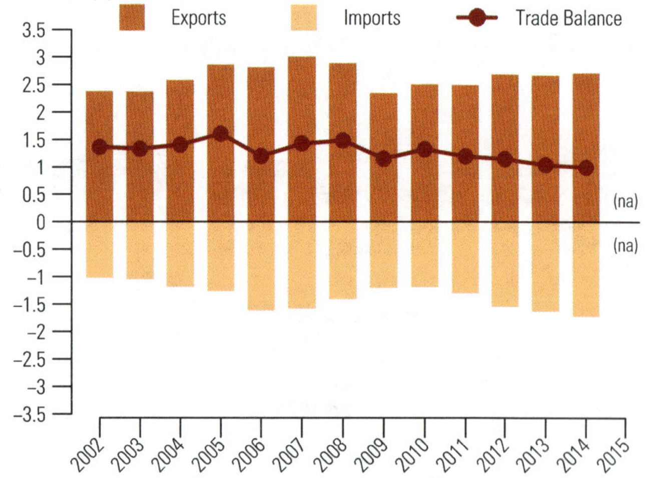

Exports Profile:

"Chemicals" (SITC section 5), "Mineral fuels, lubricants" (SITC section 3) and "Machinery and transport equipment" (SITC section 7) were the largest commodity groups for exports in 2014, representing respectively 40.1, 24.0 and 11.7 percent of exported goods (see table 2). From 2012 to 2014, the largest export commodity was "Petroleum oils, other than crude" (HS code 2710) (see table 1). The top three destinations for merchandise exports were the United States, Ireland and France, accounting for respectively 82.6, 3.2 and 3.2 percent of total exports. "Travel" (EBOPS code 236) accounted for the largest share of exports of services in 2014 at 2.3 bln US$, followed by "Other business services" (EBOPS code 268) at 240.5 mln US$ (see graph 3).

Graph 3: Exports of services by EBOPS category

(% share in 2014)

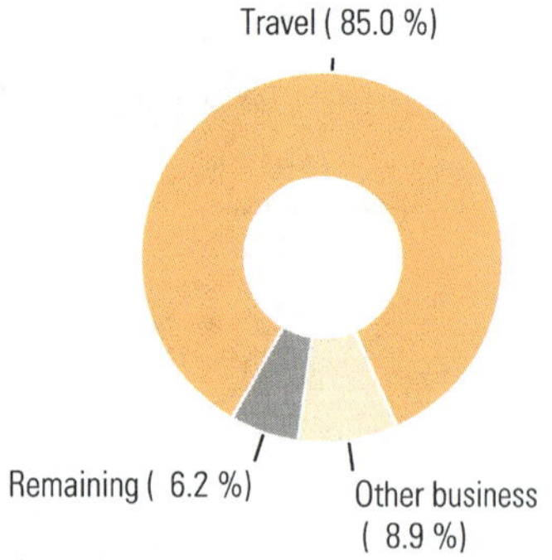

Table 1: Top 10 export commodities 2012 to 2014

HS code	4-digit heading of Harmonized System 2007	Value (million US$) 2012	2013	2014	Unit value 2012	2013	2014	Unit	SITC code
	All Commodities	828.7	811.5	689.2					
2710	Petroleum oils, other than crude	319.7	237.8	165.3					334
3903	Polymers of styrene, in primary forms	155.5	184.5	171.2	2.2	2.2	3.7	US$/kg	572
0306	Crustaceans, whether in shell or not	78.5	86.8	65.4	34.3	31.6	33.6	US$/kg	036
2933	Heterocyclic compounds with nitrogen hetero-atom(s) only	75.7	61.6	75.2	587.4	630.4	792.6	US$/kg	515
3303	Perfumes and toilet waters	38.7	34.5	18.4	83.1	72.9	54.3	US$/kg	553
2501	Salt (including table salt)	12.0	20.3	31.1	0.0	0.0	0.0	US$/kg	278
8903	Yachts and other vessels for pleasure or sports; rowing boats and canoes	2.9	30.4	18.0	23.8	178.0	27.1	thsd US$/unit	793
8205	Hand tools (including glaziers' diamonds)	5.5	6.6	16.0	8.6	11.8	19.6	US$/kg	695
7308	Structures (excluding prefabricated buildings of heading 94.06)	1.7	14.8	9.8	0.3	0.8	0.5	US$/kg	691
3304	Beauty or make-up preparations	6.5	8.4	7.7	57.0	50.3	66.6	US$/kg	553

Services Imports and Exports: EBOPS 2002 categories

Table 2: Merchandise exports by SITC

(Value in million US$, growth and shares in percentage)

SITC	2014	Avg. Growth rates 2010-2014	Avg. Growth rates 2013-2014	2014 share
Total	689.2	2.7	-15.1	100.0
0+1	72.2	-1.6	-22.4	10.5
2+4	39.8	-2.7	16.1	5.8
3	165.3	0.9	-30.5	24.0
5	276.2	6.3	-6.3	40.1
6	46.3	6.4	3.8	6.7
7	80.3	2.2	-16.3	11.7
8	9.0	-8.1	-13.1	1.3
9	0.0	-30.5	-98.2	0.0

Table 3: Merchandise imports by SITC

(Value in million US$, growth and shares in percentage)

SITC	2014	Avg. Growth rates 2010-2014	Avg. Growth rates 2013-2014	2014 share
Total	3790.4	7.3	12.6	100.0
0+1	598.1	4.9	12.5	15.8
2+4	77.2	1.9	8.8	2.0
3	868.5	6.0	19.5	22.9
5	392.7	4.8	3.1	10.4
6	554.8	10.4	21.6	14.6
7	720.1	9.9	9.5	19.0
8	426.8	7.0	6.9	11.3
9	152.3	14.1	7.1	4.0

SITC Legend

SITC Code	Description
Total	All commodities
0+1	Food, animals + beverages, tobacco
2+4	Crude materials + anim. & veg. oils
3	Mineral fuels, lubricants
5	Chemicals
6	Goods classified chiefly by material
7	Machinery and transport equipment
8	Miscellaneous manufactured articles
9	Not classified elsewhere in the SITC

Graph 4: Merchandise trade balance

(Bln US$ by MDG Regions in 2014)

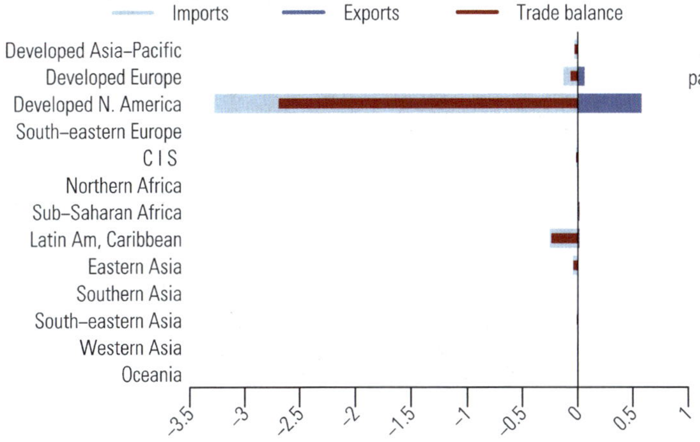

Graph 5: Partner concentration of merchandise trade

(Cumulative share by ranked partners in 2014)

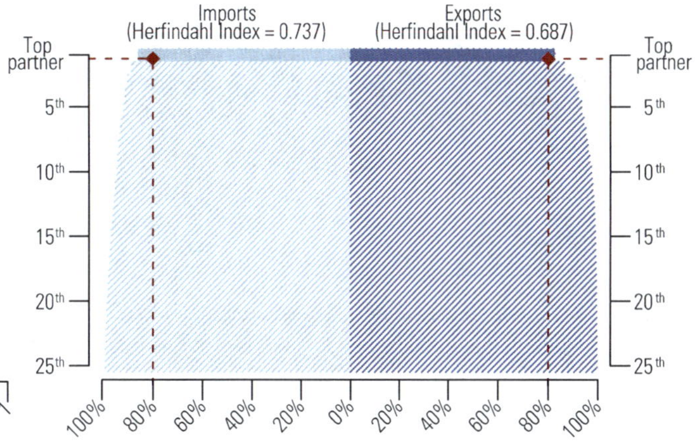

Graph 6: Imports of services by EBOPS category

(% share in 2014)

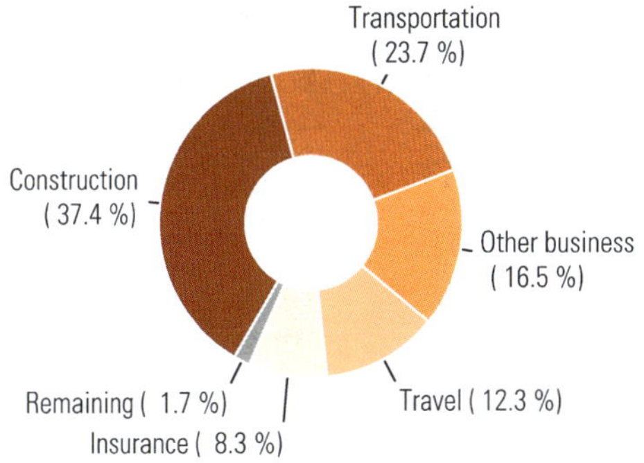

Imports Profile:

"Mineral fuels, lubricants" (SITC section 3), "Machinery and transport equipment" (SITC section 7) and "Food, animals + beverages, tobacco" (SITC section 0+1) were the largest commodity groups for imports in 2014, representing respectively 22.9, 19.0 and 15.8 percent of imported goods (see table 3). From 2012 to 2014, the largest import commodity was "Petroleum oils, other than crude" (HS code 2710) (see table 4). The top three partners for merchandise imports were the United States, Trinidad and Tobago and Areas nes, accounting for respectively 86.4, 2.6 and 1.5 percent of total imports. "Construction services" (EBOPS code 249) accounted for the largest share of imports of services in 2014 at 643.1 mln US$, followed by "Transportation" (EBOPS code 205) at 407.7 mln US$ and "Other business services" (EBOPS code 268) at 284.4 mln US$ (see graph 6).

Table 4: Top 10 import commodities 2012 to 2014

HS code	4-digit heading of Harmonized System 2007	Value (million US$) 2012	Value (million US$) 2013	Value (million US$) 2014	Unit value 2012	Unit value 2013	Unit value 2014	Unit	SITC code
	All Commodities	3646.5	3365.3	3790.4					
2710	Petroleum oils, other than crude	842.4	706.5	845.9					334
9999	Commodities not specified according to kind	133.2	142.1	152.2					931
8703	Motor cars and other motor vehicles principally designed for the transport	98.3	94.2	107.7	6.8	6.1	6.0	thsd US$/unit	781
2853	Other inorganic compounds	65.5	39.8	35.6	10.6	8.2	5.3	US$/kg	524
9403	Other furniture and parts thereof	47.6	40.2	51.5					821
3915	Waste, parings and scrap, of plastics	47.9	52.4	35.4					579
3303	Perfumes and toilet waters	51.8	43.3	25.2	25.5	20.7	20.8	US$/kg	553
0207	Meat and edible offal, of the poultry of heading 01.05	32.7	36.9	45.5	4.7	5.4	5.3	US$/kg	012
8517	Electrical apparatus for line telephony or line telegraphy	31.8	39.5	39.2					764
8903	Yachts and other vessels for pleasure or sports; rowing boats and canoes	15.1	37.3	48.5	11.4	34.1	27.2	thsd US$/unit	793

Bahrain

Goods Imports: CIF, by origin | **Goods Exports: FOB, by last known destination** | **Trade System: General**

Overview:

In 2014, the value of merchandise exports of Bahrain decreased moderately by 10.0 percent to reach 18.0 bln US$, while its merchandise imports increased moderately by 7.8 percent to reach 20.1 bln US$ (see graph 1, table 2 and table 3). The merchandise trade balance recorded a relatively small deficit of 2.0 bln US$ (see graph 1). The largest merchandise trade balance was with MDG Western Asia at -4.2 bln US$ (see graph 4). Merchandise exports in Bahrain were highly concentrated amongst partners; imports were moderately concentrated. The top 4 partners accounted for 80 percent or more of exports and 11 partners accounted for 80 percent or more of imports (see graph 5). In 2014, the value of exports of services of Bahrain increased slightly by 2.0 percent, reaching 3.0 bln US$, while its imports of services increased slightly by 3.7 percent and reached 1.6 bln US$ (see graph 2). There was a relatively large trade in services surplus of 1.4 bln US$.

Graph 1: Total merchandise trade, by value

(Bln US$ by year)

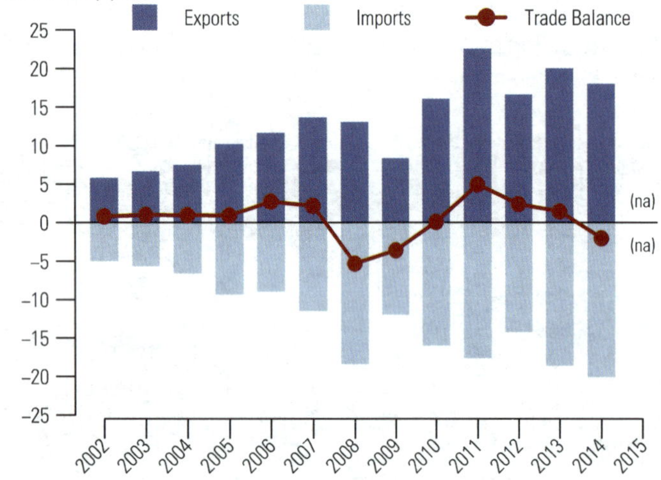

Graph 2: Total services trade, by value

(Bln US$ by year)

Exports Profile:

"Mineral fuels, lubricants" (SITC section 3), "Goods classified chiefly by material" (SITC section 6) and "Machinery and transport equipment" (SITC section 7) were the largest commodity groups for exports in 2014, representing respectively 51.5, 20.9 and 9.8 percent of exported goods (see table 2). From 2012 to 2014, the largest export commodity was "Petroleum oils, other than crude" (HS code 2710) (see table 1). The top three destinations for merchandise exports were Areas nes, Saudi Arabia and the United Arab Emirates, accounting for respectively 52.5, 16.0 and 6.8 percent of total exports. "Travel" (EBOPS code 236) accounted for the largest share of exports of services in 2014 at 1.2 bln US$, followed by "Transportation" (EBOPS code 205) at 718.1 mln US$ and "Insurance services" (EBOPS code 253) at 408.2 mln US$ (see graph 3).

Graph 3: Exports of services by EBOPS category

(% share in 2014)

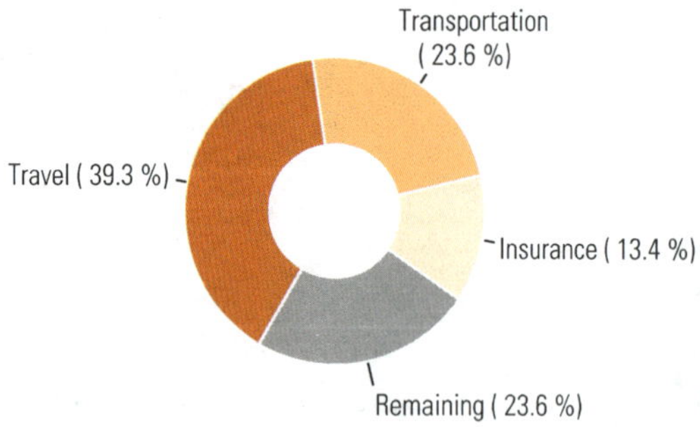

Table 1: Top 10 export commodities 2012 to 2014

HS code	4-digit heading of Harmonized System 2007	Value (million US$) 2012	2013	2014	Unit value 2012	2013	2014	Unit	SITC code
	All Commodities	16621.2	20036.2	18030.7					
2710	Petroleum oils, other than crude	9888.5	10131.5	9249.4	*1.1*	*1.1*	*1.1*	US$/kg	334
7604	Aluminium bars, rods and profiles	1301.4	1512.0	971.4	2.6	3.7	2.6	US$/kg	684
2601	Iron ores and concentrates, including roasted iron pyrites	1368.6	609.9	592.5	0.2	0.2	0.2	US$/kg	281
7605	Aluminium wire	173.3	630.9	843.5	2.5	3.0	3.7	US$/kg	684
8703	Motor cars and other motor vehicles principally designed for the transport	290.0	814.7	406.2	27.7	18.1	25.6	thsd US$/unit	781
7113	Articles of jewellery and parts thereof, of precious metal	88.4	655.6	469.7	54.7			thsd US$/kg	897
7614	Stranded wire, cables, plaited bands and the like, of aluminium	314.5	461.9	367.8	2.7	2.7	2.9	US$/kg	693
3102	Mineral or chemical fertilisers, nitrogenous	227.6	272.2	253.3	0.5		0.3	US$/kg	562
2905	Acyclic alcohols and their derivatives	343.3	201.6	203.2					512
0406	Cheese and curd	163.5	209.1	198.7	6.9	6.7	7.2	US$/kg	024

Services Imports and Exports: EBOPS 2002 categories

Table 2: Merchandise exports by SITC

(Value in million US$, growth and shares in percentage)

SITC	2014	Avg. Growth rates 2010-2014	Avg. Growth rates 2013-2014	2014 share
Total	18030.7	2.9	-10.0	100.0
0+1	628.0	19.7	-25.5	3.5
2+4	682.6	-13.9	-4.0	3.8
3	9281.3	-5.3	-8.8	51.5
5	952.5	71.1	30.5	5.3
6	3777.2	15.6	-9.9	20.9
7	1768.2	34.6	-25.2	9.8
8	884.4	42.3	-12.9	4.9
9	56.6	60.7	460.3	0.3

Table 3: Merchandise imports by SITC

(Value in million US$, growth and shares in percentage)

SITC	2014	Avg. Growth rates 2010-2014	Avg. Growth rates 2013-2014	2014 share
Total	20073.7	5.8	7.8	100.0
0+1	1834.6	11.6	10.9	9.1
2+4	1659.1	-8.9	82.1	8.3
3	8044.9	7.2	-7.3	40.1
5	1074.6	12.0	25.2	5.4
6	1691.0	6.0	9.2	8.4
7	4279.9	4.5	13.2	21.3
8	1209.9	14.0	30.8	6.0
9	279.5	237.4	6.0	1.4

SITC Legend

SITC Code	Description
Total	All commodities
0+1	Food, animals + beverages, tobacco
2+4	Crude materials + anim. & veg. oils
3	Mineral fuels, lubricants
5	Chemicals
6	Goods classified chiefly by material
7	Machinery and transport equipment
8	Miscellaneous manufactured articles
9	Not classified elsewhere in the SITC

Graph 4: Merchandise trade balance

(Bln US$ by MDG Regions in 2014)

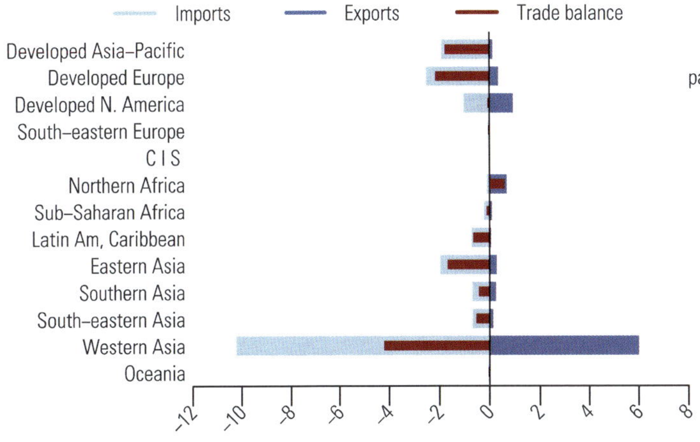

Graph 5: Partner concentration of merchandise trade

(Cumulative share by ranked partners in 2014)

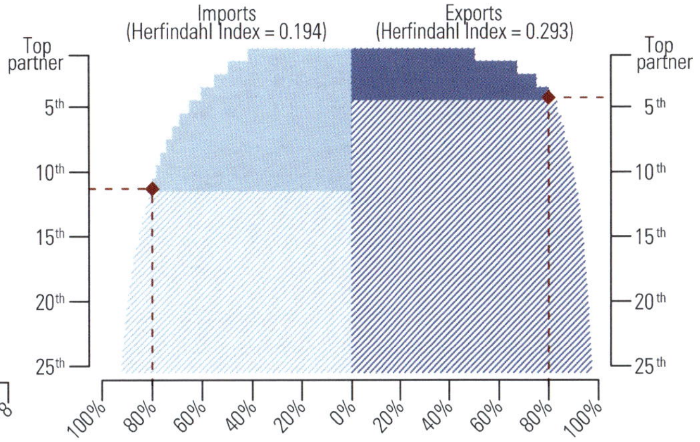

Graph 6: Imports of services by EBOPS category

(% share in 2014)

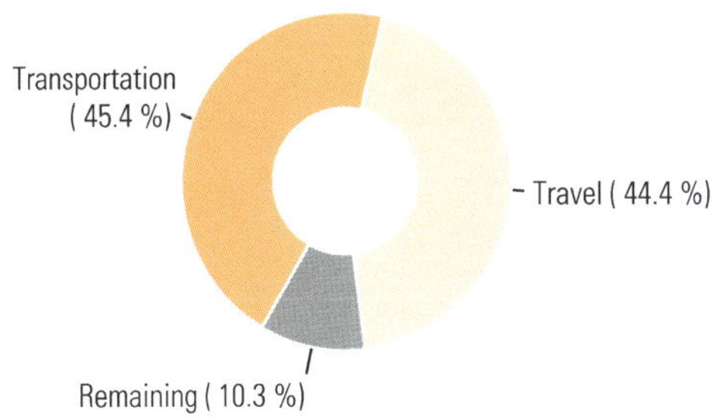

Imports Profile:

"Mineral fuels, lubricants" (SITC section 3), "Machinery and transport equipment" (SITC section 7) and "Food, animals + beverages, tobacco" (SITC section 0+1) were the largest commodity groups for imports in 2014, representing respectively 40.1, 21.3 and 9.1 percent of imported goods (see table 3). From 2012 to 2014, the largest import commodity was "Petroleum oils and oils obtained from bituminous minerals, crude" (HS code 2709) (see table 4). The top three partners for merchandise imports were Saudi Arabia, China and Areas nes, accounting for respectively 34.5, 8.1 and 6.5 percent of total imports. "Transportation" (EBOPS code 205) accounted for the largest share of imports of services in 2014 at 734.0 mln US$, followed by "Travel" (EBOPS code 236) at 718.1 mln US$ (see graph 6).

Table 4: Top 10 import commodities 2012 to 2014

HS code	4-digit heading of Harmonized System 2007	Value (million US$) 2012	Value (million US$) 2013	Value (million US$) 2014	Unit value 2012	Unit value 2013	Unit value 2014	Unit	SITC code
	All Commodities	14249.1	18617.5	20073.7					
2709	Petroleum oils and oils obtained from bituminous minerals, crude	3358.0	8486.4	7440.1	*0.8*	*0.8*	*0.8*	US$/kg	333
8703	Motor cars and other motor vehicles principally designed for the transport	1304.6	1314.2	1421.1	24.4	13.9	9.8	thsd US$/unit	781
2601	Iron ores and concentrates, including roasted iron pyrites	671.2	366.8	561.8	0.2	0.2	0.1	US$/kg	281
8517	Electrical apparatus for line telephony or line telegraphy	315.2	302.5	389.1					764
2710	Petroleum oils, other than crude	195.4	83.7	403.0	0.9	*0.9*		US$/kg	334
7108	Gold (including gold plated with platinum)	138.4	236.3	275.2	49.1	43.7	40.7	thsd US$/kg	971
2818	Artificial corundum, whether or not chemically defined	145.4	194.4	262.4	0.3	0.3	0.4	US$/kg	285
3004	Medicaments (excluding goods of heading 30.02, 30.05 or 30.06)	167.3	190.4	222.1	67.0	54.3	61.3	US$/kg	542
2606	Aluminium ores and concentrates	77.4	123.0	354.0	0.3	0.4	0.3	US$/kg	285
8471	Automatic data processing machines and units thereof	187.5	131.2	199.9	287.3	106.4	210.1	US$/unit	752

Bangladesh

Goods Imports: CIF, by consignment | **Goods Exports: FOB, by last known destination** | **Trade System: General**

Overview:

In 2011, the value of merchandise exports of Bangladesh increased substantially by 26.4 percent to reach 24.3 bln US$, while its merchandise imports increased substantially by 35.1 percent to reach 41.2 bln US$ (see graph 1, table 2 and table 3). The merchandise trade balance recorded a moderate deficit of 16.9 bln US$ (see graph 1). The largest merchandise trade balance was with MDG South-eastern Asia at -15.9 bln US$ (see graph 4). Merchandise exports in Bangladesh were diversified amongst partners; imports were also diversified. The top 13 partners accounted for 80 percent or more of exports and 15 partners accounted for 80 percent or more of imports (see graph 5). In 2014, the value of exports of services of Bangladesh increased moderately by 8.8 percent, reaching 2.8 bln US$, while its imports of services increased substantially by 22.6 percent and reached 7.1 bln US$ (see graph 2). There was a large trade in services deficit of 4.3 bln US$.

Graph 1: Total merchandise trade, by value

(Bln US$ by year)

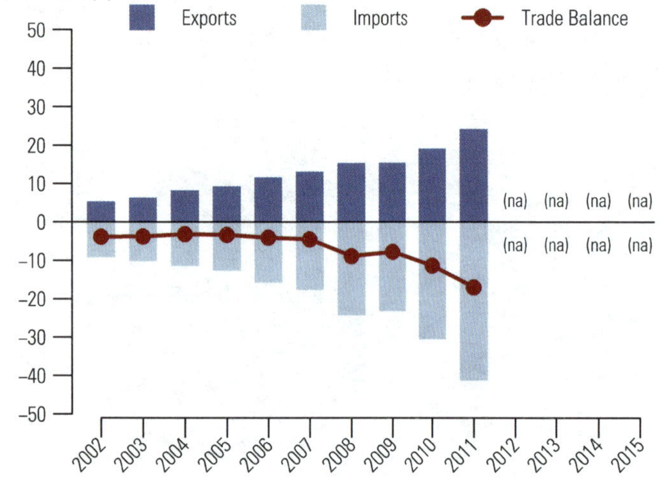

Graph 2: Total services trade, by value

(Bln US$ by year)

Exports Profile:

"Miscellaneous manufactured articles" (SITC section 8), "Goods classified chiefly by material" (SITC section 6) and "Food, animals + beverages, tobacco" (SITC section 0+1) were the largest commodity groups for exports in 2011, representing respectively 81.1, 9.8 and 3.8 percent of exported goods (see table 2). From 2009 to 2011, the largest export commodity was "T-shirts, singlets and other vests, knitted or crocheted" (HS code 6109) (see table 1). The top three destinations for merchandise exports were the United States, Germany and the United Kingdom, accounting for respectively 22.9, 14.6 and 9.3 percent of total exports. "Government services, n.i.e." (EBOPS code 291) accounted for the largest share of exports of services in 2014 at 1.2 bln US$, followed by "Other business services" (EBOPS code 268) at 433.3 mln US$ and "Transportation" (EBOPS code 205) at 388.3 mln US$ (see graph 3).

Graph 3: Exports of services by EBOPS category

(% share in 2014)

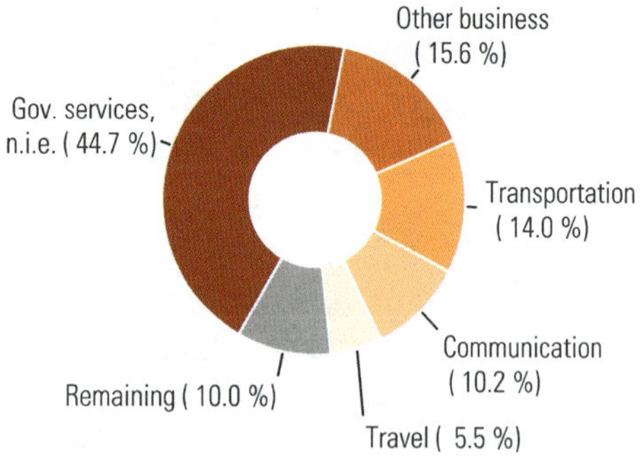

Table 1: Top 10 export commodities 2009 to 2011

HS code	4-digit heading of Harmonized System 2007	Value (million US$) 2009	2010	2011	Unit value 2009	2010	2011	Unit	SITC code
	All Commodities	15558.6	19231.0	24313.7					
6109	T-shirts, singlets and other vests, knitted or crocheted	3146.5	3845.5	4832.3		10.1	21.8	US$/unit	845
6203	Men's or boys' suits, ensembles, jackets, blazers, trousers	2954.3	3523.8	4545.9	*5.2*	11.4	*25.1*	US$/unit	841
6110	Jerseys, pullovers, cardigans, waist-coats and similar articles	1836.4	2073.7	2656.3	7.1	13.6	34.9	US$/unit	845
6204	Women's or girls' suits, ensembles, jackets, blazers, dresses, skirts	1299.6	1568.5	2076.1	5.6	13.3	*27.6*	US$/unit	842
6205	Men's or boys' shirts	950.2	1238.9	1705.6	5.5	13.5	31.4	US$/unit	841
6105	Men's or boys' shirts, knitted or crocheted	421.4	566.4	732.2	4.8	11.0	23.1	US$/unit	843
6302	Bed linen, table linen, toilet linen and kitchen linen	270.0	376.6	664.1	5.7	6.1	15.2	US$/kg	658
0306	Crustaceans, whether in shell or not	318.5	438.0	498.2	7.3	8.5	17.9	US$/kg	036
5307	Yarn of jute or of other textile bast fibres of heading 53.03	259.9	491.4	479.4	0.8	1.3	2.1	US$/kg	651
6103	Men's, boys' suits,jackets,trousers etc knitted or crocheted	300.8	300.7	424.2	*5.4*	10.8	*25.2*	US$/unit	843

Services Imports and Exports: EBOPS 2002 categories

Table 2: Merchandise exports by SITC

(Value in million US$, growth and shares in percentage)

SITC	2011	Avg. Growth rates 2007-2011	Avg. Growth rates 2010-2011	2011 share
Total	24313.7	16.6	26.4	100.0
0+1	926.2	2.0	22.7	3.8
2+4	536.0	4.3	12.7	2.2
3	280.1	7.0	-22.3	1.2
5	171.0	-0.8	44.1	0.7
6	2387.6	14.1	20.4	9.8
7	282.8	-4.2	10.0	1.2
8	19730.1	19.4	29.1	81.1
9	0.0	-72.9	-83.4	0.0

Table 3: Merchandise imports by SITC

(Value in million US$, growth and shares in percentage)

SITC	2011	Avg. Growth rates 2007-2011	Avg. Growth rates 2010-2011	2011 share
Total	41221.7	23.7	35.1	100.0
0+1	4201.3	17.3	40.0	10.2
2+4	7169.8	20.4	42.3	17.4
3	3126.4	14.1	23.5	7.6
5	5073.0	24.5	40.2	12.3
6	10495.3	37.2	26.5	25.5
7	9370.1	23.2	43.0	22.7
8	1785.2	25.2	22.1	4.3
9	0.6	-78.3	94.7	0.0

SITC Legend

SITC Code	Description
Total	All commodities
0+1	Food, animals + beverages, tobacco
2+4	Crude materials + anim. & veg. oils
3	Mineral fuels, lubricants
5	Chemicals
6	Goods classified chiefly by material
7	Machinery and transport equipment
8	Miscellaneous manufactured articles
9	Not classified elsewhere in the SITC

Graph 4: Merchandise trade balance

(Bln US$ by MDG Regions in 2011)

Graph 5: Partner concentration of merchandise trade

(Cumulative share by ranked partners in 2011)

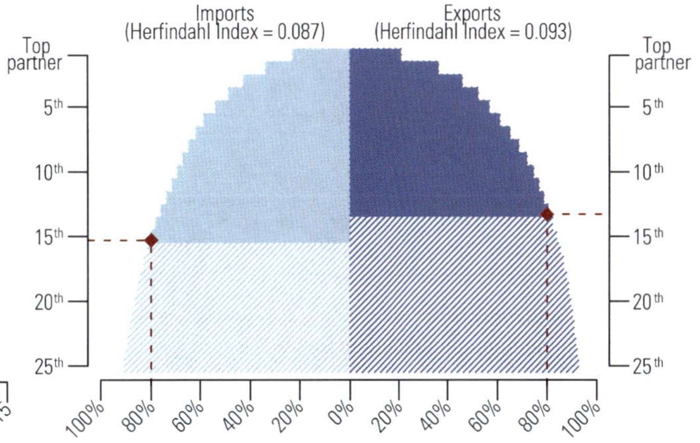

Graph 6: Imports of services by EBOPS category

(% share in 2014)

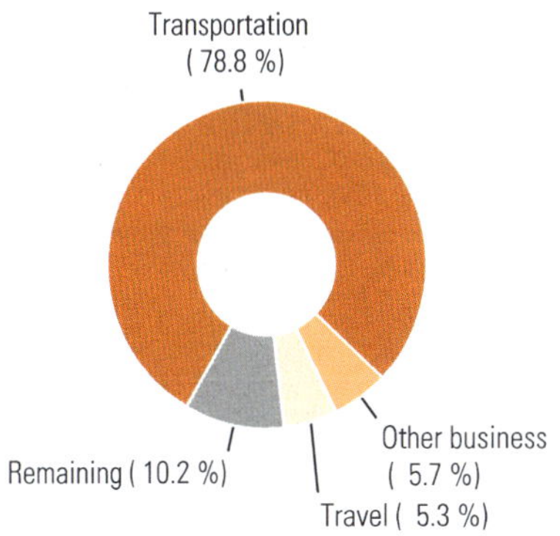

Imports Profile:

"Goods classified chiefly by material" (SITC section 6), "Machinery and transport equipment" (SITC section 7) and "Crude materials + anim. & veg. oils" (SITC section 2+4) were the largest commodity groups for imports in 2011, representing respectively 25.5, 22.7 and 17.4 percent of imported goods (see table 3). From 2009 to 2011, the largest import commodity was "Petroleum oils, other than crude" (HS code 2710) (see table 4). The top three partners for merchandise imports were China, Thailand and India, accounting for respectively 13.4, 12.4 and 11.1 percent of total imports. "Transportation" (EBOPS code 205) accounted for the largest share of imports of services in 2014 at 5.6 bln US$, followed by "Other business services" (EBOPS code 268) at 404.3 mln US$ and "Travel" (EBOPS code 236) at 380.4 mln US$ (see graph 6).

Table 4: Top 10 import commodities 2009 to 2011

HS code	4-digit heading of Harmonized System 2007	Value (million US$) 2009	Value (million US$) 2010	Value (million US$) 2011	Unit value 2009	Unit value 2010	Unit value 2011	Unit	SITC code
	All Commodities	23245.0	30503.8	41221.7					
2710	Petroleum oils, other than crude	2316.6	2103.9	2739.3	*0.4*	*0.5*	0.5	US$/kg	334
5201	Cotton, not carded or combed	1143.1	1958.8	2393.5	1.4	2.0	*3.4*	US$/kg	263
1511	Palm oil and its fractions	1278.4	1460.1	2372.3	0.7	0.8	1.1	US$/kg	422
5208	Woven fabrics of cotton, containing 85 % or more by weight of cotton	680.9	957.5	1486.5	*5.3*	*7.3*	9.7	US$/kg	652
1001	Wheat and meslin	788.3	807.5	1004.8	0.3	0.3	0.4	US$/kg	041
1701	Cane or beet sugar and chemically pure sucrose, in solid form	584.0	731.5	1157.5	0.4	0.6	0.7	US$/kg	061
5209	Woven fabrics of cotton, containing 85 % or more by weight of cotton	575.7	740.9	1131.8	4.9	5.8	8.1	US$/kg	652
5205	Cotton yarn (other than sewing thread), containing 85 % or more	409.1	793.1	1130.9	2.7	3.8	5.1	US$/kg	651
1507	Soya-bean oil and its fractions	534.0	651.7	1109.4	0.8	0.9	1.3	US$/kg	421
2523	Portland cement, aluminous cement, slag cement	301.4	1322.1	561.7	0.0	0.2	0.1	US$/kg	661

Barbados

Goods Imports: CIF, by origin | **Goods Exports: FOB, by last known destination** | **Trade System: General**

Overview:

In 2015, the value of merchandise exports of Barbados increased slightly by 0.4 percent to reach 482.8 mln US$, while its merchandise imports decreased moderately by 7.0 percent to reach 1.6 bln US$ (see graph 1, table 2 and table 3). The merchandise trade balance recorded a large deficit of 1.1 bln US$ (see graph 1). The largest merchandise trade balance was with MDG Developed North America at -505.7 mln US$ (see graph 4). Merchandise exports in Barbados were diversified amongst partners; imports were moderately concentrated. The top 10 partners accounted for 80 percent or more of exports and 12 partners accounted for 80 percent or more of imports (see graph 5). In 2013, the value of exports of services of Barbados increased substantially by 19.9 percent, reaching 1.8 bln US$, while its imports of services increased substantially by 39.1 percent and reached 688.2 mln US$ (see graph 2). There was a large trade in services surplus of 1.1 bln US$.

Graph 1: Total merchandise trade, by value

(Bln US$ by year)

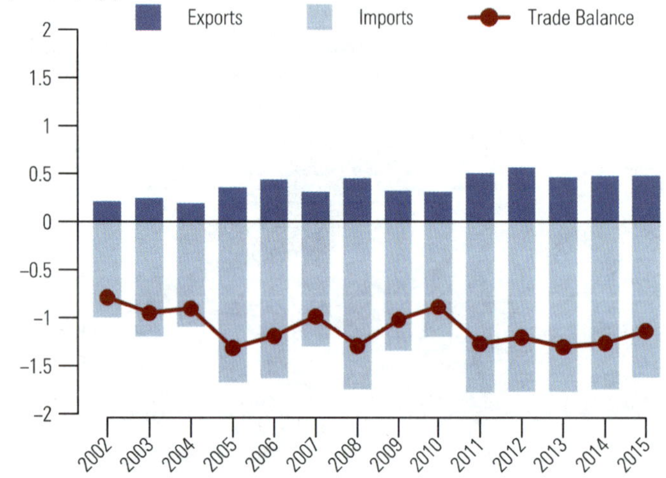

Graph 2: Total services trade, by value

(Bln US$ by year)

Exports Profile:

"Miscellaneous manufactured articles" (SITC section 8), "Food, animals + beverages, tobacco" (SITC section 0+1) and "Mineral fuels, lubricants" (SITC section 3) were the largest commodity groups for exports in 2015, representing respectively 29.0, 18.6 and 18.6 percent of exported goods (see table 2). From 2013 to 2015, the largest export commodity was "Petroleum oils, other than crude" (HS code 2710) (see table 1). The top three destinations for merchandise exports were the United States, Areas nes and Trinidad and Tobago, accounting for respectively 22.6, 22.3 and 10.7 percent of total exports. "Travel" (EBOPS code 236) accounted for the largest share of exports of services in 2013 at 972.8 mln US$, followed by "Other business services" (EBOPS code 268) at 668.0 mln US$ (see graph 3).

Graph 3: Exports of services by EBOPS category

(% share in 2013)

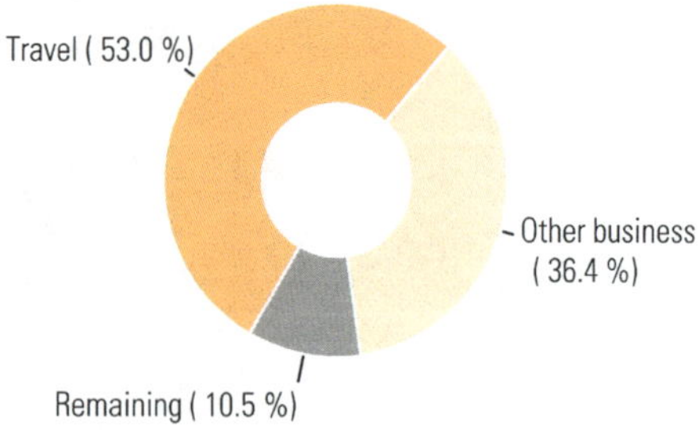

Table 1: Top 10 export commodities 2013 to 2015

HS code	4-digit heading of Harmonized System 2002	Value (million US$) 2013	2014	2015	Unit value 2013	2014	2015	Unit	SITC code
	All Commodities	467.4	480.8	482.8					
2710	Petroleum oils, other than crude	128.1	116.3	75.6	*1.0*	*1.0*	*0.5*	US$/kg	334
2208	Alcohol of a strength by volume of less than 80 % vol	49.0	45.7	45.2	*3.0*	*2.9*	*3.2*	US$/litre	112
3004	Medicaments (excluding goods of heading 30.02, 30.05 or 30.06)	45.9	45.9	47.0		*35.4*	*38.2*	US$/kg	542
2709	Petroleum oils, crude	24.3	26.4	14.0	0.7	0.6	0.3	US$/kg	333
2523	Portland cement, aluminous cement, slag cement	20.0	19.3	17.4	0.1	0.1	*0.1*	US$/kg	661
7113	Articles of jewellery and parts thereof, of precious metal	8.4	11.5	33.6	*2.3*	*2.4*	*0.6*	thsd US$/kg	897
9021	Orthopaedic appliances, including crutches, surgical belts and trusses	17.6	16.0	16.0					899
4821	Paper or paperboard lables of all kinds, whether or not printed	12.2	12.1	11.0	*25.3*	*21.9*	*24.7*	US$/kg	892
1905	Bread, pastry, cakes, biscuits and other bakers' wares	9.2	11.7	8.9	3.6	*3.2*	*3.6*	US$/kg	048
1517	Margarine; edible mixtures	10.1	10.1	9.3	2.9	2.9	2.8	US$/kg	091

Services Imports and Exports: EBOPS 2002 categories

Table 2: Merchandise exports by SITC
(Value in million US$, growth and shares in percentage)

SITC	2015	Avg. Growth rates 2011-2015	Avg. Growth rates 2014-2015	2015 share
Total	482.8	-1.3	0.4	100.0
0+1	89.7	0.3	-7.9	18.6
2+4	6.2	-1.7	-11.6	1.3
3	89.6	-18.4	-37.3	18.6
5	75.8	-5.7	6.2	15.7
6	42.5	5.4	0.5	8.8
7	33.4	9.0	16.2	6.9
8	140.0	26.9	66.4	29.0
9	5.7	8.2	-19.5	1.2

Table 3: Merchandise imports by SITC
(Value in million US$, growth and shares in percentage)

SITC	2015	Avg. Growth rates 2011-2015	Avg. Growth rates 2014-2015	2015 share
Total	1617.9	-2.3	-7.0	100.0
0+1	325.8	1.7	1.7	20.1
2+4	43.6	-4.1	-4.2	2.7
3	301.8	-11.2	-32.1	18.7
5	175.4	0.0	-4.5	10.8
6	190.9	-1.6	-1.4	11.8
7	354.8	1.0	8.2	21.9
8	218.6	1.4	0.4	13.5
9	6.8	-2.2	0.6	0.4

SITC Legend

SITC Code	Description
Total	All commodities
0+1	Food, animals + beverages, tobacco
2+4	Crude materials + anim. & veg. oils
3	Mineral fuels, lubricants
5	Chemicals
6	Goods classified chiefly by material
7	Machinery and transport equipment
8	Miscellaneous manufactured articles
9	Not classified elsewhere in the SITC

Graph 4: Merchandise trade balance
(Mln US$ by MDG Regions in 2015)

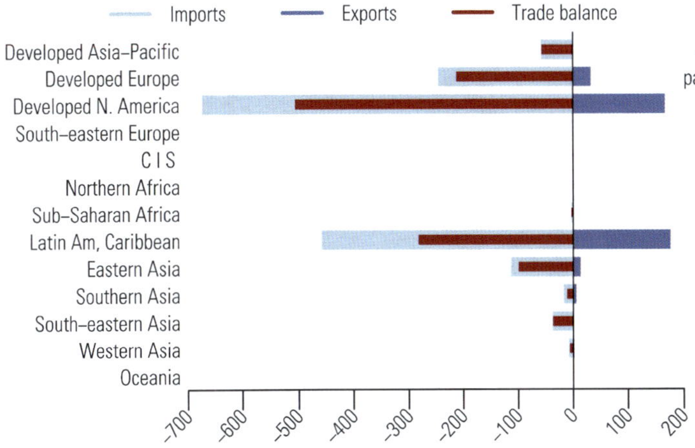

Graph 5: Partner concentration of merchandise trade
(Cumulative share by ranked partners in 2015)

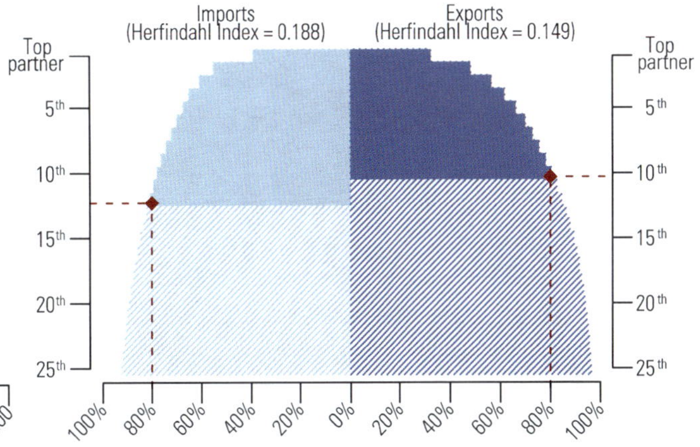

Graph 6: Imports of services by EBOPS category
(% share in 2013)

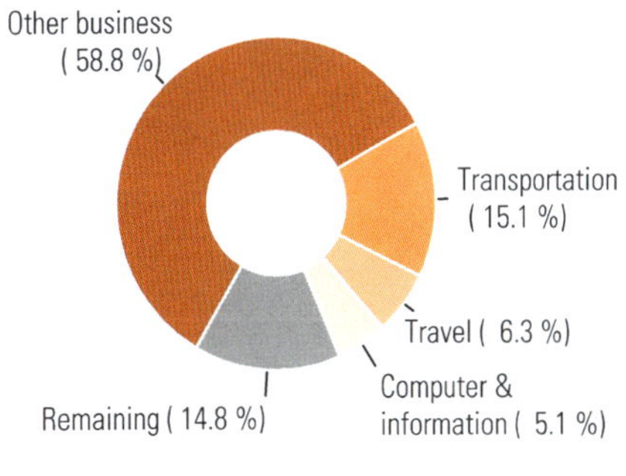

Imports Profile:

"Machinery and transport equipment" (SITC section 7), "Food, animals + beverages, tobacco" (SITC section 0+1) and "Mineral fuels, lubricants" (SITC section 3) were the largest commodity groups for imports in 2015, representing respectively 21.9, 20.1 and 18.7 percent of imported goods (see table 3). From 2013 to 2015, the largest import commodity was "Petroleum oils, other than crude" (HS code 2710) (see table 4). The top three partners for merchandise imports were the United States, Trinidad and Tobago and China, accounting for respectively 35.6, 21.0 and 5.1 percent of total imports. "Other business services" (EBOPS code 268) accounted for the largest share of imports of services in 2013 at 404.3 mln US$, followed by "Transportation" (EBOPS code 205) at 104.0 mln US$ and "Travel" (EBOPS code 236) at 43.0 mln US$ (see graph 6).

Table 4: Top 10 import commodities 2013 to 2015

HS code	4-digit heading of Harmonized System 2002	Value (million US$) 2013	Value (million US$) 2014	Value (million US$) 2015	Unit value 2013	Unit value 2014	Unit value 2015	Unit	SITC code
	All Commodities	1768.7	1740.5	1617.9					
2710	Petroleum oils, other than crude	462.9	426.6	290.7	*0.8*	*0.8*	*0.5*	US$/kg	334
3004	Medicaments (excluding goods of heading 30.02, 30.05 or 30.06)	60.1	66.1	54.6	*30.9*	*33.0*	*33.4*	US$/kg	542
8703	Motor cars and other motor vehicles principally designed for the transport	37.7	40.9	42.2	*14.7*	*14.8*	*15.1*	thsd US$/unit	781
8471	Automatic data processing machines and units thereof	27.0	25.8	23.3					752
8544	Insulated (including enamelled or anodised) wire, cable	18.3	25.7	19.4	*14.3*	*17.7*	*14.0*	US$/kg	773
8517	Electrical apparatus for line telephony or line telegraphy	19.7	17.6	24.7					764
7113	Articles of jewellery and parts thereof, of precious metal	17.1	19.8	21.6	*3.1*	*2.9*	*0.4*	thsd US$/kg	897
2106	Food preparations not elsewhere specified or included	18.2	18.3	19.2	*2.8*	*0.4*	*3.4*	US$/kg	098
3923	Articles for the conveyance or packing of goods, of plastics	17.8	17.8	17.8	*1.4*	*3.4*	*3.2*	US$/kg	893
2202	Waters with added sugar	16.9	15.0	17.3	*0.9*	*0.9*	*0.8*	US$/litre	111

Belarus

Goods Imports: CIF, by origin | **Goods Exports: FOB, by last known destination** | **Trade System: General**

Overview:

In 2015, the value of merchandise exports of Belarus decreased substantially by 25.8 percent to reach 26.8 bln US$, while its merchandise imports decreased substantially by 26.1 percent to reach 29.9 bln US$ (see graph 1, table 2 and table 3). The merchandise trade balance recorded a relatively small deficit of 3.2 bln US$ (see graph 1). The largest merchandise trade balance was with MDG CIS at -4.2 bln US$ (see graph 4). Merchandise exports in Belarus were moderately concentrated amongst partners; imports were highly concentrated. The top 9 partners accounted for 80 percent or more of exports and 9 partners accounted for 80 percent or more of imports (see graph 5). In 2014, the value of exports of services of Belarus increased moderately by 8.4 percent, reaching 7.5 bln US$, while its imports of services increased substantially by 24.4 percent and reached 5.5 bln US$ (see graph 2). There was a moderate trade in services surplus of 2.0 bln US$.

Graph 1: Total merchandise trade, by value

(Bln US$ by year)

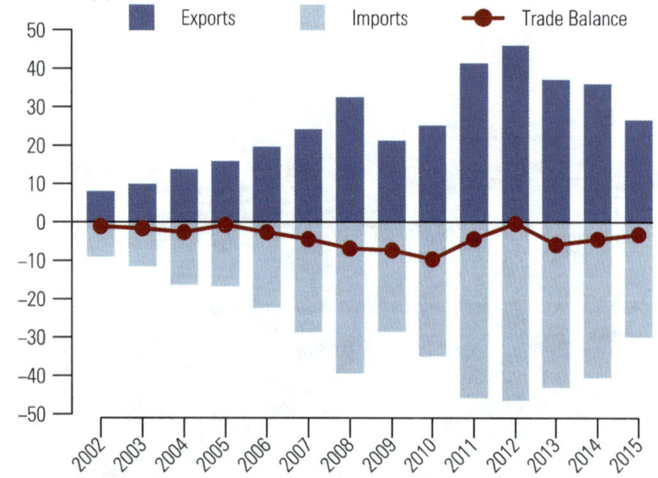

Graph 2: Total services trade, by value

(Bln US$ by year)

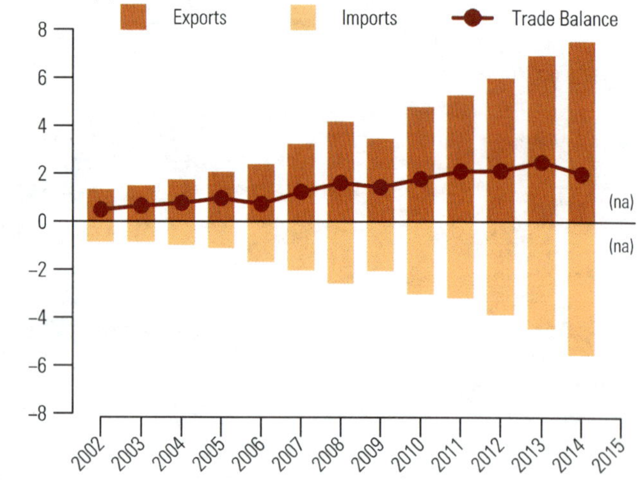

Exports Profile:

"Mineral fuels, lubricants" (SITC section 3), "Chemicals" (SITC section 5) and "Food, animals + beverages, tobacco" (SITC section 0+1) were the largest commodity groups for exports in 2015, representing respectively 29.7, 18.0 and 14.9 percent of exported goods (see table 2). From 2013 to 2015, the largest export commodity was "Petroleum oils, other than crude" (HS code 2710) (see table 1). The top three destinations for merchandise exports were the Russian Federation, Ukraine and the United Kingdom, accounting for respectively 42.0, 10.8 and 7.0 percent of total exports. "Transportation" (EBOPS code 205) accounted for the largest share of exports of services in 2014 at 3.7 bln US$, followed by "Construction services" (EBOPS code 249) at 1.2 bln US$ and "Travel" (EBOPS code 236) at 867.6 mln US$ (see graph 3).

Graph 3: Exports of services by EBOPS category

(% share in 2014)

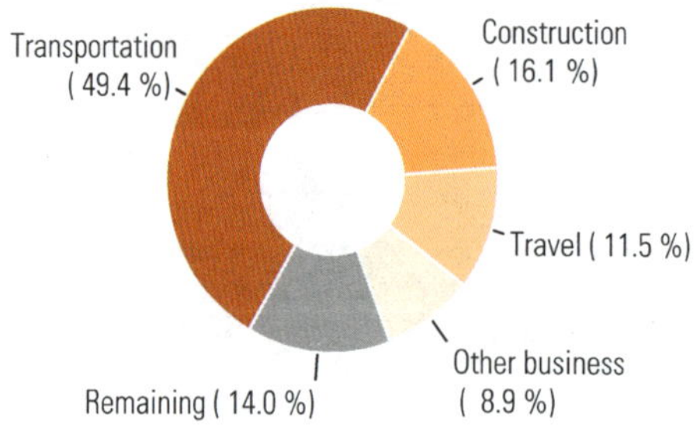

Table 1: Top 10 export commodities 2013 to 2015

HS code	4-digit heading of Harmonized System 2012	Value (million US$)			Unit value				SITC code
		2013	2014	2015	2013	2014	2015	Unit	
	All Commodities	37 203.0	36 080.5	26 757.9					
2710	Petroleum oils, other than crude	10 155.5	9 853.3	6 943.5	0.7	0.7	0.4	US$/kg	334
3104	Mineral or chemical fertilisers, potassic	2 052.4	2 668.9	2 679.7	0.4	0.3	0.3	US$/kg	562
9999	Commodities not specified according to kind	1 528.4	1 068.7	998.4					931
2709	Petroleum oils and oils obtained from bituminous minerals, crude	1 241.3	1 124.3	579.3	0.8	0.7	0.4	US$/kg	333
8704	Motor vehicles for the transport of goods	1 110.5	932.4	574.7	101.6		151.9	thsd US$/unit	782
8701	Tractors (other than tractors of heading 87.09)	1 076.3	849.9	485.1	19.7		14.8	thsd US$/unit	722
0406	Cheese and curd	649.4	802.9	620.7	4.6	4.8	3.5	US$/kg	024
0402	Milk and cream, concentrated or containing added sugar	847.0	679.8	462.0	3.6	3.4	2.1	US$/kg	022
7214	Other bars and rods of iron or non-alloy steel	468.9	480.7	335.2	0.6	0.5	0.4	US$/kg	676
4011	New pneumatic tyres, of rubber	610.9	387.5	266.3	141.8		79.5	US$/unit	625

Services Imports and Exports: EBOPS 2002 categories

Table 2: Merchandise exports by SITC

(Value in million US$, growth and shares in percentage)

SITC	2015	Avg. Growth rates 2011-2015	Avg. Growth rates 2014-2015	2015 share
Total	26757.9	-10.3	-25.8	100.0
0+1	3985.2	1.5	-23.1	14.9
2+4	745.2	-2.2	-19.0	2.8
3	7943.0	-14.0	-34.3	29.7
5	4807.6	-9.3	-3.0	18.0
6	3451.7	-8.1	-27.0	12.9
7	3320.9	-15.0	-32.9	12.4
8	1505.8	-5.4	-31.3	5.6
9	998.4	-17.4	-6.6	3.7

Table 3: Merchandise imports by SITC

(Value in million US$, growth and shares in percentage)

SITC	2015	Avg. Growth rates 2011-2015	Avg. Growth rates 2014-2015	2015 share
Total	29940.9	-10.1	-26.1	100.0
0+1	4106.1	9.5	-7.8	13.7
2+4	977.4	-14.8	-22.3	3.3
3	9208.7	-16.3	-22.3	30.8
5	3315.4	-5.1	-27.9	11.1
6	3824.0	-11.0	-33.2	12.8
7	5599.2	-8.4	-32.3	18.7
8	1689.3	1.5	-29.9	5.6
9	1220.8	-17.1	-36.9	4.1

SITC Legend

SITC Code	Description
Total	All commodities
0+1	Food, animals + beverages, tobacco
2+4	Crude materials + anim. & veg. oils
3	Mineral fuels, lubricants
5	Chemicals
6	Goods classified chiefly by material
7	Machinery and transport equipment
8	Miscellaneous manufactured articles
9	Not classified elsewhere in the SITC

Graph 4: Merchandise trade balance

(Bln US$ by MDG Regions in 2015)

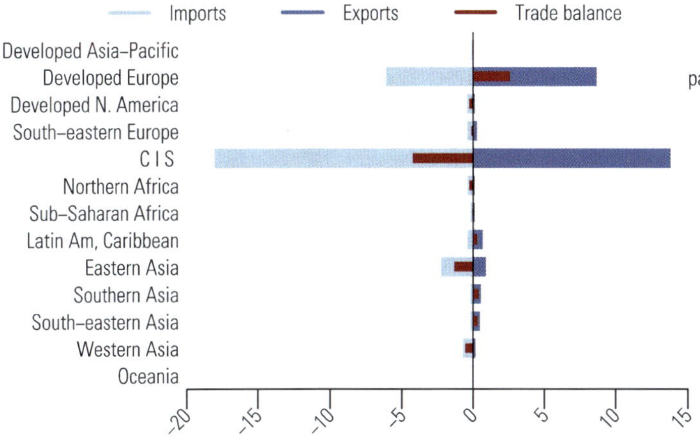

Graph 5: Partner concentration of merchandise trade

(Cumulative share by ranked partners in 2015)

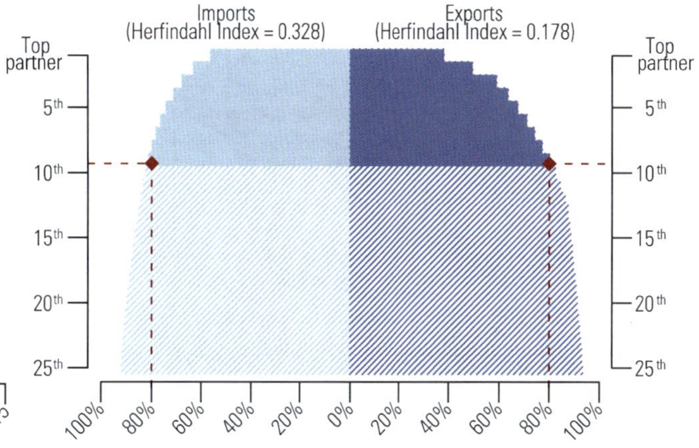

Graph 6: Imports of services by EBOPS category

(% share in 2014)

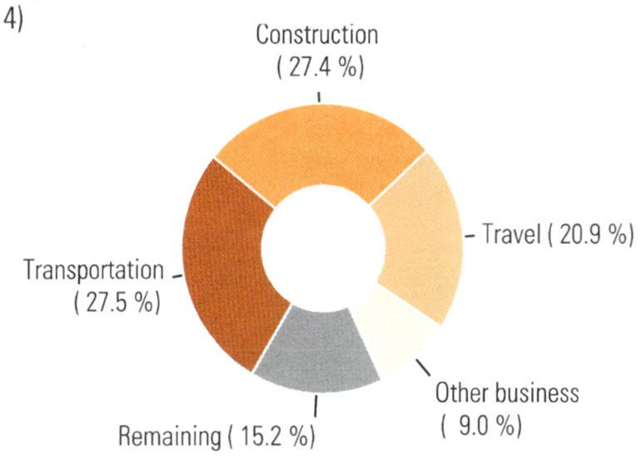

Imports Profile:

"Mineral fuels, lubricants" (SITC section 3), "Machinery and transport equipment" (SITC section 7) and "Food, animals + beverages, tobacco" (SITC section 0+1) were the largest commodity groups for imports in 2015, representing respectively 30.8, 18.7 and 13.7 percent of imported goods (see table 3). From 2013 to 2015, the largest import commodity was "Petroleum oils and oils obtained from bituminous minerals, crude" (HS code 2709) (see table 4). The top three partners for merchandise imports were the Russian Federation, Germany and China, accounting for respectively 54.0, 6.0 and 5.1 percent of total imports. "Transportation" (EBOPS code 205) accounted for the largest share of imports of services in 2014 at 1.5 bln US$, followed by "Construction services" (EBOPS code 249) at 1.5 bln US$ and "Travel" (EBOPS code 236) at 1.2 bln US$ (see graph 6).

Table 4: Top 10 import commodities 2013 to 2015

HS code	4-digit heading of Harmonized System 2012	Value (million US$) 2013	2014	2015	Unit value 2013	2014	2015	Unit	SITC code
	All Commodities	43022.7	40502.4	29940.9					
2709	Petroleum oils and oils obtained from bituminous minerals, crude	8392.1	7629.3	5667.3	0.4	0.3		US$/kg	333
2711	Petroleum gases and other gaseous hydrocarbons	3512.2	3594.6	2817.7	*0.2*	0.3	0.2	US$/kg	343
9999	Commodities not specified according to kind	1341.3	1933.7	1220.8					931
3004	Medicaments (excluding goods of heading 30.02, 30.05 or 30.06)	523.6	579.6	405.1	*67.4*	*71.3*	*62.4*	US$/kg	542
8517	Electrical apparatus for line telephony or line telegraphy	493.3	403.6	341.6					764
8703	Motor cars and other motor vehicles principally designed for the transport	491.6	419.2	285.6	16.9	*19.2*	11.4	thsd US$/unit	781
7204	Ferrous waste and scrap; remelting scrap ingots of iron or steel	386.9	374.8	294.0	0.3	0.3	0.2	US$/kg	282
8708	Parts and accessories of the motor vehicles of headings 87.01 to 87.05	436.3	378.1	239.2	*5.1*	*5.2*	*4.6*	US$/kg	784
0808	Apples, pears and quinces, fresh	109.9	318.2	585.5	0.5	0.6	0.6	US$/kg	057
8471	Automatic data processing machines and units thereof	401.2	382.0	186.4	75.4		84.8	US$/unit	752

Belgium

Goods Imports: CIF, by origin/consignment for intra-eu **Goods Exports: FOB, by last known destination** **Trade System: Special**

Overview:

In 2015, the value of merchandise exports of Belgium decreased substantially by 15.8 percent to reach 397.7 bln US$, while its merchandise imports decreased substantially by 18.1 percent to reach 371.0 bln US$ (see graph 1, table 2 and table 3). These rates of decrease are approximately double the rates of decrease in 2014 (7.7 and 7.3 percent, respectively). The merchandise trade balance recorded a relatively small surplus of 26.7 bln US$ (see graph 1). The largest merchandise trade balance was with MDG Developed Europe at 50.6 bln US$ (see graph 4). Merchandise exports in Belgium were diversified amongst partners; imports were also diversified. The top 17 partners accounted for 80 percent or more of exports and 17 partners accounted for 80 percent or more of imports (see graph 5). In 2014, the value of exports of services of Belgium increased substantially by 10.8 percent, reaching 120.9 bln US$, while its imports of services increased substantially by 13.2 percent and reached 114.6 bln US$ (see graph 2). These rates of increase are higher than the rates of increase of 7.3 percent for both in 2013. There was a relatively small trade in services surplus of 6.3 bln US$.

Graph 1: Total merchandise trade, by value

(Bln US$ by year)

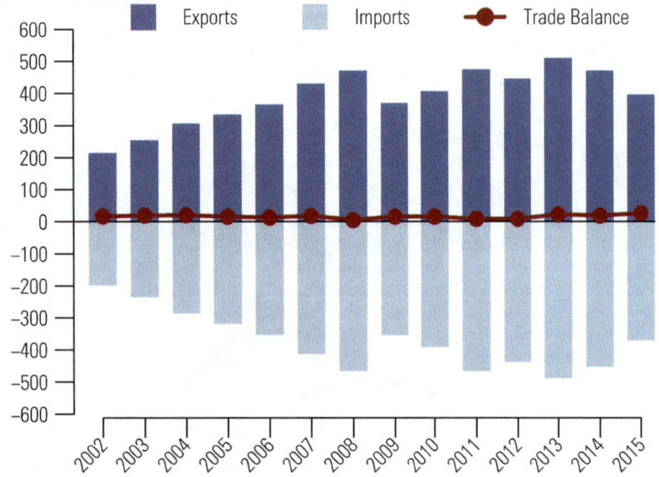

Graph 2: Total services trade, by value

(Bln US$ by year)

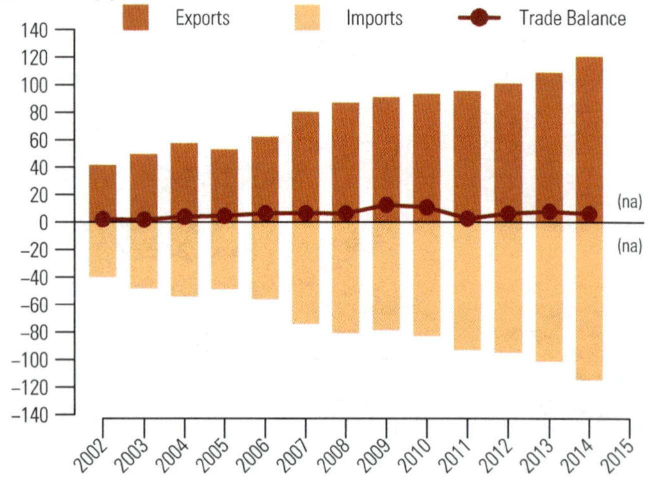

Exports Profile:

"Chemicals" (SITC section 5), "Machinery and transport equipment" (SITC section 7) and "Goods classified chiefly by material" (SITC section 6) were the largest commodity groups for exports in 2015, representing respectively 29.8, 21.5 and 15.2 percent of exported goods (see table 2). From 2013 to 2015, the largest export commodity was "Petroleum oils, other than crude" (HS code 2710) (see table 1). The top three destinations for merchandise exports were Germany, France and the Netherlands, accounting for respectively 16.9, 15.6 and 11.9 percent of total exports. "Other business services" (EBOPS code 268) accounted for the largest share of exports of services in 2014 at 49.5 bln US$, followed by "Transportation" (EBOPS code 205) at 24.9 bln US$ and "Travel" (EBOPS code 236) at 14.0 bln US$ (see graph 3).

Graph 3: Exports of services by EBOPS category

(% share in 2014)

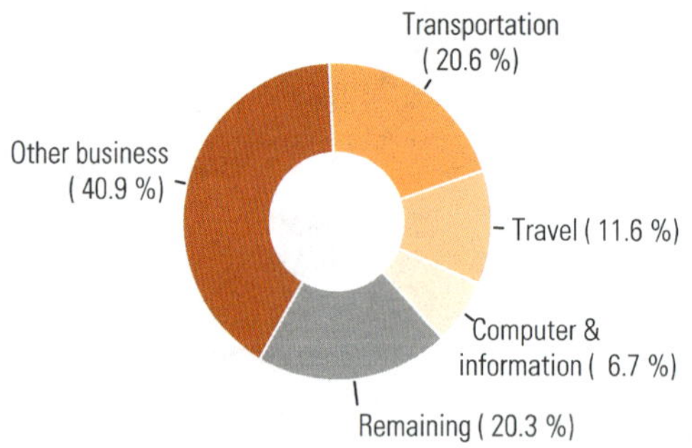

Table 1: Top 10 export commodities 2013 to 2015

HS code	4-digit heading of Harmonized System 2012	Value (million US$) 2013	2014	2015	Unit value 2013	2014	2015	Unit	SITC code
	All Commodities	511 505.0	472 201.3	397 739.2					
2710	Petroleum oils, other than crude	48 751.7	40 829.2	24 275.2	*0.9*	*0.8*	*0.5*	US$/kg	334
3004	Medicaments (excluding goods of heading 30.02, 30.05 or 30.06)	33 329.6	30 345.9	27 251.7	*164.2*	*157.0*	*146.9*	US$/kg	542
8703	Motor cars and other motor vehicles principally designed for the transport	32 125.5	30 288.7	27 740.9	16.6	17.7	16.2	thsd US$/unit	781
7102	Diamonds, whether or not worked, but not mounted or set	20 866.0	20 562.7	15 509.7					667
3002	Human blood; animal blood prepared for therapeutic uses	14 050.4	16 729.0	13 345.2	*0.9*	*1.5*	*1.2*	thsd US$/kg	541
9999	Commodities not specified according to kind	12 165.8	12 471.3	10 228.6					931
2933	Heterocyclic compounds with nitrogen hetero-atom(s) only	10 982.5	8 101.2	8 953.3	*19.3*	*16.6*	*20.2*	US$/kg	515
2711	Petroleum gases and other gaseous hydrocarbons	11 991.5	8 239.5	6 217.8	*0.5*	*0.7*	*0.5*	US$/kg	343
9018	Instruments and appliances used in medical, surgical, dental or veterinary	6 303.3	7 018.7	6 261.4					872
3901	Polymers of ethylene, in primary forms	6 770.4	6 218.7	5 711.7	*1.9*	*1.9*	*1.6*	US$/kg	571

Services Imports and Exports: EBOPS 2002 categories

Table 2: Merchandise exports by SITC

(Value in million US$, growth and shares in percentage)

SITC	2015	Avg. Growth rates 2011-2015	Avg. Growth rates 2014-2015	2015 share
Total	397739.2	-4.4	-15.8	100.0
0+1	36907.1	-1.8	-12.7	9.3
2+4	11009.4	-7.4	-20.1	2.8
3	33315.3	-10.3	-38.2	8.4
5	118366.0	-3.1	-12.3	29.8
6	60328.7	-8.2	-17.6	15.2
7	85658.6	-3.4	-10.6	21.5
8	40453.5	-0.2	-8.1	10.2
9	11700.8	0.3	-17.9	2.9

Table 3: Merchandise imports by SITC

(Value in million US$, growth and shares in percentage)

SITC	2015	Avg. Growth rates 2011-2015	Avg. Growth rates 2014-2015	2015 share
Total	371025.0	-5.6	-18.1	100.0
0+1	30743.8	-2.7	-16.4	8.3
2+4	15177.0	-10.0	-23.8	4.1
3	45655.1	-12.0	-38.6	12.3
5	96537.4	-2.0	-10.8	26.0
6	52867.8	-8.1	-18.2	14.2
7	88442.7	-4.4	-12.0	23.8
8	36786.3	-2.4	-14.2	9.9
9	4814.9	-10.6	-12.7	1.3

SITC Legend

SITC Code	Description
Total	All commodities
0+1	Food, animals + beverages, tobacco
2+4	Crude materials + anim. & veg. oils
3	Mineral fuels, lubricants
5	Chemicals
6	Goods classified chiefly by material
7	Machinery and transport equipment
8	Miscellaneous manufactured articles
9	Not classified elsewhere in the SITC

Graph 4: Merchandise trade balance

(Bln US$ by MDG Regions in 2015)

Graph 5: Partner concentration of merchandise trade

(Cumulative share by ranked partners in 2015)

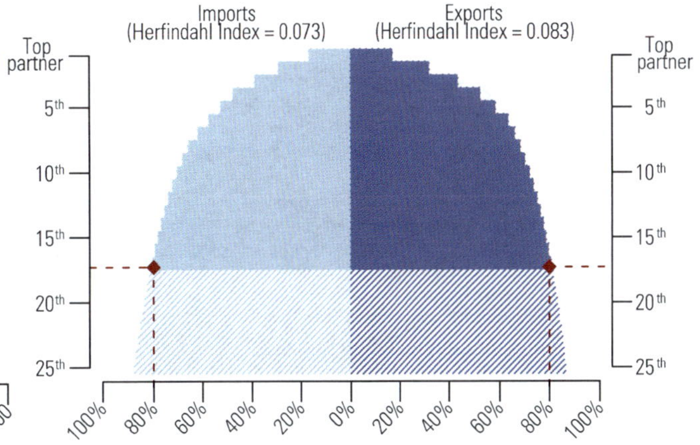

Graph 6: Imports of services by EBOPS category

(% share in 2014)

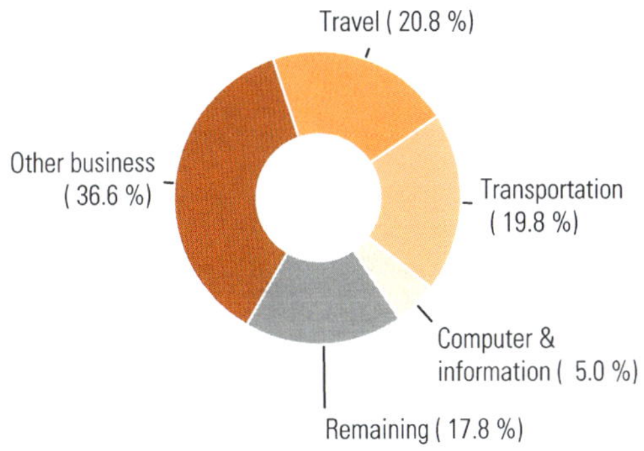

Imports Profile:

"Chemicals" (SITC section 5), "Machinery and transport equipment" (SITC section 7) and "Goods classified chiefly by material" (SITC section 6) were the largest commodity groups for imports in 2015, representing respectively 26.0, 23.8 and 14.2 percent of imported goods (see table 3). From 2013 to 2015, the largest import commodity was "Motor cars and other motor vehicles principally designed for the transport" (HS code 8703) (see table 4). The top three partners for merchandise imports were the Netherlands, Germany and France, accounting for respectively 19.2, 13.2 and 10.1 percent of total imports. "Other business services" (EBOPS code 268) accounted for the largest share of imports of services in 2014 at 41.9 bln US$, followed by "Travel" (EBOPS code 236) at 23.8 bln US$ and "Transportation" (EBOPS code 205) at 22.7 bln US$ (see graph 6).

Table 4: Top 10 import commodities 2013 to 2015

HS code	4-digit heading of Harmonized System 2012	Value (million US$) 2013	Value (million US$) 2014	Value (million US$) 2015	Unit value 2013	Unit value 2014	Unit value 2015	Unit	SITC code
	All Commodities	488527.2	452772.5	371025.0					
8703	Motor cars and other motor vehicles principally designed for the transport	30018.4	26947.4	28418.0	19.7	20.4	18.4	thsd US$/unit	781
2710	Petroleum oils, other than crude	36997.6	29191.2	17586.9	*0.8*	*0.8*	*0.5*	US$/kg	334
3004	Medicaments (excluding goods of heading 30.02, 30.05 or 30.06)	25317.7	23413.4	21999.4	*126.5*	*109.0*	*103.0*	US$/kg	542
2709	Petroleum oils and oils obtained from bituminous minerals, crude	28489.1	27379.6	14525.0	*0.8*	0.7	*0.4*	US$/kg	333
7102	Diamonds, whether or not worked, but not mounted or set	20913.1	19755.4	15594.4					667
2711	Petroleum gases and other gaseous hydrocarbons	20792.3	13803.4	10723.9	*0.6*	*0.6*	*0.5*	US$/kg	343
3002	Human blood; animal blood prepared for therapeutic uses	12671.5	13811.8	12218.1	*1.3*	*0.7*	*1.0*	thsd US$/kg	541
8708	Parts and accessories of the motor vehicles of headings 87.01 to 87.05	10539.9	9396.8	7098.8	*8.1*	*8.1*	*6.9*	US$/kg	784
2933	Heterocyclic compounds with nitrogen hetero-atom(s) only	7822.7	7405.7	9448.8	*62.5*	*56.8*	*78.6*	US$/kg	515
9018	Instruments and appliances used in medical, surgical, dental or veterinary	5955.4	5814.0	5495.0					872

Source: UN Comtrade

Belize

Goods Imports: CIF, by origin | **Goods Exports: FOB, by last known destination** | **Trade System: General**

Overview:

In 2015, the value of merchandise exports of Belize decreased moderately by 9.9 percent to reach 328.9 mln US$, while its merchandise imports increased slightly by 2.6 percent to reach 1.0 bln US$ (see graph 1, table 2 and table 3). The merchandise trade balance recorded a large deficit of 699.8 mln US$ (see graph 1). The largest merchandise trade balance was with MDG Latin America and the Caribbean at -258.3 mln US$ (see graph 4). Merchandise exports in Belize were moderately concentrated amongst partners; imports were also moderately concentrated. The top 6 partners accounted for 80 percent or more of exports and 9 partners accounted for 80 percent or more of imports (see graph 5). In 2014, the value of exports of services of Belize increased substantially by 10.4 percent, reaching 494.3 mln US$, while its imports of services increased moderately by 8.1 percent and reached 224.6 mln US$ (see graph 2). There was a large trade in services surplus of 269.7 mln US$.

Graph 1: Total merchandise trade, by value

(Bln US$ by year)

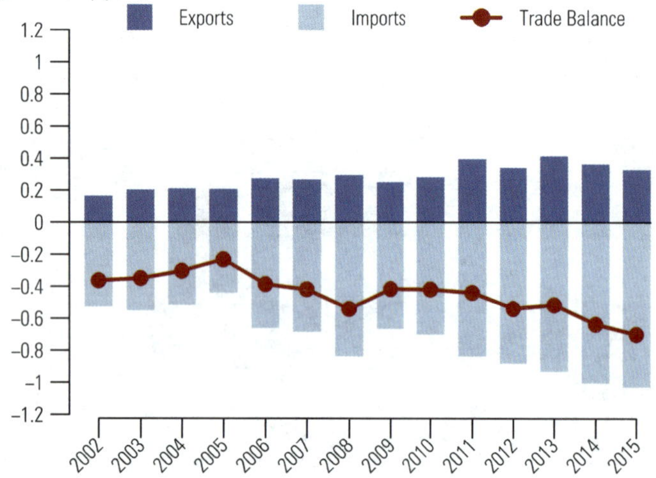

Graph 2: Total services trade, by value

(Mln US$ by year)

Exports Profile:

"Food, animals + beverages, tobacco" (SITC section 0+1), "Not classified elsewhere in the SITC" (SITC section 9) and "Mineral fuels, lubricants" (SITC section 3) were the largest commodity groups for exports in 2015, representing respectively 60.7, 15.0 and 8.2 percent of exported goods (see table 2). From 2013 to 2015, the largest export commodity was "Cane or beet sugar and chemically pure sucrose, in solid form" (HS code 1701) (see table 1). The top three destinations for merchandise exports were the United States, the United Kingdom and Mexico, accounting for respectively 38.8, 23.5 and 5.2 percent of total exports. "Travel" (EBOPS code 236) accounted for the largest share of exports of services in 2014 at 379.6 mln US$, followed by "Other business services" (EBOPS code 268) at 47.4 mln US$ and "Government services, n.i.e." (EBOPS code 291) at 29.2 mln US$ (see graph 3).

Graph 3: Exports of services by EBOPS category

(% share in 2014)

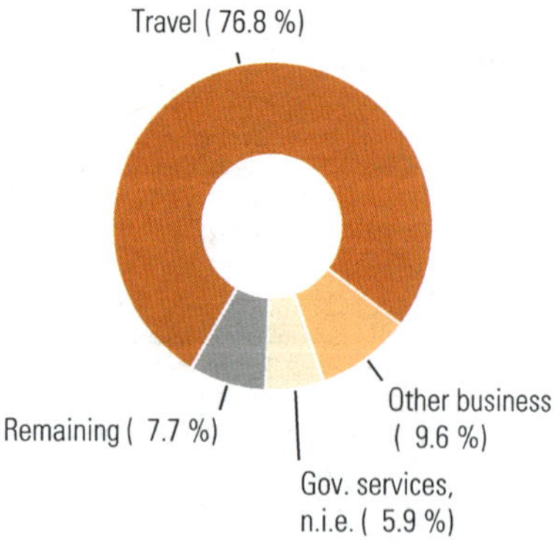

Table 1: Top 10 export commodities 2013 to 2015

HS code	4-digit heading of Harmonized System 2007	Value (million US$) 2013	2014	2015	Unit value 2013	2014	2015	Unit	SITC code
	All Commodities	415.7	364.9	328.9					
1701	Cane or beet sugar and chemically pure sucrose, in solid form	53.7	55.1	67.2	0.5	0.5	0.2	US$/kg	061
9999	Commodities not specified according to kind	46.7	62.6	49.4					931
2009	Fruit juices (including grape must) and vegetable juices	54.7	46.2	45.7	1.8	1.9	0.9	US$/kg	059
0306	Crustaceans, whether in shell or not	54.8	52.1	39.6	7.5	7.7	3.9	US$/kg	036
2709	Petroleum oils and oils obtained from bituminous minerals, crude	70.1	51.1	18.2		1.3		US$/kg	333
0803	Bananas, including plantains, fresh or dried	48.5	...	...	0.5			US$/kg	057
2309	Preparations of a kind used in animal feeding	13.6	12.5	5.9	0.3	0.2		US$/kg	081
2710	Petroleum oils, other than crude	10.6	7.3	8.6	1.0	1.0	0.3	US$/kg	334
0713	Dried leguminous vegetables, shelled, whether or not skinned or split	8.0	8.3	8.5	1.3	1.4	0.5	US$/kg	054
0807	Melons (including watermelons) and papaws (papayas), fresh	10.3	6.6	6.5	0.4	0.4	0.2	US$/kg	057

Services Imports and Exports: EBOPS 2002 categories

Table 2: Merchandise exports by SITC

(Value in million US$, growth and shares in percentage)

SITC	2015	Avg. Growth rates 2011-2015	Avg. Growth rates 2014-2015	2015 share
Total	328.9	-4.5	-9.9	100.0
0+1	199.7	1.6	-0.5	60.7
2+4	6.2	-6.8	27.1	1.9
3	26.9	-35.4	-54.0	8.2
5	7.4	7.4	65.0	2.2
6	5.9	10.4	15.7	1.8
7	19.2	28.7	6.0	5.8
8	14.2	25.1	33.5	4.3
9	49.4	20.7	-21.1	15.0

Table 3: Merchandise imports by SITC

(Value in million US$, growth and shares in percentage)

SITC	2015	Avg. Growth rates 2011-2015	Avg. Growth rates 2014-2015	2015 share
Total	1 028.7	5.3	2.6	100.0
0+1	205.4	20.0	-5.8	20.0
2+4	26.0	16.0	6.5	2.5
3	113.8	-5.8	-24.0	11.1
5	97.6	8.2	7.0	9.5
6	144.3	10.0	7.0	14.0
7	264.3	20.8	22.9	25.7
8	174.5	34.8	5.6	17.0
9	2.9	-66.6	-22.5	0.3

SITC Legend

SITC Code	Description
Total	All commodities
0+1	Food, animals + beverages, tobacco
2+4	Crude materials + anim. & veg. oils
3	Mineral fuels, lubricants
5	Chemicals
6	Goods classified chiefly by material
7	Machinery and transport equipment
8	Miscellaneous manufactured articles
9	Not classified elsewhere in the SITC

Graph 4: Merchandise trade balance

(Mln US$ by MDG Regions in 2015)

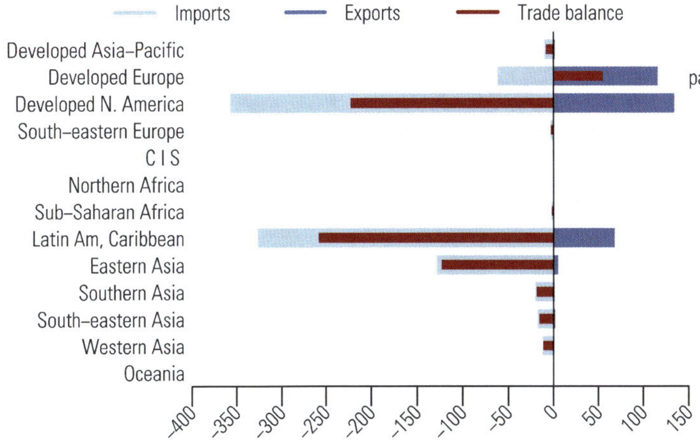

Graph 5: Partner concentration of merchandise trade

(Cumulative share by ranked partners in 2015)

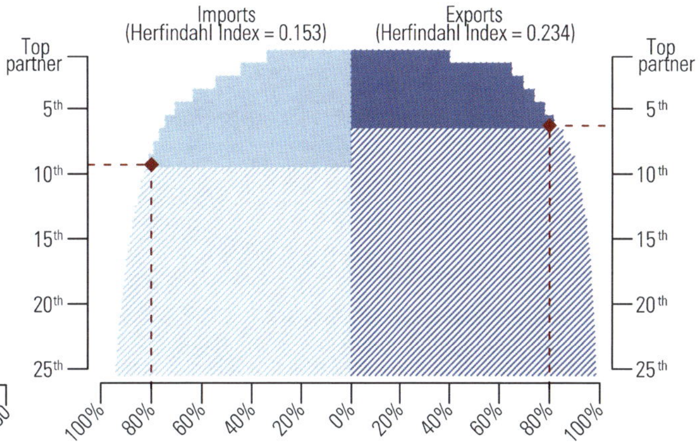

Graph 6: Imports of services by EBOPS category

(% share in 2014)

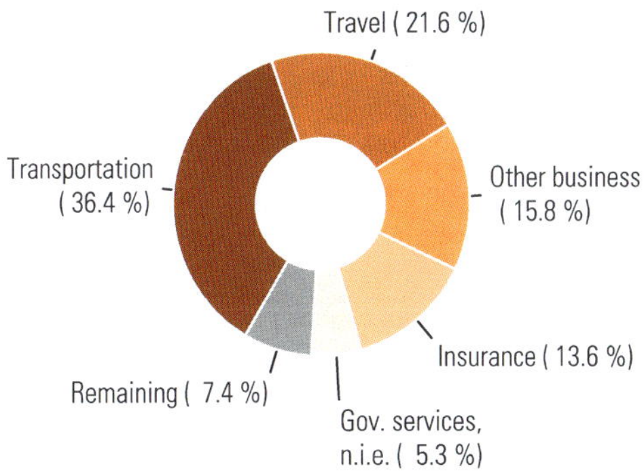

Imports Profile:

"Machinery and transport equipment" (SITC section 7), "Food, animals + beverages, tobacco" (SITC section 0+1) and "Miscellaneous manufactured articles" (SITC section 8) were the largest commodity groups for imports in 2015, representing respectively 25.7, 20.0 and 17.0 percent of imported goods (see table 3). From 2013 to 2015, the largest import commodity was "Petroleum oils, other than crude" (HS code 2710) (see table 4). The top three partners for merchandise imports were the United States, Curaçao and Mexico, accounting for respectively 32.4, 11.2 and 10.9 percent of total imports. "Transportation" (EBOPS code 205) accounted for the largest share of imports of services in 2014 at 81.6 mln US$, followed by "Travel" (EBOPS code 236) at 48.5 mln US$ and "Other business services" (EBOPS code 268) at 35.4 mln US$ (see graph 6).

Table 4: Top 10 import commodities 2013 to 2015

HS code	4-digit heading of Harmonized System 2007	Value (million US$) 2013	Value (million US$) 2014	Value (million US$) 2015	Unit value 2013	Unit value 2014	Unit value 2015	Unit	SITC code
	All Commodities	931.2	1 002.4	1 028.7					
2710	Petroleum oils, other than crude	127.3	133.0	101.2	1.0	1.1	0.3	US$/kg	334
9999	Commodities not specified according to kind	211.1	3.7	2.9					931
2402	Cigars, cheroots, cigarillos and cigarettes	8.9	59.4	56.0		5.6	2.6	US$/kg	122
8704	Motor vehicles for the transport of goods	22.3	28.1	29.0	*9.1*	*10.1*		thsd US$/unit	782
8703	Motor cars and other motor vehicles principally designed for the transport	17.1	20.8	19.5	*4.1*	*4.6*	*3.5*	thsd US$/unit	781
2309	Preparations of a kind used in animal feeding	5.8	23.7	16.1	1.0	0.9	0.5	US$/kg	081
4202	Trunks, suit-cases, vanity-cases, executive-cases, brief-cases	1.3	22.0	20.5					831
2711	Petroleum gases and other gaseous hydrocarbons	13.9	16.2	12.1	0.9	0.9	0.3	US$/kg	343
2523	Portland cement, aluminous cement, slag cement	14.9	14.2	11.5	0.1	0.1	0.0	US$/kg	661
3808	Insecticides, rodenticides, fungicides, herbicides	13.5	13.4	13.6	4.6	4.7	2.1	US$/kg	591

Benin

Goods Imports: CIF, by origin | **Goods Exports: FOB, by last known destination** | **Trade System: General**

Overview:

In 2014, the value of merchandise exports of Benin increased substantially by 58.0 percent to reach 951.0 mln US$, while its merchandise imports increased substantially by 22.3 percent to reach 3.6 bln US$ (see graph 1, table 2 and table 3). The merchandise trade balance recorded a large deficit of 2.6 bln US$ (see graph 1). The largest merchandise trade balance was with MDG Developed Europe at -916.5 mln US$ (see graph 4). Merchandise exports in Benin were diversified amongst partners; imports were also diversified. The top 15 partners accounted for 80 percent or more of exports and 16 partners accounted for 80 percent or more of imports (see graph 5). In 2013, the value of exports of services of Benin increased substantially by 25.6 percent, reaching 511.2 mln US$, while its imports of services increased substantially by 32.9 percent and reached 756.9 mln US$ (see graph 2). There was a moderate trade in services deficit of 245.7 mln US$.

Graph 1: Total merchandise trade, by value

(Bln US$ by year)

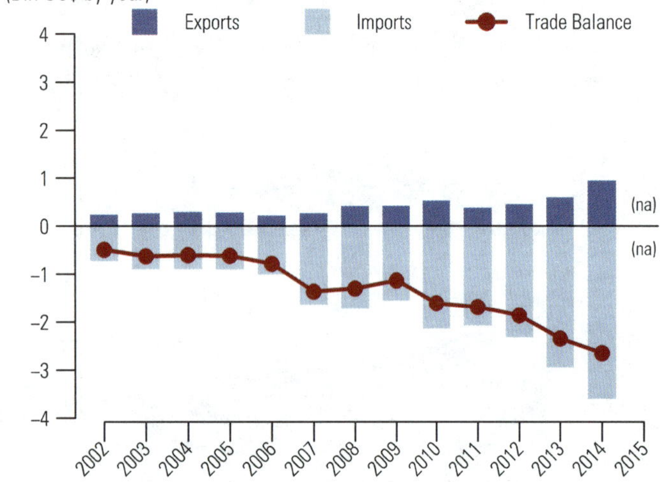

Graph 2: Total services trade, by value

(Mln US$ by year)

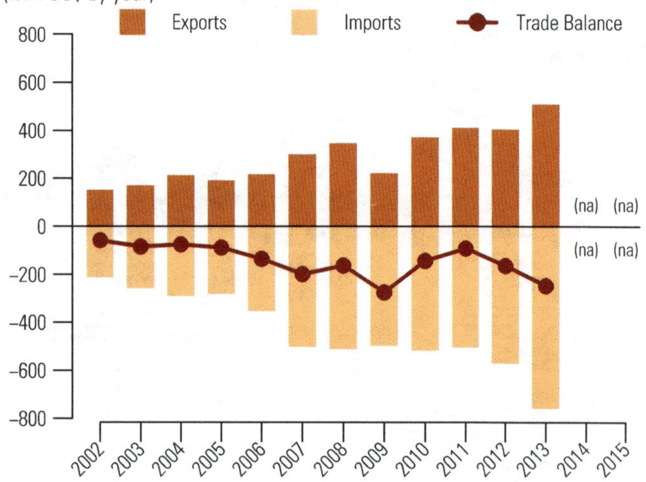

Exports Profile:

"Crude materials + anim. & veg. oils" (SITC section 2+4), "Machinery and transport equipment" (SITC section 7) and "Food, animals + beverages, tobacco" (SITC section 0+1) were the largest commodity groups for exports in 2014, representing respectively 35.0, 23.0 and 13.8 percent of exported goods (see table 2). From 2012 to 2014, the largest export commodity was "Cotton, not carded or combed" (HS code 5201) (see table 1). The top three destinations for merchandise exports were China, India and Nigeria, accounting for respectively 16.4, 10.1 and 7.9 percent of total exports. "Travel" (EBOPS code 236) accounted for the largest share of exports of services in 2012 at 169.4 mln US$, followed by "Transportation" (EBOPS code 205) at 110.6 mln US$ and "Financial services" (EBOPS code 260) at 41.2 mln US$ (see graph 3).

Graph 3: Exports of services by EBOPS category

(% share in 2012)

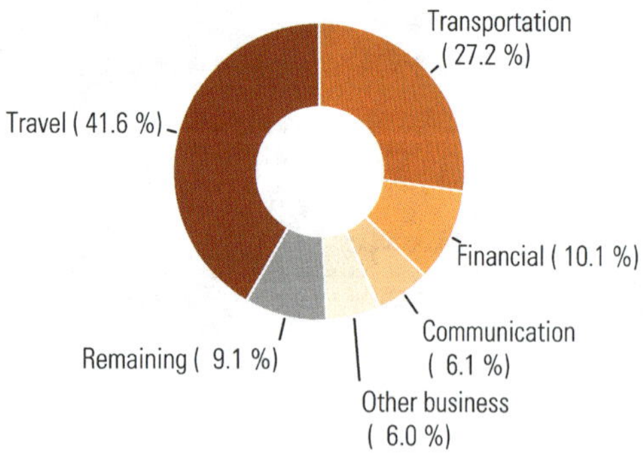

Table 1: Top 10 export commodities 2012 to 2014

HS code	4-digit heading of Harmonized System 2002	Value (million US$) 2012	2013	2014	Unit value 2012	2013	2014	Unit	SITC code
	All Commodities	460.3	602.0	951.0					
5201	Cotton, not carded or combed	148.1	235.3	287.9	1.5	1.5	1.6	US$/kg	263
0801	Coconuts, Brazil nuts and cashew nuts, fresh or dried	50.4	62.5	65.1					057
2710	Petroleum oils, other than crude	37.3	34.8	100.2	1.0	1.0	1.0	US$/kg	334
8431	Parts suitable for use principally with the machinery of headings 84.25	0.3	2.8	73.0	3.0	13.3	14.9	US$/kg	723
7213	Bars and rods, hot-rolled, in irregularly wound coils	32.1	25.3	13.0	0.8	0.7	0.6	US$/kg	676
7108	Gold (including gold plated with platinum)	19.5	21.3	21.6					971
2523	Portland cement, aluminous cement, slag cement	2.2	13.0	38.5	0.1	0.1	0.1	US$/kg	661
0802	Other nuts, fresh or dried	8.6	14.8	22.5					057
8802	Other aircraft (for example, helicopters, aeroplanes); spacecraft	...	...	44.7					792
8903	Yachts and other vessels for pleasure or sports; rowing boats and canoes	...	0.1	44.2					793

Services Imports and Exports: EBOPS 2002 categories

Table 2: Merchandise exports by SITC

(Value in million US$, growth and shares in percentage)

SITC	2014	Avg. Growth rates 2010-2014	Avg. Growth rates 2013-2014	2014 share
Total	951.0	15.5	58.0	100.0
0+1	131.1	-14.6	-4.0	13.8
2+4	332.6	23.3	15.6	35.0
3	104.0	27.1	179.4	10.9
5	9.6	20.7	72.9	1.0
6	116.3	27.7	26.6	12.2
7	219.0	63.1	1073.9	23.0
8	16.7	76.0	532.3	1.8
9	21.6	-1.7	0.2	2.3

Table 3: Merchandise imports by SITC

(Value in million US$, growth and shares in percentage)

SITC	2014	Avg. Growth rates 2010-2014	Avg. Growth rates 2013-2014	2014 share
Total	3596.1	13.9	22.3	100.0
0+1	1622.5	24.7	49.5	45.1
2+4	175.4	-5.4	-4.9	4.9
3	515.0	5.3	24.1	14.3
5	179.4	5.2	10.1	5.0
6	360.7	6.6	-13.2	10.0
7	650.1	21.5	9.9	18.1
8	91.8	-2.5	12.1	2.6
9	1.2	110.2	-71.1	0.0

SITC Legend

SITC Code	Description
Total	All commodities
0+1	Food, animals + beverages, tobacco
2+4	Crude materials + anim. & veg. oils
3	Mineral fuels, lubricants
5	Chemicals
6	Goods classified chiefly by material
7	Machinery and transport equipment
8	Miscellaneous manufactured articles
9	Not classified elsewhere in the SITC

Graph 4: Merchandise trade balance

(Bln US$ by MDG Regions in 2014)

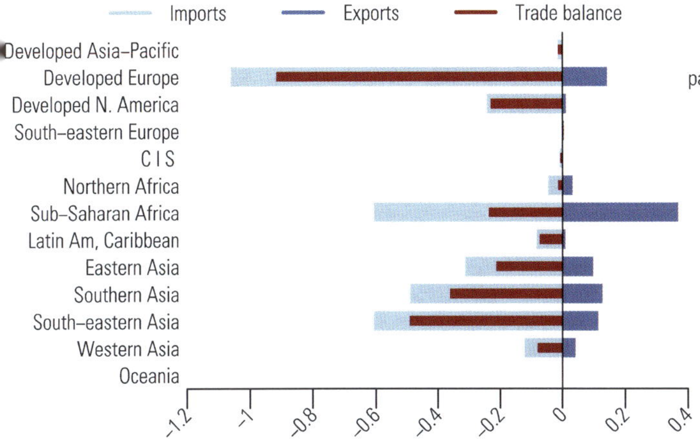

Graph 5: Partner concentration of merchandise trade

(Cumulative share by ranked partners in 2014)

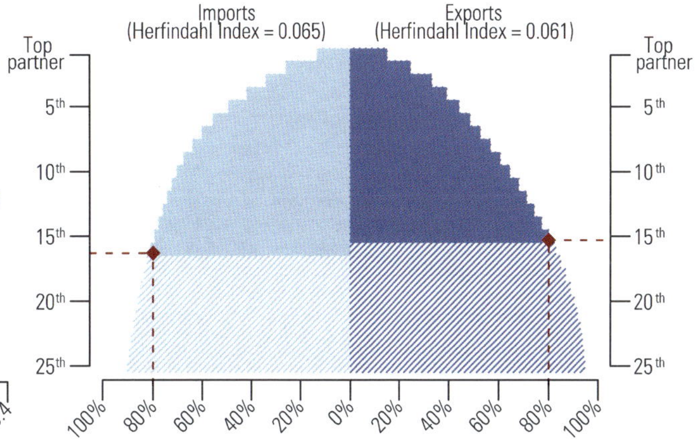

Graph 6: Imports of services by EBOPS category

(% share in 2012)

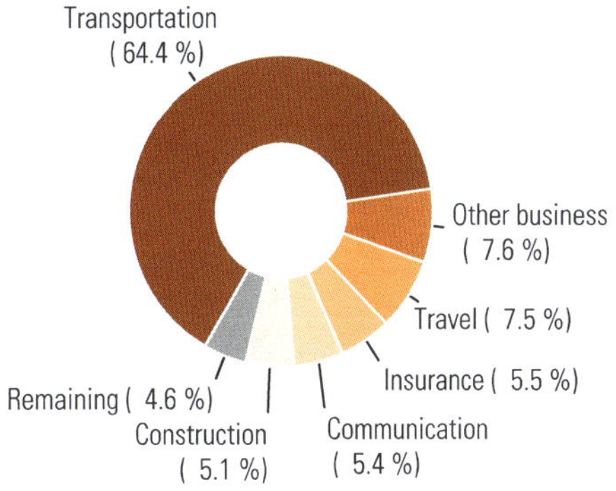

Imports Profile:

"Food, animals + beverages, tobacco" (SITC section 0+1), "Machinery and transport equipment" (SITC section 7) and "Mineral fuels, lubricants" (SITC section 3) were the largest commodity groups for imports in 2014, representing respectively 45.1, 18.1 and 14.3 percent of imported goods (see table 3). From 2012 to 2014, the largest import commodity was "Rice" (HS code 1006) (see table 4). The top three partners for merchandise imports were France, India and Togo, accounting for respectively 10.8, 10.2 and 9.0 percent of total imports. "Transportation" (EBOPS code 205) accounted for the largest share of imports of services in 2012 at 366.8 mln US$, followed by "Other business services" (EBOPS code 268) at 43.4 mln US$ and "Travel" (EBOPS code 236) at 42.5 mln US$ (see graph 6).

Table 4: Top 10 import commodities 2012 to 2014

HS code	4-digit heading of Harmonized System 2002	Value (million US$) 2012	2013	2014	Unit value 2012	2013	2014	Unit	SITC code
	All Commodities	2316.4	2940.7	3596.1					
1006	Rice	315.2	595.4	1023.4	0.6	0.4	0.7	US$/kg	042
2710	Petroleum oils, other than crude	358.0	261.5	348.8	0.7	0.8	0.7	US$/kg	334
0207	Meat and edible offal, of the poultry of heading 01.05	217.9	229.3	244.9	1.2	1.3	1.2	US$/kg	012
2716	Electrical energy	122.0	136.8	136.3	*70.2*	*66.1*	*60.6*	US$/MWh	351
3004	Medicaments (excluding goods of heading 30.02, 30.05 or 30.06)	72.8	77.9	89.8	7.3	15.1	10.8	US$/kg	542
2523	Portland cement, aluminous cement, slag cement	79.5	82.2	46.6	0.1	0.1	0.1	US$/kg	661
8905	Light-vessels, fire-floats, dredgers, floating cranes and other vessels	0.0	50.4	149.3					793
8703	Motor cars and other motor vehicles principally designed for the transport	65.1	63.6	70.1	*14.3*	*18.1*	*18.3*	thsd US$/unit	781
1511	Palm oil and its fractions	62.0	66.2	50.9	0.7	0.7	0.8	US$/kg	422
6309	Worn clothing and other worn articles	55.9	56.3	54.8	1.1	1.1	1.1	US$/kg	269

Bermuda

Goods Imports: CIF, by origin | **Goods Exports: FOB, by last known destination** | **Trade System: General**

Overview:

In 2015, the value of merchandise exports of Bermuda decreased substantially by 28.0 percent to reach 8.6 mln US$, while its merchandise imports decreased slightly by 3.3 percent to reach 928.9 mln US$ (see graph 1, table 2 and table 3). The merchandise trade balance recorded a large deficit of 920.3 mln US$ (see graph 1). The largest merchandise trade balance was with MDG Developed North America at -739.7 mln US$ (see graph 4). Merchandise exports in Bermuda were highly concentrated amongst partners; imports were also highly concentrated. The top 1 partner accounted for 80 percent or more of exports and 2 partners accounted for 80 percent or more of imports (see graph 5). In 2014, the value of exports of services of Bermuda increased slightly by 0.5 percent, reaching 1.4 bln US$, while its imports of services increased moderately by 8.9 percent and reached 977.9 mln US$ (see graph 2). There was a moderate trade in services surplus of 399.3 mln US$.

Graph 1: Total merchandise trade, by value

(Bln US$ by year)

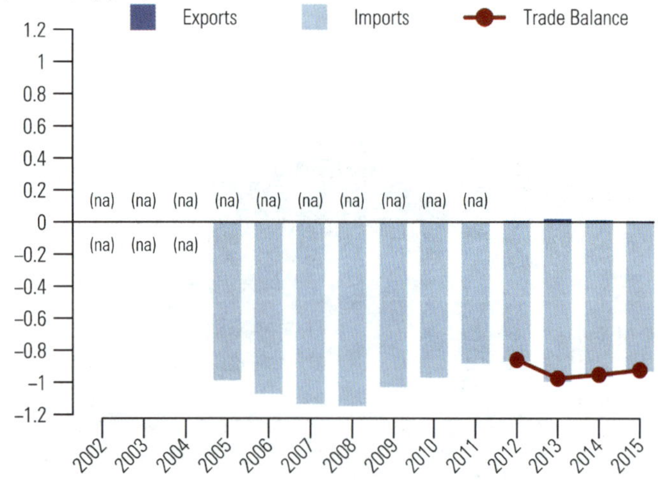

Graph 2: Total services trade, by value

(Bln US$ by year)

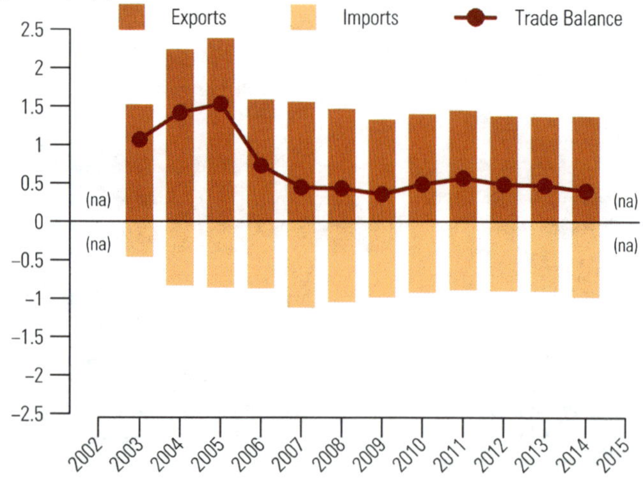

Exports Profile:

"Food, animals + beverages, tobacco" (SITC section 0+1), "Miscellaneous manufactured articles" (SITC section 8) and "Machinery and transport equipment" (SITC section 7) were the largest commodity groups for exports in 2015, representing respectively 44.8, 27.4 and 12.9 percent of exported goods (see table 2). From 2013 to 2015, the largest export commodity was "Other string musical instruments (for example, guitars, violins, harps)" (HS code 9202) (see table 1). The top three destinations for merchandise exports were the United States, the United Kingdom and Areas nes, accounting for respectively 53.9, 39.0 and 3.5 percent of total exports. "Other business services" (EBOPS code 268) accounted for the largest share of exports of services in 2014 at 505.3 mln US$, followed by "Travel" (EBOPS code 236) at 408.7 mln US$ and "Financial services" (EBOPS code 260) at 175.0 mln US$ (see graph 3).

Graph 3: Exports of services by EBOPS category

(% share in 2014)

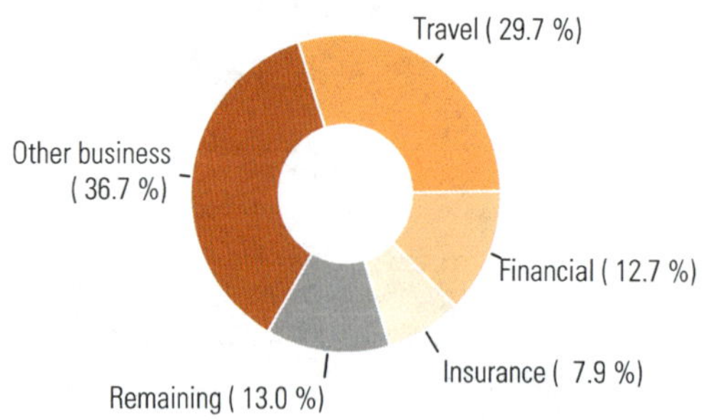

Table 1: Top 10 export commodities 2013 to 2015

HS code	4-digit heading of Harmonized System 2012	Value (million US$) 2013	2014	2015	Unit value 2013	2014	2015	Unit	SITC code
	All Commodities	21.7	12.0	8.6					
9202	Other string musical instruments (for example, guitars, violins, harps)	10.0	0.0	0.0		0.7	2.5	thsd US$/unit	898
2208	Alcohol of a strength by volume of less than 80 % vol	...	2.4	3.4		3.7	3.4	US$/litre	112
8525	Transmission apparatus for radio-telephony, radio-broadcasting	1.8	0.9	0.0	4.5	3.1	3.2	thsd US$/unit	764
9209	Parts (for example, mechanisms for musical boxes) and accessories	2.6	0.0	0.0			0.0	mln US$/kg	898
8803	Parts of goods of heading 88.01 or 88.02	1.9	0.1	0.2	2.2	0.4	0.1	thsd US$/kg	792
9705	Collections and collectors'pieces of zoological, botanical, mineralogical	...	1.3	...		1.3		mln US$/kg	896
8511	Electrical ignition or starting equipment	0.5	0.6	0.0					778
9999	Commodities not specified according to kind	0.0	0.2	1.0					931
9401	Seats (other than those of heading 94.02)	0.0	0.0	1.1					821
8414	Air or vacuum pumps, air or other gas compressors and fans	0.4	0.4	0.0					743

Services Imports and Exports: EBOPS 2002 categories

Table 2: Merchandise exports by SITC

(Value in million US$, growth and shares in percentage)

SITC	2015	Avg. Growth rates 2011-2015	Avg. Growth rates 2014-2015	2015 share
Total	8.6	...	-28.0	100.0
0+1	3.9	...	35.9	44.8
2+4	0.0	...	-18.4	0.1
3	0.0	...	...	0.0
5	0.0	...	-94.2	0.2
6	0.3	...	-78.0	3.4
7	1.1	...	-70.9	12.9
8	2.4	...	-31.9	27.4
9	1.0	...	530.1	11.1

Table 3: Merchandise imports by SITC

(Value in million US$, growth and shares in percentage)

SITC	2015	Avg. Growth rates 2011-2015	Avg. Growth rates 2014-2015	2015 share
Total	928.9	1.3	-3.3	100.0
0+1	190.0	6.7	-3.8	20.5
2+4	16.8	13.2	51.7	1.8
3	91.7	0.7	-39.9	9.9
5	63.5	4.4	0.4	6.8
6	77.6	0.1	-2.3	8.3
7	154.9	2.4	5.2	16.7
8	218.9	2.2	10.6	23.6
9	115.6	-8.1	3.1	12.4

SITC Legend

SITC Code	Description
Total	All commodities
0+1	Food, animals + beverages, tobacco
2+4	Crude materials + anim. & veg. oils
3	Mineral fuels, lubricants
5	Chemicals
6	Goods classified chiefly by material
7	Machinery and transport equipment
8	Miscellaneous manufactured articles
9	Not classified elsewhere in the SITC

Graph 4: Merchandise trade balance

(Mln US$ by MDG Regions in 2015)

Graph 5: Partner concentration of merchandise trade

(Cumulative share by ranked partners in 2015)

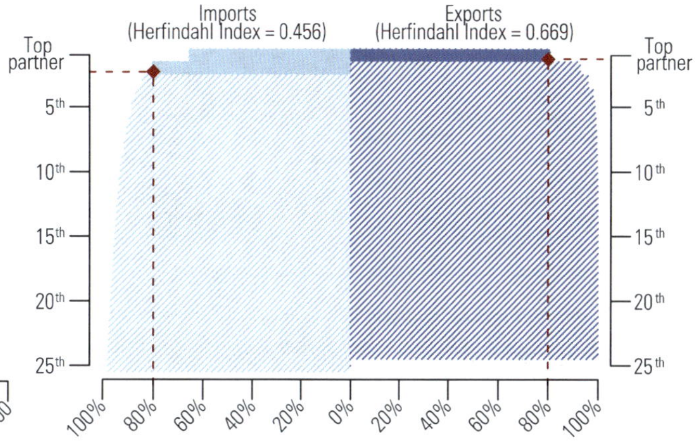

Graph 6: Imports of services by EBOPS category

(% share in 2014)

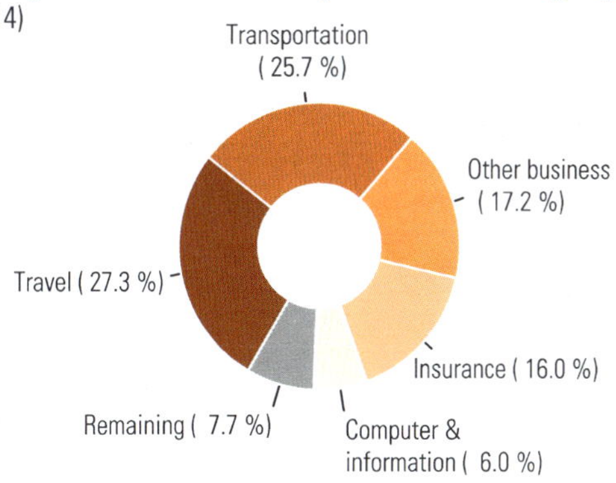

Imports Profile:

"Miscellaneous manufactured articles" (SITC section 8), "Food, animals + beverages, tobacco" (SITC section 0+1) and "Machinery and transport equipment" (SITC section 7) were the largest commodity groups for imports in 2015, representing respectively 23.6, 20.5 and 16.7 percent of imported goods (see table 3). From 2013 to 2015, the largest import commodity was "Petroleum oils, other than crude" (HS code 2710) (see table 4). The top three partners for merchandise imports were the United States, Canada and the United Kingdom, accounting for respectively 68.8, 13.3 and 3.5 percent of total imports. "Travel" (EBOPS code 236) accounted for the largest share of imports of services in 2014 at 266.7 mln US$, followed by "Transportation" (EBOPS code 205) at 251.6 mln US$ and "Other business services" (EBOPS code 268) at 168.7 mln US$ (see graph 6).

Table 4: Top 10 import commodities 2013 to 2015

HS code	4-digit heading of Harmonized System 2012	Value (million US$) 2013	Value (million US$) 2014	Value (million US$) 2015	Unit value 2013	Unit value 2014	Unit value 2015	Unit	SITC code
	All Commodities	994.6	961.1	928.9					
2710	Petroleum oils, other than crude	153.9	149.0	89.5	0.9	0.7	*0.5*	US$/kg	334
9999	Commodities not specified according to kind	111.4	111.9	115.2					931
4907	Unused postage, revenue or similar stamps of current or new issue	82.5	65.3	80.5	15.6	0.2	2.6	thsd US$/kg	892
3004	Medicaments (excluding goods of heading 30.02, 30.05 or 30.06)	23.5	20.7	17.9	34.6	27.5	23.4	US$/kg	542
9403	Other furniture and parts thereof	18.0	20.6	18.1					821
8703	Motor cars and other motor vehicles principally designed for the transport	13.3	16.8	19.6	13.4	12.3	12.4	thsd US$/unit	781
2204	Wine of fresh grapes, including fortified wines	10.9	14.3	14.0	10.0	9.7	9.5	US$/litre	112
1905	Bread, pastry, cakes, biscuits and other bakers'wares	13.1	12.7	12.4	2.2	1.6	2.0	US$/kg	048
8517	Electrical apparatus for line telephony or line telegraphy	9.7	10.4	8.4					764
2202	Waters with added sugar	8.8	9.4	9.4	0.3	0.5	0.6	US$/litre	111

Bhutan

Goods Imports: CIF, by origin | **Goods Exports: FOB, by last known destination** | **Trade System: General**

Overview:

In 2012, the value of merchandise exports of Bhutan increased substantially by 17.3 percent to reach 531.2 mln US$, while its merchandise imports decreased moderately by 5.7 percent to reach 991.7 mln US$ (see graph 1, table 2 and table 3). The merchandise trade balance recorded a large deficit of 460.5 mln US$ (see graph 1). The largest merchandise trade balance was with MDG Southern Asia at -273.9 mln US$ (see graph 4). Merchandise exports in Bhutan were highly concentrated amongst partners; imports were also highly concentrated. The top 1 partner accounted for 80 percent or more of exports and 2 partners accounted for 80 percent or more of imports (see graph 5). In 2014, the value of exports of services of Bhutan decreased slightly by 1.3 percent, reaching 130.2 mln US$, while its imports of services increased slightly by 2.6 percent and reached 184.8 mln US$ (see graph 2). There was a moderate trade in services deficit of 54.6 mln US$.

Graph 1: Total merchandise trade, by value

(Bln US$ by year)

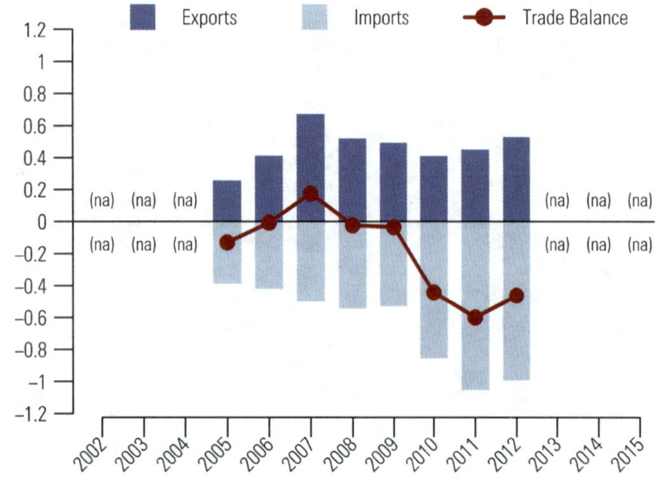

Graph 2: Total services trade, by value

(Mln US$ by year)

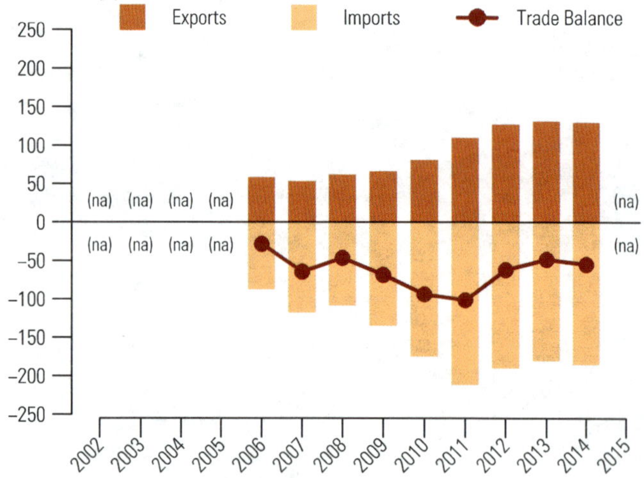

Exports Profile:

"Goods classified chiefly by material" (SITC section 6), "Mineral fuels, lubricants" (SITC section 3) and "Crude materials + anim. & veg. oils" (SITC section 2+4) were the largest commodity groups for exports in 2012, representing respectively 45.5, 32.9 and 7.6 percent of exported goods (see table 2). From 2010 to 2012, the largest export commodity was "Ferro-alloys" (HS code 7202) (see table 1). The top three destinations for merchandise exports were India, China, Hong Kong SAR and Bangladesh, accounting for respectively 84.5, 8.8 and 4.9 percent of total exports. "Travel" (EBOPS code 236) accounted for the largest share of exports of services in 2014 at 96.8 mln US$, followed by "Transportation" (EBOPS code 205) at 27.8 mln US$ (see graph 3).

Graph 3: Exports of services by EBOPS category

(% share in 2014)

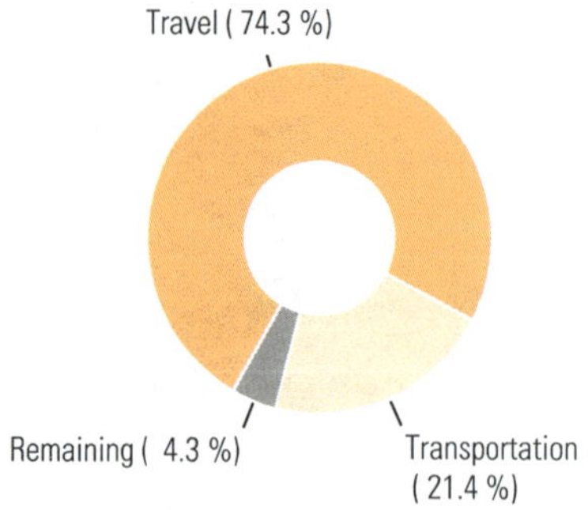

Table 1: Top 10 export commodities 2010 to 2012

HS code	4-digit heading of Harmonized System 2007	Value (million US$) 2010	2011	2012	Unit value 2010	2011	2012	Unit	SITC code
	All Commodities	413.5	453.0	531.2					
7202	Ferro-alloys	124.9	132.0	127.5					671
2716	Electrical energy	...	...	170.6					351
8523	Prepared unrecorded media for sound recording	46.9	71.9	...					898
7408	Copper wire	37.7	42.9	24.2	3.8	5.6	5.7	US$/kg	682
2849	Carbides, whether or not chemically defined	31.0	31.0	29.5					524
2523	Portland cement, aluminous cement, slag cement	30.0	22.9	25.1	0.1	0.1	0.1	US$/kg	661
7214	Other bars and rods of iron or non-alloy steel	16.1	25.1	27.1	0.7	0.8	0.8	US$/kg	676
2518	Dolomite, whether or not calcined or sintered	16.1	16.5	17.6	0.0	0.0	0.0	US$/kg	278
7207	Semi-finished products of iron or non-alloy steel	8.9	3.5	21.6	0.6	0.7	0.4	US$/kg	672
2520	Gypsum; anhydrite; plasters	10.5	12.1	10.3	0.0	0.0	0.0	US$/kg	273

Services Imports and Exports: EBOPS 2002 categories

Table 2: Merchandise exports by SITC

(Value in million US$, growth and shares in percentage)

SITC	2012	Avg. Growth rates 2008-2012	2011-2012	2012 share
Total	531.2	0.5	17.3	100.0
0+1	36.7	-38.2	-2.8	6.9
2+4	40.4	55.5	-3.3	7.6
3	174.9	-9.0	2811.2	32.9
5	36.8	463.1	-3.9	6.9
6	241.7	144.4	-5.7	45.5
7	0.1	69.0	112.1	0.0
8	0.6	-2.1	-99.1	0.1
9	0.0	-30.9	155.1	0.0

Table 3: Merchandise imports by SITC

(Value in million US$, growth and shares in percentage)

SITC	2012	Avg. Growth rates 2008-2012	2011-2012	2012 share
Total	991.7	16.2	-5.7	100.0
0+1	116.8	15.6	17.3	11.8
2+4	85.0	6.3	-0.7	8.6
3	182.6	17.8	14.6	18.4
5	56.9	16.9	3.4	5.7
6	277.8	26.3	20.9	28.0
7	225.2	10.5	-40.9	22.7
8	38.3	11.0	-2.9	3.9
9	9.0	72.7	419.2	0.9

SITC Legend

SITC Code	Description
Total	All commodities
0+1	Food, animals + beverages, tobacco
2+4	Crude materials + anim. & veg. oils
3	Mineral fuels, lubricants
5	Chemicals
6	Goods classified chiefly by material
7	Machinery and transport equipment
8	Miscellaneous manufactured articles
9	Not classified elsewhere in the SITC

Graph 4: Merchandise trade balance

(Mln US$ by MDG Regions in 2012)

Graph 5: Partner concentration of merchandise trade

(Cumulative share by ranked partners in 2012)

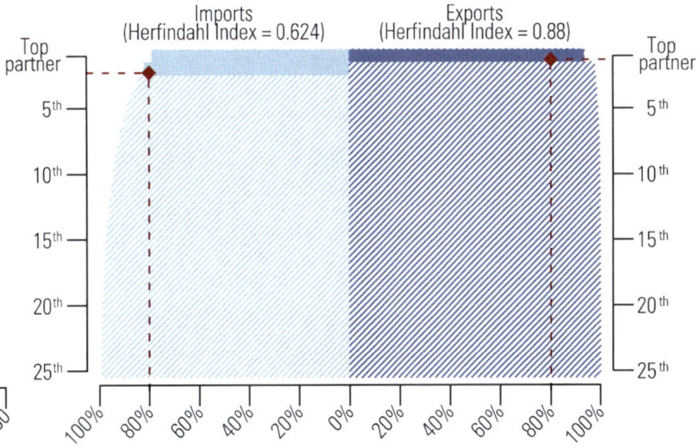

Graph 6: Imports of services by EBOPS category

(% share in 2014)

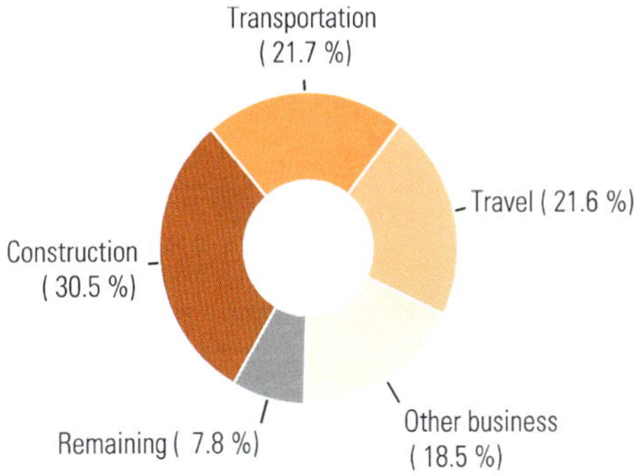

Imports Profile:

"Goods classified chiefly by material" (SITC section 6), "Machinery and transport equipment" (SITC section 7) and "Mineral fuels, lubricants" (SITC section 3) were the largest commodity groups for imports in 2012, representing respectively 28.0, 22.7 and 18.4 percent of imported goods (see table 3). From 2010 to 2012, the largest import commodity was "Petroleum oils, other than crude" (HS code 2710) (see table 4). The top three partners for merchandise imports were India, the Republic of Korea and Japan, accounting for respectively 75.3, 4.8 and 2.6 percent of total imports. "Construction services" (EBOPS code 249) accounted for the largest share of imports of services in 2014 at 56.3 mln US$, followed by "Transportation" (EBOPS code 205) at 40.0 mln US$ and "Travel" (EBOPS code 236) at 39.8 mln US$ (see graph 6).

Table 4: Top 10 import commodities 2010 to 2012

HS code	4-digit heading of Harmonized System 2007	Value (million US$) 2010	2011	2012	Unit value 2010	2011	2012	Unit	SITC code
	All Commodities	853.8	1 051.7	991.7					
2710	Petroleum oils, other than crude	91.9	120.6	130.6					334
8703	Motor cars and other motor vehicles principally designed for the transport	31.2	69.2	21.4	9.0	*10.9*	9.7	thsd US$/unit	781
7408	Copper wire	40.5	42.6	26.5	5.0	5.7	5.9	US$/kg	682
7203	Ferrous products obtained by direct reduction of iron ore	26.9	30.7	40.7	0.4	0.5	0.4	US$/kg	671
8429	Self-propelled bulldozers, angledozers, graders, levellers, scrapers	36.8	38.9	17.5	11.1	32.2	52.7	thsd US$/unit	723
8704	Motor vehicles for the transport of goods	31.6	46.6	13.4	20.5	19.7	18.7	thsd US$/unit	782
7308	Structures (excluding prefabricated buildings of heading 94.06)	19.6	15.6	30.2	1.5	1.7	1.2	US$/kg	691
1006	Rice	18.5	18.4	23.4	0.4	0.3	0.3	US$/kg	042
4402	Wood charcoal (including shell or nut charcoal), whether or not agglomerated	15.5	23.5	18.6	0.2	0.3	0.3	US$/kg	245
7204	Ferrous waste and scrap; remelting scrap ingots of iron or steel	15.4	16.9	21.4	0.4	0.5	0.5	US$/kg	282

Source: UN Comtrade

Bolivia (Plurinational State of)

Goods Imports: CIF, by origin **Goods Exports: FOB, by last known destination** **Trade System: General**

Overview:

In 2015, the value of merchandise exports of the Plurinational State of Bolivia decreased substantially by 30.7 percent to reach 8.9 bln US$, while its merchandise imports decreased moderately by 7.7 percent to reach 9.7 bln US$ (see graph 1, table 2 and table 3). The merchandise trade balance recorded a relatively small deficit of 773.8 mln US$ (see graph 1). The largest merchandise trade balance was with MDG Eastern Asia at -1.1 bln US$ (see graph 4). Merchandise exports in the Plurinational State of Bolivia were diversified amongst partners; imports were also diversified. The top 8 partners accounted for 80 percent or more of exports and 11 partners accounted for 80 percent or more of imports (see graph 5). In 2014, the value of exports of services of the Plurinational State of Bolivia increased substantially by 12.4 percent, reaching 1.2 bln US$, while its imports of services increased substantially by 29.9 percent and reached 3.0 bln US$ (see graph 2). There was a large trade in services deficit of 1.8 bln US$.

Graph 1: Total merchandise trade, by value

(Bln US$ by year)

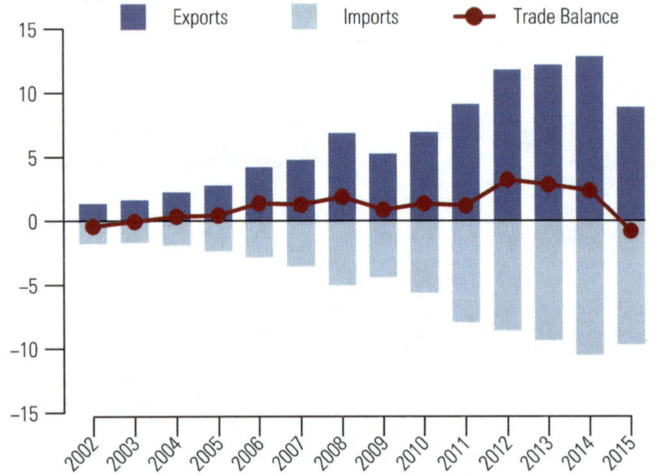

Graph 2: Total services trade, by value

(Bln US$ by year)

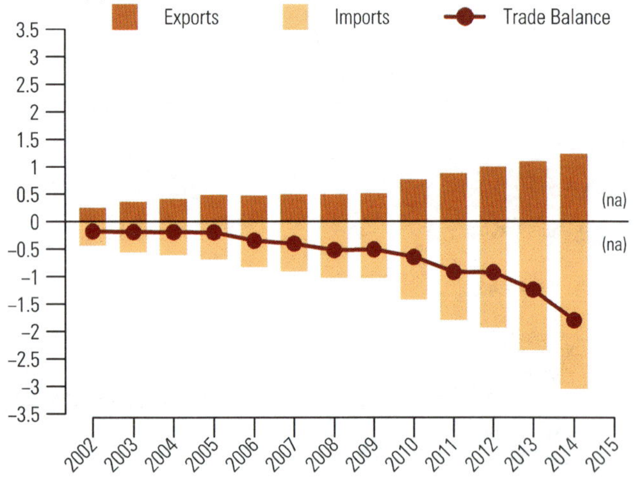

Exports Profile:

"Mineral fuels, lubricants" (SITC section 3), "Crude materials + anim. & veg. oils" (SITC section 2+4) and "Food, animals + beverages, tobacco" (SITC section 0+1) were the largest commodity groups for exports in 2015, representing respectively 45.3, 24.5 and 11.6 percent of exported goods (see table 2). From 2013 to 2015, the largest export commodity was "Petroleum gases and other gaseous hydrocarbons" (HS code 2711) (see table 1). The top three destinations for merchandise exports were Brazil, Argentina and the United States, accounting for respectively 30.3, 19.3 and 12.8 percent of total exports. "Travel" (EBOPS code 236) accounted for the largest share of exports of services in 2014 at 652.3 mln US$, followed by "Transportation" (EBOPS code 205) at 285.9 mln US$ and "Insurance services" (EBOPS code 253) at 130.5 mln US$ (see graph 3).

Graph 3: Exports of services by EBOPS category

(% share in 2014)

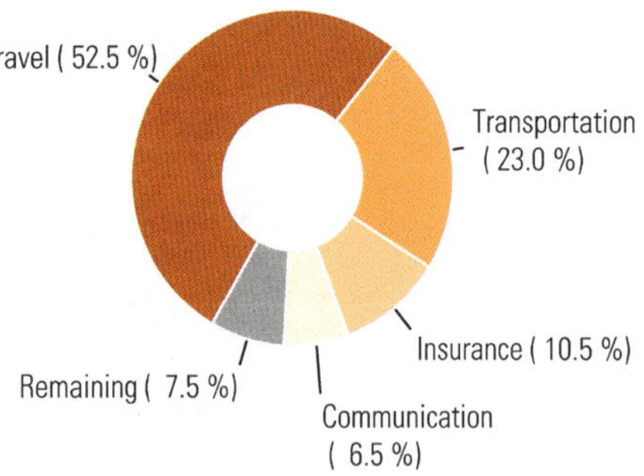

Table 1: Top 10 export commodities 2013 to 2015

HS code	4-digit heading of Harmonized System 2012	Value (million US$) 2013	2014	2015	Unit value 2013	2014	2015	Unit	SITC code
	All Commodities	12 207.5	12 856.1	8 908.7					
2711	Petroleum gases and other gaseous hydrocarbons	6 116.8	6 011.9	3 783.0	0.5	0.4	0.3	US$/kg	343
2608	Zinc ores and concentrates	756.8	980.9	865.7	1.0	1.4	1.3	US$/kg	287
7108	Gold (including gold plated with platinum)	330.8	1 360.9	725.3	40.5	38.0	35.0	thsd US$/kg	971
2616	Precious metal ores and concentrates	866.5	725.9	589.6	54.1	48.1	37.4	US$/kg	289
2304	Oil-cake and other solid residues	612.2	662.2	512.9	0.4	0.4	0.3	US$/kg	081
2709	Petroleum oils and oils obtained from bituminous minerals, crude	511.1	582.5	202.7	0.8	0.8	0.4	US$/kg	333
8001	Unwrought tin	335.5	346.8	254.5	22.4	22.0	16.3	US$/kg	687
1507	Soya-bean oil and its fractions	278.1	293.7	256.0	0.9	0.8	0.7	US$/kg	421
0801	Coconuts, Brazil nuts and cashew nuts, fresh or dried	129.5	175.1	192.0	6.4	6.9	7.8	US$/kg	057
2607	Lead ores and concentrates	168.2	160.3	133.5	1.1	1.4	1.2	US$/kg	287

Table 2: Merchandise exports by SITC

(Value in million US$, growth and shares in percentage)

SITC	2015	Avg. Growth rates 2011-2015	Avg. Growth rates 2014-2015	2015 share
Total	8908.7	-0.7	-30.7	100.0
0+1	1032.9	8.3	-19.9	11.6
2+4	2180.8	-7.0	-17.7	24.5
3	4032.8	-0.7	-39.3	45.3
5	119.2	-3.9	-11.7	1.3
6	472.1	-12.3	-23.8	5.3
7	161.1	108.7	2296.3	1.8
8	182.7	11.9	23.9	2.1
9	727.0	28.6	-46.6	8.2

Table 3: Merchandise imports by SITC

(Value in million US$, growth and shares in percentage)

SITC	2015	Avg. Growth rates 2011-2015	Avg. Growth rates 2014-2015	2015 share
Total	9682.4	5.1	-7.7	100.0
0+1	647.8	1.3	-16.4	6.7
2+4	94.0	2.4	1.9	1.0
3	1087.2	-0.5	-12.3	11.2
5	1386.1	5.4	-2.3	14.3
6	1678.9	4.3	-8.5	17.3
7	3950.2	7.3	-8.1	40.8
8	789.9	8.3	0.2	8.2
9	48.3	14.6	7.9	0.5

SITC Legend

SITC Code	Description
Total	All commodities
0+1	Food, animals + beverages, tobacco
2+4	Crude materials + anim. & veg. oils
3	Mineral fuels, lubricants
5	Chemicals
6	Goods classified chiefly by material
7	Machinery and transport equipment
8	Miscellaneous manufactured articles
9	Not classified elsewhere in the SITC

Graph 4: Merchandise trade balance

(Bln US$ by MDG Regions in 2015)

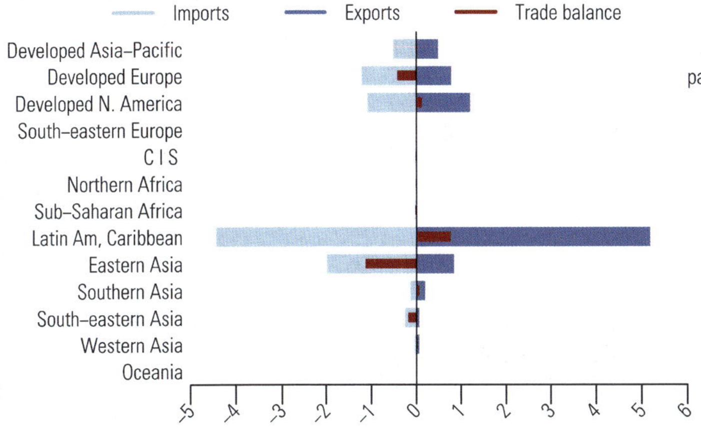

Graph 5: Partner concentration of merchandise trade

(Cumulative share by ranked partners in 2015)

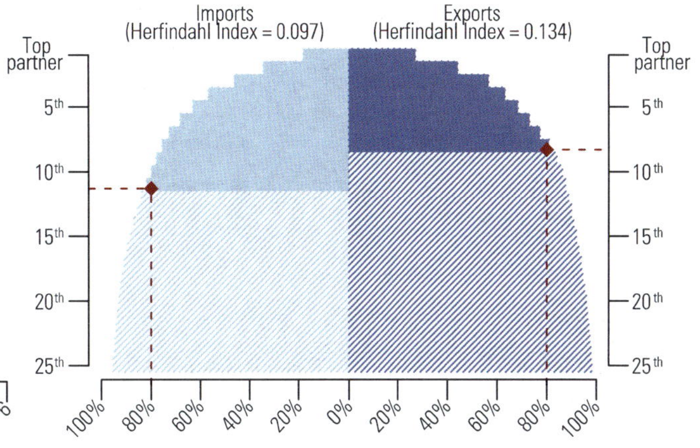

Graph 6: Imports of services by EBOPS category

(% share in 2014)

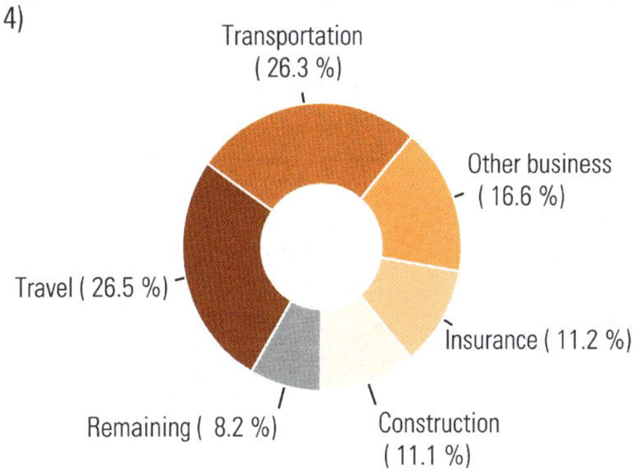

Imports Profile:

"Machinery and transport equipment" (SITC section 7), "Goods classified chiefly by material" (SITC section 6) and "Chemicals" (SITC section 5) were the largest commodity groups for imports in 2015, representing respectively 40.8, 17.3 and 14.3 percent of imported goods (see table 3). From 2013 to 2015, the largest import commodity was "Petroleum oils, other than crude" (HS code 2710) (see table 4). The top three partners for merchandise imports were Brazil, China and the United States, accounting for respectively 16.4, 16.3 and 11.6 percent of total imports. "Travel" (EBOPS code 236) accounted for the largest share of imports of services in 2014 at 804.8 mln US$, followed by "Transportation" (EBOPS code 205) at 800.4 mln US$ and "Other business services" (EBOPS code 268) at 505.4 mln US$ (see graph 6).

Table 4: Top 10 import commodities 2013 to 2015

HS code	4-digit heading of Harmonized System 2012	Value (million US$) 2013	Value (million US$) 2014	Value (million US$) 2015	Unit value 2013	Unit value 2014	Unit value 2015	Unit	SITC code
	All Commodities	9353.0	10492.1	9682.4					
2710	Petroleum oils, other than crude	1222.7	1169.6	1030.8	1.1	1.1	0.8	US$/kg	334
8703	Motor cars and other motor vehicles principally designed for the transport	456.1	494.1	547.8	12.2	12.0	13.7	thsd US$/unit	781
8704	Motor vehicles for the transport of goods	319.9	319.5	316.0	17.0	17.4	18.4	thsd US$/unit	782
3808	Insecticides, rodenticides, fungicides, herbicides	245.6	248.8	227.1	5.2	5.5	5.2	US$/kg	591
7214	Other bars and rods of iron or non-alloy steel	226.3	257.6	202.8	0.9	0.8	0.7	US$/kg	676
8419	Machinery, plant or laboratory equipment	329.6	249.3	75.8					741
8429	Self-propelled bulldozers, angledozers, graders, levellers, scrapers	215.7	224.5	204.2	67.5	72.1	63.6	thsd US$/unit	723
8517	Electrical apparatus for line telephony or line telegraphy	126.5	168.4	221.0					764
8701	Tractors (other than tractors of heading 87.09)	193.3	165.1	130.6	27.1	9.7	17.5	thsd US$/unit	722
8479	Machines and mechanical appliances having individual functions	42.0	186.1	226.3					728

Bosnia and Herzegovina

Goods Imports: CIF, by origin | **Goods Exports: FOB, by last known destination** | **Trade System: Special**

Overview:

In 2015, the value of merchandise exports of Bosnia and Herzegovina decreased substantially by 13.4 percent to reach 5.1 bln US$, while its merchandise imports decreased substantially by 18.2 percent to reach 9.0 bln US$ (see graph 1, table 2 and table 3). The merchandise trade balance recorded a moderate deficit of 3.9 bln US$ (see graph 1). The largest merchandise trade balance was with MDG Developed Europe at -1.7 bln US$ (see graph 4). Merchandise exports in Bosnia and Herzegovina were diversified amongst partners; imports were also diversified. The top 11 partners accounted for 80 percent or more of exports and 14 partners accounted for 80 percent or more of imports (see graph 5). In 2014, the value of exports of services of Bosnia and Herzegovina decreased substantially by 35.3 percent, reaching 1.3 bln US$, while its imports of services increased moderately by 9.6 percent and reached 529.8 mln US$ (see graph 2). There was a large trade in services surplus of 762.5 mln US$.

Graph 1: Total merchandise trade, by value

(Bln US$ by year)

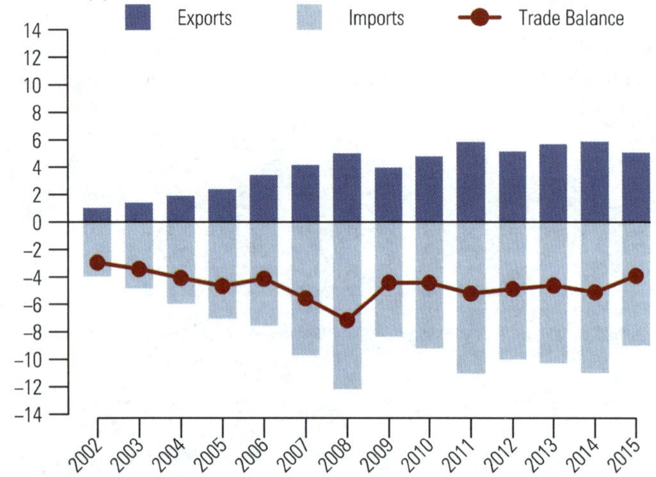

Graph 2: Total services trade, by value

(Bln US$ by year)

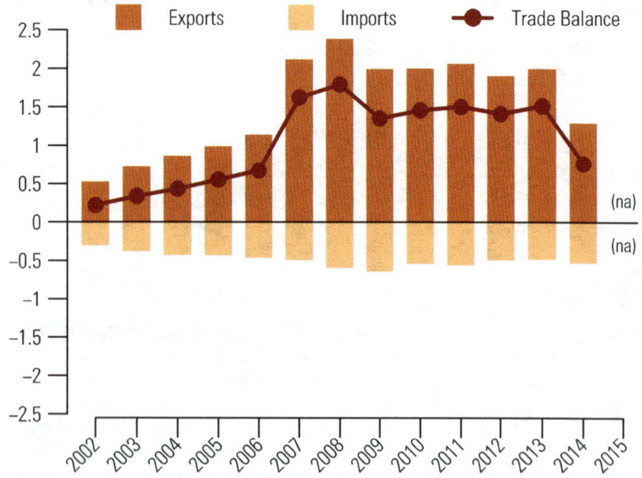

Exports Profile:

"Miscellaneous manufactured articles" (SITC section 8), "Goods classified chiefly by material" (SITC section 6) and "Machinery and transport equipment" (SITC section 7) were the largest commodity groups for exports in 2015, representing respectively 26.0, 22.8 and 14.6 percent of exported goods (see table 2). From 2013 to 2015, the largest export commodity was "Seats (other than those of heading 94.02)" (HS code 9401) (see table 1). The top three destinations for merchandise exports were Germany, Italy and Croatia, accounting for respectively 15.5, 13.1 and 11.9 percent of total exports. "Travel" (EBOPS code 236) accounted for the largest share of exports of services in 2014 at 707.1 mln US$, followed by "Transportation" (EBOPS code 205) at 354.4 mln US$ and "Communications services" (EBOPS code 245) at 89.1 mln US$ (see graph 3).

Graph 3: Exports of services by EBOPS category

(% share in 2014)

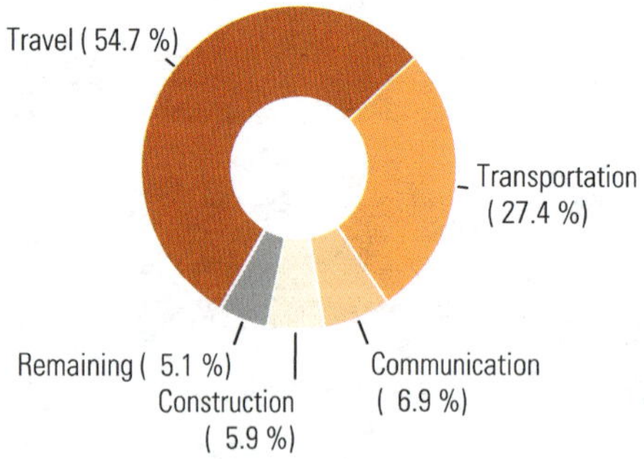

Table 1: Top 10 export commodities 2013 to 2015

HS code	4-digit heading of Harmonized System 2012	Value (million US$) 2013	2014	2015	Unit value 2013	2014	2015	Unit	SITC code
	All Commodities	5687.5	5890.7	5099.1					
9401	Seats (other than those of heading 94.02)	391.5	416.3	349.7					821
7601	Unwrought aluminium	269.5	249.5	195.3	2.2	2.3	2.2	US$/kg	684
2716	Electrical energy	320.3	209.4	161.4	*65.6*	*59.5*	*54.1*	US$/MWh	351
6403	Footwear with outer soles of rubber, plastics, leather	204.9	229.0	174.6	*36.1*			US$/pair	851
4407	Wood sawn or chipped lengthwise, sliced or peeled	164.7	193.6	178.9	*320.3*			US$/m³	248
9999	Commodities not specified according to kind	151.2	145.3	157.5					931
8708	Parts and accessories of the motor vehicles of headings 87.01 to 87.05	144.3	166.7	142.4	4.2	4.4	3.9	US$/kg	784
9403	Other furniture and parts thereof	148.3	151.4	144.0					821
2710	Petroleum oils, other than crude	164.6	152.4	61.7	1.0	0.9	0.6	US$/kg	334
7214	Other bars and rods of iron or non-alloy steel	94.2	104.3	89.9	0.6	0.6	0.5	US$/kg	676

Services Imports and Exports: EBOPS 2002 categories

Table 2: Merchandise exports by SITC

(Value in million US$, growth and shares in percentage)

SITC	2015	Avg. Growth rates 2011-2015	Avg. Growth rates 2014-2015	2015 share
Total	5 099.1	-3.4	-13.4	100.0
0+1	369.9	0.9	5.6	7.3
2+4	623.2	-6.9	-16.4	12.2
3	357.5	-18.7	-36.6	7.0
5	358.9	3.1	-6.3	7.0
6	1 163.0	-5.8	-15.5	22.8
7	745.0	1.4	-9.6	14.6
8	1 323.5	2.6	-11.8	26.0
9	158.2	1.1	7.6	3.1

Table 3: Merchandise imports by SITC

(Value in million US$, growth and shares in percentage)

SITC	2015	Avg. Growth rates 2011-2015	Avg. Growth rates 2014-2015	2015 share
Total	8 993.9	-5.0	-18.2	100.0
0+1	1 488.8	-4.8	-13.0	16.6
2+4	345.2	-6.3	-12.5	3.8
3	1 215.6	-15.4	-33.6	13.5
5	1 178.3	-1.9	-15.0	13.1
6	2 030.4	-1.4	-14.3	22.6
7	1 849.0	-2.6	-18.8	20.6
8	876.1	-1.4	-13.6	9.7
9	10.5	17.2	6.2	0.1

SITC Legend

SITC Code	Description
Total	All commodities
0+1	Food, animals + beverages, tobacco
2+4	Crude materials + anim. & veg. oils
3	Mineral fuels, lubricants
5	Chemicals
6	Goods classified chiefly by material
7	Machinery and transport equipment
8	Miscellaneous manufactured articles
9	Not classified elsewhere in the SITC

Graph 4: Merchandise trade balance

(Bln US$ by MDG Regions in 2015)

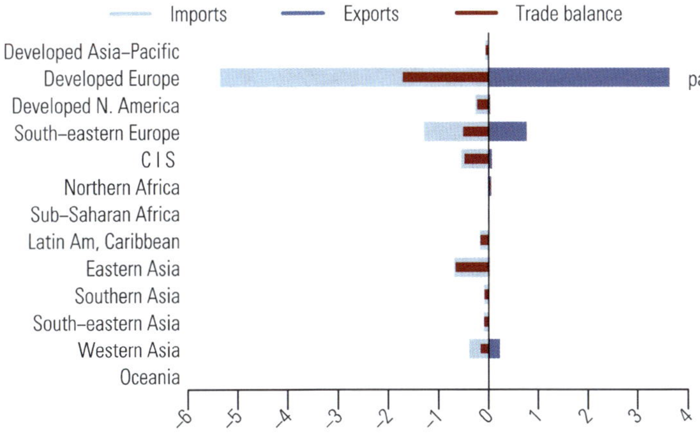

Graph 5: Partner concentration of merchandise trade

(Cumulative share by ranked partners in 2015)

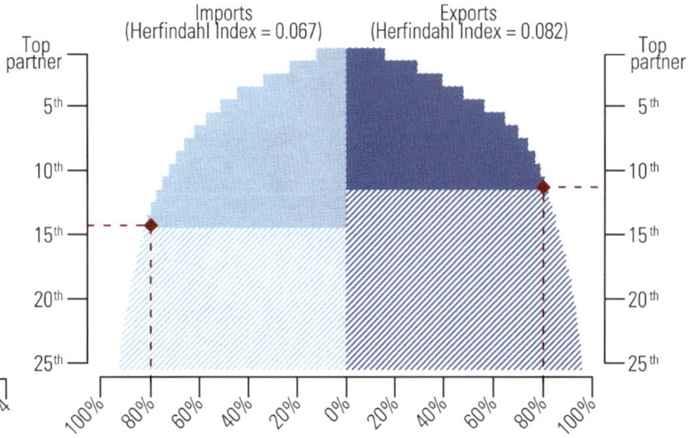

Graph 6: Imports of services by EBOPS category

(% share in 2014)

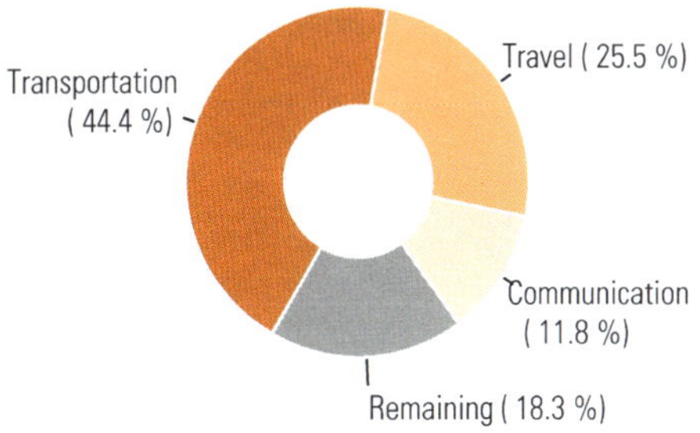

Imports Profile:

"Goods classified chiefly by material" (SITC section 6), "Machinery and transport equipment" (SITC section 7) and "Food, animals + beverages, tobacco" (SITC section 0+1) were the largest commodity groups for imports in 2015, representing respectively 22.6, 20.6 and 16.6 percent of imported goods (see table 3). From 2013 to 2015, the largest import commodity was "Petroleum oils and oils obtained from bituminous minerals, crude" (HS code 2709) (see table 4). The top three partners for merchandise imports were Croatia, Germany and Italy, accounting for respectively 11.7, 11.7 and 10.3 percent of total imports. "Transportation" (EBOPS code 205) accounted for the largest share of imports of services in 2014 at 235.0 mln US$, followed by "Travel" (EBOPS code 236) at 135.2 mln US$ and "Communications services" (EBOPS code 245) at 62.5 mln US$ (see graph 6).

Table 4: Top 10 import commodities 2013 to 2015

HS code	4-digit heading of Harmonized System 2012	Value (million US$) 2013	Value (million US$) 2014	Value (million US$) 2015	Unit value 2013	Unit value 2014	Unit value 2015	Unit	SITC code
	All Commodities	10 295.2	10 990.4	8 993.9					
2709	Petroleum oils and oils obtained from bituminous minerals, crude	814.2	701.9	359.7	0.8	0.7	0.4	US$/kg	333
2710	Petroleum oils, other than crude	690.2	664.1	474.1	1.0	0.9	0.6	US$/kg	334
8703	Motor cars and other motor vehicles principally designed for the transport	333.4	356.5	311.3	*20.6*	*20.5*	*21.4*	thsd US$/unit	781
3004	Medicaments (excluding goods of heading 30.02, 30.05 or 30.06)	272.7	323.8	246.5	40.6	47.9	39.2	US$/kg	542
2701	Coal; briquettes, ovoids and similar solid fuels manufactured from coal	210.0	215.9	172.3	0.2	0.2	0.1	US$/kg	321
2711	Petroleum gases and other gaseous hydrocarbons	158.1	148.6	117.8	0.8	0.8	0.5	US$/kg	343
8517	Electrical apparatus for line telephony or line telegraphy	115.6	119.4	112.0					764
8708	Parts and accessories of the motor vehicles of headings 87.01 to 87.05	112.2	122.9	103.1	2.6	2.6	2.4	US$/kg	784
4107	Leather further prepared after tanning or crusting	99.4	125.1	112.4	33.5	34.2	30.9	US$/kg	611
6406	Parts of footwear	87.7	115.5	85.9	19.6	20.9	18.0	US$/kg	851

Botswana

Goods Imports: CIF, by origin | **Goods Exports: FOB, by last known destination** | **Trade System: General**

Overview:

In 2014, the value of merchandise exports of Botswana increased slightly by 4.5 percent to reach 7.9 bln US$, while its merchandise imports increased moderately by 5.3 percent to reach 7.8 bln US$ (see graph 1, table 2 and table 3). The merchandise trade balance recorded a relatively small surplus of 85.0 mln US$ (see graph 1). The largest merchandise trade balance was with MDG Sub-Saharan Africa at -4.3 bln US$ (see graph 4). Merchandise exports in Botswana were diversified amongst partners; imports were highly concentrated. The top 8 partners accounted for 80 percent or more of exports and 3 partners accounted for 80 percent or more of imports (see graph 5). In 2014, the value of exports of services of Botswana increased moderately by 8.8 percent, reaching 1.4 bln US$, while its imports of services decreased substantially by 13.4 percent and reached 775.0 mln US$ (see graph 2). There was a moderate trade in services surplus of 578.3 mln US$.

Graph 1: Total merchandise trade, by value

(Bln US$ by year)

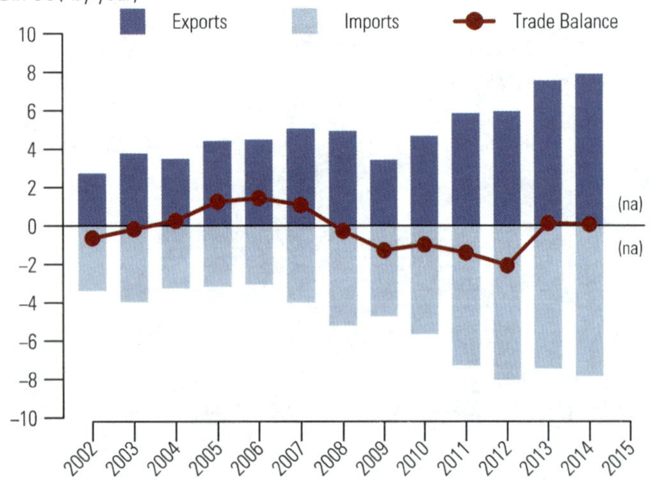

Graph 2: Total services trade, by value

(Bln US$ by year)

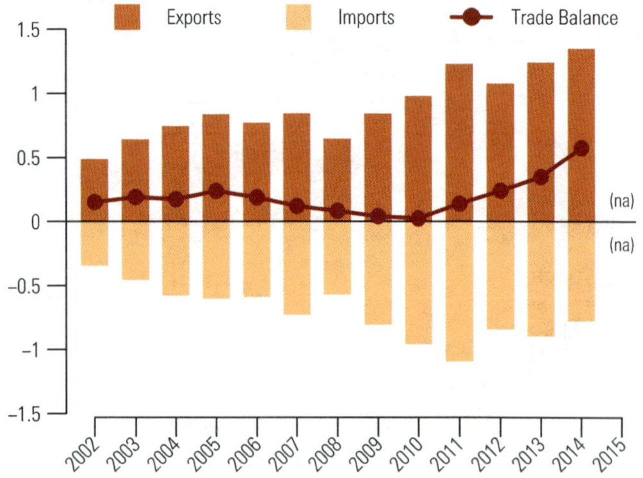

Exports Profile:

"Goods classified chiefly by material" (SITC section 6), "Crude materials + anim. & veg. oils" (SITC section 2+4) and "Machinery and transport equipment" (SITC section 7) were the largest commodity groups for exports in 2014, representing respectively 85.4, 7.1 and 2.5 percent of exported goods (see table 2). From 2012 to 2014, the largest export commodity was "Diamonds, whether or not worked, but not mounted or set" (HS code 7102) (see table 1). The top three destinations for merchandise exports were the United Kingdom, Belgium and South Africa, accounting for respectively 34.5, 15.3 and 11.7 percent of total exports. "Travel" (EBOPS code 236) accounted for the largest share of exports of services in 2014 at 977.4 mln US$, followed by "Other business services" (EBOPS code 268) at 159.8 mln US$ and "Government services, n.i.e." (EBOPS code 291) at 106.9 mln US$ (see graph 3).

Graph 3: Exports of services by EBOPS category

(% share in 2014)

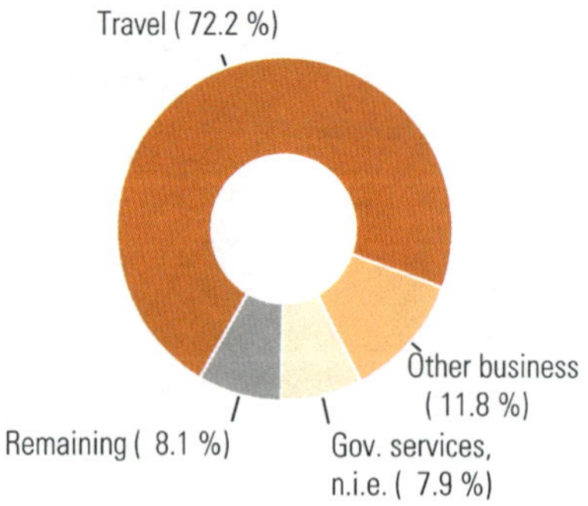

Table 1: Top 10 export commodities 2012 to 2014

HS code	4-digit heading of Harmonized System 2002	Value (million US$) 2012	2013	2014	Unit value 2012	2013	2014	Unit	SITC code
	All Commodities	5971.2	7573.3	7915.5					
7102	Diamonds, whether or not worked, but not mounted or set	4743.8	6279.2	6721.3					667
7501	Nickel mattes, nickel oxide sinters and other intermediate products	333.1	418.6	334.1	7.4	7.5	8.5	US$/kg	284
2603	Copper ores and concentrates	96.4	128.2	133.8	1.6	1.4	1.2	US$/kg	283
0202	Meat of bovine animals, frozen	46.6	74.7	64.4	3.7	3.7	3.6	US$/kg	011
7108	Gold (including gold plated with platinum)	84.2	56.1	41.6	54.1	42.2	40.8	thsd US$/kg	971
8544	Insulated (including enamelled or anodised) wire, cable	48.6	37.4	35.0	*15.6*		10.3	US$/kg	773
2836	Carbonates; peroxocarbonates (percarbonates)	37.3	36.3	37.0					523
0201	Meat of bovine animals, fresh or chilled	17.9	40.9	50.3	4.8	6.3	5.8	US$/kg	011
8703	Motor cars and other motor vehicles principally designed for the transport	41.8	25.1	17.6	*17.3*	*16.8*		thsd US$/unit	781
9999	Commodities not specified according to kind	7.1	25.9	39.3					931

Table 2: Merchandise exports by SITC

(Value in million US$, growth and shares in percentage)

SITC	2014	Avg. Growth rates 2010-2014	Avg. Growth rates 2013-2014	2014 share
Total	7 915.5	14.0	4.5	100.0
0+1	152.8	-9.6	-12.4	1.9
2+4	562.0	-5.0	-19.8	7.1
3	38.6	23.3	22.0	0.5
5	81.7	-4.2	7.3	1.0
6	6 760.8	20.1	7.9	85.4
7	198.9	2.4	-2.8	2.5
8	39.7	-29.7	-0.4	0.5
9	81.0	2.2	-1.3	1.0

Table 3: Merchandise imports by SITC

(Value in million US$, growth and shares in percentage)

SITC	2014	Avg. Growth rates 2010-2014	Avg. Growth rates 2013-2014	2014 share
Total	7 830.5	8.5	5.3	100.0
0+1	657.3	-0.3	-7.5	8.4
2+4	96.7	-12.6	-40.7	1.2
3	1 209.9	9.9	-5.4	15.5
5	481.7	1.6	-4.2	6.2
6	3 323.6	22.1	20.8	42.4
7	1 504.9	0.2	2.6	19.2
8	461.3	-1.1	-0.8	5.9
9	94.9	4.9	1.9	1.2

SITC Legend

SITC Code	Description
Total	All commodities
0+1	Food, animals + beverages, tobacco
2+4	Crude materials + anim. & veg. oils
3	Mineral fuels, lubricants
5	Chemicals
6	Goods classified chiefly by material
7	Machinery and transport equipment
8	Miscellaneous manufactured articles
9	Not classified elsewhere in the SITC

Graph 4: Merchandise trade balance

(Bln US$ by MDG Regions in 2014)

Graph 5: Partner concentration of merchandise trade

(Cumulative share by ranked partners in 2014)

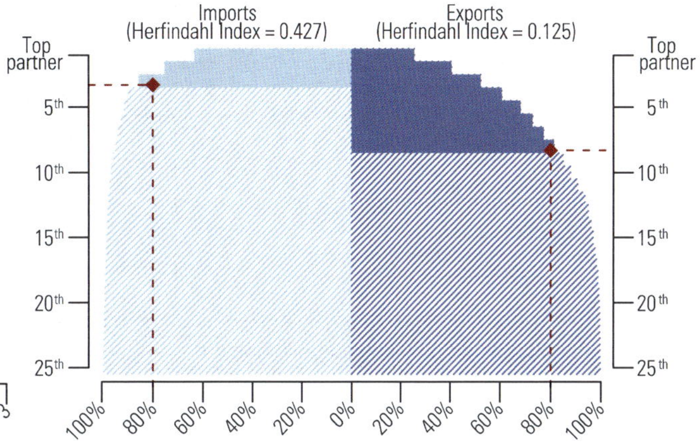

Graph 6: Imports of services by EBOPS category

(% share in 2014)

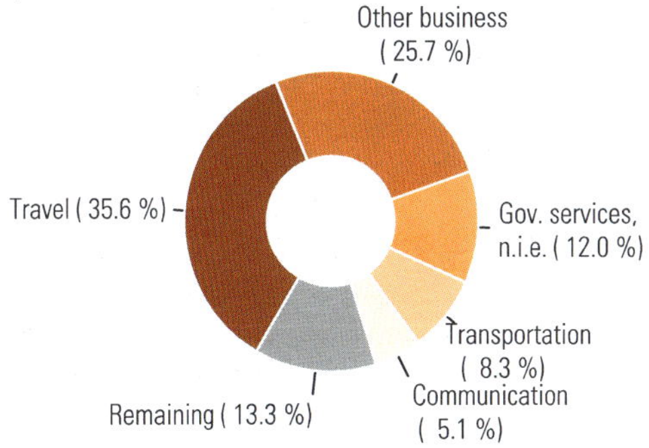

Imports Profile:

"Goods classified chiefly by material" (SITC section 6), "Machinery and transport equipment" (SITC section 7) and "Mineral fuels, lubricants" (SITC section 3) were the largest commodity groups for imports in 2014, representing respectively 42.4, 19.2 and 15.5 percent of imported goods (see table 3). From 2012 to 2014, the largest import commodity was "Diamonds, whether or not worked, but not mounted or set" (HS code 7102) (see table 4). The top three partners for merchandise imports were South Africa, the United Kingdom and Namibia, accounting for respectively 63.9, 8.4 and 8.2 percent of total imports. "Travel" (EBOPS code 236) accounted for the largest share of imports of services in 2014 at 275.9 mln US$, followed by "Other business services" (EBOPS code 268) at 199.2 mln US$ and "Government services, n.i.e." (EBOPS code 291) at 93.3 mln US$ (see graph 6).

Table 4: Top 10 import commodities 2012 to 2014

HS code	4-digit heading of Harmonized System 2002	Value (million US$) 2012	2013	2014	Unit value 2012	2013	2014	Unit	SITC code
	All Commodities	8 025.3	7 433.5	7 830.5					
7102	Diamonds, whether or not worked, but not mounted or set	2 160.3	2 026.5	2 658.3					667
2710	Petroleum oils, other than crude	1 031.1	1 017.2	1 038.5	1.0	*1.0*	1.0	US$/kg	334
8704	Motor vehicles for the transport of goods	236.1	214.7	212.3			*31.8*	thsd US$/unit	782
2716	Electrical energy	236.2	240.2	149.0	*70.2*	*66.1*	17.4	US$/MWh	351
8703	Motor cars and other motor vehicles principally designed for the transport	226.1	189.0	189.2	*19.7*	*19.4*	*5.7*	thsd US$/unit	781
9999	Commodities not specified according to kind	125.7	89.6	91.7					931
3004	Medicaments (excluding goods of heading 30.02, 30.05 or 30.06)	100.6	95.0	83.6	*40.8*	31.9	27.9	US$/kg	542
8431	Parts suitable for use principally with the machinery of headings 84.25	101.6	72.9	71.7	*13.6*	10.3	*9.2*	US$/kg	723
4011	New pneumatic tyres, of rubber	73.3	83.3	67.4			*78.7*	US$/unit	625
8708	Parts and accessories of the motor vehicles of headings 87.01 to 87.05	79.8	70.1	64.7	*13.1*	*10.0*	8.7	US$/kg	784

Brazil

Goods Imports: FOB, by origin | **Goods Exports: FOB, by last known destination** | **Trade System: Special**

Overview:

In 2015, the value of merchandise exports of Brazil decreased substantially by 15.1 percent to reach 191.1 bln US$, while its merchandise imports decreased substantially by 25.2 percent to reach 171.4 bln US$ (see graph 1, table 2 and table 3). The merchandise trade balance recorded a relatively small surplus of 19.7 bln US$ (see graph 1). The largest merchandise trade balance was with MDG Latin America and the Caribbean at 11.5 bln US$ (see graph 4). Merchandise exports in Brazil were diversified amongst partners; imports were also diversified. The top 29 partners accounted for 80 percent or more of exports and 22 partners accounted for 80 percent or more of imports (see graph 5). In 2014, the value of exports of services of Brazil increased slightly by 1.2 percent, reaching 39.6 bln US$, while its imports of services increased slightly by 1.9 percent and reached 87.9 bln US$ (see graph 2). There was a large trade in services deficit of 48.3 bln US$.

Graph 1: Total merchandise trade, by value
(Bln US$ by year)

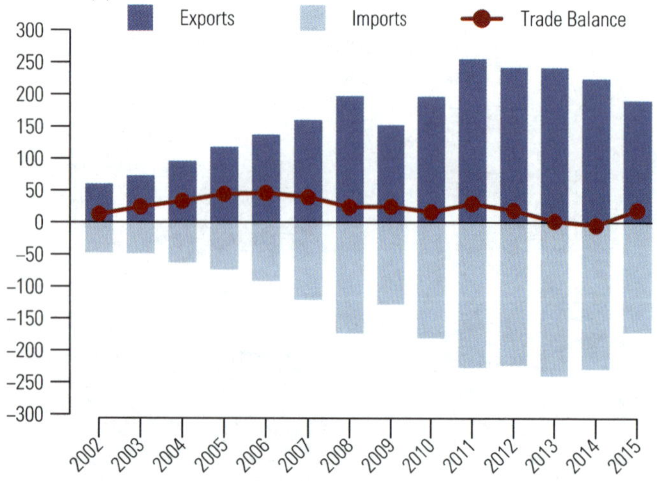

Graph 2: Total services trade, by value
(Bln US$ by year)

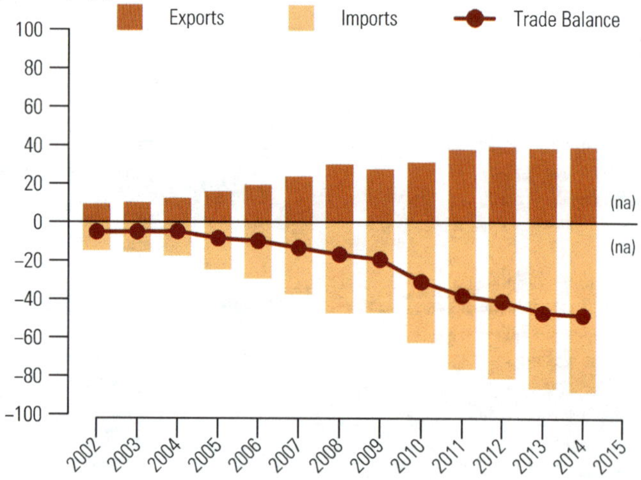

Exports Profile:

"Crude materials + anim. & veg. oils" (SITC section 2+4), "Food, animals + beverages, tobacco" (SITC section 0+1) and "Machinery and transport equipment" (SITC section 7) were the largest commodity groups for exports in 2015, representing respectively 27.2, 25.3 and 16.4 percent of exported goods (see table 2). From 2013 to 2015, the largest export commodity was "Iron ores and concentrates, including roasted iron pyrites" (HS code 2601) (see table 1). The top three destinations for merchandise exports were China, the United States and Argentina, accounting for respectively 18.6, 11.6 and 7.1 percent of total exports. "Other business services" (EBOPS code 268) accounted for the largest share of exports of services in 2014 at 21.4 bln US$, followed by "Travel" (EBOPS code 236) at 6.8 bln US$ and "Communications services" (EBOPS code 245) at 3.3 bln US$ (see graph 3).

Graph 3: Exports of services by EBOPS category
(% share in 2014)

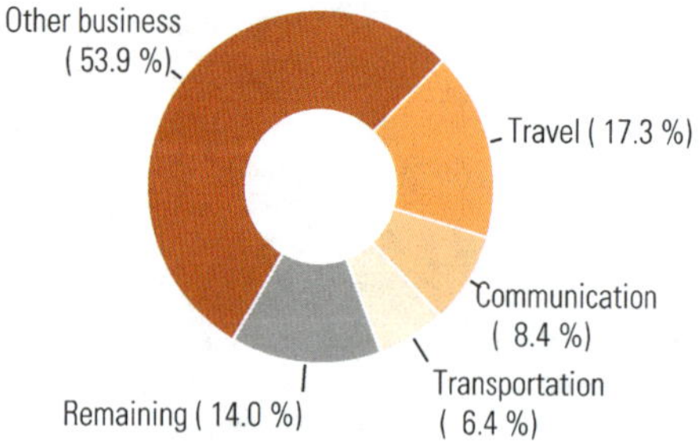

Table 1: Top 10 export commodities 2013 to 2015

HS code	4-digit heading of Harmonized System 2012	Value (million US$) 2013	2014	2015	Unit value 2013	2014	2015	Unit	SITC code
	All Commodities	242 178.1	225 098.4	191 126.9					
2601	Iron ores and concentrates, including roasted iron pyrites	32 491.5	25 819.1	14 076.1	0.1	0.1	0.0	US$/kg	281
1201	Soya beans, whether or not broken	22 810.0	23 277.4	20 983.6	0.5	0.5	*0.4*	US$/kg	222
2709	Petroleum oils and oils obtained from bituminous minerals, crude	12 956.6	16 356.8	11 781.3	0.7	*0.6*	0.3	US$/kg	333
1701	Cane or beet sugar and chemically pure sucrose, in solid form	11 842.5	9 459.2	7 641.5	0.4	0.4	0.3	US$/kg	061
0207	Meat and edible offal, of the poultry of heading 01.05	7 201.4	7 050.1	6 378.9	2.0	1.9	1.6	US$/kg	012
2304	Oil-cake and other solid residues	6 787.3	7 000.6	5 821.1	0.5	0.5	0.4	US$/kg	081
0901	Coffee, whether or not roasted or decaffeinated	4 598.1	6 052.7	5 565.6	2.7	3.0	2.8	US$/kg	071
1005	Maize (corn)	6 307.6	3 931.9	5 009.0	0.2	0.2		US$/kg	044
4703	Chemical wood pulp, soda or sulphate, other than dissolving grades	4 824.8	4 914.4	5 343.3	0.5	0.5	0.5	US$/kg	251
0202	Meat of bovine animals, frozen	4 503.9	4 960.2	3 973.4	4.3	4.5	4.1	US$/kg	011

Services Imports and Exports: EBOPS 2002 categories

Table 2: Merchandise exports by SITC

(Value in million US$, growth and shares in percentage)

SITC	2015	Avg. Growth rates 2011-2015	Avg. Growth rates 2014-2015	2015 share
Total	191 126.9	-7.0	-15.1	100.0
0+1	48 285.0	-4.6	-10.5	25.3
2+4	52 066.6	-9.0	-21.1	27.2
3	13 748.0	-15.4	-33.4	7.2
5	11 440.3	-6.6	-13.5	6.0
6	24 877.1	-3.6	-6.4	13.0
7	31 265.7	-5.3	-5.5	16.4
8	4 102.0	-4.5	-8.8	2.1
9	5 342.3	-7.8	-25.1	2.8

Table 3: Merchandise imports by SITC

(Value in million US$, growth and shares in percentage)

SITC	2015	Avg. Growth rates 2011-2015	Avg. Growth rates 2014-2015	2015 share
Total	171 446.2	-6.7	-25.2	100.0
0+1	7 855.4	-3.7	-20.8	4.6
2+4	4 950.9	-8.5	-15.9	2.9
3	24 919.7	-12.2	-44.7	14.5
5	37 907.9	-2.4	-15.9	22.1
6	18 705.5	-7.7	-23.3	10.9
7	64 050.6	-7.3	-23.1	37.4
8	13 053.1	-1.2	-15.5	7.6
9	3.1	-5.0	-69.3	0.0

SITC Legend

SITC Code	Description
Total	All commodities
0+1	Food, animals + beverages, tobacco
2+4	Crude materials + anim. & veg. oils
3	Mineral fuels, lubricants
5	Chemicals
6	Goods classified chiefly by material
7	Machinery and transport equipment
8	Miscellaneous manufactured articles
9	Not classified elsewhere in the SITC

Graph 4: Merchandise trade balance

(Bln US$ by MDG Regions in 2015)

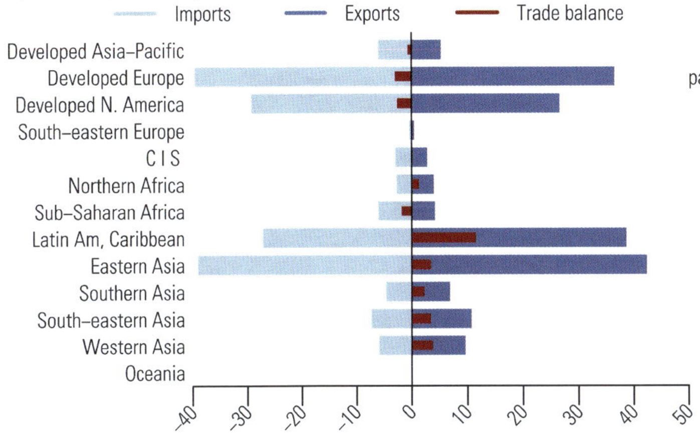

Graph 5: Partner concentration of merchandise trade

(Cumulative share by ranked partners in 2015)

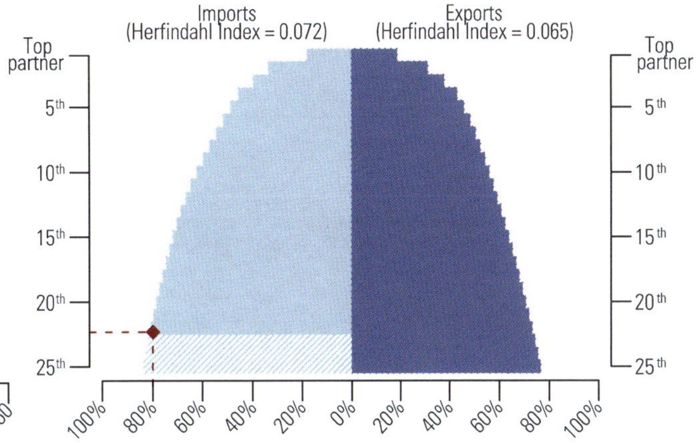

Graph 6: Imports of services by EBOPS category

(% share in 2014)

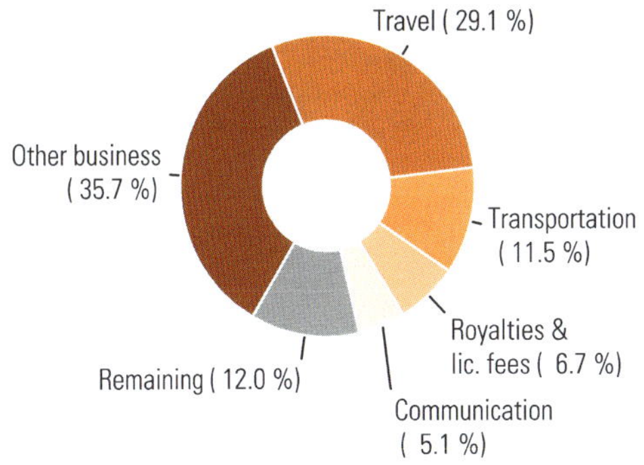

Imports Profile:

"Machinery and transport equipment" (SITC section 7), "Chemicals" (SITC section 5) and "Mineral fuels, lubricants" (SITC section 3) were the largest commodity groups for imports in 2015, representing respectively 37.4, 22.1 and 14.5 percent of imported goods (see table 3). From 2013 to 2015, the largest import commodity was "Petroleum oils, other than crude" (HS code 2710) (see table 4). The top three partners for merchandise imports were China, the United States and Argentina, accounting for respectively 16.5, 15.4 and 6.4 percent of total imports. "Other business services" (EBOPS code 268) accounted for the largest share of imports of services in 2014 at 31.3 bln US$, followed by "Travel" (EBOPS code 236) at 25.6 bln US$ and "Transportation" (EBOPS code 205) at 10.1 bln US$ (see graph 6).

Table 4: Top 10 import commodities 2013 to 2015

HS code	4-digit heading of Harmonized System 2012	Value (million US$) 2013	Value (million US$) 2014	Value (million US$) 2015	Unit value 2013	Unit value 2014	Unit value 2015	Unit	SITC code
	All Commodities	239 620.9	229 060.1	171 446.2					
2710	Petroleum oils, other than crude	17 757.0	17 630.0	8 628.6	*1.0*	*0.9*	*0.6*	US$/kg	334
2709	Petroleum oils and oils obtained from bituminous minerals, crude	16 320.0	15 533.1	7 380.8	0.8	0.8	0.5	US$/kg	333
2711	Petroleum gases and other gaseous hydrocarbons	7 997.9	8 474.6	5 919.3	*0.6*	*0.6*		US$/kg	343
8703	Motor cars and other motor vehicles principally designed for the transport	9 081.2	7 675.6	5 019.5	15.2	16.0	15.7	thsd US$/unit	781
8708	Parts and accessories of the motor vehicles of headings 87.01 to 87.05	8 296.7	7 143.5	5 361.3	*8.0*	*8.1*	*7.7*	US$/kg	784
8517	Electrical apparatus for line telephony or line telegraphy	5 036.2	5 677.0	4 282.8					764
8542	Electronic integrated circuits	4 748.7	4 444.8	2 962.0					776
3004	Medicaments (excluding goods of heading 30.02, 30.05 or 30.06)	3 734.3	3 682.5	3 252.6	*152.1*	*140.5*	*112.0*	US$/kg	542
3808	Insecticides, rodenticides, fungicides, herbicides	2 999.8	3 464.1	3 080.9	*10.6*	*11.8*	*10.5*	US$/kg	591
3002	Human blood; animal blood prepared for therapeutic uses	3 187.0	3 242.9	2 734.4	*315.4*	*343.3*	*315.4*	US$/kg	541

Brunei Darussalam

Goods Imports: CIF, by origin | **Goods Exports: FOB, by last known destination** | **Trade System: Special**

Overview:

In 2014, the value of merchandise exports of Brunei Darussalam decreased moderately by 8.2 percent to reach 10.5 bln US$, while its merchandise imports decreased slightly by 0.4 percent to reach 3.6 bln US$ (see graph 1, table 2 and table 3). The merchandise trade balance recorded a large surplus of 6.9 bln US$ (see graph 1). The largest merchandise trade balance was with MDG Developed Asia-Pacific at 4.9 bln US$ (see graph 4). Merchandise exports in Brunei Darussalam were moderately concentrated amongst partners; imports were diversified. The top 7 partners accounted for 80 percent or more of exports and 8 partners accounted for 80 percent or more of imports (see graph 5). In 2014, the value of exports of services of Brunei Darussalam increased substantially by 13.0 percent, reaching 556.8 mln US$, while its imports of services decreased substantially by 23.5 percent and reached 2.2 bln US$ (see graph 2). There was a large trade in services deficit of 1.6 bln US$.

Graph 1: Total merchandise trade, by value

(Bln US$ by year)

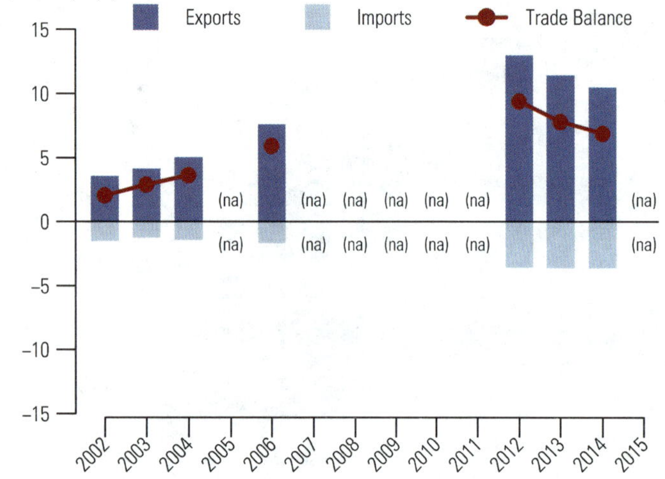

Graph 2: Total services trade, by value

(Bln US$ by year)

Exports Profile:

"Mineral fuels, lubricants" (SITC section 3), "Chemicals" (SITC section 5) and "Machinery and transport equipment" (SITC section 7) were the largest commodity groups for exports in 2014, representing respectively 92.5, 4.5 and 1.4 percent of exported goods (see table 2). From 2012 to 2014, the largest export commodity was "Petroleum gases and other gaseous hydrocarbons" (HS code 2711) (see table 1). The top three destinations for merchandise exports were Japan, the Republic of Korea and India, accounting for respectively 40.6, 14.5 and 8.5 percent of total exports. "Transportation" (EBOPS code 205) accounted for the largest share of exports of services in 2009 at 451.7 mln US$, followed by "Travel" (EBOPS code 236) at 254.4 mln US$ and "Other business services" (EBOPS code 268) at 174.0 mln US$ (see graph 3).

Graph 3: Exports of services by EBOPS category

(% share in 2009)

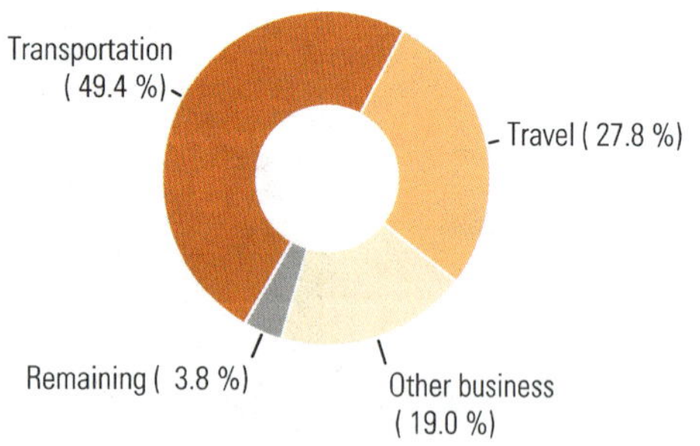

Table 1: Top 10 export commodities 2012 to 2014

HS code	4-digit heading of Harmonized System 2007	Value (million US$)			Unit value				SITC code
		2012	2013	2014	2012	2013	2014	Unit	
	All Commodities	13000.8	11447.2	10508.8					
2711	Petroleum gases and other gaseous hydrocarbons	6176.4	5930.9	5345.8		0.9	0.9	US$/kg	343
2709	Petroleum oils and oils obtained from bituminous minerals, crude	6271.3	5118.0	4378.6	*0.7*	0.9	0.8	US$/kg	333
2905	Acyclic alcohols and their derivatives	243.4	82.0	201.4					512
2936	Provitamins and vitamins, natural or reproduced by synthesis	0.0	0.0	243.1		0.0		thsd US$/kg	541
8803	Parts of goods of heading 88.01 or 88.02	24.1	17.3	23.1		379.0	199.3	US$/kg	792
9999	Commodities not specified according to kind	18.5	17.7	14.6					931
8517	Electrical apparatus for line telephony or line telegraphy	21.4	4.9	11.3					764
8431	Parts suitable for use principally with the machinery of headings 84.25	8.3	10.6	14.0	*22.9*	9.1	12.2	US$/kg	723
7304	Tubes, pipes and hollow profiles, seamless, of iron (other than cast iron)	8.4	19.4	4.9		8.1	2.2	US$/kg	679
8207	Interchangeable tools for hand tools, whether or not power-operated	12.6	11.1	4.4		4.8	11.4	US$/kg	695

Services Imports and Exports: EBOPS 2002 categories

Table 2: Merchandise exports by SITC

(Value in million US$, growth and shares in percentage)

SITC	2014	Avg. Growth rates 2010-2014	Avg. Growth rates 2013-2014	2014 share
Total	10 508.8	...	-8.2	100.0
0+1	40.9	...	123.3	0.4
2+4	14.0	...	14.9	0.1
3	9 724.9	...	-12.0	92.5
5	471.9	...	411.3	4.5
6	53.2	...	-33.0	0.5
7	143.0	...	10.9	1.4
8	46.4	...	-5.0	0.4
9	14.6	...	-18.0	0.1

Table 3: Merchandise imports by SITC

(Value in million US$, growth and shares in percentage)

SITC	2014	Avg. Growth rates 2010-2014	Avg. Growth rates 2013-2014	2014 share
Total	3 598.7	...	-0.4	100.0
0+1	537.9	...	1.7	14.9
2+4	49.9	...	-4.3	1.4
3	365.4	...	34.8	10.2
5	303.6	...	5.4	8.4
6	540.8	...	-26.4	15.0
7	1 387.4	...	4.7	38.6
8	394.8	...	3.1	11.0
9	19.0	...	-35.7	0.5

SITC Legend

SITC Code	Description
Total	All commodities
0+1	Food, animals + beverages, tobacco
2+4	Crude materials + anim. & veg. oils
3	Mineral fuels, lubricants
5	Chemicals
6	Goods classified chiefly by material
7	Machinery and transport equipment
8	Miscellaneous manufactured articles
9	Not classified elsewhere in the SITC

Graph 4: Merchandise trade balance

(Bln US$ by MDG Regions in 2014)

Graph 5: Partner concentration of merchandise trade

(Cumulative share by ranked partners in 2014)

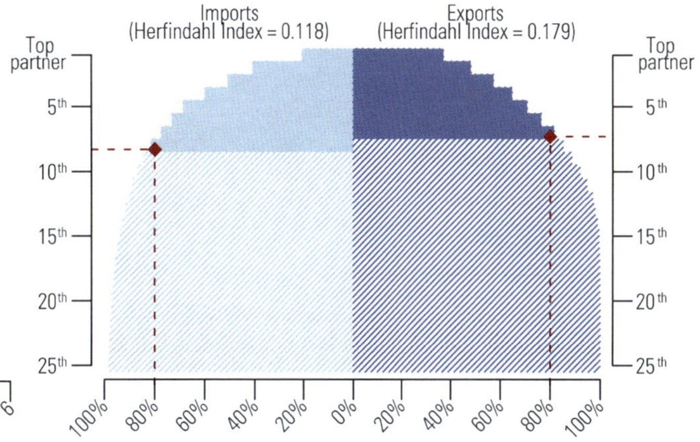

Graph 6: Imports of services by EBOPS category

(% share in 2009)

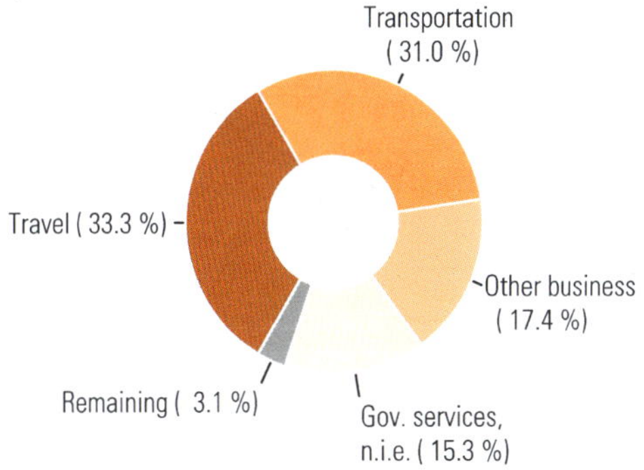

Imports Profile:

"Machinery and transport equipment" (SITC section 7), "Goods classified chiefly by material" (SITC section 6) and "Food, animals + beverages, tobacco" (SITC section 0+1) were the largest commodity groups for imports in 2014, representing respectively 38.6, 15.0 and 14.9 percent of imported goods (see table 3). From 2012 to 2014, the largest import commodity was "Petroleum oils, other than crude" (HS code 2710) (see table 4). The top three partners for merchandise imports were Singapore, Malaysia and China, accounting for respectively 21.0, 20.8 and 10.9 percent of total imports. "Travel" (EBOPS code 236) accounted for the largest share of imports of services in 2009 at 477.1 mln US$, followed by "Transportation" (EBOPS code 205) at 444.7 mln US$ and "Other business services" (EBOPS code 268) at 248.8 mln US$ (see graph 6).

Table 4: Top 10 import commodities 2012 to 2014

HS code	4-digit heading of Harmonized System 2007	Value (million US$) 2012	2013	2014	Unit value 2012	2013	2014	Unit	SITC code
	All Commodities	3 572.2	3 612.4	3 598.7					
2710	Petroleum oils, other than crude	342.7	268.3	362.2		1.1	1.0	US$/kg	334
8703	Motor cars and other motor vehicles principally designed for the transport	303.6	319.4	301.7	*17.5*	17.3	*16.0*	thsd US$/unit	781
7304	Tubes, pipes and hollow profiles, seamless, of iron (other than cast iron)	89.0	88.7	46.0		0.8	2.1	US$/kg	679
8517	Electrical apparatus for line telephony or line telegraphy	54.8	77.6	79.9					764
8901	Cruise ships, excursion boats, ferry-boats, cargo ships, barges	0.0	0.1	209.7			69.9	mln US$/unit	793
2309	Preparations of a kind used in animal feeding	54.4	79.1	58.4	*1.7*	0.8	0.8	US$/kg	081
8481	Taps, cocks, valves and similar appliances for pipes, boiler shells	63.5	66.3	59.1		33.0	30.3	US$/kg	747
7307	Tube or pipe fittings (for example, couplings, elbows, sleeves)	51.3	71.6	41.8		3.5	*3.3*	US$/kg	679
3004	Medicaments (excluding goods of heading 30.02, 30.05 or 30.06)	51.5	52.4	58.7		34.2	34.4	US$/kg	542
7326	Other articles of iron or steel	75.4	45.7	32.2		*1.3*	1.5	US$/kg	699

Bulgaria

Goods Imports: CIF, by consignment	Goods Exports: FOB, by last known destination	Trade System: Special

Overview:

In 2015, the value of merchandise exports of Bulgaria decreased substantially by 12.3 percent to reach 25.8 bln US$, while its merchandise imports decreased substantially by 15.8 percent to reach 29.3 bln US$ (see graph 1, table 2 and table 3). The merchandise trade balance recorded a relatively small deficit of 3.5 bln US$ (see graph 1). The largest merchandise trade balance was with MDG CIS at -3.3 bln US$ (see graph 4). Merchandise exports in Bulgaria were diversified amongst partners; imports were also diversified. The top 21 partners accounted for 80 percent or more of exports and 16 partners accounted for 80 percent or more of imports (see graph 5). In 2014, the value of exports of services of Bulgaria increased substantially by 14.6 percent, reaching 8.5 bln US$, while its imports of services increased substantially by 30.4 percent and reached 5.5 bln US$ (see graph 2). There was a moderate trade in services surplus of 3.0 bln US$.

Graph 1: Total merchandise trade, by value

(Bln US$ by year)

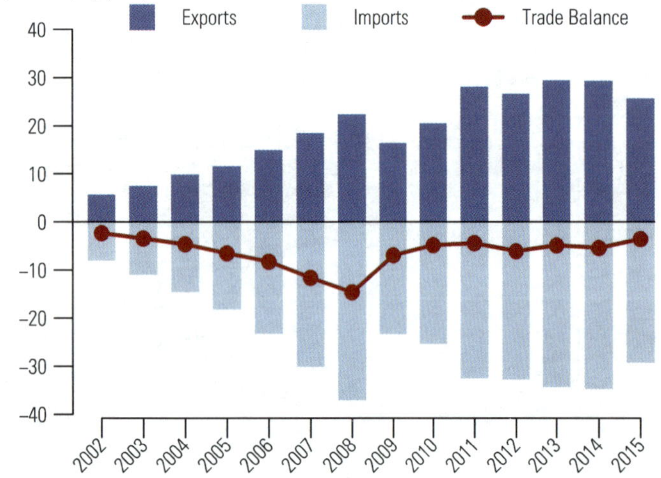

Graph 2: Total services trade, by value

(Bln US$ by year)

Exports Profile:

"Goods classified chiefly by material" (SITC section 6), "Machinery and transport equipment" (SITC section 7) and "Miscellaneous manufactured articles" (SITC section 8) were the largest commodity groups for exports in 2015, representing respectively 21.9, 20.4 and 13.6 percent of exported goods (see table 2). From 2013 to 2015, the largest export commodity was "Petroleum oils, other than crude" (HS code 2710) (see table 1). The top three destinations for merchandise exports were Germany, Turkey and Italy, accounting for respectively 12.3, 9.0 and 8.9 percent of total exports. "Travel" (EBOPS code 236) accounted for the largest share of exports of services in 2014 at 4.0 bln US$, followed by "Transportation" (EBOPS code 205) at 2.1 bln US$ and "Other business services" (EBOPS code 268) at 1.0 bln US$ (see graph 3).

Graph 3: Exports of services by EBOPS category

(% share in 2014)

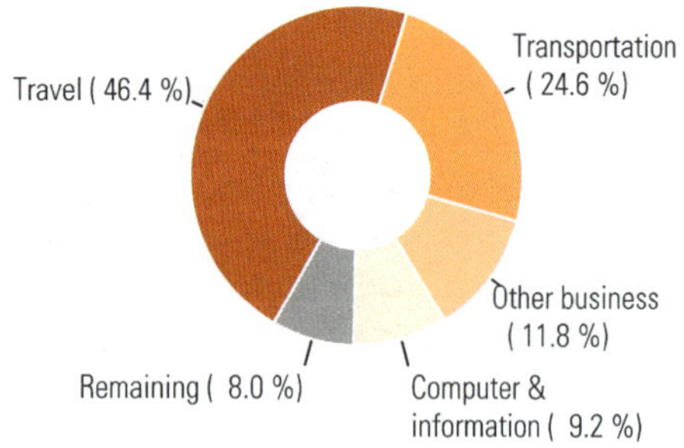

Table 1: Top 10 export commodities 2013 to 2015

HS code	4-digit heading of Harmonized System 2012	Value (million US$) 2013	2014	2015	Unit value 2013	2014	2015	Unit	SITC code
	All Commodities	29 510.6	29 386.5	25 778.7					
2710	Petroleum oils, other than crude	3 855.0	2 718.7	1 713.8	0.8	0.8	0.5	US$/kg	334
7403	Refined copper and copper alloys, unwrought	1 479.6	1 362.6	1 175.0	7.4	6.9	5.6	US$/kg	682
7402	Unrefined copper; copper anodes for electrolytic refining	1 028.0	924.8	761.0	8.5	8.0	6.4	US$/kg	682
9999	Commodities not specified according to kind	678.6	915.3	998.1					931
3004	Medicaments (excluding goods of heading 30.02, 30.05 or 30.06)	780.7	939.8	806.1	*52.5*	57.5	*46.7*	US$/kg	542
1001	Wheat and meslin	950.7	691.3	652.9	0.3	0.2	0.2	US$/kg	041
1206	Sunflower seeds, whether or not broken	741.8	496.3	402.5	0.6	0.6	0.6	US$/kg	222
2716	Electrical energy	452.8	526.6	601.3	59.0	57.7	44.9	US$/MWh	351
8544	Insulated (including enamelled or anodised) wire, cable	374.2	464.3	485.7	*13.8*	*14.8*	*12.5*	US$/kg	773
1005	Maize (corn)	490.4	386.4	214.2	0.2	0.2		US$/kg	044

Services Imports and Exports: EBOPS 2002 categories

Table 2: Merchandise exports by SITC

(Value in million US$, growth and shares in percentage)

SITC	2015	Avg. Growth rates 2011-2015	2014-2015	2015 share
Total	25778.7	-2.2	-12.3	100.0
0+1	3165.4	0.0	-14.4	12.3
2+4	1941.1	-10.4	-19.3	7.5
3	2736.6	-7.3	-26.1	10.6
5	2501.4	3.5	-4.8	9.7
6	5647.3	-5.1	-13.0	21.9
7	5262.7	3.1	-5.3	20.4
8	3506.1	-1.0	-11.4	13.6
9	1018.2	5.0	7.7	3.9

Table 3: Merchandise imports by SITC

(Value in million US$, growth and shares in percentage)

SITC	2015	Avg. Growth rates 2011-2015	2014-2015	2015 share
Total	29265.1	-2.6	-15.8	100.0
0+1	2592.0	-1.9	-9.1	8.9
2+4	2574.5	-6.3	-14.9	8.8
3	4555.9	-11.7	-34.4	15.6
5	3963.5	2.6	-7.7	13.5
6	4751.7	-3.0	-19.3	16.2
7	7321.7	0.8	-9.7	25.0
8	2091.0	1.6	-8.5	7.1
9	1414.8	12.6	5.3	4.8

SITC Legend

SITC Code	Description
Total	All commodities
0+1	Food, animals + beverages, tobacco
2+4	Crude materials + anim. & veg. oils
3	Mineral fuels, lubricants
5	Chemicals
6	Goods classified chiefly by material
7	Machinery and transport equipment
8	Miscellaneous manufactured articles
9	Not classified elsewhere in the SITC

Graph 4: Merchandise trade balance

(Bln US$ by MDG Regions in 2015)

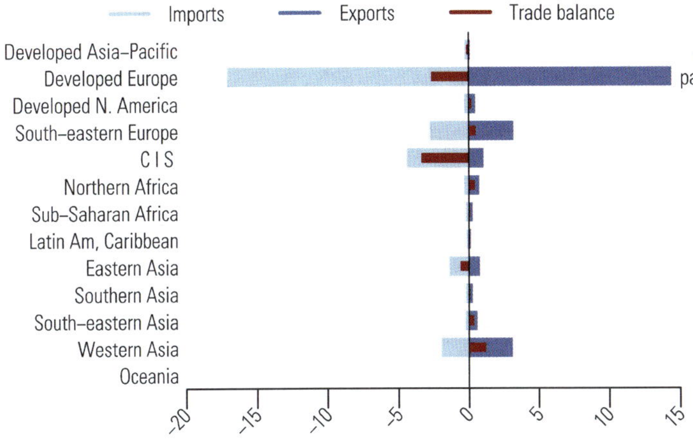

Graph 5: Partner concentration of merchandise trade

(Cumulative share by ranked partners in 2015)

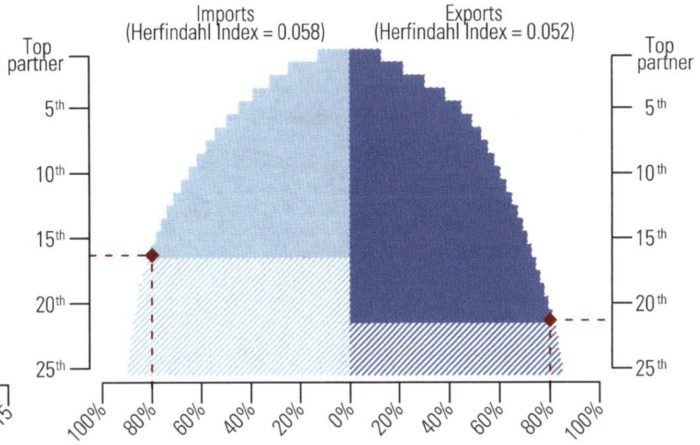

Graph 6: Imports of services by EBOPS category

(% share in 2014)

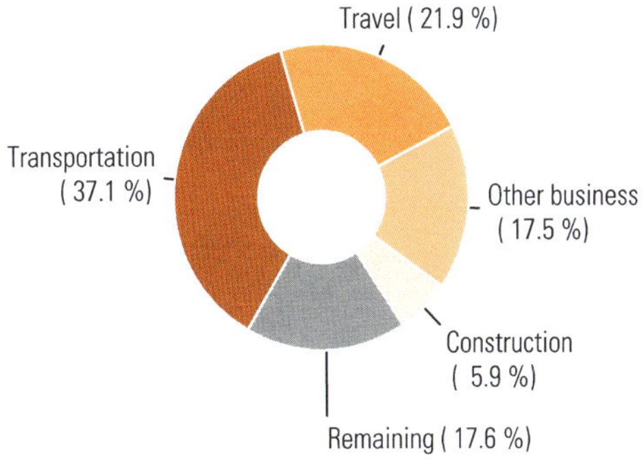

Imports Profile:

"Machinery and transport equipment" (SITC section 7), "Goods classified chiefly by material" (SITC section 6) and "Mineral fuels, lubricants" (SITC section 3) were the largest commodity groups for imports in 2015, representing respectively 25.0, 16.2 and 15.6 percent of imported goods (see table 3). From 2013 to 2015, the largest import commodity was "Petroleum oils and oils obtained from bituminous minerals, crude" (HS code 2709) (see table 4). The top three partners for merchandise imports were the Russian Federation, Germany and Italy, accounting for respectively 15.4, 11.9 and 7.3 percent of total imports. "Transportation" (EBOPS code 205) accounted for the largest share of imports of services in 2014 at 2.0 bln US$, followed by "Travel" (EBOPS code 236) at 1.2 bln US$ and "Other business services" (EBOPS code 268) at 961.2 mln US$ (see graph 6).

Table 4: Top 10 import commodities 2013 to 2015

HS code	4-digit heading of Harmonized System 2012	Value (million US$) 2013	2014	2015	Unit value 2013	2014	2015	Unit	SITC code
	All Commodities	34316.6	34740.0	29265.1					
2709	Petroleum oils and oils obtained from bituminous minerals, crude	4487.7	3515.4	2245.0	0.8	0.7	0.4	US$/kg	333
2603	Copper ores and concentrates	1951.0	1601.0	1337.8	1.9	1.8	1.4	US$/kg	283
2710	Petroleum oils, other than crude	1710.2	1496.1	727.3	*0.9*	*0.8*	*0.5*	US$/kg	334
9999	Commodities not specified according to kind	1028.8	1325.5	1400.6					931
2711	Petroleum gases and other gaseous hydrocarbons	1283.2	1265.9	1043.3	*0.6*	0.6	0.4	US$/kg	343
3004	Medicaments (excluding goods of heading 30.02, 30.05 or 30.06)	1002.2	1136.1	997.2	*62.6*	*59.0*	*49.4*	US$/kg	542
8703	Motor cars and other motor vehicles principally designed for the transport	761.4	826.9	808.2	10.2	12.4	10.6	thsd US$/unit	781
8517	Electrical apparatus for line telephony or line telegraphy	443.9	540.5	484.9					764
8701	Tractors (other than tractors of heading 87.09)	361.7	369.1	410.1	42.3	40.7	42.3	thsd US$/unit	722
7404	Copper waste and scrap	374.5	384.3	307.1	6.7	6.4	5.1	US$/kg	288

Source: UN Comtrade

Burkina Faso

Goods Imports: CIF, by origin | **Goods Exports: FOB, by last known destination** | **Trade System: General**

Overview:

In 2014, the value of merchandise exports of Burkina Faso increased moderately by 7.4 percent to reach 2.8 bln US$, while its merchandise imports decreased substantially by 18.1 percent to reach 3.6 bln US$ (see graph 1, table 2 and table 3). The merchandise trade balance recorded a moderate deficit of 729.5 mln US$ (see graph 1). The largest merchandise trade balance was with MDG Sub-Saharan Africa at -1.1 bln US$ (see graph 4). Merchandise exports in Burkina Faso were highly concentrated amongst partners; imports were diversified. The top 7 partners accounted for 80 percent or more of exports and 12 partners accounted for 80 percent or more of imports (see graph 5). In 2014, the value of exports of services of Burkina Faso decreased slightly by 3.8 percent, reaching 458.4 mln US$, while its imports of services decreased moderately by 10.0 percent and reached 1.3 bln US$ (see graph 2). There was a large trade in services deficit of 810.3 mln US$.

Graph 1: Total merchandise trade, by value

(Bln US$ by year)

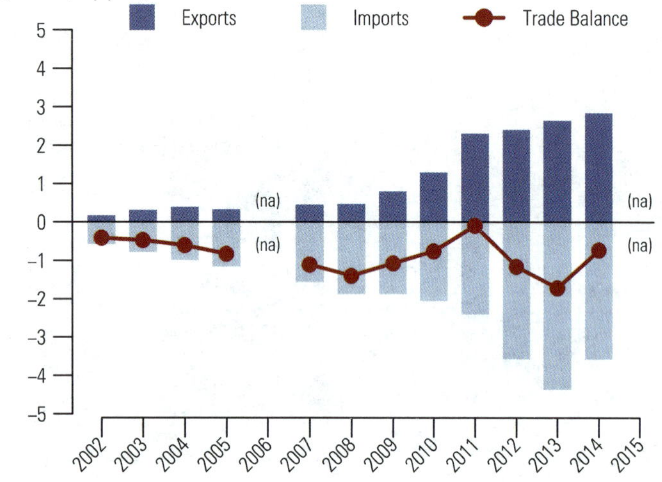

Graph 2: Total services trade, by value

(Bln US$ by year)

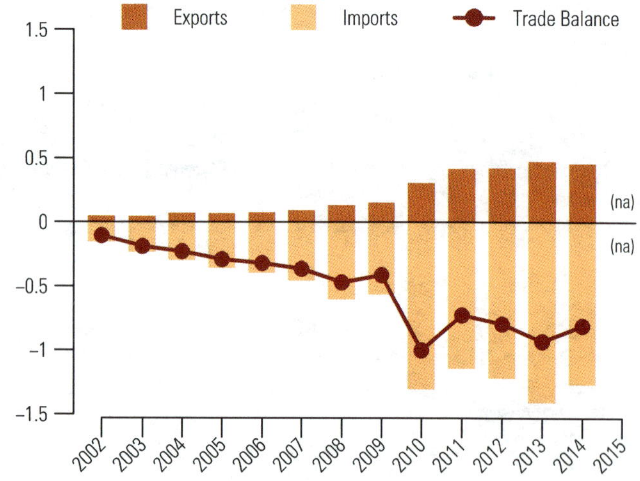

Exports Profile:

"Not classified elsewhere in the SITC" (SITC section 9), "Crude materials + anim. & veg. oils" (SITC section 2+4) and "Mineral fuels, lubricants" (SITC section 3) were the largest commodity groups for exports in 2014, representing respectively 51.4, 25.5 and 9.7 percent of exported goods (see table 2). From 2012 to 2014, the largest export commodity was "Gold (including gold plated with platinum)" (HS code 7108) (see table 1). The top three destinations for merchandise exports were Switzerland, Mali and South Africa, accounting for respectively 53.3, 6.5 and 6.1 percent of total exports. "Travel" (EBOPS code 236) accounted for the largest share of exports of services in 2014 at 134.8 mln US$, followed by "Construction services" (EBOPS code 249) at 86.3 mln US$ and "Financial services" (EBOPS code 260) at 75.1 mln US$ (see graph 3).

Graph 3: Exports of services by EBOPS category

(% share in 2014)

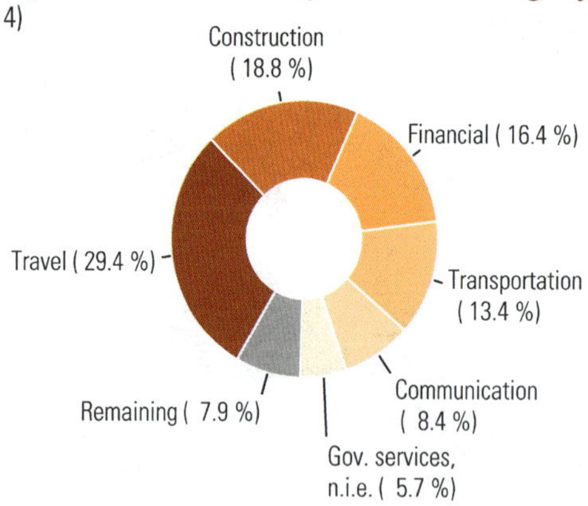

Table 1: Top 10 export commodities 2012 to 2014

HS code	4-digit heading of Harmonized System 2007	Value (million US$) 2012	2013	2014	Unit value 2012	2013	2014	Unit	SITC code
	All Commodities	2411.0	2650.5	2845.6					
7108	Gold (including gold plated with platinum)	1582.3	1484.4	1462.9	44.5	38.1	34.4	thsd US$/kg	971
5201	Cotton, not carded or combed	294.3	439.3	494.9	1.6	1.6	1.6	US$/kg	263
2710	Petroleum oils, other than crude	141.6	231.4	275.3	1.0	1.1	1.1	US$/kg	334
1207	Other oil seeds and oleaginous fruits, whether or not broken	109.1	207.2	194.5	0.6	0.7	0.6	US$/kg	222
0801	Coconuts, Brazil nuts and cashew nuts, fresh or dried	33.2	52.2	43.2					057
7901	Unwrought zinc	...	25.4	87.2					686
8502	Electric generating sets and rotary converters	60.5	0.3	1.5					716
8429	Self-propelled bulldozers, angledozers, graders, levellers, scrapers	9.8	13.5	29.5					723
8430	Other moving, grading, levelling, scraping, excavating, tamping, compacting	14.9	15.2	15.9					723
8704	Motor vehicles for the transport of goods	6.4	4.7	21.8					782

Services Imports and Exports: EBOPS 2002 categories

Table 2: Merchandise exports by SITC

(Value in million US$, growth and shares in percentage)

SITC	2014	Avg. Growth rates 2010-2014	Avg. Growth rates 2013-2014	2014 share
Total	2 845.6	21.9	7.4	100.0
0+1	101.7	14.2	6.4	3.6
2+4	724.4	23.9	9.6	25.5
3	275.3	503.1	19.0	9.7
5	12.0	22.0	1.6	0.4
6	130.8	66.4	98.9	4.6
7	123.1	83.8	46.1	4.3
8	15.4	44.6	-5.2	0.5
9	1 462.9	13.4	-1.4	51.4

Table 3: Merchandise imports by SITC

(Value in million US$, growth and shares in percentage)

SITC	2014	Avg. Growth rates 2010-2014	Avg. Growth rates 2013-2014	2014 share
Total	3 575.1	14.9	-18.1	100.0
0+1	415.6	9.5	-13.1	11.6
2+4	65.4	7.6	-20.3	1.8
3	1 118.3	25.5	-1.6	31.3
5	505.2	15.5	-15.7	14.1
6	576.0	10.8	-23.0	16.1
7	731.4	11.7	-35.7	20.5
8	163.2	6.9	-10.7	4.6
9	0.0	35.4	20.4	0.0

SITC Legend

SITC Code	Description
Total	All commodities
0+1	Food, animals + beverages, tobacco
2+4	Crude materials + anim. & veg. oils
3	Mineral fuels, lubricants
5	Chemicals
6	Goods classified chiefly by material
7	Machinery and transport equipment
8	Miscellaneous manufactured articles
9	Not classified elsewhere in the SITC

Graph 4: Merchandise trade balance

(Bln US$ by MDG Regions in 2014)

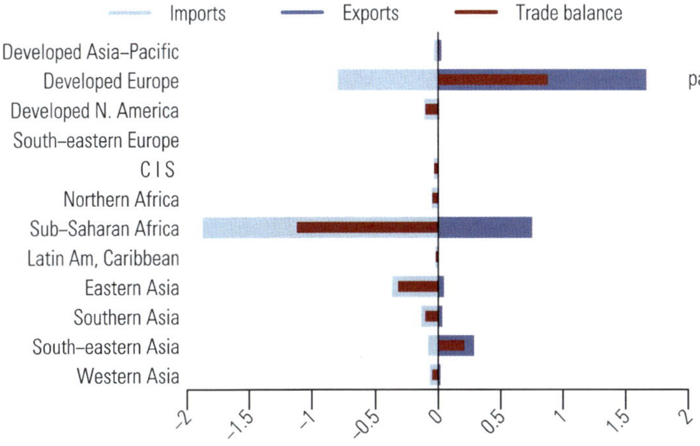

Graph 5: Partner concentration of merchandise trade

(Cumulative share by ranked partners in 2014)

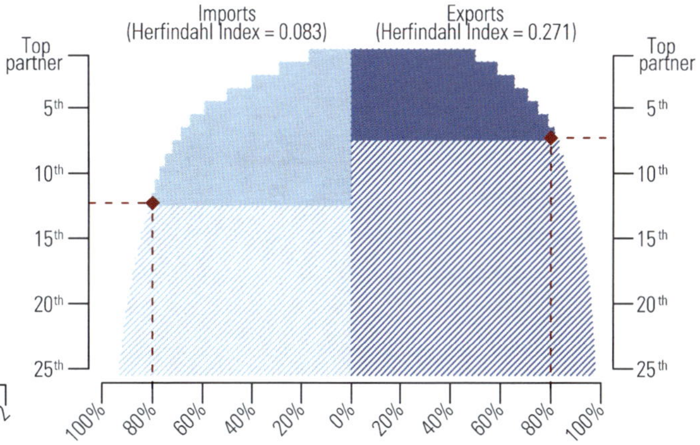

Graph 6: Imports of services by EBOPS category

(% share in 2014)

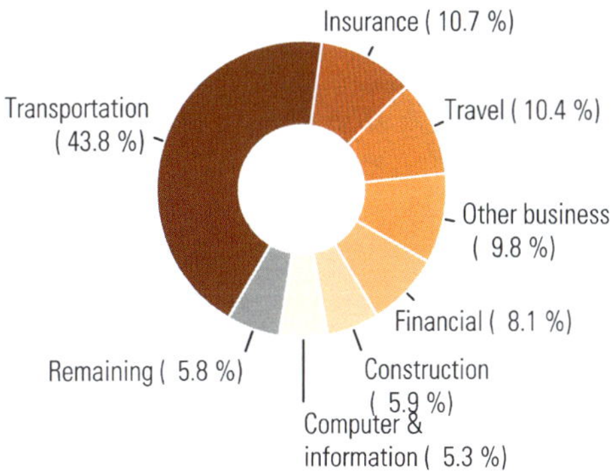

Imports Profile:

"Mineral fuels, lubricants" (SITC section 3), "Machinery and transport equipment" (SITC section 7) and "Goods classified chiefly by material" (SITC section 6) were the largest commodity groups for imports in 2014, representing respectively 31.3, 20.5 and 16.1 percent of imported goods (see table 3). From 2012 to 2014, the largest import commodity was "Petroleum oils, other than crude" (HS code 2710) (see table 4). The top three partners for merchandise imports were Côte d'Ivoire, France and China, accounting for respectively 11.5, 9.3 and 9.2 percent of total imports. "Transportation" (EBOPS code 205) accounted for the largest share of imports of services in 2014 at 555.7 mln US$, followed by "Insurance services" (EBOPS code 253) at 136.2 mln US$ and "Travel" (EBOPS code 236) at 132.1 mln US$ (see graph 6).

Table 4: Top 10 import commodities 2012 to 2014

HS code	4-digit heading of Harmonized System 2007	Value (million US$) 2012	2013	2014	Unit value 2012	2013	2014	Unit	SITC code
	All Commodities	3 568.0	4 365.4	3 575.1					
2710	Petroleum oils, other than crude	867.8	1 071.9	1 049.6	1.0	1.1	1.0	US$/kg	334
3004	Medicaments (excluding goods of heading 30.02, 30.05 or 30.06)	100.0	176.9	155.8	16.2	18.4	24.4	US$/kg	542
1006	Rice	115.1	125.4	99.1	0.3	0.3	0.3	US$/kg	042
2523	Portland cement, aluminous cement, slag cement	93.1	108.9	95.0	0.1	0.1	0.1	US$/kg	661
8703	Motor cars and other motor vehicles principally designed for the transport	86.0	93.3	82.7	*22.8*	*21.5*	*21.2*	thsd US$/unit	781
3105	Mineral or chemical fertilisers	86.0	101.7	58.9	0.7	0.7	0.5	US$/kg	562
8704	Motor vehicles for the transport of goods	81.8	93.3	45.9					782
7213	Bars and rods, hot-rolled, in irregularly wound coils	69.4	58.0	72.8	0.7	0.6	0.5	US$/kg	676
8711	Motorcycles (including mopeds) and cycles fitted with an auxiliary motor	71.4	70.8	57.8			*2.1*	thsd US$/unit	785
8429	Self-propelled bulldozers, angledozers, graders, levellers, scrapers	61.8	89.5	30.8					723

Burundi

Goods Imports: CIF, by origin | **Goods Exports: FOB, by last known destination** | **Trade System: General**

Overview:

In 2015, the value of merchandise exports of Burundi decreased substantially by 19.6 percent to reach 113.8 mln US$, while its merchandise imports decreased substantially by 16.7 percent to reach 560.6 mln US$ (see graph 1, table 2 and table 3). The merchandise trade balance recorded a large deficit of 446.8 mln US$ (see graph 1). The largest merchandise trade balance was with MDG Sub-Saharan Africa at -97.0 mln US$ (see graph 4). Merchandise exports in Burundi were diversified amongst partners; imports were also diversified. The top 7 partners accounted for 80 percent or more of exports and 13 partners accounted for 80 percent or more of imports (see graph 5). In 2013, the value of exports of services of Burundi increased substantially by 41.4 percent, reaching 131.2 mln US$, while its imports of services increased substantially by 10.7 percent and reached 234.1 mln US$ (see graph 2). There was a moderate trade in services deficit of 102.9 mln US$.

Graph 1: Total merchandise trade, by value

(Bln US$ by year)

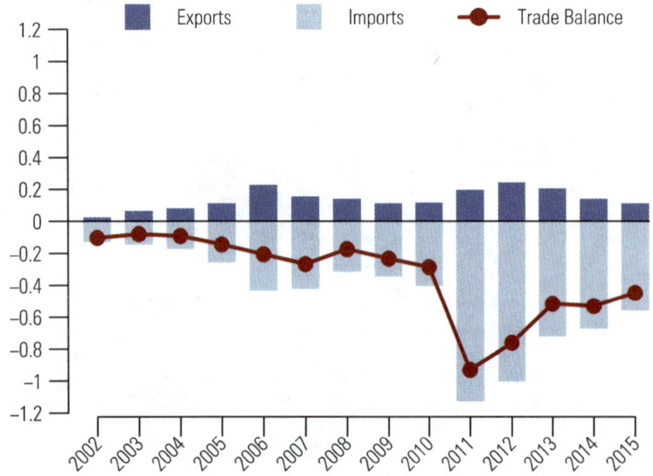

Graph 2: Total services trade, by value

(Mln US$ by year)

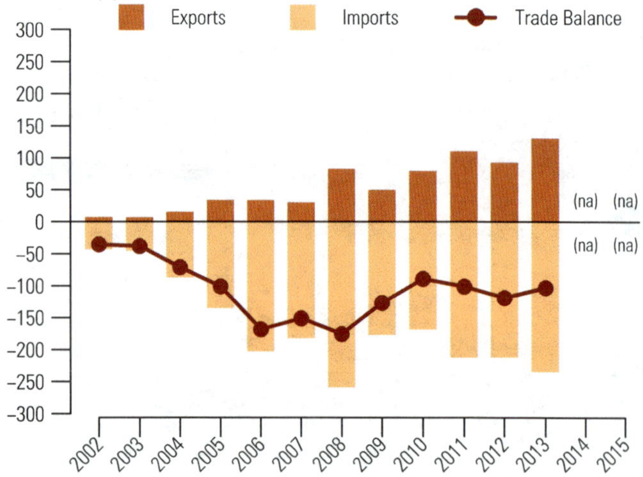

Exports Profile:

"Food, animals + beverages, tobacco" (SITC section 0+1), "Not classified elsewhere in the SITC" (SITC section 9) and "Goods classified chiefly by material" (SITC section 6) were the largest commodity groups for exports in 2015, representing respectively 62.5, 12.1 and 7.3 percent of exported goods (see table 2). From 2013 to 2015, the largest export commodity was "Gold (including gold plated with platinum)" (HS code 7108) (see table 1). The top three destinations for merchandise exports were the United Arab Emirates, Democratic Republic of the Congo and Switzerland, accounting for respectively 34.5, 14.9 and 13.3 percent of total exports. "Government services, n.i.e." (EBOPS code 291) accounted for the largest share of exports of services in 2013 at 98.9 mln US$, followed by "Communications services" (EBOPS code 245) at 12.8 mln US$ (see graph 3).

Graph 3: Exports of services by EBOPS category

(% share in 2013)

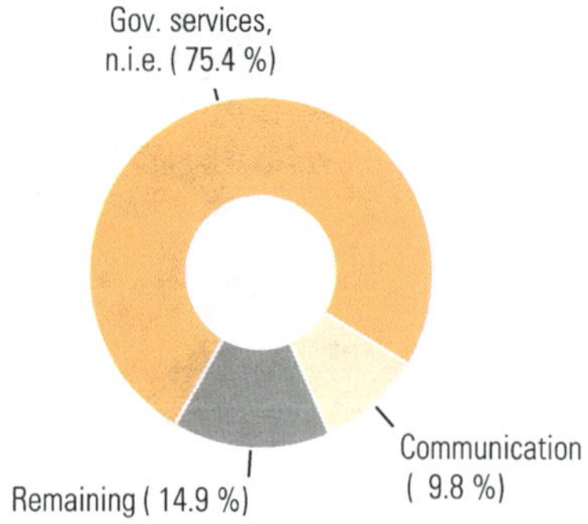

Table 1: Top 10 export commodities 2013 to 2015

HS code	4-digit heading of Harmonized System 2007	Value (million US$) 2013	2014	2015	Unit value 2013	2014	2015	Unit	SITC code
	All Commodities	205.7	141.5	113.8					
7108	Gold (including gold plated with platinum)	119.8	24.4	13.8	41.1	36.2	35.3	thsd US$/kg	971
0901	Coffee, whether or not roasted or decaffeinated	28.7	51.7	38.4	2.4	3.6	2.9	US$/kg	071
0902	Tea, whether or not flavoured	14.5	13.5	14.1	1.4	1.3	1.4	US$/kg	074
3401	Soap; organic surface-active products	7.9	7.3	6.1	1.0	1.1	0.8	US$/kg	554
2203	Beer made from malt	2.7	5.5	6.1	*0.5*	*0.5*	*0.9*	US$/litre	112
1101	Wheat or meslin flour	2.9	4.6	5.6	0.8	0.8	0.7	US$/kg	046
2402	Cigars, cheroots, cigarillos and cigarettes	4.1	3.2	5.3	7.5	7.0	6.6	US$/kg	122
3923	Articles for the conveyance or packing of goods, of plastics	0.0	5.6	3.9	0.9	3.6	4.0	US$/kg	893
7010	Carboys, bottles, flasks, jars, pots, phials, ampoules	0.1	3.8	3.9	1.0	1.9	2.2	US$/kg	665
2615	Niobium, tantalum, vanadium or zirconium ores and concentrates	2.7	1.7	1.4	35.3	23.6	14.4	US$/kg	287

Services Imports and Exports: EBOPS 2002 categories

Table 2: Merchandise exports by SITC

(Value in million US$, growth and shares in percentage)

SITC	2015	Avg. Growth rates 2011-2015	Avg. Growth rates 2014-2015	2015 share
Total	113.8	-12.9	-19.6	100.0
0+1	71.1	-6.3	-11.5	62.5
2+4	5.1	-27.2	24.7	4.5
3	0.4	-10.1	-39.7	0.4
5	6.9	10.7	-19.6	6.0
6	8.3	5.6	-20.7	7.3
7	2.9	-33.6	-53.6	2.6
8	5.3	50.7	-20.2	4.7
9	13.8	-30.6	-43.6	12.1

Table 3: Merchandise imports by SITC

(Value in million US$, growth and shares in percentage)

SITC	2015	Avg. Growth rates 2011-2015	Avg. Growth rates 2014-2015	2015 share
Total	560.6	-16.0	-16.7	100.0
0+1	62.5	-19.4	-17.9	11.2
2+4	21.1	-39.6	3.2	3.8
3	115.1	-22.9	-29.7	20.5
5	87.7	-1.0	-8.9	15.6
6	78.4	-16.5	-20.6	14.0
7	148.2	-3.5	-17.2	26.4
8	46.9	-2.0	27.7	8.4
9	0.6	-57.6	-57.5	0.1

SITC Legend

SITC Code	Description
Total	All commodities
0+1	Food, animals + beverages, tobacco
2+4	Crude materials + anim. & veg. oils
3	Mineral fuels, lubricants
5	Chemicals
6	Goods classified chiefly by material
7	Machinery and transport equipment
8	Miscellaneous manufactured articles
9	Not classified elsewhere in the SITC

Graph 4: Merchandise trade balance

(Mln US$ by MDG Regions in 2015)

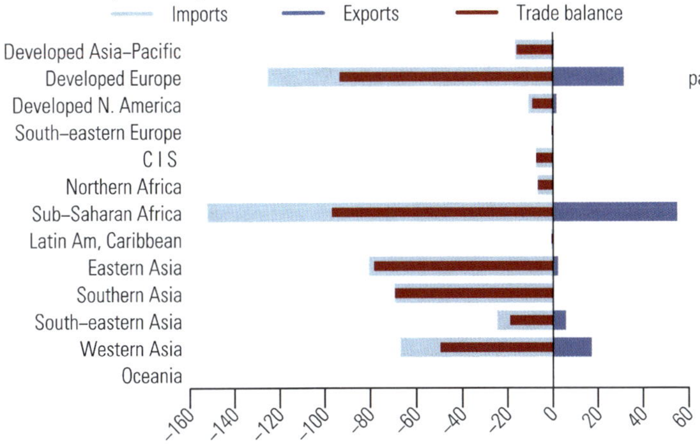

Graph 5: Partner concentration of merchandise trade

(Cumulative share by ranked partners in 2015)

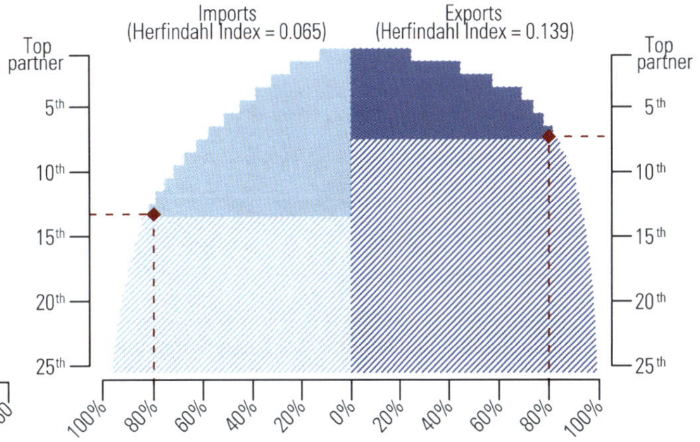

Graph 6: Imports of services by EBOPS category

(% share in 2013)

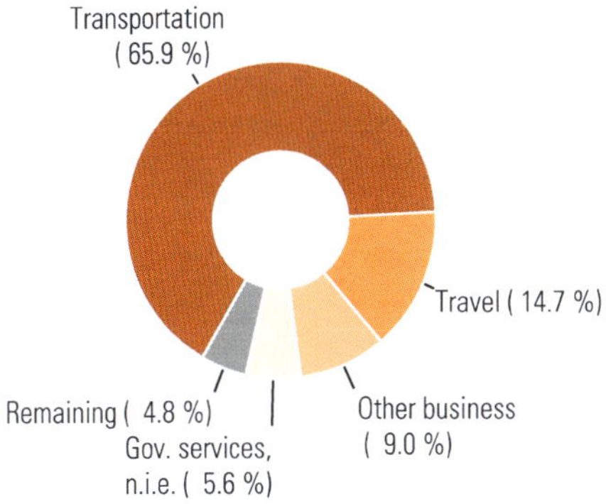

Imports Profile:

"Machinery and transport equipment" (SITC section 7), "Mineral fuels, lubricants" (SITC section 3) and "Chemicals" (SITC section 5) were the largest commodity groups for imports in 2015, representing respectively 26.4, 20.5 and 15.6 percent of imported goods (see table 3). From 2013 to 2015, the largest import commodity was "Petroleum oils, other than crude" (HS code 2710) (see table 4). The top three partners for merchandise imports were India, China and Saudi Arabia, accounting for respectively 11.2, 10.5 and 10.0 percent of total imports. "Transportation" (EBOPS code 205) accounted for the largest share of imports of services in 2013 at 154.2 mln US$, followed by "Travel" (EBOPS code 236) at 34.5 mln US$ and "Other business services" (EBOPS code 268) at 21.1 mln US$ (see graph 6).

Table 4: Top 10 import commodities 2013 to 2015

HS code	4-digit heading of Harmonized System 2007	Value (million US$) 2013	Value (million US$) 2014	Value (million US$) 2015	Unit value 2013	Unit value 2014	Unit value 2015	Unit	SITC code
	All Commodities	721.7	672.6	560.6					
2710	Petroleum oils, other than crude	162.8	160.9	112.6	1.3	1.3	0.9	US$/kg	334
3004	Medicaments (excluding goods of heading 30.02, 30.05 or 30.06)	41.8	37.2	34.1	10.6	10.4	9.6	US$/kg	542
8703	Motor cars and other motor vehicles principally designed for the transport	19.9	28.6	15.9	*11.3*	*17.2*		thsd US$/unit	781
8517	Electrical apparatus for line telephony or line telegraphy	11.8	18.7	32.8					764
8704	Motor vehicles for the transport of goods	8.1	27.4	15.9					782
2523	Portland cement, aluminous cement, slag cement	20.6	19.7	10.3	0.1	0.1	0.1	US$/kg	661
3105	Mineral or chemical fertilisers	18.7	17.6	13.0	0.8	0.7	0.7	US$/kg	562
1001	Wheat and meslin	14.6	19.0	9.6	0.4	0.3	0.3	US$/kg	041
3002	Human blood; animal blood prepared for therapeutic uses	10.3	7.8	14.4	160.3	92.6	218.1	US$/kg	541
8429	Self-propelled bulldozers, angledozers, graders, levellers, scrapers	0.3	14.5	17.0	*56.0*			thsd US$/unit	723

Cabo Verde

Goods Imports: CIF, by origin | **Goods Exports: FOB, by last known destination** | **Trade System: General**

Overview:

In 2015, the value of merchandise exports of Cabo Verde decreased substantially by 39.7 percent to reach 215.2 mln US$, while its merchandise imports decreased substantially by 21.1 percent to reach 606.3 mln US$ (see graph 1, table 2 and table 3). The merchandise trade balance recorded a large deficit of 391.1 mln US$ (see graph 1). The largest merchandise trade balance was with MDG Developed Europe at -320.8 mln US$ (see graph 4). Merchandise exports in Cabo Verde were moderately concentrated amongst partners; imports were also moderately concentrated. The top 4 partners accounted for 80 percent or more of exports and 9 partners accounted for 80 percent or more of imports (see graph 5). In 2014, the value of exports of services of Cabo Verde decreased slightly by 2.7 percent, reaching 626.7 mln US$, while its imports of services increased moderately by 6.4 percent and reached 351.1 mln US$ (see graph 2). There was a moderate trade in services surplus of 275.6 mln US$.

Graph 1: Total merchandise trade, by value
(Mln US$ by year)

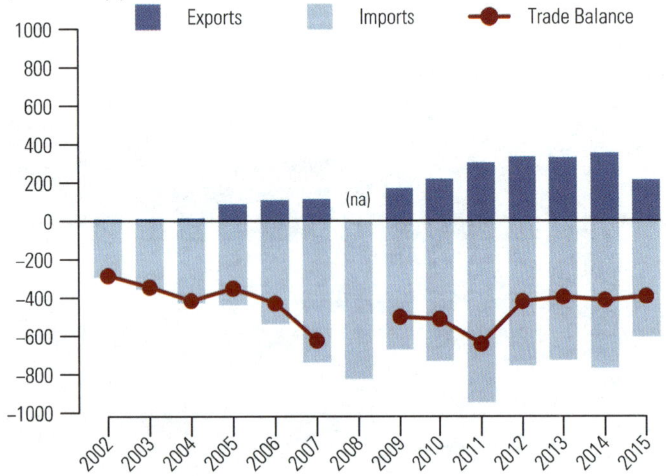

Graph 2: Total services trade, by value
(Mln US$ by year)

Exports Profile:

"Food, animals + beverages, tobacco" (SITC section 0+1), "Mineral fuels, lubricants" (SITC section 3) and "Machinery and transport equipment" (SITC section 7) were the largest commodity groups for exports in 2015, representing respectively 39.8, 36.9 and 16.4 percent of exported goods (see table 2). From 2013 to 2015, the largest export commodity was "Petroleum oils, other than crude" (HS code 2710) (see table 1). The top three destinations for merchandise exports were Portugal, Areas nes and Spain, accounting for respectively 28.7, 27.8 and 18.9 percent of total exports. "Travel" (EBOPS code 236) accounted for the largest share of exports of services in 2014 at 404.9 mln US$, followed by "Transportation" (EBOPS code 205) at 114.9 mln US$ (see graph 3).

Graph 3: Exports of services by EBOPS category
(% share in 2014)

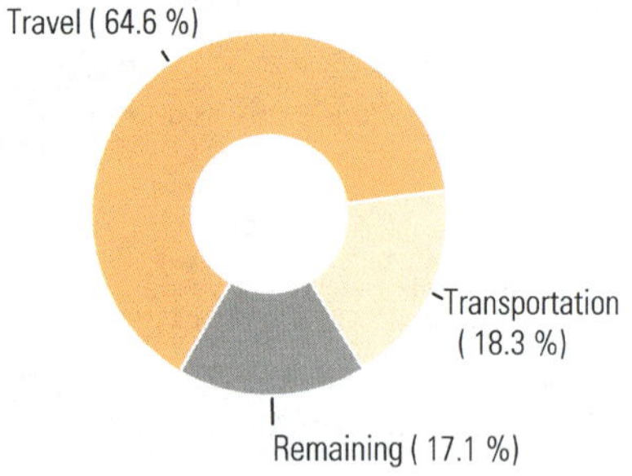

Table 1: Top 10 export commodities 2013 to 2015

HS code	4-digit heading of Harmonized System 2012	Value (million US$) 2013	2014	2015	Unit value 2013	2014	2015	Unit	SITC code
	All Commodities	332.5	356.8	215.2					
2710	Petroleum oils, other than crude	118.6	119.0	79.4	1.0	0.9	0.6	US$/kg	334
0303	Fish, frozen, excluding fish fillets and other fish meat of heading 03.04	62.3	51.3	48.6	2.4	1.7	1.5	US$/kg	034
8609	Containers (including containers for the transport of fluids)	26.9	83.8	12.8					786
1604	Prepared or preserved fish; caviar	26.9	32.2	27.1	7.6	7.3	5.1	US$/kg	037
8429	Self-propelled bulldozers, angledozers, graders, levellers, scrapers	39.5	0.3	2.0	*46.0*	*47.5*	*48.9*	thsd US$/unit	723
8802	Other aircraft (for example, helicopters, aeroplanes); spacecraft	...	32.6	...		*32.6*		mln US$/unit	792
8426	Ships'derricks; cranes, including cable cranes; mobile lifting frames	11.6	2.8	3.5					744
6406	Parts of footwear	5.1	5.4	3.8	67.1	79.3	61.1	US$/kg	851
2208	Alcohol of a strength by volume of less than 80 % vol	1.0	0.8	7.1	*4.4*	*4.5*		US$/litre	112
6203	Men's or boys'suits, ensembles, jackets, blazers, trousers	1.4	3.1	2.9					841

Services Imports and Exports: EBOPS 2002 categories

Table 2: Merchandise exports by SITC

(Value in million US$, growth and shares in percentage)

SITC	2015	Avg. Growth rates 2011-2015	Avg. Growth rates 2014-2015	2015 share
Total	215.2	-8.4	-39.7	100.0
0+1	85.7	-3.1	-2.6	39.8
2+4	1.1	1.7	-28.0	0.5
3	79.4	-7.2	-33.5	36.9
5	0.7	-18.6	-53.5	0.3
6	1.7	-15.9	-37.7	0.8
7	35.4	-17.9	-72.3	16.4
8	11.3	-10.3	-29.3	5.2

Table 3: Merchandise imports by SITC

(Value in million US$, growth and shares in percentage)

SITC	2015	Avg. Growth rates 2011-2015	Avg. Growth rates 2014-2015	2015 share
Total	606.3	-10.5	-21.1	100.0
0+1	185.4	-4.8	-9.4	30.6
2+4	23.0	-4.5	-10.9	3.8
3	77.9	-19.2	-34.3	12.8
5	40.8	-6.7	-18.7	6.7
6	101.9	-8.9	-18.0	16.8
7	132.6	-14.4	-27.5	21.9
8	44.7	-8.0	-28.2	7.4
9	0.0	...	914.7	0.0

SITC Legend

SITC Code	Description
Total	All commodities
0+1	Food, animals + beverages, tobacco
2+4	Crude materials + anim. & veg. oils
3	Mineral fuels, lubricants
5	Chemicals
6	Goods classified chiefly by material
7	Machinery and transport equipment
8	Miscellaneous manufactured articles
9	Not classified elsewhere in the SITC

Graph 4: Merchandise trade balance

(Mln US$ by MDG Regions in 2015)

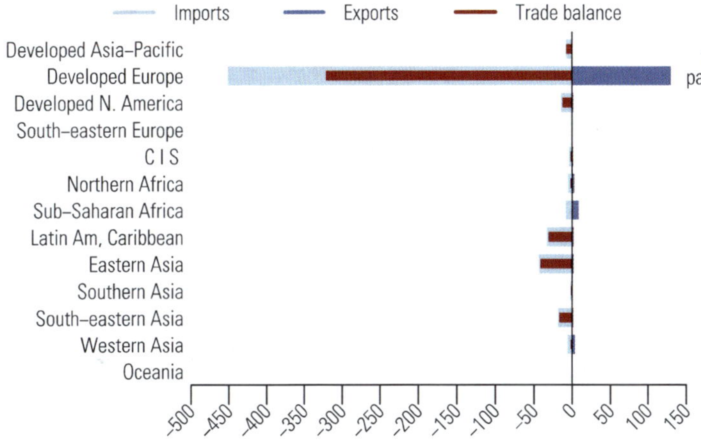

Graph 5: Partner concentration of merchandise trade

(Cumulative share by ranked partners in 2015)

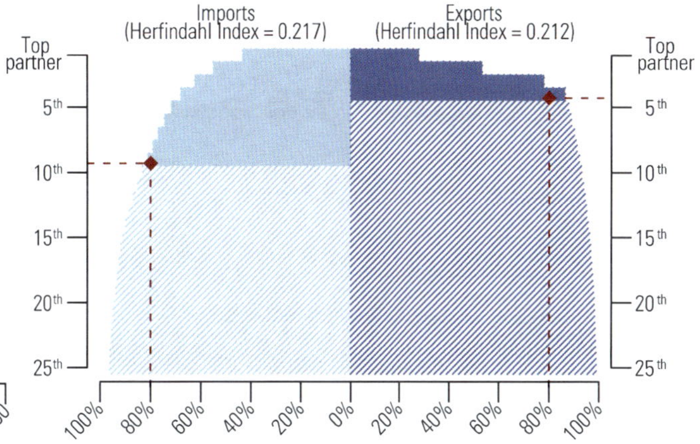

Graph 6: Imports of services by EBOPS category

(% share in 2014)

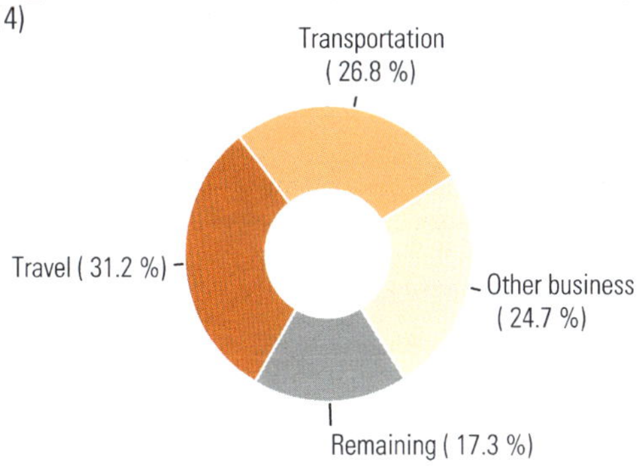

Imports Profile:

"Food, animals + beverages, tobacco" (SITC section 0+1), "Machinery and transport equipment" (SITC section 7) and "Goods classified chiefly by material" (SITC section 6) were the largest commodity groups for imports in 2015, representing respectively 30.6, 21.9 and 16.8 percent of imported goods (see table 3). From 2013 to 2015, the largest import commodity was "Petroleum oils, other than crude" (HS code 2710) (see table 4). The top three partners for merchandise imports were Portugal, the Netherlands and Spain, accounting for respectively 40.7, 15.7 and 7.9 percent of total imports. "Travel" (EBOPS code 236) accounted for the largest share of imports of services in 2014 at 109.5 mln US$, followed by "Transportation" (EBOPS code 205) at 94.2 mln US$ and "Other business services" (EBOPS code 268) at 86.7 mln US$ (see graph 6).

Table 4: Top 10 import commodities 2013 to 2015

HS code	4-digit heading of Harmonized System 2012	Value (million US$) 2013	Value (million US$) 2014	Value (million US$) 2015	Unit value 2013	Unit value 2014	Unit value 2015	Unit	SITC code
	All Commodities	726.4	768.7	606.3					
2710	Petroleum oils, other than crude	141.5	107.3	70.8	0.9	0.8	0.5	US$/kg	334
1006	Rice	27.2	20.7	21.6	0.7	0.7	0.6	US$/kg	042
2523	Portland cement, aluminous cement, slag cement	23.3	24.2	18.8	0.1	0.1	0.1	US$/kg	661
0402	Milk and cream, concentrated or containing added sugar	16.5	18.2	15.6	4.7	4.8	4.0	US$/kg	022
8517	Electrical apparatus for line telephony or line telegraphy	11.0	15.6	12.4					764
0207	Meat and edible offal, of the poultry of heading 01.05	13.3	13.0	11.2	1.8	1.7	1.3	US$/kg	012
8703	Motor cars and other motor vehicles principally designed for the transport	11.2	12.4	12.1	*18.2*	*17.1*	*17.6*	thsd US$/unit	781
7214	Other bars and rods of iron or non-alloy steel	9.4	12.7	9.3	0.8	0.8	0.6	US$/kg	676
1701	Cane or beet sugar and chemically pure sucrose, in solid form	11.9	8.9	7.2	0.7	0.6	0.5	US$/kg	061
2711	Petroleum gases and other gaseous hydrocarbons	11.0	10.2	6.6	1.0	1.0	0.6	US$/kg	343

Cambodia

Goods Imports: CIF, by origin | **Goods Exports: FOB, by last known destination** | **Trade System: General**

Overview:

In 2014, the value of merchandise exports of Cambodia increased substantially by 15.5 percent to reach 10.7 bln US$, while its merchandise imports increased substantially by 105.6 percent to reach 19.0 bln US$ (see graph 1, table 2 and table 3). The merchandise trade balance recorded a moderate deficit of 8.3 bln US$ (see graph 1). The largest merchandise trade balance was with MDG Eastern Asia at -8.4 bln US$ (see graph 4). Merchandise exports in Cambodia were diversified amongst partners; imports were moderately concentrated. The top 8 partners accounted for 80 percent or more of exports and 7 partners accounted for 80 percent or more of imports (see graph 5). In 2013, the value of exports of services of Cambodia increased moderately by 9.5 percent, reaching 2.8 bln US$, while its imports of services increased substantially by 14.4 percent and reached 1.8 bln US$ (see graph 2). There was a moderate trade in services surplus of 1.0 bln US$. See footnote*.

Graph 1: Total merchandise trade, by value

(Bln US$ by year)

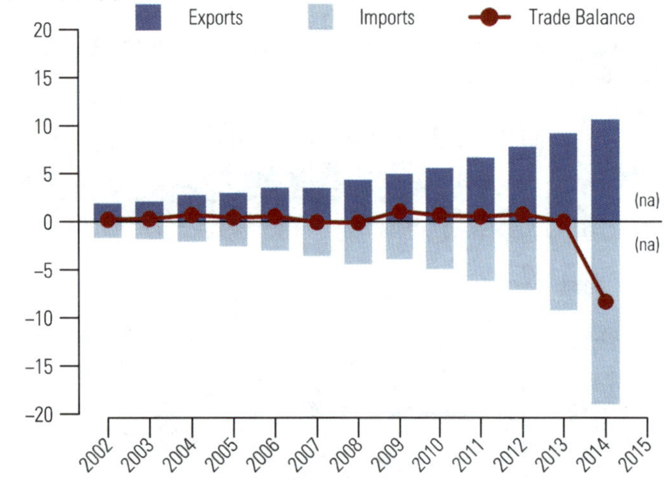

Graph 2: Total services trade, by value

(Bln US$ by year)

Exports Profile:

"Miscellaneous manufactured articles" (SITC section 8), "Food, animals + beverages, tobacco" (SITC section 0+1) and "Crude materials + anim. & veg. oils" (SITC section 2+4) were the largest commodity groups for exports in 2014, representing respectively 92.0, 3.2 and 2.7 percent of exported goods (see table 2). From 2012 to 2014, the largest export commodity was "Unused postage, revenue or similar stamps of current or new issue" (HS code 4907) (see table 1). The top three destinations for merchandise exports were the United States, China, Hong Kong SAR and Singapore, accounting for respectively 22.4, 20.2 and 11.6 percent of total exports. "Travel" (EBOPS code 236) accounted for the largest share of exports of services in 2013 at 1.9 bln US$, followed by "Transportation" (EBOPS code 205) at 343.5 mln US$ and "Other business services" (EBOPS code 268) at 251.1 mln US$ (see graph 3).

Graph 3: Exports of services by EBOPS category

(% share in 2013)

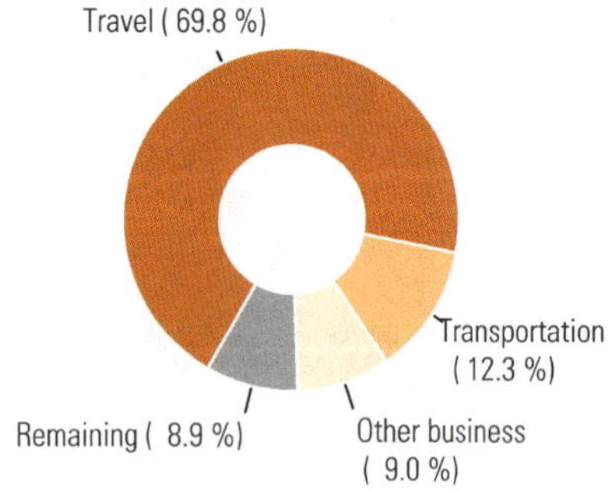

Table 1: Top 10 export commodities 2012 to 2014

HS code	4-digit heading of Harmonized System 2007	Value (million US$) 2012	2013	2014	Unit value 2012	2013	2014	Unit	SITC code
	All Commodities	7838.1	9248.1	10681.4					
4907	Unused postage, revenue or similar stamps of current or new issue	2282.1	2260.1	3932.7	55.8	56.4	62.0	thsd US$/kg	892
6104	Women's or girls' suits, ensembles, jackets, blazers, dresses, skirts	1064.8	1199.6	1324.7					844
6109	T-shirts, singlets and other vests, knitted or crocheted	586.8	1045.2	1153.7	*6.1*	*5.5*	*5.2*	US$/unit	845
6103	Men's, boys' suits,jackets,trousers etc knitted or crocheted	741.1	865.0	937.8					843
6110	Jerseys, pullovers, cardigans, waist-coats and similar articles	754.2	546.4	519.6	*18.3*	*16.9*	*17.6*	US$/unit	845
6108	Women's or girls' slips, petticoats, briefs, panties, knitted or crocheted	250.1	321.3	330.6					844
6403	Footwear with outer soles of rubber, plastics, leather	186.5	207.7	269.2	*19.2*	*21.8*	*19.4*	US$/pair	851
1006	Rice	139.5	258.2	231.5	0.7	0.7	0.7	US$/kg	042
8712	Bicycles and other cycles (including delivery tricycles), not motorised	253.4	357.6	0.7					785
6111	Babies' garments and clothing accessories, knitted or crocheted	123.1	181.4	231.4	15.4	15.0	12.7	US$/kg	845

*Increase of imports in 2014 is concentrated on inputs for clothing industry (HS chapters 60, 55, 52).

Services Imports and Exports: EBOPS 2002 categories

Table 2: Merchandise exports by SITC

(Value in million US$, growth and shares in percentage)

SITC	2014	Avg. Growth rates 2010-2014	Avg. Growth rates 2013-2014	2014 share
Total	10 681.4	17.6	15.5	100.0
0+1	343.1	49.8	-9.9	3.2
2+4	284.1	17.9	2.5	2.7
3	0.0	-75.2	-100.0	0.0
5	10.7	-8.2	-47.6	0.1
6	86.2	21.7	-38.6	0.8
7	87.2	-24.5	-87.4	0.8
8	9 830.8	18.1	27.1	92.0
9	39.3	80.5	1197.7	0.4

Table 3: Merchandise imports by SITC

(Value in million US$, growth and shares in percentage)

SITC	2014	Avg. Growth rates 2010-2014	Avg. Growth rates 2013-2014	2014 share
Total	18 973.2	40.3	105.6	100.0
0+1	1 410.0	42.6	151.4	7.4
2+4	226.1	19.6	130.5	1.2
3	690.0	18.8	-31.3	3.6
5	1 250.7	41.9	144.7	6.6
6	9 759.9	44.3	172.1	51.4
7	3 610.4	37.3	96.5	19.0
8	1 655.0	46.4	7.1	8.7
9	371.2	22.2	342.0	2.0

SITC Legend

SITC Code	Description
Total	All commodities
0+1	Food, animals + beverages, tobacco
2+4	Crude materials + anim. & veg. oils
3	Mineral fuels, lubricants
5	Chemicals
6	Goods classified chiefly by material
7	Machinery and transport equipment
8	Miscellaneous manufactured articles
9	Not classified elsewhere in the SITC

Graph 4: Merchandise trade balance

(Bln US$ by MDG Regions in 2014)

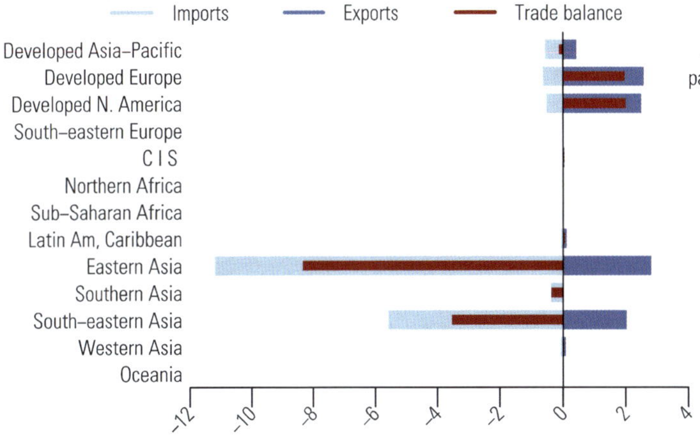

Graph 5: Partner concentration of merchandise trade

(Cumulative share by ranked partners in 2014)

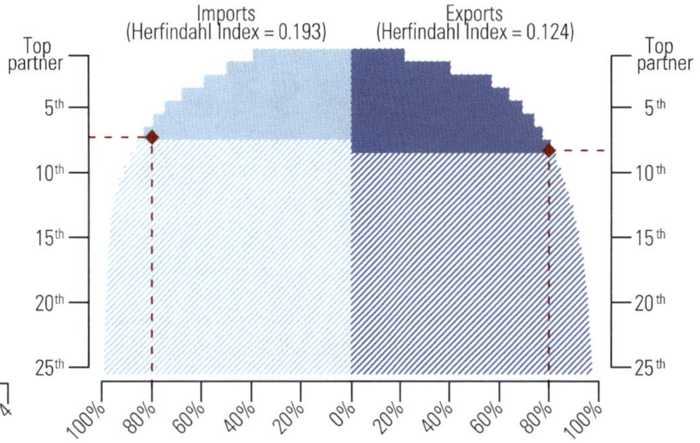

Graph 6: Imports of services by EBOPS category

(% share in 2013)

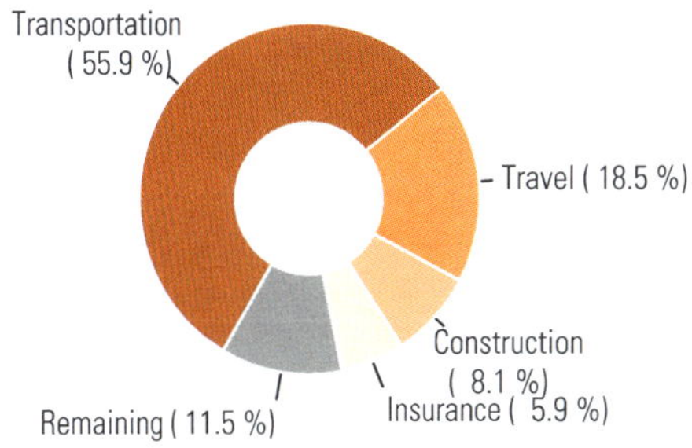

Imports Profile:

"Goods classified chiefly by material" (SITC section 6), "Machinery and transport equipment" (SITC section 7) and "Miscellaneous manufactured articles" (SITC section 8) were the largest commodity groups for imports in 2014, representing respectively 51.4, 19.0 and 8.7 percent of imported goods (see table 3). From 2012 to 2014, the largest import commodity was "Other knitted or crocheted fabrics" (HS code 6006) (see table 4). The top three partners for merchandise imports were China, Thailand and Viet Nam, accounting for respectively 35.8, 11.4 and 10.3 percent of total imports. "Transportation" (EBOPS code 205) accounted for the largest share of imports of services in 2013 at 987.9 mln US$, followed by "Travel" (EBOPS code 236) at 327.9 mln US$ and "Construction services" (EBOPS code 249) at 144.0 mln US$ (see graph 6).

Table 4: Top 10 import commodities 2012 to 2014

HS code	4-digit heading of Harmonized System 2007	Value (million US$) 2012	2013	2014	Unit value 2012	2013	2014	Unit	SITC code
	All Commodities	7 062.6	9 227.4	18 973.2					
6006	Other knitted or crocheted fabrics	768.1	815.1	2 310.0	6.7	6.7	6.9	US$/kg	655
6004	Knitted or crocheted fabrics of a width exceeding 30 cm	593.0	744.0	1 898.9	5.4	5.8	6.3	US$/kg	655
5515	Other woven fabrics of synthetic staple fibres	554.6	641.6	1 721.9	7.5	8.0	8.7	US$/kg	653
2710	Petroleum oils, other than crude	910.1	950.3	646.1	0.9	1.0	1.1	US$/kg	334
4907	Unused postage, revenue or similar stamps of current or new issue	0.1	978.5	75.3	0.0	6.6	4.8	thsd US$/kg	892
8703	Motor cars and other motor vehicles principally designed for the transport	207.6	216.6	424.8	*21.0*	*22.2*	*22.0*	thsd US$/unit	781
2402	Cigars, cheroots, cigarillos and cigarettes	155.3	184.4	395.5	4.8	5.2	5.4	US$/kg	122
7108	Gold (including gold plated with platinum)	104.9	80.4	371.2	51.9	39.8	40.4	thsd US$/kg	971
5509	Yarn (other than sewing thread) of synthetic staple fibres	131.5	155.5	241.8	5.1	5.4	5.9	US$/kg	651
8704	Motor vehicles for the transport of goods	149.3	152.5	169.3					782

Cameroon

Goods Imports: CIF, by origin	Goods Exports: FOB, by last known destination	Trade System: Special

Overview:

In 2014, the value of merchandise exports of Cameroon increased substantially by 14.1 percent to reach 5.2 bln US$, while its merchandise imports increased substantially by 13.6 percent to reach 7.6 bln US$ (see graph 1, table 2 and table 3). The merchandise trade balance recorded a moderate deficit of 2.4 bln US$ (see graph 1). The largest merchandise trade balance was with MDG Sub-Saharan Africa at -1.5 bln US$ (see graph 4). Merchandise exports in Cameroon were diversified amongst partners; imports were also diversified. The top 12 partners accounted for 80 percent or more of exports and 19 partners accounted for 80 percent or more of imports (see graph 5). In 2013, the value of exports of services of Cameroon increased substantially by 21.5 percent, reaching 2.0 bln US$, while its imports of services increased substantially by 22.1 percent and reached 2.6 bln US$ (see graph 2). There was a moderate trade in services deficit of 619.9 mln US$.

Graph 1: Total merchandise trade, by value

(Bln US$ by year)

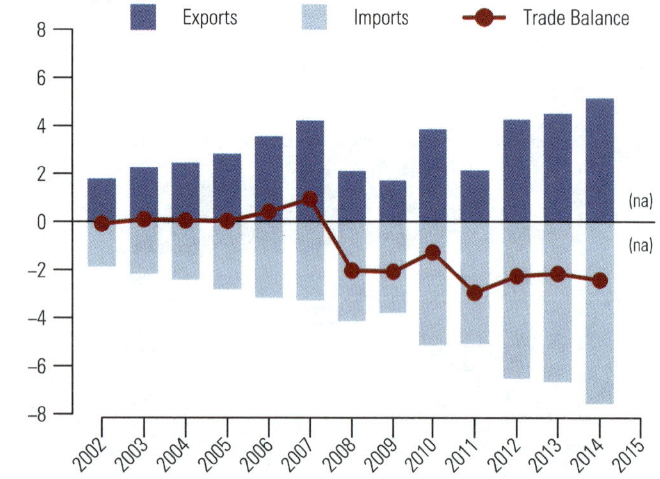

Graph 2: Total services trade, by value

(Bln US$ by year)

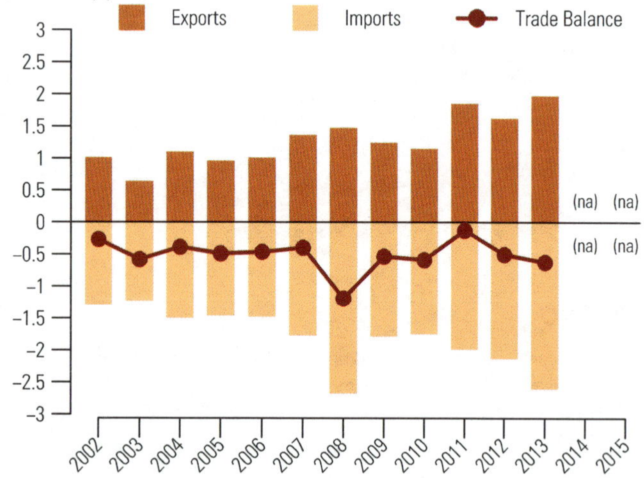

Exports Profile:

"Mineral fuels, lubricants" (SITC section 3), "Food, animals + beverages, tobacco" (SITC section 0+1) and "Crude materials + anim. & veg. oils" (SITC section 2+4) were the largest commodity groups for exports in 2014, representing respectively 56.3, 17.4 and 15.2 percent of exported goods (see table 2). From 2012 to 2014, the largest export commodity was "Petroleum oils, crude" (HS code 2709) (see table 1). The top three destinations for merchandise exports were Spain, Portugal and China, accounting for respectively 13.8, 12.7 and 12.0 percent of total exports. "Travel" (EBOPS code 236) accounted for the largest share of exports of services in 2013 at 576.0 mln US$, followed by "Transportation" (EBOPS code 205) at 567.7 mln US$ and "Other business services" (EBOPS code 268) at 437.1 mln US$ (see graph 3).

Graph 3: Exports of services by EBOPS category

(% share in 2013)

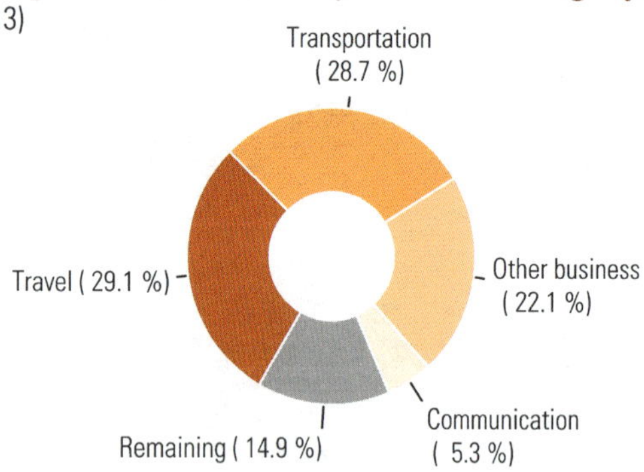

Table 1: Top 10 export commodities 2012 to 2014

HS code	4-digit heading of Harmonized System 2002	Value (million US$) 2012	2013	2014	Unit value 2012	2013	2014	Unit	SITC code
	All Commodities	4275.0	4520.9	5159.5					
2709	Petroleum oils, crude	1834.1	2204.0	2469.2	0.6	0.7	0.6	US$/kg	333
1801	Cocoa beans, whole or broken, raw or roasted	394.8	453.5	563.6	2.3	2.4	2.9	US$/kg	072
2710	Petroleum oils, other than crude	527.5	258.2	321.1	0.9	0.8	0.8	US$/kg	334
4407	Wood sawn or chipped lengthwise, sliced or peeled	279.8	274.7	300.7	*0.7*	*1.2*		thsd US$/m^3	248
5201	Cotton, not carded or combed	143.7	173.7	160.6	1.9	1.9	1.8	US$/kg	263
4403	Wood in the rough, whether or not stripped of bark or sapwood	121.8	145.9	176.7					247
4001	Natural rubber, balata, gutta-percha, guayule, chicle	121.5	122.2	91.8	2.8	2.3	1.6	US$/kg	231
7601	Unwrought aluminium	52.6	64.5	147.9	1.8	1.9	1.8	US$/kg	684
0803	Bananas, including plantains	74.9	83.5	77.1	0.3	0.3	0.3	US$/kg	057
0901	Coffee, whether or not roasted or decaffeinated	87.3	40.2	63.9	2.1	1.9	2.0	US$/kg	071

Services Imports and Exports: EBOPS 2002 categories

Table 2: Merchandise exports by SITC

(Value in million US$, growth and shares in percentage)

SITC	2014	Avg. Growth rates 2010-2014	Avg. Growth rates 2013-2014	2014 share
Total	5 159.5	7.4	14.1	100.0
0+1	897.0	-1.2	20.6	17.4
2+4	783.8	6.5	6.1	15.2
3	2 906.0	10.9	14.9	56.3
5	98.1	15.2	-12.2	1.9
6	309.1	9.3	25.3	6.0
7	118.4	10.7	-2.7	2.3
8	41.3	10.5	91.8	0.8
9	5.8	-32.6	-24.1	0.1

Table 3: Merchandise imports by SITC

(Value in million US$, growth and shares in percentage)

SITC	2014	Avg. Growth rates 2010-2014	Avg. Growth rates 2013-2014	2014 share
Total	7 561.1	10.2	13.6	100.0
0+1	1 234.5	9.0	-13.0	16.3
2+4	284.1	9.8	15.3	3.8
3	2 117.9	10.5	35.4	28.0
5	777.8	9.7	7.2	10.3
6	1 007.9	10.5	9.7	13.3
7	1 807.8	11.7	25.8	23.9
8	330.7	5.4	3.0	4.4
9	0.3	80.5	-98.6	0.0

SITC Legend

SITC Code	Description
Total	All commodities
0+1	Food, animals + beverages, tobacco
2+4	Crude materials + anim. & veg. oils
3	Mineral fuels, lubricants
5	Chemicals
6	Goods classified chiefly by material
7	Machinery and transport equipment
8	Miscellaneous manufactured articles
9	Not classified elsewhere in the SITC

Graph 4: Merchandise trade balance

(Bln US$ by MDG Regions in 2014)

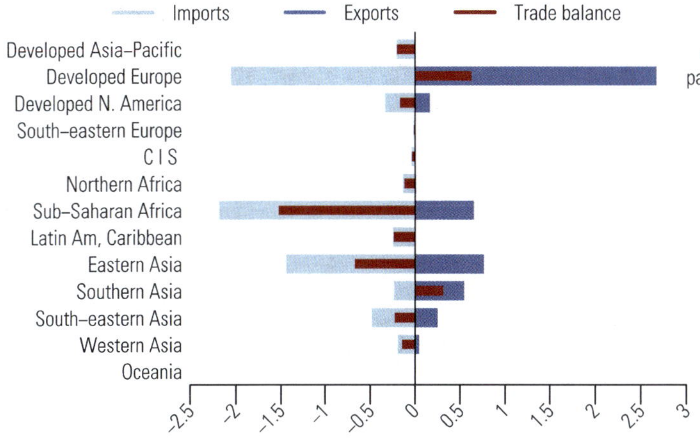

Graph 5: Partner concentration of merchandise trade

(Cumulative share by ranked partners in 2014)

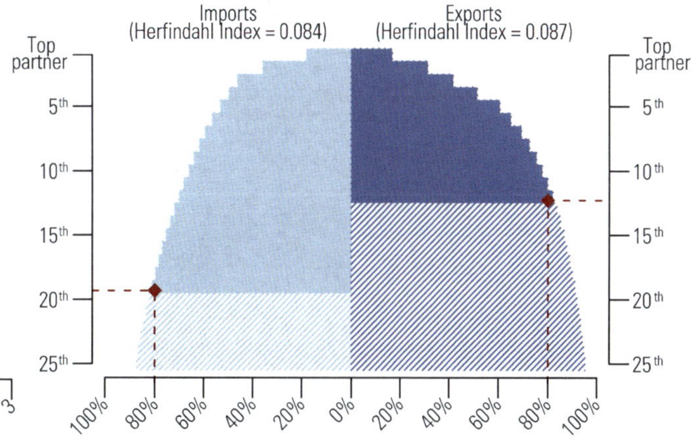

Graph 6: Imports of services by EBOPS category

(% share in 2013)

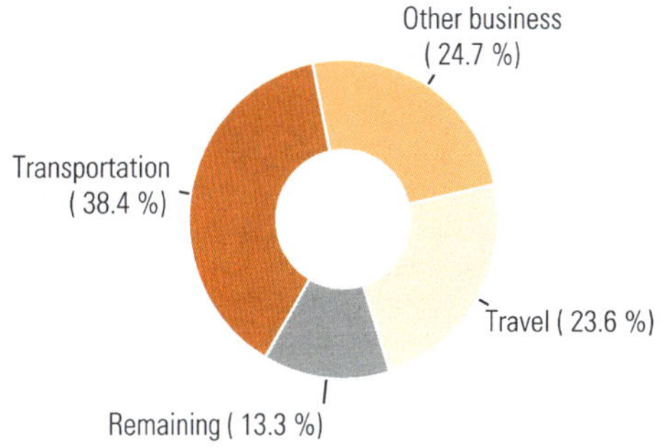

Imports Profile:

"Mineral fuels, lubricants" (SITC section 3), "Machinery and transport equipment" (SITC section 7) and "Food, animals + beverages, tobacco" (SITC section 0+1) were the largest commodity groups for imports in 2014, representing respectively 28.0, 23.9 and 16.3 percent of imported goods (see table 3). From 2012 to 2014, the largest import commodity was "Petroleum oils, crude" (HS code 2709) (see table 4). The top three partners for merchandise imports were Nigeria, China and France, accounting for respectively 16.5, 14.4 and 11.4 percent of total imports. "Transportation" (EBOPS code 205) accounted for the largest share of imports of services in 2013 at 998.9 mln US$, followed by "Other business services" (EBOPS code 268) at 642.6 mln US$ and "Travel" (EBOPS code 236) at 612.4 mln US$ (see graph 6).

Table 4: Top 10 import commodities 2012 to 2014

HS code	4-digit heading of Harmonized System 2002	Value (million US$) 2012	2013	2014	Unit value 2012	2013	2014	Unit	SITC code
	All Commodities	6 515.1	6 657.2	7 561.1					
2709	Petroleum oils, crude	1 300.9	999.4	1 429.9	0.9	0.9	0.8	US$/kg	333
2710	Petroleum oils, other than crude	565.0	445.4	551.3	1.0	1.0	1.0	US$/kg	334
1006	Rice	306.9	430.7	282.6	0.6	0.5	0.5	US$/kg	042
0303	Fish, frozen, excluding fish fillets	239.4	281.4	292.9	1.3	1.4	1.4	US$/kg	034
1001	Wheat and meslin	196.6	194.2	192.1	0.4	0.4	0.4	US$/kg	041
3004	Medicaments (excluding goods of heading 30.02, 30.05 or 30.06)	165.8	168.3	218.0	21.8	20.5	17.7	US$/kg	542
2523	Portland cement, aluminous cement, slag cement	137.8	179.4	200.9	0.1	0.1	0.1	US$/kg	661
8703	Motor cars and other motor vehicles principally designed for the transport	147.1	145.0	159.3	*20.9*	*20.3*	*20.3*	thsd US$/unit	781
8517	Electrical apparatus for line telephony or line telegraphy	62.3	154.9	222.6					764
8704	Motor vehicles for the transport of goods	100.3	106.4	108.8					782

Canada

Goods Imports: FOB, by origin | **Goods Exports: FOB, by last known destination** | **Trade System: General**

Overview:

In 2015, the value of merchandise exports of Canada decreased substantially by 14.0 percent to reach 407.1 bln US$, while its merchandise imports decreased moderately by 9.5 percent to reach 418.8 bln US$ (see graph 1, table 2 and table 3). The merchandise trade balance recorded a relatively small deficit of 11.7 bln US$ (see graph 1). The largest merchandise trade balance was with MDG Developed North America at 86.1 bln US$ (see graph 4). Merchandise exports in Canada were highly concentrated amongst partners; imports were also highly concentrated. The top 2 partners accounted for 80 percent or more of exports and 7 partners accounted for 80 percent or more of imports (see graph 5). In 2014, the value of exports of services of Canada decreased slightly by 4.2 percent, reaching 82.1 bln US$, while its imports of services decreased slightly by 4.5 percent and reached 105.9 bln US$ (see graph 2). There was a moderate trade in services deficit of 23.8 bln US$.

Graph 1: Total merchandise trade, by value

(Bln US$ by year)

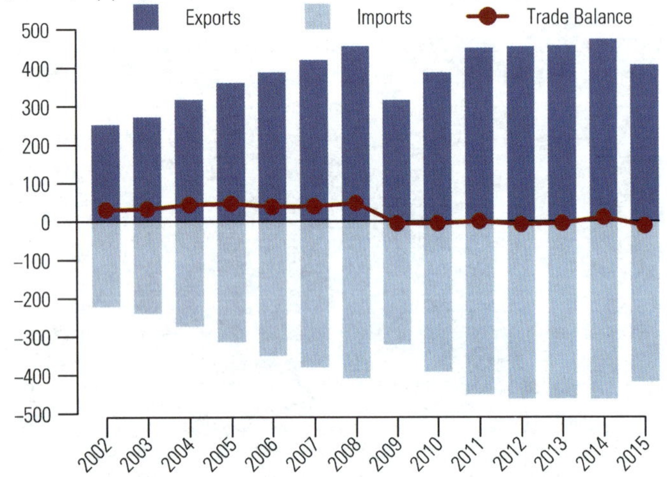

Graph 2: Total services trade, by value

(Bln US$ by year)

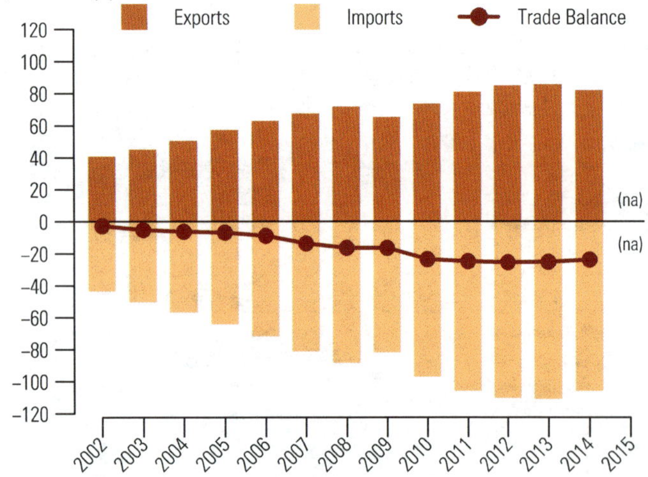

Exports Profile:

"Machinery and transport equipment" (SITC section 7), "Mineral fuels, lubricants" (SITC section 3) and "Goods classified chiefly by material" (SITC section 6) were the largest commodity groups for exports in 2015, representing respectively 28.8, 19.0 and 11.8 percent of exported goods (see table 2). From 2013 to 2015, the largest export commodity was "Petroleum oils and oils obtained from bituminous minerals, crude" (HS code 2709) (see table 1). Canada was the third largest export in the World of this commodity. The main destination for merchandise exports was the United States which accounted for 76.4 percent of total exports. It was followed by China and the United Kingdom, accounting for respectively 4.0 and 3.0 percent of total exports. "Other business services" (EBOPS code 268) accounted for the largest share of exports of services in 2014 at 27.8 bln US$, followed by "Travel" (EBOPS code 236) at 17.4 bln US$ and "Transportation" (EBOPS code 205) at 12.4 bln US$ (see graph 3).

Graph 3: Exports of services by EBOPS category

(% share in 2014)

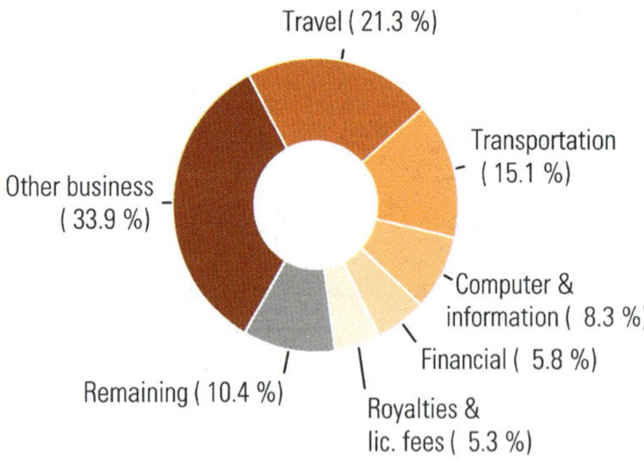

Table 1: Top 10 export commodities 2013 to 2015

HS code	4-digit heading of Harmonized System 2012	Value (million US$)			Unit value				SITC code
		2013	2014	2015	2013	2014	2015	Unit	
	All Commodities	456 598.3	473 603.1	407 140.0					
2709	Petroleum oils and oils obtained from bituminous minerals, crude	79 372.9	88 120.1	50 198.4		*0.8*	*0.8*	US$/kg	333
8703	Motor cars and other motor vehicles principally designed for the transport	45 193.3	44 877.3	44 874.1	*21.0*	*20.7*	*21.0*	thsd US$/unit	781
9999	Commodities not specified according to kind	14 619.7	16 017.7	17 914.9					931
2710	Petroleum oils, other than crude	18 455.3	15 185.3	11 427.8					334
7108	Gold (including gold plated with platinum)	15 717.6	14 972.8	12 420.5	44.2	40.2	36.1	thsd US$/kg	971
2711	Petroleum gases and other gaseous hydrocarbons	12 954.2	17 001.6	9 162.4					343
8708	Parts and accessories of the motor vehicles of headings 87.01 to 87.05	10 403.2	10 762.8	10 737.6	*10.5*	*10.2*	*10.3*	US$/kg	784
8802	Other aircraft (for example, helicopters, aeroplanes); spacecraft	6 501.7	8 148.9	8 278.2					792
4407	Wood sawn or chipped lengthwise, sliced or peeled	7 438.7	7 842.3	7 009.3	*192.0*	*192.4*		US$/m³	248
1001	Wheat and meslin	6 488.6	7 189.9	6 206.4	0.3	*0.3*		US$/kg	041

Services Imports and Exports: EBOPS 2002 categories

Table 2: Merchandise exports by SITC

(Value in million US$, growth and shares in percentage)

SITC	2015	Avg. Growth rates 2011-2015	Avg. Growth rates 2014-2015	2015 share
Total	407 140.0	-2.5	-14.0	100.0
0+1	37 781.0	3.1	-4.8	9.3
2+4	37 948.5	-4.0	-14.0	9.3
3	77 343.2	-9.6	-39.9	19.0
5	36 510.1	-1.9	-3.8	9.0
6	48 053.3	-3.8	-8.1	11.8
7	117 182.2	1.7	-1.4	28.8
8	21 480.3	1.5	5.8	5.3
9	30 841.4	0.0	-2.7	7.6

Table 3: Merchandise imports by SITC

(Value in million US$, growth and shares in percentage)

SITC	2015	Avg. Growth rates 2011-2015	Avg. Growth rates 2014-2015	2015 share
Total	418 801.1	-1.8	-9.5	100.0
0+1	32 864.3	1.9	-3.8	7.8
2+4	11 610.1	-4.4	-13.4	2.8
3	29 478.1	-13.7	-38.1	7.0
5	44 991.1	-0.4	-7.3	10.7
6	50 596.1	-2.1	-9.5	12.1
7	181 843.5	0.2	-4.9	43.4
8	52 130.7	-0.1	-5.0	12.4
9	15 287.1	-5.5	-12.1	3.7

SITC Legend

SITC Code	Description
Total	All commodities
0+1	Food, animals + beverages, tobacco
2+4	Crude materials + anim. & veg. oils
3	Mineral fuels, lubricants
5	Chemicals
6	Goods classified chiefly by material
7	Machinery and transport equipment
8	Miscellaneous manufactured articles
9	Not classified elsewhere in the SITC

Graph 4: Merchandise trade balance

(Bln US$ by MDG Regions in 2015)

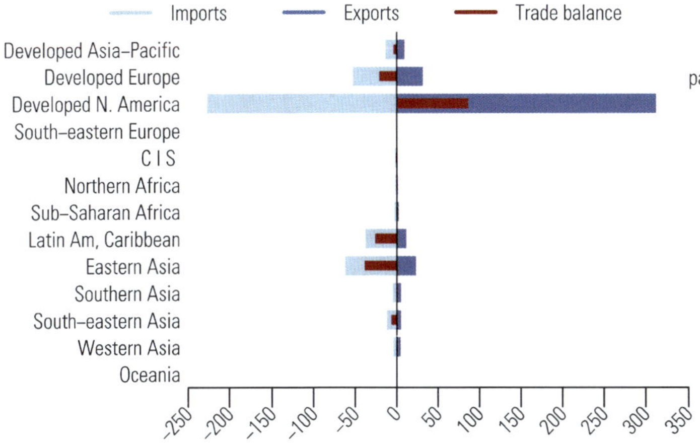

Graph 5: Partner concentration of merchandise trade

(Cumulative share by ranked partners in 2015)

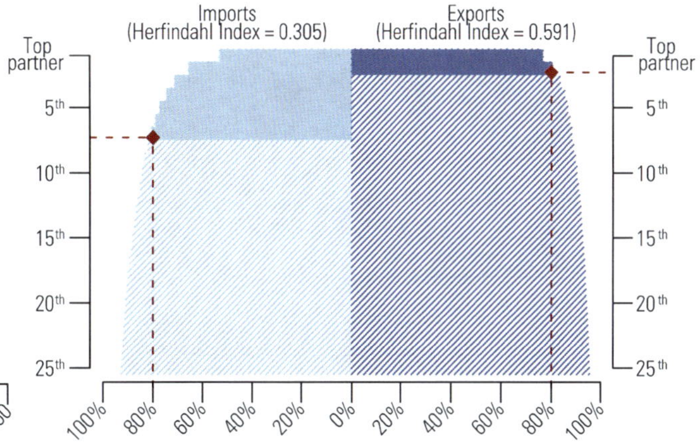

Graph 6: Imports of services by EBOPS category

(% share in 2014)

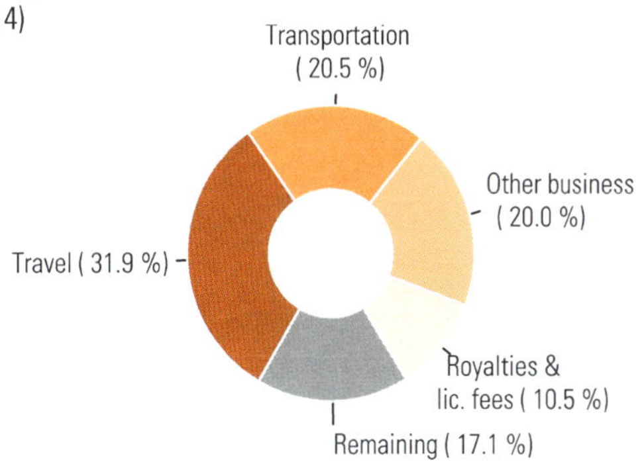

Imports Profile:

"Machinery and transport equipment" (SITC section 7), "Miscellaneous manufactured articles" (SITC section 8) and "Goods classified chiefly by material" (SITC section 6) were the largest commodity groups for imports in 2015, representing respectively 43.4, 12.4 and 12.1 percent of imported goods (see table 3). From 2013 to 2015, the largest import commodity was "Motor cars and other motor vehicles principally designed for the transport" (HS code 8703) (see table 4). The top three partners for merchandise imports were the United States, China and Mexico, accounting for respectively 53.2, 11.6 and 5.7 percent of total imports. "Travel" (EBOPS code 236) accounted for the largest share of imports of services in 2014 at 33.8 bln US$, followed by "Transportation" (EBOPS code 205) at 21.7 bln US$ and "Other business services" (EBOPS code 268) at 21.1 bln US$ (see graph 6).

Table 4: Top 10 import commodities 2013 to 2015

HS code	4-digit heading of Harmonized System 2012	Value (million US$) 2013	2014	2015	Unit value 2013	2014	2015	Unit	SITC code
	All Commodities	461 785.1	462 984.2	418 801.1					
8703	Motor cars and other motor vehicles principally designed for the transport	26 336.7	27 009.3	26 296.6	*20.9*	*20.3*	*19.0*	thsd US$/unit	781
8708	Parts and accessories of the motor vehicles of headings 87.01 to 87.05	21 552.8	20 560.0	19 906.3	*12.1*	*12.2*	*12.3*	US$/kg	784
2709	Petroleum oils and oils obtained from bituminous minerals, crude	26 237.9	21 562.1	13 161.6		*0.8*	*0.8*	US$/kg	333
2710	Petroleum oils, other than crude	17 376.4	18 294.3	11 849.4					334
8704	Motor vehicles for the transport of goods	13 189.9	12 775.8	11 878.2	*33.8*	*31.5*	*28.8*	thsd US$/unit	782
8517	Electrical apparatus for line telephony or line telegraphy	9 412.2	9 105.3	9 587.0					764
8471	Automatic data processing machines and units thereof	8 957.7	8 888.1	7 886.4					752
9999	Commodities not specified according to kind	8 497.9	8 688.0	8 058.4					931
3004	Medicaments (excluding goods of heading 30.02, 30.05 or 30.06)	8 436.2	8 611.1	7 539.8					542
7108	Gold (including gold plated with platinum)	9 281.5	7 999.4	6 532.8	*23.2*	*22.0*	*17.7*	thsd US$/kg	971

Central African Republic

Goods Imports: CIF, by origin | **Goods Exports: FOB, by last known destination** | **Trade System: General**

Overview:

In 2014, the value of merchandise exports of the Central African Republic decreased substantially by 57.3 percent to reach 20.7 mln US$, while its merchandise imports increased substantially by 137.4 percent to reach 308.0 mln US$ (see graph 1, table 2 and table 3). The merchandise trade balance recorded a large deficit of 287.3 mln US$ (see graph 1). The largest merchandise trade balance was with MDG Developed Europe at -120.6 mln US$ (see graph 4). Merchandise exports in the Central African Republic were highly concentrated amongst partners; imports were diversified. The top 3 partners accounted for 80 percent or more of exports and 13 partners accounted for 80 percent or more of imports (see graph 5). In 2012, the value of exports of services of the Central African Republic increased moderately by 6.3 percent, reaching 69.1 mln US$, while its imports of services increased substantially by 14.5 percent and reached 179.0 mln US$ (see graph 2). There was a large trade in services deficit of 109.9 mln US$.

Graph 1: Total merchandise trade, by value

(Mln US$ by year)

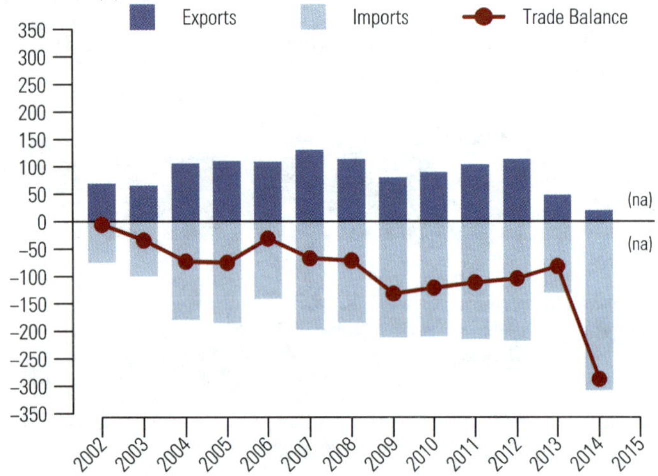

Graph 2: Total services trade, by value

(Mln US$ by year)

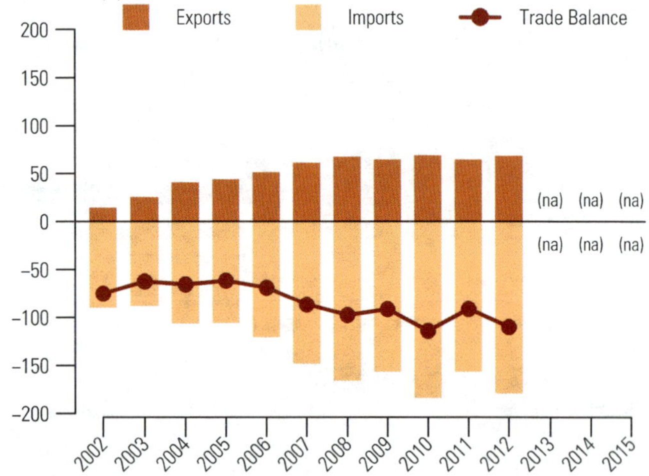

Exports Profile:

"Crude materials + anim. & veg. oils" (SITC section 2+4) was the largest commodity group for export in 2014 accounting for 99.3 percent of exported goods (see table 2). From 2012 to 2014, the largest export commodity was "Diamonds, whether or not worked, but not mounted or set" (HS code 7102) (see table 1). "Government services, n.i.e." (EBOPS code 291) accounted for the largest share of exports of services in 2012 at 47.1 mln US$, followed by "Travel" (EBOPS code 236) at 11.0 mln US$ and "Transportation" (EBOPS code 205) at 5.5 mln US$ (see graph 3).

Graph 3: Exports of services by EBOPS category

(% share in 2012)

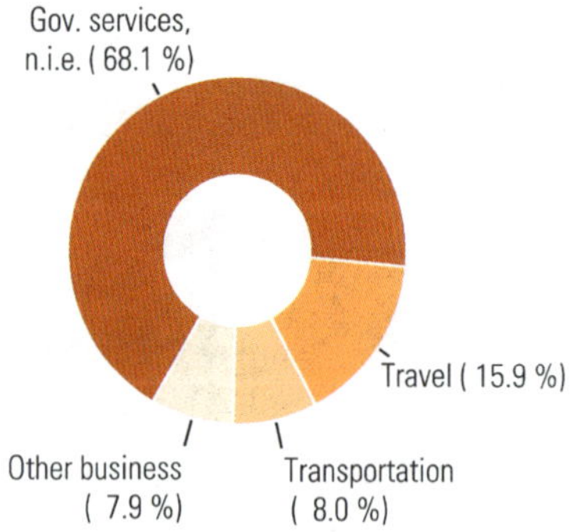

Table 1: Top 10 export commodities 2012 to 2014

HS code	4-digit heading of Harmonized System 2007	Value (million US$) 2012	2013	2014	Unit value 2012	2013	2014	Unit	SITC code
	All Commodities	114.2	48.5	20.7					
7102	Diamonds, whether or not worked, but not mounted or set	65.2	22.2	...					667
4403	Wood in the rough, whether or not stripped of bark or sapwood	18.6	14.3	12.5			*565.2*	US$/m³	247
4407	Wood sawn or chipped lengthwise, sliced or peeled	7.2	5.1	5.1		*1.2*	*1.3*	thsd US$/m³	248
5201	Cotton, not carded or combed	10.8	2.8	2.9			0.0	thsd US$/kg	263
8429	Self-propelled bulldozers, angledozers, graders, levellers, scrapers	2.0	1.0	...	*45.9*	*51.3*		thsd US$/unit	723
8704	Motor vehicles for the transport of goods	1.8	0.6	...		*25.7*		thsd US$/unit	782
8701	Tractors (other than tractors of heading 87.09)	1.5	...	...					722
7108	Gold (including gold plated with platinum)	1.1	0.3	...	10.4			thsd US$/kg	971
2714	Bitumen and asphalt, natural	0.8	...	...	1.1			US$/kg	278
8430	Other moving, grading, levelling, scraping, excavating, tamping, compacting	0.8	...	...					723

Services Imports and Exports: EBOPS 2002 categories

Table 2: Merchandise exports by SITC

(Value in million US$, growth and shares in percentage)

SITC	2014	Avg. Growth rates 2010-2014	2013-2014	2014 share
Total	20.7	-30.7	-57.3	100.0
0+1	0.0	-67.2	-67.5	0.1
2+4	20.6	-29.7	-53.7	99.3
5	0.1	26.6	1023.8	0.4
6	0.0	-38.4	-82.4	0.2
7	0.0	-75.5	-99.8	0.0
8	0.0	-80.8	-99.3	0.0

Table 3: Merchandise imports by SITC

(Value in million US$, growth and shares in percentage)

SITC	2014	Avg. Growth rates 2010-2014	2013-2014	2014 share
Total	308.0	10.1	137.4	100.0
0+1	76.0	10.1	78.9	24.7
2+4	8.0	-11.4	16.5	2.6
3	1.3	-11.5	41.2	0.4
5	54.8	11.7	72.9	17.8
6	30.9	-2.1	116.7	10.0
7	90.9	12.4	268.9	29.5
8	45.8	28.2	437.5	14.9
9	0.2	-12.9	-29.2	0.1

SITC Legend

SITC Code	Description
Total	All commodities
0+1	Food, animals + beverages, tobacco
2+4	Crude materials + anim. & veg. oils
3	Mineral fuels, lubricants
5	Chemicals
6	Goods classified chiefly by material
7	Machinery and transport equipment
8	Miscellaneous manufactured articles
9	Not classified elsewhere in the SITC

Graph 4: Merchandise trade balance

(Mln US$ by MDG Regions in 2014)

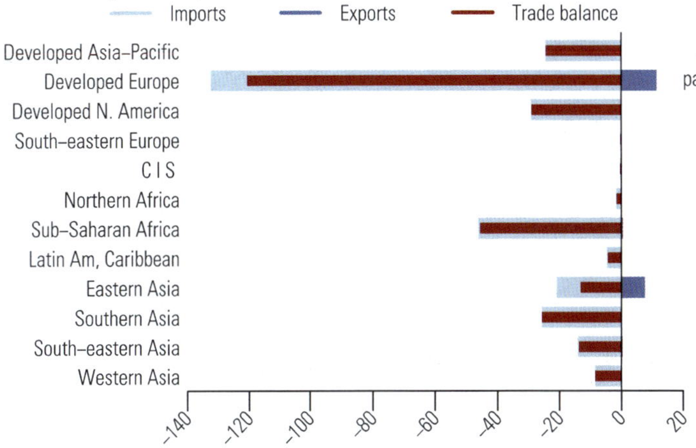

Graph 5: Partner concentration of merchandise trade

(Cumulative share by ranked partners in 2014)

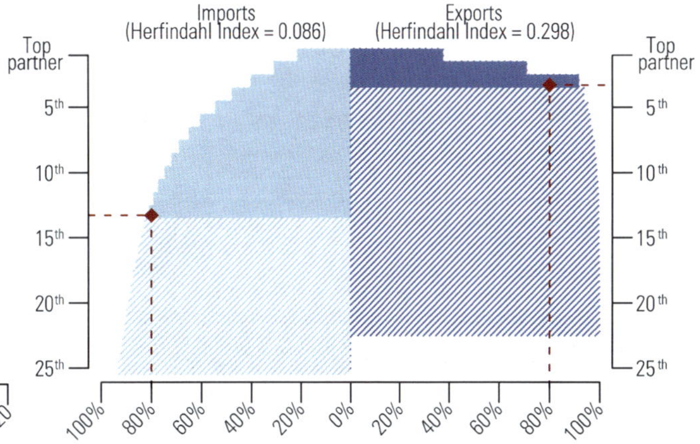

Graph 6: Imports of services by EBOPS category

(% share in 2012)

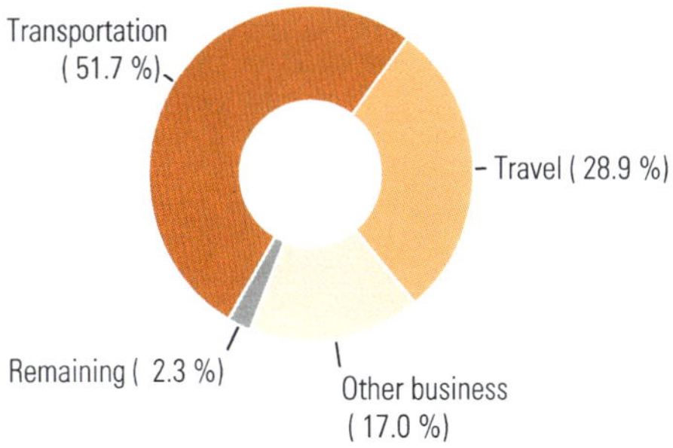

Imports Profile:

"Machinery and transport equipment" (SITC section 7), "Food, animals + beverages, tobacco" (SITC section 0+1) and "Chemicals" (SITC section 5) were the largest commodity groups for imports in 2014, representing respectively 29.5, 24.7 and 17.8 percent of imported goods (see table 3). From 2012 to 2014, the largest import commodity was "Medicaments (excluding goods of heading 30.02, 30.05 or 30.06)" (HS code 3004) (see table 4). The top three partners for merchandise imports were France, China and the United States, accounting for respectively 23.4, 8.2 and 7.6 percent of total imports. "Transportation" (EBOPS code 205) accounted for the largest share of imports of services in 2012 at 92.6 mln US$, followed by "Travel" (EBOPS code 236) at 51.8 mln US$ and "Other business services" (EBOPS code 268) at 30.5 mln US$ (see graph 6).

Table 4: Top 10 import commodities 2012 to 2014

HS code	4-digit heading of Harmonized System 2007	Value (million US$) 2012	2013	2014	Unit value 2012	2013	2014	Unit	SITC code
	All Commodities	217.5	129.7	308.0					
3004	Medicaments (excluding goods of heading 30.02, 30.05 or 30.06)	13.9	20.0	42.6	*14.0*	26.9	35.6	US$/kg	542
8703	Motor cars and other motor vehicles principally designed for the transport	12.0	3.7	20.2	*27.4*	*23.7*	*33.1*	thsd US$/unit	781
8704	Motor vehicles for the transport of goods	7.5	0.9	25.3		*23.5*	*29.3*	thsd US$/unit	782
1101	Wheat or meslin flour	17.5	10.3	5.0	0.5	0.5	0.5	US$/kg	046
1701	Cane or beet sugar and chemically pure sucrose, in solid form	10.6	6.6	5.7	0.7	0.6	0.7	US$/kg	061
8517	Electrical apparatus for line telephony or line telegraphy	7.1	3.4	6.5					764
1006	Rice	2.1	3.4	11.4	0.6	0.8	0.6	US$/kg	042
9018	Instruments and appliances used in medical, surgical, dental or veterinary	3.4	3.9	8.8					872
3002	Human blood; animal blood prepared for therapeutic uses	4.3	5.5	4.1	241.0	225.7	212.0	US$/kg	541
9301	Military weapons, other than revolvers, pistols and the arms of heading 93.07	...	...	13.2					891

Chile

Goods Imports: CIF, by consignment | **Goods Exports: FOB, by last known destination** | **Trade System: General**

Overview:

In 2015, the value of merchandise exports of Chile decreased substantially by 17.3 percent to reach 63.4 bln US$, while its merchandise imports decreased substantially by 12.9 percent to reach 63.0 bln US$ (see graph 1, table 2 and table 3). The merchandise trade balance recorded a relatively small surplus of 322.5 mln US$ (see graph 1). The largest merchandise trade balance was with MDG Eastern Asia at 5.1 bln US$ (see graph 4). Merchandise exports in Chile were diversified amongst partners; imports were also diversified. The top 15 partners accounted for 80 percent or more of exports and 14 partners accounted for 80 percent or more of imports (see graph 5). In 2014, the value of exports of services of Chile decreased substantially by 11.9 percent, reaching 11.0 bln US$, while its imports of services decreased moderately by 7.1 percent and reached 14.7 bln US$ (see graph 2). There was a moderate trade in services deficit of 3.8 bln US$.

Graph 1: Total merchandise trade, by value

(Bln US$ by year)

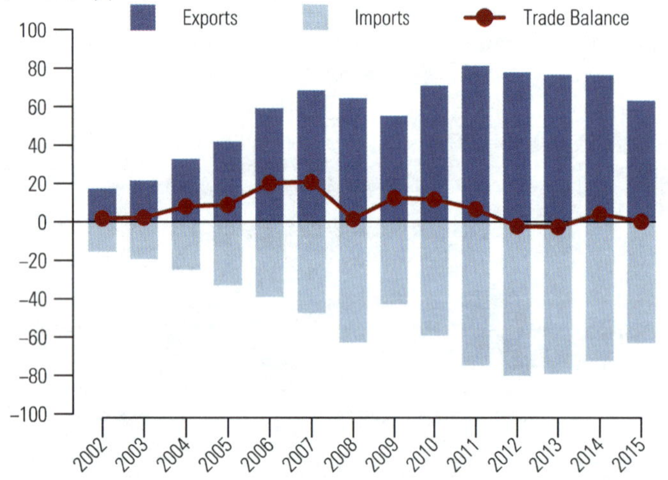

Graph 2: Total services trade, by value

(Bln US$ by year)

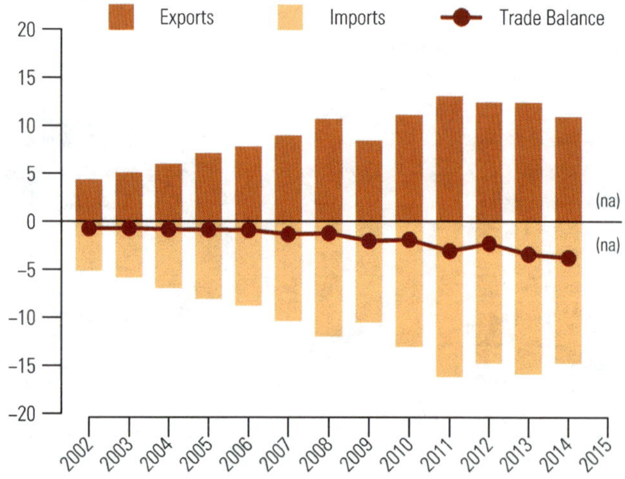

Exports Profile:

"Crude materials + anim. & veg. oils" (SITC section 2+4), "Goods classified chiefly by material" (SITC section 6) and "Food, animals + beverages, tobacco" (SITC section 0+1) were the largest commodity groups for exports in 2015, representing respectively 33.8, 31.6 and 23.5 percent of exported goods (see table 2). From 2013 to 2015, the largest export commodity was "Refined copper and copper alloys, unwrought" (HS code 7403) (see table 1). The top three destinations for merchandise exports were China, the United States and Japan, accounting for respectively 25.2, 12.6 and 9.6 percent of total exports. "Transportation" (EBOPS code 205) accounted for the largest share of exports of services in 2014 at 4.8 bln US$, followed by "Other business services" (EBOPS code 268) at 2.5 bln US$ and "Travel" (EBOPS code 236) at 2.3 bln US$ (see graph 3).

Graph 3: Exports of services by EBOPS category

(% share in 2014)

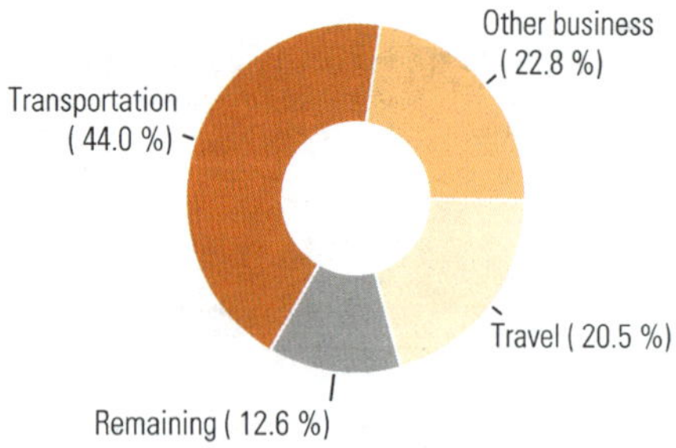

Table 1: Top 10 export commodities 2013 to 2015

HS code	4-digit heading of Harmonized System 2012	Value (million US$)			Unit value				SITC code
		2013	2014	2015	2013	2014	2015	Unit	
	All Commodities	76684.1	76639.2	63360.1					
7403	Refined copper and copper alloys, unwrought	18805.1	18105.6	14381.2	7.1	6.8	5.4	US$/kg	682
2603	Copper ores and concentrates	16883.1	16816.9	13891.0	6.8	6.4	5.1	US$/kg	283
7402	Unrefined copper; copper anodes for electrolytic refining	3552.1	3005.7	2177.4	7.5	6.9	5.4	US$/kg	682
4703	Chemical wood pulp, soda or sulphate, other than dissolving grades	2804.9	2890.1	2572.1	0.6	0.6	0.6	US$/kg	251
0304	Fish fillets and other fish meat (whether or not minced)	1988.2	2332.0	1893.0	8.3	9.5		US$/kg	034
2204	Wine of fresh grapes, including fortified wines	1968.7	1856.0	1842.7	2.2	2.3	2.1	US$/litre	112
0806	Grapes, fresh or dried	1794.0	1690.2	1486.1	1.9	2.1	1.8	US$/kg	057
0303	Fish, frozen, excluding fish fillets and other fish meat of heading 03.04	1367.6	1707.8	1325.3	3.7	4.6		US$/kg	034
7108	Gold (including gold plated with platinum)	1382.2	1066.7	796.4	43.8	38.5	36.1	thsd US$/kg	971
2601	Iron ores and concentrates, including roasted iron pyrites	1378.8	1140.2	717.6	0.1	0.1	0.1	US$/kg	281

Services Imports and Exports: EBOPS 2002 categories

Table 2: Merchandise exports by SITC

(Value in million US$, growth and shares in percentage)

SITC	2015	Avg. Growth rates 2011-2015	Avg. Growth rates 2014-2015	2015 share
Total	63360.1	-6.1	-17.3	100.0
0+1	14874.7	1.5	-10.6	23.5
2+4	21407.3	-2.8	-17.8	33.8
3	443.7	-14.4	-31.0	0.7
5	2880.3	-4.8	-15.0	4.5
6	20005.4	-12.5	-20.5	31.6
7	2004.3	-4.1	-24.1	3.2
8	944.0	-5.9	-11.2	1.5
9	800.4	-13.8	-25.0	1.3

Table 3: Merchandise imports by SITC

(Value in million US$, growth and shares in percentage)

SITC	2015	Avg. Growth rates 2011-2015	Avg. Growth rates 2014-2015	2015 share
Total	63037.6	-4.2	-12.9	100.0
0+1	5143.2	0.1	-7.0	8.2
2+4	1445.3	-11.5	-26.5	2.3
3	8920.9	-16.0	-41.8	14.2
5	7625.8	0.6	-3.1	12.1
6	8235.2	0.1	-2.6	13.1
7	23707.6	-2.6	-4.2	37.6
8	7919.9	2.3	-6.1	12.6
9	39.7	361.5	101.1	0.1

SITC Legend

SITC Code	Description
Total	All commodities
0+1	Food, animals + beverages, tobacco
2+4	Crude materials + anim. & veg. oils
3	Mineral fuels, lubricants
5	Chemicals
6	Goods classified chiefly by material
7	Machinery and transport equipment
8	Miscellaneous manufactured articles
9	Not classified elsewhere in the SITC

Graph 4: Merchandise trade balance

(Bln US$ by MDG Regions in 2015)

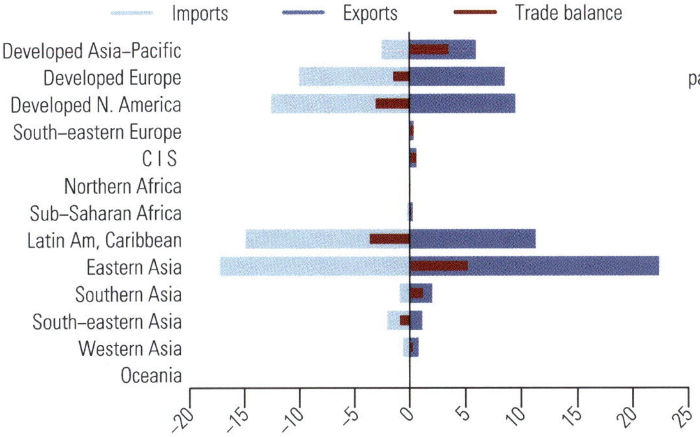

Graph 5: Partner concentration of merchandise trade

(Cumulative share by ranked partners in 2015)

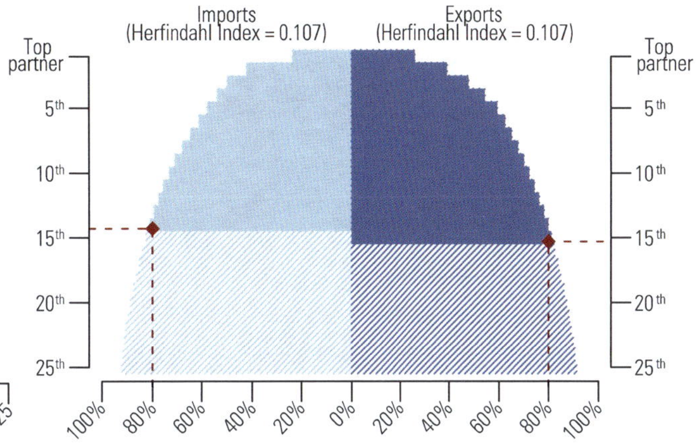

Graph 6: Imports of services by EBOPS category

(% share in 2014)

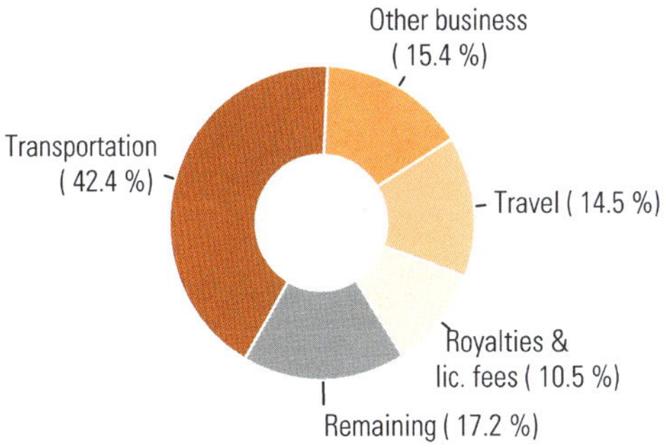

Imports Profile:

"Machinery and transport equipment" (SITC section 7), "Mineral fuels, lubricants" (SITC section 3) and "Goods classified chiefly by material" (SITC section 6) were the largest commodity groups for imports in 2015, representing respectively 37.6, 14.2 and 13.1 percent of imported goods (see table 3). From 2013 to 2015, the largest import commodity was "Petroleum oils, other than crude" (HS code 2710) (see table 4). The top three partners for merchandise imports were China, the United States and Brazil, accounting for respectively 21.2, 19.7 and 7.3 percent of total imports. "Transportation" (EBOPS code 205) accounted for the largest share of imports of services in 2014 at 6.2 bln US$, followed by "Other business services" (EBOPS code 268) at 2.3 bln US$ and "Travel" (EBOPS code 236) at 2.1 bln US$ (see graph 6).

Table 4: Top 10 import commodities 2013 to 2015

HS code	4-digit heading of Harmonized System 2012	Value (million US$) 2013	Value (million US$) 2014	Value (million US$) 2015	Unit value 2013	Unit value 2014	Unit value 2015	Unit	SITC code
	All Commodities	79172.8	72344.3	63037.6					
2710	Petroleum oils, other than crude	7088.5	6272.5	4001.0	*1.1*	*1.0*		US$/kg	334
2709	Petroleum oils and oils obtained from bituminous minerals, crude	6633.4	6040.6	2854.3	0.7	0.7	0.3	US$/kg	333
8703	Motor cars and other motor vehicles principally designed for the transport	4476.9	3744.6	3217.2	*14.7*	*15.7*	*14.8*	thsd US$/unit	781
8517	Electrical apparatus for line telephony or line telegraphy	2591.1	2017.3	2344.6					764
8704	Motor vehicles for the transport of goods	2612.8	1935.8	1712.2					782
2711	Petroleum gases and other gaseous hydrocarbons	1901.1	1950.7	1226.1	*0.5*	0.5		US$/kg	343
8471	Automatic data processing machines and units thereof	1428.1	1142.2	1191.1	*147.0*			US$/unit	752
4011	New pneumatic tyres, of rubber	1216.7	1095.7	1009.9		*149.1*	*124.5*	US$/unit	625
8802	Other aircraft (for example, helicopters, aeroplanes); spacecraft	1279.0	864.5	907.1	14.5	8.5		mln US$/unit	792
8708	Parts and accessories of the motor vehicles of headings 87.01 to 87.05	942.7	1034.2	1018.0	*12.4*	*13.1*	*12.6*	US$/kg	784

Source: UN Comtrade

China

Goods Imports: CIF, by origin | **Goods Exports: FOB, by last known destination** | **Trade System: General**

Overview:

In 2015, China was again the world's top exporter of merchandise goods. The value of merchandise exports of China decreased slightly by 2.6 percent to reach 2281.9 bln US$ in 2015, while its merchandise imports decreased substantially by 14.1 percent to reach 1681.7 bln US$ (see graph 1, table 2 and table 3). The merchandise trade balance recorded a moderate surplus of 600.2 bln US$ (see graph 1). The largest merchandise trade balance was with MDG Developed North America at 263.7 bln US$ (see graph 4). Merchandise exports in China were diversified amongst partners; imports were also diversified. The top 25 partners accounted for 80 percent or more of exports and 21 partners accounted for 80 percent or more of imports (see graph 5). In 2014, the value of exports of services of China increased substantially by 14.6 percent, reaching 210.6 bln US$, while its imports of services increased substantially by 15.8 percent and reached 382.9 bln US$ (see graph 2). There was a moderate trade in services deficit of 172.3 bln US$.

Graph 1: Total merchandise trade, by value

(Bln US$ by year)

Graph 2: Total services trade, by value

(Bln US$ by year)

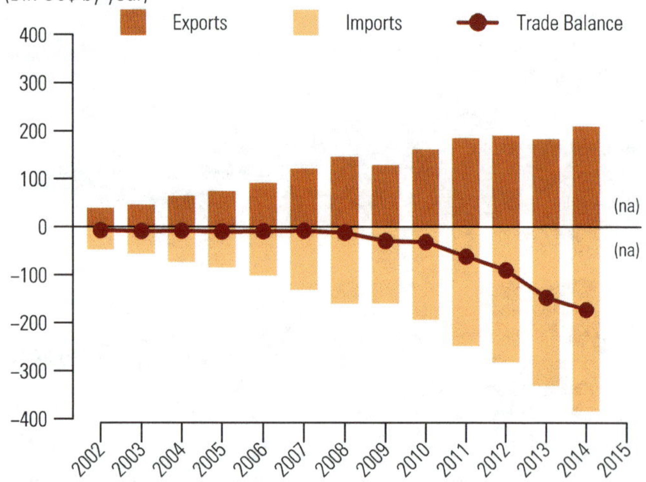

Exports Profile:

"Machinery and transport equipment" (SITC section 7), "Miscellaneous manufactured articles" (SITC section 8) and "Goods classified chiefly by material" (SITC section 6) were the largest commodity groups for exports in 2015, representing respectively 46.8, 25.7 and 17.2 percent of exported goods (see table 2). From 2013 to 2015, the largest export commodity was "Electrical apparatus for line telephony or line telegraphy" (HS code 8517). China's exports of this commodity grew by 9.2 percent from 2014 to 2015 (see table 1). The top three destinations for merchandise exports were the United States, China, Hong Kong SAR and Japan, accounting for respectively 17.2, 15.8 and 6.4 percent of total exports. "Other business services" (EBOPS code 268) accounted for the largest share of exports of services in 2014 at 68.9 bln US$, followed by "Travel" (EBOPS code 236) at 56.9 bln US$ and "Transportation" (EBOPS code 205) at 38.2 bln US$ (see graph 3).

Graph 3: Exports of services by EBOPS category

(% share in 2014)

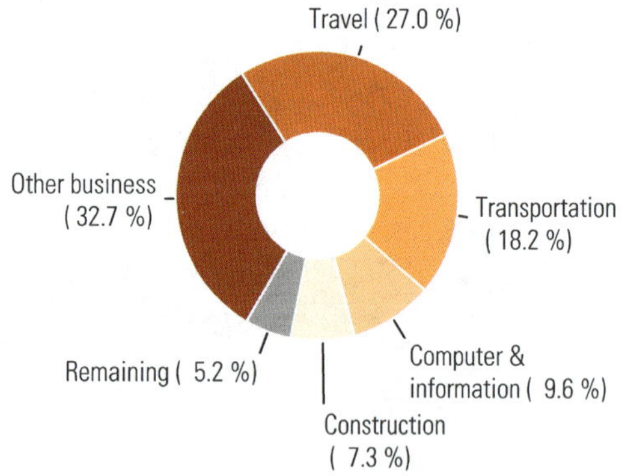

Table 1: Top 10 export commodities 2013 to 2015

HS code	4-digit heading of Harmonized System 2012	Value (billion US$) 2013	2014	2015	Unit value 2013	2014	2015	Unit	SITC code
	All Commodities	2 209.0	2 342.3	2 281.9					
8517	Electrical apparatus for line telephony or line telegraphy	174.9	195.3	213.2					764
8471	Automatic data processing machines and units thereof	161.7	163.4	137.3	92.2	90.1	84.2	US$/unit	752
8542	Electronic integrated circuits	87.9	61.2	70.1					776
9013	Liquid crystal devices	38.6	34.7	34.0					871
7113	Articles of jewellery and parts thereof, of precious metal	28.9	48.5	18.6	32.2	50.3	30.4	thsd US$/kg	897
8541	Diodes, transistors and similar semiconductor devices	27.9	30.6	33.6					776
9405	Lamps and lighting fittings	24.7	31.1	35.8	*10.3*	*14.7*	*11.8*	US$/kg	813
8473	Parts and accessories for use with machines of heading 84.69 to 84.72	29.4	31.2	28.9	*37.0*	*42.9*	*48.9*	US$/kg	759
9403	Other furniture and parts thereof	28.9	28.4	29.2					821
8528	Reception apparatus for television	26.7	30.3	28.2	98.5	98.7	93.0	US$/unit	761

Services Imports and Exports: EBOPS 2002 categories

Table 2: Merchandise exports by SITC

(Value in million US$, growth and shares in percentage)

SITC	2015	Avg. Growth rates 2011-2015	Avg. Growth rates 2014-2015	2015 share
Total	2 281 855.9	4.7	-2.6	100.0
0+1	61 527.3	3.9	-0.4	2.7
2+4	14 627.0	-1.5	-11.4	0.6
3	27 943.8	-3.5	-18.9	1.2
5	129 616.5	3.1	-3.6	5.7
6	393 489.9	5.3	-2.1	17.2
7	1 067 094.0	4.3	-0.4	46.8
8	585 526.0	6.3	-5.4	25.7
9	2 031.5	-3.5	-10.4	0.1

Table 3: Merchandise imports by SITC

(Value in million US$, growth and shares in percentage)

SITC	2015	Avg. Growth rates 2011-2015	Avg. Growth rates 2014-2015	2015 share
Total	1 681 670.8	-0.9	-14.1	100.0
0+1	56 285.2	14.8	9.4	3.3
2+4	219 255.0	-7.3	-21.5	13.0
3	198 668.2	-7.9	-37.3	11.8
5	170 887.2	-1.4	-10.9	10.2
6	135 042.5	-2.6	-22.0	8.0
7	688 286.3	2.2	-5.0	40.9
8	132 721.7	1.0	-3.8	7.9
9	80 524.7	12.9	-2.7	4.8

SITC Legend

SITC Code	Description
Total	All commodities
0+1	Food, animals + beverages, tobacco
2+4	Crude materials + anim. & veg. oils
3	Mineral fuels, lubricants
5	Chemicals
6	Goods classified chiefly by material
7	Machinery and transport equipment
8	Miscellaneous manufactured articles
9	Not classified elsewhere in the SITC

Graph 4: Merchandise trade balance

(Bln US$ by MDG Regions in 2015)

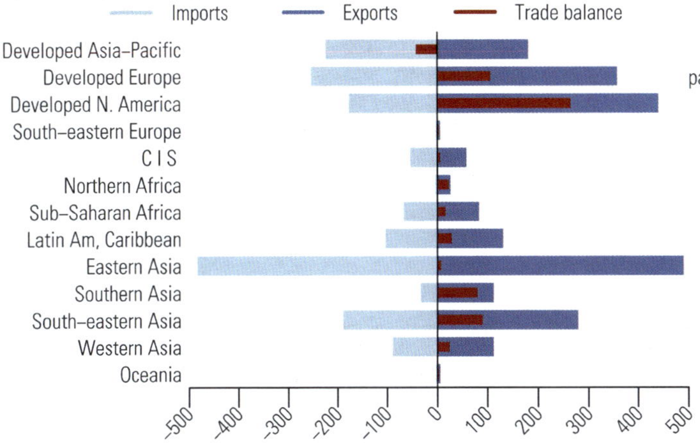

Graph 5: Partner concentration of merchandise trade

(Cumulative share by ranked partners in 2015)

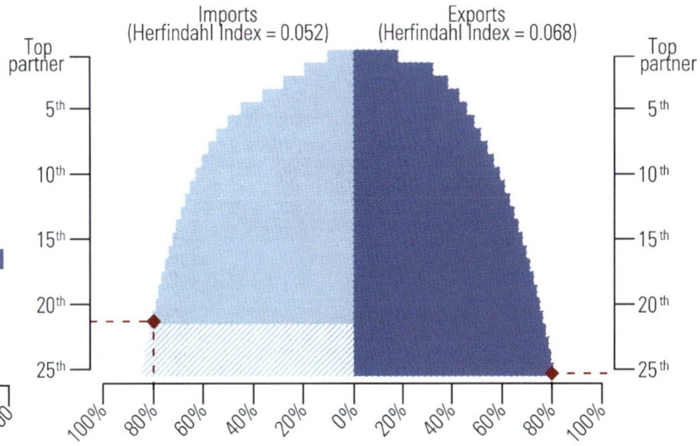

Graph 6: Imports of services by EBOPS category

(% share in 2014)

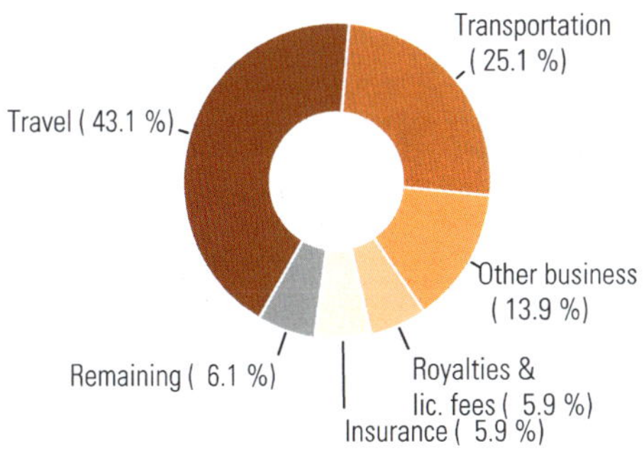

Imports Profile:

"Machinery and transport equipment" (SITC section 7), "Crude materials + anim. & veg. oils" (SITC section 2+4) and "Mineral fuels, lubricants" (SITC section 3) were the largest commodity groups for imports in 2015, representing respectively 40.9, 13.0 and 11.8 percent of imported goods (see table 3). From 2013 to 2015, the largest import commodity was "Electronic integrated circuits" (HS code 8542) (see table 4). The top three partners for merchandise imports were the Republic of Korea, Japan and the United States, accounting for respectively 9.8, 8.4 and 8.3 percent of total imports. "Travel" (EBOPS code 236) accounted for the largest share of imports of services in 2014 at 164.9 bln US$, followed by "Transportation" (EBOPS code 205) at 96.2 bln US$ and "Other business services" (EBOPS code 268) at 53.4 bln US$ (see graph 6).

Table 4: Top 10 import commodities 2013 to 2015

HS code	4-digit heading of Harmonized System 2012	Value (billion US$) 2013	Value (billion US$) 2014	Value (billion US$) 2015	Unit value 2013	Unit value 2014	Unit value 2015	Unit	SITC code
	All Commodities	1 950.0	1 958.0	1 681.7					
8542	Electronic integrated circuits	232.1	218.5	231.1					776
2709	Petroleum oils and oils obtained from bituminous minerals, crude	219.7	228.3	134.3	0.8	0.7	0.4	US$/kg	333
9999	Commodities not specified according to kind	104.7	82.8	80.5					931
2601	Iron ores and concentrates, including roasted iron pyrites	106.2	93.5	57.9	0.1	0.1	*0.1*	US$/kg	281
9013	Liquid crystal devices	55.4	50.0	46.3					871
8703	Motor cars and other motor vehicles principally designed for the transport	47.5	59.7	44.2	40.1	42.2	40.4	thsd US$/unit	781
8517	Electrical apparatus for line telephony or line telegraphy	46.9	43.9	48.9					764
1201	Soya beans, whether or not broken	38.0	40.3	34.9	0.6	0.6	0.4	US$/kg	222
8541	Diodes, transistors and similar semiconductor devices	29.2	31.4	30.7					776
8471	Automatic data processing machines and units thereof	29.1	28.7	26.1	39.5	38.1	36.8	US$/unit	752

China, Hong Kong SAR

Goods Imports: CIF, by origin | **Goods Exports: FOB, by last known destination** | **Trade System: General**

Overview:

In 2015, the value of merchandise exports of China, Hong Kong SAR decreased slightly by 4.9 percent to reach 498.6 bln US$, while its merchandise imports decreased moderately by 8.8 percent to reach 547.6 bln US$ (see graph 1, table 2 and table 3). The merchandise trade balance recorded a relatively small deficit, narrowing to 49.0 bln US$ (see graph 1). The largest merchandise trade balance was with MDG South-eastern Asia at -34.9 bln US$ (see graph 4). Merchandise exports in China, Hong Kong SAR were highly concentrated amongst partners; imports were moderately concentrated. The top 10 partners accounted for 80 percent or more of exports and 8 partners accounted for 80 percent or more of imports (see graph 5). In 2013, the value of exports of services of China, Hong Kong SAR decreased substantially by 22.3 percent, reaching 100.5 bln US$, while its imports of services increased slightly by 1.7 percent and reached 59.7 bln US$ (see graph 2). There was a moderate trade in services surplus of 40.8 bln US$, down from the trade in service surplus in 2012 of 70.6 bln US$.

Graph 1: Total merchandise trade, by value

(Bln US$ by year)

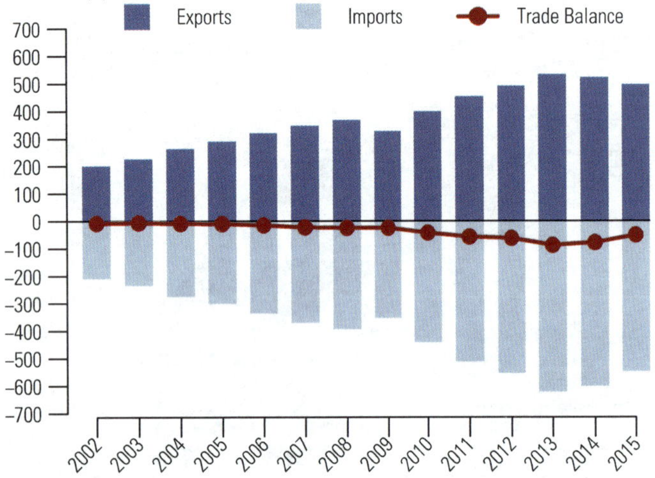

Graph 2: Total services trade, by value

(Bln US$ by year)

Exports Profile:

"Machinery and transport equipment" (SITC section 7), "Miscellaneous manufactured articles" (SITC section 8) and "Not classified elsewhere in the SITC" (SITC section 9) were the largest commodity groups for exports in 2015, representing respectively 62.6, 15.1 and 9.0 percent of exported goods (see table 2). From 2013 to 2015, the largest export commodity was "Electronic integrated circuits" (HS code 8542), accounting for 17.2 percent of total merchandise exports by value in 2015 (see table 1). The top three destinations for merchandise exports were China, the United States and Japan, accounting for respectively 58.1, 8.3 and 3.2 percent of total exports. "Travel" (EBOPS code 236) accounted for the largest share of exports of services in 2013 at 38.9 bln US$, followed by "Transportation" (EBOPS code 205) at 30.8 bln US$ and "Other business services" (EBOPS code 268) at 12.8 bln US$ (see graph 3).

Graph 3: Exports of services by EBOPS category

(% share in 2013)

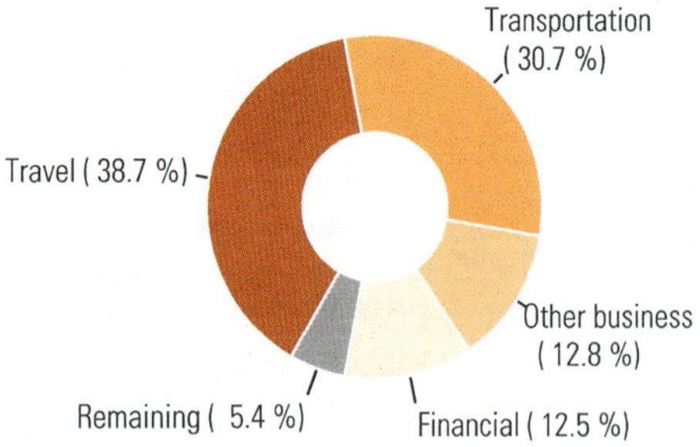

Table 1: Top 10 export commodities 2013 to 2015

HS code	4-digit heading of Harmonized System 2012	Value (million US$) 2013	2014	2015	Unit value 2013	2014	2015	Unit	SITC code
	All Commodities	535 186.7	524 064.9	498 557.6					
8542	Electronic integrated circuits	67 365.5	77 458.1	85 539.5					776
8517	Electrical apparatus for line telephony or line telegraphy	64 329.4	69 571.0	75 127.6					764
7108	Gold (including gold plated with platinum)	76 190.6	49 952.6	45 005.7	*49.3*	41.2	37.7	thsd US$/kg	971
8473	Parts and accessories for use with machines of heading 84.69 to 84.72	26 068.8	26 478.7	24 194.6		84.7	86.8	US$/kg	759
8471	Automatic data processing machines and units thereof	16 823.9	17 650.1	18 489.6		47.9	59.9	US$/unit	752
7102	Diamonds, whether or not worked, but not mounted or set	14 786.0	16 105.4	14 969.1					667
8529	Parts suitable for use with the apparatus of headings 85.25 to 85.28	12 926.1	11 607.1	11 369.1		85.6	98.0	US$/kg	764
8541	Diodes, transistors and similar semiconductor devices	10 267.3	12 857.6	10 610.1					776
8504	Electrical transformers, static converters	10 928.1	11 208.8	10 416.0					771
8534	Printed circuits	9 410.5	9 802.3	9 737.9		57.8	59.1	US$/kg	772

Services Imports and Exports: EBOPS 2002 categories

Table 2: Merchandise exports by SITC

(Value in million US$, growth and shares in percentage)

SITC	2015	Avg. Growth rates 2011-2015	Avg. Growth rates 2014-2015	2015 share
Total	498 557.6	2.3	-4.9	100.0
0+1	9 090.2	6.6	6.2	1.8
2+4	2 408.7	-8.7	-22.7	0.5
3	726.4	-6.3	-15.0	0.1
5	14 066.3	-8.4	-20.9	2.8
6	39 559.0	-5.2	-18.0	7.9
7	312 343.1	5.1	1.1	62.6
8	75 296.4	-4.9	-12.2	15.1
9	45 067.5	13.9	-11.1	9.0

Table 3: Merchandise imports by SITC

(Value in million US$, growth and shares in percentage)

SITC	2015	Avg. Growth rates 2011-2015	Avg. Growth rates 2014-2015	2015 share
Total	547 568.5	1.8	-8.8	100.0
0+1	25 021.4	4.4	-5.9	4.6
2+4	3 132.9	-7.9	-12.4	0.6
3	12 122.1	-10.4	-23.1	2.2
5	15 502.1	-10.8	-29.2	2.8
6	47 662.2	-3.8	-15.0	8.7
7	330 623.6	5.0	-0.4	60.4
8	76 774.1	-3.2	-13.7	14.0
9	36 730.0	8.0	-34.3	6.7

SITC Legend

SITC Code	Description
Total	All commodities
0+1	Food, animals + beverages, tobacco
2+4	Crude materials + anim. & veg. oils
3	Mineral fuels, lubricants
5	Chemicals
6	Goods classified chiefly by material
7	Machinery and transport equipment
8	Miscellaneous manufactured articles
9	Not classified elsewhere in the SITC

Graph 4: Merchandise trade balance

(Bln US$ by MDG Regions in 2015)

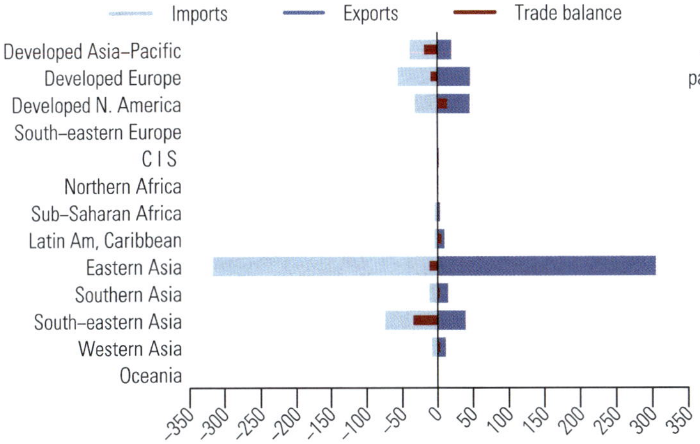

Graph 5: Partner concentration of merchandise trade

(Cumulative share by ranked partners in 2015)

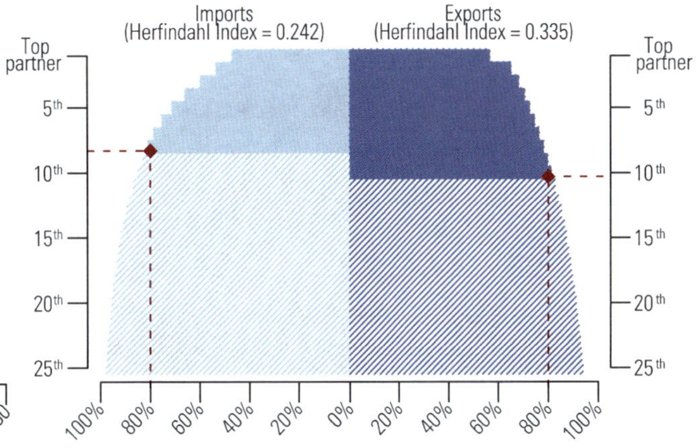

Graph 6: Imports of services by EBOPS category

(% share in 2013)

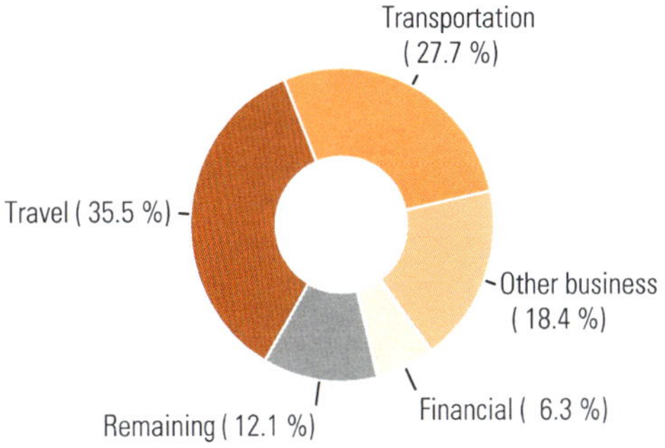

Imports Profile:

"Machinery and transport equipment" (SITC section 7), "Miscellaneous manufactured articles" (SITC section 8) and "Goods classified chiefly by material" (SITC section 6) were the largest commodity groups for imports in 2015, representing respectively 60.4, 14.0 and 8.7 percent of imported goods (see table 3). From 2013 to 2015, the largest import commodity was "Electronic integrated circuits" (HS code 8542), accounting for 18.5 percent of total merchandise imports by value in 2015 (see table 4). The top three partners for merchandise imports were China, Japan and Other Asia nes, accounting for respectively 44.8, 6.3 and 6.2 percent of total imports. "Travel" (EBOPS code 236) accounted for the largest share of imports of services in 2013 at 21.2 bln US$, followed by "Transportation" (EBOPS code 205) at 16.5 bln US$ and "Other business services" (EBOPS code 268) at 11.0 bln US$ (see graph 6).

Table 4: Top 10 import commodities 2013 to 2015

HS code	4-digit heading of Harmonized System 2012	Value (million US$) 2013	Value (million US$) 2014	Value (million US$) 2015	Unit value 2013	Unit value 2014	Unit value 2015	Unit	SITC code
	All Commodities	621 416.9	600 613.1	547 568.5					
8542	Electronic integrated circuits	81 418.9	98 116.7	101 098.9					776
8517	Electrical apparatus for line telephony or line telegraphy	61 337.1	68 951.5	77 872.6					764
7108	Gold (including gold plated with platinum)	97 142.9	54 964.5	36 212.6	43.4	37.9	33.9	thsd US$/kg	971
8471	Automatic data processing machines and units thereof	22 444.9	22 676.1	22 520.8		55.2	62.5	US$/unit	752
7102	Diamonds, whether or not worked, but not mounted or set	20 068.5	21 926.9	19 081.6					667
8473	Parts and accessories for use with machines of heading 84.69 to 84.72	21 961.3	19 339.6	17 266.8		68.0	65.2	US$/kg	759
8541	Diodes, transistors and similar semiconductor devices	12 968.7	15 532.0	12 804.3					776
7113	Articles of jewellery and parts thereof, of precious metal	12 247.2	14 156.3	10 890.3	36.4	36.6	30.6	thsd US$/kg	897
2710	Petroleum oils, other than crude	14 717.9	12 726.9	9 047.9	*1.6*	*1.7*	*1.7*	US$/kg	334
8529	Parts suitable for use with the apparatus of headings 85.25 to 85.28	11 229.7	9 693.5	8 934.2		71.4	83.4	US$/kg	764

China, Macao SAR

Goods Imports: CIF, by origin | **Goods Exports: FOB, by last known destination** | **Trade System: General**

Overview:

In 2015, the value of merchandise exports of China, Macao SAR increased moderately by 8.0 percent to reach 1.3 bln US$, while its merchandise imports decreased moderately by 7.0 percent to reach 10.6 bln US$ (see graph 1, table 2 and table 3). The merchandise trade balance recorded a large deficit of 9.3 bln US$ (see graph 1). The largest merchandise trade balance was with MDG Eastern Asia at -9.4 bln US$ (see graph 4). Merchandise exports in China, Macao SAR were highly concentrated amongst partners; imports were also highly concentrated. The top 2 partners accounted for 80 percent or more of exports and 1 partner accounted for 80 percent or more of imports (see graph 5). In 2014, the value of exports of services of China, Macao SAR decreased slightly by 0.9 percent, reaching 53.1 bln US$, while its imports of services decreased substantially by 10.9 percent and reached 10.4 bln US$ (see graph 2). There was a large trade in services surplus of 42.7 bln US$.

Graph 1: Total merchandise trade, by value

(Bln US$ by year)

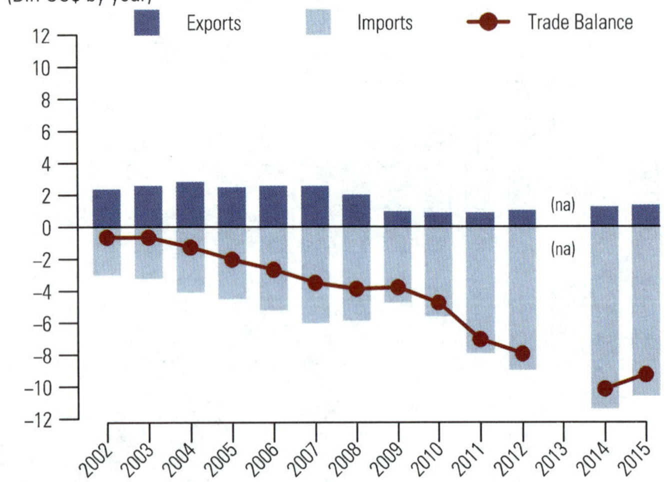

Graph 2: Total services trade, by value

(Bln US$ by year)

Exports Profile:

"Not classified elsewhere in the SITC" (SITC section 9), "Miscellaneous manufactured articles" (SITC section 8) and "Machinery and transport equipment" (SITC section 7) were the largest commodity groups for exports in 2015, representing respectively 43.5, 29.2 and 20.0 percent of exported goods (see table 2). From 2013 to 2015, the largest export commodity was "Commodities not specified according to kind" (HS code 9999) (see table 1). The top three destinations for merchandise exports were China, Hong Kong SAR, Special Categories and Areas nes, accounting for respectively 50.7, 37.7 and 25.3 percent of total exports. "Travel" (EBOPS code 236) accounted for the largest share of exports of services in 2014 at 51.0 bln US$ (see graph 3).

Graph 3: Exports of services by EBOPS category

(% share in 2014)

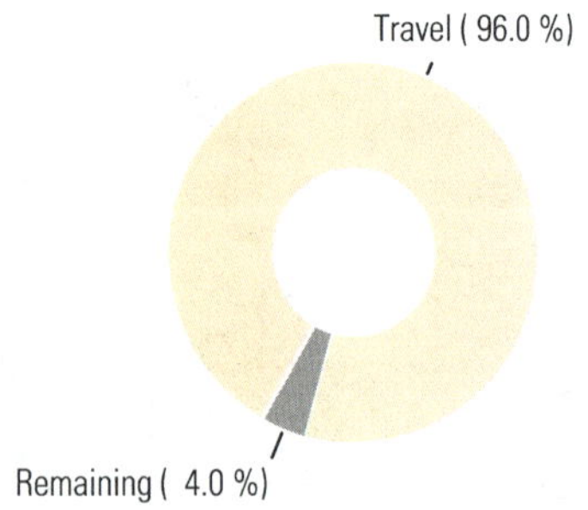

Table 1: Top 10 export commodities 2013 to 2015

HS code	4-digit heading of Harmonized System 2012	Value (million US$) 2013	2014	2015	Unit value 2013	2014	2015	Unit	SITC code
	All Commodities	...	1 240.0	1 339.0					
9999	Commodities not specified according to kind	...	447.0	582.3					931
9101	Wrist-watches, pocket-watches and other watches, precious metal	...	96.6	142.5		27.1		thsd US$/unit	885
8517	Electrical apparatus for line telephony or line telegraphy	...	116.9	66.5					764
7113	Articles of jewellery and parts thereof, of precious metal	...	66.4	86.7		*235.6*	*216.8*	thsd US$/kg	897
8538	Parts suitable for use with the apparatus of heading 85.35, 85.36 or 85.37	...	47.9	62.6		380.6	492.0	US$/kg	772
4202	Trunks, suit-cases, vanity-cases, executive-cases, brief-cases	...	33.5	45.9					831
2402	Cigars, cheroots, cigarillos and cigarettes	...	62.0	2.5		*42.3*	56.6	US$/kg	122
8502	Electric generating sets and rotary converters	...	43.1	1.5					716
8536	Electrical apparatus for switching or protecting electrical circuits	...	6.6	36.5		85.0	95.4	US$/kg	772
8703	Motor cars and other motor vehicles principally designed for the transport	...	5.2	24.9		54.7	*21.4*	thsd US$/unit	781

Services Imports and Exports: EBOPS 2002 categories

Table 2: Merchandise exports by SITC

(Value in million US$, growth and shares in percentage)

SITC	2015	Avg. Growth rates 2011-2015	Avg. Growth rates 2014-2015	2015 share
Total	1 339.0	11.4	8.0	100.0
0+1	26.4	6.2	-73.9	2.0
2+4	6.1	-4.7	-70.4	0.5
3	0.0	...	-59.4	0.0
5	38.5	59.9	172.9	2.9
6	26.8	10.8	8.9	2.0
7	268.4	34.6	-9.1	20.0
8	390.6	33.8	15.7	29.2
9	582.3	-1.3	30.3	43.5

Table 3: Merchandise imports by SITC

(Value in million US$, growth and shares in percentage)

SITC	2015	Avg. Growth rates 2011-2015	Avg. Growth rates 2014-2015	2015 share
Total	10 602.6	7.5	-7.0	100.0
0+1	1 681.8	8.3	1.9	15.9
2+4	74.1	13.7	6.5	0.7
3	735.8	3.3	-6.5	6.9
5	814.5	16.8	3.9	7.7
6	822.4	20.8	12.7	7.8
7	2 470.8	10.1	-5.6	23.3
8	3 662.0	6.0	-11.7	34.5
9	341.3	-13.3	-44.0	3.2

SITC Legend

SITC Code	Description
Total	All commodities
0+1	Food, animals + beverages, tobacco
2+4	Crude materials + anim. & veg. oils
3	Mineral fuels, lubricants
5	Chemicals
6	Goods classified chiefly by material
7	Machinery and transport equipment
8	Miscellaneous manufactured articles
9	Not classified elsewhere in the SITC

Graph 4: Merchandise trade balance

(Bln US$ by MDG Regions in 2015)

Graph 5: Partner concentration of merchandise trade

(Cumulative share by ranked partners in 2015)

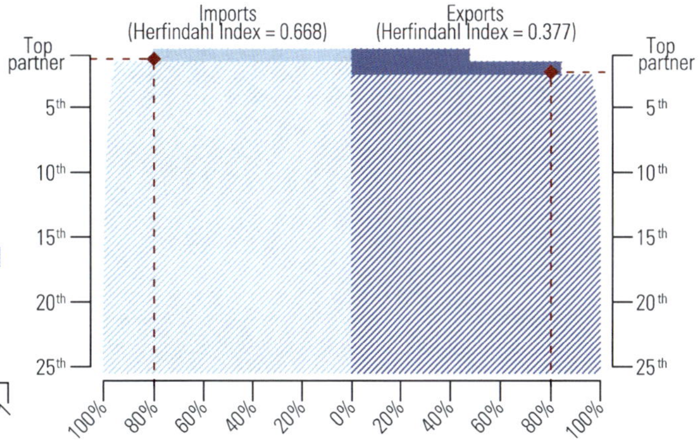

Graph 6: Imports of services by EBOPS category

(% share in 2014)

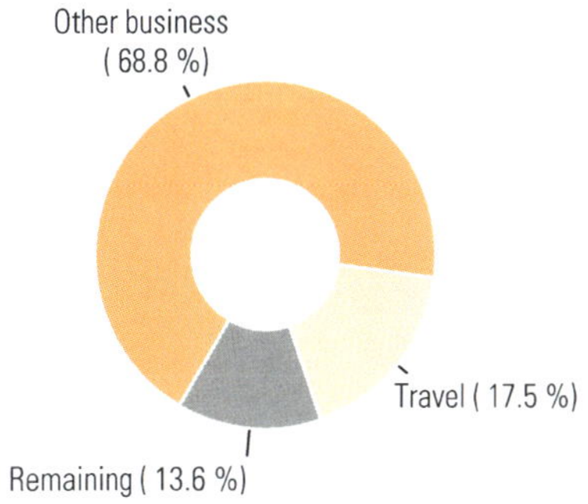

Imports Profile:

"Miscellaneous manufactured articles" (SITC section 8), "Machinery and transport equipment" (SITC section 7) and "Food, animals + beverages, tobacco" (SITC section 0+1) were the largest commodity groups for imports in 2015, representing respectively 34.5, 23.3 and 15.9 percent of imported goods (see table 3). From 2013 to 2015, the largest import commodity was "Articles of jewellery and parts thereof, of precious metal" (HS code 7113) (see table 4). The top three partners for merchandise imports were China, Hong Kong SAR, China and Switzerland, accounting for respectively 44.0, 24.2 and 4.7 percent of total imports. "Other business services" (EBOPS code 268) accounted for the largest share of imports of services in 2014 at 7.2 bln US$, followed by "Travel" (EBOPS code 236) at 1.8 bln US$ (see graph 6).

Table 4: Top 10 import commodities 2013 to 2015

HS code	4-digit heading of Harmonized System 2012	Value (million US$) 2013	Value (million US$) 2014	Value (million US$) 2015	Unit value 2013	Unit value 2014	Unit value 2015	Unit	SITC code
	All Commodities	...	11 395.9	10 602.6					
7113	Articles of jewellery and parts thereof, of precious metal	...	1 361.4	1 023.8		*66.5*	*44.3*	thsd US$/kg	897
8517	Electrical apparatus for line telephony or line telegraphy	...	998.0	1 083.4					764
9101	Wrist-watches, pocket-watches and other watches, precious metal	...	817.9	607.9		12.6		thsd US$/unit	885
9999	Commodities not specified according to kind	...	587.9	317.7					931
4202	Trunks, suit-cases, vanity-cases, executive-cases, brief-cases	...	475.9	415.6					831
2716	Electrical energy	...	432.1	429.3		105.4	*54.8*	US$/MWh	351
8703	Motor cars and other motor vehicles principally designed for the transport	...	434.3	323.1		41.5	*21.5*	thsd US$/unit	781
3304	Beauty or make-up preparations	...	380.8	370.0		*66.4*	*58.4*	US$/kg	553
1901	Malt extract; food preparations of flour	...	278.2	345.3		21.0	22.8	US$/kg	048
2710	Petroleum oils, other than crude	...	298.3	272.7		1.0	0.6	US$/kg	334

Colombia

Goods Imports: CIF, by origin | **Goods Exports: FOB, by last known destination** | **Trade System: Special**

Overview:

In 2015, the value of merchandise exports of Colombia decreased substantially by 34.9 percent to reach 35.7 bln US$, while its merchandise imports decreased substantially by 15.6 percent to reach 54.0 bln US$ (see graph 1, table 2 and table 3). The merchandise trade balance recorded a moderate deficit of 18.3 bln US$ (see graph 1). The largest merchandise trade balance was with MDG Eastern Asia at -9.2 bln US$ (see graph 4). Merchandise exports in Colombia were diversified amongst partners; imports were also diversified. The top 18 partners accounted for 80 percent or more of exports and 13 partners accounted for 80 percent or more of imports (see graph 5). In 2014, the value of exports of services of Colombia increased slightly by 0.3 percent, reaching 6.8 bln US$, while its imports of services increased slightly by 4.9 percent and reached 12.9 bln US$ (see graph 2). There was a large trade in services deficit of 6.1 bln US$.

Graph 1: Total merchandise trade, by value

(Bln US$ by year)

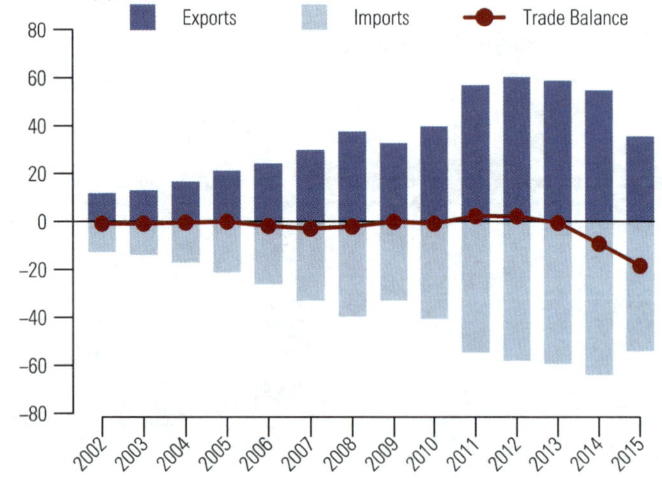

Graph 2: Total services trade, by value

(Bln US$ by year)

Exports Profile:

"Mineral fuels, lubricants" (SITC section 3), "Food, animals + beverages, tobacco" (SITC section 0+1) and "Chemicals" (SITC section 5) were the largest commodity groups for exports in 2015, representing respectively 52.8, 14.4 and 9.6 percent of exported goods (see table 2). From 2013 to 2015, the largest export commodity was "Petroleum oils and oils obtained from bituminous minerals, crude" (HS code 2709) (see table 1). The top three destinations for merchandise exports were the United States, China and Panama, accounting for respectively 28.9, 8.8 and 6.2 percent of total exports. "Travel" (EBOPS code 236) accounted for the largest share of exports of services in 2014 at 3.8 bln US$, followed by "Transportation" (EBOPS code 205) at 1.7 bln US$ and "Other business services" (EBOPS code 268) at 744.3 mln US$ (see graph 3).

Graph 3: Exports of services by EBOPS category

(% share in 2014)

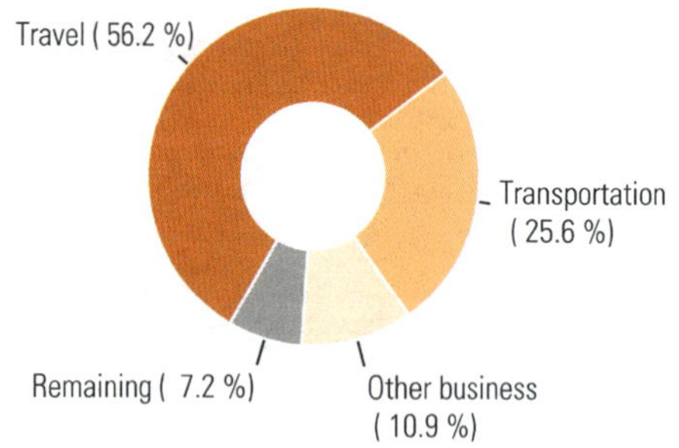

Table 1: Top 10 export commodities 2013 to 2015

HS code	4-digit heading of Harmonized System 2012	Value (million US$) 2013	2014	2015	Unit value 2013	2014	2015	Unit	SITC code
	All Commodities	58821.9	54794.8	35690.8					
2709	Petroleum oils and oils obtained from bituminous minerals, crude	27644.2	25760.8	12834.4	0.7	0.6	0.3	US$/kg	333
2701	Coal; briquettes, ovoids and similar solid fuels manufactured from coal	6253.8	6426.7	4257.4	0.1	0.1	0.1	US$/kg	321
2710	Petroleum oils, other than crude	4364.6	2855.1	1281.1	0.7	0.6	0.3	US$/kg	334
0901	Coffee, whether or not roasted or decaffeinated	1922.5	2516.7	2576.5	3.5	4.0	3.6	US$/kg	071
7108	Gold (including gold plated with platinum)	2226.5	1581.8	1089.9	38.9	33.0	29.8	thsd US$/kg	971
0603	Cut flowers and flower buds of a kind suitable for bouquets	1334.6	1374.2	1295.4	6.3	6.2	5.8	US$/kg	292
0803	Bananas, including plantains, fresh or dried	763.9	835.5	802.6	0.5	0.5	0.5	US$/kg	057
7202	Ferro-alloys	681.8	642.1	430.3	4.9	4.8	3.3	US$/kg	671
3004	Medicaments (excluding goods of heading 30.02, 30.05 or 30.06)	447.7	480.2	453.1	10.2	9.0	9.8	US$/kg	542
3808	Insecticides, rodenticides, fungicides, herbicides	442.0	392.6	456.2	8.0	6.8	7.9	US$/kg	591

Services Imports and Exports: EBOPS 2002 categories

Table 2: Merchandise exports by SITC

(Value in million US$, growth and shares in percentage)

SITC	2015	Avg. Growth rates 2011-2015	Avg. Growth rates 2014-2015	2015 share
Total	35690.8	-11.0	-34.9	100.0
0+1	5139.7	-1.3	-6.2	14.4
2+4	2140.9	-0.1	-4.9	6.0
3	18839.9	-15.2	-47.6	52.8
5	3423.0	0.8	-7.1	9.6
6	2367.7	-9.1	-20.1	6.6
7	1423.5	-4.6	-6.9	4.0
8	1255.0	-5.7	-7.7	3.5
9	1101.1	-20.8	-31.0	3.1

Table 3: Merchandise imports by SITC

(Value in million US$, growth and shares in percentage)

SITC	2015	Avg. Growth rates 2011-2015	Avg. Growth rates 2014-2015	2015 share
Total	54035.5	-0.3	-15.6	100.0
0+1	4823.2	3.0	-6.6	8.9
2+4	1349.4	-4.5	-9.9	2.5
3	5132.6	7.4	-32.1	9.5
5	10043.3	2.2	-6.9	18.6
6	7581.9	-3.0	-16.1	14.0
7	19890.6	-2.8	-16.1	36.8
8	4597.4	1.1	-18.0	8.5
9	617.1	5.2	-6.9	1.1

SITC Legend

SITC Code	Description
Total	All commodities
0+1	Food, animals + beverages, tobacco
2+4	Crude materials + anim. & veg. oils
3	Mineral fuels, lubricants
5	Chemicals
6	Goods classified chiefly by material
7	Machinery and transport equipment
8	Miscellaneous manufactured articles
9	Not classified elsewhere in the SITC

Graph 4: Merchandise trade balance

(Bln US$ by MDG Regions in 2015)

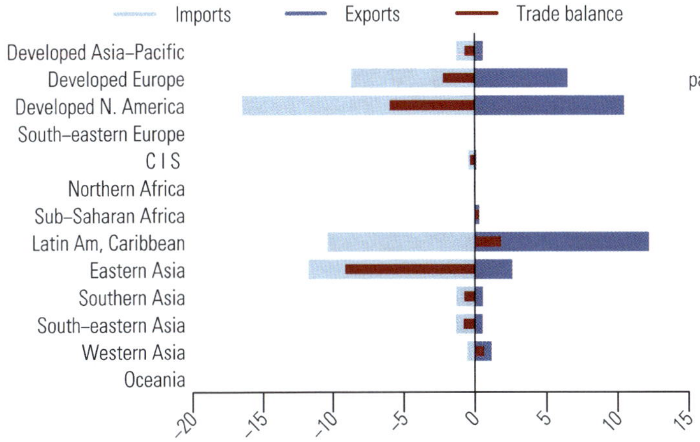

Graph 5: Partner concentration of merchandise trade

(Cumulative share by ranked partners in 2015)

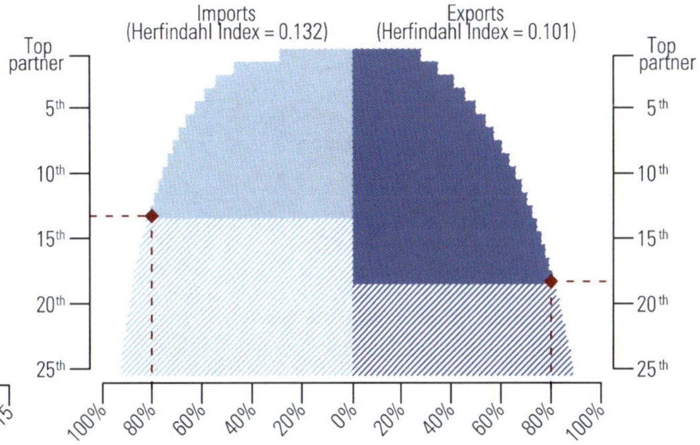

Graph 6: Imports of services by EBOPS category

(% share in 2014)

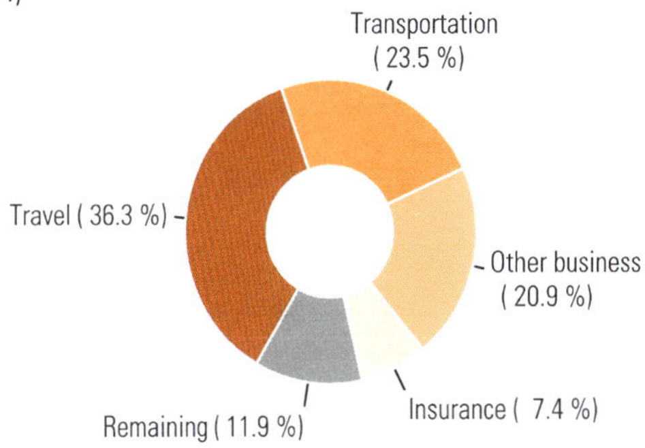

Imports Profile:

"Machinery and transport equipment" (SITC section 7), "Chemicals" (SITC section 5) and "Goods classified chiefly by material" (SITC section 6) were the largest commodity groups for imports in 2015, representing respectively 36.8, 18.6 and 14.0 percent of imported goods (see table 3). From 2013 to 2015, the largest import commodity was "Petroleum oils, other than crude" (HS code 2710) (see table 4). The top three partners for merchandise imports were the United States, China and Mexico, accounting for respectively 28.3, 18.1 and 8.2 percent of total imports. "Travel" (EBOPS code 236) accounted for the largest share of imports of services in 2014 at 4.7 bln US$, followed by "Transportation" (EBOPS code 205) at 3.0 bln US$ and "Other business services" (EBOPS code 268) at 2.7 bln US$ (see graph 6).

Table 4: Top 10 import commodities 2013 to 2015

HS code	4-digit heading of Harmonized System 2012	Value (million US$) 2013	Value (million US$) 2014	Value (million US$) 2015	Unit value 2013	Unit value 2014	Unit value 2015	Unit	SITC code
	All Commodities	59381.2	64027.6	54035.5					
2710	Petroleum oils, other than crude	6332.7	7492.4	5088.6	1.0	0.9	0.6	US$/kg	334
8703	Motor cars and other motor vehicles principally designed for the transport	2802.0	3119.4	2525.6	11.5	11.4	10.1	thsd US$/unit	781
8517	Electrical apparatus for line telephony or line telegraphy	2318.7	2613.4	2334.5					764
8802	Other aircraft (for example, helicopters, aeroplanes); spacecraft	2033.9	1963.0	2329.2	7.8	7.6	1.2	mln US$/unit	792
8471	Automatic data processing machines and units thereof	1800.1	1958.7	1347.5	163.0	145.4	123.3	US$/unit	752
3004	Medicaments (excluding goods of heading 30.02, 30.05 or 30.06)	1315.3	1445.9	1422.9	39.8	41.8	33.8	US$/kg	542
1005	Maize (corn)	1022.4	938.5	955.8	0.3	0.2	0.2	US$/kg	044
8704	Motor vehicles for the transport of goods	964.9	1218.2	474.3	24.1	22.9	16.1	thsd US$/unit	782
8528	Reception apparatus for television	809.0	917.3	566.0	203.4	233.2	143.4	US$/unit	761
3002	Human blood; animal blood prepared for therapeutic uses	820.0	744.1	713.4	97.3	76.6	78.5	US$/kg	541

Comoros

Goods Imports: CIF, by consignment | **Goods Exports: FOB, by last known destination** | **Trade System: General**

Overview:

In 2013, the value of merchandise exports of Comoros decreased substantially by 18.7 percent to reach 10.1 mln US$, while its merchandise imports decreased moderately by 8.4 percent to reach 115.2 mln US$ (see graph 1, table 2 and table 3). The merchandise trade balance recorded a large deficit of 105.1 mln US$ (see graph 1). The largest merchandise trade balance was with MDG Western Asia at -26.3 mln US$ (see graph 4). Merchandise exports in Comoros were moderately concentrated amongst partners; imports were diversified. The top 8 partners accounted for 80 percent or more of exports and 7 partners accounted for 80 percent or more of imports (see graph 5). In 2012, the value of exports of services of Comoros decreased moderately by 8.2 percent, reaching 67.8 mln US$, while its imports of services decreased slightly by 1.6 percent and reached 105.0 mln US$ (see graph 2). There was a moderate trade in services deficit of 37.2 mln US$.

Graph 1: Total merchandise trade, by value

(Mln US$ by year)

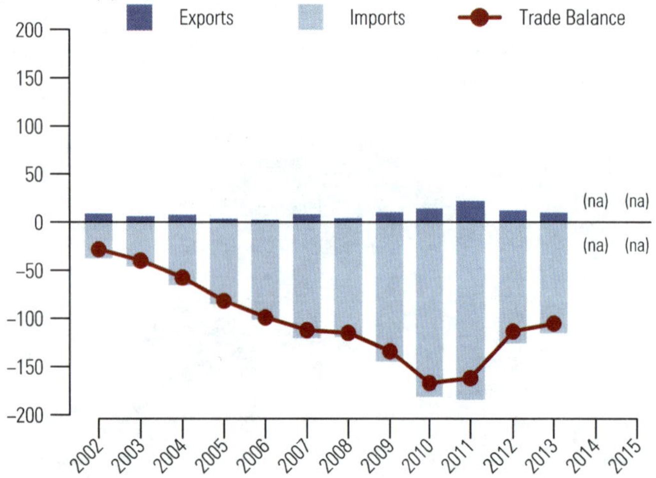

Graph 2: Total services trade, by value

(Mln US$ by year)

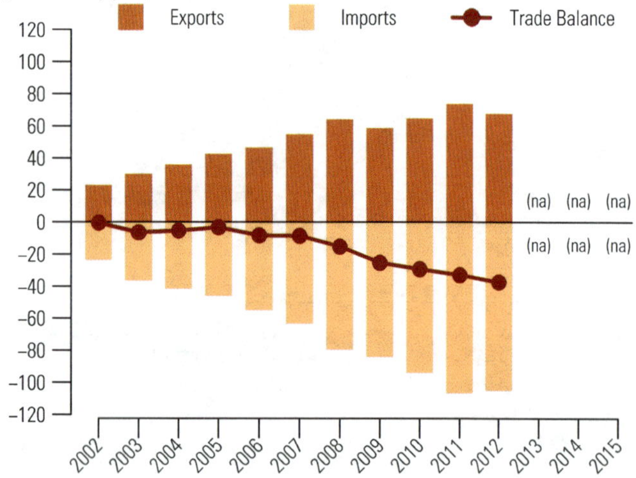

Exports Profile:

"Food, animals + beverages, tobacco" (SITC section 0+1), "Chemicals" (SITC section 5) and "Machinery and transport equipment" (SITC section 7) were the largest commodity groups for exports in 2013, representing respectively 78.3, 12.4 and 6.9 percent of exported goods (see table 2). From 2011 to 2013, the largest export commodity was "Cloves (whole fruit, cloves and stems)" (HS code 0907) (see table 1). The top three destinations for merchandise exports were Singapore, France and the Netherlands, accounting for respectively 27.3, 18.7 and 9.3 percent of total exports. "Travel" (EBOPS code 236) accounted for the largest share of exports of services in 2011 at 41.7 mln US$, followed by "Communications services" (EBOPS code 245) at 18.3 mln US$ and "Government services, n.i.e." (EBOPS code 291) at 10.3 mln US$ (see graph 3).

Graph 3: Exports of services by EBOPS category

(% share in 2011)

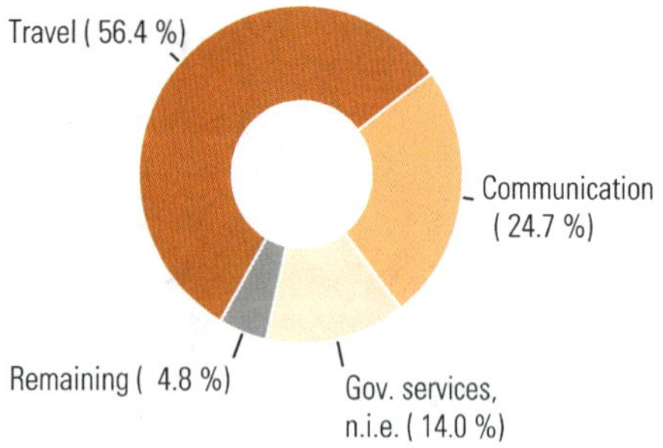

Table 1: Top 10 export commodities 2011 to 2013

HS code	4-digit heading of Harmonized System 2002	Value (million US$) 2011	2012	2013	Unit value 2011	2012	2013	Unit	SITC code
	All Commodities	22.4	12.5	10.1					
0907	Cloves (whole fruit, cloves and stems)	16.7	8.9	4.6		6.1	6.6	US$/kg	075
0905	Vanilla	0.9	1.4	3.3	24.1	18.4	39.5	US$/kg	075
3301	Essential oils (terpeneless or not), including concretes	1.5	1.3	1.2	60.3	55.0	52.1	US$/kg	551
8703	Motor cars and other motor vehicles principally designed for the transport	2.1	0.1	0.2		*6.3*	11.6	thsd US$/unit	781
9617	Vacuum flasks and other vacuum vessels, complete with cases	0.2	0.1	0.1	0.7	0.7	*0.8*	US$/kg	899
8803	Parts of goods of heading 88.01 or 88.02	0.2	...	...	31.3			US$/kg	792
8437	Machines for cleaning, sorting or grading seed, grain	...	...	0.2			199.5	thsd US$/unit	72
7407	Copper bars, rods and profiles	0.2	...	...	9.0			US$/kg	682
9108	Watch movements, complete and assembled	0.2	...	...					885
3206	Other colouring matter	...	0.1	...					533

Services Imports and Exports: EBOPS 2002 categories

Table 2: Merchandise exports by SITC

(Value in million US$, growth and shares in percentage)

SITC	2013	Avg. Growth rates 2009-2013	Avg. Growth rates 2012-2013	2013 share
Total	10.1	-1.0	-18.7	100.0
0+1	7.9	0.2	-23.3	78.3
2+4	0.0	-47.9	-95.7	0.0
3	0.0	-78.9	-99.9	0.0
5	1.3	-10.3	-10.2	12.4
6	0.1	-23.8	-61.3	0.5
7	0.7	20.1	130.6	6.9
8	0.2	-3.1	-24.8	2.0

Table 3: Merchandise imports by SITC

(Value in million US$, growth and shares in percentage)

SITC	2013	Avg. Growth rates 2009-2013	Avg. Growth rates 2012-2013	2013 share
Total	115.2	-5.5	-8.4	100.0
0+1	34.6	-9.0	-37.3	30.0
2+4	3.0	-5.6	-28.5	2.6
3	1.6	27.5	138.2	1.3
5	3.9	-8.4	-31.7	3.4
6	22.6	-12.0	-12.9	19.6
7	43.1	5.3	64.6	37.4
8	6.6	-12.9	-18.6	5.7

SITC Legend

SITC Code	Description
Total	All commodities
0+1	Food, animals + beverages, tobacco
2+4	Crude materials + anim. & veg. oils
3	Mineral fuels, lubricants
5	Chemicals
6	Goods classified chiefly by material
7	Machinery and transport equipment
8	Miscellaneous manufactured articles
9	Not classified elsewhere in the SITC

Graph 4: Merchandise trade balance

(Mln US$ by MDG Regions in 2013)

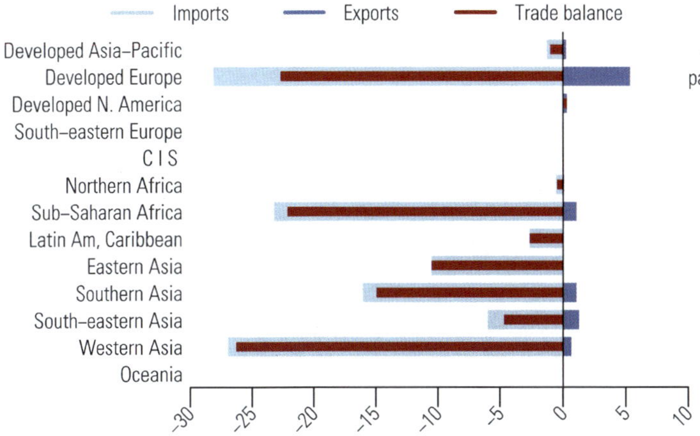

Graph 5: Partner concentration of merchandise trade

(Cumulative share by ranked partners in 2013)

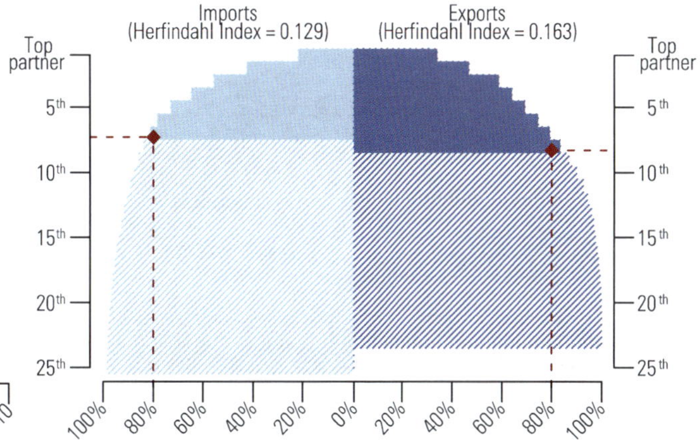

Graph 6: Imports of services by EBOPS category

(% share in 2011)

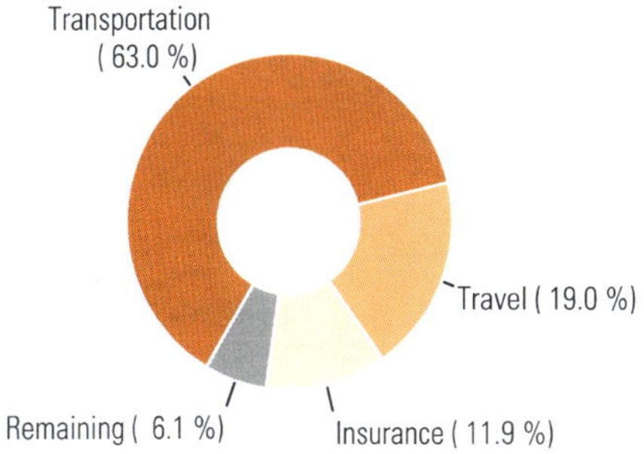

Imports Profile:

"Machinery and transport equipment" (SITC section 7), "Food, animals + beverages, tobacco" (SITC section 0+1) and "Goods classified chiefly by material" (SITC section 6) were the largest commodity groups for imports in 2013, representing respectively 37.4, 30.0 and 19.6 percent of imported goods (see table 3). From 2011 to 2013, the largest import commodity was "Rice" (HS code 1006) (see table 4). The top three partners for merchandise imports were the United Arab Emirates, France and Pakistan, accounting for respectively 27.2, 21.6 and 12.8 percent of total imports. "Transportation" (EBOPS code 205) accounted for the largest share of imports of services in 2011 at 67.2 mln US$, followed by "Travel" (EBOPS code 236) at 20.2 mln US$ and "Insurance services" (EBOPS code 253) at 12.7 mln US$ (see graph 6).

Table 4: Top 10 import commodities 2011 to 2013

HS code	4-digit heading of Harmonized System 2002	Value (million US$) 2011	Value (million US$) 2012	Value (million US$) 2013	Unit value 2011	Unit value 2012	Unit value 2013	Unit	SITC code
	All Commodities	184.1	125.8	115.2					
1006	Rice	29.4	22.8	10.7	0.7	0.5	0.5	US$/kg	042
2523	Portland cement, aluminous cement, slag cement	16.4	11.2	8.2	0.1	0.1	0.1	US$/kg	661
8703	Motor cars and other motor vehicles principally designed for the transport	14.3	7.3	13.7		*27.2*	*9.5*	thsd US$/unit	781
8705	Special purpose motor vehicles	24.9	1.0	0.5			*97.5*	thsd US$/unit	782
0207	Meat and edible offal, of the poultry of heading 01.05	10.9	6.2	5.8	1.5	1.4	1.3	US$/kg	012
7214	Other bars and rods of iron or non-alloy steel	5.1	4.6	4.9	0.9	0.8	0.9	US$/kg	676
1701	Cane or beet sugar and pure sucrose, in solid form	6.0	4.8	2.7	0.9	0.9	0.8	US$/kg	061
8531	Electric sound or visual signalling apparatus	0.0	0.0	13.4			15.8	thsd US$/unit	778
1101	Wheat or meslin flour	5.3	4.5	2.9	0.6	0.6	0.7	US$/kg	046
8517	Electrical apparatus for line telephony or line telegraphy	0.7	4.1	5.4					764

Congo

Goods Imports: CIF, by origin | **Goods Exports: FOB, by last known destination** | **Trade System: Special**

Overview:

In 2014, the value of merchandise exports of the Congo decreased substantially by 37.3 percent to reach 6.6 bln US$, while its merchandise imports decreased substantially by 60.0 percent to reach 3.3 bln US$ (see graph 1, table 2 and table 3). The merchandise trade balance recorded a large surplus of 3.2 bln US$ (see graph 1). The largest merchandise trade balance was with MDG Eastern Asia at 1.8 bln US$ (see graph 4). Merchandise exports in the Congo were moderately concentrated amongst partners; imports were diversified. The top 9 partners accounted for 80 percent or more of exports and 15 partners accounted for 80 percent or more of imports (see graph 5). In 2012, the value of exports of services of the Congo increased slightly by 3.2 percent, reaching 488.5 mln US$, while its imports of services decreased moderately by 5.9 percent and reached 5.1 bln US$ (see graph 2). There was a large trade in services deficit of 4.6 bln US$.

Graph 1: Total merchandise trade, by value

(Bln US$ by year)

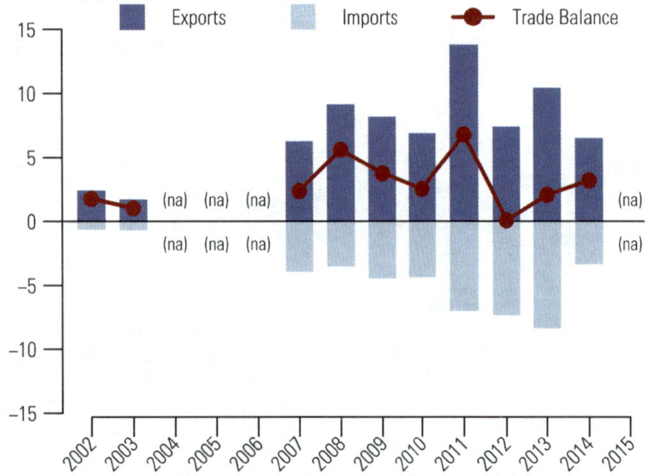

Graph 2: Total services trade, by value

(Bln US$ by year)

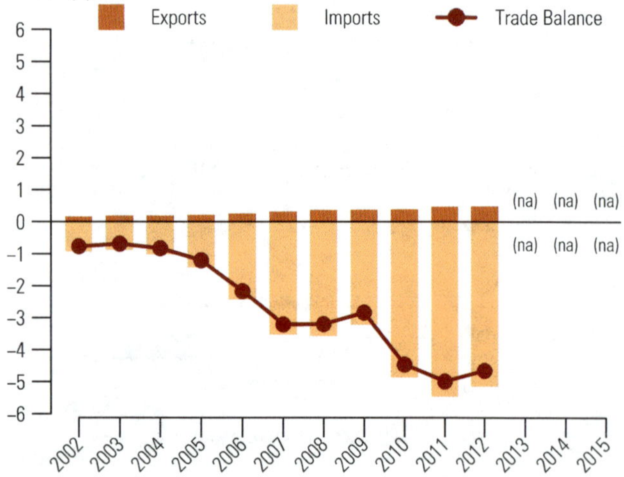

Exports Profile:

"Mineral fuels, lubricants" (SITC section 3), "Machinery and transport equipment" (SITC section 7) and "Crude materials + anim. & veg. oils" (SITC section 2+4) were the largest commodity groups for exports in 2014, representing respectively 61.9, 35.6 and 1.0 percent of exported goods (see table 2). From 2012 to 2014, the largest export commodity was "Petroleum oils, crude" (HS code 2709) (see table 1). The top three destinations for merchandise exports were China, Australia and France, accounting for respectively 33.2, 7.5 and 7.0 percent of total exports. "Other business services" (EBOPS code 268) accounted for the largest share of exports of services in 2007 at 141.0 mln US$, followed by "Insurance services" (EBOPS code 253) at 95.1 mln US$ and "Travel" (EBOPS code 236) at 54.5 mln US$ (see graph 3).

Graph 3: Exports of services by EBOPS category

(% share in 2007)

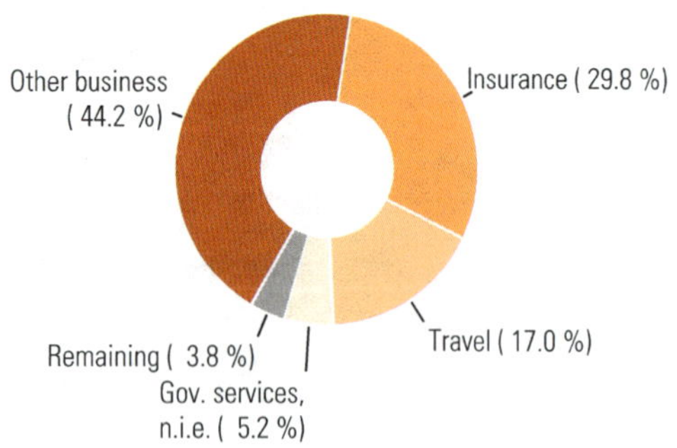

Table 1: Top 10 export commodities 2012 to 2014

HS code	4-digit heading of Harmonized System 2002	Value (million US$) 2012	2013	2014	Unit value 2012	2013	2014	Unit	SITC code
	All Commodities	7437.9	10453.1	6550.0					
2709	Petroleum oils, crude	5779.5	7666.9	4010.7	0.7	0.8	0.7	US$/kg	333
8905	Light-vessels, fire-floats, dredgers, floating cranes and other vessels	607.5	1042.7	1089.8					793
8901	Cruise ships, excursion boats, ferry-boats, cargo ships, barges	621.8	1047.2	1017.9					793
2711	Petroleum gases and other gaseous hydrocarbons	73.0	211.5	41.3	0.7	0.6	0.6	US$/kg	343
8904	Tugs and pusher craft	36.7	119.0	14.8					793
4403	Wood in the rough, whether or not stripped of bark or sapwood	57.6	64.5	40.3					247
8704	Motor vehicles for the transport of goods	1.8	2.0	97.3					782
8906	Other vessels, including warships and lifeboats other than rowing boats	9.7	51.6	12.8					793
8431	Parts suitable for use principally with the machinery of headings 84.25	21.6	29.8	19.6	16.3	18.6	16.2	US$/kg	723
2710	Petroleum oils, other than crude	15.8	35.6	0.3		0.8	1.1	US$/kg	334

Services Imports and Exports: EBOPS 2002 categories

Table 2: Merchandise exports by SITC

(Value in million US$, growth and shares in percentage)

SITC	2014	Avg. Growth rates 2010-2014	Avg. Growth rates 2013-2014	2014 share
Total	6550.0	-1.4	-37.3	100.0
0+1	16.3	-15.8	37.8	0.2
2+4	63.6	-13.0	-38.1	1.0
3	4052.4	-3.6	-48.8	61.9
5	4.8	-6.6	4.0	0.1
6	37.3	-15.7	14.4	0.6
7	2330.4	4.8	-1.3	35.6
8	34.4	-18.5	32.9	0.5
9	10.9	448.3	...	0.2

Table 3: Merchandise imports by SITC

(Value in million US$, growth and shares in percentage)

SITC	2014	Avg. Growth rates 2010-2014	Avg. Growth rates 2013-2014	2014 share
Total	3347.7	-6.4	-60.0	100.0
0+1	570.6	18.8	7.9	17.0
2+4	68.1	13.4	-12.6	2.0
3	96.1	-21.1	-26.7	2.9
5	281.7	23.1	9.1	8.4
6	802.3	27.7	32.6	24.0
7	1264.0	-21.0	-80.6	37.8
8	250.8	20.5	3.5	7.5
9	14.1	513.4	>	0.4

SITC Legend

SITC Code	Description
Total	All commodities
0+1	Food, animals + beverages, tobacco
2+4	Crude materials + anim. & veg. oils
3	Mineral fuels, lubricants
5	Chemicals
6	Goods classified chiefly by material
7	Machinery and transport equipment
8	Miscellaneous manufactured articles
9	Not classified elsewhere in the SITC

Graph 4: Merchandise trade balance

(Bln US$ by MDG Regions in 2014)

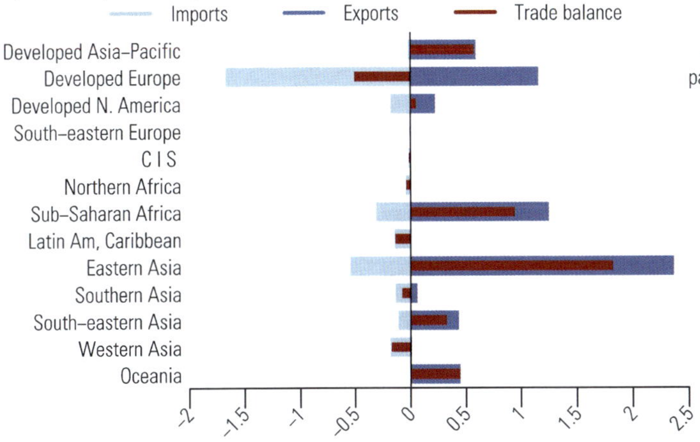

Graph 5: Partner concentration of merchandise trade

(Cumulative share by ranked partners in 2014)

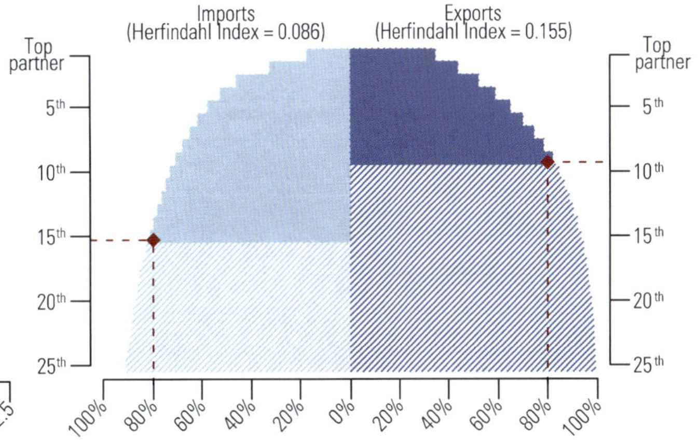

Graph 6: Imports of services by EBOPS category

(% share in 2007)

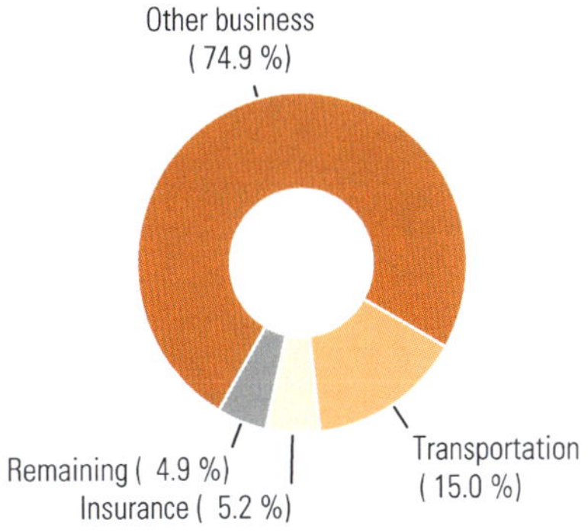

Imports Profile:

"Machinery and transport equipment" (SITC section 7), "Goods classified chiefly by material" (SITC section 6) and "Food, animals + beverages, tobacco" (SITC section 0+1) were the largest commodity groups for imports in 2014, representing respectively 37.8, 24.0 and 17.0 percent of imported goods (see table 3). From 2012 to 2014, the largest import commodity was "Cruise ships, excursion boats, ferry-boats, cargo ships, barges" (HS code 8901) (see table 4). The top three partners for merchandise imports were Angola, Gabon and France, accounting for respectively 16.8, 10.2 and 10.2 percent of total imports. "Other business services" (EBOPS code 268) accounted for the largest share of imports of services in 2007 at 2.6 bln US$, followed by "Transportation" (EBOPS code 205) at 529.1 mln US$ (see graph 6).

Table 4: Top 10 import commodities 2012 to 2014

HS code	4-digit heading of Harmonized System 2002	Value (million US$) 2012	Value (million US$) 2013	Value (million US$) 2014	Unit value 2012	Unit value 2013	Unit value 2014	Unit	SITC code
	All Commodities	7348.6	8371.6	3347.7					
8901	Cruise ships, excursion boats, ferry-boats, cargo ships, barges	2790.4	2407.2	22.8					793
8905	Light-vessels, fire-floats, dredgers, floating cranes and other vessels	1631.2	2189.2	37.3					793
8906	Other vessels, including warships and lifeboats other than rowing boats	9.6	441.2	0.0					793
8904	Tugs and pusher craft	54.8	376.0	1.4					793
8703	Motor cars and other motor vehicles principally designed for the transport	98.1	115.2	142.6	19.7	18.8	19.5	thsd US$/unit	781
2523	Portland cement, aluminous cement, slag cement	98.2	115.7	128.7	0.1	0.1	0.1	US$/kg	661
2710	Petroleum oils, other than crude	70.2	105.7	81.7	1.3	0.2	1.3	US$/kg	334
7304	Tubes, pipes and hollow profiles, seamless, of iron (other than cast iron)	65.4	75.7	114.3	3.4	3.4	3.7	US$/kg	679
8431	Parts suitable for use principally with the machinery of headings 84.25	101.8	68.6	68.7	26.6	22.6	14.3	US$/kg	723
3004	Medicaments (excluding goods of heading 30.02, 30.05 or 30.06)	70.6	71.7	87.1	21.1	22.6	13.2	US$/kg	542

Source: UN Comtrade

Cook Islands

Goods Imports: CIF, by origin | **Goods Exports: FOB, by last known destination** | **Trade System: General**

Overview:

In 2011, the value of merchandise exports of the Cook Islands decreased substantially by 39.5 percent to reach 3.1 mln US$, while its merchandise imports increased substantially by 20.6 percent to reach 109.3 mln US$ (see graph 1, table 2 and table 3). The merchandise trade balance recorded a large deficit of 106.2 mln US$ (see graph 1). The largest merchandise trade balance was with MDG Developed Asia-Pacific at -88.8 mln US$ (see graph 4). Merchandise exports in the Cook Islands were highly concentrated amongst partners; imports were also highly concentrated. The top 4 partners accounted for 80 percent or more of exports and 2 partners accounted for 80 percent or more of imports (see graph 5). No trade in services data is available.

Graph 1: Total merchandise trade, by value

(Mln US$ by year)

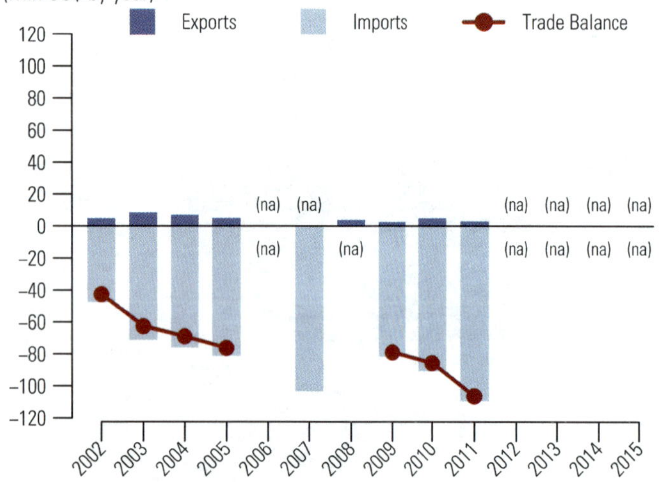

Graph 2: No Data Available

Exports Profile:

"Not classified elsewhere in the SITC" (SITC section 9), "Food, animals + beverages, tobacco" (SITC section 0+1) and "Crude materials + anim. & veg. oils" (SITC section 2+4) were the largest commodity groups for exports in 2011, representing respectively 72.0, 19.7 and 5.3 percent of exported goods (see table 2). From 2009 to 2011, the largest export commodity was "Commodities not specified according to kind" (HS code 9999) (see table 1). The top three destinations for merchandise exports were Japan, China and Indonesia, accounting for respectively 51.4, 16.2 and 8.1 percent of total exports. Services data by detailed EBOPS category is not available for exports.

Graph 3: No Data Available

Table 1: Top 10 export commodities 2009 to 2011

HS code	4-digit heading of Harmonized System 1992	Value (million US$)			Unit value				SITC code
		2009	2010	2011	2009	2010	2011	Unit	
	All Commodities	2.7	5.2	3.1					
9999	Commodities not specified according to kind	1.5	3.5	2.2					931
2009	Fruit and vegetable juices, not fermented or spirited	0.6	0.7	0.5	*3.9*	*4.7*		US$/kg	059
7101	Pearls, natural or cultured, not mounted or set	0.4	0.7	0.1					667
0301	Live fish	0.1	0.2	0.1	20.0		70.9	US$/kg	034
0508	Coral, shell, cuttle bone, etc, unworked, and waste	0.0	0.0	0.2					291
7112	Waste or scrap of precious metal	0.0	0.0	0.0					971
0807	Melons, watermelons and papaws (papayas), fresh	0.0	0.0	...	1.7	1.9		US$/kg	057
8903	Yachts, pleasure, sports vessels, rowing boats, canoes	...	0.0	...		693.0		US$/unit	793
7116	Articles of pearls, precious or semi-precious stones	0.0	0.0	0.0					897
0714	Manioc, arrowroot, salep etc, fresh, dried, sago pith	0.0	0.0	...	4.6	4.9		US$/kg	054

Services Imports and Exports: EBOPS 2002 categories

Table 2: Merchandise exports by SITC

(Value in million US$, growth and shares in percentage)

SITC	2011	Avg. Growth rates 2007-2011	Avg. Growth rates 2010-2011	2011 share
Total	3.1	...	-39.5	100.0
0+1	0.6	...	-29.7	19.7
2+4	0.2	...	354.5	5.3
6	0.1	...	-88.9	2.5
8	0.0	...	854.1	0.4
9	2.2	...	-36.1	72.0

Table 3: Merchandise imports by SITC

(Value in million US$, growth and shares in percentage)

SITC	2011	Avg. Growth rates 2007-2011	Avg. Growth rates 2010-2011	2011 share
Total	109.3	1.4	20.6	100.0
0+1	23.1	10.6	10.1	21.2
2+4	0.9	-13.1	-27.1	0.9
3	16.0	-4.6	17.9	14.7
5	2.0	4.1	20.2	1.8
6	6.0	-2.3	26.6	5.5
7	7.9	-7.9	14.7	7.3
8	4.1	-7.2	28.3	3.7
9	49.2	4.1	28.7	45.0

SITC Legend

SITC Code	Description
Total	All commodities
0+1	Food, animals + beverages, tobacco
2+4	Crude materials + anim. & veg. oils
3	Mineral fuels, lubricants
5	Chemicals
6	Goods classified chiefly by material
7	Machinery and transport equipment
8	Miscellaneous manufactured articles
9	Not classified elsewhere in the SITC

Graph 4: Merchandise trade balance

(Mln US$ by MDG Regions in 2011)

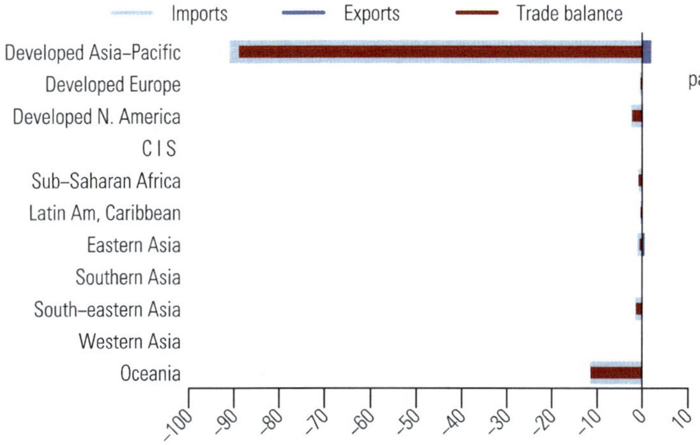

Graph 5: Partner concentration of merchandise trade

(Cumulative share by ranked partners in 2011)

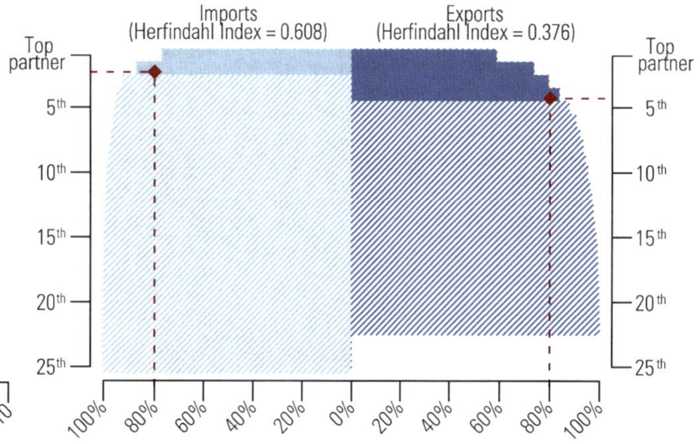

Graph 6: No Data Available

Imports Profile:

"Not classified elsewhere in the SITC" (SITC section 9), "Food, animals + beverages, tobacco" (SITC section 0+1) and "Mineral fuels, lubricants" (SITC section 3) were the largest commodity groups for imports in 2011, representing respectively 45.0, 21.2 and 14.7 percent of imported goods (see table 3). From 2009 to 2011, the largest import commodity was "Commodities not specified according to kind" (HS code 9999) (see table 4). The top three partners for merchandise imports were New Zealand, Fiji and Australia, accounting for respectively 76.2, 9.5 and 6.1 percent of total imports. Services data by detailed EBOPS category is not available for imports.

Table 4: Top 10 import commodities 2009 to 2011

HS code	4-digit heading of Harmonized System 1992	Value (million US$) 2009	2010	2011	Unit value 2009	2010	2011	Unit	SITC code
	All Commodities	81.6	90.6	109.3					
9999	Commodities not specified according to kind	34.6	38.2	49.1					931
2710	Oils petroleum, bituminous, distillates, except crude	11.9	12.5	14.6	*1.3*	*1.0*	*1.1*	US$/kg	334
1602	Prepared or preserved meat, meat offal and blood, nes	1.6	1.5	1.4	19.1	*10.3*	17.7	US$/kg	017
0202	Meat of bovine animals, frozen	1.1	1.6	1.7	4.8	3.0	*8.3*	US$/kg	011
2203	Beer made from malt	1.0	1.2	2.1	*1.2*	*1.2*	*1.1*	US$/litre	112
2202	Waters, non-alcoholic sweetened or flavoured beverages	0.7	1.8	1.8	*2.3*	*0.6*	*1.3*	US$/litre	111
8703	Motor vehicles for transport of persons (except buses)	1.3	1.4	1.6	*7.9*	*6.9*	*12.2*	thsd US$/unit	781
4818	Household, sanitary, hospital paper articles, clothing	0.9	1.1	1.1	*3.1*	*2.8*	*2.6*	US$/kg	642
8525	Radio and TV transmitters, television cameras	0.9	1.0	1.1					764
1905	Baked bread, pastry, wafers, rice paper, biscuits, etc	0.9	1.1	1.1	*3.7*	*3.4*	*3.3*	US$/kg	048

Goods Imports: CIF, by origin	Goods Exports: FOB, by last known destination	Trade System: General

Overview:

In 2015, the value of merchandise exports of Costa Rica reached 9.6 bln US$, while its merchandise imports reached 15.5 bln US$ (see graph 1, table 2 and table 3). The merchandise trade balance recorded a moderate deficit of 5.9 bln US$ (see graph 1). The largest merchandise trade balance was with MDG Eastern Asia at -2.4 bln US$ (see graph 4). Merchandise exports in Costa Rica were moderately concentrated amongst partners; imports were also moderately concentrated. The top 11 partners accounted for 80 percent or more of exports and 13 partners accounted for 80 percent or more of imports (see graph 5). In 2014, the value of exports of services of Costa Rica increased slightly by 4.7 percent, reaching 6.4 bln US$, while its imports of services increased slightly by 1.6 percent and reached 2.1 bln US$ (see graph 2). There was a large trade in services surplus of 4.4 bln US$.

Graph 1: Total merchandise trade, by value

(Bln US$ by year)

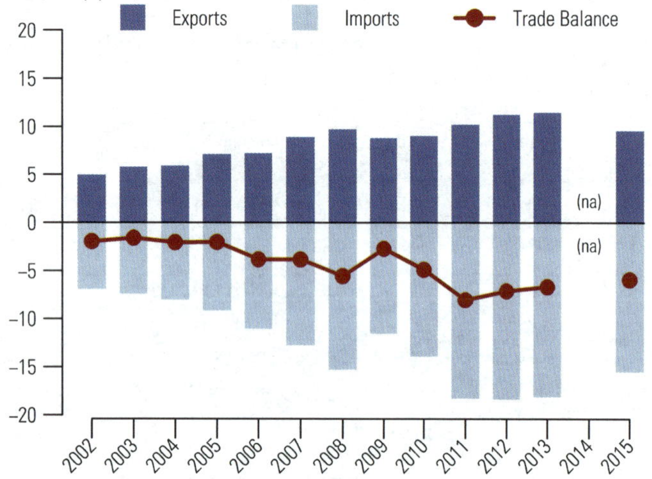

Graph 2: Total services trade, by value

(Bln US$ by year)

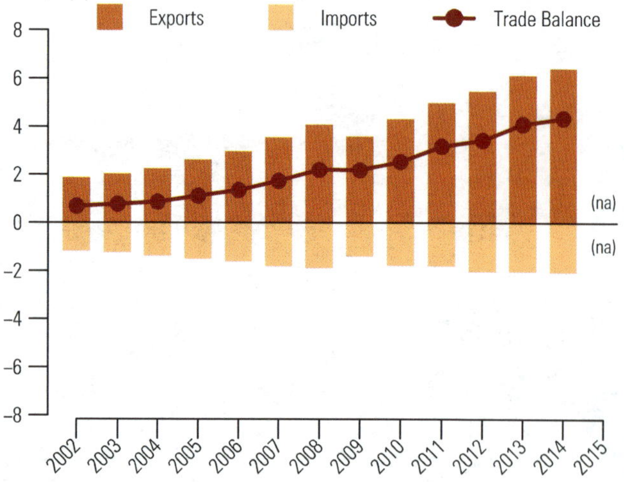

Exports Profile:

"Food, animals + beverages, tobacco" (SITC section 0+1), "Miscellaneous manufactured articles" (SITC section 8) and "Goods classified chiefly by material" (SITC section 6) were the largest commodity groups for exports in 2015, representing respectively 41.0, 26.4 and 10.0 percent of exported goods (see table 2). From 2013 to 2015, the largest export commodity was "Instruments and appliances used in medical, surgical, dental or veterinary" (HS code 9018) (see table 1). The top three destinations for merchandise exports were the United States, the Netherlands and Panama, accounting for respectively 39.4, 6.0 and 5.4 percent of total exports. "Travel" (EBOPS code 236) accounted for the largest share of exports of services in 2014 at 3.1 bln US$, followed by "Computer and information services" (EBOPS code 262) at 1.7 bln US$ and "Other business services" (EBOPS code 268) at 1.2 bln US$ (see graph 3).

Graph 3: Exports of services by EBOPS category

(% share in 2014)

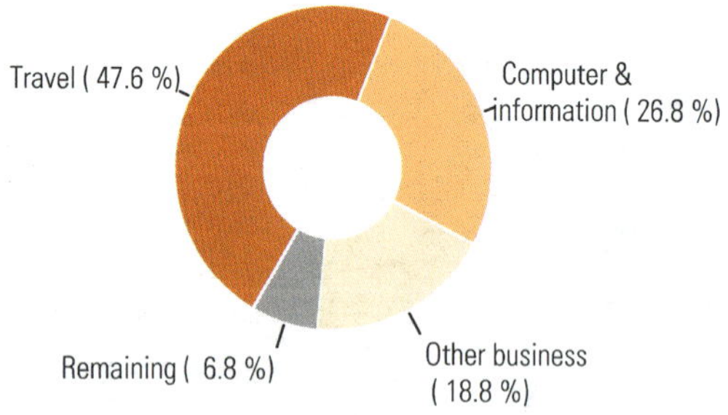

Table 1: Top 10 export commodities 2013 to 2015

HS code	4-digit heading of Harmonized System 2012	Value (million US$) 2013	2014	2015	Unit value 2013	2014	2015	Unit	SITC code
	All Commodities	11 472.1	...	9 578.3					
9018	Instruments and appliances used in medical, surgical, dental or veterinary	1 121.5	...	1 694.9					872
8542	Electronic integrated circuits	2 396.2	...	32.1					776
0804	Dates, figs, pineapples, avocados and mangosteens, fresh or dried	837.2	...	827.4	0.4		0.4	US$/kg	057
0803	Bananas, including plantains, fresh or dried	780.2	...	835.3	0.4		0.4	US$/kg	057
2106	Food preparations not elsewhere specified or included	352.2	...	402.0	11.2		*12.5*	US$/kg	098
9021	Orthopaedic appliances, including crutches, surgical belts and trusses	298.9	...	423.0					899
0901	Coffee, whether or not roasted or decaffeinated	308.1	...	309.7	3.7		4.5	US$/kg	071
8544	Insulated (including enamelled or anodised) wire, cable	274.1	...	188.5	13.4		*9.8*	US$/kg	773
2009	Fruit juices (including grape must) and vegetable juices	172.0	...	189.7	0.9		0.9	US$/kg	059
4011	New pneumatic tyres, of rubber	173.3	...	151.1					625

Services Imports and Exports: EBOPS 2002 categories

Table 2: Merchandise exports by SITC

(Value in million US$, growth and shares in percentage)

SITC	2015	Avg. Growth rates 2011-2015	Avg. Growth rates 2014-2015	2015 share
Total	9578.3	-1.6	...	100.0
0+1	3922.5	4.3	...	41.0
2+4	446.8	-7.9	...	4.7
3	3.7	-42.4	...	0.0
5	757.4	-1.8	...	7.9
6	961.6	-0.6	...	10.0
7	932.9	-23.7	...	9.7
8	2533.3	11.2	...	26.4
9	20.1	-17.4	...	0.2

Table 3: Merchandise imports by SITC

(Value in million US$, growth and shares in percentage)

SITC	2015	Avg. Growth rates 2011-2015	Avg. Growth rates 2014-2015	2015 share
Total	15504.4	-4.0	...	100.0
0+1	1689.7	4.7	...	10.9
2+4	406.6	-2.8	...	2.6
3	1312.3	-12.8	...	8.5
5	2681.6	2.7	...	17.3
6	2630.7	-2.5	...	17.0
7	4749.0	-8.4	...	30.6
8	2018.3	-0.2	...	13.0
9	16.2	10.3	...	0.1

SITC Legend

SITC Code	Description
Total	All commodities
0+1	Food, animals + beverages, tobacco
2+4	Crude materials + anim. & veg. oils
3	Mineral fuels, lubricants
5	Chemicals
6	Goods classified chiefly by material
7	Machinery and transport equipment
8	Miscellaneous manufactured articles
9	Not classified elsewhere in the SITC

Graph 4: Merchandise trade balance

(Bln US$ by MDG Regions in 2015)

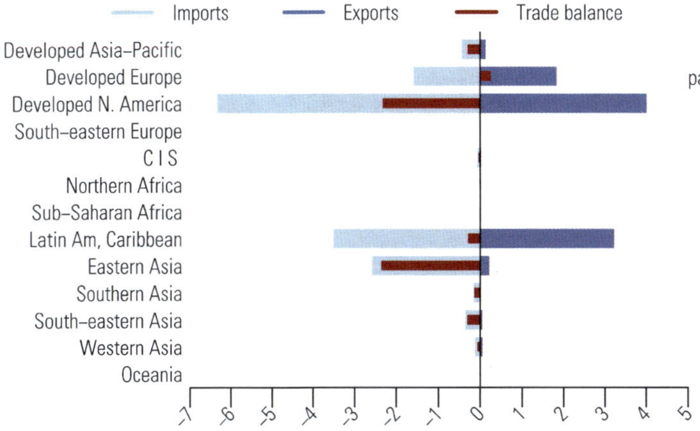

Graph 5: Partner concentration of merchandise trade

(Cumulative share by ranked partners in 2015)

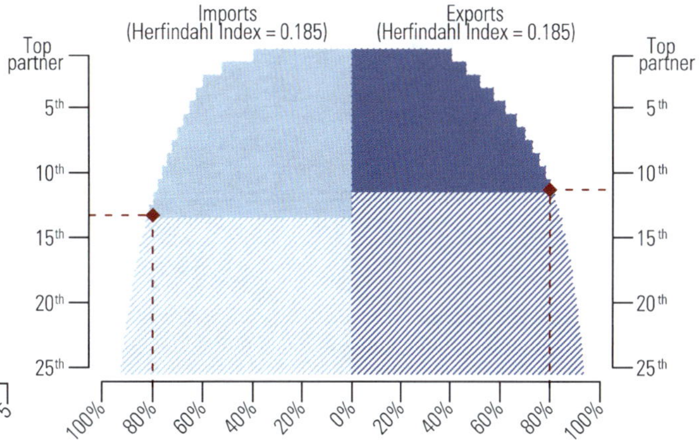

Graph 6: Imports of services by EBOPS category

(% share in 2014)

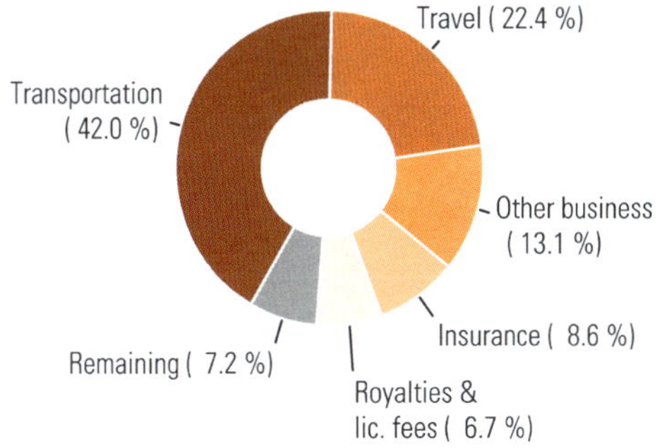

Imports Profile:

"Machinery and transport equipment" (SITC section 7), "Chemicals" (SITC section 5) and "Goods classified chiefly by material" (SITC section 6) were the largest commodity groups for imports in 2015, representing respectively 30.6, 17.3 and 17.0 percent of imported goods (see table 3). From 2013 to 2015, the largest import commodity was "Petroleum oils, other than crude" (HS code 2710) (see table 4). The top three partners for merchandise imports were the United States, China and Mexico, accounting for respectively 45.3, 11.0 and 6.9 percent of total imports. "Transportation" (EBOPS code 205) accounted for the largest share of imports of services in 2014 at 864.2 mln US$, followed by "Travel" (EBOPS code 236) at 460.9 mln US$ and "Other business services" (EBOPS code 268) at 268.7 mln US$ (see graph 6).

Table 4: Top 10 import commodities 2013 to 2015

HS code	4-digit heading of Harmonized System 2012	Value (million US$) 2013	2014	2015	Unit value 2013	2014	2015	Unit	SITC code
	All Commodities	18124.5	...	15504.4					
2710	Petroleum oils, other than crude	2154.6	...	1236.6	1.0		*0.6*	US$/kg	334
8542	Electronic integrated circuits	1698.0	...	149.4					776
8703	Motor cars and other motor vehicles principally designed for the transport	556.6	...	712.4	*18.7*		*18.6*	thsd US$/unit	781
8517	Electrical apparatus for line telephony or line telegraphy	513.0	...	642.3					764
3004	Medicaments (excluding goods of heading 30.02, 30.05 or 30.06)	442.9	...	512.5	48.1		*51.1*	US$/kg	542
9018	Instruments and appliances used in medical, surgical, dental or veterinary	261.8	...	264.6					872
8534	Printed circuits	517.3	...	5.2	438.2		*107.8*	US$/kg	772
8471	Automatic data processing machines and units thereof	263.7	...	251.2					752
8609	Containers (including containers for the transport of fluids)	219.8	...	196.8					786
8704	Motor vehicles for the transport of goods	165.0	...	213.7					782

Côte d'Ivoire

Goods Imports: CIF, by origin | **Goods Exports: FOB, by last known destination** | **Trade System: Special**

Overview:

In 2014, the value of merchandise exports of Côte d'Ivoire increased moderately by 7.5 percent to reach 13.0 bln US$, while its merchandise imports decreased substantially by 10.5 percent to reach 11.2 bln US$ (see graph 1, table 2 and table 3). The merchandise trade balance recorded a relatively small surplus of 1.8 bln US$ (see graph 1). The largest merchandise trade balance was with MDG Developed Europe at 1.9 bln US$ (see graph 4). Merchandise exports in Côte d'Ivoire were diversified amongst partners; imports were also diversified. The top 20 partners accounted for 80 percent or more of exports and 18 partners accounted for 80 percent or more of imports (see graph 5). In 2013, the value of exports of services of Côte d'Ivoire increased slightly by 4.8 percent, reaching 1.0 bln US$, while its imports of services increased substantially by 10.8 percent and reached 3.3 bln US$ (see graph 2). There was a large trade in services deficit of 2.2 bln US$.

Graph 1: Total merchandise trade, by value

(Bln US$ by year)

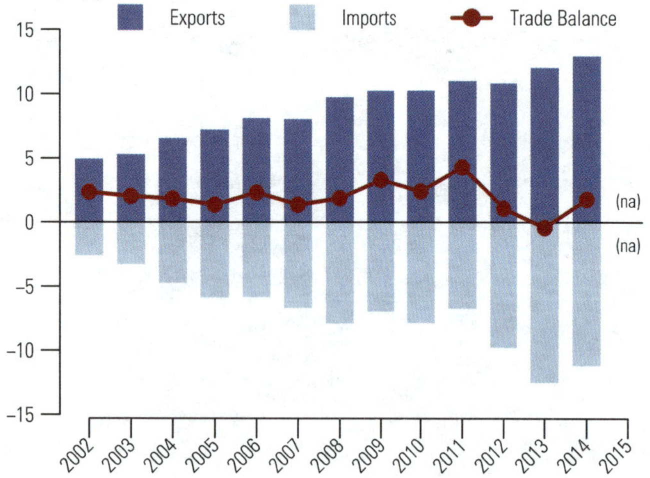

Graph 2: Total services trade, by value

(Bln US$ by year)

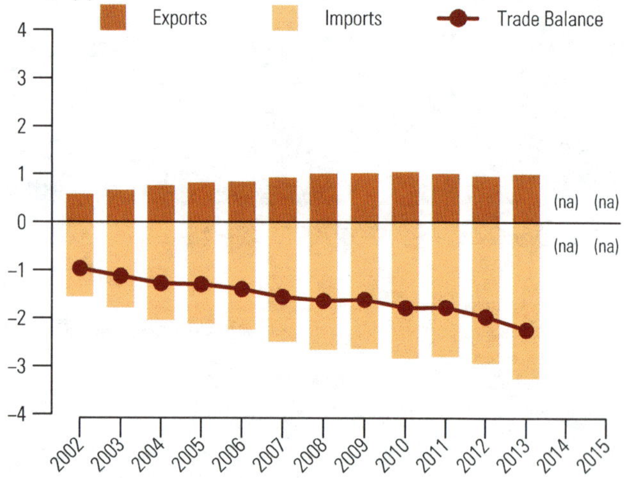

Exports Profile:

"Food, animals + beverages, tobacco" (SITC section 0+1), "Mineral fuels, lubricants" (SITC section 3) and "Crude materials + anim. & veg. oils" (SITC section 2+4) were the largest commodity groups for exports in 2014, representing respectively 47.2, 20.3 and 10.7 percent of exported goods (see table 2). From 2012 to 2014, the largest export commodity was "Cocoa beans, whole or broken, raw or roasted" (HS code 1801) (see table 1). The top three destinations for merchandise exports were the Netherlands, Ghana and the United States, accounting for respectively 8.9, 7.6 and 7.5 percent of total exports. "Other business services" (EBOPS code 268) accounted for the largest share of exports of services in 2013 at 285.5 mln US$, followed by "Transportation" (EBOPS code 205) at 194.3 mln US$ and "Travel" (EBOPS code 236) at 182.8 mln US$ (see graph 3).

Graph 3: Exports of services by EBOPS category

(% share in 2013)

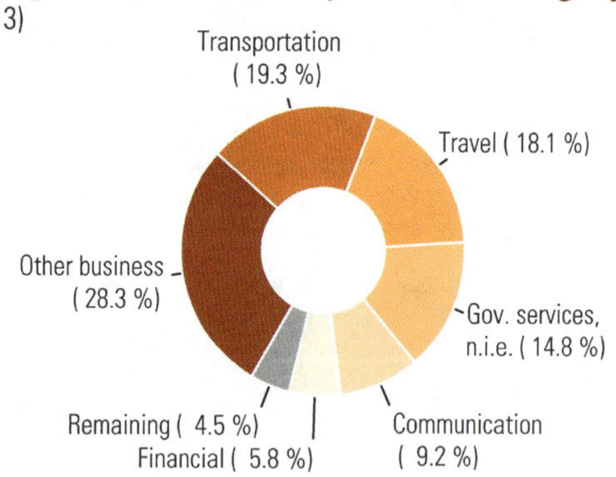

Table 1: Top 10 export commodities 2012 to 2014

HS code	4-digit heading of Harmonized System 2007	Value (million US$) 2012	2013	2014	Unit value 2012	2013	2014	Unit	SITC code
	All Commodities	10861.0	12083.8	12985.1					
1801	Cocoa beans, whole or broken, raw or roasted	2325.0	2044.5	3045.1	2.3	2.5	2.7	US$/kg	072
2710	Petroleum oils, other than crude	1766.0	1781.8	1738.8	1.0	1.0	0.9	US$/kg	334
2709	Petroleum oils and oils obtained from bituminous minerals, crude	1255.6	959.5	652.1	0.8	0.8	0.7	US$/kg	333
8905	Light-vessels, fire-floats, dredgers, floating cranes and other vessels	5.5	1730.8	568.4					793
4001	Natural rubber, balata, gutta-percha, guayule, chicle	808.6	759.6	602.7	3.0	2.9	1.7	US$/kg	231
7108	Gold (including gold plated with platinum)	641.1	575.8	702.9	48.9	40.3	36.7	thsd US$/kg	971
1803	Cocoa paste, whether or not defatted	437.3	544.1	764.5	3.1	4.1	3.6	US$/kg	072
0801	Coconuts, Brazil nuts and cashew nuts, fresh or dried	351.6	346.0	826.5			1.4	US$/kg	057
1804	Cocoa butter, fat and oil	210.4	265.6	461.8	3.0	4.8	5.1	US$/kg	072
5201	Cotton, not carded or combed	223.0	271.9	322.7	1.9	1.8	1.8	US$/kg	263

Services Imports and Exports: EBOPS 2002 categories

Table 2: Merchandise exports by SITC

(Value in million US$, growth and shares in percentage)

SITC	2014	Avg. Growth rates 2010-2014	Avg. Growth rates 2013-2014	2014 share
Total	12 985.1	6.0	7.5	100.0
0+1	6 126.3	6.2	46.1	47.2
2+4	1 386.5	3.8	-3.7	10.7
3	2 635.2	2.0	-8.5	20.3
5	421.7	7.1	27.6	3.2
6	356.3	5.5	18.0	2.7
7	897.4	0.6	-56.4	6.9
8	448.3	26.3	52.1	3.5
9	713.4	40.0	21.8	5.5

Table 3: Merchandise imports by SITC

(Value in million US$, growth and shares in percentage)

SITC	2014	Avg. Growth rates 2010-2014	Avg. Growth rates 2013-2014	2014 share
Total	11 177.7	9.2	-10.5	100.0
0+1	1 803.5	6.0	2.9	16.1
2+4	203.5	-0.5	1.9	1.8
3	2 894.3	11.7	-10.0	25.9
5	1 519.6	13.2	22.8	13.6
6	1 494.4	15.6	37.2	13.4
7	2 811.9	5.0	-39.0	25.2
8	410.4	11.3	16.5	3.7
9	40.1	44.9	40.0	0.4

SITC Legend

SITC Code	Description
Total	All commodities
0+1	Food, animals + beverages, tobacco
2+4	Crude materials + anim. & veg. oils
3	Mineral fuels, lubricants
5	Chemicals
6	Goods classified chiefly by material
7	Machinery and transport equipment
8	Miscellaneous manufactured articles
9	Not classified elsewhere in the SITC

Graph 4: Merchandise trade balance

(Bln US$ by MDG Regions in 2014)

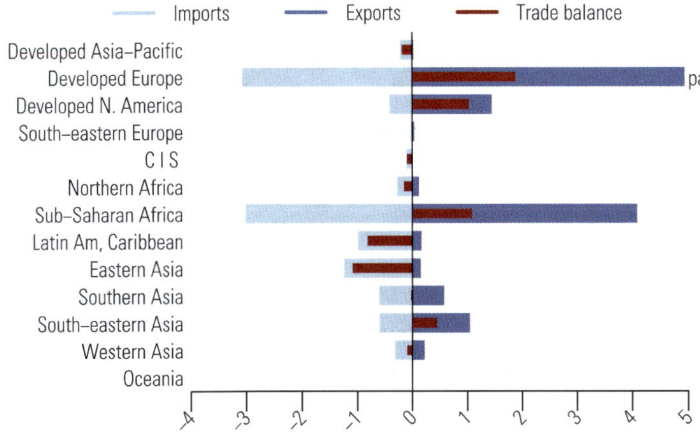

Graph 5: Partner concentration of merchandise trade

(Cumulative share by ranked partners in 2014)

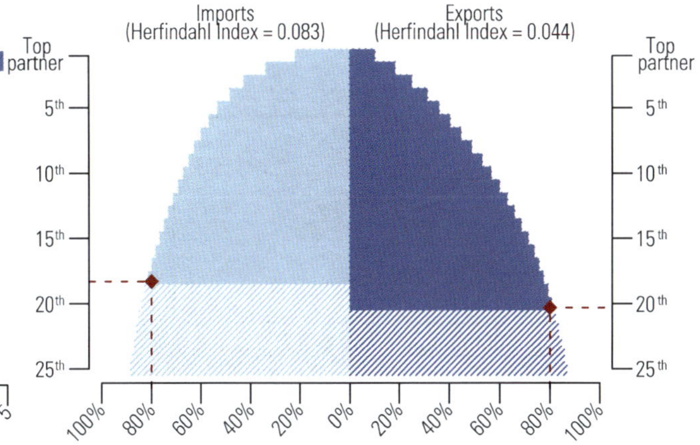

Graph 6: Imports of services by EBOPS category

(% share in 2013)

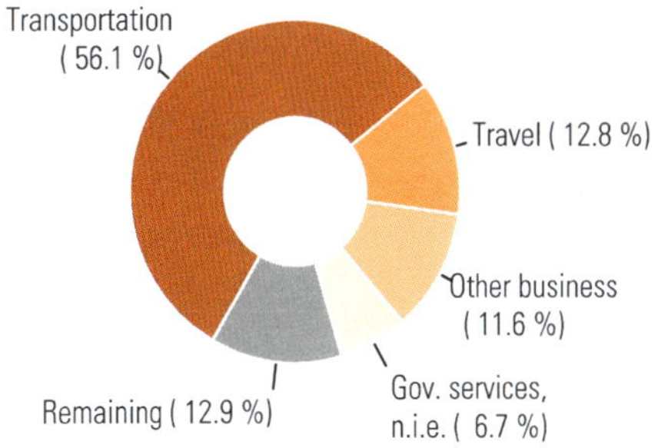

Imports Profile:

"Mineral fuels, lubricants" (SITC section 3), "Machinery and transport equipment" (SITC section 7) and "Food, animals + beverages, tobacco" (SITC section 0+1) were the largest commodity groups for imports in 2014, representing respectively 25.9, 25.2 and 16.1 percent of imported goods (see table 3). From 2012 to 2014, the largest import commodity was "Petroleum oils and oils obtained from bituminous minerals, crude" (HS code 2709) (see table 4). The top three partners for merchandise imports were Nigeria, France and China, accounting for respectively 23.4, 11.6 and 9.3 percent of total imports. "Transportation" (EBOPS code 205) accounted for the largest share of imports of services in 2013 at 1.8 bln US$, followed by "Travel" (EBOPS code 236) at 415.6 mln US$ and "Other business services" (EBOPS code 268) at 376.2 mln US$ (see graph 6).

Table 4: Top 10 import commodities 2012 to 2014

HS code	4-digit heading of Harmonized System 2007	Value (million US$) 2012	Value (million US$) 2013	Value (million US$) 2014	Unit value 2012	Unit value 2013	Unit value 2014	Unit	SITC code
	All Commodities	9 769.7	12 483.0	11 177.7					
2709	Petroleum oils and oils obtained from bituminous minerals, crude	2 752.8	2 928.1	2 612.5	0.8	0.8	0.8	US$/kg	333
8905	Light-vessels, fire-floats, dredgers, floating cranes and other vessels	398.2	2 685.7	613.1					793
1006	Rice	684.5	472.5	437.3	0.5	0.6	0.5	US$/kg	042
0303	Fish, frozen, excluding fish fillets and other fish meat of heading 03.04	329.5	358.1	386.8	1.2	1.3	1.2	US$/kg	034
3004	Medicaments (excluding goods of heading 30.02, 30.05 or 30.06)	255.5	247.5	337.9	25.1	26.2	28.7	US$/kg	542
8703	Motor cars and other motor vehicles principally designed for the transport	234.9	258.0	250.9	*19.9*	*22.1*	*20.2*	thsd US$/unit	781
1001	Wheat and meslin	218.3	210.9	189.1	0.4	0.4	0.4	US$/kg	041
2710	Petroleum oils, other than crude	149.3	151.9	129.0	1.1	1.1	1.3	US$/kg	334
3901	Polymers of ethylene, in primary forms	112.3	119.8	165.9	1.5	1.6	1.6	US$/kg	571
8704	Motor vehicles for the transport of goods	127.9	113.9	146.7					782

Croatia

Goods Imports: CIF, by origin | **Goods Exports: FOB, by last known destination** | **Trade System: Special**

Overview:

In 2015, the value of merchandise exports of Croatia decreased moderately by 7.2 percent to reach 12.8 bln US$, while its merchandise imports decreased substantially by 10.2 percent to reach 20.6 bln US$ (see graph 1, table 2 and table 3). The merchandise trade balance recorded a moderate deficit of 7.7 bln US$ (see graph 1). The largest merchandise trade balance was with MDG Developed Europe at -7.4 bln US$ (see graph 4). Merchandise exports in Croatia were diversified amongst partners; imports were also diversified. The top 18 partners accounted for 80 percent or more of exports and 15 partners accounted for 80 percent or more of imports (see graph 5). In 2014, the value of exports of services of Croatia increased slightly by 4.3 percent, reaching 13.2 bln US$, while its imports of services increased slightly by 1.1 percent and reached 3.8 bln US$ (see graph 2). There was a large trade in services surplus of 9.4 bln US$. See footnote*.

Graph 1: Total merchandise trade, by value

(Bln US$ by year)

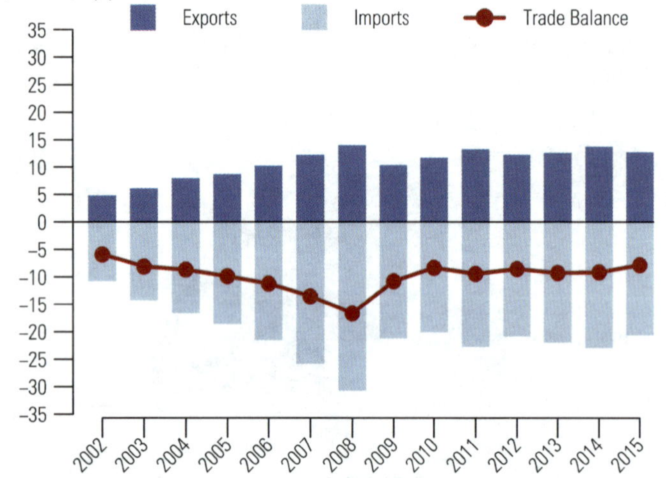

Graph 2: Total services trade, by value

(Bln US$ by year)

Exports Profile:

"Machinery and transport equipment" (SITC section 7), "Miscellaneous manufactured articles" (SITC section 8) and "Goods classified chiefly by material" (SITC section 6) were the largest commodity groups for exports in 2015, representing respectively 24.1, 16.1 and 15.7 percent of exported goods (see table 2). From 2013 to 2015, the largest export commodity was "Petroleum oils, other than crude" (HS code 2710) (see table 1). The top three destinations for merchandise exports were Italy, Germany and Slovenia, accounting for respectively 13.9, 11.4 and 11.3 percent of total exports. "Travel" (EBOPS code 236) accounted for the largest share of exports of services in 2014 at 9.8 bln US$, followed by "Transportation" (EBOPS code 205) at 1.3 bln US$ and "Other business services" (EBOPS code 268) at 1.2 bln US$ (see graph 3).

Graph 3: Exports of services by EBOPS category

(% share in 2014)

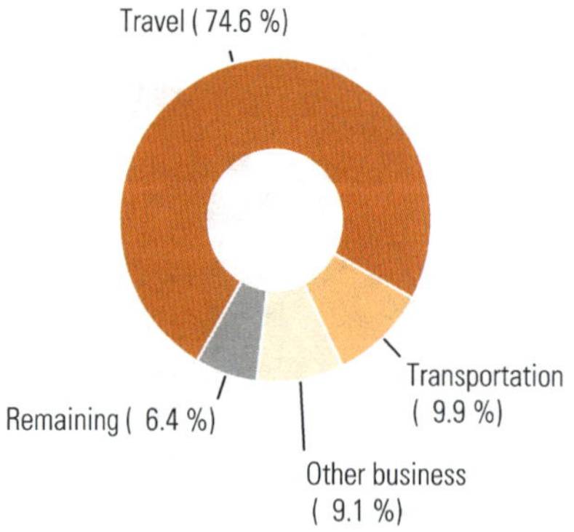

Table 1: Top 10 export commodities 2013 to 2015

HS code	4-digit heading of Harmonized System 2012	Value (million US$) 2013	2014	2015	Unit value 2013	2014	2015	Unit	SITC code
	All Commodities	12741.6	13843.9	12846.8					
2710	Petroleum oils, other than crude	1207.5	1140.4	819.7	*0.9*	0.9	0.5	US$/kg	334
3004	Medicaments (excluding goods of heading 30.02, 30.05 or 30.06)	492.0	489.0	433.7	*138.1*	148.7	100.4	US$/kg	542
4407	Wood sawn or chipped lengthwise, sliced or peeled	312.7	417.7	388.2	*456.8*	*251.7*		US$/m^3	248
2716	Electrical energy	237.4	454.0	418.0	*50.0*	54.0	45.7	US$/MWh	351
8504	Electrical transformers, static converters	315.5	352.9	269.5					771
9401	Seats (other than those of heading 94.02)	246.6	295.6	273.4					821
2711	Petroleum gases and other gaseous hydrocarbons	294.2	235.1	135.4	0.7	0.6	0.3	US$/kg	343
3102	Mineral or chemical fertilisers, nitrogenous	214.6	223.0	183.9	*0.3*	0.3	0.3	US$/kg	562
6115	Panty hose, tights, stockings, socks and other hosiery	137.7	223.4	203.5	*29.0*	33.9	31.1	US$/kg	846
6403	Footwear with outer soles of rubber, plastics, leather	151.6	171.7	159.0	*34.2*	41.3	35.4	US$/pair	851

*As of 2003, trade in services data including "travel" category.

Services Imports and Exports: EBOPS 2002 categories

Table 2: Merchandise exports by SITC

(Value in million US$, growth and shares in percentage)

SITC	2015	Avg. Growth rates 2011-2015	2014-2015	2015 share
Total	12846.8	-1.0	-7.2	100.0
0+1	1556.0	2.3	-3.0	12.1
2+4	1032.2	-0.9	-9.4	8.0
3	1401.5	-3.5	-25.1	10.9
5	1513.1	-0.3	2.5	11.8
6	2019.6	0.2	-9.4	15.7
7	3102.1	-6.0	2.1	24.1
8	2071.4	5.3	-8.3	16.1
9	151.0	21.8	-33.7	1.2

Table 3: Merchandise imports by SITC

(Value in million US$, growth and shares in percentage)

SITC	2015	Avg. Growth rates 2011-2015	2014-2015	2015 share
Total	20579.8	-2.4	-10.2	100.0
0+1	2594.2	2.4	-8.0	12.6
2+4	482.4	-0.4	-8.5	2.3
3	3132.9	-10.8	-26.6	15.2
5	2894.9	-1.9	-4.2	14.1
6	3724.8	-2.3	-8.2	18.1
7	4937.7	-0.6	-4.4	24.0
8	2800.8	1.6	-6.9	13.6
9	12.1	133.3	-69.6	0.1

SITC Legend

SITC Code	Description
Total	All commodities
0+1	Food, animals + beverages, tobacco
2+4	Crude materials + anim. & veg. oils
3	Mineral fuels, lubricants
5	Chemicals
6	Goods classified chiefly by material
7	Machinery and transport equipment
8	Miscellaneous manufactured articles
9	Not classified elsewhere in the SITC

Graph 4: Merchandise trade balance

(Bln US$ by MDG Regions in 2015)

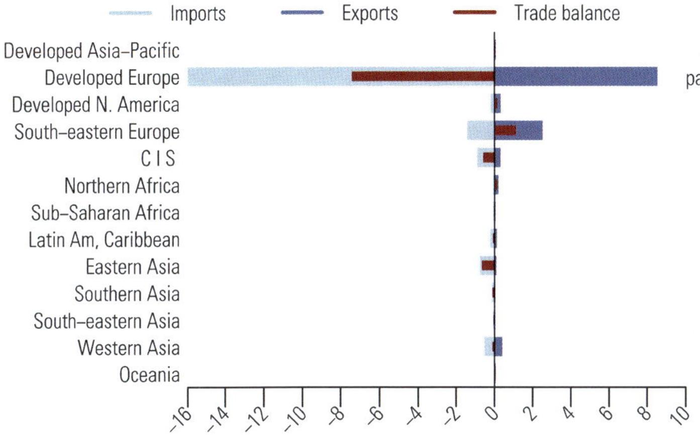

Graph 5: Partner concentration of merchandise trade

(Cumulative share by ranked partners in 2015)

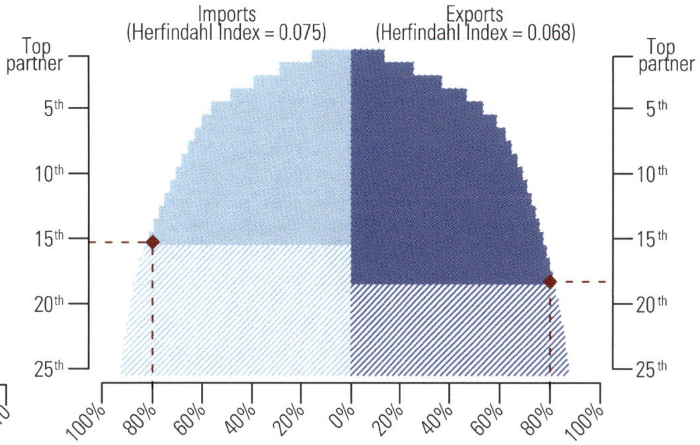

Graph 6: Imports of services by EBOPS category

(% share in 2014)

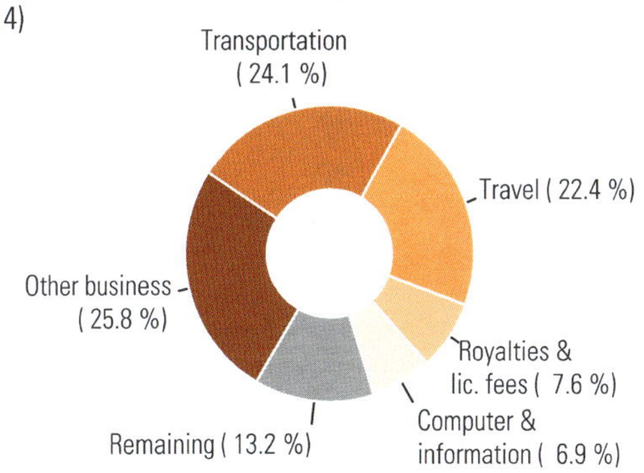

Imports Profile:

"Machinery and transport equipment" (SITC section 7), "Goods classified chiefly by material" (SITC section 6) and "Mineral fuels, lubricants" (SITC section 3) were the largest commodity groups for imports in 2015, representing respectively 24.0, 18.1 and 15.2 percent of imported goods (see table 3). From 2013 to 2015, the largest import commodity was "Petroleum oils and oils obtained from bituminous minerals, crude" (HS code 2709) (see table 4). The top three partners for merchandise imports were Germany, Italy and Slovenia, accounting for respectively 14.9, 13.5 and 11.0 percent of total imports. "Other business services" (EBOPS code 268) accounted for the largest share of imports of services in 2014 at 972.1 mln US$, followed by "Transportation" (EBOPS code 205) at 906.4 mln US$ and "Travel" (EBOPS code 236) at 842.3 mln US$ (see graph 6).

Table 4: Top 10 import commodities 2013 to 2015

HS code	4-digit heading of Harmonized System 2012	Value (million US$) 2013	2014	2015	Unit value 2013	2014	2015	Unit	SITC code
	All Commodities	21932.0	22906.9	20579.8					
2709	Petroleum oils and oils obtained from bituminous minerals, crude	1965.5	1418.8	932.4	0.8	0.8	0.4	US$/kg	333
2710	Petroleum oils, other than crude	1181.1	1509.1	972.0	*1.0*	0.9	0.5	US$/kg	334
2716	Electrical energy	624.6	689.5	747.1	*67.3*	53.8	45.3	US$/MWh	351
8703	Motor cars and other motor vehicles principally designed for the transport	566.1	695.1	692.0	*12.4*	11.7	12.9	thsd US$/unit	781
3004	Medicaments (excluding goods of heading 30.02, 30.05 or 30.06)	632.6	626.5	570.2	*71.0*	61.1	53.5	US$/kg	542
2711	Petroleum gases and other gaseous hydrocarbons	759.7	438.6	316.3	*0.7*	0.5	0.4	US$/kg	343
8517	Electrical apparatus for line telephony or line telegraphy	383.9	402.6	404.4					764
4107	Leather further prepared after tanning or crusting	189.0	290.8	349.6	36.2	36.4	35.3	US$/kg	611
8471	Automatic data processing machines and units thereof	243.1	246.7	222.5		109.1	125.3	US$/unit	752
0203	Meat of swine, fresh, chilled or frozen	184.7	211.8	176.6	3.0	2.8	2.1	US$/kg	012

Cyprus

Goods Imports: CIF, by origin/consignment for intra-eu **Goods Exports: FOB, by last known destination** **Trade System: General**

Overview:

In 2015, the value of merchandise exports of Cyprus increased slightly by 0.4 percent to reach 1.9 bln US$, while its merchandise imports decreased substantially by 17.0 percent to reach 5.7 bln US$ (see graph 1, table 2 and table 3). The merchandise trade balance recorded a large deficit of 3.7 bln US$ (see graph 1). The largest merchandise trade balance was with MDG Developed Europe at -3.2 bln US$ (see graph 4). Merchandise exports in Cyprus were diversified amongst partners; imports were also diversified. The top 25 partners accounted for 80 percent or more of exports and 14 partners accounted for 80 percent or more of imports (see graph 5). In 2014, the value of exports of services of Cyprus decreased moderately by 5.7 percent, reaching 10.0 bln US$, while its imports of services decreased slightly by 0.3 percent and reached 5.6 bln US$ (see graph 2). There was a moderate trade in services surplus of 4.4 bln US$.

Graph 1: Total merchandise trade, by value

(Bln US$ by year)

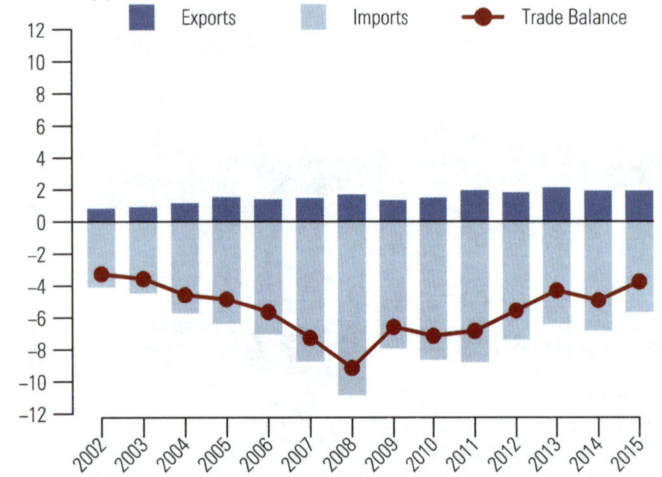

Graph 2: Total services trade, by value

(Bln US$ by year)

Exports Profile:

"Machinery and transport equipment" (SITC section 7), "Chemicals" (SITC section 5) and "Food, animals + beverages, tobacco" (SITC section 0+1) were the largest commodity groups for exports in 2015, representing respectively 22.9, 19.4 and 18.8 percent of exported goods (see table 2). From 2013 to 2015, the largest export commodity was "Medicaments (excluding goods of heading 30.02, 30.05 or 30.06)" (HS code 3004) (see table 1). The top three destinations for merchandise exports were Bunkers, ship stores, Greece and the United Kingdom, accounting for respectively 14.9, 14.3 and 9.9 percent of total exports. "Transportation" (EBOPS code 205) accounted for the largest share of exports of services in 2014 at 3.1 bln US$, followed by "Travel" (EBOPS code 236) at 2.8 bln US$ and "Financial services" (EBOPS code 260) at 2.4 bln US$ (see graph 3).

Graph 3: Exports of services by EBOPS category

(% share in 2014)

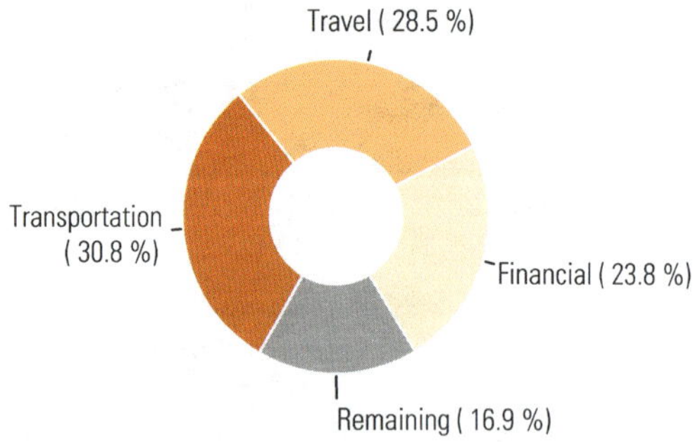

Table 1: Top 10 export commodities 2013 to 2015

HS code	4-digit heading of Harmonized System 2012	Value (million US$) 2013	2014	2015	Unit value 2013	2014	2015	Unit	SITC code
	All Commodities	2134.4	1923.5	1931.4					
3004	Medicaments (excluding goods of heading 30.02, 30.05 or 30.06)	286.3	293.2	258.7	*51.9*	55.1	*43.5*	US$/kg	542
9999	Commodities not specified according to kind	240.4	221.8	118.6					931
2710	Petroleum oils, other than crude	91.0	94.6	320.6	0.9	0.8	0.5	US$/kg	334
8802	Other aircraft (for example, helicopters, aeroplanes); spacecraft	208.5	0.1	179.3	29.8		14.9	mln US$/unit	792
0406	Cheese and curd	102.0	122.8	119.6	*8.8*	*8.9*	7.4	US$/kg	024
8517	Electrical apparatus for line telephony or line telegraphy	70.0	85.0	99.2					764
2523	Portland cement, aluminous cement, slag cement	51.9	62.6	71.5	0.0	0.1	0.1	US$/kg	661
0701	Potatoes, fresh or chilled	71.5	57.1	40.5	0.7	0.5	0.6	US$/kg	054
2402	Cigars, cheroots, cigarillos and cigarettes	63.2	52.9	42.7	31.2	45.8	93.5	US$/kg	122
7108	Gold (including gold plated with platinum)	53.4	64.5	9.3	36.3	29.8	26.0	thsd US$/kg	971

Services Imports and Exports: EBOPS 2002 categories

Table 2: Merchandise exports by SITC

(Value in million US$, growth and shares in percentage)

SITC	2015	Avg. Growth rates 2011-2015	Avg. Growth rates 2014-2015	2015 share
Total	1 931.4	-0.3	0.4	100.0
0+1	362.9	-2.3	-14.4	18.8
2+4	67.1	-16.4	-24.8	3.5
3	320.6	-2.0	238.9	16.6
5	375.4	-6.5	-11.0	19.4
6	116.8	8.8	-2.4	6.0
7	443.1	11.0	29.1	22.9
8	117.4	-8.5	-18.9	6.1
9	128.2	35.0	-55.3	6.6

Table 3: Merchandise imports by SITC

(Value in million US$, growth and shares in percentage)

SITC	2015	Avg. Growth rates 2011-2015	Avg. Growth rates 2014-2015	2015 share
Total	5 666.0	-10.4	-17.0	100.0
0+1	1 110.2	-4.4	-15.1	19.6
2+4	80.4	-11.2	-15.6	1.4
3	1 243.9	-13.3	-26.0	22.0
5	686.6	-6.3	-13.3	12.1
6	574.2	-13.4	-7.9	10.1
7	1 083.9	-13.0	-19.4	19.1
8	875.1	-8.2	-10.6	15.4
9	11.8	-40.0	126.6	0.2

SITC Legend

SITC Code	Description
Total	All commodities
0+1	Food, animals + beverages, tobacco
2+4	Crude materials + anim. & veg. oils
3	Mineral fuels, lubricants
5	Chemicals
6	Goods classified chiefly by material
7	Machinery and transport equipment
8	Miscellaneous manufactured articles
9	Not classified elsewhere in the SITC

Graph 4: Merchandise trade balance

(Bln US$ by MDG Regions in 2015)

Graph 5: Partner concentration of merchandise trade

(Cumulative share by ranked partners in 2015)

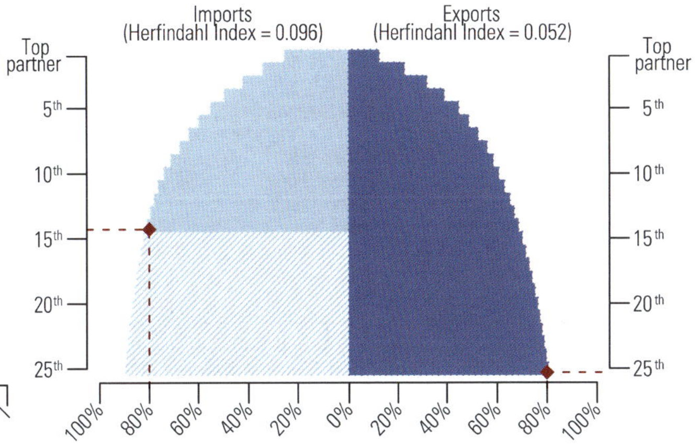

Graph 6: Imports of services by EBOPS category

(% share in 2014)

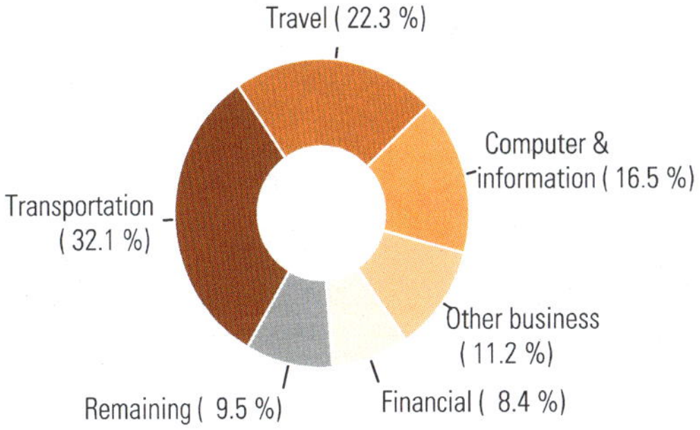

Imports Profile:

"Mineral fuels, lubricants" (SITC section 3), "Food, animals + beverages, tobacco" (SITC section 0+1) and "Machinery and transport equipment" (SITC section 7) were the largest commodity groups for imports in 2015, representing respectively 22.0, 19.6 and 19.1 percent of imported goods (see table 3). From 2013 to 2015, the largest import commodity was "Petroleum oils, other than crude" (HS code 2710) (see table 4). The top three partners for merchandise imports were Greece, Israel and the United Kingdom, accounting for respectively 24.0, 9.6 and 7.5 percent of total imports. "Transportation" (EBOPS code 205) accounted for the largest share of imports of services in 2014 at 1.8 bln US$, followed by "Travel" (EBOPS code 236) at 1.3 bln US$ and "Computer and information services" (EBOPS code 262) at 927.3 mln US$ (see graph 6).

Table 4: Top 10 import commodities 2013 to 2015

HS code	4-digit heading of Harmonized System 2012	Value (million US$) 2013	2014	2015	Unit value 2013	2014	2015	Unit	SITC code
	All Commodities	6 418.2	6 828.6	5 666.0					
2710	Petroleum oils, other than crude	1 767.8	1 606.9	1 195.3	0.9	0.8	0.4	US$/kg	334
8703	Motor cars and other motor vehicles principally designed for the transport	167.6	246.5	296.5	16.0	16.5	13.8	thsd US$/unit	781
3004	Medicaments (excluding goods of heading 30.02, 30.05 or 30.06)	212.8	206.0	174.4	59.3	48.7	43.1	US$/kg	542
8517	Electrical apparatus for line telephony or line telegraphy	132.1	120.5	107.0					764
8903	Yachts and other vessels for pleasure or sports; rowing boats and canoes	9.6	252.1	59.9	57.6	200.8	194.3	thsd US$/unit	793
2402	Cigars, cheroots, cigarillos and cigarettes	98.5	94.6	84.2	39.9	36.5	47.7	US$/kg	122
2208	Alcohol of a strength by volume of less than 80 % vol	67.3	66.2	62.4	21.3	21.0	19.3	US$/litre	112
8471	Automatic data processing machines and units thereof	59.3	60.6	60.8	163.3	152.4	160.6	US$/unit	752
6204	Women's or girls'suits, ensembles, jackets, blazers, dresses, skirts	56.4	65.6	51.0	16.1	16.7	14.1	US$/unit	842
2309	Preparations of a kind used in animal feeding	52.1	57.3	49.4	1.6	1.6	1.3	US$/kg	081

Source: UN Comtrade

Czech Republic

Goods Imports: CIF, by origin | **Goods Exports: FOB, by last known destination** | **Trade System: Special**

Overview:

In 2015, the value of merchandise exports of the Czech Republic decreased substantially by 10.7 percent to reach 155.7 bln US$, while its merchandise imports decreased substantially by 10.3 percent to reach 137.5 bln US$ (see graph 1, table 2 and table 3). The merchandise trade balance recorded a relatively small surplus of 18.2 bln US$ (see graph 1). The largest merchandise trade balance was with MDG Developed Europe at 39.8 bln US$ (see graph 4). Merchandise exports in the Czech Republic were diversified amongst partners; imports were also diversified. The top 13 partners accounted for 80 percent or more of exports and 15 partners accounted for 80 percent or more of imports (see graph 5). In 2014, the value of exports of services of the Czech Republic increased slightly by 2.8 percent, reaching 22.7 bln US$, while its imports of services increased moderately by 8.7 percent and reached 21.1 bln US$ (see graph 2). There was a relatively small trade in services surplus of 1.6 bln US$.

Graph 1: Total merchandise trade, by value

(Bln US$ by year)

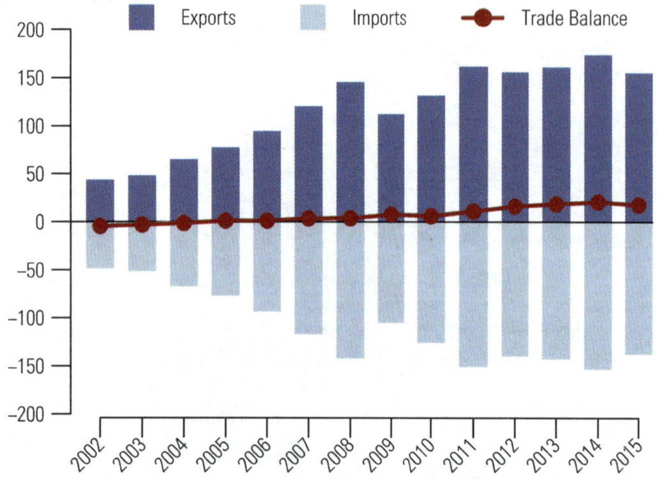

Graph 2: Total services trade, by value

(Bln US$ by year)

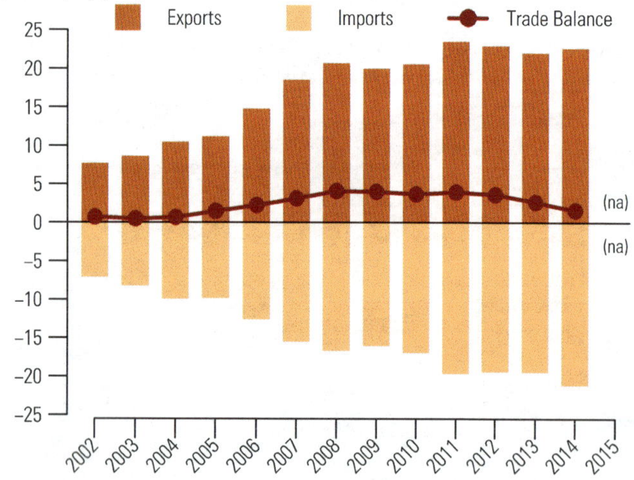

Exports Profile:

"Machinery and transport equipment" (SITC section 7), "Goods classified chiefly by material" (SITC section 6) and "Miscellaneous manufactured articles" (SITC section 8) were the largest commodity groups for exports in 2015, representing respectively 55.7, 15.9 and 12.1 percent of exported goods (see table 2). From 2013 to 2015, the largest export commodity was "Motor cars and other motor vehicles principally designed for the transport" (HS code 8703) (see table 1). The top three destinations for merchandise exports were Germany, Slovakia and Poland, accounting for respectively 31.9, 8.7 and 5.9 percent of total exports. "Travel" (EBOPS code 236) accounted for the largest share of exports of services in 2014 at 6.8 bln US$, followed by "Transportation" (EBOPS code 205) at 5.6 bln US$ and "Other business services" (EBOPS code 268) at 5.5 bln US$ (see graph 3).

Graph 3: Exports of services by EBOPS category

(% share in 2014)

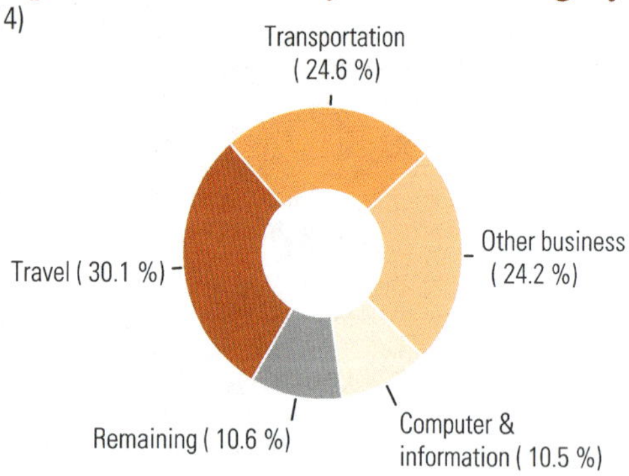

Table 1: Top 10 export commodities 2013 to 2015

HS code	4-digit heading of Harmonized System 2012	Value (million US$)			Unit value				SITC code
		2013	2014	2015	2013	2014	2015	Unit	
	All Commodities	161 524.2	174 279.5	155 677.7					
8703	Motor cars and other motor vehicles principally designed for the transport	15 345.2	17 811.6	16 919.2	15.0	15.7	14.0	thsd US$/unit	781
8708	Parts and accessories of the motor vehicles of headings 87.01 to 87.05	11 564.3	13 176.1	12 495.8	*8.1*	*8.5*	*7.3*	US$/kg	784
8471	Automatic data processing machines and units thereof	9 212.7	9 810.2	7 847.3	211.2	234.3	217.6	US$/unit	752
8517	Electrical apparatus for line telephony or line telegraphy	4 168.6	4 953.4	4 959.7					764
8544	Insulated (including enamelled or anodised) wire, cable	2 796.5	3 000.4	2 577.1	*9.0*	*9.7*	*9.2*	US$/kg	773
9503	Tricycles, scooters, wheeled toys; dolls'carriages; dolls; other toys	2 369.1	2 645.3	2 489.0	*21.9*	24.9	*20.7*	US$/kg	894
9401	Seats (other than those of heading 94.02)	2 230.7	2 624.7	2 451.8					821
8536	Electrical apparatus for switching or protecting electrical circuits	2 296.3	2 686.0	2 202.6	*18.8*	*29.9*	*21.4*	US$/kg	772
4011	New pneumatic tyres, of rubber	2 330.1	2 318.0	2 000.2	77.5	74.2	63.4	US$/unit	625
8512	Electrical lighting or signalling equipment	1 769.8	2 214.2	2 385.7					778

Services Imports and Exports: EBOPS 2002 categories

Table 2: Merchandise exports by SITC

(Value in million US$, growth and shares in percentage)

SITC	2015	Avg. Growth rates 2011-2015	Avg. Growth rates 2014-2015	2015 share
Total	155 677.7	-1.1	-10.7	100.0
0+1	7 008.5	3.4	-7.8	4.5
2+4	3 927.9	-5.3	-18.4	2.5
3	4 622.0	-6.9	0.0	3.0
5	9 328.5	-1.7	-17.0	6.0
6	24 812.5	-3.6	-14.0	15.9
7	86 694.7	-0.7	-10.0	55.7
8	18 884.2	2.5	-7.5	12.1
9	399.3	11.9	-5.6	0.3

Table 3: Merchandise imports by SITC

(Value in million US$, growth and shares in percentage)

SITC	2015	Avg. Growth rates 2011-2015	Avg. Growth rates 2014-2015	2015 share
Total	137 485.7	-2.3	-10.3	100.0
0+1	7 775.7	-0.4	-9.5	5.7
2+4	3 384.0	-8.7	-20.2	2.5
3	9 140.7	-11.9	-25.9	6.6
5	15 565.4	-1.5	-12.2	11.3
6	23 785.6	-3.8	-12.2	17.3
7	62 386.1	-0.5	-6.4	45.4
8	15 130.5	1.0	-6.4	11.0
9	317.5	1.6	-22.0	0.2

SITC Legend

SITC Code	Description
Total	All commodities
0+1	Food, animals + beverages, tobacco
2+4	Crude materials + anim. & veg. oils
3	Mineral fuels, lubricants
5	Chemicals
6	Goods classified chiefly by material
7	Machinery and transport equipment
8	Miscellaneous manufactured articles
9	Not classified elsewhere in the SITC

Graph 4: Merchandise trade balance

(Bln US$ by MDG Regions in 2015)

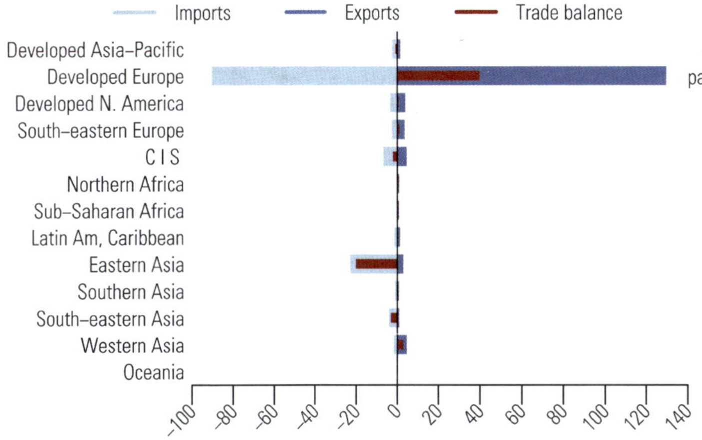

Graph 5: Partner concentration of merchandise trade

(Cumulative share by ranked partners in 2015)

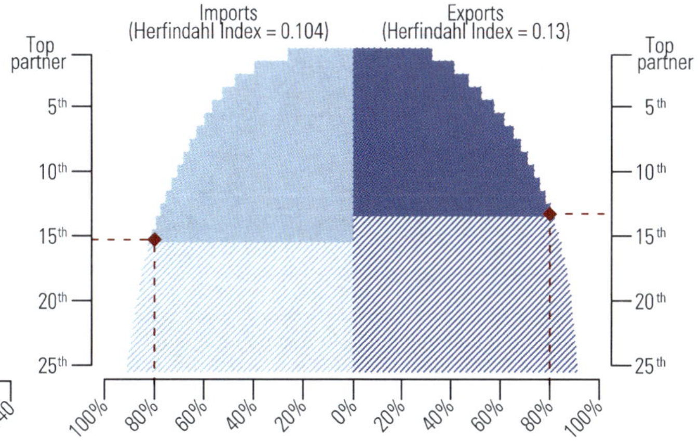

Graph 6: Imports of services by EBOPS category

(% share in 2014)

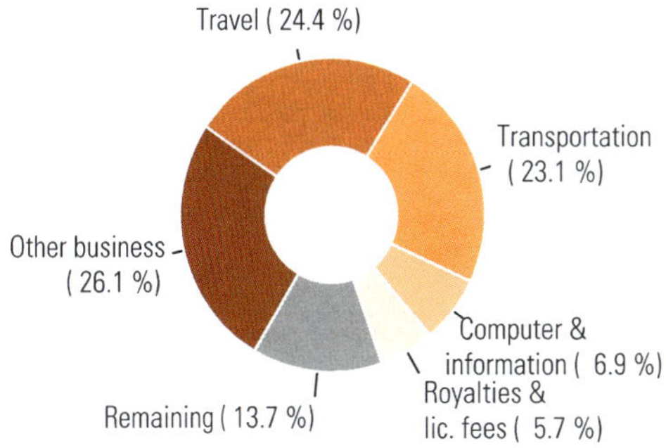

Imports Profile:

"Machinery and transport equipment" (SITC section 7), "Goods classified chiefly by material" (SITC section 6) and "Chemicals" (SITC section 5) were the largest commodity groups for imports in 2015, representing respectively 45.4, 17.3 and 11.3 percent of imported goods (see table 3). From 2013 to 2015, the largest import commodity was "Parts and accessories of the motor vehicles of headings 87.01 to 87.05" (HS code 8708) (see table 4). The top three partners for merchandise imports were Germany, China and Poland, accounting for respectively 26.1, 11.8 and 7.7 percent of total imports. "Other business services" (EBOPS code 268) accounted for the largest share of imports of services in 2014 at 5.5 bln US$, followed by "Travel" (EBOPS code 236) at 5.1 bln US$ and "Transportation" (EBOPS code 205) at 4.9 bln US$ (see graph 6).

Table 4: Top 10 import commodities 2013 to 2015

HS code	4-digit heading of Harmonized System 2012	Value (million US$) 2013	Value (million US$) 2014	Value (million US$) 2015	Unit value 2013	Unit value 2014	Unit value 2015	Unit	SITC code
	All Commodities	142 525.8	153 225.5	137 485.7					
8708	Parts and accessories of the motor vehicles of headings 87.01 to 87.05	7 479.0	8 544.7	8 035.0	*6.9*	*7.1*	*6.0*	US$/kg	784
8471	Automatic data processing machines and units thereof	5 614.2	5 682.1	6 029.6	88.3	90.4	106.1	US$/unit	752
8517	Electrical apparatus for line telephony or line telegraphy	4 062.0	4 679.6	5 494.3					764
2709	Petroleum oils and oils obtained from bituminous minerals, crude	5 414.2	5 656.8	3 115.5	0.8	0.8	*0.4*	US$/kg	333
3004	Medicaments (excluding goods of heading 30.02, 30.05 or 30.06)	3 041.2	3 669.9	3 176.2	*85.6*	*105.8*	*70.6*	US$/kg	542
2711	Petroleum gases and other gaseous hydrocarbons	4 054.9	2 608.5	2 573.2	0.6	*0.5*	*0.4*	US$/kg	343
8703	Motor cars and other motor vehicles principally designed for the transport	2 519.2	3 040.4	3 223.8	17.6	17.2	2.6	thsd US$/unit	781
8473	Parts and accessories for use with machines of heading 84.69 to 84.72	2 599.9	3 093.2	2 327.0	*45.1*	*44.6*	*45.3*	US$/kg	759
8542	Electronic integrated circuits	2 617.7	3 043.1	2 020.9					776
2710	Petroleum oils, other than crude	2 502.4	2 572.9	1 881.5	*1.0*	*0.9*	*0.6*	US$/kg	334

Denmark

Goods Imports: CIF, by origin/consignment for intra-eu **Goods Exports: FOB, by last known destination** **Trade System: General**

Overview:

In 2015, the value of merchandise exports of Denmark decreased substantially by 14.7 percent to reach 94.5 bln US$, while its merchandise imports decreased substantially by 14.1 percent to reach 85.5 bln US$ (see graph 1, table 2 and table 3). The merchandise trade balance recorded a relatively small surplus of 9.0 bln US$ (see graph 1). The largest merchandise trade balance was with MDG Developed Europe at -3.7 bln US$ (see graph 4). Merchandise exports in Denmark were diversified amongst partners; imports were also diversified. The top 17 partners accounted for 80 percent or more of exports and 15 partners accounted for 80 percent or more of imports (see graph 5). In 2014, the value of exports of services of Denmark increased by 3.0 percent, reaching 72.1 bln US$, while its imports of services increased slightly by 0.1 percent and reached 61.2 bln US$ (see graph 2). There was a relatively small trade in services surplus of 11.0 bln US$.

Graph 1: Total merchandise trade, by value

(Bln US$ by year)

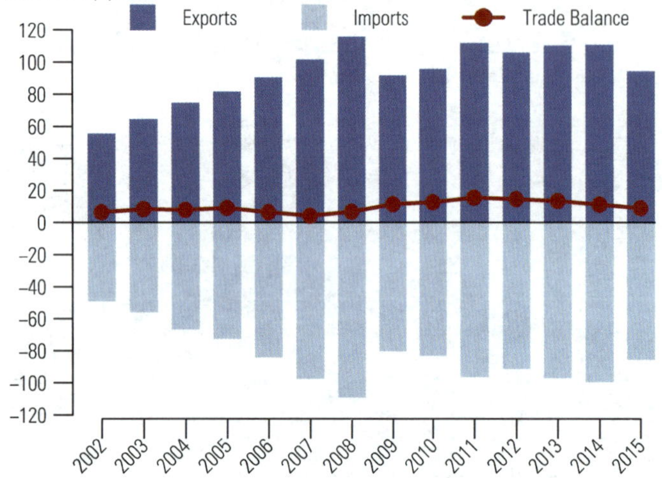

Graph 2: Total services trade, by value

(Bln US$ by year)

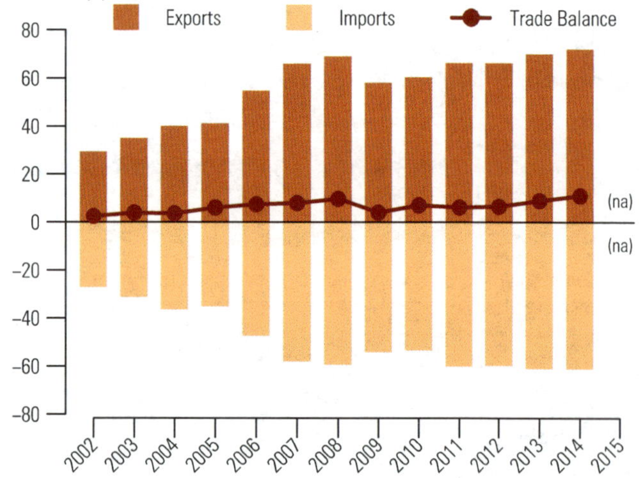

Exports Profile:

"Machinery and transport equipment" (SITC section 7), "Food, animals + beverages, tobacco" (SITC section 0+1) and "Chemicals" (SITC section 5) were the largest commodity groups for exports in 2015, representing respectively 26.3, 17.6 and 16.6 percent of exported goods (see table 2). From 2013 to 2015, the largest export commodity was "Commodities not specified according to kind" (HS code 9999) (see table 1). The top three destinations for merchandise exports were Germany, Sweden and Special Categories, accounting for respectively 16.2, 11.4 and 10.2 percent of total exports. "Transportation" (EBOPS code 205) accounted for the largest share of exports of services in 2014 at 44.3 bln US$, followed by "Other business services" (EBOPS code 268) at 8.1 bln US$ and "Travel" (EBOPS code 236) at 7.6 bln US$ (see graph 3).

Graph 3: Exports of services by EBOPS category

(% share in 2014)

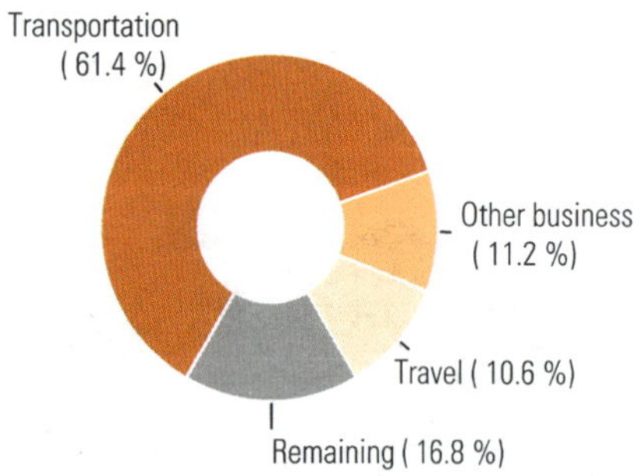

Table 1: Top 10 export commodities 2013 to 2015

HS code	4-digit heading of Harmonized System 2012	Value (million US$) 2013	Value (million US$) 2014	Value (million US$) 2015	Unit value 2013	Unit value 2014	Unit value 2015	Unit	SITC code
	All Commodities	110421.7	110748.9	94484.1					
9999	Commodities not specified according to kind	10611.7	10104.4	5977.2					931
3004	Medicaments (excluding goods of heading 30.02, 30.05 or 30.06)	3209.9	3220.6	6410.2	*224.3*	*230.2*	*350.2*	US$/kg	542
2710	Petroleum oils, other than crude	4053.5	3802.9	2548.5	*0.9*	*0.8*	*0.5*	US$/kg	334
8502	Electric generating sets and rotary converters	2921.3	3786.7	3195.5	359.1	529.0	525.4	thsd US$/unit	716
2709	Petroleum oils and oils obtained from bituminous minerals, crude	4915.1	3039.7	1779.0	0.8	0.7	0.4	US$/kg	333
0203	Meat of swine, fresh, chilled or frozen	3407.3	3227.5	2521.1	3.1	3.0	2.2	US$/kg	012
3002	Human blood; animal blood prepared for therapeutic uses	2317.0	2374.4	2402.9	*520.2*	*455.4*	*403.7*	US$/kg	541
4301	Raw furskins (including heads, tails, paws and other pieces or cuttings	2284.9	1398.5	1610.0	655.7	337.6		US$/kg	212
0406	Cheese and curd	1585.0	1697.7	1385.2	*5.4*	*5.4*	4.2	US$/kg	024
9403	Other furniture and parts thereof	1421.4	1498.5	1349.2					821

Services Imports and Exports: EBOPS 2002 categories

Table 2: Merchandise exports by SITC

(Value in million US$, growth and shares in percentage)

SITC	2015	Avg. Growth rates 2011-2015	Avg. Growth rates 2014-2015	2015 share
Total	94484.1	-4.1	-14.7	100.0
0+1	16625.0	-3.3	-15.9	17.6
2+4	4382.4	-5.2	-12.7	4.6
3	4575.4	-18.3	-37.0	4.8
5	15705.1	5.8	16.5	16.6
6	8077.5	-6.2	-16.7	8.5
7	24834.7	-3.2	-15.1	26.3
8	14288.4	-4.5	-11.4	15.1
9	5995.7	-9.0	-40.8	6.3

Table 3: Merchandise imports by SITC

(Value in million US$, growth and shares in percentage)

SITC	2015	Avg. Growth rates 2011-2015	Avg. Growth rates 2014-2015	2015 share
Total	85502.1	-3.0	-14.1	100.0
0+1	11119.9	-1.2	-12.7	13.0
2+4	3429.2	-2.6	-14.7	4.0
3	5493.7	-12.0	-34.7	6.4
5	10029.7	-1.1	-14.7	11.7
6	11618.8	-4.6	-13.1	13.6
7	27758.9	-1.0	-10.7	32.5
8	14095.6	-2.6	-10.7	16.5
9	1956.3	-8.3	-17.9	2.3

SITC Legend

SITC Code	Description
Total	All commodities
0+1	Food, animals + beverages, tobacco
2+4	Crude materials + anim. & veg. oils
3	Mineral fuels, lubricants
5	Chemicals
6	Goods classified chiefly by material
7	Machinery and transport equipment
8	Miscellaneous manufactured articles
9	Not classified elsewhere in the SITC

Graph 4: Merchandise trade balance

(Bln US$ by MDG Regions in 2015)

Graph 5: Partner concentration of merchandise trade

(Cumulative share by ranked partners in 2015)

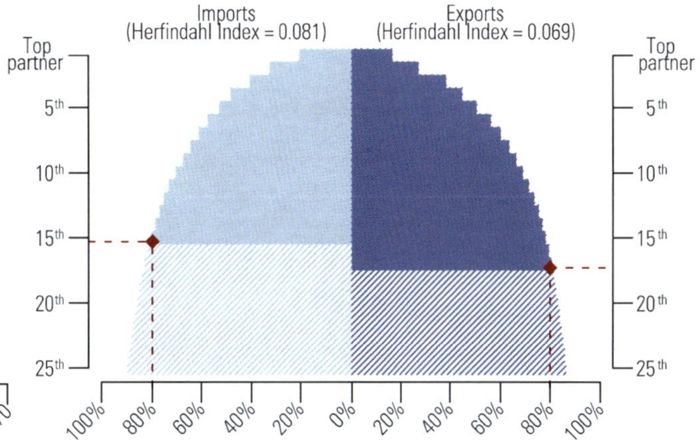

Graph 6: Imports of services by EBOPS category

(% share in 2014)

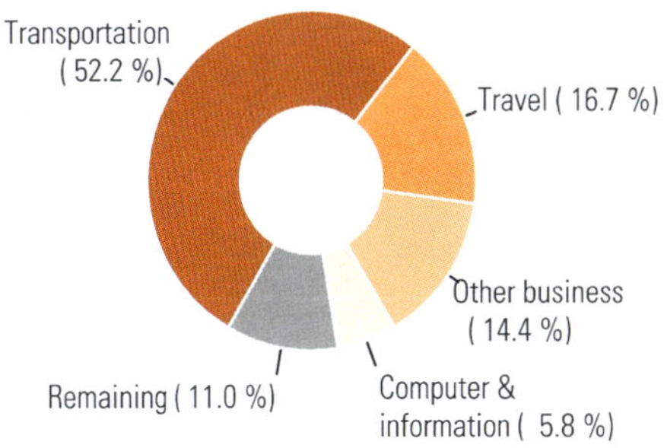

Imports Profile:

"Machinery and transport equipment" (SITC section 7), "Miscellaneous manufactured articles" (SITC section 8) and "Goods classified chiefly by material" (SITC section 6) were the largest commodity groups for imports in 2015, representing respectively 32.5, 16.5 and 13.6 percent of imported goods (see table 3). From 2013 to 2015, the largest import commodity was "Petroleum oils, other than crude" (HS code 2710) (see table 4). The top three partners for merchandise imports were Germany, Sweden and the Netherlands, accounting for respectively 20.7, 12.3 and 7.6 percent of total imports. "Transportation" (EBOPS code 205) accounted for the largest share of imports of services in 2014 at 31.9 bln US$, followed by "Travel" (EBOPS code 236) at 10.2 bln US$ and "Other business services" (EBOPS code 268) at 8.8 bln US$ (see graph 6).

Table 4: Top 10 import commodities 2013 to 2015

HS code	4-digit heading of Harmonized System 2012	Value (million US$) 2013	2014	2015	Unit value 2013	2014	2015	Unit	SITC code
	All Commodities	96978.6	99567.8	85502.1					
2710	Petroleum oils, other than crude	5407.7	4905.2	3251.7	*0.9*	*0.8*	*0.5*	US$/kg	334
8703	Motor cars and other motor vehicles principally designed for the transport	3112.9	3490.9	3652.3	14.1	15.2	14.0	thsd US$/unit	781
3004	Medicaments (excluding goods of heading 30.02, 30.05 or 30.06)	2808.0	3046.9	2430.6	*136.1*	*159.2*	*90.3*	US$/kg	542
2709	Petroleum oils and oils obtained from bituminous minerals, crude	3683.7	2705.5	1706.8	0.8	0.8	0.4	US$/kg	333
9999	Commodities not specified according to kind	2495.6	2364.7	1941.7					931
8901	Cruise ships, excursion boats, ferry-boats, cargo ships, barges	1656.3	2506.1	1758.6	43.6	57.0		mln US$/unit	793
8517	Electrical apparatus for line telephony or line telegraphy	1890.2	2067.8	1880.6					764
8471	Automatic data processing machines and units thereof	1996.7	2007.1	1705.0	233.5	228.6	152.3	US$/unit	752
8708	Parts and accessories of the motor vehicles of headings 87.01 to 87.05	933.5	967.6	877.0	*9.6*	*10.5*	*9.2*	US$/kg	784
9403	Other furniture and parts thereof	798.5	862.3	787.4					821

Dominica

Goods Imports: CIF, by origin	Goods Exports: FOB, by last known destination	Trade System: Special

Overview:

In 2012, the value of merchandise exports of Dominica was 37.0 mln US$, while its merchandise imports was 211.9 mln US$ (see graph 1, table 2 and table 3). The merchandise trade balance recorded a large deficit of 174.9 mln US$ (see graph 1). The largest merchandise trade balance was with MDG Developed North America at -81.2 mln US$ (see graph 4). Merchandise exports in Dominica were diversified amongst partners; imports were moderately concentrated. The top 8 partners accounted for 80 percent or more of exports and 11 partners accounted for 80 percent or more of imports (see graph 5, and Introduction, paragraphs 19-21). In 2013, the value of exports of services of Dominica decreased substantially by 22.7 percent, reaching 96.0 mln US$, while its imports of services decreased substantially by 44.7 percent and reached 37.4 mln US$ (see graph 2). There was a large trade in services surplus of 58.6 mln US$.

Graph 1: Total merchandise trade, by value

(Mln US$ by year)

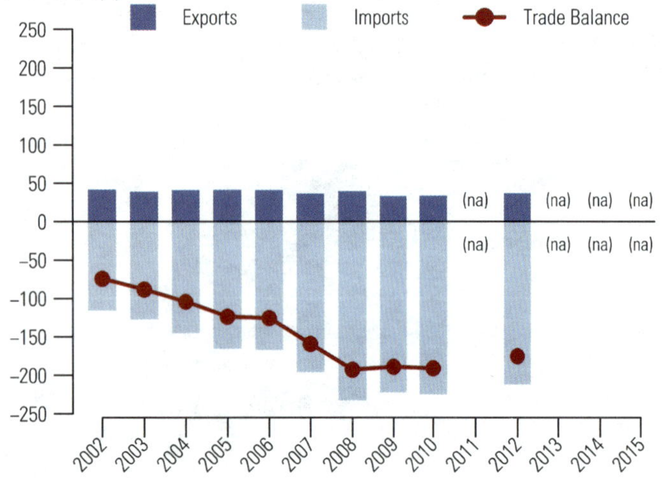

Graph 2: Total services trade, by value

(Mln US$ by year)

Exports Profile:

"Chemicals" (SITC section 5), "Miscellaneous manufactured articles" (SITC section 8) and "Machinery and transport equipment" (SITC section 7) were the largest commodity groups for exports in 2012, representing respectively 50.9, 14.6 and 11.6 percent of exported goods (see table 2). From 2010 to 2012, the largest export commodity was "Soap; organic surface-active products" (HS code 3401) (see table 1). The top three destinations for merchandise exports were Jamaica, Trinidad and Tobago and Saint Kitts and Nevis, accounting for respectively 16.9, 16.3 and 16.0 percent of total exports. "Travel" (EBOPS code 236) accounted for the largest share of exports of services in 2012 at 78.6 mln US$, followed by "Other business services" (EBOPS code 268) at 26.2 mln US$ and "Government services, n.i.e." (EBOPS code 291) at 13.5 mln US$ (see graph 3).

Graph 3: Exports of services by EBOPS category

(% share in 2012)

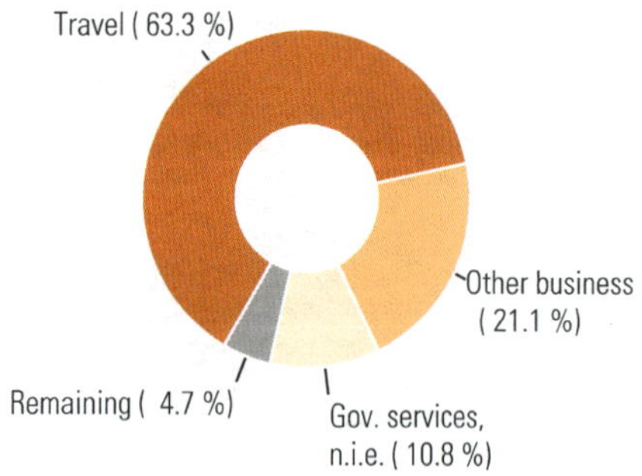

Table 1: Top 10 export commodities 2010 to 2012

HS code	4-digit heading of Harmonized System 2007	Value (million US$) 2010	2011	2012	Unit value 2010	2011	2012	Unit	SITC code
	All Commodities	34.1	...	37.0					
3401	Soap; organic surface-active products	13.8	...	16.5	*3.9*		26.0	US$/kg	554
4907	Unused postage, revenue or similar stamps of current or new issue	4.5	...	4.5			55.7	thsd US$/kg	892
0803	Bananas, including plantains, fresh or dried	3.1	...	1.1	*0.8*			US$/kg	057
3210	Other paints and varnishes	1.8	...	1.5	*4.3*		27.2	US$/kg	533
2517	Pebbles, gravel, broken or crushed stone	0.9	...	2.4	*0.0*			US$/kg	273
0714	Manioc, arrowroot, sweet potatoes and similar roots	1.7	...	1.2	*3.2*		3.2	US$/kg	054
8518	Microphones and stands therefor; loudspeakers	0.6	...	1.5					764
2505	Natural sands of all kinds	0.9	...	1.1	*0.0*		6.2	US$/kg	273
8525	Transmission apparatus for radio-telephony, radio-broadcasting	0.0	...	1.1					764
3301	Essential oils (terpeneless or not), including concretes	0.6	...	0.4	*0.1*			thsd US$/kg	551

Services Imports and Exports: EBOPS 2002 categories

Table 2: Merchandise exports by SITC
(Value in million US$, growth and shares in percentage)

SITC	2012	Avg. Growth rates 2008-2012	2011-2012	2012 share
Total	37.0	-1.9	...	100.0
0+1	4.2	-28.1	...	11.3
2+4	3.6	-9.9	...	9.7
3	0.0	-2.6	...	0.0
5	18.8	1.5	...	50.9
6	0.7	35.1	...	1.9
7	4.3	62.7	...	11.6
8	5.4	92.8	...	14.6
9	0.0	...	...	0.0

Table 3: Merchandise imports by SITC
(Value in million US$, growth and shares in percentage)

SITC	2012	Avg. Growth rates 2008-2012	2011-2012	2012 share
Total	211.9	-2.3	...	100.0
0+1	47.7	2.3	...	22.5
2+4	10.3	-4.3	...	4.8
3	46.9	6.6	...	22.1
5	17.0	-4.4	...	8.0
6	31.1	-5.5	...	14.7
7	36.1	-10.5	...	17.0
8	22.7	-0.6	...	10.7
9	0.3	-34.5	...	0.1

SITC Legend

SITC Code	Description
Total	All commodities
0+1	Food, animals + beverages, tobacco
2+4	Crude materials + anim. & veg. oils
3	Mineral fuels, lubricants
5	Chemicals
6	Goods classified chiefly by material
7	Machinery and transport equipment
8	Miscellaneous manufactured articles
9	Not classified elsewhere in the SITC

Graph 4: Merchandise trade balance
(Mln US$ by MDG Regions in 2012)

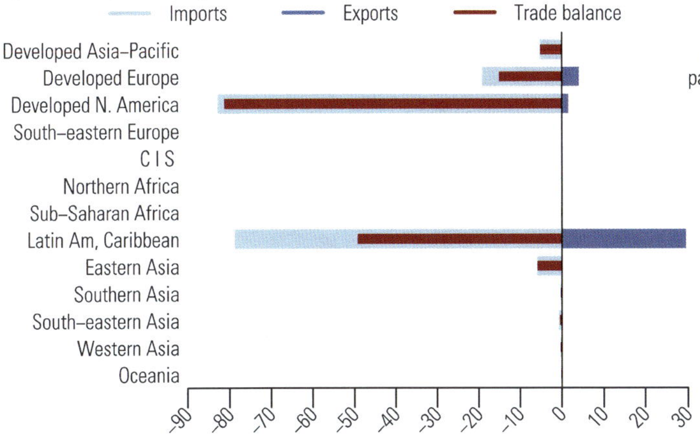

Graph 5: Partner concentration of merchandise trade
(Cumulative share by ranked partners in 2012)

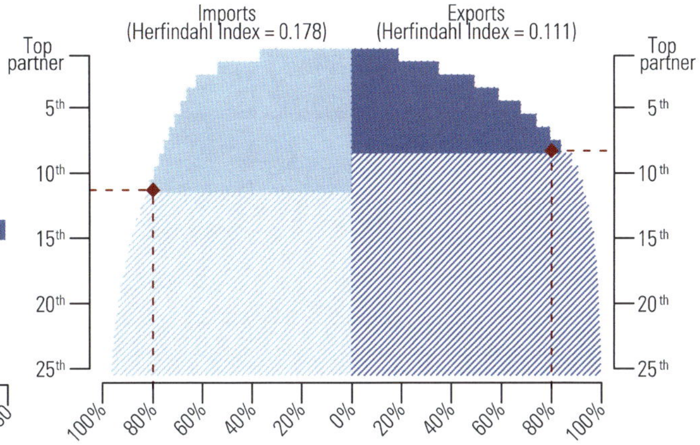

Graph 6: Imports of services by EBOPS category
(% share in 2012)

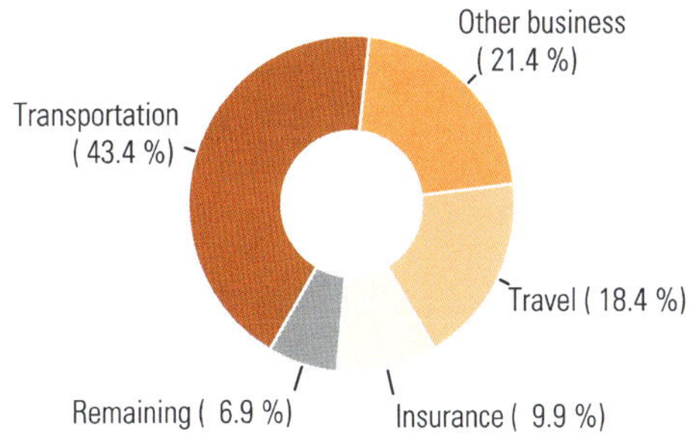

Imports Profile:

"Food, animals + beverages, tobacco" (SITC section 0+1), "Mineral fuels, lubricants" (SITC section 3) and "Machinery and transport equipment" (SITC section 7) were the largest commodity groups for imports in 2012, representing respectively 22.5, 22.1 and 17.0 percent of imported goods (see table 3). From 2010 to 2012, the largest import commodity was "Petroleum oils, other than crude" (HS code 2710) (see table 4). The top three partners for merchandise imports were the United States, Trinidad and Tobago and Areas nes, accounting for respectively 39.4, 16.1 and 4.6 percent of total imports. "Transportation" (EBOPS code 205) accounted for the largest share of imports of services in 2012 at 29.4 mln US$, followed by "Other business services" (EBOPS code 268) at 14.4 mln US$ and "Travel" (EBOPS code 236) at 12.4 mln US$ (see graph 6).

Table 4: Top 10 import commodities 2010 to 2012

HS code	4-digit heading of Harmonized System 2007	Value (million US$) 2010	2011	2012	Unit value 2010	2011	2012	Unit	SITC code
	All Commodities	224.6	...	211.9					
2710	Petroleum oils, other than crude	35.3	...	43.2	*1.2*		4.1	US$/kg	334
0207	Meat and edible offal, of the poultry of heading 01.05	5.5	...	5.4	*3.9*			US$/kg	012
8703	Motor cars and other motor vehicles principally designed for the transport	5.5	...	3.5	*16.3*		*18.2*	thsd US$/unit	781
1502	Fats of bovine animals, sheep or goats, other than those of heading 15.03	5.2	...	3.4	3.5		2.9	US$/kg	411
0402	Milk and cream, concentrated or containing added sugar	3.7	...	3.3	*4.2*			US$/kg	022
2523	Portland cement, aluminous cement, slag cement	3.1	...	3.5					661
1101	Wheat or meslin flour	3.1	...	3.4	*1.6*			US$/kg	046
2202	Waters with added sugar	2.9	...	3.6	*2.2*		*5.2*	US$/litre	111
8517	Electrical apparatus for line telephony or line telegraphy	3.4	...	2.4					764
8704	Motor vehicles for the transport of goods	3.7	...	1.8					782

Dominican Republic

Goods Imports: FOB, by origin **Goods Exports: FOB, by last known destination** **Trade System: General**

Overview:

In 2015, the value of merchandise exports of Dominican Republic decreased substantially by 15.5 percent to reach 8.4 bln US$, while its merchandise imports decreased slightly by 2.3 percent to reach 17.3 bln US$ (see graph 1, table 2 and table 3). The merchandise trade balance recorded a large deficit of 9.0 bln US$ (see graph 1). The largest merchandise trade balance was with MDG Eastern Asia at -2.5 bln US$ (see graph 4). Merchandise exports in Dominican Republic were highly concentrated amongst partners; imports were moderately concentrated. The top 4 partners accounted for 80 percent or more of exports and 13 partners accounted for 80 percent or more of imports (see graph 5). In 2014, the value of exports of services of Dominican Republic increased slightly by 4.7 percent, reaching 6.4 bln US$, while its imports of services increased slightly by 1.6 percent and reached 2.1 bln US$ (see graph 2). There was a large trade in services surplus of 4.4 bln US$.

Graph 1: Total merchandise trade, by value

(Bln US$ by year)

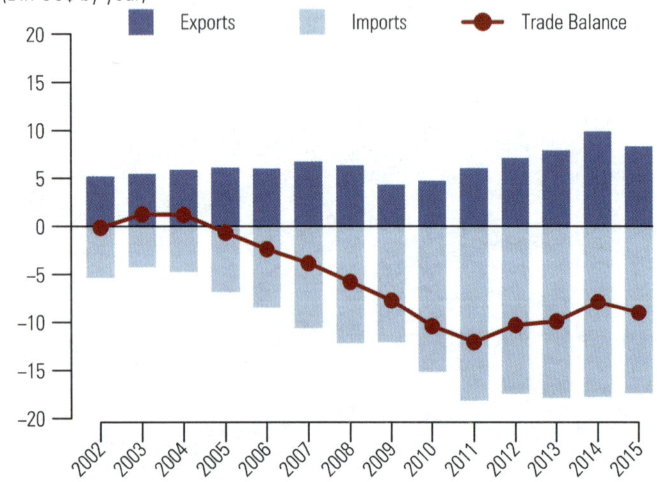

Graph 2: Total services trade, by value

(Bln US$ by year)

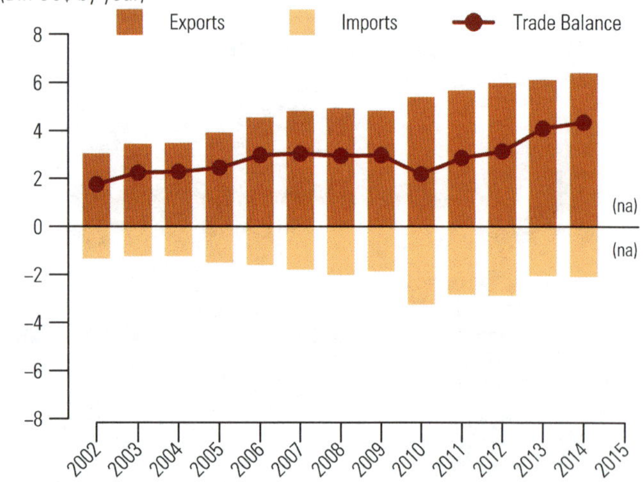

Exports Profile:

"Miscellaneous manufactured articles" (SITC section 8), "Food, animals + beverages, tobacco" (SITC section 0+1) and "Not classified elsewhere in the SITC" (SITC section 9) were the largest commodity groups for exports in 2015, representing respectively 35.3, 23.5 and 15.2 percent of exported goods (see table 2). From 2013 to 2015, the largest export commodity was "Gold (including gold plated with platinum)" (HS code 7108) (see table 1). The top three destinations for merchandise exports were the United States, Haiti and Canada, accounting for respectively 51.2, 13.2 and 9.8 percent of total exports. "Travel" (EBOPS code 236) accounted for the largest share of exports of services in 2014 at 3.1 bln US$, followed by "Computer and information services" (EBOPS code 262) at 1.7 bln US$ and "Other business services" (EBOPS code 268) at 1.2 bln US$ (see graph 3).

Graph 3: Exports of services by EBOPS category

(% share in 2014)

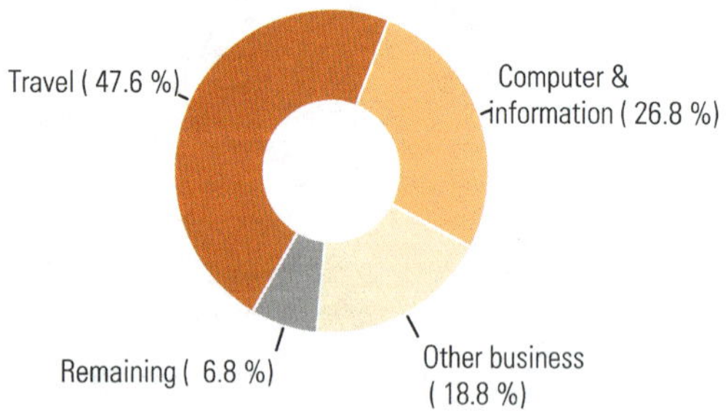

Table 1: Top 10 export commodities 2013 to 2015

HS code	4-digit heading of Harmonized System 2012	Value (million US$) 2013	2014	2015	Unit value 2013	2014	2015	Unit	SITC code
	All Commodities	7961.0	9927.8	8384.1					
7108	Gold (including gold plated with platinum)	1198.4	1582.0	1270.3	11.9			thsd US$/kg	971
9018	Instruments and appliances used in medical, surgical, dental or veterinary	752.7	874.4	933.6					872
2402	Cigars, cheroots, cigarillos and cigarettes	510.5	526.5	625.6	22.6		19.1	US$/kg	122
8536	Electrical apparatus for switching or protecting electrical circuits	367.0	484.4	402.7					772
6109	T-shirts, singlets and other vests, knitted or crocheted	204.6	313.4	378.8	5.2	4.8	5.0	US$/unit	845
7113	Articles of jewellery and parts thereof, of precious metal	194.8	250.5	374.1					897
3006	Pharmaceutical goods specified in Note 4 to this Chapter	278.2	227.0	257.4					541
2710	Petroleum oils, other than crude	153.0	558.7	29.4					334
0803	Bananas, including plantains, fresh or dried	167.9	331.6	229.4	0.5	0.6	0.6	US$/kg	057
1801	Cocoa beans, whole or broken, raw or roasted	162.3	212.1	250.8	2.6	3.1	3.2	US$/kg	072

Services Imports and Exports: EBOPS 2002 categories

Table 2: Merchandise exports by SITC

(Value in million US$, growth and shares in percentage)

SITC	2015	Avg. Growth rates 2011-2015	Avg. Growth rates 2014-2015	2015 share
Total	8384.1	8.2	-15.5	100.0
0+1	1970.7	7.6	-9.5	23.5
2+4	223.9	-3.1	-32.8	2.7
3	34.5	-33.8	-93.9	0.4
5	533.2	9.4	-6.6	6.4
6	684.4	-13.6	-33.1	8.2
7	700.6	7.7	-13.8	8.4
8	2963.7	9.3	3.7	35.3
9	1273.0	218.6	-19.8	15.2

Table 3: Merchandise imports by SITC

(Value in million US$, growth and shares in percentage)

SITC	2015	Avg. Growth rates 2011-2015	Avg. Growth rates 2014-2015	2015 share
Total	17347.8	-1.1	-2.3	100.0
0+1	2346.7	2.4	5.2	13.5
2+4	541.4	-5.6	-19.7	3.1
3	2692.3	-12.9	-33.1	15.5
5	2158.3	2.2	1.0	12.4
6	3386.3	-0.6	7.1	19.5
7	4064.6	5.1	16.7	23.4
8	2057.3	3.9	5.6	11.9
9	101.0	-3.9	11.7	0.6

SITC Legend

SITC Code	Description
Total	All commodities
0+1	Food, animals + beverages, tobacco
2+4	Crude materials + anim. & veg. oils
3	Mineral fuels, lubricants
5	Chemicals
6	Goods classified chiefly by material
7	Machinery and transport equipment
8	Miscellaneous manufactured articles
9	Not classified elsewhere in the SITC

Graph 4: Merchandise trade balance

(Bln US$ by MDG Regions in 2015)

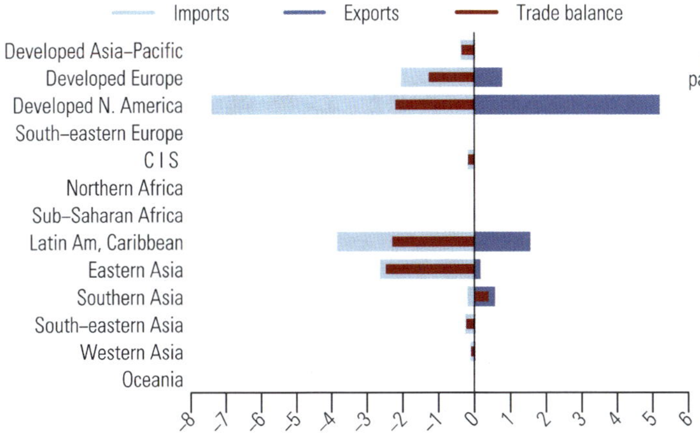

Graph 5: Partner concentration of merchandise trade

(Cumulative share by ranked partners in 2015)

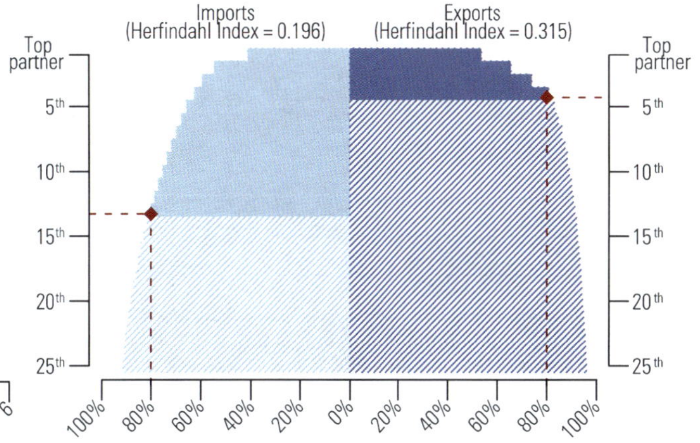

Graph 6: Imports of services by EBOPS category

(% share in 2014)

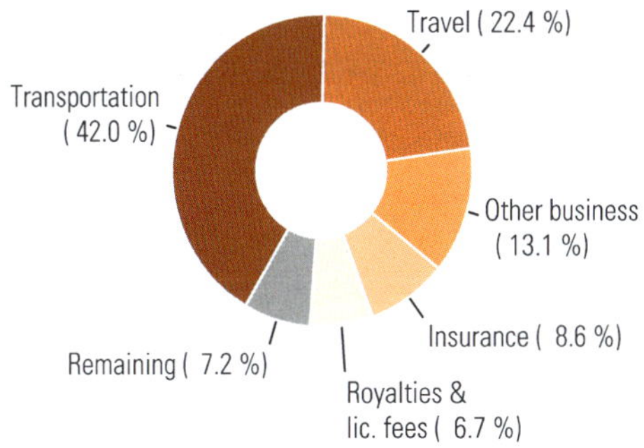

Imports Profile:

"Machinery and transport equipment" (SITC section 7), "Goods classified chiefly by material" (SITC section 6) and "Mineral fuels, lubricants" (SITC section 3) were the largest commodity groups for imports in 2015, representing respectively 23.4, 19.5 and 15.5 percent of imported goods (see table 3). From 2013 to 2015, the largest import commodity was "Petroleum oils, other than crude" (HS code 2710) (see table 4). The top three partners for merchandise imports were the United States, China and Mexico, accounting for respectively 40.1, 11.8 and 5.6 percent of total imports. "Transportation" (EBOPS code 205) accounted for the largest share of imports of services in 2014 at 864.2 mln US$, followed by "Travel" (EBOPS code 236) at 460.9 mln US$ and "Other business services" (EBOPS code 268) at 268.7 mln US$ (see graph 6).

Table 4: Top 10 import commodities 2013 to 2015

HS code	4-digit heading of Harmonized System 2012	Value (million US$) 2013	Value (million US$) 2014	Value (million US$) 2015	Unit value 2013	Unit value 2014	Unit value 2015	Unit	SITC code
	All Commodities	17845.0	17751.7	17347.8					
2710	Petroleum oils, other than crude	2869.2	2210.0	1838.7					334
2709	Petroleum oils and oils obtained from bituminous minerals, crude	1226.4	941.3	306.2	*0.8*	*0.8*	*0.8*	US$/kg	333
8703	Motor cars and other motor vehicles principally designed for the transport	518.1	617.5	759.2	*22.3*	*20.9*	*22.4*	thsd US$/unit	781
2711	Petroleum gases and other gaseous hydrocarbons	706.3	756.7	395.4					343
3004	Medicaments (excluding goods of heading 30.02, 30.05 or 30.06)	426.9	418.4	456.7					542
3926	Other articles of plastics	329.0	359.7	388.7	*12.2*	*12.7*	*14.3*	US$/kg	893
8517	Electrical apparatus for line telephony or line telegraphy	323.2	303.5	293.3					764
1005	Maize (corn)	278.7	227.9	215.7		*0.4*		US$/kg	044
3923	Articles for the conveyance or packing of goods, of plastics	152.0	166.9	186.4	*4.9*	*4.9*	*5.2*	US$/kg	893
2401	Unmanufactured tobacco; tobacco refuse	171.9	152.0	161.5	*5.3*	*5.2*	*5.4*	US$/kg	121

Ecuador

Goods Imports: CIF, by origin | **Goods Exports: FOB, by last known destination** | **Trade System: Special**

Overview:

In 2015, the value of merchandise exports of Ecuador decreased substantially by 28.8 percent to reach 18.3 bln US$, while its merchandise imports decreased substantially by 22.3 percent to reach 21.4 bln US$ (see graph 1, table 2 and table 3). The merchandise trade balance recorded a relatively small deficit of 3.1 bln US$ (see graph 1). The largest merchandise trade balance was with MDG Eastern Asia at -4.2 bln US$ (see graph 4). Merchandise exports in Ecuador were moderately concentrated amongst partners; imports were diversified. The top 13 partners accounted for 80 percent or more of exports and 14 partners accounted for 80 percent or more of imports (see graph 5). In 2014, the value of exports of services of Ecuador increased substantially by 15.0 percent, reaching 2.3 bln US$, while its imports of services increased slightly by 0.9 percent and reached 3.6 bln US$ (see graph 2). There was a moderate trade in services deficit of 1.2 bln US$.

Graph 1: Total merchandise trade, by value

(Bln US$ by year)

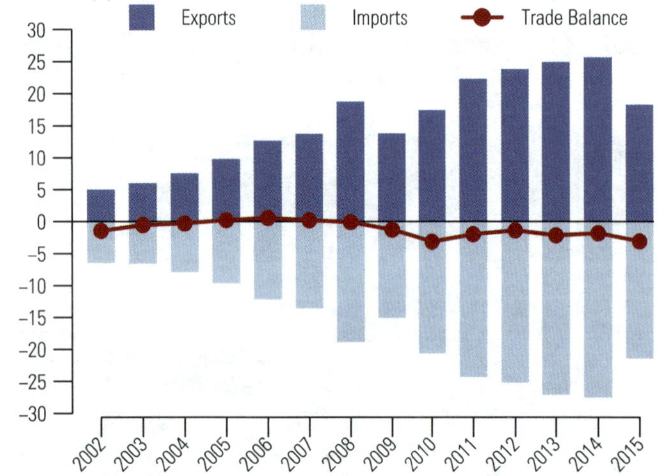

Graph 2: Total services trade, by value

(Bln US$ by year)

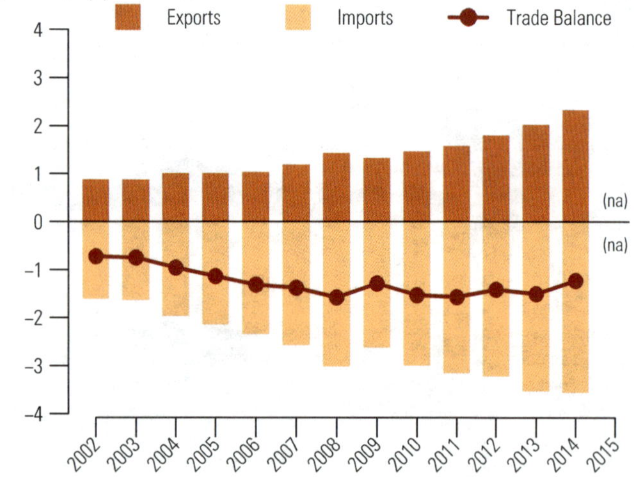

Exports Profile:

"Food, animals + beverages, tobacco" (SITC section 0+1), "Mineral fuels, lubricants" (SITC section 3) and "Crude materials + anim. & veg. oils" (SITC section 2+4) were the largest commodity groups for exports in 2015, representing respectively 44.3, 36.3 and 8.0 percent of exported goods (see table 2). From 2013 to 2015, the largest export commodity was "Petroleum oils and oils obtained from bituminous minerals, crude" (HS code 2709) (see table 1). The top three destinations for merchandise exports were the United States, Chile and Peru, accounting for respectively 42.9, 8.6 and 6.4 percent of total exports. "Travel" (EBOPS code 236) accounted for the largest share of exports of services in 2014 at 1.5 bln US$, followed by "Transportation" (EBOPS code 205) at 424.7 mln US$ and "Government services, n.i.e." (EBOPS code 291) at 121.5 mln US$ (see graph 3).

Graph 3: Exports of services by EBOPS category

(% share in 2014)

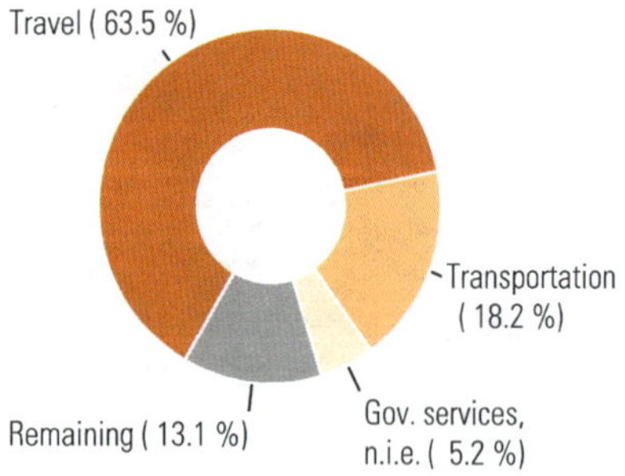

Table 1: Top 10 export commodities 2013 to 2015

HS code	4-digit heading of Harmonized System 2012	Value (million US$) 2013	2014	2015	Unit value 2013	2014	2015	Unit	SITC code
	All Commodities	24957.6	25730.1	18330.6					
2709	Petroleum oils and oils obtained from bituminous minerals, crude	13411.8	13016.0	6355.2	0.7	0.6	0.3	US$/kg	333
0803	Bananas, including plantains, fresh or dried	2332.2	2620.7	2820.1	0.4	0.4	0.4	US$/kg	057
0306	Crustaceans, whether in shell or not	1795.0	2580.6	2287.4	8.1	8.6	6.7	US$/kg	036
1604	Prepared or preserved fish; caviar	1337.9	1241.5	921.3	5.1	4.5	3.6	US$/kg	037
0603	Cut flowers and flower buds of a kind suitable for bouquets	837.3	798.4	819.9	5.3	5.7	5.6	US$/kg	292
7108	Gold (including gold plated with platinum)	467.8	854.6	681.8		34.4	32.8	thsd US$/kg	971
1801	Cocoa beans, whole or broken, raw or roasted	433.3	587.8	705.4	2.4	3.0	3.0	US$/kg	072
2710	Petroleum oils, other than crude	551.9	192.4	294.2	0.6	0.5	0.3	US$/kg	334
1511	Palm oil and its fractions	208.4	225.0	225.4	1.0	1.0	0.8	US$/kg	422
2101	Extracts, essences and concentrates, of coffee, tea or mate	190.1	152.9	126.7	7.8	6.8	7.2	US$/kg	071

Services Imports and Exports: EBOPS 2002 categories

Table 2: Merchandise exports by SITC

(Value in million US$, growth and shares in percentage)

SITC	2015	Avg. Growth rates 2011-2015	Avg. Growth rates 2014-2015	2015 share
Total	18 330.6	-4.8	-28.8	100.0
0+1	8 112.5	6.7	-4.4	44.3
2+4	1 465.9	2.5	-7.7	8.0
3	6 661.9	-15.2	-49.9	36.3
5	266.1	-3.4	-7.4	1.5
6	616.9	-0.3	-6.7	3.4
7	340.3	-12.1	0.8	1.9
8	183.0	-3.1	-14.4	1.0
9	684.1	50.4	-20.2	3.7

Table 3: Merchandise imports by SITC

(Value in million US$, growth and shares in percentage)

SITC	2015	Avg. Growth rates 2011-2015	Avg. Growth rates 2014-2015	2015 share
Total	21 387.3	-3.1	-22.3	100.0
0+1	1 720.5	-2.2	-12.2	8.0
2+4	444.3	-7.5	-27.8	2.1
3	4 195.7	-6.1	-36.9	19.6
5	3 886.6	1.1	-8.4	18.2
6	2 922.7	-4.9	-22.0	13.7
7	6 489.1	-3.3	-21.4	30.3
8	1 616.5	0.2	-16.2	7.6
9	111.8	6.2	-1.8	0.5

SITC Legend

SITC Code	Description
Total	All commodities
0+1	Food, animals + beverages, tobacco
2+4	Crude materials + anim. & veg. oils
3	Mineral fuels, lubricants
5	Chemicals
6	Goods classified chiefly by material
7	Machinery and transport equipment
8	Miscellaneous manufactured articles
9	Not classified elsewhere in the SITC

Graph 4: Merchandise trade balance

(Bln US$ by MDG Regions in 2015)

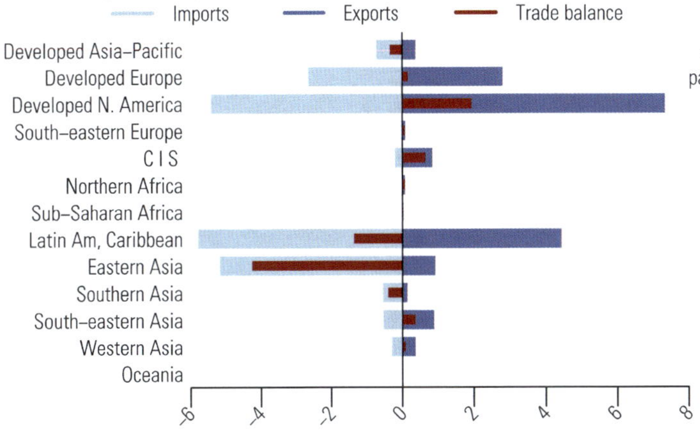

Graph 5: Partner concentration of merchandise trade

(Cumulative share by ranked partners in 2015)

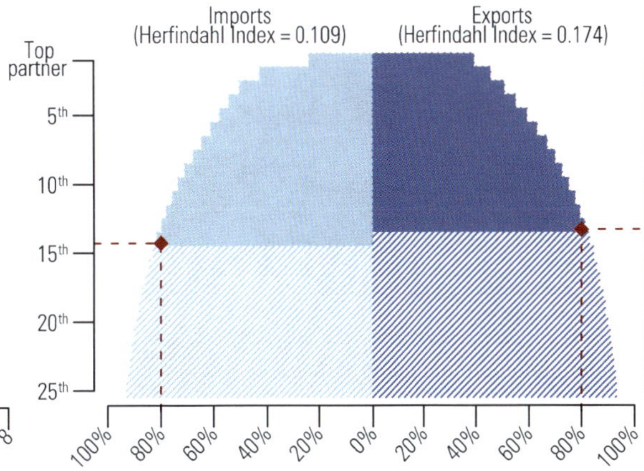

Graph 6: Imports of services by EBOPS category

(% share in 2014)

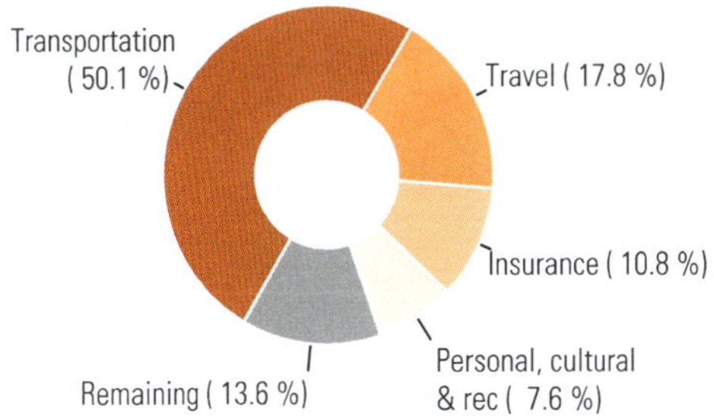

Imports Profile:

"Machinery and transport equipment" (SITC section 7), "Mineral fuels, lubricants" (SITC section 3) and "Chemicals" (SITC section 5) were the largest commodity groups for imports in 2015, representing respectively 30.3, 19.6 and 18.2 percent of imported goods (see table 3). From 2013 to 2015, the largest import commodity was "Petroleum oils, other than crude" (HS code 2710) (see table 4). The top three partners for merchandise imports were the United States, China and Colombia, accounting for respectively 25.8, 17.3 and 7.7 percent of total imports. "Transportation" (EBOPS code 205) accounted for the largest share of imports of services in 2014 at 1.8 bln US$, followed by "Travel" (EBOPS code 236) at 634.6 mln US$ and "Insurance services" (EBOPS code 253) at 383.0 mln US$ (see graph 6).

Table 4: Top 10 import commodities 2013 to 2015

HS code	4-digit heading of Harmonized System 2012	Value (million US$) 2013	2014	2015	Unit value 2013	2014	2015	Unit	SITC code
	All Commodities	27 064.5	27 515.4	21 387.3					
2710	Petroleum oils, other than crude	3 403.9	3 362.7	2 095.8	*1.0*	0.9	0.6	US$/kg	334
2707	Oils and other products of high temperature coal tar	2 113.4	2 430.4	1 604.2	1.1	1.0	0.7	US$/kg	335
3004	Medicaments (excluding goods of heading 30.02, 30.05 or 30.06)	803.1	858.7	856.5	*34.7*	34.9	30.4	US$/kg	542
8703	Motor cars and other motor vehicles principally designed for the transport	784.5	778.6	524.8	*15.8*	*16.4*	9.5	thsd US$/unit	781
2711	Petroleum gases and other gaseous hydrocarbons	657.8	698.2	394.0	0.8	0.8	0.4	US$/kg	343
8704	Motor vehicles for the transport of goods	564.8	598.9	376.1			14.9	thsd US$/unit	782
8517	Electrical apparatus for line telephony or line telegraphy	513.0	508.4	463.4					764
8471	Automatic data processing machines and units thereof	482.2	489.4	252.3			74.5	US$/unit	752
2304	Oil-cake and other solid residues	336.0	406.7	381.3	0.5	0.5	0.4	US$/kg	081
7304	Tubes, pipes and hollow profiles, seamless, of iron (other than cast iron)	358.9	406.2	175.6	*2.1*	*2.0*	1.8	US$/kg	679

Egypt

Goods Imports: CIF, by consignment | **Goods Exports: FOB, by last known destination** | **Trade System: General**

Overview:

In 2015, the value of merchandise exports of Egypt decreased substantially by 18.1 percent to reach 22.0 bln US$, while its merchandise imports increased slightly by 4.2 percent to reach 74.4 bln US$ (see graph 1, table 2 and table 3). The merchandise trade balance recorded a large deficit of 52.4 bln US$ (see graph 1). The largest merchandise trade balance was with MDG Developed Europe at -17.6 bln US$ (see graph 4). Merchandise exports in Egypt were diversified amongst partners; imports were also diversified. The top 26 partners accounted for 80 percent or more of exports and 22 partners accounted for 80 percent or more of imports (see graph 5). In 2014, the value of exports of services of Egypt increased substantially by 19.9 percent, reaching 21.9 bln US$, while its imports of services increased moderately by 6.7 percent and reached 17.5 bln US$ (see graph 2). There was a moderate trade in services surplus of 4.4 bln US$. See footnote*.

Graph 1: Total merchandise trade, by value

(Bln US$ by year)

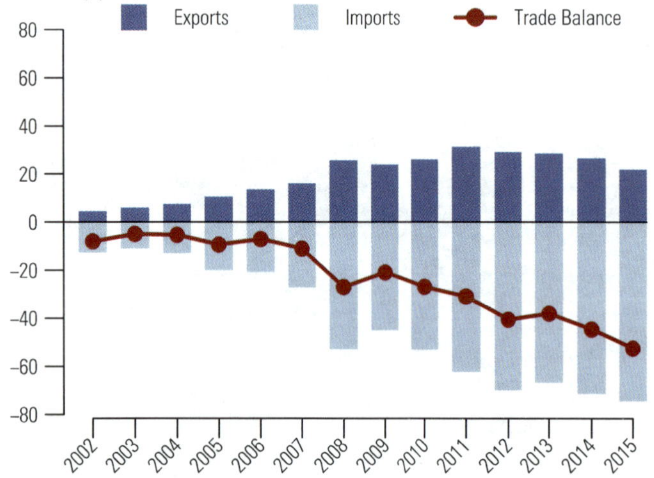

Graph 2: Total services trade, by value

(Bln US$ by year)

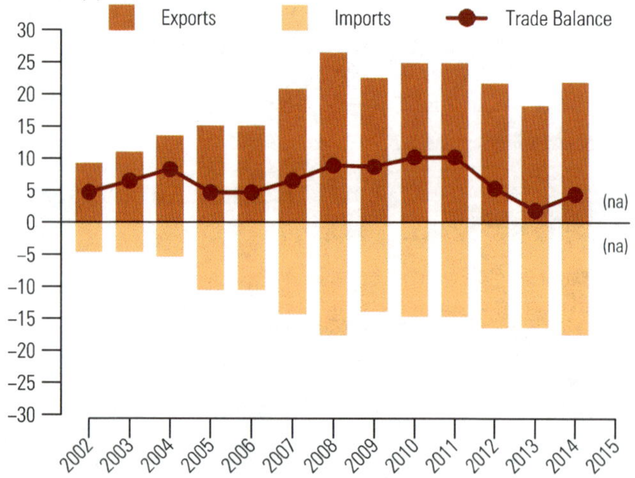

Exports Profile:

"Goods classified chiefly by material" (SITC section 6), "Food, animals + beverages, tobacco" (SITC section 0+1) and "Mineral fuels, lubricants" (SITC section 3) were the largest commodity groups for exports in 2015, representing respectively 20.2, 19.1 and 17.9 percent of exported goods (see table 2). From 2013 to 2015, the largest export commodity was "Petroleum oils and oils obtained from bituminous minerals, crude" (HS code 2709) (see table 1). The top three destinations for merchandise exports were Italy, Saudi Arabia and India, accounting for respectively 8.7, 7.7 and 6.4 percent of total exports. "Transportation" (EBOPS code 205) accounted for the largest share of exports of services in 2014 at 9.8 bln US$, followed by "Travel" (EBOPS code 236) at 7.2 bln US$ and "Government services, n.i.e." (EBOPS code 291) at 1.6 bln US$ (see graph 3).

Graph 3: Exports of services by EBOPS category

(% share in 2014)

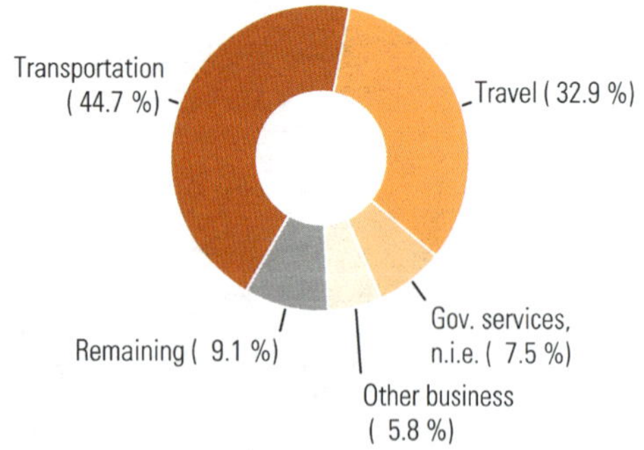

Table 1: Top 10 export commodities 2013 to 2015

HS code	4-digit heading of Harmonized System 2007	Value (million US$) 2013	2014	2015	Unit value 2013	2014	2015	Unit	SITC code
	All Commodities	28779.4	26812.2	21967.3					
2709	Petroleum oils and oils obtained from bituminous minerals, crude	3059.5	3050.5	1994.1	0.7	0.6	*0.8*	US$/kg	333
2710	Petroleum oils, other than crude	2548.9	2437.2	1485.5	0.9	0.8	*1.1*	US$/kg	334
8544	Insulated (including enamelled or anodised) wire, cable	895.9	1001.8	770.7	*8.6*	7.7		US$/kg	773
7108	Gold (including gold plated with platinum)	901.1	659.3	631.3	43.5	38.5	*39.8*	thsd US$/kg	971
2711	Petroleum gases and other gaseous hydrocarbons	1559.7	379.8	145.2	0.4	0.5		US$/kg	343
3102	Mineral or chemical fertilisers, nitrogenous	1077.1	644.7	332.4	*0.4*	0.3		US$/kg	562
8528	Reception apparatus for television	110.8	749.4	782.6		331.3		US$/unit	761
0805	Citrus fruit, fresh or dried	533.3	475.3	526.1	*0.4*	0.4	*0.7*	US$/kg	057
6203	Men's or boys' suits, ensembles, jackets, blazers, trousers	372.1	321.0	436.1		9.1		US$/unit	841
0406	Cheese and curd	374.9	378.9	340.8	*3.8*	3.3	*5.3*	US$/kg	024

*Special trade system up to 2007.

Table 2: Merchandise exports by SITC

(Value in million US$, growth and shares in percentage)

SITC	2015	Avg. Growth rates 2011-2015	Avg. Growth rates 2014-2015	2015 share
Total	21 967.3	-8.7	-18.1	100.0
0+1	4 202.0	0.7	-0.6	19.1
2+4	1 099.1	-11.9	-6.1	5.0
3	3 927.1	-19.3	-37.3	17.9
5	3 198.2	-8.5	-27.6	14.6
6	4 441.9	-8.2	-15.1	20.2
7	1 996.4	7.1	-14.2	9.1
8	2 259.1	-0.9	0.9	10.3
9	843.7	-16.8	-10.4	3.8

Table 3: Merchandise imports by SITC

(Value in million US$, growth and shares in percentage)

SITC	2015	Avg. Growth rates 2011-2015	Avg. Growth rates 2014-2015	2015 share
Total	74 361.3	4.5	4.2	100.0
0+1	12 763.6	2.3	1.4	17.2
2+4	4 681.5	-10.2	-27.7	6.3
3	11 674.5	5.9	19.0	15.7
5	9 575.1	5.5	4.5	12.9
6	13 628.4	3.6	2.7	18.3
7	18 167.9	9.6	14.0	24.4
8	3 619.0	16.2	22.7	4.9
9	251.3	61.5	-77.9	0.3

SITC Legend

SITC Code	Description
Total	All commodities
0+1	Food, animals + beverages, tobacco
2+4	Crude materials + anim. & veg. oils
3	Mineral fuels, lubricants
5	Chemicals
6	Goods classified chiefly by material
7	Machinery and transport equipment
8	Miscellaneous manufactured articles
9	Not classified elsewhere in the SITC

Graph 4: Merchandise trade balance

(Bln US$ by MDG Regions in 2015)

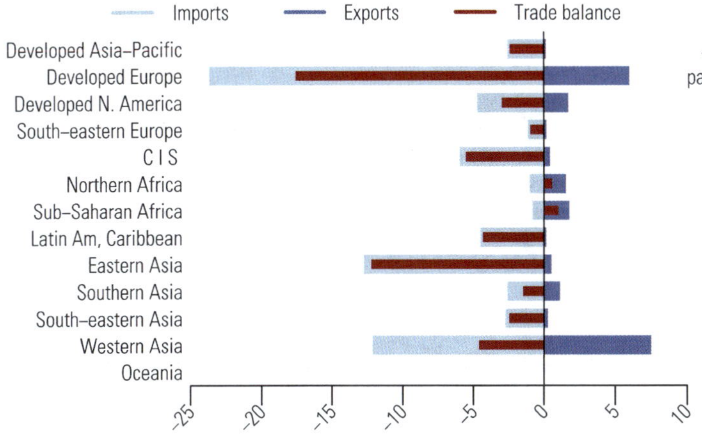

Graph 5: Partner concentration of merchandise trade

(Cumulative share by ranked partners in 2015)

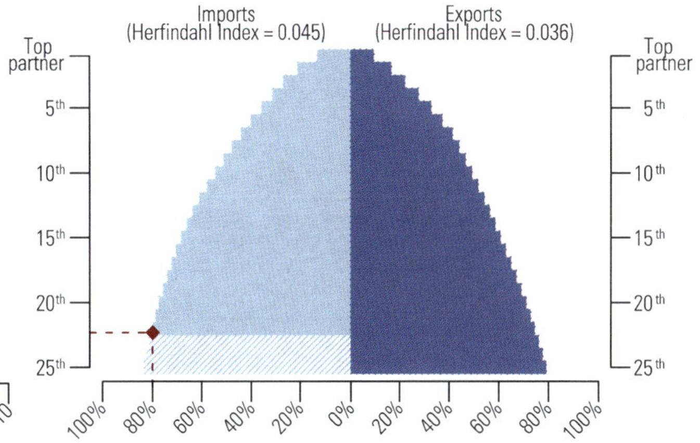

Graph 6: Imports of services by EBOPS category

(% share in 2014)

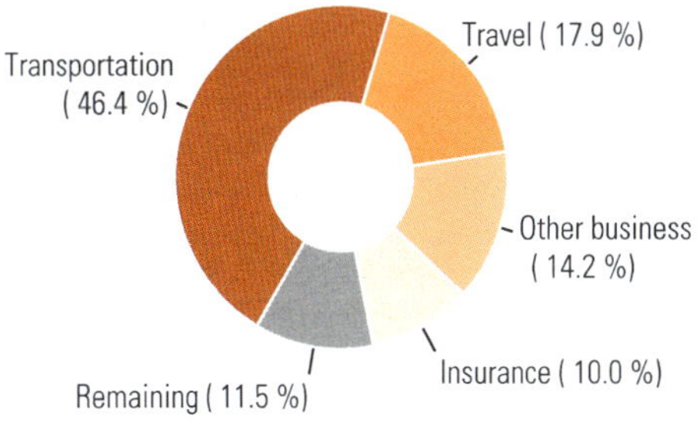

Imports Profile:

"Machinery and transport equipment" (SITC section 7), "Goods classified chiefly by material" (SITC section 6) and "Food, animals + beverages, tobacco" (SITC section 0+1) were the largest commodity groups for imports in 2015, representing respectively 24.4, 18.3 and 17.2 percent of imported goods (see table 3). From 2013 to 2015, the largest import commodity was "Petroleum oils, other than crude" (HS code 2710) (see table 4). The top three partners for merchandise imports were China, Germany and the United States, accounting for respectively 11.7, 7.8 and 7.0 percent of total imports. "Transportation" (EBOPS code 205) accounted for the largest share of imports of services in 2014 at 8.1 bln US$, followed by "Travel" (EBOPS code 236) at 3.1 bln US$ and "Other business services" (EBOPS code 268) at 2.5 bln US$ (see graph 6).

Table 4: Top 10 import commodities 2013 to 2015

HS code	4-digit heading of Harmonized System 2007	Value (million US$) 2013	Value (million US$) 2014	Value (million US$) 2015	Unit value 2013	Unit value 2014	Unit value 2015	Unit	SITC code
	All Commodities	66 666.4	71 337.7	74 361.3					
2710	Petroleum oils, other than crude	5 527.0	5 548.4	7 133.2	0.9	0.8	*1.2*	US$/kg	334
8703	Motor cars and other motor vehicles principally designed for the transport	1 266.2	2 556.6	3 301.5	*16.0*		*17.4*	thsd US$/unit	781
2709	Petroleum oils and oils obtained from bituminous minerals, crude	2 028.6	3 044.0	1 756.5	0.8	0.7	*0.8*	US$/kg	333
1001	Wheat and meslin	721.7	3 066.2	2 536.0			*0.4*	US$/kg	041
1005	Maize (corn)	1 985.0	1 951.6	1 790.3					044
3004	Medicaments (excluding goods of heading 30.02, 30.05 or 30.06)	1 599.5	1 662.3	2 018.4	39.1	127.6		US$/kg	542
2711	Petroleum gases and other gaseous hydrocarbons	1 573.5	1 022.3	2 467.6	0.9	0.8		US$/kg	343
8517	Electrical apparatus for line telephony or line telegraphy	1 278.9	1 653.2	1 895.4					764
7207	Semi-finished products of iron or non-alloy steel	1 527.6	1 513.2	1 389.5		0.5	*1.3*	US$/kg	672
7326	Other articles of iron or steel	1 135.0	1 319.7	1 189.2	12.1	7.3		US$/kg	699

El Salvador

Goods Imports: CIF, by origin | **Goods Exports: FOB, by last known destination** | **Trade System: General**

Overview:

In 2015, the value of merchandise exports of El Salvador increased slightly by 4.0 percent to reach 5.5 bln US$, while its merchandise imports decreased slightly by 0.9 percent to reach 10.4 bln US$ (see graph 1, table 2 and table 3). The merchandise trade balance recorded a large deficit of 4.9 bln US$ (see graph 1). The largest merchandise trade balance was with MDG Developed North America at -1.5 bln US$ (see graph 4). Merchandise exports in El Salvador were highly concentrated amongst partners; imports were moderately concentrated. The top 4 partners accounted for 80 percent or more of exports and 11 partners accounted for 80 percent or more of imports (see graph 5). In 2014, the value of exports of services of El Salvador increased substantially by 15.5 percent, reaching 1.7 bln US$, while its imports of services decreased slightly by 1.9 percent and reached 1.3 bln US$ (see graph 2). There was a moderate trade in services surplus of 442.4 mln US$.

Graph 1: Total merchandise trade, by value

(Bln US$ by year)

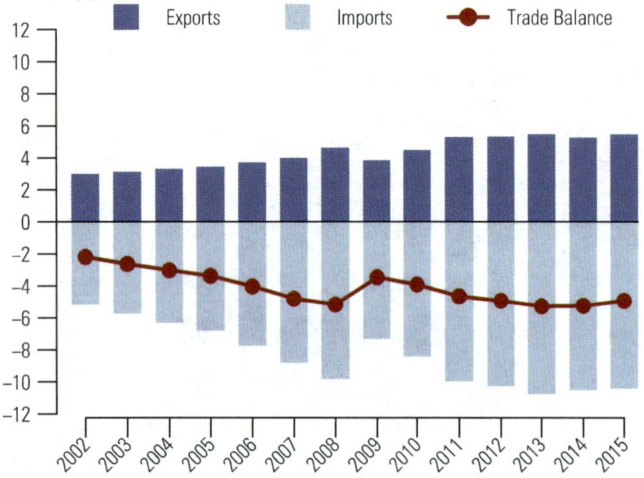

Graph 2: Total services trade, by value

(Bln US$ by year)

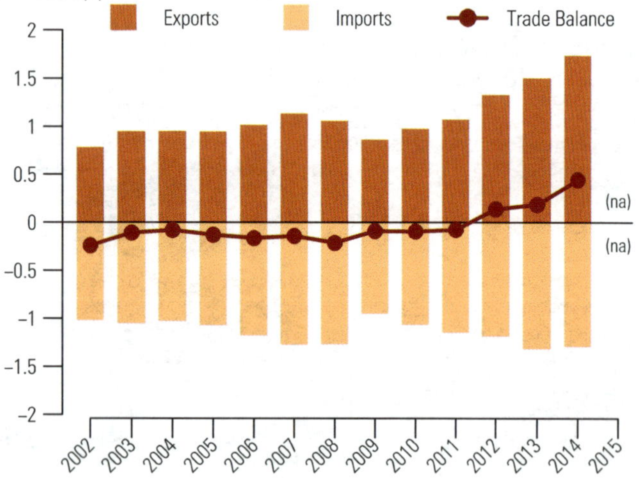

Exports Profile:

"Miscellaneous manufactured articles" (SITC section 8), "Food, animals + beverages, tobacco" (SITC section 0+1) and "Goods classified chiefly by material" (SITC section 6) were the largest commodity groups for exports in 2015, representing respectively 48.4, 19.4 and 16.9 percent of exported goods (see table 2). From 2013 to 2015, the largest export commodity was "T-shirts, singlets and other vests, knitted or crocheted" (HS code 6109) (see table 1). The top three destinations for merchandise exports were the United States, Honduras and Guatemala, accounting for respectively 46.5, 14.2 and 13.4 percent of total exports. "Travel" (EBOPS code 236) accounted for the largest share of exports of services in 2014 at 821.4 mln US$, followed by "Transportation" (EBOPS code 205) at 551.3 mln US$ and "Communications services" (EBOPS code 245) at 116.2 mln US$ (see graph 3).

Graph 3: Exports of services by EBOPS category

(% share in 2014)

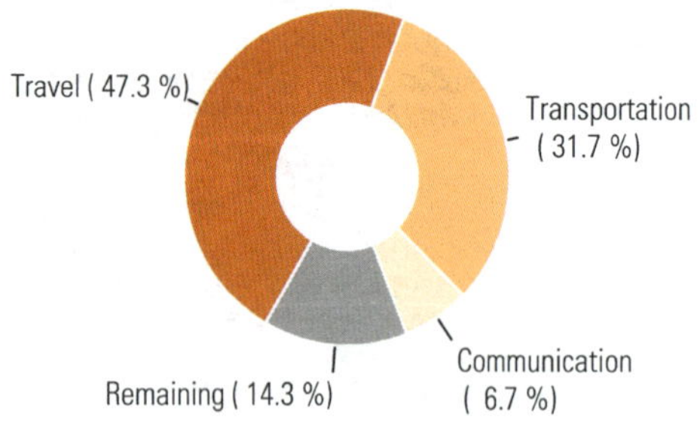

Table 1: Top 10 export commodities 2013 to 2015

HS code	4-digit heading of Harmonized System 2012	Value (million US$) 2013	2014	2015	Unit value 2013	2014	2015	Unit	SITC code
	All Commodities	5491.1	5272.7	5484.9					
6109	T-shirts, singlets and other vests, knitted or crocheted	810.7	753.3	771.7	*5.3*	*5.0*	*5.2*	US$/unit	845
6110	Jerseys, pullovers, cardigans, waist-coats and similar articles	240.8	286.3	290.4	*13.6*	*12.6*		US$/unit	845
6115	Panty hose, tights, stockings, socks and other hosiery	228.4	253.7	255.3	11.5	11.9	11.8	US$/kg	846
1701	Cane or beet sugar and chemically pure sucrose, in solid form	209.2	192.0	193.1	0.5	0.4	0.4	US$/kg	061
3923	Articles for the conveyance or packing of goods, of plastics	172.0	178.0	185.8	2.3	2.3	2.1	US$/kg	893
8532	Electrical capacitors, fixed, variable or adjustable (pre-set)	171.0	171.2	159.4	206.8	209.5	194.9	US$/kg	778
0901	Coffee, whether or not roasted or decaffeinated	233.9	110.5	149.2	3.5	3.9	4.3	US$/kg	071
6107	Men's or boys'underpants, briefs, nightshirts, pyjamas, bathrobes	109.9	122.7	214.5					843
4818	Toilet paper and similar paper	129.4	128.8	127.1	1.6	1.7	1.8	US$/kg	642
3004	Medicaments (excluding goods of heading 30.02, 30.05 or 30.06)	109.5	106.1	118.2	4.8	6.0	6.2	US$/kg	542

Services Imports and Exports: EBOPS 2002 categories

Table 2: Merchandise exports by SITC

(Value in million US$, growth and shares in percentage)

SITC	2015	Avg. Growth rates 2011-2015	Avg. Growth rates 2014-2015	2015 share
Total	5484.9	0.8	4.0	100.0
0+1	1066.8	-0.9	7.4	19.4
2+4	80.6	-10.7	-22.2	1.5
3	104.9	-11.2	-22.5	1.9
5	351.0	0.4	4.3	6.4
6	928.1	3.7	9.8	16.9
7	287.2	1.1	-4.6	5.2
8	2653.9	4.8	4.7	48.4
9	12.4	-54.1	-46.1	0.2

Table 3: Merchandise imports by SITC

(Value in million US$, growth and shares in percentage)

SITC	2015	Avg. Growth rates 2011-2015	Avg. Growth rates 2014-2015	2015 share
Total	10415.4	1.1	-0.9	100.0
0+1	1647.6	4.5	4.0	15.8
2+4	340.2	-5.7	-1.5	3.3
3	1436.9	-4.7	-21.5	13.8
5	1647.5	0.5	0.9	15.8
6	2255.6	1.2	-0.7	21.7
7	1908.9	5.5	10.4	18.3
8	1164.0	6.1	5.3	11.2
9	14.7	-47.1	0.0	0.1

SITC Legend

SITC Code	Description
Total	All commodities
0+1	Food, animals + beverages, tobacco
2+4	Crude materials + anim. & veg. oils
3	Mineral fuels, lubricants
5	Chemicals
6	Goods classified chiefly by material
7	Machinery and transport equipment
8	Miscellaneous manufactured articles
9	Not classified elsewhere in the SITC

Graph 4: Merchandise trade balance

(Bln US$ by MDG Regions in 2015)

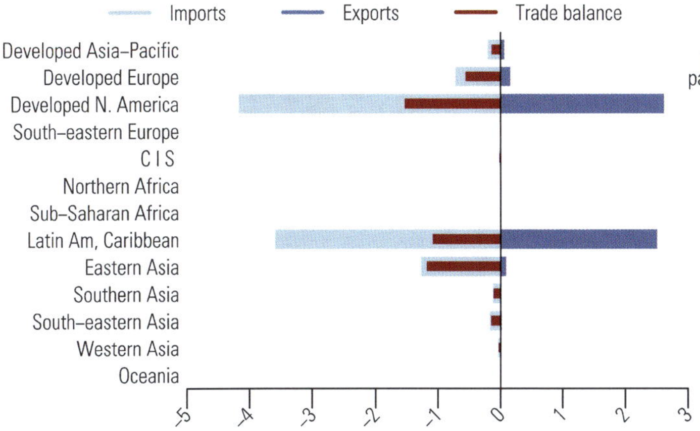

Graph 5: Partner concentration of merchandise trade

(Cumulative share by ranked partners in 2015)

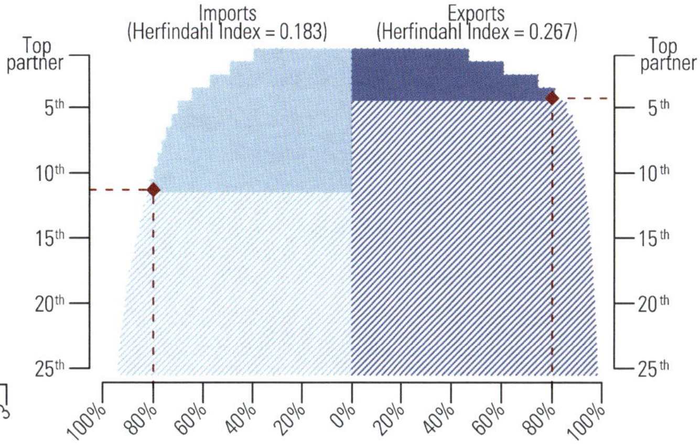

Graph 6: Imports of services by EBOPS category

(% share in 2014)

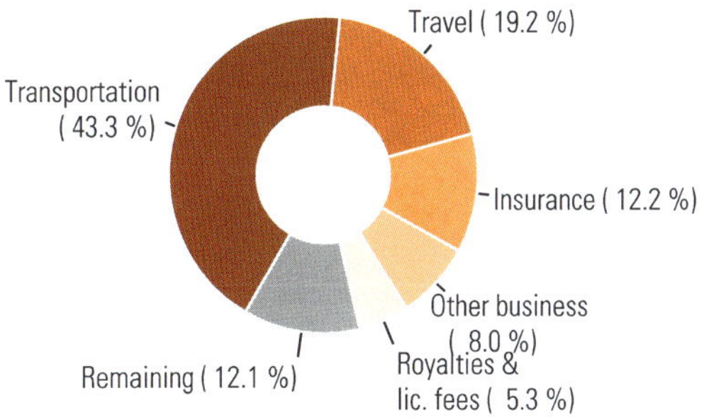

Imports Profile:

"Goods classified chiefly by material" (SITC section 6), "Machinery and transport equipment" (SITC section 7) and "Food, animals + beverages, tobacco" (SITC section 0+1) were the largest commodity groups for imports in 2015, representing respectively 21.7, 18.3 and 15.8 percent of imported goods (see table 3). From 2013 to 2015, the largest import commodity was "Petroleum oils, other than crude" (HS code 2710) (see table 4). The top three partners for merchandise imports were the United States, Guatemala and China, accounting for respectively 39.8, 9.3 and 7.3 percent of total imports. "Transportation" (EBOPS code 205) accounted for the largest share of imports of services in 2014 at 560.5 mln US$, followed by "Travel" (EBOPS code 236) at 248.2 mln US$ and "Insurance services" (EBOPS code 253) at 157.7 mln US$ (see graph 6).

Table 4: Top 10 import commodities 2013 to 2015

HS code	4-digit heading of Harmonized System 2012	Value (million US$) 2013	Value 2014	Value 2015	Unit value 2013	Unit value 2014	Unit value 2015	Unit	SITC code
	All Commodities	10772.0	10512.9	10415.4					
2710	Petroleum oils, other than crude	1790.7	1521.5	1213.8	0.9	0.9	0.6	US$/kg	334
6006	Other knitted or crocheted fabrics	349.6	325.1	263.7	5.2	5.0	5.3	US$/kg	655
3004	Medicaments (excluding goods of heading 30.02, 30.05 or 30.06)	266.1	267.0	305.5	27.9	21.8	22.7	US$/kg	542
8517	Electrical apparatus for line telephony or line telegraphy	227.3	253.1	261.9					764
2711	Petroleum gases and other gaseous hydrocarbons	171.7	216.9	135.3	0.8	0.9	0.5	US$/kg	343
5402	Synthetic filament yarn (other than sewing thread)	140.1	156.6	156.9	3.9	3.9	3.7	US$/kg	651
8703	Motor cars and other motor vehicles principally designed for the transport	147.0	136.6	162.8	*17.3*	*17.7*	*18.9*	thsd US$/unit	781
5205	Cotton yarn (other than sewing thread), containing 85 % or more	155.2	155.8	115.8	3.3	3.4	3.0	US$/kg	651
3901	Polymers of ethylene, in primary forms	121.1	125.3	111.1	1.6	1.7	1.4	US$/kg	571
1005	Maize (corn)	102.3	107.8	134.2	0.3	0.3	0.2	US$/kg	044

Source: UN Comtrade

Estonia

Goods Imports: CIF, by consignment | **Goods Exports: FOB, by last known destination** | **Trade System: General**

Overview:

In 2015, the value of merchandise exports of Estonia decreased substantially by 20.5 percent to reach 14.0 bln US$, while its merchandise imports decreased substantially by 22.1 percent to reach 15.7 bln US$ (see graph 1, table 2 and table 3). The merchandise trade balance recorded a relatively small deficit of 1.8 bln US$ (see graph 1). The largest merchandise trade balance was with MDG Eastern Asia at -1.2 bln US$ (see graph 4). Merchandise exports in Estonia were diversified amongst partners; imports were also diversified. The top 12 partners accounted for 80 percent or more of exports and 16 partners accounted for 80 percent or more of imports (see graph 5). In 2014, the value of exports of services of Estonia increased substantially by 10.9 percent, reaching 6.9 bln US$, while its imports of services increased slightly by 1.8 percent and reached 4.6 bln US$ (see graph 2). There was a moderate trade in services surplus of 2.3 bln US$.

Graph 1: Total merchandise trade, by value

(Bln US$ by year)

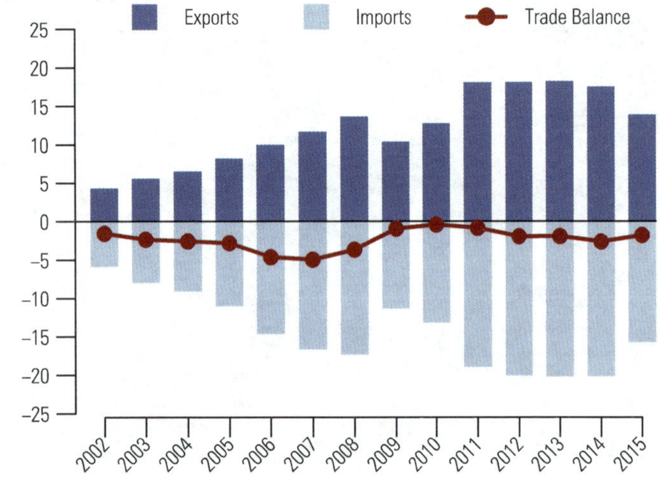

Graph 2: Total services trade, by value

(Bln US$ by year)

Exports Profile:

"Machinery and transport equipment" (SITC section 7), "Miscellaneous manufactured articles" (SITC section 8) and "Goods classified chiefly by material" (SITC section 6) were the largest commodity groups for exports in 2015, representing respectively 31.4, 15.2 and 13.6 percent of exported goods (see table 2). From 2013 to 2015, the largest export commodity was "Electrical apparatus for line telephony or line telegraphy" (HS code 8517) (see table 1). The top three destinations for merchandise exports were Sweden, Finland and the Russian Federation, accounting for respectively 16.1, 14.3 and 14.2 percent of total exports. "Transportation" (EBOPS code 205) accounted for the largest share of exports of services in 2014 at 2.3 bln US$, followed by "Travel" (EBOPS code 236) at 1.8 bln US$ and "Other business services" (EBOPS code 268) at 1.5 bln US$ (see graph 3).

Graph 3: Exports of services by EBOPS category

(% share in 2014)

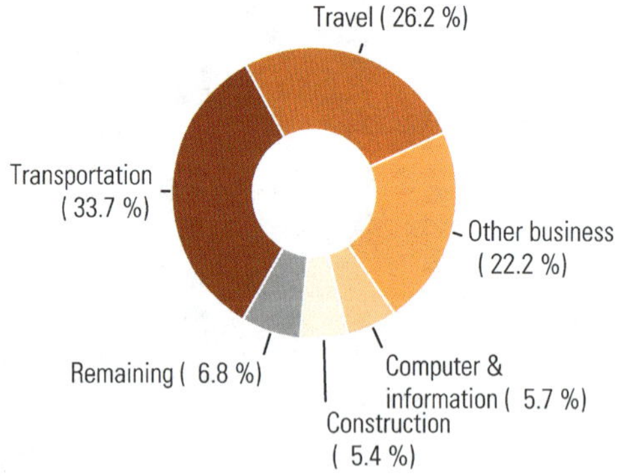

Table 1: Top 10 export commodities 2013 to 2015

HS code	4-digit heading of Harmonized System 2012	Value (million US$) 2013	2014	2015	Unit value 2013	2014	2015	Unit	SITC code
	All Commodities	18284.1	17568.9	13964.8					
8517	Electrical apparatus for line telephony or line telegraphy	1875.2	1963.0	1424.7					764
2710	Petroleum oils, other than crude	1330.0	1418.9	1099.2	0.7	0.6	0.4	US$/kg	334
9999	Commodities not specified according to kind	811.2	936.4	876.9					931
8544	Insulated (including enamelled or anodised) wire, cable	366.9	360.5	304.9	*14.9*	14.0	*12.2*	US$/kg	773
8703	Motor cars and other motor vehicles principally designed for the transport	318.8	363.6	290.1	24.3	25.3	21.8	thsd US$/unit	781
9406	Prefabricated buildings	290.3	323.1	325.2	2.1	2.1	1.9	US$/kg	811
2716	Electrical energy	365.7	326.8	237.5	58.1	50.4	37.2	US$/MWh	351
4418	Builders'joinery and carpentry of wood	288.7	310.3	269.4	2.2	2.3	1.8	US$/kg	635
4407	Wood sawn or chipped lengthwise, sliced or peeled	264.8	285.0	267.7	*327.7*	*336.6*	*293.3*	US$/m³	248
8504	Electrical transformers, static converters	215.6	257.8	230.3					771

Services Imports and Exports: EBOPS 2002 categories

Table 2: Merchandise exports by SITC
(Value in million US$, growth and shares in percentage)

SITC	2015	Avg. Growth rates 2011-2015	Avg. Growth rates 2014-2015	2015 share
Total	13 964.8	-6.3	-20.5	100.0
0+1	1 337.3	-2.8	-21.6	9.6
2+4	1 040.8	-5.0	-19.9	7.5
3	1 542.1	-15.6	-23.1	11.0
5	719.1	-8.1	-22.5	5.1
6	1 895.0	-7.5	-21.8	13.6
7	4 382.4	-5.5	-22.5	31.4
8	2 117.3	-3.8	-16.3	15.2
9	930.7	5.2	-9.1	6.7

Table 3: Merchandise imports by SITC
(Value in million US$, growth and shares in percentage)

SITC	2015	Avg. Growth rates 2011-2015	Avg. Growth rates 2014-2015	2015 share
Total	15 717.6	-4.6	-22.1	100.0
0+1	1 576.8	-3.5	-19.8	10.0
2+4	510.2	0.0	-19.4	3.2
3	2 073.1	-11.5	-34.0	13.2
5	1 524.6	-3.5	-18.4	9.7
6	2 105.2	-7.3	-23.2	13.4
7	5 147.6	-4.4	-19.9	32.8
8	1 426.0	-0.4	-20.1	9.1
9	1 354.1	7.1	-15.8	8.6

SITC Legend

SITC Code	Description
Total	All commodities
0+1	Food, animals + beverages, tobacco
2+4	Crude materials + anim. & veg. oils
3	Mineral fuels, lubricants
5	Chemicals
6	Goods classified chiefly by material
7	Machinery and transport equipment
8	Miscellaneous manufactured articles
9	Not classified elsewhere in the SITC

Graph 4: Merchandise trade balance
(Bln US$ by MDG Regions in 2015)

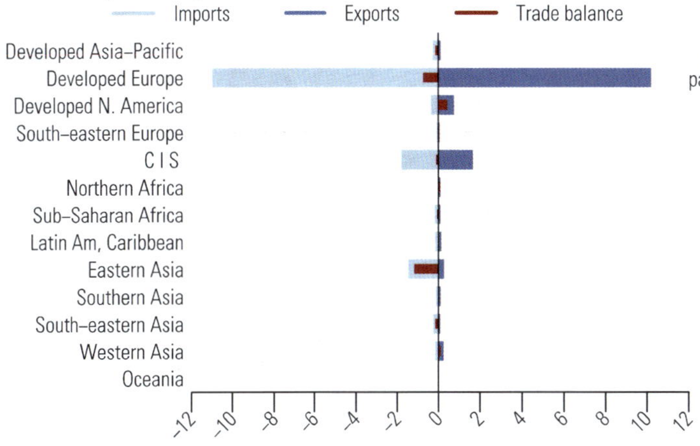

Graph 5: Partner concentration of merchandise trade
(Cumulative share by ranked partners in 2015)

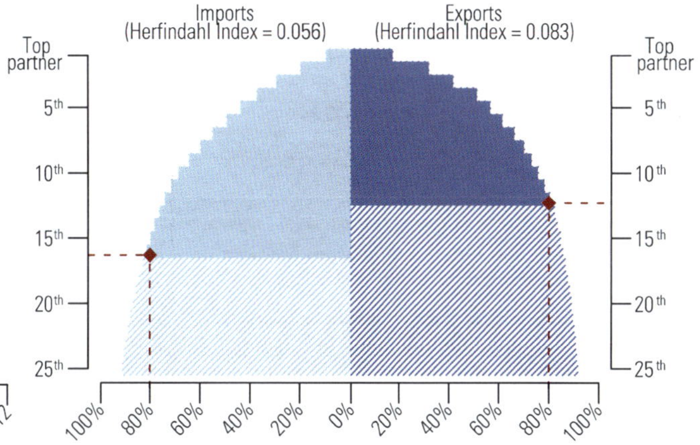

Graph 6: Imports of services by EBOPS category
(% share in 2014)

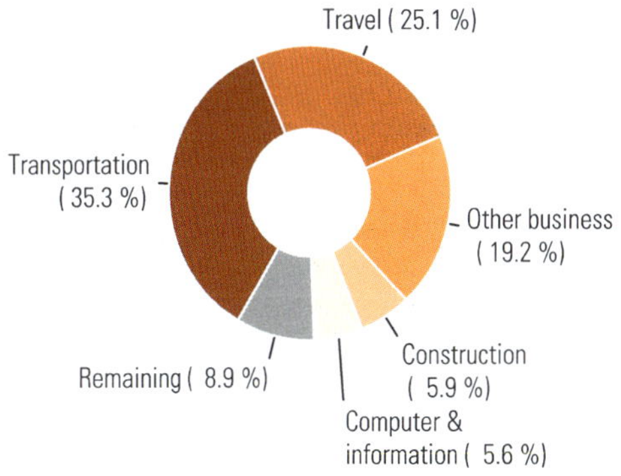

Imports Profile:

"Machinery and transport equipment" (SITC section 7), "Goods classified chiefly by material" (SITC section 6) and "Mineral fuels, lubricants" (SITC section 3) were the largest commodity groups for imports in 2015, representing respectively 32.8, 13.4 and 13.2 percent of imported goods (see table 3). From 2013 to 2015, the largest import commodity was "Petroleum oils, other than crude" (HS code 2710) (see table 4). The top three partners for merchandise imports were Finland, Germany and the Russian Federation, accounting for respectively 10.0, 9.9 and 9.9 percent of total imports. "Transportation" (EBOPS code 205) accounted for the largest share of imports of services in 2014 at 1.6 bln US$, followed by "Travel" (EBOPS code 236) at 1.2 bln US$ and "Other business services" (EBOPS code 268) at 893.2 mln US$ (see graph 6).

Table 4: Top 10 import commodities 2013 to 2015

HS code	4-digit heading of Harmonized System 2012	Value (million US$) 2013	Value (million US$) 2014	Value (million US$) 2015	Unit value 2013	Unit value 2014	Unit value 2015	Unit	SITC code
	All Commodities	20 186.2	20 169.3	15 717.6					
2710	Petroleum oils, other than crude	2 143.7	2 397.5	1 509.1	*0.8*	0.7	*0.4*	US$/kg	334
9999	Commodities not specified according to kind	1 431.8	1 535.5	1 299.0					931
8517	Electrical apparatus for line telephony or line telegraphy	1 077.9	1 209.3	937.0					764
8703	Motor cars and other motor vehicles principally designed for the transport	754.8	820.9	661.4	22.6	23.2	20.0	thsd US$/unit	781
8542	Electronic integrated circuits	430.3	434.5	280.2					776
3004	Medicaments (excluding goods of heading 30.02, 30.05 or 30.06)	322.0	345.0	312.6	*101.6*	*111.0*	*99.4*	US$/kg	542
4011	New pneumatic tyres, of rubber	342.1	275.2	152.9	72.8	57.1	51.2	US$/unit	625
4407	Wood sawn or chipped lengthwise, sliced or peeled	233.8	274.0	231.5	*266.2*	*278.3*	*214.7*	US$/m³	248
2711	Petroleum gases and other gaseous hydrocarbons	326.6	237.7	174.5	*0.6*	0.6	0.4	US$/kg	343
8544	Insulated (including enamelled or anodised) wire, cable	226.7	223.0	200.8	*9.2*	*11.1*	*10.0*	US$/kg	773

Ethiopia

Goods Imports: CIF, by origin | **Goods Exports: FOB, by last known destination** | **Trade System: General**

Overview:

In 2015, the value of merchandise exports of Ethiopia decreased substantially by 11.3 percent to reach 5.0 bln US$, while its merchandise imports increased substantially by 17.8 percent to reach 25.8 bln US$ (see graph 1, table 2 and table 3). The merchandise trade balance recorded a large deficit of 20.8 bln US$ (see graph 1). The largest merchandise trade balance was with MDG Eastern Asia at -7.1 bln US$ (see graph 4). Merchandise exports in Ethiopia were diversified amongst partners; imports were also diversified. The top 14 partners accounted for 80 percent or more of exports and 11 partners accounted for 80 percent or more of imports (see graph 5). In 2014, the value of exports of services of Ethiopia decreased slightly by 4.8 percent, reaching 3.0 bln US$, while its imports of services increased substantially by 26.1 percent and reached 4.4 bln US$ (see graph 2). There was a moderate trade in services deficit of 1.4 bln US$.

Graph 1: Total merchandise trade, by value

(Bln US$ by year)

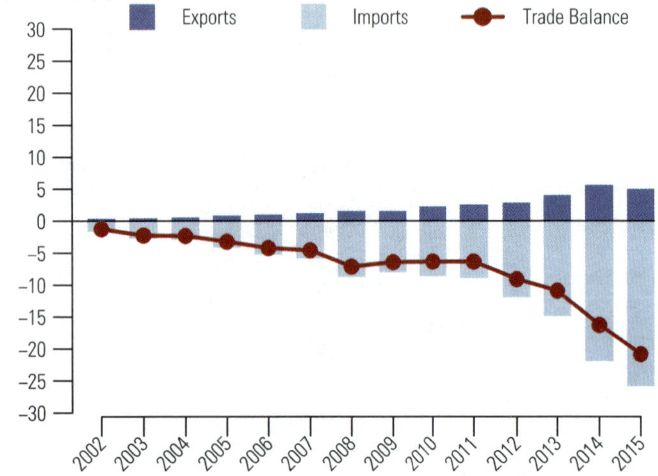

Graph 2: Total services trade, by value

(Bln US$ by year)

Exports Profile:

"Food, animals + beverages, tobacco" (SITC section 0+1), "Crude materials + anim. & veg. oils" (SITC section 2+4) and "Mineral fuels, lubricants" (SITC section 3) were the largest commodity groups for exports in 2015, representing respectively 48.5, 25.9 and 13.8 percent of exported goods (see table 2). From 2013 to 2015, the largest export commodity was "Coffee, whether or not roasted or decaffeinated" (HS code 0901) (see table 1). The top three destinations for merchandise exports were Somalia, Kuwait and the Netherlands, accounting for respectively 13.7, 10.4 and 10.4 percent of total exports. "Transportation" (EBOPS code 205) accounted for the largest share of exports of services in 2014 at 2.2 bln US$, followed by "Travel" (EBOPS code 236) at 352.1 mln US$ and "Government services, n.i.e." (EBOPS code 291) at 244.3 mln US$ (see graph 3).

Graph 3: Exports of services by EBOPS category

(% share in 2014)

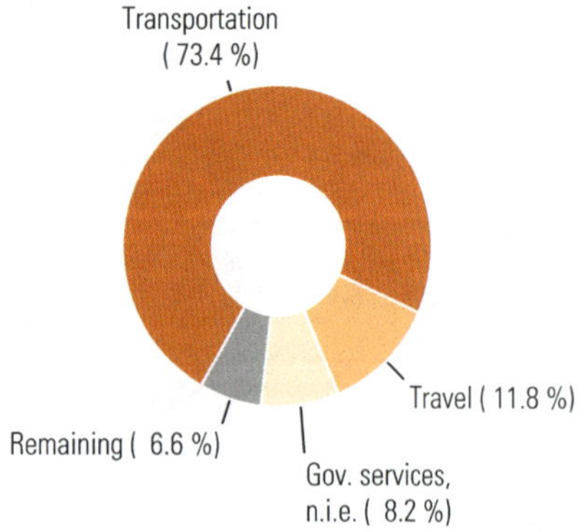

Table 1: Top 10 export commodities 2013 to 2015

HS code	4-digit heading of Harmonized System 2007	Value (million US$) 2013	2014	2015	Unit value 2013	2014	2015	Unit	SITC code
	All Commodities	4076.9	5666.9	5027.5					
0901	Coffee, whether or not roasted or decaffeinated	770.8	1023.9	1018.6	3.5	4.3	4.3	US$/kg	071
2710	Petroleum oils, other than crude	260.5	1078.4	693.2	1.1	1.1	1.0	US$/kg	334
0603	Cut flowers and flower buds of a kind suitable for bouquets	527.1	610.4	662.4	4.0	4.3	4.5	US$/kg	292
1207	Other oil seeds and oleaginous fruits, whether or not broken	527.1	744.5	506.7	1.9	2.2	1.5	US$/kg	222
0709	Other vegetables, fresh or chilled	558.8	567.6	568.4	5.5	5.7	6.0	US$/kg	054
0713	Dried leguminous vegetables, shelled, whether or not skinned or split	239.4	287.0	240.7	0.7	0.8	0.7	US$/kg	054
0102	Live bovine animals	215.2	216.0	174.8	*0.5*	*1.1*	*1.0*	thsd US$/unit	001
7108	Gold (including gold plated with platinum)	157.4	156.3	158.0	34.3	34.1	33.6	thsd US$/kg	971
0204	Meat of sheep or goats, fresh, chilled or frozen	70.5	84.1	103.6	5.3	5.5	6.0	US$/kg	012
0106	Other live animals	73.6	66.9	72.2					001

Services Imports and Exports: EBOPS 2002 categories

Table 2: Merchandise exports by SITC

(Value in million US$, growth and shares in percentage)

SITC	2015	Avg. Growth rates 2011-2015	Avg. Growth rates 2014-2015	2015 share
Total	5027.5	17.8	-11.3	100.0
0+1	2436.3	10.7	-2.0	48.5
2+4	1301.3	20.9	-12.4	25.9
3	693.2	3972.5	-35.7	13.8
5	5.0	-6.4	2.3	0.1
6	183.8	1.1	-6.6	3.7
7	119.8	43.1	21.6	2.4
8	129.7	26.7	11.4	2.6
9	158.4	6.2	-21.0	3.2

Table 3: Merchandise imports by SITC

(Value in million US$, growth and shares in percentage)

SITC	2015	Avg. Growth rates 2011-2015	Avg. Growth rates 2014-2015	2015 share
Total	25815.3	30.5	17.8	100.0
0+1	1543.5	14.2	25.2	6.0
2+4	1559.0	31.3	83.6	6.0
3	2482.1	12.0	-34.4	9.6
5	3067.9	31.5	15.2	11.9
6	5070.7	36.1	17.6	19.6
7	9307.3	35.4	31.9	36.1
8	2358.8	40.4	37.0	9.1
9	426.0	226.2	45.4	1.7

SITC Legend

SITC Code	Description
Total	All commodities
0+1	Food, animals + beverages, tobacco
2+4	Crude materials + anim. & veg. oils
3	Mineral fuels, lubricants
5	Chemicals
6	Goods classified chiefly by material
7	Machinery and transport equipment
8	Miscellaneous manufactured articles
9	Not classified elsewhere in the SITC

Graph 4: Merchandise trade balance

(Bln US$ by MDG Regions in 2015)

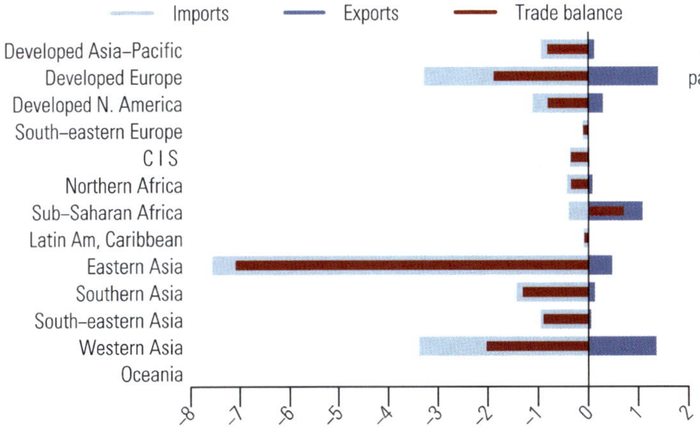

Graph 5: Partner concentration of merchandise trade

(Cumulative share by ranked partners in 2015)

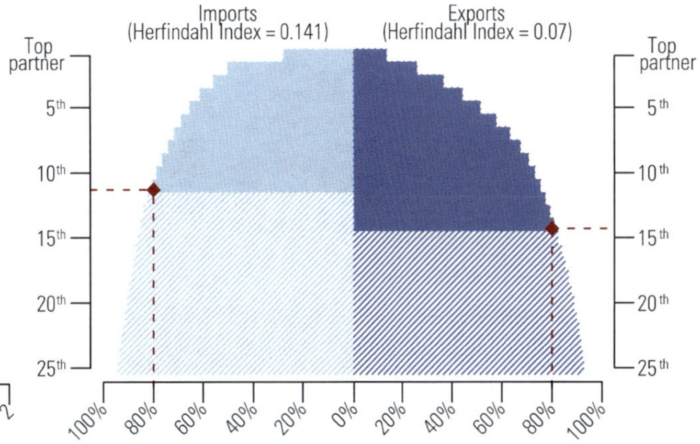

Graph 6: Imports of services by EBOPS category

(% share in 2014)

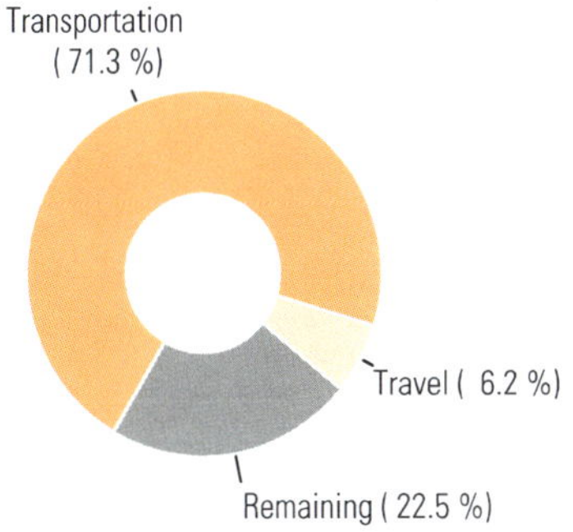

Imports Profile:

"Machinery and transport equipment" (SITC section 7), "Goods classified chiefly by material" (SITC section 6) and "Chemicals" (SITC section 5) were the largest commodity groups for imports in 2015, representing respectively 36.1, 19.6 and 11.9 percent of imported goods (see table 3). From 2013 to 2015, the largest import commodity was "Petroleum oils, other than crude" (HS code 2710) (see table 4). The top three partners for merchandise imports were China, Areas nes and Kuwait, accounting for respectively 25.9, 19.4 and 6.2 percent of total imports. "Transportation" (EBOPS code 205) accounted for the largest share of imports of services in 2014 at 3.1 bln US$, followed by "Travel" (EBOPS code 236) at 272.4 mln US$ (see graph 6).

Table 4: Top 10 import commodities 2013 to 2015

HS code	4-digit heading of Harmonized System 2007	Value (million US$) 2013	Value (million US$) 2014	Value (million US$) 2015	Unit value 2013	Unit value 2014	Unit value 2015	Unit	SITC code
	All Commodities	14899.1	21914.4	25815.3					
2710	Petroleum oils, other than crude	1687.1	3639.4	2316.5	1.0	1.0	0.9	US$/kg	334
8704	Motor vehicles for the transport of goods	762.3	750.1	1059.8					782
1511	Palm oil and its fractions	375.0	452.1	1018.3	1.1	1.2	1.4	US$/kg	422
8517	Electrical apparatus for line telephony or line telegraphy	73.2	571.2	1058.9					764
1001	Wheat and meslin	527.6	339.1	433.1	0.4	0.4	0.3	US$/kg	041
3004	Medicaments (excluding goods of heading 30.02, 30.05 or 30.06)	410.5	274.3	522.6	33.2	21.0	30.8	US$/kg	542
8429	Self-propelled bulldozers, angledozers, graders, levellers, scrapers	449.0	360.9	355.8					723
8703	Motor cars and other motor vehicles principally designed for the transport	313.0	375.8	414.6	*15.3*	*16.8*	*17.1*	thsd US$/unit	781
7308	Structures (excluding prefabricated buildings of heading 94.06)	169.0	442.3	437.2	2.3	2.7	3.3	US$/kg	691
4011	New pneumatic tyres, of rubber	258.8	284.6	281.5					625

Source: UN Comtrade

Fiji

Goods Imports: CIF, by purchase	Goods Exports: FOB, by sale	Trade System: General

Overview:

In 2014, the value of merchandise exports of Fiji increased substantially by 23.9 percent to reach 1.4 bln US$, while its merchandise imports increased substantially by 15.0 percent to reach 3.3 bln US$ (see graph 1, table 2 and table 3). The merchandise trade balance recorded a large deficit of 1.9 bln US$ (see graph 1). The largest merchandise trade balance was with MDG South-eastern Asia at -1.0 bln US$ (see graph 4). Merchandise exports in Fiji were diversified amongst partners; imports were also diversified. The top 14 partners accounted for 80 percent or more of exports and 8 partners accounted for 80 percent or more of imports (see graph 5). In 2013, the value of exports of services of Fiji increased slightly by 0.3 percent, reaching 1.2 bln US$, while its imports of services decreased slightly by 1.4 percent and reached 562.6 mln US$ (see graph 2). There was a large trade in services surplus of 649.4 mln US$.

Graph 1: Total merchandise trade, by value

(Bln US$ by year)

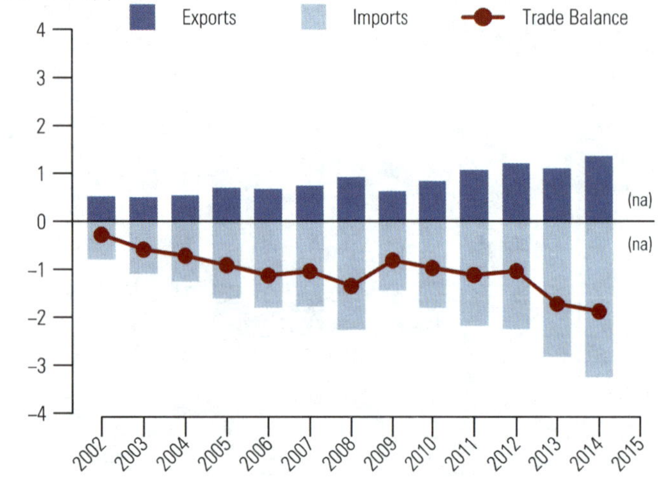

Graph 2: Total services trade, by value

(Bln US$ by year)

Exports Profile:

"Food, animals + beverages, tobacco" (SITC section 0+1), "Mineral fuels, lubricants" (SITC section 3) and "Machinery and transport equipment" (SITC section 7) were the largest commodity groups for exports in 2014, representing respectively 40.1, 25.1 and 9.6 percent of exported goods (see table 2). From 2012 to 2014, the largest export commodity was "Petroleum oils, other than crude" (HS code 2710) (see table 1). The top three destinations for merchandise exports were Bunkers, ship stores, Australia and the United States, accounting for respectively 17.0, 13.2 and 12.7 percent of total exports. "Travel" (EBOPS code 236) accounted for the largest share of exports of services in 2013 at 722.4 mln US$, followed by "Transportation" (EBOPS code 205) at 306.7 mln US$ and "Government services, n.i.e." (EBOPS code 291) at 115.1 mln US$ (see graph 3).

Graph 3: Exports of services by EBOPS category

(% share in 2013)

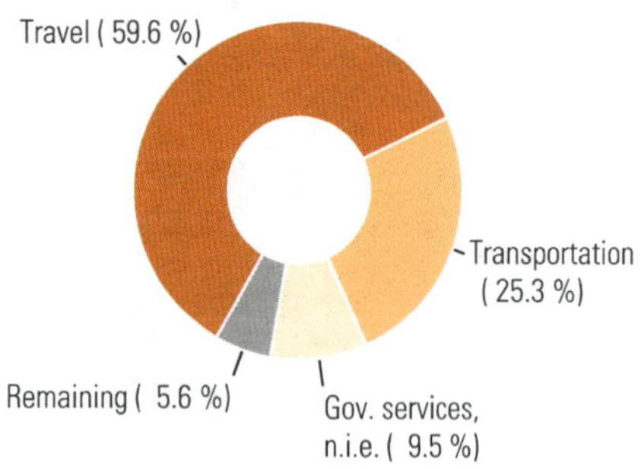

Table 1: Top 10 export commodities 2012 to 2014

HS code	4-digit heading of Harmonized System 2012	Value (million US$) 2012	2013	2014	Unit value 2012	2013	2014	Unit	SITC code
	All Commodities	1 220.6	1 108.0	1 373.3					
2710	Petroleum oils, other than crude	327.3	316.9	343.6			*1.1*	US$/kg	334
0303	Fish, frozen, excluding fish fillets and other fish meat of heading 03.04	120.4	89.7	126.8	2.7		2.2	US$/kg	034
2201	Waters, including natural or artificial mineral waters	89.7	85.4	113.1		0.5		US$/litre	111
1701	Cane or beet sugar and chemically pure sucrose, in solid form	97.6	64.3	111.1	0.7	*2.1*	0.5	US$/kg	061
7108	Gold (including gold plated with platinum)	77.0	45.2	48.7	48.6	41.1	39.1	thsd US$/kg	971
1905	Bread, pastry, cakes, biscuits and other bakers'wares	30.6	27.6	28.4		2.1	1.9	US$/kg	048
0302	Fish, fresh or chilled, excluding fish fillets	35.9	16.8	20.4	2.3		3.6	US$/kg	034
4407	Wood sawn or chipped lengthwise, sliced or peeled	19.0	21.7	22.4		*403.6*	*249.4*	US$/m^3	248
6203	Men's or boys'suits, ensembles, jackets, blazers, trousers	16.6	19.5	20.4		18.5		US$/unit	841
8802	Other aircraft (for example, helicopters, aeroplanes); spacecraft	27.2	20.3	5.2					792

Source: UN Comtrade

Services Imports and Exports: EBOPS 2002 categories

Table 2: Merchandise exports by SITC

(Value in million US$, growth and shares in percentage)

SITC	2014	Avg. Growth rates 2010-2014	Avg. Growth rates 2013-2014	2014 share
Total	1 373.3	13.0	23.9	100.0
0+1	550.9	13.3	28.4	40.1
2+4	87.2	13.0	43.9	6.3
3	344.6	12.8	8.3	25.1
5	37.1	10.2	11.8	2.7
6	78.0	14.6	38.3	5.7
7	132.2	54.4	85.3	9.6
8	82.7	5.4	3.5	6.0
9	60.5	-6.8	2.3	4.4

Table 3: Merchandise imports by SITC

(Value in million US$, growth and shares in percentage)

SITC	2014	Avg. Growth rates 2010-2014	Avg. Growth rates 2013-2014	2014 share
Total	3 250.5	15.8	15.0	100.0
0+1	548.3	14.7	28.8	16.9
2+4	55.3	16.3	9.7	1.7
3	787.7	8.2	19.2	24.2
5	213.8	9.3	19.0	6.6
6	388.8	12.1	26.7	12.0
7	992.9	31.9	0.3	30.5
8	239.5	11.6	22.9	7.4
9	24.3	29.3	35.7	0.7

SITC Legend

SITC Code	Description
Total	All commodities
0+1	Food, animals + beverages, tobacco
2+4	Crude materials + anim. & veg. oils
3	Mineral fuels, lubricants
5	Chemicals
6	Goods classified chiefly by material
7	Machinery and transport equipment
8	Miscellaneous manufactured articles
9	Not classified elsewhere in the SITC

Graph 4: Merchandise trade balance

(Bln US$ by MDG Regions in 2014)

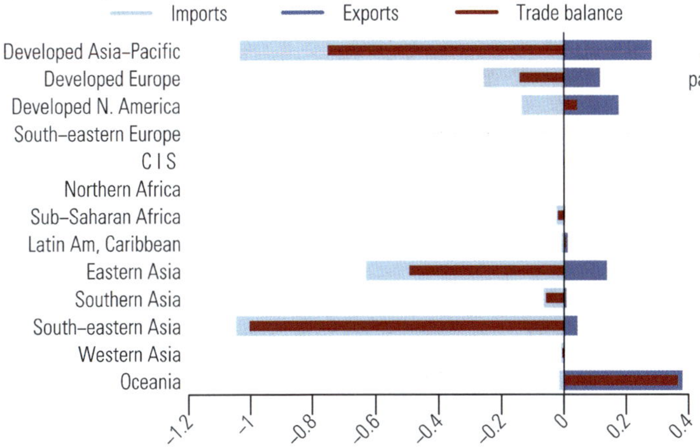

Graph 5: Partner concentration of merchandise trade

(Cumulative share by ranked partners in 2014)

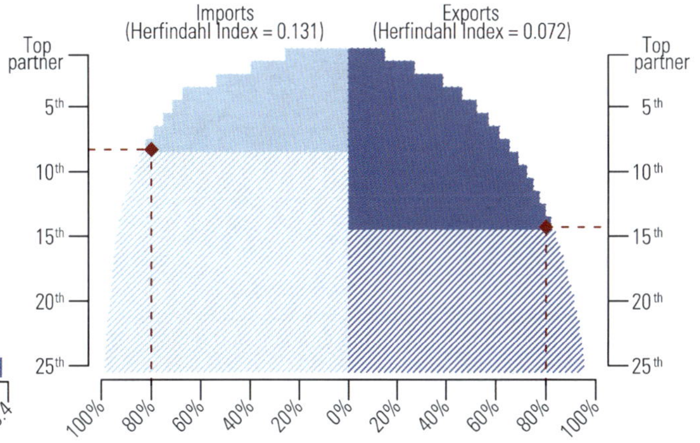

Graph 6: Imports of services by EBOPS category

(% share in 2013)

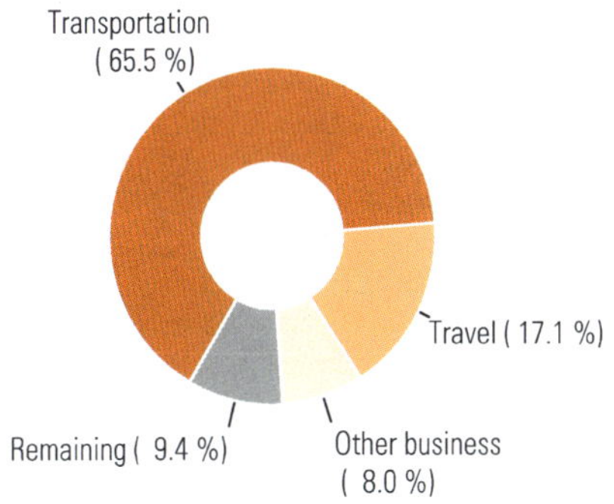

Imports Profile:

"Machinery and transport equipment" (SITC section 7), "Mineral fuels, lubricants" (SITC section 3) and "Food, animals + beverages, tobacco" (SITC section 0+1) were the largest commodity groups for imports in 2014, representing respectively 30.5, 24.2 and 16.9 percent of imported goods (see table 3). From 2012 to 2014, the largest import commodity was "Petroleum oils, other than crude" (HS code 2710) (see table 4). The top three partners for merchandise imports were Singapore, Australia and New Zealand, accounting for respectively 25.8, 15.0 and 13.3 percent of total imports. "Transportation" (EBOPS code 205) accounted for the largest share of imports of services in 2013 at 368.3 mln US$, followed by "Travel" (EBOPS code 236) at 96.4 mln US$ and "Other business services" (EBOPS code 268) at 45.0 mln US$ (see graph 6).

Table 4: Top 10 import commodities 2012 to 2014

HS code	4-digit heading of Harmonized System 2012	Value (million US$) 2012	Value (million US$) 2013	Value (million US$) 2014	Unit value 2012	Unit value 2013	Unit value 2014	Unit	SITC code
	All Commodities	2 252.6	2 825.7	3 250.5					
2710	Petroleum oils, other than crude	651.6	634.3	754.9			*1.1*	US$/kg	334
8802	Other aircraft (for example, helicopters, aeroplanes); spacecraft	8.1	443.8	175.8					792
0303	Fish, frozen, excluding fish fillets and other fish meat of heading 03.04	124.2	92.8	177.1	1.9		1.6	US$/kg	034
1001	Wheat and meslin	60.6	68.9	61.4	0.4	0.4	0.7	US$/kg	041
8703	Motor cars and other motor vehicles principally designed for the transport	31.4	50.6	72.4		*12.2*	*10.9*	thsd US$/unit	781
8704	Motor vehicles for the transport of goods	27.1	52.5	60.2					782
8517	Electrical apparatus for line telephony or line telegraphy	34.7	40.7	62.5					764
8803	Parts of goods of heading 88.01 or 88.02	21.7	34.5	28.5	47.5	46.8	131.9	US$/kg	792
2711	Petroleum gases and other gaseous hydrocarbons	25.0	26.0	32.2	1.3	1.2	1.2	US$/kg	343
0402	Milk and cream, concentrated or containing added sugar	20.5	20.8	38.0	4.2	5.0	5.2	US$/kg	022

Finland

Goods Imports: CIF, by origin | **Goods Exports: FOB, by last known destination** | **Trade System: Special**

Overview:

In 2015, the value of merchandise exports of Finland decreased substantially by 19.7 percent to reach 59.7 bln US$, while its merchandise imports decreased substantially by 21.6 percent to reach 60.2 bln US$ (see graph 1, table 2 and table 3). The merchandise trade balance recorded a relatively small deficit of 492.1 mln US$ (see graph 1). The largest merchandise trade balance was with MDG CIS at -2.9 bln US$ (see graph 4). Merchandise exports in Finland were diversified amongst partners; imports were also diversified. The top 20 partners accounted for 80 percent or more of exports and 16 partners accounted for 80 percent or more of imports (see graph 5). In 2014, the value of exports of services of Finland decreased slightly by 4.5 percent, reaching 28.6 bln US$, while its imports of services decreased slightly by 3.0 percent and reached 30.6 bln US$ (see graph 2). There was a relatively small trade in services deficit of 1.9 bln US$.

Graph 1: Total merchandise trade, by value

(Bln US$ by year)

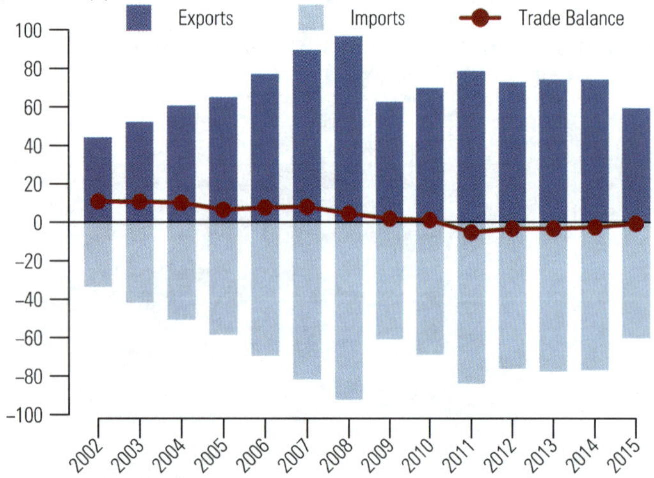

Graph 2: Total services trade, by value

(Bln US$ by year)

Exports Profile:

"Machinery and transport equipment" (SITC section 7), "Goods classified chiefly by material" (SITC section 6) and "Crude materials + anim. & veg. oils" (SITC section 2+4) were the largest commodity groups for exports in 2015, representing respectively 31.1, 28.2 and 8.8 percent of exported goods (see table 2). From 2013 to 2015, the largest export commodity was "Petroleum oils, other than crude" (HS code 2710) (see table 1). The top three destinations for merchandise exports were Germany, Sweden and the Russian Federation, accounting for respectively 11.3, 10.9 and 7.9 percent of total exports. "Other business services" (EBOPS code 268) accounted for the largest share of exports of services in 2012 at 9.5 bln US$, followed by "Computer and information services" (EBOPS code 262) at 6.0 bln US$ and "Travel" (EBOPS code 236) at 4.0 bln US$ (see graph 3).

Graph 3: Exports of services by EBOPS category

(% share in 2012)

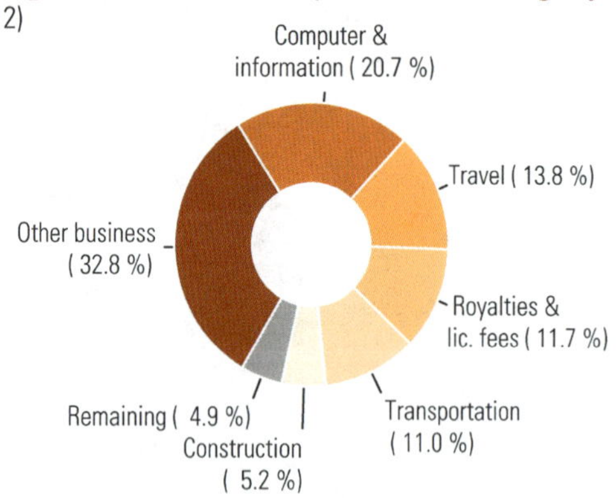

Table 1: Top 10 export commodities 2013 to 2015

HS code	4-digit heading of Harmonized System 2012	Value (million US$) 2013	2014	2015	Unit value 2013	2014	2015	Unit	SITC code
	All Commodities	74445.4	74338.8	59682.3					
2710	Petroleum oils, other than crude	8880.3	7724.0	3765.9	*1.0*	*0.9*	*0.6*	US$/kg	334
4810	Paper and paperboard, coated on one or both sides with kaolin	5201.3	5092.1	4438.0	*0.9*	*0.9*	*0.8*	US$/kg	641
9999	Commodities not specified according to kind	1508.6	4223.5	4828.7					931
7219	Flat-rolled products of stainless steel, of a width of 600 mm or more	2699.2	2794.3	2433.2	*3.1*	*2.8*	*2.1*	US$/kg	675
4407	Wood sawn or chipped lengthwise, sliced or peeled	1892.8	2045.3	1722.2	*264.6*	273.4	218.6	US$/m³	248
4703	Chemical wood pulp, soda or sulphate, other than dissolving grades	1824.5	1905.8	1783.9	0.7	0.7	*0.6*	US$/kg	251
4802	Uncoated paper and paperboard, of a kind used for writing	1725.9	1619.5	1231.0	*0.8*	*0.8*	*0.7*	US$/kg	641
8703	Motor cars and other motor vehicles principally designed for the transport	580.2	1459.7	1845.3	15.1	19.7	17.6	thsd US$/unit	781
8504	Electrical transformers, static converters	1369.4	1321.7	1050.7					771
9018	Instruments and appliances used in medical, surgical, dental or veterinary	1099.4	1364.1	1138.3					872

Services Imports and Exports: EBOPS 2002 categories

Table 2: Merchandise exports by SITC

(Value in million US$, growth and shares in percentage)

SITC	2015	Avg. Growth rates 2011-2015	Avg. Growth rates 2014-2015	2015 share
Total	59682.3	-6.7	-19.7	100.0
0+1	1443.7	-9.0	-27.7	2.4
2+4	5274.9	-2.2	-12.4	8.8
3	4036.4	-14.3	-49.6	6.8
5	4581.8	-14.9	-31.9	7.7
6	16857.8	-9.5	-18.3	28.2
7	18565.9	-5.4	-13.2	31.1
8	3850.7	-2.9	-21.6	6.5
9	5071.0	24.2	9.0	8.5

Table 3: Merchandise imports by SITC

(Value in million US$, growth and shares in percentage)

SITC	2015	Avg. Growth rates 2011-2015	Avg. Growth rates 2014-2015	2015 share
Total	60174.4	-8.0	-21.6	100.0
0+1	4739.3	-2.5	-14.3	7.9
2+4	3849.6	-15.6	-39.5	6.4
3	7689.9	-19.4	-47.8	12.8
5	6876.1	-7.0	-18.7	11.4
6	6492.7	-9.9	-22.7	10.8
7	18795.7	-5.2	-10.1	31.2
8	6101.5	-5.6	-16.6	10.1
9	5629.5	19.1	11.4	9.4

SITC Legend

SITC Code	Description
Total	All commodities
0+1	Food, animals + beverages, tobacco
2+4	Crude materials + anim. & veg. oils
3	Mineral fuels, lubricants
5	Chemicals
6	Goods classified chiefly by material
7	Machinery and transport equipment
8	Miscellaneous manufactured articles
9	Not classified elsewhere in the SITC

Graph 4: Merchandise trade balance

(Bln US$ by MDG Regions in 2015)

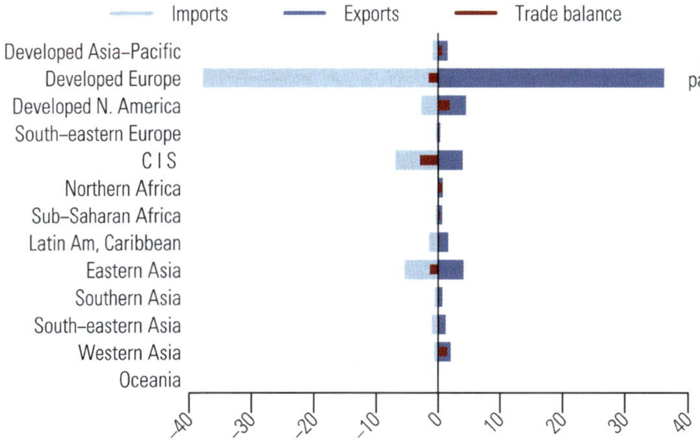

Graph 5: Partner concentration of merchandise trade

(Cumulative share by ranked partners in 2015)

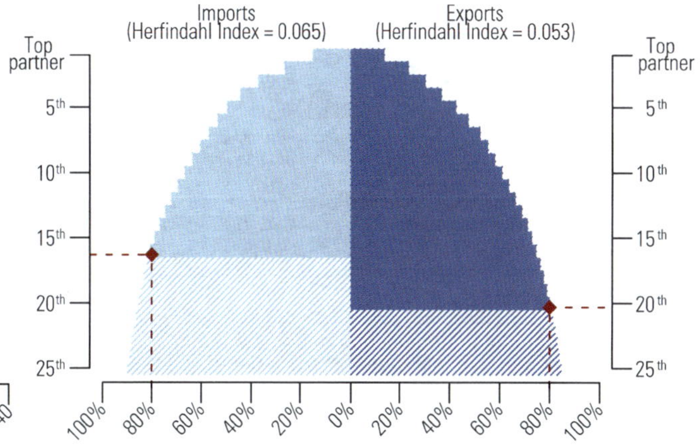

Graph 6: Imports of services by EBOPS category

(% share in 2012)

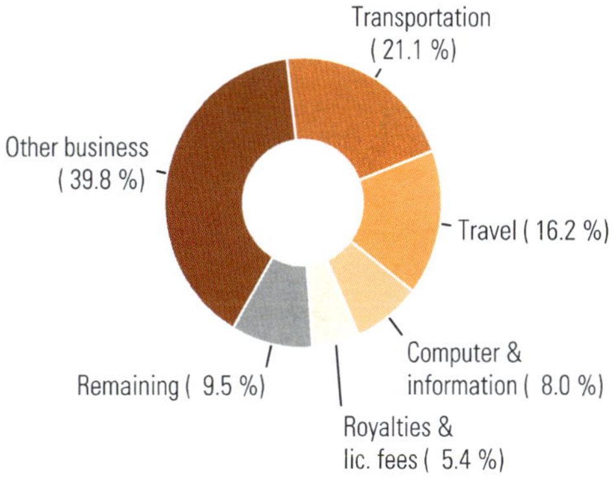

Imports Profile:

"Machinery and transport equipment" (SITC section 7), "Mineral fuels, lubricants" (SITC section 3) and "Chemicals" (SITC section 5) were the largest commodity groups for imports in 2015, representing respectively 31.2, 12.8 and 11.4 percent of imported goods (see table 3). From 2013 to 2015, the largest import commodity was "Petroleum oils and oils obtained from bituminous minerals, crude" (HS code 2709) (see table 4). The top three partners for merchandise imports were the Russian Federation, Germany and Sweden, accounting for respectively 14.9, 13.4 and 11.3 percent of total imports. "Other business services" (EBOPS code 268) accounted for the largest share of imports of services in 2012 at 12.3 bln US$, followed by "Transportation" (EBOPS code 205) at 6.5 bln US$ and "Travel" (EBOPS code 236) at 5.0 bln US$ (see graph 6).

Table 4: Top 10 import commodities 2013 to 2015

HS code	4-digit heading of Harmonized System 2012	Value (million US$) 2013	Value (million US$) 2014	Value (million US$) 2015	Unit value 2013	Unit value 2014	Unit value 2015	Unit	SITC code
	All Commodities	77587.0	76773.3	60174.4					
2709	Petroleum oils and oils obtained from bituminous minerals, crude	9342.2	8396.7	3994.5	0.8	0.7	*0.4*	US$/kg	333
9999	Commodities not specified according to kind	2648.6	5021.8	5601.6					931
2710	Petroleum oils, other than crude	5131.1	4319.5	2418.8	*1.0*	*0.9*	*0.6*	US$/kg	334
8703	Motor cars and other motor vehicles principally designed for the transport	2581.3	2651.2	2460.5	20.3	21.1	18.1	thsd US$/unit	781
3004	Medicaments (excluding goods of heading 30.02, 30.05 or 30.06)	1884.7	1891.3	1718.4	*139.4*	*142.1*	*127.2*	US$/kg	542
8517	Electrical apparatus for line telephony or line telegraphy	1322.2	1414.4	1357.9					764
8471	Automatic data processing machines and units thereof	1310.0	1319.4	1148.3	269.6	279.1	275.0	US$/unit	752
8708	Parts and accessories of the motor vehicles of headings 87.01 to 87.05	789.5	1117.4	1167.2	*10.0*	*9.8*	*8.3*	US$/kg	784
2716	Electrical energy	940.9	1025.3	705.0	53.5	47.1	32.8	US$/MWh	351
7204	Ferrous waste and scrap; remelting scrap ingots of iron or steel	1028.9	1193.4	50.9	*1.9*	*1.5*	*0.4*	US$/kg	282

France including Monaco

Goods Imports: CIF, by origin | **Goods Exports: FOB, by last known destination** | **Trade System: Special**

Overview:

In 2015, France became the world's fifth largest exporter of merchandise goods, climbing up two spots from 2014, and the fourth largest importer of merchandise goods, climbing up one spots from 2014. The value of merchandise exports of France increased slightly by 1.1 percent to reach 573.1 bln US$, while its merchandise imports decreased slightly by 1.3 percent to reach 651.5 bln US$ (see graph 1, table 2 and table 3). The merchandise trade balance recorded a relatively small deficit of 78.4 bln US$ (see graph 1). The largest merchandise trade balance was with MDG Developed Europe at -49.8 bln US$ (see graph 4). Merchandise exports in France were diversified amongst partners; imports were also diversified. The top 29 partners accounted for 80 percent or more of exports and 22 partners accounted for 80 percent or more of imports (see graph 5). In 2014, the value of exports of services of France increased moderately by 7.6 percent, reaching 280.7 bln US$, while its imports of services increased substantially by 11.6 percent and reached 238.2 bln US$ (see graph 2). France has maintained its position as the world's fourth largest exporter and importer of services. There was a relatively small trade in services surplus of 42.5 bln US$.

Graph 1: Total merchandise trade, by value

(Bln US$ by year)

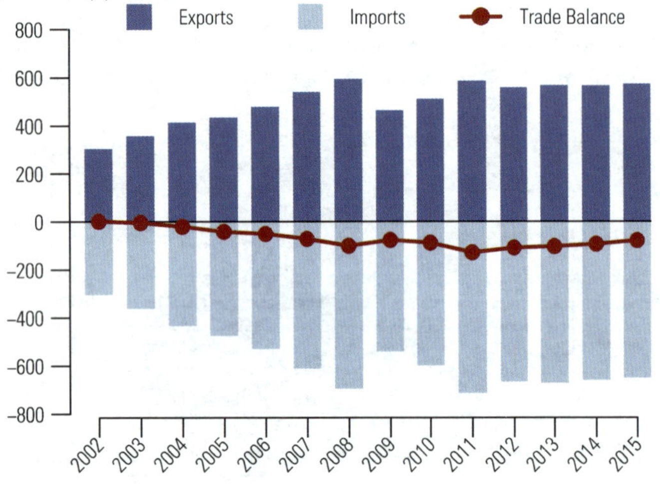

Graph 2: Total services trade, by value

(Bln US$ by year)

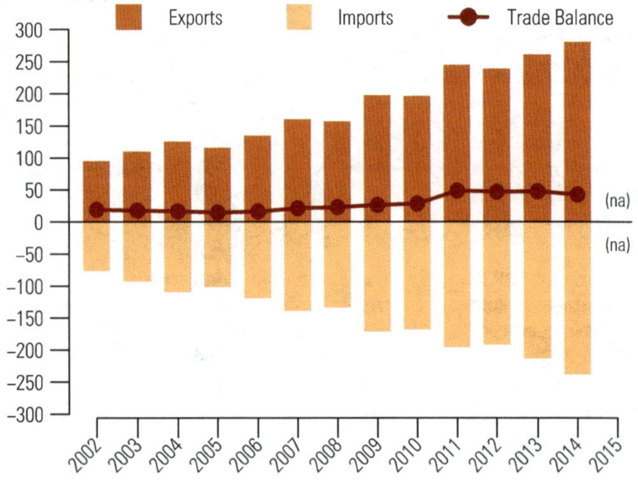

Exports Profile:

"Machinery and transport equipment" (SITC section 7), "Chemicals" (SITC section 5) and "Miscellaneous manufactured articles" (SITC section 8) were the largest commodity groups for exports in 2015, representing respectively 41.7, 16.5 and 14.5 percent of exported goods (see table 2). From 2013 to 2015, the largest export commodity was "Other aircraft (for example, helicopters, aeroplanes); spacecraft" (HS code 8802) (see table 1). The top three destinations for merchandise exports were Germany, the United States and Belgium, accounting for respectively 15.6, 7.0 and 6.9 percent of total exports. "Other business services" (EBOPS code 268) accounted for the largest share of exports of services in 2014 at 113.8 bln US$, followed by "Travel" (EBOPS code 236) at 57.4 bln US$ and "Transportation" (EBOPS code 205) at 52.3 bln US$ (see graph 3).

Graph 3: Exports of services by EBOPS category

(% share in 2014)

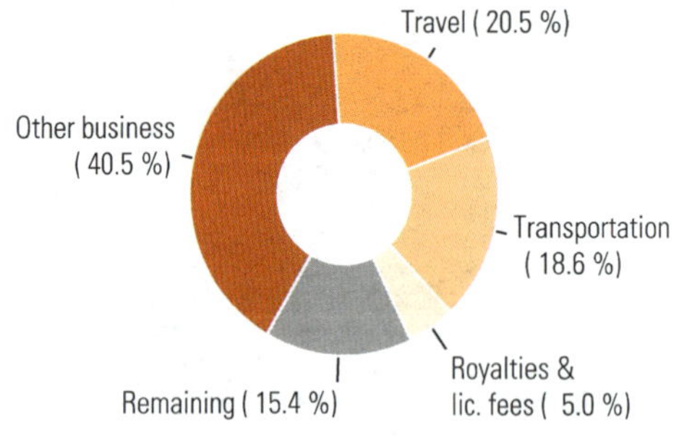

Table 1: Top 10 export commodities 2013 to 2015

HS code	4-digit heading of Harmonized System 2012	Value (million US$) 2013	2014	2015	Unit value 2013	2014	2015	Unit	SITC code
	All Commodities	567 987.7	566 656.2	573 055.5					
8802	Other aircraft (for example, helicopters, aeroplanes); spacecraft	48 756.2	49 798.6	65 894.1	41.7	43.4	19.1	mln US$/unit	792
3004	Medicaments (excluding goods of heading 30.02, 30.05 or 30.06)	27 848.9	25 725.4	23 133.3	*87.7*	*79.6*	*66.5*	US$/kg	542
8703	Motor cars and other motor vehicles principally designed for the transport	18 664.3	19 192.7	18 334.0	14.2	14.4	12.5	thsd US$/unit	781
8708	Parts and accessories of the motor vehicles of headings 87.01 to 87.05	17 364.5	16 771.9	14 473.0	*8.8*	*9.0*	*7.7*	US$/kg	784
2710	Petroleum oils, other than crude	14 396.1	13 627.2	12 215.3	*0.9*	*0.8*	*0.5*	US$/kg	334
8411	Turbo-jets, turbo-propellers and other gas turbines	11 632.8	12 404.1	15 487.5					714
9999	Commodities not specified according to kind	13 872.7	14 160.6	5 075.7					931
2204	Wine of fresh grapes, including fortified wines	10 396.1	10 262.3	9 216.1	7.1	7.1	6.5	US$/litre	112
8803	Parts of goods of heading 88.01 or 88.02	7 772.6	7 820.7	10 838.5	*443.2*	*396.3*	*366.3*	US$/kg	792
3304	Beauty or make-up preparations	7 319.8	7 781.4	7 000.5	*29.7*	*30.7*	*26.5*	US$/kg	553

Services Imports and Exports: EBOPS 2002 categories

Table 2: Merchandise exports by SITC

(Value in million US$, growth and shares in percentage)

SITC	2015	Avg. Growth rates 2011-2015	Avg. Growth rates 2014-2015	2015 share
Total	573055.5	-0.5	1.1	100.0
0+1	61725.2	-3.1	-10.7	10.8
2+4	12247.9	-8.4	-14.6	2.1
3	19760.4	-7.2	-10.1	3.4
5	94298.4	-1.6	-6.4	16.5
6	56697.9	-5.1	-8.7	9.9
7	239121.2	2.0	9.9	41.7
8	83079.6	7.4	26.8	14.5
9	6125.1	-23.2	-59.8	1.1

Table 3: Merchandise imports by SITC

(Value in million US$, growth and shares in percentage)

SITC	2015	Avg. Growth rates 2011-2015	Avg. Growth rates 2014-2015	2015 share
Total	651495.6	-2.3	-1.3	100.0
0+1	52673.7	-1.0	-8.2	8.1
2+4	14495.4	-8.7	-13.1	2.2
3	68065.9	-12.3	-29.2	10.4
5	80749.1	-4.7	-13.4	12.4
6	70555.5	-6.2	-11.3	10.8
7	249464.2	1.3	14.0	38.3
8	114394.8	4.5	18.1	17.6
9	1097.1	-1.4	-1.5	0.2

SITC Legend

SITC Code	Description
Total	All commodities
0+1	Food, animals + beverages, tobacco
2+4	Crude materials + anim. & veg. oils
3	Mineral fuels, lubricants
5	Chemicals
6	Goods classified chiefly by material
7	Machinery and transport equipment
8	Miscellaneous manufactured articles
9	Not classified elsewhere in the SITC

Graph 4: Merchandise trade balance

(Bln US$ by MDG Regions in 2015)

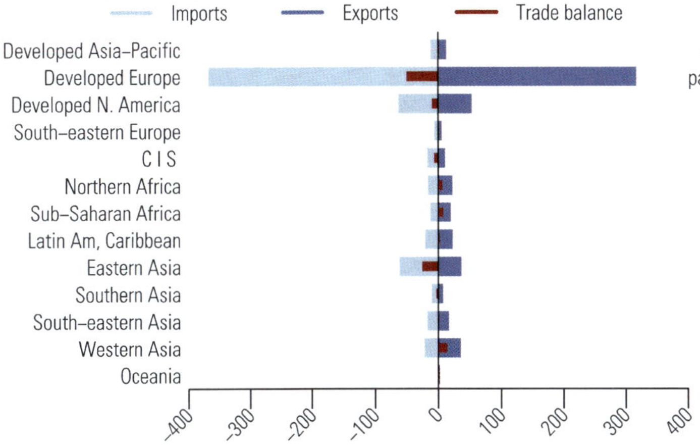

Graph 5: Partner concentration of merchandise trade

(Cumulative share by ranked partners in 2015)

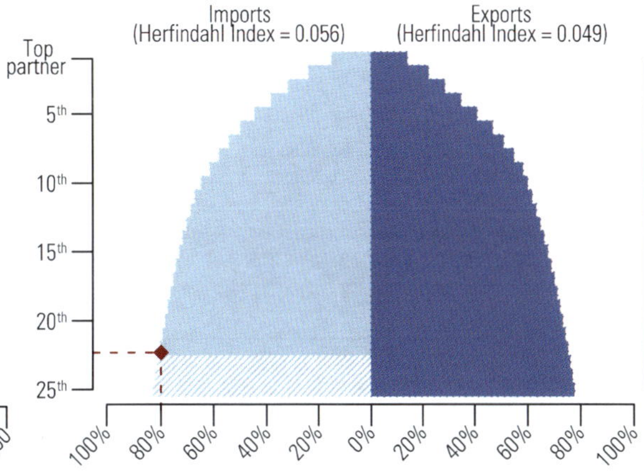

Graph 6: Imports of services by EBOPS category

(% share in 2014)

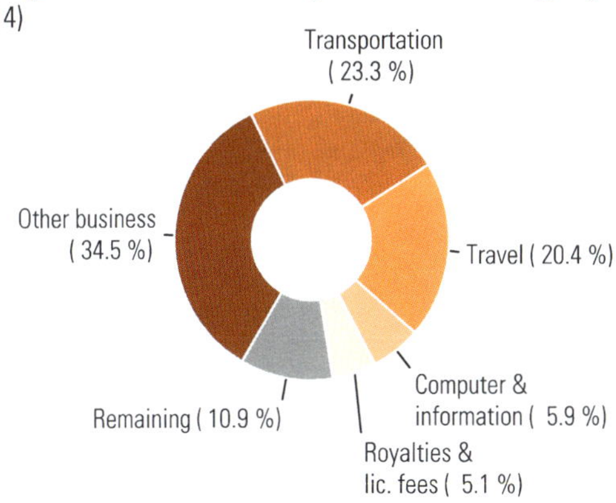

Imports Profile:

"Machinery and transport equipment" (SITC section 7), "Miscellaneous manufactured articles" (SITC section 8) and "Chemicals" (SITC section 5) were the largest commodity groups for imports in 2015, representing respectively 38.3, 17.6 and 12.4 percent of imported goods (see table 3). From 2013 to 2015, the largest import commodity was "Petroleum oils and oils obtained from bituminous minerals, crude" (HS code 2709) (see table 4). The top three partners for merchandise imports were Germany, China and Belgium, accounting for respectively 16.4, 8.2 and 7.4 percent of total imports. "Other business services" (EBOPS code 268) accounted for the largest share of imports of services in 2014 at 82.1 bln US$, followed by "Transportation" (EBOPS code 205) at 55.4 bln US$ and "Travel" (EBOPS code 236) at 48.7 bln US$ (see graph 6).

Table 4: Top 10 import commodities 2013 to 2015

HS code	4-digit heading of Harmonized System 2012	Value (million US$) 2013	Value (million US$) 2014	Value (million US$) 2015	Unit value 2013	Unit value 2014	Unit value 2015	Unit	SITC code
	All Commodities	671253.6	659872.1	651495.6					
2709	Petroleum oils and oils obtained from bituminous minerals, crude	45645.0	38874.2	22874.3	0.8	0.8	*0.4*	US$/kg	333
8703	Motor cars and other motor vehicles principally designed for the transport	29712.2	30969.1	31097.6	17.8	18.8	16.0	thsd US$/unit	781
2710	Petroleum oils, other than crude	35165.8	32474.2	21588.6	*0.9*	*0.9*	*0.5*	US$/kg	334
2711	Petroleum gases and other gaseous hydrocarbons	24777.4	20835.0	20313.7	*0.6*	*0.6*	*0.4*	US$/kg	343
8803	Parts of goods of heading 88.01 or 88.02	15774.5	16581.1	24979.6	*277.0*	*299.5*	*434.1*	US$/kg	792
8802	Other aircraft (for example, helicopters, aeroplanes); spacecraft	14034.0	12987.9	29533.3	35.8	16.6	1.0	mln US$/unit	792
3004	Medicaments (excluding goods of heading 30.02, 30.05 or 30.06)	18298.2	18290.5	15853.5	*84.3*	*73.3*	*65.9*	US$/kg	542
8708	Parts and accessories of the motor vehicles of headings 87.01 to 87.05	12778.1	13195.6	12362.5	*7.7*	*8.3*	*7.2*	US$/kg	784
8517	Electrical apparatus for line telephony or line telegraphy	11594.5	11645.7	11364.4					764
8411	Turbo-jets, turbo-propellers and other gas turbines	9081.3	9113.2	13600.3					714

French Polynesia

Goods Imports: CIF, by origin | **Goods Exports: FOB, by last known destination** | **Trade System: Special**

Overview:

In 2014, the value of merchandise exports of French Polynesia increased substantially by 12.3 percent to reach 170.1 mln US$, while its merchandise imports decreased slightly by 2.9 percent to reach 1.8 bln US$ (see graph 1, table 2 and table 3). The merchandise trade balance recorded a large deficit of 1.6 bln US$ (see graph 1). The largest merchandise trade balance was with MDG Developed Europe at -687.1 mln US$ (see graph 4). Merchandise exports in French Polynesia were moderately concentrated amongst partners; imports were diversified. The top 5 partners accounted for 80 percent or more of exports and 10 partners accounted for 80 percent or more of imports (see graph 5). In 2013, the value of exports of services of French Polynesia decreased slightly by 0.2 percent, reaching 1.1 bln US$, while its imports of services decreased slightly by 1.9 percent and reached 496.0 mln US$ (see graph 2). There was a large trade in services surplus of 590.0 mln US$.

Graph 1: Total merchandise trade, by value

(Bln US$ by year)

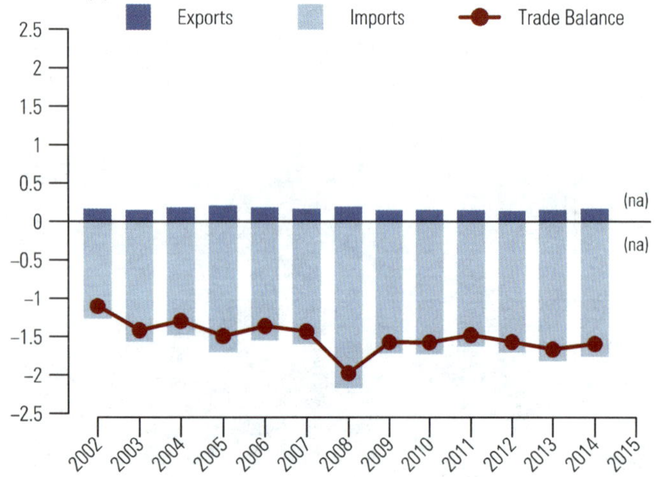

Graph 2: Total services trade, by value

(Bln US$ by year)

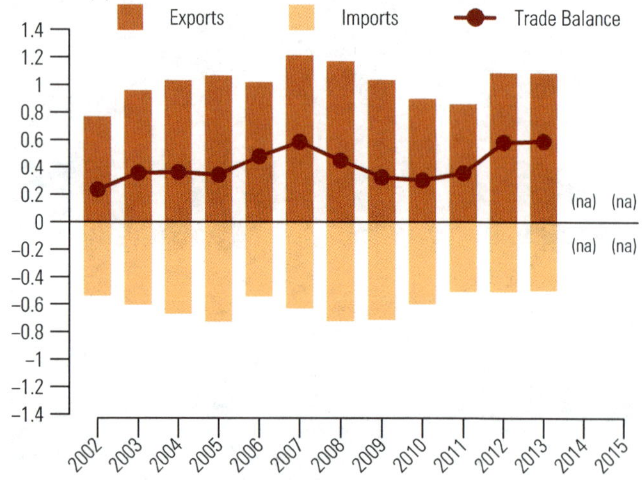

Exports Profile:

"Goods classified chiefly by material" (SITC section 6), "Machinery and transport equipment" (SITC section 7) and "Food, animals + beverages, tobacco" (SITC section 0+1) were the largest commodity groups for exports in 2014, representing respectively 57.5, 15.4 and 15.0 percent of exported goods (see table 2). From 2012 to 2014, the largest export commodity was "Pearls, natural or cultured" (HS code 7101) (see table 1). The top three destinations for merchandise exports were Japan, China, Hong Kong SAR and the United States, accounting for respectively 28.3, 27.9 and 14.3 percent of total exports. "Travel" (EBOPS code 236) accounted for the largest share of exports of services in 2013 at 458.0 mln US$, followed by "Transportation" (EBOPS code 205) at 322.1 mln US$ and "Government services, n.i.e." (EBOPS code 291) at 223.3 mln US$ (see graph 3).

Graph 3: Exports of services by EBOPS category

(% share in 2013)

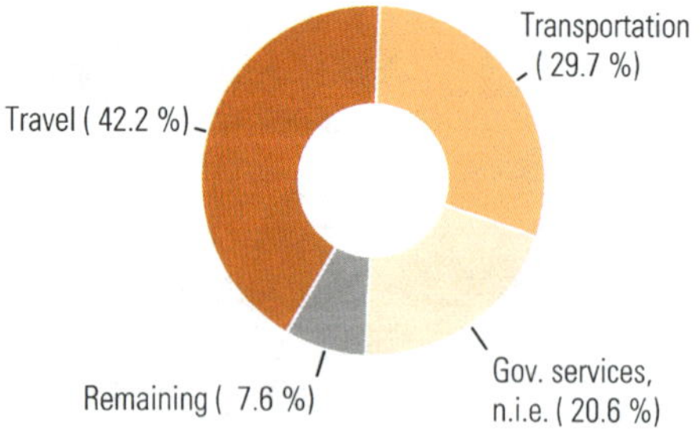

Table 1: Top 10 export commodities 2012 to 2014

HS code	4-digit heading of Harmonized System 2012	Value (million US$) 2012	2013	2014	Unit value 2012	2013	2014	Unit	SITC code
	All Commodities	139.0	151.5	170.1					
7101	Pearls, natural or cultured	76.2	86.6	96.7	*5.3*		6.6	thsd US$/kg	667
0302	Fish, fresh or chilled, excluding fish fillets	9.6	7.9	9.7	9.0	8.7	8.9	US$/kg	034
8802	Other aircraft (for example, helicopters, aeroplanes); spacecraft	0.6	6.7	15.3			5.1	mln US$/unit	792
1513	Coconut (copra), palm kernel or babassu oil	7.7	4.7	5.4	1.1	*0.8*	1.1	US$/kg	422
2007	Jams, fruit jellies, marmalades, fruit or nut pastes	5.4	4.1	4.9	3.0	*3.1*	3.1	US$/kg	058
0905	Vanilla	3.2	3.5	4.1	188.1	201.2	230.3	US$/kg	075
0508	Coral and similar materials, unworked or simply prepared	2.9	4.3	3.1	*1.1*	*1.4*	1.4	US$/kg	291
0304	Fish fillets and other fish meat (whether or not minced)	3.9	3.5	2.5	12.6	13.6	10.7	US$/kg	034
7112	Waste and scrap of precious metal or of metal clad with precious metal	3.7	4.2	1.2	31.0	25.4	*18.9*	thsd US$/kg	971
3304	Beauty or make-up preparations	2.6	2.4	2.9	9.3	9.9	*9.7*	US$/kg	553

Services Imports and Exports: EBOPS 2002 categories

Table 2: Merchandise exports by SITC

(Value in million US$, growth and shares in percentage)

SITC	2014	Avg. Growth rates 2010-2014	Avg. Growth rates 2013-2014	2014 share
Total	170.1	2.7	12.3	100.0
0+1	25.4	6.6	6.9	15.0
2+4	10.0	2.0	-5.0	5.9
3	0.0	-32.7	-56.5	0.0
5	3.7	6.6	24.1	2.2
6	97.7	3.7	10.0	57.5
7	26.2	-1.3	87.3	15.4
8	5.6	-12.1	5.4	3.3
9	1.5	496.9	-75.4	0.9

Table 3: Merchandise imports by SITC

(Value in million US$, growth and shares in percentage)

SITC	2014	Avg. Growth rates 2010-2014	Avg. Growth rates 2013-2014	2014 share
Total	1 761.7	0.5	-2.9	100.0
0+1	437.5	2.4	2.2	24.8
2+4	32.7	1.6	0.1	1.9
3	277.6	5.5	-10.6	15.8
5	175.5	0.6	-1.0	10.0
6	191.5	-1.5	-3.8	10.9
7	443.2	-2.1	-5.0	25.2
8	203.3	-1.3	1.3	11.5
9	0.4	20.9	279.5	0.0

SITC Legend

SITC Code	Description
Total	All commodities
0+1	Food, animals + beverages, tobacco
2+4	Crude materials + anim. & veg. oils
3	Mineral fuels, lubricants
5	Chemicals
6	Goods classified chiefly by material
7	Machinery and transport equipment
8	Miscellaneous manufactured articles
9	Not classified elsewhere in the SITC

Graph 4: Merchandise trade balance

(Mln US$ by MDG Regions in 2014)

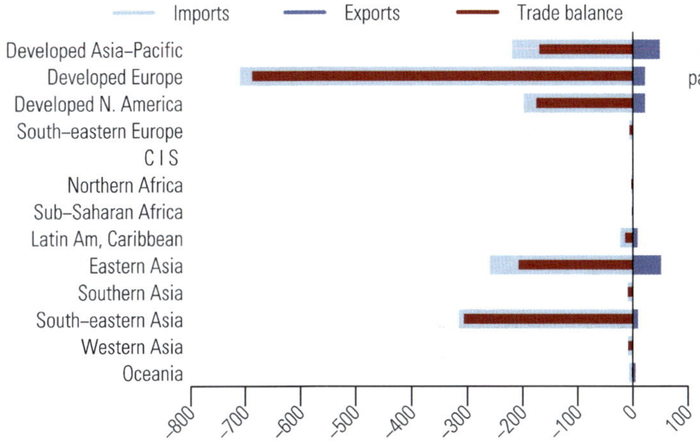

Graph 5: Partner concentration of merchandise trade

(Cumulative share by ranked partners in 2014)

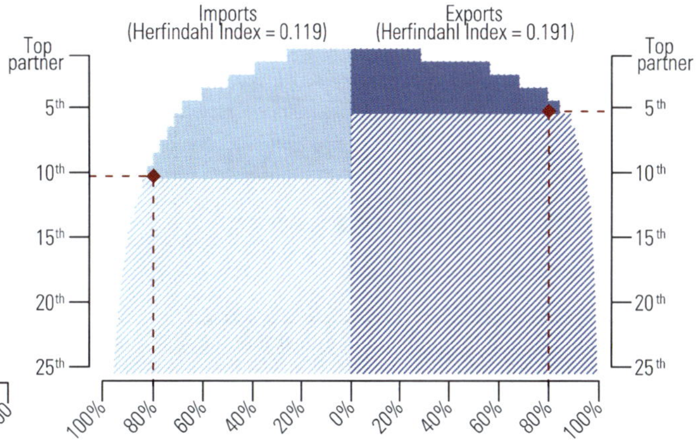

Graph 6: Imports of services by EBOPS category

(% share in 2013)

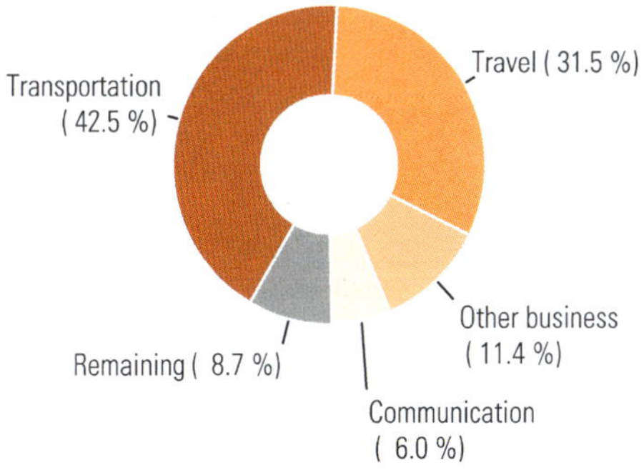

Imports Profile:

"Machinery and transport equipment" (SITC section 7), "Food, animals + beverages, tobacco" (SITC section 0+1) and "Mineral fuels, lubricants" (SITC section 3) were the largest commodity groups for imports in 2014, representing respectively 25.2, 24.8 and 15.8 percent of imported goods (see table 3). From 2012 to 2014, the largest import commodity was "Petroleum oils, other than crude" (HS code 2710) (see table 4). The top three partners for merchandise imports were France, China and the United States, accounting for respectively 24.9, 10.0 and 10.0 percent of total imports. "Transportation" (EBOPS code 205) accounted for the largest share of imports of services in 2013 at 210.6 mln US$, followed by "Travel" (EBOPS code 236) at 156.2 mln US$ and "Other business services" (EBOPS code 268) at 56.4 mln US$ (see graph 6).

Table 4: Top 10 import commodities 2012 to 2014

HS code	4-digit heading of Harmonized System 2012	Value (million US$) 2012	Value (million US$) 2013	Value (million US$) 2014	Unit value 2012	Unit value 2013	Unit value 2014	Unit	SITC code
	All Commodities	1 706.3	1 814.8	1 761.7					
2710	Petroleum oils, other than crude	279.0	292.1	257.6	*1.0*	*1.0*	*1.0*	US$/kg	334
8703	Motor cars and other motor vehicles principally designed for the transport	63.9	69.0	73.1		*18.9*	16.7	thsd US$/unit	781
3004	Medicaments (excluding goods of heading 30.02, 30.05 or 30.06)	64.9	70.9	69.9	*58.8*	*63.5*	*63.7*	US$/kg	542
0207	Meat and edible offal, of the poultry of heading 01.05	32.0	32.9	33.3	2.3	2.2	2.1	US$/kg	012
8517	Electrical apparatus for line telephony or line telegraphy	27.8	29.6	27.4					764
1905	Bread, pastry, cakes, biscuits and other bakers'wares	27.5	26.4	28.4	5.6	*5.7*	*5.7*	US$/kg	048
8471	Automatic data processing machines and units thereof	25.0	28.6	23.8			214.7	US$/unit	752
0202	Meat of bovine animals, frozen	22.8	22.8	25.2	5.2	5.4	5.6	US$/kg	011
0201	Meat of bovine animals, fresh or chilled	23.1	22.8	21.4	9.6	9.7	9.9	US$/kg	011
8901	Cruise ships, excursion boats, ferry-boats, cargo ships, barges	21.0	46.2	...					793

Gambia

Goods Imports: CIF, by origin | **Goods Exports: FOB, by last known destination** | **Trade System: General**

Overview:

In 2014, the value of merchandise exports of the Gambia decreased slightly by 2.1 percent to reach 103.9 mln US$, while its merchandise imports increased substantially by 10.6 percent to reach 387.2 mln US$ (see graph 1, table 2 and table 3). The merchandise trade balance recorded a large deficit of 283.3 mln US$ (see graph 1). The largest merchandise trade balance was with MDG Developed Europe at -98.3 mln US$ (see graph 4). Merchandise exports in the Gambia were moderately concentrated amongst partners; imports were diversified. The top 4 partners accounted for 80 percent or more of exports and 14 partners accounted for 80 percent or more of imports (see graph 5). In 2012, the value of exports of services of the Gambia increased moderately by 5.4 percent, reaching 151.5 mln US$, while its imports of services increased substantially by 17.3 percent and reached 80.3 mln US$ (see graph 2). There was a large trade in services surplus of 71.2 mln US$. See footnote*.

Graph 1: Total merchandise trade, by value

(Mln US$ by year)

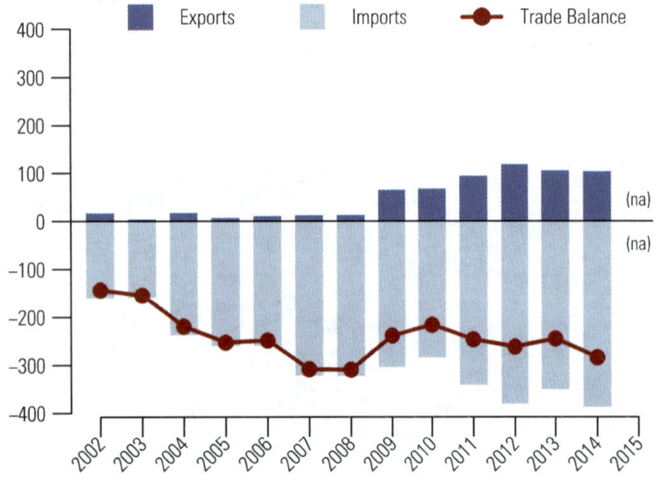

Graph 2: Total services trade, by value

(Mln US$ by year)

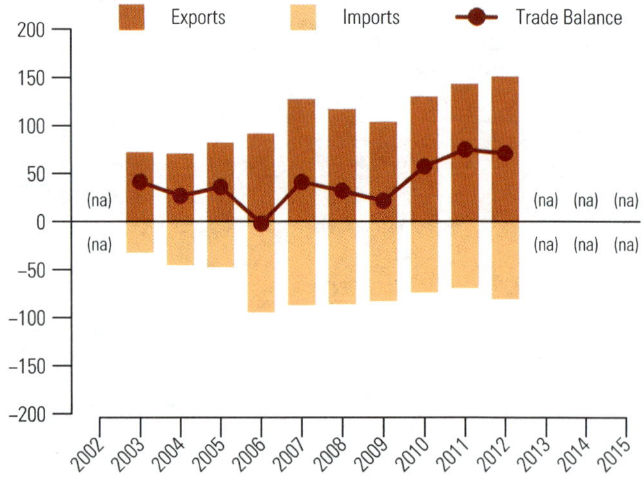

Exports Profile:

"Goods classified chiefly by material" (SITC section 6), "Food, animals + beverages, tobacco" (SITC section 0+1) and "Crude materials + anim. & veg. oils" (SITC section 2+4) were the largest commodity groups for exports in 2014, representing respectively 62.0, 17.8 and 10.0 percent of exported goods (see table 2). From 2012 to 2014, the largest export commodity was "Woven fabrics of artificial filament yarn" (HS code 5408) (see table 1). The top three destinations for merchandise exports were Mali, Guinea and Senegal, accounting for respectively 34.9, 28.6 and 16.0 percent of total exports. "Travel" (EBOPS code 236) accounted for the largest share of exports of services in 2012 at 87.6 mln US$, followed by "Transportation" (EBOPS code 205) at 50.4 mln US$ and "Insurance services" (EBOPS code 253) at 9.1 mln US$ (see graph 3).

Graph 3: Exports of services by EBOPS category

(% share in 2012)

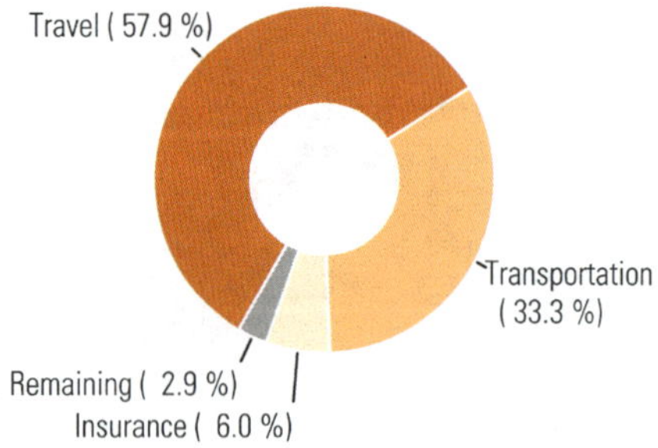

Table 1: Top 10 export commodities 2012 to 2014

HS code	4-digit heading of Harmonized System 2007	Value (million US$) 2012	2013	2014	Unit value 2012	2013	2014	Unit	SITC code
	All Commodities	118.8	106.2	103.9					
5408	Woven fabrics of artificial filament yarn	58.3	67.3	60.9		1.8	9.0	US$/kg	653
0801	Coconuts, Brazil nuts and cashew nuts, fresh or dried	3.0	5.3	4.9					057
2710	Petroleum oils, other than crude	6.3	2.3	0.9	0.4	0.4	1.0	US$/kg	334
0402	Milk and cream, concentrated or containing added sugar	5.1	2.5	1.3	3.0	2.6	2.0	US$/kg	022
4401	Fuel wood, in logs, in billets, in twigs, in faggots or in similar forms	0.4	0.1	7.5	0.1	0.1	0.1	US$/kg	246
6309	Worn clothing and other worn articles	5.1	1.3	1.3	4.3	2.7	3.3	US$/kg	269
8429	Self-propelled bulldozers, angledozers, graders, levellers, scrapers	0.1	1.3	5.2	*58.9*	*54.7*	472.5	thsd US$/unit	723
4408	Sheets for veneering	5.7	0.4	0.0					634
1701	Cane or beet sugar and chemically pure sucrose, in solid form	1.8	3.3	1.0	0.8	1.2	1.2	US$/kg	061
8704	Motor vehicles for the transport of goods	0.2	3.7	2.0			63.8	thsd US$/unit	782

*As of 2009, merchandise trade includes re-exports.

Services Imports and Exports: EBOPS 2002 categories

Table 2: Merchandise exports by SITC

(Value in million US$, growth and shares in percentage)

SITC	2014	Avg. Growth rates 2010-2014	Avg. Growth rates 2013-2014	2014 share
Total	103.9	11.1	-2.1	100.0
0+1	18.5	-0.6	-6.0	17.8
2+4	10.4	-16.9	63.4	10.0
3	0.9	-24.4	-63.0	0.8
5	0.4	5.1	-53.7	0.3
6	64.5	38.0	-6.4	62.0
7	8.9	51.6	27.6	8.5
8	0.5	-43.6	-59.0	0.5

Table 3: Merchandise imports by SITC

(Value in million US$, growth and shares in percentage)

SITC	2014	Avg. Growth rates 2010-2014	Avg. Growth rates 2013-2014	2014 share
Total	387.2	8.1	10.6	100.0
0+1	130.4	11.5	15.2	33.7
2+4	33.5	10.4	45.2	8.6
3	82.4	9.0	-0.3	21.3
5	13.9	7.5	-1.7	3.6
6	45.7	3.6	18.3	11.8
7	59.4	4.9	0.9	15.4
8	21.9	5.6	11.4	5.7
9	0.0	-87.7	-98.9	0.0

SITC Legend

SITC Code	Description
Total	All commodities
0+1	Food, animals + beverages, tobacco
2+4	Crude materials + anim. & veg. oils
3	Mineral fuels, lubricants
5	Chemicals
6	Goods classified chiefly by material
7	Machinery and transport equipment
8	Miscellaneous manufactured articles
9	Not classified elsewhere in the SITC

Graph 4: Merchandise trade balance

(Mln US$ by MDG Regions in 2014)

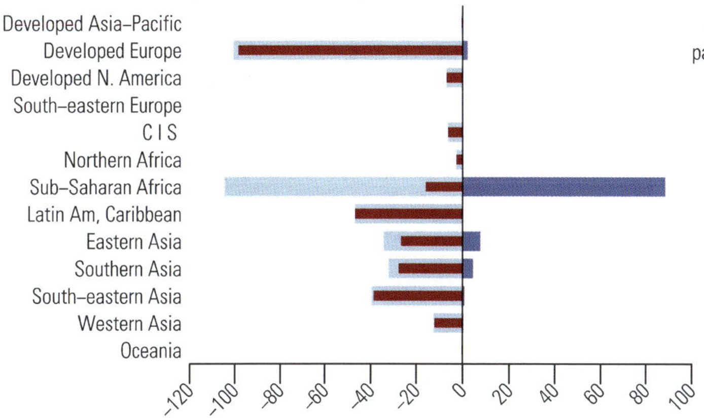

Graph 5: Partner concentration of merchandise trade

(Cumulative share by ranked partners in 2014)

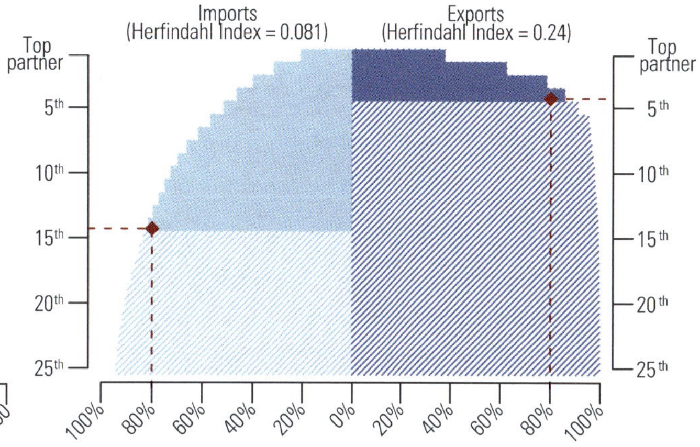

Graph 6: Imports of services by EBOPS category

(% share in 2012)

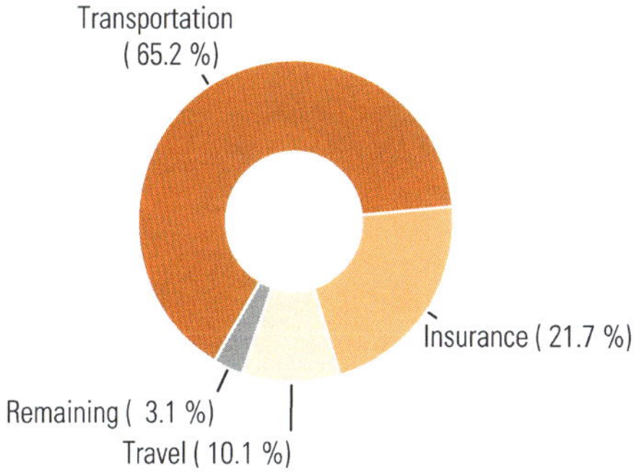

Imports Profile:

"Food, animals + beverages, tobacco" (SITC section 0+1), "Mineral fuels, lubricants" (SITC section 3) and "Machinery and transport equipment" (SITC section 7) were the largest commodity groups for imports in 2014, representing respectively 33.7, 21.3 and 15.4 percent of imported goods (see table 3). From 2012 to 2014, the largest import commodity was "Petroleum oils, other than crude" (HS code 2710) (see table 4). The top three partners for merchandise imports were Côte d'Ivoire, Brazil and China, accounting for respectively 23.4, 9.6 and 7.9 percent of total imports. "Transportation" (EBOPS code 205) accounted for the largest share of imports of services in 2012 at 52.3 mln US$, followed by "Insurance services" (EBOPS code 253) at 17.4 mln US$ and "Travel" (EBOPS code 236) at 8.1 mln US$ (see graph 6).

Table 4: Top 10 import commodities 2012 to 2014

HS code	4-digit heading of Harmonized System 2007	Value (million US$) 2012	2013	2014	Unit value 2012	2013	2014	Unit	SITC code
	All Commodities	380.0	350.2	387.2					
2710	Petroleum oils, other than crude	102.5	82.4	82.0	1.1	1.0	0.9	US$/kg	334
1006	Rice	44.2	31.7	46.4	0.5	0.4	0.3	US$/kg	042
1701	Cane or beet sugar and chemically pure sucrose, in solid form	16.6	27.2	26.2	0.3	0.4	0.2	US$/kg	061
1515	Other fixed vegetable fats and oils	18.0	16.6	27.3	0.4	0.4	0.5	US$/kg	42
8703	Motor cars and other motor vehicles principally designed for the transport	20.5	22.2	17.7	*18.4*	*18.1*		thsd US$/unit	781
2523	Portland cement, aluminous cement, slag cement	12.9	10.3	12.8	0.1	0.1	0.3	US$/kg	661
1101	Wheat or meslin flour	14.1	18.7	1.5	0.2	0.4	0.3	US$/kg	046
1001	Wheat and meslin	0.0	5.2	22.6	0.1	1.6	0.7	US$/kg	041
5408	Woven fabrics of artificial filament yarn	7.5	7.4	7.8					653
3004	Medicaments (excluding goods of heading 30.02, 30.05 or 30.06)	5.0	3.4	5.6	7.4			US$/kg	542

Georgia

Goods Imports: CIF, by consignment | **Goods Exports: FOB, by last known destination** | **Trade System: General**

Overview:

In 2015, the value of merchandise exports of Georgia decreased substantially by 23.0 percent to reach 2.2 bln US$, while its merchandise imports decreased substantially by 10.1 percent to reach 7.7 bln US$ (see graph 1, table 2 and table 3). The merchandise trade balance recorded a large deficit of 5.5 bln US$ (see graph 1). The largest merchandise trade balance was with MDG Developed Europe at -1.8 bln US$ (see graph 4). Merchandise exports in Georgia were diversified amongst partners; imports were also diversified. The top 18 partners accounted for 80 percent or more of exports and 18 partners accounted for 80 percent or more of imports (see graph 5). In 2014, the value of exports of services of Georgia increased slightly by 1.8 percent, reaching 3.0 bln US$, while its imports of services increased moderately by 7.7 percent and reached 1.7 bln US$ (see graph 2). There was a moderate trade in services surplus of 1.3 bln US$.

Graph 1: Total merchandise trade, by value

(Bln US$ by year)

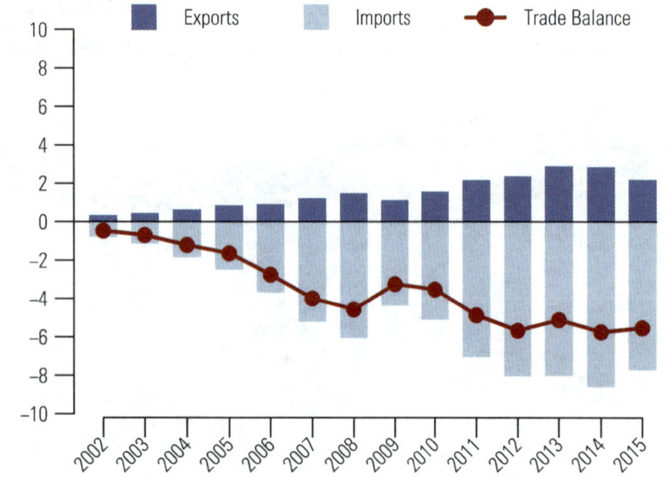

Graph 2: Total services trade, by value

(Bln US$ by year)

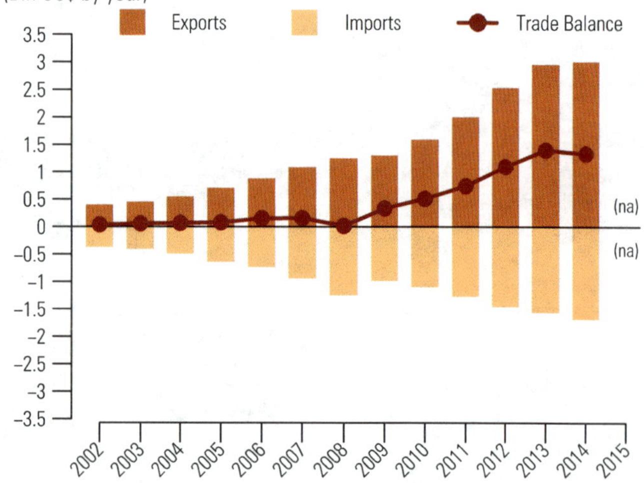

Exports Profile:

"Food, animals + beverages, tobacco" (SITC section 0+1), "Crude materials + anim. & veg. oils" (SITC section 2+4) and "Goods classified chiefly by material" (SITC section 6) were the largest commodity groups for exports in 2015, representing respectively 27.2, 15.3 and 14.5 percent of exported goods (see table 2). From 2013 to 2015, the largest export commodity was "Motor cars and other motor vehicles principally designed for the transport" (HS code 8703) (see table 1). The top three destinations for merchandise exports were Azerbaijan, Armenia and the Russian Federation, accounting for respectively 18.7, 9.4 and 7.6 percent of total exports. "Travel" (EBOPS code 236) accounted for the largest share of exports of services in 2014 at 1.8 bln US$, followed by "Transportation" (EBOPS code 205) at 967.1 mln US$ (see graph 3).

Graph 3: Exports of services by EBOPS category

(% share in 2014)

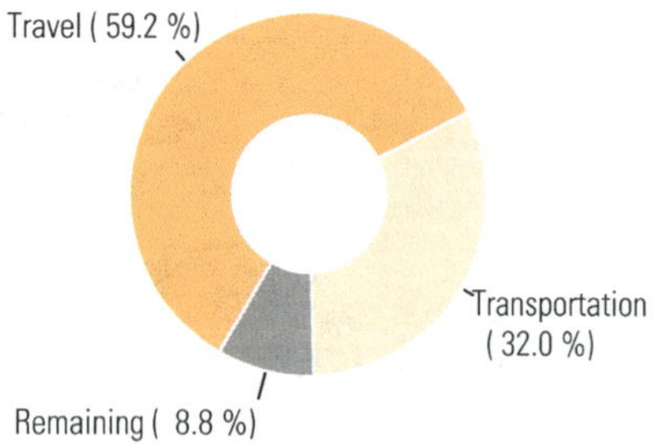

Table 1: Top 10 export commodities 2013 to 2015

HS code	4-digit heading of Harmonized System 2012	Value (million US$) 2013	2014	2015	Unit value 2013	2014	2015	Unit	SITC code
	All Commodities	2909.5	2860.7	2203.6					
8703	Motor cars and other motor vehicles principally designed for the transport	703.8	517.8	179.6	9.6	11.4	9.9	thsd US$/unit	781
7202	Ferro-alloys	230.7	285.8	194.5					671
2603	Copper ores and concentrates	161.6	248.0	270.6	1.3	1.3	1.1	US$/kg	283
0802	Other nuts, fresh or dried, whether or not shelled or peeled	166.7	183.4	176.4	5.5	9.2	9.1	US$/kg	057
2204	Wine of fresh grapes, including fortified wines	127.9	180.4	95.8	3.6	3.9	3.5	US$/litre	112
3102	Mineral or chemical fertilisers, nitrogenous	130.6	137.6	109.8	0.3	0.3	0.2	US$/kg	562
2201	Waters, including natural or artificial mineral waters	106.9	137.1	82.2	0.8	0.9	0.8	US$/litre	111
3004	Medicaments (excluding goods of heading 30.02, 30.05 or 30.06)	52.1	92.1	140.7	23.6	33.3	42.3	US$/kg	542
2208	Alcohol of a strength by volume of less than 80 % vol	99.8	95.2	64.9	8.7	10.1	8.0	US$/litre	112
7108	Gold (including gold plated with platinum)	73.3	39.3	62.1	17.1	17.3	20.2	thsd US$/kg	971

Services Imports and Exports: EBOPS 2002 categories

Table 2: Merchandise exports by SITC

(Value in million US$, growth and shares in percentage)

SITC	2015	Avg. Growth rates 2011-2015	Avg. Growth rates 2014-2015	2015 share
Total	2 203.6	0.2	-23.0	100.0
0+1	598.3	12.1	-26.3	27.2
2+4	338.1	2.5	3.1	15.3
3	135.8	17.1	76.4	6.2
5	317.0	8.0	6.1	14.4
6	320.5	-4.7	-37.0	14.5
7	295.3	-16.1	-55.3	13.4
8	130.6	26.0	0.9	5.9
9	68.1	-19.4	46.3	3.1

Table 3: Merchandise imports by SITC

(Value in million US$, growth and shares in percentage)

SITC	2015	Avg. Growth rates 2011-2015	Avg. Growth rates 2014-2015	2015 share
Total	7 724.4	2.4	-10.1	100.0
0+1	1 004.9	6.1	-17.5	13.0
2+4	397.5	18.6	3.6	5.1
3	1 243.2	-0.4	-13.2	16.1
5	1 284.7	18.6	40.5	16.6
6	1 145.0	1.4	-14.4	14.8
7	1 891.6	-1.3	-22.5	24.5
8	714.4	1.2	-12.7	9.2
9	43.1	-41.7	-9.6	0.6

SITC Legend

SITC Code	Description
Total	All commodities
0+1	Food, animals + beverages, tobacco
2+4	Crude materials + anim. & veg. oils
3	Mineral fuels, lubricants
5	Chemicals
6	Goods classified chiefly by material
7	Machinery and transport equipment
8	Miscellaneous manufactured articles
9	Not classified elsewhere in the SITC

Graph 4: Merchandise trade balance

(Bln US$ by MDG Regions in 2015)

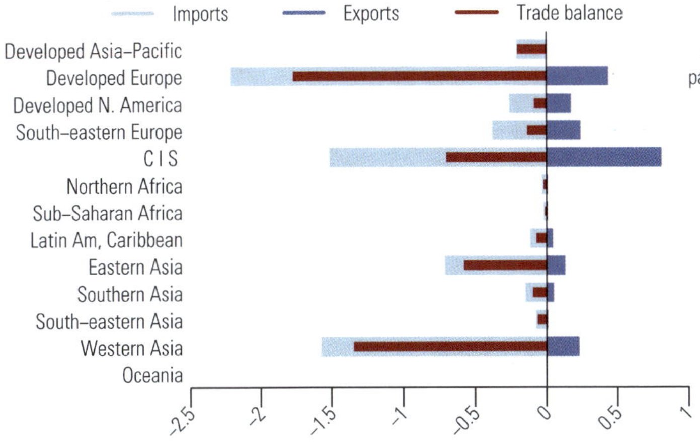

Graph 5: Partner concentration of merchandise trade

(Cumulative share by ranked partners in 2015)

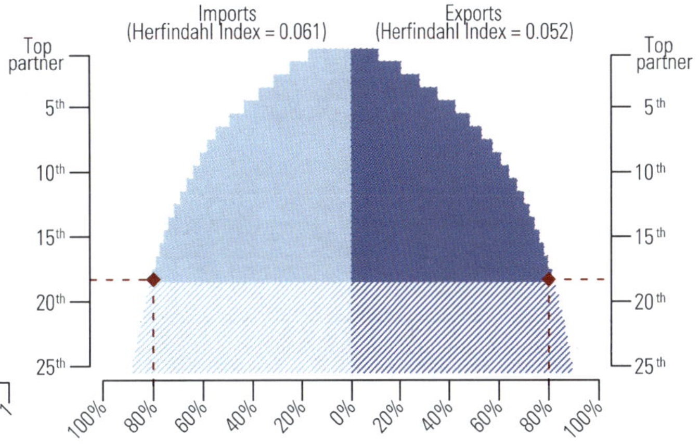

Graph 6: Imports of services by EBOPS category

(% share in 2014)

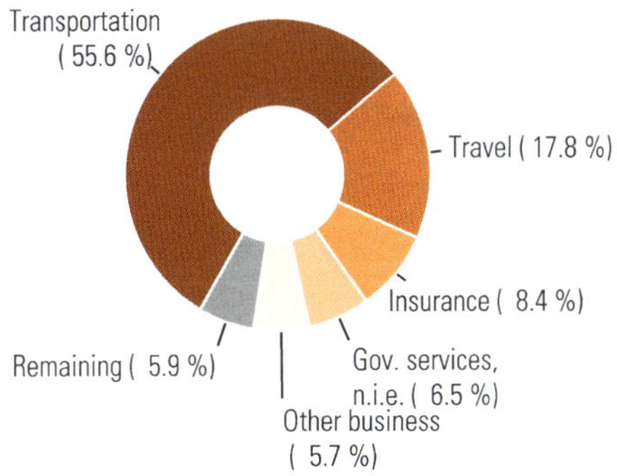

Imports Profile:

"Machinery and transport equipment" (SITC section 7), "Chemicals" (SITC section 5) and "Mineral fuels, lubricants" (SITC section 3) were the largest commodity groups for imports in 2015, representing respectively 24.5, 16.6 and 16.1 percent of imported goods (see table 3). From 2013 to 2015, the largest import commodity was "Petroleum oils, other than crude" (HS code 2710) (see table 4). The top three partners for merchandise imports were Turkey, China and Ukraine, accounting for respectively 18.3, 7.9 and 6.6 percent of total imports. "Transportation" (EBOPS code 205) accounted for the largest share of imports of services in 2014 at 932.7 mln US$, followed by "Travel" (EBOPS code 236) at 298.5 mln US$ and "Insurance services" (EBOPS code 253) at 141.7 mln US$ (see graph 6).

Table 4: Top 10 import commodities 2013 to 2015

HS code	4-digit heading of Harmonized System 2012	Value (million US$) 2013	2014	2015	Unit value 2013	2014	2015	Unit	SITC code
	All Commodities	8 011.1	8 593.3	7 724.4					
2710	Petroleum oils, other than crude	954.3	918.4	657.4	1.0	0.9	0.5	US$/kg	334
8703	Motor cars and other motor vehicles principally designed for the transport	710.5	715.1	461.3	8.7	7.4	5.5	thsd US$/unit	781
3004	Medicaments (excluding goods of heading 30.02, 30.05 or 30.06)	280.7	314.6	745.4	34.6	33.6	73.1	US$/kg	542
2711	Petroleum gases and other gaseous hydrocarbons	316.7	368.5	419.4	*0.6*	*0.6*	*0.5*	US$/kg	343
8517	Electrical apparatus for line telephony or line telegraphy	152.5	195.5	148.9					764
2603	Copper ores and concentrates	113.1	165.3	207.9	1.5	0.8	1.2	US$/kg	283
1001	Wheat and meslin	184.8	151.8	118.7	0.3	0.3	0.2	US$/kg	041
2402	Cigars, cheroots, cigarillos and cigarettes	95.7	115.5	103.6	12.5	12.8	11.9	US$/kg	122
8471	Automatic data processing machines and units thereof	90.6	104.1	58.8	98.6	111.1	88.5	US$/unit	752
7308	Structures (excluding prefabricated buildings of heading 94.06)	65.4	90.8	63.5	2.4	2.5	1.9	US$/kg	691

Germany

Goods Imports: CIF, by origin | **Goods Exports: FOB, by last known destination** | **Trade System: Special**

Overview:

In 2015, the value of merchandise exports of Germany decreased substantially by 11.1 percent to reach 1331.2 bln US$, while its merchandise imports decreased substantially by 13.1 percent to reach 1056.3 bln US$ (see graph 1, table 2 and table 3). Germany was the third largest trader in the World in 2015, behind China and US. The merchandise trade balance recorded a moderate surplus of 274.9 bln US$ (see graph 1). The largest merchandise trade balance was with MDG Developed Europe at 162.9 bln US$ (see graph 4). Merchandise exports in Germany were diversified amongst partners; imports were also diversified. The top 21 partners accounted for 80 percent or more of exports and 20 partners accounted for 80 percent or more of imports (see graph 5). In 2014, the value of exports of services of Germany increased slightly by 4.5 percent, reaching 285.4 bln US$, while its imports of services increased slightly by 2.6 percent and reached 312.5 bln US$ (see graph 2). There was a relatively small trade in services deficit of 27.1 bln US$.

Graph 1: Total merchandise trade, by value

(Bln US$ by year)

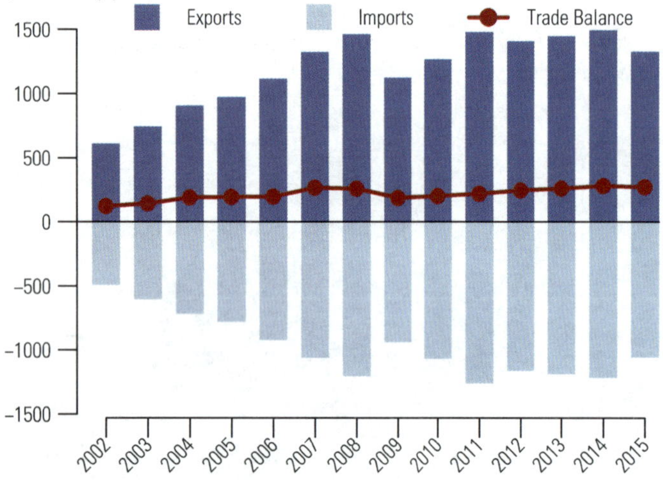

Graph 2: Total services trade, by value

(Bln US$ by year)

Exports Profile:

"Machinery and transport equipment" (SITC section 7), "Chemicals" (SITC section 5) and "Goods classified chiefly by material" (SITC section 6) were the largest commodity groups for exports in 2015, representing respectively 48.0, 14.9 and 11.7 percent of exported goods (see table 2). From 2013 to 2015, the largest export commodity was "Motor cars and other motor vehicles principally designed for the transport" (HS code 8703) (see table 1). Germany is the World's largest exporter of this commodity. The top three destinations for merchandise exports were France, the United States and the United Kingdom, accounting for respectively 8.9, 8.7 and 7.0 percent of total exports. "Other business services" (EBOPS code 268) accounted for the largest share of exports of services in 2014 at 107.1 bln US$, followed by "Transportation" (EBOPS code 205) at 56.1 bln US$ and "Travel" (EBOPS code 236) at 43.3 bln US$ (see graph 3).

Graph 3: Exports of services by EBOPS category

(% share in 2014)

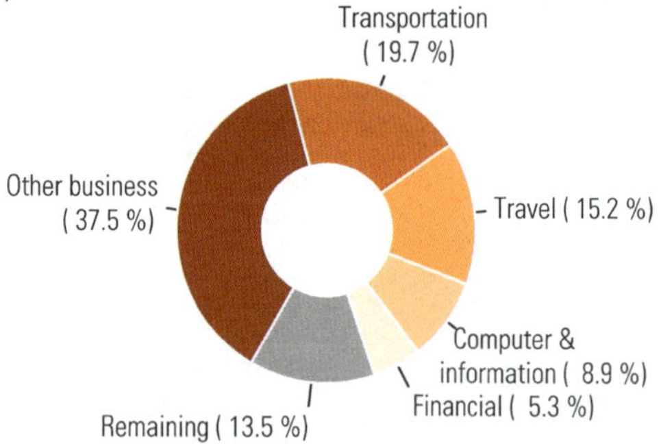

Table 1: Top 10 export commodities 2013 to 2015

HS code	4-digit heading of Harmonized System 2012	Value (billion US$) 2013	2014	2015	Unit value 2013	2014	2015	Unit	SITC code
	All Commodities	1 451.0	1 498.2	1 331.2					
8703	Motor cars and other motor vehicles principally designed for the transport	148.6	160.3	152.7	*19.7*	*19.1*	*19.5*	thsd US$/unit	781
9999	Commodities not specified according to kind	65.8	72.1	76.5					931
8708	Parts and accessories of the motor vehicles of headings 87.01 to 87.05	56.1	60.3	53.3	*10.6*	*10.9*	*9.4*	US$/kg	784
3004	Medicaments (excluding goods of heading 30.02, 30.05 or 30.06)	48.5	51.6	48.9	*80.9*	*86.5*	*79.1*	US$/kg	542
8802	Other aircraft (for example, helicopters, aeroplanes); spacecraft	34.8	33.9	34.0					792
3002	Human blood; animal blood prepared for therapeutic uses	20.8	22.3	22.1	*1.0*	*1.0*	*1.0*	thsd US$/kg	541
2710	Petroleum oils, other than crude	18.4	18.1	12.4	*1.0*	*1.0*	*0.6*	US$/kg	334
8409	Parts suitable for use with the engines of heading 84	14.8	15.5	13.5	*14.5*	*15.1*	*12.7*	US$/kg	713
8479	Machines and mechanical appliances having individual functions	13.7	14.3	12.9					728
9018	Instruments and appliances used in medical, surgical, dental or veterinary	13.8	14.0	12.6					872

Source: UN Comtrade

Services Imports and Exports: EBOPS 2002 categories

Table 2: Merchandise exports by SITC

(Value in million US$, growth and shares in percentage)

SITC	2015	Avg. Growth rates 2011-2015	Avg. Growth rates 2014-2015	2015 share
Total	1 331 193.7	-2.7	-11.1	100.0
0+1	68 765.8	-2.3	-15.9	5.2
2+4	22 324.3	-9.4	-20.4	1.7
3	28 276.3	-4.0	-16.2	2.1
5	198 978.8	-1.7	-11.7	14.9
6	156 167.4	-5.9	-15.8	11.7
7	639 033.9	-2.1	-10.2	48.0
8	136 421.7	-2.6	-11.8	10.2
9	81 225.5	0.3	4.5	6.1

Table 3: Merchandise imports by SITC

(Value in million US$, growth and shares in percentage)

SITC	2015	Avg. Growth rates 2011-2015	Avg. Growth rates 2014-2015	2015 share
Total	1 056 340.5	-4.3	-13.1	100.0
0+1	73 760.3	-2.6	-13.9	7.0
2+4	38 994.7	-9.5	-20.5	3.7
3	97 251.4	-12.6	-34.3	9.2
5	138 740.4	-3.2	-10.7	13.1
6	132 537.5	-6.2	-15.4	12.5
7	371 832.7	-2.8	-9.8	35.2
8	136 060.1	-0.7	-9.0	12.9
9	67 163.5	-0.4	14.7	6.4

SITC Legend

SITC Code	Description
Total	All commodities
0+1	Food, animals + beverages, tobacco
2+4	Crude materials + anim. & veg. oils
3	Mineral fuels, lubricants
5	Chemicals
6	Goods classified chiefly by material
7	Machinery and transport equipment
8	Miscellaneous manufactured articles
9	Not classified elsewhere in the SITC

Graph 4: Merchandise trade balance

(Bln US$ by MDG Regions in 2015)

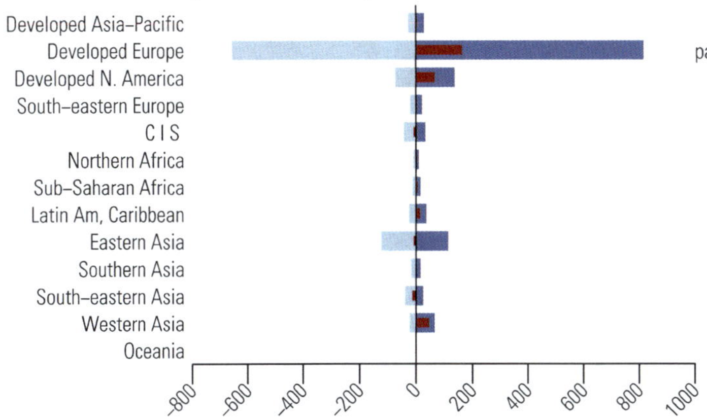

Graph 5: Partner concentration of merchandise trade

(Cumulative share by ranked partners in 2015)

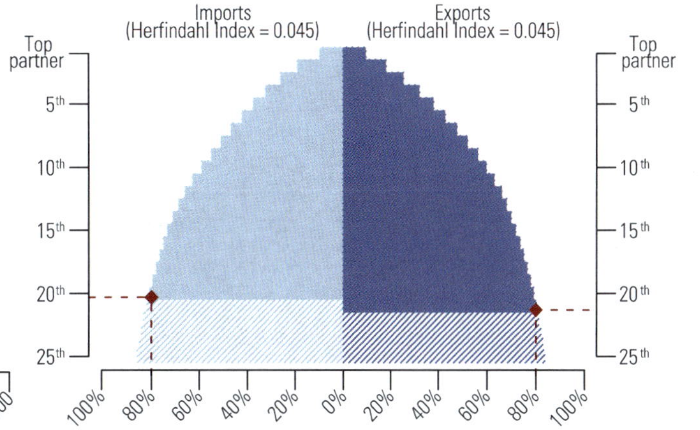

Graph 6: Imports of services by EBOPS category

(% share in 2014)

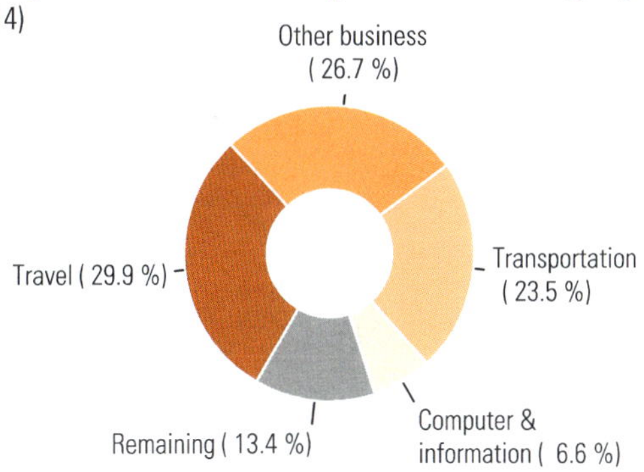

Imports Profile:

"Machinery and transport equipment" (SITC section 7), "Chemicals" (SITC section 5) and "Miscellaneous manufactured articles" (SITC section 8) were the largest commodity groups for imports in 2015, representing respectively 35.2, 13.1 and 12.9 percent of imported goods (see table 3). From 2013 to 2015, the largest import commodity was "Petroleum oils and oils obtained from bituminous minerals, crude" (HS code 2709) (see table 4). The top three partners for merchandise imports were the Netherlands, China and France, accounting for respectively 9.6, 9.0 and 7.2 percent of total imports. "Travel" (EBOPS code 236) accounted for the largest share of imports of services in 2014 at 93.3 bln US$, followed by "Other business services" (EBOPS code 268) at 83.5 bln US$ and "Transportation" (EBOPS code 205) at 73.3 bln US$ (see graph 6).

Table 4: Top 10 import commodities 2013 to 2015

HS code	4-digit heading of Harmonized System 2012	Value (billion US$) 2013	Value (billion US$) 2014	Value (billion US$) 2015	Unit value 2013	Unit value 2014	Unit value 2015	Unit	SITC code
	All Commodities	1 187.3	1 215.0	1 056.3					
2709	Petroleum oils and oils obtained from bituminous minerals, crude	75.7	65.7	36.4	0.8	0.8	0.4	US$/kg	333
9999	Commodities not specified according to kind	48.5	53.0	61.6					931
8703	Motor cars and other motor vehicles principally designed for the transport	41.1	46.5	45.5	*17.6*	*17.7*	*19.0*	thsd US$/unit	781
2711	Petroleum gases and other gaseous hydrocarbons	43.2	37.8	32.0	0.5	0.4	0.3	US$/kg	343
8708	Parts and accessories of the motor vehicles of headings 87.01 to 87.05	35.4	37.9	34.1	*8.4*	*8.4*	*7.4*	US$/kg	784
2710	Petroleum oils, other than crude	36.9	33.0	20.4	1.0	*0.9*	*0.5*	US$/kg	334
3004	Medicaments (excluding goods of heading 30.02, 30.05 or 30.06)	24.2	26.3	24.2	*90.8*	*99.5*	*90.3*	US$/kg	542
8471	Automatic data processing machines and units thereof	18.1	21.5	21.1					752
8517	Electrical apparatus for line telephony or line telegraphy	19.3	20.1	19.9					764
8802	Other aircraft (for example, helicopters, aeroplanes); spacecraft	18.4	19.7	16.2					792

Ghana

Goods Imports: CIF, by origin | **Goods Exports: FOB, by last known destination** | **Trade System: General**

Overview:

In 2013, the value of merchandise exports of Ghana decreased substantially by 19.8 percent to reach 12.6 bln US$, while its merchandise imports decreased moderately by 5.8 percent to reach 12.8 bln US$ (see graph 1, table 2 and table 3). The merchandise trade balance recorded a relatively small deficit of 143.3 mln US$ (see graph 1). The largest merchandise trade balance was with MDG Sub-Saharan Africa at 2.8 bln US$ (see graph 4). Merchandise exports in Ghana were diversified amongst partners; imports were also diversified. The top 10 partners accounted for 80 percent or more of exports and 21 partners accounted for 80 percent or more of imports (see graph 5). In 2014, the value of exports of services of Ghana decreased substantially by 16.7 percent, reaching 2.0 bln US$, while its imports of services decreased moderately by 5.4 percent and reached 4.6 bln US$ (see graph 2). There was a large trade in services deficit of 2.6 bln US$. See footnote*.

Graph 1: Total merchandise trade, by value

(Bln US$ by year)

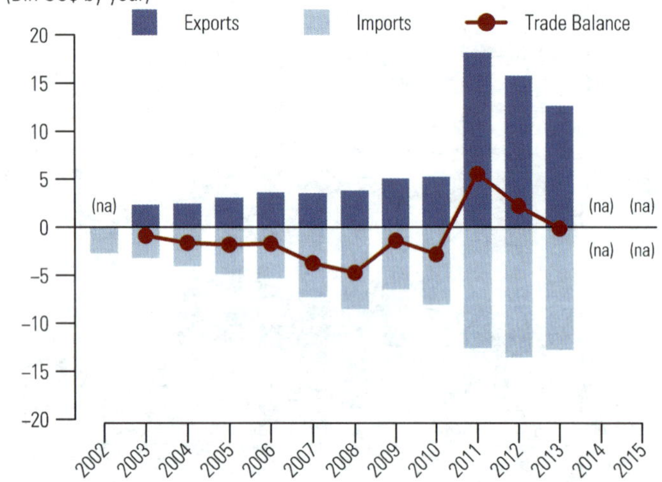

Graph 2: Total services trade, by value

(Bln US$ by year)

Exports Profile:

"Not classified elsewhere in the SITC" (SITC section 9), "Mineral fuels, lubricants" (SITC section 3) and "Food, animals + beverages, tobacco" (SITC section 0+1) were the largest commodity groups for exports in 2013, representing respectively 42.6, 24.7 and 16.3 percent of exported goods (see table 2). From 2011 to 2013, the largest export commodity was "Gold (including gold plated with platinum)" (HS code 7108) (see table 1). The top three destinations for merchandise exports were South Africa, Togo and the United Arab Emirates, accounting for respectively 22.6, 11.9 and 9.2 percent of total exports. "Travel" (EBOPS code 236) accounted for the largest share of exports of services in 2014 at 896.8 mln US$, followed by "Transportation" (EBOPS code 205) at 616.0 mln US$ and "Other business services" (EBOPS code 268) at 429.7 mln US$ (see graph 3).

Graph 3: Exports of services by EBOPS category

(% share in 2014)

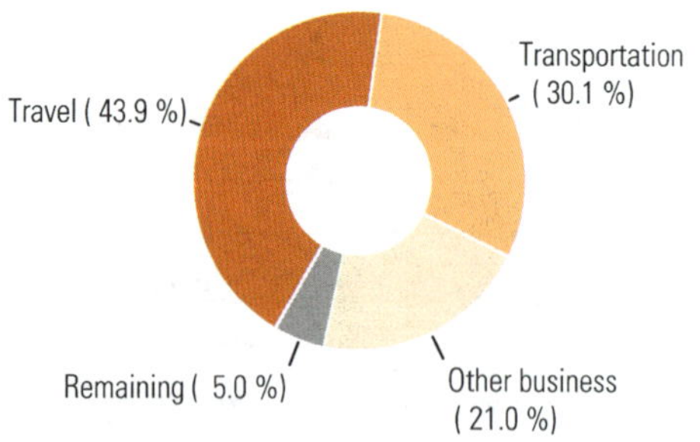

Table 1: Top 10 export commodities 2011 to 2013

HS code	4-digit heading of Harmonized System 2007	Value (million US$) 2011	2012	2013	Unit value 2011	2012	2013	Unit	SITC code
	All Commodities	18146.7	15761.2	12643.9					
7108	Gold (including gold plated with platinum)	4836.6	7093.2	5364.6	41.7	31.7	38.4	thsd US$/kg	971
2709	Petroleum oils and oils obtained from bituminous minerals, crude	2862.0	3683.9	3015.4	0.7	0.6	0.5	US$/kg	333
1801	Cocoa beans, whole or broken, raw or roasted	2071.6	1967.8	1380.5	3.3	3.4	2.6	US$/kg	072
2711	Petroleum gases and other gaseous hydrocarbons	4330.8	620.2	10.6			2.2	US$/kg	343
0801	Coconuts, Brazil nuts and cashew nuts, fresh or dried	512.4	160.8	417.8	3.2	1.4	2.2	US$/kg	057
0714	Manioc, arrowroot, sweet potatoes and similar roots	422.0	11.2	19.7		0.5	0.8	US$/kg	054
3304	Beauty or make-up preparations	78.2	124.8	238.5	6.0	59.0	151.0	US$/kg	553
4407	Wood sawn or chipped lengthwise, sliced or peeled	127.8	79.7	231.2					248
2710	Petroleum oils, other than crude	76.1	214.8	101.6	1.0	1.4		US$/kg	334
2602	Manganese ores and concentrates	107.4	104.3	134.6					287

*In 2011, Ghana exported crude petroleum & natural gas in large quantities.

Services Imports and Exports: EBOPS 2002 categories

Table 2: Merchandise exports by SITC

(Value in million US$, growth and shares in percentage)

SITC	2013	Avg. Growth rates 2009-2013	Avg. Growth rates 2012-2013	2013 share
Total	12643.9	25.7	-19.8	100.0
0+1	2059.1	13.0	-15.9	16.3
2+4	771.3	37.1	29.1	6.1
3	3128.7	143.6	-31.5	24.7
5	417.7	53.1	66.8	3.3
6	532.7	17.8	5.3	4.2
7	220.7	28.6	16.1	1.7
8	121.8	1.2	9.9	1.0
9	5391.9	16.3	-24.0	42.6

Table 3: Merchandise imports by SITC

(Value in million US$, growth and shares in percentage)

SITC	2013	Avg. Growth rates 2009-2013	Avg. Growth rates 2012-2013	2013 share
Total	12787.2	18.6	-5.8	100.0
0+1	1986.5	19.0	12.9	15.5
2+4	308.8	14.4	-4.5	2.4
3	471.9	24.5	-14.3	3.7
5	1650.6	17.3	-5.8	12.9
6	2398.0	17.4	-10.2	18.8
7	5057.1	20.6	-11.8	39.5
8	795.1	20.8	2.1	6.2
9	119.4	-11.7	1379.7	0.9

SITC Legend

SITC Code	Description
Total	All commodities
0+1	Food, animals + beverages, tobacco
2+4	Crude materials + anim. & veg. oils
3	Mineral fuels, lubricants
5	Chemicals
6	Goods classified chiefly by material
7	Machinery and transport equipment
8	Miscellaneous manufactured articles
9	Not classified elsewhere in the SITC

Graph 4: Merchandise trade balance

(Bln US$ by MDG Regions in 2013)

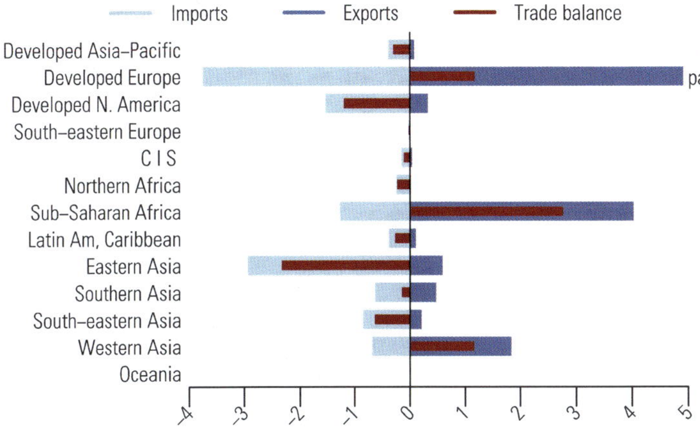

Graph 5: Partner concentration of merchandise trade

(Cumulative share by ranked partners in 2013)

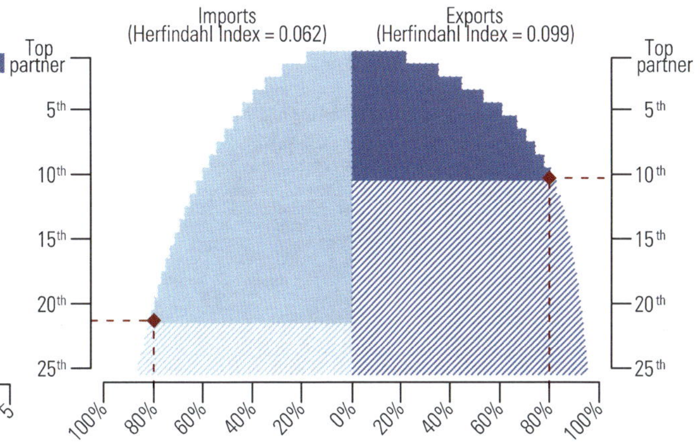

Graph 6: Imports of services by EBOPS category

(% share in 2014)

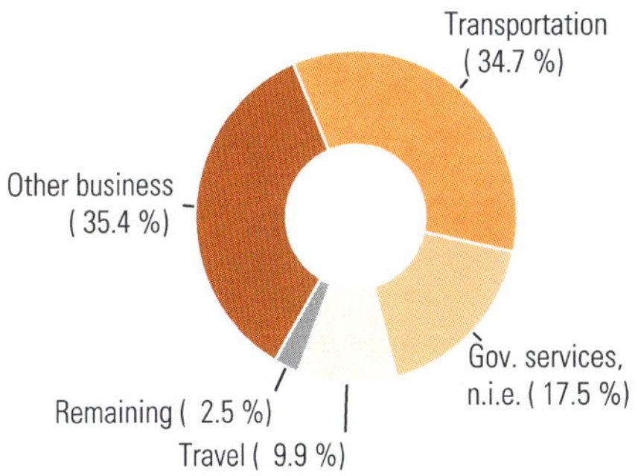

Imports Profile:

"Machinery and transport equipment" (SITC section 7), "Goods classified chiefly by material" (SITC section 6) and "Food, animals + beverages, tobacco" (SITC section 0+1) were the largest commodity groups for imports in 2013, representing respectively 39.5, 18.8 and 15.5 percent of imported goods (see table 3). From 2011 to 2013, the largest import commodity was "Motor cars and other motor vehicles principally designed for the transport" (HS code 8703) (see table 4). The top three partners for merchandise imports were China, the United States and Belgium, accounting for respectively 17.3, 10.6 and 6.8 percent of total imports. "Other business services" (EBOPS code 268) accounted for the largest share of imports of services in 2014 at 1.6 bln US$, followed by "Transportation" (EBOPS code 205) at 1.6 bln US$ and "Government services, n.i.e." (EBOPS code 291) at 813.7 mln US$ (see graph 6).

Table 4: Top 10 import commodities 2011 to 2013

HS code	4-digit heading of Harmonized System 2007	Value (million US$) 2011	Value (million US$) 2012	Value (million US$) 2013	Unit value 2011	Unit value 2012	Unit value 2013	Unit	SITC code
	All Commodities	12602.7	13578.1	12787.2					
8703	Motor cars and other motor vehicles principally designed for the transport	860.4	1070.9	1093.0		*19.7*	*19.2*	thsd US$/unit	781
8704	Motor vehicles for the transport of goods	628.0	802.7	612.2					782
2709	Petroleum oils and oils obtained from bituminous minerals, crude	787.7	430.7	308.7					333
1006	Rice	390.6	356.3	421.3	0.7	0.7	0.7	US$/kg	042
2523	Portland cement, aluminous cement, slag cement	308.0	353.6	303.5		0.1	0.1	US$/kg	661
3808	Insecticides, rodenticides, fungicides, herbicides	370.9	336.6	241.2	5.0	4.3	4.0	US$/kg	591
8517	Electrical apparatus for line telephony or line telegraphy	400.3	291.0	193.5					764
8429	Self-propelled bulldozers, angledozers, graders, levellers, scrapers	219.4	358.7	286.0	*62.1*			thsd US$/unit	723
0303	Fish, frozen, excluding fish fillets and other fish meat of heading 03.04	237.1	216.2	257.8	0.8	1.0	1.1	US$/kg	034
0207	Meat and edible offal, of the poultry of heading 01.05	178.1	188.0	200.4	1.1	1.2	1.2	US$/kg	012

Greece

Goods Imports: CIF, by origin/consignment for intra-eu **Goods Exports: FOB, by last known destination** **Trade System: Special**

Overview:

In 2015, the value of merchandise exports of Greece decreased substantially by 20.9 percent to reach 28.3 bln US$, while its merchandise imports decreased substantially by 24.0 percent to reach 47.3 bln US$ (see graph 1, table 2 and table 3). The merchandise trade balance recorded a moderate deficit of 19.0 bln US$ (see graph 1). The largest merchandise trade balance was with MDG Developed Europe at -10.5 bln US$ (see graph 4). Merchandise exports in Greece were diversified amongst partners; imports were also diversified. The top 27 partners accounted for 80 percent or more of exports and 19 partners accounted for 80 percent or more of imports (see graph 5). In 2014, the value of exports of services of Greece increased moderately by 6.5 percent, reaching 41.1 bln US$, while its imports of services increased substantially by 10.2 percent and reached 16.6 bln US$ (see graph 2). There was a large trade in services surplus of 24.4 bln US$.

Graph 1: Total merchandise trade, by value

(Bln US$ by year)

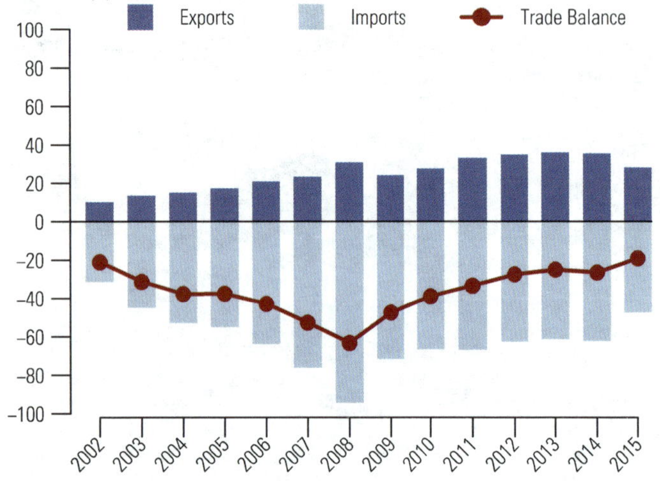

Graph 2: Total services trade, by value

(Bln US$ by year)

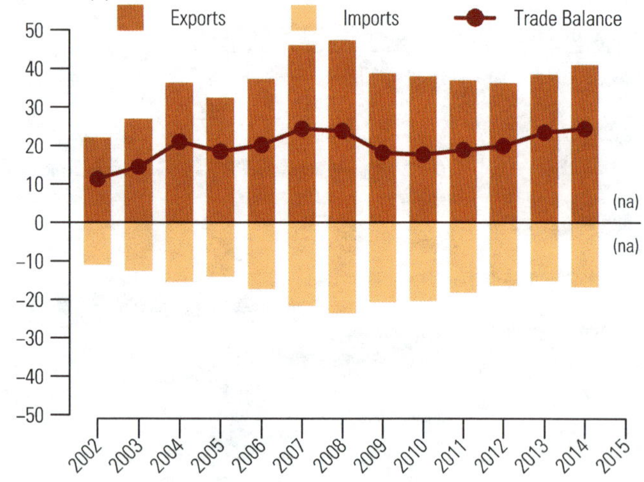

Exports Profile:

"Mineral fuels, lubricants" (SITC section 3), "Food, animals + beverages, tobacco" (SITC section 0+1) and "Goods classified chiefly by material" (SITC section 6) were the largest commodity groups for exports in 2015, representing respectively 29.8, 17.6 and 16.0 percent of exported goods (see table 2). From 2013 to 2015, the largest export commodity was "Petroleum oils, other than crude" (HS code 2710) (see table 1). The top three destinations for merchandise exports were Turkey, Italy and Germany, accounting for respectively 10.5, 9.7 and 6.7 percent of total exports. "Travel" (EBOPS code 236) accounted for the largest share of exports of services in 2014 at 17.8 bln US$, followed by "Transportation" (EBOPS code 205) at 17.4 bln US$ and "Other business services" (EBOPS code 268) at 2.2 bln US$ (see graph 3).

Graph 3: Exports of services by EBOPS category

(% share in 2014)

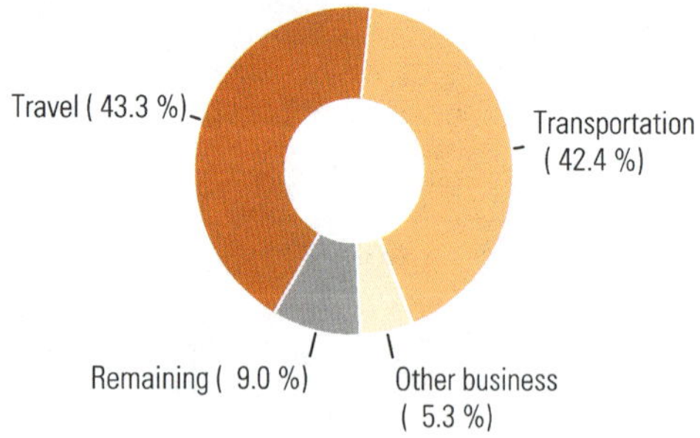

Table 1: Top 10 export commodities 2013 to 2015

HS code	4-digit heading of Harmonized System 2012	Value (million US$) 2013	2014	2015	Unit value 2013	2014	2015	Unit	SITC code
	All Commodities	36 261.6	35 755.4	28 289.2					
2710	Petroleum oils, other than crude	13 639.5	13 212.3	7 973.1	0.9	0.8	0.5	US$/kg	334
3004	Medicaments (excluding goods of heading 30.02, 30.05 or 30.06)	1 284.3	1 263.6	1 030.1	58.5	49.1	39.0	US$/kg	542
9999	Commodities not specified according to kind	699.4	724.0	631.5					931
7606	Aluminium plates, sheets and strip, of a thickness exceeding 0.2 mm	661.0	723.7	631.2	3.7	3.5	3.3	US$/kg	684
1509	Olive oil and its fractions	656.5	345.9	702.5	3.9	4.7	4.0	US$/kg	421
0302	Fish, fresh or chilled, excluding fish fillets	582.6	578.3	511.1	6.0	6.7	5.9	US$/kg	034
2005	Other vegetables prepared or preserved	449.0	467.1	433.5	3.0	3.5	2.6	US$/kg	056
0406	Cheese and curd	394.8	443.5	413.9	7.5	7.6	6.3	US$/kg	024
7411	Copper tubes and pipes	429.5	419.8	398.9	8.3	7.6	6.3	US$/kg	682
5201	Cotton, not carded or combed	492.1	410.0	326.6	1.9	1.7	1.5	US$/kg	263

Services Imports and Exports: EBOPS 2002 categories

Table 2: Merchandise exports by SITC

(Value in million US$, growth and shares in percentage)

SITC	2015	Avg. Growth rates 2011-2015	Avg. Growth rates 2014-2015	2015 share
Total	28 289.2	-4.1	-20.9	100.0
0+1	4 978.6	-2.8	-12.5	17.6
2+4	1 924.5	0.8	7.3	6.8
3	8 430.9	-4.9	-38.7	29.8
5	2 972.4	-3.1	-15.5	10.5
6	4 522.9	-6.5	-8.6	16.0
7	2 865.4	-2.0	-4.4	10.1
8	1 928.1	-4.5	-15.9	6.8
9	666.3	-8.4	-13.0	2.4

Table 3: Merchandise imports by SITC

(Value in million US$, growth and shares in percentage)

SITC	2015	Avg. Growth rates 2011-2015	Avg. Growth rates 2014-2015	2015 share
Total	47 264.0	-8.2	-24.0	100.0
0+1	6 122.6	-7.0	-16.2	13.0
2+4	1 490.8	-10.0	-21.9	3.2
3	12 600.5	-11.6	-41.0	26.7
5	7 378.9	-7.1	-14.3	15.6
6	5 162.1	-8.1	-16.7	10.9
7	9 474.2	-5.5	-13.8	20.0
8	4 920.4	-7.0	-14.9	10.4
9	114.6	46.0	303.4	0.2

SITC Legend

SITC Code	Description
Total	All commodities
0+1	Food, animals + beverages, tobacco
2+4	Crude materials + anim. & veg. oils
3	Mineral fuels, lubricants
5	Chemicals
6	Goods classified chiefly by material
7	Machinery and transport equipment
8	Miscellaneous manufactured articles
9	Not classified elsewhere in the SITC

Graph 4: Merchandise trade balance

(Bln US$ by MDG Regions in 2015)

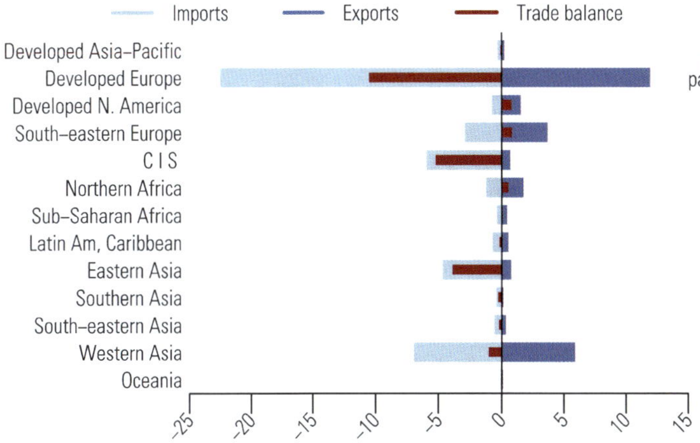

Graph 5: Partner concentration of merchandise trade

(Cumulative share by ranked partners in 2015)

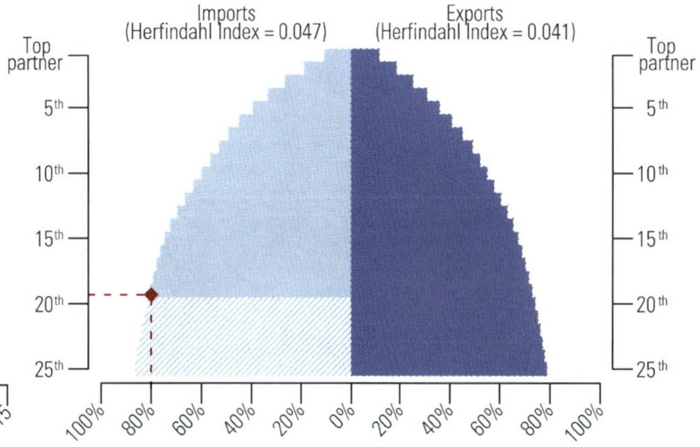

Graph 6: Imports of services by EBOPS category

(% share in 2014)

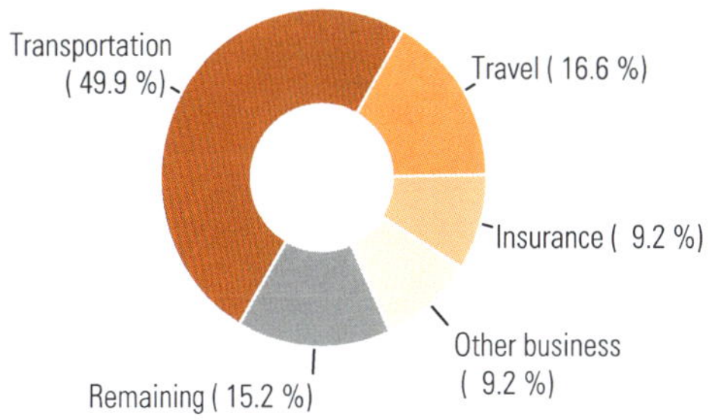

Imports Profile:

"Mineral fuels, lubricants" (SITC section 3), "Machinery and transport equipment" (SITC section 7) and "Chemicals" (SITC section 5) were the largest commodity groups for imports in 2015, representing respectively 26.7, 20.0 and 15.6 percent of imported goods (see table 3). From 2013 to 2015, the largest import commodity was "Petroleum oils and oils obtained from bituminous minerals, crude" (HS code 2709) (see table 4). The top three partners for merchandise imports were the Russian Federation, Germany and Iraq, accounting for respectively 11.1, 10.0 and 7.8 percent of total imports. "Transportation" (EBOPS code 205) accounted for the largest share of imports of services in 2014 at 8.3 bln US$, followed by "Travel" (EBOPS code 236) at 2.8 bln US$ and "Insurance services" (EBOPS code 253) at 1.5 bln US$ (see graph 6).

Table 4: Top 10 import commodities 2013 to 2015

HS code	4-digit heading of Harmonized System 2012	Value (million US$) 2013	Value (million US$) 2014	Value (million US$) 2015	Unit value 2013	Unit value 2014	Unit value 2015	Unit	SITC code
	All Commodities	61 148.1	62 180.6	47 264.0					
2709	Petroleum oils and oils obtained from bituminous minerals, crude	16 052.2	14 928.0	8 070.3	0.8	0.7	0.4	US$/kg	333
2710	Petroleum oils, other than crude	4 371.4	4 473.2	3 031.8	0.8	0.7	0.4	US$/kg	334
3004	Medicaments (excluding goods of heading 30.02, 30.05 or 30.06)	2 953.5	2 865.4	2 380.5	116.1	98.0	77.5	US$/kg	542
8901	Cruise ships, excursion boats, ferry-boats, cargo ships, barges	1 579.0	2 390.2	1 696.3	1.0	2.1	7.1	mln US$/unit	793
2711	Petroleum gases and other gaseous hydrocarbons	1 894.3	1 263.2	844.2	0.7	0.6	0.4	US$/kg	343
8703	Motor cars and other motor vehicles principally designed for the transport	787.1	1 117.3	1 023.5	7.6	6.5	7.5	thsd US$/unit	781
8517	Electrical apparatus for line telephony or line telegraphy	691.6	690.0	723.2					764
8471	Automatic data processing machines and units thereof	430.4	798.2	744.6	97.4	154.9	131.5	US$/unit	752
0203	Meat of swine, fresh, chilled or frozen	576.8	566.4	438.6	2.9	2.9	2.2	US$/kg	012
0406	Cheese and curd	568.9	578.7	430.6	5.0	4.9	3.6	US$/kg	024

Source: UN Comtrade

Greenland

Goods Imports: CIF, by origin	Goods Exports: FOB, by last known destination	Trade System: General

Overview:

In 2015, the value of merchandise exports of Greenland decreased substantially by 26.9 percent to reach 394.9 mln US$, while its merchandise imports decreased substantially by 23.7 percent to reach 586.2 mln US$ (see graph 1, table 2 and table 3). The merchandise trade balance recorded a moderate deficit of 191.3 mln US$ (see graph 1). The largest merchandise trade balance was with MDG Developed Europe at -168.0 mln US$ (see graph 4). Merchandise exports in Greenland were highly concentrated amongst partners; imports were also highly concentrated. The top 1 partner accounted for 80 percent or more of exports and 2 partners accounted for 80 percent or more of imports (see graph 5). In 2006, the value of exports of services of Greenland decreased moderately by 9.8 percent, reaching 203.0 mln US$, while its imports of services increased moderately by 6.4 percent and reached 315.1 mln US$ (see graph 2). There was a moderate trade in services deficit of 112.1 mln US$.

Graph 1: Total merchandise trade, by value

(Mln US$ by year)

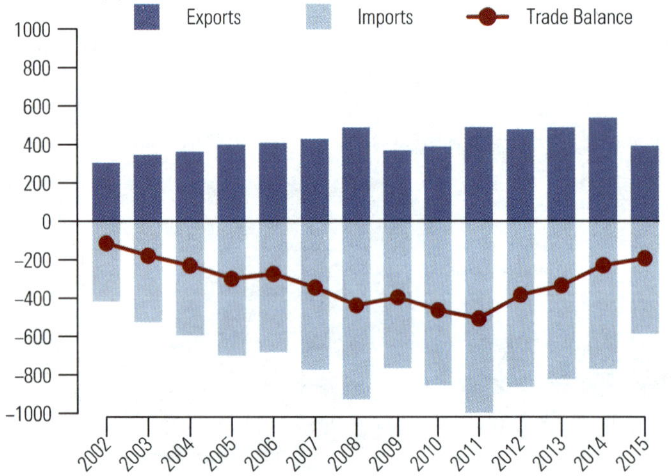

Graph 2: Total services trade, by value

(Mln US$ by year)

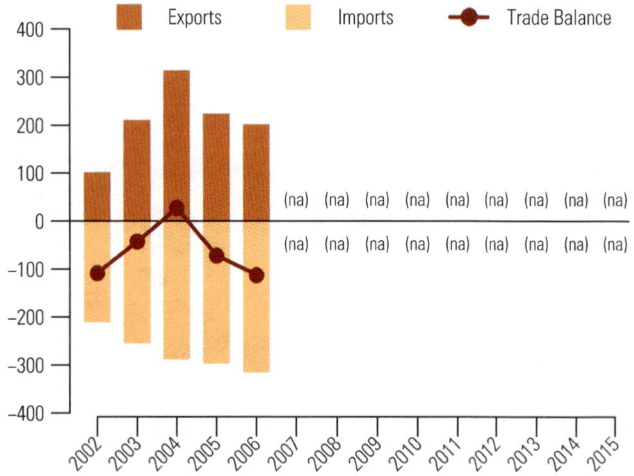

Exports Profile:

"Food, animals + beverages, tobacco" (SITC section 0+1), "Not classified elsewhere in the SITC" (SITC section 9) and "Miscellaneous manufactured articles" (SITC section 8) were the largest commodity groups for exports in 2015, representing respectively 89.7, 9.1 and 0.5 percent of exported goods (see table 2). From 2013 to 2015, the largest export commodity was "Fish, frozen, excluding fish fillets and other fish meat of heading 03.04" (HS code 0303) (see table 1). The top three destinations for merchandise exports were Denmark, Portugal and Areas nes, accounting for respectively 82.3, 5.6 and 5.0 percent of total exports. "Transportation" (EBOPS code 205) accounted for the largest share of exports of services in 2006 at 169.0 mln US$, followed by "Travel" (EBOPS code 236) at 13.5 mln US$ and "Communications services" (EBOPS code 245) at 11.7 mln US$ (see graph 3).

Graph 3: Exports of services by EBOPS category

(% share in 2006)

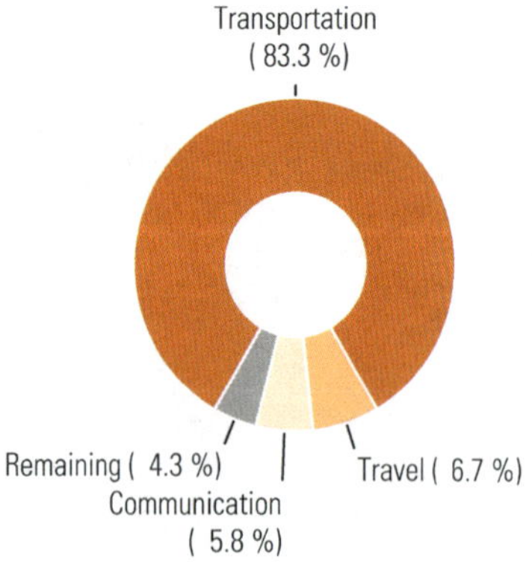

Table 1: Top 10 export commodities 2013 to 2015

HS code	4-digit heading of Harmonized System 2012	Value (million US$) 2013	2014	2015	Unit value 2013	2014	2015	Unit	SITC code
	All Commodities	490.1	540.5	394.9					
0303	Fish, frozen, excluding fish fillets and other fish meat of heading 03.04	128.9	203.2	131.6	1.8	1.8	2.0	US$/kg	034
0306	Crustaceans, whether in shell or not	120.2	133.5	100.7	3.2	3.4	3.3	US$/kg	036
1605	Crustaceans, molluscs and other aquatic invertebrates, prepared or preserved	120.4	114.0	72.5	6.4	7.0	6.3	US$/kg	037
9999	Commodities not specified according to kind	50.6	39.3	35.9					931
0304	Fish fillets and other fish meat (whether or not minced)	28.2	28.7	39.1	5.6	5.1	4.8	US$/kg	034
0305	Fish, dried, salted or in brine	14.1	9.8	7.1	7.5	5.3	4.6	US$/kg	035
7108	Gold (including gold plated with platinum)	12.2	0.0	...	38.9	15.0		thsd US$/kg	971
0302	Fish, fresh or chilled, excluding fish fillets	1.9	2.2	1.6					034
8902	Fishing vessels; factory ships and other vessels for processing	5.3	...	...					793
0307	Molluscs, whether in shell or not	1.3	1.8	1.2	9.2	12.0	10.2	US$/kg	036

Services Imports and Exports: EBOPS 2002 categories

Table 2: Merchandise exports by SITC

(Value in million US$, growth and shares in percentage)

SITC	2015	Avg. Growth rates 2011-2015	Avg. Growth rates 2014-2015	2015 share
Total	394.9	-5.3	-26.9	100.0
0+1	354.2	-4.1	-28.3	89.7
2+4	0.8	-14.7	-72.5	0.2
3	0.0	-8.4	380.7	0.0
5	0.0	-6.6	8.7	0.0
6	0.6	-28.4	-56.1	0.1
7	1.4	-45.6	-2.1	0.3
8	2.1	-0.7	14.0	0.5
9	35.9	-8.3	-8.7	9.1

Table 3: Merchandise imports by SITC

(Value in million US$, growth and shares in percentage)

SITC	2015	Avg. Growth rates 2011-2015	Avg. Growth rates 2014-2015	2015 share
Total	586.2	-12.4	-23.7	100.0
0+1	148.6	-4.7	-14.4	25.4
2+4	8.4	-6.1	-20.3	1.4
3	53.4	-30.2	-66.7	9.1
5	49.0	-2.2	-10.6	8.4
6	90.1	-7.3	-7.7	15.4
7	141.4	-16.1	-9.5	24.1
8	70.7	-7.7	-19.2	12.1
9	24.5	1.9	-11.4	4.2

SITC Legend

SITC Code	Description
Total	All commodities
0+1	Food, animals + beverages, tobacco
2+4	Crude materials + anim. & veg. oils
3	Mineral fuels, lubricants
5	Chemicals
6	Goods classified chiefly by material
7	Machinery and transport equipment
8	Miscellaneous manufactured articles
9	Not classified elsewhere in the SITC

Graph 4: Merchandise trade balance

(Mln US$ by MDG Regions in 2015)

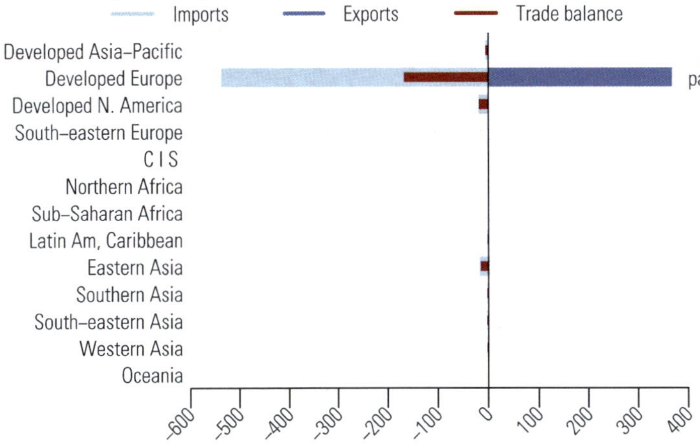

Graph 5: Partner concentration of merchandise trade

(Cumulative share by ranked partners in 2015)

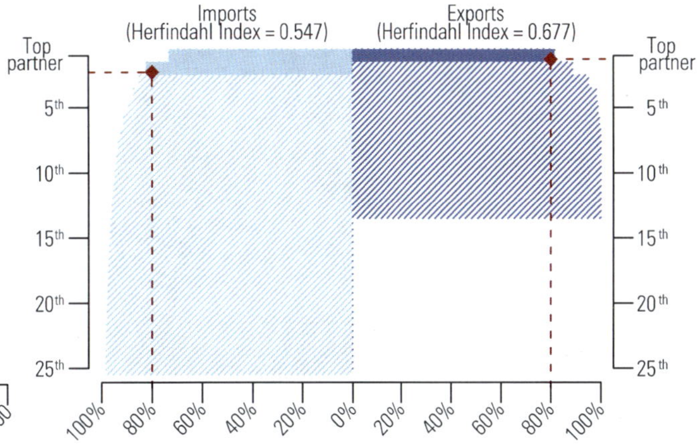

Graph 6: Imports of services by EBOPS category

(% share in 2006)

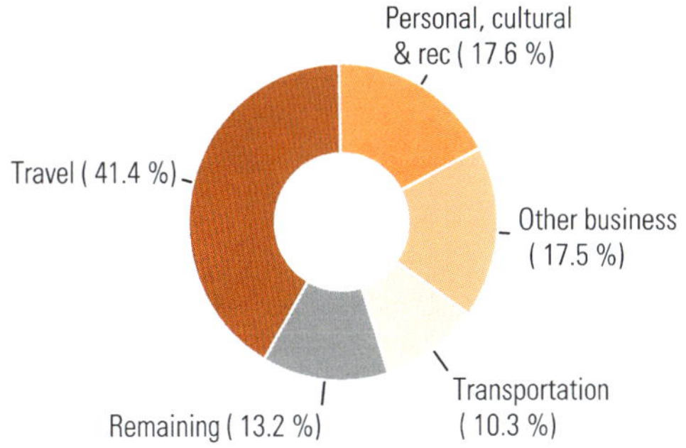

Imports Profile:

"Food, animals + beverages, tobacco" (SITC section 0+1), "Machinery and transport equipment" (SITC section 7) and "Goods classified chiefly by material" (SITC section 6) were the largest commodity groups for imports in 2015, representing respectively 25.4, 24.1 and 15.4 percent of imported goods (see table 3). From 2013 to 2015, the largest import commodity was "Petroleum oils, other than crude" (HS code 2710) (see table 4). The top three partners for merchandise imports were Denmark, Sweden and China, accounting for respectively 66.4, 18.6 and 2.6 percent of total imports. "Travel" (EBOPS code 236) accounted for the largest share of imports of services in 2006 at 130.4 mln US$, followed by "Personal, cultural, and recreational services" (EBOPS code 287) at 55.5 mln US$ and "Other business services" (EBOPS code 268) at 55.1 mln US$ (see graph 6).

Table 4: Top 10 import commodities 2013 to 2015

HS code	4-digit heading of Harmonized System 2012	Value (million US$) 2013	2014	2015	Unit value 2013	2014	2015	Unit	SITC code
	All Commodities	822.1	768.3	586.2					
2710	Petroleum oils, other than crude	195.5	159.4	51.7	1.1	1.0	0.7	US$/kg	334
9999	Commodities not specified according to kind	27.8	27.7	24.5					931
3004	Medicaments (excluding goods of heading 30.02, 30.05 or 30.06)	17.7	17.8	17.2	63.8	63.6	46.7	US$/kg	542
8803	Parts of goods of heading 88.01 or 88.02	13.0	14.5	17.1	438.4	486.3	699.5	US$/kg	792
8517	Electrical apparatus for line telephony or line telegraphy	14.6	12.0	10.6					764
1905	Bread, pastry, cakes, biscuits and other bakers'wares	12.8	12.9	10.9	5.8	5.8	4.9	US$/kg	048
9403	Other furniture and parts thereof	13.6	11.8	8.5					821
8429	Self-propelled bulldozers, angledozers, graders, levellers, scrapers	5.8	9.8	11.3	*74.8*	*74.6*	134.0	thsd US$/unit	723
0203	Meat of swine, fresh, chilled or frozen	8.8	9.2	8.1	6.3	6.5	5.5	US$/kg	012
7324	Sanitary ware and parts thereof, of iron or steel	9.1	9.0	7.2	12.8	10.6	9.5	US$/kg	697

Source: UN Comtrade

Guatemala

Goods Imports: CIF, by origin | **Goods Exports: FOB, by last known destination** | **Trade System: General**

Overview:

In 2015, the value of merchandise exports of Guatemala decreased slightly by 0.9 percent to reach 10.8 bln US$, while its merchandise imports decreased slightly by 3.5 percent to reach 17.6 bln US$ (see graph 1, table 2 and table 3). The merchandise trade balance recorded a moderate deficit of 6.8 bln US$ (see graph 1). The largest merchandise trade balance was with MDG Developed North America at -2.5 bln US$ (see graph 4). Merchandise exports in Guatemala were moderately concentrated amongst partners; imports were also moderately concentrated. The top 12 partners accounted for 80 percent or more of exports and 11 partners accounted for 80 percent or more of imports (see graph 5). In 2014, the value of exports of services of Guatemala increased moderately by 8.1 percent, reaching 2.7 bln US$, while its imports of services increased substantially by 10.1 percent and reached 2.9 bln US$ (see graph 2). There was a relatively small trade in services deficit of 138.8 mln US$.

Graph 1: Total merchandise trade, by value
(Bln US$ by year)

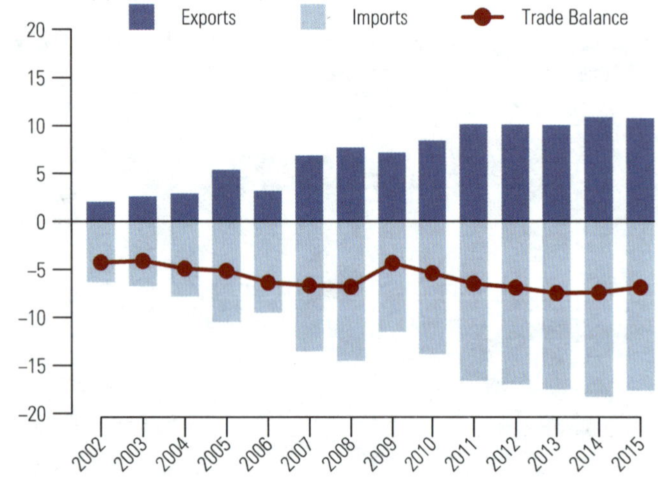

Graph 2: Total services trade, by value
(Bln US$ by year)

Exports Profile:

"Food, animals + beverages, tobacco" (SITC section 0+1), "Miscellaneous manufactured articles" (SITC section 8) and "Crude materials + anim. & veg. oils" (SITC section 2+4) were the largest commodity groups for exports in 2015, representing respectively 39.7, 16.8 and 13.5 percent of exported goods (see table 2). From 2013 to 2015, the largest export commodity was "Cane or beet sugar and chemically pure sucrose, in solid form" (HS code 1701) (see table 1). The top three destinations for merchandise exports were the United States, El Salvador and Honduras, accounting for respectively 36.8, 11.4 and 8.1 percent of total exports. "Travel" (EBOPS code 236) accounted for the largest share of exports of services in 2014 at 1.6 bln US$, followed by "Transportation" (EBOPS code 205) at 383.3 mln US$ and "Communications services" (EBOPS code 245) at 343.0 mln US$ (see graph 3).

Graph 3: Exports of services by EBOPS category
(% share in 2014)

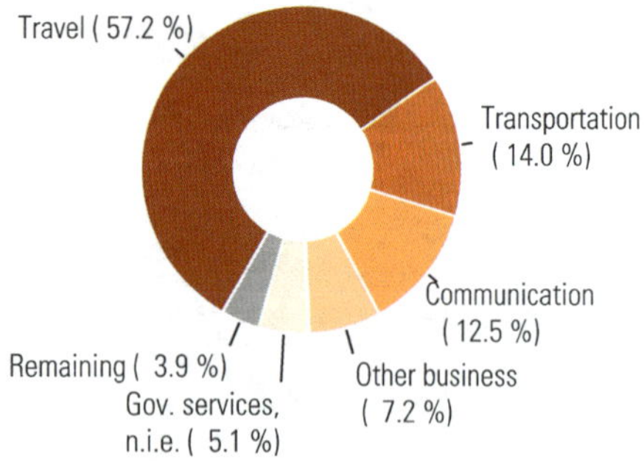

Table 1: Top 10 export commodities 2013 to 2015

HS code	4-digit heading of Harmonized System 2012	Value (million US$) 2013	2014	2015	Unit value 2013	2014	2015	Unit	SITC code
	All Commodities	10065.3	10890.7	10797.0					
1701	Cane or beet sugar and chemically pure sucrose, in solid form	941.9	952.2	852.0	0.5	0.4	0.4	US$/kg	061
0803	Bananas, including plantains, fresh or dried	652.0	721.4	833.9	0.3	0.3	0.3	US$/kg	057
0901	Coffee, whether or not roasted or decaffeinated	716.0	668.0	664.5	3.3	3.6	3.6	US$/kg	071
6106	Women's or girls'blouses, shirts and shirt-blouses, knitted or crocheted	457.8	419.9	396.5	*8.2*	*7.4*	*7.8*	US$/unit	844
2616	Precious metal ores and concentrates	448.5	359.3	310.9	1.8	1.3	0.2	thsd US$/kg	289
1511	Palm oil and its fractions	269.8	288.2	282.6	0.7	0.7	0.6	US$/kg	422
6105	Men's or boys'shirts, knitted or crocheted	264.2	263.7	275.0	*10.3*			US$/unit	843
3004	Medicaments (excluding goods of heading 30.02, 30.05 or 30.06)	229.7	256.0	304.3	30.9	*35.9*	41.7	US$/kg	542
0908	Nutmeg, mace and cardamoms	217.5	240.6	243.5	5.6	6.2	7.3	US$/kg	075
2607	Lead ores and concentrates	30.7	349.3	306.2	15.8	14.3	11.5	US$/kg	287

Services Imports and Exports: EBOPS 2002 categories

Table 2: Merchandise exports by SITC

(Value in million US$, growth and shares in percentage)

SITC	2015	Avg. Growth rates 2011-2015	Avg. Growth rates 2014-2015	2015 share
Total	10797.0	1.5	-0.9	100.0
0+1	4284.4	3.2	1.6	39.7
2+4	1454.3	-5.8	-10.6	13.5
3	439.8	-3.9	-38.3	4.1
5	1285.5	4.5	4.3	11.9
6	1203.5	4.0	13.6	11.1
7	270.1	0.8	16.0	2.5
8	1814.7	2.7	3.8	16.8
9	44.8	9.8	-28.3	0.4

Table 3: Merchandise imports by SITC

(Value in million US$, growth and shares in percentage)

SITC	2015	Avg. Growth rates 2011-2015	Avg. Growth rates 2014-2015	2015 share
Total	17631.1	1.5	-3.5	100.0
0+1	2329.6	4.7	2.8	13.2
2+4	471.3	-4.3	-5.0	2.7
3	2511.7	-6.7	-29.5	14.2
5	3219.7	3.5	2.9	18.3
6	3305.1	0.9	3.3	18.7
7	4284.2	4.8	4.7	24.3
8	1482.6	4.9	0.4	8.4
9	26.8	17.8	-35.4	0.2

SITC Legend

SITC Code	Description
Total	All commodities
0+1	Food, animals + beverages, tobacco
2+4	Crude materials + anim. & veg. oils
3	Mineral fuels, lubricants
5	Chemicals
6	Goods classified chiefly by material
7	Machinery and transport equipment
8	Miscellaneous manufactured articles
9	Not classified elsewhere in the SITC

Graph 4: Merchandise trade balance

(Bln US$ by MDG Regions in 2015)

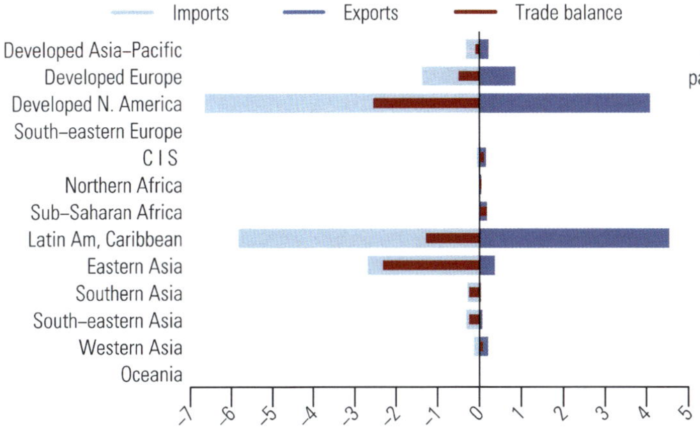

Graph 5: Partner concentration of merchandise trade

(Cumulative share by ranked partners in 2015)

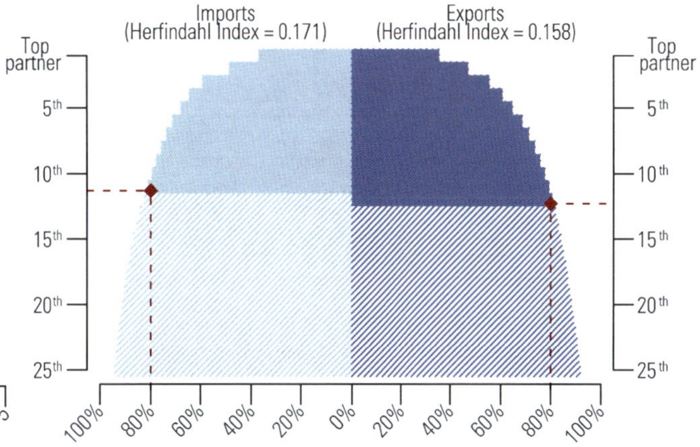

Graph 6: Imports of services by EBOPS category

(% share in 2014)

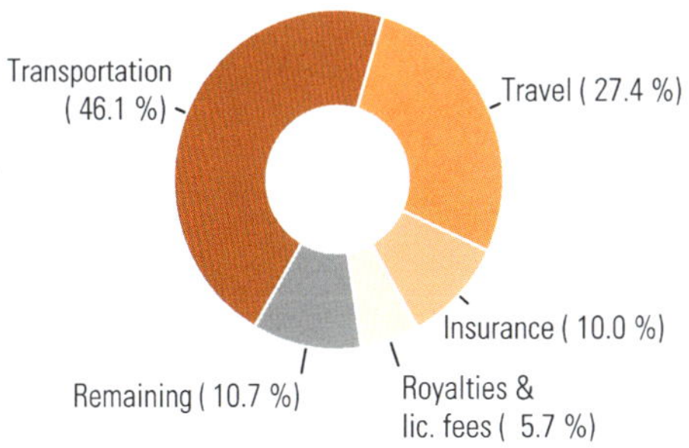

Imports Profile:

"Machinery and transport equipment" (SITC section 7), "Goods classified chiefly by material" (SITC section 6) and "Chemicals" (SITC section 5) were the largest commodity groups for imports in 2015, representing respectively 24.3, 18.7 and 18.3 percent of imported goods (see table 3). From 2013 to 2015, the largest import commodity was "Petroleum oils, other than crude" (HS code 2710) (see table 4). The top three partners for merchandise imports were the United States, Mexico and China, accounting for respectively 38.2, 11.0 and 9.6 percent of total imports. "Transportation" (EBOPS code 205) accounted for the largest share of imports of services in 2014 at 1.3 bln US$, followed by "Travel" (EBOPS code 236) at 788.3 mln US$ and "Insurance services" (EBOPS code 253) at 287.8 mln US$ (see graph 6).

Table 4: Top 10 import commodities 2013 to 2015

HS code	4-digit heading of Harmonized System 2012	Value (million US$) 2013	Value (million US$) 2014	Value (million US$) 2015	Unit value 2013	Unit value 2014	Unit value 2015	Unit	SITC code
	All Commodities	17504.0	18263.2	17631.1					
2710	Petroleum oils, other than crude	2868.1	2970.8	2017.6	0.9	*0.9*	0.5	US$/kg	334
3004	Medicaments (excluding goods of heading 30.02, 30.05 or 30.06)	470.8	501.5	568.6	19.8	19.8	21.2	US$/kg	542
8517	Electrical apparatus for line telephony or line telegraphy	472.9	484.6	548.0					764
8703	Motor cars and other motor vehicles principally designed for the transport	392.7	458.2	545.0	*18.3*	*17.9*	*19.8*	thsd US$/unit	781
2711	Petroleum gases and other gaseous hydrocarbons	297.4	334.7	236.6	0.7	0.8	0.5	US$/kg	343
8704	Motor vehicles for the transport of goods	247.4	265.5	311.9					782
3901	Polymers of ethylene, in primary forms	193.6	226.6	211.5	1.6	1.8	1.5	US$/kg	571
1005	Maize (corn)	205.8	212.6	212.9	0.3	0.2	0.2	US$/kg	044
8471	Automatic data processing machines and units thereof	197.7	193.3	178.3					752
6006	Other knitted or crocheted fabrics	179.6	189.6	199.8	7.9	7.5	6.7	US$/kg	655

Guinea

Goods Imports: CIF, by origin | **Goods Exports: FOB, by last known destination** | **Trade System: Special**

Overview:

In 2015, the value of merchandise exports of Guinea decreased substantially by 19.2 percent to reach 1.6 bln US$, while its merchandise imports decreased substantially by 14.8 percent to reach 2.1 bln US$ (see graph 1, table 2 and table 3). The merchandise trade balance recorded a moderate deficit of 565.0 mln US$ (see graph 1). The largest merchandise trade balance was with MDG Eastern Asia at -317.9 mln US$ (see graph 4). Merchandise exports in Guinea were diversified amongst partners; imports were also diversified. The top 8 partners accounted for 80 percent or more of exports and 16 partners accounted for 80 percent or more of imports (see graph 5). In 2013, the value of exports of services of Guinea decreased substantially by 34.9 percent, reaching 103.5 mln US$, while its imports of services decreased substantially by 21.3 percent and reached 694.4 mln US$ (see graph 2). There was a large trade in services deficit of 590.9 mln US$.

Graph 1: Total merchandise trade, by value

(Bln US$ by year)

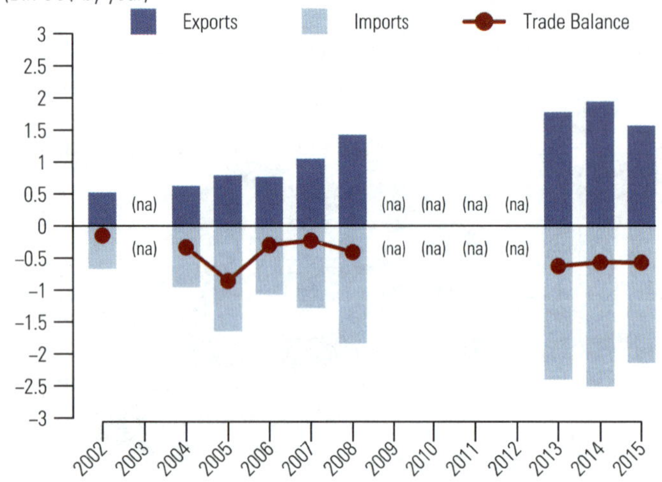

Graph 2: Total services trade, by value

(Mln US$ by year)

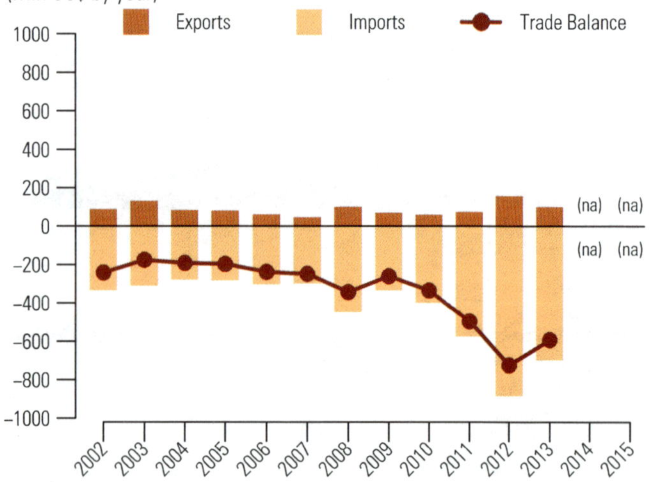

Exports Profile:

"Not classified elsewhere in the SITC" (SITC section 9), "Crude materials + anim. & veg. oils" (SITC section 2+4) and "Miscellaneous manufactured articles" (SITC section 8) were the largest commodity groups for exports in 2015, representing respectively 40.3, 38.9 and 8.5 percent of exported goods (see table 2). From 2013 to 2015, the largest export commodity was "Gold (including gold plated with platinum)" (HS code 7108) (see table 1). The top three destinations for merchandise exports were Ghana, France and the United Arab Emirates, accounting for respectively 14.6, 13.4 and 13.1 percent of total exports. "Communications services" (EBOPS code 245) accounted for the largest share of exports of services in 2013 at 63.6 mln US$, followed by "Personal, cultural, and recreational services" (EBOPS code 287) at 12.2 mln US$ and "Transportation" (EBOPS code 205) at 9.8 mln US$ (see graph 3).

Graph 3: Exports of services by EBOPS category

(% share in 2013)

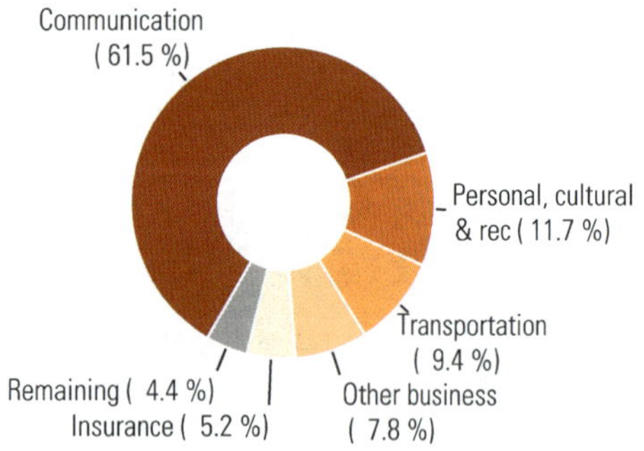

Table 1: Top 10 export commodities 2013 to 2015

HS code	4-digit heading of Harmonized System 2012	Value (million US$) 2013	2014	2015	Unit value 2013	2014	2015	Unit	SITC code
	All Commodities	1780.5	1946.7	1573.7					
7108	Gold (including gold plated with platinum)	942.3	973.7	631.5					971
2606	Aluminium ores and concentrates	432.5	587.6	576.3	0.0	0.0	0.0	US$/kg	285
4907	Unused postage, revenue or similar stamps of current or new issue	201.0	187.7	119.5	85.5	59.0	76.6	thsd US$/kg	892
8905	Light-vessels, fire-floats, dredgers, floating cranes and other vessels	...	...	81.0					793
4001	Natural rubber, balata, gutta-percha, guayule, chicle	21.4	26.4	26.0	1.8	1.9	1.6	US$/kg	231
0801	Coconuts, Brazil nuts and cashew nuts, fresh or dried	9.6	25.5	20.6		1.8	1.2	US$/kg	057
2601	Iron ores and concentrates, including roasted iron pyrites	26.7	11.6	0.0	0.1	0.1		US$/kg	281
7102	Diamonds, whether or not worked, but not mounted or set	5.5	27.8	...					667
8429	Self-propelled bulldozers, angledozers, graders, levellers, scrapers	24.4	1.6	2.0					723
1801	Cocoa beans, whole or broken, raw or roasted	2.2	5.6	18.9					072

Services Imports and Exports: EBOPS 2002 categories

Table 2: Merchandise exports by SITC

(Value in million US$, growth and shares in percentage)

SITC	2015	Avg. Growth rates 2011-2015	Avg. Growth rates 2014-2015	2015 share
Total	1 573.7	...	-19.2	100.0
0+1	68.8	...	20.5	4.4
2+4	611.5	...	-3.9	38.9
3	3.4	...	-67.7	0.2
5	3.0	...	50.0	0.2
6	2.8	...	-90.5	0.2
7	115.9	...	282.3	7.4
8	134.2	...	-34.4	8.5
9	634.0	...	-35.1	40.3

Table 3: Merchandise imports by SITC

(Value in million US$, growth and shares in percentage)

SITC	2015	Avg. Growth rates 2011-2015	Avg. Growth rates 2014-2015	2015 share
Total	2 138.6	...	-14.8	100.0
0+1	455.8	...	-23.4	21.3
2+4	85.8	...	41.5	4.0
3	322.7	...	-59.3	15.1
5	231.1	...	10.3	10.8
6	261.4	...	2.5	12.2
7	643.8	...	37.1	30.1
8	126.0	...	9.5	5.9
9	12.0	...	8.2	0.6

SITC Legend

SITC Code	Description
Total	All commodities
0+1	Food, animals + beverages, tobacco
2+4	Crude materials + anim. & veg. oils
3	Mineral fuels, lubricants
5	Chemicals
6	Goods classified chiefly by material
7	Machinery and transport equipment
8	Miscellaneous manufactured articles
9	Not classified elsewhere in the SITC

Graph 4: Merchandise trade balance

(Mln US$ by MDG Regions in 2015)

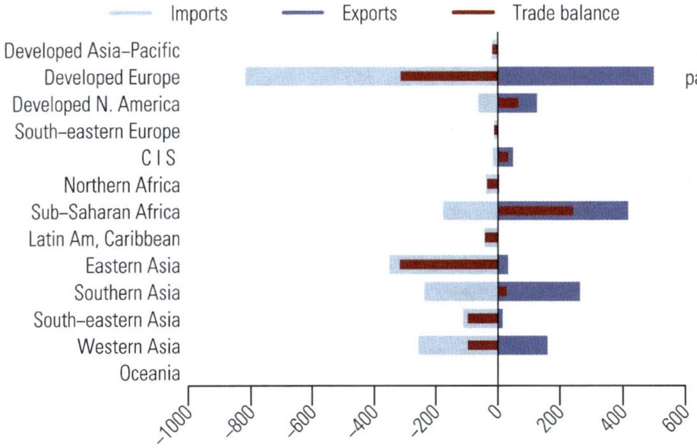

Graph 5: Partner concentration of merchandise trade

(Cumulative share by ranked partners in 2015)

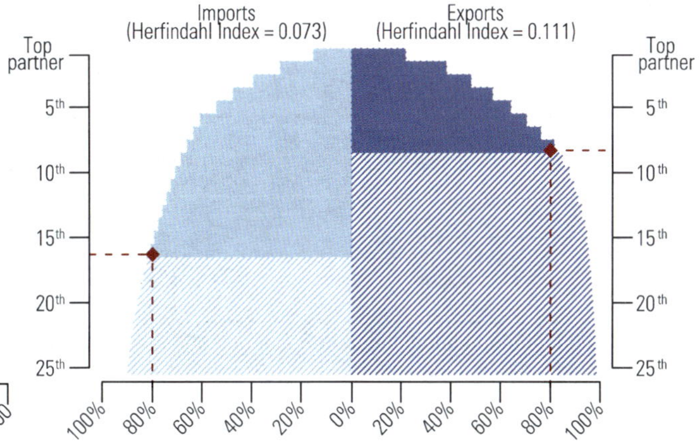

Graph 6: Imports of services by EBOPS category

(% share in 2013)

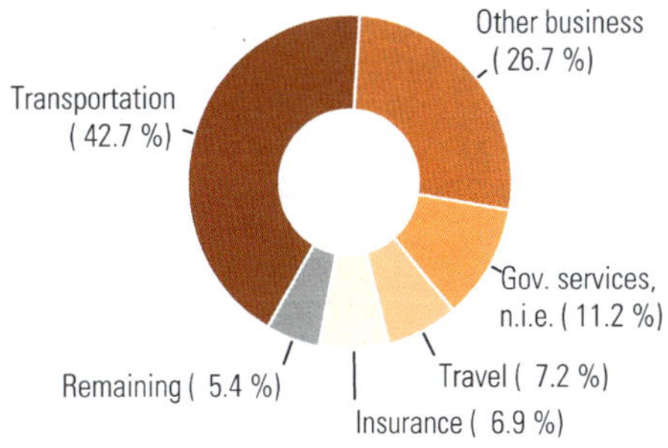

Imports Profile:

"Machinery and transport equipment" (SITC section 7), "Food, animals + beverages, tobacco" (SITC section 0+1) and "Mineral fuels, lubricants" (SITC section 3) were the largest commodity groups for imports in 2015, representing respectively 30.1, 21.3 and 15.1 percent of imported goods (see table 3). From 2013 to 2015, the largest import commodity was "Petroleum oils, other than crude" (HS code 2710) (see table 4). The top three partners for merchandise imports were the Netherlands, China and India, accounting for respectively 25.4, 13.5 and 9.3 percent of total imports. "Transportation" (EBOPS code 205) accounted for the largest share of imports of services in 2013 at 296.4 mln US$, followed by "Other business services" (EBOPS code 268) at 185.1 mln US$ and "Government services, n.i.e." (EBOPS code 291) at 77.9 mln US$ (see graph 6).

Table 4: Top 10 import commodities 2013 to 2015

HS code	4-digit heading of Harmonized System 2012	Value (million US$) 2013	Value (million US$) 2014	Value (million US$) 2015	Unit value 2013	Unit value 2014	Unit value 2015	Unit	SITC code
	All Commodities	2 401.0	2 509.2	2 138.6					
2710	Petroleum oils, other than crude	725.5	783.6	310.2	0.8	0.8	0.5	US$/kg	334
1006	Rice	239.5	286.4	227.9	0.5	0.5	0.4	US$/kg	042
3004	Medicaments (excluding goods of heading 30.02, 30.05 or 30.06)	73.1	84.3	117.1			8.3	US$/kg	542
1101	Wheat or meslin flour	75.0	78.2	20.3	0.4	0.4	0.4	US$/kg	046
8431	Parts suitable for use principally with the machinery of headings 84.25	64.2	52.6	35.3	15.7	14.4	9.1	US$/kg	723
8703	Motor cars and other motor vehicles principally designed for the transport	34.6	43.1	67.3	*19.6*	*19.3*	*22.6*	thsd US$/unit	781
1701	Cane or beet sugar and chemically pure sucrose, in solid form	37.5	58.9	47.6	0.3	0.4	0.4	US$/kg	061
2402	Cigars, cheroots, cigarillos and cigarettes	39.2	39.0	34.7	3.6	3.8	4.2	US$/kg	122
2523	Portland cement, aluminous cement, slag cement	55.5	27.2	27.3	0.1			US$/kg	661
1511	Palm oil and its fractions	33.0	35.6	40.0	0.6	0.5	0.5	US$/kg	422

Goods Imports: CIF, by origin | **Goods Exports: FOB, by last known destination** | **Trade System: Special**

Overview:

In 2015, the value of merchandise exports of Guyana increased moderately by 9.5 percent to reach 1.3 bln US$, while its merchandise imports increased substantially by 22.6 percent to reach 2.2 bln US$ (see graph 1, table 2 and table 3). The merchandise trade balance recorded a moderate deficit of 899.9 mln US$ (see graph 1). The largest merchandise trade balance was with MDG Eastern Asia at -801.8 mln US$ (see graph 4). Merchandise exports in Guyana were diversified amongst partners; imports were moderately concentrated. The top 11 partners accounted for 80 percent or more of exports and 9 partners accounted for 80 percent or more of imports (see graph 5). In 2014, the value of exports of services of Guyana increased moderately by 9.8 percent, reaching 180.8 mln US$, while its imports of services decreased substantially by 14.8 percent and reached 426.2 mln US$ (see graph 2). There was a large trade in services deficit of 245.4 mln US$.

Graph 1: Total merchandise trade, by value

(Bln US$ by year)

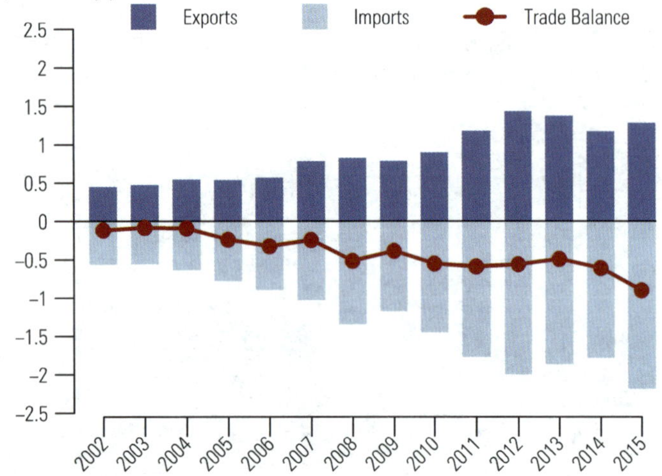

Graph 2: Total services trade, by value

(Mln US$ by year)

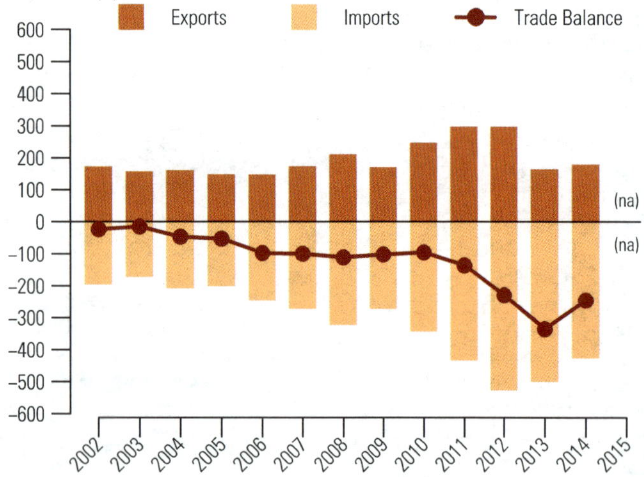

Exports Profile:

"Food, animals + beverages, tobacco" (SITC section 0+1), "Not classified elsewhere in the SITC" (SITC section 9) and "Machinery and transport equipment" (SITC section 7) were the largest commodity groups for exports in 2015, representing respectively 38.6, 27.8 and 14.7 percent of exported goods (see table 2). From 2013 to 2015, the largest export commodity was "Gold (including gold plated with platinum)" (HS code 7108) (see table 1). The top three destinations for merchandise exports were the United States, Canada and the Bolivarian Republic of Venezuela, accounting for respectively 25.4, 21.8 and 8.5 percent of total exports. "Travel" (EBOPS code 236) accounted for the largest share of exports of services in 2014 at 78.7 mln US$, followed by "Other business services" (EBOPS code 268) at 38.3 mln US$ and "Transportation" (EBOPS code 205) at 25.5 mln US$ (see graph 3).

Graph 3: Exports of services by EBOPS category

(% share in 2014)

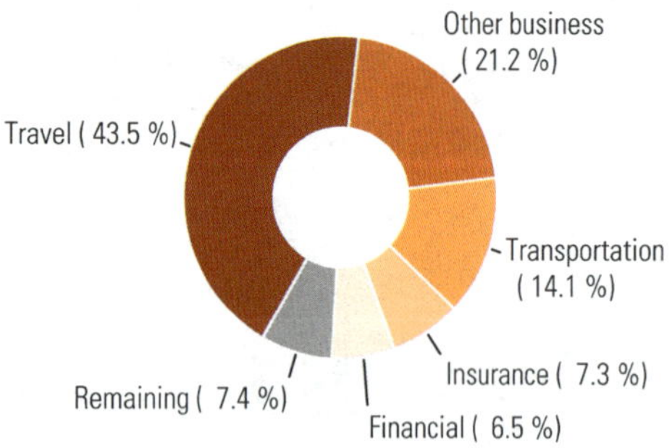

Table 1: Top 10 export commodities 2013 to 2015

HS code	4-digit heading of Harmonized System 2007	Value (million US$) 2013	2014	2015	Unit value 2013	2014	2015	Unit	SITC code
	All Commodities	1 375.9	1 174.0	1 285.8					
7108	Gold (including gold plated with platinum)	644.2	471.1	357.9	42.9	39.3	18.9	thsd US$/kg	971
1006	Rice	239.0	247.4	212.0	0.6	0.5	0.2	US$/kg	042
2606	Aluminium ores and concentrates	133.4	123.4	138.4	0.1	0.1	0.2	US$/kg	285
1701	Cane or beet sugar and chemically pure sucrose, in solid form	114.2	87.8	111.7	0.7	0.5	0.3	US$/kg	061
0306	Crustaceans, whether in shell or not	53.3	33.2	42.8	3.7	3.9	4.4	US$/kg	036
8609	Containers (including containers for the transport of fluids)	...	0.0	126.1		0.2	*1.7*	thsd US$/unit	786
2208	Alcohol of a strength by volume of less than 80 % vol	42.9	41.7	36.5	2.1	*3.9*		US$/litre	112
0302	Fish, fresh or chilled, excluding fish fillets	13.1	14.8	16.0	2.3	2.4	2.5	US$/kg	034
7102	Diamonds, whether or not worked, but not mounted or set	11.8	14.7	16.8	180.0	161.9	154.0	US$/carat	667
4404	Hoopwood; split poles; piles, pickets and stakes of wood	8.7	16.9	17.2	0.2			US$/kg	634

Services Imports and Exports: EBOPS 2002 categories

Table 2: Merchandise exports by SITC

(Value in million US$, growth and shares in percentage)

SITC	2015	Avg. Growth rates 2011-2015	Avg. Growth rates 2014-2015	2015 share
Total	1 285.8	2.2	9.5	100.0
0+1	496.7	3.9	3.4	38.6
2+4	170.1	-1.2	3.2	13.2
3	0.1	150.2	2120.6	0.0
5	13.1	28.4	103.1	1.0
6	54.3	16.6	36.7	4.2
7	189.0	100.8	3706.7	14.7
8	4.6	-23.3	-27.6	0.4
9	357.9	-8.7	-24.0	27.8

Table 3: Merchandise imports by SITC

(Value in million US$, growth and shares in percentage)

SITC	2015	Avg. Growth rates 2011-2015	Avg. Growth rates 2014-2015	2015 share
Total	2 185.7	5.4	22.6	100.0
0+1	237.6	0.7	-2.2	10.9
2+4	31.3	4.1	2.5	1.4
3	312.4	-14.4	-46.3	14.3
5	154.7	-1.3	5.3	7.1
6	219.8	3.4	1.3	10.1
7	1 115.9	24.6	159.0	51.1
8	114.0	1.0	-14.2	5.2
9	0.0	-4.4	-66.7	0.0

SITC Legend

SITC Code	Description
Total	All commodities
0+1	Food, animals + beverages, tobacco
2+4	Crude materials + anim. & veg. oils
3	Mineral fuels, lubricants
5	Chemicals
6	Goods classified chiefly by material
7	Machinery and transport equipment
8	Miscellaneous manufactured articles
9	Not classified elsewhere in the SITC

Graph 4: Merchandise trade balance

(Mln US$ by MDG Regions in 2015)

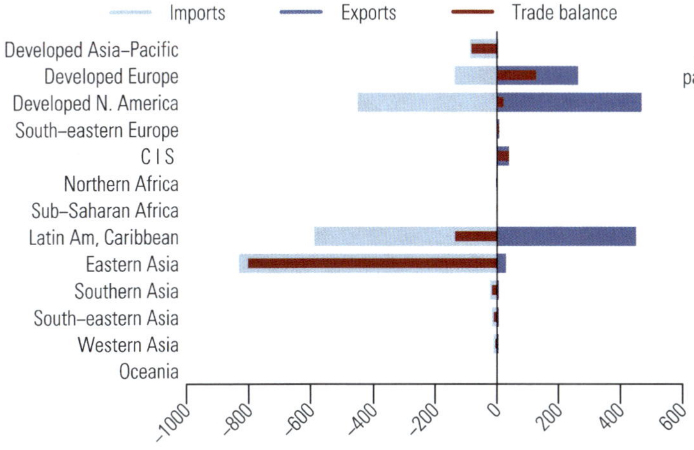

Graph 5: Partner concentration of merchandise trade

(Cumulative share by ranked partners in 2015)

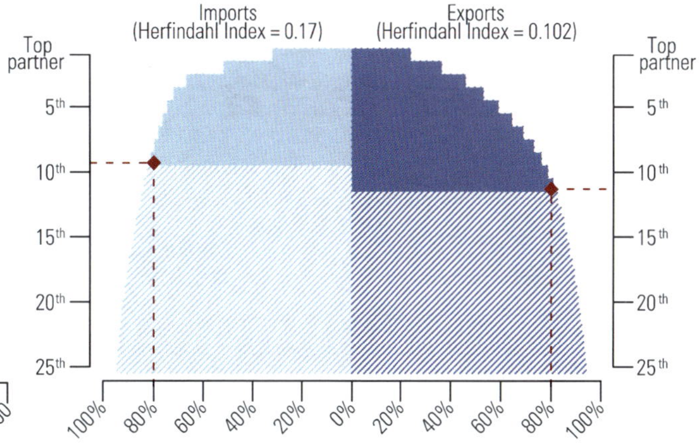

Graph 6: Imports of services by EBOPS category

(% share in 2014)

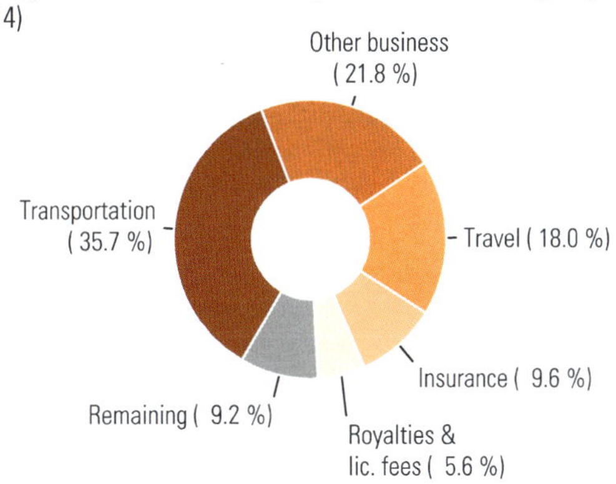

Imports Profile:

"Machinery and transport equipment" (SITC section 7), "Mineral fuels, lubricants" (SITC section 3) and "Food, animals + beverages, tobacco" (SITC section 0+1) were the largest commodity groups for imports in 2015, representing respectively 51.1, 14.3 and 10.9 percent of imported goods (see table 3). From 2013 to 2015, the largest import commodity was "Petroleum oils, other than crude" (HS code 2710) (see table 4). The top three partners for merchandise imports were the United States, Trinidad and Tobago and the Republic of Korea, accounting for respectively 21.6, 18.3 and 12.5 percent of total imports. "Transportation" (EBOPS code 205) accounted for the largest share of imports of services in 2014 at 152.3 mln US$, followed by "Other business services" (EBOPS code 268) at 92.7 mln US$ and "Travel" (EBOPS code 236) at 76.9 mln US$ (see graph 6).

Table 4: Top 10 import commodities 2013 to 2015

HS code	4-digit heading of Harmonized System 2007	Value (million US$) 2013	2014	2015	Unit value 2013	2014	2015	Unit	SITC code
	All Commodities	1 866.3	1 783.3	2 185.7					
2710	Petroleum oils, other than crude	561.1	555.6	297.2	0.7	0.8	1.4	US$/kg	334
8430	Other moving, grading, levelling, scraping, excavating, tamping, compacting	1.7	2.7	694.2		21.8		thsd US$/unit	723
8703	Motor cars and other motor vehicles principally designed for the transport	43.6	40.7	38.9	4.6	*5.9*	*4.1*	thsd US$/unit	781
8429	Self-propelled bulldozers, angledozers, graders, levellers, scrapers	51.9	42.1	25.7	74.0	*42.5*	4.1	thsd US$/unit	723
8704	Motor vehicles for the transport of goods	39.5	36.6	31.2	17.3	*19.8*	*17.0*	thsd US$/unit	782
2523	Portland cement, aluminous cement, slag cement	32.7	30.6	33.4	0.1	0.1	0.1	US$/kg	661
3102	Mineral or chemical fertilisers, nitrogenous	40.7	23.4	26.8	0.9	0.6	0.5	US$/kg	562
0402	Milk and cream, concentrated or containing added sugar	33.8	24.4	25.9	*5.9*	3.5	3.0	US$/kg	022
3923	Articles for the conveyance or packing of goods, of plastics	24.8	25.7	25.5	*3.1*	0.9	2.9	US$/kg	893
8431	Parts suitable for use principally with the machinery of headings 84.25	14.8	14.7	38.2	*7.3*	7.1	11.8	US$/kg	723

Honduras

Goods Imports: CIF, by origin | **Goods Exports: FOB, by last known destination** | **Trade System: Special**

Overview:

In 2014, the value of merchandise exports of Honduras increased substantially by 24.2 percent to reach 4.5 bln US$, while its merchandise imports decreased moderately by 6.8 percent to reach 8.0 bln US$ (see graph 1, table 2 and table 3). The merchandise trade balance recorded a moderate deficit of 3.5 bln US$ (see graph 1). The largest merchandise trade balance was with MDG Developed North America at -1.3 bln US$ (see graph 4). Merchandise exports in Honduras were moderately concentrated amongst partners; imports were also moderately concentrated. The top 11 partners accounted for 80 percent or more of exports and 10 partners accounted for 80 percent or more of imports (see graph 5). In 2014, the value of exports of services of Honduras decreased slightly by 4.3 percent, reaching 1.1 bln US$, while its imports of services increased moderately by 8.8 percent and reached 1.8 bln US$ (see graph 2). There was a moderate trade in services deficit of 697.5 mln US$.

Graph 1: Total merchandise trade, by value

(Bln US$ by year)

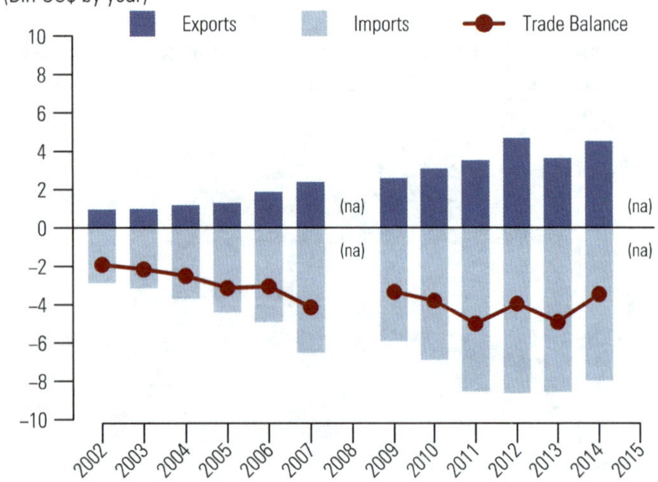

Graph 2: Total services trade, by value

(Bln US$ by year)

Exports Profile:

"Food, animals + beverages, tobacco" (SITC section 0+1), "Machinery and transport equipment" (SITC section 7) and "Goods classified chiefly by material" (SITC section 6) were the largest commodity groups for exports in 2014, representing respectively 46.8, 15.6 and 11.0 percent of exported goods (see table 2). From 2012 to 2014, the largest export commodity was "Coffee, whether or not roasted or decaffeinated" (HS code 0901) (see table 1). The top three destinations for merchandise exports were the United States, Germany and El Salvador, accounting for respectively 42.6, 8.5 and 6.1 percent of total exports. "Travel" (EBOPS code 236) accounted for the largest share of exports of services in 2014 at 629.5 mln US$, followed by "Communications services" (EBOPS code 245) at 230.0 mln US$ and "Transportation" (EBOPS code 205) at 98.3 mln US$ (see graph 3).

Graph 3: Exports of services by EBOPS category

(% share in 2014)

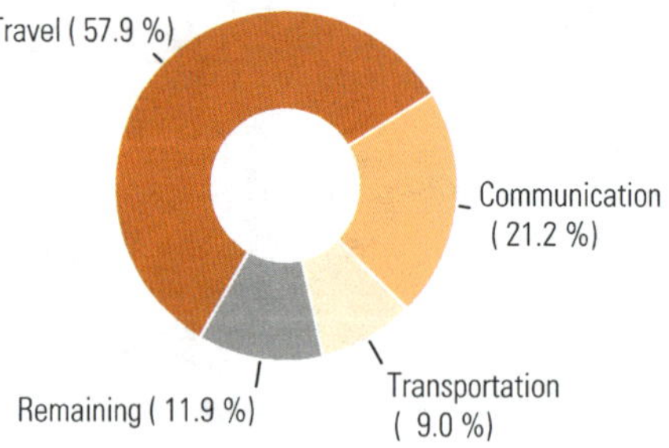

Table 1: Top 10 export commodities 2012 to 2014

HS code	4-digit heading of Harmonized System 2012	Value (million US$) 2012	2013	2014	Unit value 2012	2013	2014	Unit	SITC code
	All Commodities	4696.2	3648.8	4533.3					
0901	Coffee, whether or not roasted or decaffeinated	1339.1	796.8	783.3	4.2		3.2	US$/kg	071
8544	Insulated (including enamelled or anodised) wire, cable	497.8	14.5	580.7	17.9		*18.1*	US$/kg	773
0306	Crustaceans, whether in shell or not	197.6	281.1	345.3	6.4	*9.4*	6.2	US$/kg	036
1511	Palm oil and its fractions	279.6	253.9	230.1	1.0	*1.1*	0.8	US$/kg	422
0803	Bananas, including plantains, fresh or dried	75.4	269.9	221.6	0.3	*0.6*	0.3	US$/kg	057
2711	Petroleum gases and other gaseous hydrocarbons	179.8	138.1	...	0.8			US$/kg	343
7108	Gold (including gold plated with platinum)	102.2	99.3	104.4	30.3	*49.6*	34.2	thsd US$/kg	971
7112	Waste and scrap of precious metal or of metal clad with precious metal	99.7	98.9	74.0	24.4		2.2	thsd US$/kg	971
2402	Cigars, cheroots, cigarillos and cigarettes	99.5	51.7	109.6	11.2	*21.2*	16.5	US$/kg	122
3401	Soap; organic surface-active products	50.8	96.0	81.5	1.2	*2.0*	1.1	US$/kg	554

Services Imports and Exports: EBOPS 2002 categories

Table 2: Merchandise exports by SITC
(Value in million US$, growth and shares in percentage)

SITC	2014	Avg. Growth rates 2010-2014	Avg. Growth rates 2013-2014	2014 share
Total	4533.3	9.9	24.2	100.0
0+1	2120.8	9.1	5.6	46.8
2+4	495.6	5.1	11.7	10.9
3	1.2	-73.8	-99.2	0.0
5	312.9	16.4	13.9	6.9
6	498.4	33.4	18.4	11.0
7	705.5	26.6	2001.4	15.6
8	218.6	11.4	180.9	4.8
9	180.3	-3.2	-27.9	4.0

Table 3: Merchandise imports by SITC
(Value in million US$, growth and shares in percentage)

SITC	2014	Avg. Growth rates 2010-2014	Avg. Growth rates 2013-2014	2014 share
Total	7983.6	3.7	-6.8	100.0
0+1	1370.9	6.9	-3.8	17.2
2+4	160.0	-1.7	-5.2	2.0
3	1862.6	4.8	-16.0	23.3
5	1239.5	0.6	-9.9	15.5
6	1077.3	3.5	-3.8	13.5
7	1642.9	4.2	3.2	20.6
8	630.3	1.7	-5.3	7.9
9	0.1	26.1	-97.2	0.0

SITC Legend

SITC Code	Description
Total	All commodities
0+1	Food, animals + beverages, tobacco
2+4	Crude materials + anim. & veg. oils
3	Mineral fuels, lubricants
5	Chemicals
6	Goods classified chiefly by material
7	Machinery and transport equipment
8	Miscellaneous manufactured articles
9	Not classified elsewhere in the SITC

Graph 4: Merchandise trade balance
(Bln US$ by MDG Regions in 2014)

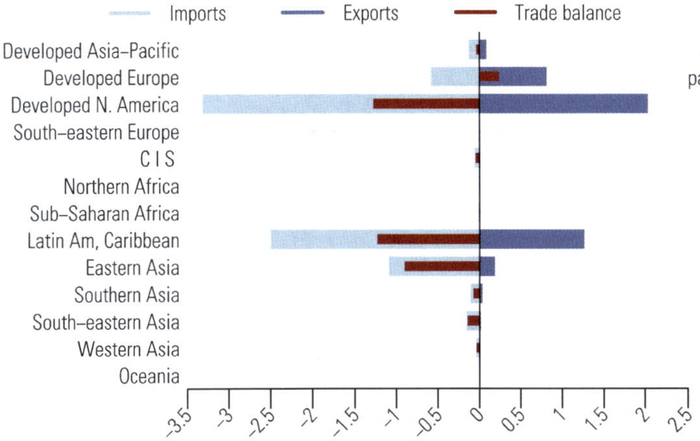

Graph 5: Partner concentration of merchandise trade
(Cumulative share by ranked partners in 2014)

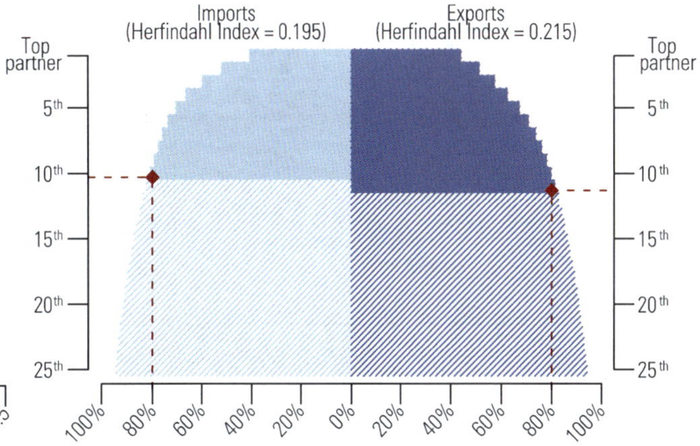

Graph 6: Imports of services by EBOPS category
(% share in 2014)

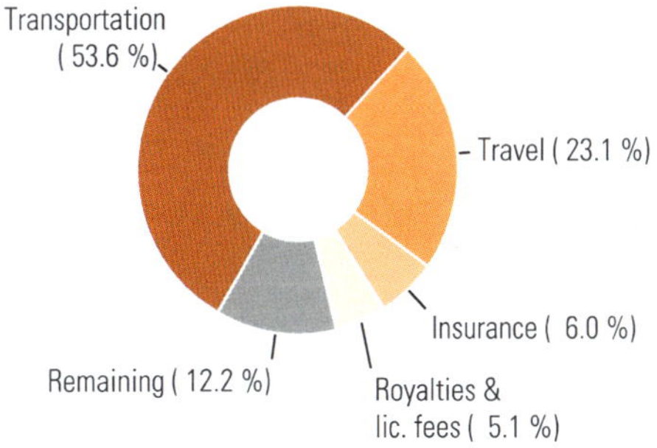

Imports Profile:

"Mineral fuels, lubricants" (SITC section 3), "Machinery and transport equipment" (SITC section 7) and "Food, animals + beverages, tobacco" (SITC section 0+1) were the largest commodity groups for imports in 2014, representing respectively 23.3, 20.6 and 17.2 percent of imported goods (see table 3). From 2012 to 2014, the largest import commodity was "Petroleum oils, other than crude" (HS code 2710) (see table 4). The top three partners for merchandise imports were the United States, China and Guatemala, accounting for respectively 40.4, 10.0 and 7.2 percent of total imports. "Transportation" (EBOPS code 205) accounted for the largest share of imports of services in 2014 at 955.7 mln US$, followed by "Travel" (EBOPS code 236) at 412.2 mln US$ and "Insurance services" (EBOPS code 253) at 107.2 mln US$ (see graph 6).

Table 4: Top 10 import commodities 2012 to 2014

HS code	4-digit heading of Harmonized System 2012	Value (million US$) 2012	2013	2014	Unit value 2012	2013	2014	Unit	SITC code
	All Commodities	8646.8	8566.1	7983.6					
2710	Petroleum oils, other than crude	2096.6	2156.5	1819.4	1.3		0.8	US$/kg	334
3004	Medicaments (excluding goods of heading 30.02, 30.05 or 30.06)	392.4	341.8	311.1	40.6		33.1	US$/kg	542
8517	Electrical apparatus for line telephony or line telegraphy	157.9	173.1	195.5					764
8704	Motor vehicles for the transport of goods	195.0	158.4	134.6					782
2106	Food preparations not elsewhere specified or included	132.0	145.2	140.2	4.3		4.5	US$/kg	098
8703	Motor cars and other motor vehicles principally designed for the transport	148.2	142.1	116.6	*19.2*	*18.5*	*18.4*	thsd US$/unit	781
1005	Maize (corn)	121.6	113.7	99.9	0.3		0.3	US$/kg	044
2304	Oil-cake and other solid residues	95.5	105.9	106.7	0.5	*0.6*	0.6	US$/kg	081
8471	Automatic data processing machines and units thereof	108.9	116.9	59.9					752
1905	Bread, pastry, cakes, biscuits and other bakers'wares	90.0	95.4	93.4	1.8	*3.4*	1.7	US$/kg	048

Hungary

Goods Imports: CIF, by consignment | **Goods Exports: FOB, by last known destination** | **Trade System: Special**

Overview:

In 2015, the value of merchandise exports of Hungary decreased substantially by 10.7 percent to reach 100.2 bln US$, while its merchandise imports decreased substantially by 12.4 percent to reach 90.4 bln US$ (see graph 1, table 2 and table 3). The merchandise trade balance recorded a relatively small surplus of 9.8 bln US$ (see graph 1). The largest merchandise trade balance was with MDG Developed Europe at 7.6 bln US$ (see graph 4). Merchandise exports in Hungary were diversified amongst partners; imports were also diversified. The top 16 partners accounted for 80 percent or more of exports and 14 partners accounted for 80 percent or more of imports (see graph 5). In 2014, the value of exports of services of Hungary increased moderately by 8.0 percent, reaching 23.6 bln US$, while its imports of services increased slightly by 3.2 percent and reached 17.2 bln US$ (see graph 2). There was a moderate trade in services surplus of 6.4 bln US$.

Graph 1: Total merchandise trade, by value

(Bln US$ by year)

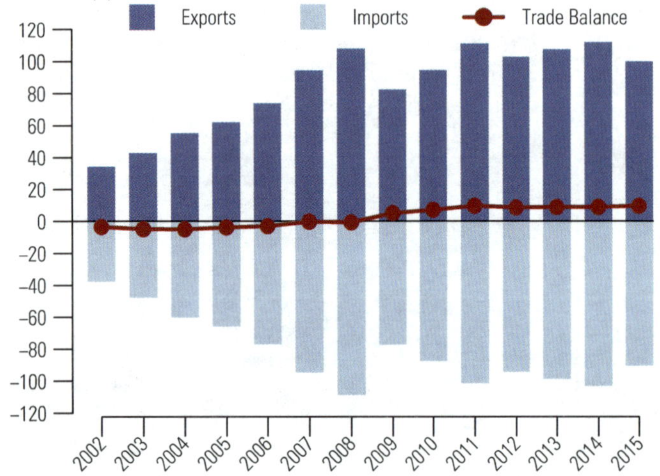

Graph 2: Total services trade, by value

(Bln US$ by year)

Exports Profile:

"Machinery and transport equipment" (SITC section 7), "Chemicals" (SITC section 5) and "Goods classified chiefly by material" (SITC section 6) were the largest commodity groups for exports in 2015, representing respectively 56.3, 10.8 and 10.3 percent of exported goods (see table 2). From 2013 to 2015, the largest export commodity was "Motor cars and other motor vehicles principally designed for the transport" (HS code 8703) (see table 1). The top three destinations for merchandise exports were Germany, Romania and Austria, accounting for respectively 26.9, 5.5 and 5.3 percent of total exports. "Other business services" (EBOPS code 268) accounted for the largest share of exports of services in 2014 at 6.4 bln US$, followed by "Transportation" (EBOPS code 205) at 6.0 bln US$ and "Travel" (EBOPS code 236) at 5.9 bln US$ (see graph 3).

Graph 3: Exports of services by EBOPS category

(% share in 2014)

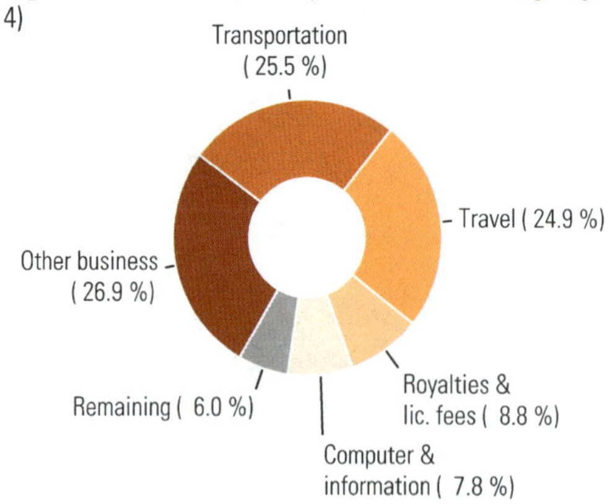

Table 1: Top 10 export commodities 2013 to 2015

HS code	4-digit heading of Harmonized System 2012	Value (million US$) 2013	2014	2015	Unit value 2013	2014	2015	Unit	SITC code
	All Commodities	107 730.0	112 196.3	100 166.5					
8703	Motor cars and other motor vehicles principally designed for the transport	7 399.1	11 031.2	11 207.7	19.0	21.0	18.7	thsd US$/unit	781
8708	Parts and accessories of the motor vehicles of headings 87.01 to 87.05	4 576.0	5 301.7	5 264.1	*9.6*	*9.8*	*8.1*	US$/kg	784
8517	Electrical apparatus for line telephony or line telegraphy	5 938.0	3 447.0	2 655.3					764
8407	Spark-ignition reciprocating or rotary internal combustion piston engines	4 070.0	4 052.0	3 262.5	2.7	2.6	2.2	thsd US$/unit	713
3004	Medicaments (excluding goods of heading 30.02, 30.05 or 30.06)	3 852.1	3 655.4	3 370.6	*124.7*	*89.1*	*54.6*	US$/kg	542
8471	Automatic data processing machines and units thereof	3 014.7	2 971.5	2 498.9	464.9	466.4	429.9	US$/unit	752
8528	Reception apparatus for television	3 149.2	2 701.1	2 455.7	265.9	227.7	204.9	US$/unit	761
8408	Compression-ignition internal combustion piston engines	2 444.5	2 509.9	3 073.9	3.3	3.5	3.1	thsd US$/unit	713
9999	Commodities not specified according to kind	2 920.9	2 566.6	2 340.1					931
8544	Insulated (including enamelled or anodised) wire, cable	2 125.0	2 279.4	2 028.2	*15.1*	*15.1*	*13.1*	US$/kg	773

Services Imports and Exports: EBOPS 2002 categories

Table 2: Merchandise exports by SITC

(Value in million US$, growth and shares in percentage)

SITC	2015	Avg. Growth rates 2011-2015	Avg. Growth rates 2014-2015	2015 share
Total	100 166.5	-2.6	-10.7	100.0
0+1	6 981.4	-2.4	-14.0	7.0
2+4	2 171.6	-8.8	-23.8	2.2
3	2 328.7	-12.0	-38.3	2.3
5	10 792.5	1.2	-7.6	10.8
6	10 340.9	-1.6	-12.1	10.3
7	56 344.3	-2.1	-7.1	56.3
8	8 810.3	-1.3	-17.9	8.8
9	2 396.8	-15.3	-8.7	2.4

Table 3: Merchandise imports by SITC

(Value in million US$, growth and shares in percentage)

SITC	2015	Avg. Growth rates 2011-2015	Avg. Growth rates 2014-2015	2015 share
Total	90 374.3	-2.8	-12.4	100.0
0+1	4 346.6	-1.9	-11.1	4.8
2+4	1 830.2	-6.4	-13.9	2.0
3	7 419.9	-12.2	-40.3	8.2
5	10 746.1	-0.3	-7.4	11.9
6	12 298.8	-2.0	-12.6	13.6
7	42 561.9	-1.0	-7.2	47.1
8	6 904.7	2.9	-6.3	7.6
9	4 266.0	-12.3	-10.4	4.7

SITC Legend

SITC Code	Description
Total	All commodities
0+1	Food, animals + beverages, tobacco
2+4	Crude materials + anim. & veg. oils
3	Mineral fuels, lubricants
5	Chemicals
6	Goods classified chiefly by material
7	Machinery and transport equipment
8	Miscellaneous manufactured articles
9	Not classified elsewhere in the SITC

Graph 4: Merchandise trade balance

(Bln US$ by MDG Regions in 2015)

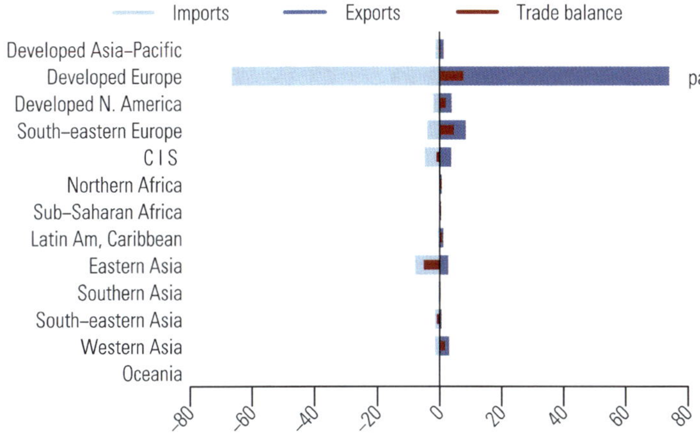

Graph 5: Partner concentration of merchandise trade

(Cumulative share by ranked partners in 2015)

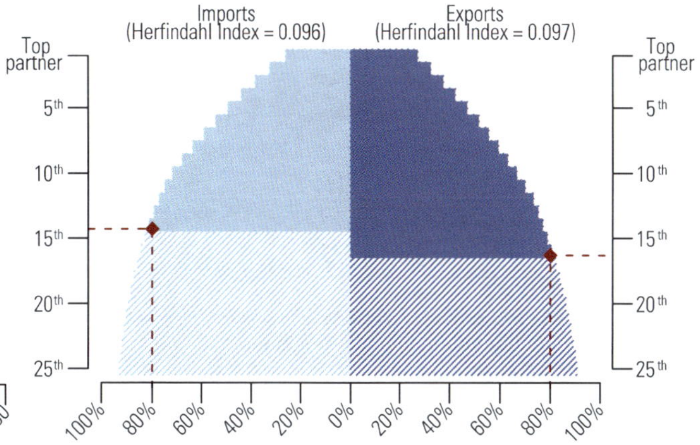

Graph 6: Imports of services by EBOPS category

(% share in 2014)

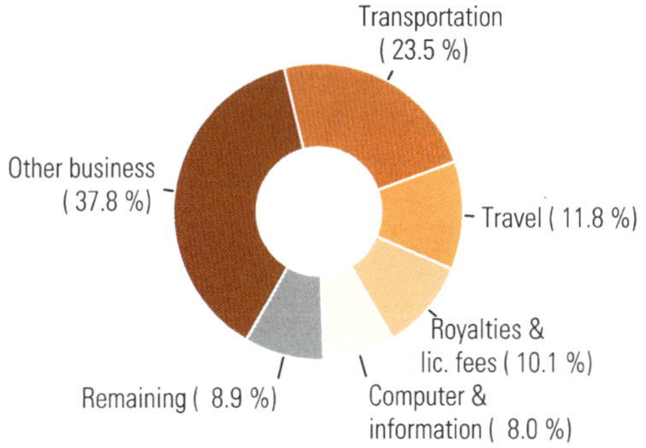

Imports Profile:

"Machinery and transport equipment" (SITC section 7), "Goods classified chiefly by material" (SITC section 6) and "Chemicals" (SITC section 5) were the largest commodity groups for imports in 2015, representing respectively 47.1, 13.6 and 11.9 percent of imported goods (see table 3). From 2013 to 2015, the largest import commodity was "Commodities not specified according to kind" (HS code 9999) (see table 4). The top three partners for merchandise imports were Germany, Austria and the Russian Federation, accounting for respectively 25.5, 6.9 and 6.7 percent of total imports. "Other business services" (EBOPS code 268) accounted for the largest share of imports of services in 2014 at 6.5 bln US$, followed by "Transportation" (EBOPS code 205) at 4.0 bln US$ and "Travel" (EBOPS code 236) at 2.0 bln US$ (see graph 6).

Table 4: Top 10 import commodities 2013 to 2015

HS code	4-digit heading of Harmonized System 2012	Value (million US$) 2013	2014	2015	Unit value 2013	2014	2015	Unit	SITC code
	All Commodities	98 661.8	103 111.0	90 374.3					
9999	Commodities not specified according to kind	5 367.6	4 727.3	4 231.9					931
8708	Parts and accessories of the motor vehicles of headings 87.01 to 87.05	3 862.6	5 232.1	5 227.0	*10.4*	*10.5*	*8.9*	US$/kg	784
2709	Petroleum oils and oils obtained from bituminous minerals, crude	4 488.6	4 309.0	2 178.4	0.8	0.7	0.4	US$/kg	333
8517	Electrical apparatus for line telephony or line telegraphy	4 908.0	3 015.2	2 857.8					764
2711	Petroleum gases and other gaseous hydrocarbons	3 884.7	4 056.8	2 265.3	0.6	*0.5*	*0.4*	US$/kg	343
3004	Medicaments (excluding goods of heading 30.02, 30.05 or 30.06)	2 672.7	2 667.3	2 578.9	*74.4*	*47.1*	*61.3*	US$/kg	542
8409	Parts suitable for use with the engines of heading 84	2 342.6	2 546.7	2 280.2	*9.3*	*9.7*	*7.9*	US$/kg	713
8542	Electronic integrated circuits	2 141.6	2 228.5	2 116.7					776
8703	Motor cars and other motor vehicles principally designed for the transport	1 947.6	2 316.7	2 189.0	16.5	16.8	14.8	thsd US$/unit	781
2710	Petroleum oils, other than crude	2 263.4	2 195.3	1 365.3	*1.0*	*0.9*	*0.6*	US$/kg	334

Iceland

Goods Imports: CIF, by origin | **Goods Exports: FOB, by last known destination** | **Trade System: Special**

Overview:

In 2015, the value of merchandise exports of Iceland decreased moderately by 6.5 percent to reach 4.7 bln US$, while its merchandise imports decreased slightly by 1.6 percent to reach 5.3 bln US$ (see graph 1, table 2 and table 3). The merchandise trade balance recorded a relatively small deficit of 562.5 mln US$ (see graph 1). The largest merchandise trade balance was with MDG Developed Europe at 573.1 mln US$ (see graph 4). Merchandise exports in Iceland were diversified amongst partners; imports were also diversified. The top 11 partners accounted for 80 percent or more of exports and 18 partners accounted for 80 percent or more of imports (see graph 5). In 2013, the value of exports of services of Iceland increased substantially by 13.7 percent, reaching 3.5 bln US$, while its imports of services decreased substantially by 11.8 percent and reached 2.5 bln US$ (see graph 2). There was a moderate trade in services surplus of 976.9 mln US$.

Graph 1: Total merchandise trade, by value

(Bln US$ by year)

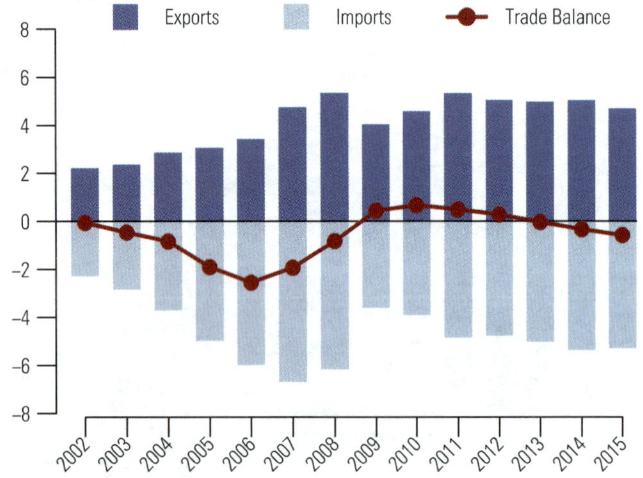

Graph 2: Total services trade, by value

(Bln US$ by year)

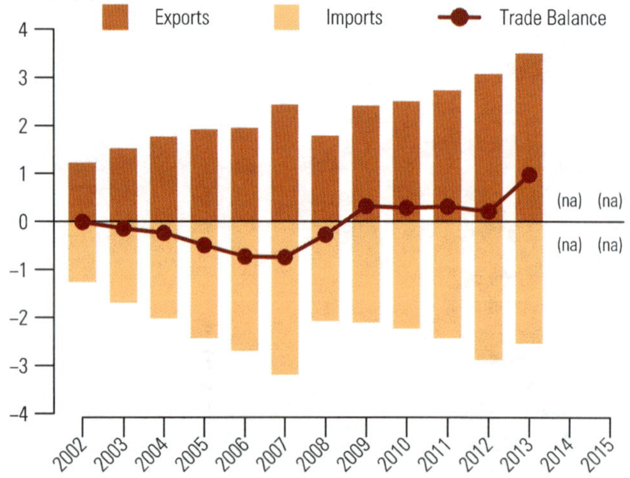

Exports Profile:

"Goods classified chiefly by material" (SITC section 6), "Food, animals + beverages, tobacco" (SITC section 0+1) and "Machinery and transport equipment" (SITC section 7) were the largest commodity groups for exports in 2015, representing respectively 43.1, 43.0 and 4.2 percent of exported goods (see table 2). From 2013 to 2015, the largest export commodity was "Unwrought aluminium" (HS code 7601) (see table 1). The top three destinations for merchandise exports were the Netherlands, the United Kingdom and Germany, accounting for respectively 28.5, 10.8 and 8.6 percent of total exports. "Transportation" (EBOPS code 205) accounted for the largest share of exports of services in 2013 at 1.6 bln US$, followed by "Travel" (EBOPS code 236) at 1.1 bln US$ and "Other business services" (EBOPS code 268) at 422.8 mln US$ (see graph 3).

Graph 3: Exports of services by EBOPS category

(% share in 2013)

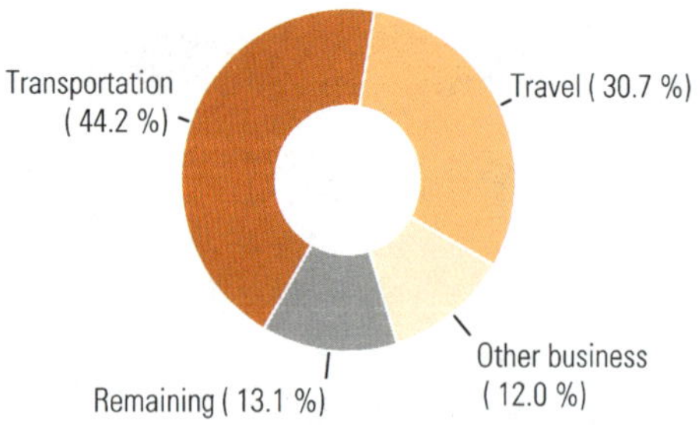

Table 1: Top 10 export commodities 2013 to 2015

HS code	4-digit heading of Harmonized System 2012	Value (million US$) 2013	2014	2015	Unit value 2013	2014	2015	Unit	SITC code
	All Commodities	4997.7	5051.3	4723.3					
7601	Unwrought aluminium	1665.1	1503.6	1493.5	2.1	2.2	2.1	US$/kg	684
0304	Fish fillets and other fish meat (whether or not minced)	847.2	838.7	780.8	5.1	5.5	6.0	US$/kg	034
0303	Fish, frozen, excluding fish fillets and other fish meat of heading 03.04	524.1	471.0	366.9	1.8	1.9	2.0	US$/kg	034
0305	Fish, dried, salted or in brine	334.7	354.7	326.5	5.0	5.3	*4.9*	US$/kg	035
2301	Flours, meals and pellets, of meat or meat offal	217.9	136.1	222.3	1.8	1.7	1.5	US$/kg	081
7202	Ferro-alloys	163.8	157.6	143.6					671
7605	Aluminium wire	96.0	173.4	140.3	2.2	2.3	2.0	US$/kg	684
7604	Aluminium bars, rods and profiles	0.6	160.3	164.0	14.1	2.3	2.0	US$/kg	684
1504	Fats and oils and their fractions, of fish or marine mammals	135.5	90.9	93.0	2.3	2.5	2.5	US$/kg	411
7607	Aluminium foil (whether or not printed or backed with paper, paperboard	103.2	97.5	76.5	*51.1*	*48.6*	*40.9*	US$/kg	684

Services Imports and Exports: EBOPS 2002 categories

Table 2: Merchandise exports by SITC

(Value in million US$, growth and shares in percentage)

SITC	2015	Avg. Growth rates 2011-2015	Avg. Growth rates 2014-2015	2015 share
Total	4723.3	-3.1	-6.5	100.0
0+1	2030.6	-1.7	-4.3	43.0
2+4	152.6	-4.0	-6.0	3.2
3	76.1	-7.4	-24.4	1.6
5	97.8	-11.5	-10.5	2.1
6	2035.5	-3.5	-4.1	43.1
7	200.7	-4.9	-31.0	4.2
8	94.6	-4.3	-16.2	2.0
9	35.4	8.1	14.2	0.8

Table 3: Merchandise imports by SITC

(Value in million US$, growth and shares in percentage)

SITC	2015	Avg. Growth rates 2011-2015	Avg. Growth rates 2014-2015	2015 share
Total	5285.8	2.2	-1.6	100.0
0+1	558.4	4.1	4.4	10.6
2+4	655.2	-1.8	5.3	12.4
3	660.1	-1.5	-28.4	12.5
5	474.8	1.4	-3.0	9.0
6	555.7	-0.9	-3.7	10.5
7	1849.5	6.6	10.5	35.0
8	522.9	1.2	-4.4	9.9
9	9.2	10.1	44.2	0.2

SITC Legend

SITC Code	Description
Total	All commodities
0+1	Food, animals + beverages, tobacco
2+4	Crude materials + anim. & veg. oils
3	Mineral fuels, lubricants
5	Chemicals
6	Goods classified chiefly by material
7	Machinery and transport equipment
8	Miscellaneous manufactured articles
9	Not classified elsewhere in the SITC

Graph 4: Merchandise trade balance

(Bln US$ by MDG Regions in 2015)

Graph 5: Partner concentration of merchandise trade

(Cumulative share by ranked partners in 2015)

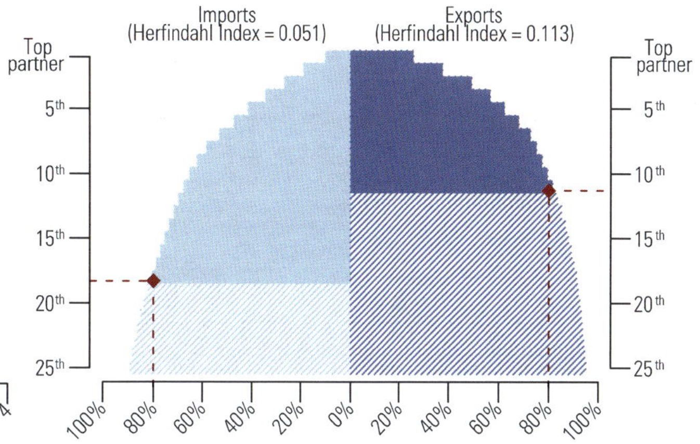

Graph 6: Imports of services by EBOPS category

(% share in 2013)

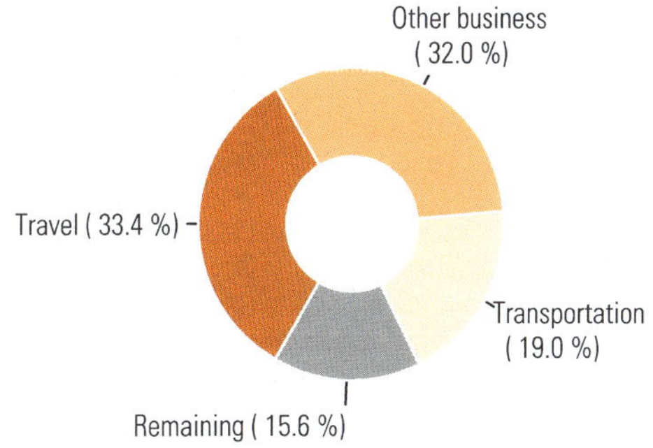

Imports Profile:

"Machinery and transport equipment" (SITC section 7), "Mineral fuels, lubricants" (SITC section 3) and "Crude materials + anim. & veg. oils" (SITC section 2+4) were the largest commodity groups for imports in 2015, representing respectively 35.0, 12.5 and 12.4 percent of imported goods (see table 3). From 2013 to 2015, the largest import commodity was "Petroleum oils, other than crude" (HS code 2710) (see table 4). The top three partners for merchandise imports were Norway, the United States and Germany, accounting for respectively 13.3, 9.2 and 8.1 percent of total imports. "Travel" (EBOPS code 236) accounted for the largest share of imports of services in 2013 at 846.1 mln US$, followed by "Other business services" (EBOPS code 268) at 809.5 mln US$ and "Transportation" (EBOPS code 205) at 481.2 mln US$ (see graph 6).

Table 4: Top 10 import commodities 2013 to 2015

HS code	4-digit heading of Harmonized System 2012	Value (million US$) 2013	Value (million US$) 2014	Value (million US$) 2015	Unit value 2013	Unit value 2014	Unit value 2015	Unit	SITC code
	All Commodities	5019.2	5371.9	5285.8					
2710	Petroleum oils, other than crude	896.0	881.8	617.7	*1.0*	*0.9*	*0.6*	US$/kg	334
2818	Artificial corundum, whether or not chemically defined	502.6	494.9	518.4	*0.3*	0.3	0.3	US$/kg	522
8545	Carbon electrodes, carbon brushes, lamp carbons, battery carbons	365.9	373.1	312.2					778
8703	Motor cars and other motor vehicles principally designed for the transport	156.2	216.5	291.1		*17.4*	*17.9*	thsd US$/unit	781
3004	Medicaments (excluding goods of heading 30.02, 30.05 or 30.06)	124.3	129.2	113.5	*134.1*	*138.8*	122.0	US$/kg	542
8471	Automatic data processing machines and units thereof	88.4	105.8	97.8					752
8517	Electrical apparatus for line telephony or line telegraphy	76.3	92.2	94.2					764
8802	Other aircraft (for example, helicopters, aeroplanes); spacecraft	39.4	46.5	156.7					792
8902	Fishing vessels; factory ships and other vessels for processing	26.9	73.5	103.1	0.0		9.4	mln US$/unit	793
0306	Crustaceans, whether in shell or not	34.4	56.9	93.9	*3.0*	3.7	3.8	US$/kg	036

India

Goods Imports: CIF, by origin | **Goods Exports: FOB, by last known destination** | **Trade System: General**

Overview:

In 2015, the value of merchandise exports of India decreased substantially by 16.7 percent to reach 264.4 bln US$, while its merchandise imports decreased substantially by 14.9 percent to reach 390.7 bln US$ (see graph 1, table 2 and table 3). The merchandise trade balance recorded a moderate deficit of 126.4 bln US$ (see graph 1). The largest merchandise trade balance was with MDG Eastern Asia at -57.4 bln US$, much higher than that with Western Asia with which India had the largest deficit in 2014 (see graph 4). Merchandise exports in India were diversified amongst partners; imports were also diversified. The top 31 partners accounted for 80 percent or more of exports and 25 partners accounted for 80 percent or more of imports (see graph 5). In 2014, the value of exports of services of India increased slightly by 4.5 percent, reaching 155.3 bln US$, while its imports of services increased slightly by 1.7 percent and reached 79.7 bln US$ (see graph 2). There was a large trade in services surplus of 75.6 bln US$.

Graph 1: Total merchandise trade, by value

(Bln US$ by year)

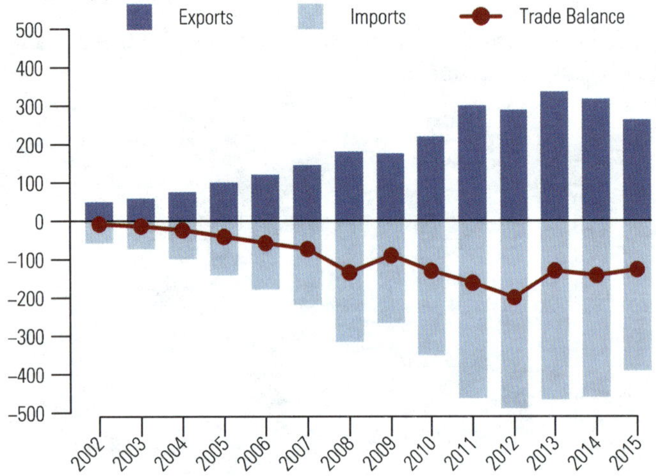

Graph 2: Total services trade, by value

(Bln US$ by year)

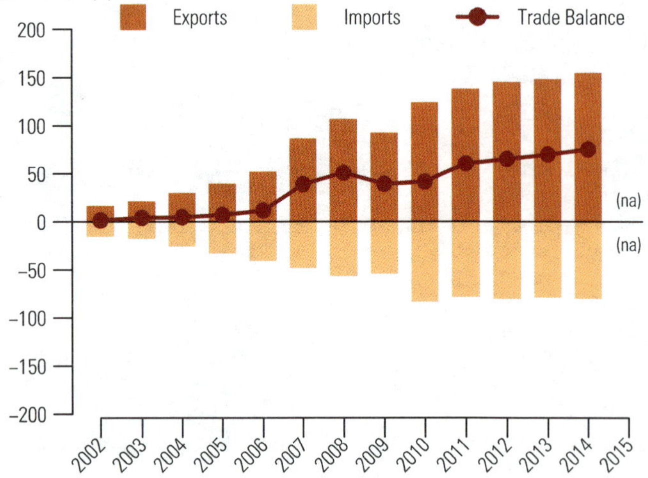

Exports Profile:

"Goods classified chiefly by material" (SITC section 6), "Machinery and transport equipment" (SITC section 7) and "Miscellaneous manufactured articles" (SITC section 8) were the largest commodity groups for exports in 2015, representing respectively 26.0, 16.4 and 14.9 percent of exported goods (see table 2). From 2013 to 2015, the largest export commodity was "Petroleum oils, other than crude" (HS code 2710) (see table 1). The top three destinations for merchandise exports were the United States, the United Arab Emirates and China, accounting for respectively 13.6, 10.5 and 4.3 percent of total exports. "Computer and information services" (EBOPS code 262) accounted for the largest share of exports of services in 2014 at 72.6 bln US$, followed by "Other business services" (EBOPS code 268) at 30.7 bln US$ and "Travel" (EBOPS code 236) at 19.7 bln US$ (see graph 3).

Graph 3: Exports of services by EBOPS category

(% share in 2014)

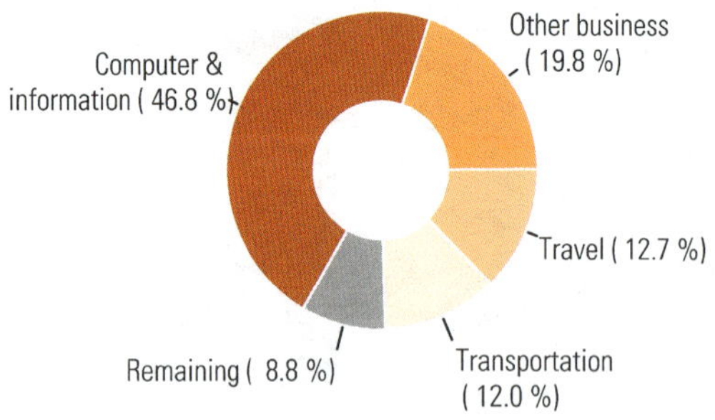

Table 1: Top 10 export commodities 2013 to 2015

HS code	4-digit heading of Harmonized System 2012	Value (million US$) 2013	2014	2015	Unit value 2013	2014	2015	Unit	SITC code
	All Commodities	336611.4	317544.6	264381.0					
2710	Petroleum oils, other than crude	67075.2	60838.6	30455.0		0.9	0.5	US$/kg	334
7102	Diamonds, whether or not worked, but not mounted or set	28952.1	24064.5	21873.3					667
7113	Articles of jewellery and parts thereof, of precious metal	10603.3	13087.6	9991.7			26.0	thsd US$/kg	897
3004	Medicaments (excluding goods of heading 30.02, 30.05 or 30.06)	10314.0	10302.7	11235.6	26.4	26.7	31.1	US$/kg	542
1006	Rice	8169.5	7905.7	6380.1	0.7	0.7	0.6	US$/kg	042
8703	Motor cars and other motor vehicles principally designed for the transport	5556.5	5769.0	5392.9	5.5	5.5	5.1	thsd US$/unit	781
0202	Meat of bovine animals, frozen	4411.0	4719.1	4030.6	2.9	3.2	3.2	US$/kg	011
5205	Cotton yarn (other than sewing thread), containing 85 % or more	4773.1	4095.4	3736.7	3.5	3.3	2.8	US$/kg	651
8708	Parts and accessories of the motor vehicles of headings 87.01 to 87.05	3912.8	4001.3	3885.5	5.9	5.7	5.7	US$/kg	784
8802	Other aircraft (for example, helicopters, aeroplanes); spacecraft	2590.3	5247.8	2437.7	16.5		0.5	mln US$/unit	792

Services Imports and Exports: EBOPS 2002 categories

Table 2: Merchandise exports by SITC

(Value in million US$, growth and shares in percentage)

SITC	2015	Avg. Growth rates 2011-2015	Avg. Growth rates 2014-2015	2015 share
Total	264 381.0	-3.2	-16.7	100.0
0+1	27 483.3	3.2	-17.1	10.4
2+4	10 342.9	-12.4	-24.9	3.9
3	31 387.1	-13.7	-49.7	11.9
5	35 945.8	3.6	-3.2	13.6
6	68 750.6	-2.4	-10.5	26.0
7	43 324.6	0.8	-10.8	16.4
8	39 522.3	-0.3	-6.6	14.9
9	7 624.5	-14.6	122.5	2.9

Table 3: Merchandise imports by SITC

(Value in million US$, growth and shares in percentage)

SITC	2015	Avg. Growth rates 2011-2015	Avg. Growth rates 2014-2015	2015 share
Total	390 744.7	-4.1	-14.9	100.0
0+1	9 664.0	13.9	20.2	2.5
2+4	32 347.1	0.1	-9.3	8.3
3	104 631.1	-9.7	-40.9	26.8
5	46 818.9	2.6	-2.6	12.0
6	55 980.7	-5.2	-6.0	14.3
7	80 444.6	1.2	7.6	20.6
8	15 006.5	2.8	1.7	3.8
9	45 851.9	-8.5	10.1	11.7

SITC Legend

SITC Code	Description
Total	All commodities
0+1	Food, animals + beverages, tobacco
2+4	Crude materials + anim. & veg. oils
3	Mineral fuels, lubricants
5	Chemicals
6	Goods classified chiefly by material
7	Machinery and transport equipment
8	Miscellaneous manufactured articles
9	Not classified elsewhere in the SITC

Graph 4: Merchandise trade balance

(Bln US$ by MDG Regions in 2015)

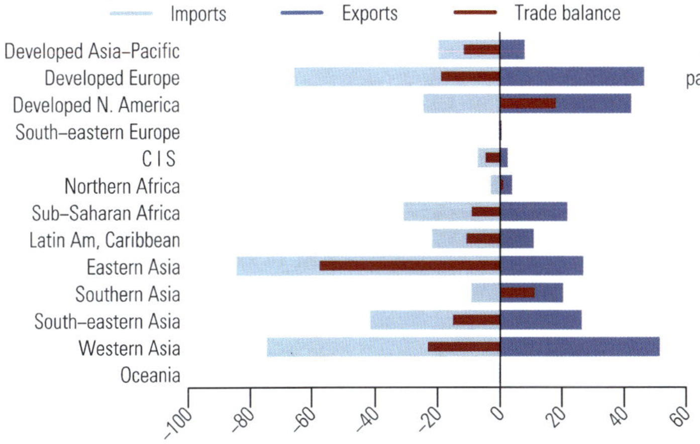

Graph 5: Partner concentration of merchandise trade

(Cumulative share by ranked partners in 2015)

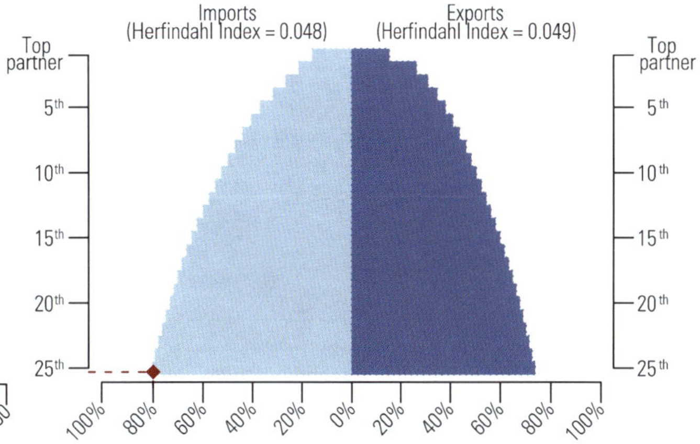

Graph 6: Imports of services by EBOPS category

(% share in 2014)

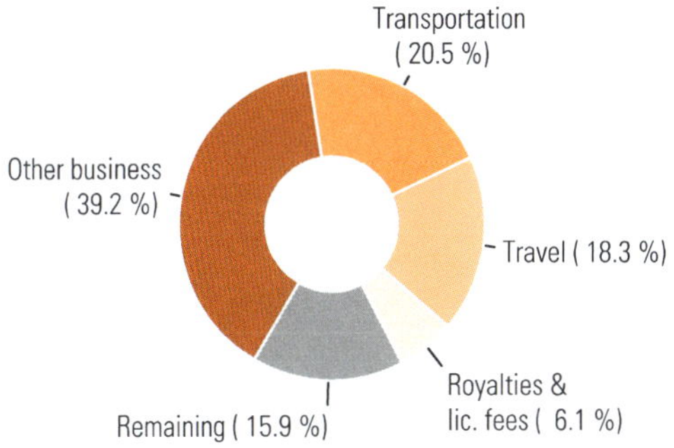

Imports Profile:

"Mineral fuels, lubricants" (SITC section 3), "Machinery and transport equipment" (SITC section 7) and "Goods classified chiefly by material" (SITC section 6) were the largest commodity groups for imports in 2015, representing respectively 26.8, 20.6 and 14.3 percent of imported goods (see table 3). From 2013 to 2015, the largest import commodity was "Petroleum oils and oils obtained from bituminous minerals, crude" (HS code 2709) (see table 4). The top three partners for merchandise imports were China, Saudi Arabia and the United Arab Emirates, accounting for respectively 13.0, 6.9 and 6.1 percent of total imports. "Other business services" (EBOPS code 268) accounted for the largest share of imports of services in 2014 at 31.2 bln US$, followed by "Transportation" (EBOPS code 205) at 16.3 bln US$ and "Travel" (EBOPS code 236) at 14.6 bln US$ (see graph 6).

Table 4: Top 10 import commodities 2013 to 2015

HS code	4-digit heading of Harmonized System 2012	Value (million US$) 2013	Value (million US$) 2014	Value (million US$) 2015	Unit value 2013	Unit value 2014	Unit value 2015	Unit	SITC code
	All Commodities	466 045.6	459 369.5	390 744.7					
2709	Petroleum oils and oils obtained from bituminous minerals, crude	148 046.7	135 826.2	72 321.7	0.8	0.7	*0.4*	US$/kg	333
7108	Gold (including gold plated with platinum)	37 711.8	31 039.7	34 999.5	*45.1*		*33.5*	thsd US$/kg	971
7102	Diamonds, whether or not worked, but not mounted or set	22 649.6	21 609.7	16 405.1					667
2701	Coal; briquettes, ovoids and similar solid fuels manufactured from coal	14 931.2	16 395.3	14 115.0	0.1	0.1	0.1	US$/kg	321
2711	Petroleum gases and other gaseous hydrocarbons	14 272.7	17 627.2	11 868.1	0.7	0.8	*0.5*	US$/kg	343
8517	Electrical apparatus for line telephony or line telegraphy	10 916.4	13 432.3	15 814.0					764
9999	Commodities not specified according to kind	11 504.7	10 599.3	10 852.2					931
1511	Palm oil and its fractions	6 966.8	6 551.4	5 922.1	0.8	0.8	0.6	US$/kg	422
2603	Copper ores and concentrates	7 443.4	5 320.2	4 093.6	2.5	2.7	2.4	US$/kg	283
8471	Automatic data processing machines and units thereof	4 600.9	4 530.2	5 220.5	*80.0*	*81.6*	89.8	US$/unit	752

Indonesia

Goods Imports: CIF, by origin	Goods Exports: FOB, by last known destination	Trade System: General

Overview:

In 2014, the value of merchandise exports of Indonesia decreased slightly by 3.6 percent to reach 176.0 bln US$, while its merchandise imports decreased slightly by 4.5 percent to reach 178.2 bln US$ (see graph 1, table 2 and table 3). The merchandise trade balance recorded a relatively small deficit of 2.1 bln US$ (see graph 1). The largest merchandise trade balance was with MDG Southern Asia at 12.3 bln US$ (see graph 4). Merchandise exports in Indonesia were diversified amongst partners; imports were also diversified. The top 16 partners accounted for 80 percent or more of exports and 14 partners accounted for 80 percent or more of imports (see graph 5). In 2014, the value of exports of services of Indonesia increased slightly by 3.0 percent, reaching 23.0 bln US$, while its imports of services decreased slightly by 3.9 percent and reached 33.1 bln US$ (see graph 2). There was a moderate trade in services deficit of 10.1 bln US$. See footnote*.

Graph 1: Total merchandise trade, by value

(Bln US$ by year)

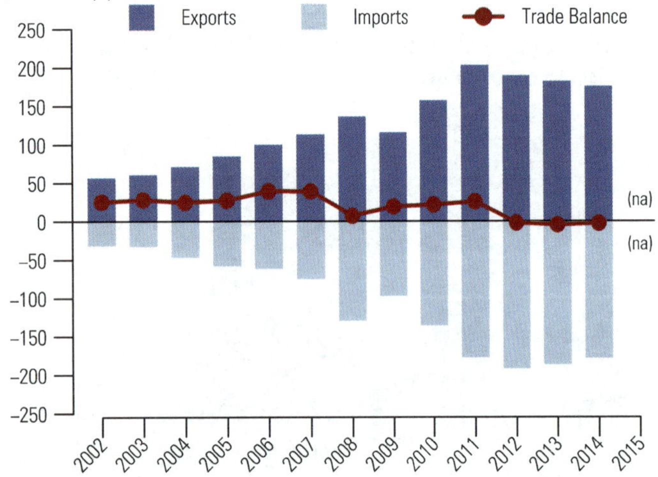

Graph 2: Total services trade, by value

(Bln US$ by year)

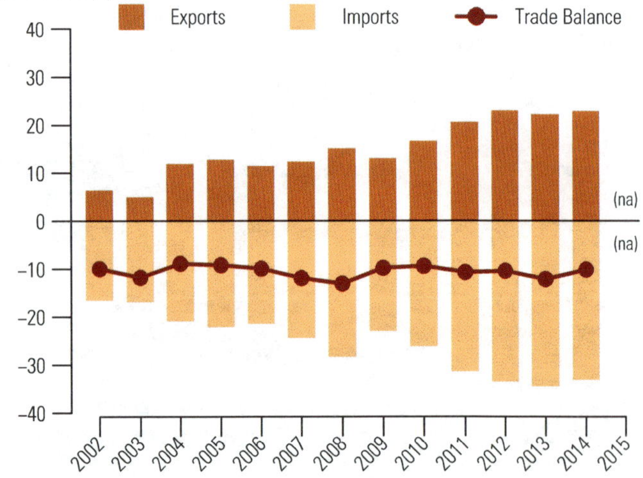

Exports Profile:

"Mineral fuels, lubricants" (SITC section 3), "Crude materials + anim. & veg. oils" (SITC section 2+4) and "Goods classified chiefly by material" (SITC section 6) were the largest commodity groups for exports in 2014, representing respectively 29.0, 20.0 and 12.9 percent of exported goods (see table 2). From 2012 to 2014, the largest export commodity was "Coal; briquettes, ovoids and similar solid fuels manufactured from coal" (HS code 2701) (see table 1). The top three destinations for merchandise exports were Japan, China and Singapore, accounting for respectively 14.6, 11.3 and 9.2 percent of total exports. "Travel" (EBOPS code 236) accounted for the largest share of exports of services in 2014 at 10.3 bln US$, followed by "Other business services" (EBOPS code 268) at 6.0 bln US$ and "Transportation" (EBOPS code 205) at 3.8 bln US$ (see graph 3).

Graph 3: Exports of services by EBOPS category

(% share in 2014)

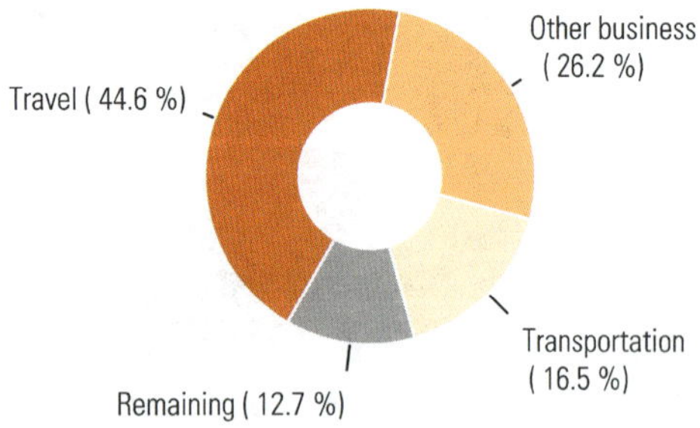

Table 1: Top 10 export commodities 2012 to 2014

HS code	4-digit heading of Harmonized System 2012	Value (million US$) 2012	2013	2014	Unit value 2012	2013	2014	Unit	SITC code
	All Commodities	190031.8	182551.8	176036.2					
2701	Coal; briquettes, ovoids and similar solid fuels manufactured from coal	24293.2	22773.2	18697.8	0.1	0.1	0.1	US$/kg	321
2711	Petroleum gases and other gaseous hydrocarbons	20520.5	18129.2	17180.3	0.7	0.7	0.7	US$/kg	343
1511	Palm oil and its fractions	17602.2	15838.9	17464.9	0.9	0.8	0.8	US$/kg	422
2709	Petroleum oils and oils obtained from bituminous minerals, crude	12293.4	10204.7	9271.2	0.8	0.8	0.7	US$/kg	333
4001	Natural rubber, balata, gutta-percha, guayule, chicle	7864.5	6910.7	4744.8	3.2	2.6	1.8	US$/kg	231
2713	Petroleum coke and other residues	2379.2	2674.3	2309.6	0.7	0.7	0.6	US$/kg	335
2603	Copper ores and concentrates	2594.7	3006.8	1683.6	2.3	2.1	2.4	US$/kg	283
8703	Motor cars and other motor vehicles principally designed for the transport	2264.3	2116.0	2641.6	*14.0*	*14.9*	*14.8*	thsd US$/unit	781
1513	Coconut (copra), palm kernel or babassu oil	2458.2	1829.5	2484.4	1.1	0.8	1.1	US$/kg	422
6403	Footwear with outer soles of rubber, plastics, leather	2195.9	2272.1	2233.3	*29.4*	*29.5*		US$/pair	851

*Merchandise imports data follows special trade system up to 2007.

Services Imports and Exports: EBOPS 2002 categories

Table 2: Merchandise exports by SITC

(Value in million US$, growth and shares in percentage)

SITC	2014	Avg. Growth rates 2010-2014	Avg. Growth rates 2013-2014	2014 share
Total	176 036.2	2.8	-3.6	100.0
0+1	13 171.7	10.0	10.0	7.5
2+4	35 195.2	-1.2	-10.2	20.0
3	51 125.9	2.3	-10.9	29.0
5	11 246.2	8.3	2.4	6.4
6	22 683.9	0.8	3.1	12.9
7	21 786.9	2.7	-1.6	12.4
8	19 293.5	7.9	13.2	11.0
9	1 532.8	6.7	-15.7	0.9

Table 3: Merchandise imports by SITC

(Value in million US$, growth and shares in percentage)

SITC	2014	Avg. Growth rates 2010-2014	Avg. Growth rates 2013-2014	2014 share
Total	178 179.3	7.1	-4.5	100.0
0+1	15 376.6	10.8	4.7	8.6
2+4	9 346.0	5.8	-1.4	5.2
3	43 928.7	12.4	-3.5	24.7
5	23 754.6	9.2	0.8	13.3
6	26 981.4	7.2	-5.6	15.1
7	51 218.0	2.2	-9.3	28.7
8	6 571.2	9.0	-4.7	3.7
9	1 002.8	-13.1	-30.7	0.6

SITC Legend

SITC Code	Description
Total	All commodities
0+1	Food, animals + beverages, tobacco
2+4	Crude materials + anim. & veg. oils
3	Mineral fuels, lubricants
5	Chemicals
6	Goods classified chiefly by material
7	Machinery and transport equipment
8	Miscellaneous manufactured articles
9	Not classified elsewhere in the SITC

Graph 4: Merchandise trade balance

(Bln US$ by MDG Regions in 2014)

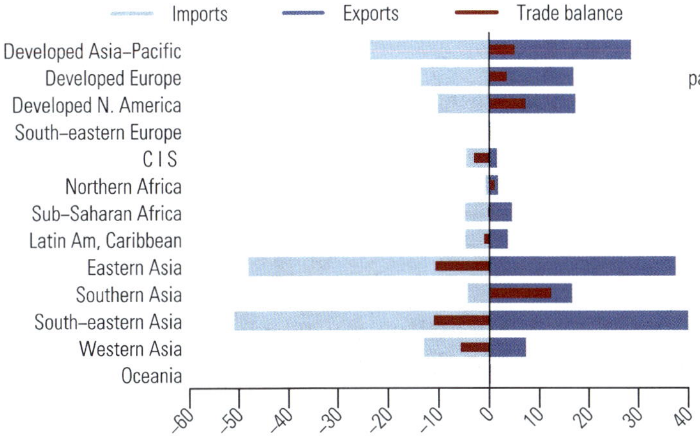

Graph 5: Partner concentration of merchandise trade

(Cumulative share by ranked partners in 2014)

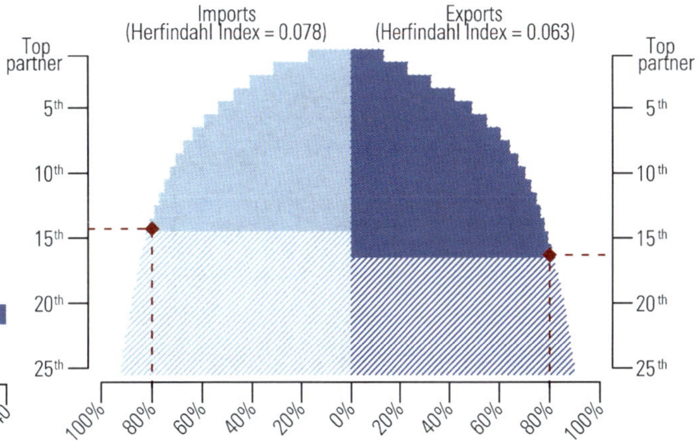

Graph 6: Imports of services by EBOPS category

(% share in 2014)

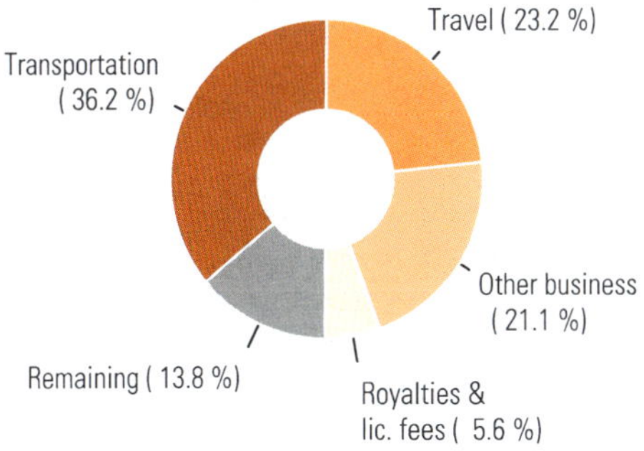

Imports Profile:

"Machinery and transport equipment" (SITC section 7), "Mineral fuels, lubricants" (SITC section 3) and "Goods classified chiefly by material" (SITC section 6) were the largest commodity groups for imports in 2014, representing respectively 28.7, 24.7 and 15.1 percent of imported goods (see table 3). From 2012 to 2014, the largest import commodity was "Petroleum oils, other than crude" (HS code 2710) (see table 4). The top three partners for merchandise imports were China, Singapore and Japan, accounting for respectively 16.1, 13.8 and 10.6 percent of total imports. "Transportation" (EBOPS code 205) accounted for the largest share of imports of services in 2014 at 12.0 bln US$, followed by "Travel" (EBOPS code 236) at 7.7 bln US$ and "Other business services" (EBOPS code 268) at 7.0 bln US$ (see graph 6).

Table 4: Top 10 import commodities 2012 to 2014

HS code	4-digit heading of Harmonized System 2012	Value (million US$) 2012	2013	2014	Unit value 2012	2013	2014	Unit	SITC code
	All Commodities	191 690.9	186 628.6	178 179.3					
2710	Petroleum oils, other than crude	28 038.2	27 850.9	26 717.3	1.0	1.0	1.0	US$/kg	334
2709	Petroleum oils and oils obtained from bituminous minerals, crude	10 803.2	13 585.8	13 072.4	0.9	0.8	0.8	US$/kg	333
8517	Electrical apparatus for line telephony or line telegraphy	5 113.4	5 291.2	4 855.4					764
2711	Petroleum gases and other gaseous hydrocarbons	3 081.6	3 113.0	3 025.0	1.0	0.9	0.8	US$/kg	343
8708	Parts and accessories of the motor vehicles of headings 87.01 to 87.05	2 982.3	3 218.3	2 908.5	10.1	9.5	9.8	US$/kg	784
1001	Wheat and meslin	2 253.9	2 440.0	2 387.3	0.4	0.4	0.3	US$/kg	041
8471	Automatic data processing machines and units thereof	2 299.4	2 443.8	2 106.8					752
8703	Motor cars and other motor vehicles principally designed for the transport	2 728.2	2 231.2	1 480.9	*15.6*	*15.8*	*16.3*	thsd US$/unit	781
7207	Semi-finished products of iron or non-alloy steel	2 292.3	2 048.4	1 879.8	0.6	0.5	0.5	US$/kg	672
2304	Oil-cake and other solid residues	1 828.5	1 927.0	2 194.9	0.5	0.5	0.6	US$/kg	081

Iran (Islamic Republic of)

Goods Imports: CIF, by origin | **Goods Exports: FOB, by last known destination** | **Trade System: Special**

Overview:

In 2011, the value of merchandise exports of the Islamic Republic of Iran increased substantially by 55.8 percent to reach 130.5 bln US$, while its merchandise imports increased substantially by 24.9 percent to reach 68.3 bln US$ (see graph 1, table 2 and table 3). The merchandise trade balance recorded a large surplus of 62.2 bln US$ (see graph 1). The largest merchandise trade balance was with MDG Eastern Asia at 55.8 bln US$ (see graph 4). Merchandise exports in the Islamic Republic of Iran were highly concentrated amongst partners; imports were diversified. The top 5 partners accounted for 80 percent or more of exports and 11 partners accounted for 80 percent or more of imports (see graph 5). In 2012, the value of exports of services of the Islamic Republic of Iran decreased substantially by 22.4 percent, reaching 6.7 bln US$, while its imports of services decreased substantially by 23.9 percent and reached 13.0 bln US$ (see graph 2). There was a large trade in services deficit of 6.3 bln US$.

Graph 1: Total merchandise trade, by value

(Bln US$ by year)

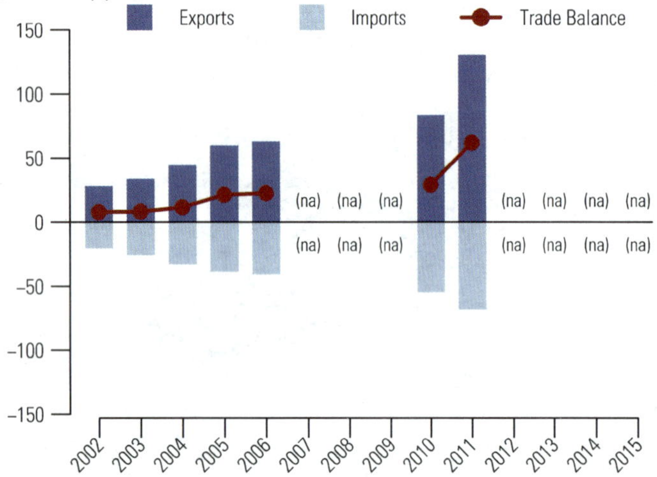

Graph 2: Total services trade, by value

(Bln US$ by year)

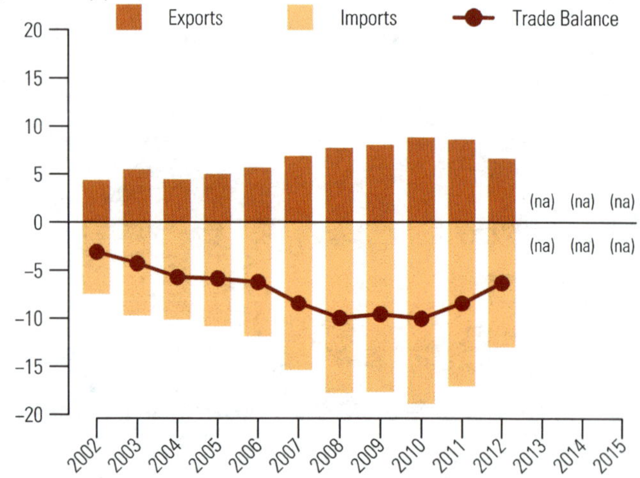

Exports Profile:

"Mineral fuels, lubricants" (SITC section 3), "Not classified elsewhere in the SITC" (SITC section 9) and "Chemicals" (SITC section 5) were the largest commodity groups for exports in 2011, representing respectively 70.5, 11.3 and 7.0 percent of exported goods (see table 2). From 2009 to 2011, the largest export commodity was "Petroleum oils, crude" (HS code 2709) (see table 1). The top three destinations for merchandise exports were Other Asia nes, Rest of Europe nes and Areas nes, accounting for respectively 45.6, 18.9 and 5.9 percent of total exports. "Transportation" (EBOPS code 205) accounted for the largest share of exports of services in 2006 at 2.9 bln US$, followed by "Travel" (EBOPS code 236) at 1.2 bln US$ and "Construction services" (EBOPS code 249) at 996.0 mln US$ (see graph 3).

Graph 3: Exports of services by EBOPS category

(% share in 2006)

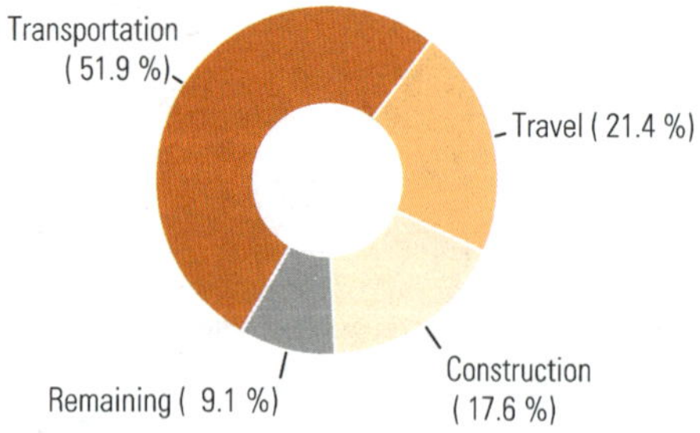

Table 1: Top 10 export commodities 2009 to 2011

HS code	4-digit heading of Harmonized System 2002	Value (million US$) 2009	2010	2011	Unit value 2009	2010	2011	Unit	SITC code
	All Commodities	...	83785.0	130544.0					
2709	Petroleum oils, crude	...	46709.4	84381.6		0.4	0.7	US$/kg	333
9999	Commodities not specified according to kind	...	3326.2	14755.6					931
2710	Petroleum oils, other than crude	...	8482.5	1075.7		*0.7*	0.9	US$/kg	334
2711	Petroleum gases and other gaseous hydrocarbons	...	3167.2	5544.8		0.7	0.9	US$/kg	343
3901	Polymers of ethylene, in primary forms	...	1814.4	2074.8		1.1	1.3	US$/kg	571
2905	Acyclic alcohols and their derivatives	...	1220.1	1672.7					512
0802	Other nuts, fresh or dried	...	1175.3	1034.8		7.6	7.8	US$/kg	057
2902	Cyclic hydrocarbons	...	831.6	1130.0		1.0	1.1	US$/kg	511
2601	Iron ores and concentrates	...	1124.3	789.9		0.1	0.0	US$/kg	281
2713	Petroleum coke and other residues	...	668.1	713.8		0.5	0.5	US$/kg	335

Table 2: Merchandise exports by SITC

(Value in million US$, growth and shares in percentage)

SITC	2011	Avg. Growth rates 2007-2011	Avg. Growth rates 2010-2011	2011 share
Total	130 544.0	...	55.8	100.0
0+1	4 694.5	...	-7.8	3.6
2+4	1 620.2	...	-13.9	1.2
3	92 038.9	...	55.2	70.5
5	9 113.4	...	26.4	7.0
6	5 555.6	...	21.2	4.3
7	1 425.0	...	-6.1	1.1
8	1 329.7	...	58.0	1.0
9	14 766.7	...	342.7	11.3

Table 3: Merchandise imports by SITC

(Value in million US$, growth and shares in percentage)

SITC	2011	Avg. Growth rates 2007-2011	Avg. Growth rates 2010-2011	2011 share
Total	68 319.0	...	24.9	100.0
0+1	7 391.3	...	9.8	10.8
2+4	4 192.3	...	32.6	6.1
3	973.9	...	-33.9	1.4
5	7 449.4	...	12.0	10.9
6	14 125.5	...	5.3	20.7
7	19 334.6	...	14.9	28.3
8	2 078.9	...	3.6	3.0
9	12 773.2	...	188.4	18.7

SITC Legend

SITC Code	Description
Total	All commodities
0+1	Food, animals + beverages, tobacco
2+4	Crude materials + anim. & veg. oils
3	Mineral fuels, lubricants
5	Chemicals
6	Goods classified chiefly by material
7	Machinery and transport equipment
8	Miscellaneous manufactured articles
9	Not classified elsewhere in the SITC

Graph 4: Merchandise trade balance

(Bln US$ by MDG Regions in 2011)

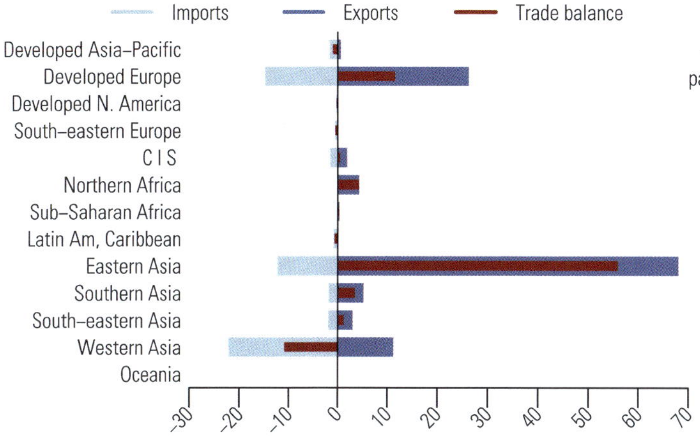

Graph 5: Partner concentration of merchandise trade

(Cumulative share by ranked partners in 2011)

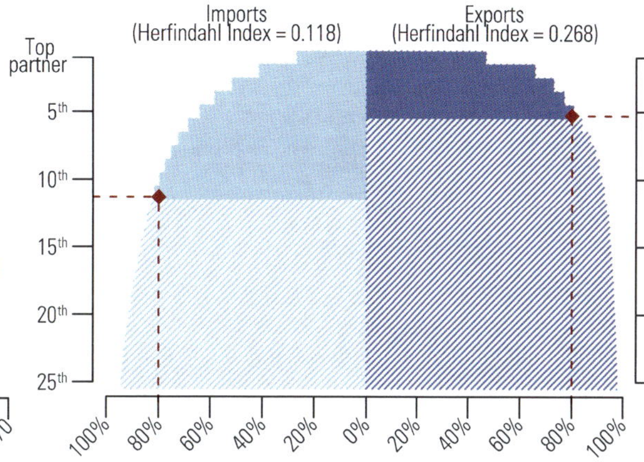

Graph 6: Imports of services by EBOPS category

(% share in 2006)

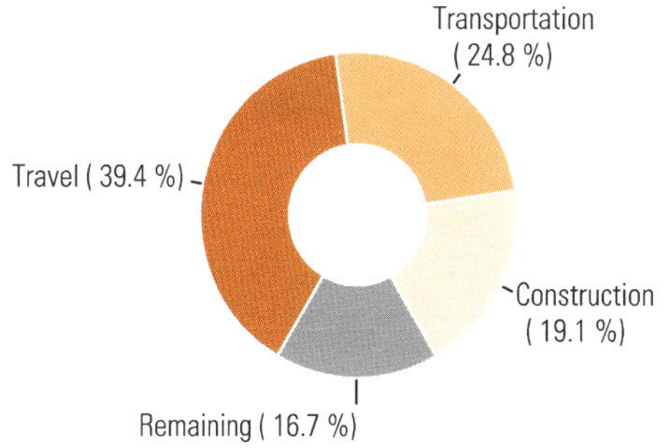

Imports Profile:

"Machinery and transport equipment" (SITC section 7), "Goods classified chiefly by material" (SITC section 6) and "Not classified elsewhere in the SITC" (SITC section 9) were the largest commodity groups for imports in 2011, representing respectively 28.3, 20.7 and 18.7 percent of imported goods (see table 3). From 2009 to 2011, the largest import commodity was "Commodities not specified according to kind" (HS code 9999) (see table 4). The top three partners for merchandise imports were the United Arab Emirates, China and Areas nes, accounting for respectively 27.5, 10.4 and 8.2 percent of total imports. "Travel" (EBOPS code 236) accounted for the largest share of imports of services in 2006 at 4.7 bln US$, followed by "Transportation" (EBOPS code 205) at 3.0 bln US$ and "Construction services" (EBOPS code 249) at 2.3 bln US$ (see graph 6).

Table 4: Top 10 import commodities 2009 to 2011

HS code	4-digit heading of Harmonized System 2002	Value (million US$) 2009	2010	2011	Unit value 2009	2010	2011	Unit	SITC code
	All Commodities	...	54 697.2	68 319.0					
9999	Commodities not specified according to kind	...	3 977.2	12 773.2					931
7206	Iron and non-alloy steel in ingots or other primary forms	...	2 479.3	2 867.7		0.6	0.7	US$/kg	672
7208	Flat-rolled products of iron or non-alloy steel	...	1 977.8	1 613.8		0.7	0.8	US$/kg	673
1005	Maize (corn)	...	919.6	1 294.0		0.3	0.4	US$/kg	044
3004	Medicaments (excluding goods of heading 30.02, 30.05 or 30.06)	...	943.4	1 120.0		130.5	130.2	US$/kg	542
1006	Rice	...	942.0	975.4		0.8	0.9	US$/kg	042
8471	Automatic data processing machines and units thereof	...	873.0	1 013.9					752
8411	Turbo-jets, turbo-propellers and other gas turbines	...	1 192.2	629.7					714
2304	Oil-cake and other solid residues	...	735.5	844.8		0.4	0.5	US$/kg	081
0202	Meat of bovine animals, frozen	...	777.4	769.3		4.1	5.3	US$/kg	011

Ireland

Goods Imports: CIF, by origin | **Goods Exports: FOB, by last known destination** | **Trade System: General**

Overview:

In 2015, the value of merchandise exports of Ireland increased slightly by 4.1 percent to reach 123.2 bln US$, while its merchandise imports increased slightly by 4.6 percent to reach 74.3 bln US$ (see graph 1, table 2 and table 3). The merchandise trade balance recorded a moderate surplus of 48.8 bln US$ (see graph 1). The largest merchandise trade balance was with MDG Developed Europe at 25.2 bln US$ (see graph 4). Merchandise exports in Ireland were diversified amongst partners; imports were also diversified. The top 10 partners accounted for 80 percent or more of exports and 11 partners accounted for 80 percent or more of imports (see graph 5). In 2014, the value of exports of services of Ireland increased moderately by 8.5 percent, reaching 141.6 bln US$, while its imports of services increased substantially by 17.5 percent and reached 143.8 bln US$ (see graph 2). There was a relatively small trade in services deficit of 2.2 bln US$.

Graph 1: Total merchandise trade, by value

(Bln US$ by year)

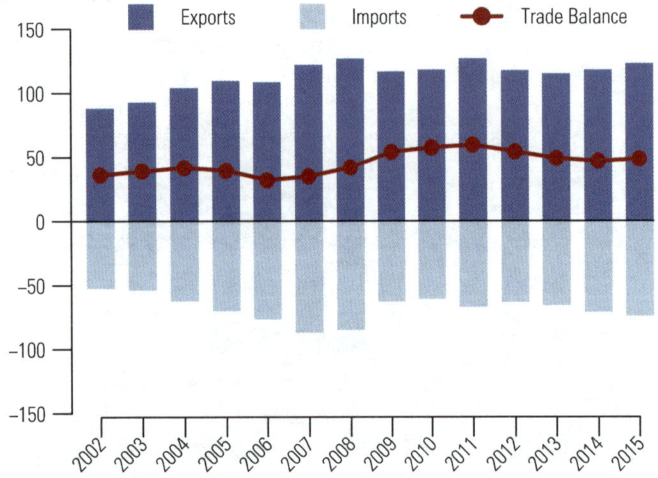

Graph 2: Total services trade, by value

(Bln US$ by year)

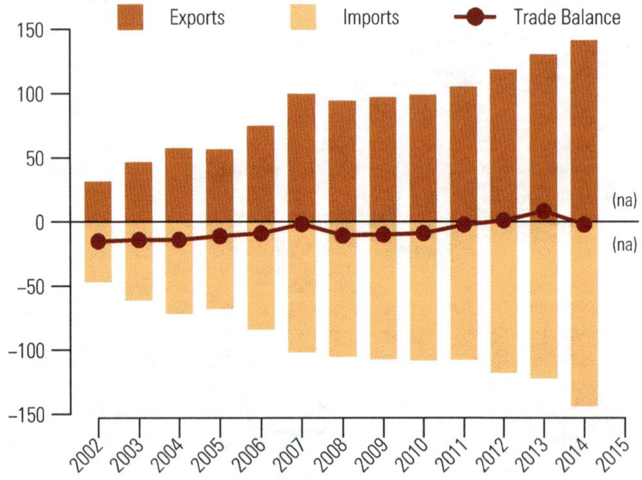

Exports Profile:

"Chemicals" (SITC section 5), "Machinery and transport equipment" (SITC section 7) and "Miscellaneous manufactured articles" (SITC section 8) were the largest commodity groups for exports in 2015, representing respectively 57.7, 14.0 and 12.9 percent of exported goods (see table 2). From 2013 to 2015, the largest export commodity was "Medicaments (excluding goods of heading 30.02, 30.05 or 30.06)" (HS code 3004) (see table 1). The top three destinations for merchandise exports were the United States, the United Kingdom and Belgium, accounting for respectively 22.4, 15.0 and 13.1 percent of total exports. "Computer and information services" (EBOPS code 262) accounted for the largest share of exports of services in 2014 at 63.7 bln US$, followed by "Other business services" (EBOPS code 268) at 31.8 bln US$ and "Insurance services" (EBOPS code 253) at 12.3 bln US$ (see graph 3).

Graph 3: Exports of services by EBOPS category

(% share in 2014)

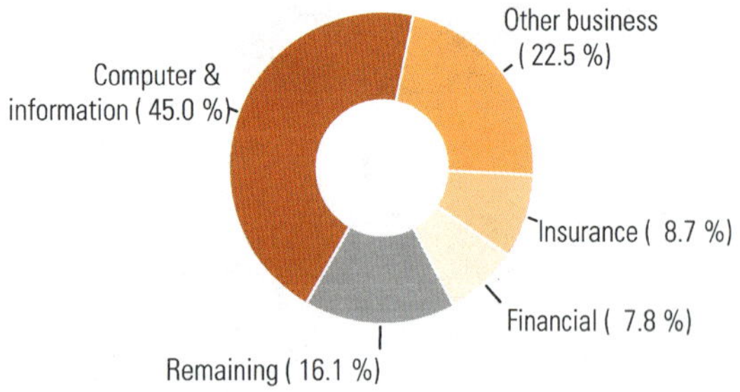

Table 1: Top 10 export commodities 2013 to 2015

HS code	4-digit heading of Harmonized System 2012	Value (million US$) 2013	2014	2015	Unit value 2013	2014	2015	Unit	SITC code
	All Commodities	115 323.5	118 287.4	123 152.3					
3004	Medicaments (excluding goods of heading 30.02, 30.05 or 30.06)	18 152.6	19 662.2	21 811.0	*115.6*	*121.1*	*137.2*	US$/kg	542
2933	Heterocyclic compounds with nitrogen hetero-atom(s) only	15 128.0	13 926.1	13 558.2					515
3302	Mixtures of odoriferous substances and mixtures	7 388.0	8 306.9	8 150.1	*56.0*	*62.3*	59.2	US$/kg	551
3002	Human blood; animal blood prepared for therapeutic uses	6 216.4	5 961.0	8 719.3	*5.1*	*4.8*	*2.9*	thsd US$/kg	541
9021	Orthopaedic appliances, including crutches, surgical belts and trusses	4 881.2	4 865.2	4 803.1					899
9018	Instruments and appliances used in medical, surgical, dental or veterinary	3 990.8	4 386.3	5 634.1					872
2934	Nucleic acids and their salts	4 233.0	4 478.7	3 700.4		*18.9*	*17.7*	thsd US$/kg	515
8471	Automatic data processing machines and units thereof	3 396.8	3 738.9	3 534.0	*1.0*	*1.3*	*1.2*	thsd US$/unit	752
2935	Sulphonamides	2 277.9	3 357.2	4 176.2	*21.2*	*19.1*	*20.6*	thsd US$/kg	515
3824	Prepared binders for foundry moulds or cores	2 760.6	2 688.4	2 261.9	*24.6*	*24.1*	*17.4*	US$/kg	598

Services Imports and Exports: EBOPS 2002 categories

Table 2: Merchandise exports by SITC

(Value in million US$, growth and shares in percentage)

SITC	2015	Avg. Growth rates 2011-2015	Avg. Growth rates 2014-2015	2015 share
Total	123152.3	-0.8	4.1	100.0
0+1	12357.5	-0.5	-11.1	10.0
2+4	2028.8	-4.5	-16.3	1.6
3	881.2	-17.3	-19.6	0.7
5	71032.8	-2.3	3.9	57.7
6	2319.4	0.1	-5.7	1.9
7	17201.4	4.5	29.6	14.0
8	15907.3	2.5	5.4	12.9
9	1423.9	7.2	-15.3	1.2

Table 3: Merchandise imports by SITC

(Value in million US$, growth and shares in percentage)

SITC	2015	Avg. Growth rates 2011-2015	Avg. Growth rates 2014-2015	2015 share
Total	74334.5	2.6	4.6	100.0
0+1	8358.8	0.8	-9.8	11.2
2+4	1228.2	-2.7	-3.0	1.7
3	5687.0	-12.4	-33.7	7.7
5	15421.1	1.6	2.2	20.7
6	5222.1	0.3	-6.4	7.0
7	27672.6	12.5	44.0	37.2
8	9047.5	2.0	0.0	12.2
9	1697.3	-11.7	-43.5	2.3

SITC Legend

SITC Code	Description
Total	All commodities
0+1	Food, animals + beverages, tobacco
2+4	Crude materials + anim. & veg. oils
3	Mineral fuels, lubricants
5	Chemicals
6	Goods classified chiefly by material
7	Machinery and transport equipment
8	Miscellaneous manufactured articles
9	Not classified elsewhere in the SITC

Graph 4: Merchandise trade balance

(Bln US$ by MDG Regions in 2015)

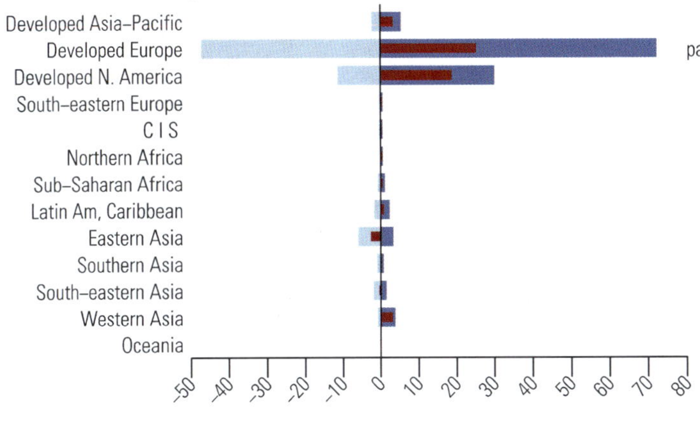

Graph 5: Partner concentration of merchandise trade

(Cumulative share by ranked partners in 2015)

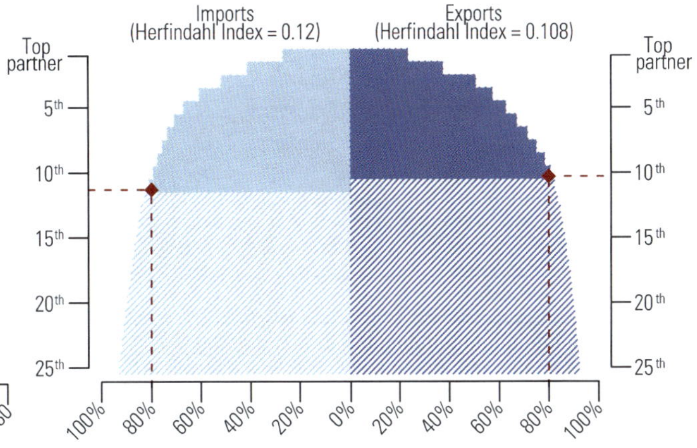

Graph 6: Imports of services by EBOPS category

(% share in 2014)

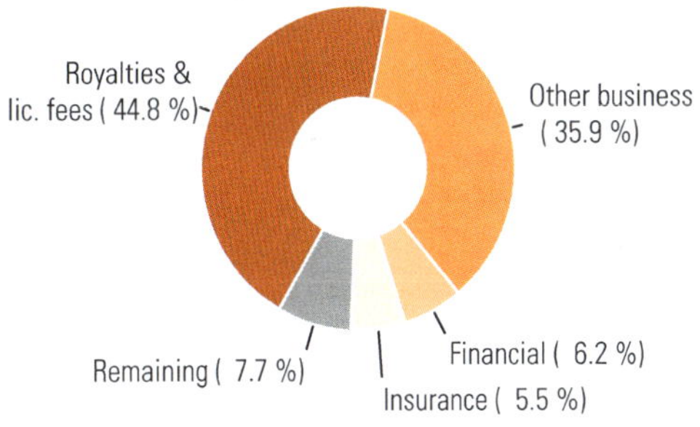

Imports Profile:

"Machinery and transport equipment" (SITC section 7), "Chemicals" (SITC section 5) and "Miscellaneous manufactured articles" (SITC section 8) were the largest commodity groups for imports in 2015, representing respectively 37.2, 20.7 and 12.2 percent of imported goods (see table 3). From 2013 to 2015, the largest import commodity was "Other aircraft (for example, helicopters, aeroplanes); spacecraft" (HS code 8802) (see table 4). The top three partners for merchandise imports were the United Kingdom, the United States and Germany, accounting for respectively 30.7, 12.1 and 8.3 percent of total imports. "Royalties and license fees" (EBOPS code 266) accounted for the largest share of imports of services in 2014 at 64.4 bln US$, followed by "Other business services" (EBOPS code 268) at 51.6 bln US$ and "Financial services" (EBOPS code 260) at 8.9 bln US$ (see graph 6).

Table 4: Top 10 import commodities 2013 to 2015

HS code	4-digit heading of Harmonized System 2012	Value (million US$) 2013	Value (million US$) 2014	Value (million US$) 2015	Unit value 2013	Unit value 2014	Unit value 2015	Unit	SITC code
	All Commodities	65950.7	71049.0	74334.5					
8802	Other aircraft (for example, helicopters, aeroplanes); spacecraft	1037.4	950.7	9554.8					792
2710	Petroleum oils, other than crude	4016.0	4318.6	2473.5	*1.0*	*1.0*	0.6	US$/kg	334
3004	Medicaments (excluding goods of heading 30.02, 30.05 or 30.06)	3478.6	3216.1	3619.6	*122.3*	*64.3*	*69.4*	US$/kg	542
9999	Commodities not specified according to kind	2875.8	2991.9	1674.5					931
8471	Automatic data processing machines and units thereof	1973.1	2345.1	2603.3	*113.6*	*272.6*	*273.0*	US$/unit	752
8703	Motor cars and other motor vehicles principally designed for the transport	1528.2	2220.1	2501.5	*5.5*	*9.4*	8.6	thsd US$/unit	781
2709	Petroleum oils and oils obtained from bituminous minerals, crude	2492.1	2114.3	1548.6	0.8	0.8	0.4	US$/kg	333
2711	Petroleum gases and other gaseous hydrocarbons	2093.7	1698.3	1279.2	0.5	0.4	0.3	US$/kg	343
8473	Parts and accessories for use with machines of heading 84.69 to 84.72	1567.7	1517.6	1399.1	*136.5*	*149.4*	*162.4*	US$/kg	759
2933	Heterocyclic compounds with nitrogen hetero-atom(s) only	1182.2	1627.0	1616.3			*249.2*	US$/kg	515

Israel

Goods Imports: CIF, by origin | **Goods Exports: FOB, by sale** | **Trade System: Special**

Overview:

In 2015, the value of merchandise exports of Israel decreased moderately by 7.6 percent to reach 63.8 bln US$, while its merchandise imports decreased substantially by 14.2 percent to reach 62.1 bln US$ (see graph 1, table 2 and table 3). The merchandise trade balance recorded a relatively small surplus of 1.7 bln US$ (see graph 1). The largest merchandise trade balance was with MDG Developed North America at 10.6 bln US$ (see graph 4). Merchandise exports in Israel were diversified amongst partners; imports were also diversified. The top 15 partners accounted for 80 percent or more of exports and 17 partners accounted for 80 percent or more of imports (see graph 5). In 2014, the value of exports of services of Israel increased slightly by 2.6 percent, reaching 35.4 bln US$, while its imports of services increased moderately by 8.0 percent and reached 22.5 bln US$ (see graph 2). There was a moderate trade in services surplus of 12.9 bln US$.

Graph 1: Total merchandise trade, by value

(Bln US$ by year)

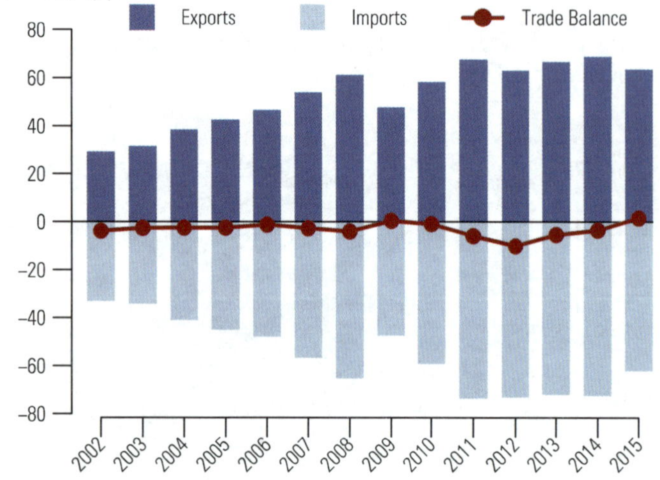

Graph 2: Total services trade, by value

(Bln US$ by year)

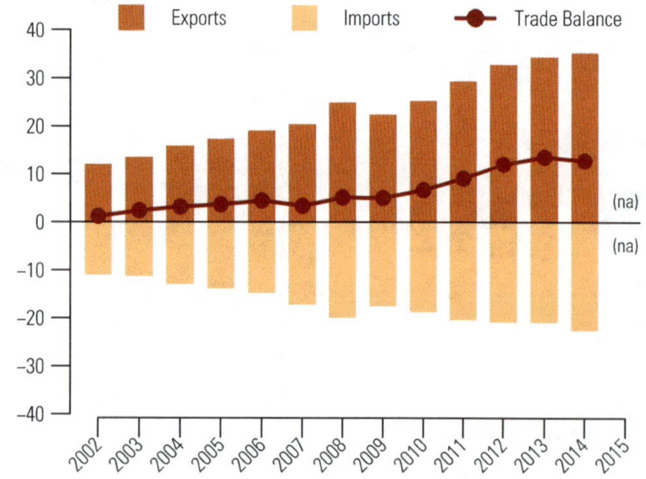

Exports Profile:

"Goods classified chiefly by material" (SITC section 6), "Machinery and transport equipment" (SITC section 7) and "Chemicals" (SITC section 5) were the largest commodity groups for exports in 2015, representing respectively 33.0, 28.7 and 24.3 percent of exported goods (see table 2). From 2013 to 2015, the largest export commodity was "Diamonds, whether or not worked, but not mounted or set" (HS code 7102) (see table 1). The top three destinations for merchandise exports were the United States, China, Hong Kong SAR and the United Kingdom, accounting for respectively 27.3, 8.4 and 5.9 percent of total exports. "Computer and information services" (EBOPS code 262) accounted for the largest share of exports of services in 2014 at 14.3 bln US$, followed by "Other business services" (EBOPS code 268) at 7.9 bln US$ and "Travel" (EBOPS code 236) at 5.7 bln US$ (see graph 3).

Graph 3: Exports of services by EBOPS category

(% share in 2014)

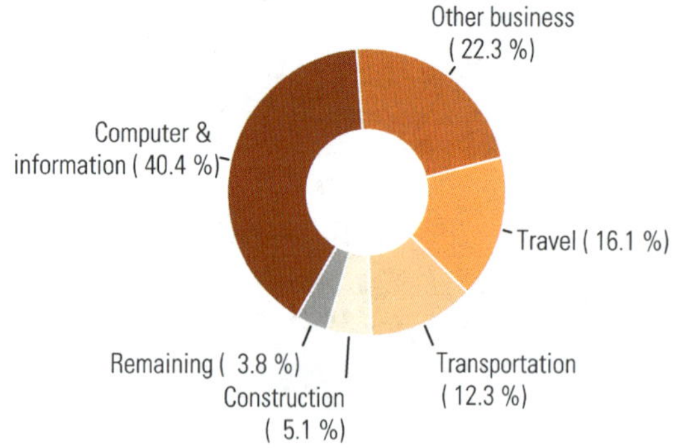

Table 1: Top 10 export commodities 2013 to 2015

HS code	4-digit heading of Harmonized System 2012	Value (million US$) 2013	2014	2015	Unit value 2013	2014	2015	Unit	SITC code
	All Commodities	66781.2	68965.0	63750.6					
7102	Diamonds, whether or not worked, but not mounted or set	19016.2	20546.6	17554.2					667
8542	Electronic integrated circuits	4075.4	3910.2	5609.8					776
3004	Medicaments (excluding goods of heading 30.02, 30.05 or 30.06)	3284.1	3846.1	3785.9					542
3824	Prepared binders for foundry moulds or cores	4039.9	4167.8	2151.4					598
3003	Medicaments (excluding goods of heading 30.02, 30.05 or 30.06)	2592.1	2160.0	2539.4					542
8803	Parts of goods of heading 88.01 or 88.02	1865.3	1534.1	2576.1					792
8517	Electrical apparatus for line telephony or line telegraphy	1788.2	1790.5	1591.0					764
9018	Instruments and appliances used in medical, surgical, dental or veterinary	1320.9	1506.5	1443.2					872
3105	Mineral or chemical fertilisers	1439.9	1260.6	990.0	*0.5*	*1.5*		US$/kg	562
9031	Measuring or checking instruments, appliances and machines	1186.2	939.8	709.8					874

Services Imports and Exports: EBOPS 2002 categories

Table 2: Merchandise exports by SITC

(Value in million US$, growth and shares in percentage)

SITC	2015	Avg. Growth rates 2011-2015	Avg. Growth rates 2014-2015	2015 share
Total	63 750.6	-1.5	-7.6	100.0
0+1	1 717.5	-3.3	-15.6	2.7
2+4	858.4	-7.7	-17.0	1.3
3	275.2	-19.6	-65.1	0.4
5	15 479.2	-4.7	-14.4	24.3
6	21 065.0	-3.6	-12.4	33.0
7	18 274.9	4.9	10.6	28.7
8	5 409.3	-0.9	-1.8	8.5
9	671.1	35.4	-27.3	1.1

Table 3: Merchandise imports by SITC

(Value in million US$, growth and shares in percentage)

SITC	2015	Avg. Growth rates 2011-2015	Avg. Growth rates 2014-2015	2015 share
Total	62 058.2	-4.2	-14.2	100.0
0+1	4 733.9	0.0	-5.3	7.6
2+4	1 411.7	-4.3	-11.6	2.3
3	7 390.5	-14.2	-42.1	11.9
5	7 575.5	-1.0	-7.4	12.2
6	13 603.1	-6.8	-17.6	21.9
7	20 197.1	-1.1	-4.3	32.5
8	6 638.0	2.5	-1.2	10.7
9	508.3	7.9	11.4	0.8

SITC Legend

SITC Code	Description
Total	All commodities
0+1	Food, animals + beverages, tobacco
2+4	Crude materials + anim. & veg. oils
3	Mineral fuels, lubricants
5	Chemicals
6	Goods classified chiefly by material
7	Machinery and transport equipment
8	Miscellaneous manufactured articles
9	Not classified elsewhere in the SITC

Graph 4: Merchandise trade balance

(Bln US$ by MDG Regions in 2015)

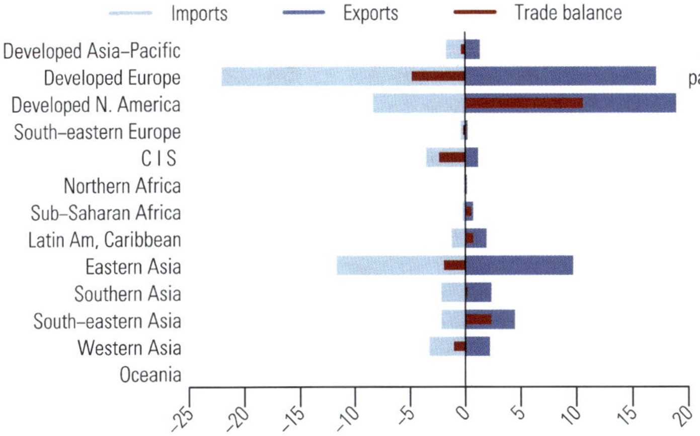

Graph 5: Partner concentration of merchandise trade

(Cumulative share by ranked partners in 2015)

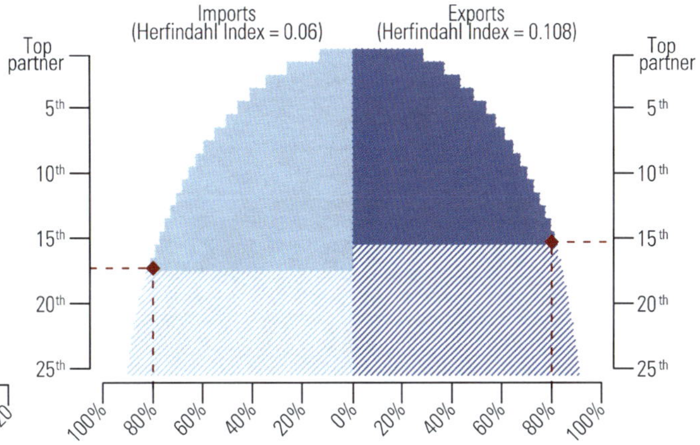

Graph 6: Imports of services by EBOPS category

(% share in 2014)

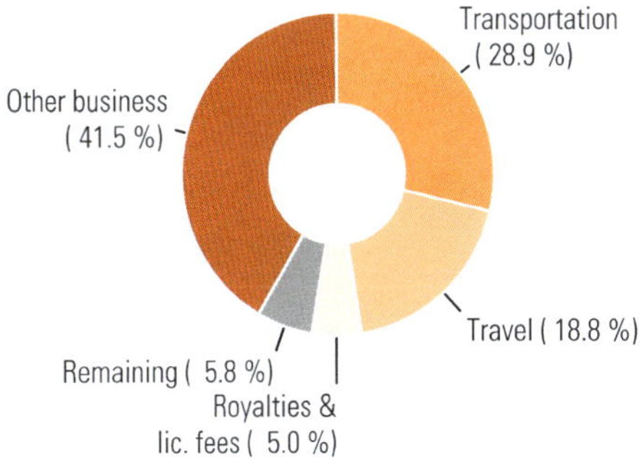

Imports Profile:

"Machinery and transport equipment" (SITC section 7), "Goods classified chiefly by material" (SITC section 6) and "Chemicals" (SITC section 5) were the largest commodity groups for imports in 2015, representing respectively 32.5, 21.9 and 12.2 percent of imported goods (see table 3). From 2013 to 2015, the largest import commodity was "Diamonds, whether or not worked, but not mounted or set" (HS code 7102) (see table 4). The top three partners for merchandise imports were Areas nes, the United States and China, accounting for respectively 15.4, 12.0 and 9.5 percent of total imports. "Other business services" (EBOPS code 268) accounted for the largest share of imports of services in 2014 at 9.3 bln US$, followed by "Transportation" (EBOPS code 205) at 6.5 bln US$ and "Travel" (EBOPS code 236) at 4.2 bln US$ (see graph 6).

Table 4: Top 10 import commodities 2013 to 2015

HS code	4-digit heading of Harmonized System 2012	Value (million US$) 2013	2014	2015	Unit value 2013	2014	2015	Unit	SITC code
	All Commodities	71 995.0	72 331.8	62 058.2					
7102	Diamonds, whether or not worked, but not mounted or set	9 014.2	9 301.2	6 892.2					667
2709	Petroleum oils and oils obtained from bituminous minerals, crude	9 062.5	8 459.6	4 552.2		*0.8*	*0.8*	US$/kg	333
8703	Motor cars and other motor vehicles principally designed for the transport	3 220.1	4 062.9	3 128.4	*14.1*	*14.6*	*16.3*	thsd US$/unit	781
2710	Petroleum oils, other than crude	3 698.8	3 031.8	1 790.4					334
8542	Electronic integrated circuits	1 846.6	1 735.4	2 531.3					776
8517	Electrical apparatus for line telephony or line telegraphy	1 450.9	1 642.9	1 656.7					764
3004	Medicaments (excluding goods of heading 30.02, 30.05 or 30.06)	1 471.4	1 363.9	1 295.1					542
8471	Automatic data processing machines and units thereof	1 298.3	1 345.9	1 284.8					752
2701	Coal; briquettes, ovoids and similar solid fuels manufactured from coal	1 157.1	929.1	730.1	*0.1*	*0.1*	*0.1*	US$/kg	321
8704	Motor vehicles for the transport of goods	773.1	613.5	766.0		40.2		thsd US$/unit	782

Italy

Goods Imports: CIF, by origin | **Goods Exports: FOB, by last known destination** | **Trade System: Special**

Overview:

In 2015, the value of merchandise exports of Italy fell for the first time since 2012, decreasing substantially by 13.4 percent to reach 458.8 bln US$, while its merchandise imports also decreased substantially by 13.7 percent to reach 409.0 bln US$ (see graph 1, table 2 and table 3). The merchandise trade balance recorded a relatively small surplus of 49.8 bln US$ (see graph 1). The largest merchandise trade balance was with MDG Developed North America at 26.6 bln US$ (see graph 4). Merchandise exports in Italy were diversified amongst partners; imports were also diversified. The top 28 partners accounted for 80 percent or more of exports and 25 partners accounted for 80 percent or more of imports (see graph 5). In 2014, the value of exports of services of Italy increased slightly by 1.9 percent, reaching 111.0 bln US$, while its imports of services increased slightly by 4.6 percent and reached 111.3 bln US$ (see graph 2). There was a relatively small trade in services deficit of 227.9 mln US$.

Graph 1: Total merchandise trade, by value

(Bln US$ by year)

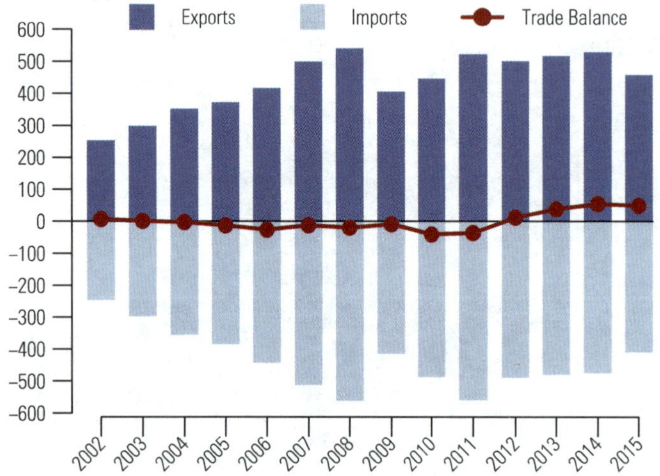

Graph 2: Total services trade, by value

(Bln US$ by year)

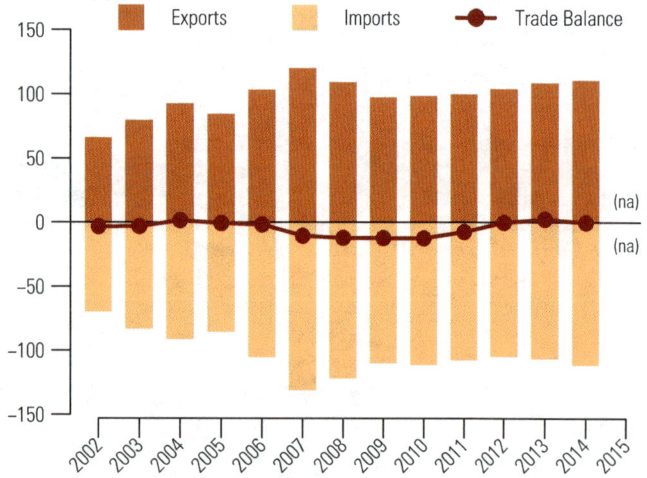

Exports Profile:

"Machinery and transport equipment" (SITC section 7), "Miscellaneous manufactured articles" (SITC section 8) and "Goods classified chiefly by material" (SITC section 6) were the largest commodity groups for exports in 2015, representing respectively 36.1, 18.0 and 17.8 percent of exported goods (see table 2). From 2013 to 2015, the largest export commodity was "Medicaments (excluding goods of heading 30.02, 30.05 or 30.06)" (HS code 3004), although it decreased by 16.1 percent in 2015 (see table 1). The top three destinations for merchandise exports were Germany, France and the United States, accounting for respectively 12.4, 10.6 and 7.7 percent of total exports. "Travel" (EBOPS code 236) continued to account for the largest share of exports of services in 2014 at 45.5 bln US$, followed by "Other business services" (EBOPS code 268) at 29.6 bln US$ and "Transportation" (EBOPS code 205) at 14.7 bln US$ (see graph 3).

Graph 3: Exports of services by EBOPS category

(% share in 2014)

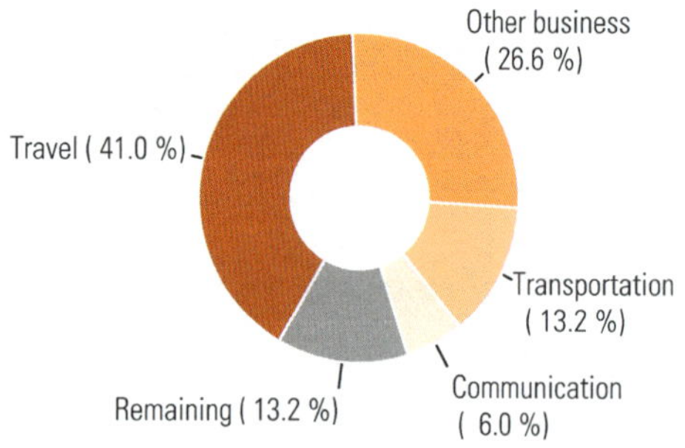

Table 1: Top 10 export commodities 2013 to 2015

HS code	4-digit heading of Harmonized System 2012	Value (million US$) 2013	2014	2015	Unit value 2013	2014	2015	Unit	SITC code
	All Commodities	518095.1	529528.7	458751.2					
3004	Medicaments (excluding goods of heading 30.02, 30.05 or 30.06)	20898.5	22088.8	18523.2	*112.4*	111.2	*94.4*	US$/kg	542
2710	Petroleum oils, other than crude	20432.5	17491.0	13087.8	0.9	0.9	0.5	US$/kg	334
8708	Parts and accessories of the motor vehicles of headings 87.01 to 87.05	15000.2	14550.9	12568.4	*8.0*	8.0	*6.9*	US$/kg	784
8703	Motor cars and other motor vehicles principally designed for the transport	10021.0	11616.4	13989.9	23.1	26.7	20.7	thsd US$/unit	781
9999	Commodities not specified according to kind	11430.0	11175.5	8904.6					931
6403	Footwear with outer soles of rubber, plastics, leather	8839.2	9141.0	7695.3	*66.3*	69.2	61.5	US$/pair	851
8481	Taps, cocks, valves and similar appliances for pipes, boiler shells	8814.9	9026.9	7577.2	*22.7*	*23.0*	*19.3*	US$/kg	747
9403	Other furniture and parts thereof	7726.3	7918.9	7012.6					821
4202	Trunks, suit-cases, vanity-cases, executive-cases, brief-cases	6818.6	7310.9	6450.0					831
7113	Articles of jewellery and parts thereof, of precious metal	6982.6	6937.9	6298.9	*8.3*	7.5	*6.0*	thsd US$/kg	897

Source: UN Comtrade

Services Imports and Exports: EBOPS 2002 categories

Table 2: Merchandise exports by SITC

(Value in million US$, growth and shares in percentage)

SITC	2015	Avg. Growth rates 2011-2015	Avg. Growth rates 2014-2015	2015 share
Total	458751.2	-3.2	-13.4	100.0
0+1	36701.1	-0.3	-10.2	8.0
2+4	7634.0	-4.6	-12.6	1.7
3	14716.9	-12.3	-24.9	3.2
5	57793.8	-0.6	-12.5	12.6
6	81645.2	-5.3	-16.5	17.8
7	165813.2	-2.6	-11.1	36.1
8	82475.6	-1.6	-13.1	18.0
9	11971.5	-11.3	-20.8	2.6

Table 3: Merchandise imports by SITC

(Value in million US$, growth and shares in percentage)

SITC	2015	Avg. Growth rates 2011-2015	Avg. Growth rates 2014-2015	2015 share
Total	408971.0	-7.5	-13.7	100.0
0+1	38622.3	-4.2	-14.2	9.4
2+4	20978.3	-8.3	-16.9	5.1
3	51882.5	-17.1	-32.9	12.7
5	64461.1	-4.5	-11.4	15.8
6	62438.8	-6.9	-13.0	15.3
7	109592.7	-6.0	-4.6	26.8
8	51120.2	-3.5	-8.4	12.5
9	9875.3	-7.2	-12.1	2.4

SITC Legend

SITC Code	Description
Total	All commodities
0+1	Food, animals + beverages, tobacco
2+4	Crude materials + anim. & veg. oils
3	Mineral fuels, lubricants
5	Chemicals
6	Goods classified chiefly by material
7	Machinery and transport equipment
8	Miscellaneous manufactured articles
9	Not classified elsewhere in the SITC

Graph 4: Merchandise trade balance

(Bln US$ by MDG Regions in 2015)

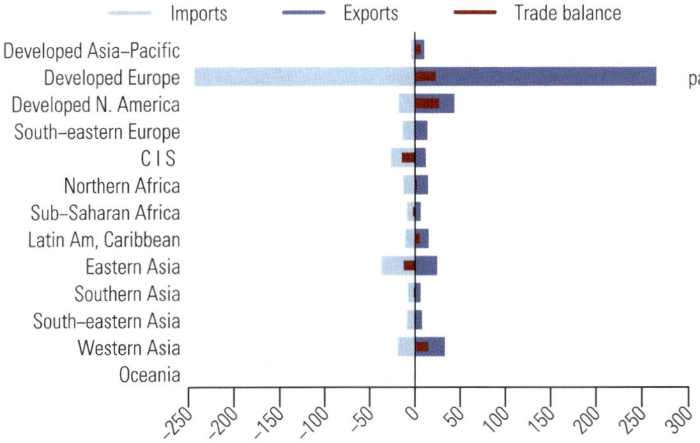

Graph 5: Partner concentration of merchandise trade

(Cumulative share by ranked partners in 2015)

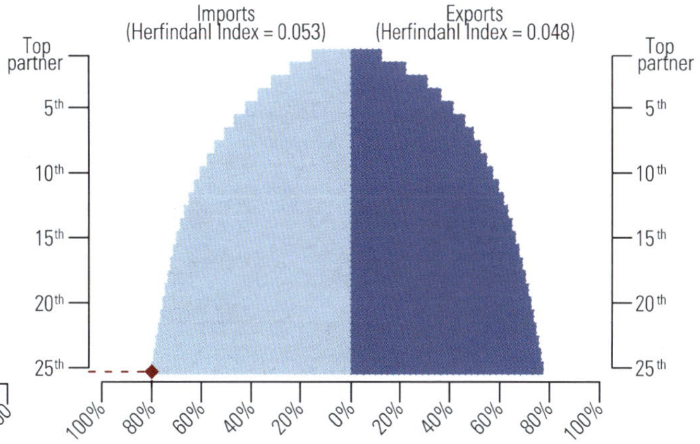

Graph 6: Imports of services by EBOPS category

(% share in 2014)

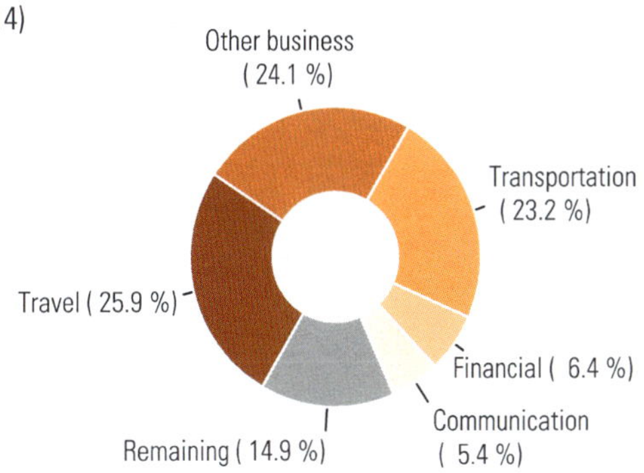

Imports Profile:

"Machinery and transport equipment" (SITC section 7), "Chemicals" (SITC section 5) and "Goods classified chiefly by material" (SITC section 6) were the largest commodity groups for imports in 2015, representing respectively 26.8, 15.8 and 15.3 percent of imported goods (see table 3). From 2013 to 2015, the largest import commodity was "Petroleum oils and oils obtained from bituminous minerals, crude" (HS code 2709), although it decreased by 38.4 percent in 2015 (see table 4). The top three partners for merchandise imports were Germany, France and China, accounting for respectively 15.1, 8.6 and 7.0 percent of total imports. "Travel" (EBOPS code 236) accounted for the largest share of imports of services in 2014 at 28.8 bln US$, followed by "Other business services" (EBOPS code 268) at 26.8 bln US$ and "Transportation" (EBOPS code 205) at 25.9 bln US$ (see graph 6).

Table 4: Top 10 import commodities 2013 to 2015

HS code	4-digit heading of Harmonized System 2012	Value (million US$) 2013	Value (million US$) 2014	Value (million US$) 2015	Unit value 2013	Unit value 2014	Unit value 2015	Unit	SITC code
	All Commodities	479336.4	474082.6	408971.0					
2709	Petroleum oils and oils obtained from bituminous minerals, crude	46459.8	38523.9	23749.8	0.8	0.7	0.4	US$/kg	333
2711	Petroleum gases and other gaseous hydrocarbons	29068.4	22202.8	16652.3	0.6	0.5	0.4	US$/kg	343
8703	Motor cars and other motor vehicles principally designed for the transport	20206.4	22865.4	22575.0	17.0	17.5	15.1	thsd US$/unit	781
3004	Medicaments (excluding goods of heading 30.02, 30.05 or 30.06)	15528.0	14905.7	14060.4	*108.3*	*107.0*	*104.7*	US$/kg	542
2710	Petroleum oils, other than crude	13821.5	11598.1	7010.0	0.8	0.8	0.5	US$/kg	334
8517	Electrical apparatus for line telephony or line telegraphy	7723.7	7782.3	7869.4					764
8708	Parts and accessories of the motor vehicles of headings 87.01 to 87.05	6584.8	6956.0	7370.0	*8.4*	*8.4*	8.2	US$/kg	784
9999	Commodities not specified according to kind	5991.6	6326.6	5662.8					931
8471	Automatic data processing machines and units thereof	5717.5	5755.0	4652.1			157.2	US$/unit	752
7108	Gold (including gold plated with platinum)	5611.4	4785.7	4027.5	32.0	33.0	30.6	thsd US$/kg	971

Jamaica

Goods Imports: CIF, by origin **Goods Exports: FOB, by last known destination** **Trade System: Special**

Overview:

In 2014, the value of merchandise exports of Jamaica decreased moderately by 7.5 percent to reach 1.5 bln US$, while its merchandise imports decreased moderately by 6.1 percent to reach 5.8 bln US$ (see graph 1, table 2 and table 3). The merchandise trade balance recorded a large deficit of 4.4 bln US$ (see graph 1). The largest merchandise trade balance was with MDG Latin America and the Caribbean at -1.8 bln US$ (see graph 4). Merchandise exports in Jamaica were moderately concentrated amongst partners; imports were also moderately concentrated. The top 8 partners accounted for 80 percent or more of exports and 11 partners accounted for 80 percent or more of imports (see graph 5). In 2014, the value of exports of services of Jamaica increased moderately by 7.3 percent, reaching 2.9 bln US$, while its imports of services increased moderately by 8.0 percent and reached 2.2 bln US$ (see graph 2). There was a moderate trade in services surplus of 626.1 mln US$.

Graph 1: Total merchandise trade, by value

(Bln US$ by year)

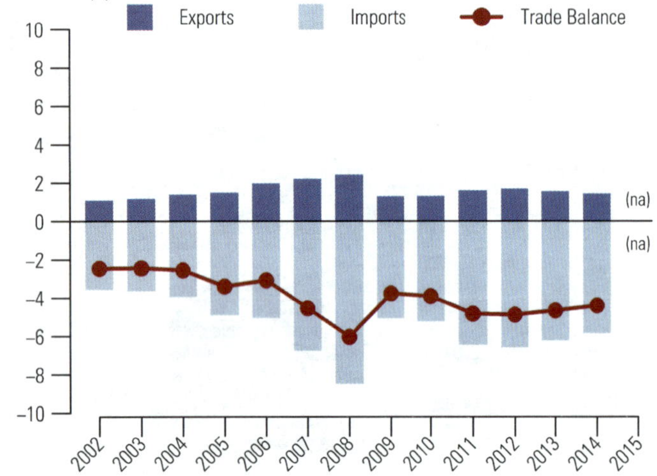

Graph 2: Total services trade, by value

(Bln US$ by year)

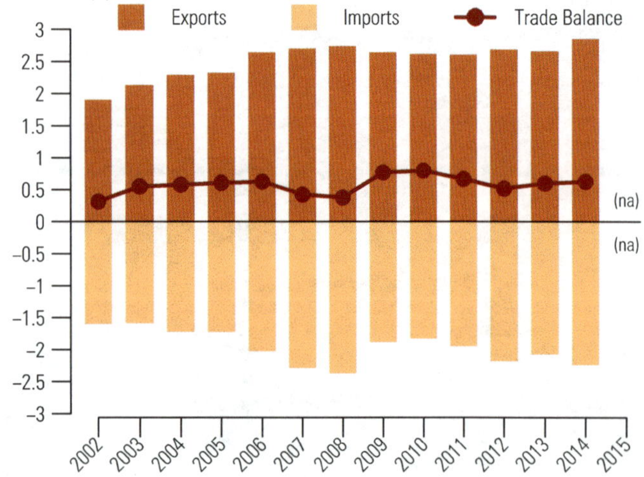

Exports Profile:

"Crude materials + anim. & veg. oils" (SITC section 2+4), "Mineral fuels, lubricants" (SITC section 3) and "Food, animals + beverages, tobacco" (SITC section 0+1) were the largest commodity groups for exports in 2014, representing respectively 47.6, 21.2 and 18.1 percent of exported goods (see table 2). From 2012 to 2014, the largest export commodity was "Artificial corundum, whether or not chemically defined" (HS code 2818) (see table 1). The top three destinations for merchandise exports were the United States, Canada and the Netherlands, accounting for respectively 45.8, 12.0 and 5.5 percent of total exports. "Travel" (EBOPS code 236) accounted for the largest share of exports of services in 2014 at 2.3 bln US$, followed by "Transportation" (EBOPS code 205) at 218.2 mln US$ (see graph 3).

Graph 3: Exports of services by EBOPS category

(% share in 2014)

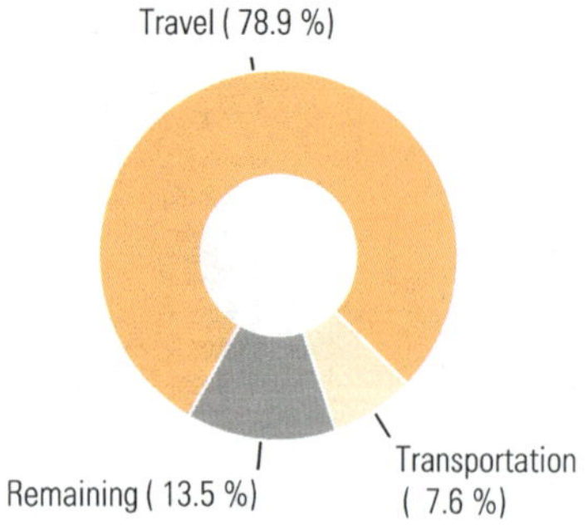

Table 1: Top 10 export commodities 2012 to 2014

HS code	4-digit heading of Harmonized System 2007	Value (million US$) 2012	2013	2014	Unit value 2012	2013	2014	Unit	SITC code
	All Commodities	1711.8	1569.1	1452.0					
2818	Artificial corundum, whether or not chemically defined	515.6	535.8	537.3	0.3	0.3	0.3	US$/kg	285
2710	Petroleum oils, other than crude	365.6	333.7	298.6	0.9	0.8	0.8	US$/kg	334
2606	Aluminium ores and concentrates	130.4	129.4	131.2	0.0	0.0	0.0	US$/kg	285
2207	Alcohol of a strength by volume of 80 % vol or higher	179.2	85.2	0.1	*0.9*	*0.9*	*0.9*	US$/litre	512
2208	Alcohol of a strength by volume of less than 80 % vol	59.5	52.4	50.7	*2.7*	*2.5*	*2.9*	US$/litre	112
1701	Cane or beet sugar and chemically pure sucrose, in solid form	92.6	52.7	0.1	0.9	0.9	1.5	US$/kg	061
0714	Manioc, arrowroot, sweet potatoes and similar roots	24.6	28.0	26.8	2.0	2.3	2.1	US$/kg	054
9999	Commodities not specified according to kind	5.8	6.1	64.0					931
0901	Coffee, whether or not roasted or decaffeinated	17.0	19.0	15.8	21.0	22.9	28.8	US$/kg	071
2103	Sauces and preparations therefor	15.4	16.3	17.6	4.2	4.1	3.7	US$/kg	098

Services Imports and Exports: EBOPS 2002 categories

Table 2: Merchandise exports by SITC

(Value in million US$, growth and shares in percentage)

SITC	2014	Avg. Growth rates 2010-2014	Avg. Growth rates 2013-2014	2014 share
Total	1 452.0	2.3	-7.5	100.0
0+1	263.0	-4.2	-19.6	18.1
2+4	691.1	5.6	1.4	47.6
3	307.4	2.2	-13.3	21.2
5	28.2	-23.7	-74.4	1.9
6	50.5	32.7	283.1	3.5
7	21.8	-11.2	-44.3	1.5
8	16.3	-8.4	-32.4	1.1
9	73.5	40.0	292.2	5.1

Table 3: Merchandise imports by SITC

(Value in million US$, growth and shares in percentage)

SITC	2014	Avg. Growth rates 2010-2014	Avg. Growth rates 2013-2014	2014 share
Total	5 835.5	2.8	-6.1	100.0
0+1	932.0	1.2	-10.1	16.0
2+4	104.5	2.5	4.6	1.8
3	1 936.3	5.1	-14.3	33.2
5	615.6	-3.1	-19.1	10.5
6	614.3	1.1	2.1	10.5
7	967.6	5.0	7.6	16.6
8	493.4	0.6	11.0	8.5
9	171.9	16.5	51.3	2.9

SITC Legend

SITC Code	Description
Total	All commodities
0+1	Food, animals + beverages, tobacco
2+4	Crude materials + anim. & veg. oils
3	Mineral fuels, lubricants
5	Chemicals
6	Goods classified chiefly by material
7	Machinery and transport equipment
8	Miscellaneous manufactured articles
9	Not classified elsewhere in the SITC

Graph 4: Merchandise trade balance

(Bln US$ by MDG Regions in 2014)

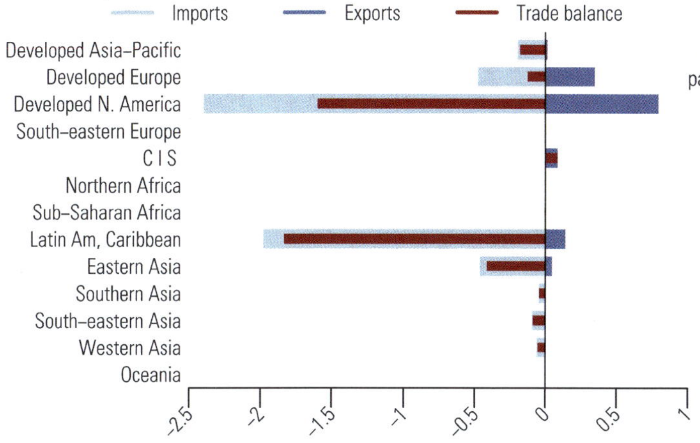

Graph 5: Partner concentration of merchandise trade

(Cumulative share by ranked partners in 2014)

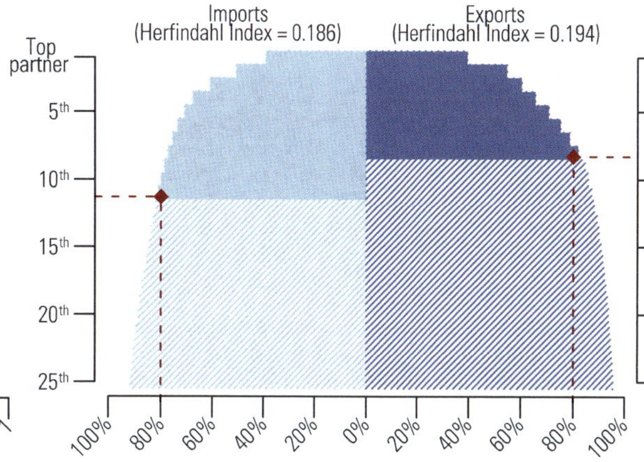

Graph 6: Imports of services by EBOPS category

(% share in 2014)

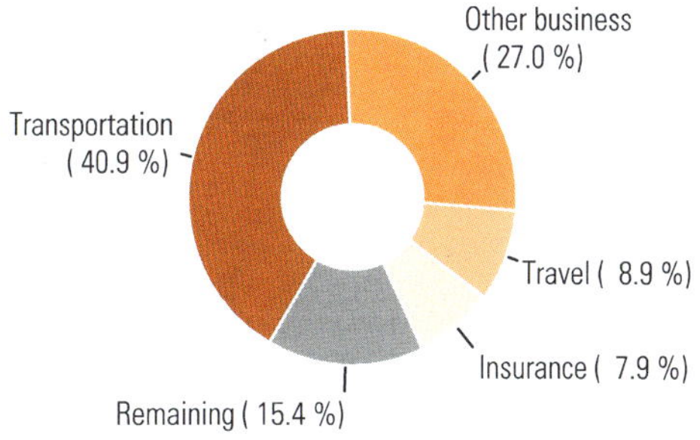

Imports Profile:

"Mineral fuels, lubricants" (SITC section 3), "Machinery and transport equipment" (SITC section 7) and "Food, animals + beverages, tobacco" (SITC section 0+1) were the largest commodity groups for imports in 2014, representing respectively 33.2, 16.6 and 16.0 percent of imported goods (see table 3). From 2012 to 2014, the largest import commodity was "Petroleum oils, other than crude" (HS code 2710) (see table 4). The top three partners for merchandise imports were the United States, the Bolivarian Republic of Venezuela and Trinidad and Tobago, accounting for respectively 36.3, 14.0 and 11.1 percent of total imports. "Transportation" (EBOPS code 205) accounted for the largest share of imports of services in 2014 at 914.3 mln US$, followed by "Other business services" (EBOPS code 268) at 602.4 mln US$ and "Travel" (EBOPS code 236) at 197.9 mln US$ (see graph 6).

Table 4: Top 10 import commodities 2012 to 2014

HS code	4-digit heading of Harmonized System 2007	Value (million US$) 2012	2013	2014	Unit value 2012	2013	2014	Unit	SITC code
	All Commodities	6 580.4	6 216.2	5 835.5					
2710	Petroleum oils, other than crude	1 362.0	1 265.7	1 218.1	0.9	0.8	0.8	US$/kg	334
2709	Petroleum oils and oils obtained from bituminous minerals, crude	939.3	921.2	642.6	0.7	0.8	0.7	US$/kg	333
2207	Alcohol of a strength by volume of 80 % vol or higher	384.3	231.8	82.7	*1.0*	*1.0*	*0.9*	US$/litre	512
8703	Motor cars and other motor vehicles principally designed for the transport	224.4	210.0	173.4	*17.5*	*16.8*	*17.0*	thsd US$/unit	781
9999	Commodities not specified according to kind	116.3	113.6	171.9					931
3004	Medicaments (excluding goods of heading 30.02, 30.05 or 30.06)	132.6	122.5	137.6	43.7	49.2	22.5	US$/kg	542
8517	Electrical apparatus for line telephony or line telegraphy	59.7	66.2	103.4					764
2815	Sodium hydroxide (caustic soda)	85.5	79.7	63.7	0.3	0.8	0.2	US$/kg	522
1005	Maize (corn)	77.6	81.3	69.4	0.5	0.5	0.3	US$/kg	044
2106	Food preparations not elsewhere specified or included	64.5	71.1	71.6	9.0	6.1	5.5	US$/kg	098

Japan

Goods Imports: CIF, by origin | **Goods Exports: FOB, by last known destination** | **Trade System: General**

Overview:

In 2015, the value of merchandise exports of Japan decreased moderately by 9.4 percent to reach 625.0 bln US$, while its merchandise imports decreased substantially by 22.9 percent to reach 626.1 bln US$ (see graph 1, table 2 and table 3). The merchandise trade balance recorded a relatively small deficit of 1.1 bln US$, narrowing substantially from the merchandise trade deficit in 2014 of 122.0 bln US$ (see graph 1). The largest merchandise trade balance was with MDG Developed North America at 56.6 bln US$ (see graph 4). Merchandise exports in Japan were diversified amongst partners; imports were also diversified. The top 16 partners accounted for 80 percent or more of exports and 17 partners accounted for 80 percent or more of imports (see graph 5). In 2014, the value of exports of services of Japan increased substantially by 15.5 percent, reaching 169.8 bln US$, and its imports of services also increased substantially by 10.9 percent and reached 180.1 bln US$ (see graph 2). There was a relatively small trade in services deficit of 10.3 bln US$.

Graph 1: Total merchandise trade, by value

(Bln US$ by year)

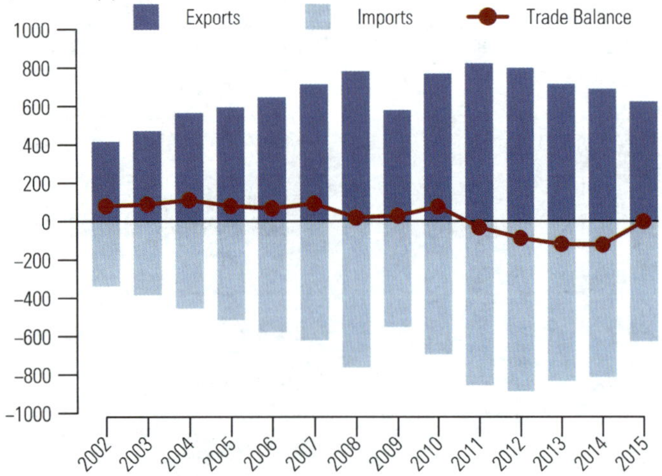

Graph 2: Total services trade, by value

(Bln US$ by year)

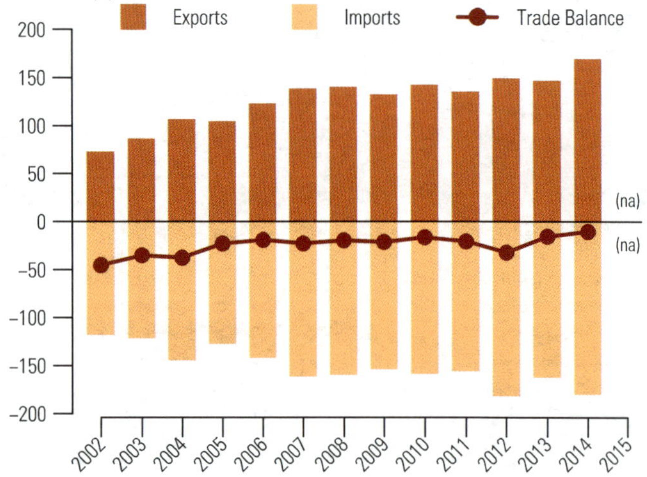

Exports Profile:

"Machinery and transport equipment" (SITC section 7), "Goods classified chiefly by material" (SITC section 6) and "Chemicals" (SITC section 5) were the largest commodity groups for exports in 2015, representing respectively 58.7, 12.4 and 10.1 percent of exported goods (see table 2). From 2013 to 2015, the largest export commodity was "Motor cars and other motor vehicles principally designed for the transport" (HS code 8703), but exports of this commodity dropped by 2.8 percent from 2014 to 2015 (see table 1). The top three destinations for merchandise exports were the United States, China and the Republic of Korea, accounting for respectively 19.3, 18.0 and 7.5 percent of total exports. "Other business services" (EBOPS code 268) accounted for the largest share of exports of services in 2014 at 46.3 bln US$, followed by "Transportation" (EBOPS code 205) at 39.6 bln US$ and "Royalties and license fees" (EBOPS code 266) at 36.9 bln US$ (see graph 3).

Graph 3: Exports of services by EBOPS category

(% share in 2014)

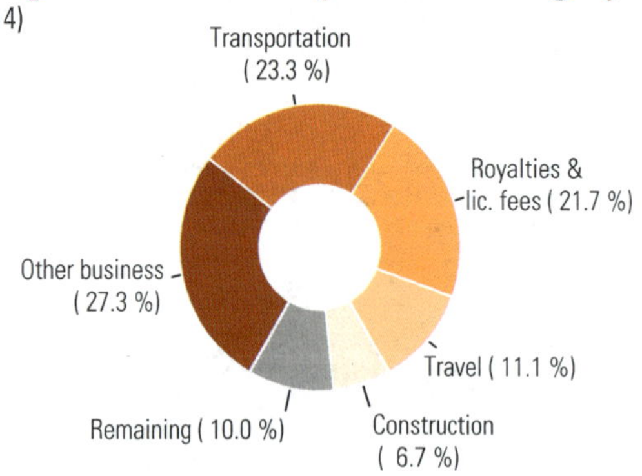

Table 1: Top 10 export commodities 2013 to 2015

HS code	4-digit heading of Harmonized System 2012	Value (million US$) 2013	2014	2015	Unit value 2013	2014	2015	Unit	SITC code
	All Commodities	715097.2	690217.5	625024.8					
8703	Motor cars and other motor vehicles principally designed for the transport	91688.8	88542.8	86050.9	*18.5*	*18.2*	*17.3*	thsd US$/unit	781
9999	Commodities not specified according to kind	35791.4	35844.4	37086.4					931
8708	Parts and accessories of the motor vehicles of headings 87.01 to 87.05	35301.2	32493.0	28616.9	12.7	12.1	11.2	US$/kg	784
8542	Electronic integrated circuits	26994.8	25477.7	23643.3					776
8486	Machines and apparatus used for the manufacture of semiconductor devices	12691.2	13021.3	13137.7					728
8901	Cruise ships, excursion boats, ferry-boats, cargo ships, barges	14867.8	12245.6	11000.3					793
2710	Petroleum oils, other than crude	14665.6	13373.9	9616.6	*0.9*	0.9	*0.5*	US$/kg	334
8443	Printing machinery used for printing by means of the printing type, blocks	12512.5	11512.6	10405.1					726
8704	Motor vehicles for the transport of goods	10105.1	10492.5	9676.6	*18.5*	*17.4*	*15.7*	thsd US$/unit	782
8541	Diodes, transistors and similar semiconductor devices	9062.4	9046.2	8419.1					776

Services Imports and Exports: EBOPS 2002 categories

Table 2: Merchandise exports by SITC

(Value in million US$, growth and shares in percentage)

SITC	2015	Avg. Growth rates 2011-2015	Avg. Growth rates 2014-2015	2015 share
Total	625 024.8	-6.7	-9.4	100.0
0+1	4 933.6	2.4	8.9	0.8
2+4	9 554.6	-6.3	-16.5	1.5
3	11 403.3	-8.5	-27.9	1.8
5	62 861.9	-7.1	-12.8	10.1
6	77 204.1	-8.4	-14.1	12.4
7	366 811.3	-6.5	-8.3	58.7
8	49 768.9	-6.8	-10.8	8.0
9	42 487.2	-3.7	4.9	6.8

Table 3: Merchandise imports by SITC

(Value in million US$, growth and shares in percentage)

SITC	2015	Avg. Growth rates 2011-2015	Avg. Growth rates 2014-2015	2015 share
Total	626 082.8	-7.5	-22.9	100.0
0+1	57 823.9	-5.8	-9.1	9.2
2+4	42 926.8	-11.2	-22.2	6.9
3	128 458.8	-17.3	-51.0	20.5
5	63 585.6	-4.3	-1.1	10.2
6	55 804.9	-6.6	-12.4	8.9
7	176 607.5	-0.2	-9.3	28.2
8	89 729.9	-2.1	-7.8	14.3
9	11 145.5	-4.3	-0.8	1.8

SITC Legend

SITC Code	Description
Total	All commodities
0+1	Food, animals + beverages, tobacco
2+4	Crude materials + anim. & veg. oils
3	Mineral fuels, lubricants
5	Chemicals
6	Goods classified chiefly by material
7	Machinery and transport equipment
8	Miscellaneous manufactured articles
9	Not classified elsewhere in the SITC

Graph 4: Merchandise trade balance

(Bln US$ by MDG Regions in 2015)

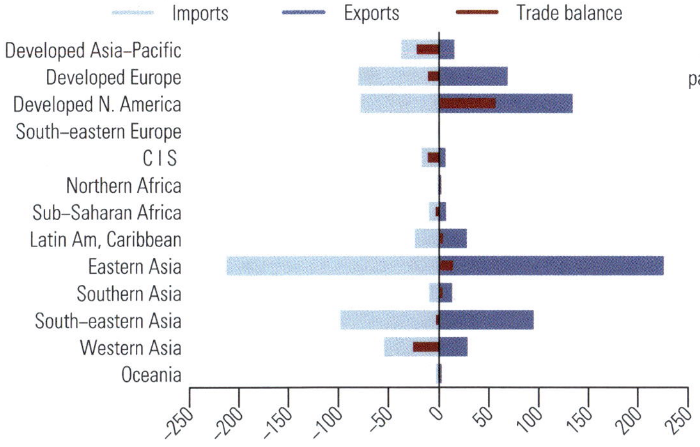

Graph 5: Partner concentration of merchandise trade

(Cumulative share by ranked partners in 2015)

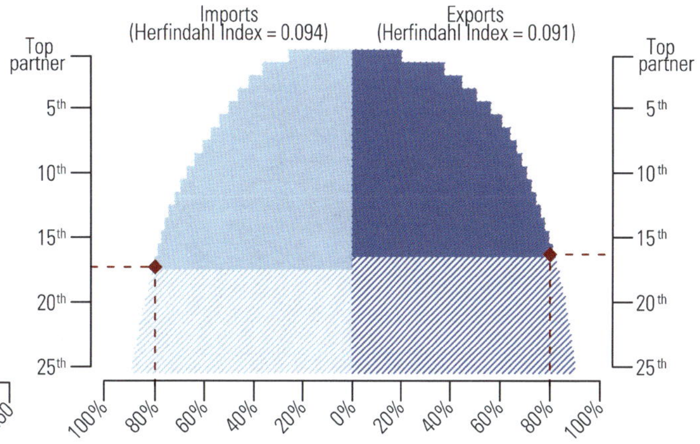

Graph 6: Imports of services by EBOPS category

(% share in 2014)

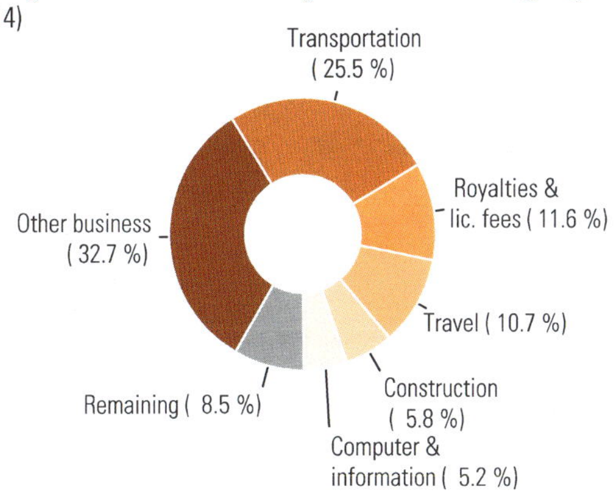

Imports Profile:

"Machinery and transport equipment" (SITC section 7), "Mineral fuels, lubricants" (SITC section 3) and "Miscellaneous manufactured articles" (SITC section 8) were the largest commodity groups for imports in 2015, representing respectively 28.2, 20.5 and 14.3 percent of imported goods (see table 3). From 2013 to 2015, the largest import commodity was "Petroleum oils and oils obtained from bituminous minerals, crude" (HS code 2709), although imports of this commodity fell by 65.6 percent in value terms from 2014 to 2015 (see table 4). The top three partners for merchandise imports were China, the United States and Australia, accounting for respectively 23.0, 9.4 and 5.9 percent of total imports. "Other business services" (EBOPS code 268) accounted for the largest share of imports of services in 2014 at 58.9 bln US$, followed by "Transportation" (EBOPS code 205) at 45.9 bln US$ and "Royalties and license fees" (EBOPS code 266) at 20.9 bln US$ (see graph 6).

Table 4: Top 10 import commodities 2013 to 2015

HS code	4-digit heading of Harmonized System 2012	Value (million US$) 2013	2014	2015	Unit value 2013	2014	2015	Unit	SITC code
	All Commodities	833 166.1	812 184.8	626 082.8					
2709	Petroleum oils and oils obtained from bituminous minerals, crude	145 720.8	130 657.5	44 998.8	0.8	0.8	*0.7*	US$/kg	333
2711	Petroleum gases and other gaseous hydrocarbons	83 330.4	84 493.9	51 141.7					343
8517	Electrical apparatus for line telephony or line telegraphy	25 991.0	25 512.8	22 680.3					764
2710	Petroleum oils, other than crude	26 882.1	24 963.4	14 489.5	*0.9*	0.9	*0.5*	US$/kg	334
2701	Coal; briquettes, ovoids and similar solid fuels manufactured from coal	23 608.1	19 748.7	16 312.3	*0.1*	0.1	0.1	US$/kg	321
8542	Electronic integrated circuits	16 501.6	16 780.9	16 913.3					776
8471	Automatic data processing machines and units thereof	16 473.9	16 808.2	13 500.2	179.8	189.0	184.2	US$/unit	752
3004	Medicaments (excluding goods of heading 30.02, 30.05 or 30.06)	14 790.8	13 718.1	17 270.3	*278.6*	*267.1*	*339.4*	US$/kg	542
2601	Iron ores and concentrates, including roasted iron pyrites	17 391.5	15 917.2	9 263.5	*0.1*	*0.1*	*0.1*	US$/kg	281
9999	Commodities not specified according to kind	10 484.6	10 460.8	10 687.6					931

Jordan

Goods Imports: CIF, by origin | **Goods Exports: FOB, by last known destination** | **Trade System: Special**

Overview:

In 2015, the value of merchandise exports of Jordan decreased moderately by 6.3 percent to reach 7.9 bln US$, while its merchandise imports decreased substantially by 11.9 percent to reach 20.0 bln US$ (see graph 1, table 2 and table 3). The merchandise trade balance recorded a large deficit of 12.2 bln US$ (see graph 1). The largest merchandise trade balance was with MDG Developed Europe at -4.4 bln US$ (see graph 4). Merchandise exports in Jordan were diversified amongst partners; imports were also diversified. The top 12 partners accounted for 80 percent or more of exports and 21 partners accounted for 80 percent or more of imports (see graph 5). In 2013, the value of exports of services of Jordan decreased slightly by 1.0 percent, reaching 6.4 bln US$, while its imports of services increased slightly by 0.7 percent and reached 4.6 bln US$ (see graph 2). There was a moderate trade in services surplus of 1.8 bln US$.

Graph 1: Total merchandise trade, by value

(Bln US$ by year)

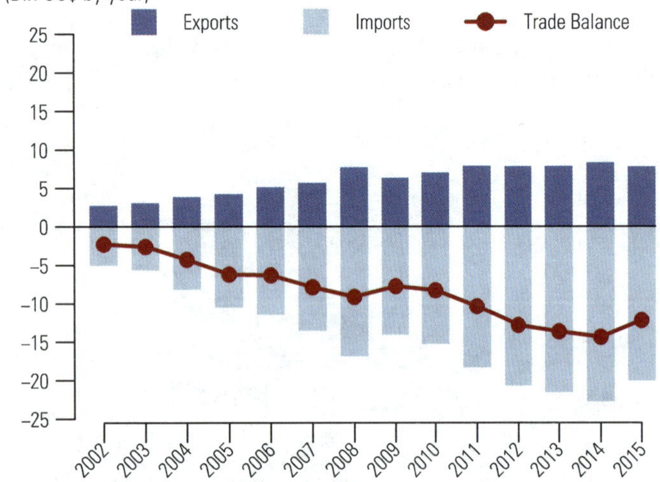

Graph 2: Total services trade, by value

(Bln US$ by year)

Exports Profile:

"Chemicals" (SITC section 5), "Miscellaneous manufactured articles" (SITC section 8) and "Food, animals + beverages, tobacco" (SITC section 0+1) were the largest commodity groups for exports in 2015, representing respectively 29.2, 23.9 and 19.5 percent of exported goods (see table 2). From 2013 to 2015, the largest export commodity was "Other garments, knitted or crocheted" (HS code 6114) (see table 1). The top three destinations for merchandise exports were the United States, Iraq and Saudi Arabia, accounting for respectively 16.5, 14.2 and 13.1 percent of total exports. "Travel" (EBOPS code 236) accounted for the largest share of exports of services in 2013 at 4.1 bln US$, followed by "Transportation" (EBOPS code 205) at 1.4 bln US$ and "Government services, n.i.e." (EBOPS code 291) at 331.4 mln US$ (see graph 3).

Graph 3: Exports of services by EBOPS category

(% share in 2013)

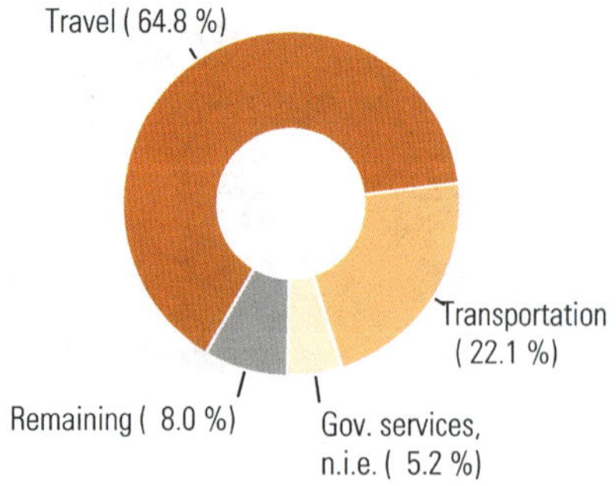

Table 1: Top 10 export commodities 2013 to 2015

HS code	4-digit heading of Harmonized System 2012	Value (million US$) 2013	2014	2015	Unit value 2013	2014	2015	Unit	SITC code
	All Commodities	7 919.6	8 385.3	7 860.3					
6114	Other garments, knitted or crocheted	905.6	1 021.2	1 129.9	23.1	23.5	24.5	US$/kg	845
3104	Mineral or chemical fertilisers, potassic	604.7	602.5	641.6		*0.9*		US$/kg	562
2510	Natural calcium phosphates	376.7	469.7	520.8	0.1	0.1	0.1	US$/kg	272
3004	Medicaments (excluding goods of heading 30.02, 30.05 or 30.06)	451.8	386.9	405.2	56.4	50.1	50.7	US$/kg	542
0702	Tomatoes, fresh or chilled	316.3	399.0	332.1	0.5	0.8	0.8	US$/kg	054
3003	Medicaments (excluding goods of heading 30.02, 30.05 or 30.06)	256.8	256.2	216.9	21.3	20.8	20.2	US$/kg	542
3102	Mineral or chemical fertilisers, nitrogenous	220.9	297.1	153.0	0.5	0.5	0.5	US$/kg	562
0104	Live sheep and goats	218.0	206.0	200.4			350.0	US$/unit	001
8544	Insulated (including enamelled or anodised) wire, cable	185.3	205.2	128.6	5.4	5.5	4.1	US$/kg	773
6109	T-shirts, singlets and other vests, knitted or crocheted	116.2	141.6	153.7	*5.2*	*4.8*	*5.0*	US$/unit	845

Services Imports and Exports: EBOPS 2002 categories

Table 2: Merchandise exports by SITC

(Value in million US$, growth and shares in percentage)

SITC	2015	Avg. Growth rates 2011-2015	Avg. Growth rates 2014-2015	2015 share
Total	7 860.3	-0.3	-6.3	100.0
0+1	1 536.0	5.6	-5.5	19.5
2+4	650.5	-5.8	6.7	8.3
3	10.2	-13.3	-37.2	0.1
5	2 294.1	-2.8	-14.0	29.2
6	692.1	-3.7	-12.8	8.8
7	743.7	-1.8	-11.4	9.5
8	1 875.3	6.7	3.5	23.9
9	58.4	-31.9	157.5	0.7

Table 3: Merchandise imports by SITC

(Value in million US$, growth and shares in percentage)

SITC	2015	Avg. Growth rates 2011-2015	Avg. Growth rates 2014-2015	2015 share
Total	20 043.0	2.3	-11.9	100.0
0+1	3 494.9	6.6	-7.4	17.4
2+4	526.9	-1.0	-10.6	2.6
3	3 331.4	-10.9	-46.2	16.6
5	2 166.3	1.9	-5.9	10.8
6	3 140.6	2.3	-4.8	15.7
7	4 693.8	8.5	12.5	23.4
8	1 433.6	4.7	-3.5	7.2
9	1 255.6	42.9	36.4	6.3

SITC Legend

SITC Code	Description
Total	All commodities
0+1	Food, animals + beverages, tobacco
2+4	Crude materials + anim. & veg. oils
3	Mineral fuels, lubricants
5	Chemicals
6	Goods classified chiefly by material
7	Machinery and transport equipment
8	Miscellaneous manufactured articles
9	Not classified elsewhere in the SITC

Graph 4: Merchandise trade balance

(Bln US$ by MDG Regions in 2015)

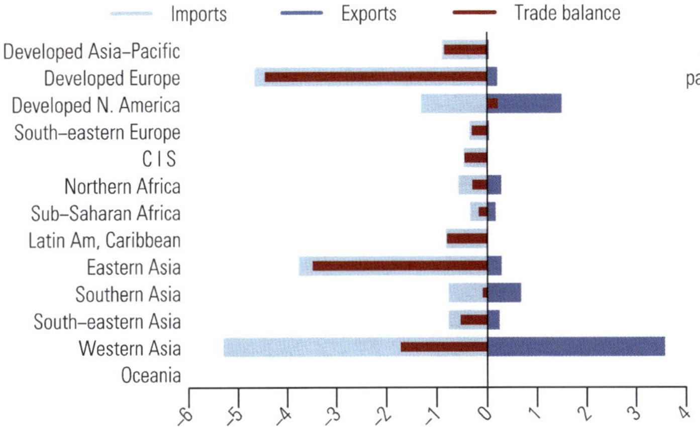

Graph 5: Partner concentration of merchandise trade

(Cumulative share by ranked partners in 2015)

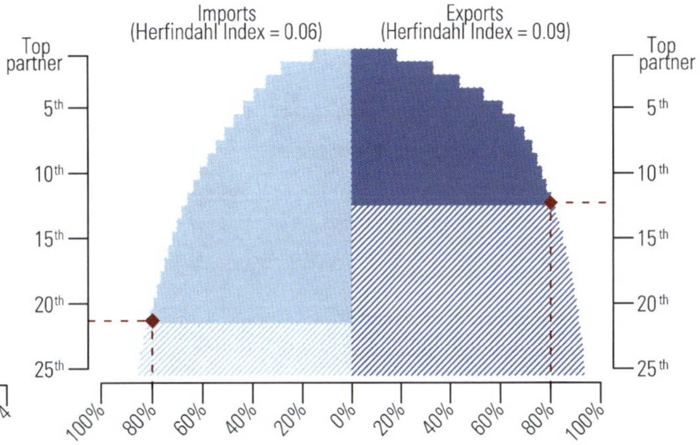

Graph 6: Imports of services by EBOPS category

(% share in 2013)

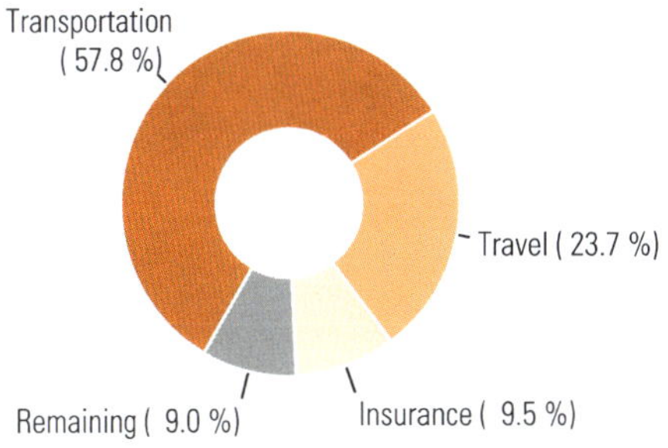

Imports Profile:

"Machinery and transport equipment" (SITC section 7), "Food, animals + beverages, tobacco" (SITC section 0+1) and "Mineral fuels, lubricants" (SITC section 3) were the largest commodity groups for imports in 2015, representing respectively 23.4, 17.4 and 16.6 percent of imported goods (see table 3). From 2013 to 2015, the largest import commodity was "Petroleum oils, other than crude" (HS code 2710) (see table 4). The top three partners for merchandise imports were Saudi Arabia, China and the United States, accounting for respectively 18.0, 11.2 and 6.1 percent of total imports. "Transportation" (EBOPS code 205) accounted for the largest share of imports of services in 2013 at 2.6 bln US$, followed by "Travel" (EBOPS code 236) at 1.1 bln US$ and "Insurance services" (EBOPS code 253) at 435.7 mln US$ (see graph 6).

Table 4: Top 10 import commodities 2013 to 2015

HS code	4-digit heading of Harmonized System 2012	Value (million US$) 2013	2014	2015	Unit value 2013	2014	2015	Unit	SITC code
	All Commodities	21 549.0	22 740.3	20 043.0					
2710	Petroleum oils, other than crude	2 634.8	3 421.1	1 351.6	0.9	0.8	0.5	US$/kg	334
2709	Petroleum oils and oils obtained from bituminous minerals, crude	2 284.7	2 313.6	1 313.2	0.8	0.7	0.4	US$/kg	333
8703	Motor cars and other motor vehicles principally designed for the transport	733.6	975.3	1 050.5	*18.9*	*18.5*	*13.4*	thsd US$/unit	781
7108	Gold (including gold plated with platinum)	522.3	543.9	867.0	44.3	39.5	39.4	thsd US$/kg	971
2711	Petroleum gases and other gaseous hydrocarbons	464.3	295.0	539.5	0.4	0.6	0.4	US$/kg	343
8517	Electrical apparatus for line telephony or line telegraphy	388.7	374.1	474.4					764
3004	Medicaments (excluding goods of heading 30.02, 30.05 or 30.06)	390.9	405.0	421.7	43.8	41.3	44.2	US$/kg	542
9999	Commodities not specified according to kind	329.9	376.6	388.5					931
6006	Other knitted or crocheted fabrics	245.0	321.1	330.6	8.4	8.4	8.5	US$/kg	655
8704	Motor vehicles for the transport of goods	227.9	251.5	402.1			*18.5*	thsd US$/unit	782

Kazakhstan

Goods Imports: CIF, by origin | **Goods Exports: FOB, by last known destination** | **Trade System: General**

Overview:

In 2014, the value of merchandise exports of Kazakhstan decreased moderately by 6.2 percent to reach 79.5 bln US$, while its merchandise imports decreased substantially by 15.4 percent to reach 41.3 bln US$ (see graph 1, table 2 and table 3). The merchandise trade balance recorded a large surplus of 38.2 bln US$ (see graph 1). The largest merchandise trade balance was with MDG Developed Europe at 37.4 bln US$ (see graph 4). Merchandise exports in Kazakhstan were diversified amongst partners; imports were moderately concentrated. The top 12 partners accounted for 80 percent or more of exports and 12 partners accounted for 80 percent or more of imports (see graph 5). In 2014, the value of exports of services of Kazakhstan increased substantially by 24.0 percent, reaching 6.3 bln US$, while its imports of services increased slightly by 4.7 percent and reached 12.8 bln US$ (see graph 2). There was a large trade in services deficit of 6.4 bln US$.

Graph 1: Total merchandise trade, by value

(Bln US$ by year)

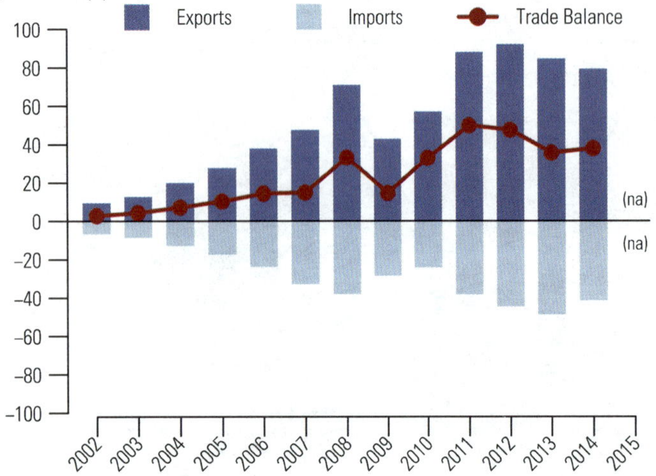

Graph 2: Total services trade, by value

(Bln US$ by year)

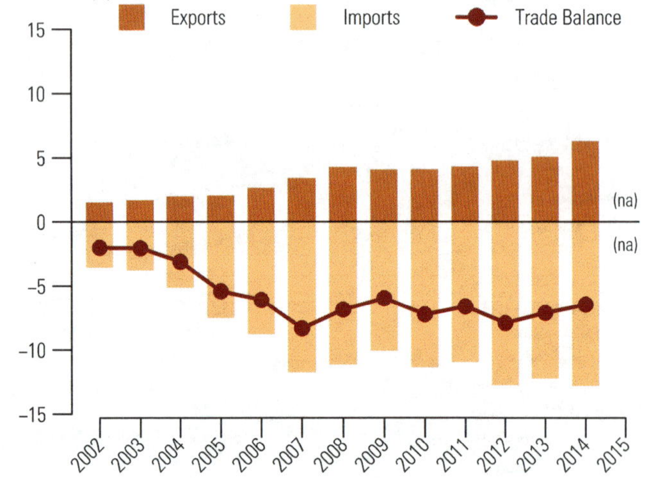

Exports Profile:

"Mineral fuels, lubricants" (SITC section 3), "Goods classified chiefly by material" (SITC section 6) and "Crude materials + anim. & veg. oils" (SITC section 2+4) were the largest commodity groups for exports in 2014, representing respectively 76.4, 9.1 and 5.0 percent of exported goods (see table 2). From 2012 to 2014, the largest export commodity was "Petroleum oils and oils obtained from bituminous minerals, crude" (HS code 2709) (see table 1). The top three destinations for merchandise exports were Italy, China and the Netherlands, accounting for respectively 18.7, 15.9 and 10.2 percent of total exports. "Transportation" (EBOPS code 205) accounted for the largest share of exports of services in 2014 at 3.8 bln US$, followed by "Travel" (EBOPS code 236) at 1.3 bln US$ and "Other business services" (EBOPS code 268) at 557.1 mln US$ (see graph 3).

Graph 3: Exports of services by EBOPS category

(% share in 2014)

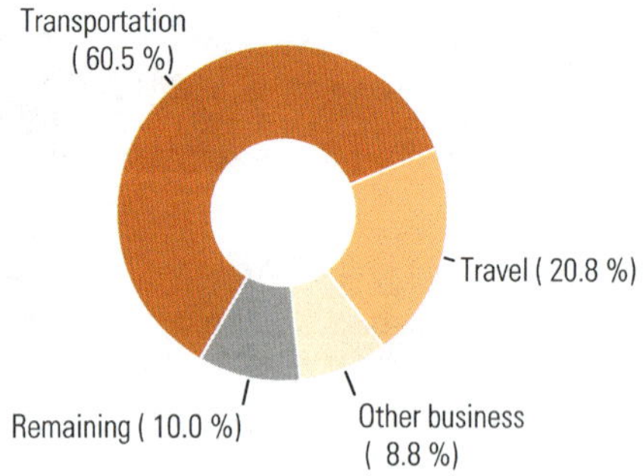

Table 1: Top 10 export commodities 2012 to 2014

HS code	4-digit heading of Harmonized System 2012	Value (million US$) 2012	2013	2014	Unit value 2012	2013	2014	Unit	SITC code
	All Commodities	92 281.5	84 698.5	79 458.7					
2709	Petroleum oils and oils obtained from bituminous minerals, crude	56 442.4	57 249.5	53 626.9	0.8	0.8	0.8	US$/kg	333
2711	Petroleum gases and other gaseous hydrocarbons	3 620.0	3 384.4	3 296.6	0.2	0.2	0.2	US$/kg	343
2710	Petroleum oils, other than crude	3 226.8	3 151.8	2 977.2	*0.6*	0.6	0.6	US$/kg	334
7403	Refined copper and copper alloys, unwrought	3 427.9	2 693.5	1 711.6	*7.6*	7.1	6.6	US$/kg	682
7202	Ferro-alloys	3 893.0	1 722.3	1 839.5					671
2844	Radioactive chemical elements and radioactive isotopes	2 752.9	2 332.1	2 082.9		81.4	69.4	US$/kg	525
2601	Iron ores and concentrates, including roasted iron pyrites	2 416.2	1 566.3	1 108.5	0.1	0.1	0.1	US$/kg	281
1001	Wheat and meslin	1 599.1	1 253.9	960.1	*0.2*	0.2	0.2	US$/kg	041
2603	Copper ores and concentrates	818.1	587.3	825.2		1.1	1.3	US$/kg	283
7901	Unwrought zinc	1 030.9	487.0	587.6	1.8	1.8	2.1	US$/kg	686

Services Imports and Exports: EBOPS 2002 categories

Table 2: Merchandise exports by SITC

(Value in million US$, growth and shares in percentage)

SITC	2014	Avg. Growth rates 2010-2014	Avg. Growth rates 2013-2014	2014 share
Total	79 458.7	8.5	-6.2	100.0
0+1	2 295.8	5.4	-6.8	2.9
2+4	3 994.3	6.3	-6.1	5.0
3	60 700.6	10.3	-6.1	76.4
5	2 851.7	3.2	-7.7	3.6
6	7 269.2	-0.5	-12.6	9.1
7	1 859.8	52.3	50.5	2.3
8	225.3	41.5	-10.5	0.3
9	262.0	-26.0	-43.4	0.3

Table 3: Merchandise imports by SITC

(Value in million US$, growth and shares in percentage)

SITC	2014	Avg. Growth rates 2010-2014	Avg. Growth rates 2013-2014	2014 share
Total	41 295.5	14.5	-15.4	100.0
0+1	4 058.3	17.1	-5.8	9.8
2+4	974.7	23.0	8.1	2.4
3	2 317.2	-0.7	-57.6	5.6
5	4 651.0	12.9	-9.4	11.3
6	7 497.6	14.6	-23.7	18.2
7	16 993.0	15.1	-7.1	41.1
8	4 742.7	21.7	-0.6	11.5
9	60.9	39.0	-35.7	0.1

SITC Legend

SITC Code	Description
Total	All commodities
0+1	Food, animals + beverages, tobacco
2+4	Crude materials + anim. & veg. oils
3	Mineral fuels, lubricants
5	Chemicals
6	Goods classified chiefly by material
7	Machinery and transport equipment
8	Miscellaneous manufactured articles
9	Not classified elsewhere in the SITC

Graph 4: Merchandise trade balance

(Bln US$ by MDG Regions in 2014)

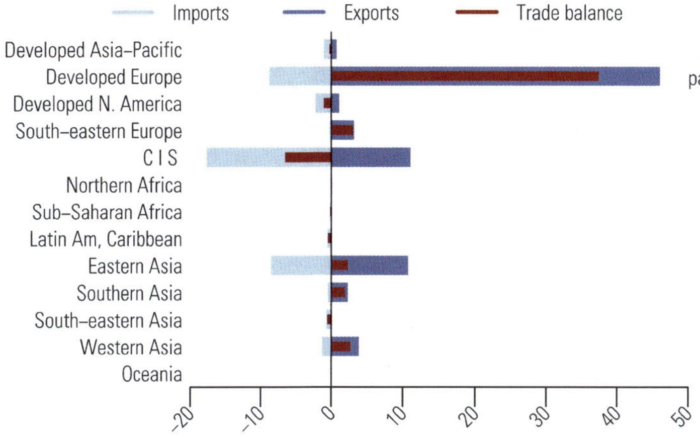

Graph 5: Partner concentration of merchandise trade

(Cumulative share by ranked partners in 2014)

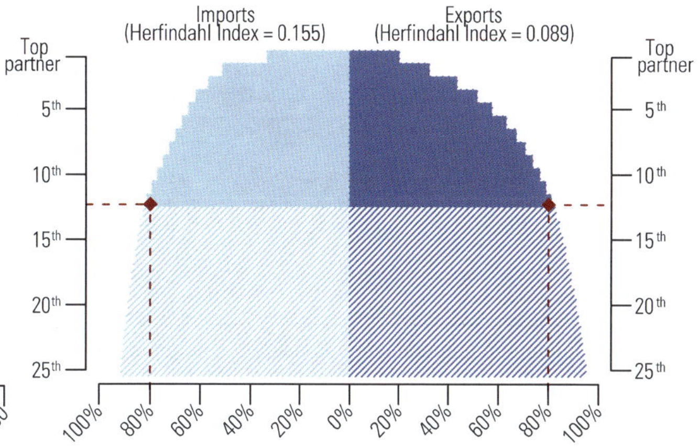

Graph 6: Imports of services by EBOPS category

(% share in 2014)

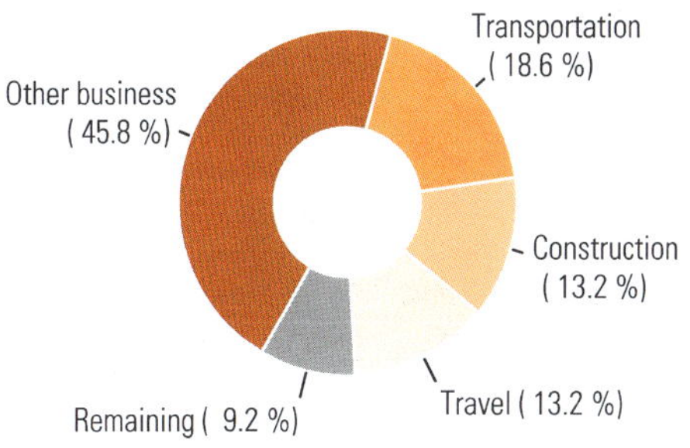

Imports Profile:

"Machinery and transport equipment" (SITC section 7), "Goods classified chiefly by material" (SITC section 6) and "Miscellaneous manufactured articles" (SITC section 8) were the largest commodity groups for imports in 2014, representing respectively 41.1, 18.2 and 11.5 percent of imported goods (see table 3). From 2012 to 2014, the largest import commodity was "Motor cars and other motor vehicles principally designed for the transport" (HS code 8703) (see table 4). The top three partners for merchandise imports were the Russian Federation, China and Germany, accounting for respectively 36.3, 17.2 and 5.2 percent of total imports. "Other business services" (EBOPS code 268) accounted for the largest share of imports of services in 2014 at 5.9 bln US$, followed by "Transportation" (EBOPS code 205) at 2.4 bln US$ and "Construction services" (EBOPS code 249) at 1.7 bln US$ (see graph 6).

Table 4: Top 10 import commodities 2012 to 2014

HS code	4-digit heading of Harmonized System 2012	Value (million US$) 2012	Value (million US$) 2013	Value (million US$) 2014	Unit value 2012	Unit value 2013	Unit value 2014	Unit	SITC code
	All Commodities	44 538.1	48 804.6	41 295.5					
8703	Motor cars and other motor vehicles principally designed for the transport	1 384.1	2 190.0	2 330.0	11.4	*19.9*	*18.1*	thsd US$/unit	781
2709	Petroleum oils and oils obtained from bituminous minerals, crude	2 198.9	2 841.3	188.0	0.4	0.4	0.4	US$/kg	333
2710	Petroleum oils, other than crude	1 455.0	1 599.3	1 412.5	*0.7*	0.6	0.7	US$/kg	334
3004	Medicaments (excluding goods of heading 30.02, 30.05 or 30.06)	1 018.1	1 285.5	1 108.4	*32.6*	35.0	34.5	US$/kg	542
7305	Other tubes and pipes (for example, welded, riveted or similarly closed)	997.6	1 754.1	269.7	*2.3*	1.1	1.6	US$/kg	679
8517	Electrical apparatus for line telephony or line telegraphy	779.6	1 024.8	1 064.9					764
8471	Automatic data processing machines and units thereof	906.9	1 062.9	630.4	78.5			US$/unit	752
8606	Railway or tramway goods vans and wagons, not self-propelled	1 642.2	373.9	287.4	75.9	*68.4*		thsd US$/unit	791
7304	Tubes, pipes and hollow profiles, seamless, of iron (other than cast iron)	565.8	800.2	688.6		0.9	*1.9*	US$/kg	679
8704	Motor vehicles for the transport of goods	588.3	657.0	524.4	28.3			thsd US$/unit	782

Kenya

Goods Imports: CIF, by origin | **Goods Exports: FOB, by last known destination** | **Trade System: General**

Overview:

In 2013, the value of merchandise exports of Kenya was 5.5 bln US$, while its merchandise imports was 16.4 bln US$ (see graph 1, table 2 and table 3). The merchandise trade balance recorded a large deficit of 10.9 bln US$ (see graph 1). The largest merchandise trade balance was with MDG Southern Asia at -2.6 bln US$ (see graph 4). Merchandise exports in Kenya were diversified amongst partners; imports were also diversified. The top 21 partners accounted for 80 percent or more of exports and 18 partners accounted for 80 percent or more of imports (see graph 5). In 2014, the value of exports of services of Kenya decreased slightly by 0.8 percent, reaching 4.9 bln US$, while its imports of services increased substantially by 20.5 percent and reached 2.9 bln US$ (see graph 2). There was a moderate trade in services surplus of 2.1 bln US$.

Graph 1: Total merchandise trade, by value

(Bln US$ by year)

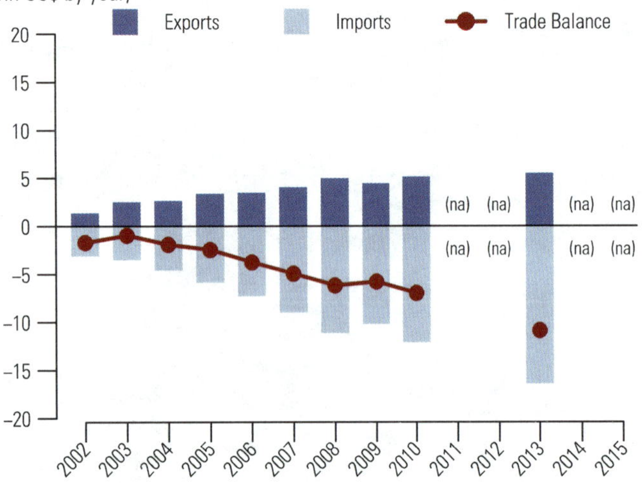

Graph 2: Total services trade, by value

(Bln US$ by year)

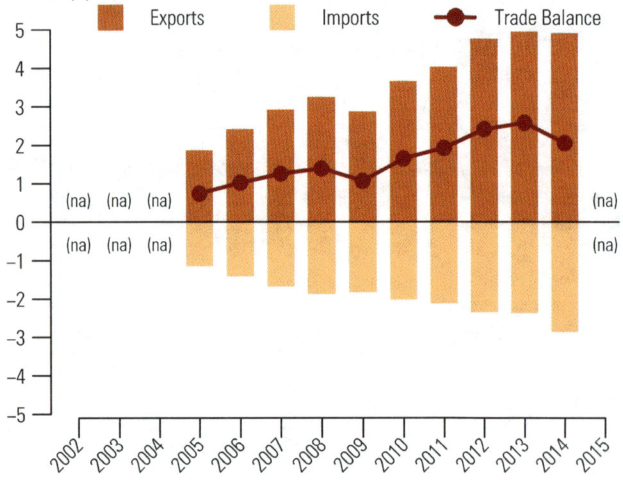

Exports Profile:

"Food, animals + beverages, tobacco" (SITC section 0+1), "Crude materials + anim. & veg. oils" (SITC section 2+4) and "Goods classified chiefly by material" (SITC section 6) were the largest commodity groups for exports in 2013, representing respectively 42.0, 15.0 and 12.8 percent of exported goods (see table 2). From 2011 to 2013, the largest export commodity was "Tea, whether or not flavoured" (HS code 0902) (see table 1). The top three destinations for merchandise exports were Uganda, the United Kingdom and the United Republic of Tanzania, accounting for respectively 11.9, 7.9 and 7.7 percent of total exports. "Transportation" (EBOPS code 205) accounted for the largest share of exports of services in 2014 at 2.2 bln US$, followed by "Government services, n.i.e." (EBOPS code 291) at 908.1 mln US$ and "Travel" (EBOPS code 236) at 810.7 mln US$ (see graph 3).

Graph 3: Exports of services by EBOPS category

(% share in 2014)

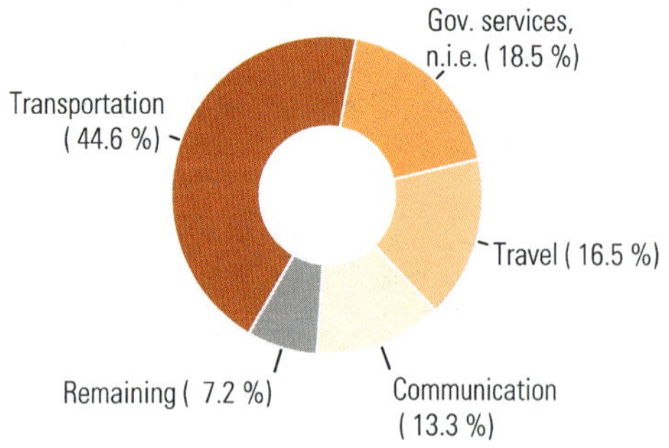

Table 1: Top 10 export commodities 2011 to 2013

HS code	4-digit heading of Harmonized System 2007	Value (million US$) 2011	2012	2013	Unit value 2011	2012	2013	Unit	SITC code
	All Commodities	...	...	5 537.0					
0902	Tea, whether or not flavoured	...	...	1 218.2			2.7	US$/kg	074
0603	Cut flowers and flower buds of a kind suitable for bouquets	...	...	480.0			*4.0*	US$/kg	292
2710	Petroleum oils, other than crude	...	...	203.7					334
0901	Coffee, whether or not roasted or decaffeinated	...	...	190.8			3.8	US$/kg	071
0708	Leguminous vegetables, shelled or unshelled, fresh or chilled	...	...	126.7			*3.0*	US$/kg	054
2836	Carbonates; peroxocarbonates (percarbonates)	...	...	107.8					523
2523	Portland cement, aluminous cement, slag cement	...	...	103.6			0.1	US$/kg	661
2402	Cigars, cheroots, cigarillos and cigarettes	...	...	103.4					122
3923	Articles for the conveyance or packing of goods, of plastics	...	...	90.6			2.6	US$/kg	893
7108	Gold (including gold plated with platinum)	...	...	88.9					971

Services Imports and Exports: EBOPS 2002 categories

Table 2: Merchandise exports by SITC

(Value in million US$, growth and shares in percentage)

SITC	2013	Avg. Growth rates 2009-2013	Avg. Growth rates 2012-2013	2013 share
Total	5537.0	5.5	...	100.0
0+1	2327.2	5.6	...	42.0
2+4	830.1	3.8	...	15.0
3	218.3	3.9	...	3.9
5	485.8	1.5	...	8.8
6	710.0	6.7	...	12.8
7	213.8	-1.8	...	3.9
8	586.2	8.1	...	10.6
9	165.5	56.9	...	3.0

Table 3: Merchandise imports by SITC

(Value in million US$, growth and shares in percentage)

SITC	2013	Avg. Growth rates 2009-2013	Avg. Growth rates 2012-2013	2013 share
Total	16394.5	12.6	...	100.0
0+1	1170.7	-0.3	...	7.1
2+4	859.1	10.3	...	5.2
3	3870.3	15.3	...	23.6
5	2282.5	14.5	...	13.9
6	2627.4	16.9	...	16.0
7	4623.7	10.5	...	28.2
8	794.6	17.5	...	4.8
9	166.0	276.9	...	1.0

SITC Legend

SITC Code	Description
Total	All commodities
0+1	Food, animals + beverages, tobacco
2+4	Crude materials + anim. & veg. oils
3	Mineral fuels, lubricants
5	Chemicals
6	Goods classified chiefly by material
7	Machinery and transport equipment
8	Miscellaneous manufactured articles
9	Not classified elsewhere in the SITC

Graph 4: Merchandise trade balance

(Bln US$ by MDG Regions in 2013)

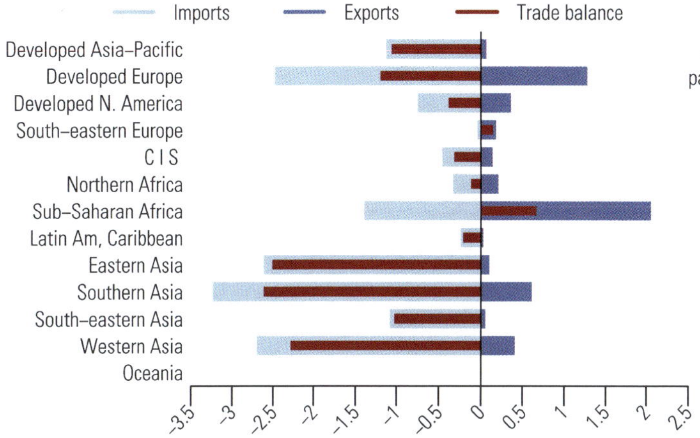

Graph 5: Partner concentration of merchandise trade

(Cumulative share by ranked partners in 2013)

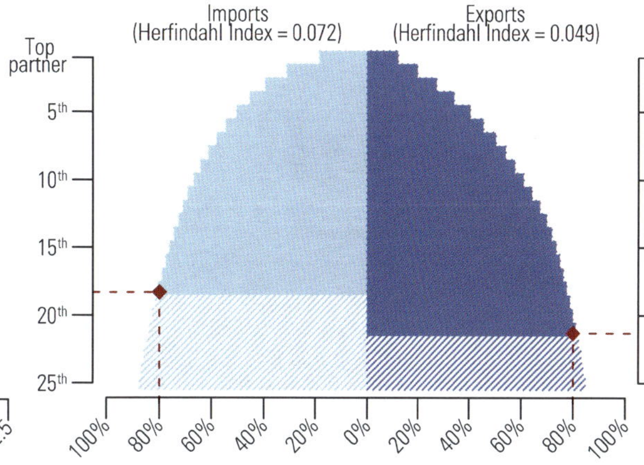

Graph 6: Imports of services by EBOPS category

(% share in 2014)

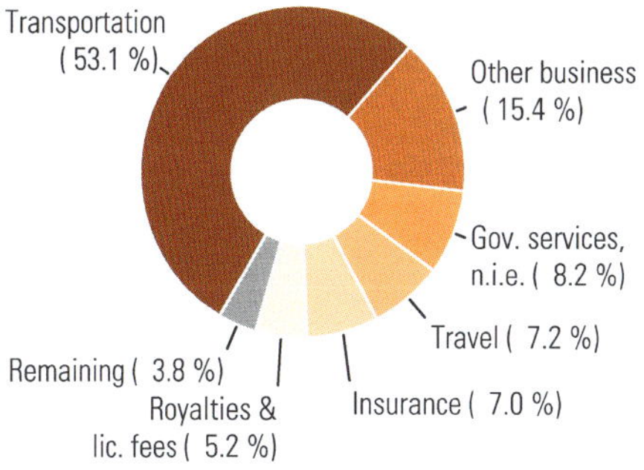

Imports Profile:

"Machinery and transport equipment" (SITC section 7), "Mineral fuels, lubricants" (SITC section 3) and "Goods classified chiefly by material" (SITC section 6) were the largest commodity groups for imports in 2013, representing respectively 28.2, 23.6 and 16.0 percent of imported goods (see table 3). From 2011 to 2013, the largest import commodity was "Petroleum oils, other than crude" (HS code 2710) (see table 4). The top three partners for merchandise imports were India, China and the United Arab Emirates, accounting for respectively 18.3, 12.9 and 8.3 percent of total imports. "Transportation" (EBOPS code 205) accounted for the largest share of imports of services in 2014 at 1.5 bln US$, followed by "Other business services" (EBOPS code 268) at 440.4 mln US$ and "Government services, n.i.e." (EBOPS code 291) at 235.2 mln US$ (see graph 6).

Table 4: Top 10 import commodities 2011 to 2013

HS code	4-digit heading of Harmonized System 2007	Value (million US$) 2011	Value (million US$) 2012	Value (million US$) 2013	Unit value 2011	Unit value 2012	Unit value 2013	Unit	SITC code
	All Commodities	...	...	16394.5					
2710	Petroleum oils, other than crude	...	...	3231.6					334
1511	Palm oil and its fractions	...	...	518.9			0.9	US$/kg	422
8703	Motor cars and other motor vehicles principally designed for the transport	...	...	496.4			6.7	thsd US$/unit	781
2709	Petroleum oils and oils obtained from bituminous minerals, crude	...	...	476.5			0.8	US$/kg	333
8517	Electrical apparatus for line telephony or line telegraphy	...	...	407.2					764
7208	Flat-rolled products of iron or non-alloy steel	...	...	381.3			0.7	US$/kg	673
3004	Medicaments (excluding goods of heading 30.02, 30.05 or 30.06)	...	...	355.0			24.8	US$/kg	542
1001	Wheat and meslin	...	...	256.3			0.4	US$/kg	041
8701	Tractors (other than tractors of heading 87.09)	...	...	231.4			36.2	thsd US$/unit	722
3105	Mineral or chemical fertilisers	...	...	230.7			0.5	US$/kg	562

Kiribati

Goods Imports: CIF, by origin | **Goods Exports: FOB, by last known destination** | **Trade System: Special**

Overview:

In 2013, the value of merchandise exports of Kiribati increased substantially by 14.8 percent to reach 6.7 mln US$, while its merchandise imports decreased substantially by 10.5 percent to reach 97.1 mln US$ (see graph 1, table 2 and table 3). The merchandise trade balance recorded a large deficit of 90.4 mln US$ (see graph 1). The largest merchandise trade balance was with MDG Developed Asia-Pacific at -41.9 mln US$ (see graph 4). Merchandise exports in Kiribati were diversified amongst partners; imports were moderately concentrated. The top 7 partners accounted for 80 percent or more of exports and 5 partners accounted for 80 percent or more of imports (see graph 5). In 2014, the value of exports of services of Kiribati decreased substantially by 12.5 percent, reaching 12.0 mln US$, while its imports of services decreased substantially by 21.6 percent and reached 53.7 mln US$ (see graph 2). There was a large trade in services deficit of 41.7 mln US$.

Graph 1: Total merchandise trade, by value

(Mln US$ by year)

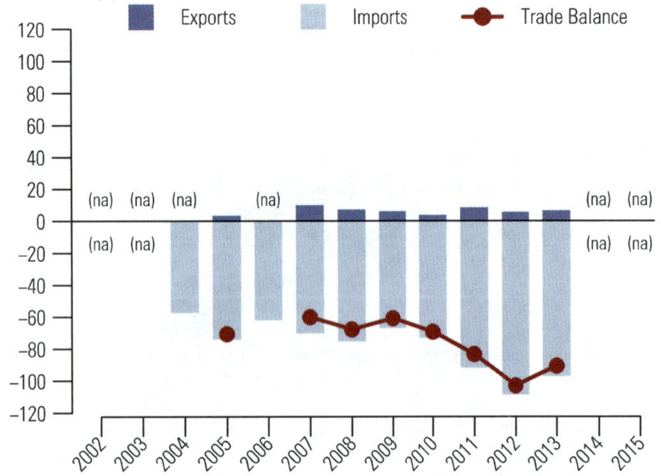

Graph 2: Total services trade, by value

(Mln US$ by year)

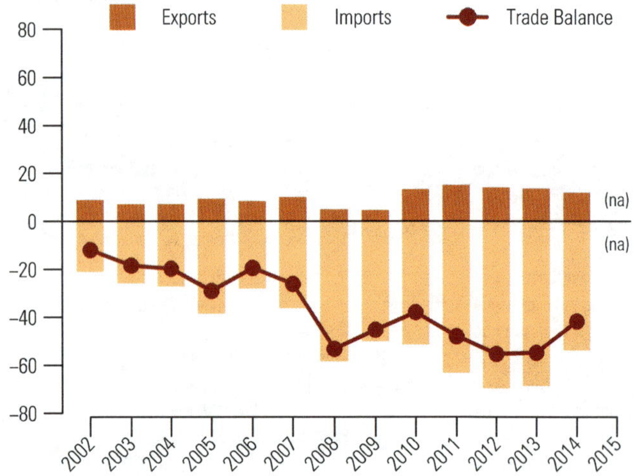

Exports Profile:

"Crude materials + anim. & veg. oils" (SITC section 2+4), "Mineral fuels, lubricants" (SITC section 3) and "Food, animals + beverages, tobacco" (SITC section 0+1) were the largest commodity groups for exports in 2013, representing respectively 49.4, 32.5 and 11.6 percent of exported goods (see table 2). From 2011 to 2013, the largest export commodity was "Coconut (copra), palm kernel or babassu oil" (HS code 1513) (see table 1). The top three destinations for merchandise exports were Other Asia nes, Morocco and Marshall Islands, accounting for respectively 30.0, 27.1 and 12.9 percent of total exports. "Financial services" (EBOPS code 260) accounted for the largest share of exports of services in 2014 at 3.5 mln US$, followed by "Travel" (EBOPS code 236) at 2.9 mln US$ and "Construction services" (EBOPS code 249) at 2.2 mln US$ (see graph 3).

Graph 3: Exports of services by EBOPS category

(% share in 2014)

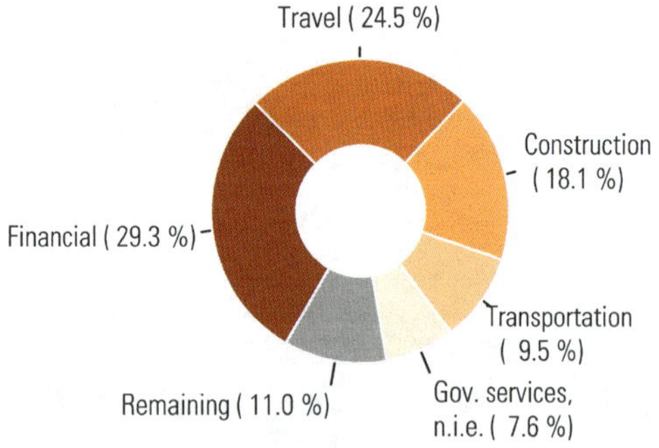

Table 1: Top 10 export commodities 2011 to 2013

HS code	4-digit heading of Harmonized System 2002	Value (million US$) 2011	2012	2013	Unit value 2011	2012	2013	Unit	SITC code
	All Commodities	8.6	5.8	6.7					
1513	Coconut (copra), palm kernel or babassu oil	5.8	3.8	2.3	*1.1*	*2.1*		US$/kg	422
2710	Petroleum oils, other than crude	0.0	0.0	2.2					334
0305	Fish, dried, salted or in brine	0.8	0.9	0.3	7.9	7.6	18.0	US$/kg	035
1203	Copra	...	...	0.8			2.0	US$/kg	223
2306	Oil-cake and other solid residues	0.3	0.2	0.1	0.6	0.6	1.7	US$/kg	081
1212	Locust beans, seaweeds and other algae	0.4	...	0.2	8.3		0.9	US$/kg	292
8903	Yachts and other vessels for pleasure or sports; rowing boats and canoes	0.6	...	...	624.4			thsd US$/unit	793
9999	Commodities not specified according to kind	0.3	0.1	0.1					931
0302	Fish, fresh or chilled, excluding fish fillets	...	0.0	0.3					034
7616	Other articles of aluminium	0.0	0.1	0.1	0.5	0.5		US$/kg	699

Services Imports and Exports: EBOPS 2002 categories

Table 2: Merchandise exports by SITC

(Value in million US$, growth and shares in percentage)

SITC	2013	Avg. Growth rates 2009-2013	Avg. Growth rates 2012-2013	2013 share
Total	6.7	1.6	14.8	100.0
0+1	0.8	-25.3	-41.2	11.6
2+4	3.3	11.2	-13.2	49.4
3	2.2	...	>	32.5
6	0.1	-4.4	-49.4	1.0
7	0.3	-32.3	38.2	4.1
8	0.0	-3.9	-84.5	0.6
9	0.1	-24.4	-32.1	0.8

Table 3: Merchandise imports by SITC

(Value in million US$, growth and shares in percentage)

SITC	2013	Avg. Growth rates 2009-2013	Avg. Growth rates 2012-2013	2013 share
Total	97.1	9.7	-10.5	100.0
0+1	34.5	5.4	-3.9	35.6
2+4	2.3	20.2	8.2	2.4
3	18.8	14.6	5.3	19.4
5	3.4	2.6	-21.8	3.5
6	9.7	10.8	-50.5	9.9
7	22.0	11.9	-1.1	22.6
8	5.2	12.7	0.6	5.3
9	1.3	40.0	-11.8	1.3

SITC Legend

SITC Code	Description
Total	All commodities
0+1	Food, animals + beverages, tobacco
2+4	Crude materials + anim. & veg. oils
3	Mineral fuels, lubricants
5	Chemicals
6	Goods classified chiefly by material
7	Machinery and transport equipment
8	Miscellaneous manufactured articles
9	Not classified elsewhere in the SITC

Graph 4: Merchandise trade balance

(Mln US$ by MDG Regions in 2013)

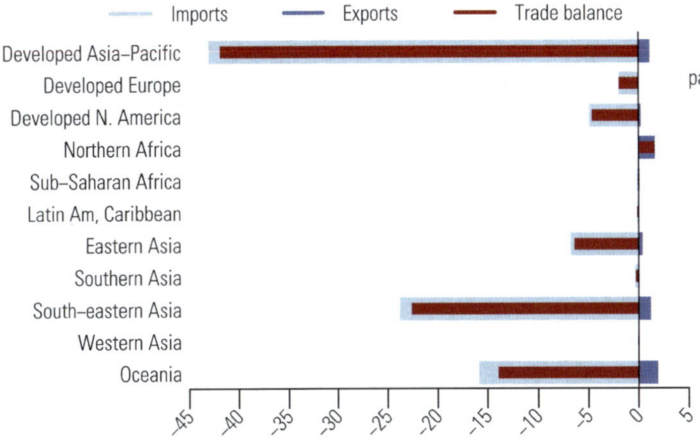

Graph 5: Partner concentration of merchandise trade

(Cumulative share by ranked partners in 2013)

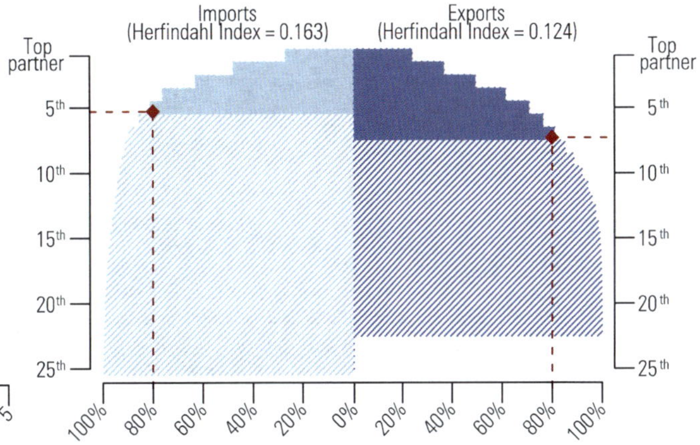

Graph 6: Imports of services by EBOPS category

(% share in 2014)

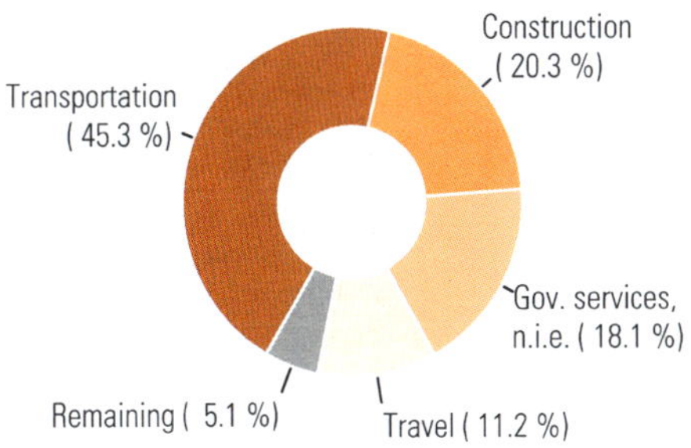

Imports Profile:

"Food, animals + beverages, tobacco" (SITC section 0+1), "Machinery and transport equipment" (SITC section 7) and "Mineral fuels, lubricants" (SITC section 3) were the largest commodity groups for imports in 2013, representing respectively 35.6, 22.6 and 19.4 percent of imported goods (see table 3). From 2011 to 2013, the largest import commodity was "Petroleum oils, other than crude" (HS code 2710) (see table 4). The top three partners for merchandise imports were Australia, Singapore and Fiji, accounting for respectively 28.8, 18.0 and 14.1 percent of total imports. "Transportation" (EBOPS code 205) accounted for the largest share of imports of services in 2014 at 24.3 mln US$, followed by "Construction services" (EBOPS code 249) at 10.9 mln US$ and "Government services, n.i.e." (EBOPS code 291) at 9.7 mln US$ (see graph 6).

Table 4: Top 10 import commodities 2011 to 2013

HS code	4-digit heading of Harmonized System 2002	Value (million US$) 2011	2012	2013	Unit value 2011	2012	2013	Unit	SITC code
	All Commodities	91.7	108.6	97.1					
2710	Petroleum oils, other than crude	17.3	17.6	18.5					334
1006	Rice	10.3	8.4	8.5	1.0	0.9	0.8	US$/kg	042
2403	Other manufactured tobacco and tobacco substitutes	3.8	5.0	3.7	43.4	48.0	45.4	US$/kg	122
1701	Cane or beet sugar and pure sucrose, in solid form	5.5	2.7	3.0	0.9	0.8	0.7	US$/kg	061
1602	Other prepared or preserved meat, meat offal or blood	3.2	2.1	2.2	*6.5*	*15.7*	*6.1*	US$/kg	017
1101	Wheat or meslin flour	2.7	2.3	2.1	0.8	0.7	0.7	US$/kg	046
8903	Yachts and other vessels for pleasure or sports; rowing boats and canoes	0.1	6.9	0.2	6.8	7.0	8.2	thsd US$/unit	793
1212	Locust beans, seaweeds and other algae	2.0	2.2	2.0	20.8	17.6	20.5	US$/kg	292
8901	Cruise ships, excursion boats, ferry-boats, cargo ships, barges	0.6	1.1	3.4	304.5	90.0	427.6	thsd US$/unit	793
0207	Meat and edible offal, of the poultry of heading 01.05	1.7	1.5	1.5	2.3	2.3	2.2	US$/kg	012

Source: UN Comtrade

Korea, Republic of

Goods Imports: CIF, by origin | **Goods Exports: FOB, by last known destination** | **Trade System: General**

Overview:

In 2014, the value of merchandise exports of the Republic of Korea increased slightly by 2.4 percent to reach 573.1 bln US$, while its merchandise imports increased slightly by 1.9 percent to reach 525.6 bln US$ (see graph 1, table 2 and table 3). The merchandise trade balance recorded a relatively small surplus of 47.5 bln US$ (see graph 1). The largest merchandise trade balance was with MDG Eastern Asia at 80.7 bln US$ (see graph 4). Merchandise exports in the Republic of Korea were diversified amongst partners; imports were also diversified. The top 21 partners accounted for 80 percent or more of exports and 18 partners accounted for 80 percent or more of imports (see graph 5). In 2014, the value of exports of services of the Republic of Korea increased substantially by 15.8 percent, reaching 116.7 bln US$, while its imports of services increased slightly by 4.0 percent and reached 105.6 bln US$ (see graph 2). There was a relatively small trade in services surplus of 11.1 bln US$.

Graph 1: Total merchandise trade, by value

(Bln US$ by year)

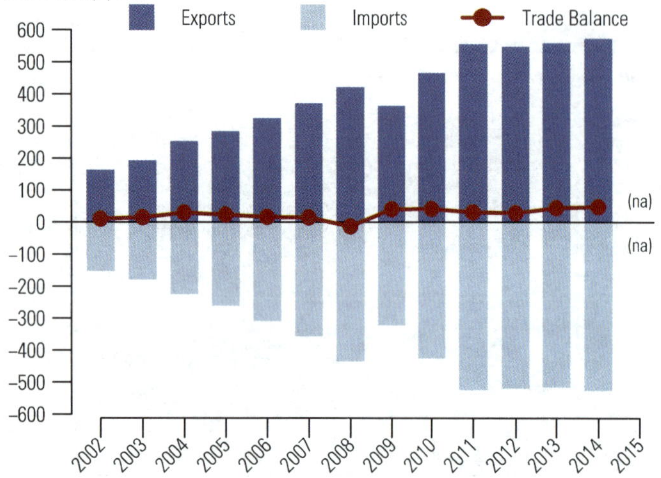

Graph 2: Total services trade, by value

(Bln US$ by year)

Exports Profile:

"Machinery and transport equipment" (SITC section 7), "Goods classified chiefly by material" (SITC section 6) and "Chemicals" (SITC section 5) were the largest commodity groups for exports in 2014, representing respectively 55.0, 13.2 and 11.8 percent of exported goods (see table 2). From 2012 to 2014, the largest export commodity was "Petroleum oils, other than crude" (HS code 2710) (see table 1). The top three destinations for merchandise exports were China, the United States and Japan, accounting for respectively 25.3, 11.4 and 6.3 percent of total exports. "Transportation" (EBOPS code 205) accounted for the largest share of exports of services in 2014 at 35.0 bln US$, followed by "Other business services" (EBOPS code 268) at 34.3 bln US$ and "Travel" (EBOPS code 236) at 18.1 bln US$ (see graph 3).

Graph 3: Exports of services by EBOPS category

(% share in 2014)

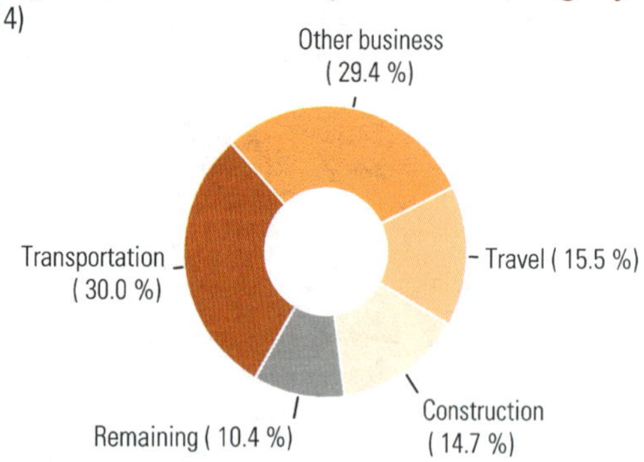

Table 1: Top 10 export commodities 2012 to 2014

HS code	4-digit heading of Harmonized System 2012	Value (million US$) 2012	2013	2014	Unit value 2012	2013	2014	Unit	SITC code
	All Commodities	547854.4	559618.6	573074.8					
2710	Petroleum oils, other than crude	54726.3	51003.4	49097.8	1.0	0.9	0.9	US$/kg	334
8542	Electronic integrated circuits	41346.6	47118.0	51543.9					776
8703	Motor cars and other motor vehicles principally designed for the transport	42387.5	44283.4	44816.4		15.9	16.4	thsd US$/unit	781
9013	Liquid crystal devices	27525.0	25308.8	24884.2					871
8901	Cruise ships, excursion boats, ferry-boats, cargo ships, barges	30566.1	24365.5	21838.1					793
8517	Electrical apparatus for line telephony or line telegraphy	20962.1	25604.6	27665.7					764
8708	Parts and accessories of the motor vehicles of headings 87.01 to 87.05	22632.1	23840.0	24265.3	8.1	8.3	8.3	US$/kg	784
8905	Light-vessels, fire-floats, dredgers, floating cranes and other vessels	7216.0	11328.8	16329.6					793
2902	Cyclic hydrocarbons	9065.8	10408.3	10659.4	1.3	1.4	1.3	US$/kg	511
8529	Parts suitable for use with the apparatus of headings 85.25 to 85.28	7091.8	7951.8	7240.0	23.2	29.1	28.3	US$/kg	764

Services Imports and Exports: EBOPS 2002 categories

Table 2: Merchandise exports by SITC

(Value in million US$, growth and shares in percentage)

SITC	2014	Avg. Growth rates 2010-2014	Avg. Growth rates 2013-2014	2014 share
Total	573 074.8	5.3	2.4	100.0
0+1	6 456.0	7.0	5.4	1.1
2+4	6 502.0	3.4	-4.1	1.1
3	52 670.6	12.8	-2.7	9.2
5	67 726.0	8.5	2.4	11.8
6	75 652.2	5.8	5.5	13.2
7	315 169.0	4.5	3.1	55.0
8	47 739.2	0.5	0.1	8.3
9	1 159.7	-21.4	-18.6	0.2

Table 3: Merchandise imports by SITC

(Value in million US$, growth and shares in percentage)

SITC	2014	Avg. Growth rates 2010-2014	Avg. Growth rates 2013-2014	2014 share
Total	525 557.0	5.4	1.9	100.0
0+1	24 384.0	9.1	6.5	4.6
2+4	35 888.6	3.0	0.2	6.8
3	175 718.0	9.4	-2.6	33.4
5	47 194.8	3.6	1.1	9.0
6	58 039.0	0.8	5.3	11.0
7	141 752.2	3.5	5.2	27.0
8	41 218.7	6.9	7.2	7.8
9	1 361.7	-3.5	-3.2	0.3

SITC Legend

SITC Code	Description
Total	All commodities
0+1	Food, animals + beverages, tobacco
2+4	Crude materials + anim. & veg. oils
3	Mineral fuels, lubricants
5	Chemicals
6	Goods classified chiefly by material
7	Machinery and transport equipment
8	Miscellaneous manufactured articles
9	Not classified elsewhere in the SITC

Graph 4: Merchandise trade balance

(Bln US$ by MDG Regions in 2014)

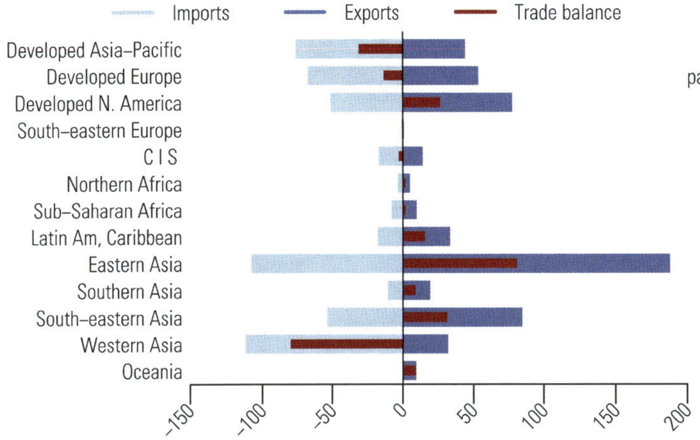

Graph 5: Partner concentration of merchandise trade

(Cumulative share by ranked partners in 2014)

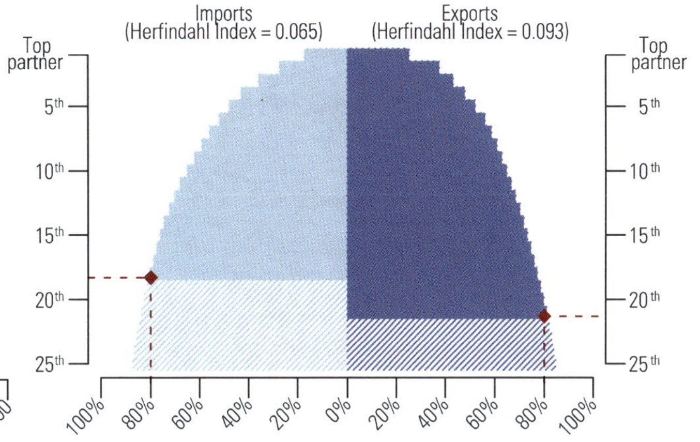

Graph 6: Imports of services by EBOPS category

(% share in 2014)

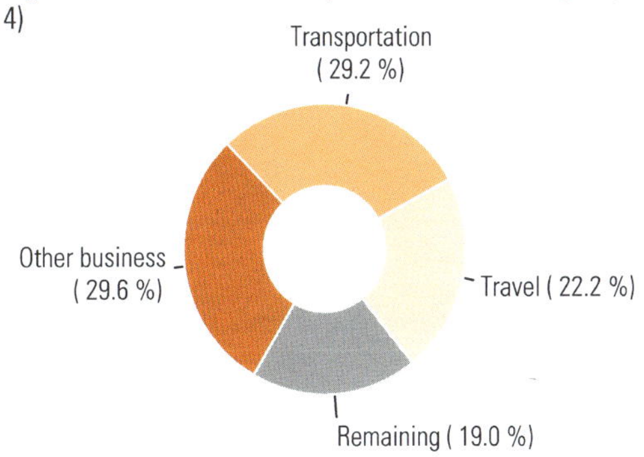

Imports Profile:

"Mineral fuels, lubricants" (SITC section 3), "Machinery and transport equipment" (SITC section 7) and "Goods classified chiefly by material" (SITC section 6) were the largest commodity groups for imports in 2014, representing respectively 33.4, 27.0 and 11.0 percent of imported goods (see table 3). From 2012 to 2014, the largest import commodity was "Petroleum oils and oils obtained from bituminous minerals, crude" (HS code 2709) (see table 4). The top three partners for merchandise imports were China, Japan and the United States, accounting for respectively 16.3, 11.4 and 8.4 percent of total imports. "Other business services" (EBOPS code 268) accounted for the largest share of imports of services in 2014 at 31.2 bln US$, followed by "Transportation" (EBOPS code 205) at 30.8 bln US$ and "Travel" (EBOPS code 236) at 23.5 bln US$ (see graph 6).

Table 4: Top 10 import commodities 2012 to 2014

HS code	4-digit heading of Harmonized System 2012	Value (million US$) 2012	2013	2014	Unit value 2012	2013	2014	Unit	SITC code
	All Commodities	519 575.6	515 573.0	525 557.0					
2709	Petroleum oils and oils obtained from bituminous minerals, crude	108 298.2	99 333.2	94 971.6	0.8	*0.8*	0.8	US$/kg	333
2711	Petroleum gases and other gaseous hydrocarbons	33 834.1	36 320.7	36 585.9	*0.8*	*0.8*	*0.9*	US$/kg	343
2710	Petroleum oils, other than crude	25 700.6	28 842.4	29 661.9	*0.9*	*0.9*	*0.8*	US$/kg	334
8542	Electronic integrated circuits	25 421.6	27 808.5	29 927.3					776
2701	Coal; briquettes, ovoids and similar solid fuels manufactured from coal	15 908.0	12 951.0	11 995.4	0.1	*0.1*	*0.1*	US$/kg	321
2601	Iron ores and concentrates, including roasted iron pyrites	9 531.7	8 354.2	8 492.0	*0.1*	*0.1*	*0.1*	US$/kg	281
8486	Machines and apparatus used for the manufacture of semiconductor devices	8 219.3	6 436.7	7 735.6					728
8517	Electrical apparatus for line telephony or line telegraphy	5 373.1	5 857.8	9 569.4					764
8703	Motor cars and other motor vehicles principally designed for the transport	4 567.4	5 572.6	8 086.5		*24.3*	*23.7*	thsd US$/unit	781
7208	Flat-rolled products of iron or non-alloy steel	5 994.8	4 233.6	4 727.1	0.7	*0.6*	*0.6*	US$/kg	673

Kuwait

Goods Imports: CIF, by origin | **Goods Exports: FOB, by last known destination** | **Trade System: Special**

Overview:

In 2015, the value of merchandise exports of Kuwait decreased substantially by 45.5 percent to reach 55.2 bln US$, while its merchandise imports increased slightly by 1.3 percent to reach 31.9 bln US$ (see graph 1, table 2 and table 3). The merchandise trade balance recorded a moderate surplus of 23.3 bln US$ (see graph 1). The largest merchandise trade balance was with MDG Developed Europe at -7.1 bln US$ (see graph 4). Merchandise exports in Kuwait were highly concentrated amongst partners; imports were diversified. The top 1 partner accounted for 80 percent or more of exports and 19 partners accounted for 80 percent or more of imports (see graph 5). In 2014, the value of exports of services of Kuwait increased slightly by 1.8 percent, reaching 5.9 bln US$, while its imports of services increased substantially by 13.6 percent and reached 22.4 bln US$ (see graph 2). There was a large trade in services deficit of 16.5 bln US$.

Graph 1: Total merchandise trade, by value

(Bln US$ by year)

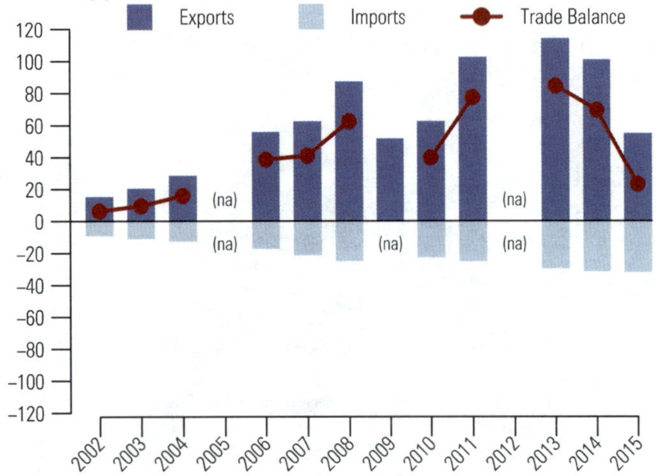

Graph 2: Total services trade, by value

(Bln US$ by year)

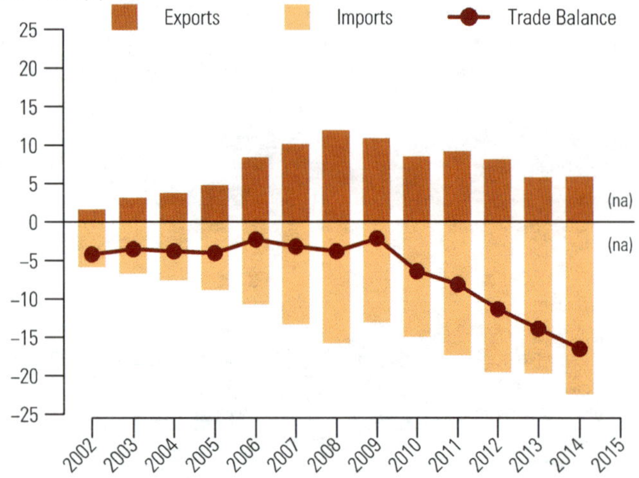

Exports Profile:

"Mineral fuels, lubricants" (SITC section 3), "Chemicals" (SITC section 5) and "Machinery and transport equipment" (SITC section 7) were the largest commodity groups for exports in 2015, representing respectively 89.1, 5.0 and 2.7 percent of exported goods (see table 2). From 2013 to 2015, the largest export commodity was "Petroleum oils and oils obtained from bituminous minerals, crude" (HS code 2709) (see table 1). The top three destinations for merchandise exports were Areas nes, China and the United Arab Emirates, accounting for respectively 92.8, 1.1 and 0.9 percent of total exports. "Communications services" (EBOPS code 245) accounted for the largest share of exports of services in 2014 at 2.9 bln US$, followed by "Transportation" (EBOPS code 205) at 1.6 bln US$ and "Government services, n.i.e." (EBOPS code 291) at 549.9 mln US$ (see graph 3).

Graph 3: Exports of services by EBOPS category

(% share in 2014)

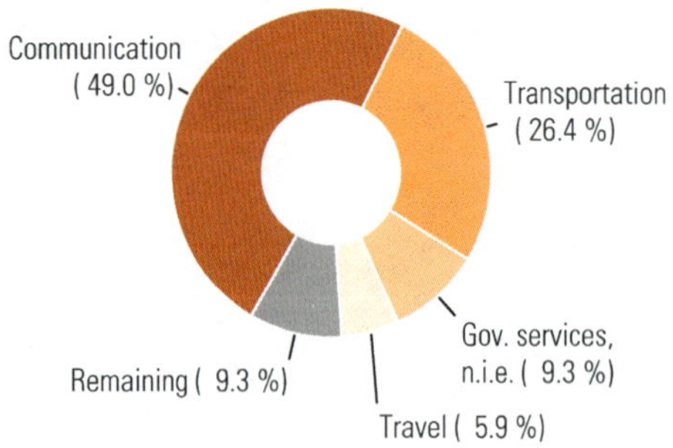

Table 1: Top 10 export commodities 2013 to 2015

HS code	4-digit heading of Harmonized System 2012	Value (million US$) 2013	2014	2015	Unit value 2013	2014	2015	Unit	SITC code
	All Commodities	114404.1	101132.0	55161.6					
2709	Petroleum oils and oils obtained from bituminous minerals, crude	79041.0	69298.2	34142.7	0.8	0.7		US$/kg	333
2710	Petroleum oils, other than crude	24980.5	22828.9	12986.0	0.9	0.8		US$/kg	334
2711	Petroleum gases and other gaseous hydrocarbons	3764.8	2386.1	1856.5					343
2905	Acyclic alcohols and their derivatives	1149.9	994.6	834.2	1.1	1.0	0.7	US$/kg	512
3901	Polymers of ethylene, in primary forms	1419.2	823.6	649.4	1.1	1.0	1.0	US$/kg	571
8703	Motor cars and other motor vehicles principally designed for the transport	506.6	569.6	652.1	19.5	6.1	19.0	thsd US$/unit	781
2902	Cyclic hydrocarbons	34.5	714.3	288.8	1.3	1.3	0.9	US$/kg	511
3102	Mineral or chemical fertilisers, nitrogenous	402.7	328.6	262.6	0.4	0.3	0.3	US$/kg	562
8704	Motor vehicles for the transport of goods	236.8	324.3	204.9	14.9	8.1	15.4	thsd US$/unit	782
7113	Articles of jewellery and parts thereof, of precious metal	290.0	217.6	183.7	45.6	43.2	*3.4*	thsd US$/kg	897

Services Imports and Exports: EBOPS 2002 categories

Table 2: Merchandise exports by SITC

(Value in million US$, growth and shares in percentage)

SITC	2015	Avg. Growth rates 2011-2015	Avg. Growth rates 2014-2015	2015 share
Total	55 161.6	-14.4	-45.5	100.0
0+1	512.1	16.2	5.7	0.9
2+4	152.8	-12.1	-30.4	0.3
3	49 145.5	-15.7	-48.0	89.1
5	2 780.6	-3.7	-15.6	5.0
6	356.4	-7.6	-38.8	0.6
7	1 480.8	17.3	-1.8	2.7
8	514.7	19.2	-0.5	0.9
9	218.6	153.7	>	0.4

Table 3: Merchandise imports by SITC

(Value in million US$, growth and shares in percentage)

SITC	2015	Avg. Growth rates 2011-2015	Avg. Growth rates 2014-2015	2015 share
Total	31 907.2	6.1	1.3	100.0
0+1	4 887.5	5.0	3.8	15.3
2+4	833.1	11.3	14.8	2.6
3	194.2	5.3	-4.7	0.6
5	3 367.2	6.7	5.2	10.6
6	4 702.0	-0.1	-4.3	14.7
7	12 398.4	7.0	1.1	38.9
8	4 819.1	10.2	2.0	15.1
9	705.8	17.7	-5.4	2.2

SITC Legend

SITC Code	Description
Total	All commodities
0+1	Food, animals + beverages, tobacco
2+4	Crude materials + anim. & veg. oils
3	Mineral fuels, lubricants
5	Chemicals
6	Goods classified chiefly by material
7	Machinery and transport equipment
8	Miscellaneous manufactured articles
9	Not classified elsewhere in the SITC

Graph 4: Merchandise trade balance

(Bln US$ by MDG Regions in 2015)

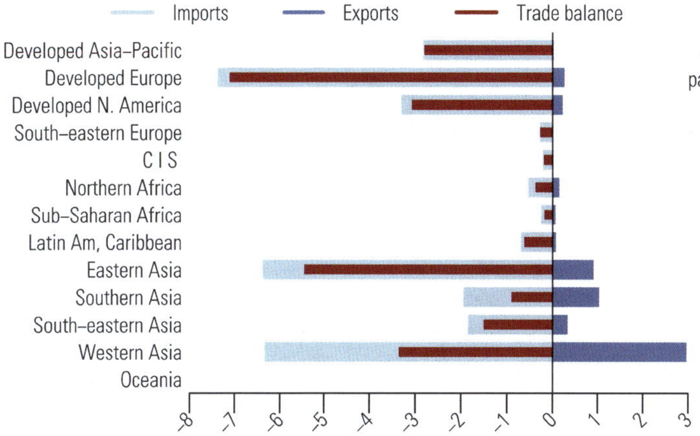

Graph 5: Partner concentration of merchandise trade

(Cumulative share by ranked partners in 2015)

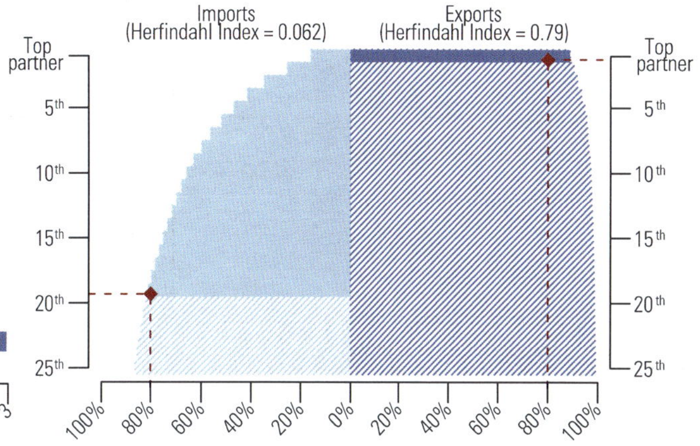

Graph 6: Imports of services by EBOPS category

(% share in 2014)

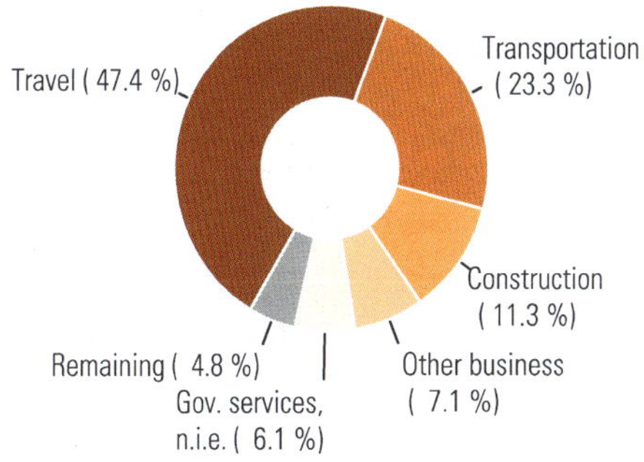

Imports Profile:

"Machinery and transport equipment" (SITC section 7), "Food, animals + beverages, tobacco" (SITC section 0+1) and "Miscellaneous manufactured articles" (SITC section 8) were the largest commodity groups for imports in 2015, representing respectively 38.9, 15.3 and 15.1 percent of imported goods (see table 3). From 2013 to 2015, the largest import commodity was "Motor cars and other motor vehicles principally designed for the transport" (HS code 8703) (see table 4). The top three partners for merchandise imports were China, the United States and the United Arab Emirates, accounting for respectively 14.6, 9.7 and 9.2 percent of total imports. "Travel" (EBOPS code 236) accounted for the largest share of imports of services in 2014 at 10.6 bln US$, followed by "Transportation" (EBOPS code 205) at 5.2 bln US$ and "Construction services" (EBOPS code 249) at 2.5 bln US$ (see graph 6).

Table 4: Top 10 import commodities 2013 to 2015

HS code	4-digit heading of Harmonized System 2012	Value (million US$) 2013	2014	2015	Unit value 2013	2014	2015	Unit	SITC code
	All Commodities	29 645.6	31 488.7	31 907.2					
8703	Motor cars and other motor vehicles principally designed for the transport	4 055.9	3 871.7	3 566.8	27.6	*27.8*	25.4	thsd US$/unit	781
8517	Electrical apparatus for line telephony or line telegraphy	1 164.0	1 327.2	1 551.9					764
3004	Medicaments (excluding goods of heading 30.02, 30.05 or 30.06)	771.3	757.9	838.6	113.0	117.3	*110.5*	US$/kg	542
7108	Gold (including gold plated with platinum)	795.9	740.1	657.2	54.7	39.4		thsd US$/kg	971
7113	Articles of jewellery and parts thereof, of precious metal	554.9	665.1	679.7	49.2	51.9	*15.3*	thsd US$/kg	897
8704	Motor vehicles for the transport of goods	479.1	492.6	540.5	11.2	19.1	*14.6*	thsd US$/unit	782
8471	Automatic data processing machines and units thereof	428.9	467.0	458.2	293.2	233.8	250.0	US$/unit	752
8544	Insulated (including enamelled or anodised) wire, cable	506.5	455.9	353.6	6.1	5.9	*5.7*	US$/kg	773
7304	Tubes, pipes and hollow profiles, seamless, of iron (other than cast iron)	383.0	346.4	387.3	1.5	1.6	0.7	US$/kg	679
8431	Parts suitable for use principally with the machinery of headings 84.25	274.9	374.1	368.8	17.8	11.7	13.3	US$/kg	723

Kyrgyzstan

Goods Imports: CIF, by origin **Goods Exports: FOB, by last known destination** **Trade System: General**

Overview:

In 2015, the value of merchandise exports of Kyrgyzstan was 1.4 bln US$, while its merchandise imports was 4.1 bln US$ (see graph 1, table 2 and table 3). The merchandise trade balance recorded a large deficit of 2.6 bln US$ (see graph 1). The largest merchandise trade balance was with MDG CIS at -1.6 bln US$ (see graph 4). Merchandise exports in Kyrgyzstan were moderately concentrated amongst partners; imports were also moderately concentrated. The top 6 partners accounted for 80 percent or more of exports and 5 partners accounted for 80 percent or more of imports (see graph 5). In 2014, the value of exports of services of Kyrgyzstan decreased substantially by 34.2 percent, reaching 896.6 mln US$, while its imports of services decreased moderately by 6.6 percent and reached 1.2 bln US$ (see graph 2). There was a moderate trade in services deficit of 334.5 mln US$.

Graph 1: Total merchandise trade, by value

(Bln US$ by year)

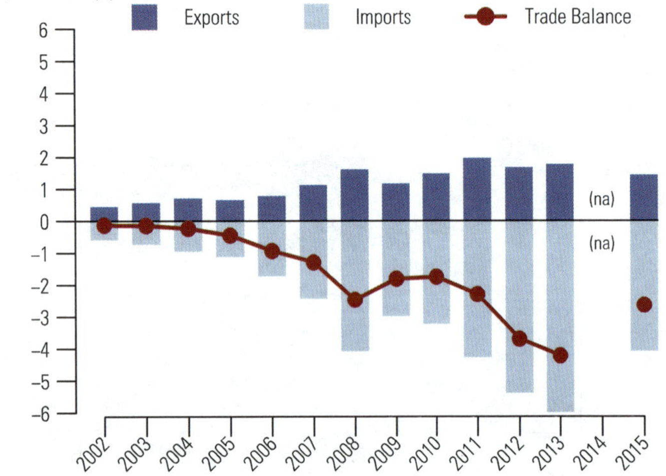

Graph 2: Total services trade, by value

(Bln US$ by year)

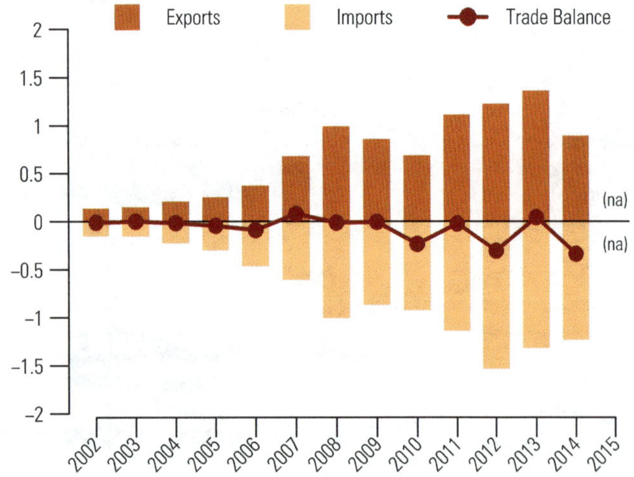

Exports Profile:

"Not classified elsewhere in the SITC" (SITC section 9), "Machinery and transport equipment" (SITC section 7) and "Food, animals + beverages, tobacco" (SITC section 0+1) were the largest commodity groups for exports in 2015, representing respectively 55.3, 13.0 and 9.8 percent of exported goods (see table 2). From 2013 to 2015, the largest export commodity was "Gold (including gold plated with platinum)" (HS code 7108) (see table 1). The top three destinations for merchandise exports were Switzerland, Kazakhstan and the United Arab Emirates, accounting for respectively 33.5, 19.0 and 10.0 percent of total exports. "Travel" (EBOPS code 236) accounted for the largest share of exports of services in 2014 at 422.7 mln US$, followed by "Transportation" (EBOPS code 205) at 158.5 mln US$ and "Other business services" (EBOPS code 268) at 108.3 mln US$ (see graph 3).

Graph 3: Exports of services by EBOPS category

(% share in 2014)

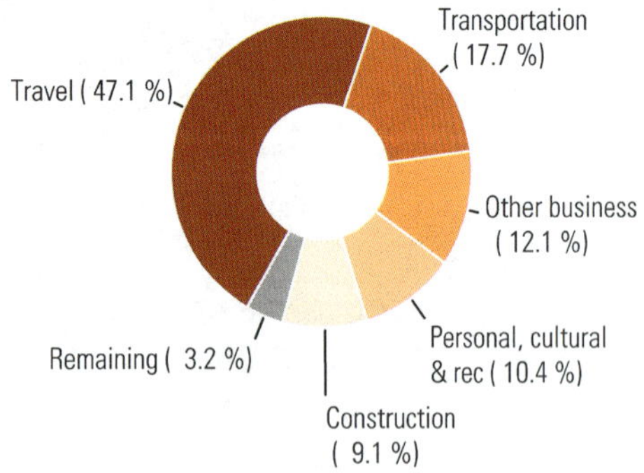

Table 1: Top 10 export commodities 2013 to 2015

HS code	4-digit heading of Harmonized System 2007	Value (million US$) 2013	2014	2015	Unit value 2013	2014	2015	Unit	SITC code
	All Commodities	1773.2	...	1441.5					
7108	Gold (including gold plated with platinum)	736.8	...	665.4	43.5		37.8	thsd US$/kg	971
2710	Petroleum oils, other than crude	140.0	...	69.0	1.0		0.7	US$/kg	334
9999	Commodities not specified according to kind	46.3	...	131.5					931
0713	Dried leguminous vegetables, shelled, whether or not skinned or split	73.7	...	43.8	1.2		0.7	US$/kg	054
8708	Parts and accessories of the motor vehicles of headings 87.01 to 87.05	33.4	...	31.6	6.6		*8.7*	US$/kg	784
6204	Women's or girls' suits, ensembles, jackets, blazers, dresses, skirts	41.0	...	17.1	9.8			US$/unit	842
8704	Motor vehicles for the transport of goods	26.0	...	23.5	155.8		301.3	thsd US$/unit	782
8802	Other aircraft (for example, helicopters, aeroplanes); spacecraft	8.4	...	38.9	0.6		1.8	mln US$/unit	792
7005	Float glass and surface ground or polished glass, in sheets	28.4	...	10.8			2.9	US$/m²	664
8539	Electric filament or discharge lamps, including sealed beam lamp units	23.7	...	15.5					778

Services Imports and Exports: EBOPS 2002 categories

Table 2: Merchandise exports by SITC

(Value in million US$, growth and shares in percentage)

SITC	2015	Avg. Growth rates 2011-2015	Avg. Growth rates 2014-2015	2015 share
Total	1 441.5	-7.6	...	100.0
0+1	141.3	-10.5	...	9.8
2+4	64.9	-7.3	...	4.5
3	75.2	-20.1	...	5.2
5	15.7	-4.4	...	1.1
6	74.5	-8.2	...	5.2
7	187.2	10.6	...	13.0
8	85.7	-15.9	...	5.9
9	796.9	-7.0	...	55.3

Table 3: Merchandise imports by SITC

(Value in million US$, growth and shares in percentage)

SITC	2015	Avg. Growth rates 2011-2015	Avg. Growth rates 2014-2015	2015 share
Total	4 068.1	-1.1	...	100.0
0+1	511.8	-5.7	...	12.6
2+4	120.9	-4.0	...	3.0
3	778.1	-5.4	...	19.1
5	447.4	-0.3	...	11.0
6	874.5	7.2	...	21.5
7	797.2	-4.8	...	19.6
8	407.2	1.2	...	10.0
9	131.1	51.7	...	3.2

SITC Legend

SITC Code	Description
Total	All commodities
0+1	Food, animals + beverages, tobacco
2+4	Crude materials + anim. & veg. oils
3	Mineral fuels, lubricants
5	Chemicals
6	Goods classified chiefly by material
7	Machinery and transport equipment
8	Miscellaneous manufactured articles
9	Not classified elsewhere in the SITC

Graph 4: Merchandise trade balance

(Bln US$ by MDG Regions in 2015)

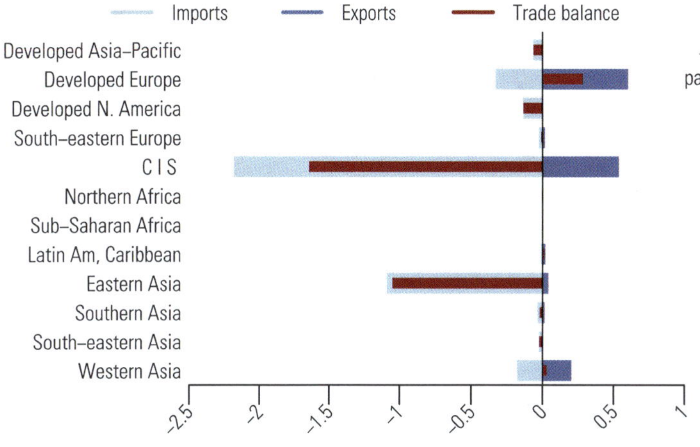

Graph 5: Partner concentration of merchandise trade

(Cumulative share by ranked partners in 2015)

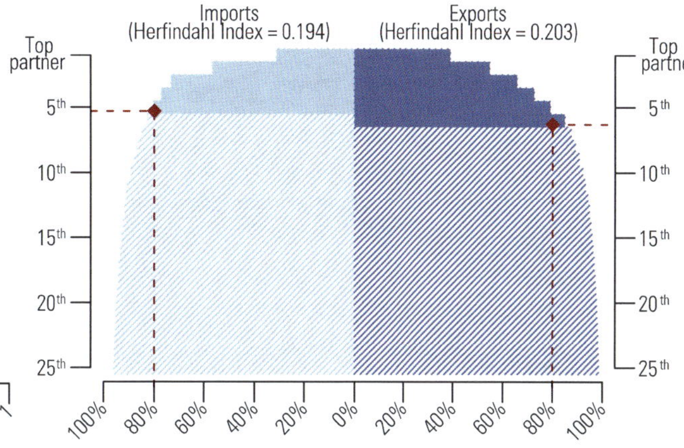

Graph 6: Imports of services by EBOPS category

(% share in 2014)

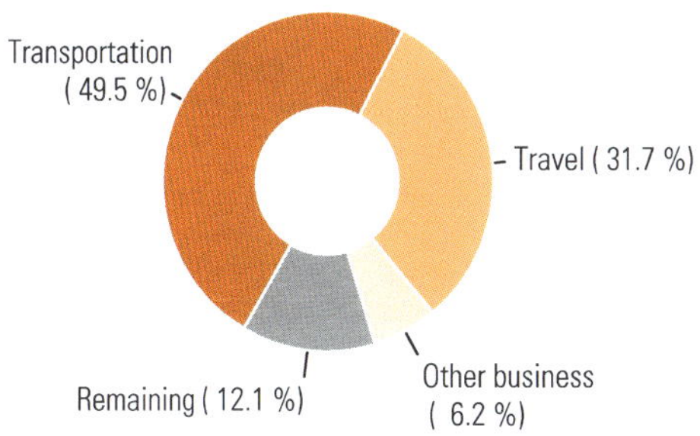

Imports Profile:

"Goods classified chiefly by material" (SITC section 6), "Machinery and transport equipment" (SITC section 7) and "Mineral fuels, lubricants" (SITC section 3) were the largest commodity groups for imports in 2015, representing respectively 21.5, 19.6 and 19.1 percent of imported goods (see table 3). From 2013 to 2015, the largest import commodity was "Petroleum oils, other than crude" (HS code 2710) (see table 4). The top three partners for merchandise imports were the Russian Federation, China and Kazakhstan, accounting for respectively 32.4, 24.5 and 12.3 percent of total imports. "Transportation" (EBOPS code 205) accounted for the largest share of imports of services in 2014 at 608.9 mln US$, followed by "Travel" (EBOPS code 236) at 390.0 mln US$ and "Other business services" (EBOPS code 268) at 76.7 mln US$ (see graph 6).

Table 4: Top 10 import commodities 2013 to 2015

HS code	4-digit heading of Harmonized System 2007	Value (million US$) 2013	2014	2015	Unit value 2013	2014	2015	Unit	SITC code
	All Commodities	5 983.0	...	4 068.1					
2710	Petroleum oils, other than crude	1 139.7	...	643.3	*0.7*		*0.4*	US$/kg	334
8703	Motor cars and other motor vehicles principally designed for the transport	372.4	...	43.7	5.2		*16.2*	thsd US$/unit	781
3004	Medicaments (excluding goods of heading 30.02, 30.05 or 30.06)	169.6	...	134.2	*19.9*		*20.1*	US$/kg	542
8704	Motor vehicles for the transport of goods	156.3	...	56.1	15.3		*14.9*	thsd US$/unit	782
7210	Flat-rolled products of iron or non-alloy steel	54.9	...	124.6	1.0		2.2	US$/kg	674
1001	Wheat and meslin	89.8	...	61.3	0.2		0.2	US$/kg	041
9999	Commodities not specified according to kind	20.9	...	113.7					931
8517	Electrical apparatus for line telephony or line telegraphy	73.1	...	59.3					764
7308	Structures (excluding prefabricated buildings of heading 94.06)	108.0	...	19.2	2.1		1.8	US$/kg	691
2402	Cigars, cheroots, cigarillos and cigarettes	64.8	...	53.2	*11.4*		*9.5*	US$/kg	122

Source: UN Comtrade

Goods Imports: CIF, by origin | **Goods Exports: FOB, by last known destination** | **Trade System: Special**

Overview:

In 2015, the value of merchandise exports of Latvia decreased substantially by 15.5 percent to reach 11.5 bln US$, while its merchandise imports decreased substantially by 17.6 percent to reach 13.8 bln US$ (see graph 1, table 2 and table 3). The merchandise trade balance recorded a relatively small deficit of 2.3 bln US$ (see graph 1). The largest merchandise trade balance was with MDG Developed Europe at -2.4 bln US$ (see graph 4). Merchandise exports in Latvia were diversified amongst partners; imports were also diversified. The top 16 partners accounted for 80 percent or more of exports and 13 partners accounted for 80 percent or more of imports (see graph 5). In 2014, the value of exports of services of Latvia increased slightly by 0.4 percent, reaching 4.9 bln US$, while its imports of services decreased slightly by 0.9 percent and reached 2.7 bln US$ (see graph 2). There was a moderate trade in services surplus of 2.2 bln US$.

Graph 1: Total merchandise trade, by value

(Bln US$ by year)

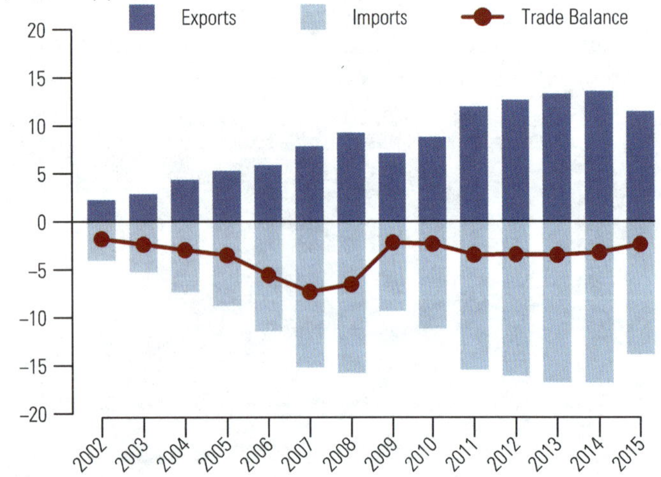

Graph 2: Total services trade, by value

(Bln US$ by year)

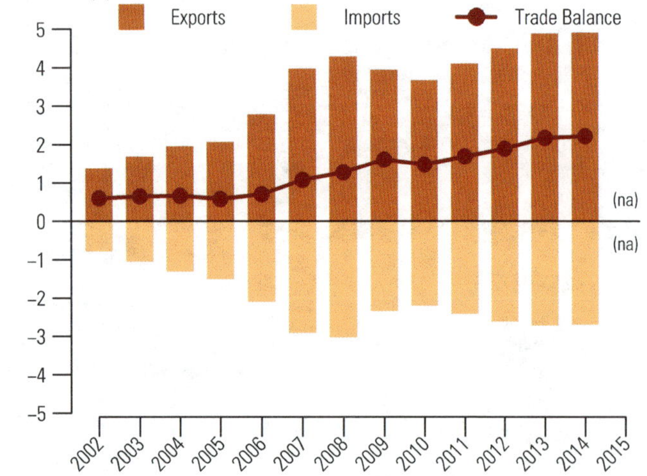

Exports Profile:

"Machinery and transport equipment" (SITC section 7), "Goods classified chiefly by material" (SITC section 6) and "Food, animals + beverages, tobacco" (SITC section 0+1) were the largest commodity groups for exports in 2015, representing respectively 21.6, 17.7 and 16.0 percent of exported goods (see table 2). From 2013 to 2015, the largest export commodity was "Commodities not specified according to kind" (HS code 9999) (see table 1). The top three destinations for merchandise exports were Lithuania, Estonia and the Russian Federation, accounting for respectively 18.3, 12.1 and 10.2 percent of total exports. "Transportation" (EBOPS code 205) accounted for the largest share of exports of services in 2014 at 2.1 bln US$, followed by "Travel" (EBOPS code 236) at 955.2 mln US$ and "Other business services" (EBOPS code 268) at 821.7 mln US$ (see graph 3).

Graph 3: Exports of services by EBOPS category

(% share in 2014)

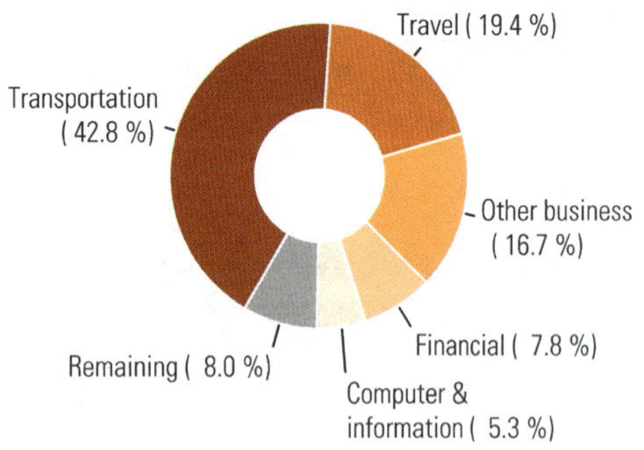

Table 1: Top 10 export commodities 2013 to 2015

HS code	4-digit heading of Harmonized System 2012	Value (million US$)			Unit value				SITC code
		2013	2014	2015	2013	2014	2015	Unit	
	All Commodities	13324.7	13602.8	11500.4					
9999	Commodities not specified according to kind	931.5	816.3	959.0					931
4407	Wood sawn or chipped lengthwise, sliced or peeled	640.0	743.1	627.9	*253.6*	*266.4*	*214.4*	US$/$m^3$	248
8517	Electrical apparatus for line telephony or line telegraphy	552.2	801.3	649.9					764
2710	Petroleum oils, other than crude	708.5	693.7	494.5	*1.0*	*0.9*		US$/kg	334
2208	Alcohol of a strength by volume of less than 80 % vol	513.4	519.6	323.4	*18.4*	*16.8*	*11.0*	US$/litre	112
1001	Wheat and meslin	340.2	357.0	354.6	0.3	0.3	0.2	US$/kg	041
3004	Medicaments (excluding goods of heading 30.02, 30.05 or 30.06)	343.0	356.4	312.2	*151.5*	*157.0*	*141.6*	US$/kg	542
4401	Fuel wood, in logs, in billets, in twigs, in faggots or in similar forms	317.3	329.0	305.8	0.1	0.1	0.1	US$/kg	246
8528	Reception apparatus for television	225.0	266.8	232.0	435.4	421.7	328.0	US$/unit	761
4403	Wood in the rough, whether or not stripped of bark or sapwood	247.8	261.2	161.9	*66.3*	68.1	55.7	US$/$m^3$	247

Services Imports and Exports: EBOPS 2002 categories

Table 2: Merchandise exports by SITC

(Value in million US$, growth and shares in percentage)

SITC	2015	Avg. Growth rates 2011-2015	Avg. Growth rates 2014-2015	2015 share
Total	11 500.4	-1.0	-15.5	100.0
0+1	1 835.2	2.4	-21.6	16.0
2+4	1 523.4	-5.3	-18.7	13.2
3	705.3	-8.1	-30.2	6.1
5	864.1	-2.9	-14.6	7.5
6	2 030.4	-6.0	-15.7	17.7
7	2 479.0	2.9	-11.7	21.6
8	1 071.2	0.6	-16.7	9.3
9	991.9	12.9	15.1	8.6

Table 3: Merchandise imports by SITC

(Value in million US$, growth and shares in percentage)

SITC	2015	Avg. Growth rates 2011-2015	Avg. Growth rates 2014-2015	2015 share
Total	13 846.1	-2.7	-17.6	100.0
0+1	1 739.5	-1.8	-21.5	12.6
2+4	569.0	-3.1	-20.9	4.1
3	1 540.7	-11.8	-34.0	11.1
5	1 579.9	-2.2	-14.4	11.4
6	1 932.9	-6.0	-20.8	14.0
7	3 655.3	-0.3	-13.6	26.4
8	1 311.7	0.3	-20.1	9.5
9	1 517.1	6.7	10.6	11.0

SITC Legend

SITC Code	Description
Total	All commodities
0+1	Food, animals + beverages, tobacco
2+4	Crude materials + anim. & veg. oils
3	Mineral fuels, lubricants
5	Chemicals
6	Goods classified chiefly by material
7	Machinery and transport equipment
8	Miscellaneous manufactured articles
9	Not classified elsewhere in the SITC

Graph 4: Merchandise trade balance

(Bln US$ by MDG Regions in 2015)

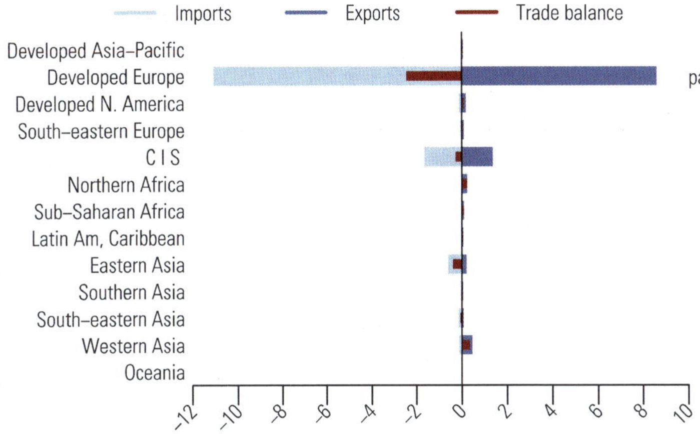

Graph 5: Partner concentration of merchandise trade

(Cumulative share by ranked partners in 2015)

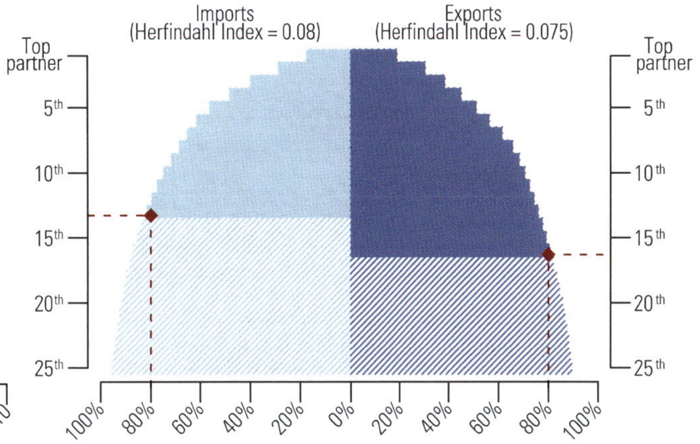

Graph 6: Imports of services by EBOPS category

(% share in 2014)

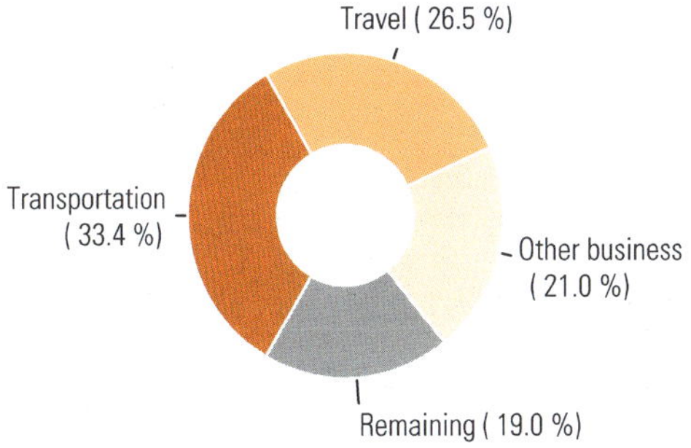

Imports Profile:

"Machinery and transport equipment" (SITC section 7), "Goods classified chiefly by material" (SITC section 6) and "Food, animals + beverages, tobacco" (SITC section 0+1) were the largest commodity groups for imports in 2015, representing respectively 26.4, 14.0 and 12.6 percent of imported goods (see table 3). From 2013 to 2015, the largest import commodity was "Commodities not specified according to kind" (HS code 9999) (see table 4). The top three partners for merchandise imports were Lithuania, Germany and Poland, accounting for respectively 18.5, 11.5 and 10.7 percent of total imports. "Transportation" (EBOPS code 205) accounted for the largest share of imports of services in 2014 at 898.1 mln US$, followed by "Travel" (EBOPS code 236) at 713.4 mln US$ and "Other business services" (EBOPS code 268) at 565.9 mln US$ (see graph 6).

Table 4: Top 10 import commodities 2013 to 2015

HS code	4-digit heading of Harmonized System 2012	Value (million US$) 2013	Value (million US$) 2014	Value (million US$) 2015	Unit value 2013	Unit value 2014	Unit value 2015	Unit	SITC code
	All Commodities	16 778.9	16 798.4	13 846.1					
9999	Commodities not specified according to kind	1 733.6	1 339.8	1 505.3					931
2710	Petroleum oils, other than crude	1 713.3	1 568.3	1 097.8	*1.0*	*0.9*		US$/kg	334
8517	Electrical apparatus for line telephony or line telegraphy	543.3	797.1	643.4					764
2711	Petroleum gases and other gaseous hydrocarbons	755.2	628.6	385.3	*0.6*	*0.6*	*0.4*	US$/kg	343
8703	Motor cars and other motor vehicles principally designed for the transport	468.7	570.6	447.9	23.8	23.1	19.3	thsd US$/unit	781
3004	Medicaments (excluding goods of heading 30.02, 30.05 or 30.06)	483.9	506.0	431.4	*77.8*	*91.2*	*79.4*	US$/kg	542
8528	Reception apparatus for television	217.9	258.4	222.2	299.0	326.6	279.2	US$/unit	761
8471	Automatic data processing machines and units thereof	201.4	213.8	191.3	105.0	154.1	128.3	US$/unit	752
8708	Parts and accessories of the motor vehicles of headings 87.01 to 87.05	186.9	186.8	168.0	*10.1*	*9.3*	*8.5*	US$/kg	784
4011	New pneumatic tyres, of rubber	165.8	185.9	137.8	85.9	81.7	65.6	US$/unit	625

Lebanon

Goods Imports: CIF, by origin | **Goods Exports: FOB, by last known destination** | **Trade System: Special**

Overview:

In 2014, the value of merchandise exports of Lebanon decreased substantially by 15.9 percent to reach 3.3 bln US$, while its merchandise imports decreased slightly by 3.5 percent to reach 20.5 bln US$ (see graph 1, table 2 and table 3). The merchandise trade balance recorded a large deficit of 17.2 bln US$ (see graph 1). The largest merchandise trade balance was with MDG Developed Europe at -8.2 bln US$ (see graph 4). Merchandise exports in Lebanon were diversified amongst partners; imports were also diversified. The top 23 partners accounted for 80 percent or more of exports and 23 partners accounted for 80 percent or more of imports (see graph 5). In 2014, the value of exports of services of Lebanon decreased moderately by 6.9 percent, reaching 13.7 bln US$, while its imports of services decreased slightly by 4.6 percent and reached 12.5 bln US$ (see graph 2). There was a relatively small trade in services surplus of 1.2 bln US$.

Graph 1: Total merchandise trade, by value

(Bln US$ by year)

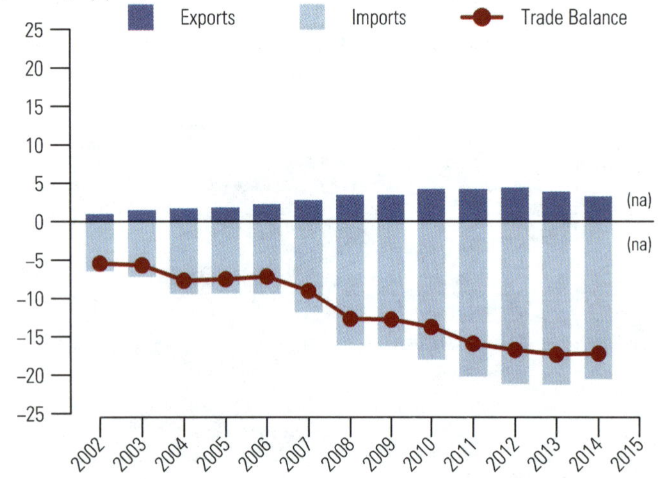

Graph 2: Total services trade, by value

(Bln US$ by year)

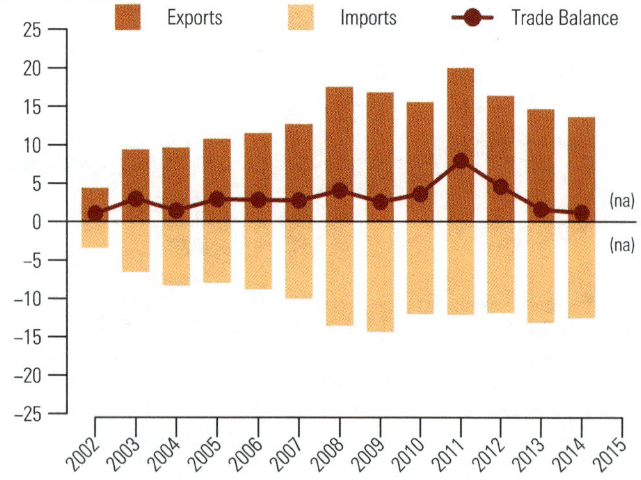

Exports Profile:

"Food, animals + beverages, tobacco" (SITC section 0+1), "Miscellaneous manufactured articles" (SITC section 8) and "Goods classified chiefly by material" (SITC section 6) were the largest commodity groups for exports in 2014, representing respectively 22.3, 14.6 and 14.5 percent of exported goods (see table 2). From 2012 to 2014, the largest export commodity was "Gold (including gold plated with platinum)" (HS code 7108) (see table 1). The top three destinations for merchandise exports were South Africa, Saudi Arabia and the Syrian Arab Republic, accounting for respectively 13.3, 9.2 and 9.1 percent of total exports. "Travel" (EBOPS code 236) accounted for the largest share of exports of services in 2014 at 6.3 bln US$, followed by "Other business services" (EBOPS code 268) at 3.0 bln US$ and "Financial services" (EBOPS code 260) at 1.8 bln US$ (see graph 3).

Graph 3: Exports of services by EBOPS category

(% share in 2014)

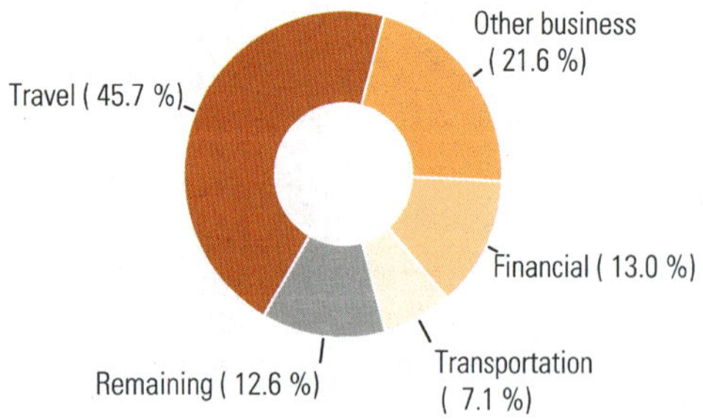

Table 1: Top 10 export commodities 2012 to 2014

HS code	4-digit heading of Harmonized System 2012	Value (million US$) 2012	2013	2014	Unit value 2012	2013	2014	Unit	SITC code
	All Commodities	4446.2	3937.1	3312.2					
7108	Gold (including gold plated with platinum)	1396.1	558.7	365.8	*46.5*	*41.4*	36.1	thsd US$/kg	971
7404	Copper waste and scrap	157.2	187.9	96.9	6.4	5.9	5.3	US$/kg	288
7102	Diamonds, whether or not worked, but not mounted or set	197.5	110.2	91.1					667
2710	Petroleum oils, other than crude	72.4	298.6	19.2	1.0	1.0	1.0	US$/kg	334
8502	Electric generating sets and rotary converters	144.0	136.4	109.3					716
7204	Ferrous waste and scrap; remelting scrap ingots of iron or steel	133.8	147.0	85.5	0.4	0.3	0.3	US$/kg	282
4901	Printed books, brochures, leaflets and similar printed matter	74.7	73.8	112.5	1.5	1.5	2.2	US$/kg	892
7113	Articles of jewellery and parts thereof, of precious metal	105.9	81.8	56.9	*43.5*	*44.3*	*27.5*	thsd US$/kg	897
3103	Mineral or chemical fertilisers, phosphatic	85.2	72.9	72.5	0.4	0.3	0.3	US$/kg	562
8418	Refrigerators, freezers and other refrigerating or freezing equipment	57.1	53.8	54.7					741

Services Imports and Exports: EBOPS 2002 categories

Table 2: Merchandise exports by SITC

(Value in million US$, growth and shares in percentage)

SITC	2014	Avg. Growth rates 2010-2014	Avg. Growth rates 2013-2014	2014 share
Total	3312.2	-6.1	-15.9	100.0
0+1	739.0	11.0	7.9	22.3
2+4	267.7	-7.7	-38.2	8.1
3	32.3	54.8	-90.4	1.0
5	462.2	4.9	10.7	14.0
6	480.6	-6.2	-6.1	14.5
7	476.3	-10.7	-11.8	14.4
8	483.4	-11.9	7.4	14.6
9	370.8	-18.4	-34.1	11.2

Table 3: Merchandise imports by SITC

(Value in million US$, growth and shares in percentage)

SITC	2014	Avg. Growth rates 2010-2014	Avg. Growth rates 2013-2014	2014 share
Total	20487.4	3.3	-3.5	100.0
0+1	3276.0	5.8	5.9	16.0
2+4	648.3	6.6	10.9	3.2
3	4746.2	6.6	-5.1	23.2
5	2522.7	7.1	3.2	12.3
6	3099.2	3.2	-0.7	15.1
7	3717.2	-2.4	-14.7	18.1
8	1808.7	2.9	2.3	8.8
9	669.0	-4.6	-22.4	3.3

SITC Legend

SITC Code	Description
Total	All commodities
0+1	Food, animals + beverages, tobacco
2+4	Crude materials + anim. & veg. oils
3	Mineral fuels, lubricants
5	Chemicals
6	Goods classified chiefly by material
7	Machinery and transport equipment
8	Miscellaneous manufactured articles
9	Not classified elsewhere in the SITC

Graph 4: Merchandise trade balance

(Bln US$ by MDG Regions in 2014)

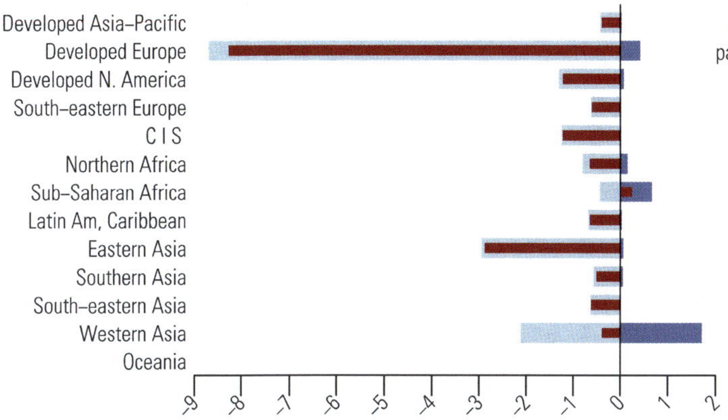

Graph 5: Partner concentration of merchandise trade

(Cumulative share by ranked partners in 2014)

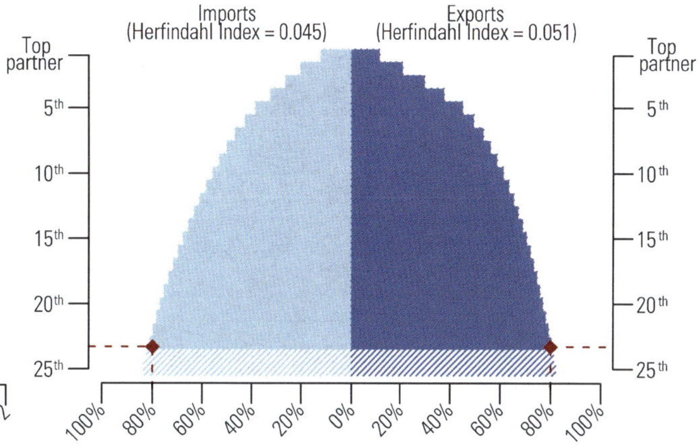

Graph 6: Imports of services by EBOPS category

(% share in 2014)

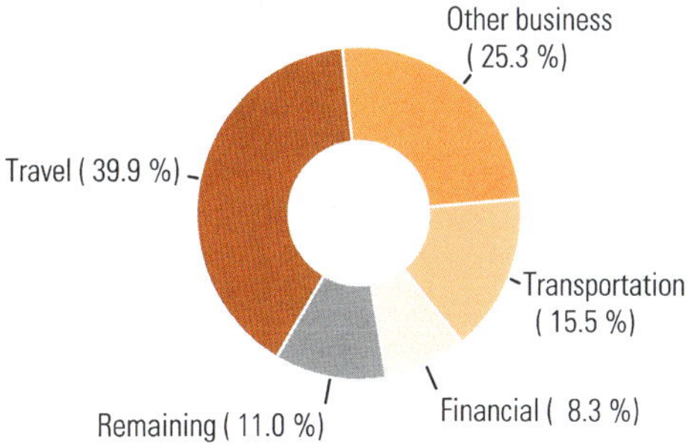

Imports Profile:

"Mineral fuels, lubricants" (SITC section 3), "Machinery and transport equipment" (SITC section 7) and "Food, animals + beverages, tobacco" (SITC section 0+1) were the largest commodity groups for imports in 2014, representing respectively 23.2, 18.1 and 16.0 percent of imported goods (see table 3). From 2012 to 2014, the largest import commodity was "Petroleum oils, other than crude" (HS code 2710) (see table 4). The top three partners for merchandise imports were China, Italy and the United States, accounting for respectively 10.3, 8.3 and 8.1 percent of total imports. "Travel" (EBOPS code 236) accounted for the largest share of imports of services in 2014 at 5.0 bln US$, followed by "Other business services" (EBOPS code 268) at 3.2 bln US$ and "Transportation" (EBOPS code 205) at 1.9 bln US$ (see graph 6).

Table 4: Top 10 import commodities 2012 to 2014

HS code	4-digit heading of Harmonized System 2012	Value (million US$) 2012	2013	2014	Unit value 2012	2013	2014	Unit	SITC code
	All Commodities	21146.5	21234.2	20487.4					
2710	Petroleum oils, other than crude	5517.5	4664.7	4418.3	*1.0*	*1.0*	0.9	US$/kg	334
8703	Motor cars and other motor vehicles principally designed for the transport	1101.5	1168.2	1086.3		*21.4*	*20.8*	thsd US$/unit	781
3004	Medicaments (excluding goods of heading 30.02, 30.05 or 30.06)	831.4	935.7	973.2	115.7	116.7	*110.6*	US$/kg	542
7108	Gold (including gold plated with platinum)	1186.4	852.1	657.9	*47.6*	*43.6*	*38.7*	thsd US$/kg	971
7228	Other bars and rods of other alloy steel	280.9	478.2	492.7	0.6	0.6	0.5	US$/kg	676
0102	Live bovine animals	270.3	277.3	342.7		*1.0*	*1.1*	thsd US$/unit	001
2402	Cigars, cheroots, cigarillos and cigarettes	309.2	242.1	188.4	21.5	21.9	20.9	US$/kg	122
7102	Diamonds, whether or not worked, but not mounted or set	279.7	198.8	224.2					667
2711	Petroleum gases and other gaseous hydrocarbons	224.0	226.1	225.5	1.1	1.0	0.9	US$/kg	343
8517	Electrical apparatus for line telephony or line telegraphy	139.0	314.1	174.2					764

Source: UN Comtrade

Lesotho

Goods Imports: CIF, by consignment | **Goods Exports: FOB, by last known destination** | **Trade System: General**

Overview:

In 2012, the value of merchandise exports of Lesotho decreased substantially by 11.9 percent to reach 678.2 mln US$, while its merchandise imports increased moderately by 9.2 percent to reach 1.6 bln US$ (see graph 1, table 2 and table 3). The merchandise trade balance recorded a large deficit of 916.1 mln US$ (see graph 1). The largest merchandise trade balance was with MDG Sub-Saharan Africa at -1.1 bln US$ (see graph 4). Merchandise exports in Lesotho were highly concentrated amongst partners; imports were also highly concentrated. The top 2 partners accounted for 80 percent or more of exports and 1 partner accounted for 80 percent or more of imports (see graph 5). In 2012, the value of exports of services of Lesotho increased substantially by 41.3 percent, reaching 63.5 mln US$, while its imports of services decreased moderately by 6.1 percent and reached 174.9 mln US$ (see graph 2). There was a large trade in services deficit of 111.4 mln US$.

Graph 1: Total merchandise trade, by value

(Bln US$ by year)

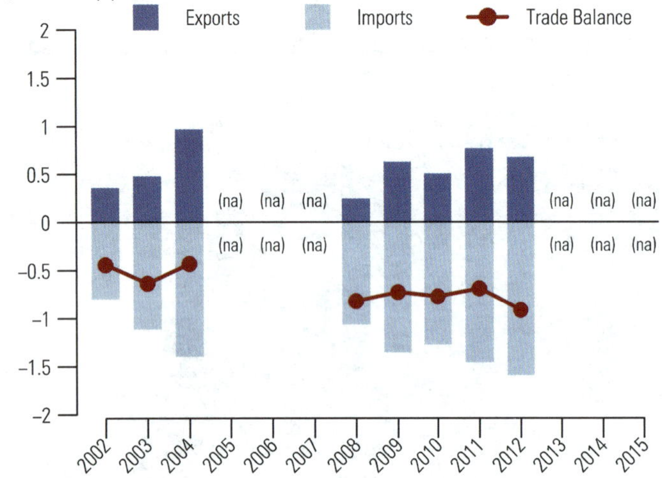

Graph 2: Total services trade, by value

(Mln US$ by year)

Exports Profile:

"Miscellaneous manufactured articles" (SITC section 8), "Food, animals + beverages, tobacco" (SITC section 0+1) and "Machinery and transport equipment" (SITC section 7) were the largest commodity groups for exports in 2012, representing respectively 60.1, 14.3 and 11.4 percent of exported goods (see table 2). From 2010 to 2012, the largest export commodity was "Men's or boys' suits, jackets, trousers etc" (HS code 6203) (see table 1). The top three destinations for merchandise exports were South Africa, the United States and Belgium, accounting for respectively 53.5, 36.8 and 3.4 percent of total exports. "Travel" (EBOPS code 236) accounted for the largest share of exports of services in 2012 at 46.2 mln US$, followed by "Communications services" (EBOPS code 245) at 6.2 mln US$ and "Other business services" (EBOPS code 268) at 5.6 mln US$ (see graph 3).

Graph 3: Exports of services by EBOPS category

(% share in 2012)

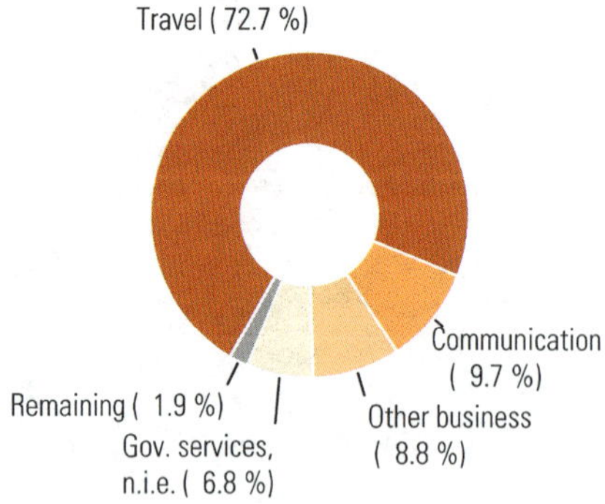

Table 1: Top 10 export commodities 2010 to 2012

HS code	4-digit heading of Harmonized System 1996	Value (million US$) 2010	2011	2012	Unit value 2010	2011	2012	Unit	SITC code
	All Commodities	503.3	770.1	678.2					
6203	Men's or boys' suits, jackets, trousers etc	52.0	139.5	110.4					841
2201	Unsweetened beverage waters, ice and snow	60.1	67.5	64.5					111
6104	Womens, girls suit, dress, skirt, etc, knit or crocheted	29.8	64.9	77.7					844
6110	Jerseys, pullovers, cardigans, etc, knitted or crocheted	26.1	56.2	33.1	*11.7*	*12.1*	*12.6*	US$/unit	845
9999	Commodities not elsewhere specified	78.2	34.5	2.1					931
8538	Parts for electrical switches, protectors, connectors	39.7	40.2	34.7					772
6204	Women's or girls' suits, jacket, dress, skirt, etc	24.9	53.2	33.0					842
6105	Men's or boys' shirts, knitted or crocheted	13.0	36.0	43.7					843
5101	Wool, not carded or combed	16.5	17.3	36.1	*1.8*			US$/kg	268
6109	T-shirts, singlets and other vests, knitted or crocheted	11.4	21.4	33.3	*5.2*	*5.4*	*6.5*	US$/unit	845

Services Imports and Exports: EBOPS 2002 categories

Table 2: Merchandise exports by SITC

(Value in million US$, growth and shares in percentage)

SITC	2012	Avg. Growth rates 2008-2012	Avg. Growth rates 2011-2012	2012 share
Total	678.2	29.0	-11.9	100.0
0+1	97.3	31.1	-10.8	14.3
2+4	41.4	10.2	46.6	6.1
3	0.8	-2.9	-27.1	0.1
5	0.6	-18.5	-30.3	0.1
6	50.9	33.0	-21.3	7.5
7	77.6	-6.2	22.3	11.4
8	407.7	58.4	-12.9	60.1
9	2.1	59.3	-94.1	0.3

Table 3: Merchandise imports by SITC

(Value in million US$, growth and shares in percentage)

SITC	2012	Avg. Growth rates 2008-2012	Avg. Growth rates 2011-2012	2012 share
Total	1 594.2	10.6	9.2	100.0
0+1	314.3	10.7	-4.3	19.7
2+4	69.9	22.4	2.6	4.4
3	193.5	14.2	-4.0	12.1
5	161.6	15.8	7.9	10.1
6	316.0	27.3	26.3	19.8
7	290.1	8.6	18.1	18.2
8	187.8	5.4	22.1	11.8
9	61.1	-18.9	-1.9	3.8

SITC Legend

SITC Code	Description
Total	All commodities
0+1	Food, animals + beverages, tobacco
2+4	Crude materials + anim. & veg. oils
3	Mineral fuels, lubricants
5	Chemicals
6	Goods classified chiefly by material
7	Machinery and transport equipment
8	Miscellaneous manufactured articles
9	Not classified elsewhere in the SITC

Graph 4: Merchandise trade balance

(Bln US$ by MDG Regions in 2012)

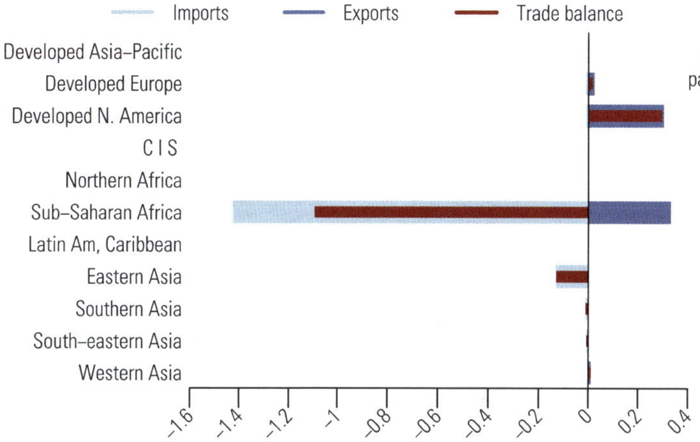

Graph 5: Partner concentration of merchandise trade

(Cumulative share by ranked partners in 2012)

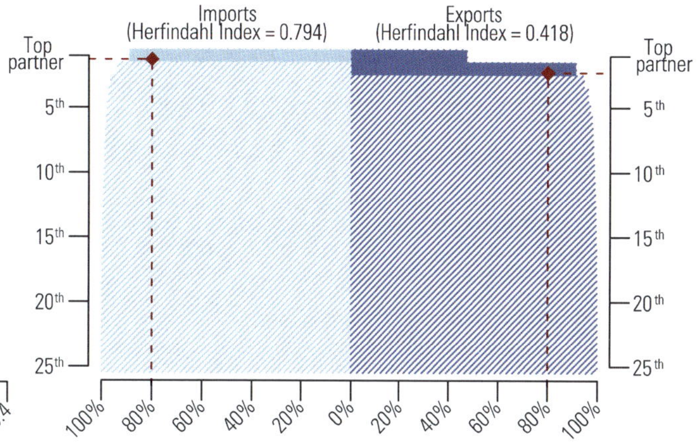

Graph 6: Imports of services by EBOPS category

(% share in 2012)

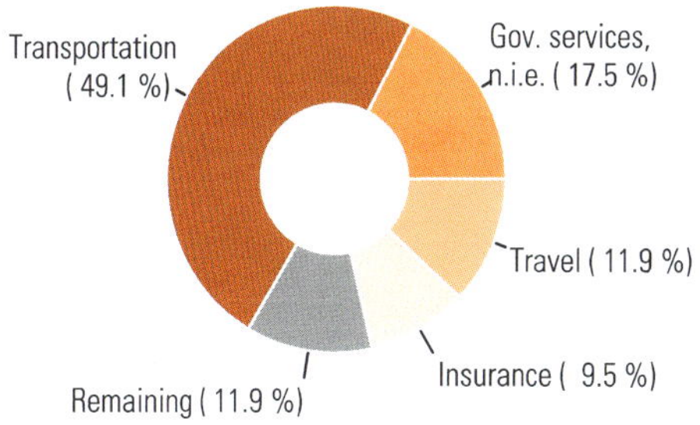

Imports Profile:

"Goods classified chiefly by material" (SITC section 6), "Food, animals + beverages, tobacco" (SITC section 0+1) and "Machinery and transport equipment" (SITC section 7) were the largest commodity groups for imports in 2012, representing respectively 19.8, 19.7 and 18.2 percent of imported goods (see table 3). From 2010 to 2012, the largest import commodity was "Oils petroleum, bituminous, distillates, except crude" (HS code 2710) (see table 4). The top three partners for merchandise imports were South Africa, Other Asia nes and China, accounting for respectively 88.5, 3.4 and 1.9 percent of total imports. "Transportation" (EBOPS code 205) accounted for the largest share of imports of services in 2012 at 85.9 mln US$, followed by "Government services, n.i.e." (EBOPS code 291) at 30.6 mln US$ and "Travel" (EBOPS code 236) at 20.8 mln US$ (see graph 6).

Table 4: Top 10 import commodities 2010 to 2012

HS code	4-digit heading of Harmonized System 1996	Value (million US$) 2010	2011	2012	Unit value 2010	2011	2012	Unit	SITC code
	All Commodities	1 276.6	1 459.7	1 594.2					
2710	Oils petroleum, bituminous, distillates, except crude	61.4	156.0	150.9	*1.0*	*0.8*	*1.2*	US$/kg	334
9999	Commodities not elsewhere specified	31.0	62.3	61.1					931
8703	Motor vehicles for transport of persons (except buses)	20.3	30.9	44.1	*12.0*		*12.4*	thsd US$/unit	781
8708	Parts and accessories for motor vehicles	26.7	25.4	26.2	*12.2*		*13.5*	US$/kg	784
5201	Cotton, not carded or combed	16.0	32.1	29.1	*1.4*	*1.9*	*3.3*	US$/kg	263
2711	Petroleum gases and other gaseous hydrocarbons	31.2	29.9	14.0					343
0207	Meat, edible offal of domestic poultry	21.7	26.2	24.5		*1.8*	*1.7*	US$/kg	012
8704	Motor vehicles for the transport of goods	17.2	24.7	29.5					782
5209	Woven cotton nes, >85% cotton, >200g/m2	31.4	10.4	29.6	*6.5*	*6.6*	*8.5*	US$/kg	652
3923	Containers, bobbins and packages, of plastics	15.9	14.1	38.8	*4.0*	*4.4*	*3.9*	US$/kg	893

Lithuania

Goods Imports: CIF, by origin | **Goods Exports: FOB, by last known destination** | **Trade System: Special**

Overview:

In 2015, the value of merchandise exports of Lithuania decreased substantially by 21.3 percent to reach 25.5 bln US$, while its merchandise imports decreased substantially by 20.0 percent to reach 28.2 bln US$ (see graph 1, table 2 and table 3). The merchandise trade balance recorded a relatively small deficit of 2.7 bln US$ (see graph 1). The largest merchandise trade balance was with MDG Developed Europe at -2.8 bln US$ (see graph 4). Merchandise exports in Lithuania were diversified amongst partners; imports were also diversified. The top 15 partners accounted for 80 percent or more of exports and 14 partners accounted for 80 percent or more of imports (see graph 5). In 2014, the value of exports of services of Lithuania increased moderately by 6.2 percent, reaching 7.5 bln US$, while its imports of services increased slightly by 4.1 percent and reached 5.4 bln US$ (see graph 2). There was a moderate trade in services surplus of 2.1 bln US$.

Graph 1: Total merchandise trade, by value

(Bln US$ by year)

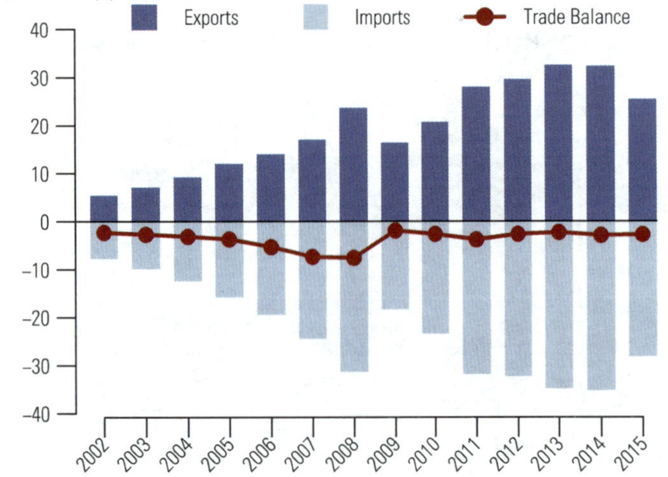

Graph 2: Total services trade, by value

(Bln US$ by year)

Exports Profile:

"Machinery and transport equipment" (SITC section 7), "Food, animals + beverages, tobacco" (SITC section 0+1) and "Mineral fuels, lubricants" (SITC section 3) were the largest commodity groups for exports in 2015, representing respectively 18.0, 16.9 and 16.4 percent of exported goods (see table 2). From 2013 to 2015, the largest export commodity was "Petroleum oils, other than crude" (HS code 2710) (see table 1). The top three destinations for merchandise exports were the Russian Federation, Latvia and Poland, accounting for respectively 18.5, 9.6 and 8.4 percent of total exports. "Transportation" (EBOPS code 205) accounted for the largest share of exports of services in 2014 at 4.7 bln US$, followed by "Travel" (EBOPS code 236) at 1.4 bln US$ and "Other business services" (EBOPS code 268) at 635.0 mln US$ (see graph 3).

Graph 3: Exports of services by EBOPS category

(% share in 2014)

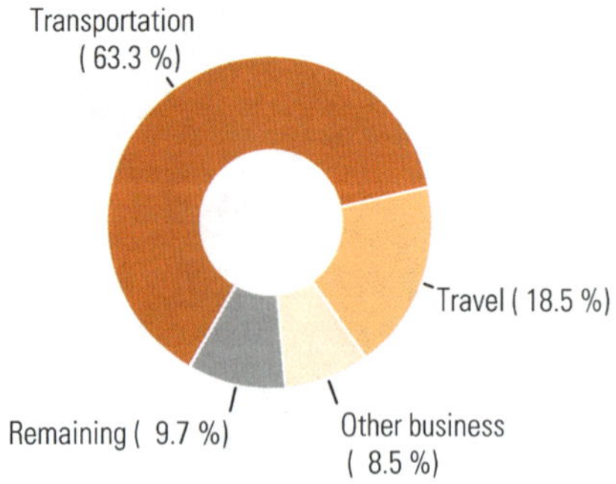

Table 1: Top 10 export commodities 2013 to 2015

HS code	4-digit heading of Harmonized System 2012	Value (million US$) 2013	2014	2015	Unit value 2013	2014	2015	Unit	SITC code
	All Commodities	32 599.7	32 394.3	25 499.0					
2710	Petroleum oils, other than crude	7 104.8	5 372.1	3 939.1	0.9	0.8	0.5	US$/kg	334
9403	Other furniture and parts thereof	1 044.0	1 206.4	1 051.4					821
9999	Commodities not specified according to kind	583.5	799.4	628.8					931
3102	Mineral or chemical fertilisers, nitrogenous	593.8	656.1	578.0	0.3	0.3	0.2	US$/kg	562
3907	Polyacetals, other polyethers and epoxide resins, in primary forms	706.7	646.3	449.8	1.6	1.5	1.1	US$/kg	574
1001	Wheat and meslin	594.0	646.0	503.1	0.3	0.3	0.2	US$/kg	041
3004	Medicaments (excluding goods of heading 30.02, 30.05 or 30.06)	452.0	570.7	564.2	153.4	147.6	137.2	US$/kg	542
8703	Motor cars and other motor vehicles principally designed for the transport	738.0	553.5	245.6	5.0	5.5	7.9	thsd US$/unit	781
3105	Mineral or chemical fertilisers	459.6	458.1	434.8	0.5	0.5	0.5	US$/kg	562
9401	Seats (other than those of heading 94.02)	382.5	416.2	361.0					821

Services Imports and Exports: EBOPS 2002 categories

Table 2: Merchandise exports by SITC

(Value in million US$, growth and shares in percentage)

SITC	2015	Avg. Growth rates 2011-2015	Avg. Growth rates 2014-2015	2015 share
Total	25 499.0	-2.4	-21.3	100.0
0+1	4 313.8	0.4	-22.6	16.9
2+4	1 336.8	1.3	-10.3	5.2
3	4 191.3	-12.3	-26.3	16.4
5	3 728.8	-0.5	-12.1	14.6
6	2 708.9	0.0	-18.6	10.6
7	4 591.0	-1.8	-27.9	18.0
8	3 995.2	2.9	-18.5	15.7
9	633.2	9.0	-21.1	2.5

Table 3: Merchandise imports by SITC

(Value in million US$, growth and shares in percentage)

SITC	2015	Avg. Growth rates 2011-2015	Avg. Growth rates 2014-2015	2015 share
Total	28 172.8	-3.0	-20.0	100.0
0+1	3 416.3	-0.4	-21.0	12.1
2+4	1 238.3	0.3	-8.6	4.4
3	5 693.3	-14.1	-33.6	20.2
5	4 195.6	1.1	-9.6	14.9
6	3 505.1	0.0	-18.5	12.4
7	6 696.3	0.5	-19.3	23.8
8	2 255.4	5.4	-14.0	8.0
9	1 172.6	13.0	6.5	4.2

SITC Legend

SITC Code	Description
Total	All commodities
0+1	Food, animals + beverages, tobacco
2+4	Crude materials + anim. & veg. oils
3	Mineral fuels, lubricants
5	Chemicals
6	Goods classified chiefly by material
7	Machinery and transport equipment
8	Miscellaneous manufactured articles
9	Not classified elsewhere in the SITC

Graph 4: Merchandise trade balance

(Bln US$ by MDG Regions in 2015)

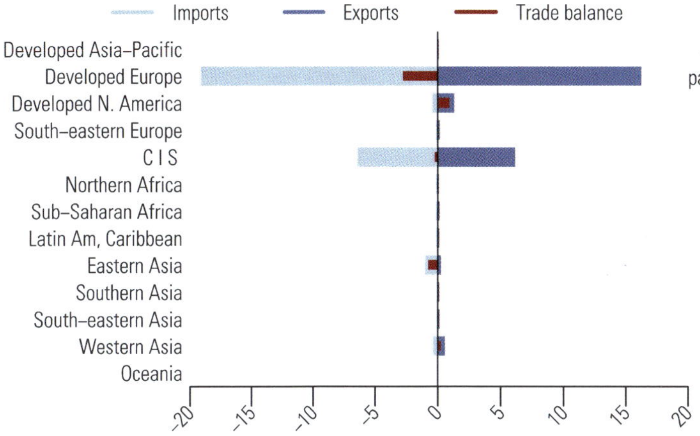

Graph 5: Partner concentration of merchandise trade

(Cumulative share by ranked partners in 2015)

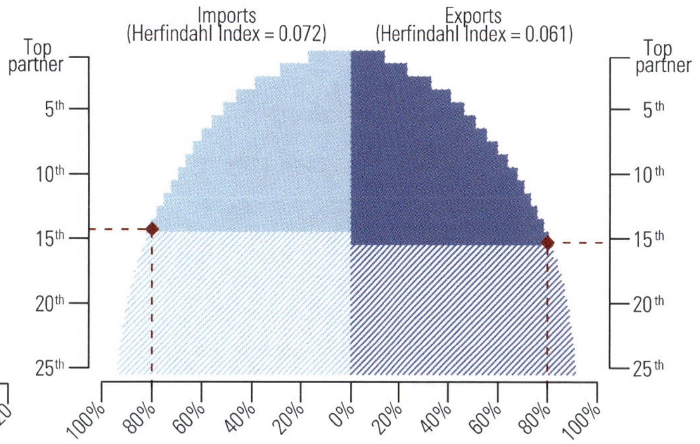

Graph 6: Imports of services by EBOPS category

(% share in 2014)

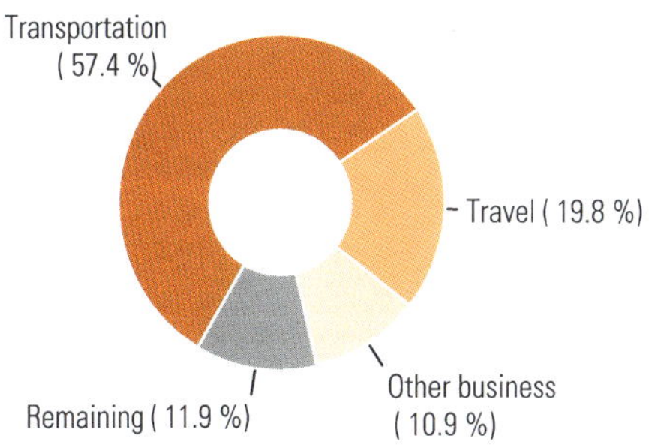

Imports Profile:

"Machinery and transport equipment" (SITC section 7), "Mineral fuels, lubricants" (SITC section 3) and "Chemicals" (SITC section 5) were the largest commodity groups for imports in 2015, representing respectively 23.8, 20.2 and 14.9 percent of imported goods (see table 3). From 2013 to 2015, the largest import commodity was "Petroleum oils and oils obtained from bituminous minerals, crude" (HS code 2709) (see table 4). The top three partners for merchandise imports were the Russian Federation, Germany and Poland, accounting for respectively 22.6, 10.9 and 9.7 percent of total imports. "Transportation" (EBOPS code 205) accounted for the largest share of imports of services in 2014 at 3.1 bln US$, followed by "Travel" (EBOPS code 236) at 1.1 bln US$ and "Other business services" (EBOPS code 268) at 583.2 mln US$ (see graph 6).

Table 4: Top 10 import commodities 2013 to 2015

HS code	4-digit heading of Harmonized System 2012	Value (million US$) 2013	Value (million US$) 2014	Value (million US$) 2015	Unit value 2013	Unit value 2014	Unit value 2015	Unit	SITC code
	All Commodities	34 813.2	35 217.4	28 172.8					
2709	Petroleum oils and oils obtained from bituminous minerals, crude	7 170.5	5 643.5	3 420.5	0.8	0.8	0.4	US$/kg	333
2710	Petroleum oils, other than crude	1 407.6	1 415.3	1 169.0	1.0	0.9	0.6	US$/kg	334
2711	Petroleum gases and other gaseous hydrocarbons	1 392.4	1 203.6	879.5	0.7	0.6	0.4	US$/kg	343
9999	Commodities not specified according to kind	940.0	1 093.8	1 167.3					931
8703	Motor cars and other motor vehicles principally designed for the transport	1 026.6	969.2	749.1	7.8	8.6	8.9	thsd US$/unit	781
3004	Medicaments (excluding goods of heading 30.02, 30.05 or 30.06)	790.1	866.4	856.1	78.3	80.5	74.1	US$/kg	542
2917	Polycarboxylic acids, their anhydrides	496.9	468.6	319.4	1.2	1.0	0.7	US$/kg	513
8517	Electrical apparatus for line telephony or line telegraphy	374.3	416.4	478.3					764
8701	Tractors (other than tractors of heading 87.09)	510.9	284.8	401.8	46.6	38.9	40.7	thsd US$/unit	722
8471	Automatic data processing machines and units thereof	331.6	342.8	318.6	136.1	139.7	119.8	US$/unit	752

Luxembourg

Goods Imports: CIF, by origin/consignment for intra-eu **Goods Exports: FOB, by last known destination** **Trade System: Special**

Overview:

In 2015, the value of merchandise exports of Luxembourg decreased substantially by 14.5 percent to reach 12.6 bln US$, while its merchandise imports decreased substantially by 19.1 percent to reach 19.3 bln US$ (see graph 1, table 2 and table 3). The merchandise trade balance recorded a moderate deficit of 6.7 bln US$ (see graph 1). The largest merchandise trade balance was with MDG Developed Europe at -5.2 bln US$ (see graph 4). Merchandise exports in Luxembourg were diversified amongst partners; imports were also diversified. The top 12 partners accounted for 80 percent or more of exports and 7 partners accounted for 80 percent or more of imports (see graph 5). In 2014, the value of exports of services of Luxembourg increased substantially by 12.8 percent, reaching 105.0 bln US$, while its imports of services increased substantially by 14.5 percent and reached 76.4 bln US$ (see graph 2). There was a moderate trade in services surplus of 28.6 bln US$.

Graph 1: Total merchandise trade, by value

(Bln US$ by year)

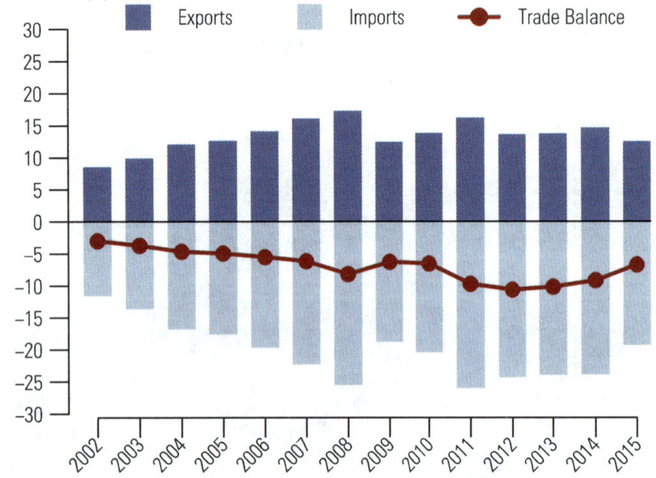

Graph 2: Total services trade, by value

(Bln US$ by year)

Exports Profile:

"Goods classified chiefly by material" (SITC section 6), "Machinery and transport equipment" (SITC section 7) and "Chemicals" (SITC section 5) were the largest commodity groups for exports in 2015, representing respectively 39.3, 24.1 and 11.1 percent of exported goods (see table 2). From 2013 to 2015, the largest export commodity was "Angles, shapes and sections of iron or non-alloy steel" (HS code 7216) (see table 1). The top three destinations for merchandise exports were Germany, France and Belgium, accounting for respectively 27.5, 14.2 and 13.0 percent of total exports. "Financial services" (EBOPS code 260) accounted for the largest share of exports of services in 2014 at 54.3 bln US$, followed by "Other business services" (EBOPS code 268) at 23.4 bln US$ and "Personal, cultural, and recreational services" (EBOPS code 287) at 6.1 bln US$ (see graph 3).

Graph 3: Exports of services by EBOPS category

(% share in 2014)

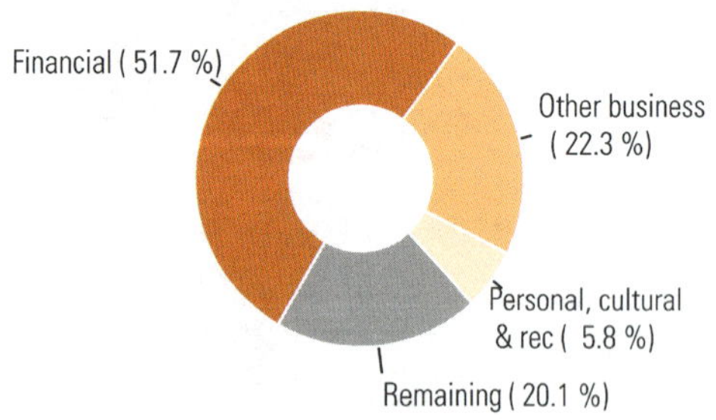

Table 1: Top 10 export commodities 2013 to 2015

HS code	4-digit heading of Harmonized System 2012	Value (million US$) 2013	2014	2015	Unit value 2013	2014	2015	Unit	SITC code
	All Commodities	13 826.0	14 767.6	12 625.7					
7216	Angles, shapes and sections of iron or non-alloy steel	983.5	1 066.9	839.7	0.8	0.7	0.6	US$/kg	676
4011	New pneumatic tyres, of rubber	675.4	638.0	527.1	*321.0*	*305.0*	*237.5*	US$/unit	625
7301	Sheet piling of iron or steel	598.0	565.0	408.9	1.0	1.0	0.8	US$/kg	676
7210	Flat-rolled products of iron or non-alloy steel	504.6	588.4	432.5	0.9	0.9	0.7	US$/kg	674
8703	Motor cars and other motor vehicles principally designed for the transport	472.5	526.4	442.6	16.0	18.0	*7.7*	thsd US$/unit	781
9999	Commodities not specified according to kind	416.6	448.6	365.9					931
0406	Cheese and curd	327.0	441.0	331.9	6.7	8.6	*7.0*	US$/kg	024
4811	Paper, paperboard, cellulose wadding and webs of cellulose fibres	363.6	365.1	291.4	2.8	2.8	2.2	US$/kg	641
7601	Unwrought aluminium	340.6	332.0	264.7	2.3	2.3	2.1	US$/kg	684
5603	Nonwovens, whether or not impregnated, coated, covered or laminated	239.7	268.6	299.8	6.3	6.7	5.8	US$/kg	657

Services Imports and Exports: EBOPS 2002 categories

Table 2: Merchandise exports by SITC

(Value in million US$, growth and shares in percentage)

SITC	2015	Avg. Growth rates 2011-2015	Avg. Growth rates 2014-2015	2015 share
Total	12 625.7	-6.2	-14.5	100.0
0+1	1 345.7	1.2	-13.8	10.7
2+4	313.2	-18.1	-15.6	2.5
3	60.7	-17.9	-48.2	0.5
5	1 397.5	4.4	2.0	11.1
6	4 965.6	-9.3	-18.2	39.3
7	3 047.0	-3.7	-7.7	24.1
8	1 063.1	-5.7	-17.6	8.4
9	433.0	-13.8	-36.8	3.4

Table 3: Merchandise imports by SITC

(Value in million US$, growth and shares in percentage)

SITC	2015	Avg. Growth rates 2011-2015	Avg. Growth rates 2014-2015	2015 share
Total	19 296.3	-7.2	-19.1	100.0
0+1	2 324.3	-1.6	-16.2	12.0
2+4	1 313.8	-15.1	-23.4	6.8
3	1 363.4	-16.3	-41.7	7.1
5	2 215.6	-1.5	-6.0	11.5
6	2 989.1	-8.1	-19.3	15.5
7	6 346.0	-3.0	-15.7	32.9
8	1 847.0	-5.5	-16.6	9.6
9	897.2	-19.6	-26.9	4.6

SITC Legend

SITC Code	Description
Total	All commodities
0+1	Food, animals + beverages, tobacco
2+4	Crude materials + anim. & veg. oils
3	Mineral fuels, lubricants
5	Chemicals
6	Goods classified chiefly by material
7	Machinery and transport equipment
8	Miscellaneous manufactured articles
9	Not classified elsewhere in the SITC

Graph 4: Merchandise trade balance

(Bln US$ by MDG Regions in 2015)

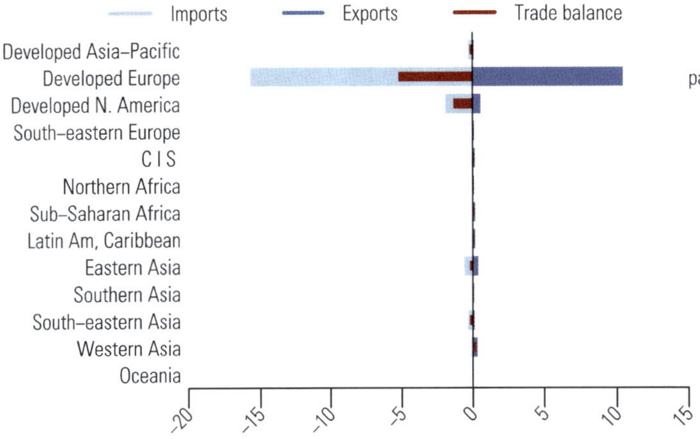

Graph 5: Partner concentration of merchandise trade

(Cumulative share by ranked partners in 2015)

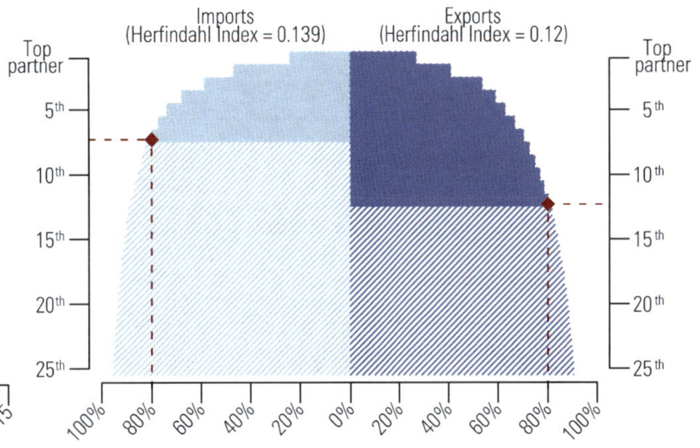

Graph 6: Imports of services by EBOPS category

(% share in 2014)

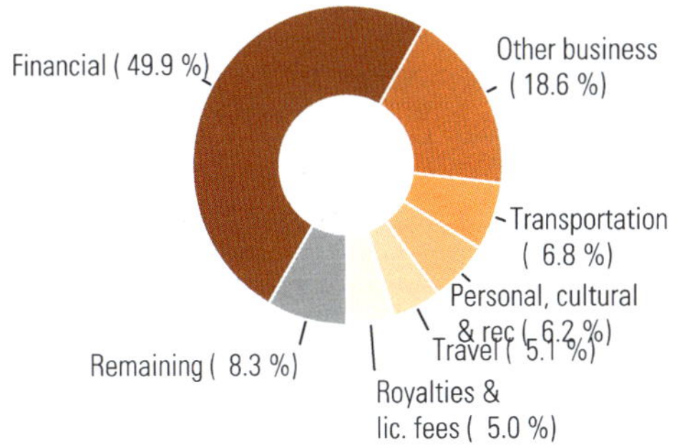

Imports Profile:

"Machinery and transport equipment" (SITC section 7), "Goods classified chiefly by material" (SITC section 6) and "Food, animals + beverages, tobacco" (SITC section 0+1) were the largest commodity groups for imports in 2015, representing respectively 32.9, 15.5 and 12.0 percent of imported goods (see table 3). From 2013 to 2015, the largest import commodity was "Petroleum oils, other than crude" (HS code 2710) (see table 4). The top three partners for merchandise imports were Germany, Belgium and France, accounting for respectively 23.9, 23.9 and 13.2 percent of total imports. "Financial services" (EBOPS code 260) accounted for the largest share of imports of services in 2014 at 38.1 bln US$, followed by "Other business services" (EBOPS code 268) at 14.2 bln US$ and "Transportation" (EBOPS code 205) at 5.2 bln US$ (see graph 6).

Table 4: Top 10 import commodities 2013 to 2015

HS code	4-digit heading of Harmonized System 2012	Value (million US$) 2013	2014	2015	Unit value 2013	2014	2015	Unit	SITC code
	All Commodities	23 934.1	23 846.8	19 296.3					
2710	Petroleum oils, other than crude	2 559.1	2 289.1	1 334.4	*1.0*	0.9	*0.5*	US$/kg	334
8703	Motor cars and other motor vehicles principally designed for the transport	1 841.1	2 070.4	1 663.4	*29.7*	*30.7*	*11.4*	thsd US$/unit	781
8802	Other aircraft (for example, helicopters, aeroplanes); spacecraft	1 649.5	1 411.4	1 106.3	58.9	52.3	*46.1*	mln US$/unit	792
9999	Commodities not specified according to kind	1 363.3	1 177.0	830.1					931
7204	Ferrous waste and scrap; remelting scrap ingots of iron or steel	812.0	765.7	494.6	0.4	0.3	0.2	US$/kg	282
3004	Medicaments (excluding goods of heading 30.02, 30.05 or 30.06)	358.9	389.9	343.9	*15.8*	14.1	*10.2*	US$/kg	542
0406	Cheese and curd	375.2	398.3	303.7	6.5	6.7	*5.4*	US$/kg	024
8517	Electrical apparatus for line telephony or line telegraphy	316.6	369.6	304.2					764
7602	Aluminium waste and scrap	299.3	272.4	243.6	1.8	2.0	1.6	US$/kg	288
7209	Flat-rolled products of iron or non-alloy steel	285.8	243.3	187.6	0.6	0.6	0.5	US$/kg	673

Source: UN Comtrade

Madagascar

Goods Imports: CIF, by origin | **Goods Exports: FOB, by last known destination** | **Trade System: General**

Overview:

In 2014, the value of merchandise exports of Madagascar increased substantially by 37.9 percent to reach 2.2 bln US$, while its merchandise imports increased substantially by 24.3 percent to reach 3.4 bln US$ (see graph 1, table 2 and table 3). The merchandise trade balance recorded a moderate deficit of 1.1 bln US$ (see graph 1). The largest merchandise trade balance was with MDG Western Asia at -842.2 mln US$ (see graph 4). Merchandise exports in Madagascar were diversified amongst partners; imports were also diversified. The top 12 partners accounted for 80 percent or more of exports and 15 partners accounted for 80 percent or more of imports (see graph 5). In 2013, the value of exports of services of Madagascar decreased moderately by 7.0 percent, reaching 1.3 bln US$, while its imports of services decreased slightly by 3.2 percent and reached 1.3 bln US$ (see graph 2). There was a relatively small trade in services deficit of 70.8 mln US$.

Graph 1: Total merchandise trade, by value

(Bln US$ by year)

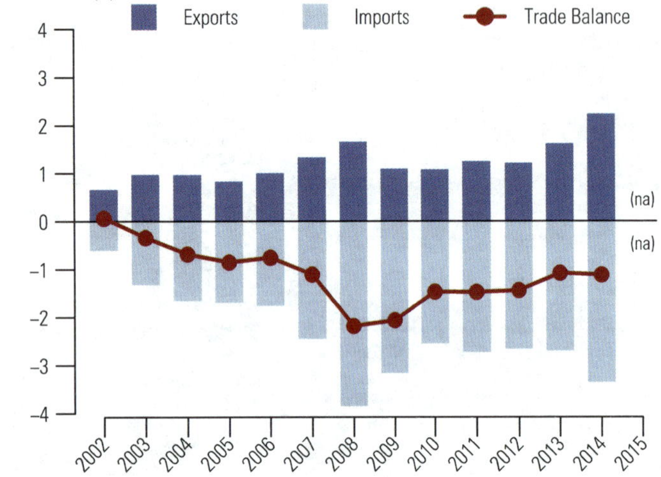

Graph 2: Total services trade, by value

(Bln US$ by year)

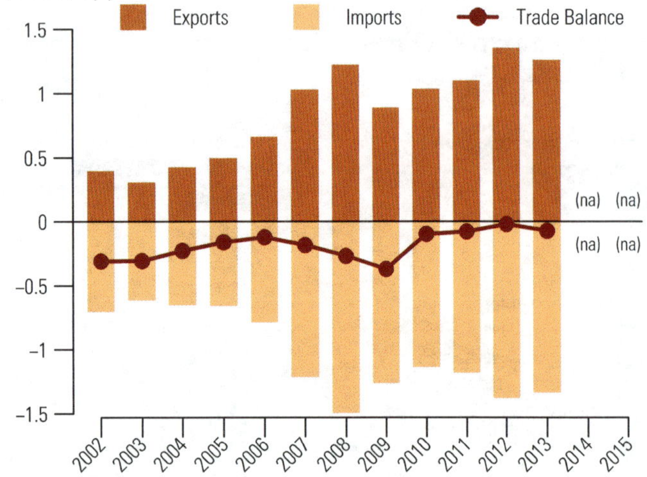

Exports Profile:

"Goods classified chiefly by material" (SITC section 6), "Food, animals + beverages, tobacco" (SITC section 0+1) and "Miscellaneous manufactured articles" (SITC section 8) were the largest commodity groups for exports in 2014, representing respectively 35.5, 24.7 and 23.2 percent of exported goods (see table 2). From 2012 to 2014, the largest export commodity was "Unwrought nickel" (HS code 7502) (see table 1). The top three destinations for merchandise exports were France, the United States and China, accounting for respectively 25.5, 7.2 and 6.2 percent of total exports. "Travel" (EBOPS code 236) accounted for the largest share of exports of services in 2013 at 573.7 mln US$, followed by "Transportation" (EBOPS code 205) at 427.6 mln US$ and "Other business services" (EBOPS code 268) at 131.9 mln US$ (see graph 3).

Graph 3: Exports of services by EBOPS category

(% share in 2013)

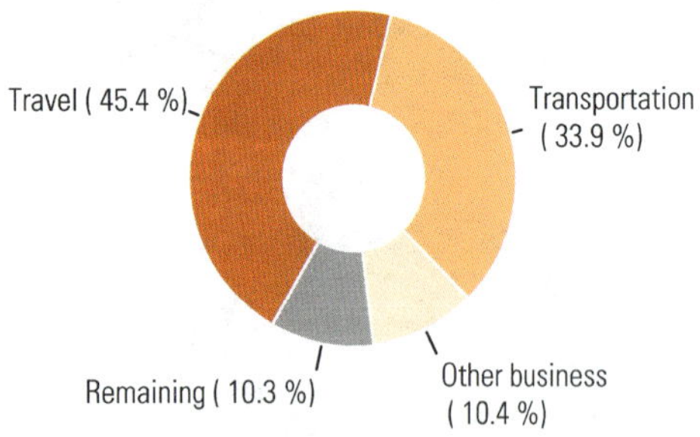

Table 1: Top 10 export commodities 2012 to 2014

HS code	4-digit heading of Harmonized System 2012	Value (million US$) 2012	2013	2014	Unit value 2012	2013	2014	Unit	SITC code
	All Commodities	1 224.5	1 626.9	2 243.2					
7502	Unwrought nickel	59.4	321.3	601.3	17.3	14.6	16.6	US$/kg	683
6110	Jerseys, pullovers, cardigans, waist-coats and similar articles	116.4	125.9	139.6		*32.7*	*33.1*	US$/unit	845
0907	Cloves (whole fruit, cloves and stems)	167.7	87.2	114.2	8.8	8.8	9.7	US$/kg	075
0306	Crustaceans, whether in shell or not	65.6	78.7	98.6	8.9	10.0	9.4	US$/kg	036
2710	Petroleum oils, other than crude	81.0	70.6	83.7	1.3	1.3	1.3	US$/kg	334
2614	Titanium ores and concentrates	72.2	68.5	60.7	0.1	0.1	0.2	US$/kg	287
0905	Vanilla	10.2	40.7	118.2	19.3	39.4	50.2	US$/kg	075
6214	Shawls, scarves, mufflers, mantillas, veils and the like	38.2	49.7	66.0					846
6203	Men's or boys'suits, ensembles, jackets, blazers, trousers	32.6	51.4	65.6					841
8105	Cobalt mattes and other intermediate products of cobalt metallurgy	10.2	46.8	87.5	26.9	26.6	30.1	US$/kg	689

Services Imports and Exports: EBOPS 2002 categories

Table 2: Merchandise exports by SITC

(Value in million US$, growth and shares in percentage)

SITC	2014	Avg. Growth rates 2010-2014	Avg. Growth rates 2013-2014	2014 share
Total	2 243.2	20.0	37.9	100.0
0+1	553.9	21.8	37.5	24.7
2+4	169.6	8.9	4.0	7.6
3	84.4	7.7	16.8	3.8
5	66.2	19.7	45.7	2.9
6	796.4	81.8	74.6	35.5
7	33.0	-27.6	-49.5	1.5
8	519.6	9.3	24.4	23.2
9	20.0	-23.3	402.3	0.9

Table 3: Merchandise imports by SITC

(Value in million US$, growth and shares in percentage)

SITC	2014	Avg. Growth rates 2010-2014	Avg. Growth rates 2013-2014	2014 share
Total	3 354.8	7.1	24.3	100.0
0+1	460.9	12.8	13.5	13.7
2+4	274.9	32.3	28.5	8.2
3	734.3	17.4	15.0	21.9
5	348.2	12.0	33.3	10.4
6	741.0	4.0	28.0	22.1
7	594.8	-5.7	32.2	17.7
8	187.2	2.2	28.3	5.6
9	13.4	16.1	179.6	0.4

SITC Legend

SITC Code	Description
Total	All commodities
0+1	Food, animals + beverages, tobacco
2+4	Crude materials + anim. & veg. oils
3	Mineral fuels, lubricants
5	Chemicals
6	Goods classified chiefly by material
7	Machinery and transport equipment
8	Miscellaneous manufactured articles
9	Not classified elsewhere in the SITC

Graph 4: Merchandise trade balance

(Bln US$ by MDG Regions in 2014)

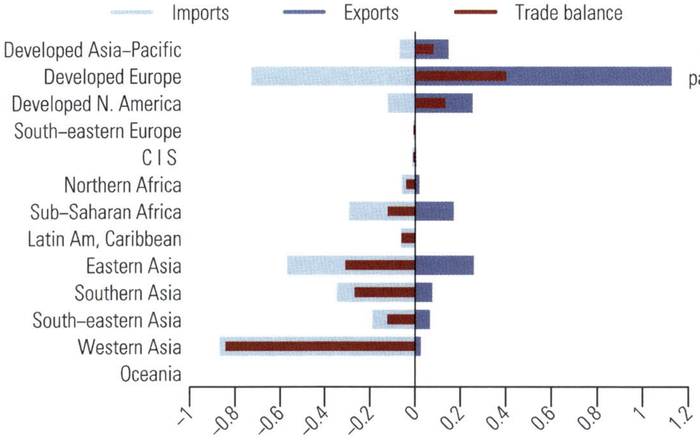

Graph 5: Partner concentration of merchandise trade

(Cumulative share by ranked partners in 2014)

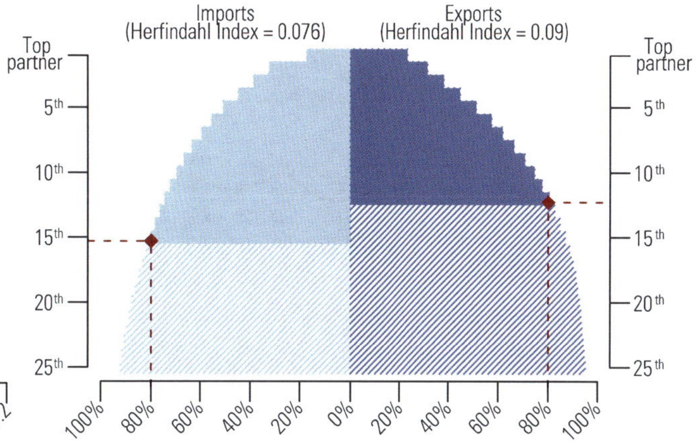

Graph 6: Imports of services by EBOPS category

(% share in 2013)

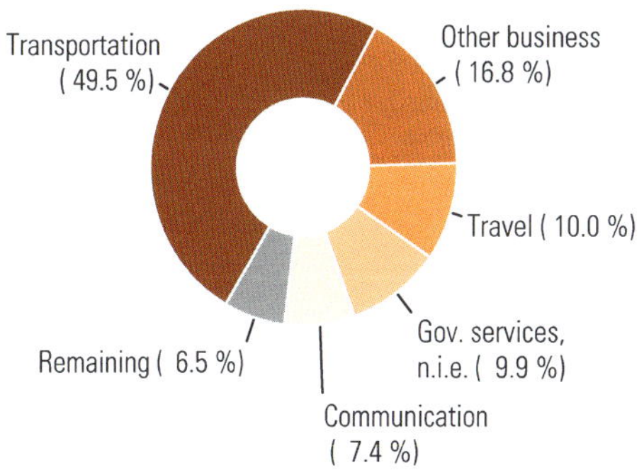

Imports Profile:

"Goods classified chiefly by material" (SITC section 6), "Mineral fuels, lubricants" (SITC section 3) and "Machinery and transport equipment" (SITC section 7) were the largest commodity groups for imports in 2014, representing respectively 22.1, 21.9 and 17.7 percent of imported goods (see table 3). From 2012 to 2014, the largest import commodity was "Petroleum oils, other than crude" (HS code 2710) (see table 4). The top three partners for merchandise imports were the United Arab Emirates, China and Rest of Europe nes, accounting for respectively 17.5, 14.8 and 6.7 percent of total imports. "Transportation" (EBOPS code 205) accounted for the largest share of imports of services in 2013 at 660.5 mln US$, followed by "Other business services" (EBOPS code 268) at 223.7 mln US$ and "Travel" (EBOPS code 236) at 133.7 mln US$ (see graph 6).

Table 4: Top 10 import commodities 2012 to 2014

HS code	4-digit heading of Harmonized System 2012	Value (million US$) 2012	2013	2014	Unit value 2012	2013	2014	Unit	SITC code
	All Commodities	2 659.0	2 699.4	3 354.8					
2710	Petroleum oils, other than crude	569.3	582.5	668.8	1.0	1.0	0.9	US$/kg	334
1006	Rice	85.9	143.3	149.6	0.5	0.5	0.4	US$/kg	042
8703	Motor cars and other motor vehicles principally designed for the transport	81.6	54.8	72.3		*19.1*	*19.5*	thsd US$/unit	781
8704	Motor vehicles for the transport of goods	68.6	53.6	60.7					782
1701	Cane or beet sugar and chemically pure sucrose, in solid form	57.5	54.7	69.5	0.7	0.6	0.5	US$/kg	061
3004	Medicaments (excluding goods of heading 30.02, 30.05 or 30.06)	49.3	49.8	71.5	12.0	11.8	12.1	US$/kg	542
2503	Sulphur of all kinds	24.7	55.4	73.2	0.2	0.2	0.2	US$/kg	274
1101	Wheat or meslin flour	48.6	44.6	51.4	0.5	0.5	0.5	US$/kg	046
5105	Wool and fine or coarse animal hair, carded or combed	27.1	45.5	61.9	199.6	143.0	157.4	US$/kg	268
5208	Woven fabrics of cotton, containing 85 % or more by weight of cotton	29.2	41.4	49.3	15.6	15.5	13.7	US$/kg	652

Malawi

Goods Imports: CIF, by origin | **Goods Exports: FOB, by last known destination** | **Trade System: General**

Overview:

In 2014, the value of merchandise exports of Malawi increased substantially by 11.1 percent to reach 1.3 bln US$, while its merchandise imports decreased slightly by 2.5 percent to reach 2.8 bln US$ (see graph 1, table 2 and table 3). The merchandise trade balance recorded a large deficit of 1.4 bln US$ (see graph 1). The largest merchandise trade balance was with MDG Sub-Saharan Africa at -687.2 mln US$ (see graph 4). Merchandise exports in Malawi were diversified amongst partners; imports were also diversified. The top 18 partners accounted for 80 percent or more of exports and 14 partners accounted for 80 percent or more of imports (see graph 5). In 2014, the value of exports of services of Malawi decreased moderately by 9.6 percent, reaching 100.4 mln US$, while its imports of services increased moderately by 9.6 percent and reached 268.8 mln US$ (see graph 2). There was a large trade in services deficit of 168.3 mln US$.

Graph 1: Total merchandise trade, by value

(Bln US$ by year)

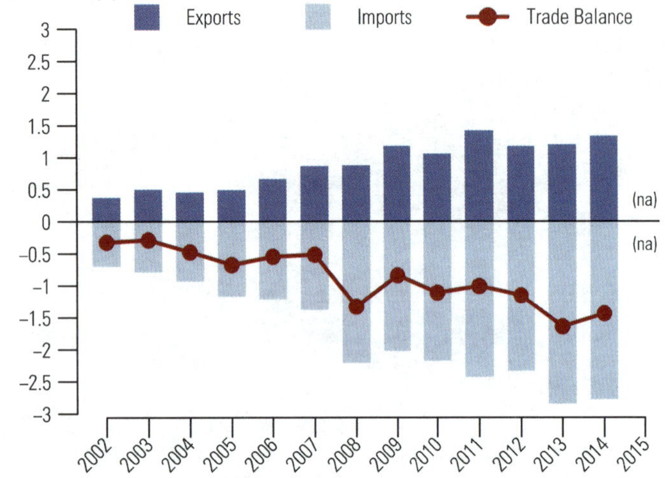

Graph 2: Total services trade, by value

(Mln US$ by year)

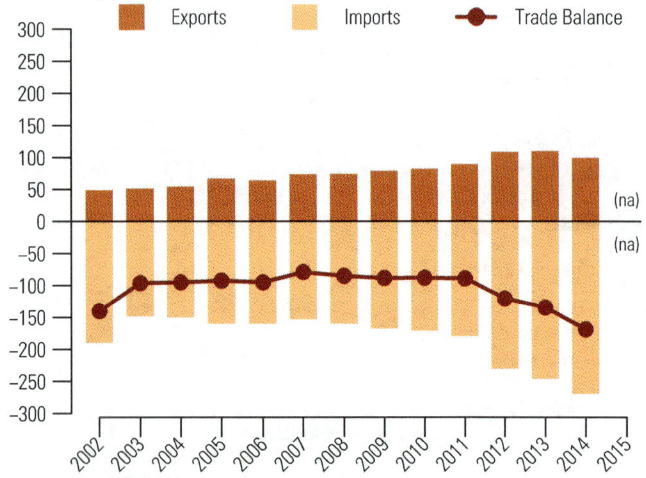

Exports Profile:

"Food, animals + beverages, tobacco" (SITC section 0+1), "Machinery and transport equipment" (SITC section 7) and "Crude materials + anim. & veg. oils" (SITC section 2+4) were the largest commodity groups for exports in 2014, representing respectively 64.5, 11.9 and 11.9 percent of exported goods (see table 2). From 2012 to 2014, the largest export commodity was "Unmanufactured tobacco; tobacco refuse" (HS code 2401) (see table 1). The top three destinations for merchandise exports were Belgium, Canada and South Africa, accounting for respectively 9.5, 8.1 and 7.7 percent of total exports. "Travel" (EBOPS code 236) accounted for the largest share of exports of services in 2014 at 32.4 mln US$, followed by "Communications services" (EBOPS code 245) at 23.3 mln US$ and "Transportation" (EBOPS code 205) at 18.5 mln US$ (see graph 3).

Graph 3: Exports of services by EBOPS category

(% share in 2014)

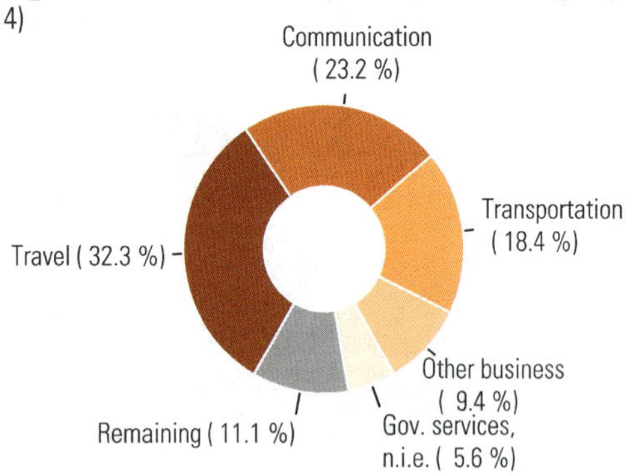

Table 1: Top 10 export commodities 2012 to 2014

HS code	4-digit heading of Harmonized System 2007	Value (million US$) 2012	2013	2014	Unit value 2012	2013	2014	Unit	SITC code
	All Commodities	1 182.9	1 208.0	1 341.9					
2401	Unmanufactured tobacco; tobacco refuse	636.1	562.6	639.3	3.4	4.1	2.5	US$/kg	121
2612	Uranium or thorium ores and concentrates	131.3	136.6	40.1	87.6	81.0	62.1	US$/kg	286
0902	Tea, whether or not flavoured	70.0	86.0	74.3	1.5	2.0	1.6	US$/kg	074
1701	Cane or beet sugar and chemically pure sucrose, in solid form	41.8	114.2	60.9	0.4	0.6	0.7	US$/kg	061
1202	Ground-nuts, not roasted or otherwise cooked, whether or not shelled or broken	41.7	60.3	46.1	1.0	1.3	1.3	US$/kg	222
0713	Dried leguminous vegetables, shelled, whether or not skinned or split	42.6	29.0	26.5	0.6	0.7	1.0	US$/kg	054
5201	Cotton, not carded or combed	40.8	19.4	16.5	1.6	1.7	1.9	US$/kg	263
9999	Commodities not specified according to kind	0.0	0.3	63.1					931
8426	Ships' derricks; cranes, including cable cranes; mobile lifting frames	0.0	0.1	52.2		0.1		mln US$/unit	744
8429	Self-propelled bulldozers, angledozers, graders, levellers, scrapers	2.9	5.2	37.4	*58.0*	5.5		thsd US$/unit	723

Services Imports and Exports: EBOPS 2002 categories

Table 2: Merchandise exports by SITC

(Value in million US$, growth and shares in percentage)

SITC	2014	Avg. Growth rates 2010-2014	Avg. Growth rates 2013-2014	2014 share
Total	1 341.9	5.9	11.1	100.0
0+1	866.2	2.1	3.3	64.5
2+4	159.9	-1.6	-40.9	11.9
3	0.6	-26.5	31.2	0.0
5	28.0	15.6	112.1	2.1
6	33.1	20.0	78.0	2.5
7	160.0	55.9	478.6	11.9
8	31.1	-4.9	-19.7	2.3
9	63.1	...	18058.1	4.7

Table 3: Merchandise imports by SITC

(Value in million US$, growth and shares in percentage)

SITC	2014	Avg. Growth rates 2010-2014	Avg. Growth rates 2013-2014	2014 share
Total	2 774.4	6.3	-2.5	100.0
0+1	228.4	-1.9	-15.6	8.2
2+4	119.5	7.2	-2.0	4.3
3	374.0	14.6	-9.1	13.5
5	732.8	8.3	-13.3	26.4
6	446.8	6.6	3.9	16.1
7	586.6	3.3	3.7	21.1
8	242.3	2.2	23.7	8.7
9	43.9	98.4	1086.4	1.6

SITC Legend

SITC Code	Description
Total	All commodities
0+1	Food, animals + beverages, tobacco
2+4	Crude materials + anim. & veg. oils
3	Mineral fuels, lubricants
5	Chemicals
6	Goods classified chiefly by material
7	Machinery and transport equipment
8	Miscellaneous manufactured articles
9	Not classified elsewhere in the SITC

Graph 4: Merchandise trade balance

(Bln US$ by MDG Regions in 2014)

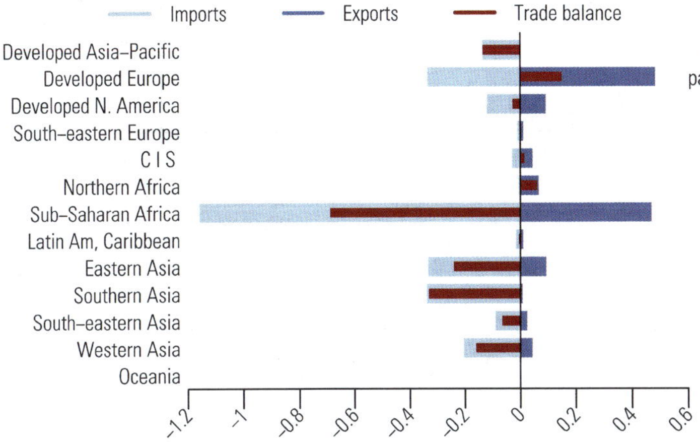

Graph 5: Partner concentration of merchandise trade

(Cumulative share by ranked partners in 2014)

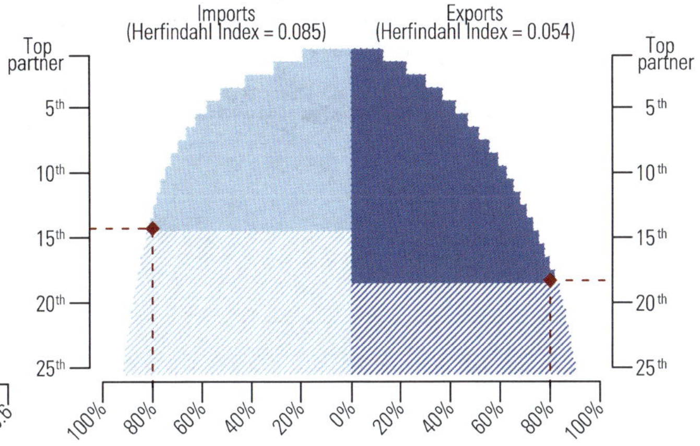

Graph 6: Imports of services by EBOPS category

(% share in 2014)

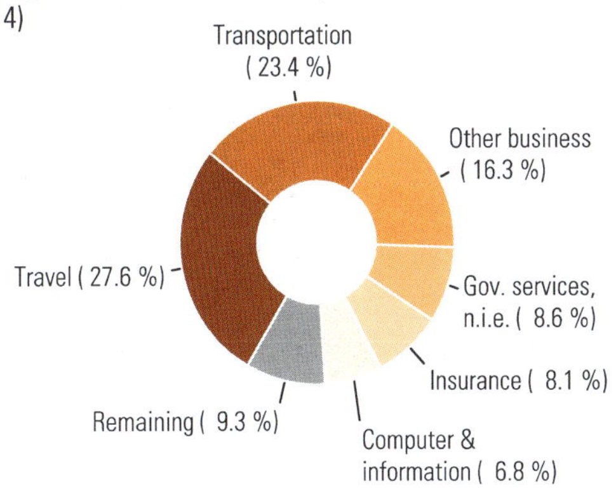

Imports Profile:

"Chemicals" (SITC section 5), "Machinery and transport equipment" (SITC section 7) and "Goods classified chiefly by material" (SITC section 6) were the largest commodity groups for imports in 2014, representing respectively 26.4, 21.1 and 16.1 percent of imported goods (see table 3). From 2012 to 2014, the largest import commodity was "Petroleum oils, other than crude" (HS code 2710) (see table 4). The top three partners for merchandise imports were South Africa, Mozambique and China, accounting for respectively 21.6, 10.6 and 10.0 percent of total imports. "Travel" (EBOPS code 236) accounted for the largest share of imports of services in 2014 at 74.1 mln US$, followed by "Transportation" (EBOPS code 205) at 62.9 mln US$ and "Other business services" (EBOPS code 268) at 43.8 mln US$ (see graph 6).

Table 4: Top 10 import commodities 2012 to 2014

HS code	4-digit heading of Harmonized System 2007	Value (million US$) 2012	Value (million US$) 2013	Value (million US$) 2014	Unit value 2012	Unit value 2013	Unit value 2014	Unit	SITC code
	All Commodities	2 330.4	2 844.6	2 774.4					
2710	Petroleum oils, other than crude	314.2	389.2	359.2	1.2	1.4	1.4	US$/kg	334
3102	Mineral or chemical fertilisers, nitrogenous	185.9	211.8	134.3	0.8	0.7	0.6	US$/kg	562
3004	Medicaments (excluding goods of heading 30.02, 30.05 or 30.06)	156.4	161.7	184.5	38.4	38.0	44.8	US$/kg	542
3105	Mineral or chemical fertilisers	77.9	119.8	69.2	0.7	0.8	0.7	US$/kg	562
2523	Portland cement, aluminous cement, slag cement	52.7	63.7	58.9	0.2	0.2	0.2	US$/kg	661
8703	Motor cars and other motor vehicles principally designed for the transport	52.6	58.9	54.5	*9.3*	7.0	5.6	thsd US$/unit	781
2401	Unmanufactured tobacco; tobacco refuse	23.6	86.0	54.5	1.9	3.5	3.2	US$/kg	121
1001	Wheat and meslin	31.7	87.4	40.6	0.5	0.5	0.5	US$/kg	041
4907	Unused postage, revenue or similar stamps of current or new issue	29.5	55.6	54.5	64.8	117.7	165.4	US$/kg	892
8704	Motor vehicles for the transport of goods	48.9	40.8	39.2	*8.7*	11.8	14.0	thsd US$/unit	782

Source: UN Comtrade

Malaysia

Goods Imports: CIF, by origin | **Goods Exports: FOB, by last known destination** | **Trade System: General**

Overview:

In 2015, the value of merchandise exports of Malaysia decreased substantially by 14.5 percent to reach 200.2 bln US$, while its merchandise imports decreased substantially by 15.6 percent to reach 176.2 bln US$ (see graph 1, table 2 and table 3). The merchandise trade balance recorded a relatively small surplus of 24.0 bln US$ (see graph 1). The largest merchandise trade balance was with MDG South-eastern Asia at 9.5 bln US$ (see graph 4). Merchandise exports in Malaysia were diversified amongst partners; imports were also diversified. The top 14 partners accounted for 80 percent or more of exports and 14 partners accounted for 80 percent or more of imports (see graph 5). In 2014, the value of exports of services of Malaysia decreased slightly by 0.7 percent, reaching 39.1 bln US$, while its imports of services increased slightly by 0.5 percent and reached 45.0 bln US$ (see graph 2). There was a relatively small trade in services deficit of 5.8 bln US$.

Graph 1: Total merchandise trade, by value

(Bln US$ by year)

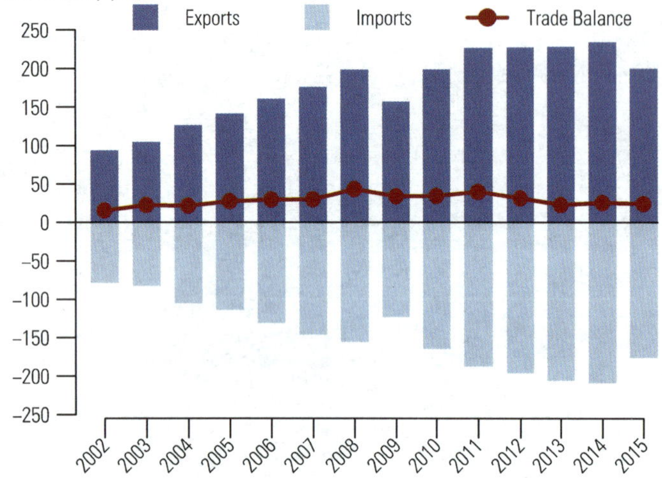

Graph 2: Total services trade, by value

(Bln US$ by year)

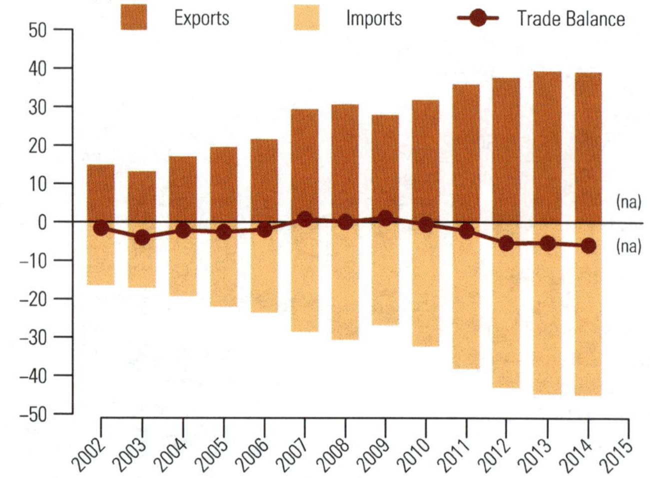

Exports Profile:

"Machinery and transport equipment" (SITC section 7), "Mineral fuels, lubricants" (SITC section 3) and "Miscellaneous manufactured articles" (SITC section 8) were the largest commodity groups for exports in 2015, representing respectively 41.9, 16.5 and 10.8 percent of exported goods (see table 2). From 2013 to 2015, the largest export commodity was "Electronic integrated circuits" (HS code 8542) (see table 1). The top three destinations for merchandise exports were Singapore, China and Japan, accounting for respectively 14.0, 12.8 and 10.5 percent of total exports. "Travel" (EBOPS code 236) accounted for the largest share of exports of services in 2014 at 22.6 bln US$, followed by "Other business services" (EBOPS code 268) at 7.0 bln US$ and "Transportation" (EBOPS code 205) at 4.8 bln US$ (see graph 3).

Graph 3: Exports of services by EBOPS category

(% share in 2014)

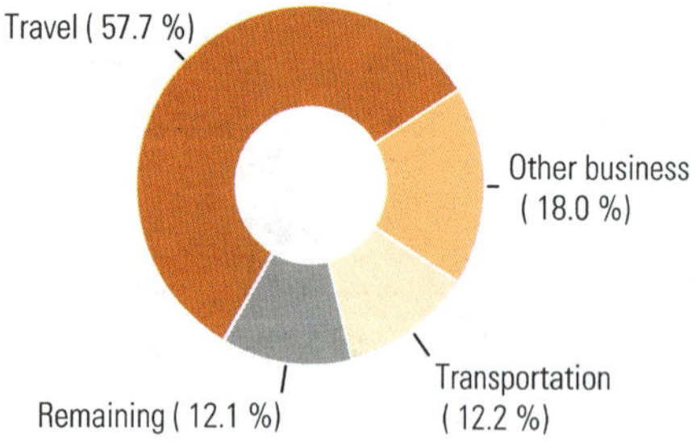

Table 1: Top 10 export commodities 2013 to 2015

HS code	4-digit heading of Harmonized System 2012	Value (million US$) 2013	2014	2015	Unit value 2013	2014	2015	Unit	SITC code
	All Commodities	228316.1	234135.0	200210.9					
8542	Electronic integrated circuits	27791.4	31028.2	27208.0					776
2711	Petroleum gases and other gaseous hydrocarbons	20467.7	20876.8	12713.2	0.8	0.8	0.5	US$/kg	343
2710	Petroleum oils, other than crude	19433.7	18463.8	10637.2	0.9	0.8	0.5	US$/kg	334
1511	Palm oil and its fractions	12288.9	11994.8	9501.1	0.8	0.8	0.6	US$/kg	422
2709	Petroleum oils and oils obtained from bituminous minerals, crude	10220.8	10518.3	6852.9	0.8	0.8	0.4	US$/kg	333
8471	Automatic data processing machines and units thereof	8867.2	8260.0	7632.7	82.8	62.6	59.4	US$/unit	752
8541	Diodes, transistors and similar semiconductor devices	7523.3	7864.2	8055.6					776
8473	Parts and accessories for use with machines of heading 84.69 to 84.72	5424.7	4493.0	3820.9	49.3	48.3	44.6	US$/kg	759
8517	Electrical apparatus for line telephony or line telegraphy	3537.9	4186.0	3751.1					764
4015	Articles of apparel and clothing accessories	3390.7	3312.1	3383.9	5.6	4.7	5.1	US$/kg	848

Services Imports and Exports: EBOPS 2002 categories

Table 2: Merchandise exports by SITC

(Value in million US$, growth and shares in percentage)

SITC	2015	Avg. Growth rates 2011-2015	Avg. Growth rates 2014-2015	2015 share
Total	200210.9	-3.1	-14.5	100.0
0+1	8208.3	1.5	-9.7	4.1
2+4	18912.4	-12.4	-14.6	9.4
3	32962.2	-4.9	-36.3	16.5
5	14411.6	-1.2	-9.1	7.2
6	19284.9	-2.4	-7.0	9.6
7	83848.0	-1.2	-7.7	41.9
8	21549.1	0.6	-3.8	10.8
9	1034.5	-6.7	-25.6	0.5

Table 3: Merchandise imports by SITC

(Value in million US$, growth and shares in percentage)

SITC	2015	Avg. Growth rates 2011-2015	Avg. Growth rates 2014-2015	2015 share
Total	176174.6	-1.6	-15.6	100.0
0+1	12855.2	1.1	-10.0	7.3
2+4	7909.6	-9.6	-7.6	4.5
3	21758.1	-0.3	-38.1	12.4
5	17632.1	0.0	-10.6	10.0
6	23032.9	-1.6	-13.8	13.1
7	76383.2	-2.3	-12.6	43.4
8	12924.3	2.5	1.7	7.3
9	3679.3	-0.9	-14.0	2.1

SITC Legend

SITC Code	Description
Total	All commodities
0+1	Food, animals + beverages, tobacco
2+4	Crude materials + anim. & veg. oils
3	Mineral fuels, lubricants
5	Chemicals
6	Goods classified chiefly by material
7	Machinery and transport equipment
8	Miscellaneous manufactured articles
9	Not classified elsewhere in the SITC

Graph 4: Merchandise trade balance

(Bln US$ by MDG Regions in 2015)

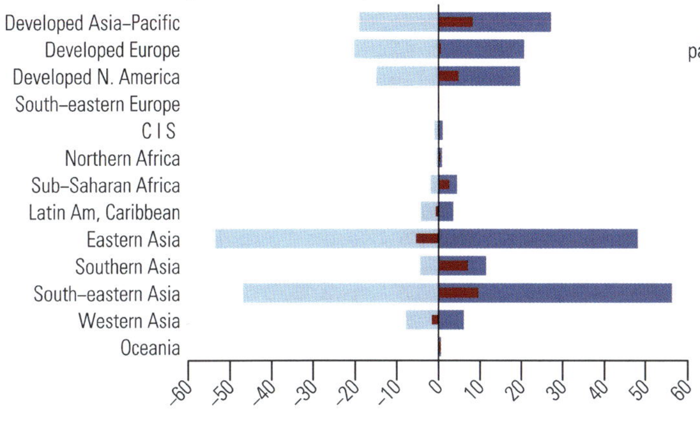

Graph 5: Partner concentration of merchandise trade

(Cumulative share by ranked partners in 2015)

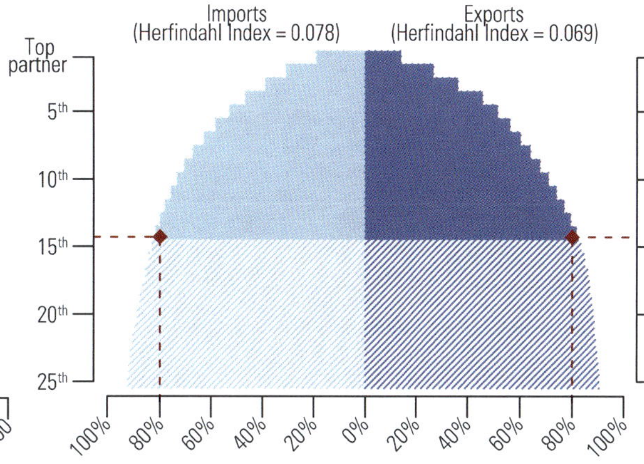

Graph 6: Imports of services by EBOPS category

(% share in 2014)

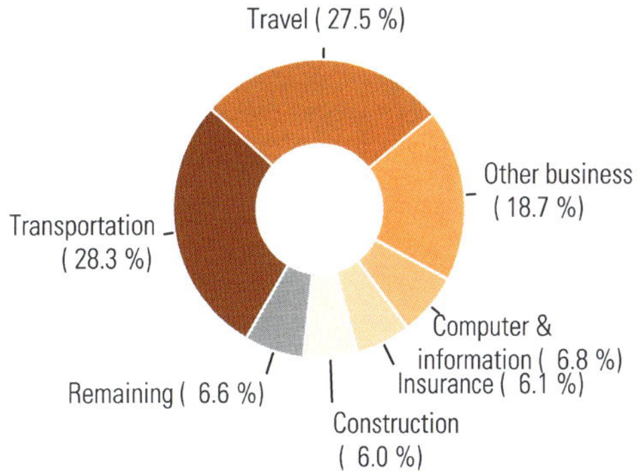

Imports Profile:

"Machinery and transport equipment" (SITC section 7), "Goods classified chiefly by material" (SITC section 6) and "Mineral fuels, lubricants" (SITC section 3) were the largest commodity groups for imports in 2015, representing respectively 43.4, 13.1 and 12.4 percent of imported goods (see table 3). From 2013 to 2015, the largest import commodity was "Electronic integrated circuits" (HS code 8542) (see table 4). The top three partners for merchandise imports were China, Singapore and Japan, accounting for respectively 17.3, 12.3 and 8.2 percent of total imports. "Transportation" (EBOPS code 205) accounted for the largest share of imports of services in 2014 at 12.7 bln US$, followed by "Travel" (EBOPS code 236) at 12.4 bln US$ and "Other business services" (EBOPS code 268) at 8.4 bln US$ (see graph 6).

Table 4: Top 10 import commodities 2013 to 2015

HS code	4-digit heading of Harmonized System 2012	Value (million US$) 2013	2014	2015	Unit value 2013	2014	2015	Unit	SITC code
	All Commodities	205813.5	208823.4	176174.6					
8542	Electronic integrated circuits	26553.8	29270.1	24788.2					776
2710	Petroleum oils, other than crude	22082.0	22802.1	14718.8	0.9	0.9	0.5	US$/kg	334
2709	Petroleum oils and oils obtained from bituminous minerals, crude	7152.9	7713.5	3282.2	0.8	0.7	0.4	US$/kg	333
8541	Diodes, transistors and similar semiconductor devices	3885.1	4171.2	3853.1					776
8517	Electrical apparatus for line telephony or line telegraphy	3883.5	3839.8	3810.8					764
8473	Parts and accessories for use with machines of heading 84.69 to 84.72	3647.7	3219.2	2695.2	49.9	73.9	47.4	US$/kg	759
7108	Gold (including gold plated with platinum)	3427.1	3209.8	2848.3	43.9	40.0	36.7	thsd US$/kg	971
8802	Other aircraft (for example, helicopters, aeroplanes); spacecraft	4177.0	3156.3	1148.5	49.7	43.8	25.0	mln US$/unit	792
8471	Automatic data processing machines and units thereof	2955.7	2630.5	2569.9	61.9	92.6		US$/unit	752
7403	Refined copper and copper alloys, unwrought	3932.4	1872.4	2026.6	7.5	7.1	5.7	US$/kg	682

Maldives

Goods Imports: CIF, by origin **Goods Exports: FOB, by last known destination** **Trade System: General**

Overview:

In 2015, the value of merchandise exports of Maldives decreased very slightly by 0.4 percent to reach 144.2 mln US$, while its merchandise imports decreased slightly by 4.0 percent to reach 1.9 bln US$ (see graph 1, table 2 and table 3). The merchandise trade balance recorded a large deficit of 1.8 bln US$ (see graph 1). The largest merchandise trade balance was with MDG South-eastern Asia at -546.4 mln US$ (see graph 4). Merchandise exports in Maldives were diversified amongst partners; imports were also diversified. The top 8 partners accounted for 80 percent or more of exports and 10 partners accounted for 80 percent or more of imports (see graph 5). In 2014, the value of exports of services of Maldives increased substantially by 20.9 percent, reaching 3.0 bln US$, while its imports of services increased substantially by 22.1 percent and reached 796.6 mln US$ (see graph 2). There was a large trade in services surplus of 2.2 bln US$. See footnote*.

Graph 1: Total merchandise trade, by value

(Bln US$ by year)

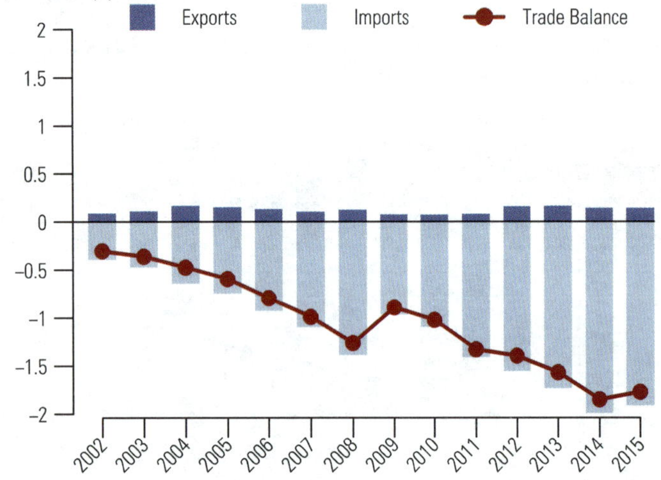

Graph 2: Total services trade, by value

(Bln US$ by year)

Exports Profile:

"Food, animals + beverages, tobacco" (SITC section 0+1), "Crude materials + anim. & veg. oils" (SITC section 2+4) and "Machinery and transport equipment" (SITC section 7) were the largest commodity groups for exports in 2015, representing respectively 97.4, 2.1 and 0.5 percent of exported goods (see table 2). From 2013 to 2015, the largest export commodity was "Fish, frozen, excluding fish fillets and other fish meat of heading 03.04" (HS code 0303) (see table 1). The top three destinations for merchandise exports were Thailand, France and Sri Lanka, accounting for respectively 31.8, 12.8 and 7.8 percent of total exports. "Travel" (EBOPS code 236) accounted for the largest share of exports of services in 2014 at 2.7 bln US$, followed by "Transportation" (EBOPS code 205) at 224.9 mln US$ (see graph 3).

Graph 3: Exports of services by EBOPS category

(% share in 2014)

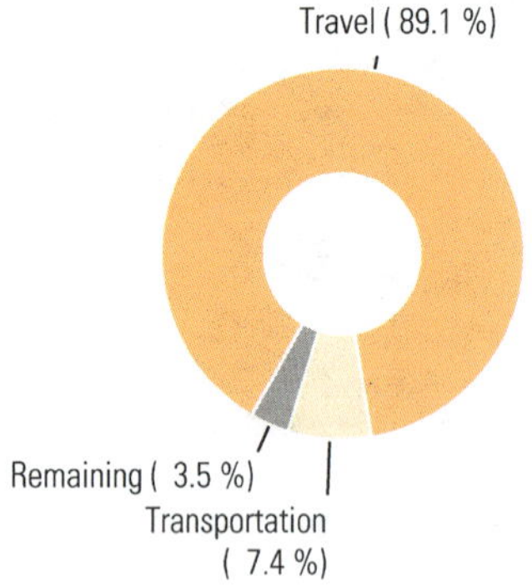

Table 1: Top 10 export commodities 2013 to 2015

HS code	4-digit heading of Harmonized System 2012	Value (million US$) 2013	2014	2015	Unit value 2013	2014	2015	Unit	SITC code
	All Commodities	166.5	144.8	144.2					
0303	Fish, frozen, excluding fish fillets and other fish meat of heading 03.04	72.0	49.7	37.7	2.0	1.5	1.5	US$/kg	034
0302	Fish, fresh or chilled, excluding fish fillets	31.4	35.9	38.8	5.6	5.2	5.2	US$/kg	034
0304	Fish fillets and other fish meat (whether or not minced)	33.0	30.8	37.2	7.6	7.5	6.5	US$/kg	034
1604	Prepared or preserved fish; caviar	16.5	15.8	13.9	7.0	6.1	4.7	US$/kg	037
0305	Fish, dried, salted or in brine	8.5	7.4	10.6	3.7	2.8	3.0	US$/kg	035
7204	Ferrous waste and scrap; remelting scrap ingots of iron or steel	1.7	1.6	1.1	0.3	0.3	0.2	US$/kg	282
0301	Live fish	1.0	1.1	1.3					034
7404	Copper waste and scrap	0.7	1.0	1.4	4.9	4.8	4.5	US$/kg	288
2301	Flours, meals and pellets, of meat or meat offal	0.7	0.5	0.4	0.9	1.0	1.0	US$/kg	081
0308	Aquatic invertebrates other than crustaceans and molluscs	0.6	0.3	0.6	4.9		4.8	US$/kg	036

*Merchandise trade data does not include re-exports. As of 2011, trade in services data reflect the improvement of the coverage of balance of payments statistics that was implemented in September 2012.

Services Imports and Exports: EBOPS 2002 categories

Table 2: Merchandise exports by SITC

(Value in million US$, growth and shares in percentage)

SITC	2015	Avg. Growth rates 2011-2015	Avg. Growth rates 2014-2015	2015 share
Total	144.2	14.7	-0.4	100.0
0+1	140.4	14.9	-0.8	97.4
2+4	3.0	4.1	1.5	2.1
3	0.0	10.9	-45.6	0.0
5	0.0	-9.9	-61.0	0.0
6	0.0	25.0	135.6	0.0
7	0.7	373.4	360.4	0.5
8	0.0	5.1	-23.1	0.0

Table 3: Merchandise imports by SITC

(Value in million US$, growth and shares in percentage)

SITC	2015	Avg. Growth rates 2011-2015	Avg. Growth rates 2014-2015	2015 share
Total	1 913.8	7.9	-4.0	100.0
0+1	409.4	9.1	0.6	21.4
2+4	122.6	22.0	38.4	6.4
3	308.4	-3.3	-46.0	16.1
5	128.1	13.2	7.3	6.7
6	279.1	12.1	27.9	14.6
7	485.7	9.9	13.7	25.4
8	179.5	8.8	11.3	9.4
9	1.0	283.3	9849.9	0.1

SITC Legend

SITC Code	Description
Total	All commodities
0+1	Food, animals + beverages, tobacco
2+4	Crude materials + anim. & veg. oils
3	Mineral fuels, lubricants
5	Chemicals
6	Goods classified chiefly by material
7	Machinery and transport equipment
8	Miscellaneous manufactured articles
9	Not classified elsewhere in the SITC

Graph 4: Merchandise trade balance

(Mln US$ by MDG Regions in 2015)

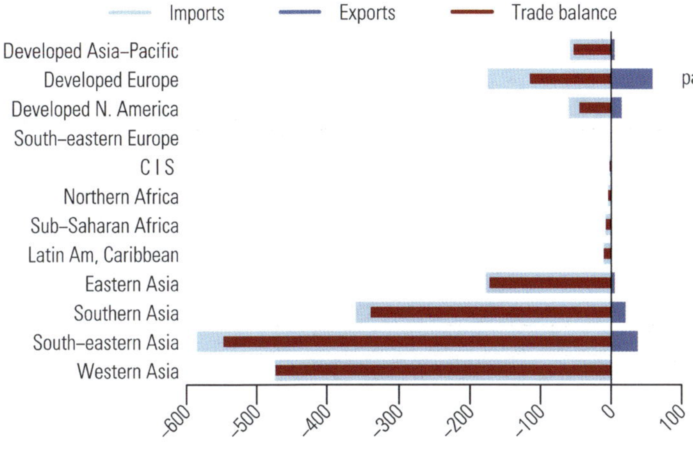

Graph 5: Partner concentration of merchandise trade

(Cumulative share by ranked partners in 2015)

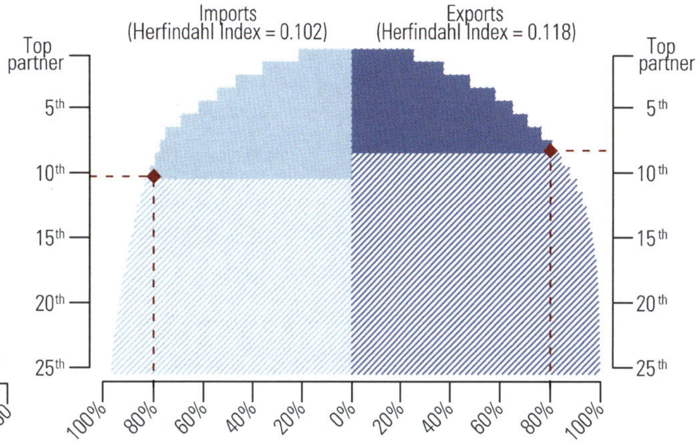

Graph 6: Imports of services by EBOPS category

(% share in 2014)

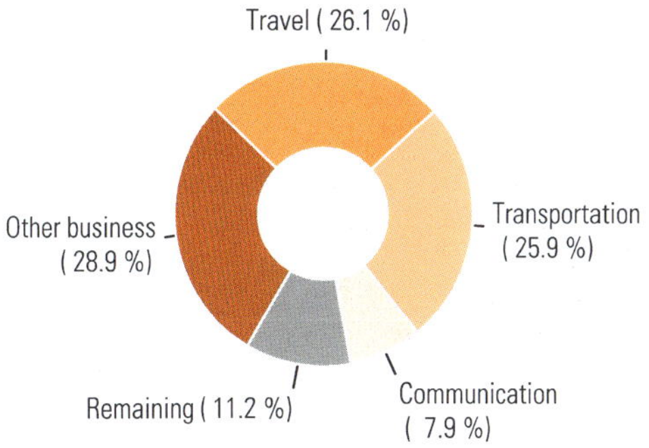

Imports Profile:

"Machinery and transport equipment" (SITC section 7), "Food, animals + beverages, tobacco" (SITC section 0+1) and "Mineral fuels, lubricants" (SITC section 3) were the largest commodity groups for imports in 2015, representing respectively 25.4, 21.4 and 16.1 percent of imported goods (see table 3). From 2013 to 2015, the largest import commodity was "Petroleum oils, other than crude" (HS code 2710) (see table 4). The top three partners for merchandise imports were the United Arab Emirates, Singapore and India, accounting for respectively 24.3, 16.2 and 9.5 percent of total imports. "Other business services" (EBOPS code 268) accounted for the largest share of imports of services in 2014 at 229.9 mln US$, followed by "Travel" (EBOPS code 236) at 207.6 mln US$ and "Transportation" (EBOPS code 205) at 206.7 mln US$ (see graph 6).

Table 4: Top 10 import commodities 2013 to 2015

HS code	4-digit heading of Harmonized System 2012	Value (million US$) 2013	2014	2015	Unit value 2013	2014	2015	Unit	SITC code
	All Commodities	1 733.3	1 992.7	1 913.8					
2710	Petroleum oils, other than crude	445.2	500.2	295.0	*1.0*	*0.8*	*0.5*	US$/kg	334
8802	Other aircraft (for example, helicopters, aeroplanes); spacecraft	40.2	39.8	59.2	20.1	4.0	7.4	mln US$/unit	792
2711	Petroleum gases and other gaseous hydrocarbons	57.8	70.5	8.3	*1.0*	*1.2*		US$/kg	343
8517	Electrical apparatus for line telephony or line telegraphy	36.8	34.7	48.4					764
9403	Other furniture and parts thereof	22.7	25.1	24.1					821
0207	Meat and edible offal, of the poultry of heading 01.05	23.5	21.9	22.4	2.3	2.4	2.1	US$/kg	012
4407	Wood sawn or chipped lengthwise, sliced or peeled	19.4	17.8	29.2	*747.0*	*733.8*	*736.7*	US$/m³	248
0402	Milk and cream, concentrated or containing added sugar	20.9	22.5	22.0	*3.2*	*3.3*		US$/kg	022
8803	Parts of goods of heading 88.01 or 88.02	16.4	21.2	26.2	*579.3*		*573.5*	US$/kg	792
2202	Waters with added sugar	17.5	22.6	21.4	1.6	*1.7*	*0.8*	US$/litre	111

Mali

Goods Imports: CIF, by origin | **Goods Exports: FOB, by last known destination** | **Trade System: General**

Overview:

In 2012, the value of merchandise exports of Mali increased moderately by 9.9 percent to reach 2.6 bln US$, while its merchandise imports increased slightly by 3.3 percent to reach 3.5 bln US$ (see graph 1, table 2 and table 3). The merchandise trade balance recorded a moderate deficit of 852.3 mln US$ (see graph 1). The largest merchandise trade balance was with MDG Developed Europe at -264.8 mln US$ (see graph 4). Merchandise exports in Mali were highly concentrated amongst partners; imports were diversified. The top 5 partners accounted for 80 percent or more of exports and 14 partners accounted for 80 percent or more of imports (see graph 5). In 2013, the value of exports of services of Mali increased substantially by 21.7 percent, reaching 428.6 mln US$, while its imports of services increased substantially by 97.7 percent and reached 2.1 bln US$ (see graph 2). There was a large trade in services deficit of 1.7 bln US$.

Graph 1: Total merchandise trade, by value

(Bln US$ by year)

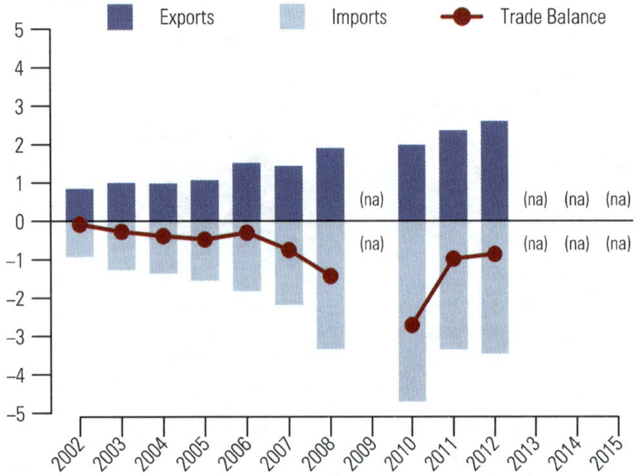

Graph 2: Total services trade, by value

(Bln US$ by year)

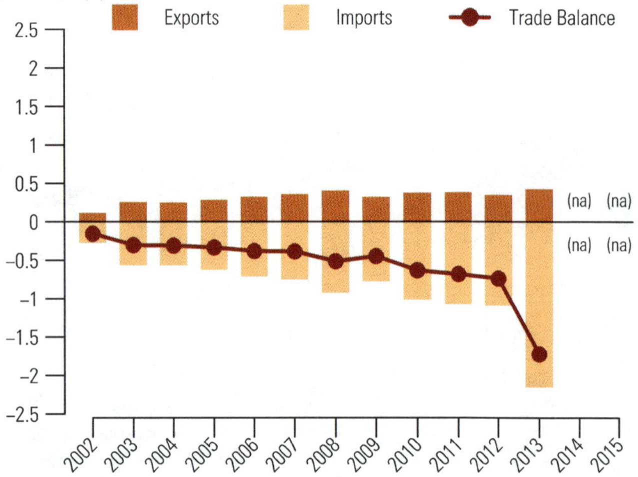

Exports Profile:

"Not classified elsewhere in the SITC" (SITC section 9), "Crude materials + anim. & veg. oils" (SITC section 2+4) and "Chemicals" (SITC section 5) were the largest commodity groups for exports in 2012, representing respectively 65.6, 16.1 and 6.7 percent of exported goods (see table 2). From 2010 to 2012, the largest export commodity was "Gold (including gold plated with platinum)" (HS code 7108) (see table 1). The top three destinations for merchandise exports were South Africa, Switzerland and China, accounting for respectively 55.0, 11.8 and 4.7 percent of total exports. "Travel" (EBOPS code 236) accounted for the largest share of exports of services in 2013 at 178.5 mln US$, followed by "Communications services" (EBOPS code 245) at 173.6 mln US$ and "Government services, n.i.e." (EBOPS code 291) at 56.3 mln US$ (see graph 3).

Graph 3: Exports of services by EBOPS category

(% share in 2013)

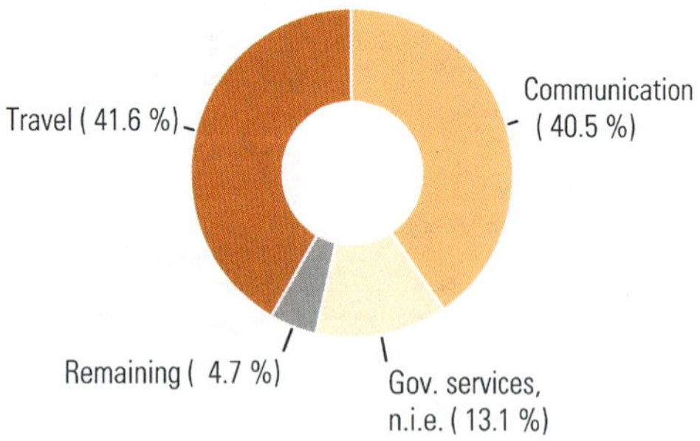

Table 1: Top 10 export commodities 2010 to 2012

HS code	4-digit heading of Harmonized System 2007	Value (million US$)			Unit value				SITC code
		2010	2011	2012	2010	2011	2012	Unit	
	All Commodities	1 996.3	2 374.5	2 610.4					
7108	Gold (including gold plated with platinum)	1 578.7	1 691.1	1 709.3	32.5	39.9	38.0	thsd US$/kg	971
5203	Cotton, carded or combed	139.4	55.6	372.2	1.5	1.7	2.6	US$/kg	263
3105	Mineral or chemical fertilisers	30.0	113.7	119.0	0.6	0.7	0.6	US$/kg	562
5201	Cotton, not carded or combed	27.9	149.3	13.2	1.1	1.6	1.1	US$/kg	263
0102	Live bovine animals	48.6	54.7	84.2	*0.8*	*1.1*	*2.3*	thsd US$/unit	001
2710	Petroleum oils, other than crude	28.4	55.5	14.1	0.8	1.1	1.0	US$/kg	334
0104	Live sheep and goats	20.5	15.9	27.9					001
0804	Dates, figs, pineapples, avocados and mangosteens, fresh or dried	14.9	17.8	13.2	1.1	0.9	0.6	US$/kg	057
3102	Mineral or chemical fertilisers, nitrogenous	0.1	17.6	25.1	0.7	0.4	0.5	US$/kg	562
3104	Mineral or chemical fertilisers, potassic	...	23.8	16.0		0.6	0.6	US$/kg	562

Services Imports and Exports: EBOPS 2002 categories

Table 2: Merchandise exports by SITC

(Value in million US$, growth and shares in percentage)

SITC	2012	Avg. Growth rates 2008-2012	2011-2012	2012 share
Total	2610.4	8.0	9.9	100.0
0+1	147.9	3.4	24.0	5.7
2+4	420.0	18.5	76.6	16.1
3	16.0	-13.5	-71.1	0.6
5	174.3	57.2	1.4	6.7
6	44.5	40.6	64.4	1.7
7	87.6	10.6	51.1	3.4
8	8.2	3.8	-17.2	0.3
9	1711.8	4.4	1.0	65.6

Table 3: Merchandise imports by SITC

(Value in million US$, growth and shares in percentage)

SITC	2012	Avg. Growth rates 2008-2012	2011-2012	2012 share
Total	3462.7	0.9	3.3	100.0
0+1	440.3	5.2	4.7	12.7
2+4	62.1	-7.3	-12.0	1.8
3	993.6	8.6	1.2	28.7
5	508.3	1.9	19.7	14.7
6	560.0	-4.8	-7.2	16.2
7	765.4	-2.9	3.3	22.1
8	130.4	-5.4	21.7	3.8
9	2.6	-10.6	1.9	0.1

SITC Legend

SITC Code	Description
Total	All commodities
0+1	Food, animals + beverages, tobacco
2+4	Crude materials + anim. & veg. oils
3	Mineral fuels, lubricants
5	Chemicals
6	Goods classified chiefly by material
7	Machinery and transport equipment
8	Miscellaneous manufactured articles
9	Not classified elsewhere in the SITC

Graph 4: Merchandise trade balance

(Bln US$ by MDG Regions in 2012)

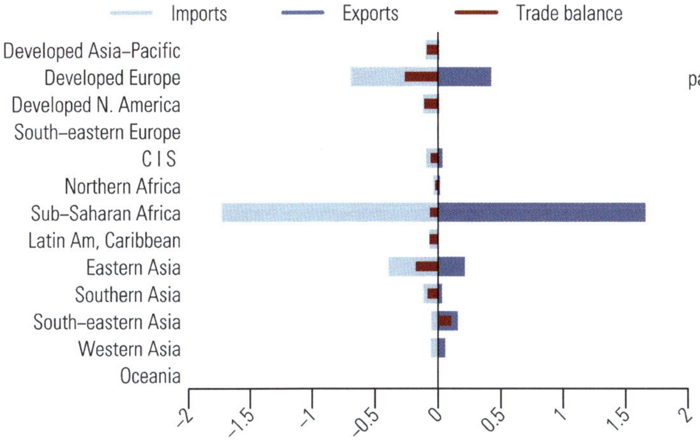

Graph 5: Partner concentration of merchandise trade

(Cumulative share by ranked partners in 2012)

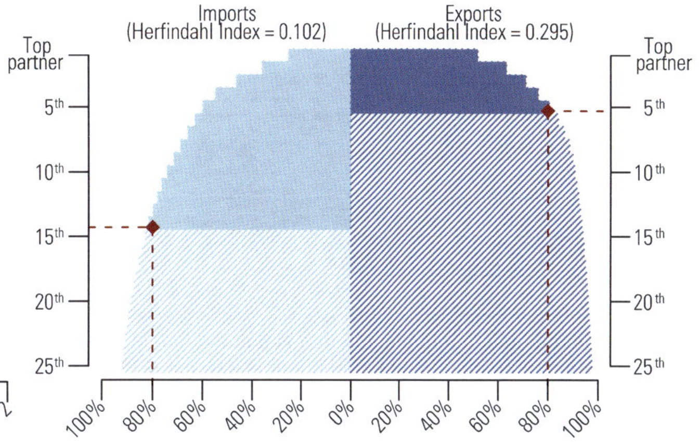

Graph 6: Imports of services by EBOPS category

(% share in 2013)

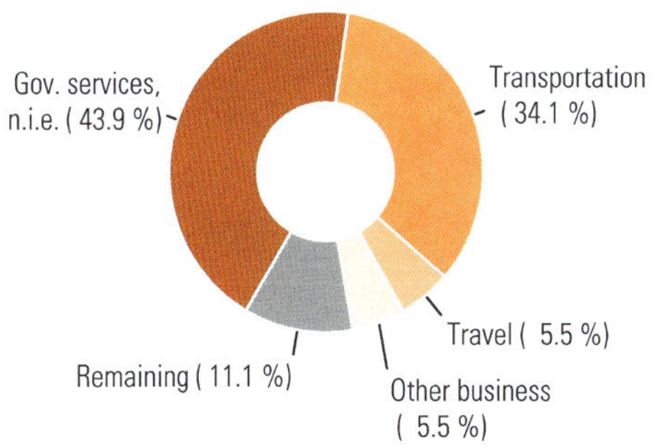

Imports Profile:

"Mineral fuels, lubricants" (SITC section 3), "Machinery and transport equipment" (SITC section 7) and "Goods classified chiefly by material" (SITC section 6) were the largest commodity groups for imports in 2012, representing respectively 28.7, 22.1 and 16.2 percent of imported goods (see table 3). From 2010 to 2012, the largest import commodity was "Petroleum oils, other than crude" (HS code 2710) (see table 4). The top three partners for merchandise imports were Senegal, France and China, accounting for respectively 19.3, 11.7 and 10.4 percent of total imports. "Government services, n.i.e." (EBOPS code 291) accounted for the largest share of imports of services in 2013 at 943.0 mln US$, followed by "Transportation" (EBOPS code 205) at 732.1 mln US$ and "Travel" (EBOPS code 236) at 117.8 mln US$ (see graph 6).

Table 4: Top 10 import commodities 2010 to 2012

HS code	4-digit heading of Harmonized System 2007	Value (million US$) 2010	2011	2012	Unit value 2010	2011	2012	Unit	SITC code
	All Commodities	4703.5	3351.5	3462.7					
2710	Petroleum oils, other than crude	1201.2	961.1	963.3	0.8	1.1	1.1	US$/kg	334
2523	Portland cement, aluminous cement, slag cement	185.3	201.2	176.2	0.1	0.1	0.1	US$/kg	661
3004	Medicaments (excluding goods of heading 30.02, 30.05 or 30.06)	309.5	97.2	141.5	43.0	13.1	20.9	US$/kg	542
8431	Parts suitable for use principally with the machinery of headings 84.25	100.5	73.8	69.1	26.6	18.1	18.7	US$/kg	723
3102	Mineral or chemical fertilisers, nitrogenous	56.2	92.8	93.1	0.3	0.4	0.4	US$/kg	562
8703	Motor cars and other motor vehicles principally designed for the transport	101.1	66.4	51.7	*15.9*		*14.0*	thsd US$/unit	781
8704	Motor vehicles for the transport of goods	81.5	67.2	47.2					782
8517	Electrical apparatus for line telephony or line telegraphy	56.8	52.1	76.2					764
1001	Wheat and meslin	63.5	60.5	60.0	0.3	0.5	0.4	US$/kg	041
1006	Rice	50.0	44.9	87.8	0.2	0.2	0.2	US$/kg	042

Malta

Goods Imports: CIF, by origin | **Goods Exports: FOB, by last known destination** | **Trade System: General**

Overview:

In 2015, the value of merchandise exports of Malta decreased substantially by 48.1 percent to reach 2.6 bln US$, while its merchandise imports decreased substantially by 31.4 percent to reach 5.8 bln US$ (see graph 1, table 2 and table 3). The merchandise trade balance recorded a large deficit of 3.2 bln US$ (see graph 1). The largest merchandise trade balance was with MDG Developed Europe at -2.7 bln US$ (see graph 4). Merchandise exports in Malta were diversified amongst partners; imports were also diversified. The top 17 partners accounted for 80 percent or more of exports and 16 partners accounted for 80 percent or more of imports (see graph 5). In 2013, the value of exports of services of Malta increased slightly by 4.5 percent, reaching 5.2 bln US$, while its imports of services increased slightly by 4.0 percent and reached 3.3 bln US$ (see graph 2). There was a moderate trade in services surplus of 2.0 bln US$.

Graph 1: Total merchandise trade, by value

(Bln US$ by year)

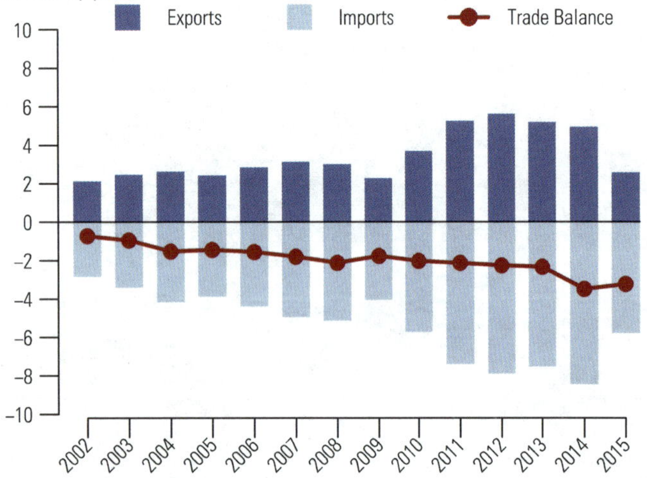

Graph 2: Total services trade, by value

(Bln US$ by year)

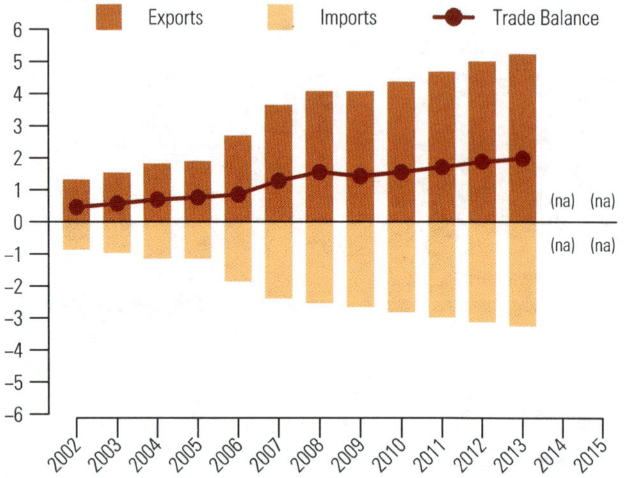

Exports Profile:

"Machinery and transport equipment" (SITC section 7), "Miscellaneous manufactured articles" (SITC section 8) and "Mineral fuels, lubricants" (SITC section 3) were the largest commodity groups for exports in 2015, representing respectively 39.9, 17.5 and 13.3 percent of exported goods (see table 2). From 2013 to 2015, the largest export commodity was "Petroleum oils, other than crude" (HS code 2710) (see table 1). The top three destinations for merchandise exports were Bunkers, ship stores, Germany and Egypt, accounting for respectively 12.0, 9.5 and 7.3 percent of total exports. "Personal, cultural, and recreational services" (EBOPS code 287) accounted for the largest share of exports of services in 2013 at 2.3 bln US$, followed by "Travel" (EBOPS code 236) at 1.5 bln US$ and "Other business services" (EBOPS code 268) at 482.7 mln US$ (see graph 3).

Graph 3: Exports of services by EBOPS category

(% share in 2013)

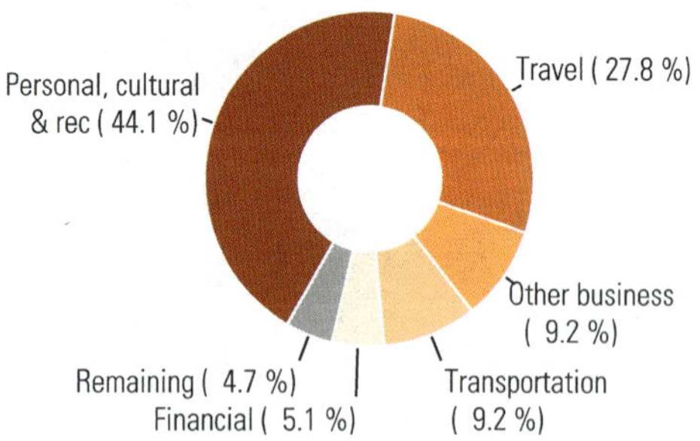

Table 1: Top 10 export commodities 2013 to 2015

HS code	4-digit heading of Harmonized System 2012	Value (million US$)			Unit value				SITC code
		2013	2014	2015	2013	2014	2015	Unit	
	All Commodities	5206.2	4970.8	2580.8					
2710	Petroleum oils, other than crude	2209.6	2139.4	316.8	0.7	0.6		US$/kg	334
8542	Electronic integrated circuits	720.4	396.3	327.3					776
3004	Medicaments (excluding goods of heading 30.02, 30.05 or 30.06)	341.6	328.7	263.1	104.7	103.7		US$/kg	542
8541	Diodes, transistors and similar semiconductor devices	217.8	316.5	223.5					776
8536	Electrical apparatus for switching or protecting electrical circuits	194.3	185.3	134.1	54.0	59.1	*51.1*	US$/kg	772
9503	Tricycles, scooters, wheeled toys; dolls'carriages; dolls; other toys	143.1	131.7	100.3	30.2	36.6	*29.6*	US$/kg	894
4907	Unused postage, revenue or similar stamps of current or new issue	113.6	98.9	145.1	54.2	61.1	*59.3*	US$/kg	892
8803	Parts of goods of heading 88.01 or 88.02	106.0	94.0	92.5	657.0	656.4	*798.6*	US$/kg	792
0303	Fish, frozen, excluding fish fillets and other fish meat of heading 03.04	119.4	110.5	58.4	21.5	18.5	11.6	US$/kg	034
2106	Food preparations not elsewhere specified or included	69.3	73.3	67.9	3.2	3.3	*3.2*	US$/kg	098

Services Imports and Exports: EBOPS 2002 categories

Table 2: Merchandise exports by SITC

(Value in million US$, growth and shares in percentage)

SITC	2015	Avg. Growth rates 2011-2015	Avg. Growth rates 2014-2015	2015 share
Total	2580.8	-16.4	-48.1	100.0
0+1	264.9	8.2	-12.2	10.3
2+4	17.7	-10.4	-17.7	0.7
3	343.1	-37.5	-84.0	13.3
5	325.5	-2.3	-35.0	12.6
6	117.1	-10.6	-23.0	4.5
7	1028.6	-12.0	-22.7	39.9
8	451.7	-3.5	-7.0	17.5
9	32.2	-5.3	-16.0	1.2

Table 3: Merchandise imports by SITC

(Value in million US$, growth and shares in percentage)

SITC	2015	Avg. Growth rates 2011-2015	Avg. Growth rates 2014-2015	2015 share
Total	5793.7	-5.9	-31.4	100.0
0+1	614.2	-2.3	-21.6	10.6
2+4	38.7	-3.4	-11.0	0.7
3	1297.3	-16.7	-61.8	22.4
5	488.4	-5.1	-26.6	8.4
6	360.7	-5.9	-19.8	6.2
7	2497.6	1.5	-1.5	43.1
8	444.4	-3.6	-18.8	7.7
9	52.4	-0.4	158.6	0.9

SITC Legend

SITC Code	Description
Total	All commodities
0+1	Food, animals + beverages, tobacco
2+4	Crude materials + anim. & veg. oils
3	Mineral fuels, lubricants
5	Chemicals
6	Goods classified chiefly by material
7	Machinery and transport equipment
8	Miscellaneous manufactured articles
9	Not classified elsewhere in the SITC

Graph 4: Merchandise trade balance

(Bln US$ by MDG Regions in 2015)

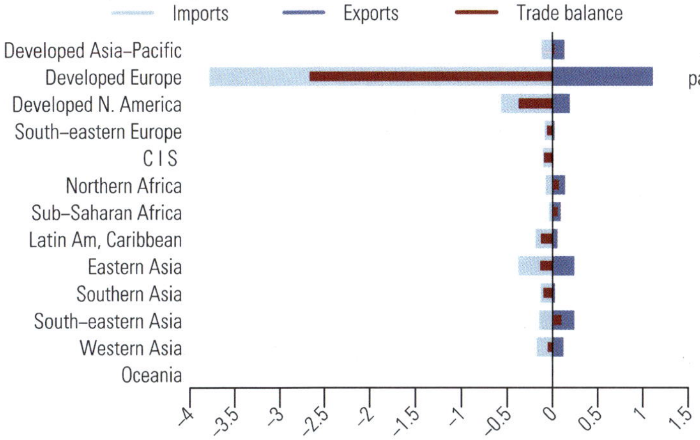

Graph 5: Partner concentration of merchandise trade

(Cumulative share by ranked partners in 2015)

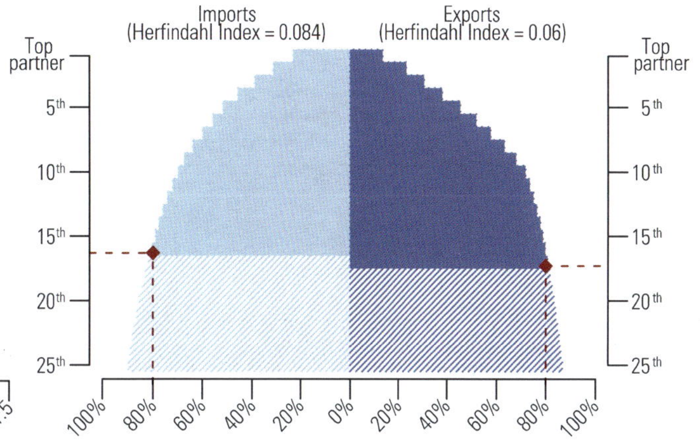

Graph 6: Imports of services by EBOPS category

(% share in 2013)

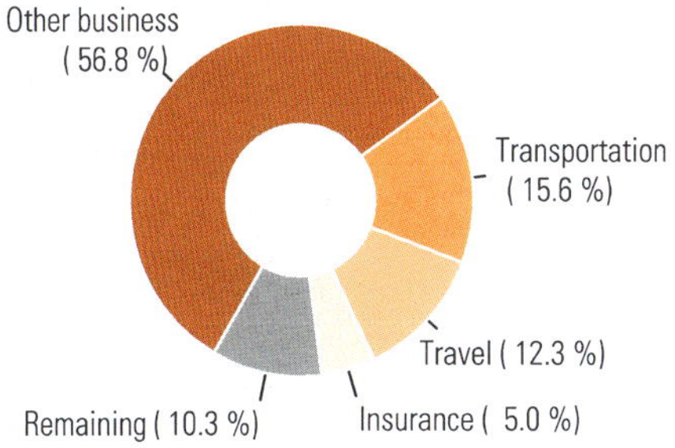

Imports Profile:

"Machinery and transport equipment" (SITC section 7), "Mineral fuels, lubricants" (SITC section 3) and "Food, animals + beverages, tobacco" (SITC section 0+1) were the largest commodity groups for imports in 2015, representing respectively 43.1, 22.4 and 10.6 percent of imported goods (see table 3). From 2013 to 2015, the largest import commodity was "Petroleum oils, other than crude" (HS code 2710) (see table 4). The top three partners for merchandise imports were Italy, the United Kingdom and the United States, accounting for respectively 21.8, 6.2 and 5.8 percent of total imports. "Other business services" (EBOPS code 268) accounted for the largest share of imports of services in 2013 at 1.8 bln US$, followed by "Transportation" (EBOPS code 205) at 507.5 mln US$ and "Travel" (EBOPS code 236) at 398.6 mln US$ (see graph 6).

Table 4: Top 10 import commodities 2013 to 2015

HS code	4-digit heading of Harmonized System 2012	Value (million US$) 2013	2014	2015	Unit value 2013	2014	2015	Unit	SITC code
	All Commodities	7525.4	8445.2	5793.7					
2710	Petroleum oils, other than crude	2930.4	3375.8	1207.9	0.7	0.7		US$/kg	334
8903	Yachts and other vessels for pleasure or sports; rowing boats and canoes	461.6	647.8	831.8	202.5	191.4	698.4	thsd US$/unit	793
8542	Electronic integrated circuits	655.9	351.8	238.4					776
8802	Other aircraft (for example, helicopters, aeroplanes); spacecraft	140.1	444.7	362.9	17.5	29.6	20.2	mln US$/unit	792
3004	Medicaments (excluding goods of heading 30.02, 30.05 or 30.06)	138.4	141.8	129.1	56.2	51.4		US$/kg	542
8803	Parts of goods of heading 88.01 or 88.02	135.6	119.3	148.1	459.3	553.5	*556.5*	US$/kg	792
8703	Motor cars and other motor vehicles principally designed for the transport	89.8	119.9	132.9	11.4	4.4	5.3	thsd US$/unit	781
2933	Heterocyclic compounds with nitrogen hetero-atom(s) only	61.5	54.0	47.8	275.7	250.3		US$/kg	515
8534	Printed circuits	58.3	49.2	54.5	300.6	282.5	*321.7*	US$/kg	772
8541	Diodes, transistors and similar semiconductor devices	26.4	57.3	75.2					776

Source: UN Comtrade

Mauritania

Goods Imports: CIF, by origin | **Goods Exports: FOB, by last known destination** | **Trade System: General**

Overview:

In 2014, the value of merchandise exports of Mauritania decreased substantially by 13.1 percent to reach 2.1 bln US$, while its merchandise imports decreased moderately by 8.5 percent to reach 3.6 bln US$ (see graph 1, table 2 and table 3). The merchandise trade balance recorded a moderate deficit of 1.5 bln US$ (see graph 1). The largest merchandise trade balance was with MDG Developed North America at -870.7 mln US$ (see graph 4). Merchandise exports in Mauritania were moderately concentrated amongst partners; imports were diversified. The top 8 partners accounted for 80 percent or more of exports and 11 partners accounted for 80 percent or more of imports (see graph 5). In 2014, the value of exports of services of Mauritania increased substantially by 49.4 percent, reaching 278.4 mln US$, while its imports of services decreased substantially by 10.2 percent and reached 899.1 mln US$ (see graph 2). There was a large trade in services deficit of 620.7 mln US$.

Graph 1: Total merchandise trade, by value

(Bln US$ by year)

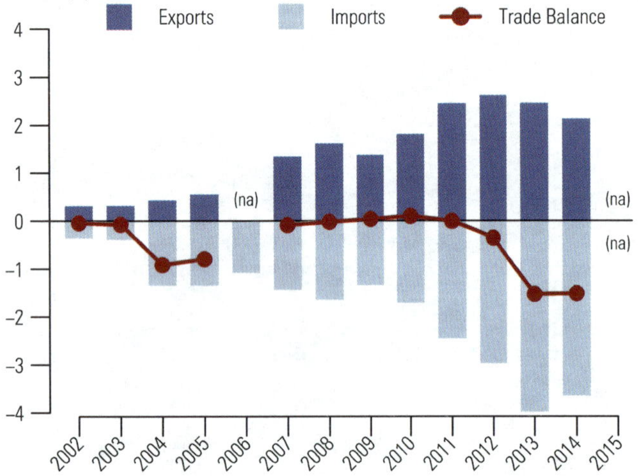

Graph 2: Total services trade, by value

(Bln US$ by year)

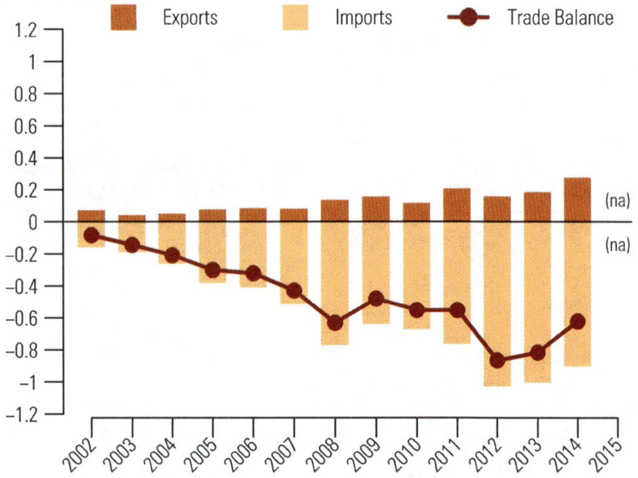

Exports Profile:

"Crude materials + anim. & veg. oils" (SITC section 2+4), "Food, animals + beverages, tobacco" (SITC section 0+1) and "Not classified elsewhere in the SITC" (SITC section 9) were the largest commodity groups for exports in 2014, representing respectively 51.4, 30.7 and 15.1 percent of exported goods (see table 2). From 2012 to 2014, the largest export commodity was "Iron ores and concentrates, including roasted iron pyrites" (HS code 2601) (see table 1). The top three destinations for merchandise exports were China, Switzerland and Italy, accounting for respectively 42.9, 13.6 and 6.1 percent of total exports. "Other business services" (EBOPS code 268) accounted for the largest share of exports of services in 2014 at 163.8 mln US$, followed by "Travel" (EBOPS code 236) at 36.5 mln US$ and "Transportation" (EBOPS code 205) at 34.9 mln US$ (see graph 3).

Graph 3: Exports of services by EBOPS category

(% share in 2014)

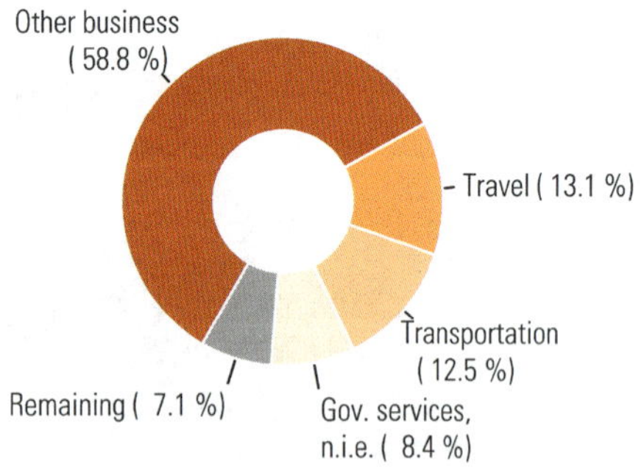

Table 1: Top 10 export commodities 2012 to 2014

HS code	4-digit heading of Harmonized System 2007	Value (million US$) 2012	2013	2014	Unit value 2012	2013	2014	Unit	SITC code
	All Commodities	2 623.8	2 462.5	2 139.8					
2601	Iron ores and concentrates, including roasted iron pyrites	1 011.1	1 269.2	854.2	0.1	0.1	0.1	US$/kg	281
7108	Gold (including gold plated with platinum)	317.4	352.9	322.2	50.2	42.6	37.3	thsd US$/kg	971
2603	Copper ores and concentrates	312.2	303.5	216.5	1.6	1.6	1.4	US$/kg	283
0307	Molluscs, whether in shell or not	380.4	199.4	227.1	6.7	4.9	7.0	US$/kg	036
0303	Fish, frozen, excluding fish fillets and other fish meat of heading 03.04	144.1	167.5	288.3		0.6	0.5	US$/kg	034
2709	Petroleum oils and oils obtained from bituminous minerals, crude	271.3	...	...	0.8			US$/kg	333
2710	Petroleum oils, other than crude	73.8	62.6	59.3	1.0	0.8	0.3	US$/kg	334
2301	Flours, meals and pellets, of meat or meat offal	36.1	43.1	76.1	1.0	1.1	1.1	US$/kg	081
0302	Fish, fresh or chilled, excluding fish fillets	28.5	25.0	25.9		1.5	1.4	US$/kg	034
0306	Crustaceans, whether in shell or not	12.8	6.4	24.3	5.8	6.0	7.7	US$/kg	036

Services Imports and Exports: EBOPS 2002 categories

Table 2: Merchandise exports by SITC

(Value in million US$, growth and shares in percentage)

SITC	2014	Avg. Growth rates 2010-2014	Avg. Growth rates 2013-2014	2014 share
Total	2139.8	4.1	-13.1	100.0
0+1	657.8	25.7	46.4	30.7
2+4	1099.9	14.3	-31.1	51.4
3	59.7	-31.0	-4.7	2.8
6	0.3	53.4	4.2	0.0
9	322.2	-16.1	-8.7	15.1

Table 3: Merchandise imports by SITC

(Value in million US$, growth and shares in percentage)

SITC	2014	Avg. Growth rates 2010-2014	Avg. Growth rates 2013-2014	2014 share
Total	3641.8	20.8	-8.5	100.0
0+1	392.3	7.1	1.4	10.8
2+4	63.6	9.4	-6.2	1.7
3	750.3	13.4	-6.3	20.6
5	149.8	18.7	-4.8	4.1
6	450.7	24.4	25.9	12.4
7	1766.3	31.0	-17.1	48.5
8	68.7	15.2	-11.0	1.9
9	0.0	-86.5	...	0.0

SITC Legend

SITC Code	Description
Total	All commodities
0+1	Food, animals + beverages, tobacco
2+4	Crude materials + anim. & veg. oils
3	Mineral fuels, lubricants
5	Chemicals
6	Goods classified chiefly by material
7	Machinery and transport equipment
8	Miscellaneous manufactured articles
9	Not classified elsewhere in the SITC

Graph 4: Merchandise trade balance

(Bln US$ by MDG Regions in 2014)

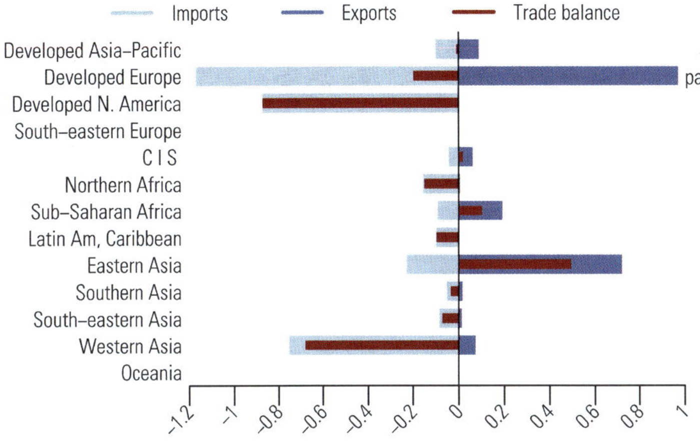

Graph 5: Partner concentration of merchandise trade

(Cumulative share by ranked partners in 2014)

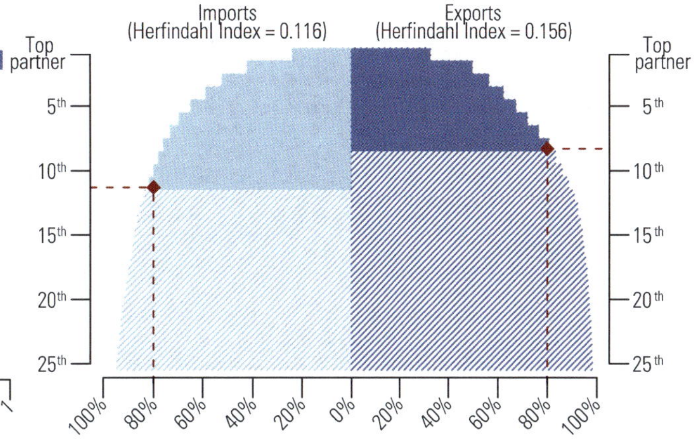

Graph 6: Imports of services by EBOPS category

(% share in 2014)

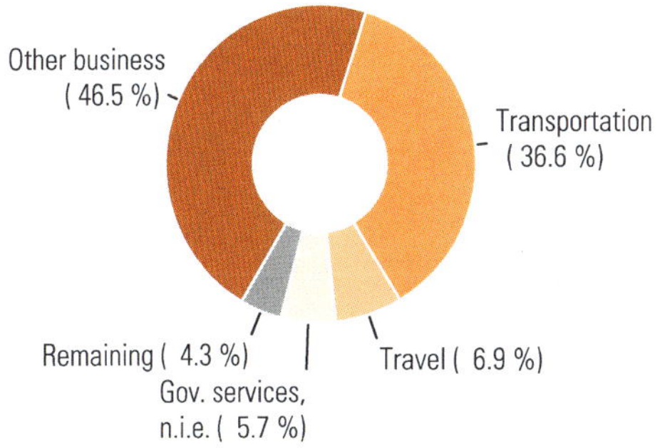

Imports Profile:

"Machinery and transport equipment" (SITC section 7), "Mineral fuels, lubricants" (SITC section 3) and "Goods classified chiefly by material" (SITC section 6) were the largest commodity groups for imports in 2014, representing respectively 48.5, 20.6 and 12.4 percent of imported goods (see table 3). From 2012 to 2014, the largest import commodity was "Petroleum oils, other than crude" (HS code 2710) (see table 4). The top three partners for merchandise imports were the United Arab Emirates, the United States and France, accounting for respectively 20.1, 11.7 and 10.2 percent of total imports. "Other business services" (EBOPS code 268) accounted for the largest share of imports of services in 2014 at 418.1 mln US$, followed by "Transportation" (EBOPS code 205) at 328.9 mln US$ and "Travel" (EBOPS code 236) at 61.9 mln US$ (see graph 6).

Table 4: Top 10 import commodities 2012 to 2014

HS code	4-digit heading of Harmonized System 2007	Value (million US$) 2012	Value (million US$) 2013	Value (million US$) 2014	Unit value 2012	Unit value 2013	Unit value 2014	Unit	SITC code
	All Commodities	2970.6	3978.5	3641.8					
2710	Petroleum oils, other than crude	730.3	733.6	686.2	0.9	1.0	0.9	US$/kg	334
8905	Light-vessels, fire-floats, dredgers, floating cranes and other vessels	19.4	926.9	687.3					793
8431	Parts suitable for use principally with the machinery of headings 84.25	195.1	247.0	204.2	14.0	12.2	17.5	US$/kg	723
1001	Wheat and meslin	139.0	107.2	110.4	0.3	0.3	0.2	US$/kg	041
8703	Motor cars and other motor vehicles principally designed for the transport	108.3	103.8	105.4	*22.2*	*21.7*	*22.6*	thsd US$/unit	781
8474	Machinery for sorting, screening, separating, washing, crushing, grinding	87.5	62.9	41.7					728
8429	Self-propelled bulldozers, angledozers, graders, levellers, scrapers	85.8	81.8	24.4					723
1006	Rice	54.0	59.8	60.1	0.3	0.3	0.4	US$/kg	042
8904	Tugs and pusher craft	...	76.0	92.5					793
8428	Other lifting, handling, loading or unloading machinery	36.2	91.9	22.2					744

Goods Imports: CIF, by origin	Goods Exports: FOB, by last known destination	Trade System: General

Overview:

In 2015, the value of merchandise exports of Mauritius decreased moderately by 6.8 percent to reach 2.5 bln US$, while its merchandise imports decreased substantially by 20.5 percent to reach 4.5 bln US$ (see graph 1, table 2 and table 3). The merchandise trade balance recorded a moderate deficit of 2.0 bln US$ (see graph 1). The largest merchandise trade balance was with MDG Eastern Asia at -913.2 mln US$ (see graph 4). Merchandise exports in Mauritius were diversified amongst partners; imports were also diversified. The top 11 partners accounted for 80 percent or more of exports and 17 partners accounted for 80 percent or more of imports (see graph 5). In 2014, the value of exports of services of Mauritius increased substantially by 14.9 percent, reaching 3.2 bln US$, while its imports of services increased substantially by 13.0 percent and reached 2.5 bln US$ (see graph 2). There was a moderate trade in services surplus of 692.4 mln US$.

Graph 1: Total merchandise trade, by value

(Bln US$ by year)

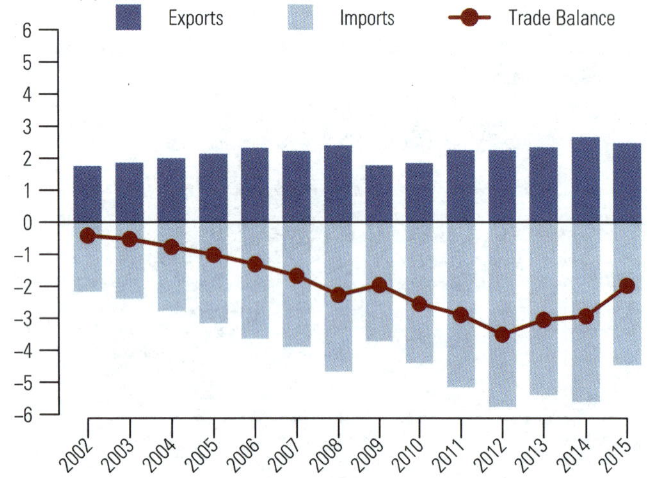

Graph 2: Total services trade, by value

(Bln US$ by year)

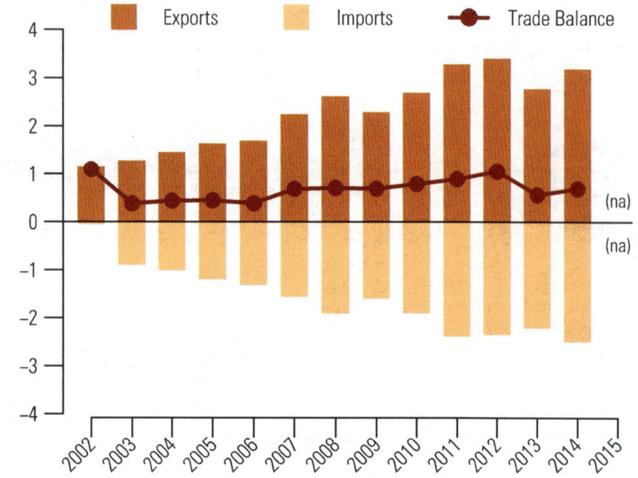

Exports Profile:

"Miscellaneous manufactured articles" (SITC section 8), "Food, animals + beverages, tobacco" (SITC section 0+1) and "Machinery and transport equipment" (SITC section 7) were the largest commodity groups for exports in 2015, representing respectively 38.7, 29.7 and 15.3 percent of exported goods (see table 2). From 2013 to 2015, the largest export commodity was "Prepared or preserved fish; caviar" (HS code 1604) (see table 1). The top three destinations for merchandise exports were the United Kingdom, France and the United States, accounting for respectively 14.4, 13.7 and 10.4 percent of total exports. "Travel" (EBOPS code 236) accounted for the largest share of exports of services in 2014 at 1.4 bln US$, followed by "Other business services" (EBOPS code 268) at 906.2 mln US$ and "Transportation" (EBOPS code 205) at 364.4 mln US$ (see graph 3).

Graph 3: Exports of services by EBOPS category

(% share in 2014)

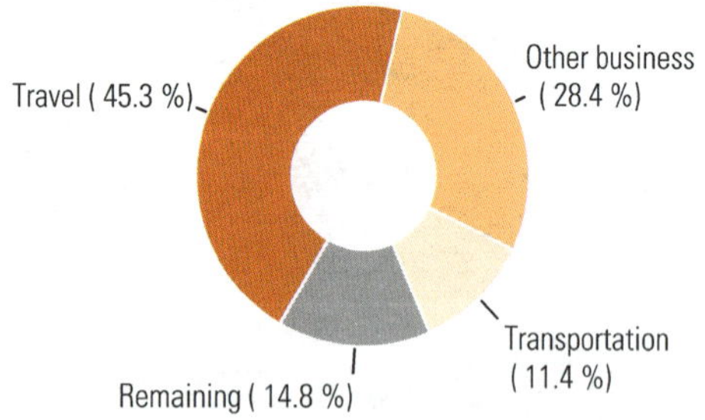

Table 1: Top 10 export commodities 2013 to 2015

HS code	4-digit heading of Harmonized System 2012	Value (million US$) 2013	2014	2015	Unit value 2013	2014	2015	Unit	SITC code
	All Commodities	2341.3	2663.0	2481.1					
1604	Prepared or preserved fish; caviar	375.6	320.3	255.9	5.6	4.7	4.0	US$/kg	037
1701	Cane or beet sugar and chemically pure sucrose, in solid form	308.9	254.0	218.6	0.7	0.6	0.5	US$/kg	061
6109	T-shirts, singlets and other vests, knitted or crocheted	208.1	232.6	204.9	4.3	4.3	4.1	US$/unit	845
8517	Electrical apparatus for line telephony or line telegraphy	55.3	299.8	287.1					764
6205	Men's or boys'shirts	168.1	167.6	166.0	10.1	10.2	10.0	US$/unit	841
6203	Men's or boys'suits, ensembles, jackets, blazers, trousers	106.5	117.1	125.9	13.6	13.3	13.4	US$/unit	841
7102	Diamonds, whether or not worked, but not mounted or set	83.4	112.8	115.2					667
0303	Fish, frozen, excluding fish fillets and other fish meat of heading 03.04	82.9	89.0	95.9	2.3	1.7	1.5	US$/kg	034
6110	Jerseys, pullovers, cardigans, waist-coats and similar articles	68.9	65.3	55.3	11.0	10.6	9.2	US$/unit	845
6104	Women's or girls'suits, ensembles, jackets, blazers, dresses, skirts	58.7	59.3	52.3	6.6	6.7	7.2	US$/unit	844

Source: UN Comtrade

Services Imports and Exports: EBOPS 2002 categories

Table 2: Merchandise exports by SITC

(Value in million US$, growth and shares in percentage)

SITC	2015	Avg. Growth rates 2011-2015	Avg. Growth rates 2014-2015	2015 share
Total	2 481.1	2.4	-6.8	100.0
0+1	736.6	-0.5	-12.7	29.7
2+4	37.4	-4.3	-10.1	1.5
3	6.1	24.4	291.9	0.2
5	94.9	5.8	-5.1	3.8
6	257.9	3.0	-7.5	10.4
7	379.5	65.5	-0.3	15.3
8	959.2	-3.2	-4.6	38.7
9	9.5	-2.7	-19.3	0.4

Table 3: Merchandise imports by SITC

(Value in million US$, growth and shares in percentage)

SITC	2015	Avg. Growth rates 2011-2015	Avg. Growth rates 2014-2015	2015 share
Total	4 458.3	-3.6	-20.5	100.0
0+1	941.7	-2.2	-16.8	21.1
2+4	148.7	-10.7	-21.6	3.3
3	674.8	-11.8	-37.2	15.1
5	380.5	-2.5	-13.3	8.5
6	791.5	-4.8	-12.5	17.8
7	1 117.3	4.7	-18.7	25.1
8	382.5	-4.0	-18.9	8.6
9	21.4	7.2	-9.3	0.5

SITC Legend

SITC Code	Description
Total	All commodities
0+1	Food, animals + beverages, tobacco
2+4	Crude materials + anim. & veg. oils
3	Mineral fuels, lubricants
5	Chemicals
6	Goods classified chiefly by material
7	Machinery and transport equipment
8	Miscellaneous manufactured articles
9	Not classified elsewhere in the SITC

Graph 4: Merchandise trade balance

(Bln US$ by MDG Regions in 2015)

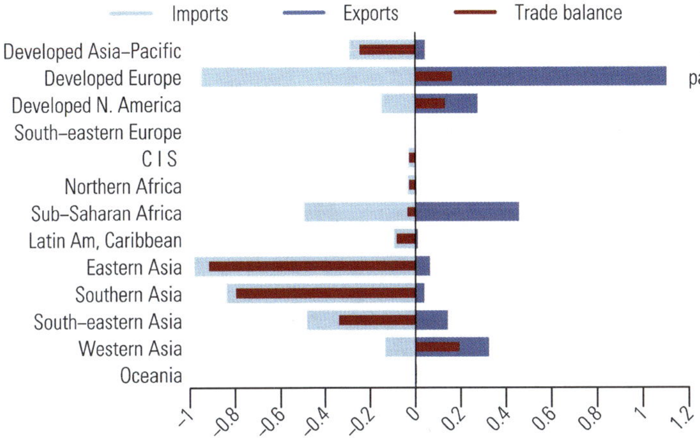

Graph 5: Partner concentration of merchandise trade

(Cumulative share by ranked partners in 2015)

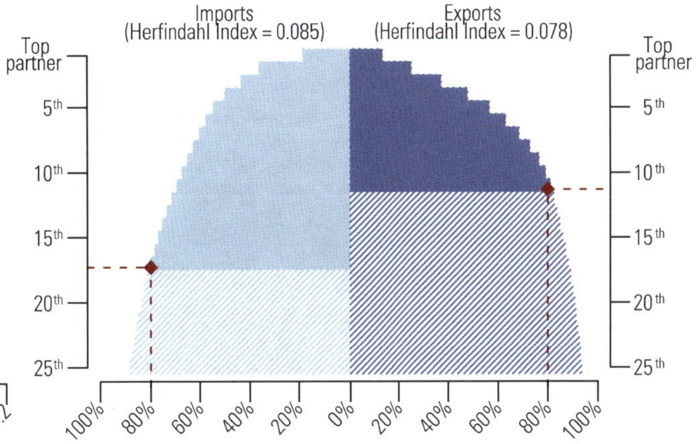

Graph 6: Imports of services by EBOPS category

(% share in 2014)

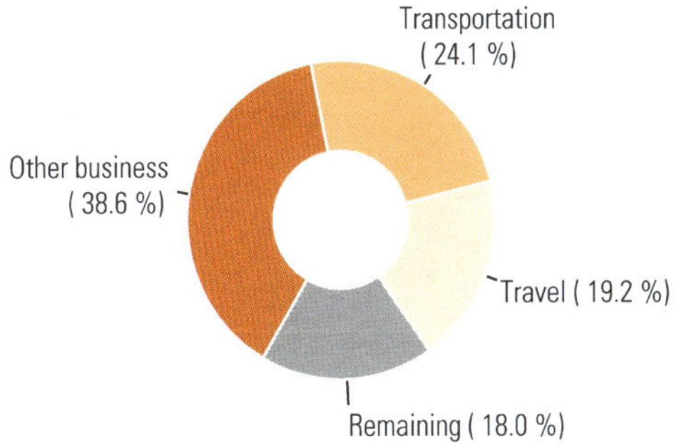

Imports Profile:

"Machinery and transport equipment" (SITC section 7), "Food, animals + beverages, tobacco" (SITC section 0+1) and "Goods classified chiefly by material" (SITC section 6) were the largest commodity groups for imports in 2015, representing respectively 25.1, 21.1 and 17.8 percent of imported goods (see table 3). From 2013 to 2015, the largest import commodity was "Petroleum oils, other than crude" (HS code 2710) (see table 4). The top three partners for merchandise imports were India, China and France, accounting for respectively 21.5, 16.2 and 7.7 percent of total imports. "Other business services" (EBOPS code 268) accounted for the largest share of imports of services in 2014 at 964.9 mln US$, followed by "Transportation" (EBOPS code 205) at 603.0 mln US$ and "Travel" (EBOPS code 236) at 480.7 mln US$ (see graph 6).

Table 4: Top 10 import commodities 2013 to 2015

HS code	4-digit heading of Harmonized System 2012	Value (million US$) 2013	Value (million US$) 2014	Value (million US$) 2015	Unit value 2013	Unit value 2014	Unit value 2015	Unit	SITC code
	All Commodities	5 395.5	5 607.2	4 458.3					
2710	Petroleum oils, other than crude	1 018.6	890.0	553.9	*1.6*	*1.8*	*1.8*	US$/kg	334
8517	Electrical apparatus for line telephony or line telegraphy	129.0	374.0	341.4					764
0303	Fish, frozen, excluding fish fillets and other fish meat of heading 03.04	337.4	283.7	201.9	2.1	1.7	1.2	US$/kg	034
8703	Motor cars and other motor vehicles principally designed for the transport	166.0	182.6	168.1	11.0	11.6	9.9	thsd US$/unit	781
7102	Diamonds, whether or not worked, but not mounted or set	91.0	116.0	104.8					667
3004	Medicaments (excluding goods of heading 30.02, 30.05 or 30.06)	93.2	106.0	103.9	23.2	19.8	18.4	US$/kg	542
2711	Petroleum gases and other gaseous hydrocarbons	68.1	105.3	69.9	1.0	0.9	0.5	US$/kg	343
5208	Woven fabrics of cotton, containing 85 % or more by weight of cotton	79.7	78.6	71.4	13.6	14.3	12.9	US$/kg	652
8471	Automatic data processing machines and units thereof	73.2	75.5	63.1	230.7	187.5	156.8	US$/unit	752
0402	Milk and cream, concentrated or containing added sugar	64.6	85.0	55.2	4.8	5.1	3.8	US$/kg	022

Source: UN Comtrade

Goods Imports: FOB, by origin	Goods Exports: FOB, by last known destination	Trade System: General

Overview:

In 2015, the value of merchandise exports of Mexico decreased slightly by 4.1 percent to reach 380.7 bln US$, while its merchandise imports decreased slightly by 1.2 percent to reach 395.2 bln US$ (see graph 1, table 2 and table 3). While the overall merchandise trade deficit of 14.5 bln US$ was relatively small, it reflected a substantial increase from the deficit in 2014 of 2.9 bln US$ (see graph 1). Mexico recorded a merchandise trade surplus of 121.8 bln US$ with its largest partner, the United States, a very slight decrease of 0.8 percent compared to the surplus with the United States in 2014. The largest merchandise trade balance was with MDG Developed North America at 122.4 bln US$ (see graph 4). Merchandise exports in Mexico were highly concentrated amongst partners; imports were also highly concentrated. The top 1 partner accounted for 80 percent or more of exports and 7 partners accounted for 80 percent or more of imports (see graph 5). In 2014, the value of exports of services of Mexico increased slightly by 4.6 percent, reaching 21.0 bln US$, while its imports of services increased moderately by 8.8 percent and reached 34.7 bln US$ (see graph 2). There was a moderate trade in services deficit of 13.7 bln US$.

Graph 1: Total merchandise trade, by value

(Bln US$ by year)

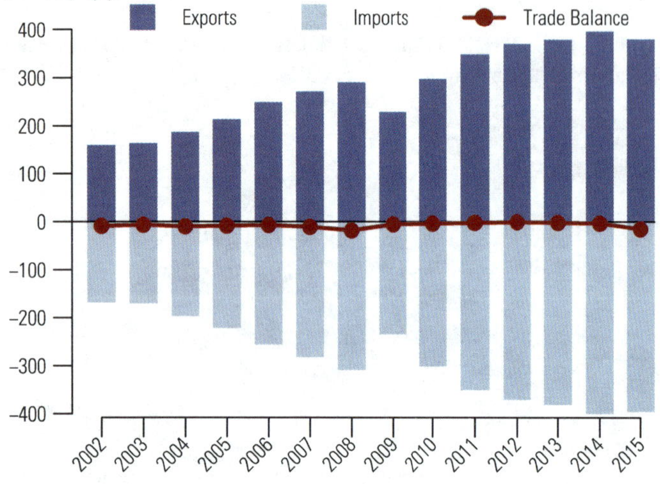

Graph 2: Total services trade, by value

(Bln US$ by year)

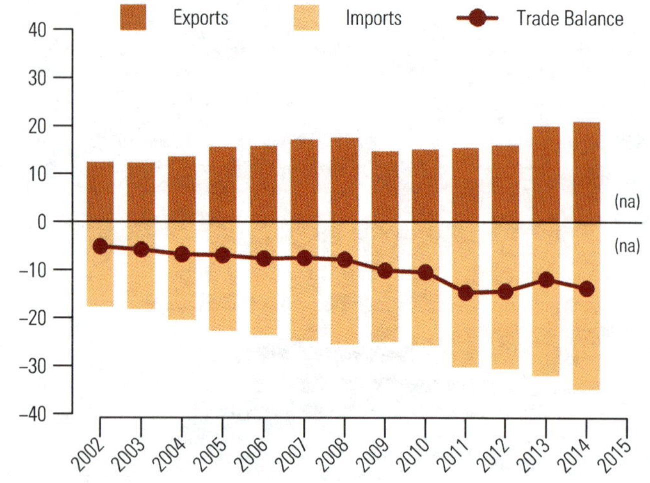

Exports Profile:

"Machinery and transport equipment" (SITC section 7), "Miscellaneous manufactured articles" (SITC section 8) and "Goods classified chiefly by material" (SITC section 6) were the largest commodity groups for exports in 2015, representing respectively 61.9, 10.3 and 7.0 percent of exported goods (see table 2). In 2015, the largest export commodity was "Motor cars and other motor vehicles principally designed for the transport" (HS code 8703), overtaking "Petroleum oils and oils obtained from bituminous minerals, crude" (HS code 2709), which was the largest export commodity in 2014 (see table 1). The top three destinations for merchandise exports were the United States, Canada and China, accounting for respectively 80.1, 2.7 and 1.5 percent of total exports. "Travel" (EBOPS code 236) accounted for the largest share of exports of services in 2014 at 16.3 bln US$, followed by "Insurance services" (EBOPS code 253) at 3.6 bln US$ (see graph 3).

Graph 3: Exports of services by EBOPS category

(% share in 2014)

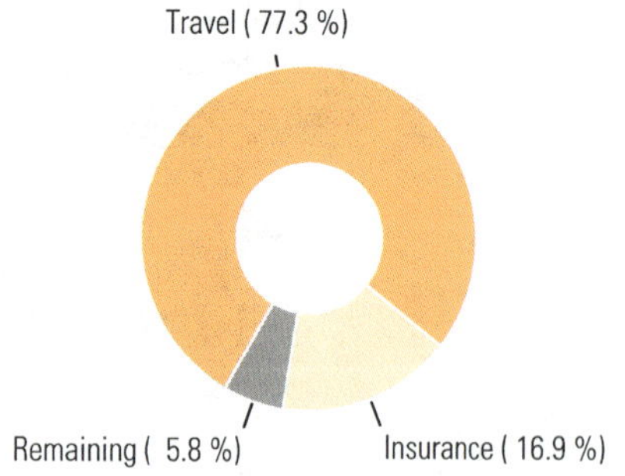

Table 1: Top 10 export commodities 2013 to 2015

HS code	4-digit heading of Harmonized System 2012	Value (million US$) 2013	2014	2015	Unit value 2013	2014	2015	Unit	SITC code
	All Commodities	379 949.3	397 098.8	380 749.9					
8703	Motor cars and other motor vehicles principally designed for the transport	32 389.4	32 391.3	32 843.3	16.8	16.1	16.1	thsd US$/unit	781
2709	Petroleum oils and oils obtained from bituminous minerals, crude	42 711.7	35 855.4	18 779.4	0.7	*0.6*	*0.8*	US$/kg	333
8708	Parts and accessories of the motor vehicles of headings 87.01 to 87.05	20 521.9	22 820.3	25 132.3	*10.7*	*10.7*	*10.7*	US$/kg	784
8704	Motor vehicles for the transport of goods	17 560.5	21 503.5	21 752.0	24.9	25.2	22.7	thsd US$/unit	782
8471	Automatic data processing machines and units thereof	17 401.3	20 737.9	18 381.4	458.0	630.0	643.2	US$/unit	752
8528	Reception apparatus for television	16 688.9	16 869.5	16 783.9	273.2	263.2	268.9	US$/unit	761
8517	Electrical apparatus for line telephony or line telegraphy	17 975.6	15 750.8	15 859.5					764
8544	Insulated (including enamelled or anodised) wire, cable	10 161.1	11 110.6	11 416.4	*13.7*	*5.8*	*14.3*	US$/kg	773
8701	Tractors (other than tractors of heading 87.09)	5 565.7	7 777.2	8 902.2	24.4	83.3	59.0	thsd US$/unit	722
9401	Seats (other than those of heading 94.02)	5 270.2	6 241.0	6 278.1					821

Services Imports and Exports: EBOPS 2002 categories

Table 2: Merchandise exports by SITC

(Value in million US$, growth and shares in percentage)

SITC	2015	Avg. Growth rates 2011-2015	Avg. Growth rates 2014-2015	2015 share
Total	380749.9	2.2	-4.1	100.0
0+1	25860.0	5.1	4.1	6.8
2+4	6824.9	-1.5	-13.0	1.8
3	22837.0	-20.0	-45.4	6.0
5	14414.7	0.4	-8.3	3.8
6	26737.0	-1.4	-6.9	7.0
7	235693.8	6.4	1.8	61.9
8	39179.6	8.0	3.5	10.3
9	9203.0	-2.5	5.7	2.4

Table 3: Merchandise imports by SITC

(Value in million US$, growth and shares in percentage)

SITC	2015	Avg. Growth rates 2011-2015	Avg. Growth rates 2014-2015	2015 share
Total	395232.2	3.0	-1.2	100.0
0+1	19686.6	0.1	-7.4	5.0
2+4	9727.1	-5.5	-9.3	2.5
3	26450.9	-6.8	-20.4	6.7
5	42799.1	2.0	-6.0	10.8
6	54646.2	3.4	-0.3	13.8
7	192029.6	4.8	2.0	48.6
8	37993.3	6.1	7.4	9.6
9	11899.4	12.1	10.4	3.0

SITC Legend

SITC Code	Description
Total	All commodities
0+1	Food, animals + beverages, tobacco
2+4	Crude materials + anim. & veg. oils
3	Mineral fuels, lubricants
5	Chemicals
6	Goods classified chiefly by material
7	Machinery and transport equipment
8	Miscellaneous manufactured articles
9	Not classified elsewhere in the SITC

Graph 4: Merchandise trade balance

(Bln US$ by MDG Regions in 2015)

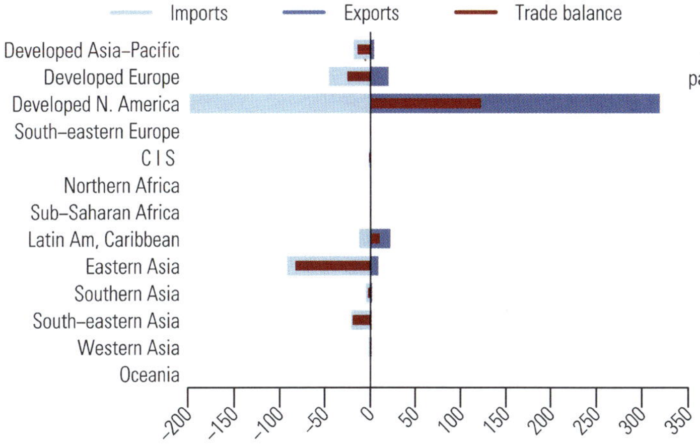

Graph 5: Partner concentration of merchandise trade

(Cumulative share by ranked partners in 2015)

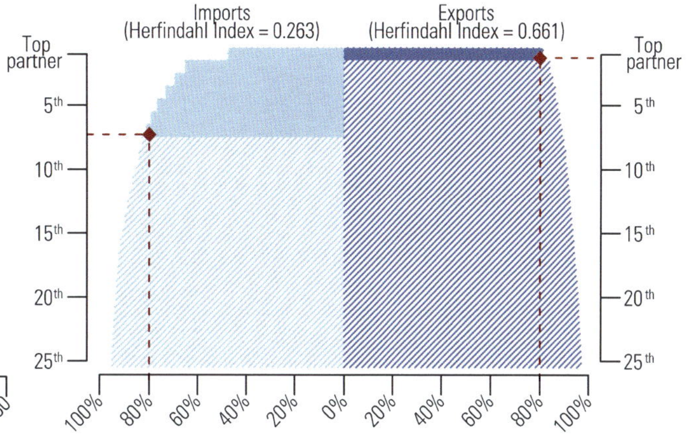

Graph 6: Imports of services by EBOPS category

(% share in 2014)

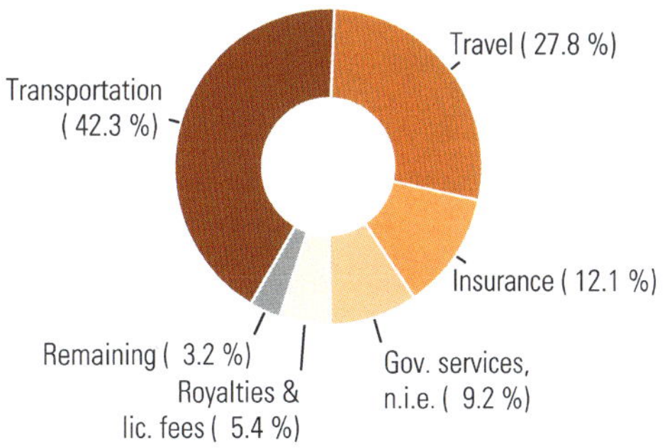

Imports Profile:

"Machinery and transport equipment" (SITC section 7), "Goods classified chiefly by material" (SITC section 6) and "Chemicals" (SITC section 5) were the largest commodity groups for imports in 2015, representing respectively 48.6, 13.8 and 10.8 percent of imported goods (see table 3). From 2013 to 2015, the largest import commodity was "Petroleum oils, other than crude" (HS code 2710), although "Parts and accessories of the motor vehicles of headings 87.01 to 87.05" (HS code 8708) became the largest import commodity in 2015 (see table 4). The top three partners for merchandise imports were the United States, China and Japan, accounting for respectively 48.5, 16.8 and 4.4 percent of total imports. "Transportation" (EBOPS code 205) accounted for the largest share of imports of services in 2014 at 14.7 bln US$, followed by "Travel" (EBOPS code 236) at 9.7 bln US$ and "Insurance services" (EBOPS code 253) at 4.2 bln US$ (see graph 6).

Table 4: Top 10 import commodities 2013 to 2015

HS code	4-digit heading of Harmonized System 2012	Value (million US$) 2013	2014	2015	Unit value 2013	2014	2015	Unit	SITC code
	All Commodities	381210.1	399976.9	395232.2					
2710	Petroleum oils, other than crude	25329.9	24352.5	19974.2					334
8708	Parts and accessories of the motor vehicles of headings 87.01 to 87.05	20611.1	22921.5	23432.9	*12.2*	*12.5*	*12.7*	US$/kg	784
8517	Electrical apparatus for line telephony or line telegraphy	15060.0	13436.2	14724.8					764
8542	Electronic integrated circuits	13359.8	13933.6	14793.1					776
9999	Commodities not specified according to kind	8583.1	10672.9	11701.8					931
8471	Automatic data processing machines and units thereof	8832.6	8973.9	9339.4	*74.9*	*77.3*	*92.6*	US$/unit	752
8703	Motor cars and other motor vehicles principally designed for the transport	8452.6	8574.9	9463.8	8.7	*10.3*	11.3	thsd US$/unit	781
8529	Parts suitable for use with the apparatus of headings 85.25 to 85.28	9555.5	9535.1	6107.5	*25.7*	*24.5*		US$/kg	764
2711	Petroleum gases and other gaseous hydrocarbons	5568.6	7142.4	4978.8					343
8536	Electrical apparatus for switching or protecting electrical circuits	5608.3	5949.6	6097.1	*17.2*	*11.0*	*14.2*	US$/kg	772

Micronesia (Federated states of)

Goods Imports: CIF, by origin | **Goods Exports: FOB, by last known destination** | **Trade System: General**

Overview:

In 2013, the value of merchandise exports of Micronesia (Federated states of) decreased substantially by 38.7 percent to reach 27.6 mln US$, while its merchandise imports decreased slightly by 3.1 percent to reach 187.7 mln US$ (see graph 1, table 2 and table 3). The merchandise trade balance recorded a large deficit of 160.1 mln US$ (see graph 1). The largest merchandise trade balance was with MDG Developed North America at -68.6 mln US$ (see graph 4). Merchandise exports in Micronesia (Federated states of) were highly concentrated amongst partners; imports were moderately concentrated. The top 2 partners accounted for 80 percent or more of exports and 6 partners accounted for 80 percent or more of imports (see graph 5). In 2008, the value of exports of services of Micronesia (Federated states of) increased moderately by 7.3 percent, reaching 26.3 mln US$, while its imports of services increased moderately by 7.9 percent and reached 64.1 mln US$ (see graph 2). There was a large trade in services deficit of 37.8 mln US$.

Graph 1: Total merchandise trade, by value

(Mln US$ by year)

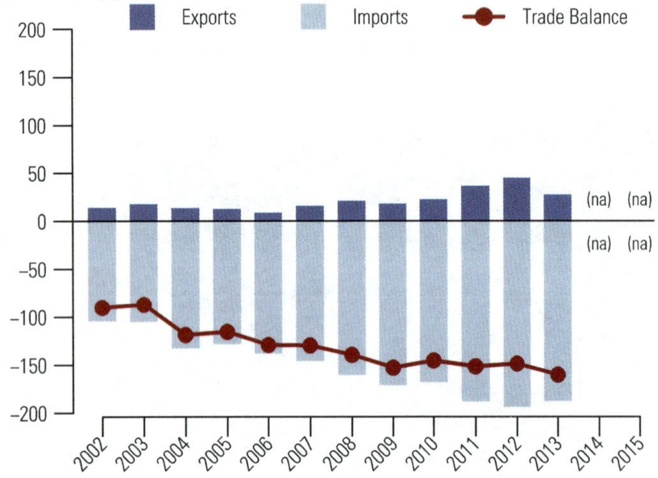

Graph 2: Total services trade, by value

(Mln US$ by year)

Exports Profile:

"Food, animals + beverages, tobacco" (SITC section 0+1), "Crude materials + anim. & veg. oils" (SITC section 2+4) and "Goods classified chiefly by material" (SITC section 6) were the largest commodity groups for exports in 2013, representing respectively 99.1, 0.5 and 0.4 percent of exported goods (see table 2). From 2011 to 2013, the largest export commodity was "Fish, frozen, excluding fish fillets" (HS code 0303) (see table 1). The top three destinations for merchandise exports were Areas nes, Guam and Northern Mariana Islands, accounting for respectively 83.6, 11.0 and 3.0 percent of total exports. "Travel" (EBOPS code 236) accounted for the largest share of exports of services in 2008 at 19.7 mln US$, followed by "Transportation" (EBOPS code 205) at 4.9 mln US$ and "Communications services" (EBOPS code 245) at 1.8 mln US$ (see graph 3).

Graph 3: Exports of services by EBOPS category

(% share in 2008)

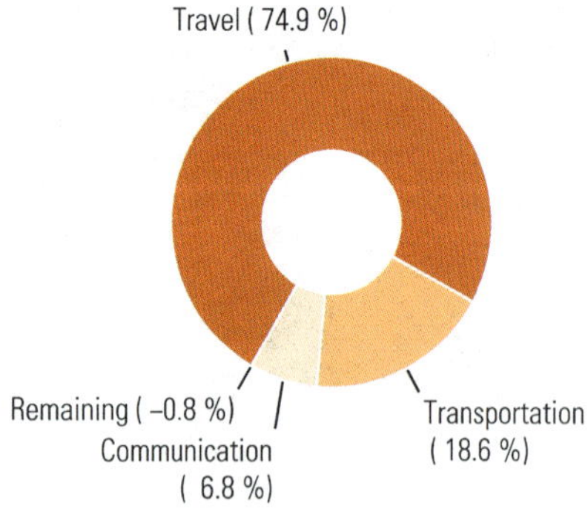

Table 1: Top 10 export commodities 2011 to 2013

HS code	4-digit heading of Harmonized System 2002	Value (million US$) 2011	2012	2013	Unit value 2011	2012	2013	Unit	SITC code
	All Commodities	36.7	45.1	27.6					
0303	Fish, frozen, excluding fish fillets	30.6	39.9	22.8	1.5	1.9		US$/kg	034
0802	Other nuts, fresh or dried	4.5	3.5	3.4	13.7	13.8		US$/kg	057
1212	Locust beans, seaweeds and other algae	0.2	0.5	0.5					292
2106	Food preparations not elsewhere specified or included	0.4	0.3	0.4	5.2			US$/kg	098
0307	Molluscs, whether in shell or not	0.4	0.2	0.2			43.4	US$/kg	036
0604	Foliage, branches and other parts of plants	0.2	0.2	0.1	6.4	6.3		US$/kg	292
0301	Live fish	0.1	0.1	0.1	12.1			US$/kg	034
1203	Copra	0.1	0.2	0.0		0.5		US$/kg	223
4421	Other articles of wood	0.1	0.1	0.1	10.2	9.3	10.8	US$/kg	635
0306	Crustaceans, whether in shell or not	0.1	0.0	0.0	6.1	3.9	5.7	US$/kg	036

Services Imports and Exports: EBOPS 2002 categories

Table 2: Merchandise exports by SITC

(Value in million US$, growth and shares in percentage)

SITC	2013	Avg. Growth rates 2009-2013	Avg. Growth rates 2012-2013	2013 share
Total	27.6	10.8	-38.7	100.0
0+1	27.4	10.9	-38.7	99.1
2+4	0.1	7.1	-62.0	0.5
6	0.1	0.6	17.2	0.4
8	0.0	195.8	200.2	0.1

Table 3: Merchandise imports by SITC

(Value in million US$, growth and shares in percentage)

SITC	2013	Avg. Growth rates 2009-2013	Avg. Growth rates 2012-2013	2013 share
Total	187.7	2.4	-3.1	100.0
0+1	51.1	-0.1	-9.6	27.2
2+4	4.7	-6.7	-42.0	2.5
3	56.4	9.2	-0.9	30.1
5	8.8	-3.8	-14.6	4.7
6	18.4	-0.5	-17.1	9.8
7	27.7	0.9	19.2	14.7
8	14.1	-1.7	-10.6	7.5
9	6.5	20.5	955.9	3.5

SITC Legend

SITC Code	Description
Total	All commodities
0+1	Food, animals + beverages, tobacco
2+4	Crude materials + anim. & veg. oils
3	Mineral fuels, lubricants
5	Chemicals
6	Goods classified chiefly by material
7	Machinery and transport equipment
8	Miscellaneous manufactured articles
9	Not classified elsewhere in the SITC

Graph 4: Merchandise trade balance

(Mln US$ by MDG Regions in 2013)

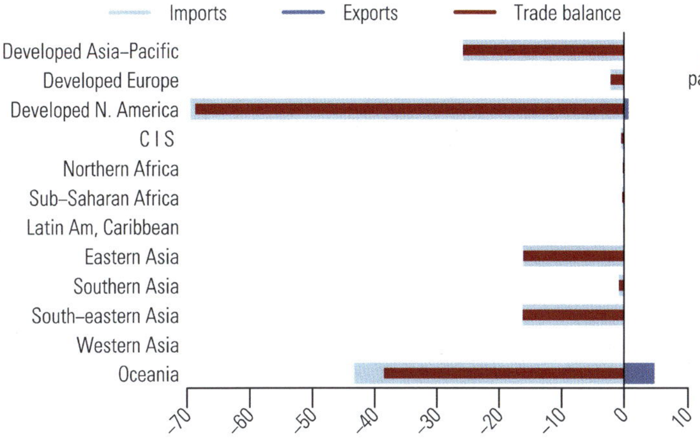

Graph 5: Partner concentration of merchandise trade

(Cumulative share by ranked partners in 2013)

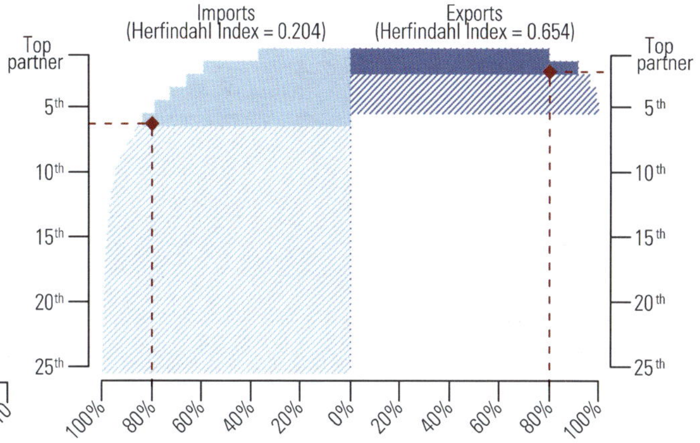

Graph 6: Imports of services by EBOPS category

(% share in 2008)

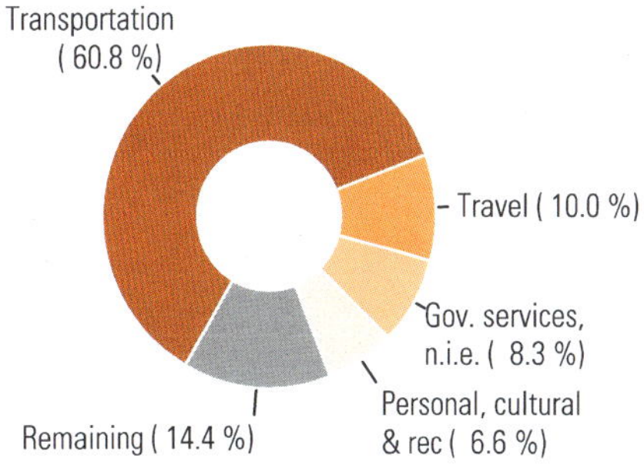

Imports Profile:

"Mineral fuels, lubricants" (SITC section 3), "Food, animals + beverages, tobacco" (SITC section 0+1) and "Machinery and transport equipment" (SITC section 7) were the largest commodity groups for imports in 2013, representing respectively 30.1, 27.2 and 14.7 percent of imported goods (see table 3). From 2011 to 2013, the largest import commodity was "Petroleum oils, other than crude" (HS code 2710) (see table 4). The top three partners for merchandise imports were the United States, Guam and Japan, accounting for respectively 37.3, 24.2 and 7.1 percent of total imports. "Transportation" (EBOPS code 205) accounted for the largest share of imports of services in 2008 at 39.0 mln US$, followed by "Travel" (EBOPS code 236) at 6.4 mln US$ and "Government services, n.i.e." (EBOPS code 291) at 5.3 mln US$ (see graph 6).

Table 4: Top 10 import commodities 2011 to 2013

HS code	4-digit heading of Harmonized System 2002	Value (million US$) 2011	2012	2013	Unit value 2011	2012	2013	Unit	SITC code
	All Commodities	188.1	193.6	187.7					
2710	Petroleum oils, other than crude	44.1	54.8	54.8					334
1006	Rice	8.2	10.3	9.4	*0.4*	*0.5*	*0.5*	US$/kg	042
8703	Motor cars and other motor vehicles principally designed for the transport	6.6	6.2	6.1		*7.5*	*8.5*	thsd US$/unit	781
0207	Meat and edible offal, of the poultry of heading 01.05	5.5	6.7	6.0	*1.6*	*1.8*		US$/kg	012
9999	Commodities not specified according to kind	10.0	0.6	6.5					931
1604	Prepared or preserved fish; caviar	3.3	3.8	3.0	*3.2*		*3.8*	US$/kg	037
1602	Other prepared or preserved meat, meat offal or blood	2.6	2.7	2.5	*5.1*	*5.7*	*5.7*	US$/kg	017
1902	Pasta, whether or not cooked or stuffed	2.6	2.5	2.4	*1.5*		*1.6*	US$/kg	048
1905	Bread, pastry, cakes, biscuits and other bakers' wares	2.5	2.5	2.3	*3.2*	*3.5*	*3.4*	US$/kg	048
2202	Waters with added sugar	2.3	2.5	2.1	*1.0*	*1.0*	*1.0*	US$/litre	111

Mongolia

Goods Imports: CIF, by origin | **Goods Exports: FOB, by last known destination** | **Trade System: General**

Overview:

In 2015, the value of merchandise exports of Mongolia decreased substantially by 19.1 percent to reach 4.7 bln US$, while its merchandise imports decreased substantially by 26.0 percent to reach 3.8 bln US$ (see graph 1, table 2 and table 3). The merchandise trade balance recorded a moderate surplus of 872.7 mln US$ (see graph 1). The largest merchandise trade balance was with MDG Eastern Asia at 2.3 bln US$ (see graph 4). Merchandise exports in Mongolia were highly concentrated amongst partners; imports were moderately concentrated. The top 1 partner accounted for 80 percent or more of exports and 5 partners accounted for 80 percent or more of imports (see graph 5). In 2014, the value of exports of services of Mongolia decreased substantially by 19.2 percent, reaching 573.4 mln US$, while its imports of services increased moderately by 5.1 percent and reached 2.1 bln US$ (see graph 2). There was a large trade in services deficit of 1.6 bln US$.

Graph 1: Total merchandise trade, by value

(Bln US$ by year)

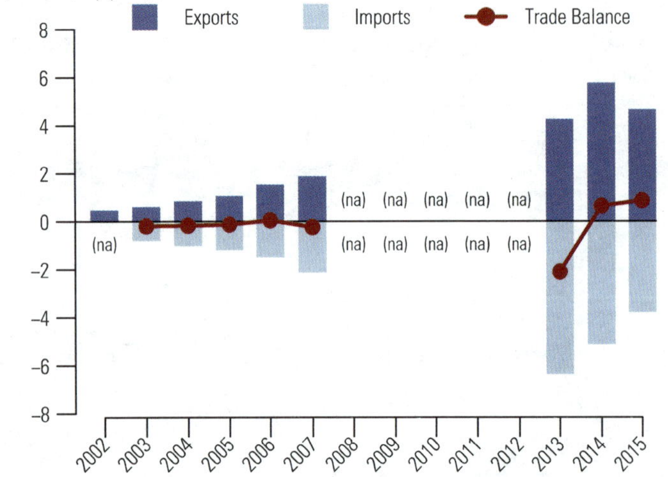

Graph 2: Total services trade, by value

(Bln US$ by year)

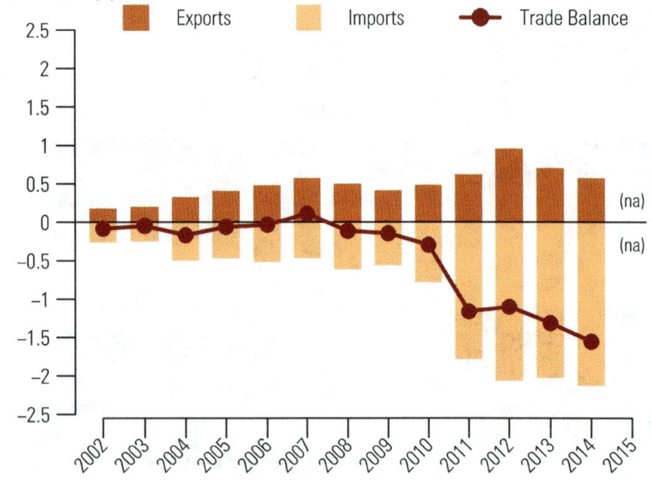

Exports Profile:

"Crude materials + anim. & veg. oils" (SITC section 2+4), "Mineral fuels, lubricants" (SITC section 3) and "Not classified elsewhere in the SITC" (SITC section 9) were the largest commodity groups for exports in 2015, representing respectively 65.0, 20.3 and 9.0 percent of exported goods (see table 2). From 2013 to 2015, the largest export commodity was "Copper ores and concentrates" (HS code 2603) (see table 1). The top three destinations for merchandise exports were China, the United Kingdom and the Russian Federation, accounting for respectively 86.1, 6.4 and 1.4 percent of total exports. "Transportation" (EBOPS code 205) accounted for the largest share of exports of services in 2014 at 204.8 mln US$, followed by "Travel" (EBOPS code 236) at 172.6 mln US$ and "Other business services" (EBOPS code 268) at 142.9 mln US$ (see graph 3).

Graph 3: Exports of services by EBOPS category

(% share in 2014)

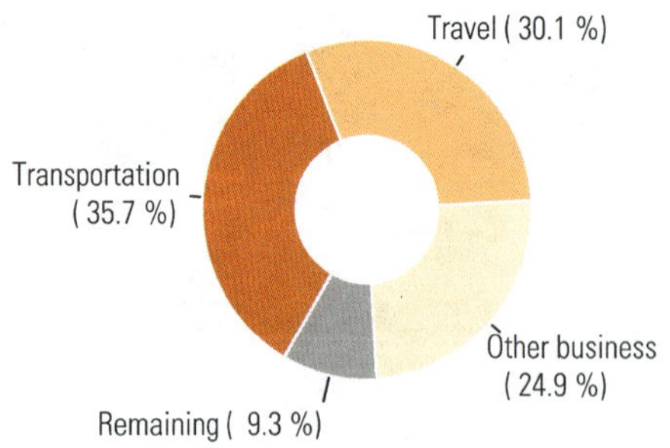

Table 1: Top 10 export commodities 2013 to 2015

HS code	4-digit heading of Harmonized System 2007	Value (million US$) 2013	2014	2015	Unit value 2013	2014	2015	Unit	SITC code
	All Commodities	4269.1	5774.3	4669.3					
2603	Copper ores and concentrates	949.0	2574.7	2280.1	1.5	1.9	1.5	US$/kg	283
2701	Coal; briquettes, ovoids and similar solid fuels manufactured from coal	1116.2	848.6	555.0	0.1	0.0	0.0	US$/kg	321
2709	Petroleum oils and oils obtained from bituminous minerals, crude	515.5	634.6	387.2	0.7	0.7	0.4	US$/kg	333
2601	Iron ores and concentrates, including roasted iron pyrites	654.3	446.4	227.2	0.1	0.1	0.0	US$/kg	281
7108	Gold (including gold plated with platinum)	309.8	405.2	420.6	41.0	40.4	37.1	thsd US$/kg	971
5102	Fine or coarse animal hair, not carded or combed	193.9	235.7	212.9	30.0	32.6	30.2	US$/kg	268
2608	Zinc ores and concentrates	119.1	113.2	101.7	0.9	1.1	1.2	US$/kg	287
2529	Feldspar; leucite, nepheline and nepheline syenite; fluorspar	83.3	71.5	65.5	0.2	0.2	0.2	US$/kg	278
5105	Wool and fine or coarse animal hair, carded or combed	58.0	63.4	43.1	74.9	81.9	37.2	US$/kg	268
7403	Refined copper and copper alloys, unwrought	16.1	41.9	66.7	7.3	6.6	5.4	US$/kg	682

Services Imports and Exports: EBOPS 2002 categories

Table 2: Merchandise exports by SITC

(Value in million US$, growth and shares in percentage)

SITC	2015	Avg. Growth rates 2011-2015	2014-2015	2015 share
Total	4669.3	...	-19.1	100.0
0+1	46.9	...	130.1	1.0
2+4	3033.9	...	-16.6	65.0
3	949.7	...	-36.5	20.3
5	2.4	...	8.6	0.1
6	111.4	...	28.5	2.4
7	71.4	...	-23.7	1.5
8	32.9	...	3.3	0.7
9	420.6	...	3.8	9.0

Table 3: Merchandise imports by SITC

(Value in million US$, growth and shares in percentage)

SITC	2015	Avg. Growth rates 2011-2015	2014-2015	2015 share
Total	3796.6	...	-26.0	100.0
0+1	447.5	...	3.1	11.8
2+4	48.1	...	-14.7	1.3
3	874.5	...	-35.6	23.0
5	315.2	...	-14.3	8.3
6	699.9	...	-30.1	18.4
7	1146.1	...	-28.6	30.2
8	265.0	...	-14.4	7.0
9	0.2	...	-43.9	0.0

SITC Legend

SITC Code	Description
Total	All commodities
0+1	Food, animals + beverages, tobacco
2+4	Crude materials + anim. & veg. oils
3	Mineral fuels, lubricants
5	Chemicals
6	Goods classified chiefly by material
7	Machinery and transport equipment
8	Miscellaneous manufactured articles
9	Not classified elsewhere in the SITC

Graph 4: Merchandise trade balance

(Bln US$ by MDG Regions in 2015)

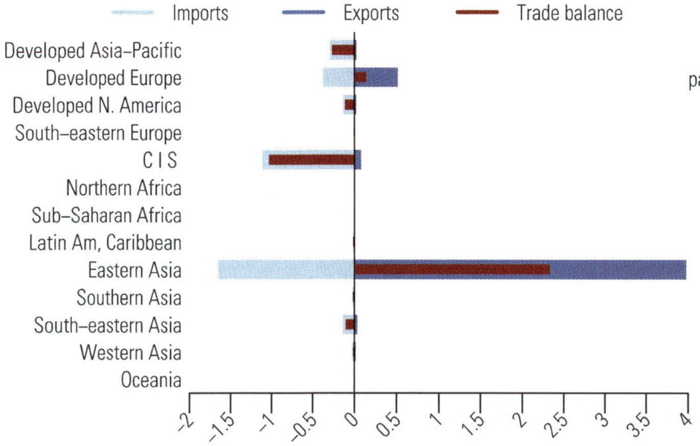

Graph 5: Partner concentration of merchandise trade

(Cumulative share by ranked partners in 2015)

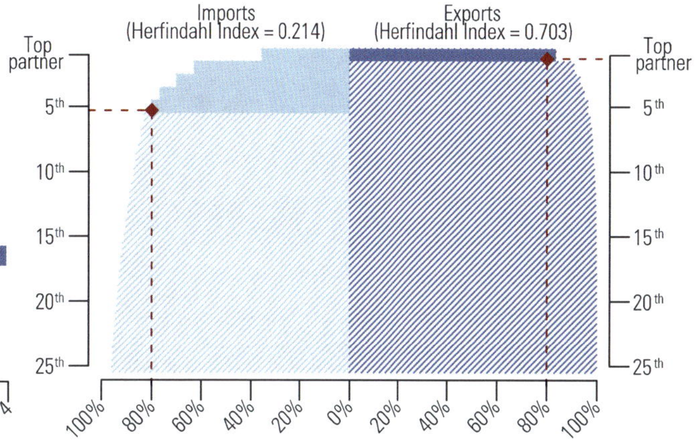

Graph 6: Imports of services by EBOPS category

(% share in 2014)

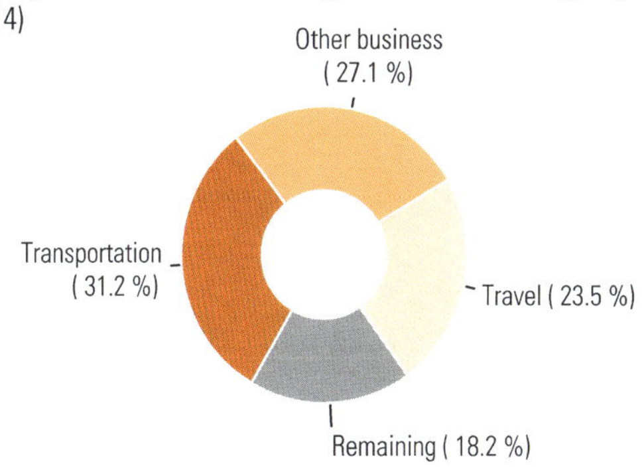

Imports Profile:

"Machinery and transport equipment" (SITC section 7), "Mineral fuels, lubricants" (SITC section 3) and "Goods classified chiefly by material" (SITC section 6) were the largest commodity groups for imports in 2015, representing respectively 30.2, 23.0 and 18.4 percent of imported goods (see table 3). From 2013 to 2015, the largest import commodity was "Petroleum oils, other than crude" (HS code 2710) (see table 4). The top three partners for merchandise imports were China, the Russian Federation and the Republic of Korea, accounting for respectively 31.7, 26.9 and 7.3 percent of total imports. "Transportation" (EBOPS code 205) accounted for the largest share of imports of services in 2014 at 662.8 mln US$, followed by "Other business services" (EBOPS code 268) at 576.6 mln US$ and "Travel" (EBOPS code 236) at 500.7 mln US$ (see graph 6).

Table 4: Top 10 import commodities 2013 to 2015

HS code	4-digit heading of Harmonized System 2007	Value (million US$) 2013	2014	2015	Unit value 2013	2014	2015	Unit	SITC code
	All Commodities	6357.8	5131.5	3796.6					
2710	Petroleum oils, other than crude	1409.8	1154.6	707.6	1.2	1.0	0.6	US$/kg	334
8703	Motor cars and other motor vehicles principally designed for the transport	373.0	289.2	210.0	8.3	7.0	5.7	thsd US$/unit	781
8704	Motor vehicles for the transport of goods	307.0	107.8	49.9	17.1	8.6	6.5	thsd US$/unit	782
2716	Electrical energy	112.8	130.0	129.2	94.4	96.4	93.3	US$/MWh	351
8474	Machinery for sorting, screening, separating, washing, crushing, grinding	117.5	113.7	64.2					728
8429	Self-propelled bulldozers, angledozers, graders, levellers, scrapers	168.8	51.4	45.0	124.3	72.1	104.3	thsd US$/unit	723
8517	Electrical apparatus for line telephony or line telegraphy	87.8	83.0	80.6					764
2523	Portland cement, aluminous cement, slag cement	97.8	91.6	49.3	0.1	0.1	0.1	US$/kg	661
7214	Other bars and rods of iron or non-alloy steel	90.2	81.7	39.0	0.6	0.6	0.4	US$/kg	676
7308	Structures (excluding prefabricated buildings of heading 94.06)	95.5	82.6	32.1	*1.5*	*1.5*	1.5	US$/kg	691

Source: UN Comtrade

Montenegro

Goods Imports: CIF, by origin | **Goods Exports: FOB, by last known destination** | **Trade System: Special**

Overview:

In 2015, the value of merchandise exports of Montenegro decreased substantially by 19.9 percent to reach 353.1 mln US$, while its merchandise imports decreased substantially by 13.4 percent to reach 2.1 bln US$ (see graph 1, table 2 and table 3). The merchandise trade balance recorded a large deficit of 1.7 bln US$ (see graph 1). The largest merchandise trade balance was with MDG Developed Europe at -697.1 mln US$ (see graph 4). Merchandise exports in Montenegro were diversified amongst partners; imports were also diversified. The top 11 partners accounted for 80 percent or more of exports and 12 partners accounted for 80 percent or more of imports (see graph 5). In 2014, the value of exports of services of Montenegro increased slightly by 4.3 percent, reaching 1.4 bln US$, while its imports of services increased slightly by 0.6 percent and reached 444.3 mln US$ (see graph 2). There was a large trade in services surplus of 923.9 mln US$.

Graph 1: Total merchandise trade, by value

(Bln US$ by year)

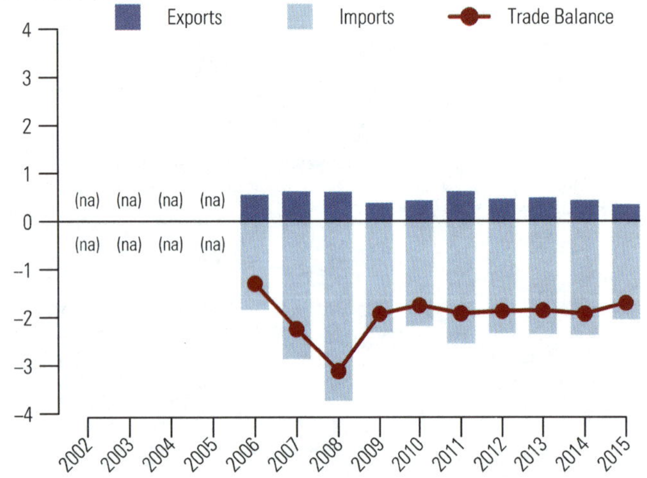

Graph 2: Total services trade, by value

(Bln US$ by year)

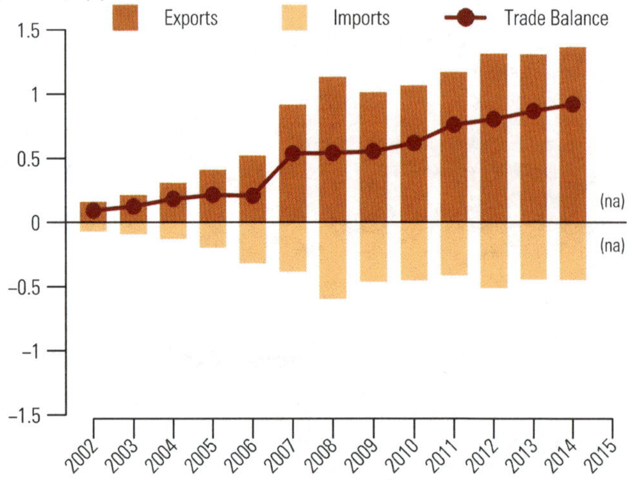

Exports Profile:

"Goods classified chiefly by material" (SITC section 6), "Crude materials + anim. & veg. oils" (SITC section 2+4) and "Food, animals + beverages, tobacco" (SITC section 0+1) were the largest commodity groups for exports in 2015, representing respectively 30.4, 20.2 and 16.8 percent of exported goods (see table 2). From 2013 to 2015, the largest export commodity was "Unwrought aluminium" (HS code 7601) (see table 1). The top three destinations for merchandise exports were Serbia, Belarus and Croatia, accounting for respectively 28.0, 10.2 and 9.8 percent of total exports. "Travel" (EBOPS code 236) accounted for the largest share of exports of services in 2014 at 906.5 mln US$, followed by "Transportation" (EBOPS code 205) at 234.2 mln US$ and "Other business services" (EBOPS code 268) at 81.0 mln US$ (see graph 3).

Graph 3: Exports of services by EBOPS category

(% share in 2014)

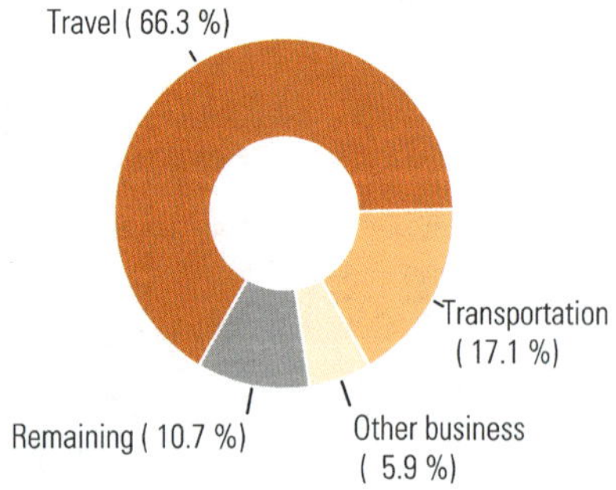

Table 1: Top 10 export commodities 2013 to 2015

HS code	4-digit heading of Harmonized System 2012	Value (million US$) 2013	2014	2015	Unit value 2013	2014	2015	Unit	SITC code
	All Commodities	494.4	440.7	353.1					
7601	Unwrought aluminium	105.9	94.9	76.1	2.2	2.2	1.9	US$/kg	684
2716	Electrical energy	126.8	49.9	33.0	64.1	74.1	61.1	US$/MWh	351
2204	Wine of fresh grapes, including fortified wines	17.5	18.2	17.2	*2.5*	3.0	2.3	US$/litre	112
4407	Wood sawn or chipped lengthwise, sliced or peeled	14.5	18.5	19.4					248
2710	Petroleum oils, other than crude	14.9	12.1	16.9	1.1	1.0	0.7	US$/kg	334
0203	Meat of swine, fresh, chilled or frozen	0.1	43.3	0.2	3.4	3.8	1.8	US$/kg	012
7204	Ferrous waste and scrap; remelting scrap ingots of iron or steel	19.1	16.8	4.2	0.3	0.3	0.3	US$/kg	282
8483	Transmission shafts (including cam shafts and crank shafts) and cranks	12.7	13.5	13.5					748
7214	Other bars and rods of iron or non-alloy steel	10.3	4.2	17.0	1.2	1.2	1.0	US$/kg	676
3004	Medicaments (excluding goods of heading 30.02, 30.05 or 30.06)	8.3	7.4	7.3	7.8	7.5	6.0	US$/kg	542

Services Imports and Exports: EBOPS 2002 categories

Table 2: Merchandise exports by SITC

(Value in million US$, growth and shares in percentage)

SITC	2015	Avg. Growth rates 2011-2015	Avg. Growth rates 2014-2015	2015 share
Total	353.1	-13.4	-19.9	100.0
0+1	59.2	-4.2	-47.5	16.8
2+4	71.4	-5.9	-22.4	20.2
3	52.3	-12.1	-18.4	14.8
5	14.3	-3.9	-15.1	4.1
6	107.4	-23.0	-1.9	30.4
7	33.1	-0.1	9.4	9.4
8	15.3	-10.2	5.6	4.3

Table 3: Merchandise imports by SITC

(Value in million US$, growth and shares in percentage)

SITC	2015	Avg. Growth rates 2011-2015	Avg. Growth rates 2014-2015	2015 share
Total	2 050.2	-5.3	-13.4	100.0
0+1	497.3	-3.9	-18.7	24.3
2+4	65.2	-17.2	-13.0	3.2
3	221.7	-16.7	-29.3	10.8
5	215.3	-2.3	-9.9	10.5
6	315.0	-3.9	-12.5	15.4
7	455.5	0.7	1.0	22.2
8	280.2	-2.7	-11.5	13.7
9	0.0	-29.8	-20.5	0.0

SITC Legend

SITC Code	Description
Total	All commodities
0+1	Food, animals + beverages, tobacco
2+4	Crude materials + anim. & veg. oils
3	Mineral fuels, lubricants
5	Chemicals
6	Goods classified chiefly by material
7	Machinery and transport equipment
8	Miscellaneous manufactured articles
9	Not classified elsewhere in the SITC

Graph 4: Merchandise trade balance

(Mln US$ by MDG Regions in 2015)

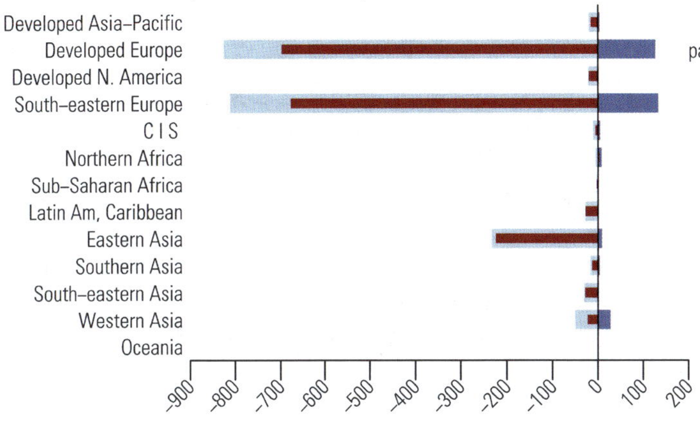

Graph 5: Partner concentration of merchandise trade

(Cumulative share by ranked partners in 2015)

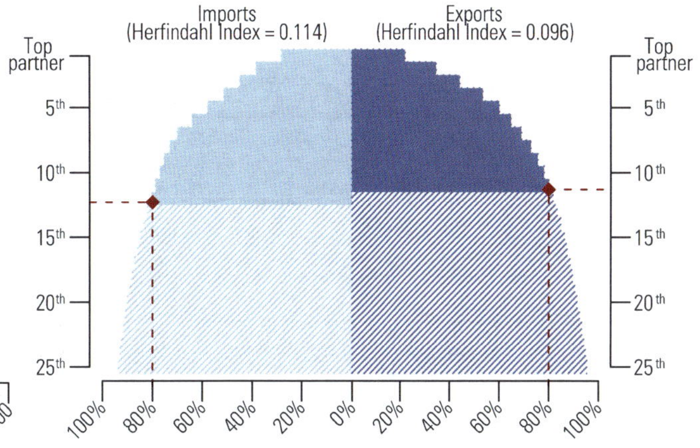

Graph 6: Imports of services by EBOPS category

(% share in 2014)

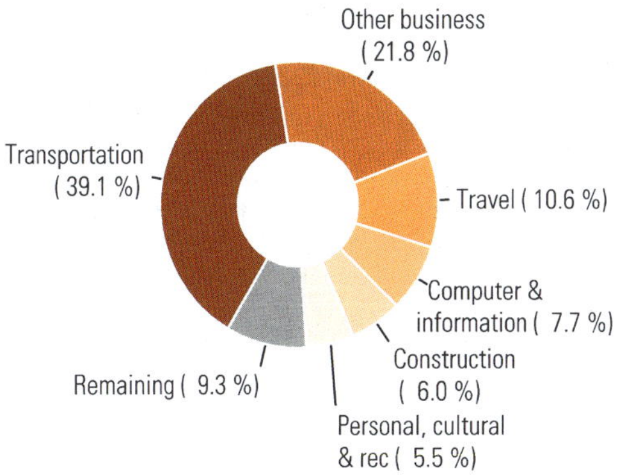

Imports Profile:

"Food, animals + beverages, tobacco" (SITC section 0+1), "Machinery and transport equipment" (SITC section 7) and "Goods classified chiefly by material" (SITC section 6) were the largest commodity groups for imports in 2015, representing respectively 24.3, 22.2 and 15.4 percent of imported goods (see table 3). From 2013 to 2015, the largest import commodity was "Petroleum oils, other than crude" (HS code 2710) (see table 4). The top three partners for merchandise imports were Serbia, China and Greece, accounting for respectively 27.9, 8.5 and 7.7 percent of total imports. "Transportation" (EBOPS code 205) accounted for the largest share of imports of services in 2014 at 173.6 mln US$, followed by "Other business services" (EBOPS code 268) at 96.7 mln US$ and "Travel" (EBOPS code 236) at 47.2 mln US$ (see graph 6).

Table 4: Top 10 import commodities 2013 to 2015

HS code	4-digit heading of Harmonized System 2012	Value (million US$) 2013	2014	2015	Unit value 2013	2014	2015	Unit	SITC code
	All Commodities	2 348.9	2 366.8	2 050.2					
2710	Petroleum oils, other than crude	239.6	231.5	154.8	1.0	0.9	0.6	US$/kg	334
8703	Motor cars and other motor vehicles principally designed for the transport	83.3	83.7	76.8	4.6	4.5	3.6	thsd US$/unit	781
0203	Meat of swine, fresh, chilled or frozen	64.1	100.4	47.2	3.2	3.1	2.3	US$/kg	012
3004	Medicaments (excluding goods of heading 30.02, 30.05 or 30.06)	60.7	59.2	55.1	61.5	68.3	54.6	US$/kg	542
2716	Electrical energy	72.3	51.2	45.1	49.7	48.3	41.4	US$/MWh	351
8517	Electrical apparatus for line telephony or line telegraphy	32.9	43.3	43.5					764
9403	Other furniture and parts thereof	32.7	37.8	30.5					821
2202	Waters with added sugar	37.7	34.8	28.0	0.6	0.6	0.6	US$/litre	111
2818	Artificial corundum, whether or not chemically defined	35.8	32.3	28.3	0.4	0.4	0.4	US$/kg	522
2523	Portland cement, aluminous cement, slag cement	29.9	30.1	27.0	0.1	0.1	0.1	US$/kg	661

Montserrat

Goods Imports: CIF, by origin | **Goods Exports: FOB, by last known destination** | **Trade System: Special**

Overview:

In 2014, the value of merchandise exports of Montserrat decreased substantially by 43.4 percent to reach 3.4 mln US$, while its merchandise imports decreased slightly by 0.4 percent to reach 41.9 mln US$ (see graph 1, table 2 and table 3). The merchandise trade balance recorded a large deficit of 38.5 mln US$ (see graph 1). The largest merchandise trade balance was with MDG Developed North America at -30.5 mln US$ (see graph 4). Merchandise exports in Montserrat were moderately concentrated amongst partners; imports were highly concentrated. The top 4 partners accounted for 80 percent or more of exports and 3 partners accounted for 80 percent or more of imports (see graph 5). In 2013, the value of exports of services of Montserrat increased slightly by 4.9 percent, reaching 13.9 mln US$, while its imports of services increased slightly by 2.9 percent and reached 18.7 mln US$ (see graph 2). There was a moderate trade in services deficit of 4.8 mln US$.

Graph 1: Total merchandise trade, by value

(Mln US$ by year)

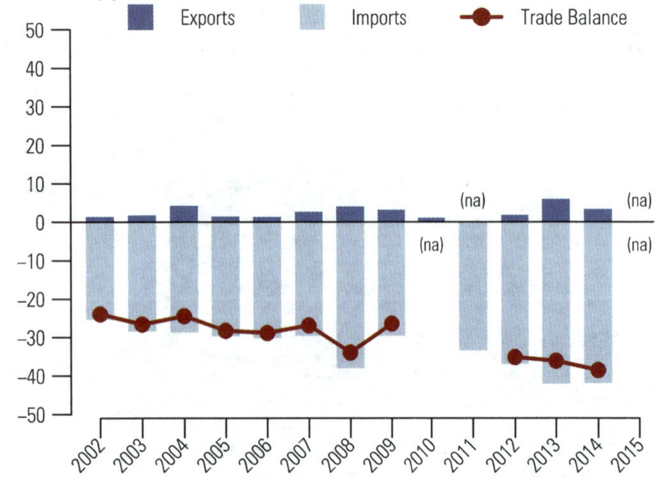

Graph 2: Total services trade, by value

(Mln US$ by year)

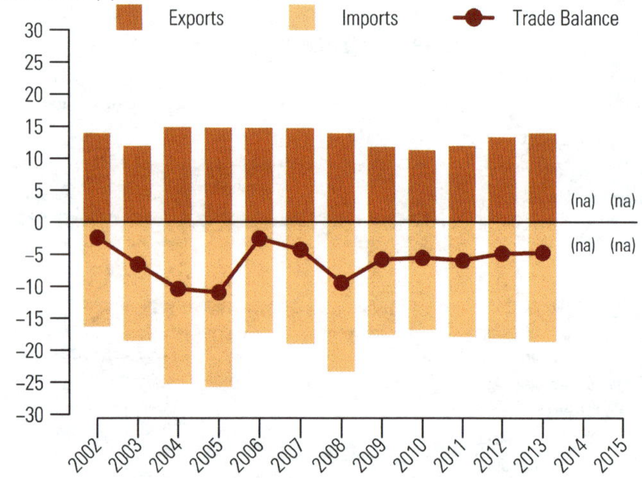

Exports Profile:

"Crude materials + anim. & veg. oils" (SITC section 2+4), "Machinery and transport equipment" (SITC section 7) and "Food, animals + beverages, tobacco" (SITC section 0+1) were the largest commodity groups for exports in 2014, representing respectively 59.6, 24.9 and 9.2 percent of exported goods (see table 2). From 2012 to 2014, the largest export commodity was "Natural sands of all kinds" (HS code 2505) (see table 1). The top three destinations for merchandise exports were Dominica, the United States and Saint Kitts and Nevis, accounting for respectively 29.7, 21.6 and 10.8 percent of total exports. "Travel" (EBOPS code 236) accounted for the largest share of exports of services in 2013 at 7.6 mln US$, followed by "Computer and information services" (EBOPS code 262) at 3.4 mln US$ and "Transportation" (EBOPS code 205) at 1.9 mln US$ (see graph 3).

Graph 3: Exports of services by EBOPS category

(% share in 2013)

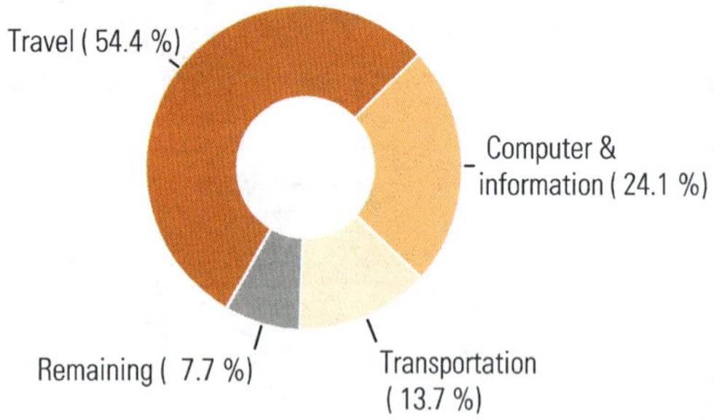

Table 1: Top 10 export commodities 2012 to 2014

HS code	4-digit heading of Harmonized System 2007	Value (million US$) 2012	2013	2014	Unit value 2012	2013	2014	Unit	SITC code
	All Commodities	1.8	6.0	3.4					
2505	Natural sands of all kinds	1.1	0.9	1.5	0.0	0.0	0.0	US$/kg	273
8716	Trailers and semi-trailers	...	1.1	...					786
8431	Parts suitable for use principally with the machinery of headings 84.25	0.0	0.6	0.0	20.9	2.3	49.6	US$/kg	723
8307	Flexible tubing of base metal, with or without fittings	...	0.6	...		9.6		US$/kg	699
2517	Pebbles, gravel, broken or crushed stone	0.0	0.1	0.4	0.0	0.0	0.0	US$/kg	273
8430	Other moving, grading, levelling, scraping, excavating, tamping, compacting	0.1	0.0	0.4					723
9031	Measuring or checking instruments, appliances and machines	0.2	0.2	...					874
8207	Interchangeable tools for hand tools, whether or not power-operated	0.0	0.4	...	25.1	9.1		US$/kg	695
7304	Tubes, pipes and hollow profiles, seamless, of iron (other than cast iron)	...	0.4	...		4.8		US$/kg	679
2402	Cigars, cheroots, cigarillos and cigarettes	...	...	0.3			8.2	US$/kg	122

Services Imports and Exports: EBOPS 2002 categories

Table 2: Merchandise exports by SITC

(Value in million US$, growth and shares in percentage)

SITC	2014	Avg. Growth rates 2010-2014	Avg. Growth rates 2013-2014	2014 share
Total	3.4	32.4	-43.4	100.0
0+1	0.3	626.7	9339.7	9.2
2+4	2.0	34.0	79.6	59.6
3	0.0	...	-98.7	0.0
5	0.0	140.2	196.9	0.7
6	0.1	85.7	-94.4	2.8
7	0.8	25.2	-70.4	24.9
8	0.0	31.8	-85.6	1.2
9	0.1	-16.2	140.0	1.6

Table 3: Merchandise imports by SITC

(Value in million US$, growth and shares in percentage)

SITC	2014	Avg. Growth rates 2010-2014	Avg. Growth rates 2013-2014	2014 share
Total	41.9	...	-0.4	100.0
0+1	6.9	...	1.5	16.5
2+4	0.8	...	-7.5	2.0
3	14.5	...	2.1	34.7
5	1.9	...	-19.2	4.5
6	5.6	...	-4.8	13.4
7	8.2	...	-7.3	19.5
8	3.8	...	41.3	9.0
9	0.2	...	-57.3	0.4

SITC Legend

SITC Code	Description
Total	All commodities
0+1	Food, animals + beverages, tobacco
2+4	Crude materials + anim. & veg. oils
3	Mineral fuels, lubricants
5	Chemicals
6	Goods classified chiefly by material
7	Machinery and transport equipment
8	Miscellaneous manufactured articles
9	Not classified elsewhere in the SITC

Graph 4: Merchandise trade balance

(Mln US$ by MDG Regions in 2014)

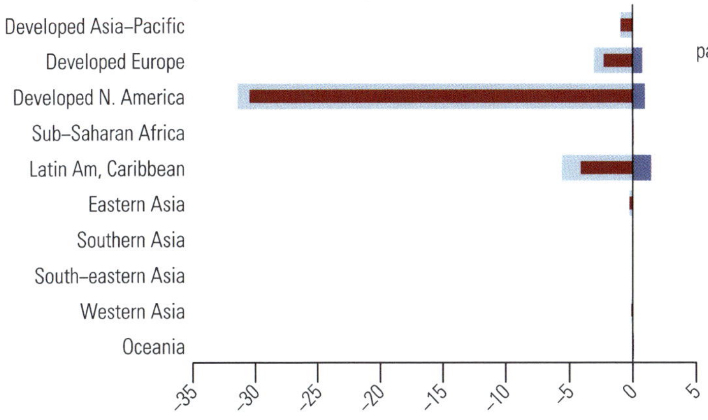

Graph 5: Partner concentration of merchandise trade

(Cumulative share by ranked partners in 2014)

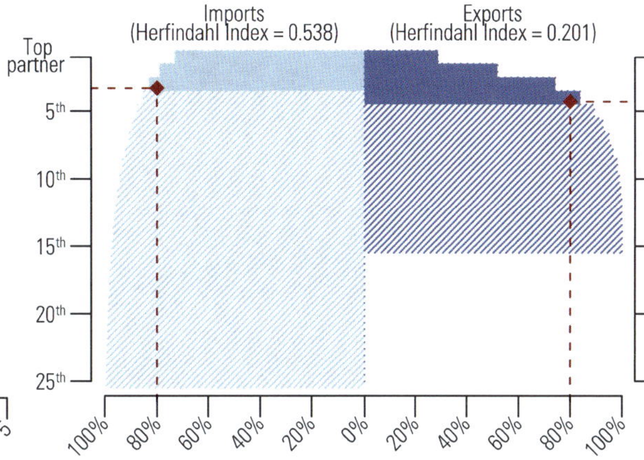

Graph 6: Imports of services by EBOPS category

(% share in 2013)

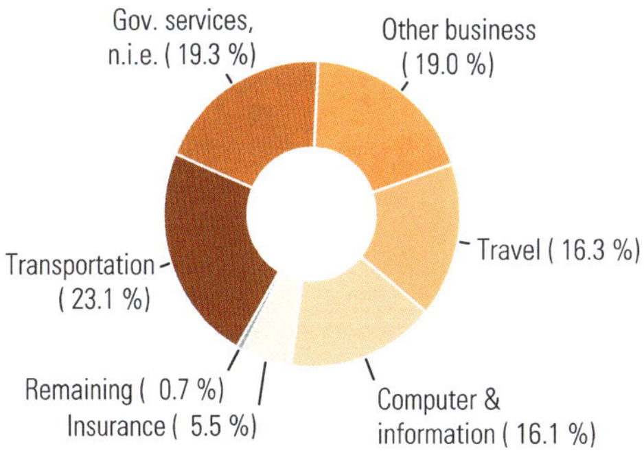

Imports Profile:

"Mineral fuels, lubricants" (SITC section 3), "Machinery and transport equipment" (SITC section 7) and "Food, animals + beverages, tobacco" (SITC section 0+1) were the largest commodity groups for imports in 2014, representing respectively 34.7, 19.5 and 16.5 percent of imported goods (see table 3). From 2012 to 2014, the largest import commodity was "Petroleum oils, other than crude" (HS code 2710) (see table 4). The top three partners for merchandise imports were the United States, Trinidad and Tobago and the United Kingdom, accounting for respectively 71.7, 6.5 and 4.0 percent of total imports. "Transportation" (EBOPS code 205) accounted for the largest share of imports of services in 2013 at 4.3 mln US$, followed by "Government services, n.i.e." (EBOPS code 291) at 3.6 mln US$ and "Other business services" (EBOPS code 268) at 3.5 mln US$ (see graph 6).

Table 4: Top 10 import commodities 2012 to 2014

HS code	4-digit heading of Harmonized System 2007	Value (million US$) 2012	2013	2014	Unit value 2012	2013	2014	Unit	SITC code
	All Commodities	36.9	42.1	41.9					
2710	Petroleum oils, other than crude	11.5	13.5	13.9	0.9	0.8	0.9	US$/kg	334
8703	Motor cars and other motor vehicles principally designed for the transport	1.0	1.2	1.3	*19.0*	*18.8*	*18.6*	thsd US$/unit	781
0207	Meat and edible offal, of the poultry of heading 01.05	0.7	0.7	0.7	2.3	2.1	2.5	US$/kg	012
2711	Petroleum gases and other gaseous hydrocarbons	0.7	0.7	0.7	1.0	1.0	1.1	US$/kg	343
8471	Automatic data processing machines and units thereof	0.6	0.5	0.7					752
2106	Food preparations not elsewhere specified or included	0.6	0.5	0.5	1.7	2.1	2.0	US$/kg	098
2523	Portland cement, aluminous cement, slag cement	0.5	0.5	0.5	0.1	0.2	0.2	US$/kg	661
2202	Waters with added sugar	0.6	0.5	0.4	*1.4*	*1.2*	*1.2*	US$/litre	111
2203	Beer made from malt	0.5	0.5	0.5	*1.2*	*1.2*	*1.1*	US$/litre	112
8517	Electrical apparatus for line telephony or line telegraphy	0.3	0.2	0.9					764

Source: UN Comtrade

Morocco

Goods Imports: CIF, by origin | **Goods Exports: FOB, by last known destination** | **Trade System: Special**

Overview:

In 2014, the value of merchandise exports of Morocco increased moderately by 8.4 percent to reach 23.8 bln US$, while its merchandise imports increased slightly by 2.2 percent to reach 46.2 bln US$ (see graph 1, table 2 and table 3). The merchandise trade balance recorded a large deficit of 22.4 bln US$ (see graph 1). The largest merchandise trade balance was with MDG Developed Europe at -8.4 bln US$ (see graph 4). Merchandise exports in Morocco were diversified amongst partners; imports were also diversified. The top 19 partners accounted for 80 percent or more of exports and 17 partners accounted for 80 percent or more of imports (see graph 5). In 2013, the value of exports of services of Morocco decreased slightly by 1.1 percent, reaching 13.5 bln US$, while its imports of services decreased slightly by 1.0 percent and reached 8.1 bln US$ (see graph 2). There was a moderate trade in services surplus of 5.4 bln US$.

Graph 1: Total merchandise trade, by value

(Bln US$ by year)

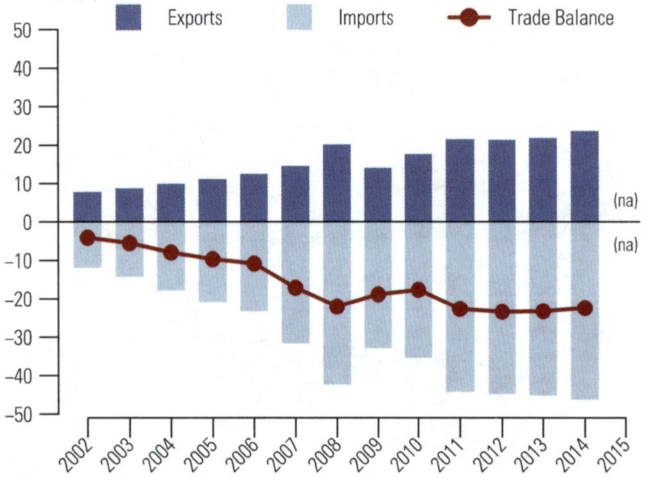

Graph 2: Total services trade, by value

(Bln US$ by year)

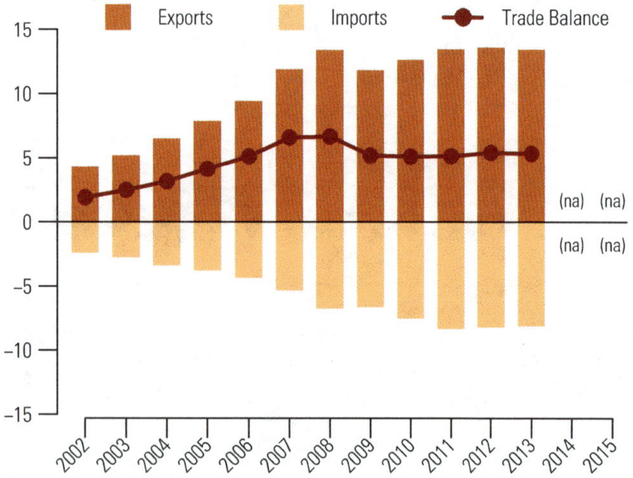

Exports Profile:

"Machinery and transport equipment" (SITC section 7), "Food, animals + beverages, tobacco" (SITC section 0+1) and "Miscellaneous manufactured articles" (SITC section 8) were the largest commodity groups for exports in 2014, representing respectively 29.3, 18.1 and 17.0 percent of exported goods (see table 2). From 2012 to 2014, the largest export commodity was "Insulated (including enamelled or anodised) wire, cable" (HS code 8544) (see table 1). The top three destinations for merchandise exports were France, Spain and Brazil, accounting for respectively 21.3, 19.2 and 5.5 percent of total exports. "Travel" (EBOPS code 236) accounted for the largest share of exports of services in 2013 at 6.9 bln US$, followed by "Transportation" (EBOPS code 205) at 2.6 bln US$ and "Other business services" (EBOPS code 268) at 2.1 bln US$ (see graph 3).

Graph 3: Exports of services by EBOPS category

(% share in 2013)

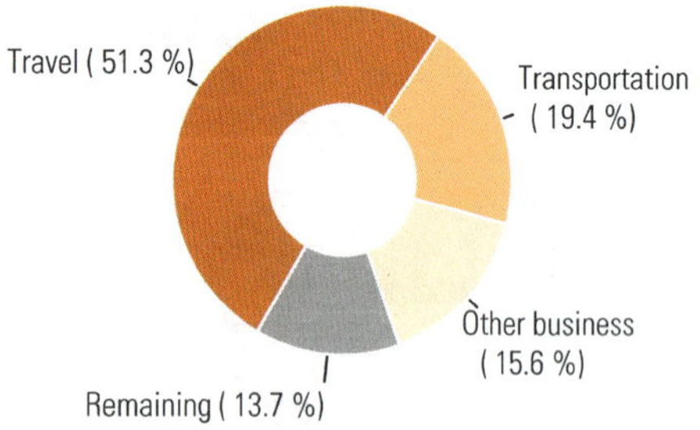

Table 1: Top 10 export commodities 2012 to 2014

HS code	4-digit heading of Harmonized System 2002	Value (million US$) 2012	2013	2014	Unit value 2012	2013	2014	Unit	SITC code
	All Commodities	21417.2	21965.4	23815.8					
8544	Insulated (including enamelled or anodised) wire, cable	1761.4	2084.8	2426.3	17.8	19.4	18.6	US$/kg	773
3105	Mineral or chemical fertilisers	2036.5	1504.0	1647.0	0.6	0.5	0.4	US$/kg	562
8703	Motor cars and other motor vehicles principally designed for the transport	836.6	1500.9	2293.2	*15.7*	*14.8*	*13.6*	thsd US$/unit	781
2809	Diphosphorus pentaoxide; phosphoric acid	1649.8	1433.5	1523.1	0.9	0.7	0.7	US$/kg	522
2510	Natural calcium phosphates	1543.5	1082.0	977.6	0.2	0.1	0.1	US$/kg	272
6204	Women's or girls' suits, ensembles, jackets, blazers, dresses, skirts	987.3	1046.5	1128.7					842
2710	Petroleum oils, other than crude	792.3	1068.0	743.0	1.0	0.9	0.9	US$/kg	334
1604	Prepared or preserved fish; caviar	643.7	679.4	702.8	4.6	4.7	4.4	US$/kg	037
0307	Molluscs, whether in shell or not	491.0	537.5	560.5	6.5	5.0	6.4	US$/kg	036
8541	Diodes, transistors and similar semiconductor devices	517.6	496.8	508.1					776

Services Imports and Exports: EBOPS 2002 categories

Table 2: Merchandise exports by SITC

(Value in million US$, growth and shares in percentage)

SITC	2014	Avg. Growth rates 2010-2014	Avg. Growth rates 2013-2014	2014 share
Total	23815.8	7.6	8.4	100.0
0+1	4301.4	7.6	6.9	18.1
2+4	2061.4	-1.0	-0.9	8.7
3	1206.3	19.7	-23.9	5.1
5	3944.2	3.2	7.6	16.6
6	1193.4	2.0	-2.1	5.0
7	6967.8	19.8	25.1	29.3
8	4039.3	2.5	6.5	17.0
9	102.0	-15.7	262.1	0.4

Table 3: Merchandise imports by SITC

(Value in million US$, growth and shares in percentage)

SITC	2014	Avg. Growth rates 2010-2014	Avg. Growth rates 2013-2014	2014 share
Total	46191.7	6.9	2.2	100.0
0+1	4972.4	9.4	17.0	10.8
2+4	2419.7	5.9	12.4	5.2
3	11067.1	8.0	-8.9	24.0
5	4698.9	7.6	4.0	10.2
6	8373.1	8.0	5.1	18.1
7	11938.6	4.9	0.7	25.8
8	2621.5	3.6	16.4	5.7
9	100.4	11.2	115.5	0.2

SITC Legend

SITC Code	Description
Total	All commodities
0+1	Food, animals + beverages, tobacco
2+4	Crude materials + anim. & veg. oils
3	Mineral fuels, lubricants
5	Chemicals
6	Goods classified chiefly by material
7	Machinery and transport equipment
8	Miscellaneous manufactured articles
9	Not classified elsewhere in the SITC

Graph 4: Merchandise trade balance

(Bln US$ by MDG Regions in 2014)

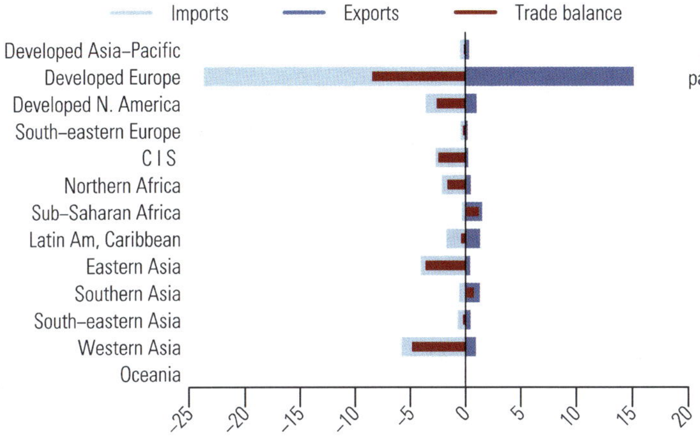

Graph 5: Partner concentration of merchandise trade

(Cumulative share by ranked partners in 2014)

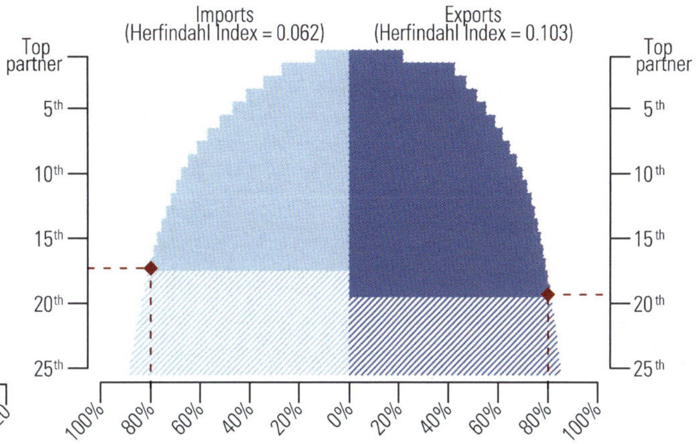

Graph 6: Imports of services by EBOPS category

(% share in 2013)

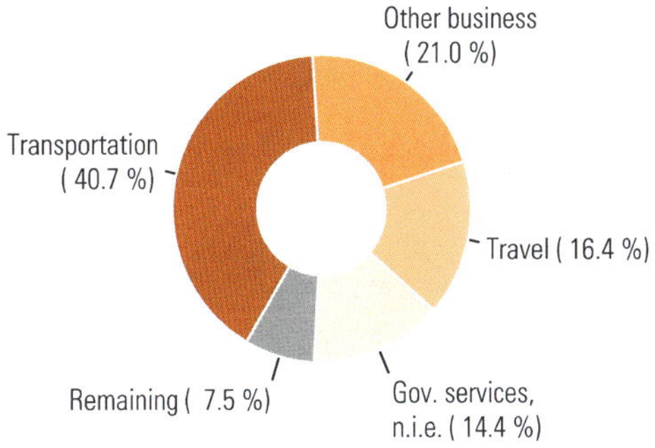

Imports Profile:

"Machinery and transport equipment" (SITC section 7), "Mineral fuels, lubricants" (SITC section 3) and "Goods classified chiefly by material" (SITC section 6) were the largest commodity groups for imports in 2014, representing respectively 25.8, 24.0 and 18.1 percent of imported goods (see table 3). From 2012 to 2014, the largest import commodity was "Petroleum oils, other than crude" (HS code 2710) (see table 4). The top three partners for merchandise imports were Spain, France and China, accounting for respectively 13.4, 12.9 and 7.1 percent of total imports. "Transportation" (EBOPS code 205) accounted for the largest share of imports of services in 2013 at 3.3 bln US$, followed by "Other business services" (EBOPS code 268) at 1.7 bln US$ and "Travel" (EBOPS code 236) at 1.3 bln US$ (see graph 6).

Table 4: Top 10 import commodities 2012 to 2014

HS code	4-digit heading of Harmonized System 2002	Value (million US$) 2012	2013	2014	Unit value 2012	2013	2014	Unit	SITC code
	All Commodities	44789.8	45186.4	46191.7					
2710	Petroleum oils, other than crude	4607.9	4533.4	4271.4	0.9	0.9	0.9	US$/kg	334
2709	Petroleum oils, crude	4352.0	4320.7	3374.2	0.8	0.7	0.7	US$/kg	333
2711	Petroleum gases and other gaseous hydrocarbons	2338.8	2274.8	2291.9	0.8	0.7	0.7	US$/kg	343
8703	Motor cars and other motor vehicles principally designed for the transport	1609.0	1502.5	1647.4	*18.2*	*18.4*	*19.3*	thsd US$/unit	781
1001	Wheat and meslin	1399.8	977.9	1514.3	0.3	0.4	0.3	US$/kg	041
8544	Insulated (including enamelled or anodised) wire, cable	609.6	788.6	1059.6	14.7	16.7	16.1	US$/kg	773
2503	Sulphur of all kinds	827.4	522.4	699.8	0.2	0.1	0.2	US$/kg	274
8708	Parts and accessories of the motor vehicles of headings 87.01 to 87.05	604.9	600.4	448.2	6.7	7.8	7.4	US$/kg	784
1005	Maize (corn)	636.2	484.2	506.6	0.3	0.3	0.2	US$/kg	044
2701	Coal; briquettes, ovoids and similar solid fuels manufactured from coal	540.3	437.1	591.6	0.1	0.1	0.1	US$/kg	321

Mozambique

Goods Imports: CIF, by origin	Goods Exports: FOB, by last known destination	Trade System: General

Overview:

In 2015, the value of merchandise exports of Mozambique decreased substantially by 32.4 percent to reach 3.2 bln US$, while its merchandise imports decreased moderately by 9.6 percent to reach 7.9 bln US$ (see graph 1, table 2 and table 3). The merchandise trade balance recorded a large deficit of 4.7 bln US$ (see graph 1). The largest merchandise trade balance was with MDG Sub-Saharan Africa at -1.9 bln US$ (see graph 4). Merchandise exports in Mozambique were diversified amongst partners; imports were also diversified. The top 11 partners accounted for 80 percent or more of exports and 12 partners accounted for 80 percent or more of imports (see graph 5). In 2014, the value of exports of services of Mozambique increased substantially by 12.3 percent, reaching 724.8 mln US$, while its imports of services decreased moderately by 6.3 percent and reached 3.7 bln US$ (see graph 2). There was a large trade in services deficit of 2.9 bln US$.

Graph 1: Total merchandise trade, by value

(Bln US$ by year)

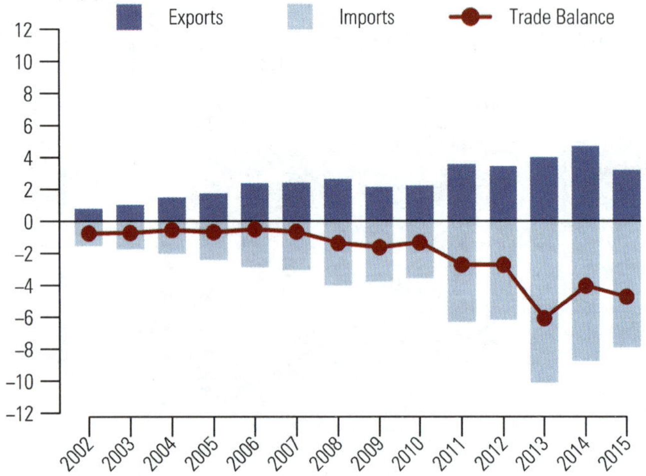

Graph 2: Total services trade, by value

(Bln US$ by year)

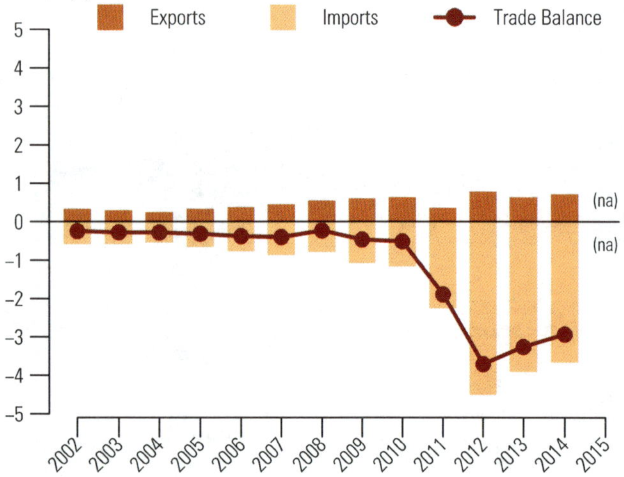

Exports Profile:

"Goods classified chiefly by material" (SITC section 6), "Mineral fuels, lubricants" (SITC section 3) and "Food, animals + beverages, tobacco" (SITC section 0+1) were the largest commodity groups for exports in 2015, representing respectively 37.4, 30.4 and 18.5 percent of exported goods (see table 2). From 2013 to 2015, the largest export commodity was "Aluminium bars, rods and profiles" (HS code 7604) (see table 1). The top three destinations for merchandise exports were the Netherlands, South Africa and India, accounting for respectively 26.9, 20.4 and 11.8 percent of total exports. "Transportation" (EBOPS code 205) accounted for the largest share of exports of services in 2014 at 432.5 mln US$, followed by "Travel" (EBOPS code 236) at 206.6 mln US$ and "Other business services" (EBOPS code 268) at 59.6 mln US$ (see graph 3).

Graph 3: Exports of services by EBOPS category

(% share in 2014)

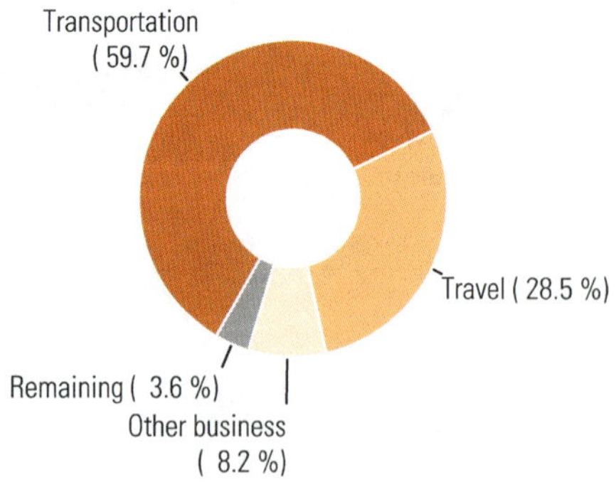

Table 1: Top 10 export commodities 2013 to 2015

HS code	4-digit heading of Harmonized System 2007	Value (million US$) 2013	2014	2015	Unit value 2013	2014	2015	Unit	SITC code
	All Commodities	4 023.7	4 725.3	3 196.1					
7604	Aluminium bars, rods and profiles	1 063.2	1 045.7	910.9	*13.3*		1.2	US$/kg	684
2704	Coke and semi-coke of coal, of lignite or of peat	526.6	484.1	387.3	0.3	0.2	0.1	US$/kg	325
2711	Petroleum gases and other gaseous hydrocarbons	445.4	568.7	231.1			2.2	US$/kg	343
2716	Electrical energy	275.5	301.2	316.9	27.7	36.8	*60.8*	US$/MWh	351
2401	Unmanufactured tobacco; tobacco refuse	257.3	258.0	292.6	4.4	4.4	4.3	US$/kg	121
7601	Unwrought aluminium	...	366.6	143.3		1.8	2.0	US$/kg	684
3802	Activated carbon; activated natural mineral products	52.5	442.4	...					598
1701	Cane or beet sugar and chemically pure sucrose, in solid form	185.7	81.7	118.3	0.6	0.6	0.4	US$/kg	061
2614	Titanium ores and concentrates	126.6	134.3	110.1	0.1		0.3	US$/kg	287
2710	Petroleum oils, other than crude	97.3	64.0	29.8	1.5	0.3	0.8	US$/kg	334

Table 2: Merchandise exports by SITC

(Value in million US$, growth and shares in percentage)

SITC	2015	Avg. Growth rates 2011-2015	Avg. Growth rates 2014-2015	2015 share
Total	3 196.1	-3.0	-32.4	100.0
0+1	590.3	-4.2	-4.9	18.5
2+4	297.0	-8.5	-40.1	9.3
3	970.9	13.4	-31.6	30.4
5	15.9	6.4	-96.7	0.5
6	1 194.9	-7.7	-23.2	37.4
7	86.6	-19.4	-17.0	2.7
8	40.5	9.6	-21.1	1.3
9	0.0	-47.3	-78.5	0.0

Table 3: Merchandise imports by SITC

(Value in million US$, growth and shares in percentage)

SITC	2015	Avg. Growth rates 2011-2015	Avg. Growth rates 2014-2015	2015 share
Total	7 907.6	5.8	-9.6	100.0
0+1	840.1	7.2	-10.3	10.6
2+4	223.8	1.6	-26.6	2.8
3	1 026.7	-8.9	-39.7	13.0
5	808.7	13.5	12.6	10.2
6	1 568.7	2.9	-12.3	19.8
7	3 002.7	13.0	6.9	38.0
8	436.9	15.6	-9.5	5.5
9	0.0	...	48.2	0.0

SITC Legend

SITC Code	Description
Total	All commodities
0+1	Food, animals + beverages, tobacco
2+4	Crude materials + anim. & veg. oils
3	Mineral fuels, lubricants
5	Chemicals
6	Goods classified chiefly by material
7	Machinery and transport equipment
8	Miscellaneous manufactured articles
9	Not classified elsewhere in the SITC

Graph 4: Merchandise trade balance

(Bln US$ by MDG Regions in 2015)

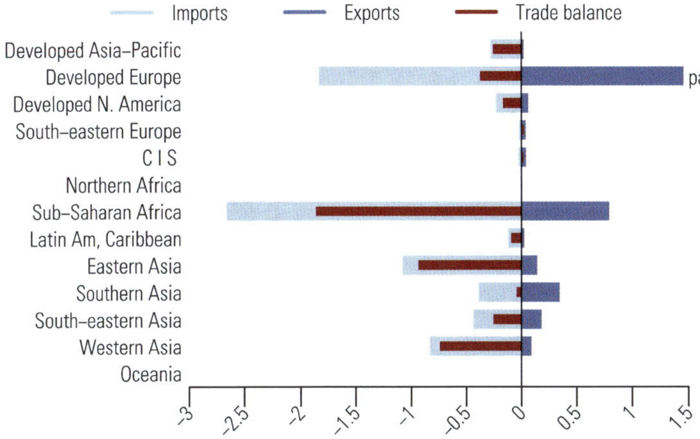

Graph 5: Partner concentration of merchandise trade

(Cumulative share by ranked partners in 2015)

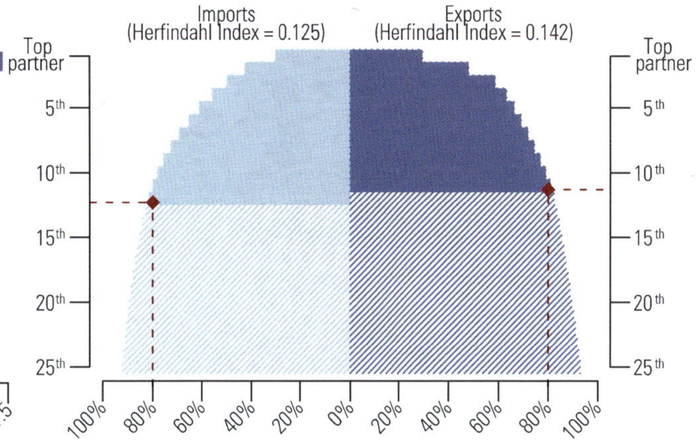

Graph 6: Imports of services by EBOPS category

(% share in 2014)

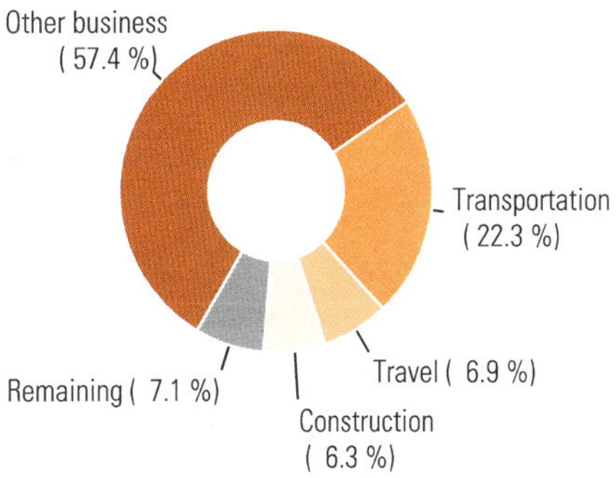

Imports Profile:

"Machinery and transport equipment" (SITC section 7), "Goods classified chiefly by material" (SITC section 6) and "Mineral fuels, lubricants" (SITC section 3) were the largest commodity groups for imports in 2015, representing respectively 38.0, 19.8 and 13.0 percent of imported goods (see table 3). From 2013 to 2015, the largest import commodity was "Petroleum oils, other than crude" (HS code 2710) (see table 4). The top three partners for merchandise imports were South Africa, China and Bahrain, accounting for respectively 32.0, 8.7 and 6.7 percent of total imports. "Other business services" (EBOPS code 268) accounted for the largest share of imports of services in 2014 at 2.1 bln US$, followed by "Transportation" (EBOPS code 205) at 815.4 mln US$ and "Travel" (EBOPS code 236) at 252.8 mln US$ (see graph 6).

Table 4: Top 10 import commodities 2013 to 2015

HS code	4-digit heading of Harmonized System 2007	Value (million US$) 2013	2014	2015	Unit value 2013	2014	2015	Unit	SITC code
	All Commodities	10 099.1	8 743.1	7 907.6					
2710	Petroleum oils, other than crude	2 063.1	1 350.2	713.1	1.1	1.0	0.7	US$/kg	334
7601	Unwrought aluminium	488.2	529.0	469.8					684
8704	Motor vehicles for the transport of goods	331.7	348.3	324.9			3.1	thsd US$/unit	782
9027	Instruments and apparatus for physical or chemical analysis	973.5	6.2	6.5					874
2716	Electrical energy	292.4	269.7	245.0	0.0			thsd US$/MWh	351
2711	Petroleum gases and other gaseous hydrocarbons	570.3	39.4	27.0		2.0	1.0	US$/kg	343
1006	Rice	248.7	187.4	152.4		0.1	0.2	US$/kg	042
3004	Medicaments (excluding goods of heading 30.02, 30.05 or 30.06)	136.9	143.6	277.1	24.2	17.6	24.4	US$/kg	542
8902	Fishing vessels; factory ships and other vessels for processing	0.0	0.0	527.1					793
8703	Motor cars and other motor vehicles principally designed for the transport	178.0	184.9	161.3					781

Namibia

Goods Imports: CIF, by origin	Goods Exports: FOB, by last known destination	Trade System: General

Overview:

In 2014, the value of merchandise exports of Namibia decreased moderately by 5.6 percent to reach 6.0 bln US$, while its merchandise imports increased substantially by 12.6 percent to reach 8.5 bln US$ (see graph 1, table 2 and table 3). The merchandise trade balance recorded a moderate deficit of 2.5 bln US$ (see graph 1). The largest merchandise trade balance was with MDG Sub-Saharan Africa at -2.7 bln US$ (see graph 4). Merchandise exports in Namibia were diversified amongst partners; imports were highly concentrated. The top 12 partners accounted for 80 percent or more of exports and 8 partners accounted for 80 percent or more of imports (see graph 5). In 2013, the value of exports of services of Namibia decreased substantially by 15.9 percent, reaching 570.3 mln US$, while its imports of services increased substantially by 15.2 percent and reached 804.8 mln US$ (see graph 2). There was a moderate trade in services deficit of 234.5 mln US$.

Graph 1: Total merchandise trade, by value

(Bln US$ by year)

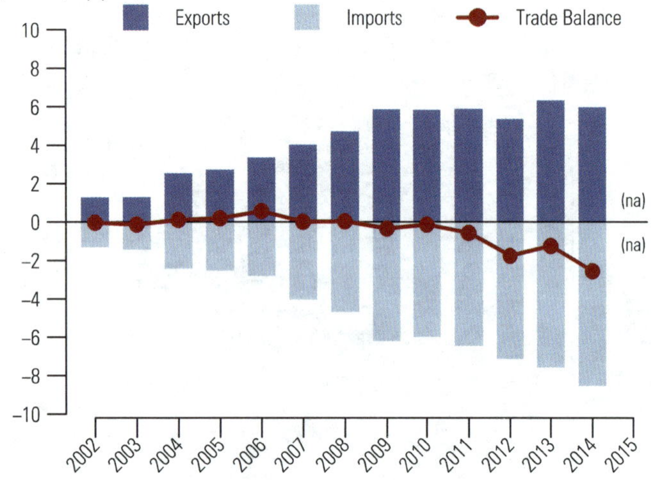

Graph 2: Total services trade, by value

(Mln US$ by year)

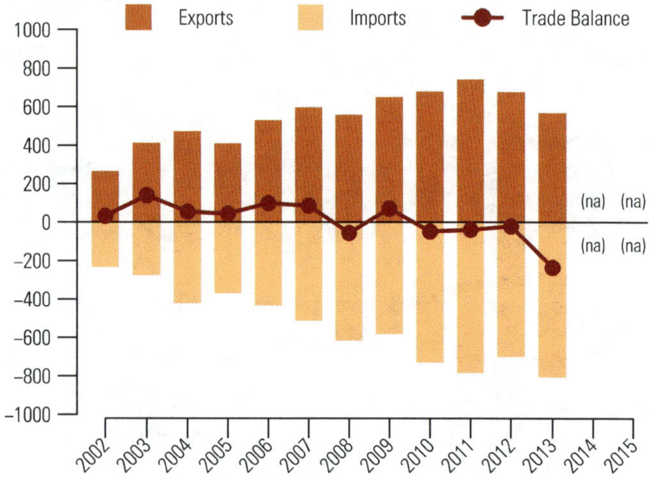

Exports Profile:

"Goods classified chiefly by material" (SITC section 6), "Machinery and transport equipment" (SITC section 7) and "Food, animals + beverages, tobacco" (SITC section 0+1) were the largest commodity groups for exports in 2014, representing respectively 37.0, 22.7 and 19.3 percent of exported goods (see table 2). From 2012 to 2014, the largest export commodity was "Diamonds, whether or not worked, but not mounted or set" (HS code 7102) (see table 1). The top three destinations for merchandise exports were South Africa, Botswana and Switzerland, accounting for respectively 19.2, 12.6 and 8.4 percent of total exports. "Travel" (EBOPS code 236) accounted for the largest share of exports of services in 2013 at 409.8 mln US$, followed by "Transportation" (EBOPS code 205) at 112.3 mln US$ (see graph 3).

Graph 3: Exports of services by EBOPS category

(% share in 2013)

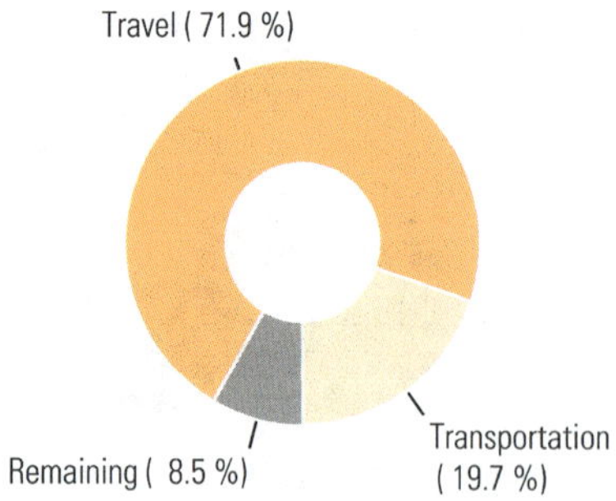

Table 1: Top 10 export commodities 2012 to 2014

HS code	4-digit heading of Harmonized System 2012	Value (million US$) 2012	2013	2014	Unit value 2012	2013	2014	Unit	SITC code
	All Commodities	5377.0	6337.2	5983.8					
7102	Diamonds, whether or not worked, but not mounted or set	1344.2	1338.6	1433.2					667
2612	Uranium or thorium ores and concentrates	613.0	639.1	417.0	100.9	88.1	79.4	US$/kg	286
0303	Fish, frozen, excluding fish fillets and other fish meat of heading 03.04	444.0	498.5	413.2	1.7	1.6	1.4	US$/kg	034
8905	Light-vessels, fire-floats, dredgers, floating cranes and other vessels	7.9	612.3	542.8	17.1			thsd US$/unit	793
7901	Unwrought zinc	272.0	274.1	301.4	2.0	2.2	2.4	US$/kg	686
2603	Copper ores and concentrates	176.6	215.0	227.4	4.3	4.3	4.7	US$/kg	283
7403	Refined copper and copper alloys, unwrought	91.5	194.1	317.2	8.7	12.0	7.2	US$/kg	682
0304	Fish fillets and other fish meat (whether or not minced)	197.4	168.4	167.7	4.2	4.0	4.1	US$/kg	034
2203	Beer made from malt	159.1	148.9	100.4	1.3	*1.0*	*1.0*	US$/litre	112
8904	Tugs and pusher craft	76.9	278.5	0.0	7.7			mln US$/unit	793

Services Imports and Exports: EBOPS 2002 categories

Table 2: Merchandise exports by SITC

(Value in million US$, growth and shares in percentage)

SITC	2014	Avg. Growth rates 2010-2014	Avg. Growth rates 2013-2014	2014 share
Total	5983.8	0.6	-5.6	100.0
0+1	1153.1	-5.5	-14.6	19.3
2+4	894.7	-3.5	-21.0	15.0
3	87.1	4.1	23.5	1.5
5	41.3	-5.5	5.8	0.7
6	2215.1	3.5	13.2	37.0
7	1359.2	38.1	-10.8	22.7
8	131.5	-36.6	-20.7	2.2
9	101.8	-5.1	4.1	1.7

Table 3: Merchandise imports by SITC

(Value in million US$, growth and shares in percentage)

SITC	2014	Avg. Growth rates 2010-2014	Avg. Growth rates 2013-2014	2014 share
Total	8531.0	9.3	12.6	100.0
0+1	942.4	2.4	-1.1	11.0
2+4	353.2	26.4	-40.0	4.1
3	537.2	-0.5	-28.3	6.3
5	653.8	0.7	3.7	7.7
6	1590.7	8.0	9.8	18.6
7	3677.6	17.6	47.2	43.1
8	766.1	2.5	9.7	9.0
9	10.0	-5.0	50.8	0.1

SITC Legend

SITC Code	Description
Total	All commodities
0+1	Food, animals + beverages, tobacco
2+4	Crude materials + anim. & veg. oils
3	Mineral fuels, lubricants
5	Chemicals
6	Goods classified chiefly by material
7	Machinery and transport equipment
8	Miscellaneous manufactured articles
9	Not classified elsewhere in the SITC

Graph 4: Merchandise trade balance

(Bln US$ by MDG Regions in 2014)

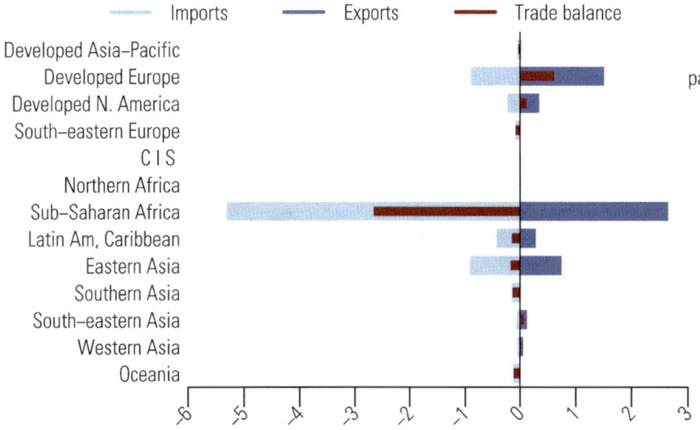

Graph 5: Partner concentration of merchandise trade

(Cumulative share by ranked partners in 2014)

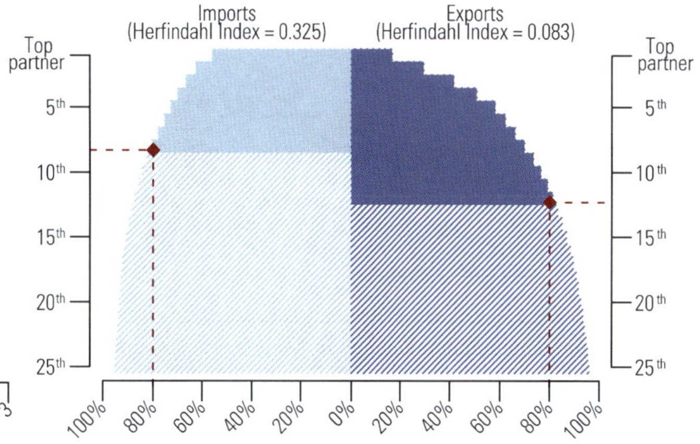

Graph 6: Imports of services by EBOPS category

(% share in 2013)

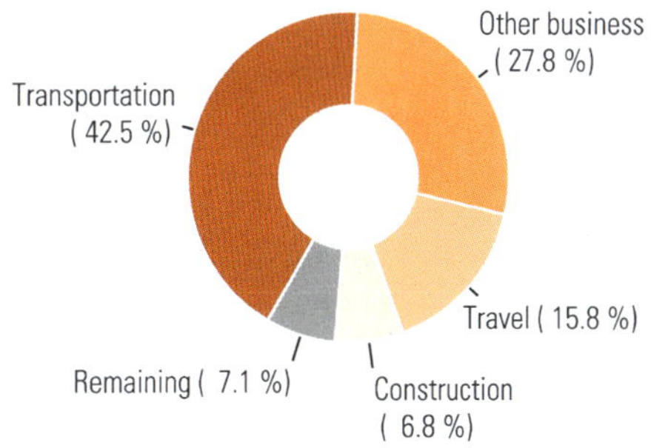

Imports Profile:

"Machinery and transport equipment" (SITC section 7), "Goods classified chiefly by material" (SITC section 6) and "Food, animals + beverages, tobacco" (SITC section 0+1) were the largest commodity groups for imports in 2014, representing respectively 43.1, 18.6 and 11.0 percent of imported goods (see table 3). From 2012 to 2014, the largest import commodity was "Petroleum oils, other than crude" (HS code 2710) (see table 4). The top three partners for merchandise imports were South Africa, Switzerland and China, accounting for respectively 62.1, 4.3 and 3.7 percent of total imports. "Transportation" (EBOPS code 205) accounted for the largest share of imports of services in 2013 at 342.3 mln US$, followed by "Other business services" (EBOPS code 268) at 223.6 mln US$ and "Travel" (EBOPS code 236) at 127.3 mln US$ (see graph 6).

Table 4: Top 10 import commodities 2012 to 2014

HS code	4-digit heading of Harmonized System 2012	Value (million US$) 2012	2013	2014	Unit value 2012	2013	2014	Unit	SITC code
	All Commodities	7132.0	7574.5	8531.0					
2710	Petroleum oils, other than crude	816.2	715.9	489.0	1.0	0.9	1.7	US$/kg	334
8703	Motor cars and other motor vehicles principally designed for the transport	423.6	379.9	377.9		*18.7*	*17.8*	thsd US$/unit	781
7102	Diamonds, whether or not worked, but not mounted or set	368.8	407.3	345.5					667
2603	Copper ores and concentrates	348.4	478.7	236.2	2.5	2.3	2.0	US$/kg	283
8905	Light-vessels, fire-floats, dredgers, floating cranes and other vessels	16.2	334.0	600.2	267.0			US$/unit	793
8704	Motor vehicles for the transport of goods	172.8	259.2	404.3					782
7403	Refined copper and copper alloys, unwrought	92.3	156.3	251.4	8.3	10.0	7.4	US$/kg	682
8429	Self-propelled bulldozers, angledozers, graders, levellers, scrapers	69.0	140.7	164.3	60.2			thsd US$/unit	723
3004	Medicaments (excluding goods of heading 30.02, 30.05 or 30.06)	128.3	115.9	116.6	24.6	31.1	25.5	US$/kg	542
8906	Other vessels, including warships and lifeboats other than rowing boats	9.2	0.1	331.4					793

Nepal

Goods Imports: CIF, by origin | **Goods Exports: FOB, by last known destination** | **Trade System: General**

Overview:

In 2015, the value of merchandise exports of Nepal decreased substantially by 26.7 percent to reach 660.2 mln US$, while its merchandise imports decreased substantially by 12.9 percent to reach 6.6 bln US$ (see graph 1, table 2 and table 3). The merchandise trade balance recorded a large deficit of 6.0 bln US$ (see graph 1). The largest merchandise trade balance was with MDG Southern Asia at -3.6 bln US$ (see graph 4). Merchandise exports in Nepal were highly concentrated amongst partners; imports were also highly concentrated. The top 4 partners accounted for 80 percent or more of exports and 4 partners accounted for 80 percent or more of imports (see graph 5). In 2014, the value of exports of services of Nepal increased substantially by 15.1 percent, reaching 1.4 bln US$, while its imports of services increased substantially by 19.9 percent and reached 1.2 bln US$ (see graph 2). There was a relatively small trade in services surplus of 188.4 mln US$.

Graph 1: Total merchandise trade, by value

(Bln US$ by year)

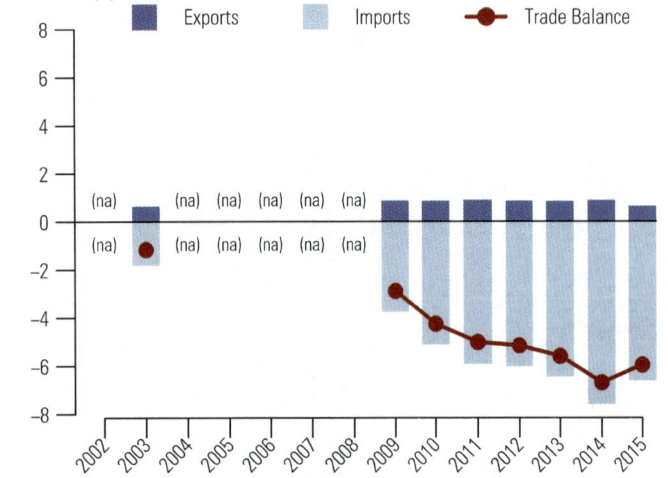

Graph 2: Total services trade, by value

(Bln US$ by year)

Exports Profile:

"Goods classified chiefly by material" (SITC section 6), "Food, animals + beverages, tobacco" (SITC section 0+1) and "Miscellaneous manufactured articles" (SITC section 8) were the largest commodity groups for exports in 2015, representing respectively 47.2, 26.7 and 16.6 percent of exported goods (see table 2). From 2013 to 2015, the largest export commodity was "Carpets and other textile floor coverings, knotted, whether or not made up" (HS code 5701) (see table 1). The top three destinations for merchandise exports were India, the United States and Germany, accounting for respectively 65.2, 8.8 and 3.8 percent of total exports. "Travel" (EBOPS code 236) accounted for the largest share of exports of services in 2014 at 477.6 mln US$, followed by "Government services, n.i.e." (EBOPS code 291) at 283.3 mln US$ and "Other business services" (EBOPS code 268) at 215.4 mln US$ (see graph 3).

Graph 3: Exports of services by EBOPS category

(% share in 2014)

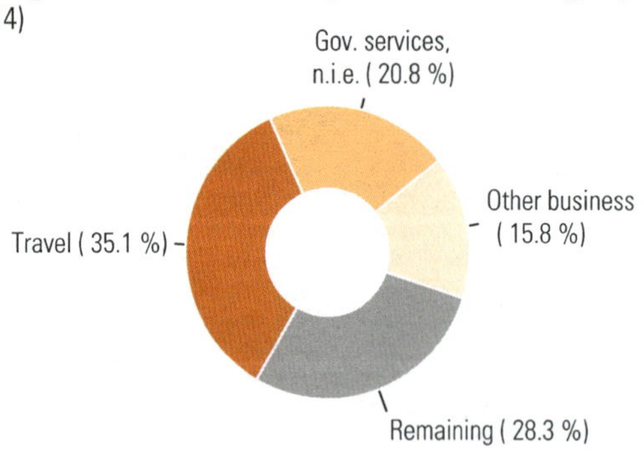

Table 1: Top 10 export commodities 2013 to 2015

HS code	4-digit heading of Harmonized System 2012	Value (million US$) 2013	2014	2015	Unit value 2013	2014	2015	Unit	SITC code
	All Commodities	863.3	900.9	660.2					
5701	Carpets and other textile floor coverings, knotted, whether or not made up	71.8	73.6	63.6	73.7	118.7	113.7	US$/m^2	659
5509	Yarn (other than sewing thread) of synthetic staple fibres	60.7	67.7	50.7	2.3	2.3	2.1	US$/kg	651
5407	Woven fabrics of synthetic filament yarn	59.2	56.7	35.3					653
7210	Flat-rolled products of iron or non-alloy steel	66.7	54.9	23.5	0.9	1.0	0.9	US$/kg	674
2009	Fruit juices (including grape must) and vegetable juices	44.8	43.3	36.2	*0.8*	*0.7*	*0.7*	US$/kg	059
6305	Sacks and bags, of a kind used for the packing of goods	32.9	34.1	29.1					658
0908	Nutmeg, mace and cardamoms	19.2	32.9	42.9	8.8	9.3	14.2	US$/kg	075
7306	Other tubes, pipes and hollow profiles	31.8	36.3	19.5	0.7	0.7	0.6	US$/kg	679
0802	Other nuts, fresh or dried, whether or not shelled or peeled	18.3	36.9	17.1	1.8	1.8	2.1	US$/kg	057
6204	Women's or girls'suits, ensembles, jackets, blazers, dresses, skirts	21.8	24.9	20.0	3.1	3.3	3.4	US$/unit	842

*Merchandise trade data up to 2009 reported by fiscal year and beginning 2010 reported by calendar year.

Services Imports and Exports: EBOPS 2002 categories

Table 2: Merchandise exports by SITC

(Value in million US$, growth and shares in percentage)

SITC	2015	Avg. Growth rates 2011-2015	Avg. Growth rates 2014-2015	2015 share
Total	660.2	-7.6	-26.7	100.0
0+1	176.3	1.6	-21.6	26.7
2+4	22.1	-18.1	-51.3	3.4
3	0.0	285.0	-73.2	0.0
5	34.5	-8.9	-28.2	5.2
6	311.9	-10.8	-29.1	47.2
7	5.6	-11.4	14.5	0.9
8	109.4	-6.2	-19.7	16.6
9	0.2	80.9	-87.1	0.0

Table 3: Merchandise imports by SITC

(Value in million US$, growth and shares in percentage)

SITC	2015	Avg. Growth rates 2011-2015	Avg. Growth rates 2014-2015	2015 share
Total	6612.1	2.8	-12.9	100.0
0+1	943.0	16.2	-6.1	14.3
2+4	437.5	-4.7	-23.0	6.6
3	881.0	-7.9	-41.2	13.3
5	855.4	4.6	3.7	12.9
6	1506.9	5.5	-2.3	22.8
7	1478.3	8.0	-0.9	22.4
8	369.5	0.8	-10.5	5.6
9	140.7	-14.9	-43.5	2.1

SITC Legend

SITC Code	Description
Total	All commodities
0+1	Food, animals + beverages, tobacco
2+4	Crude materials + anim. & veg. oils
3	Mineral fuels, lubricants
5	Chemicals
6	Goods classified chiefly by material
7	Machinery and transport equipment
8	Miscellaneous manufactured articles
9	Not classified elsewhere in the SITC

Graph 4: Merchandise trade balance

(Bln US$ by MDG Regions in 2015)

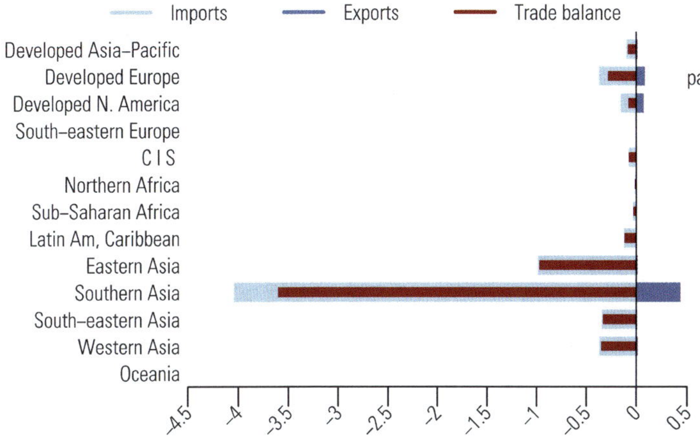

Graph 5: Partner concentration of merchandise trade

(Cumulative share by ranked partners in 2015)

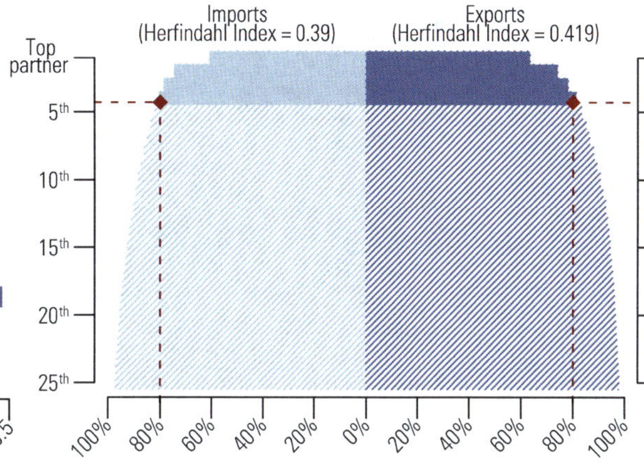

Graph 6: Imports of services by EBOPS category

(% share in 2014)

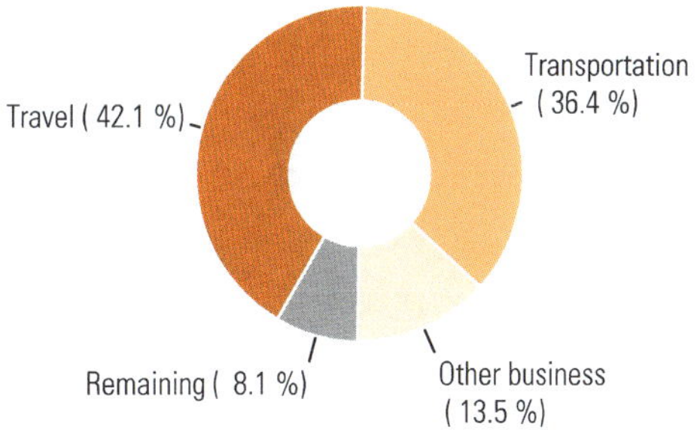

Imports Profile:

"Goods classified chiefly by material" (SITC section 6), "Machinery and transport equipment" (SITC section 7) and "Food, animals + beverages, tobacco" (SITC section 0+1) were the largest commodity groups for imports in 2015, representing respectively 22.8, 22.4 and 14.3 percent of imported goods (see table 3). From 2013 to 2015, the largest import commodity was "Petroleum oils, other than crude" (HS code 2710) (see table 4). The top three partners for merchandise imports were India, China and the United Arab Emirates, accounting for respectively 63.2, 11.9 and 5.2 percent of total imports. "Travel" (EBOPS code 236) accounted for the largest share of imports of services in 2014 at 493.3 mln US$, followed by "Transportation" (EBOPS code 205) at 426.5 mln US$ and "Other business services" (EBOPS code 268) at 158.1 mln US$ (see graph 6).

Table 4: Top 10 import commodities 2013 to 2015

HS code	4-digit heading of Harmonized System 2012	Value (million US$) 2013	2014	2015	Unit value 2013	2014	2015	Unit	SITC code
	All Commodities	6451.7	7590.1	6612.1					
2710	Petroleum oils, other than crude	866.0	1081.3	606.2	*1.7*	*5.1*	*1.6*	US$/kg	334
7207	Semi-finished products of iron or non-alloy steel	297.2	296.2	235.7	0.5	0.5	0.4	US$/kg	672
7108	Gold (including gold plated with platinum)	275.9	248.9	140.7	47.5	40.1	36.4	thsd US$/kg	971
2711	Petroleum gases and other gaseous hydrocarbons	221.8	284.0	148.3	1.2	1.0	0.7	US$/kg	343
1006	Rice	124.4	215.4	213.8	0.3	0.4	0.3	US$/kg	042
1507	Soya-bean oil and its fractions	302.8	140.3	104.4	1.0	1.0	0.9	US$/kg	421
8517	Electrical apparatus for line telephony or line telegraphy	97.9	181.9	186.8					764
7208	Flat-rolled products of iron or non-alloy steel	163.4	149.2	133.3	0.5	*0.6*	0.5	US$/kg	673
7106	Silver (including silver plated with gold or platinum)	93.2	132.2	197.7	697.6	608.1	532.2	US$/kg	681
2523	Portland cement, aluminous cement, slag cement	113.9	104.7	89.8	0.1	0.1	0.1	US$/kg	661

Netherlands

Goods Imports: CIF, by origin/consignment for intra-eu **Goods Exports: FOB, by last known destination** **Trade System: Special**

Overview:

In 2015, the value of merchandise exports of the Netherlands decreased substantially by 17.4 percent to reach 472.0 bln US$, while its merchandise imports decreased substantially by 17.5 percent to reach 419.1 bln US$ (see graph 1, table 2 and table 3). The merchandise trade balance recorded a relatively small surplus of 52.9 bln US$ (see graph 1). The largest merchandise trade balance was with MDG Developed Europe at 111.2 bln US$ (see graph 4). Merchandise exports in the Netherlands were diversified amongst partners; imports were also diversified. The top 21 partners accounted for 80 percent or more of exports and 20 partners accounted for 80 percent or more of imports (see graph 5). In 2014, the value of exports of services of the Netherlands increased moderately by 5.1 percent, reaching 188.3 bln US$, while its imports of services increased moderately by 9.6 percent and reached 166.1 bln US$ (see graph 2). There was a relatively small trade in services surplus of 22.1 bln US$.

Graph 1: Total merchandise trade, by value

(Bln US$ by year)

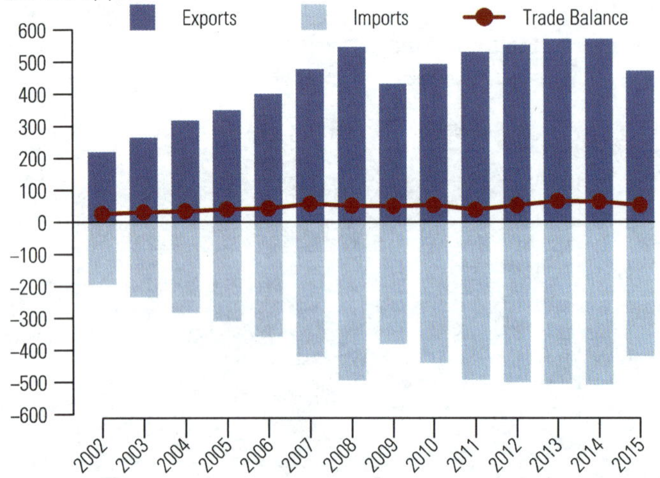

Graph 2: Total services trade, by value

(Bln US$ by year)

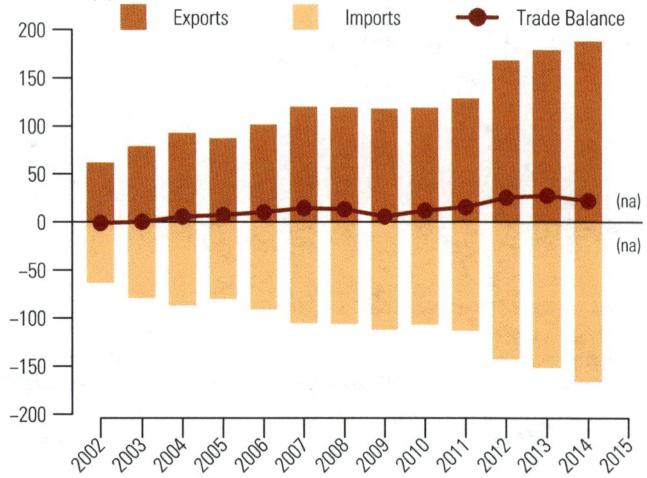

Exports Profile:

"Machinery and transport equipment" (SITC section 7), "Chemicals" (SITC section 5) and "Food, animals + beverages, tobacco" (SITC section 0+1) were the largest commodity groups for exports in 2015, representing respectively 28.0, 17.8 and 14.6 percent of exported goods (see table 2). From 2013 to 2015, the largest export commodity was "Petroleum oils, other than crude" (HS code 2710) (see table 1). The top three destinations for merchandise exports were Germany, Belgium and the United Kingdom, accounting for respectively 24.1, 10.9 and 8.6 percent of total exports. "Other business services" (EBOPS code 268) accounted for the largest share of exports of services in 2014 at 49.3 bln US$, followed by "Transportation" (EBOPS code 205) at 41.3 bln US$ and "Computer and information services" (EBOPS code 262) at 38.9 bln US$ (see graph 3).

Graph 3: Exports of services by EBOPS category

(% share in 2014)

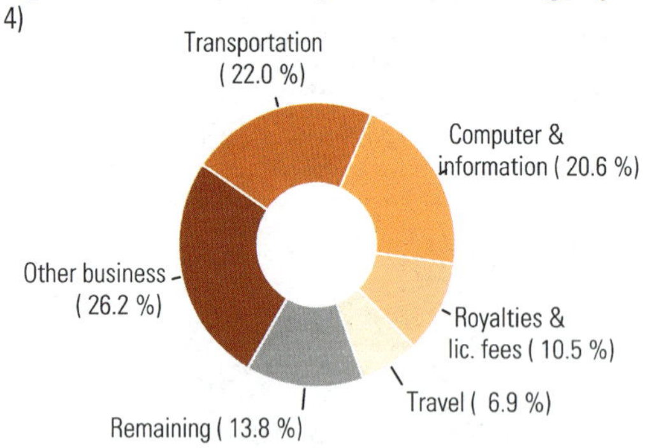

Table 1: Top 10 export commodities 2013 to 2015

HS code	4-digit heading of Harmonized System 2012	Value (million US$) 2013	2014	2015	Unit value 2013	2014	2015	Unit	SITC code
	All Commodities	571 246.9	571 347.5	471 957.7					
2710	Petroleum oils, other than crude	75 502.3	64 906.1	41 919.5	*0.9*	*0.8*	*0.5*	US$/kg	334
2711	Petroleum gases and other gaseous hydrocarbons	24 755.7	19 775.2	12 390.5	0.6	0.5	*0.4*	US$/kg	343
8517	Electrical apparatus for line telephony or line telegraphy	14 425.7	16 850.8	15 571.5					764
3004	Medicaments (excluding goods of heading 30.02, 30.05 or 30.06)	13 480.7	15 967.0	15 723.9	*228.5*	253.8	*218.6*	US$/kg	542
8471	Automatic data processing machines and units thereof	15 591.5	15 232.8	10 418.0	191.3	176.1	*160.9*	US$/unit	752
8443	Printing machinery used for printing by means of the printing type, blocks	9 958.8	9 936.3	8 439.6					726
8473	Parts and accessories for use with machines of heading 84.69 to 84.72	9 347.0	9 299.0	7 572.8	185.2	192.0	*267.0*	US$/kg	759
9018	Instruments and appliances used in medical, surgical, dental or veterinary	8 107.2	8 668.6	7 829.3					872
3002	Human blood; animal blood prepared for therapeutic uses	7 263.0	7 665.6	6 938.1	426.0	923.4	*821.5*	US$/kg	541
8486	Machines and apparatus used for the manufacture of semiconductor devices	6 861.2	7 920.1	6 596.4					728

Services Imports and Exports: EBOPS 2002 categories

Table 2: Merchandise exports by SITC

(Value in million US$, growth and shares in percentage)

SITC	2015	Avg. Growth rates 2011-2015	Avg. Growth rates 2014-2015	2015 share
Total	471 957.7	-2.9	-17.4	100.0
0+1	69 137.8	-2.4	-16.5	14.6
2+4	25 884.9	-6.8	-18.0	5.5
3	62 476.9	-3.8	-35.2	13.2
5	84 131.1	-1.2	-14.4	17.8
6	40 586.1	-5.0	-18.1	8.6
7	132 192.6	-3.8	-13.7	28.0
8	50 956.9	0.0	-10.5	10.8
9	6 591.4	14.0	138.7	1.4

Table 3: Merchandise imports by SITC

(Value in million US$, growth and shares in percentage)

SITC	2015	Avg. Growth rates 2011-2015	Avg. Growth rates 2014-2015	2015 share
Total	419 077.2	-4.0	-17.5	100.0
0+1	45 660.2	-2.1	-12.8	10.9
2+4	19 833.2	-8.0	-16.2	4.7
3	66 208.3	-10.7	-38.3	15.8
5	55 668.3	-1.9	-10.9	13.3
6	39 154.9	-6.8	-18.9	9.3
7	128 302.8	-2.6	-11.7	30.6
8	52 906.9	-0.9	-7.3	12.6
9	11 342.7	47.5	-3.0	2.7

SITC Legend

SITC Code	Description
Total	All commodities
0+1	Food, animals + beverages, tobacco
2+4	Crude materials + anim. & veg. oils
3	Mineral fuels, lubricants
5	Chemicals
6	Goods classified chiefly by material
7	Machinery and transport equipment
8	Miscellaneous manufactured articles
9	Not classified elsewhere in the SITC

Graph 4: Merchandise trade balance

(Bln US$ by MDG Regions in 2015)

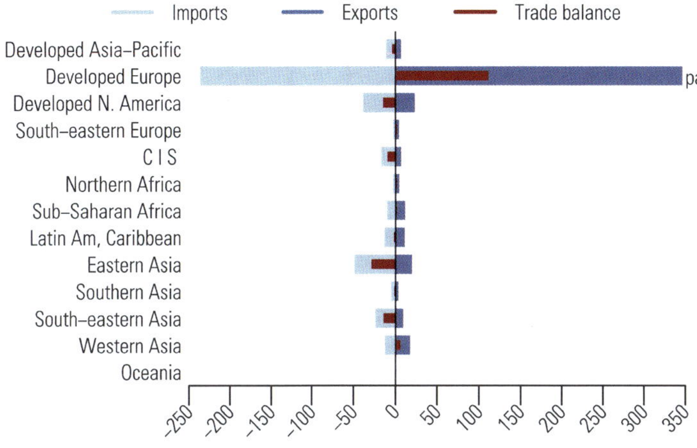

Graph 5: Partner concentration of merchandise trade

(Cumulative share by ranked partners in 2015)

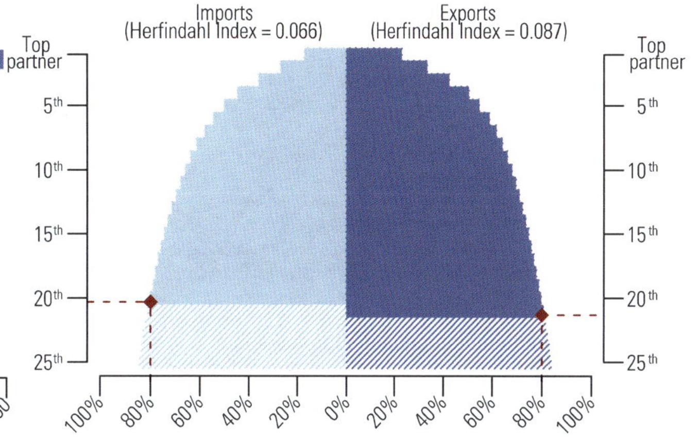

Graph 6: Imports of services by EBOPS category

(% share in 2014)

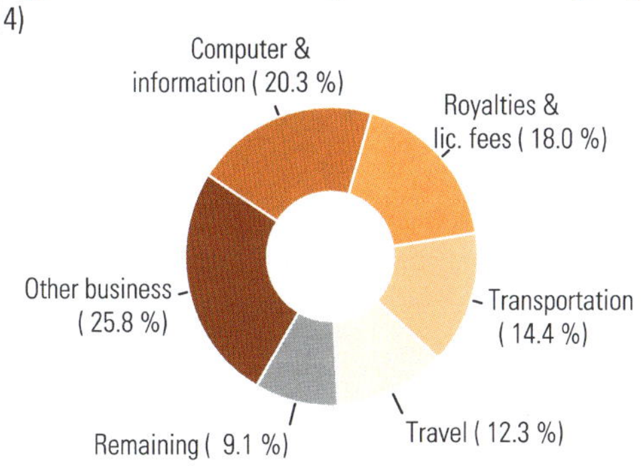

Imports Profile:

"Machinery and transport equipment" (SITC section 7), "Mineral fuels, lubricants" (SITC section 3) and "Chemicals" (SITC section 5) were the largest commodity groups for imports in 2015, representing respectively 30.6, 15.8 and 13.3 percent of imported goods (see table 3). From 2013 to 2015, the largest import commodity was "Petroleum oils and oils obtained from bituminous minerals, crude" (HS code 2709) (see table 4). The top three partners for merchandise imports were Germany, Belgium and China, accounting for respectively 16.7, 9.7 and 8.9 percent of total imports. "Other business services" (EBOPS code 268) accounted for the largest share of imports of services in 2014 at 42.9 bln US$, followed by "Computer and information services" (EBOPS code 262) at 33.7 bln US$ and "Royalties and license fees" (EBOPS code 266) at 30.0 bln US$ (see graph 6).

Table 4: Top 10 import commodities 2013 to 2015

HS code	4-digit heading of Harmonized System 2012	Value (million US$) 2013	Value (million US$) 2014	Value (million US$) 2015	Unit value 2013	Unit value 2014	Unit value 2015	Unit	SITC code
	All Commodities	506 162.3	508 032.9	419 077.2					
2709	Petroleum oils and oils obtained from bituminous minerals, crude	52 164.0	46 622.3	25 234.0	0.8	0.8	0.4	US$/kg	333
2710	Petroleum oils, other than crude	50 573.8	40 159.1	26 029.4	*0.9*	*0.8*	*0.5*	US$/kg	334
8517	Electrical apparatus for line telephony or line telegraphy	17 873.7	18 752.2	19 730.7					764
8471	Automatic data processing machines and units thereof	17 645.4	18 101.6	12 081.8	172.1	*166.0*	*158.4*	US$/unit	752
2711	Petroleum gases and other gaseous hydrocarbons	12 897.9	12 396.6	10 046.4	*1.9*	0.6	*0.4*	US$/kg	343
3004	Medicaments (excluding goods of heading 30.02, 30.05 or 30.06)	12 142.0	11 241.7	11 172.7	*163.1*	140.0	*148.5*	US$/kg	542
8703	Motor cars and other motor vehicles principally designed for the transport	11 015.3	11 562.0	9 507.4	*18.7*	*18.5*	*16.4*	thsd US$/unit	781
8443	Printing machinery used for printing by means of the printing type, blocks	8 740.8	8 405.6	8 204.9					726
8473	Parts and accessories for use with machines of heading 84.69 to 84.72	8 477.1	8 360.6	7 464.0	190.5	*184.0*	*221.9*	US$/kg	759
9999	Commodities not specified according to kind	263.2	10 881.2	10 463.8					931

New Caledonia

Goods Imports: CIF, by consignment | **Goods Exports: FOB, by last known destination** | **Trade System: General**

Overview:

In 2014, the value of merchandise exports of New Caledonia increased substantially by 30.8 percent to reach 1.6 bln US$, while its merchandise imports increased slightly by 2.4 percent to reach 3.3 bln US$ (see graph 1, table 2 and table 3). The merchandise trade balance recorded a large deficit of 1.7 bln US$ (see graph 1). The largest merchandise trade balance was with MDG Developed Europe at -899.5 mln US$ (see graph 4). Merchandise exports in New Caledonia were diversified amongst partners; imports were also diversified. The top 7 partners accounted for 80 percent or more of exports and 11 partners accounted for 80 percent or more of imports (see graph 5). In 2011, the value of exports of services of New Caledonia increased slightly by 2.3 percent, reaching 497.7 mln US$, while its imports of services decreased slightly by 1.2 percent and reached 1.4 bln US$ (see graph 2). There was a large trade in services deficit of 876.0 mln US$.

Graph 1: Total merchandise trade, by value

(Bln US$ by year)

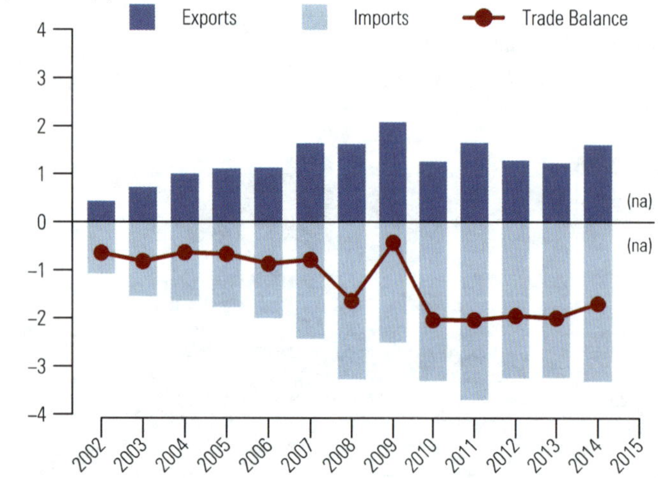

Graph 2: Total services trade, by value

(Bln US$ by year)

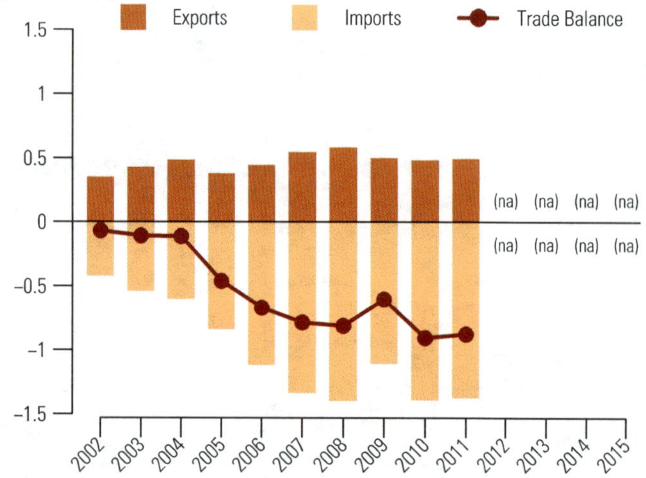

Exports Profile:

"Goods classified chiefly by material" (SITC section 6), "Crude materials + anim. & veg. oils" (SITC section 2+4) and "Chemicals" (SITC section 5) were the largest commodity groups for exports in 2014, representing respectively 53.3, 32.2 and 9.1 percent of exported goods (see table 2). From 2012 to 2014, the largest export commodity was "Ferro-alloys" (HS code 7202) (see table 1). The top three destinations for merchandise exports were Japan, France and China, accounting for respectively 15.2, 14.7 and 14.0 percent of total exports. "Travel" (EBOPS code 236) accounted for the largest share of exports of services in 2011 at 146.8 mln US$, followed by "Transportation" (EBOPS code 205) at 132.7 mln US$ and "Government services, n.i.e." (EBOPS code 291) at 106.9 mln US$ (see graph 3).

Graph 3: Exports of services by EBOPS category

(% share in 2011)

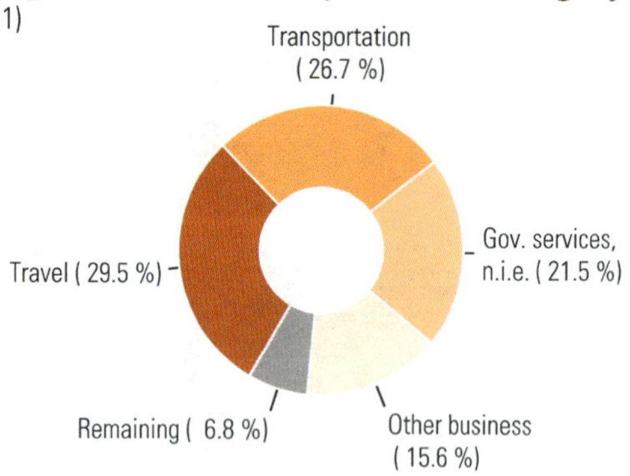

Table 1: Top 10 export commodities 2012 to 2014

HS code	4-digit heading of Harmonized System 2007	Value (million US$) 2012	2013	2014	Unit value 2012	2013	2014	Unit	SITC code
	All Commodities	1 292.9	1 237.4	1 619.0					
7202	Ferro-alloys	674.4	546.0	853.2	3.6	3.2	3.8	US$/kg	671
7501	Nickel mattes, nickel oxide sinters and other intermediate products	202.8	259.1	246.1	10.4	9.1	11.4	US$/kg	284
2604	Nickel ores and concentrates	243.4	195.3	264.8	0.1	0.0	0.0	US$/kg	284
2825	Hydrazine and hydroxylamine and their inorganic salts	79.3	88.0	130.4	3.8			US$/kg	522
9999	Commodities not specified according to kind	18.0	18.5	23.4					931
0306	Crustaceans, whether in shell or not	12.3	14.5	15.9	15.1	16.7	16.6	US$/kg	036
7204	Ferrous waste and scrap; remelting scrap ingots of iron or steel	3.3	14.3	6.7	0.6	0.6	1.8	US$/kg	282
2836	Carbonates; peroxocarbonates (percarbonates)	1.2	13.2	9.1	9.3	8.8	9.1	US$/kg	523
8609	Containers (including containers for the transport of fluids)	3.0	6.3	3.4					786
3301	Essential oils (terpeneless or not), including concretes	3.2	4.2	5.0	453.2	637.2	620.7	US$/kg	551

Source: UN Comtrade

Services Imports and Exports: EBOPS 2002 categories

Table 2: Merchandise exports by SITC

(Value in million US$, growth and shares in percentage)

SITC	2014	Avg. Growth rates 2010-2014	Avg. Growth rates 2013-2014	2014 share
Total	1619.0	6.3	30.8	100.0
0+1	26.4	4.8	3.9	1.6
2+4	521.9	0.3	7.7	32.2
3	0.0	-56.9	-80.9	0.0
5	147.8	117.8	36.2	9.1
6	863.4	5.8	56.5	53.3
7	28.8	15.1	-28.1	1.8
8	6.9	-13.9	-7.3	0.4
9	23.7	51.1	21.5	1.5

Table 3: Merchandise imports by SITC

(Value in million US$, growth and shares in percentage)

SITC	2014	Avg. Growth rates 2010-2014	Avg. Growth rates 2013-2014	2014 share
Total	3315.2	0.1	2.4	100.0
0+1	436.7	5.1	1.8	13.2
2+4	76.9	11.3	8.4	2.3
3	869.9	13.4	2.3	26.2
5	261.5	0.6	-6.2	7.9
6	376.6	-2.1	9.0	11.4
7	930.6	0.2	9.1	28.1
8	320.9	1.6	1.5	9.7
9	42.1	-45.6	-54.7	1.3

SITC Legend

SITC Code	Description
Total	All commodities
0+1	Food, animals + beverages, tobacco
2+4	Crude materials + anim. & veg. oils
3	Mineral fuels, lubricants
5	Chemicals
6	Goods classified chiefly by material
7	Machinery and transport equipment
8	Miscellaneous manufactured articles
9	Not classified elsewhere in the SITC

Graph 4: Merchandise trade balance

(Bln US$ by MDG Regions in 2014)

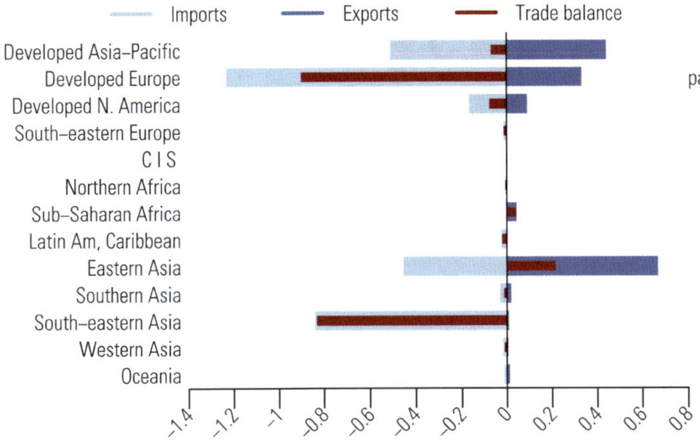

Graph 5: Partner concentration of merchandise trade

(Cumulative share by ranked partners in 2014)

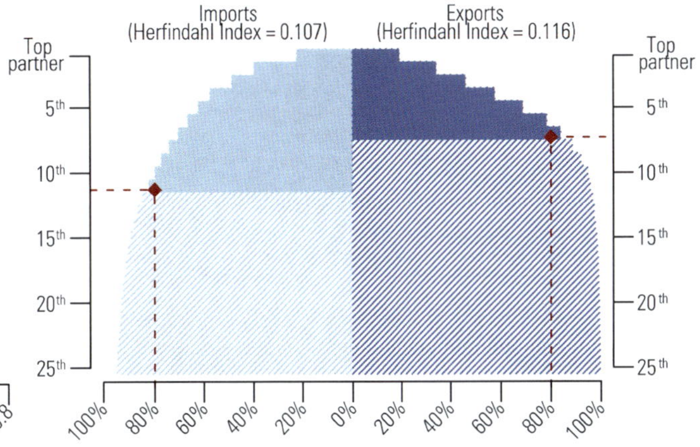

Graph 6: Imports of services by EBOPS category

(% share in 2011)

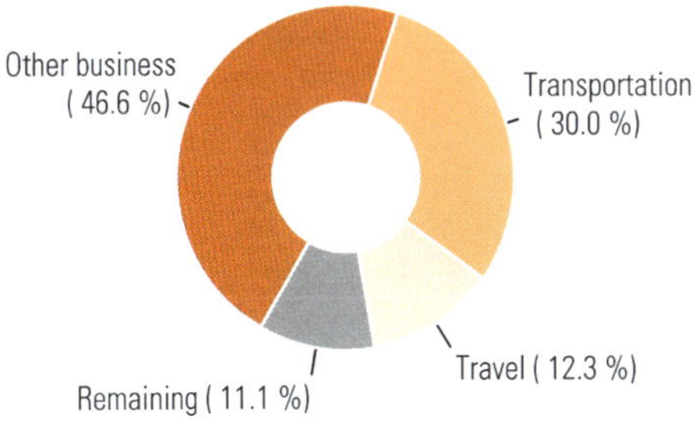

Imports Profile:

"Machinery and transport equipment" (SITC section 7), "Mineral fuels, lubricants" (SITC section 3) and "Food, animals + beverages, tobacco" (SITC section 0+1) were the largest commodity groups for imports in 2014, representing respectively 28.1, 26.2 and 13.2 percent of imported goods (see table 3). From 2012 to 2014, the largest import commodity was "Petroleum oils, other than crude" (HS code 2710) (see table 4). The top three partners for merchandise imports were France, Singapore and Australia, accounting for respectively 22.6, 18.5 and 9.6 percent of total imports. "Other business services" (EBOPS code 268) accounted for the largest share of imports of services in 2011 at 640.6 mln US$, followed by "Transportation" (EBOPS code 205) at 412.4 mln US$ and "Travel" (EBOPS code 236) at 168.5 mln US$ (see graph 6).

Table 4: Top 10 import commodities 2012 to 2014

HS code	4-digit heading of Harmonized System 2007	Value (million US$) 2012	Value (million US$) 2013	Value (million US$) 2014	Unit value 2012	Unit value 2013	Unit value 2014	Unit	SITC code
	All Commodities	3245.0	3237.0	3315.2					
2710	Petroleum oils, other than crude	641.3	742.9	762.7	0.9	0.8	0.8	US$/kg	334
8703	Motor cars and other motor vehicles principally designed for the transport	185.1	166.1	169.5	*19.4*	*18.9*	*19.4*	thsd US$/unit	781
9999	Commodities not specified according to kind	188.1	92.8	41.9					931
3004	Medicaments (excluding goods of heading 30.02, 30.05 or 30.06)	76.5	74.8	75.0	63.1	60.9	54.2	US$/kg	542
2701	Coal; briquettes, ovoids and similar solid fuels manufactured from coal	79.3	70.3	63.4	0.2	0.1	0.1	US$/kg	321
8704	Motor vehicles for the transport of goods	64.6	43.5	83.8					782
8429	Self-propelled bulldozers, angledozers, graders, levellers, scrapers	36.3	22.7	51.0		*77.9*		thsd US$/unit	723
8471	Automatic data processing machines and units thereof	34.1	35.4	35.6					752
4011	New pneumatic tyres, of rubber	32.9	36.0	34.7					625
8708	Parts and accessories of the motor vehicles of headings 87.01 to 87.05	31.1	32.2	34.9	21.1	22.2	20.6	US$/kg	784

New Zealand

Goods Imports: CIF, by origin | **Goods Exports: FOB, by last known destination** | **Trade System: General**

Overview:

In 2015, the value of merchandise exports of New Zealand decreased substantially by 17.9 percent to reach 34.2 bln US$, while its merchandise imports decreased substantially by 14.5 percent to reach 36.3 bln US$ (see graph 1, table 2 and table 3). The merchandise trade balance recorded a relatively small deficit of 2.2 bln US$ (see graph 1). The largest merchandise trade balance was with MDG Developed Europe at -2.9 bln US$ (see graph 4). Merchandise exports in New Zealand were diversified amongst partners; imports were also diversified. The top 19 partners accounted for 80 percent or more of exports and 15 partners accounted for 80 percent or more of imports (see graph 5). In 2014, the value of exports of services of New Zealand increased moderately by 6.9 percent, reaching 14.3 bln US$, while its imports of services increased slightly by 4.1 percent and reached 13.0 bln US$ (see graph 2). There was a relatively small trade in services surplus of 1.3 bln US$.

Graph 1: Total merchandise trade, by value

(Bln US$ by year)

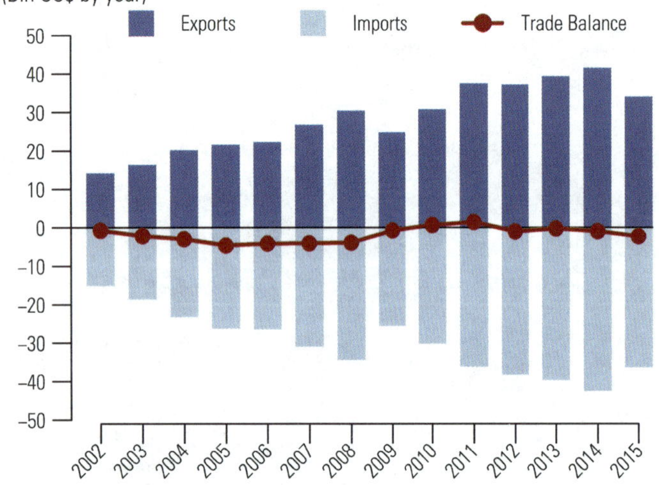

Graph 2: Total services trade, by value

(Bln US$ by year)

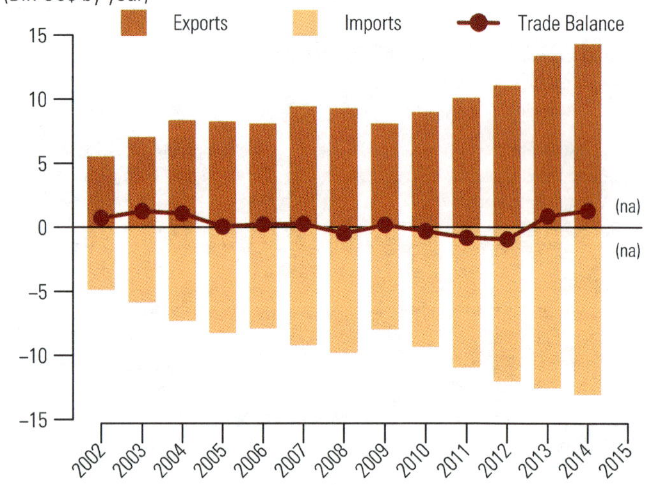

Exports Profile:

"Food, animals + beverages, tobacco" (SITC section 0+1), "Crude materials + anim. & veg. oils" (SITC section 2+4) and "Goods classified chiefly by material" (SITC section 6) were the largest commodity groups for exports in 2015, representing respectively 57.3, 12.3 and 7.5 percent of exported goods (see table 2). From 2013 to 2015, the largest export commodity was "Milk and cream, concentrated or containing added sugar" (HS code 0402) (see table 1). The top three destinations for merchandise exports were China, Australia and the United States, accounting for respectively 19.5, 17.9 and 9.8 percent of total exports. "Travel" (EBOPS code 236) accounted for the largest share of exports of services in 2014 at 8.4 bln US$, followed by "Transportation" (EBOPS code 205) at 2.1 bln US$ and "Other business services" (EBOPS code 268) at 1.6 bln US$ (see graph 3).

Graph 3: Exports of services by EBOPS category

(% share in 2014)

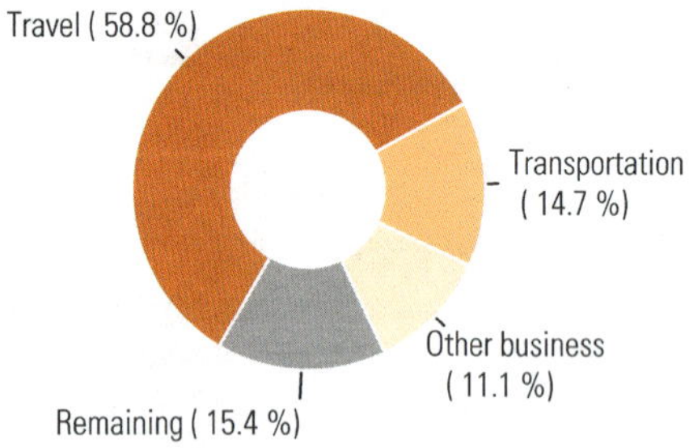

Table 1: Top 10 export commodities 2013 to 2015

HS code	4-digit heading of Harmonized System 2012	Value (million US$) 2013	2014	2015	Unit value 2013	2014	2015	Unit	SITC code
	All Commodities	39443.6	41635.6	34166.8					
0402	Milk and cream, concentrated or containing added sugar	7142.5	7647.9	4439.2	4.2	4.2	2.4	US$/kg	022
0204	Meat of sheep or goats, fresh, chilled or frozen	2240.1	2494.4	2135.7	5.4	6.0	5.1	US$/kg	012
0405	Butter and other fats and oils derived from milk; dairy spreads	1824.7	2149.8	1629.1	3.8	4.0	3.1	US$/kg	023
0202	Meat of bovine animals, frozen	1508.7	1825.1	2044.4	4.3	4.7	4.8	US$/kg	011
4403	Wood in the rough, whether or not stripped of bark or sapwood	1931.3	1890.5	1388.7	*116.3*	113.9	90.2	US$/m³	247
9999	Commodities not specified according to kind	1325.8	1482.1	1083.0					931
0406	Cheese and curd	1156.1	1280.8	1158.7	4.0	4.4	3.4	US$/kg	024
2204	Wine of fresh grapes, including fortified wines	1030.3	1123.5	1071.2	*5.9*	*5.8*	5.0	US$/litre	112
2709	Petroleum oils and oils obtained from bituminous minerals, crude	1176.4	1128.6	506.9	0.8	0.8	0.4	US$/kg	333
0810	Other fruit, fresh	692.2	869.4	1034.9	1.9	*2.2*	*2.0*	US$/kg	057

Services Imports and Exports: EBOPS 2002 categories

Table 2: Merchandise exports by SITC

(Value in million US$, growth and shares in percentage)

SITC	2015	Avg. Growth rates 2011-2015	Avg. Growth rates 2014-2015	2015 share
Total	34 166.8	-2.4	-17.9	100.0
0+1	19 592.4	-0.5	-19.1	57.3
2+4	4 208.2	-1.5	-16.9	12.3
3	626.7	-24.7	-52.4	1.8
5	1 913.4	3.7	-8.5	5.6
6	2 554.6	-6.7	-15.8	7.5
7	2 462.2	-4.5	-3.9	7.2
8	1 393.0	0.0	-8.7	4.1
9	1 416.3	-6.9	-22.7	4.1

Table 3: Merchandise imports by SITC

(Value in million US$, growth and shares in percentage)

SITC	2015	Avg. Growth rates 2011-2015	Avg. Growth rates 2014-2015	2015 share
Total	36 333.7	0.2	-14.5	100.0
0+1	3 960.9	1.8	-10.4	10.9
2+4	941.5	-1.0	-2.0	2.6
3	3 614.8	-12.7	-43.3	9.9
5	3 976.7	-1.2	-10.0	10.9
6	4 033.6	-0.6	-10.0	11.1
7	14 352.8	4.9	-11.0	39.5
8	5 187.4	2.2	-4.3	14.3
9	266.1	-3.1	-10.7	0.7

SITC Legend

SITC Code	Description
Total	All commodities
0+1	Food, animals + beverages, tobacco
2+4	Crude materials + anim. & veg. oils
3	Mineral fuels, lubricants
5	Chemicals
6	Goods classified chiefly by material
7	Machinery and transport equipment
8	Miscellaneous manufactured articles
9	Not classified elsewhere in the SITC

Graph 4: Merchandise trade balance

(Bln US$ by MDG Regions in 2015)

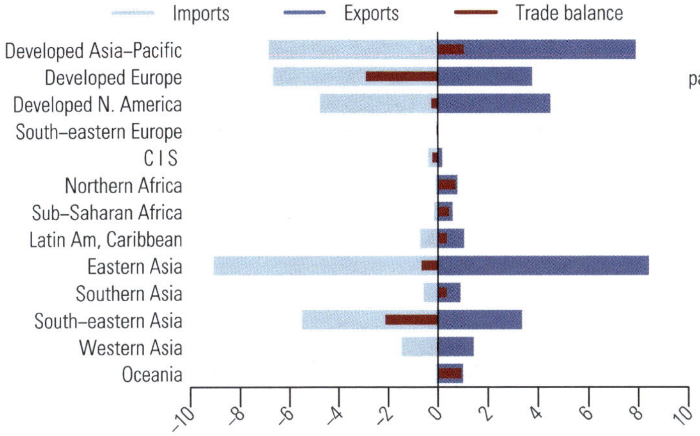

Graph 5: Partner concentration of merchandise trade

(Cumulative share by ranked partners in 2015)

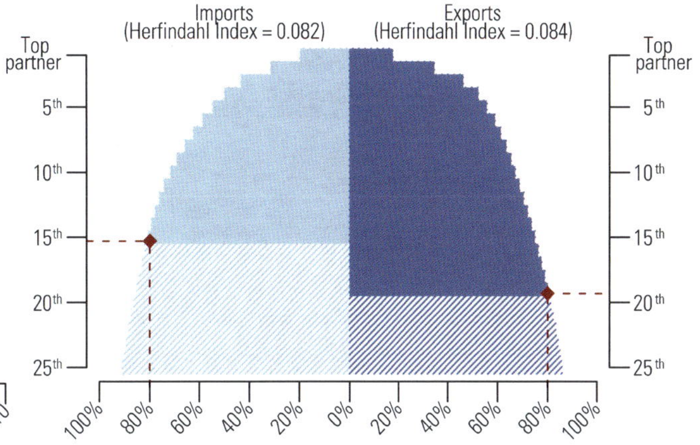

Graph 6: Imports of services by EBOPS category

(% share in 2014)

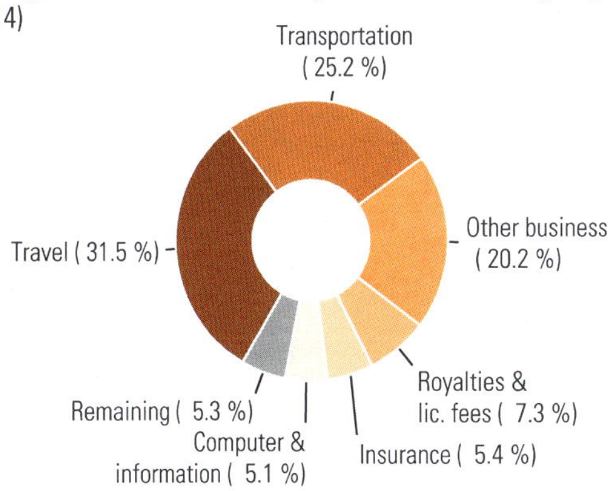

Imports Profile:

"Machinery and transport equipment" (SITC section 7), "Miscellaneous manufactured articles" (SITC section 8) and "Goods classified chiefly by material" (SITC section 6) were the largest commodity groups for imports in 2015, representing respectively 39.5, 14.3 and 11.1 percent of imported goods (see table 3). From 2013 to 2015, the largest import commodity was "Petroleum oils and oils obtained from bituminous minerals, crude" (HS code 2709) (see table 4). The top three partners for merchandise imports were China, Australia and the United States, accounting for respectively 17.8, 12.5 and 10.9 percent of total imports. "Travel" (EBOPS code 236) accounted for the largest share of imports of services in 2014 at 4.1 bln US$, followed by "Transportation" (EBOPS code 205) at 3.3 bln US$ and "Other business services" (EBOPS code 268) at 2.6 bln US$ (see graph 6).

Table 4: Top 10 import commodities 2013 to 2015

HS code	4-digit heading of Harmonized System 2012	Value (million US$) 2013	2014	2015	Unit value 2013	2014	2015	Unit	SITC code
	All Commodities	39 619.2	42 497.7	36 333.7					
2709	Petroleum oils and oils obtained from bituminous minerals, crude	4 399.5	3 966.8	2 213.5	0.9	0.8	0.4	US$/kg	333
8703	Motor cars and other motor vehicles principally designed for the transport	3 067.5	3 387.7	3 002.0	14.5	12.9	11.4	thsd US$/unit	781
2710	Petroleum oils, other than crude	2 169.2	2 303.6	1 317.2	*1.1*	*1.1*	*0.7*	US$/kg	334
8704	Motor vehicles for the transport of goods	837.5	1 185.8	1 013.2	28.8	32.4	24.5	thsd US$/unit	782
8802	Other aircraft (for example, helicopters, aeroplanes); spacecraft	446.2	1 331.5	1 101.2	2.6	2.0	5.3	mln US$/unit	792
8471	Automatic data processing machines and units thereof	989.7	970.3	898.8					752
8517	Electrical apparatus for line telephony or line telegraphy	922.8	926.5	981.6					764
3004	Medicaments (excluding goods of heading 30.02, 30.05 or 30.06)	646.7	653.3	588.5	*38.7*	*36.8*		US$/kg	542
8411	Turbo-jets, turbo-propellers and other gas turbines	379.0	451.8	506.4					714
2106	Food preparations not elsewhere specified or included	338.1	379.5	388.9	8.5	*7.8*	*7.6*	US$/kg	098

Nicaragua

Goods Imports: CIF, by origin | **Goods Exports: FOB, by last known destination** | **Trade System: General**

Overview:

In 2014, the value of merchandise exports of Nicaragua increased moderately by 8.3 percent to reach 5.0 bln US$, while its merchandise imports increased slightly by 4.5 percent to reach 5.7 bln US$ (see graph 1, table 2 and table 3). The merchandise trade balance recorded a relatively small deficit of 772.9 mln US$ (see graph 1). The largest merchandise trade balance was with MDG Developed North America at 1.7 bln US$ (see graph 4). Merchandise exports in Nicaragua were highly concentrated amongst partners; imports were diversified. The top 6 partners accounted for 80 percent or more of exports and 11 partners accounted for 80 percent or more of imports (see graph 5). In 2014, the value of exports of services of Nicaragua increased slightly by 2.1 percent, reaching 746.9 mln US$, while its imports of services increased substantially by 10.9 percent and reached 1.0 bln US$ (see graph 2). There was a moderate trade in services deficit of 289.1 mln US$.

Graph 1: Total merchandise trade, by value

(Bln US$ by year)

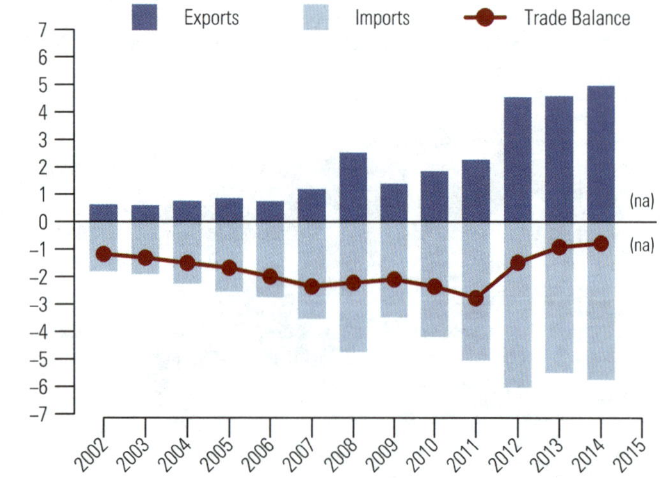

Graph 2: Total services trade, by value

(Bln US$ by year)

Exports Profile:

"Food, animals + beverages, tobacco" (SITC section 0+1), "Miscellaneous manufactured articles" (SITC section 8) and "Machinery and transport equipment" (SITC section 7) were the largest commodity groups for exports in 2014, representing respectively 42.7, 28.6 and 11.7 percent of exported goods (see table 2). From 2012 to 2014, the largest export commodity was "Insulated (including enamelled or anodised) wire, cable" (HS code 8544) (see table 1). The top three destinations for merchandise exports were the United States, Mexico and the Bolivarian Republic of Venezuela, accounting for respectively 46.6, 12.1 and 8.6 percent of total exports. "Travel" (EBOPS code 236) accounted for the largest share of exports of services in 2014 at 445.4 mln US$, followed by "Communications services" (EBOPS code 245) at 157.9 mln US$ and "Government services, n.i.e." (EBOPS code 291) at 86.2 mln US$ (see graph 3).

Graph 3: Exports of services by EBOPS category

(% share in 2014)

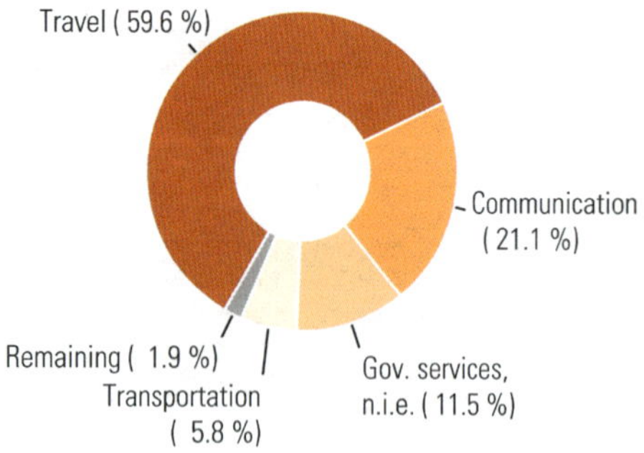

Table 1: Top 10 export commodities 2012 to 2014

HS code	4-digit heading of Harmonized System 2012	Value (million US$) 2012	2013	2014	Unit value 2012	2013	2014	Unit	SITC code
	All Commodities	4550.6	4594.1	4973.5					
8544	Insulated (including enamelled or anodised) wire, cable	451.0	572.8	562.1	14.2	15.2	15.7	US$/kg	773
0901	Coffee, whether or not roasted or decaffeinated	525.5	352.9	399.5	4.2	3.6	3.5	US$/kg	071
7108	Gold (including gold plated with platinum)	432.0	436.6	387.0	31.9	29.6	27.0	thsd US$/kg	971
0202	Meat of bovine animals, frozen	368.0	288.9	330.3	4.2	4.2	4.7	US$/kg	011
6206	Women's or girls'blouses, shirts and shirt-blouses	300.2	309.6	277.1					842
6104	Women's or girls'suits, ensembles, jackets, blazers, dresses, skirts	291.5	398.2	64.0					844
0306	Crustaceans, whether in shell or not	175.4	225.5	261.5	6.2	7.2	7.7	US$/kg	036
6109	T-shirts, singlets and other vests, knitted or crocheted	127.4	142.3	373.9	*7.3*	*7.3*	*5.5*	US$/unit	845
1701	Cane or beet sugar and chemically pure sucrose, in solid form	195.0	186.8	207.5	0.6	0.5	0.5	US$/kg	061
6203	Men's or boys'suits, ensembles, jackets, blazers, trousers	146.8	149.0	127.9					841

Services Imports and Exports: EBOPS 2002 categories

Table 2: Merchandise exports by SITC

(Value in million US$, growth and shares in percentage)

SITC	2014	Avg. Growth rates 2010-2014	Avg. Growth rates 2013-2014	2014 share
Total	4973.5	28.1	8.3	100.0
0+1	2123.6	12.4	15.3	42.7
2+4	312.1	20.3	18.6	6.3
3	15.6	-8.9	-21.2	0.3
5	35.3	7.4	-3.3	0.7
6	91.1	30.0	-7.9	1.8
7	584.0	153.6	-2.0	11.7
8	1423.6	132.4	9.5	28.6
9	388.2	14.9	-11.3	7.8

Table 3: Merchandise imports by SITC

(Value in million US$, growth and shares in percentage)

SITC	2014	Avg. Growth rates 2010-2014	Avg. Growth rates 2013-2014	2014 share
Total	5746.4	8.2	4.5	100.0
0+1	840.5	9.6	0.4	14.6
2+4	176.9	6.3	2.9	3.1
3	1008.9	2.6	-2.5	17.6
5	947.4	5.8	1.7	16.5
6	832.7	11.8	1.5	14.5
7	1378.5	10.8	14.0	24.0
8	556.4	12.3	13.7	9.7
9	5.2	-2.3	-1.4	0.1

SITC Legend

SITC Code	Description
Total	All commodities
0+1	Food, animals + beverages, tobacco
2+4	Crude materials + anim. & veg. oils
3	Mineral fuels, lubricants
5	Chemicals
6	Goods classified chiefly by material
7	Machinery and transport equipment
8	Miscellaneous manufactured articles
9	Not classified elsewhere in the SITC

Graph 4: Merchandise trade balance

(Bln US$ by MDG Regions in 2014)

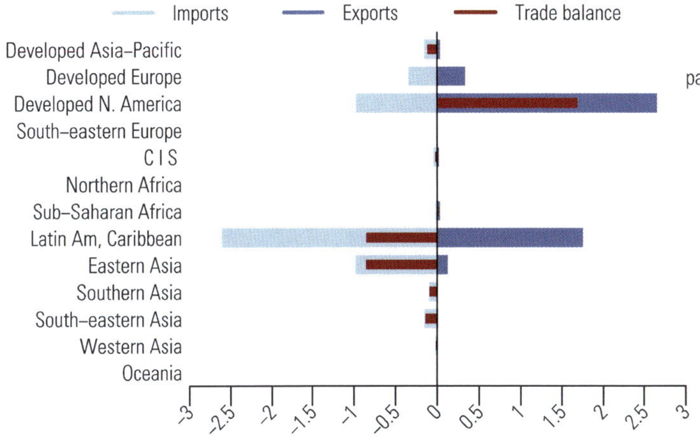

Graph 5: Partner concentration of merchandise trade

(Cumulative share by ranked partners in 2014)

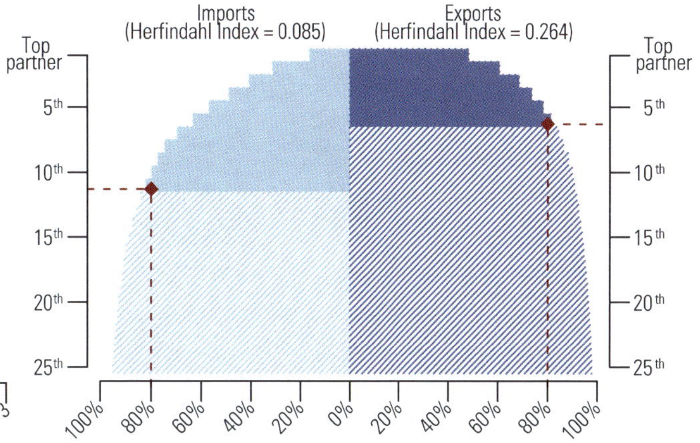

Graph 6: Imports of services by EBOPS category

(% share in 2014)

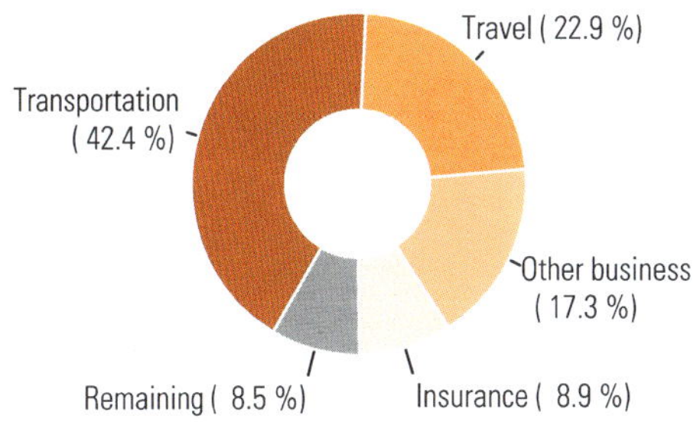

Imports Profile:

"Machinery and transport equipment" (SITC section 7), "Mineral fuels, lubricants" (SITC section 3) and "Chemicals" (SITC section 5) were the largest commodity groups for imports in 2014, representing respectively 24.0, 17.6 and 16.5 percent of imported goods (see table 3). From 2012 to 2014, the largest import commodity was "Petroleum oils, other than crude" (HS code 2710) (see table 4). The top three partners for merchandise imports were the United States, China and Curaçao, accounting for respectively 17.0, 12.0 and 10.0 percent of total imports. "Transportation" (EBOPS code 205) accounted for the largest share of imports of services in 2014 at 439.7 mln US$, followed by "Travel" (EBOPS code 236) at 236.8 mln US$ and "Other business services" (EBOPS code 268) at 179.2 mln US$ (see graph 6).

Table 4: Top 10 import commodities 2012 to 2014

HS code	4-digit heading of Harmonized System 2012	Value (million US$) 2012	2013	2014	Unit value 2012	2013	2014	Unit	SITC code
	All Commodities	6029.7	5498.8	5746.4					
2710	Petroleum oils, other than crude	960.4	457.0	429.8	0.9	1.0	1.0	US$/kg	334
2709	Petroleum oils and oils obtained from bituminous minerals, crude	440.5	505.5	508.1	0.8	0.8	0.7	US$/kg	333
3004	Medicaments (excluding goods of heading 30.02, 30.05 or 30.06)	299.4	298.8	311.3	28.9	27.2	23.5	US$/kg	542
8704	Motor vehicles for the transport of goods	131.1	150.2	157.0					782
8517	Electrical apparatus for line telephony or line telegraphy	118.2	99.1	158.5					764
8703	Motor cars and other motor vehicles principally designed for the transport	124.4	118.2	116.2	*16.1*	*15.0*	*14.7*	thsd US$/unit	781
3808	Insecticides, rodenticides, fungicides, herbicides	87.6	94.2	93.1	4.9	5.1	4.9	US$/kg	591
3923	Articles for the conveyance or packing of goods, of plastics	78.8	78.0	84.4	2.5	2.3	2.3	US$/kg	893
2106	Food preparations not elsewhere specified or included	60.1	65.2	70.0	6.1	6.6	6.2	US$/kg	098
2711	Petroleum gases and other gaseous hydrocarbons	55.9	62.0	66.4	0.8	0.8	0.9	US$/kg	343

Niger

Goods Imports: CIF, by origin | **Goods Exports: FOB, by last known destination** | **Trade System: General**

Overview:

In 2014, the value of merchandise exports of the Niger decreased substantially by 21.5 percent to reach 1.0 bln US$, while its merchandise imports increased substantially by 25.5 percent to reach 2.2 bln US$ (see graph 1, table 2 and table 3). The merchandise trade balance recorded a large deficit of 1.1 bln US$ (see graph 1). The largest merchandise trade balance was with MDG Eastern Asia at -440.1 mln US$ (see graph 4). Merchandise exports in the Niger were moderately concentrated amongst partners; imports were diversified. The top 6 partners accounted for 80 percent or more of exports and 14 partners accounted for 80 percent or more of imports (see graph 5). In 2013, the value of exports of services of the Niger increased substantially by 53.4 percent, reaching 115.2 mln US$, while its imports of services increased substantially by 16.1 percent and reached 958.7 mln US$ (see graph 2). There was a large trade in services deficit of 843.5 mln US$.

Graph 1: Total merchandise trade, by value

(Bln US$ by year)

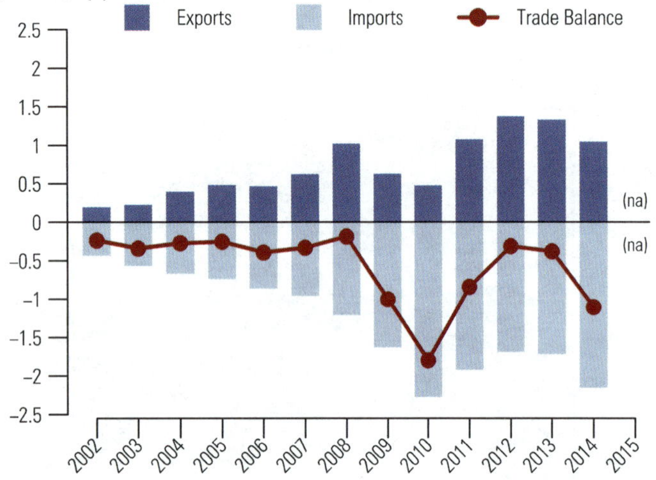

Graph 2: Total services trade, by value

(Mln US$ by year)

Exports Profile:

"Crude materials + anim. & veg. oils" (SITC section 2+4), "Mineral fuels, lubricants" (SITC section 3) and "Food, animals + beverages, tobacco" (SITC section 0+1) were the largest commodity groups for exports in 2014, representing respectively 49.3, 27.0 and 9.5 percent of exported goods (see table 2). From 2013 to 2014, the largest export commodity was "Uranium or thorium ores and concentrates" (HS code 2612) (see table 1). The top three destinations for merchandise exports were France, Nigeria and Burkina Faso, accounting for respectively 36.8, 12.9 and 11.2 percent of total exports. "Travel" (EBOPS code 236) accounted for the largest share of exports of services in 2013 at 87.8 mln US$, followed by "Transportation" (EBOPS code 205) at 7.3 mln US$ and "Other business services" (EBOPS code 268) at 7.2 mln US$ (see graph 3).

Graph 3: Exports of services by EBOPS category

(% share in 2013)

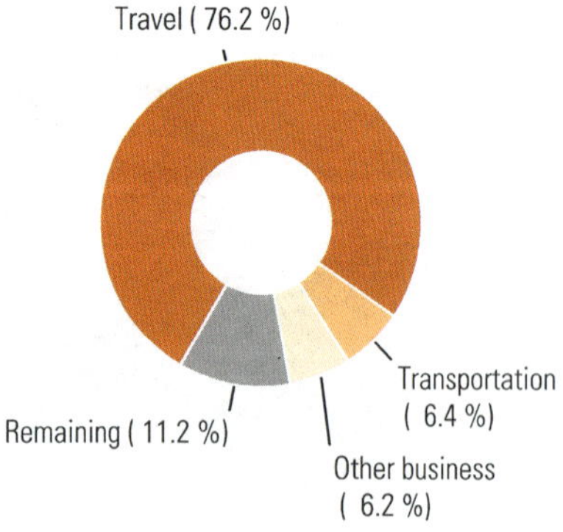

Table 1: Top 10 export commodities 2012 to 2014

HS code	4-digit heading of Harmonized System 2007	Value (million US$) 2012	2013	2014	Unit value 2012	2013	2014	Unit	SITC code
	All Commodities	1379.8	1337.2	1049.7					
2612	Uranium or thorium ores and concentrates	...	659.4	478.2		140.8	116.7	US$/kg	286
2710	Petroleum oils, other than crude	230.3	383.9	271.8	1.1	1.0	1.0	US$/kg	334
9999	Commodities not specified according to kind	749.1	...	27.1					931
6309	Worn clothing and other worn articles	71.9	20.3	14.9	1.8	1.2	0.8	US$/kg	269
9015	Surveying (including photogrammetrical surveying), hydrographic	0.7	21.1	68.4					874
0703	Onions, shallots, garlic, leeks and other alliaceous vegetables	48.9	16.0	13.4	0.6	0.2	0.2	US$/kg	054
1006	Rice	30.8	22.7	23.4	0.7	0.6	0.6	US$/kg	042
5208	Woven fabrics of cotton, containing 85 % or more by weight of cotton	30.0	16.9	15.0	25.6	34.9	26.7	US$/kg	652
1701	Cane or beet sugar and chemically pure sucrose, in solid form	36.5	8.6	10.3	0.8	0.6	0.6	US$/kg	061
7108	Gold (including gold plated with platinum)	...	54.9	...		48.5		thsd US$/kg	971

Services Imports and Exports: EBOPS 2002 categories

Table 2: Merchandise exports by SITC

(Value in million US$, growth and shares in percentage)

SITC	2014	Avg. Growth rates 2010-2014	Avg. Growth rates 2013-2014	2014 share
Total	1 049.7	21.7	-21.5	100.0
0+1	99.9	4.4	13.1	9.5
2+4	518.0	19.3	-25.7	49.3
3	283.7	148.1	-29.7	27.0
5	1.5	10.3	-93.6	0.1
6	16.8	5.1	-11.4	1.6
7	31.7	-4.4	23.5	3.0
8	71.0	101.3	194.3	6.8
9	27.1	-22.3	-50.7	2.6

Table 3: Merchandise imports by SITC

(Value in million US$, growth and shares in percentage)

SITC	2014	Avg. Growth rates 2010-2014	Avg. Growth rates 2013-2014	2014 share
Total	2 151.1	-1.4	25.5	100.0
0+1	459.5	10.1	-9.0	21.4
2+4	128.4	7.0	0.4	6.0
3	78.1	-27.6	2.9	3.6
5	194.3	8.2	15.3	9.0
6	306.8	-14.2	8.3	14.3
7	800.7	1.6	74.4	37.2
8	183.3	11.8	94.1	8.5

SITC Legend

SITC Code	Description
Total	All commodities
0+1	Food, animals + beverages, tobacco
2+4	Crude materials + anim. & veg. oils
3	Mineral fuels, lubricants
5	Chemicals
6	Goods classified chiefly by material
7	Machinery and transport equipment
8	Miscellaneous manufactured articles
9	Not classified elsewhere in the SITC

Graph 4: Merchandise trade balance

(Mln US$ by MDG Regions in 2014)

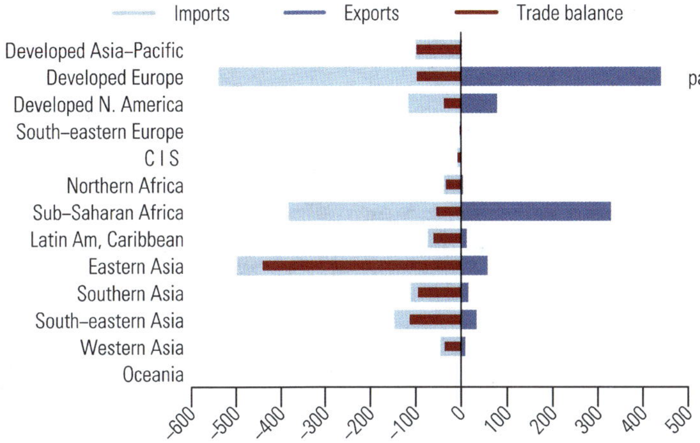

Graph 5: Partner concentration of merchandise trade

(Cumulative share by ranked partners in 2014)

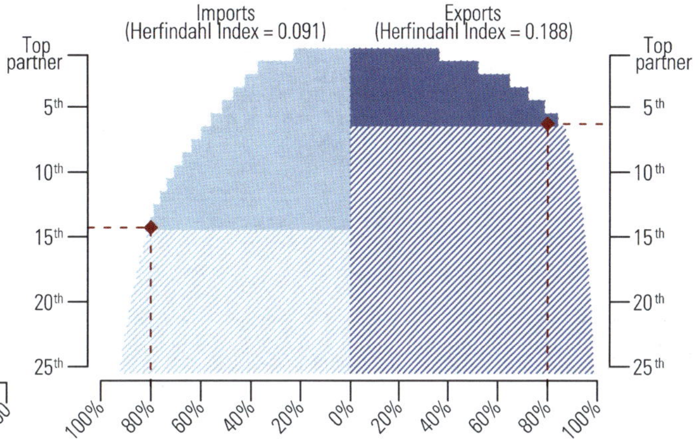

Graph 6: Imports of services by EBOPS category

(% share in 2013)

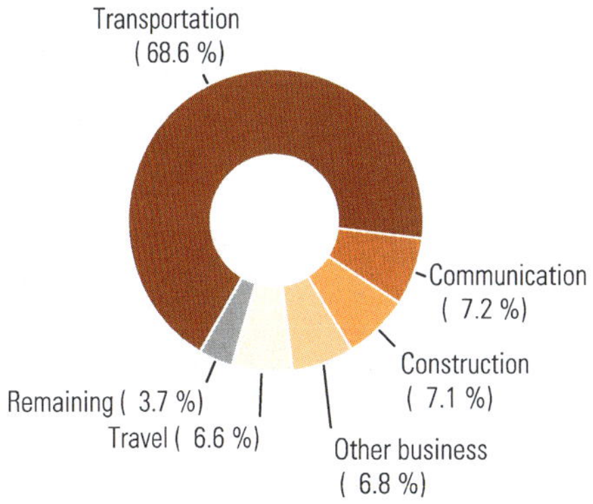

Imports Profile:

"Machinery and transport equipment" (SITC section 7), "Food, animals + beverages, tobacco" (SITC section 0+1) and "Goods classified chiefly by material" (SITC section 6) were the largest commodity groups for imports in 2014, representing respectively 37.2, 21.4 and 14.3 percent of imported goods (see table 3). From 2012 to 2014, the largest import commodity was "Rice" (HS code 1006) (see table 4). The top three partners for merchandise imports were China, France and the United States, accounting for respectively 22.5, 12.3 and 5.9 percent of total imports. "Transportation" (EBOPS code 205) accounted for the largest share of imports of services in 2013 at 657.5 mln US$, followed by "Communications services" (EBOPS code 245) at 69.4 mln US$ and "Construction services" (EBOPS code 249) at 68.0 mln US$ (see graph 6).

Table 4: Top 10 import commodities 2012 to 2014

HS code	4-digit heading of Harmonized System 2007	Value (million US$) 2012	2013	2014	Unit value 2012	2013	2014	Unit	SITC code
	All Commodities	1 687.5	1 714.1	2 151.1					
1006	Rice	169.1	195.6	160.5	0.5	0.5	0.4	US$/kg	042
2523	Portland cement, aluminous cement, slag cement	66.2	81.5	106.2	0.2	0.2	0.2	US$/kg	661
8431	Parts suitable for use principally with the machinery of headings 84.25	71.7	64.6	89.9	29.9	37.7	27.3	US$/kg	723
8704	Motor vehicles for the transport of goods	89.0	42.3	47.8					782
8703	Motor cars and other motor vehicles principally designed for the transport	42.6	53.2	66.9	*16.8*	*14.8*	*16.6*	thsd US$/unit	781
8803	Parts of goods of heading 88.01 or 88.02	5.7	20.5	131.7	893.3	557.2	18.7	US$/kg	792
3004	Medicaments (excluding goods of heading 30.02, 30.05 or 30.06)	44.5	53.5	57.4	7.9	14.9	14.1	US$/kg	542
1511	Palm oil and its fractions	42.3	44.5	57.4	0.8	0.9	0.9	US$/kg	422
2402	Cigars, cheroots, cigarillos and cigarettes	41.3	51.1	48.4	9.6	10.5	8.0	US$/kg	122
2710	Petroleum oils, other than crude	36.9	52.4	45.4	1.2	1.4	1.2	US$/kg	334

Nigeria

Goods Imports: CIF, by origin | **Goods Exports: FOB, by last known destination** | **Trade System: General**

Overview:

In 2014, the value of merchandise exports of Nigeria increased substantially by 13.6 percent to reach 102.9 bln US$, while its merchandise imports increased slightly by 4.3 percent to reach 46.5 bln US$ (see graph 1, table 2 and table 3). The merchandise trade balance recorded a large surplus of 56.3 bln US$ (see graph 1). The largest merchandise trade balance was with MDG Developed Europe at 26.1 bln US$ (see graph 4). Merchandise exports in Nigeria were diversified amongst partners; imports were also diversified. The top 14 partners accounted for 80 percent or more of exports and 17 partners accounted for 80 percent or more of imports (see graph 5). In 2014, the value of exports of services of Nigeria increased substantially by 15.9 percent, reaching 2.8 bln US$, while its imports of services increased substantially by 11.3 percent and reached 24.3 bln US$ (see graph 2). There was a large trade in services deficit of 21.5 bln US$.

Graph 1: Total merchandise trade, by value

(Bln US$ by year)

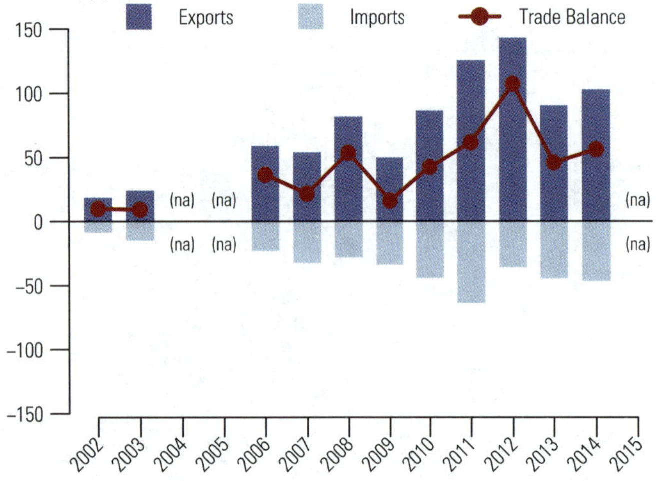

Graph 2: Total services trade, by value

(Bln US$ by year)

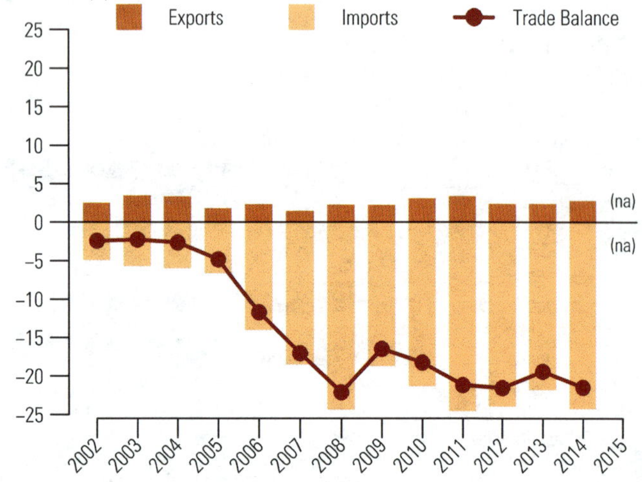

Exports Profile:

"Mineral fuels, lubricants" (SITC section 3), "Machinery and transport equipment" (SITC section 7) and "Miscellaneous manufactured articles" (SITC section 8) were the largest commodity groups for exports in 2014, representing respectively 90.9, 2.8 and 2.0 percent of exported goods (see table 2). From 2012 to 2014, the largest export commodity was "Petroleum oils and oils obtained from bituminous minerals, crude" (HS code 2709) (see table 1). The top three destinations for merchandise exports were India, the United States and the Netherlands, accounting for respectively 12.6, 10.6 and 8.9 percent of total exports. "Transportation" (EBOPS code 205) accounted for the largest share of exports of services in 2014 at 1.4 bln US$, followed by "Government services, n.i.e." (EBOPS code 291) at 588.0 mln US$ and "Travel" (EBOPS code 236) at 552.0 mln US$ (see graph 3).

Graph 3: Exports of services by EBOPS category

(% share in 2014)

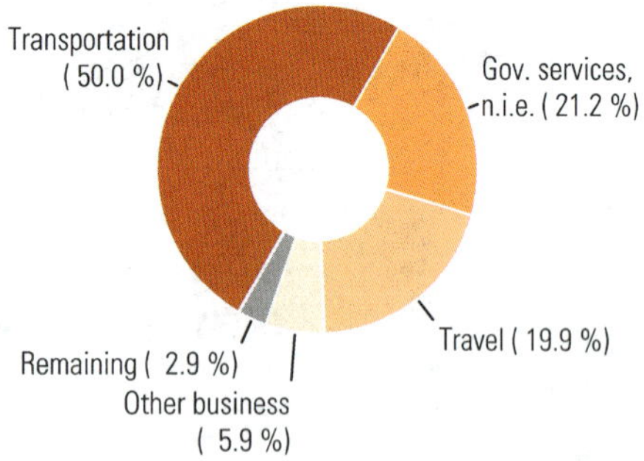

Table 1: Top 10 export commodities 2012 to 2014

HS code	4-digit heading of Harmonized System 2007	Value (million US$) 2012	2013	2014	Unit value 2012	2013	2014	Unit	SITC code
	All Commodities	143 151.2	90 554.5	102 878.5					
2709	Petroleum oils and oils obtained from bituminous minerals, crude	99 054.5	74 953.8	75 033.4			*0.8*	US$/kg	333
2711	Petroleum gases and other gaseous hydrocarbons	8 968.5	1 963.7	12 178.8					343
2710	Petroleum oils, other than crude	12 279.1	2 426.1	6 257.1					334
4001	Natural rubber, balata, gutta-percha, guayule, chicle	10 067.7	2 427.3	94.1		25.0	*2.6*	US$/kg	231
1801	Cocoa beans, whole or broken, raw or roasted	3 033.0	1 542.7	627.0		8.4		US$/kg	072
8905	Light-vessels, fire-floats, dredgers, floating cranes and other vessels	603.7	403.2	1 552.7					793
1207	Other oil seeds and oleaginous fruits, whether or not broken	497.6	867.4	556.5	2.1	4.8		US$/kg	222
3606	Ferro-cerium and other pyrophoric alloys in all forms	3.7	...	1 898.9	5.3		*4.1*	US$/kg	899
4113	Leather further prepared after tanning or crusting	686.1	413.1	526.9	20.7	10.2	*37.5*	US$/kg	611
0401	Milk and cream, not concentrated nor containing added sugar	1 076.7	0.5	0.0		1.4	*1.0*	US$/kg	022

Services Imports and Exports: EBOPS 2002 categories

Table 2: Merchandise exports by SITC
(Value in million US$, growth and shares in percentage)

SITC	2014	Avg. Growth rates 2010-2014	Avg. Growth rates 2013-2014	2014 share
Total	102 878.5	4.4	13.6	100.0
0+1	1 361.3	-11.8	-62.8	1.3
2+4	1 058.8	-20.0	-72.8	1.0
3	93 469.5	5.5	17.8	90.9
5	151.8	-26.8	-56.2	0.1
6	1 864.0	-17.1	5.3	1.8
7	2 925.8	30.1	247.1	2.8
8	2 043.8	30.7	244.0	2.0
9	3.5	-57.9	-96.2	0.0

Table 3: Merchandise imports by SITC
(Value in million US$, growth and shares in percentage)

SITC	2014	Avg. Growth rates 2010-2014	Avg. Growth rates 2013-2014	2014 share
Total	46 532.3	1.3	4.3	100.0
0+1	7 347.7	14.7	-3.2	15.8
2+4	1 127.6	10.0	-37.2	2.4
3	7 584.6	90.1	-15.6	16.3
5	5 797.1	5.0	6.5	12.5
6	6 865.8	-7.4	13.9	14.8
7	16 237.8	-7.5	22.3	34.9
8	1 555.0	-9.7	6.6	3.3
9	16.7	14.0	54.9	0.0

SITC Legend

SITC Code	Description
Total	All commodities
0+1	Food, animals + beverages, tobacco
2+4	Crude materials + anim. & veg. oils
3	Mineral fuels, lubricants
5	Chemicals
6	Goods classified chiefly by material
7	Machinery and transport equipment
8	Miscellaneous manufactured articles
9	Not classified elsewhere in the SITC

Graph 4: Merchandise trade balance
(Bln US$ by MDG Regions in 2014)

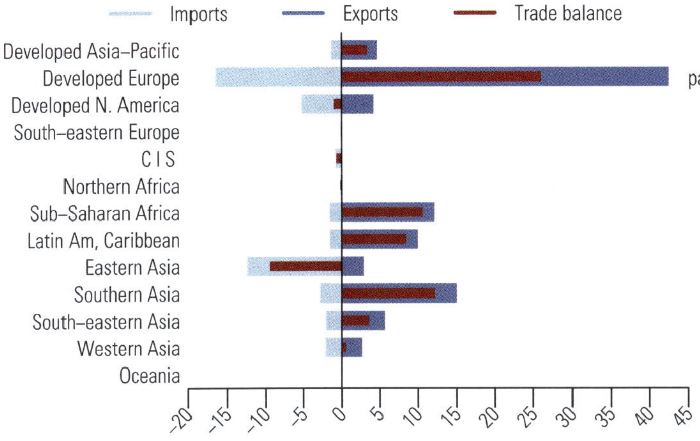

Graph 5: Partner concentration of merchandise trade
(Cumulative share by ranked partners in 2014)

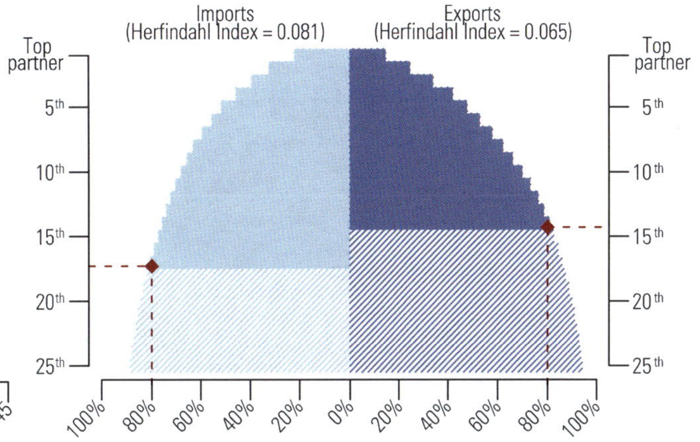

Graph 6: Imports of services by EBOPS category
(% share in 2014)

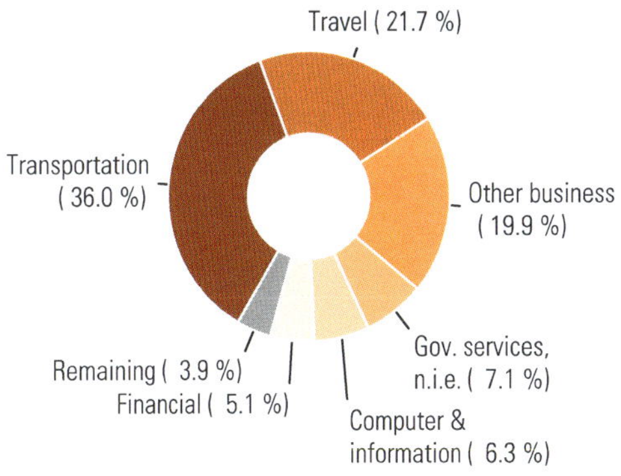

Imports Profile:

"Machinery and transport equipment" (SITC section 7), "Mineral fuels, lubricants" (SITC section 3) and "Food, animals + beverages, tobacco" (SITC section 0+1) were the largest commodity groups for imports in 2014, representing respectively 34.9, 16.3 and 15.8 percent of imported goods (see table 3). From 2012 to 2014, the largest import commodity was "Petroleum oils, other than crude" (HS code 2710) (see table 4). The top three partners for merchandise imports were China, the United States and India, accounting for respectively 21.7, 10.7 and 6.1 percent of total imports. "Transportation" (EBOPS code 205) accounted for the largest share of imports of services in 2014 at 8.7 bln US$, followed by "Travel" (EBOPS code 236) at 5.3 bln US$ and "Other business services" (EBOPS code 268) at 4.8 bln US$ (see graph 6).

Table 4: Top 10 import commodities 2012 to 2014

HS code	4-digit heading of Harmonized System 2007	Value (million US$) 2012	2013	2014	Unit value 2012	2013	2014	Unit	SITC code
	All Commodities	35 872.5	44 598.2	46 532.3					
2710	Petroleum oils, other than crude	534.0	8 598.6	7 103.4	3.5	10.6		US$/kg	334
8703	Motor cars and other motor vehicles principally designed for the transport	3 607.0	1 071.6	1 822.4	*20.2*	*18.7*	*21.8*	thsd US$/unit	781
1001	Wheat and meslin	1 491.3	1 294.9	1 740.4	0.8	0.7		US$/kg	041
0303	Fish, frozen, excluding fish fillets and other fish meat of heading 03.04	1 231.0	970.3	899.3	2.9	2.9		US$/kg	034
1701	Cane or beet sugar and chemically pure sucrose, in solid form	948.4	873.3	853.6	0.8	0.6	*0.6*	US$/kg	061
1006	Rice	1 920.2	38.0	679.3	4.0	1.9	*0.9*	US$/kg	042
8711	Motorcycles (including mopeds) and cycles fitted with an auxiliary motor	670.4	636.2	1 047.6			*2.0*	thsd US$/unit	785
8704	Motor vehicles for the transport of goods	1 078.9	598.3	558.4					782
8517	Electrical apparatus for line telephony or line telegraphy	947.5	633.5	590.1					764
8502	Electric generating sets and rotary converters	420.8	552.9	649.0					716

Norway, including Svalbard and Jan Mayen Islands

Goods Imports: CIF, by origin | **Goods Exports: FOB, by last known destination** | **Trade System: General**

Overview:

In 2015, the value of merchandise exports of Norway decreased substantially by 26.1 percent to reach 106.3 bln US$, while its merchandise imports decreased substantially by 13.7 percent to reach 77.0 bln US$ (see graph 1, table 2 and table 3). The merchandise trade balance recorded a moderate surplus of 29.3 bln US$ (see graph 1). The largest merchandise trade balance was with MDG Developed Europe at 37.6 bln US$ (see graph 4). Merchandise exports in Norway were diversified amongst partners; imports were also diversified. The top 11 partners accounted for 80 percent or more of exports and 17 partners accounted for 80 percent or more of imports (see graph 5). In 2014, the value of exports of services of Norway increased substantially by 12.1 percent, reaching 47.5 bln US$, while its imports of services increased slightly by 4.4 percent and reached 54.2 bln US$ (see graph 2). There was a relatively small trade in services deficit of 6.7 bln US$.

Graph 1: Total merchandise trade, by value

(Bln US$ by year)

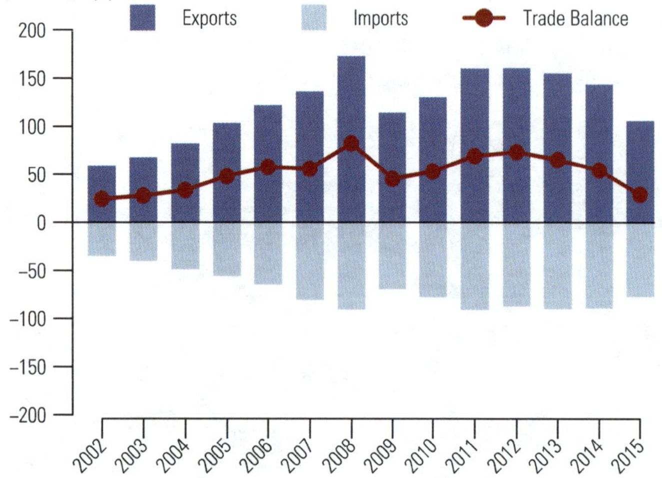

Graph 2: Total services trade, by value

(Bln US$ by year)

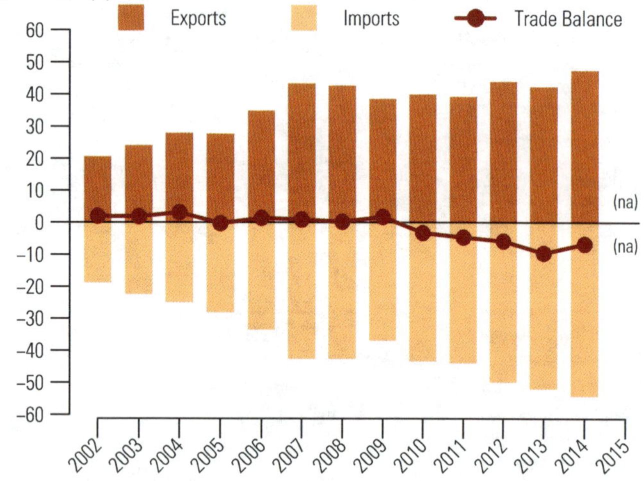

Exports Profile:

"Mineral fuels, lubricants" (SITC section 3), "Machinery and transport equipment" (SITC section 7) and "Food, animals + beverages, tobacco" (SITC section 0+1) were the largest commodity groups for exports in 2015, representing respectively 58.0, 11.7 and 9.2 percent of exported goods (see table 2). From 2013 to 2015, the largest export commodity was "Petroleum oils and oils obtained from bituminous minerals, crude" (HS code 2709) (see table 1). The top three destinations for merchandise exports were the United Kingdom, Germany and the Netherlands, accounting for respectively 22.9, 17.2 and 11.5 percent of total exports. "Transportation" (EBOPS code 205) accounted for the largest share of exports of services in 2014 at 22.2 bln US$, followed by "Other business services" (EBOPS code 268) at 13.9 bln US$ and "Travel" (EBOPS code 236) at 5.7 bln US$ (see graph 3).

Graph 3: Exports of services by EBOPS category

(% share in 2014)

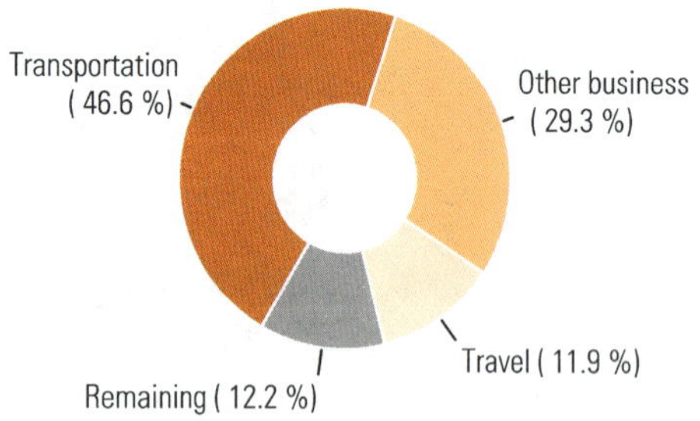

Table 1: Top 10 export commodities 2013 to 2015

HS code	4-digit heading of Harmonized System 2012	Value (million US$) 2013	2014	2015	Unit value 2013	2014	2015	Unit	SITC code
	All Commodities	155350.6	143791.3	106251.1					
2709	Petroleum oils and oils obtained from bituminous minerals, crude	49721.2	45527.1	25692.2	0.8	0.7	0.4	US$/kg	333
2711	Petroleum gases and other gaseous hydrocarbons	46100.8	39044.6	30273.0	0.5	0.4	0.3	US$/kg	343
2710	Petroleum oils, other than crude	8418.3	7511.3	5045.7	0.9	0.8	0.5	US$/kg	334
0302	Fish, fresh or chilled, excluding fish fillets	5991.1	6003.0	5208.5	5.6	5.0	4.1	US$/kg	034
9999	Commodities not specified according to kind	4995.9	4670.0	4213.8					931
7601	Unwrought aluminium	2972.9	3185.6	2673.6	2.4	2.4	2.2	US$/kg	684
0304	Fish fillets and other fish meat (whether or not minced)	1526.4	1727.6	1453.3	6.0	6.4	6.1	US$/kg	034
0303	Fish, frozen, excluding fish fillets and other fish meat of heading 03.04	1656.2	1763.8	1284.9	2.1	2.1	1.9	US$/kg	034
7502	Unwrought nickel	1378.3	1450.2	1175.7	15.4	16.8	12.4	US$/kg	683
8431	Parts suitable for use principally with the machinery of headings 84.25	1368.3	1241.7	1121.7	38.0	38.6	36.2	US$/kg	723

Services Imports and Exports: EBOPS 2002 categories

Table 2: Merchandise exports by SITC

(Value in million US$, growth and shares in percentage)

SITC	2015	Avg. Growth rates 2011-2015	Avg. Growth rates 2014-2015	2015 share
Total	106 251.1	-9.8	-26.1	100.0
0+1	9 735.3	-0.4	-15.2	9.2
2+4	2 013.2	-3.6	-19.8	1.9
3	61 671.6	-13.3	-33.7	58.0
5	3 498.1	-6.5	-9.0	3.3
6	9 119.8	-7.7	-13.5	8.6
7	12 407.7	-0.1	-9.1	11.7
8	3 463.2	-1.3	-11.4	3.3
9	4 342.2	-7.1	-9.9	4.1

Table 3: Merchandise imports by SITC

(Value in million US$, growth and shares in percentage)

SITC	2015	Avg. Growth rates 2011-2015	Avg. Growth rates 2014-2015	2015 share
Total	76 979.3	-4.0	-13.7	100.0
0+1	6 298.7	-0.6	-13.4	8.2
2+4	4 969.7	-9.9	-14.6	6.5
3	3 330.3	-12.9	-29.4	4.3
5	7 035.6	-4.2	-13.6	9.1
6	10 975.3	-4.9	-19.5	14.3
7	31 153.8	-2.7	-10.9	40.5
8	12 255.1	-1.7	-9.5	15.9
9	960.9	-7.5	-9.1	1.2

SITC Legend

SITC Code	Description
Total	All commodities
0+1	Food, animals + beverages, tobacco
2+4	Crude materials + anim. & veg. oils
3	Mineral fuels, lubricants
5	Chemicals
6	Goods classified chiefly by material
7	Machinery and transport equipment
8	Miscellaneous manufactured articles
9	Not classified elsewhere in the SITC

Graph 4: Merchandise trade balance

(Bln US$ by MDG Regions in 2015)

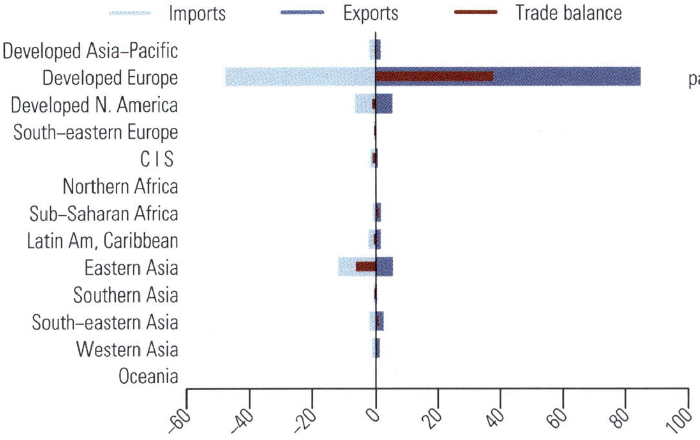

Graph 5: Partner concentration of merchandise trade

(Cumulative share by ranked partners in 2015)

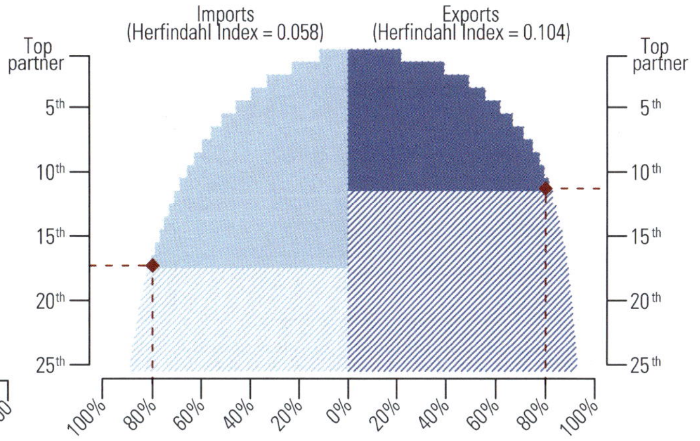

Graph 6: Imports of services by EBOPS category

(% share in 2014)

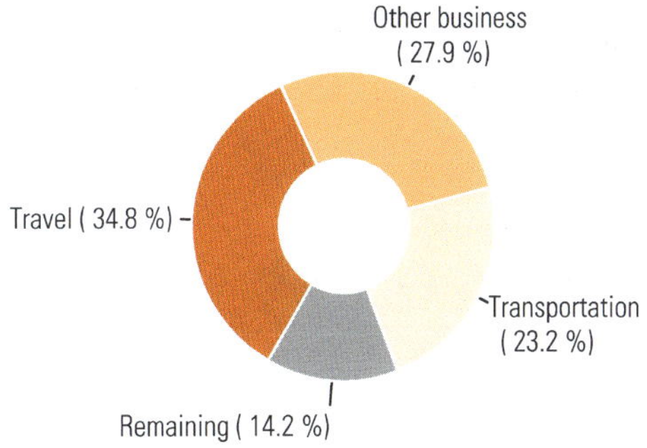

Imports Profile:

"Machinery and transport equipment" (SITC section 7), "Miscellaneous manufactured articles" (SITC section 8) and "Goods classified chiefly by material" (SITC section 6) were the largest commodity groups for imports in 2015, representing respectively 40.5, 15.9 and 14.3 percent of imported goods (see table 3). From 2013 to 2015, the largest import commodity was "Motor cars and other motor vehicles principally designed for the transport" (HS code 8703) (see table 4). The top three partners for merchandise imports were Sweden, Germany and China, accounting for respectively 12.4, 11.9 and 9.7 percent of total imports. "Travel" (EBOPS code 236) accounted for the largest share of imports of services in 2014 at 18.9 bln US$, followed by "Other business services" (EBOPS code 268) at 15.1 bln US$ and "Transportation" (EBOPS code 205) at 12.6 bln US$ (see graph 6).

Table 4: Top 10 import commodities 2013 to 2015

HS code	4-digit heading of Harmonized System 2012	Value (million US$) 2013	Value (million US$) 2014	Value (million US$) 2015	Unit value 2013	Unit value 2014	Unit value 2015	Unit	SITC code
	All Commodities	89 807.2	89 170.0	76 979.3					
8703	Motor cars and other motor vehicles principally designed for the transport	5 682.6	5 547.2	4 956.8	28.3	28.6	24.6	thsd US$/unit	781
2710	Petroleum oils, other than crude	3 680.0	2 854.1	2 191.0	0.9	0.9	0.5	US$/kg	334
8517	Electrical apparatus for line telephony or line telegraphy	1 925.2	1 885.9	1 707.8					764
7501	Nickel mattes, nickel oxide sinters and other intermediate products	1 846.3	1 859.8	1 326.6	10.3	11.5	8.4	US$/kg	284
8471	Automatic data processing machines and units thereof	1 787.0	1 742.5	1 391.6	249.4	303.1	289.4	US$/unit	752
3004	Medicaments (excluding goods of heading 30.02, 30.05 or 30.06)	1 402.9	1 529.2	1 307.5	136.2	136.3	104.3	US$/kg	542
8704	Motor vehicles for the transport of goods	1 431.8	1 304.0	1 102.6	51.9	49.9	38.6	thsd US$/unit	782
9403	Other furniture and parts thereof	1 254.9	1 296.7	1 109.3					821
7308	Structures (excluding prefabricated buildings of heading 94.06)	1 120.1	1 255.6	1 177.3	3.8	4.4	3.8	US$/kg	691
8431	Parts suitable for use principally with the machinery of headings 84.25	1 111.9	1 127.1	978.6	14.1	15.8	15.7	US$/kg	723

Source: UN Comtrade

Oman

Goods Imports: CIF, by origin | **Goods Exports: FOB, by last known destination** | **Trade System: General**

Overview:

In 2014, the value of merchandise exports of Oman decreased moderately by 8.6 percent to reach 50.7 bln US$, while its merchandise imports decreased substantially by 14.6 percent to reach 29.3 bln US$ (see graph 1, table 2 and table 3). The merchandise trade balance recorded a moderate surplus of 21.4 bln US$ (see graph 1). The largest merchandise trade balance was with MDG Eastern Asia at 31.0 bln US$ (see graph 4). Merchandise exports in Oman were moderately concentrated amongst partners; imports were diversified. The top 6 partners accounted for 80 percent or more of exports and 14 partners accounted for 80 percent or more of imports (see graph 5). In 2013, the value of exports of services of Oman increased substantially by 11.5 percent, reaching 2.9 bln US$, while its imports of services increased substantially by 14.4 percent and reached 10.0 bln US$ (see graph 2). There was a large trade in services deficit of 7.1 bln US$.

Graph 1: Total merchandise trade, by value

(Bln US$ by year)

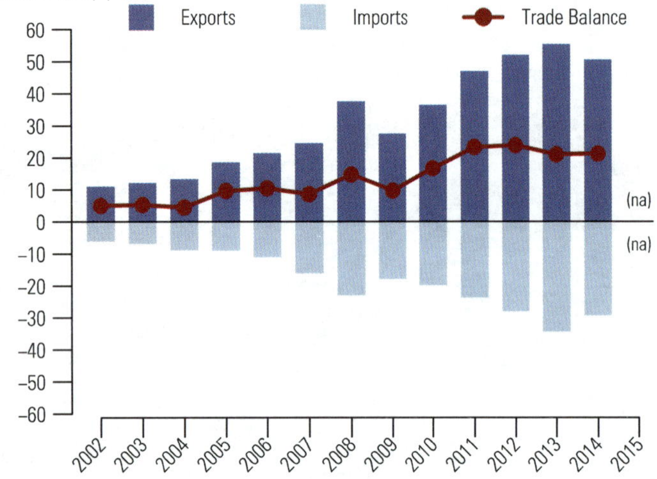

Graph 2: Total services trade, by value

(Bln US$ by year)

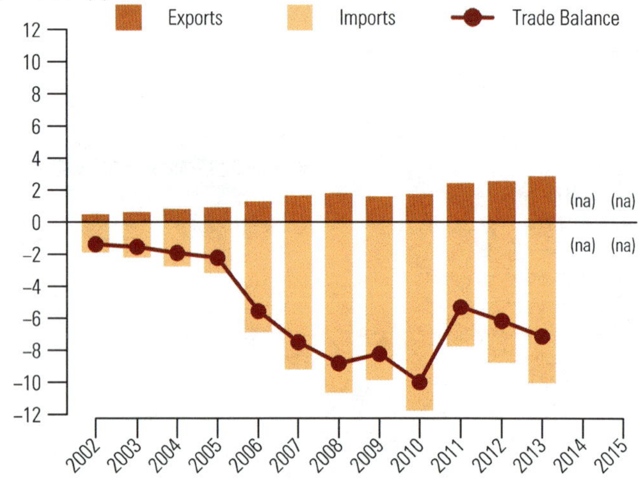

Exports Profile:

"Mineral fuels, lubricants" (SITC section 3), "Chemicals" (SITC section 5) and "Goods classified chiefly by material" (SITC section 6) were the largest commodity groups for exports in 2014, representing respectively 83.5, 6.6 and 4.7 percent of exported goods (see table 2). From 2012 to 2014, the largest export commodity was "Petroleum oils and oils obtained from bituminous minerals, crude" (HS code 2709) (see table 1). The top three destinations for merchandise exports were Areas nes, China and the Republic of Korea, accounting for respectively 46.2, 15.7 and 6.6 percent of total exports. "Travel" (EBOPS code 236) accounted for the largest share of exports of services in 2013 at 1.2 bln US$, followed by "Transportation" (EBOPS code 205) at 1.2 bln US$ and "Other business services" (EBOPS code 268) at 342.9 mln US$ (see graph 3).

Graph 3: Exports of services by EBOPS category

(% share in 2013)

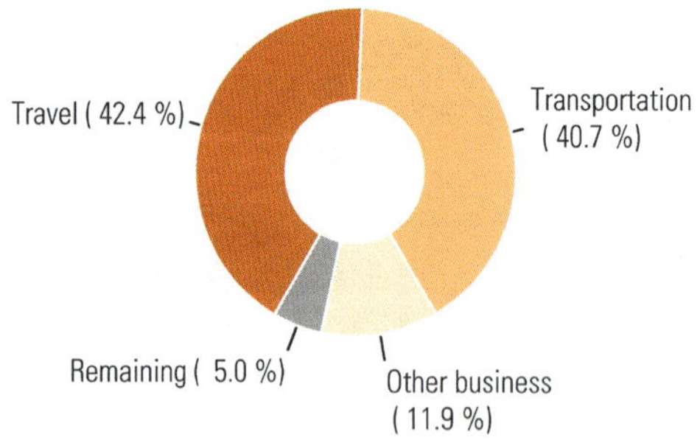

Table 1: Top 10 export commodities 2012 to 2014

HS code	4-digit heading of Harmonized System 2012	Value (million US$) 2012	2013	2014	Unit value 2012	2013	2014	Unit	SITC code
	All Commodities	52 138.2	55 497.1	50 718.3					
2709	Petroleum oils and oils obtained from bituminous minerals, crude	30 676.6	32 087.1	34 834.5			*0.8*	US$/kg	333
2711	Petroleum gases and other gaseous hydrocarbons	4 215.5	4 369.1	5 311.1		0.5	3.0	US$/kg	343
2710	Petroleum oils, other than crude	4 411.2	4 959.8	2 217.3	*1.0*	1.1	0.9	US$/kg	334
9999	Commodities not specified according to kind	4 011.1	4 543.6	1.5					931
2601	Iron ores and concentrates, including roasted iron pyrites	816.7	1 259.6	619.5	0.5	0.2	0.2	US$/kg	281
3102	Mineral or chemical fertilisers, nitrogenous	990.6	905.9	657.5	0.3	0.2	0.4	US$/kg	562
2902	Cyclic hydrocarbons	948.2	380.2	959.9	1.1	0.5	1.4	US$/kg	511
7601	Unwrought aluminium	733.2	691.2	770.5	1.5	1.0	2.5	US$/kg	684
2905	Acyclic alcohols and their derivatives	620.3	609.4	615.8			0.4	US$/kg	512
7203	Ferrous products obtained by direct reduction of iron ore	438.0	619.1	390.5	0.7	0.3	0.4	US$/kg	671

Services Imports and Exports: EBOPS 2002 categories

Table 2: Merchandise exports by SITC

(Value in million US$, growth and shares in percentage)

SITC	2014	Avg. Growth rates 2010-2014	Avg. Growth rates 2013-2014	2014 share
Total	50718.3	8.5	-8.6	100.0
0+1	1006.5	4.7	-18.6	2.0
2+4	1036.1	29.2	-40.5	2.0
3	42367.7	14.4	2.1	83.5
5	3329.1	7.3	6.3	6.6
6	2390.9	18.9	2.3	4.7
7	441.1	-13.8	-45.7	0.9
8	142.6	-17.4	-30.2	0.3
9	4.2	-83.6	-99.9	0.0

Table 3: Merchandise imports by SITC

(Value in million US$, growth and shares in percentage)

SITC	2014	Avg. Growth rates 2010-2014	Avg. Growth rates 2013-2014	2014 share
Total	29303.1	10.3	-14.6	100.0
0+1	3359.1	10.7	14.9	11.5
2+4	1809.5	27.4	-13.1	6.2
3	1806.8	5.6	-76.4	6.2
5	2993.7	14.5	0.7	10.2
6	5322.8	13.0	4.0	18.2
7	11724.7	7.3	1.8	40.0
8	2068.5	16.4	12.7	7.1
9	218.0	-14.2	-10.8	0.7

SITC Legend

SITC Code	Description
Total	All commodities
0+1	Food, animals + beverages, tobacco
2+4	Crude materials + anim. & veg. oils
3	Mineral fuels, lubricants
5	Chemicals
6	Goods classified chiefly by material
7	Machinery and transport equipment
8	Miscellaneous manufactured articles
9	Not classified elsewhere in the SITC

Graph 4: Merchandise trade balance

(Bln US$ by MDG Regions in 2014)

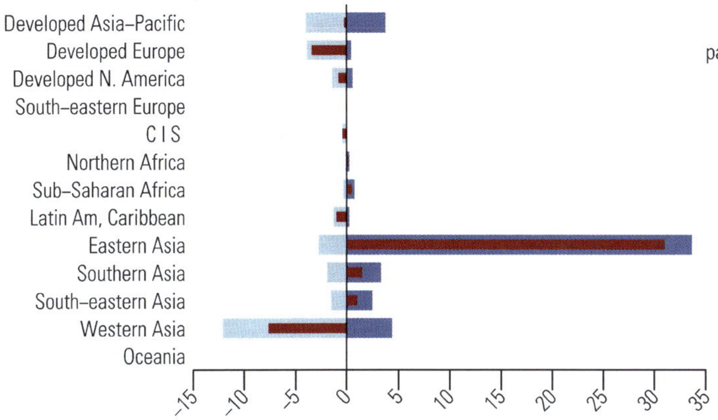

Graph 5: Partner concentration of merchandise trade

(Cumulative share by ranked partners in 2014)

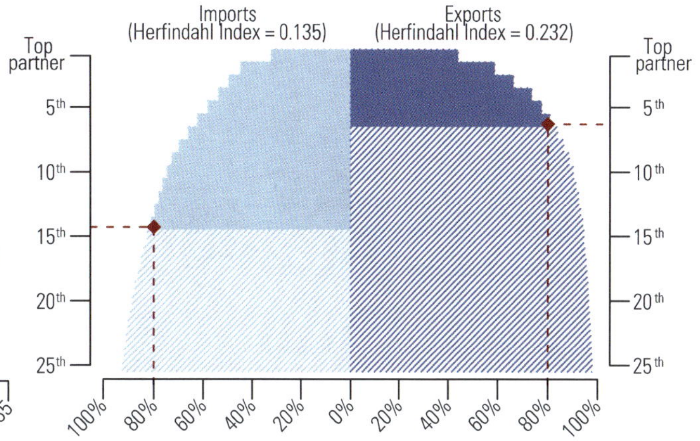

Graph 6: Imports of services by EBOPS category

(% share in 2013)

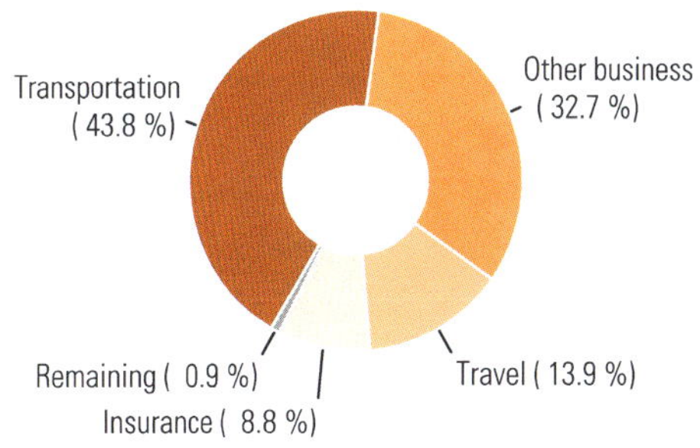

Imports Profile:

"Machinery and transport equipment" (SITC section 7), "Goods classified chiefly by material" (SITC section 6) and "Food, animals + beverages, tobacco" (SITC section 0+1) were the largest commodity groups for imports in 2014, representing respectively 40.0, 18.2 and 11.5 percent of imported goods (see table 3). From 2012 to 2014, the largest import commodity was "Petroleum oils, other than crude" (HS code 2710) (see table 4). The top three partners for merchandise imports were the United Arab Emirates, Areas nes and Japan, accounting for respectively 28.5, 10.6 and 8.1 percent of total imports. "Transportation" (EBOPS code 205) accounted for the largest share of imports of services in 2013 at 4.4 bln US$, followed by "Other business services" (EBOPS code 268) at 3.3 bln US$ and "Travel" (EBOPS code 236) at 1.4 bln US$ (see graph 6).

Table 4: Top 10 import commodities 2012 to 2014

HS code	4-digit heading of Harmonized System 2012	Value (million US$) 2012	Value (million US$) 2013	Value (million US$) 2014	Unit value 2012	Unit value 2013	Unit value 2014	Unit	SITC code
	All Commodities	28117.6	34331.2	29303.1					
2710	Petroleum oils, other than crude	2027.9	7184.3	1547.1	1.5	1.0	1.1	US$/kg	334
8703	Motor cars and other motor vehicles principally designed for the transport	...	3885.0	4392.2		*28.5*	*27.5*	thsd US$/unit	781
9999	Commodities not specified according to kind	6496.6	17.3	10.1					931
2601	Iron ores and concentrates, including roasted iron pyrites	1034.9	1235.9	938.8	0.5	0.2	0.2	US$/kg	281
8704	Motor vehicles for the transport of goods	...	781.5	836.2					782
7304	Tubes, pipes and hollow profiles, seamless, of iron (other than cast iron)	701.3	527.6	291.6	1.8	2.0	2.0	US$/kg	679
2917	Polycarboxylic acids, their anhydrides	374.2	467.9	486.1	1.2	1.2	1.0	US$/kg	513
8431	Parts suitable for use principally with the machinery of headings 84.25	463.6	441.6	367.9	10.0	10.4	9.6	US$/kg	723
8708	Parts and accessories of the motor vehicles of headings 87.01 to 87.05	...	653.3	562.2		15.2	16.3	US$/kg	784
8517	Electrical apparatus for line telephony or line telegraphy	387.7	376.4	427.8					764

Pakistan

Goods Imports: CIF, by origin	Goods Exports: FOB, by last known destination	Trade System: General

Overview:

In 2015, the value of merchandise exports of Pakistan decreased substantially by 10.7 percent to reach 22.1 bln US$, while its merchandise imports decreased moderately by 7.5 percent to reach 44.0 bln US$ (see graph 1, table 2 and table 3). The merchandise trade balance recorded a large deficit of 21.9 bln US$ (see graph 1). The largest merchandise trade balance was with MDG Eastern Asia at -9.7 bln US$ (see graph 4). Merchandise exports in Pakistan were diversified amongst partners; imports were also diversified. The top 24 partners accounted for 80 percent or more of exports and 17 partners accounted for 80 percent or more of imports (see graph 5). In 2014, the value of exports of services of Pakistan increased substantially by 17.3 percent, reaching 5.8 bln US$, while its imports of services increased slightly by 3.5 percent and reached 8.1 bln US$ (see graph 2). There was a moderate trade in services deficit of 2.4 bln US$.

Graph 1: Total merchandise trade, by value

(Bln US$ by year)

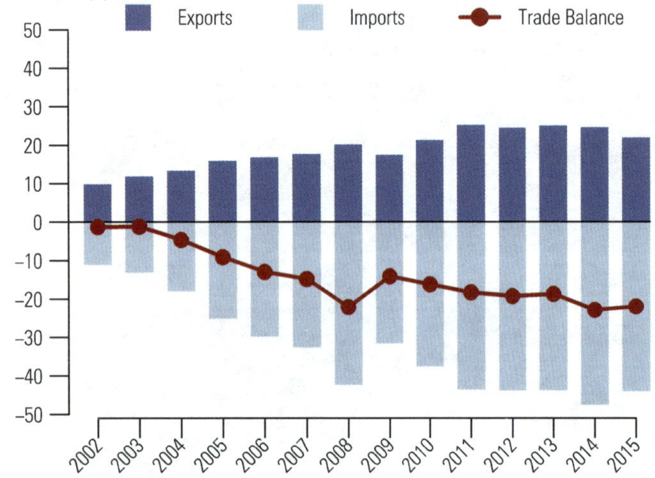

Graph 2: Total services trade, by value

(Bln US$ by year)

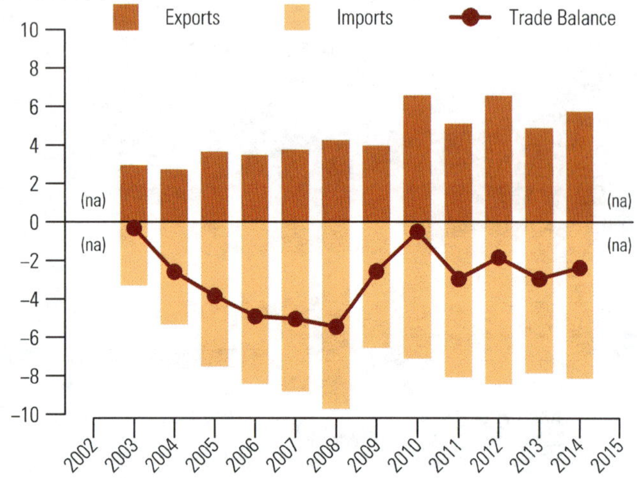

Exports Profile:

"Goods classified chiefly by material" (SITC section 6), "Miscellaneous manufactured articles" (SITC section 8) and "Food, animals + beverages, tobacco" (SITC section 0+1) were the largest commodity groups for exports in 2015, representing respectively 43.0, 27.7 and 19.3 percent of exported goods (see table 2). From 2013 to 2015, the largest export commodity was "Bed linen, table linen, toilet linen and kitchen linen" (HS code 6302) (see table 1). The top three destinations for merchandise exports were the United States, China and Afghanistan, accounting for respectively 15.4, 9.5 and 7.8 percent of total exports. "Government services, n.i.e." (EBOPS code 291) accounted for the largest share of exports of services in 2014 at 2.3 bln US$, followed by "Transportation" (EBOPS code 205) at 1.3 bln US$ and "Other business services" (EBOPS code 268) at 845.3 mln US$ (see graph 3).

Graph 3: Exports of services by EBOPS category

(% share in 2014)

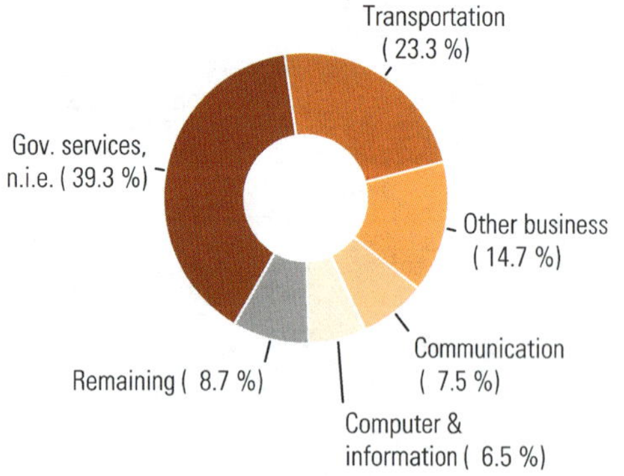

Table 1: Top 10 export commodities 2013 to 2015

HS code	4-digit heading of Harmonized System 2012	Value (million US$) 2013	2014	2015	Unit value 2013	2014	2015	Unit	SITC code
	All Commodities	25120.9	24722.2	22089.0					
6302	Bed linen, table linen, toilet linen and kitchen linen	2852.5	3026.7	2908.1	5.9	5.9	*5.7*	US$/kg	658
1006	Rice	2111.0	2199.6	1927.2	0.5	0.6	0.5	US$/kg	042
5205	Cotton yarn (other than sewing thread), containing 85 % or more	2205.4	1871.6	1529.8	3.1	2.9	3.0	US$/kg	651
5209	Woven fabrics of cotton, containing 85 % or more by weight of cotton	1210.2	1059.3	1006.2	*8.6*	*8.9*		US$/kg	652
6203	Men's or boys'suits, ensembles, jackets, blazers, trousers	969.6	1084.5	1173.4	6.6	*6.0*	6.0	US$/unit	841
6204	Women's or girls'suits, ensembles, jackets, blazers, dresses, skirts	691.2	698.8	781.2	*6.7*	*6.7*	*6.4*	US$/unit	842
5208	Woven fabrics of cotton, containing 85 % or more by weight of cotton	746.7	730.7	627.9			*10.0*	US$/kg	652
4203	Articles of apparel and clothing accessories, of leather	696.6	703.5	640.9					848
6105	Men's or boys'shirts, knitted or crocheted	506.5	565.6	518.9	4.0	4.3	4.1	US$/unit	843
2523	Portland cement, aluminous cement, slag cement	529.7	516.9	345.2	0.1	*0.1*	*0.1*	US$/kg	661

Services Imports and Exports: EBOPS 2002 categories

Table 2: Merchandise exports by SITC

(Value in million US$, growth and shares in percentage)

SITC	2015	Avg. Growth rates 2011-2015	Avg. Growth rates 2014-2015	2015 share
Total	22089.0	-3.4	-10.7	100.0
0+1	4255.5	-2.4	-5.1	19.3
2+4	738.5	-11.3	-31.5	3.3
3	265.1	-32.9	-59.1	1.2
5	882.0	-4.7	-17.4	4.0
6	9489.8	-2.7	-12.0	43.0
7	331.8	-7.0	-24.0	1.5
8	6121.4	0.3	-1.6	27.7
9	4.8	94.6	237.0	0.0

Table 3: Merchandise imports by SITC

(Value in million US$, growth and shares in percentage)

SITC	2015	Avg. Growth rates 2011-2015	Avg. Growth rates 2014-2015	2015 share
Total	43989.6	0.2	-7.5	100.0
0+1	2750.7	8.5	1.5	6.3
2+4	5664.1	-1.8	-2.7	12.9
3	10030.2	-9.4	-32.3	22.8
5	7425.0	1.2	1.8	16.9
6	5956.8	6.9	7.8	13.5
7	10515.5	8.4	10.6	23.9
8	1581.3	6.9	-13.4	3.6
9	66.1	-20.9	92.0	0.2

SITC Legend

SITC Code	Description
Total	All commodities
0+1	Food, animals + beverages, tobacco
2+4	Crude materials + anim. & veg. oils
3	Mineral fuels, lubricants
5	Chemicals
6	Goods classified chiefly by material
7	Machinery and transport equipment
8	Miscellaneous manufactured articles
9	Not classified elsewhere in the SITC

Graph 4: Merchandise trade balance

(Bln US$ by MDG Regions in 2015)

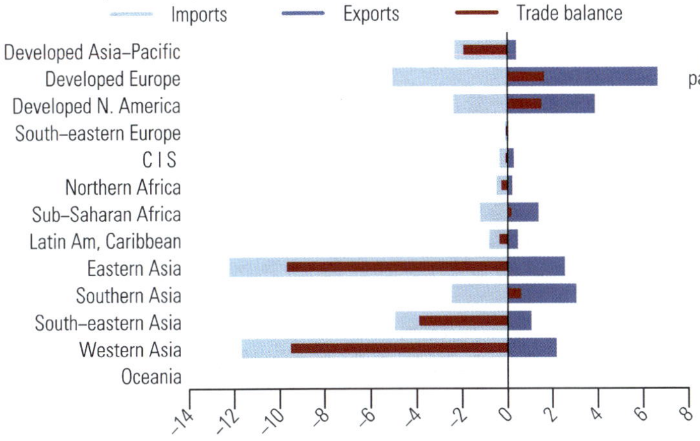

Graph 5: Partner concentration of merchandise trade

(Cumulative share by ranked partners in 2015)

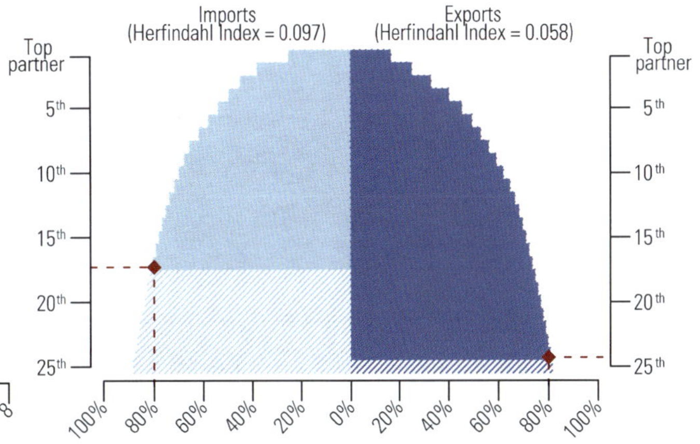

Graph 6: Imports of services by EBOPS category

(% share in 2014)

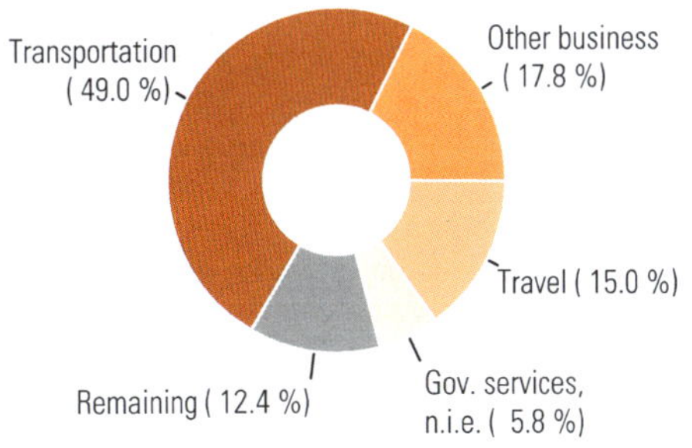

Imports Profile:

"Machinery and transport equipment" (SITC section 7), "Mineral fuels, lubricants" (SITC section 3) and "Chemicals" (SITC section 5) were the largest commodity groups for imports in 2015, representing respectively 23.9, 22.8 and 16.9 percent of imported goods (see table 3). From 2013 to 2015, the largest import commodity was "Petroleum oils, other than crude" (HS code 2710) (see table 4). The top three partners for merchandise imports were China, the United Arab Emirates and Saudi Arabia, accounting for respectively 20.1, 15.2 and 8.3 percent of total imports. "Transportation" (EBOPS code 205) accounted for the largest share of imports of services in 2014 at 4.0 bln US$, followed by "Other business services" (EBOPS code 268) at 1.4 bln US$ and "Travel" (EBOPS code 236) at 1.2 bln US$ (see graph 6).

Table 4: Top 10 import commodities 2013 to 2015

HS code	4-digit heading of Harmonized System 2012	Value (million US$) 2013	2014	2015	Unit value 2013	2014	2015	Unit	SITC code
	All Commodities	43775.2	47544.9	43989.6					
2710	Petroleum oils, other than crude	9258.0	8558.1	5898.3	0.8	0.7	*0.6*	US$/kg	334
2709	Petroleum oils and oils obtained from bituminous minerals, crude	5473.3	5609.1	3022.9	0.8	0.8	0.6	US$/kg	333
1511	Palm oil and its fractions	1842.9	1943.6	1653.4	0.8	0.8	0.7	US$/kg	422
8517	Electrical apparatus for line telephony or line telegraphy	1161.2	1353.8	1192.2					764
7204	Ferrous waste and scrap; remelting scrap ingots of iron or steel	662.2	908.4	1024.7	0.4	*0.4*	0.3	US$/kg	282
8703	Motor cars and other motor vehicles principally designed for the transport	689.4	703.3	891.5					781
8908	Vessels and other floating structures for breaking up	962.8	581.1	474.8	6.6		*4.7*	mln US$/unit	793
5201	Cotton, not carded or combed	757.3	521.6	543.7	2.0	2.2	2.0	US$/kg	263
3901	Polymers of ethylene, in primary forms	456.0	572.2	600.8	1.5	1.6	1.5	US$/kg	571
3902	Polymers of propylene or of other olefins, in primary forms	476.1	586.3	533.4	1.6	1.6	1.4	US$/kg	575

Panama

Goods Imports: CIF, by origin | **Goods Exports: FOB, by last known destination** | **Trade System: Special**

Overview:

In 2015, the value of merchandise exports of Panama decreased substantially by 15.0 percent to reach 695.7 mln US$, while its merchandise imports decreased substantially by 11.5 percent to reach 12.1 bln US$ (see graph 1, table 2 and table 3). The merchandise trade balance recorded a large deficit of 11.4 bln US$ (see graph 1). The largest merchandise trade balance was with MDG Developed North America at -3.1 bln US$ (see graph 4). Merchandise exports in Panama were diversified amongst partners; imports were also diversified. The top 17 partners accounted for 80 percent or more of exports and 13 partners accounted for 80 percent or more of imports (see graph 5). In 2014, the value of exports of services of Panama increased substantially by 30.2 percent, reaching 12.7 bln US$, while its imports of services decreased slightly by 2.1 percent and reached 4.6 bln US$ (see graph 2). There was a large trade in services surplus of 8.1 bln US$. See footnote*.

Graph 1: Total merchandise trade, by value

(Bln US$ by year)

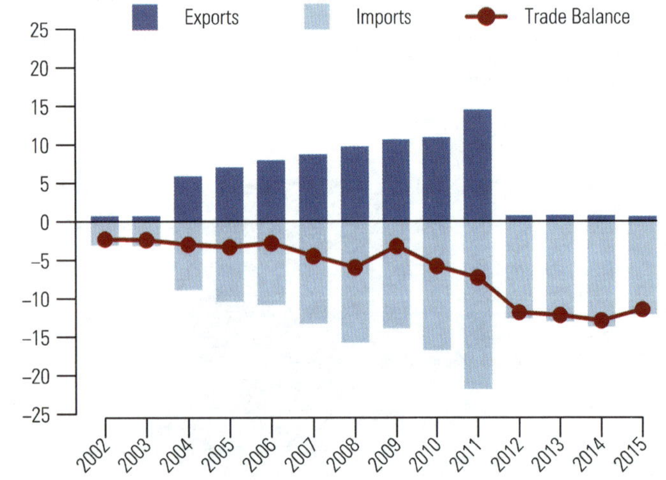

Graph 2: Total services trade, by value

(Bln US$ by year)

Exports Profile:

"Food, animals + beverages, tobacco" (SITC section 0+1), "Crude materials + anim. & veg. oils" (SITC section 2+4) and "Goods classified chiefly by material" (SITC section 6) were the largest commodity groups for exports in 2015, representing respectively 66.7, 17.9 and 8.8 percent of exported goods (see table 2). From 2013 to 2015, the largest export commodity was "Bananas, including plantains, fresh or dried" (HS code 0803) (see table 1). The top three destinations for merchandise exports were the United States, Germany and China, accounting for respectively 19.4, 9.7 and 6.9 percent of total exports. "Transportation" (EBOPS code 205) accounted for the largest share of exports of services in 2014 at 5.4 bln US$, followed by "Travel" (EBOPS code 236) at 3.7 bln US$ and "Other business services" (EBOPS code 268) at 2.4 bln US$ (see graph 3).

Graph 3: Exports of services by EBOPS category

(% share in 2014)

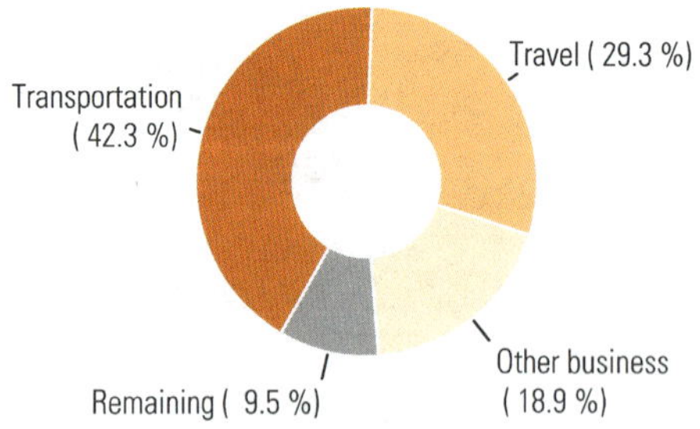

Table 1: Top 10 export commodities 2013 to 2015

HS code	4-digit heading of Harmonized System 2012	Value (million US$) 2013	2014	2015	Unit value 2013	2014	2015	Unit	SITC code
	All Commodities	843.9	818.2	695.7					
0803	Bananas, including plantains, fresh or dried	95.6	97.9	99.8	0.4	0.4	0.4	US$/kg	057
0306	Crustaceans, whether in shell or not	75.3	80.9	68.7	8.1	6.9	5.8	US$/kg	036
0302	Fish, fresh or chilled, excluding fish fillets	47.2	54.2	51.9	2.8	2.8	3.0	US$/kg	034
7204	Ferrous waste and scrap; remelting scrap ingots of iron or steel	45.9	45.7	28.1	0.1	0.2	0.1	US$/kg	282
2301	Flours, meals and pellets, of meat or meat offal	28.4	41.0	28.7	1.0	1.0	1.1	US$/kg	081
0804	Dates, figs, pineapples, avocados and mangosteens, fresh or dried	44.1	31.9	21.8	0.5	0.5	0.5	US$/kg	057
4403	Wood in the rough, whether or not stripped of bark or sapwood	28.7	28.2	30.0					247
1701	Cane or beet sugar and chemically pure sucrose, in solid form	24.0	27.7	20.1	0.5	0.5	0.6	US$/kg	061
7108	Gold (including gold plated with platinum)	66.5	1.1	...	33.3	23.7		thsd US$/kg	971
2208	Alcohol of a strength by volume of less than 80 % vol	25.2	20.9	19.5		*2.4*	*2.6*	US$/litre	112

*From 2004 to 2011 merchandise data including Zona Libre de Colon.

Services Imports and Exports: EBOPS 2002 categories

Table 2: Merchandise exports by SITC

(Value in million US$, growth and shares in percentage)

SITC	2015	Avg. Growth rates 2011-2015	Avg. Growth rates 2014-2015	2015 share
Total	695.7	-53.2	-15.0	100.0
0+1	464.2	-12.1	-10.7	66.7
2+4	124.8	-5.0	-26.0	17.9
3	0.7	-13.2	-46.4	0.1
5	26.3	-74.0	-15.0	3.8
6	61.0	-50.3	-19.8	8.8
8	14.9	-76.0	-7.3	2.1
9	3.7	-60.0	-30.5	0.5

Table 3: Merchandise imports by SITC

(Value in million US$, growth and shares in percentage)

SITC	2015	Avg. Growth rates 2011-2015	Avg. Growth rates 2014-2015	2015 share
Total	12 129.0	-13.6	-11.5	100.0
0+1	1 579.8	0.5	1.8	13.0
2+4	120.7	-3.2	-8.6	1.0
3	1 656.4	62.1	-40.9	13.7
5	1 356.3	-31.3	8.8	11.2
6	1 861.3	-7.3	-13.5	15.3
7	3 673.2	-9.3	-6.9	30.3
8	1 859.2	-24.7	0.3	15.3
9	22.2	-12.7	12.0	0.2

SITC Legend

SITC Code	Description
Total	All commodities
0+1	Food, animals + beverages, tobacco
2+4	Crude materials + anim. & veg. oils
3	Mineral fuels, lubricants
5	Chemicals
6	Goods classified chiefly by material
7	Machinery and transport equipment
8	Miscellaneous manufactured articles
9	Not classified elsewhere in the SITC

Graph 4: Merchandise trade balance

(Bln US$ by MDG Regions in 2015)

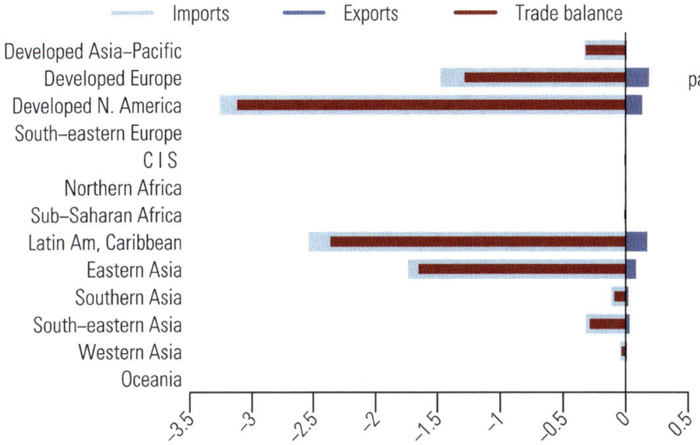

Graph 5: Partner concentration of merchandise trade

(Cumulative share by ranked partners in 2015)

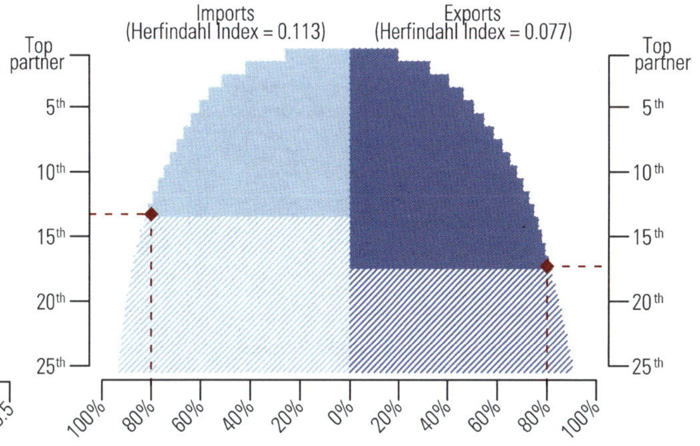

Graph 6: Imports of services by EBOPS category

(% share in 2014)

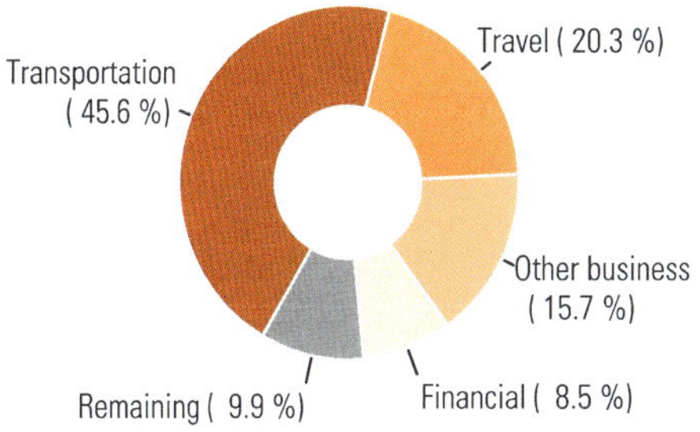

Imports Profile:

"Machinery and transport equipment" (SITC section 7), "Goods classified chiefly by material" (SITC section 6) and "Miscellaneous manufactured articles" (SITC section 8) were the largest commodity groups for imports in 2015, representing respectively 30.3, 15.3 and 15.3 percent of imported goods (see table 3). From 2013 to 2015, the largest import commodity was "Petroleum oils, other than crude" (HS code 2710) (see table 4). The top three partners for merchandise imports were the United States, Free zones and China, accounting for respectively 25.1, 16.8 and 8.5 percent of total imports. "Transportation" (EBOPS code 205) accounted for the largest share of imports of services in 2014 at 2.1 bln US$, followed by "Travel" (EBOPS code 236) at 938.8 mln US$ and "Other business services" (EBOPS code 268) at 724.4 mln US$ (see graph 6).

Table 4: Top 10 import commodities 2013 to 2015

HS code	4-digit heading of Harmonized System 2012	Value (million US$) 2013	2014	2015	Unit value 2013	2014	2015	Unit	SITC code
	All Commodities	13 024.0	13 705.3	12 129.0					
2710	Petroleum oils, other than crude	2 530.7	2 639.2	1 539.9	1.0	1.0	0.6	US$/kg	334
8703	Motor cars and other motor vehicles principally designed for the transport	794.2	840.2	921.3	*18.4*	*18.0*	*19.2*	thsd US$/unit	781
3004	Medicaments (excluding goods of heading 30.02, 30.05 or 30.06)	336.1	289.6	400.2	*39.1*	30.5	48.6	US$/kg	542
7308	Structures (excluding prefabricated buildings of heading 94.06)	179.7	454.3	312.5	3.6	4.6	3.4	US$/kg	691
8517	Electrical apparatus for line telephony or line telegraphy	206.3	206.9	194.2					764
7214	Other bars and rods of iron or non-alloy steel	192.3	186.4	126.6	0.7	0.6	0.5	US$/kg	676
8471	Automatic data processing machines and units thereof	180.4	169.2	128.0					752
9403	Other furniture and parts thereof	138.5	149.4	144.6					821
8704	Motor vehicles for the transport of goods	185.5	121.6	123.6					782
6402	Other footwear with outer soles and uppers of rubber or plastics	120.4	120.0	128.5	*9.9*	*10.4*	*10.9*	US$/pair	851

Papua New Guinea

Goods Imports: CIF, by origin	Goods Exports: FOB, by consignment	Trade System: General

Overview:

In 2012, the value of merchandise exports of Papua New Guinea decreased substantially by 17.9 percent to reach 4.5 bln US$, while its merchandise imports increased substantially by 36.6 percent to reach 8.3 bln US$ (see graph 1, table 2 and table 3). The merchandise trade balance recorded a moderate deficit of 3.8 bln US$ (see graph 1). The largest merchandise trade balance was with MDG South-eastern Asia at -1.8 bln US$ (see graph 4). Merchandise exports in Papua New Guinea were moderately concentrated amongst partners; imports were also moderately concentrated. The top 9 partners accounted for 80 percent or more of exports and 8 partners accounted for 80 percent or more of imports (see graph 5). In 2014, the value of exports of services of Papua New Guinea decreased substantially by 49.9 percent, reaching 209.4 mln US$, while its imports of services decreased substantially by 41.2 percent and reached 2.3 bln US$ (see graph 2). There was a large trade in services deficit of 2.1 bln US$.

Graph 1: Total merchandise trade, by value

(Bln US$ by year)

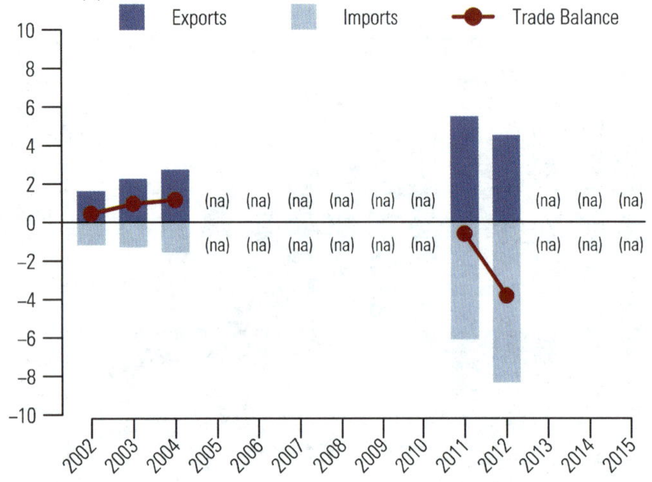

Graph 2: Total services trade, by value

(Bln US$ by year)

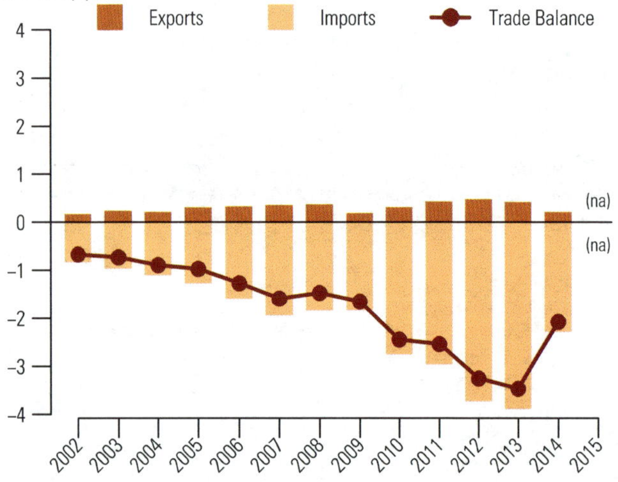

Exports Profile:

"Crude materials+anim. & veg. oils" (SITC section 2+4), "Goods classified chiefly by material" (SITC section 6) and "Food, animals + beverages, tobacco" (SITC section 0+1) were the largest commodity groups for exports in 2012, representing respectively 41.3, 33.6 and 13.5 percent of exported goods (see table 2). From 2010 to 2012, the largest export commodity was "Base metals, silver or gold, clad with platinum" (HS code 7111) (see table 1). The top three destinations for merchandise exports were Australia, Japan and Germany, accounting for respectively 39.7, 9.1 and 6.6 percent of total exports. "Other business services" (EBOPS code 268) accounted for the largest share of exports of services in 2014 at 122.7 mln US$, followed by "Government services, n.i.e." (EBOPS code 291) at 32.7 mln US$ and "Transportation" (EBOPS code 205) at 19.7 mln US$ (see graph 3).

Graph 3: Exports of services by EBOPS category

(% share in 2014)

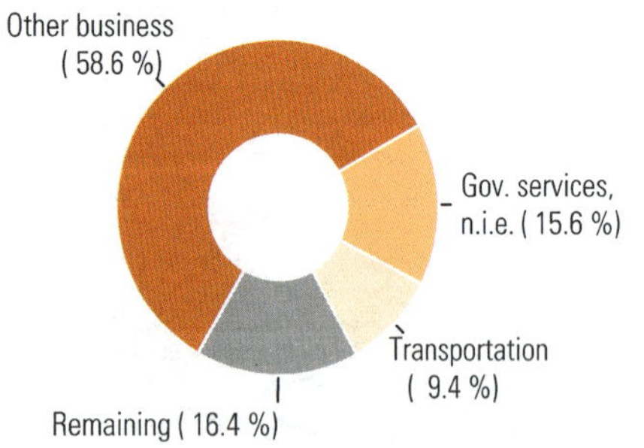

Table 1: Top 10 export commodities 2010 to 2012

HS code	4-digit heading of Harmonized System 2007	Value (million US$) 2010	2011	2012	Unit value 2010	2011	2012	Unit	SITC code
	All Commodities	...	5499.3	4517.7					
7111	Base metals, silver or gold, clad with platinum	...	2291.9	1493.4		301.8	302.4	thsd US$/kg	681
1511	Palm oil and its fractions	...	629.0	506.7		*0.9*		US$/kg	422
2603	Copper ores and concentrates	...	444.6	406.2			34.2	US$/kg	283
0901	Coffee, whether or not roasted or decaffeinated	...	404.2	254.1		31.4	31.6	US$/kg	071
2616	Precious metal ores and concentrates	...	298.2	320.5		1.3	17.4	thsd US$/kg	289
4403	Wood in the rough, whether or not stripped of bark or sapwood	...	209.5	240.5		84.4	90.7	US$/$m^3$	247
1513	Coconut (copra), palm kernel or babassu oil	...	165.5	81.3		*1.1*		US$/kg	422
2707	Oils and other products of high temperature coal tar	...	175.9	57.2		*1.3*		US$/kg	335
1801	Cocoa beans, whole or broken, raw or roasted	...	147.8	83.9					072
1604	Prepared or preserved fish; caviar	...	80.0	102.9		5.1	5.3	US$/kg	037

Services Imports and Exports: EBOPS 2002 categories

Table 2: Merchandise exports by SITC
(Value in million US$, growth and shares in percentage)

SITC	2012	Avg. Growth rates 2008-2012	Avg. Growth rates 2011-2012	2012 share
Total	4517.7	...	-17.9	100.0
0+1	607.9	...	-19.6	13.5
2+4	1866.4	...	-2.1	41.3
3	132.1	...	-36.8	2.9
5	219.6	...	476.2	4.9
6	1519.4	...	-34.6	33.6
7	135.6	...	-32.4	3.0
8	13.2	...	-11.6	0.3
9	23.4	...	-53.6	0.5

Table 3: Merchandise imports by SITC
(Value in million US$, growth and shares in percentage)

SITC	2012	Avg. Growth rates 2008-2012	Avg. Growth rates 2011-2012	2012 share
Total	8340.7	...	36.6	100.0
0+1	860.4	...	27.4	10.3
2+4	114.8	...	54.5	1.4
3	1445.9	...	165.1	17.3
5	484.4	...	23.6	5.8
6	1229.7	...	6.5	14.7
7	3538.3	...	34.7	42.4
8	551.0	...	15.1	6.6
9	116.1	...	-26.7	1.4

SITC Legend

SITC Code	Description
Total	All commodities
0+1	Food, animals + beverages, tobacco
2+4	Crude materials + anim. & veg. oils
3	Mineral fuels, lubricants
5	Chemicals
6	Goods classified chiefly by material
7	Machinery and transport equipment
8	Miscellaneous manufactured articles
9	Not classified elsewhere in the SITC

Graph 4: Merchandise trade balance
(Bln US$ by MDG Regions in 2012)

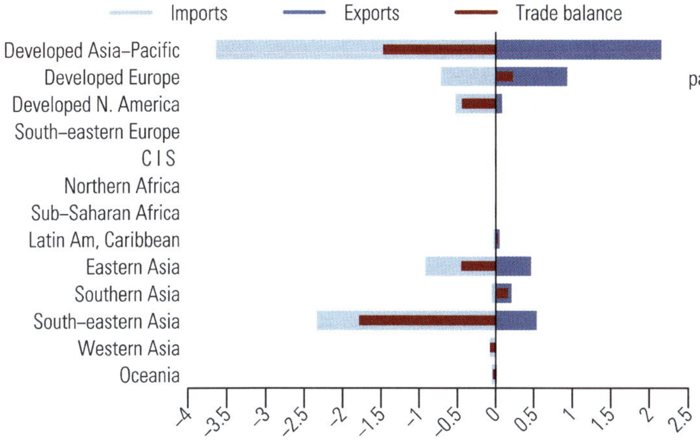

Graph 5: Partner concentration of merchandise trade
(Cumulative share by ranked partners in 2012)

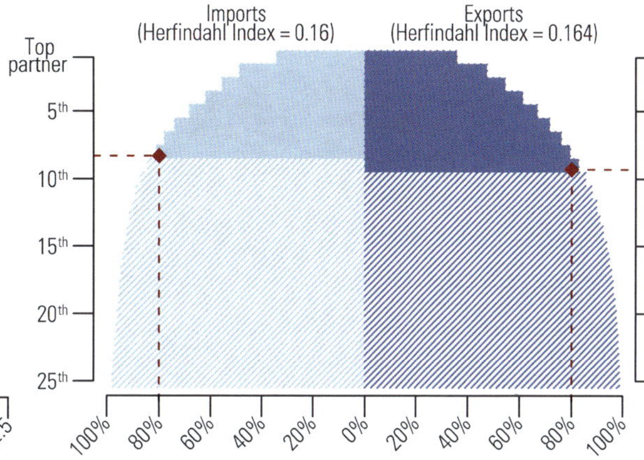

Graph 6: Imports of services by EBOPS category
(% share in 2014)

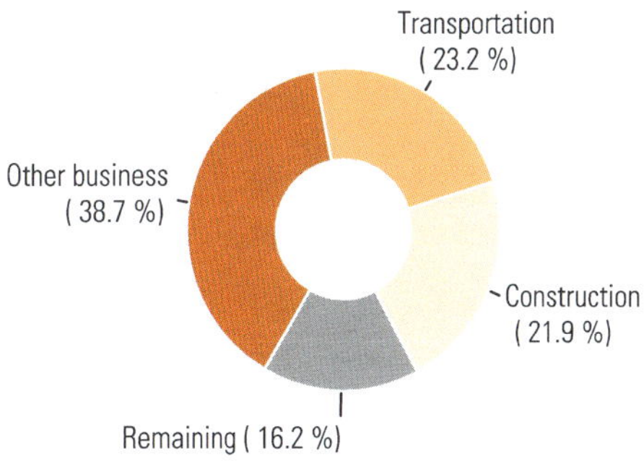

Imports Profile:

"Machinery and transport equipment" (SITC section 7), "Mineral fuels, lubricants" (SITC section 3) and "Goods classified chiefly by material" (SITC section 6) were the largest commodity groups for imports in 2012, representing respectively 42.4, 17.3 and 14.7 percent of imported goods (see table 3). From 2010 to 2012, the largest import commodity was "Petroleum oils, other than crude" (HS code 2710) (see table 4). The top three partners for merchandise imports were Australia, Singapore and China, accounting for respectively 36.5, 12.9 and 7.0 percent of total imports. "Other business services" (EBOPS code 268) accounted for the largest share of imports of services in 2014 at 884.8 mln US$, followed by "Transportation" (EBOPS code 205) at 529.5 mln US$ and "Construction services" (EBOPS code 249) at 501.7 mln US$ (see graph 6).

Table 4: Top 10 import commodities 2010 to 2012

HS code	4-digit heading of Harmonized System 2007	Value (million US$) 2010	2011	2012	Unit value 2010	2011	2012	Unit	SITC code
	All Commodities	...	6105.5	8340.7					
2710	Petroleum oils, other than crude	...	465.0	561.1					334
2709	Petroleum oils and oils obtained from bituminous minerals, crude	...	65.7	846.0		*0.8*		US$/kg	333
8704	Motor vehicles for the transport of goods	...	211.3	288.5			33.9	thsd US$/unit	782
8431	Parts suitable for use principally with the machinery of headings 84.25	...	214.1	240.0		*12.9*		US$/kg	723
1006	Rice	...	126.1	218.0		7.1		US$/kg	042
7308	Structures (excluding prefabricated buildings of heading 94.06)	...	106.1	193.5					691
9999	Commodities not specified according to kind	...	158.3	116.1					931
8481	Taps, cocks, valves and similar appliances for pipes, boiler shells	...	59.9	186.5					747
8702	Motor vehicles for the transport of ten or more persons, including the driver	...	96.8	149.5		30.4		thsd US$/unit	783
8414	Air or vacuum pumps, air or other gas compressors and fans	...	18.5	219.5					743

Source: UN Comtrade

Goods Imports: CIF, by origin | **Goods Exports: FOB, by last known destination** | **Trade System: General**

Overview:

In 2015, the value of merchandise exports of Paraguay decreased substantially by 13.2 percent to reach 8.4 bln US$, while its merchandise imports decreased substantially by 15.4 percent to reach 10.3 bln US$ (see graph 1, table 2 and table 3). The merchandise trade balance recorded a moderate deficit of 1.9 bln US$ (see graph 1). The largest merchandise trade balance was with MDG Eastern Asia at -2.7 bln US$ (see graph 4). Merchandise exports in Paraguay were diversified amongst partners; imports were moderately concentrated. The top 16 partners accounted for 80 percent or more of exports and 8 partners accounted for 80 percent or more of imports (see graph 5). In 2014, the value of exports of services of Paraguay increased moderately by 5.9 percent, reaching 891.6 mln US$, while its imports of services increased slightly by 4.1 percent and reached 1.1 bln US$ (see graph 2). There was a moderate trade in services deficit of 222.3 mln US$.

Graph 1: Total merchandise trade, by value

(Bln US$ by year)

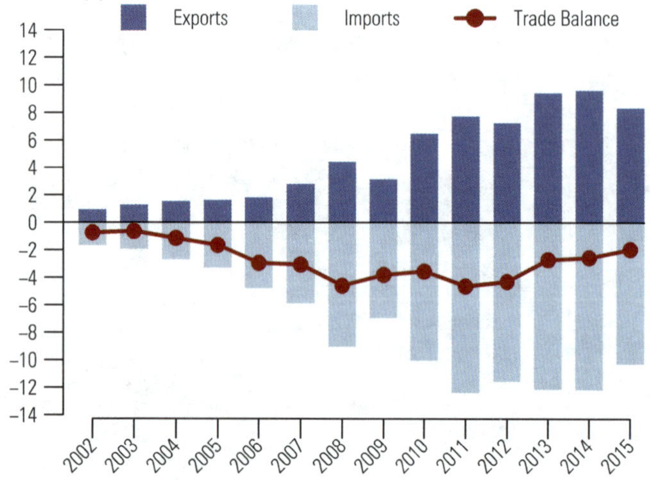

Graph 2: Total services trade, by value

(Bln US$ by year)

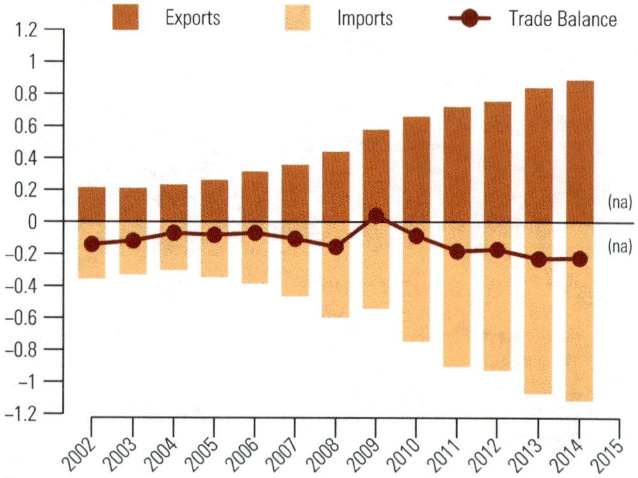

Exports Profile:

"Food, animals + beverages, tobacco" (SITC section 0+1), "Crude materials + anim. & veg. oils" (SITC section 2+4) and "Mineral fuels, lubricants" (SITC section 3) were the largest commodity groups for exports in 2015, representing respectively 35.9, 28.2 and 25.4 percent of exported goods (see table 2). From 2013 to 2015, the largest export commodity was "Electrical energy" (HS code 2716) (see table 1). The top three destinations for merchandise exports were Brazil, the Russian Federation and Argentina, accounting for respectively 30.8, 10.0 and 7.3 percent of total exports. "Transportation" (EBOPS code 205) accounted for the largest share of exports of services in 2014 at 388.4 mln US$, followed by "Travel" (EBOPS code 236) at 288.2 mln US$ and "Government services, n.i.e." (EBOPS code 291) at 166.5 mln US$ (see graph 3).

Graph 3: Exports of services by EBOPS category

(% share in 2014)

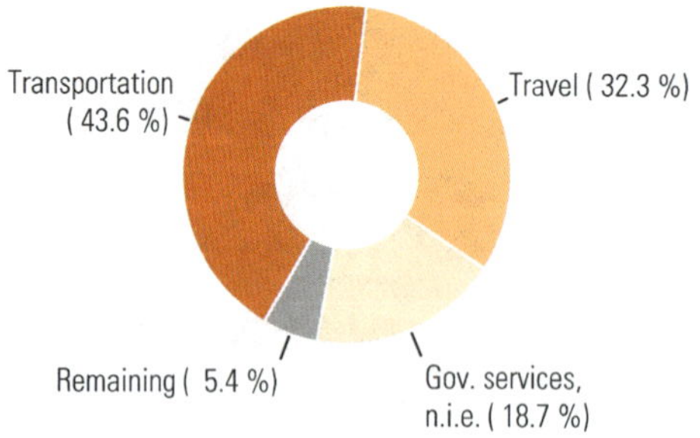

Table 1: Top 10 export commodities 2013 to 2015

HS code	4-digit heading of Harmonized System 2012	Value (million US$) 2013	2014	2015	Unit value 2013	2014	2015	Unit	SITC code
	All Commodities	9456.3	9635.7	8361.2					
2716	Electrical energy	2245.2	2143.7	2069.2	*65.6*	*59.5*	*54.1*	US$/MWh	351
1201	Soya beans, whether or not broken	2509.1	2305.1	1594.2	0.5	0.5	0.3	US$/kg	222
2304	Oil-cake and other solid residues	923.0	1107.4	904.7	0.5	0.5	0.4	US$/kg	081
0202	Meat of bovine animals, frozen	771.5	831.1	659.3	4.1	4.3	3.7	US$/kg	011
1507	Soya-bean oil and its fractions	467.5	481.1	445.2	0.9	0.8	0.6	US$/kg	421
1005	Maize (corn)	463.7	356.9	441.2					044
0201	Meat of bovine animals, fresh or chilled	233.2	453.8	462.6	5.3	5.5	5.0	US$/kg	011
4104	Tanned or crust hides and skins of bovine (including buffalo)	153.2	195.3	150.0	3.1	3.7	2.9	US$/kg	611
1006	Rice	165.4	177.6	129.8	0.4	0.4	0.3	US$/kg	042
1001	Wheat and meslin	146.1	79.4	152.9	0.3	0.2	0.2	US$/kg	041

Services Imports and Exports: EBOPS 2002 categories

Table 2: Merchandise exports by SITC

(Value in million US$, growth and shares in percentage)

SITC	2015	Avg. Growth rates 2011-2015	Avg. Growth rates 2014-2015	2015 share
Total	8 361.2	1.9	-13.2	100.0
0+1	3 000.2	11.4	-9.3	35.9
2+4	2 357.1	-5.1	-26.4	28.2
3	2 122.9	-1.8	-2.9	25.4
5	147.9	1.9	-21.5	1.8
6	323.9	4.9	-10.8	3.9
7	203.2	49.4	26.4	2.4
8	168.4	-0.6	-16.7	2.0
9	37.7	52.6	44.5	0.5

Table 3: Merchandise imports by SITC

(Value in million US$, growth and shares in percentage)

SITC	2015	Avg. Growth rates 2011-2015	Avg. Growth rates 2014-2015	2015 share
Total	10 291.2	-4.5	-15.4	100.0
0+1	865.3	-0.3	-10.5	8.4
2+4	152.4	1.3	-7.6	1.5
3	1 409.1	-3.8	-24.9	13.7
5	1 910.9	1.9	-4.8	18.6
6	1 418.1	-1.7	-12.1	13.8
7	3 591.5	-8.2	-17.9	34.9
8	942.4	-8.8	-19.0	9.2
9	1.5	9.7	271.9	0.0

SITC Legend

SITC Code	Description
Total	All commodities
0+1	Food, animals + beverages, tobacco
2+4	Crude materials + anim. & veg. oils
3	Mineral fuels, lubricants
5	Chemicals
6	Goods classified chiefly by material
7	Machinery and transport equipment
8	Miscellaneous manufactured articles
9	Not classified elsewhere in the SITC

Graph 4: Merchandise trade balance

(Bln US$ by MDG Regions in 2015)

Graph 5: Partner concentration of merchandise trade

(Cumulative share by ranked partners in 2015)

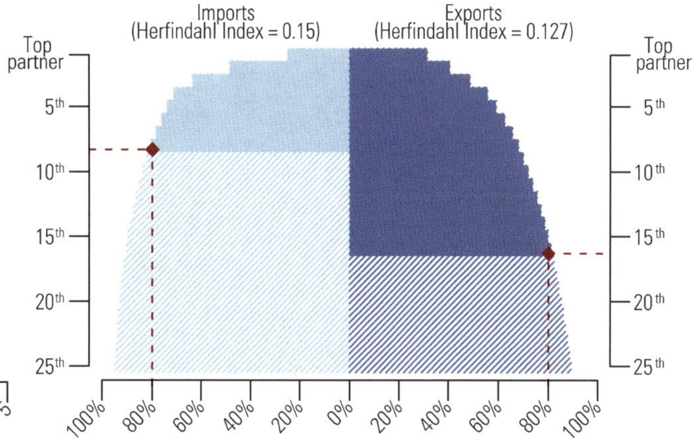

Graph 6: Imports of services by EBOPS category

(% share in 2014)

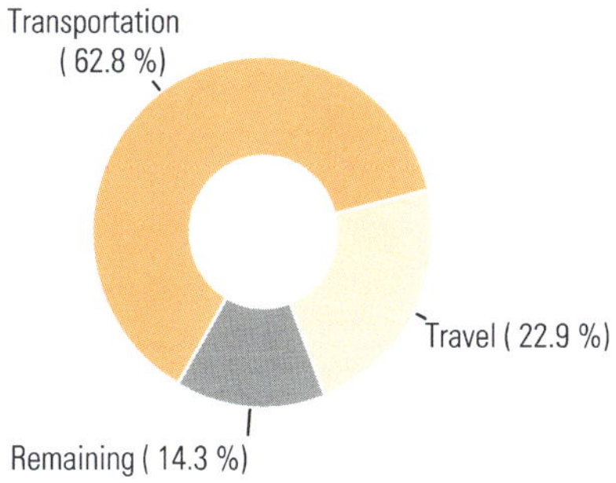

Imports Profile:

"Machinery and transport equipment" (SITC section 7), "Chemicals" (SITC section 5) and "Goods classified chiefly by material" (SITC section 6) were the largest commodity groups for imports in 2015, representing respectively 34.9, 18.6 and 13.8 percent of imported goods (see table 3). From 2013 to 2015, the largest import commodity was "Petroleum oils, other than crude" (HS code 2710) (see table 4). The top three partners for merchandise imports were Brazil, China and Argentina, accounting for respectively 26.5, 25.8 and 14.2 percent of total imports. "Transportation" (EBOPS code 205) accounted for the largest share of imports of services in 2014 at 699.3 mln US$, followed by "Travel" (EBOPS code 236) at 255.5 mln US$ (see graph 6).

Table 4: Top 10 import commodities 2013 to 2015

HS code	4-digit heading of Harmonized System 2012	Value (million US$) 2013	2014	2015	Unit value 2013	2014	2015	Unit	SITC code
	All Commodities	12 142.0	12 168.6	10 291.2					
2710	Petroleum oils, other than crude	1 639.1	1 793.5	1 324.2	1.1	1.1	0.7	US$/kg	334
8517	Electrical apparatus for line telephony or line telegraphy	783.3	644.6	512.1					764
8703	Motor cars and other motor vehicles principally designed for the transport	489.6	538.9	452.7	*16.1*	*16.6*	*18.1*	thsd US$/unit	781
3105	Mineral or chemical fertilisers	421.7	414.9	341.0	0.6	0.5	0.5	US$/kg	562
3808	Insecticides, rodenticides, fungicides, herbicides	310.5	323.5	335.0	*8.4*	9.3	*8.6*	US$/kg	591
8471	Automatic data processing machines and units thereof	361.9	284.1	172.0					752
8704	Motor vehicles for the transport of goods	252.3	257.3	232.3					782
9504	Articles for funfair, table or parlour games, including pintables	253.1	240.6	141.9					894
4011	New pneumatic tyres, of rubber	211.5	196.8	166.5					625
8528	Reception apparatus for television	210.3	196.6	137.0					761

Source: UN Comtrade

Peru

Goods Imports: CIF, by origin | **Goods Exports: FOB, by last known destination** | **Trade System: Special**

Overview:

In 2015, the value of merchandise exports of Peru decreased substantially by 13.6 percent to reach 33.2 bln US$, while its merchandise imports decreased moderately by 9.7 percent to reach 38.1 bln US$ (see graph 1, table 2 and table 3). The merchandise trade balance recorded a relatively small deficit of 4.9 bln US$ (see graph 1). The largest merchandise trade balance was with MDG Latin America and the Caribbean at -3.4 bln US$ (see graph 4). Merchandise exports in Peru were diversified amongst partners; imports were also diversified. The top 14 partners accounted for 80 percent or more of exports and 15 partners accounted for 80 percent or more of imports (see graph 5). In 2013, the value of exports of services of Peru increased substantially by 13.3 percent, reaching 5.8 bln US$, while its imports of services increased slightly by 3.1 percent and reached 7.6 bln US$ (see graph 2). There was a moderate trade in services deficit of 1.8 bln US$.

Graph 1: Total merchandise trade, by value

(Bln US$ by year)

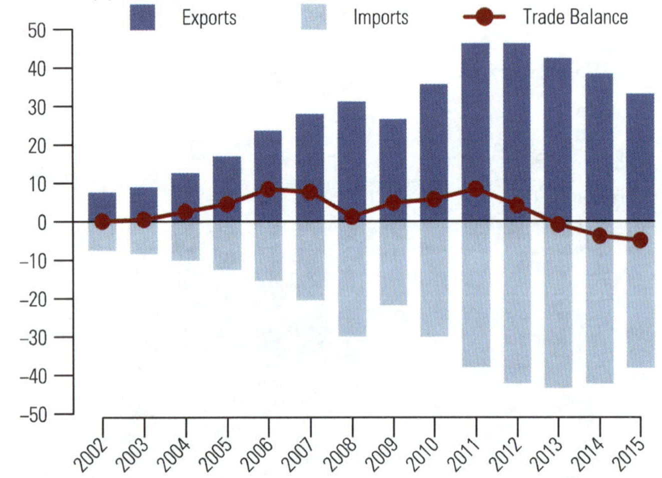

Graph 2: Total services trade, by value

(Bln US$ by year)

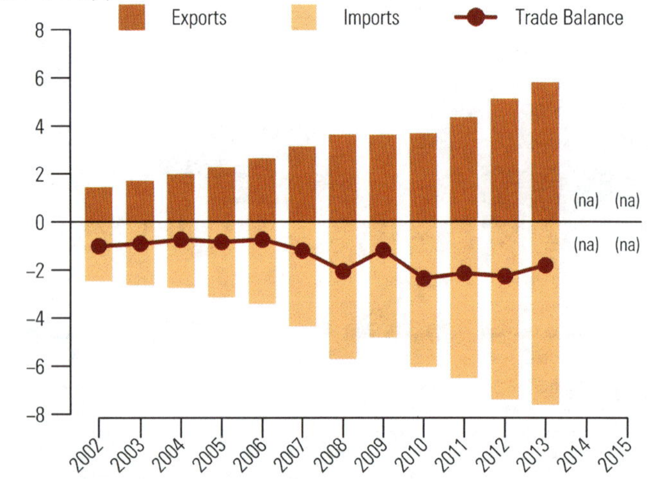

Exports Profile:

"Crude materials + anim. & veg. oils" (SITC section 2+4), "Food, animals + beverages, tobacco" (SITC section 0+1) and "Not classified elsewhere in the SITC" (SITC section 9) were the largest commodity groups for exports in 2015, representing respectively 33.6, 20.6 and 17.0 percent of exported goods (see table 2). From 2013 to 2015, the largest export commodity was "Copper ores and concentrates" (HS code 2603) (see table 1). The top three destinations for merchandise exports were China, the United States and Switzerland, accounting for respectively 19.0, 16.7 and 7.3 percent of total exports. "Travel" (EBOPS code 236) accounted for the largest share of exports of services in 2013 at 3.0 bln US$, followed by "Transportation" (EBOPS code 205) at 1.5 bln US$ and "Other business services" (EBOPS code 268) at 482.5 mln US$ (see graph 3).

Graph 3: Exports of services by EBOPS category

(% share in 2013)

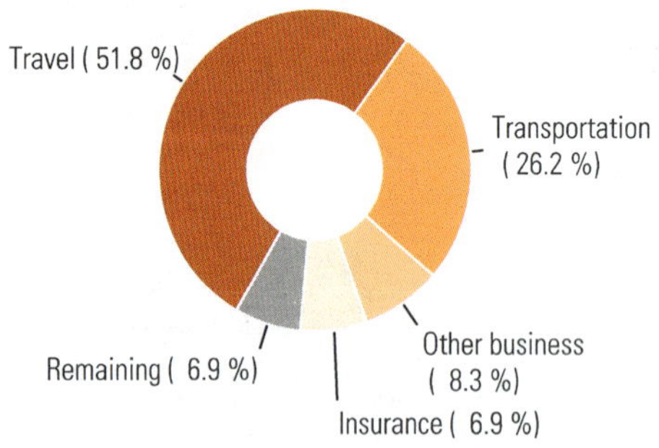

Table 1: Top 10 export commodities 2013 to 2015

HS code	4-digit heading of Harmonized System 2012	Value (million US$) 2013	2014	2015	Unit value 2013	2014	2015	Unit	SITC code
	All Commodities	42 568.9	38 459.3	33 244.9					
2603	Copper ores and concentrates	7 601.5	6 926.2	6 568.1	2.0	1.8	1.3	US$/kg	283
7108	Gold (including gold plated with platinum)	8 207.4	5 627.8	5 655.8	27.7	22.1	19.4	thsd US$/kg	971
2710	Petroleum oils, other than crude	3 352.8	3 290.3	1 771.2	0.8	0.8	0.4	US$/kg	334
7403	Refined copper and copper alloys, unwrought	2 111.9	1 863.3	1 502.5	7.4	7.0	5.6	US$/kg	682
2301	Flours, meals and pellets, of meat or meat offal	1 388.9	1 357.1	1 176.1	1.6	1.6	1.7	US$/kg	081
2608	Zinc ores and concentrates	1 038.2	1 165.6	1 202.0	0.6	0.6	0.6	US$/kg	287
2607	Lead ores and concentrates	1 145.1	1 016.7	1 081.0	3.0	2.5	1.9	US$/kg	287
2711	Petroleum gases and other gaseous hydrocarbons	1 599.6	930.6	483.7	0.4	0.2		US$/kg	343
0901	Coffee, whether or not roasted or decaffeinated	699.1	734.1	584.5	2.9	4.0	3.3	US$/kg	071
2601	Iron ores and concentrates, including roasted iron pyrites	856.8	646.7	350.0	0.1	0.1	0.0	US$/kg	281

Services Imports and Exports: EBOPS 2002 categories

Table 2: Merchandise exports by SITC

(Value in million US$, growth and shares in percentage)

SITC	2015	Avg. Growth rates 2011-2015	Avg. Growth rates 2014-2015	2015 share
Total	33 244.9	-8.0	-13.6	100.0
0+1	6 852.5	-1.0	-5.2	20.6
2+4	11 160.9	-6.0	-7.2	33.6
3	2 411.1	-16.2	-49.3	7.3
5	1 136.6	-4.8	-5.6	3.4
6	4 230.9	-8.8	-21.8	12.7
7	446.0	3.1	-10.6	1.3
8	1 350.9	-9.4	-20.8	4.1
9	5 656.1	-13.6	0.5	17.0

Table 3: Merchandise imports by SITC

(Value in million US$, growth and shares in percentage)

SITC	2015	Avg. Growth rates 2011-2015	Avg. Growth rates 2014-2015	2015 share
Total	38 104.6	0.1	-9.7	100.0
0+1	3 702.9	3.4	-2.2	9.7
2+4	1 254.8	-4.7	-18.5	3.3
3	3 934.0	-9.8	-34.3	10.3
5	5 859.1	1.7	-3.3	15.4
6	6 257.4	1.1	-2.9	16.4
7	13 704.0	1.0	-8.2	36.0
8	3 383.3	7.3	-2.2	8.9
9	9.2	9.8	5685.5	0.0

SITC Legend

SITC Code	Description
Total	All commodities
0+1	Food, animals + beverages, tobacco
2+4	Crude materials + anim. & veg. oils
3	Mineral fuels, lubricants
5	Chemicals
6	Goods classified chiefly by material
7	Machinery and transport equipment
8	Miscellaneous manufactured articles
9	Not classified elsewhere in the SITC

Graph 4: Merchandise trade balance

(Bln US$ by MDG Regions in 2015)

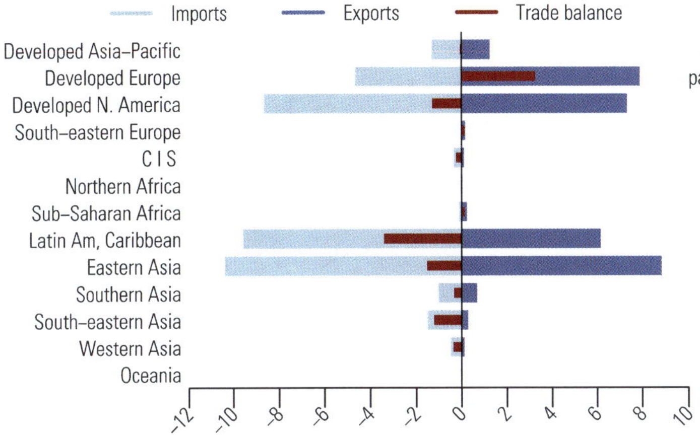

Graph 5: Partner concentration of merchandise trade

(Cumulative share by ranked partners in 2015)

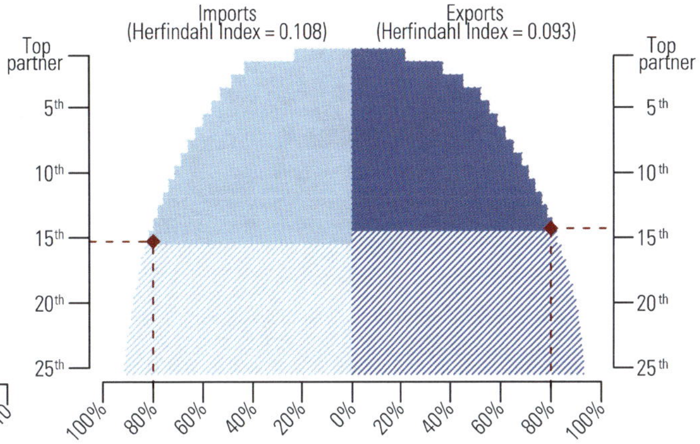

Graph 6: Imports of services by EBOPS category

(% share in 2013)

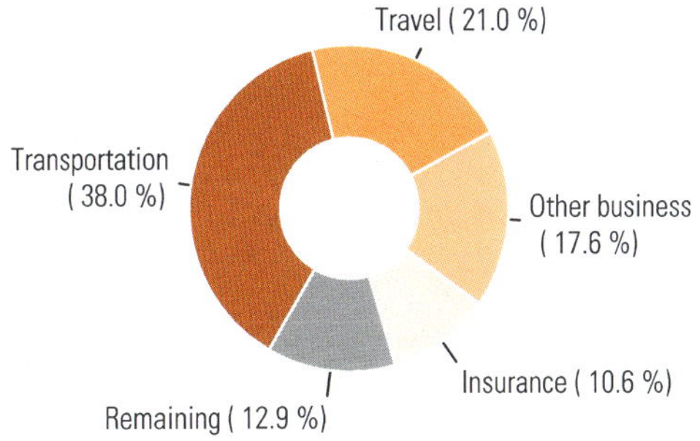

Imports Profile:

"Machinery and transport equipment" (SITC section 7), "Goods classified chiefly by material" (SITC section 6) and "Chemicals" (SITC section 5) were the largest commodity groups for imports in 2015, representing respectively 36.0, 16.4 and 15.4 percent of imported goods (see table 3). From 2013 to 2015, the largest import commodity was "Petroleum oils, other than crude" (HS code 2710) (see table 4). The top three partners for merchandise imports were China, the United States and Brazil, accounting for respectively 21.0, 20.6 and 5.1 percent of total imports. "Transportation" (EBOPS code 205) accounted for the largest share of imports of services in 2013 at 2.9 bln US$, followed by "Travel" (EBOPS code 236) at 1.6 bln US$ and "Other business services" (EBOPS code 268) at 1.3 bln US$ (see graph 6).

Table 4: Top 10 import commodities 2013 to 2015

HS code	4-digit heading of Harmonized System 2012	Value (million US$) 2013	2014	2015	Unit value 2013	2014	2015	Unit	SITC code
	All Commodities	43 321.7	42 193.6	38 104.6					
2710	Petroleum oils, other than crude	3 177.7	2 861.1	2 195.8	1.0	1.0	0.6	US$/kg	334
2709	Petroleum oils and oils obtained from bituminous minerals, crude	3 355.5	3 017.6	1 631.0	0.8	0.7	0.4	US$/kg	333
8703	Motor cars and other motor vehicles principally designed for the transport	1 766.9	1 764.7	1 591.6	10.9	10.7	10.7	thsd US$/unit	781
8517	Electrical apparatus for line telephony or line telegraphy	1 239.2	1 661.7	1 626.9					764
8704	Motor vehicles for the transport of goods	1 561.0	863.0	746.7	31.6	29.5	27.3	thsd US$/unit	782
8471	Automatic data processing machines and units thereof	797.4	791.9	750.9	88.7	75.7	*94.5*	US$/unit	752
8429	Self-propelled bulldozers, angledozers, graders, levellers, scrapers	798.7	714.7	476.1	102.4	137.3	20.7	thsd US$/unit	723
1001	Wheat and meslin	625.9	609.4	533.9	0.3	0.3	0.3	US$/kg	041
1005	Maize (corn)	581.1	567.7	576.0	0.3	0.2	0.2	US$/kg	044
8528	Reception apparatus for television	587.0	595.3	530.2	185.3	171.6	114.6	US$/unit	761

Philippines

Goods Imports: CIF, by origin | **Goods Exports: FOB, by last known destination** | **Trade System: General**

Overview:

In 2015, the value of merchandise exports of the Philippines decreased moderately by 5.1 percent to reach 58.6 bln US$, while its merchandise imports increased slightly by 3.6 percent to reach 70.2 bln US$ (see graph 1, table 2 and table 3). The merchandise trade balance recorded a relatively small deficit of 11.5 bln US$ (see graph 1). The largest merchandise trade balance was with MDG South-eastern Asia at -8.5 bln US$ (see graph 4). Merchandise exports in the Philippines were diversified amongst partners; imports were also diversified. The top 9 partners accounted for 80 percent or more of exports and 12 partners accounted for 80 percent or more of imports (see graph 5). In 2014, the value of exports of services of the Philippines increased substantially by 13.9 percent, reaching 24.7 bln US$, while its imports of services increased substantially by 34.1 percent and reached 19.6 bln US$ (see graph 2). There was a moderate trade in services surplus of 5.1 bln US$.

Graph 1: Total merchandise trade, by value

(Bln US$ by year)

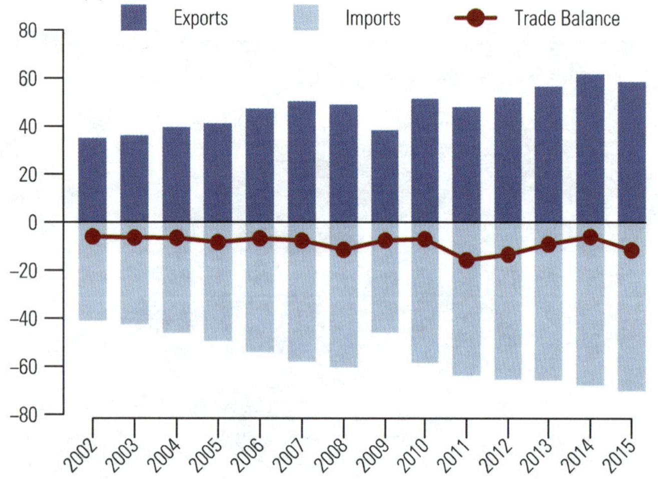

Graph 2: Total services trade, by value

(Bln US$ by year)

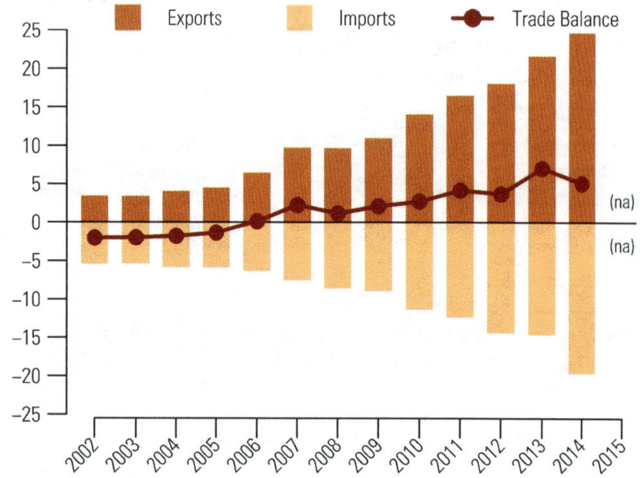

Exports Profile:

"Machinery and transport equipment" (SITC section 7), "Miscellaneous manufactured articles" (SITC section 8) and "Goods classified chiefly by material" (SITC section 6) were the largest commodity groups for exports in 2015, representing respectively 64.6, 9.7 and 8.5 percent of exported goods (see table 2). From 2013 to 2015, the largest export commodity was "Electronic integrated circuits and microassemblies" (HS code 8542) (see table 1). The top three destinations for merchandise exports were Japan, the United States and China, accounting for respectively 21.6, 14.6 and 12.1 percent of total exports. "Other business services" (EBOPS code 268) accounted for the largest share of exports of services in 2014 at 14.3 bln US$, followed by "Travel" (EBOPS code 236) at 4.8 bln US$ and "Computer and information services" (EBOPS code 262) at 3.1 bln US$ (see graph 3).

Graph 3: Exports of services by EBOPS category

(% share in 2014)

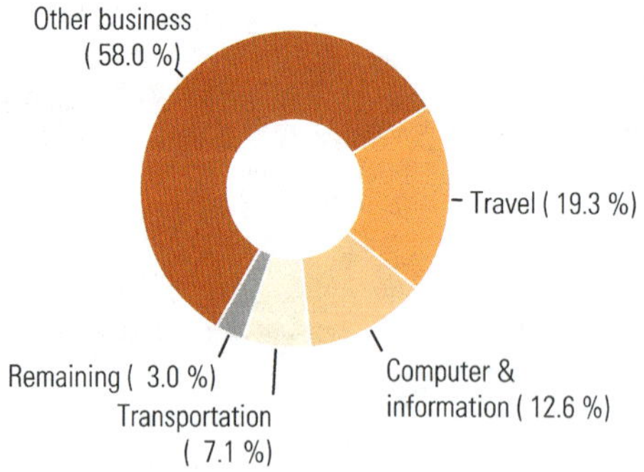

Table 1: Top 10 export commodities 2013 to 2015

HS code	4-digit heading of Harmonized System 2002	Value (million US$)			Unit value				SITC code
		2013	2014	2015	2013	2014	2015	Unit	
	All Commodities	56 697.8	61 809.8	58 648.1					
8542	Electronic integrated circuits and microassemblies	11 099.4	12 157.7	14 352.4					776
8471	Automatic data processing machines and units thereof	3 890.2	4 793.0	4 687.4	135.1	*58.4*	*36.4*	US$/unit	752
4418	Builders' joinery and carpentry of wood	3 032.3	2 925.3	2 750.2	3.3	3.0	2.0	US$/kg	635
8541	Diodes, transistors and similar semiconductor devices	2 535.6	2 954.6	3 038.8					776
8544	Insulated (including enamelled or anodised) wire, cable	1 825.4	2 174.5	2 263.3	*14.3*	*2.1*	*13.1*	US$/kg	773
8473	Parts and accessories for use with machines of heading 84.69 to 84.72	2 001.4	2 199.4	1 949.0		7.6	2.8	US$/kg	759
8504	Electrical transformers, static converters (for example, rectifiers)	1 904.6	1 557.4	1 544.2					771
8708	Parts and accessories of the motor vehicles of headings 87.01 to 87.05	1 489.6	1 472.3	1 306.9	15.2	*12.3*	*13.7*	US$/kg	784
2604	Nickel ores and concentrates	1 018.1	1 717.4	739.8	0.0	0.0	0.0	US$/kg	284
1513	Coconut (copra), palm kernel or babassu oil	1 006.0	1 345.9	1 122.6	0.9	1.5	1.3	US$/kg	422

Services Imports and Exports: EBOPS 2002 categories

Table 2: Merchandise exports by SITC

(Value in million US$, growth and shares in percentage)

SITC	2015	Avg. Growth rates 2011-2015	2014-2015	2015 share
Total	58648.1	5.1	-5.1	100.0
0+1	3324.9	-0.9	-30.7	5.7
2+4	3885.2	4.7	-29.6	6.6
3	774.6	-13.8	-57.8	1.3
5	1652.6	-3.1	-25.3	2.8
6	4984.1	2.2	-10.1	8.5
7	37871.3	17.5	6.4	64.6
8	5704.0	18.4	-5.4	9.7
9	451.4	-54.7	54.8	0.8

Table 3: Merchandise imports by SITC

(Value in million US$, growth and shares in percentage)

SITC	2015	Avg. Growth rates 2011-2015	2014-2015	2015 share
Total	70153.5	2.4	3.6	100.0
0+1	7467.6	6.2	-0.6	10.6
2+4	1656.6	-6.9	6.9	2.4
3	8292.0	-10.3	-39.0	11.8
5	7112.9	1.3	-4.6	10.1
6	7519.6	6.7	11.2	10.7
7	34355.6	17.5	24.5	49.0
8	3522.7	12.8	21.1	5.0
9	226.5	-61.2	-34.6	0.3

SITC Legend

SITC Code	Description
Total	All commodities
0+1	Food, animals + beverages, tobacco
2+4	Crude materials + anim. & veg. oils
3	Mineral fuels, lubricants
5	Chemicals
6	Goods classified chiefly by material
7	Machinery and transport equipment
8	Miscellaneous manufactured articles
9	Not classified elsewhere in the SITC

Graph 4: Merchandise trade balance

(Bln US$ by MDG Regions in 2015)

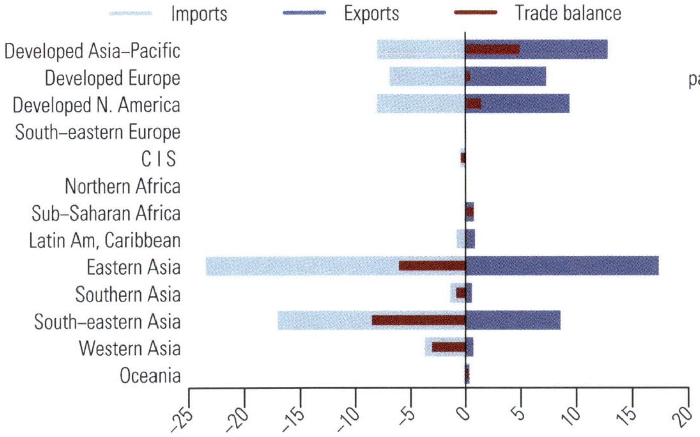

Graph 5: Partner concentration of merchandise trade

(Cumulative share by ranked partners in 2015)

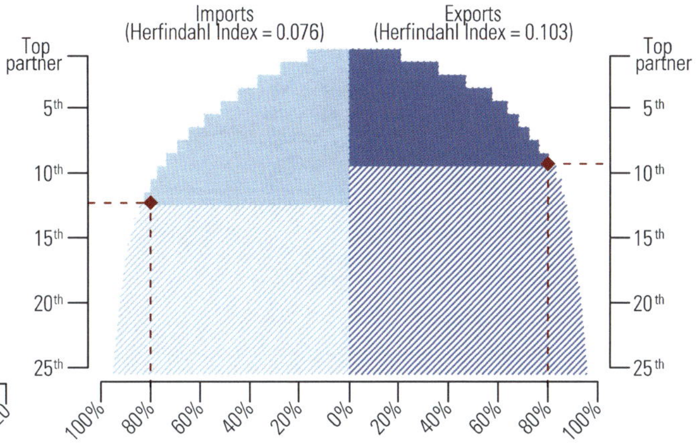

Graph 6: Imports of services by EBOPS category

(% share in 2014)

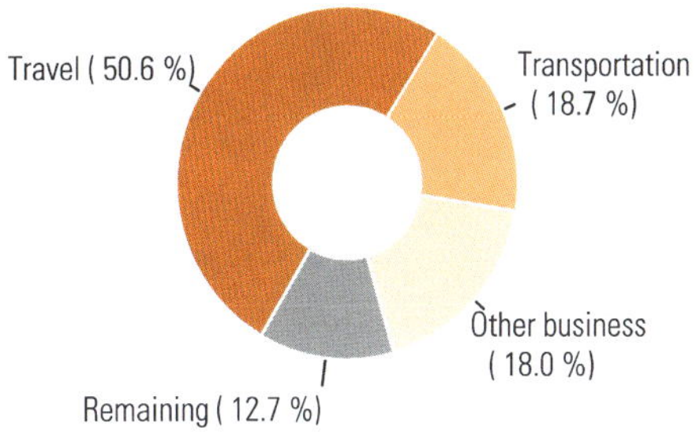

Imports Profile:

"Machinery and transport equipment" (SITC section 7), "Mineral fuels, lubricants" (SITC section 3) and "Goods classified chiefly by material" (SITC section 6) were the largest commodity groups for imports in 2015, representing respectively 49.0, 11.8 and 10.7 percent of imported goods (see table 3). From 2013 to 2015, the largest import commodity was "Electronic integrated circuits and microassemblies" (HS code 8542) (see table 4). The top three partners for merchandise imports were China, the United States and Japan, accounting for respectively 14.9, 10.3 and 8.8 percent of total imports. "Travel" (EBOPS code 236) accounted for the largest share of imports of services in 2014 at 9.9 bln US$, followed by "Transportation" (EBOPS code 205) at 3.7 bln US$ and "Other business services" (EBOPS code 268) at 3.5 bln US$ (see graph 6).

Table 4: Top 10 import commodities 2013 to 2015

HS code	4-digit heading of Harmonized System 2002	Value (million US$) 2013	2014	2015	Unit value 2013	2014	2015	Unit	SITC code
	All Commodities	65705.4	67718.9	70153.5					
8542	Electronic integrated circuits and microassemblies	10585.5	9915.8	13617.4					776
2709	Petroleum oils, crude	6611.6	6340.0	3952.4	0.8	0.8	0.4	US$/kg	333
2710	Petroleum oils, other than crude	5285.1	5857.4	3337.0	1.0	0.9	*0.5*	US$/kg	334
8473	Parts and accessories for use with machines of heading 84.69 to 84.72	2181.9	1803.1	2077.2	25.1	22.3	*30.4*	US$/kg	759
8703	Motor cars and other motor vehicles principally designed for the transport	1714.9	1720.6	2322.3	*8.8*	*3.3*	*6.6*	thsd US$/unit	781
8802	Other aircraft (for example, helicopters, aeroplanes); spacecraft	2316.3	2128.5	825.5	46.3	34.3		mln US$/unit	792
1001	Wheat and meslin	868.9	922.5	982.1	0.4	0.3	0.3	US$/kg	041
3004	Medicaments (excluding goods of heading 30.02, 30.05 or 30.06)	833.2	799.6	985.9	26.5	22.1	21.8	US$/kg	542
2304	Oil-cake and other solid residues	758.9	969.5	707.2	0.5	0.5	0.5	US$/kg	081
2701	Coal; briquettes, ovoids and similar solid fuels manufactured from coal	821.6	762.0	670.5	0.1	0.1	0.1	US$/kg	321

Poland

Goods Imports: CIF, by origin | **Goods Exports: FOB, by last known destination** | **Trade System: Special**

Overview:

In 2015, the value of merchandise exports of Poland decreased moderately by 9.3 percent to reach 194.5 bln US$, while its merchandise imports decreased substantially by 12.5 percent to reach 189.7 bln US$ (see graph 1, table 2 and table 3). The merchandise trade balance recorded a relatively small surplus of 4.8 bln US$ (see graph 1). The largest merchandise trade balance was with MDG Developed Europe at 39.8 bln US$ (see graph 4). Merchandise exports in Poland were diversified amongst partners; imports were also diversified. The top 18 partners accounted for 80 percent or more of exports and 19 partners accounted for 80 percent or more of imports (see graph 5). In 2014, the value of exports of services of Poland increased moderately by 7.2 percent, reaching 43.1 bln US$, while its imports of services increased moderately by 6.0 percent and reached 34.9 bln US$ (see graph 2). There was a moderate trade in services surplus of 8.3 bln US$.

Graph 1: Total merchandise trade, by value

(Bln US$ by year)

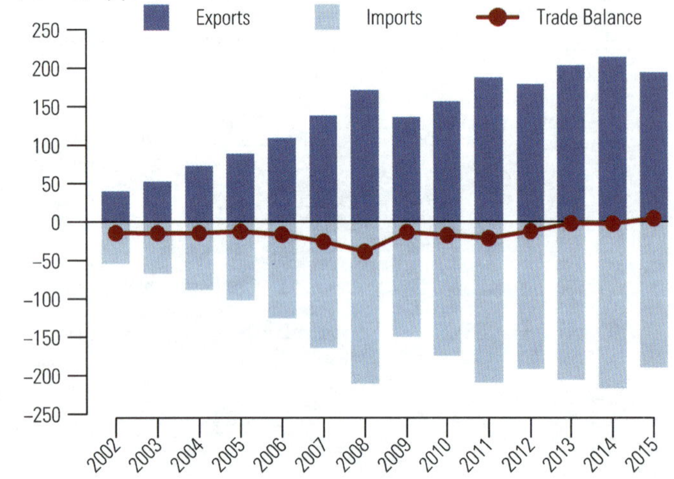

Graph 2: Total services trade, by value

(Bln US$ by year)

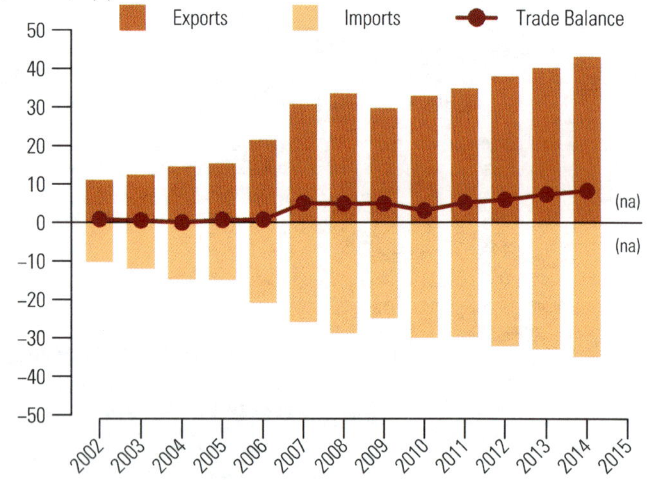

Exports Profile:

"Machinery and transport equipment" (SITC section 7), "Goods classified chiefly by material" (SITC section 6) and "Miscellaneous manufactured articles" (SITC section 8) were the largest commodity groups for exports in 2015, representing respectively 39.1, 18.8 and 15.0 percent of exported goods (see table 2). From 2013 to 2015, the largest export commodity was "Parts and accessories of the motor vehicles of headings 87.01 to 87.05" (HS code 8708) (see table 1). The top three destinations for merchandise exports were Germany, the United Kingdom and the Czech Republic, accounting for respectively 25.9, 6.6 and 6.3 percent of total exports. "Transportation" (EBOPS code 205) accounted for the largest share of exports of services in 2014 at 13.2 bln US$, followed by "Travel" (EBOPS code 236) at 11.2 bln US$ and "Other business services" (EBOPS code 268) at 10.8 bln US$ (see graph 3).

Graph 3: Exports of services by EBOPS category

(% share in 2014)

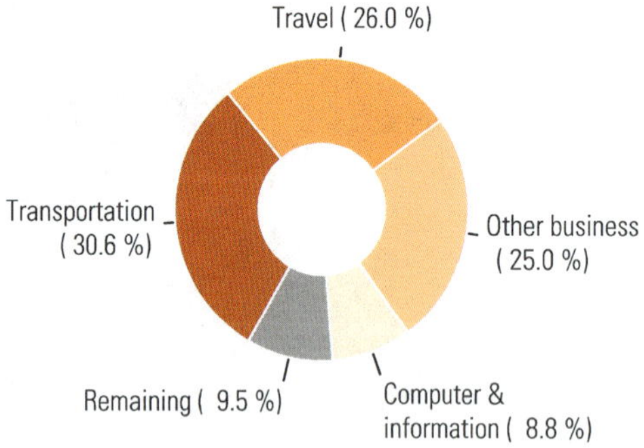

Table 1: Top 10 export commodities 2013 to 2015

HS code	4-digit heading of Harmonized System 2012	Value (million US$) 2013	2014	2015	Unit value 2013	2014	2015	Unit	SITC code
	All Commodities	203 847.9	214 476.8	194 461.2					
8708	Parts and accessories of the motor vehicles of headings 87.01 to 87.05	9 613.4	10 537.7	9 934.8	*7.4*	*7.6*	*6.7*	US$/kg	784
8703	Motor cars and other motor vehicles principally designed for the transport	6 900.9	6 554.7	6 491.5	12.5	12.6	11.1	thsd US$/unit	781
9401	Seats (other than those of heading 94.02)	4 982.3	5 519.6	5 154.5					821
8528	Reception apparatus for television	4 744.7	5 068.0	5 073.0	282.7	289.5	279.2	US$/unit	761
2710	Petroleum oils, other than crude	4 622.4	4 607.2	3 251.1	*0.8*	*0.8*	*0.5*	US$/kg	334
8901	Cruise ships, excursion boats, ferry-boats, cargo ships, barges	3 720.2	4 061.9	4 541.4	*14.2*	*13.5*	*0.5*	mln US$/unit	793
9403	Other furniture and parts thereof	3 693.9	4 234.3	3 602.5					821
8517	Electrical apparatus for line telephony or line telegraphy	3 483.8	4 804.0	3 153.5					764
8471	Automatic data processing machines and units thereof	2 794.6	3 423.6	3 679.7	*209.1*	*202.2*	185.0	US$/unit	752
3004	Medicaments (excluding goods of heading 30.02, 30.05 or 30.06)	2 700.5	3 171.8	2 674.4	*51.7*	*51.2*	*39.9*	US$/kg	542

Source: UN Comtrade

Services Imports and Exports: EBOPS 2002 categories

Table 2: Merchandise exports by SITC

(Value in million US$, growth and shares in percentage)

SITC	2015	Avg. Growth rates 2011-2015	Avg. Growth rates 2014-2015	2015 share
Total	194 461.2	0.8	-9.3	100.0
0+1	24 035.3	5.0	-8.8	12.4
2+4	4 761.2	0.3	-16.7	2.4
3	6 434.2	-8.6	-27.5	3.3
5	17 194.1	0.6	-12.2	8.8
6	36 506.6	-2.2	-13.9	18.8
7	75 955.0	0.7	-7.5	39.1
8	29 233.5	5.5	0.5	15.0
9	341.3	2.3	14.9	0.2

Table 3: Merchandise imports by SITC

(Value in million US$, growth and shares in percentage)

SITC	2015	Avg. Growth rates 2011-2015	Avg. Growth rates 2014-2015	2015 share
Total	189 696.5	-2.4	-12.5	100.0
0+1	15 158.7	0.5	-10.5	8.0
2+4	6 639.7	-5.2	-15.8	3.5
3	14 269.7	-14.5	-39.0	7.5
5	26 385.0	-2.8	-15.4	13.9
6	32 588.9	-3.7	-13.4	17.2
7	69 438.1	1.1	-5.1	36.6
8	22 374.9	2.4	0.3	11.8
9	2 841.5	-14.0	-31.3	1.5

SITC Legend

SITC Code	Description
Total	All commodities
0+1	Food, animals + beverages, tobacco
2+4	Crude materials + anim. & veg. oils
3	Mineral fuels, lubricants
5	Chemicals
6	Goods classified chiefly by material
7	Machinery and transport equipment
8	Miscellaneous manufactured articles
9	Not classified elsewhere in the SITC

Graph 4: Merchandise trade balance

(Bln US$ by MDG Regions in 2015)

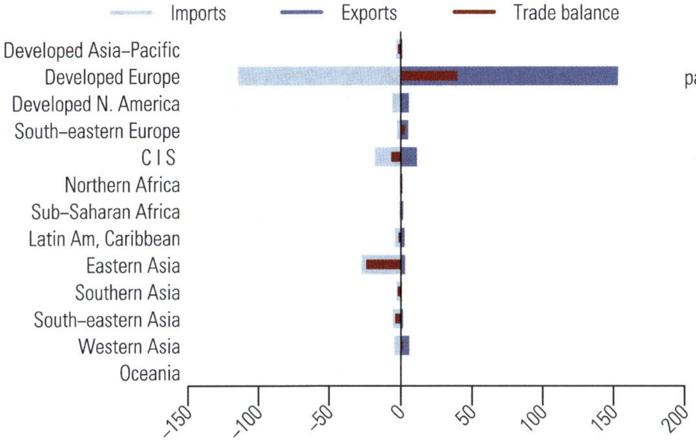

Graph 5: Partner concentration of merchandise trade

(Cumulative share by ranked partners in 2015)

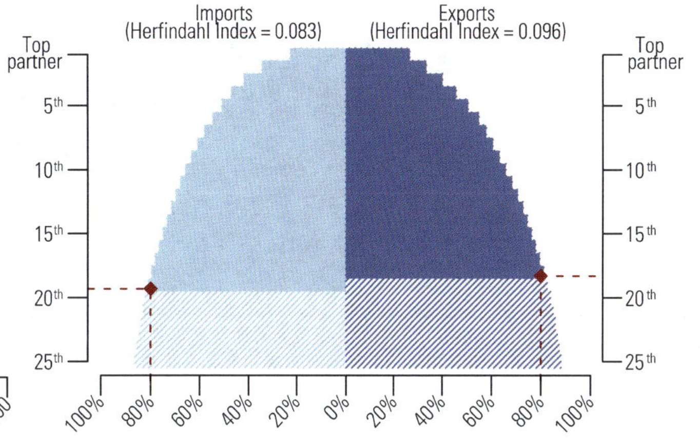

Graph 6: Imports of services by EBOPS category

(% share in 2014)

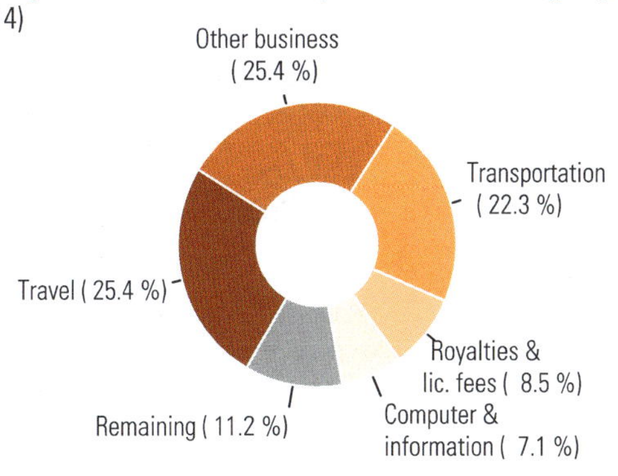

Imports Profile:

"Machinery and transport equipment" (SITC section 7), "Goods classified chiefly by material" (SITC section 6) and "Chemicals" (SITC section 5) were the largest commodity groups for imports in 2015, representing respectively 36.6, 17.2 and 13.9 percent of imported goods (see table 3). From 2013 to 2015, the largest import commodity was "Petroleum oils and oils obtained from bituminous minerals, crude" (HS code 2709) (see table 4). The top three partners for merchandise imports were Germany, China and the Russian Federation, accounting for respectively 21.9, 10.6 and 10.3 percent of total imports. "Travel" (EBOPS code 236) accounted for the largest share of imports of services in 2014 at 8.9 bln US$, followed by "Other business services" (EBOPS code 268) at 8.9 bln US$ and "Transportation" (EBOPS code 205) at 7.8 bln US$ (see graph 6).

Table 4: Top 10 import commodities 2013 to 2015

HS code	4-digit heading of Harmonized System 2012	Value (million US$) 2013	2014	2015	Unit value 2013	2014	2015	Unit	SITC code
	All Commodities	205 613.8	216 687.3	189 696.5					
2709	Petroleum oils and oils obtained from bituminous minerals, crude	18 048.9	17 195.1	9 855.4	0.8	0.7	0.4	US$/kg	333
8708	Parts and accessories of the motor vehicles of headings 87.01 to 87.05	5 995.1	6 357.7	5 931.4	*7.7*	*7.5*	*6.2*	US$/kg	784
8703	Motor cars and other motor vehicles principally designed for the transport	5 208.3	5 986.9	5 389.9	15.9	16.6	15.4	thsd US$/unit	781
3004	Medicaments (excluding goods of heading 30.02, 30.05 or 30.06)	4 456.7	4 517.0	3 893.1	*64.8*	*65.2*	*68.4*	US$/kg	542
9999	Commodities not specified according to kind	5 036.9	4 055.3	2 779.7					931
8517	Electrical apparatus for line telephony or line telegraphy	3 504.2	3 719.7	3 738.2					764
8901	Cruise ships, excursion boats, ferry-boats, cargo ships, barges	3 351.1	3 549.2	3 960.9	*13.5*	*12.9*	*13.8*	mln US$/unit	793
8471	Automatic data processing machines and units thereof	3 437.4	3 529.7	3 526.4	68.0	70.8	75.2	US$/unit	752
8529	Parts suitable for use with the apparatus of headings 85.25 to 85.28	2 934.3	2 934.5	2 553.7	*39.3*	*34.6*	*29.5*	US$/kg	764
8542	Electronic integrated circuits	1 972.8	2 176.2	2 110.1					776

Source: UN Comtrade

Portugal

Goods Imports: CIF, by origin/consignment for intra-eu **Goods Exports: FOB, by last known destination** **Trade System: Special**

Overview:

In 2015, the value of merchandise exports of Portugal decreased substantially by 13.5 percent to reach 55.2 bln US$, while its merchandise imports decreased substantially by 14.9 percent to reach 66.7 bln US$ (see graph 1, table 2 and table 3). The merchandise trade balance recorded a relatively small deficit of 11.4 bln US$ (see graph 1). The largest merchandise trade balance was with MDG Developed Europe at -5.2 bln US$ (see graph 4). Merchandise exports in Portugal were diversified amongst partners; imports were also diversified. The top 13 partners accounted for 80 percent or more of exports and 19 partners accounted for 80 percent or more of imports (see graph 5). In 2014, the value of exports of services of Portugal increased moderately by 8.7 percent, reaching 30.5 bln US$, while its imports of services increased substantially by 10.9 percent and reached 15.4 bln US$ (see graph 2). There was a large trade in services surplus of 15.1 bln US$.

Graph 1: Total merchandise trade, by value

(Bln US$ by year)

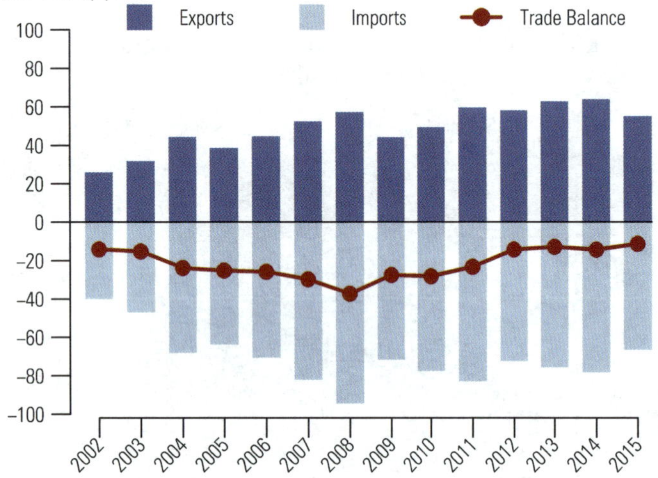

Graph 2: Total services trade, by value

(Bln US$ by year)

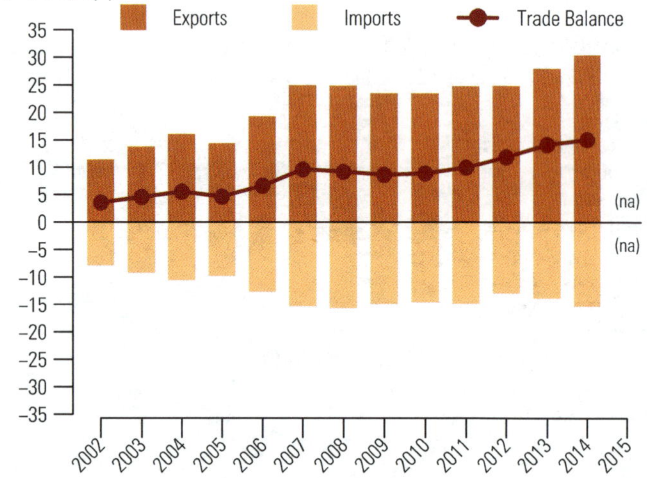

Exports Profile:

"Machinery and transport equipment" (SITC section 7), "Goods classified chiefly by material" (SITC section 6) and "Miscellaneous manufactured articles" (SITC section 8) were the largest commodity groups for exports in 2015, representing respectively 25.9, 23.0 and 17.6 percent of exported goods (see table 2). From 2013 to 2015, the largest export commodity was "Petroleum oils, other than crude" (HS code 2710) (see table 1). The top three destinations for merchandise exports were Spain, France and Germany, accounting for respectively 24.0, 11.8 and 11.7 percent of total exports. "Travel" (EBOPS code 236) accounted for the largest share of exports of services in 2014 at 13.8 bln US$, followed by "Transportation" (EBOPS code 205) at 7.6 bln US$ and "Other business services" (EBOPS code 268) at 5.6 bln US$ (see graph 3).

Graph 3: Exports of services by EBOPS category

(% share in 2014)

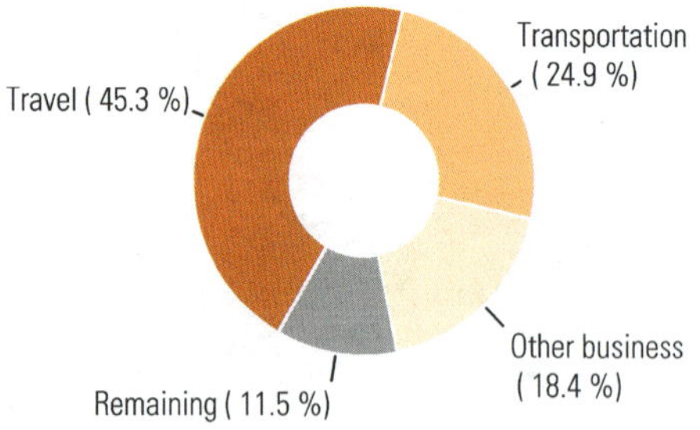

Table 1: Top 10 export commodities 2013 to 2015

HS code	4-digit heading of Harmonized System 2012	Value (million US$) 2013	2014	2015	Unit value 2013	2014	2015	Unit	SITC code
	All Commodities	62794.1	63885.6	55241.1					
2710	Petroleum oils, other than crude	5834.1	4749.7	3769.1	0.9	*0.8*	*0.5*	US$/kg	334
8708	Parts and accessories of the motor vehicles of headings 87.01 to 87.05	2359.2	2613.8	2502.5	*7.8*	*7.8*	*7.0*	US$/kg	784
8703	Motor cars and other motor vehicles principally designed for the transport	2461.4	2631.3	2304.8	21.0	21.2	18.7	thsd US$/unit	781
6403	Footwear with outer soles of rubber, plastics, leather	2031.0	2174.7	1840.2	36.1	36.6	31.0	US$/pair	851
4802	Uncoated paper and paperboard, of a kind used for writing	1535.4	1529.8	1334.5	*1.1*	*1.0*	*0.9*	US$/kg	641
4011	New pneumatic tyres, of rubber	1130.1	1104.5	1023.4	66.8	62.8	56.4	US$/unit	625
6109	T-shirts, singlets and other vests, knitted or crocheted	942.7	1019.2	876.8	6.3	6.5	5.7	US$/unit	845
2204	Wine of fresh grapes, including fortified wines	956.9	963.5	817.7	*3.1*	3.4	2.9	US$/litre	112
3004	Medicaments (excluding goods of heading 30.02, 30.05 or 30.06)	836.9	997.5	816.8	*39.8*	*44.5*	*38.5*	US$/kg	542
8544	Insulated (including enamelled or anodised) wire, cable	894.1	871.5	766.1	*9.0*	*8.8*	*7.1*	US$/kg	773

Services Imports and Exports: EBOPS 2002 categories

Table 2: Merchandise exports by SITC

(Value in million US$, growth and shares in percentage)

SITC	2015	Avg. Growth rates 2011-2015	Avg. Growth rates 2014-2015	2015 share
Total	55 241.1	-1.9	-13.5	100.0
0+1	6 186.7	0.7	-12.3	11.2
2+4	2 920.3	-5.2	-12.9	5.3
3	4 226.4	-0.3	-21.9	7.7
5	4 844.3	-2.3	-14.4	8.8
6	12 723.3	-1.8	-13.5	23.0
7	14 297.4	-3.3	-11.6	25.9
8	9 739.3	0.4	-12.9	17.6
9	303.4	-21.0	-11.4	0.5

Table 3: Merchandise imports by SITC

(Value in million US$, growth and shares in percentage)

SITC	2015	Avg. Growth rates 2011-2015	Avg. Growth rates 2014-2015	2015 share
Total	66 657.7	-5.3	-14.9	100.0
0+1	8 818.1	-4.5	-13.3	13.2
2+4	3 033.5	-6.7	-14.0	4.6
3	8 839.0	-11.7	-34.7	13.3
5	9 602.8	-3.3	-9.6	14.4
6	10 269.1	-4.9	-12.2	15.4
7	18 355.2	-3.7	-9.1	27.5
8	7 699.5	-3.3	-9.3	11.6
9	40.5	-20.8	-31.3	0.1

SITC Legend

SITC Code	Description
Total	All commodities
0+1	Food, animals + beverages, tobacco
2+4	Crude materials + anim. & veg. oils
3	Mineral fuels, lubricants
5	Chemicals
6	Goods classified chiefly by material
7	Machinery and transport equipment
8	Miscellaneous manufactured articles
9	Not classified elsewhere in the SITC

Graph 4: Merchandise trade balance

(Bln US$ by MDG Regions in 2015)

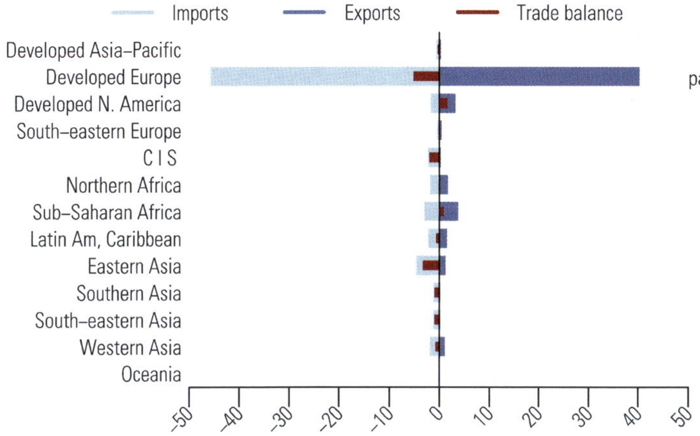

Graph 5: Partner concentration of merchandise trade

(Cumulative share by ranked partners in 2015)

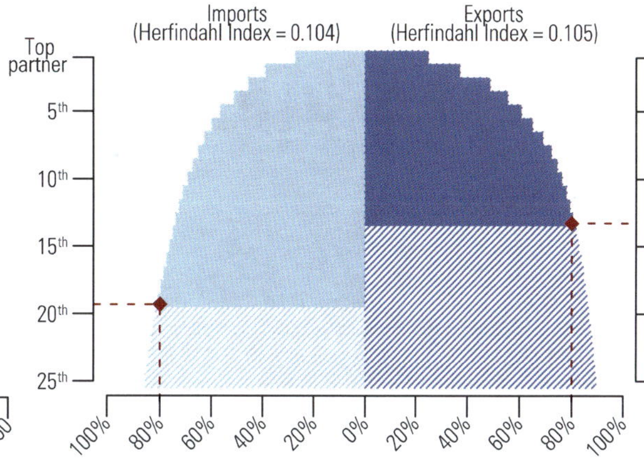

Graph 6: Imports of services by EBOPS category

(% share in 2014)

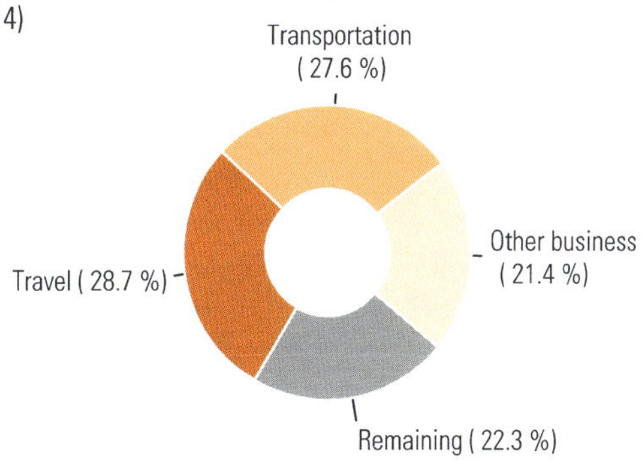

Imports Profile:

"Machinery and transport equipment" (SITC section 7), "Goods classified chiefly by material" (SITC section 6) and "Chemicals" (SITC section 5) were the largest commodity groups for imports in 2015, representing respectively 27.5, 15.4 and 14.4 percent of imported goods (see table 3). From 2013 to 2015, the largest import commodity was "Petroleum oils and oils obtained from bituminous minerals, crude" (HS code 2709) (see table 4). The top three partners for merchandise imports were Spain, Germany and France, accounting for respectively 30.8, 11.8 and 6.8 percent of total imports. "Travel" (EBOPS code 236) accounted for the largest share of imports of services in 2014 at 4.4 bln US$, followed by "Transportation" (EBOPS code 205) at 4.2 bln US$ and "Other business services" (EBOPS code 268) at 3.3 bln US$ (see graph 6).

Table 4: Top 10 import commodities 2013 to 2015

HS code	4-digit heading of Harmonized System 2012	Value (million US$) 2013	Value (million US$) 2014	Value (million US$) 2015	Unit value 2013	Unit value 2014	Unit value 2015	Unit	SITC code
	All Commodities	75 713.9	78 294.9	66 657.7					
2709	Petroleum oils and oils obtained from bituminous minerals, crude	9 355.1	8 158.6	5 465.9	0.8	0.7	0.4	US$/kg	333
8703	Motor cars and other motor vehicles principally designed for the transport	2 438.1	3 460.3	3 787.8	18.9	18.6	15.6	thsd US$/unit	781
8708	Parts and accessories of the motor vehicles of headings 87.01 to 87.05	2 682.3	2 760.0	2 475.0	10.0	10.2	9.3	US$/kg	784
3004	Medicaments (excluding goods of heading 30.02, 30.05 or 30.06)	2 169.0	2 195.1	2 157.9	64.6	64.7	60.0	US$/kg	542
2711	Petroleum gases and other gaseous hydrocarbons	2 470.7	2 398.9	1 552.4	0.6	0.6	0.4	US$/kg	343
2710	Petroleum oils, other than crude	1 960.8	2 104.2	1 124.5	0.9	0.8	0.5	US$/kg	334
8517	Electrical apparatus for line telephony or line telegraphy	923.6	1 027.5	923.2					764
8471	Automatic data processing machines and units thereof	778.2	793.0	659.2	144.2	154.3	136.1	US$/unit	752
7208	Flat-rolled products of iron or non-alloy steel	555.9	534.3	451.9	0.7	0.6	0.5	US$/kg	673
7204	Ferrous waste and scrap; remelting scrap ingots of iron or steel	515.5	531.3	367.6	0.4	0.3	0.2	US$/kg	282

Qatar

Goods Imports: CIF, by origin | **Goods Exports: FOB, by last known destination** | **Trade System: Special**

Overview:

In 2015, the value of merchandise exports of Qatar decreased substantially by 40.7 percent to reach 78.0 bln US$, while its merchandise imports increased moderately by 7.1 percent to reach 32.6 bln US$ (see graph 1, table 2 and table 3). The merchandise trade balance recorded a large surplus of 45.4 bln US$ (see graph 1). The largest merchandise trade balance was with MDG Eastern Asia at 17.0 bln US$ (see graph 4). Merchandise exports in Qatar were diversified amongst partners; imports were also diversified. The top 10 partners accounted for 80 percent or more of exports and 17 partners accounted for 80 percent or more of imports (see graph 5). In 2014, the value of exports of services of Qatar increased substantially by 21.0 percent, reaching 49.2 bln US$, while its imports of services increased substantially by 19.6 percent and reached 119.6 bln US$ (see graph 2). There was a large trade in services deficit of 70.4 bln US$.

Graph 1: Total merchandise trade, by value

(Bln US$ by year)

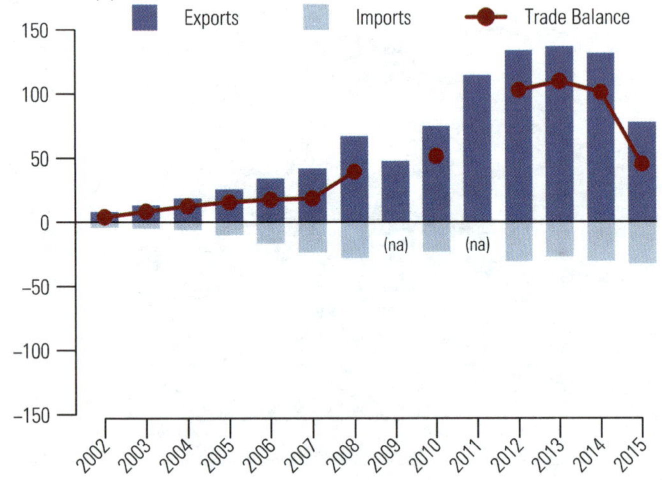

Graph 2: Total services trade, by value

(Bln US$ by year)

Exports Profile:

"Mineral fuels, lubricants" (SITC section 3), "Not classified elsewhere in the SITC" (SITC section 9) and "Machinery and transport equipment" (SITC section 7) were the largest commodity groups for exports in 2015, representing respectively 82.8, 11.2 and 2.6 percent of exported goods (see table 2). From 2013 to 2015, the largest export commodity was "Petroleum gases and other gaseous hydrocarbons" (HS code 2711) (see table 1). The top three destinations for merchandise exports were Japan, the Republic of Korea and India, accounting for respectively 25.8, 18.1 and 11.6 percent of total exports. "Transportation" (EBOPS code 205) accounted for the largest share of exports of services in 2014 at 23.4 bln US$, followed by "Travel" (EBOPS code 236) at 16.7 bln US$ and "Insurance services" (EBOPS code 253) at 3.1 bln US$ (see graph 3).

Graph 3: Exports of services by EBOPS category

(% share in 2014)

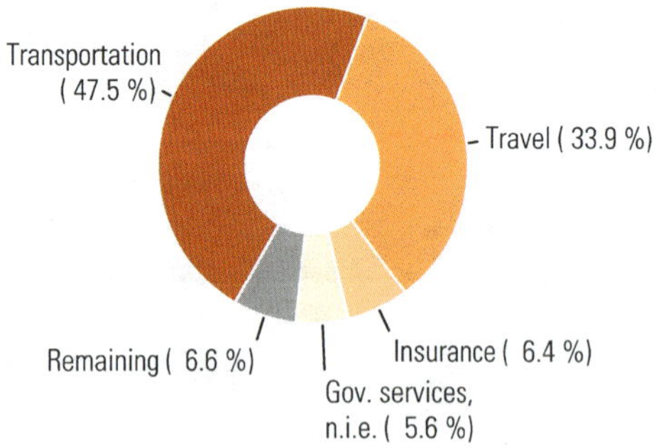

Table 1: Top 10 export commodities 2013 to 2015

HS code	4-digit heading of Harmonized System 2012	Value (million US$) 2013	2014	2015	Unit value 2013	2014	2015	Unit	SITC code
	All Commodities	136 855.1	131 591.6	77 971.1					
2711	Petroleum gases and other gaseous hydrocarbons	87 538.4	86 040.0	50 522.9	0.8	0.8	0.4	US$/kg	343
2709	Petroleum oils and oils obtained from bituminous minerals, crude	24 877.7	21 484.3	10 603.5	0.8	0.7	0.4	US$/kg	333
9999	Commodities not specified according to kind	11 656.7	17 137.3	8 733.9					931
2710	Petroleum oils, other than crude	7 544.1	6 375.0	3 407.1	0.9	0.9	0.5	US$/kg	334
3901	Polymers of ethylene, in primary forms	4 632.0	...	0.0	1.5		1.9	US$/kg	571
2503	Sulphur of all kinds	270.2	324.2	331.4	0.1	0.2	0.1	US$/kg	274
8703	Motor cars and other motor vehicles principally designed for the transport	...	...	514.9			*15.5*	thsd US$/unit	781
2903	Halogenated derivatives of hydrocarbons	...	...	486.5			0.5	US$/kg	511
7214	Other bars and rods of iron or non-alloy steel	...	...	396.2			0.5	US$/kg	676
8905	Light-vessels, fire-floats, dredgers, floating cranes and other vessels	...	...	327.4					793

Services Imports and Exports: EBOPS 2002 categories

Table 2: Merchandise exports by SITC

(Value in million US$, growth and shares in percentage)

SITC	2015	Avg. Growth rates 2011-2015	Avg. Growth rates 2014-2015	2015 share
Total	77971.1	-9.1	-40.7	100.0
0+1	160.6	149.1	1976.4	0.2
2+4	556.9	7.8	56.0	0.7
3	64534.0	-11.5	-43.3	82.8
5	956.4	-17.3	1313.0	1.2
6	729.6	128.3	2528.8	0.9
7	2021.1	350.7	41345.8	2.6
8	278.5	44.7	209.6	0.4
9	8733.9	6.1	-49.0	11.2

Table 3: Merchandise imports by SITC

(Value in million US$, growth and shares in percentage)

SITC	2015	Avg. Growth rates 2011-2015	Avg. Growth rates 2014-2015	2015 share
Total	32610.5	...	7.1	100.0
0+1	3176.7	...	8.8	9.7
2+4	1763.3	...	10.9	5.4
3	382.0	...	13.8	1.2
5	2506.9	...	3.4	7.7
6	5423.2	...	11.3	16.6
7	14831.0	...	3.7	45.5
8	4260.7	...	14.1	13.1
9	266.8	...	-1.0	0.8

SITC Legend

SITC Code	Description
Total	All commodities
0+1	Food, animals + beverages, tobacco
2+4	Crude materials + anim. & veg. oils
3	Mineral fuels, lubricants
5	Chemicals
6	Goods classified chiefly by material
7	Machinery and transport equipment
8	Miscellaneous manufactured articles
9	Not classified elsewhere in the SITC

Graph 4: Merchandise trade balance

(Bln US$ by MDG Regions in 2015)

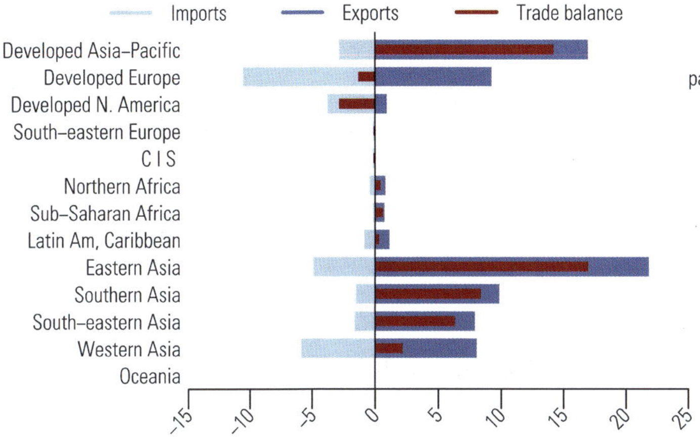

Graph 5: Partner concentration of merchandise trade

(Cumulative share by ranked partners in 2015)

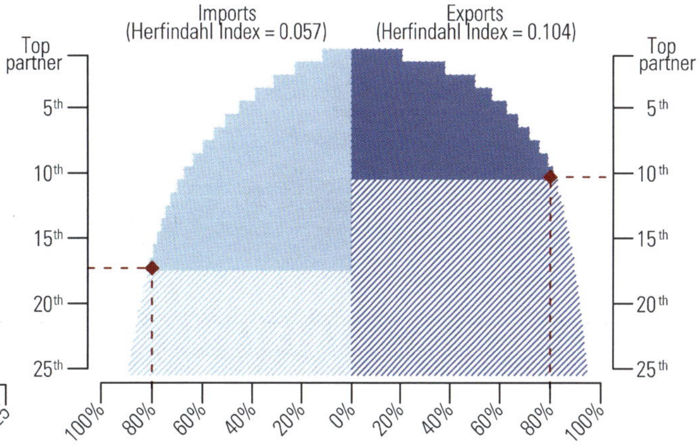

Graph 6: Imports of services by EBOPS category

(% share in 2014)

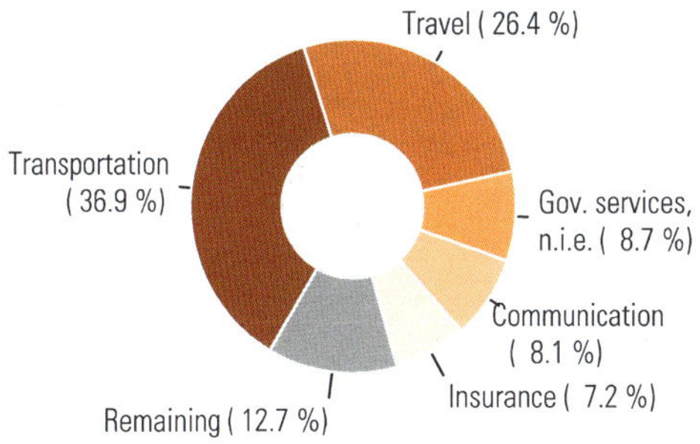

Imports Profile:

"Machinery and transport equipment" (SITC section 7), "Goods classified chiefly by material" (SITC section 6) and "Miscellaneous manufactured articles" (SITC section 8) were the largest commodity groups for imports in 2015, representing respectively 45.5, 16.6 and 13.1 percent of imported goods (see table 3). From 2013 to 2015, the largest import commodity was "Motor cars and other motor vehicles principally designed for the transport" (HS code 8703) (see table 4). The top three partners for merchandise imports were the United States, China and the United Arab Emirates, accounting for respectively 11.4, 10.7 and 8.1 percent of total imports. "Transportation" (EBOPS code 205) accounted for the largest share of imports of services in 2014 at 44.1 bln US$, followed by "Travel" (EBOPS code 236) at 31.6 bln US$ and "Government services, n.i.e." (EBOPS code 291) at 10.4 bln US$ (see graph 6).

Table 4: Top 10 import commodities 2013 to 2015

HS code	4-digit heading of Harmonized System 2012	Value (million US$) 2013	2014	2015	Unit value 2013	2014	2015	Unit	SITC code
	All Commodities	27034.1	30447.7	32610.5					
8703	Motor cars and other motor vehicles principally designed for the transport	2534.7	2625.3	2981.0	*12.7*	*15.0*	*16.3*	thsd US$/unit	781
8803	Parts of goods of heading 88.01 or 88.02	1435.6	1769.4	1896.9	465.1	426.8	425.2	US$/kg	792
8517	Electrical apparatus for line telephony or line telegraphy	665.9	786.7	879.1					764
8544	Insulated (including enamelled or anodised) wire, cable	449.9	631.7	659.0	*7.3*	*7.1*	6.7	US$/kg	773
2601	Iron ores and concentrates, including roasted iron pyrites	593.9	460.0	502.8	0.2	0.2	0.1	US$/kg	281
8704	Motor vehicles for the transport of goods	443.0	514.2	481.8					782
8471	Automatic data processing machines and units thereof	415.4	436.6	508.9					752
8481	Taps, cocks, valves and similar appliances for pipes, boiler shells	468.0	393.2	391.2	*23.2*	*27.5*	18.6	US$/kg	747
7113	Articles of jewellery and parts thereof, of precious metal	389.2	443.3	389.6		19.4	11.9	thsd US$/kg	897
8905	Light-vessels, fire-floats, dredgers, floating cranes and other vessels	678.4	529.9	0.0					793

Source: UN Comtrade

Republic of Moldova

Goods Imports: CIF, by origin | **Goods Exports: FOB, by last known destination** | **Trade System: General**

Overview:

In 2015, the value of merchandise exports of the Republic of Moldova decreased substantially by 15.9 percent to reach 2.0 bln US$, while its merchandise imports decreased substantially by 25.0 percent to reach 4.0 bln US$ (see graph 1, table 2 and table 3). The merchandise trade balance recorded a large deficit of 2.0 bln US$ (see graph 1). The largest merchandise trade balance was with MDG Developed Europe at -602.6 mln US$ (see graph 4). Merchandise exports in the Republic of Moldova were diversified amongst partners; imports were also diversified. The top 12 partners accounted for 80 percent or more of exports and 13 partners accounted for 80 percent or more of imports (see graph 5). In 2013, the value of exports of services of the Republic of Moldova increased slightly by 2.0 percent, reaching 954.6 mln US$, while its imports of services increased slightly by 1.5 percent and reached 972.2 mln US$ (see graph 2). There was a relatively small trade in services deficit of 17.5 mln US$.

Graph 1: Total merchandise trade, by value

(Bln US$ by year)

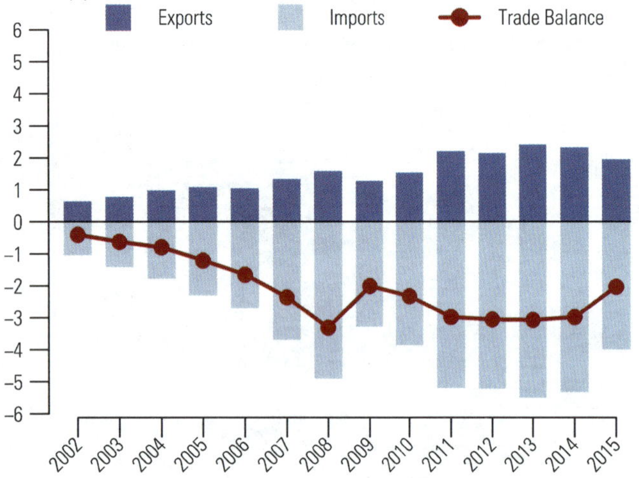

Graph 2: Total services trade, by value

(Mln US$ by year)

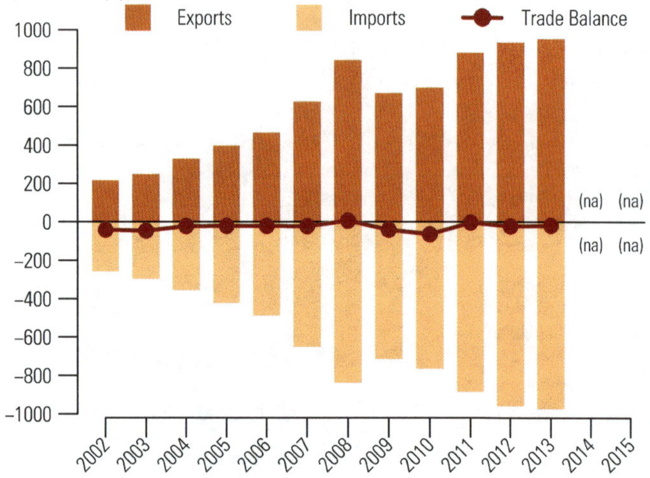

Exports Profile:

"Food, animals + beverages, tobacco" (SITC section 0+1), "Miscellaneous manufactured articles" (SITC section 8) and "Machinery and transport equipment" (SITC section 7) were the largest commodity groups for exports in 2015, representing respectively 33.4, 21.7 and 15.9 percent of exported goods (see table 2). From 2013 to 2015, the largest export commodity was "Insulated (including enamelled or anodised) wire, cable" (HS code 8544) (see table 1). The top three destinations for merchandise exports were the Russian Federation, Romania and Italy, accounting for respectively 19.2, 19.2 and 9.3 percent of total exports. "Transportation" (EBOPS code 205) accounted for the largest share of exports of services in 2013 at 403.6 mln US$, followed by "Travel" (EBOPS code 236) at 225.5 mln US$ and "Communications services" (EBOPS code 245) at 137.4 mln US$ (see graph 3).

Graph 3: Exports of services by EBOPS category

(% share in 2013)

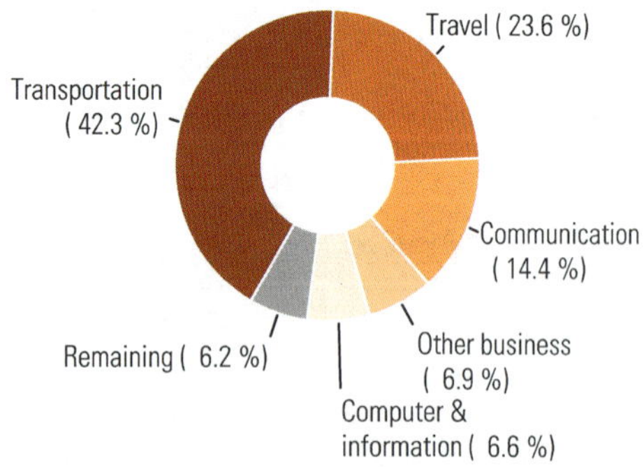

Table 1: Top 10 export commodities 2013 to 2015

HS code	4-digit heading of Harmonized System 2007	Value (million US$) 2013	2014	2015	Unit value 2013	2014	2015	Unit	SITC code
	All Commodities	2 428.3	2 339.5	1 966.9					
8544	Insulated (including enamelled or anodised) wire, cable	213.1	216.8	212.6		*13.7*	*11.3*	US$/kg	773
1206	Sunflower seeds, whether or not broken	136.2	105.6	143.7	0.5	0.4	0.4	US$/kg	222
2204	Wine of fresh grapes, including fortified wines	149.6	111.8	97.7	1.2	1.1	*0.9*	US$/litre	112
3004	Medicaments (excluding goods of heading 30.02, 30.05 or 30.06)	112.4	124.5	75.6	*66.9*	*74.7*	*63.5*	US$/kg	542
0802	Other nuts, fresh or dried, whether or not shelled or peeled	97.5	110.8	101.1	7.3	7.7	6.7	US$/kg	057
9401	Seats (other than those of heading 94.02)	75.7	86.7	81.0					821
2208	Alcohol of a strength by volume of less than 80 % vol	92.2	68.9	47.5	*6.6*	*6.5*	*6.1*	US$/litre	112
1001	Wheat and meslin	65.9	81.3	52.5	0.2	0.2	0.2	US$/kg	041
1512	Sunflower-seed, safflower or cotton-seed oil	41.6	74.1	69.0	1.0	0.8	0.7	US$/kg	421
1005	Maize (corn)	28.1	82.0	43.9	0.2	0.2		US$/kg	044

Services Imports and Exports: EBOPS 2002 categories

Table 2: Merchandise exports by SITC
(Value in million US$, growth and shares in percentage)

SITC	2015	Avg. Growth rates 2011-2015	2014-2015	2015 share
Total	1 966.9	-2.9	-15.9	100.0
0+1	656.5	0.0	-20.7	33.4
2+4	291.6	-5.3	0.3	14.8
3	10.1	-19.6	-37.4	0.5
5	130.8	1.3	-25.7	6.6
6	137.4	-10.5	-20.9	7.0
7	313.5	-1.1	-7.0	15.9
8	426.5	-4.0	-17.5	21.7
9	0.6	-42.3	-39.3	0.0

Table 3: Merchandise imports by SITC
(Value in million US$, growth and shares in percentage)

SITC	2015	Avg. Growth rates 2011-2015	2014-2015	2015 share
Total	3 986.8	-6.4	-25.0	100.0
0+1	530.1	-4.7	-19.8	13.3
2+4	108.8	-2.2	-13.3	2.7
3	458.4	-11.1	-33.5	11.5
5	626.1	-1.8	-21.4	15.7
6	807.9	-4.6	-18.6	20.3
7	825.0	-8.2	-26.7	20.7
8	364.5	-5.2	-23.4	9.1
9	266.0	-11.7	-41.0	6.7

SITC Legend

SITC Code	Description
Total	All commodities
0+1	Food, animals + beverages, tobacco
2+4	Crude materials + anim. & veg. oils
3	Mineral fuels, lubricants
5	Chemicals
6	Goods classified chiefly by material
7	Machinery and transport equipment
8	Miscellaneous manufactured articles
9	Not classified elsewhere in the SITC

Graph 4: Merchandise trade balance
(Bln US$ by MDG Regions in 2015)

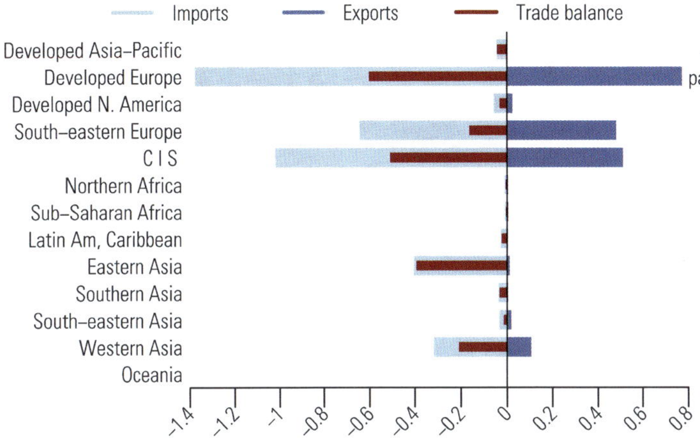

Graph 5: Partner concentration of merchandise trade
(Cumulative share by ranked partners in 2015)

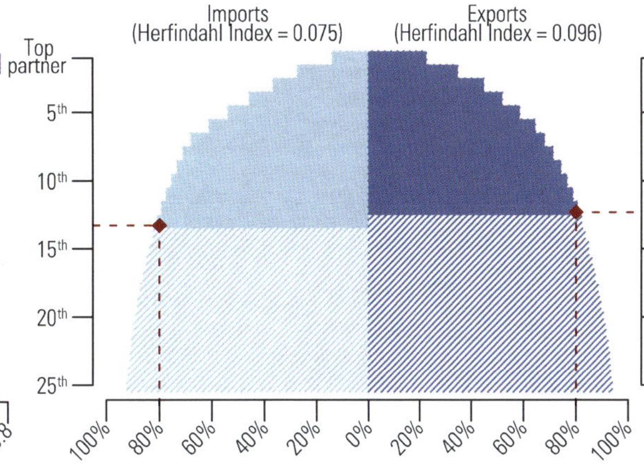

Graph 6: Imports of services by EBOPS category
(% share in 2013)

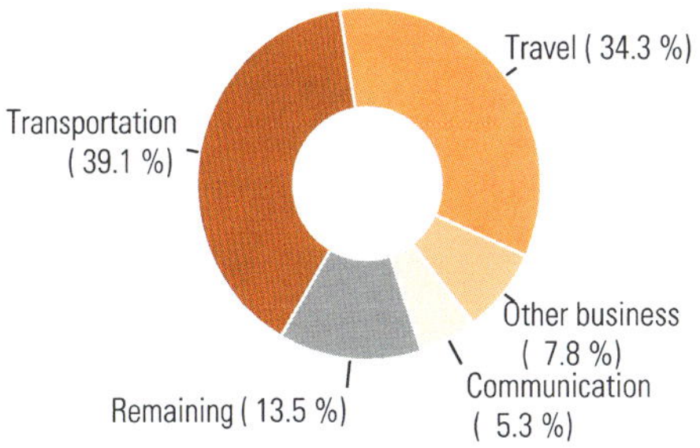

Imports Profile:

"Machinery and transport equipment" (SITC section 7), "Goods classified chiefly by material" (SITC section 6) and "Chemicals" (SITC section 5) were the largest commodity groups for imports in 2015, representing respectively 20.7, 20.3 and 15.7 percent of imported goods (see table 3). From 2013 to 2015, the largest import commodity was "Petroleum oils, other than crude" (HS code 2710) (see table 4). The top three partners for merchandise imports were Romania, the Russian Federation and Ukraine, accounting for respectively 14.1, 13.8 and 10.7 percent of total imports. "Transportation" (EBOPS code 205) accounted for the largest share of imports of services in 2013 at 379.9 mln US$, followed by "Travel" (EBOPS code 236) at 333.6 mln US$ and "Other business services" (EBOPS code 268) at 76.0 mln US$ (see graph 6).

Table 4: Top 10 import commodities 2013 to 2015

HS code	4-digit heading of Harmonized System 2007	Value (million US$) 2013	2014	2015	Unit value 2013	2014	2015	Unit	SITC code
	All Commodities	5 492.4	5 317.0	3 986.8					
2710	Petroleum oils, other than crude	620.7	581.2	396.3	*1.0*	*0.9*	*0.6*	US$/kg	334
9999	Commodities not specified according to kind	493.7	450.9	266.0					931
3004	Medicaments (excluding goods of heading 30.02, 30.05 or 30.06)	225.4	249.1	171.5	*35.8*	*37.9*	*31.4*	US$/kg	542
8703	Motor cars and other motor vehicles principally designed for the transport	131.8	132.2	87.1	18.7	20.2	18.9	thsd US$/unit	781
8544	Insulated (including enamelled or anodised) wire, cable	125.3	91.4	82.2		*8.2*	*7.2*	US$/kg	773
8517	Electrical apparatus for line telephony or line telegraphy	76.2	62.8	59.5					764
3808	Insecticides, rodenticides, fungicides, herbicides	61.4	58.1	54.1	*12.4*	*12.5*	*12.1*	US$/kg	591
2402	Cigars, cheroots, cigarillos and cigarettes	65.6	51.6	54.3	*14.0*	*13.6*	*11.3*	US$/kg	122
2711	Petroleum gases and other gaseous hydrocarbons	66.4	61.3	30.9	*0.7*	*0.8*	0.4	US$/kg	343
8701	Tractors (other than tractors of heading 87.09)	48.9	60.7	31.8	6.8	4.3	7.5	thsd US$/unit	722

Romania

Goods Imports: CIF, by origin/consignment for intra-eu | **Goods Exports: FOB, by last known destination** | **Trade System: Special**

Overview:

In 2015, the value of merchandise exports of Romania decreased substantially by 13.3 percent to reach 60.6 bln US$, while its merchandise imports decreased substantially by 10.3 percent to reach 69.9 bln US$ (see graph 1, table 2 and table 3). The merchandise trade balance recorded a relatively small deficit of 9.3 bln US$ (see graph 1). The largest merchandise trade balance was with MDG Developed Europe at -8.9 bln US$ (see graph 4). Merchandise exports in Romania were diversified amongst partners; imports were also diversified. The top 19 partners accounted for 80 percent or more of exports and 15 partners accounted for 80 percent or more of imports (see graph 5). In 2014, the value of exports of services of Romania increased substantially by 13.2 percent, reaching 16.4 bln US$, while its imports of services increased moderately by 7.5 percent and reached 11.6 bln US$ (see graph 2). There was a moderate trade in services surplus of 4.8 bln US$.

Graph 1: Total merchandise trade, by value
(Bln US$ by year)

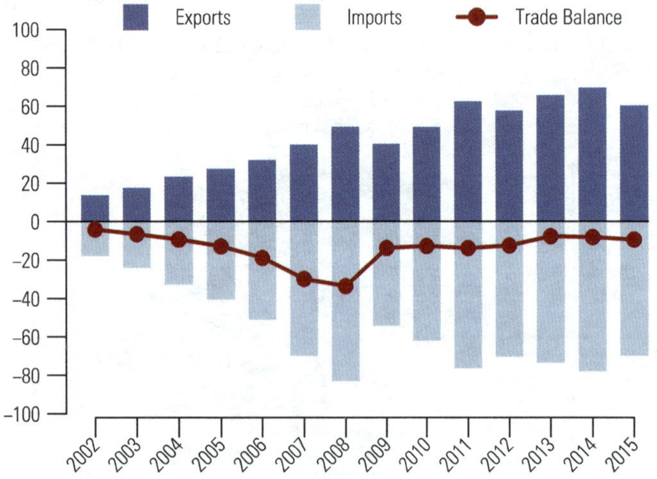

Graph 2: Total services trade, by value
(Bln US$ by year)

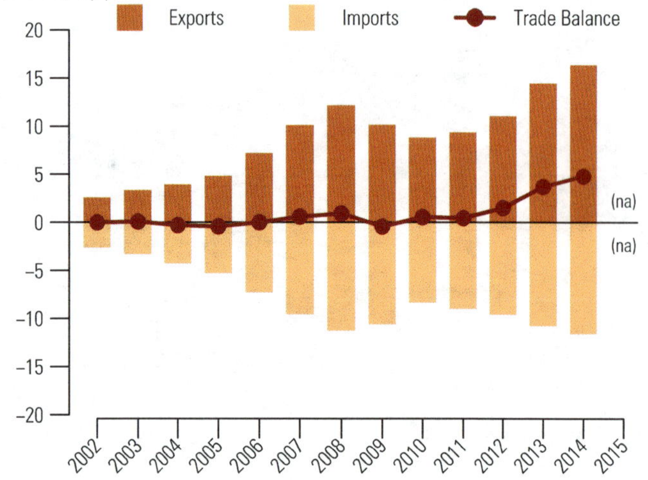

Exports Profile:

"Machinery and transport equipment" (SITC section 7), "Goods classified chiefly by material" (SITC section 6) and "Miscellaneous manufactured articles" (SITC section 8) were the largest commodity groups for exports in 2015, representing respectively 43.8, 16.2 and 14.7 percent of exported goods (see table 2). From 2013 to 2015, the largest export commodity was "Parts and accessories of the motor vehicles of headings 87.01 to 87.05" (HS code 8708) (see table 1). The top three destinations for merchandise exports were Germany, Italy and France, accounting for respectively 19.2, 11.9 and 6.8 percent of total exports. "Transportation" (EBOPS code 205) accounted for the largest share of exports of services in 2014 at 5.8 bln US$, followed by "Other business services" (EBOPS code 268) at 4.5 bln US$ and "Computer and information services" (EBOPS code 262) at 2.4 bln US$ (see graph 3).

Graph 3: Exports of services by EBOPS category
(% share in 2014)

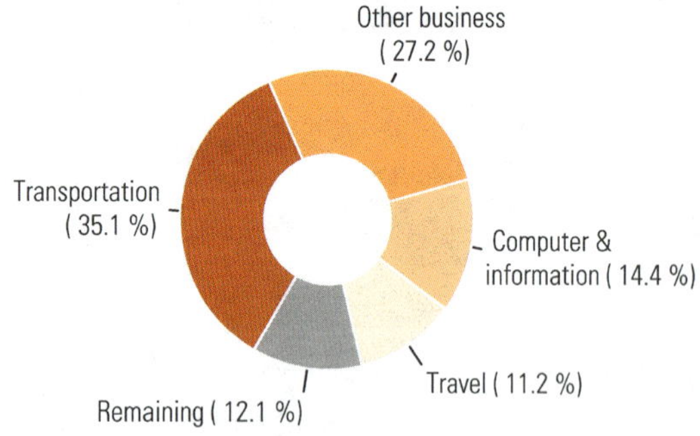

Table 1: Top 10 export commodities 2013 to 2015

HS code	4-digit heading of Harmonized System 2012	Value (million US$)			Unit value				SITC code
		2013	2014	2015	2013	2014	2015	Unit	
	All Commodities	65881.4	69877.9	60605.0					
8708	Parts and accessories of the motor vehicles of headings 87.01 to 87.05	4530.0	5267.3	4950.7	9.6	10.4	9.7	US$/kg	784
8703	Motor cars and other motor vehicles principally designed for the transport	4208.3	3974.0	3233.0	10.3	10.3	8.7	thsd US$/unit	781
8544	Insulated (including enamelled or anodised) wire, cable	3576.5	3841.8	3648.1	16.3	14.9	12.2	US$/kg	773
2710	Petroleum oils, other than crude	2675.1	3242.6	2022.4	1.0	0.9	0.5	US$/kg	334
9999	Commodities not specified according to kind	2413.7	2136.9	1997.9					931
9401	Seats (other than those of heading 94.02)	1339.9	1702.4	1523.7					821
4011	New pneumatic tyres, of rubber	1510.5	1606.8	1377.8	57.1	58.1	46.4	US$/unit	625
8517	Electrical apparatus for line telephony or line telegraphy	1149.6	1264.0	1118.4					764
1001	Wheat and meslin	1303.0	1280.7	769.3	0.3	0.3	0.2	US$/kg	041
8537	Boards, panels, consoles, desks, cabinets and other bases	729.8	1080.3	1383.1	52.7	68.8	68.4	US$/kg	772

Services Imports and Exports: EBOPS 2002 categories

Table 2: Merchandise exports by SITC

(Value in million US$, growth and shares in percentage)

SITC	2015	Avg. Growth rates 2011-2015	Avg. Growth rates 2014-2015	2015 share
Total	60605.0	-0.8	-13.3	100.0
0+1	5207.9	7.3	-9.8	8.6
2+4	2627.1	-12.1	-27.7	4.3
3	2703.9	-5.9	-35.4	4.5
5	2802.2	-7.8	-20.2	4.6
6	9818.2	-2.7	-12.4	16.2
7	26527.6	0.9	-8.9	43.8
8	8920.1	-0.9	-13.4	14.7
9	1997.9	14.0	-6.5	3.3

Table 3: Merchandise imports by SITC

(Value in million US$, growth and shares in percentage)

SITC	2015	Avg. Growth rates 2011-2015	Avg. Growth rates 2014-2015	2015 share
Total	69857.7	-2.2	-10.3	100.0
0+1	5733.6	3.3	-0.3	8.2
2+4	2081.2	-5.6	-11.0	3.0
3	4454.1	-15.2	-38.5	6.4
5	9216.6	-1.7	-10.1	13.2
6	14197.0	-3.4	-10.5	20.3
7	25127.2	-0.7	-5.6	36.0
8	6480.6	1.4	-4.8	9.3
9	2567.3	6.8	-14.7	3.7

SITC Legend

SITC Code	Description
Total	All commodities
0+1	Food, animals + beverages, tobacco
2+4	Crude materials + anim. & veg. oils
3	Mineral fuels, lubricants
5	Chemicals
6	Goods classified chiefly by material
7	Machinery and transport equipment
8	Miscellaneous manufactured articles
9	Not classified elsewhere in the SITC

Graph 4: Merchandise trade balance

(Bln US$ by MDG Regions in 2015)

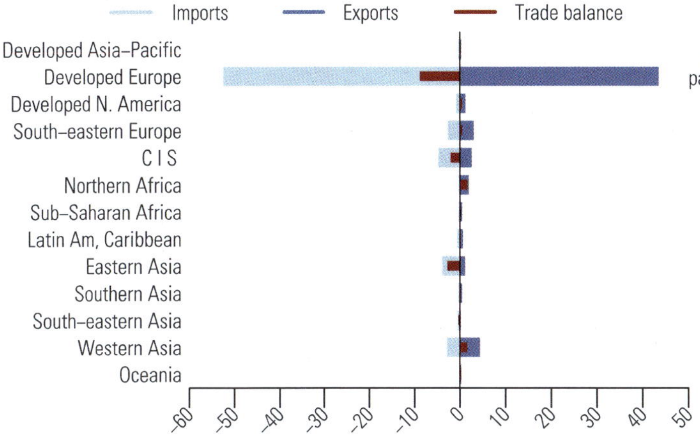

Graph 5: Partner concentration of merchandise trade

(Cumulative share by ranked partners in 2015)

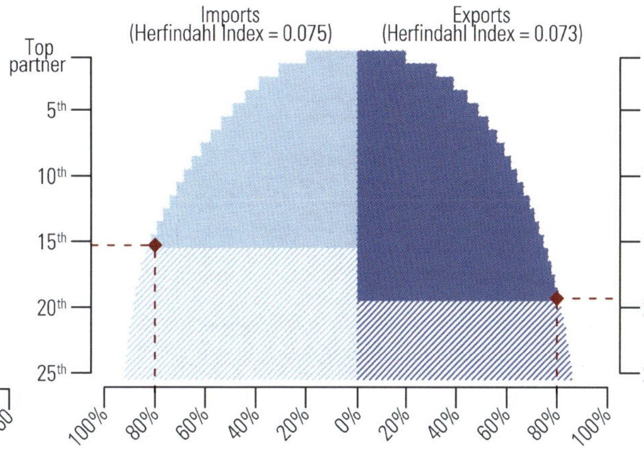

Graph 6: Imports of services by EBOPS category

(% share in 2014)

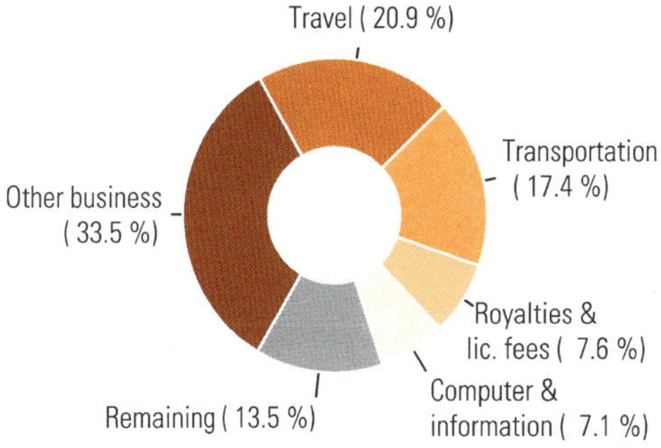

Imports Profile:

"Machinery and transport equipment" (SITC section 7), "Goods classified chiefly by material" (SITC section 6) and "Chemicals" (SITC section 5) were the largest commodity groups for imports in 2015, representing respectively 36.0, 20.3 and 13.2 percent of imported goods (see table 3). From 2013 to 2015, the largest import commodity was "Petroleum oils and oils obtained from bituminous minerals, crude" (HS code 2709) (see table 4). The top three partners for merchandise imports were Germany, Italy and Hungary, accounting for respectively 19.2, 10.9 and 8.0 percent of total imports. "Other business services" (EBOPS code 268) accounted for the largest share of imports of services in 2014 at 3.9 bln US$, followed by "Travel" (EBOPS code 236) at 2.4 bln US$ and "Transportation" (EBOPS code 205) at 2.0 bln US$ (see graph 6).

Table 4: Top 10 import commodities 2013 to 2015

HS code	4-digit heading of Harmonized System 2012	Value (million US$) 2013	2014	2015	Unit value 2013	2014	2015	Unit	SITC code
	All Commodities	73452.2	77889.1	69857.7					
2709	Petroleum oils and oils obtained from bituminous minerals, crude	4190.1	4795.5	2518.0	0.8	0.7	0.4	US$/kg	333
8708	Parts and accessories of the motor vehicles of headings 87.01 to 87.05	2637.5	3028.5	2820.2	*7.2*	*8.1*	*7.2*	US$/kg	784
3004	Medicaments (excluding goods of heading 30.02, 30.05 or 30.06)	2886.3	2872.9	2400.5	*75.7*	*71.1*	*62.2*	US$/kg	542
9999	Commodities not specified according to kind	2555.9	3010.8	2567.3					931
8517	Electrical apparatus for line telephony or line telegraphy	1402.4	1704.3	1559.8					764
8544	Insulated (including enamelled or anodised) wire, cable	1566.8	1577.0	1487.4	*11.1*	*11.5*	*9.6*	US$/kg	773
2710	Petroleum oils, other than crude	1644.8	1539.8	1210.0	*1.1*	*1.0*	*0.6*	US$/kg	334
8703	Motor cars and other motor vehicles principally designed for the transport	1188.1	1433.1	1452.4	19.1	19.1	17.1	thsd US$/unit	781
8536	Electrical apparatus for switching or protecting electrical circuits	994.3	1091.7	1049.1	*27.7*	*29.4*	*22.4*	US$/kg	772
8542	Electronic integrated circuits	734.0	866.7	840.8					776

Goods Imports: CIF, by origin	Goods Exports: FOB, by last known destination	Trade System: General

Overview:

In 2015, the value of merchandise exports of the Russian Federation decreased substantially by 30.9 percent to reach 343.9 bln US$, while its merchandise imports decreased substantially by 36.2 percent to reach 182.8 bln US$ (see graph 1, table 2 and table 3). The merchandise trade balance recorded a large surplus of 161.1 bln US$ (see graph 1). The largest merchandise trade balance was with MDG Developed Europe at 65.7 bln US$ (see graph 4). Merchandise exports in the Russian Federation were diversified amongst partners; imports were also diversified. The top 20 partners accounted for 80 percent or more of exports and 24 partners accounted for 80 percent or more of imports (see graph 5). In 2014, the value of exports of services of the Russian Federation decreased moderately by 5.2 percent, reaching 62.5 bln US$, while its imports of services decreased moderately by 5.7 percent and reached 119.2 bln US$ (see graph 2). There was a large trade in services deficit of 56.6 bln US$.

Graph 1: Total merchandise trade, by value

(Bln US$ by year)

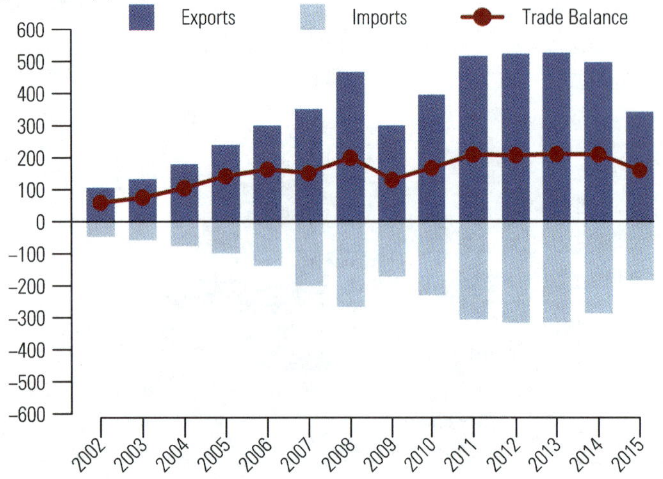

Graph 2: Total services trade, by value

(Bln US$ by year)

Exports Profile:

"Mineral fuels, lubricants" (SITC section 3), "Goods classified chiefly by material" (SITC section 6) and "Chemicals" (SITC section 5) were the largest commodity groups for exports in 2015, representing respectively 62.8, 12.6 and 5.8 percent of exported goods (see table 2). From 2013 to 2015, the largest export commodity was "Petroleum oils and oils obtained from bituminous minerals, crude" (HS code 2709) (see table 1). The top three destinations for merchandise exports were Areas nes, the Netherlands and China, accounting for respectively 13.7, 12.9 and 7.4 percent of total exports. "Transportation" (EBOPS code 205) accounted for the largest share of exports of services in 2014 at 20.5 bln US$, followed by "Travel" (EBOPS code 236) at 11.8 bln US$ and "Construction services" (EBOPS code 249) at 4.7 bln US$ (see graph 3).

Graph 3: Exports of services by EBOPS category

(% share in 2014)

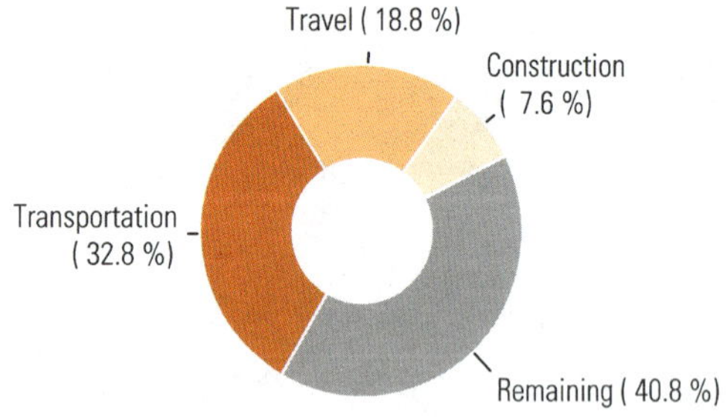

Table 1: Top 10 export commodities 2013 to 2015

HS code	4-digit heading of Harmonized System 2012	Value (million US$)			Unit value				SITC code
		2013	2014	2015	2013	2014	2015	Unit	
	All Commodities	527265.9	497833.5	343907.7					
2709	Petroleum oils and oils obtained from bituminous minerals, crude	173669.6	153887.9	89576.5	0.7	0.7	0.4	US$/kg	333
2710	Petroleum oils, other than crude	109415.4	115807.7	67403.1	0.7	0.7	*0.4*	US$/kg	334
2711	Petroleum gases and other gaseous hydrocarbons	74639.1	62647.9	47517.7	*0.5*	*0.6*	*0.5*	US$/kg	343
9999	Commodities not specified according to kind	13208.2	11647.0	10796.9					931
2701	Coal; briquettes, ovoids and similar solid fuels manufactured from coal	11821.2	11642.3	9480.3	0.1	0.1	0.1	US$/kg	321
7207	Semi-finished products of iron or non-alloy steel	6471.4	6587.4	4636.7	0.5	0.5	0.3	US$/kg	672
7601	Unwrought aluminium	6132.8	5251.7	6075.7	1.8	1.8	*1.8*	US$/kg	684
7102	Diamonds, whether or not worked, but not mounted or set	4969.3	5310.5	3945.3					667
1001	Wheat and meslin	3482.7	5423.1	3948.7	0.3	0.2	0.2	US$/kg	041
4407	Wood sawn or chipped lengthwise, sliced or peeled	3651.8	3738.4	3073.5	*171.3*	*165.5*	*125.8*	US$/m³	248

Services Imports and Exports: EBOPS 2002 categories

Table 2: Merchandise exports by SITC

(Value in million US$, growth and shares in percentage)

SITC	2015	Avg. Growth rates 2011-2015	Avg. Growth rates 2014-2015	2015 share
Total	343 907.7	-9.7	-30.9	100.0
0+1	13 891.1	8.3	-15.0	4.0
2+4	13 915.8	-6.3	-22.6	4.0
3	216 101.1	-11.1	-37.6	62.8
5	19 950.4	-2.2	-15.2	5.8
6	43 493.6	-3.7	-17.6	12.6
7	18 509.1	12.0	-7.9	5.4
8	5 737.3	26.1	-8.0	1.7
9	12 309.3	-31.5	-16.7	3.6

Table 3: Merchandise imports by SITC

(Value in million US$, growth and shares in percentage)

SITC	2015	Avg. Growth rates 2011-2015	Avg. Growth rates 2014-2015	2015 share
Total	182 782.0	-12.1	-36.2	100.0
0+1	22 974.4	-10.0	-35.8	12.6
2+4	7 985.7	-1.0	-21.1	4.4
3	2 990.2	-11.6	-26.0	1.6
5	27 436.3	-6.3	-26.6	15.0
6	22 442.5	-10.8	-37.9	12.3
7	76 382.1	-12.1	-39.9	41.8
8	21 538.0	-8.5	-38.9	11.8
9	1 032.7	-56.1	19.9	0.6

SITC Legend

SITC Code	Description
Total	All commodities
0+1	Food, animals + beverages, tobacco
2+4	Crude materials + anim. & veg. oils
3	Mineral fuels, lubricants
5	Chemicals
6	Goods classified chiefly by material
7	Machinery and transport equipment
8	Miscellaneous manufactured articles
9	Not classified elsewhere in the SITC

Graph 4: Merchandise trade balance

(Bln US$ by MDG Regions in 2015)

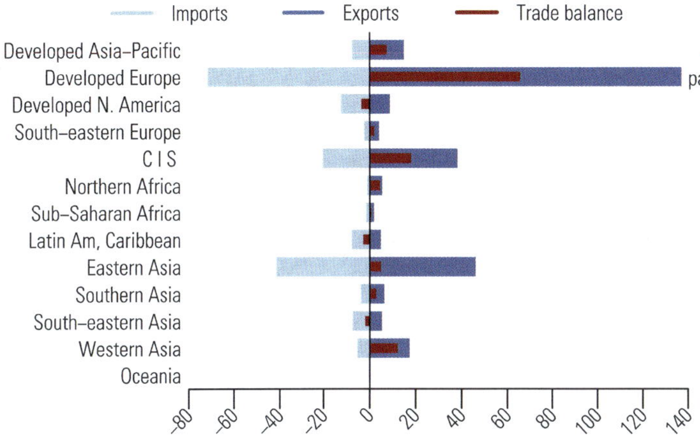

Graph 5: Partner concentration of merchandise trade

(Cumulative share by ranked partners in 2015)

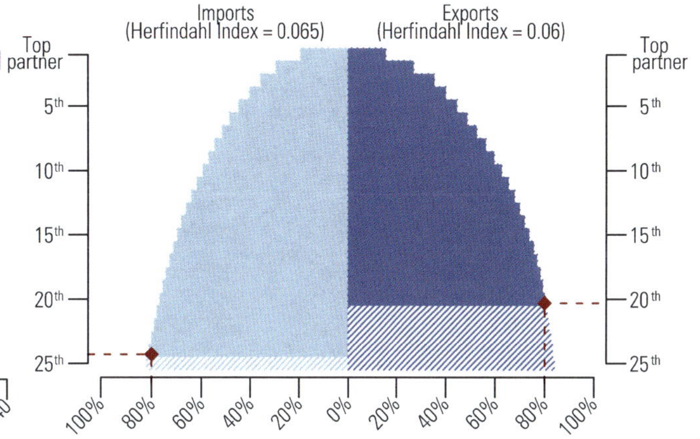

Graph 6: Imports of services by EBOPS category

(% share in 2014)

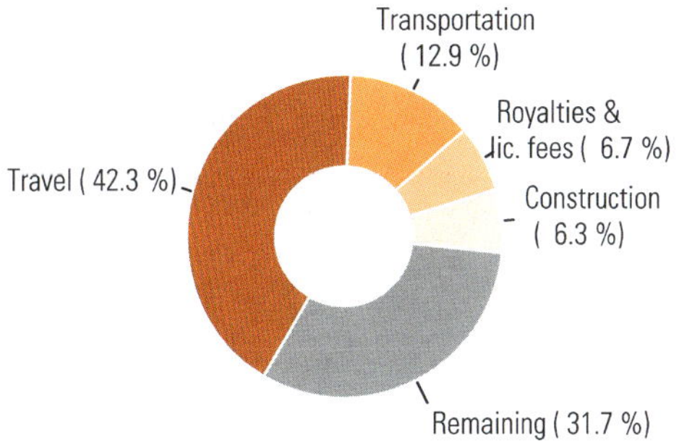

Imports Profile:

"Machinery and transport equipment" (SITC section 7), "Chemicals" (SITC section 5) and "Food, animals + beverages, tobacco" (SITC section 0+1) were the largest commodity groups for imports in 2015, representing respectively 41.8, 15.0 and 12.6 percent of imported goods (see table 3). From 2013 to 2015, the largest import commodity was "Motor cars and other motor vehicles principally designed for the transport" (HS code 8703) (see table 4). The top three partners for merchandise imports were China, Germany and the United States, accounting for respectively 17.7, 11.5 and 6.0 percent of total imports. "Travel" (EBOPS code 236) accounted for the largest share of imports of services in 2014 at 50.4 bln US$, followed by "Transportation" (EBOPS code 205) at 15.4 bln US$ and "Royalties and license fees" (EBOPS code 266) at 8.0 bln US$ (see graph 6).

Table 4: Top 10 import commodities 2013 to 2015

HS code	4-digit heading of Harmonized System 2012	Value (million US$) 2013	Value (million US$) 2014	Value (million US$) 2015	Unit value 2013	Unit value 2014	Unit value 2015	Unit	SITC code
	All Commodities	314 945.1	286 648.8	182 782.0					
8703	Motor cars and other motor vehicles principally designed for the transport	16 996.9	13 161.9	6 490.2	19.0	18.7	18.5	thsd US$/unit	781
3004	Medicaments (excluding goods of heading 30.02, 30.05 or 30.06)	11 629.5	10 108.8	6 796.5	77.1	68.2	*48.4*	US$/kg	542
8708	Parts and accessories of the motor vehicles of headings 87.01 to 87.05	11 488.9	9 802.7	5 377.4	7.6	7.2	*6.2*	US$/kg	784
8517	Electrical apparatus for line telephony or line telegraphy	7 685.1	8 236.4	6 335.0					764
8802	Other aircraft (for example, helicopters, aeroplanes); spacecraft	4 459.4	7 268.9	3 170.0	16.7	19.4	14.0	mln US$/unit	792
8471	Automatic data processing machines and units thereof	4 864.6	5 082.6	4 034.0	78.8	89.0	100.8	US$/unit	752
8419	Machinery, plant or laboratory equipment	2 509.8	3 190.2	2 558.3					741
8707	Bodies (including cabs), for the motor vehicles of headings 87.01 to 87.05	4 060.5	2 818.3	1 078.1	10.6	9.5	7.5	thsd US$/unit	784
8502	Electric generating sets and rotary converters	3 239.8	2 711.2	1 383.3	*6.4*	*5.1*	4.1	thsd US$/unit	716
9018	Instruments and appliances used in medical, surgical, dental or veterinary	2 418.2	2 412.3	1 574.7					872

Source: UN Comtrade

Rwanda

Goods Imports: CIF, by origin | **Goods Exports: FOB, by last known destination** | **Trade System: General**

Overview:

In 2014, the value of merchandise exports of Rwanda increased moderately by 7.4 percent to reach 653.4 mln US$, while its merchandise imports decreased slightly by 1.8 percent to reach 2.0 bln US$ (see graph 1, table 2 and table 3). The merchandise trade balance recorded a large deficit of 1.3 bln US$ (see graph 1). The largest merchandise trade balance was with MDG Eastern Asia at -387.5 mln US$ (see graph 4). Merchandise exports in Rwanda were moderately concentrated amongst partners; imports were diversified. The top 6 partners accounted for 80 percent or more of exports and 14 partners accounted for 80 percent or more of imports (see graph 5). In 2014, the value of exports of services of Rwanda decreased substantially by 11.0 percent, reaching 516.9 mln US$, while its imports of services decreased substantially by 24.9 percent and reached 663.1 mln US$ (see graph 2). There was a moderate trade in services deficit of 146.2 mln US$.

Graph 1: Total merchandise trade, by value

(Bln US$ by year)

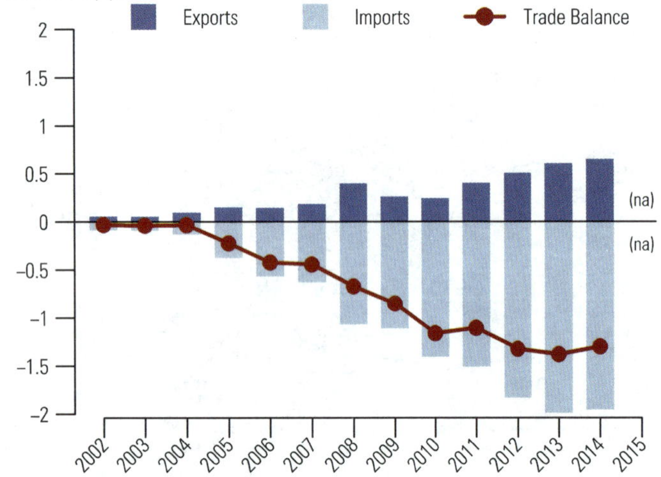

Graph 2: Total services trade, by value

(Mln US$ by year)

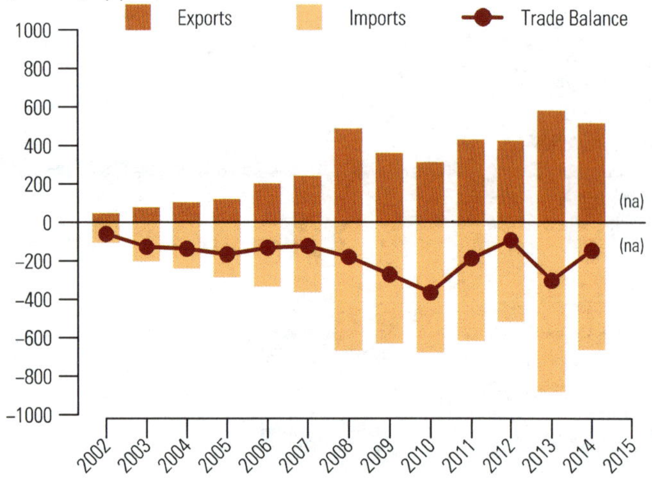

Exports Profile:

"Crude materials + anim. & veg. oils" (SITC section 2+4), "Food, animals + beverages, tobacco" (SITC section 0+1) and "Mineral fuels, lubricants" (SITC section 3) were the largest commodity groups for exports in 2014, representing respectively 36.0, 30.1 and 15.8 percent of exported goods (see table 2). From 2012 to 2014, the largest export commodity was "Niobium, tantalum, vanadium or zirconium ores and concentrates" (HS code 2615) (see table 1). The top three destinations for merchandise exports were the United Republic of Tanzania, Democratic Republic of the Congo and Kenya, accounting for respectively 34.4, 21.4 and 14.3 percent of total exports. "Travel" (EBOPS code 236) accounted for the largest share of exports of services in 2014 at 303.7 mln US$, followed by "Government services, n.i.e." (EBOPS code 291) at 191.6 mln US$ (see graph 3).

Graph 3: Exports of services by EBOPS category

(% share in 2014)

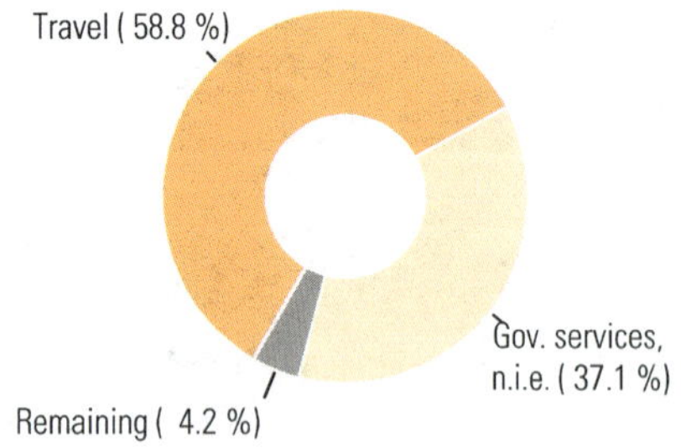

Table 1: Top 10 export commodities 2012 to 2014

HS code	4-digit heading of Harmonized System 2007	Value (million US$) 2012	2013	2014	Unit value 2012	2013	2014	Unit	SITC code
	All Commodities	507.0	608.1	653.4					
2615	Niobium, tantalum, vanadium or zirconium ores and concentrates	56.7	134.9	103.3	49.6	54.7	45.7	US$/kg	287
2710	Petroleum oils, other than crude	45.7	72.4	103.3	1.2	1.3	2.0	US$/kg	334
0902	Tea, whether or not flavoured	86.6	61.6	57.8	3.8	2.8	2.4	US$/kg	074
0901	Coffee, whether or not roasted or decaffeinated	71.2	52.2	60.8	3.6	2.8	3.7	US$/kg	071
2609	Tin ores and concentrates	52.9	58.2	71.7	11.4	12.1	12.0	US$/kg	287
2611	Tungsten ores and concentrates	21.4	29.1	25.9	15.6	13.7	11.9	US$/kg	287
1101	Wheat or meslin flour	17.0	13.2	20.4	0.8	0.8	0.8	US$/kg	046
8703	Motor cars and other motor vehicles principally designed for the transport	24.7	8.1	7.9	*30.6*	*23.9*	*24.2*	thsd US$/unit	781
1006	Rice	3.6	12.3	14.9	0.8	0.8	0.7	US$/kg	042
2203	Beer made from malt	8.9	17.8	1.3	*1.1*	*3.6*	*0.6*	US$/litre	112

Services Imports and Exports: EBOPS 2002 categories

Table 2: Merchandise exports by SITC

(Value in million US$, growth and shares in percentage)

SITC	2014	Avg. Growth rates 2010-2014	2013-2014	2014 share
Total	653.4	28.2	7.4	100.0
0+1	196.8	16.1	-7.9	30.1
2+4	235.3	22.3	-9.3	36.0
3	103.5	178.7	42.6	15.8
5	8.1	35.7	78.1	1.2
6	30.3	41.9	58.0	4.6
7	56.4	50.9	120.1	8.6
8	15.5	27.6	17.6	2.4
9	7.6	158.0	>	1.2

Table 3: Merchandise imports by SITC

(Value in million US$, growth and shares in percentage)

SITC	2014	Avg. Growth rates 2010-2014	2013-2014	2014 share
Total	1 954.2	8.6	-1.8	100.0
0+1	276.9	13.3	0.6	14.2
2+4	145.2	8.2	7.2	7.4
3	79.2	5.8	-32.8	4.1
5	315.2	14.5	22.3	16.1
6	405.8	7.8	-0.2	20.8
7	506.3	1.9	-19.3	25.9
8	225.4	18.7	33.8	11.5
9	0.2	57.0	22108.1	0.0

SITC Legend

SITC Code	Description
Total	All commodities
0+1	Food, animals + beverages, tobacco
2+4	Crude materials + anim. & veg. oils
3	Mineral fuels, lubricants
5	Chemicals
6	Goods classified chiefly by material
7	Machinery and transport equipment
8	Miscellaneous manufactured articles
9	Not classified elsewhere in the SITC

Graph 4: Merchandise trade balance

(Mln US$ by MDG Regions in 2014)

Graph 5: Partner concentration of merchandise trade

(Cumulative share by ranked partners in 2014)

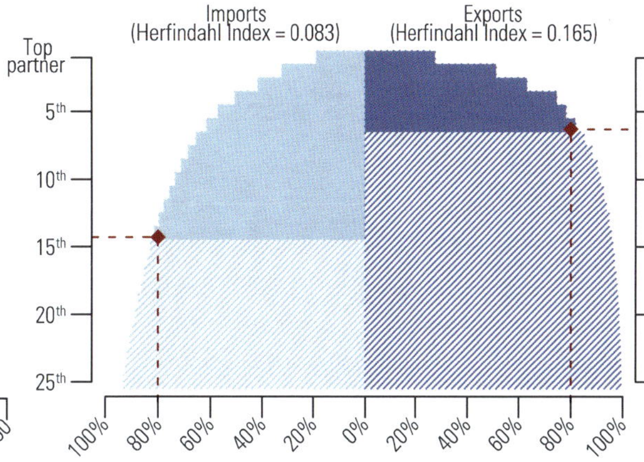

Graph 6: Imports of services by EBOPS category

(% share in 2014)

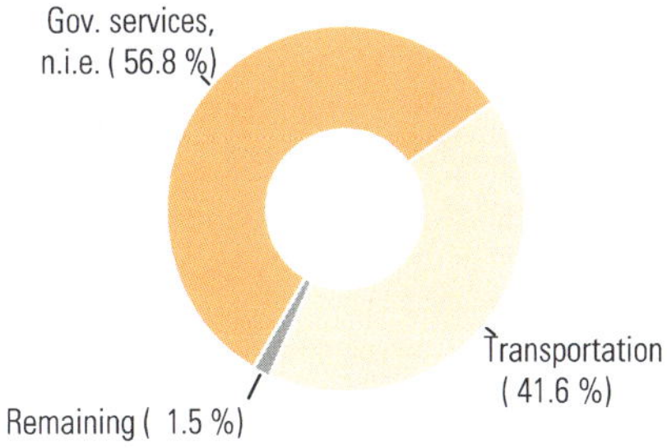

Imports Profile:

"Machinery and transport equipment" (SITC section 7), "Goods classified chiefly by material" (SITC section 6) and "Chemicals" (SITC section 5) were the largest commodity groups for imports in 2014, representing respectively 25.9, 20.8 and 16.1 percent of imported goods (see table 3). From 2012 to 2014, the largest import commodity was "Petroleum oils, other than crude" (HS code 2710) (see table 4). The top three partners for merchandise imports were China, Uganda and Kenya, accounting for respectively 15.6, 13.2 and 8.2 percent of total imports. "Government services, n.i.e." (EBOPS code 291) accounted for the largest share of imports of services in 2014 at 376.9 mln US$, followed by "Transportation" (EBOPS code 205) at 275.9 mln US$ (see graph 6).

Table 4: Top 10 import commodities 2012 to 2014

HS code	4-digit heading of Harmonized System 2007	Value (million US$) 2012	2013	2014	Unit value 2012	2013	2014	Unit	SITC code
	All Commodities	1 832.0	1 989.1	1 954.2					
2710	Petroleum oils, other than crude	124.8	109.9	68.0	1.3	1.2	1.1	US$/kg	334
8703	Motor cars and other motor vehicles principally designed for the transport	61.1	173.0	34.6	*21.6*	*34.5*	*22.3*	thsd US$/unit	781
2523	Portland cement, aluminous cement, slag cement	86.0	88.7	83.7	0.2	0.2	0.2	US$/kg	661
8517	Electrical apparatus for line telephony or line telegraphy	51.8	63.3	98.7					764
3004	Medicaments (excluding goods of heading 30.02, 30.05 or 30.06)	54.3	52.3	67.2	9.8	17.3	20.3	US$/kg	542
1701	Cane or beet sugar and chemically pure sucrose, in solid form	54.2	52.7	55.7	0.9	0.8	0.7	US$/kg	061
1001	Wheat and meslin	39.7	58.9	53.9	0.4	0.4	0.4	US$/kg	041
1516	Animal or vegetable fats and oils	31.5	36.3	50.5	1.7	1.4	1.4	US$/kg	431
7210	Flat-rolled products of iron or non-alloy steel	26.1	33.4	42.8	1.4	1.2	1.1	US$/kg	674
8471	Automatic data processing machines and units thereof	36.2	27.3	30.3					752

Source: UN Comtrade

Saint Kitts and Nevis

Goods Imports: CIF, by origin	Goods Exports: FOB, by last known destination	Trade System: Special

Overview:

In 2011, the value of merchandise exports of Saint Kitts and Nevis increased substantially by 40.2 percent to reach 44.9 mln US$, while its merchandise imports decreased moderately by 8.6 percent to reach 246.7 mln US$ (see graph 1, table 2 and table 3). The merchandise trade balance recorded a large deficit of 201.8 mln US$ (see graph 1). The largest merchandise trade balance was with MDG Developed North America at -134.8 mln US$ (see graph 4). Merchandise exports in Saint Kitts and Nevis were highly concentrated amongst partners; imports were also highly concentrated. The top 1 partner accounted for 80 percent or more of exports and 4 partners accounted for 80 percent or more of imports (see graph 5). In 2013, the value of exports of services of Saint Kitts and Nevis increased substantially by 21.5 percent, reaching 236.1 mln US$, while its imports of services increased moderately by 5.4 percent and reached 126.1 mln US$ (see graph 2). There was a large trade in services surplus of 110.0 mln US$.

Graph 1: Total merchandise trade, by value

(Mln US$ by year)

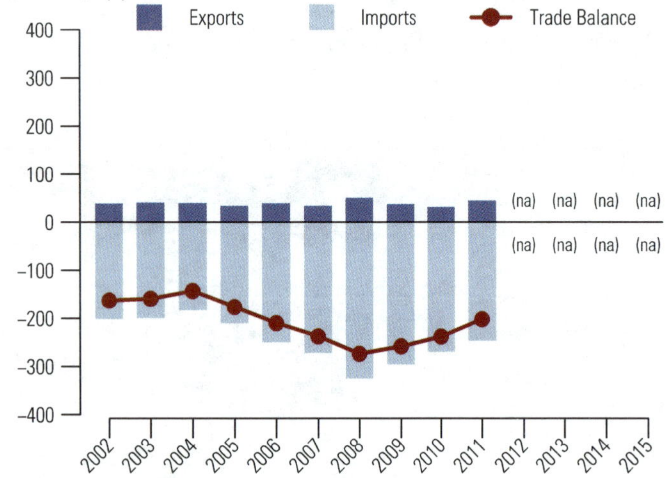

Graph 2: Total services trade, by value

(Mln US$ by year)

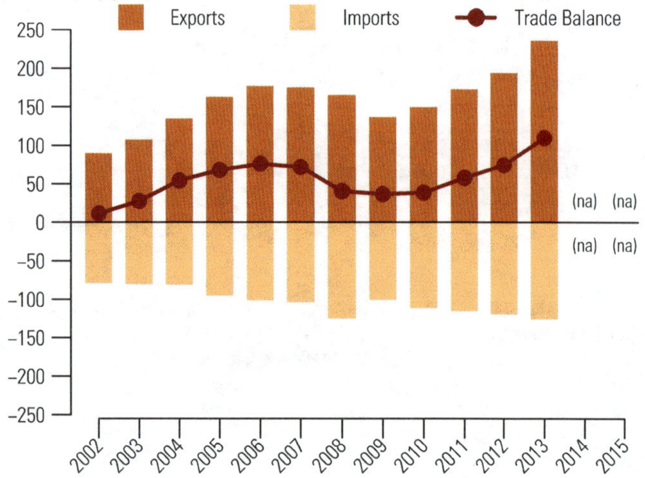

Exports Profile:

"Machinery and transport equipment" (SITC section 7), "Miscellaneous manufactured articles" (SITC section 8) and "Food, animals + beverages, tobacco" (SITC section 0+1) were the largest commodity groups for exports in 2011, representing respectively 67.6, 20.4 and 10.4 percent of exported goods (see table 2). From 2009 to 2011, the largest export commodity was "Electrical apparatus for switching or protecting electrical circuits" (HS code 8536) (see table 1). The top three destinations for merchandise exports were the United States, Antigua and Barbuda and Saint Lucia, accounting for respectively 79.3, 3.4 and 2.6 percent of total exports. "Travel" (EBOPS code 236) accounted for the largest share of exports of services in 2013 at 101.0 mln US$, followed by "Government services, n.i.e." (EBOPS code 291) at 91.6 mln US$ and "Other business services" (EBOPS code 268) at 19.0 mln US$ (see graph 3).

Graph 3: Exports of services by EBOPS category

(% share in 2013)

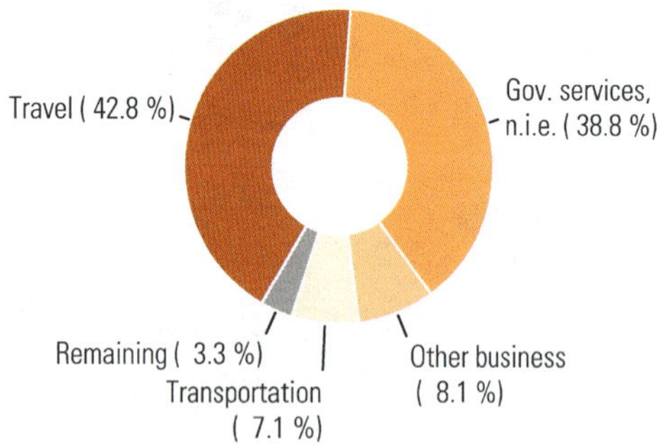

Table 1: Top 10 export commodities 2009 to 2011

HS code	4-digit heading of Harmonized System 2007	Value (million US$) 2009	2010	2011	Unit value 2009	2010	2011	Unit	SITC code
	All Commodities	37.7	32.0	44.9					
8536	Electrical apparatus for switching or protecting electrical circuits	14.2	13.4	15.2	29.7	15.8	7.8	US$/kg	772
8529	Parts suitable for use with the apparatus of headings 85.25 to 85.28	12.5	6.1	10.1	67.8	71.9	76.4	US$/kg	764
4907	Unused postage, revenue or similar stamps of current or new issue	2.6	3.0	7.6	132.2	108.4	298.0	US$/kg	892
8707	Bodies (including cabs), for the motor vehicles of headings 87.01 to 87.05	0.1	0.6	3.0					784
2203	Beer made from malt	1.5	0.9	1.2	*0.7*	*0.6*	*0.6*	US$/litre	112
2202	Waters with added sugar	0.6	0.8	1.4	*0.9*	*0.8*	*0.5*	US$/litre	111
3925	Builders' ware of plastics, not elsewhere specified or included	0.7	0.9	0.8	11.2	17.3	15.5	US$/kg	893
0306	Crustaceans, whether in shell or not	0.4	0.4	0.7	5.8	3.3		US$/kg	036
2208	Alcohol of a strength by volume of less than 80 % vol	0.1	0.5	0.6	*1.9*	*2.8*	*4.3*	US$/litre	112
8311	Wire, rods, tubes, plates, electrodes and similar products, of base metal	0.0	1.1	...	5.5	41.7		US$/kg	699

Services Imports and Exports: EBOPS 2002 categories

Table 2: Merchandise exports by SITC

(Value in million US$, growth and shares in percentage)

SITC	2011	Avg. Growth rates 2007-2011	2010-2011	2011 share
Total	44.9	7.1	40.2	100.0
0+1	4.7	8.3	32.9	10.4
2+4	0.0	37.6	2.5	0.1
3	0.0	-13.7	-77.6	0.0
5	0.3	26.3	9.1	0.6
6	0.4	-15.9	-74.6	0.8
7	30.4	1.6	39.6	67.6
8	9.2	63.0	85.0	20.4

Table 3: Merchandise imports by SITC

(Value in million US$, growth and shares in percentage)

SITC	2011	Avg. Growth rates 2007-2011	2010-2011	2011 share
Total	246.7	-2.4	-8.6	100.0
0+1	57.6	3.5	9.7	23.3
2+4	6.7	1.6	-14.2	2.7
3	6.9	-22.1	-30.3	2.8
5	20.4	1.7	3.0	8.3
6	46.3	-1.5	-7.8	18.8
7	66.5	-5.8	-8.5	27.0
8	42.3	-0.7	-25.7	17.2
9	0.0	56.3	258.2	0.0

SITC Legend

SITC Code	Description
Total	All commodities
0+1	Food, animals + beverages, tobacco
2+4	Crude materials + anim. & veg. oils
3	Mineral fuels, lubricants
5	Chemicals
6	Goods classified chiefly by material
7	Machinery and transport equipment
8	Miscellaneous manufactured articles
9	Not classified elsewhere in the SITC

Graph 4: Merchandise trade balance

(Mln US$ by MDG Regions in 2011)

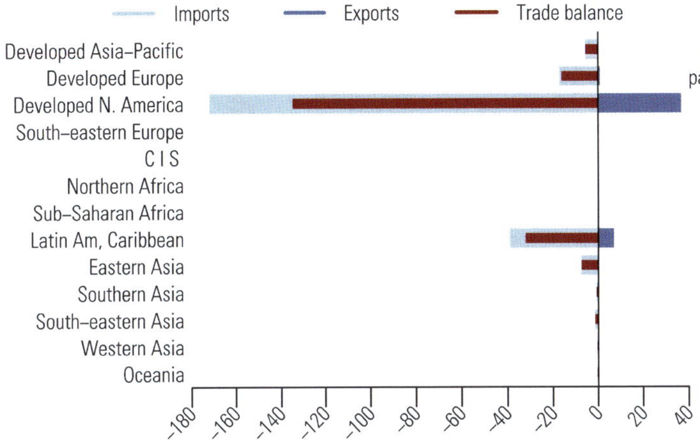

Graph 5: Partner concentration of merchandise trade

(Cumulative share by ranked partners in 2011)

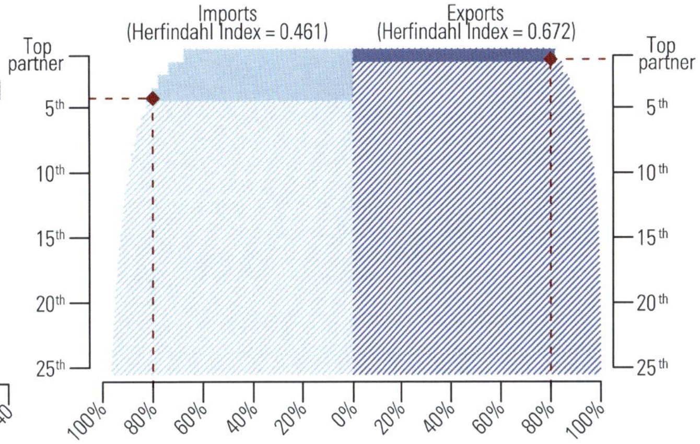

Graph 6: Imports of services by EBOPS category

(% share in 2013)

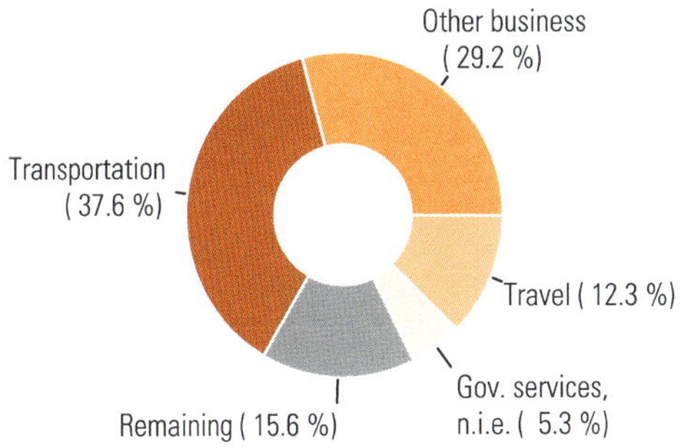

Imports Profile:

"Machinery and transport equipment" (SITC section 7), "Food, animals + beverages, tobacco" (SITC section 0+1) and "Goods classified chiefly by material" (SITC section 6) were the largest commodity groups for imports in 2011, representing respectively 27.0, 23.3 and 18.8 percent of imported goods (see table 3). From 2009 to 2011, the largest import commodity was "Articles of jewellery and parts thereof, of precious metal" (HS code 7113) (see table 4). The top three partners for merchandise imports were the United States, Trinidad and Tobago and the United Kingdom, accounting for respectively 67.1, 6.8 and 3.7 percent of total imports. "Transportation" (EBOPS code 205) accounted for the largest share of imports of services in 2013 at 47.3 mln US$, followed by "Other business services" (EBOPS code 268) at 36.8 mln US$ and "Travel" (EBOPS code 236) at 15.5 mln US$ (see graph 6).

Table 4: Top 10 import commodities 2009 to 2011

HS code	4-digit heading of Harmonized System 2007	Value (million US$) 2009	2010	2011	Unit value 2009	2010	2011	Unit	SITC code
	All Commodities	295.8	269.8	246.7					
7113	Articles of jewellery and parts thereof, of precious metal	23.7	17.3	5.3	*13.5*	*11.3*	*5.6*	thsd US$/kg	897
8703	Motor cars and other motor vehicles principally designed for the transport	10.0	9.2	7.1	*15.7*	*17.0*		thsd US$/unit	781
2710	Petroleum oils, other than crude	10.7	9.0	6.3	0.6	0.7	*1.1*	US$/kg	334
9403	Other furniture and parts thereof	7.7	6.9	5.9					821
7326	Other articles of iron or steel	6.2	5.7	6.1	*17.6*	*12.9*	16.4	US$/kg	699
2106	Food preparations not elsewhere specified or included	6.2	3.8	7.4	*2.3*	*3.3*	*5.0*	US$/kg	098
0207	Meat and edible offal, of the poultry of heading 01.05	5.5	5.4	5.8	*1.5*	*1.3*	*1.5*	US$/kg	012
8538	Parts suitable for use with the apparatus of heading 85.35, 85.36 or 85.37	1.5	3.9	7.5	21.2	21.4	17.7	US$/kg	772
8502	Electric generating sets and rotary converters	3.9	8.2	0.7					716
2523	Portland cement, aluminous cement, slag cement	5.9	3.5	2.9	0.1	0.1	0.1	US$/kg	661

Saint Lucia

Goods Imports: CIF, by origin **Goods Exports: FOB, by last known destination** **Trade System: General**

Overview:

In 2014, the value of merchandise exports of Saint Lucia was 146.3 mln US$, while its merchandise imports was 642.1 mln US$ (see graph 1, table 2 and table 3). The merchandise trade balance recorded a large deficit of 495.8 mln US$ (see graph 1). The largest merchandise trade balance was with MDG Developed North America at -234.8 mln US$ (see graph 4). Merchandise exports in Saint Lucia were moderately concentrated amongst partners; imports were highly concentrated. The top 5 partners accounted for 80 percent or more of exports and 8 partners accounted for 80 percent or more of imports (see graph 5, and Introduction, paragraphs 19-21). In 2013, the value of exports of services of Saint Lucia increased moderately by 5.0 percent, reaching 409.0 mln US$, while its imports of services decreased slightly by 1.4 percent and reached 187.4 mln US$ (see graph 2). There was a large trade in services surplus of 221.6 mln US$.

Graph 1: Total merchandise trade, by value

(Mln US$ by year)

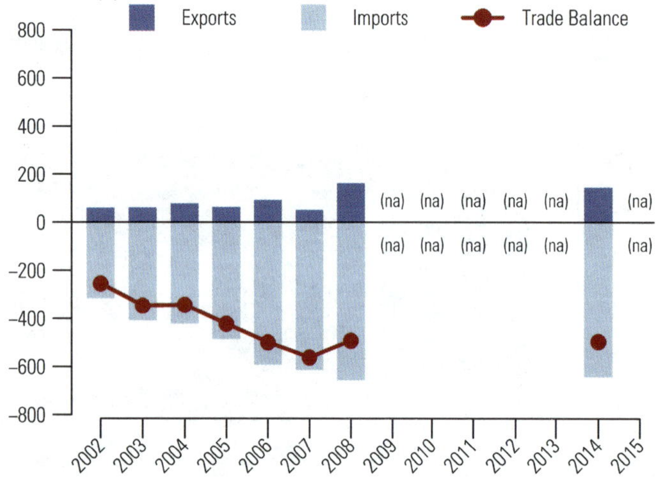

Graph 2: Total services trade, by value

(Mln US$ by year)

Exports Profile:

"Mineral fuels, lubricants" (SITC section 3), "Food, animals + beverages, tobacco" (SITC section 0+1) and "Miscellaneous manufactured articles" (SITC section 8) were the largest commodity groups for exports in 2014, representing respectively 20.8, 20.2 and 19.7 percent of exported goods (see table 2). The largest export commodity was "Petroleum oils, other than crude" (HS code 2710) (see table 1). The top three destinations for merchandise exports were the United States, Trinidad and Tobago and the United Kingdom, accounting for respectively 44.4, 14.6 and 11.5 percent of total exports. "Travel" (EBOPS code 236) accounted for the largest share of exports of services in 2013 at 354.0 mln US$, followed by "Other business services" (EBOPS code 268) at 26.1 mln US$ (see graph 3).

Graph 3: Exports of services by EBOPS category

(% share in 2013)

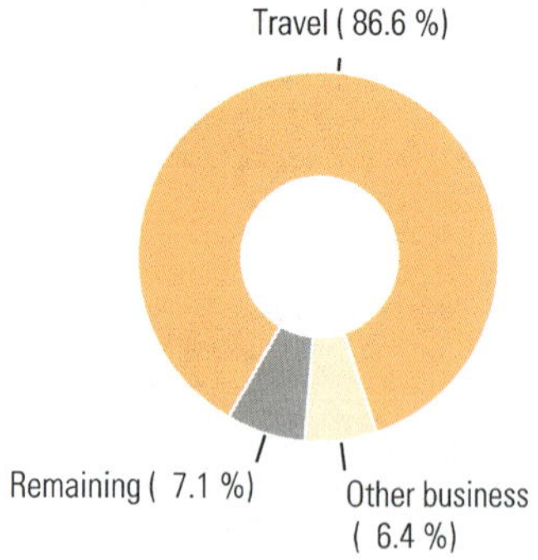

Table 1: Top 10 export commodities 2012 to 2014

HS code	4-digit heading of Harmonized System 2012	Value (million US$) 2012	2013	2014	Unit value 2012	2013	2014	Unit	SITC code
	All Commodities	...	...	146.3					
2710	Petroleum oils, other than crude	...	...	30.2			1.2	US$/kg	334
2203	Beer made from malt	...	...	14.2			*0.9*	US$/litre	112
7113	Articles of jewellery and parts thereof, of precious metal	...	...	12.5			5.3	thsd US$/kg	897
8529	Parts suitable for use with the apparatus of headings 85.25 to 85.28	...	...	11.5			52.3	US$/kg	764
2208	Alcohol of a strength by volume of less than 80 % vol	...	...	7.2			*5.1*	US$/litre	112
9999	Commodities not specified according to kind	...	...	6.0					931
2517	Pebbles, gravel, broken or crushed stone	...	...	5.8			0.0	US$/kg	273
4819	Cartons, boxes, cases, bags and other packing containers, of paper	...	...	4.0			1.6	US$/kg	642
2202	Waters with added sugar	...	...	3.4			*0.5*	US$/litre	111
7117	Imitation jewellery	...	...	2.9			118.4	US$/kg	897

Services Imports and Exports: EBOPS 2002 categories

Table 2: Merchandise exports by SITC

(Value in million US$, growth and shares in percentage)

SITC	2014	Avg. Growth rates 2010-2014	Avg. Growth rates 2013-2014	2014 share
Total	146.3	...	...	100.0
0+1	29.6	...	...	20.2
2+4	7.5	...	...	5.1
3	30.4	...	...	20.8
5	7.3	...	...	5.0
6	11.7	...	...	8.0
7	24.9	...	...	17.0
8	28.9	...	...	19.7
9	6.0	...	...	4.1

Table 3: Merchandise imports by SITC

(Value in million US$, growth and shares in percentage)

SITC	2014	Avg. Growth rates 2010-2014	Avg. Growth rates 2013-2014	2014 share
Total	642.1	...	...	100.0
0+1	148.9	...	...	23.2
2+4	11.8	...	...	1.8
3	158.1	...	...	24.6
5	43.7	...	...	6.8
6	76.8	...	...	12.0
7	121.3	...	...	18.9
8	61.7	...	...	9.6
9	19.8	...	...	3.1

SITC Legend

SITC Code	Description
Total	All commodities
0+1	Food, animals + beverages, tobacco
2+4	Crude materials + anim. & veg. oils
3	Mineral fuels, lubricants
5	Chemicals
6	Goods classified chiefly by material
7	Machinery and transport equipment
8	Miscellaneous manufactured articles
9	Not classified elsewhere in the SITC

Graph 4: Merchandise trade balance

(Mln US$ by MDG Regions in 2014)

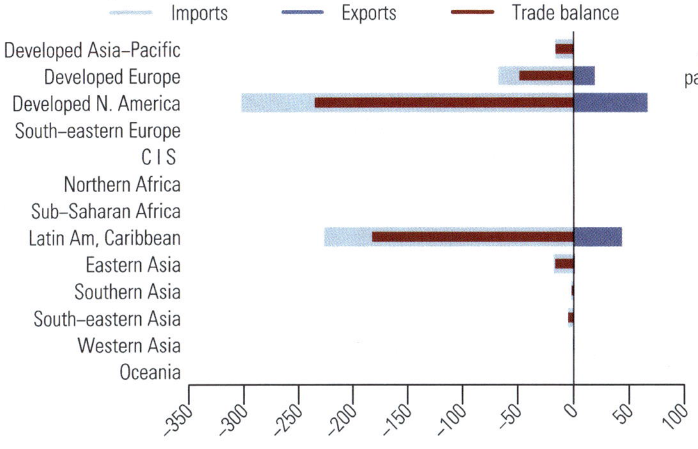

Graph 5: Partner concentration of merchandise trade

(Cumulative share by ranked partners in 2014)

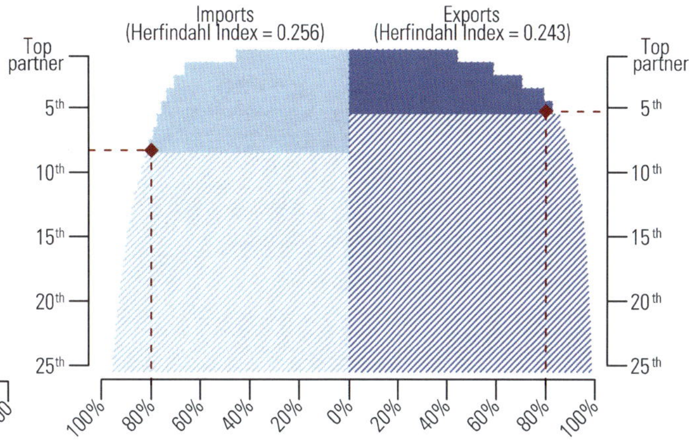

Graph 6: Imports of services by EBOPS category

(% share in 2013)

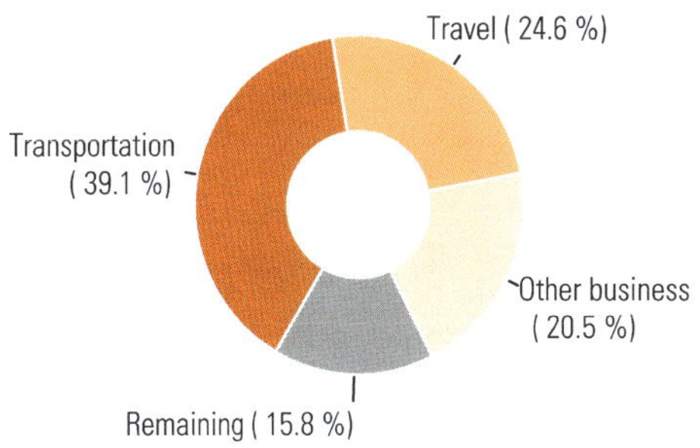

Imports Profile:

"Mineral fuels, lubricants" (SITC section 3), "Food, animals + beverages, tobacco" (SITC section 0+1) and "Machinery and transport equipment" (SITC section 7) were the largest commodity groups for imports in 2014, representing respectively 24.6, 23.2 and 18.9 percent of imported goods (see table 3). The largest import commodity was "Petroleum oils, other than crude" (HS code 2710) (see table 4). The top three partners for merchandise imports were the United States, Trinidad and Tobago and the United Kingdom, accounting for respectively 45.5, 20.8 and 4.5 percent of total imports. "Transportation" (EBOPS code 205) accounted for the largest share of imports of services in 2013 at 73.3 mln US$, followed by "Travel" (EBOPS code 236) at 46.1 mln US$ and "Other business services" (EBOPS code 268) at 38.5 mln US$ (see graph 6).

Table 4: Top 10 import commodities 2012 to 2014

HS code	4-digit heading of Harmonized System 2012	Value (million US$) 2012	2013	2014	Unit value 2012	2013	2014	Unit	SITC code
	All Commodities	...	...	642.1					
2710	Petroleum oils, other than crude	...	...	145.3			3.9	US$/kg	334
9999	Commodities not specified according to kind	...	...	19.8					931
8703	Motor cars and other motor vehicles principally designed for the transport	...	...	15.3			*16.1*	thsd US$/unit	781
0207	Meat and edible offal, of the poultry of heading 01.05	...	...	14.3			1.5	US$/kg	012
2711	Petroleum gases and other gaseous hydrocarbons	...	...	12.6					343
8517	Electrical apparatus for line telephony or line telegraphy	...	...	12.0					764
1101	Wheat or meslin flour	...	...	10.3			0.9	US$/kg	046
2523	Portland cement, aluminous cement, slag cement	...	...	8.3			0.2	US$/kg	661
3923	Articles for the conveyance or packing of goods, of plastics	...	...	8.1			3.3	US$/kg	893
0402	Milk and cream, concentrated or containing added sugar	...	...	7.0			2.4	US$/kg	022

Saint Vincent and the Grenadines

Goods Imports: CIF, by origin | **Goods Exports: FOB, by last known destination** | **Trade System: Special**

Overview:

In 2012, the value of merchandise exports of Saint Vincent and the Grenadines increased substantially by 12.0 percent to reach 43.0 mln US$, while its merchandise imports increased moderately by 5.2 percent to reach 403.2 mln US$ (see graph 1, table 2 and table 3). The merchandise trade balance recorded a large deficit of 360.2 mln US$ (see graph 1). The largest merchandise trade balance was with MDG Latin America and the Caribbean at -148.3 mln US$ (see graph 4). Merchandise exports in Saint Vincent and the Grenadines were diversified amongst partners; imports were moderately concentrated. The top 6 partners accounted for 80 percent or more of exports and 7 partners accounted for 80 percent or more of imports (see graph 5). In 2013, exports of services of Saint Vincent and the Grenadines increased slightly by 0.1 percent, reaching 140.7 mln US$, while its imports of services increased by 4.9 percent and reached 91.4 mln US$ (see graph 2). There was a moderate trade in services surplus of 49.3 mln US$.

Graph 1: Total merchandise trade, by value

(Mln US$ by year)

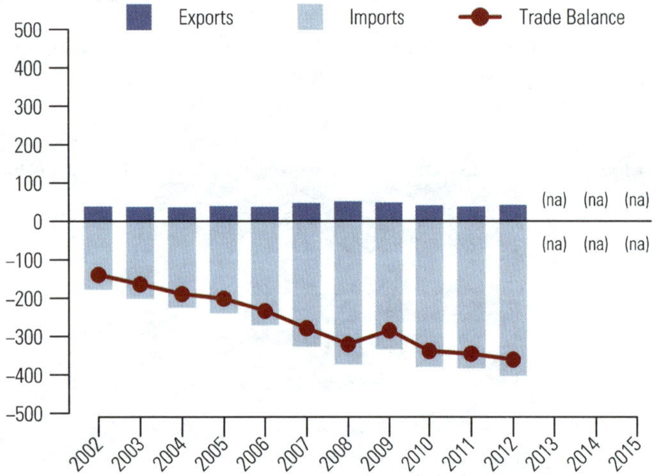

Graph 2: Total services trade, by value

(Mln US$ by year)

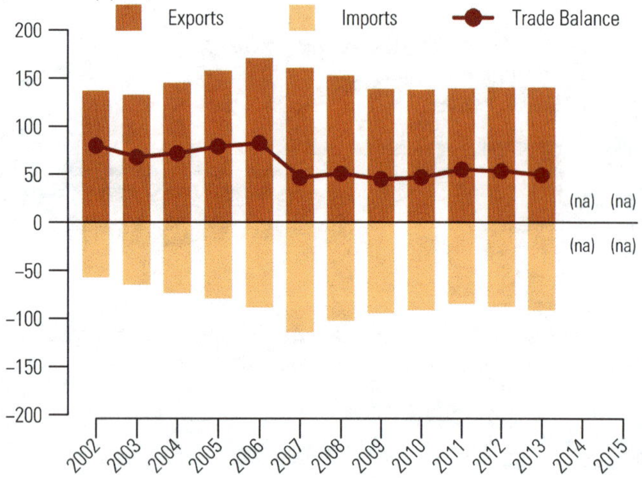

Exports Profile:

"Food, animals + beverages, tobacco" (SITC section 0+1), "Goods classified chiefly by material" (SITC section 6) and "Machinery and transport equipment" (SITC section 7) were the largest commodity groups for exports in 2012, representing respectively 74.7, 11.6 and 5.8 percent of exported goods (see table 2). From 2010 to 2012, the largest export commodity was "Wheat or meslin flour" (HS code 1101) (see table 1). The top three destinations for merchandise exports were Saint Lucia, Trinidad and Tobago and Barbados, accounting for respectively 22.9, 15.6 and 12.7 percent of total exports. "Travel" (EBOPS code 236) accounted for the largest share of exports of services in 2013 at 92.3 mln US$, followed by "Other business services" (EBOPS code 268) at 25.4 mln US$ and "Communications services" (EBOPS code 245) at 9.9 mln US$ (see graph 3).

Graph 3: Exports of services by EBOPS category

(% share in 2013)

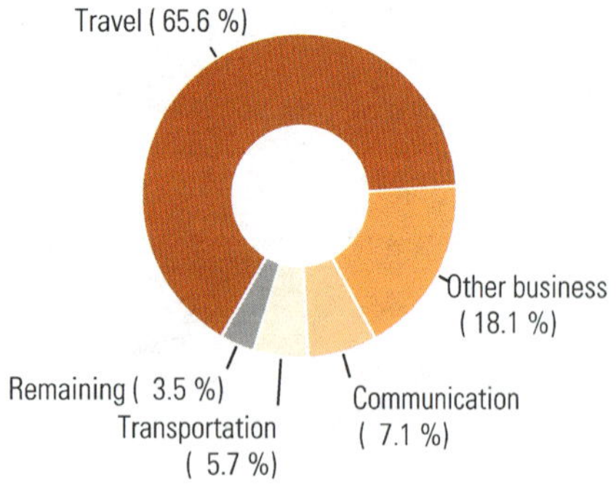

Table 1: Top 10 export commodities 2010 to 2012

HS code	4-digit heading of Harmonized System 2007	Value (million US$) 2010	2011	2012	Unit value 2010	2011	2012	Unit	SITC code
	All Commodities	41.5	38.4	43.0					
1101	Wheat or meslin flour	8.6	10.3	11.6	0.7	0.8	0.8	US$/kg	046
0714	Manioc, arrowroot, sweet potatoes and similar roots	3.9	4.3	5.0	0.6	0.6	0.6	US$/kg	054
1006	Rice	3.8	4.1	4.4	1.1	0.9	1.1	US$/kg	042
0803	Bananas, including plantains, fresh or dried	5.9	1.2	1.5	0.5	0.4	0.5	US$/kg	057
2309	Preparations of a kind used in animal feeding	1.8	2.8	3.6	0.4	0.4	0.4	US$/kg	081
2202	Waters with added sugar	2.2	1.7	2.0	*1.3*	*1.5*	*1.1*	US$/litre	111
4819	Cartons, boxes, cases, bags and other packing containers, of paper	1.8	2.0	1.7	1.7	1.8	1.8	US$/kg	642
7210	Flat-rolled products of iron or non-alloy steel	1.8	1.7	1.6	2.1	2.1	2.2	US$/kg	674
2203	Beer made from malt	0.0	1.1	2.3	*1.0*	*1.0*	*0.8*	US$/litre	112
7610	Aluminium structures (excluding prefabricated buildings of heading 94.06)	0.8	0.7	0.6	5.7	6.7	5.5	US$/kg	691

Table 2: Merchandise exports by SITC

(Value in million US$, growth and shares in percentage)

SITC	2012	Avg. Growth rates 2008-2012	Avg. Growth rates 2011-2012	2012 share
Total	43.0	-4.7	12.0	100.0
0+1	32.2	0.0	17.6	74.7
2+4	1.1	22.9	-16.2	2.5
3	0.5	-10.5	699.7	1.1
5	0.2	4.3	-15.5	0.5
6	5.0	1.8	-1.5	11.6
7	2.5	-32.4	-13.8	5.8
8	1.6	-3.1	7.0	3.7

Table 3: Merchandise imports by SITC

(Value in million US$, growth and shares in percentage)

SITC	2012	Avg. Growth rates 2008-2012	Avg. Growth rates 2011-2012	2012 share
Total	403.2	2.0	5.2	100.0
0+1	96.6	3.4	7.1	24.0
2+4	9.7	-4.4	6.6	2.4
3	114.9	20.1	8.7	28.5
5	27.3	-1.3	6.1	6.8
6	59.3	-3.1	4.2	14.7
7	61.2	-8.2	-0.4	15.2
8	34.4	-3.6	-0.2	8.5

SITC Legend

SITC Code	Description
Total	All commodities
0+1	Food, animals + beverages, tobacco
2+4	Crude materials + anim. & veg. oils
3	Mineral fuels, lubricants
5	Chemicals
6	Goods classified chiefly by material
7	Machinery and transport equipment
8	Miscellaneous manufactured articles
9	Not classified elsewhere in the SITC

Graph 4: Merchandise trade balance

(Mln US$ by MDG Regions in 2012)

Graph 5: Partner concentration of merchandise trade

(Cumulative share by ranked partners in 2012)

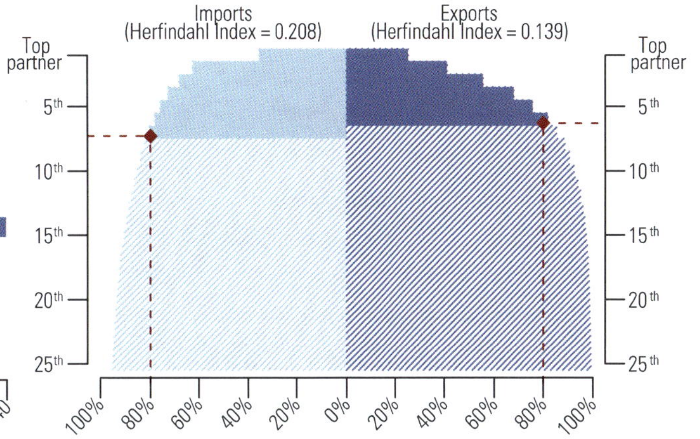

Graph 6: Imports of services by EBOPS category

(% share in 2013)

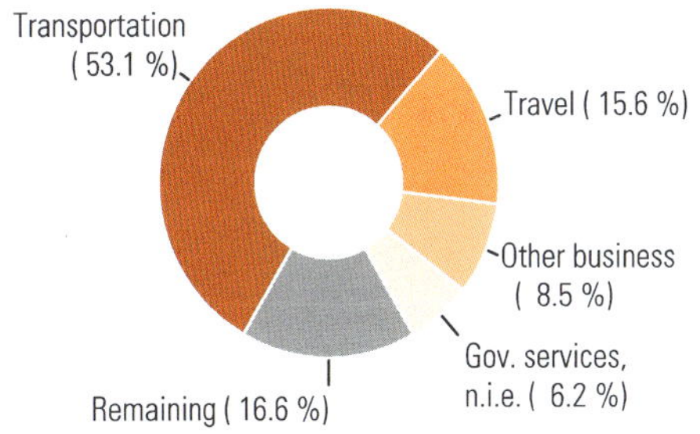

Imports Profile:

"Mineral fuels, lubricants" (SITC section 3), "Food, animals + beverages, tobacco" (SITC section 0+1) and "Machinery and transport equipment" (SITC section 7) were the largest commodity groups for imports in 2012, representing respectively 28.5, 24.0 and 15.2 percent of imported goods (see table 3). From 2010 to 2012, the largest import commodity was "Petroleum oils, other than crude" (HS code 2710) (see table 4). The top three partners for merchandise imports were the United States, Trinidad and Tobago and the United Kingdom, accounting for respectively 34.2, 28.3 and 5.2 percent of total imports. "Transportation" (EBOPS code 205) accounted for the largest share of imports of services in 2013 at 48.5 mln US$, followed by "Travel" (EBOPS code 236) at 14.2 mln US$ and "Other business services" (EBOPS code 268) at 7.8 mln US$ (see graph 6).

Table 4: Top 10 import commodities 2010 to 2012

HS code	4-digit heading of Harmonized System 2007	Value (million US$) 2010	Value (million US$) 2011	Value (million US$) 2012	Unit value 2010	Unit value 2011	Unit value 2012	Unit	SITC code
	All Commodities	379.5	383.5	403.2					
2710	Petroleum oils, other than crude	78.1	98.0	109.0	0.6	0.8	0.8	US$/kg	334
0207	Meat and edible offal, of the poultry of heading 01.05	10.0	10.9	11.6	1.5	1.5	1.8	US$/kg	012
1001	Wheat and meslin	8.4	10.3	13.0	0.4	0.5	0.5	US$/kg	041
2523	Portland cement, aluminous cement, slag cement	7.2	7.7	7.1	0.1	0.1	0.4	US$/kg	661
8703	Motor cars and other motor vehicles principally designed for the transport	7.5	5.9	5.0	*14.0*		*17.4*	thsd US$/unit	781
2711	Petroleum gases and other gaseous hydrocarbons	4.9	7.6	5.8	1.2	2.0	0.8	US$/kg	343
2106	Food preparations not elsewhere specified or included	5.0	6.6	6.4	1.3	1.5	1.8	US$/kg	098
9403	Other furniture and parts thereof	8.0	4.6	4.4					821
1006	Rice	4.3	4.7	6.0	0.8	0.7	0.8	US$/kg	042
2202	Waters with added sugar	3.8	4.8	4.8	*1.9*	*0.9*	*1.4*	US$/litre	111

Source: UN Comtrade

Samoa

Goods Imports: CIF, by origin | **Goods Exports: FOB, by last known destination** | **Trade System: General**

Overview:

In 2015, the value of merchandise exports of Samoa increased substantially by 15.7 percent to reach 58.9 mln US$, while its merchandise imports decreased slightly by 4.5 percent to reach 370.6 mln US$ (see graph 1, table 2 and table 3). The merchandise trade balance recorded a large deficit of 311.7 mln US$ (see graph 1). The largest merchandise trade balance was with MDG Developed Asia-Pacific at -115.9 mln US$ (see graph 4). Merchandise exports in Samoa were moderately concentrated amongst partners; imports were diversified. The top 4 partners accounted for 80 percent or more of exports and 6 partners accounted for 80 percent or more of imports (see graph 5). In 2014, the value of exports of services of Samoa increased slightly by 2.4 percent, reaching 196.3 mln US$, while its imports of services decreased substantially by 14.5 percent and reached 74.8 mln US$ (see graph 2). There was a large trade in services surplus of 121.6 mln US$.

Graph 1: Total merchandise trade, by value

(Mln US$ by year)

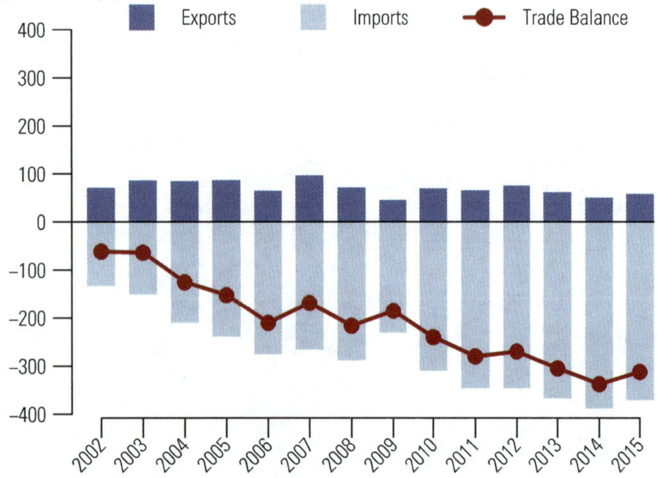

Graph 2: Total services trade, by value

(Mln US$ by year)

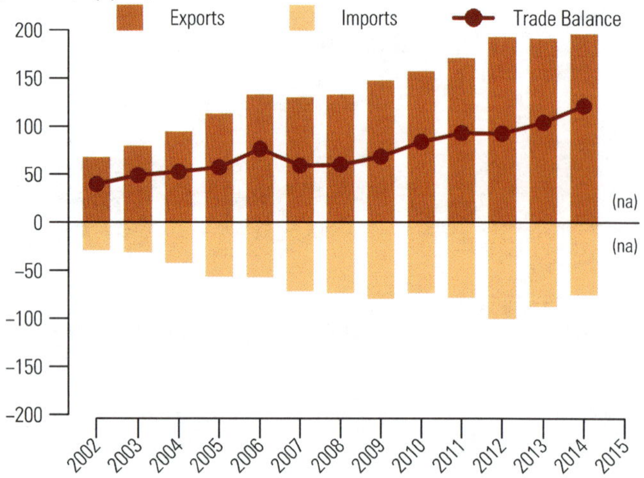

Exports Profile:

"Food, animals + beverages, tobacco" (SITC section 0+1), "Machinery and transport equipment" (SITC section 7) and "Mineral fuels, lubricants" (SITC section 3) were the largest commodity groups for exports in 2015, representing respectively 39.6, 28.6 and 25.3 percent of exported goods (see table 2). From 2013 to 2015, the largest export commodity was "Insulated (including enamelled or anodised) wire, cable" (HS code 8544) (see table 1). The top three destinations for merchandise exports were Australia, New Zealand and American Samoa, accounting for respectively 48.0, 14.0 and 11.3 percent of total exports. "Travel" (EBOPS code 236) accounted for the largest share of exports of services in 2014 at 144.7 mln US$, followed by "Other business services" (EBOPS code 268) at 12.5 mln US$ (see graph 3).

Graph 3: Exports of services by EBOPS category

(% share in 2014)

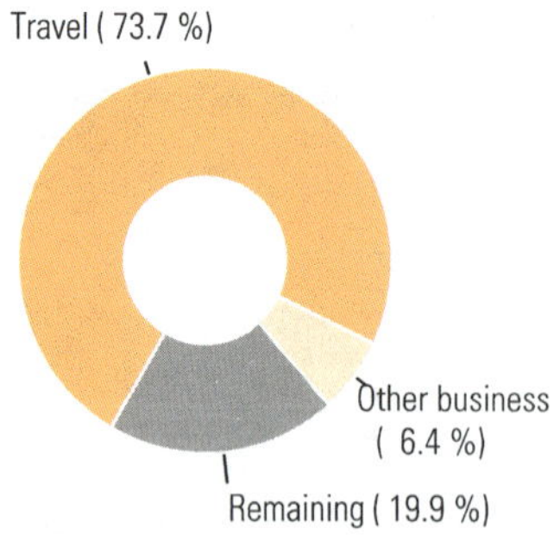

Table 1: Top 10 export commodities 2013 to 2015

HS code	4-digit heading of Harmonized System 2012	Value (million US$) 2013	2014	2015	Unit value 2013	2014	2015	Unit	SITC code
	All Commodities	62.1	50.9	58.9					
8544	Insulated (including enamelled or anodised) wire, cable	27.8	19.4	16.2					773
2710	Petroleum oils, other than crude	15.0	0.0	14.9	*1.1*		*1.0*	US$/kg	334
9999	Commodities not specified according to kind	1.0	17.1	0.0					931
0303	Fish, frozen, excluding fish fillets and other fish meat of heading 03.04	4.3	1.8	11.6	1.6	1.8	2.4	US$/kg	034
2203	Beer made from malt	4.9	2.5	2.6	2.5	1.7	0.6	US$/litre	112
2009	Fruit juices (including grape must) and vegetable juices	1.4	1.5	3.0			*2.7*	US$/kg	059
0714	Manioc, arrowroot, sweet potatoes and similar roots	0.6	1.1	2.3	0.7	1.0	1.1	US$/kg	054
1513	Coconut (copra), palm kernel or babassu oil	0.6	1.5	1.2					422
0302	Fish, fresh or chilled, excluding fish fillets	0.2	0.6	1.4		2.1	2.8	US$/kg	034
0801	Coconuts, Brazil nuts and cashew nuts, fresh or dried	0.8	0.8	0.3					057

Services Imports and Exports: EBOPS 2002 categories

Table 2: Merchandise exports by SITC

(Value in million US$, growth and shares in percentage)

SITC	2015	Avg. Growth rates 2011-2015	Avg. Growth rates 2014-2015	2015 share
Total	58.9	-2.9	15.7	100.0
0+1	23.3	14.6	137.7	39.6
2+4	2.7	-10.4	24.3	4.6
3	14.9	5.8	>	25.3
5	0.1	-8.7	71.7	0.2
6	0.3	-6.2	98.8	0.6
7	16.8	-16.1	-19.1	28.6
8	0.7	-9.8	-10.2	1.1
9	0.0	-56.9	-99.8	0.1

Table 3: Merchandise imports by SITC

(Value in million US$, growth and shares in percentage)

SITC	2015	Avg. Growth rates 2011-2015	Avg. Growth rates 2014-2015	2015 share
Total	370.6	1.7	-4.5	100.0
0+1	97.4	2.6	5.7	26.3
2+4	10.8	-3.4	-16.6	2.9
3	55.0	-7.0	-41.4	14.8
5	29.9	12.4	13.3	8.1
6	68.9	7.2	15.3	18.6
7	68.3	-2.2	4.8	18.4
8	40.2	12.8	10.2	10.9
9	0.1	-57.2	-95.1	0.0

SITC Legend

SITC Code	Description
Total	All commodities
0+1	Food, animals + beverages, tobacco
2+4	Crude materials + anim. & veg. oils
3	Mineral fuels, lubricants
5	Chemicals
6	Goods classified chiefly by material
7	Machinery and transport equipment
8	Miscellaneous manufactured articles
9	Not classified elsewhere in the SITC

Graph 4: Merchandise trade balance

(Mln US$ by MDG Regions in 2015)

Graph 5: Partner concentration of merchandise trade

(Cumulative share by ranked partners in 2015)

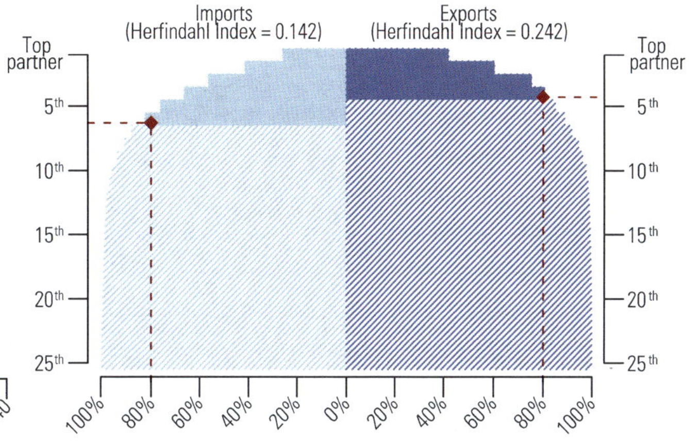

Graph 6: Imports of services by EBOPS category

(% share in 2014)

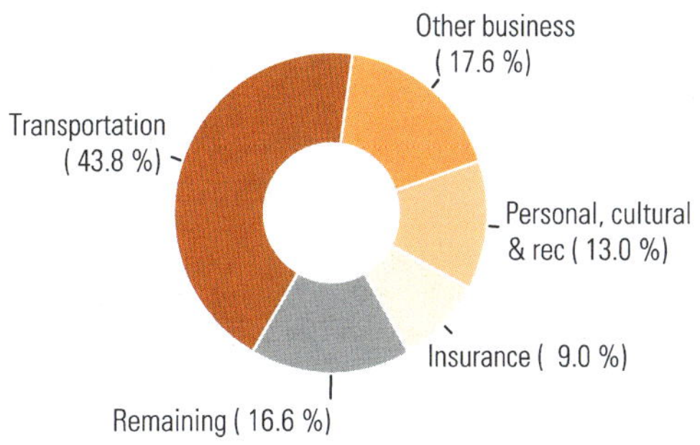

Imports Profile:

"Food, animals + beverages, tobacco" (SITC section 0+1), "Goods classified chiefly by material" (SITC section 6) and "Machinery and transport equipment" (SITC section 7) were the largest commodity groups for imports in 2015, representing respectively 26.3, 18.6 and 18.4 percent of imported goods (see table 3). From 2013 to 2015, the largest import commodity was "Petroleum oils, other than crude" (HS code 2710) (see table 4). The top three partners for merchandise imports were New Zealand, Singapore and China, accounting for respectively 26.9, 21.1 and 11.9 percent of total imports. "Transportation" (EBOPS code 205) accounted for the largest share of imports of services in 2014 at 32.8 mln US$, followed by "Other business services" (EBOPS code 268) at 13.2 mln US$ and "Personal, cultural, and recreational services" (EBOPS code 287) at 9.7 mln US$ (see graph 6).

Table 4: Top 10 import commodities 2013 to 2015

HS code	4-digit heading of Harmonized System 2012	Value (million US$) 2013	2014	2015	Unit value 2013	2014	2015	Unit	SITC code
	All Commodities	366.6	388.0	370.6					
2710	Petroleum oils, other than crude	78.4	90.6	52.2	*1.2*	*1.1*	*1.1*	US$/kg	334
0207	Meat and edible offal, of the poultry of heading 01.05	19.8	19.9	17.0	1.5	1.2	1.4	US$/kg	012
8703	Motor cars and other motor vehicles principally designed for the transport	6.3	8.2	8.2	52.8	2.7	8.9	thsd US$/unit	781
3926	Other articles of plastics	5.2	6.4	8.1	*11.6*	*12.6*	*14.5*	US$/kg	893
2523	Portland cement, aluminous cement, slag cement	5.7	5.9	6.9	0.7	0.2	0.2	US$/kg	661
1604	Prepared or preserved fish; caviar	6.3	5.6	6.2	*2.8*	*1.8*	2.0	US$/kg	037
8704	Motor vehicles for the transport of goods	5.7	5.6	6.1	2.4	19.7	23.1	thsd US$/unit	782
4407	Wood sawn or chipped lengthwise, sliced or peeled	6.4	6.4	4.3	97.8		134.4	US$/m³	248
1006	Rice	6.4	4.4	6.2	*0.5*	*0.5*	*0.6*	US$/kg	042
1701	Cane or beet sugar and chemically pure sucrose, in solid form	5.8	5.4	4.4	0.1	0.2	0.4	US$/kg	061

Source: UN Comtrade

Sao Tome and Principe

Goods Imports: CIF, by origin | **Goods Exports: FOB, by last known destination** | **Trade System: Special**

Overview:

In 2014, the value of merchandise exports of Sao Tome and Principe increased substantially by 51.3 percent to reach 10.5 mln US$, while its merchandise imports increased substantially by 11.6 percent to reach 169.7 mln US$ (see graph 1, table 2 and table 3). The merchandise trade balance recorded a large deficit of 159.2 mln US$ (see graph 1). The largest merchandise trade balance was with MDG Developed Europe at -103.7 mln US$ (see graph 4). Merchandise exports in Sao Tome and Principe were moderately concentrated amongst partners; imports were highly concentrated. The top 5 partners accounted for 80 percent or more of exports and 2 partners accounted for 80 percent or more of imports (see graph 5). In 2014, the value of exports of services of Sao Tome and Principe increased substantially by 93.3 percent, reaching 69.9 mln US$, while its imports of services increased substantially by 75.7 percent and reached 84.4 mln US$ (see graph 2). There was a relatively small trade in services deficit of 14.4 mln US$.

Graph 1: Total merchandise trade, by value

(Mln US$ by year)

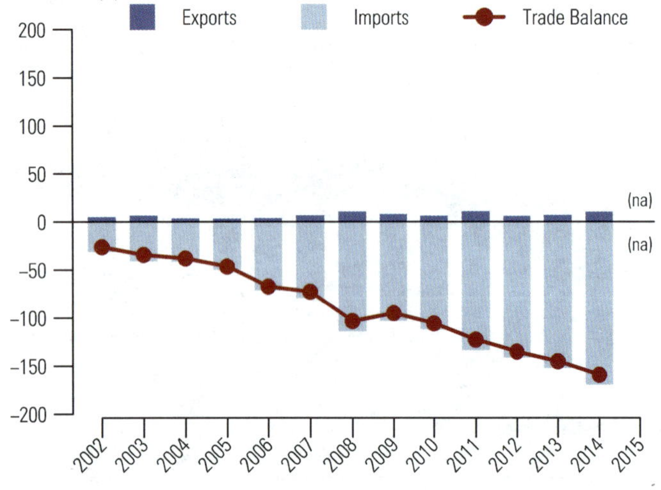

Graph 2: Total services trade, by value

(Mln US$ by year)

Exports Profile:

"Food, animals + beverages, tobacco" (SITC section 0+1), "Machinery and transport equipment" (SITC section 7) and "Miscellaneous manufactured articles" (SITC section 8) were the largest commodity groups for exports in 2014, representing respectively 96.9, 1.4 and 0.9 percent of exported goods (see table 2). From 2012 to 2014, the largest export commodity was "Cocoa beans, whole or broken, raw or roasted" (HS code 1801) (see table 1). The top three destinations for merchandise exports were the Netherlands, Belgium and Spain, accounting for respectively 29.5, 17.9 and 15.4 percent of total exports. "Travel" (EBOPS code 236) accounted for the largest share of exports of services in 2014 at 56.0 mln US$, followed by "Other business services" (EBOPS code 268) at 12.0 mln US$ (see graph 3).

Graph 3: Exports of services by EBOPS category

(% share in 2014)

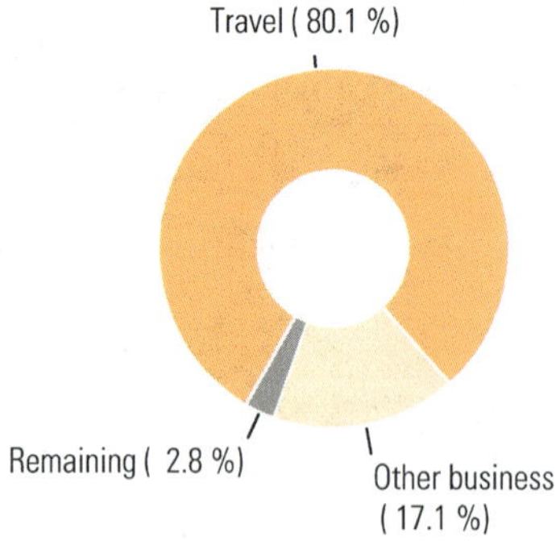

Table 1: Top 10 export commodities 2012 to 2014

HS code	4-digit heading of Harmonized System 2007	Value (million US$) 2012	2013	2014	Unit value 2012	2013	2014	Unit	SITC code
	All Commodities	6.0	6.9	10.5					
1801	Cocoa beans, whole or broken, raw or roasted	4.8	5.4	9.3	2.2	2.1	2.9	US$/kg	072
1806	Chocolate and other food preparations containing cocoa	0.2	0.2	0.3	33.6	31.1	40.9	US$/kg	073
0801	Coconuts, Brazil nuts and cashew nuts, fresh or dried	0.1	0.1	0.2					057
8422	Dish washing machines; machinery for cleaning or drying bottles	...	0.3	0.0					745
8703	Motor cars and other motor vehicles principally designed for the transport	0.1	0.0	0.1	*24.0*	*48.2*	*14.7*	thsd US$/unit	781
0904	Pepper of the genus Piper	0.1	0.0	0.1	8.3	13.2	14.5	US$/kg	075
7326	Other articles of iron or steel	0.2	0.0	0.0	0.2	30.7		US$/kg	699
1006	Rice	...	...	0.2			0.6	US$/kg	042
6309	Worn clothing and other worn articles	0.0	0.1	0.0	5.6		7.2	US$/kg	269
0901	Coffee, whether or not roasted or decaffeinated	0.0	0.0	0.0	4.4	9.5	3.8	US$/kg	071

Services Imports and Exports: EBOPS 2002 categories

Table 2: Merchandise exports by SITC

(Value in million US$, growth and shares in percentage)

SITC	2014	Avg. Growth rates 2010-2014	2013-2014	2014 share
Total	10.5	13.3	51.3	100.0
0+1	10.2	15.1	73.7	96.9
2+4	0.0	-45.1	-89.3	0.2
5	0.0	...	-96.3	0.0
6	0.1	14.1	-64.9	0.5
7	0.1	-8.4	-74.9	1.4
8	0.1	13.0	10.3	0.9
9	0.0	-48.1	...	0.0

Table 3: Merchandise imports by SITC

(Value in million US$, growth and shares in percentage)

SITC	2014	Avg. Growth rates 2010-2014	2013-2014	2014 share
Total	169.7	10.9	11.6	100.0
0+1	51.2	13.5	20.1	30.2
2+4	5.7	8.4	-8.1	3.4
3	38.7	21.0	-2.9	22.8
5	8.7	10.8	3.9	5.1
6	22.7	14.2	25.8	13.4
7	31.1	0.5	12.2	18.3
8	11.5	5.5	25.3	6.8
9	0.0	-36.1	130.8	0.0

SITC Legend

SITC Code	Description
Total	All commodities
0+1	Food, animals + beverages, tobacco
2+4	Crude materials + anim. & veg. oils
3	Mineral fuels, lubricants
5	Chemicals
6	Goods classified chiefly by material
7	Machinery and transport equipment
8	Miscellaneous manufactured articles
9	Not classified elsewhere in the SITC

Graph 4: Merchandise trade balance

(Mln US$ by MDG Regions in 2014)

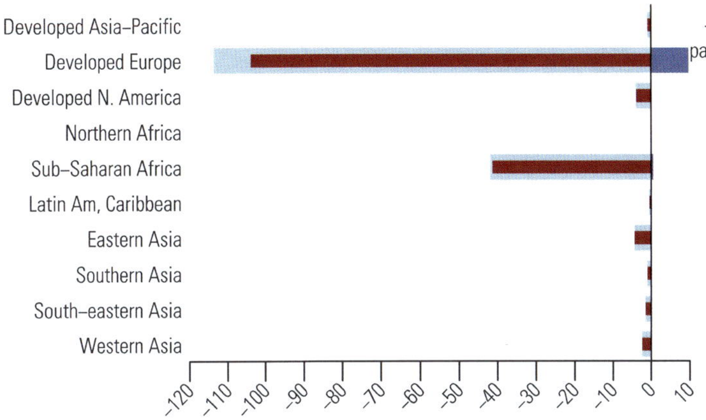

Graph 5: Partner concentration of merchandise trade

(Cumulative share by ranked partners in 2014)

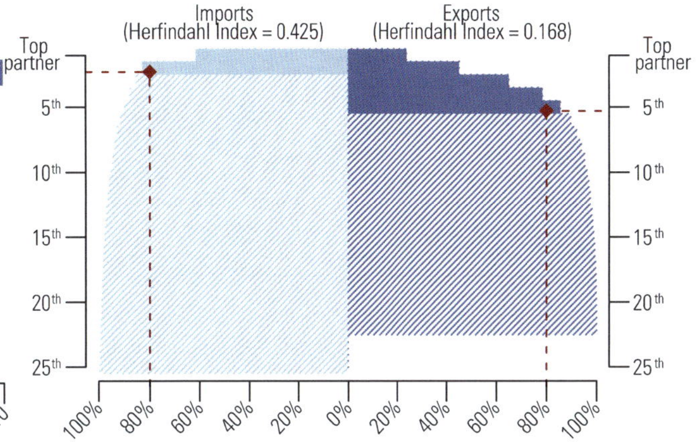

Graph 6: Imports of services by EBOPS category

(% share in 2014)

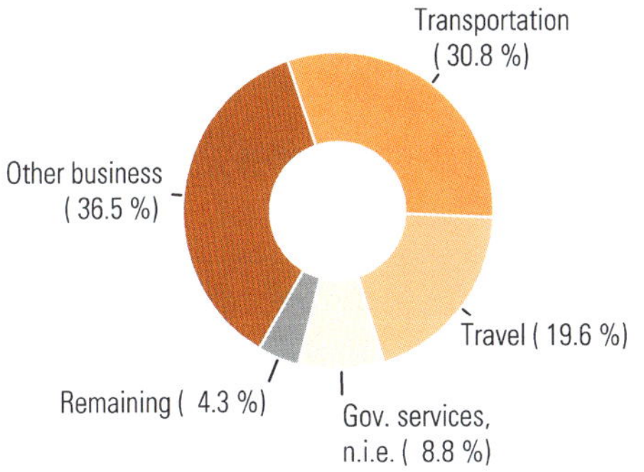

Imports Profile:

"Food, animals + beverages, tobacco" (SITC section 0+1), "Mineral fuels, lubricants" (SITC section 3) and "Machinery and transport equipment" (SITC section 7) were the largest commodity groups for imports in 2014, representing respectively 30.2, 22.8 and 18.3 percent of imported goods (see table 3). From 2012 to 2014, the largest import commodity was "Petroleum oils, other than crude" (HS code 2710) (see table 4). The top three partners for merchandise imports were Portugal, Angola and Belgium, accounting for respectively 57.8, 22.9 and 2.3 percent of total imports. "Other business services" (EBOPS code 268) accounted for the largest share of imports of services in 2014 at 30.8 mln US$, followed by "Transportation" (EBOPS code 205) at 26.0 mln US$ and "Travel" (EBOPS code 236) at 16.5 mln US$ (see graph 6).

Table 4: Top 10 import commodities 2012 to 2014

HS code	4-digit heading of Harmonized System 2007	Value (million US$) 2012	2013	2014	Unit value 2012	2013	2014	Unit	SITC code
	All Commodities	141.3	152.1	169.7					
2710	Petroleum oils, other than crude	35.2	39.5	37.9	1.1	1.5	1.0	US$/kg	334
8703	Motor cars and other motor vehicles principally designed for the transport	6.5	4.7	7.0	*21.8*	*17.7*	*20.7*	thsd US$/unit	781
2204	Wine of fresh grapes, including fortified wines	5.2	5.4	6.1	*1.3*	*1.3*	*1.5*	US$/litre	112
1006	Rice	5.2	4.9	6.5	0.8	0.7	0.8	US$/kg	042
2523	Portland cement, aluminous cement, slag cement	3.3	3.8	5.7	0.2	0.1	0.2	US$/kg	661
1101	Wheat or meslin flour	4.2	4.3	4.0	0.6	0.6	0.6	US$/kg	046
1507	Soya-bean oil and its fractions	3.9	3.6	3.1	1.5	1.4	1.4	US$/kg	421
0207	Meat and edible offal, of the poultry of heading 01.05	2.3	2.7	4.6	1.9	2.0	2.1	US$/kg	012
2202	Waters with added sugar	2.4	3.1	3.4	*0.9*	*0.1*	*1.0*	US$/litre	111
8517	Electrical apparatus for line telephony or line telegraphy	1.0	3.3	3.6					764

Saudi Arabia

Goods Imports: CIF, by origin | **Goods Exports: FOB, by last known destination** | **Trade System: General**

Overview:

In 2015, the value of merchandise exports of Saudi Arabia decreased substantially by 41.1 percent to reach 201.5 bln US$, while its merchandise imports decreased slightly by 2.6 percent to reach 163.8 bln US$ (see graph 1, table 2 and table 3). The merchandise trade balance recorded a moderate surplus of 37.7 bln US$ (see graph 1). The largest merchandise trade balance was with MDG Eastern Asia at 68.3 bln US$ (see graph 4). Merchandise exports in Saudi Arabia were highly concentrated amongst partners; imports were diversified. The top 6 partners accounted for 80 percent or more of exports and 20 partners accounted for 80 percent or more of imports (see graph 5). In 2014, the value of exports of services of Saudi Arabia increased moderately by 5.7 percent, reaching 12.5 bln US$, while its imports of services increased substantially by 31.2 percent and reached 100.5 bln US$ (see graph 2). There was a large trade in services deficit of 88.0 bln US$. See footnote*.

Graph 1: Total merchandise trade, by value

(Bln US$ by year)

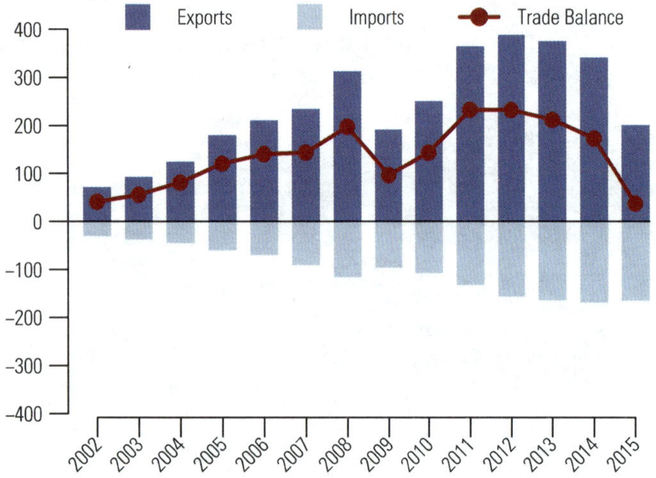

Graph 2: Total services trade, by value

(Bln US$ by year)

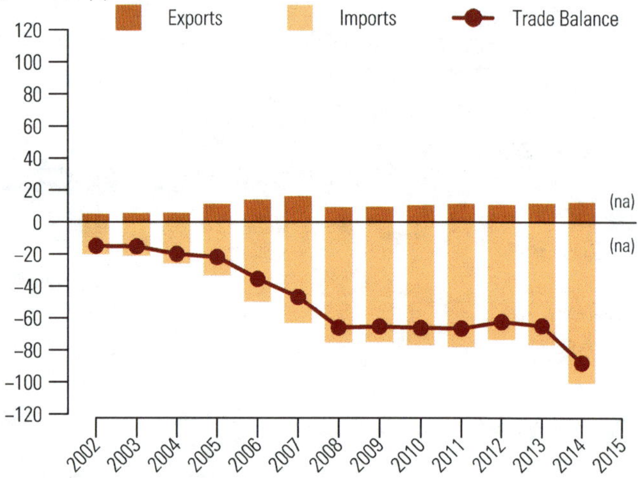

Exports Profile:

"Mineral fuels, lubricants" (SITC section 3), "Chemicals" (SITC section 5) and "Machinery and transport equipment" (SITC section 7) were the largest commodity groups for exports in 2015, representing respectively 75.9, 14.8 and 3.6 percent of exported goods (see table 2). From 2013 to 2015, the largest export commodity was "Petroleum oils and oils obtained from bituminous minerals, crude" (HS code 2709) (see table 1). The top three destinations for merchandise exports were Other Asia nes, North and Central America, Caribbean nes and Rest of Europe nes, accounting for respectively 54.8, 13.2 and 10.7 percent of total exports. "Travel" (EBOPS code 236) accounted for the largest share of exports of services in 2014 at 8.2 bln US$, followed by "Transportation" (EBOPS code 205) at 2.9 bln US$ (see graph 3).

Graph 3: Exports of services by EBOPS category

(% share in 2014)

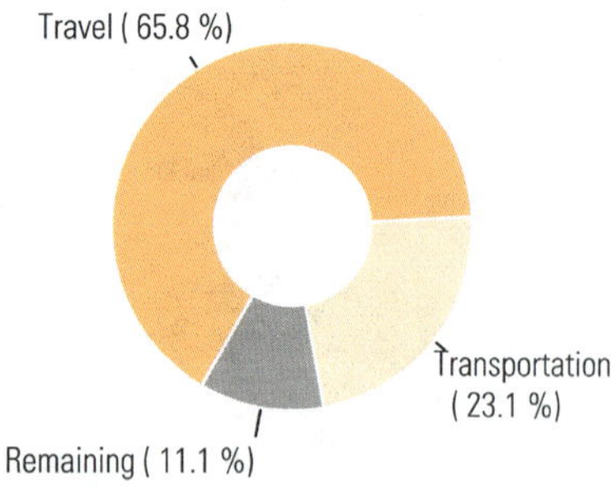

Table 1: Top 10 export commodities 2013 to 2015

HS code	4-digit heading of Harmonized System 2012	Value (million US$)			Unit value				SITC code
		2013	2014	2015	2013	2014	2015	Unit	
	All Commodities	375 873.3	341 947.2	201 491.8					
2709	Petroleum oils and oils obtained from bituminous minerals, crude	293 994.6	250 522.8	129 745.7	0.8	0.7	0.4	US$/kg	333
2710	Petroleum oils, other than crude	19 061.0	25 787.7	17 417.1	*0.8*	0.7	*0.4*	US$/kg	334
3901	Polymers of ethylene, in primary forms	9 301.0	10 336.1	8 286.4	1.3	1.3	1.1	US$/kg	571
2711	Petroleum gases and other gaseous hydrocarbons	7 849.0	6 868.6	4 090.0	0.9	0.8	0.4	US$/kg	343
3902	Polymers of propylene or of other olefins, in primary forms	5 714.9	6 465.8	5 133.3	1.4	1.4	1.1	US$/kg	575
2909	Ethers, ether-alcohols, ether-phenols, ether-alcohol-phenols	5 602.8	5 541.0	4 377.1	0.9	0.9	0.7	US$/kg	516
2905	Acyclic alcohols and their derivatives	3 405.3	3 410.7	2 377.8	0.5	0.5		US$/kg	512
2902	Cyclic hydrocarbons	2 148.8	2 393.1	1 750.4	1.4	1.5	0.9	US$/kg	511
8904	Tugs and pusher craft	1 105.5	1 748.6	2 029.3					793
2814	Ammonia, anhydrous or in aqueous solution	1 302.5	2 064.0	1 245.1	0.5	0.5	0.5	US$/kg	522

*Major export partners were defined as regions only and resulted in high partner concentration for exports in graph 5.

Services Imports and Exports: EBOPS 2002 categories

Table 2: Merchandise exports by SITC

(Value in million US$, growth and shares in percentage)

SITC	2015	Avg. Growth rates 2011-2015	Avg. Growth rates 2014-2015	2015 share
Total	201 491.8	-13.8	-41.1	100.0
0+1	3 477.7	2.1	0.3	1.7
2+4	1 331.1	15.6	-8.7	0.7
3	152 926.1	-16.7	-46.3	75.9
5	29 788.1	-0.7	-22.0	14.8
6	5 306.9	2.3	-3.5	2.6
7	7 215.3	7.1	4.0	3.6
8	1 096.9	-8.6	-17.7	0.5
9	349.7	-11.7	-3.8	0.2

Table 3: Merchandise imports by SITC

(Value in million US$, growth and shares in percentage)

SITC	2015	Avg. Growth rates 2011-2015	Avg. Growth rates 2014-2015	2015 share
Total	163 821.0	5.6	-2.6	100.0
0+1	21 206.4	3.8	-5.9	12.9
2+4	3 990.5	-4.3	-20.5	2.4
3	1 215.0	37.9	-52.5	0.7
5	16 316.4	5.6	-2.1	10.0
6	25 683.9	0.1	-14.3	15.7
7	74 984.1	8.2	4.3	45.8
8	15 325.6	8.5	2.3	9.4
9	5 099.0	7.8	9.8	3.1

SITC Legend

SITC Code	Description
Total	All commodities
0+1	Food, animals + beverages, tobacco
2+4	Crude materials + anim. & veg. oils
3	Mineral fuels, lubricants
5	Chemicals
6	Goods classified chiefly by material
7	Machinery and transport equipment
8	Miscellaneous manufactured articles
9	Not classified elsewhere in the SITC

Graph 4: Merchandise trade balance

(Bln US$ by MDG Regions in 2015)

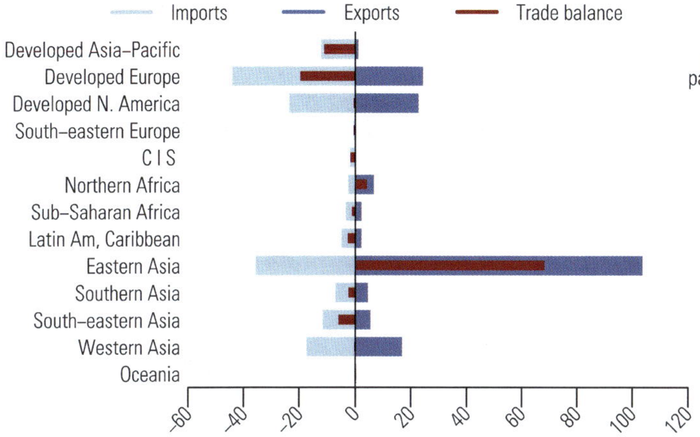

Graph 5: Partner concentration of merchandise trade

(Cumulative share by ranked partners in 2015)

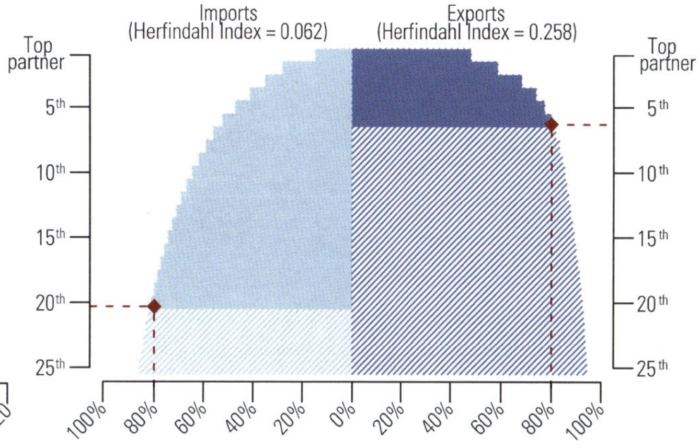

Graph 6: Imports of services by EBOPS category

(% share in 2014)

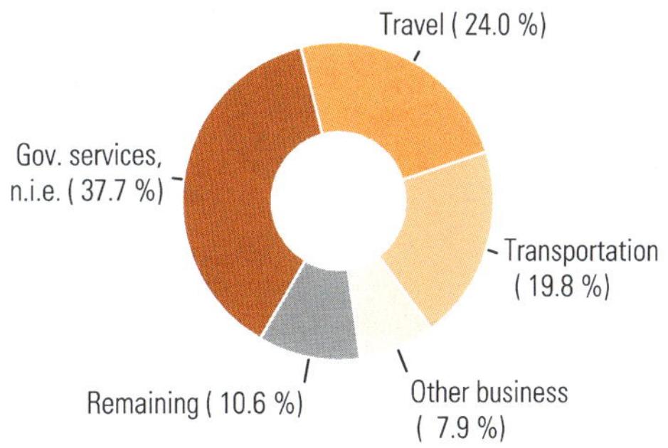

Imports Profile:

"Machinery and transport equipment" (SITC section 7), "Goods classified chiefly by material" (SITC section 6) and "Food, animals + beverages, tobacco" (SITC section 0+1) were the largest commodity groups for imports in 2015, representing respectively 45.8, 15.7 and 12.9 percent of imported goods (see table 3). From 2013 to 2015, the largest import commodity was "Motor cars and other motor vehicles principally designed for the transport" (HS code 8703) (see table 4). The top three partners for merchandise imports were China, the United States and Germany, accounting for respectively 13.7, 13.1 and 7.3 percent of total imports. "Government services, n.i.e." (EBOPS code 291) accounted for the largest share of imports of services in 2014 at 37.9 bln US$, followed by "Travel" (EBOPS code 236) at 24.1 bln US$ and "Transportation" (EBOPS code 205) at 19.9 bln US$ (see graph 6).

Table 4: Top 10 import commodities 2013 to 2015

HS code	4-digit heading of Harmonized System 2012	Value (million US$) 2013	Value (million US$) 2014	Value (million US$) 2015	Unit value 2013	Unit value 2014	Unit value 2015	Unit	SITC code
	All Commodities	163 712.8	168 239.6	163 821.0					
8703	Motor cars and other motor vehicles principally designed for the transport	16 089.8	16 050.8	17 643.3	*22.4*	*21.9*	*22.7*	thsd US$/unit	781
8517	Electrical apparatus for line telephony or line telegraphy	6 951.3	7 255.5	7 646.3					764
7108	Gold (including gold plated with platinum)	4 472.7	4 626.7	5 085.2	42.9	*41.1*	*26.3*	thsd US$/kg	971
3004	Medicaments (excluding goods of heading 30.02, 30.05 or 30.06)	3 760.2	3 550.2	3 868.2		*66.2*		US$/kg	542
8704	Motor vehicles for the transport of goods	3 653.6	3 276.7	3 484.2					782
1003	Barley	3 249.6	1 993.3	1 469.7	0.3	0.3	0.2	US$/kg	043
8471	Automatic data processing machines and units thereof	2 188.2	2 240.1	2 005.1					752
8803	Parts of goods of heading 88.01 or 88.02	1 633.2	1 697.9	2 872.7	426.0		*462.3*	US$/kg	792
8481	Taps, cocks, valves and similar appliances for pipes, boiler shells	2 060.9	2 129.1	1 835.6	17.4	*19.7*	*15.3*	US$/kg	747
8708	Parts and accessories of the motor vehicles of headings 87.01 to 87.05	1 838.4	2 018.8	1 951.4	8.7	*8.5*	*7.4*	US$/kg	784

Source: UN Comtrade

Senegal

Goods Imports: CIF, by origin | **Goods Exports: FOB, by last known destination** | **Trade System: General**

Overview:

In 2014, the value of merchandise exports of Senegal increased moderately by 5.5 percent to reach 2.8 bln US$, while its merchandise imports decreased slightly by 1.5 percent to reach 6.6 bln US$ (see graph 1, table 2 and table 3). The merchandise trade balance recorded a large deficit of 3.7 bln US$ (see graph 1). The largest merchandise trade balance was with MDG Developed Europe at -2.2 bln US$ (see graph 4). Merchandise exports in Senegal were diversified amongst partners; imports were also diversified. The top 19 partners accounted for 80 percent or more of exports and 18 partners accounted for 80 percent or more of imports (see graph 5). In 2013, the value of exports of services of Senegal increased moderately by 8.3 percent, reaching 1.3 bln US$, while its imports of services increased moderately by 8.2 percent and reached 1.4 bln US$ (see graph 2). There was a relatively small trade in services deficit of 114.7 mln US$.

Graph 1: Total merchandise trade, by value

(Bln US$ by year)

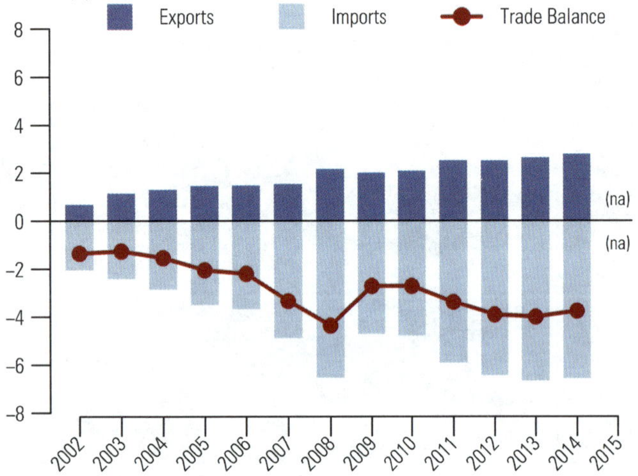

Graph 2: Total services trade, by value

(Bln US$ by year)

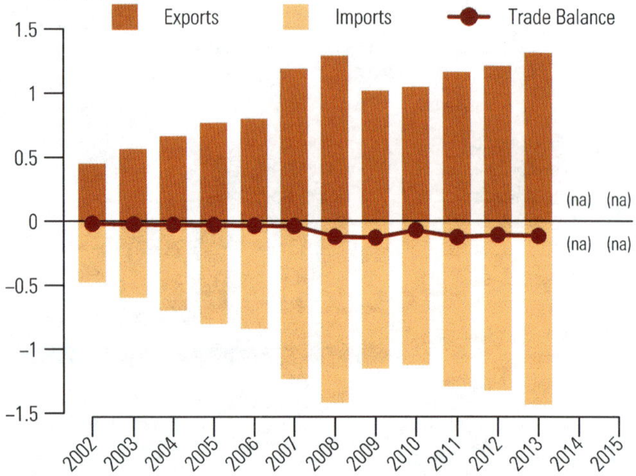

Exports Profile:

"Food, animals + beverages, tobacco" (SITC section 0+1), "Mineral fuels, lubricants" (SITC section 3) and "Goods classified chiefly by material" (SITC section 6) were the largest commodity groups for exports in 2014, representing respectively 31.8, 16.4 and 13.1 percent of exported goods (see table 2). From 2012 to 2014, the largest export commodity was "Petroleum oils, other than crude" (HS code 2710) (see table 1). The top three destinations for merchandise exports were Mali, Switzerland and Bunkers, ship stores, accounting for respectively 16.1, 10.5 and 9.1 percent of total exports. "Travel" (EBOPS code 236) accounted for the largest share of exports of services in 2013 at 438.7 mln US$, followed by "Other business services" (EBOPS code 268) at 199.9 mln US$ and "Government services, n.i.e." (EBOPS code 291) at 152.5 mln US$ (see graph 3).

Graph 3: Exports of services by EBOPS category

(% share in 2013)

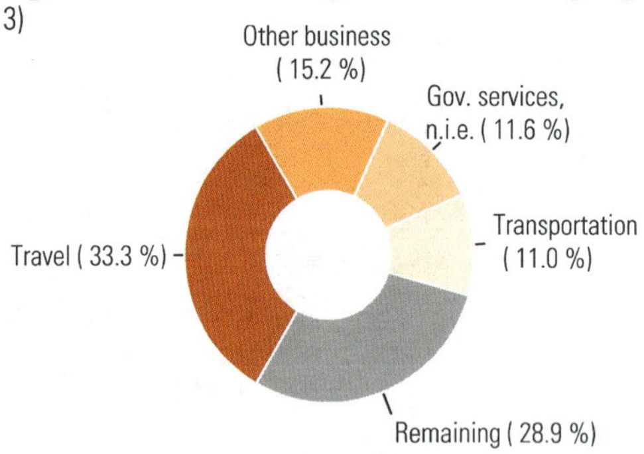

Table 1: Top 10 export commodities 2012 to 2014

HS code	4-digit heading of Harmonized System 2007	Value (million US$) 2012	2013	2014	Unit value 2012	2013	2014	Unit	SITC code
	All Commodities	2531.7	2665.9	2813.7					
2710	Petroleum oils, other than crude	351.3	431.2	446.2	1.0	1.0	0.9	US$/kg	334
7108	Gold (including gold plated with platinum)	351.0	329.0	345.6	44.5	36.1	34.1	thsd US$/kg	971
2523	Portland cement, aluminous cement, slag cement	219.2	165.4	185.7	0.1	0.1	0.1	US$/kg	661
2809	Diphosphorus pentaoxide; phosphoric acid	274.9	165.2	103.8	0.8	0.6	0.6	US$/kg	522
0303	Fish, frozen, excluding fish fillets and other fish meat of heading 03.04	107.2	151.0	212.7	1.3	1.3	1.8	US$/kg	034
2104	Soups and broths and preparations therefor	86.7	122.8	118.0	2.5	2.4	2.5	US$/kg	098
0302	Fish, fresh or chilled, excluding fish fillets	58.2	57.0	68.4	9.8	10.9	10.8	US$/kg	034
2402	Cigars, cheroots, cigarillos and cigarettes	49.1	51.0	48.5	18.3	21.5	22.5	US$/kg	122
0307	Molluscs, whether in shell or not	65.7	31.3	51.3	5.4	4.0	4.9	US$/kg	036
2403	Other manufactured tobacco and tobacco substitutes	23.9	48.3	49.8	12.6	14.3	15.7	US$/kg	122

Services Imports and Exports: EBOPS 2002 categories

Table 2: Merchandise exports by SITC

(Value in million US$, growth and shares in percentage)

SITC	2014	Avg. Growth rates 2010-2014	Avg. Growth rates 2013-2014	2014 share
Total	2 813.7	7.7	5.5	100.0
0+1	894.3	16.6	11.5	31.8
2+4	226.8	7.6	11.8	8.1
3	461.0	1.4	-0.9	16.4
5	267.5	-4.6	-10.1	9.5
6	367.8	2.8	-5.9	13.1
7	163.3	13.9	50.3	5.8
8	85.8	18.9	27.1	3.0
9	347.2	14.1	4.9	12.3

Table 3: Merchandise imports by SITC

(Value in million US$, growth and shares in percentage)

SITC	2014	Avg. Growth rates 2010-2014	Avg. Growth rates 2013-2014	2014 share
Total	6 556.7	8.2	-1.5	100.0
0+1	1 301.9	8.3	-7.6	19.9
2+4	326.3	5.9	2.9	5.0
3	1 928.3	7.8	-0.8	29.4
5	665.9	14.8	7.6	10.2
6	723.8	6.4	-2.3	11.0
7	1 285.8	6.4	-6.9	19.6
8	321.2	13.7	30.3	4.9
9	3.5	9.0	31.7	0.1

SITC Legend

SITC Code	Description
Total	All commodities
0+1	Food, animals + beverages, tobacco
2+4	Crude materials + anim. & veg. oils
3	Mineral fuels, lubricants
5	Chemicals
6	Goods classified chiefly by material
7	Machinery and transport equipment
8	Miscellaneous manufactured articles
9	Not classified elsewhere in the SITC

Graph 4: Merchandise trade balance

(Bln US$ by MDG Regions in 2014)

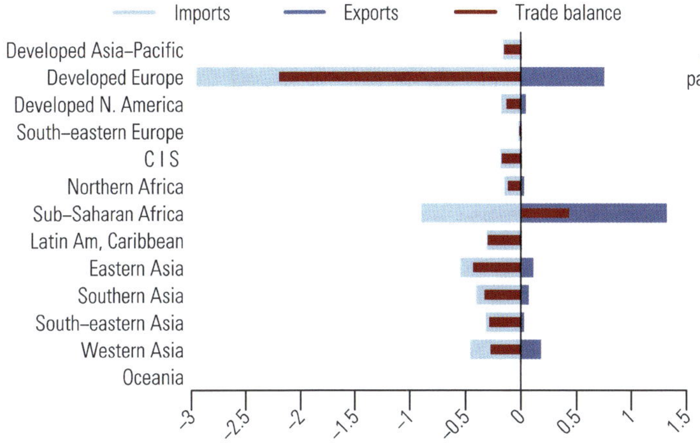

Graph 5: Partner concentration of merchandise trade

(Cumulative share by ranked partners in 2014)

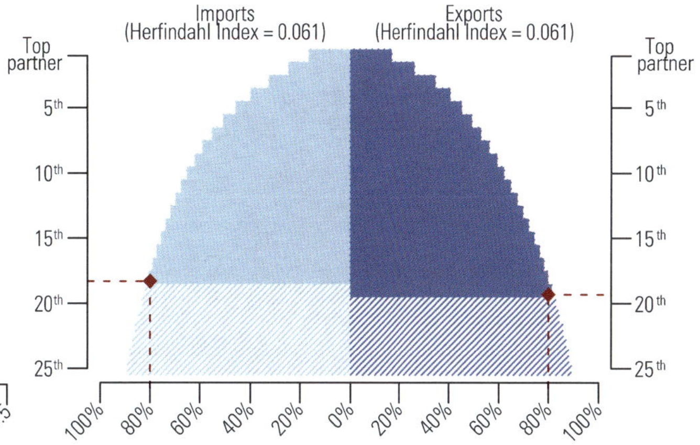

Graph 6: Imports of services by EBOPS category

(% share in 2013)

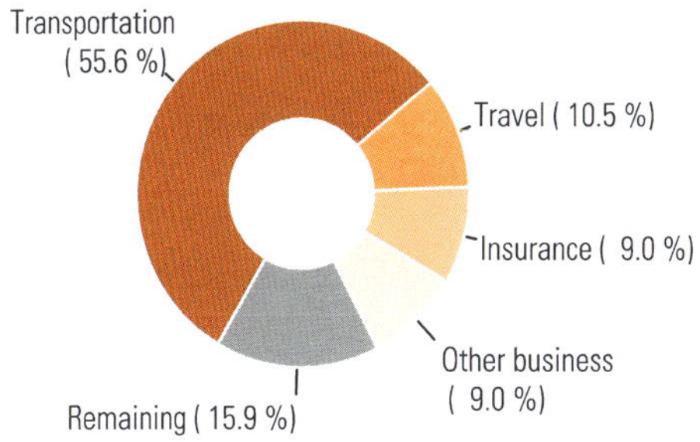

Imports Profile:

"Mineral fuels, lubricants" (SITC section 3), "Food, animals + beverages, tobacco" (SITC section 0+1) and "Machinery and transport equipment" (SITC section 7) were the largest commodity groups for imports in 2014, representing respectively 29.4, 19.9 and 19.6 percent of imported goods (see table 3). From 2012 to 2014, the largest import commodity was "Petroleum oils, other than crude" (HS code 2710) (see table 4). The top three partners for merchandise imports were France, Nigeria and China, accounting for respectively 15.5, 10.1 and 6.9 percent of total imports. "Transportation" (EBOPS code 205) accounted for the largest share of imports of services in 2013 at 796.2 mln US$, followed by "Travel" (EBOPS code 236) at 149.7 mln US$ and "Insurance services" (EBOPS code 253) at 129.5 mln US$ (see graph 6).

Table 4: Top 10 import commodities 2012 to 2014

HS code	4-digit heading of Harmonized System 2007	Value (million US$) 2012	2013	2014	Unit value 2012	2013	2014	Unit	SITC code
	All Commodities	6 434.2	6 659.4	6 556.7					
2710	Petroleum oils, other than crude	907.8	1 070.6	1 212.7	0.9	0.9	0.8	US$/kg	334
2709	Petroleum oils and oils obtained from bituminous minerals, crude	753.0	699.8	522.1	0.9	0.9	0.8	US$/kg	333
1006	Rice	449.6	461.6	414.8	0.4	0.4	0.4	US$/kg	042
1001	Wheat and meslin	189.1	191.7	176.7	0.4	0.4	0.3	US$/kg	041
3004	Medicaments (excluding goods of heading 30.02, 30.05 or 30.06)	165.4	171.3	187.1	20.2	20.0	20.1	US$/kg	542
8703	Motor cars and other motor vehicles principally designed for the transport	155.5	168.4	161.1	*24.5*	*23.8*	*23.1*	thsd US$/unit	781
1901	Malt extract; food preparations of flour	91.3	118.0	136.2	2.6	2.8	2.8	US$/kg	098
1511	Palm oil and its fractions	115.5	112.0	115.1	1.3	1.2	1.0	US$/kg	422
2711	Petroleum gases and other gaseous hydrocarbons	91.6	105.2	108.4	0.9	1.0	1.0	US$/kg	343
8704	Motor vehicles for the transport of goods	107.8	87.6	102.7					782

Serbia

Goods Imports: CIF, by origin | **Goods Exports: FOB, by last known destination** | **Trade System: General**

Overview:

In 2015, the value of merchandise exports of Serbia decreased moderately by 10.0 percent to reach 13.4 bln US$, while its merchandise imports decreased substantially by 11.6 percent to reach 18.2 bln US$ (see graph 1, table 2 and table 3). The merchandise trade balance recorded a moderate deficit of 4.9 bln US$ (see graph 1). The largest merchandise trade balance was with MDG Developed Europe at -3.1 bln US$ (see graph 4). Merchandise exports in Serbia were diversified amongst partners; imports were also diversified. The top 16 partners accounted for 80 percent or more of exports and 19 partners accounted for 80 percent or more of imports (see graph 5). In 2014, the value of exports of services of Serbia increased substantially by 10.1 percent, reaching 3.6 bln US$, while its imports of services increased moderately by 7.5 percent and reached 3.3 bln US$ (see graph 2). There was a relatively small trade in services surplus of 290.0 mln US$. See footnote*.

Graph 1: Total merchandise trade, by value

(Bln US$ by year)

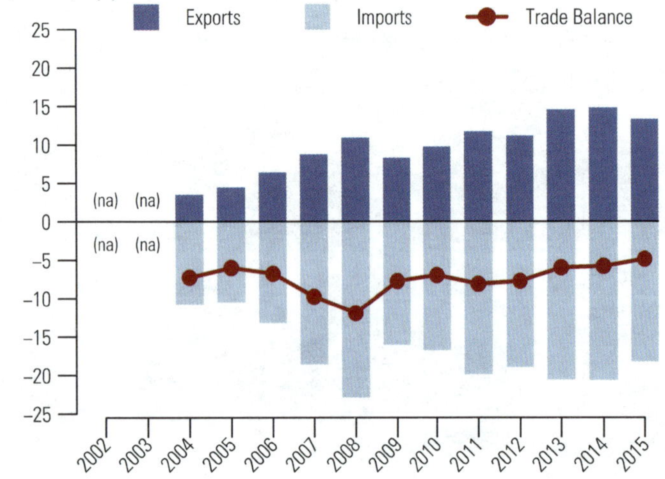

Graph 2: Total services trade, by value

(Bln US$ by year)

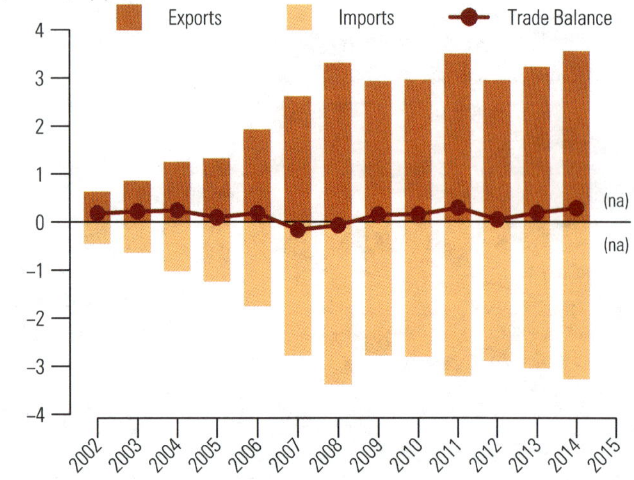

Exports Profile:

"Machinery and transport equipment" (SITC section 7), "Goods classified chiefly by material" (SITC section 6) and "Food, animals + beverages, tobacco" (SITC section 0+1) were the largest commodity groups for exports in 2015, representing respectively 29.1, 21.5 and 18.9 percent of exported goods (see table 2). From 2013 to 2015, the largest export commodity was "Motor cars and other motor vehicles principally designed for the transport" (HS code 8703) (see table 1). The top three destinations for merchandise exports were Italy, Germany and Bosnia and Herzegovina, accounting for respectively 16.6, 12.1 and 8.6 percent of total exports. "Transportation" (EBOPS code 205) accounted for the largest share of exports of services in 2014 at 881.0 mln US$, followed by "Travel" (EBOPS code 236) at 863.0 mln US$ and "Other business services" (EBOPS code 268) at 825.0 mln US$ (see graph 3).

Graph 3: Exports of services by EBOPS category

(% share in 2014)

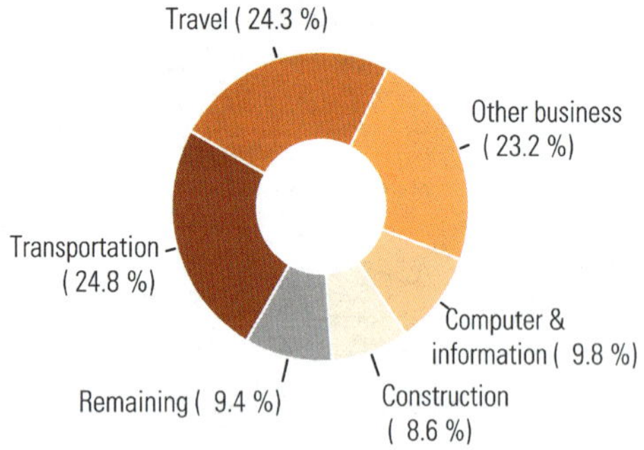

Table 1: Top 10 export commodities 2013 to 2015

HS code	4-digit heading of Harmonized System 2012	Value (million US$) 2013	2014	2015	Unit value 2013	2014	2015	Unit	SITC code
	All Commodities	14610.8	14843.3	13365.2					
8703	Motor cars and other motor vehicles principally designed for the transport	1946.6	1780.3	1301.0	12.1	12.9	13.5	thsd US$/unit	781
8544	Insulated (including enamelled or anodised) wire, cable	561.4	547.0	506.1	14.3	14.4	12.8	US$/kg	773
4011	New pneumatic tyres, of rubber	394.0	398.8	397.1					625
1005	Maize (corn)	210.7	507.2	389.3	0.3	0.2		US$/kg	044
0811	Fruit and nuts	318.9	363.3	379.4	2.3	2.2	2.1	US$/kg	058
2710	Petroleum oils, other than crude	268.2	321.3	184.9	0.8	0.8	0.6	US$/kg	334
6115	Panty hose, tights, stockings, socks and other hosiery	274.1	261.8	191.7	23.7	21.7	16.9	US$/kg	846
8503	Parts suitable for use principally with the machines of heading 85.01	222.2	258.6	245.5	8.1	8.2	6.5	US$/kg	716
3004	Medicaments (excluding goods of heading 30.02, 30.05 or 30.06)	236.7	237.4	210.4	16.1	15.5	12.4	US$/kg	542
7208	Flat-rolled products of iron or non-alloy steel	138.2	192.1	234.3	0.6	0.6	0.4	US$/kg	673

*Special trade system up to 2008.

Services Imports and Exports: EBOPS 2002 categories

Table 2: Merchandise exports by SITC

(Value in million US$, growth and shares in percentage)

SITC	2015	Avg. Growth rates 2011-2015	Avg. Growth rates 2014-2015	2015 share
Total	13 365.2	3.2	-10.0	100.0
0+1	2 526.8	4.2	-8.6	18.9
2+4	607.9	-8.0	-12.8	4.5
3	379.9	-5.2	-31.3	2.8
5	1 128.7	3.1	-5.3	8.4
6	2 870.6	-4.6	-7.7	21.5
7	3 886.5	18.6	-13.0	29.1
8	1 760.5	4.2	-9.3	13.2
9	204.2	-15.2	68.4	1.5

Table 3: Merchandise imports by SITC

(Value in million US$, growth and shares in percentage)

SITC	2015	Avg. Growth rates 2011-2015	Avg. Growth rates 2014-2015	2015 share
Total	18 215.9	-2.1	-11.6	100.0
0+1	1 299.6	2.3	-10.5	7.1
2+4	768.5	-1.7	11.2	4.2
3	2 074.3	-13.5	-28.3	11.4
5	2 617.6	-3.1	-11.8	14.4
6	3 223.7	-3.8	-11.1	17.7
7	4 807.7	1.5	-6.7	26.4
8	1 303.2	-2.9	-17.3	7.2
9	2 121.4	10.9	-5.7	11.6

SITC Legend

SITC Code	Description
Total	All commodities
0+1	Food, animals + beverages, tobacco
2+4	Crude materials + anim. & veg. oils
3	Mineral fuels, lubricants
5	Chemicals
6	Goods classified chiefly by material
7	Machinery and transport equipment
8	Miscellaneous manufactured articles
9	Not classified elsewhere in the SITC

Graph 4: Merchandise trade balance

(Bln US$ by MDG Regions in 2015)

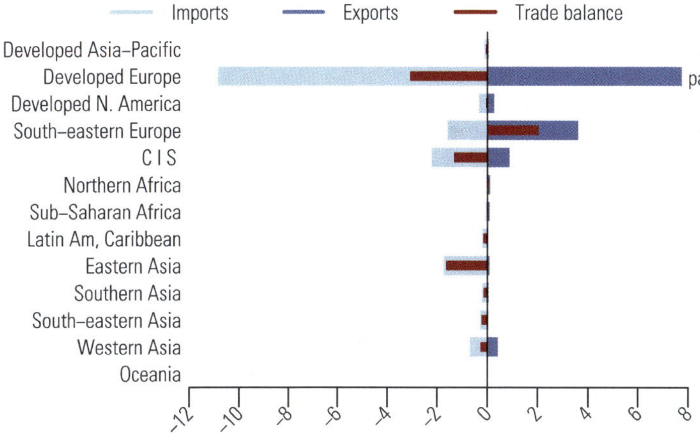

Graph 5: Partner concentration of merchandise trade

(Cumulative share by ranked partners in 2015)

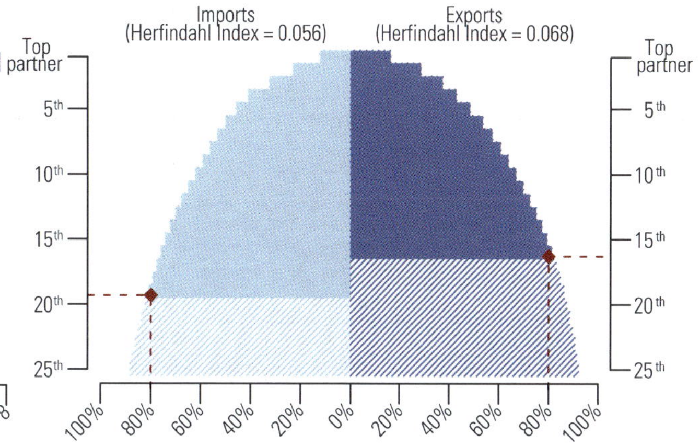

Graph 6: Imports of services by EBOPS category

(% share in 2014)

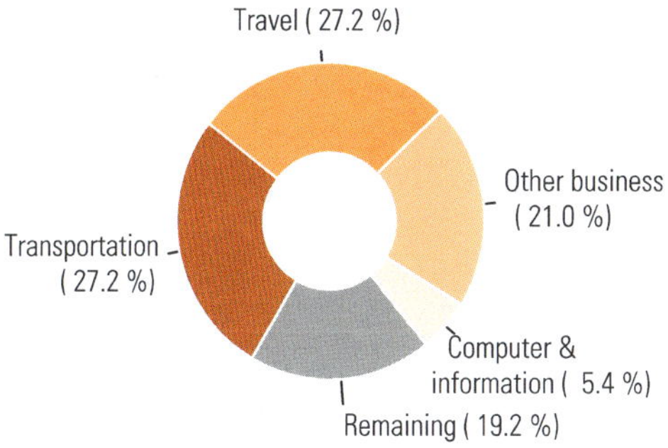

Imports Profile:

"Machinery and transport equipment" (SITC section 7), "Goods classified chiefly by material" (SITC section 6) and "Chemicals" (SITC section 5) were the largest commodity groups for imports in 2015, representing respectively 26.4, 17.7 and 14.4 percent of imported goods (see table 3). From 2013 to 2015, the largest import commodity was "Commodities not specified according to kind" (HS code 9999) (see table 4). The top three partners for merchandise imports were Germany, Italy and the Russian Federation, accounting for respectively 11.7, 11.1 and 10.1 percent of total imports. "Transportation" (EBOPS code 205) accounted for the largest share of imports of services in 2014 at 890.0 mln US$, followed by "Travel" (EBOPS code 236) at 889.0 mln US$ and "Other business services" (EBOPS code 268) at 686.0 mln US$ (see graph 6).

Table 4: Top 10 import commodities 2013 to 2015

HS code	4-digit heading of Harmonized System 2012	Value (million US$) 2013	Value (million US$) 2014	Value (million US$) 2015	Unit value 2013	Unit value 2014	Unit value 2015	Unit	SITC code
	All Commodities	20 551.0	20 608.6	18 215.9					
9999	Commodities not specified according to kind	1 295.4	2 248.5	2 121.2					931
8708	Parts and accessories of the motor vehicles of headings 87.01 to 87.05	1 646.3	1 425.9	1 059.8	*7.9*	*7.6*	*6.1*	US$/kg	784
2709	Petroleum oils and oils obtained from bituminous minerals, crude	1 321.6	1 105.7	766.1	0.8	0.8	0.4	US$/kg	333
2711	Petroleum gases and other gaseous hydrocarbons	923.8	807.5	617.6	*0.6*	*0.6*	0.5	US$/kg	343
3004	Medicaments (excluding goods of heading 30.02, 30.05 or 30.06)	636.0	569.2	477.1	*63.9*	*58.5*	*50.5*	US$/kg	542
2710	Petroleum oils, other than crude	586.0	666.5	397.8	*1.0*	*0.9*	0.6	US$/kg	334
8703	Motor cars and other motor vehicles principally designed for the transport	545.0	466.7	516.3	*17.4*	*17.3*	*18.7*	thsd US$/unit	781
8517	Electrical apparatus for line telephony or line telegraphy	311.0	281.2	297.5					764
8544	Insulated (including enamelled or anodised) wire, cable	281.4	221.1	197.1	*13.5*	*13.0*	*9.9*	US$/kg	773
3923	Articles for the conveyance or packing of goods, of plastics	191.3	203.7	80.7	*3.1*	*2.8*	*2.7*	US$/kg	893

Source: UN Comtrade

Sierra Leone

Goods Imports: CIF, by origin | **Goods Exports: FOB, by last known destination** | **Trade System: General**

Overview:

In 2014, the value of merchandise exports of Sierra Leone reached 279.3 mln US$, while its merchandise imports reached 2.1 bln US$ (see graph 1, table 2 and table 3). The merchandise trade balance recorded a large deficit of 1.8 bln US$ (see graph 1). The largest merchandise trade balance was with MDG Sub-Saharan Africa at -848.4 mln US$ (see graph 4). Merchandise exports in Sierra Leone were highly concentrated amongst partners; imports were moderately concentrated. The top 1 partner accounted for 80 percent or more of exports and 8 partners accounted for 80 percent or more of imports (see graph 5). In 2014, the value of exports of services of Sierra Leone increased slightly by 1.6 percent, reaching 187.5 mln US$, while its imports of services increased substantially by 86.1 percent and reached 1.2 bln US$ (see graph 2). There was a large trade in services deficit of 1.0 bln US$.

Graph 1: Total merchandise trade, by value

(Bln US$ by year)

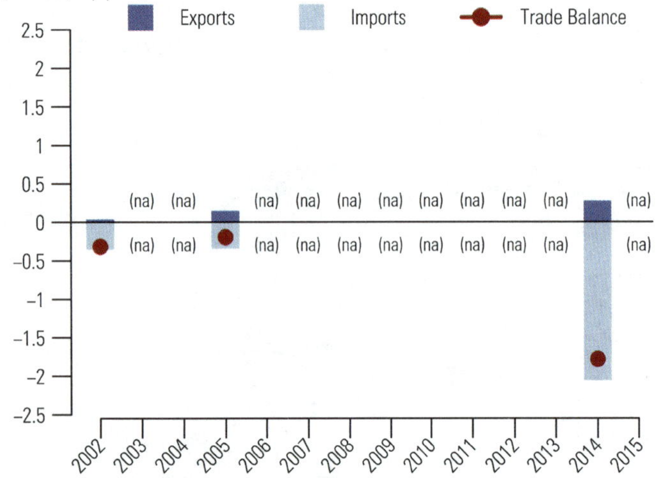

Graph 2: Total services trade, by value

(Bln US$ by year)

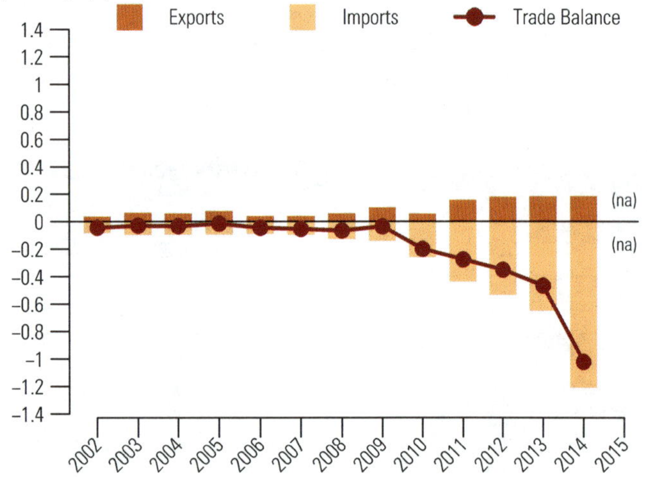

Exports Profile:

"Crude materials + anim. & veg. oils" (SITC section 2+4), "Machinery and transport equipment" (SITC section 7) and "Food, animals + beverages, tobacco" (SITC section 0+1) were the largest commodity groups for exports in 2014, representing respectively 86.5, 6.1 and 4.0 percent of exported goods (see table 2). From 2012 to 2014, the largest export commodity was "Tin ores and concentrates" (HS code 2609) (see table 1). The top three destinations for merchandise exports were China, Guinea and the Netherlands, accounting for respectively 86.4, 3.0 and 2.8 percent of total exports. "Communications services" (EBOPS code 245) accounted for the largest share of exports of services in 2014 at 126.8 mln US$, followed by "Travel" (EBOPS code 236) at 34.6 mln US$ (see graph 3).

Graph 3: Exports of services by EBOPS category

(% share in 2014)

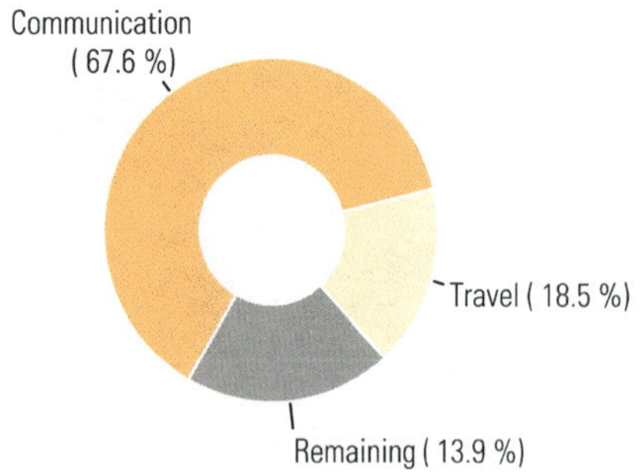

Table 1: Top 10 export commodities 2012 to 2014

HS code	4-digit heading of Harmonized System 2007	Value (million US$) 2012	2013	2014	Unit value 2012	2013	2014	Unit	SITC code
	All Commodities	...	...	279.3					
2609	Tin ores and concentrates	...	...	236.6					287
3923	Articles for the conveyance or packing of goods, of plastics	...	...	6.3			*36.4*	US$/kg	893
1802	Cocoa shells, husks, skins and other cocoa waste	...	...	5.4			15.1	US$/kg	072
8703	Motor cars and other motor vehicles principally designed for the transport	...	...	4.9			*9.1*	thsd US$/unit	781
8429	Self-propelled bulldozers, angledozers, graders, levellers, scrapers	...	...	4.2			*57.4*	thsd US$/unit	723
7204	Ferrous waste and scrap; remelting scrap ingots of iron or steel	...	...	4.1					282
8709	Works trucks, self-propelled, not fitted with lifting or handling equipment	...	...	4.0					744
2005	Other vegetables prepared or preserved	...	...	2.3			*3.6*	US$/kg	056
8427	Fork-lift trucks; other works trucks fitted with lifting or handling equipment	...	...	2.0					744
3924	Tableware, kitchenware, other household articles and toilet articles	...	...	1.8			*5.5*	US$/kg	893

Services Imports and Exports: EBOPS 2002 categories

Table 2: Merchandise exports by SITC

(Value in million US$, growth and shares in percentage)

SITC	2014	Avg. Growth rates 2010-2014	Avg. Growth rates 2013-2014	2014 share
Total	279.3	...	...	100.0
0+1	11.2	...	...	4.0
2+4	241.5	...	...	86.5
3	0.0	...	...	0.0
5	0.0	...	...	0.0
6	1.1	...	...	0.4
7	17.2	...	...	6.1
8	8.3	...	...	3.0
9	0.0	...	...	0.0

Table 3: Merchandise imports by SITC

(Value in million US$, growth and shares in percentage)

SITC	2014	Avg. Growth rates 2010-2014	Avg. Growth rates 2013-2014	2014 share
Total	2 056.8	...	...	100.0
0+1	218.8	...	...	10.6
2+4	23.5	...	...	1.1
3	787.5	...	...	38.3
5	138.1	...	...	6.7
6	221.7	...	...	10.8
7	517.1	...	...	25.1
8	149.6	...	...	7.3
9	0.5	...	...	0.0

SITC Legend

SITC Code	Description
Total	All commodities
0+1	Food, animals + beverages, tobacco
2+4	Crude materials + anim. & veg. oils
3	Mineral fuels, lubricants
5	Chemicals
6	Goods classified chiefly by material
7	Machinery and transport equipment
8	Miscellaneous manufactured articles
9	Not classified elsewhere in the SITC

Graph 4: Merchandise trade balance

(Mln US$ by MDG Regions in 2014)

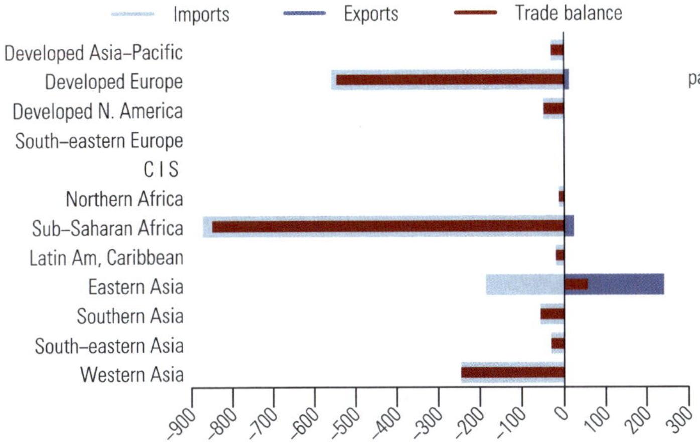

Graph 5: Partner concentration of merchandise trade

(Cumulative share by ranked partners in 2014)

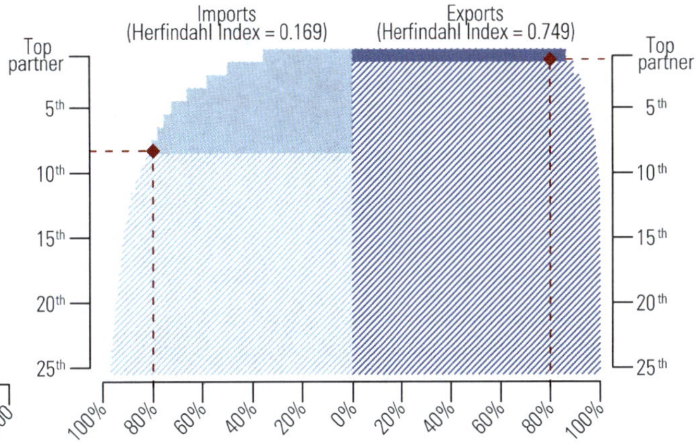

Graph 6: Imports of services by EBOPS category

(% share in 2014)

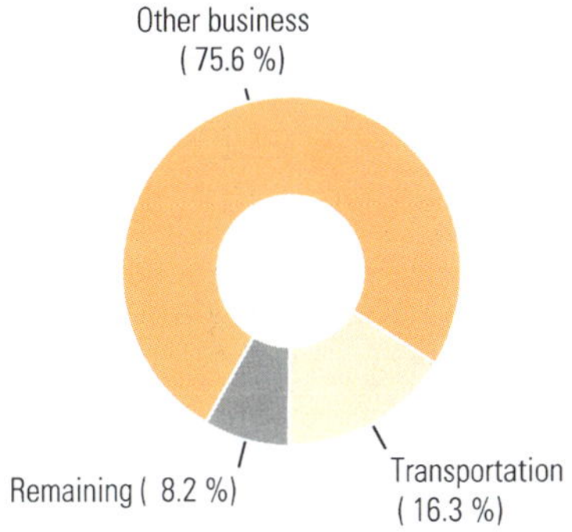

Imports Profile:

"Mineral fuels, lubricants" (SITC section 3), "Machinery and transport equipment" (SITC section 7) and "Goods classified chiefly by material" (SITC section 6) were the largest commodity groups for imports in 2014, representing respectively 38.3, 25.1 and 10.8 percent of imported goods (see table 3). From 2012 to 2014, the largest import commodity was "Petroleum oils, other than crude" (HS code 2710) (see table 4). The top three partners for merchandise imports were Benin, Belgium and China, accounting for respectively 35.6, 14.2 and 8.2 percent of total imports. "Other business services" (EBOPS code 268) accounted for the largest share of imports of services in 2014 at 912.7 mln US$, followed by "Transportation" (EBOPS code 205) at 196.5 mln US$ (see graph 6).

Table 4: Top 10 import commodities 2012 to 2014

HS code	4-digit heading of Harmonized System 2007	Value (million US$) 2012	2013	2014	Unit value 2012	2013	2014	Unit	SITC code
	All Commodities	...	...	2 056.8					
2710	Petroleum oils, other than crude	...	...	786.8			*18.1*	US$/kg	334
8703	Motor cars and other motor vehicles principally designed for the transport	...	...	116.0			*34.9*	thsd US$/unit	781
8704	Motor vehicles for the transport of goods	...	...	54.5					782
8421	Centrifuges, including centrifugal dryers	...	...	45.9					743
3004	Medicaments (excluding goods of heading 30.02, 30.05 or 30.06)	...	...	33.0					542
3917	Tubes, pipes and hoses, and fittings therefor	...	...	18.4					581
8536	Electrical apparatus for switching or protecting electrical circuits	...	...	17.1					772
8431	Parts suitable for use principally with the machinery of headings 84.25	...	...	16.6			*86.1*	US$/kg	723
8708	Parts and accessories of the motor vehicles of headings 87.01 to 87.05	...	...	15.9			*45.4*	US$/kg	784
1905	Bread, pastry, cakes, biscuits and other bakers' wares	...	...	15.7			*12.6*	US$/kg	048

Singapore

Goods Imports: CIF, by origin | **Goods Exports: FOB, by last known destination** | **Trade System: General**

Overview:

In 2015, the value of merchandise exports of Singapore decreased substantially by 15.4 percent to reach 346.6 bln US$, while its merchandise imports decreased substantially by 19.0 percent to reach 296.7 bln US$ (see graph 1, table 2 and table 3). The merchandise trade balance recorded a relatively small surplus of 49.9 bln US$ (see graph 1). The largest merchandise trade balance was with MDG South-eastern Asia at 38.7 bln US$ (see graph 4). Merchandise exports in Singapore were diversified amongst partners; imports were also diversified. The top 14 partners accounted for 80 percent or more of exports and 15 partners accounted for 80 percent or more of imports (see graph 5). In 2014, the value of exports of services of Singapore increased slightly by 2.5 percent, reaching 132.4 bln US$, while its imports of services ERROR - NO SIGNIF CHANGE slightly by 0.0 percent and reached 140.9 bln US$ (see graph 2). There was a relatively small trade in services deficit of 8.5 bln US$.

Graph 1: Total merchandise trade, by value

(Bln US$ by year)

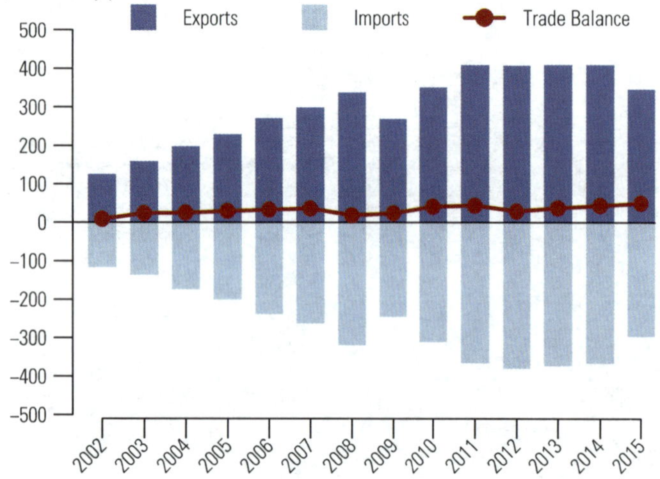

Graph 2: Total services trade, by value

(Bln US$ by year)

Exports Profile:

"Machinery and transport equipment" (SITC section 7), "Chemicals" (SITC section 5) and "Mineral fuels, lubricants" (SITC section 3) were the largest commodity groups for exports in 2015, representing respectively 51.2, 13.6 and 12.6 percent of exported goods (see table 2). From 2013 to 2015, the largest export commodity was "Electronic integrated circuits" (HS code 8542) (see table 1). The top three destinations for merchandise exports were China, Malaysia and China, Hong Kong SAR, accounting for respectively 12.6, 11.7 and 11.2 percent of total exports. "Transportation" (EBOPS code 205) accounted for the largest share of exports of services in 2014 at 44.9 bln US$, followed by "Other business services" (EBOPS code 268) at 32.8 bln US$ and "Financial services" (EBOPS code 260) at 20.5 bln US$ (see graph 3).

Graph 3: Exports of services by EBOPS category

(% share in 2014)

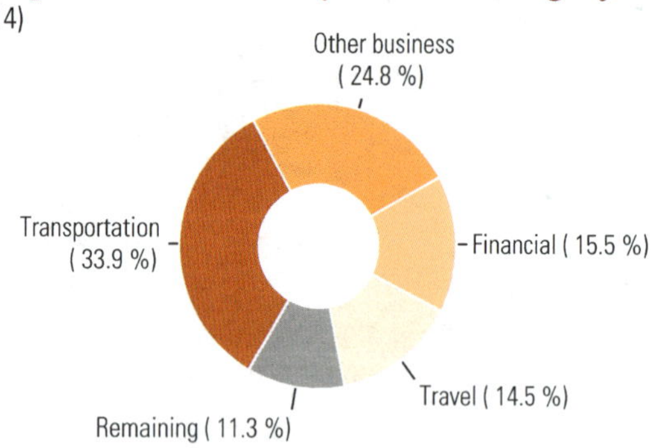

Table 1: Top 10 export commodities 2013 to 2015

HS code	4-digit heading of Harmonized System 2012	Value (million US$) 2013	2014	2015	Unit value 2013	2014	2015	Unit	SITC code
	All Commodities	410249.7	409768.7	346638.0					
8542	Electronic integrated circuits	83052.4	83704.7	75750.9					776
2710	Petroleum oils, other than crude	69253.4	66116.3	42006.7	*0.9*	*0.8*	*0.5*	US$/kg	334
9999	Commodities not specified according to kind	33134.5	32228.1	19839.0					931
8471	Automatic data processing machines and units thereof	9723.5	9293.1	10063.3	*126.8*	*82.9*	*123.8*	US$/unit	752
8517	Electrical apparatus for line telephony or line telegraphy	8628.7	8501.3	10229.9					764
8541	Diodes, transistors and similar semiconductor devices	6830.9	7962.5	8478.8					776
8443	Printing machinery used for printing by means of the printing type, blocks	6874.8	5914.5	5681.9					726
8473	Parts and accessories for use with machines of heading 84.69 to 84.72	7151.8	6371.5	4873.8					759
8803	Parts of goods of heading 88.01 or 88.02	6229.4	5571.3	6038.5					792
3004	Medicaments (excluding goods of heading 30.02, 30.05 or 30.06)	5061.9	5519.3	5104.0					542

Services Imports and Exports: EBOPS 2002 categories

Table 2: Merchandise exports by SITC

(Value in million US$, growth and shares in percentage)

SITC	2015	Avg. Growth rates 2011-2015	Avg. Growth rates 2014-2015	2015 share
Total	346 638.0	-4.1	-15.4	100.0
0+1	9 924.2	4.5	-3.3	2.9
2+4	2 793.9	-2.3	-7.1	0.8
3	43 636.1	-14.3	-36.5	12.6
5	47 126.1	-2.2	-11.0	13.6
6	14 168.4	-2.6	-16.4	4.1
7	177 531.9	-1.4	-5.4	51.2
8	30 275.0	1.5	-17.4	8.7
9	21 182.4	-11.1	-37.1	6.1

Table 3: Merchandise imports by SITC

(Value in million US$, growth and shares in percentage)

SITC	2015	Avg. Growth rates 2011-2015	Avg. Growth rates 2014-2015	2015 share
Total	296 744.6	-5.1	-19.0	100.0
0+1	11 270.2	0.6	-8.5	3.8
2+4	3 310.4	-5.8	-13.5	1.1
3	64 575.5	-14.2	-43.1	21.8
5	22 409.9	-3.0	-12.2	7.6
6	20 431.2	-4.3	-18.3	6.9
7	141 154.1	-1.5	-6.8	47.6
8	25 938.3	0.5	-6.6	8.7
9	7 655.1	5.3	10.4	2.6

SITC Legend

SITC Code	Description
Total	All commodities
0+1	Food, animals + beverages, tobacco
2+4	Crude materials + anim. & veg. oils
3	Mineral fuels, lubricants
5	Chemicals
6	Goods classified chiefly by material
7	Machinery and transport equipment
8	Miscellaneous manufactured articles
9	Not classified elsewhere in the SITC

Graph 4: Merchandise trade balance

(Bln US$ by MDG Regions in 2015)

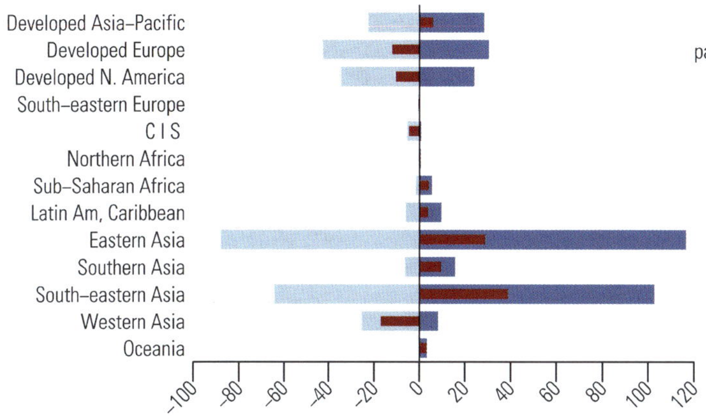

Graph 5: Partner concentration of merchandise trade

(Cumulative share by ranked partners in 2015)

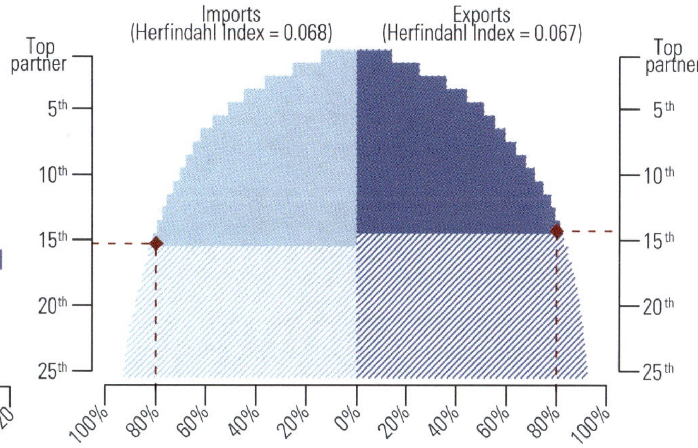

Graph 6: Imports of services by EBOPS category

(% share in 2014)

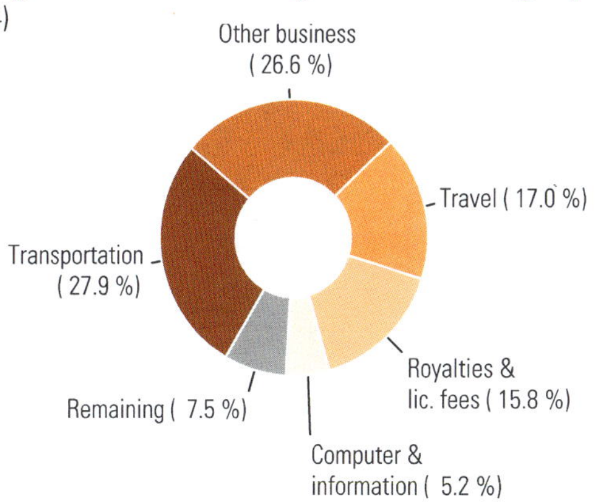

Imports Profile:

"Machinery and transport equipment" (SITC section 7), "Mineral fuels, lubricants" (SITC section 3) and "Miscellaneous manufactured articles" (SITC section 8) were the largest commodity groups for imports in 2015, representing respectively 47.6, 21.8 and 8.7 percent of imported goods (see table 3). From 2013 to 2015, the largest import commodity was "Petroleum oils, other than crude" (HS code 2710) (see table 4). The top three partners for merchandise imports were China, Malaysia and the United States, accounting for respectively 12.6, 10.9 and 10.6 percent of total imports. "Transportation" (EBOPS code 205) accounted for the largest share of imports of services in 2014 at 39.3 bln US$, followed by "Other business services" (EBOPS code 268) at 37.5 bln US$ and "Travel" (EBOPS code 236) at 23.9 bln US$ (see graph 6).

Table 4: Top 10 import commodities 2013 to 2015

HS code	4-digit heading of Harmonized System 2012	Value (million US$) 2013	Value (million US$) 2014	Value (million US$) 2015	Unit value 2013	Unit value 2014	Unit value 2015	Unit	SITC code
	All Commodities	373 015.7	366 247.3	296 744.6					
2710	Petroleum oils, other than crude	74 603.6	72 328.8	42 573.7	*0.7*	*0.7*	*0.4*	US$/kg	334
8542	Electronic integrated circuits	59 380.1	58 342.4	53 054.5					776
2709	Petroleum oils and oils obtained from bituminous minerals, crude	35 538.7	34 326.2	18 202.8	*0.8*	*0.8*	*0.4*	US$/kg	333
8517	Electrical apparatus for line telephony or line telegraphy	9 365.2	8 511.0	8 420.6					764
8411	Turbo-jets, turbo-propellers and other gas turbines	7 720.1	7 510.4	6 202.0					714
8471	Automatic data processing machines and units thereof	6 558.9	6 076.1	6 185.7	*79.0*	*71.0*	*88.1*	US$/unit	752
2711	Petroleum gases and other gaseous hydrocarbons	6 532.0	6 639.7	3 615.6	*0.7*	*0.7*	*0.4*	US$/kg	343
8473	Parts and accessories for use with machines of heading 84.69 to 84.72	5 716.7	5 351.0	4 868.9					759
9999	Commodities not specified according to kind	5 947.8	4 901.0	4 497.9					931
8541	Diodes, transistors and similar semiconductor devices	4 681.1	4 936.6	5 096.5					776

Slovakia

Goods Imports: CIF, by origin	Goods Exports: FOB, by last known destination	Trade System: Special

Overview:

In 2015, the value of merchandise exports of Slovakia decreased substantially by 12.5 percent to reach 75.3 bln US$, while its merchandise imports decreased substantially by 10.1 percent to reach 73.1 bln US$ (see graph 1, table 2 and table 3). The merchandise trade balance recorded a relatively small surplus of 2.1 bln US$ (see graph 1). The largest merchandise trade balance was with MDG Developed Europe at 15.6 bln US$ (see graph 4). Merchandise exports in Slovakia were diversified amongst partners; imports were also diversified. The top 13 partners accounted for 80 percent or more of exports and the same number of partners accounted for 80 percent or more of imports (see graph 5). In 2014, the value of exports of services of Slovakia increased slightly by 0.2 percent, reaching 8.6 bln US$, while its imports of services increased slightly by 4.8 percent and reached 8.6 bln US$ (see graph 2). There was a relatively small trade in services surplus of 37.3 mln US$.

Graph 1: Total merchandise trade, by value

(Bln US$ by year)

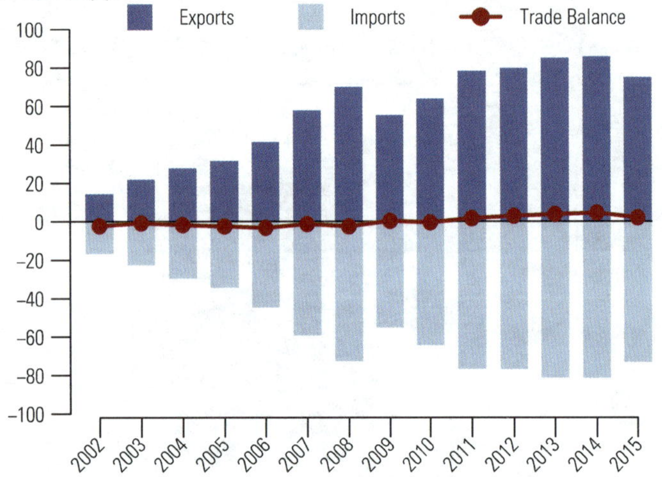

Graph 2: Total services trade, by value

(Bln US$ by year)

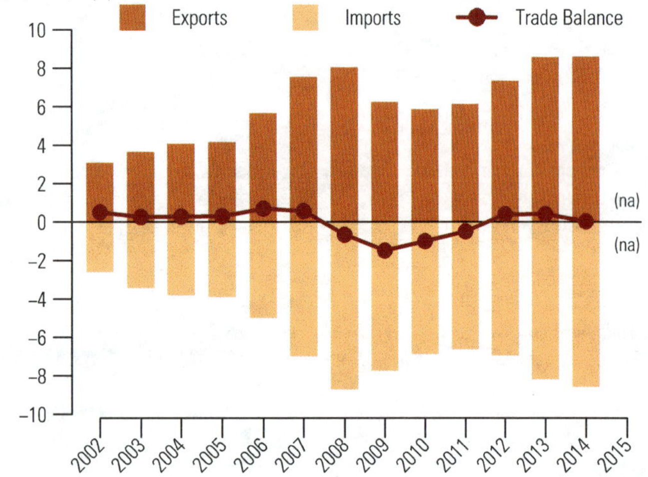

Exports Profile:

"Machinery and transport equipment" (SITC section 7), "Goods classified chiefly by material" (SITC section 6) and "Miscellaneous manufactured articles" (SITC section 8) were the largest commodity groups for exports in 2015, representing respectively 59.6, 16.7 and 9.6 percent of exported goods (see table 2). From 2013 to 2015, the largest export commodity was "Motor cars and other motor vehicles principally designed for the transport" (HS code 8703) (see table 1). The top three destinations for merchandise exports were Germany, the Czech Republic and Poland, accounting for respectively 21.8, 12.9 and 8.2 percent of total exports. "Transportation" (EBOPS code 205) accounted for the largest share of exports of services in 2014 at 2.7 bln US$, followed by "Travel" (EBOPS code 236) at 2.6 bln US$ and "Other business services" (EBOPS code 268) at 1.8 bln US$ (see graph 3).

Graph 3: Exports of services by EBOPS category

(% share in 2014)

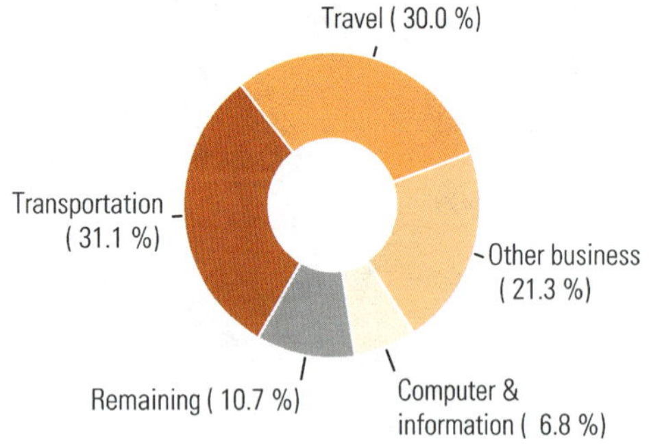

Table 1: Top 10 export commodities 2013 to 2015

HS code	4-digit heading of Harmonized System 2012	Value (million US$) 2013	2014	2015	Unit value 2013	2014	2015	Unit	SITC code
	All Commodities	85184.2	85976.3	75256.9					
8703	Motor cars and other motor vehicles principally designed for the transport	14446.9	14883.2	14058.7	*14.5*	*14.6*	*13.0*	thsd US$/unit	781
8528	Reception apparatus for television	7034.9	7238.9	5857.6	*381.0*	*379.7*	*351.2*	US$/unit	761
8517	Electrical apparatus for line telephony or line telegraphy	4082.9	4312.3	3867.2					764
8708	Parts and accessories of the motor vehicles of headings 87.01 to 87.05	3597.1	3943.0	3937.4	*9.0*	*9.0*	*8.0*	US$/kg	784
2710	Petroleum oils, other than crude	3878.6	3057.5	2071.1	*0.9*	*0.9*	*0.5*	US$/kg	334
8707	Bodies (including cabs), for the motor vehicles of headings 87.01 to 87.05	2252.9	1966.4	1978.5	*1.8*	2.1	11.8	thsd US$/unit	784
4011	New pneumatic tyres, of rubber	1716.0	1679.6	1802.0	*98.6*	*96.8*	83.9	US$/unit	625
8544	Insulated (including enamelled or anodised) wire, cable	1312.0	1355.2	1171.7	*13.4*	*16.0*	*13.3*	US$/kg	773
8471	Automatic data processing machines and units thereof	1313.1	1266.8	1018.2	*213.1*	169.8	*139.3*	US$/unit	752
7208	Flat-rolled products of iron or non-alloy steel	1239.8	1176.2	787.4	*0.7*	0.6	0.5	US$/kg	673

Services Imports and Exports: EBOPS 2002 categories

Table 2: Merchandise exports by SITC

(Value in million US$, growth and shares in percentage)

SITC	2015	Avg. Growth rates 2011-2015	Avg. Growth rates 2014-2015	2015 share
Total	75256.9	-1.0	-12.5	100.0
0+1	2572.3	-5.1	-15.7	3.4
2+4	1503.5	-9.7	-20.2	2.0
3	2801.1	-13.6	-31.0	3.7
5	3498.8	-2.5	-14.5	4.6
6	12553.2	-3.8	-13.4	16.7
7	44884.7	1.8	-9.9	59.6
8	7226.9	-1.4	-13.0	9.6
9	216.4	12.3	-25.1	0.3

Table 3: Merchandise imports by SITC

(Value in million US$, growth and shares in percentage)

SITC	2015	Avg. Growth rates 2011-2015	Avg. Growth rates 2014-2015	2015 share
Total	73147.0	-1.2	-10.1	100.0
0+1	3883.9	-3.4	-14.1	5.3
2+4	1828.5	-11.9	-26.2	2.5
3	5897.3	-15.0	-30.1	8.1
5	6456.9	-1.1	-10.1	8.8
6	10957.7	-2.0	-12.3	15.0
7	34607.5	3.1	-4.0	47.3
8	9247.5	2.4	-6.9	12.6
9	267.6	2.2	4.4	0.4

SITC Legend

SITC Code	Description
Total	All commodities
0+1	Food, animals + beverages, tobacco
2+4	Crude materials + anim. & veg. oils
3	Mineral fuels, lubricants
5	Chemicals
6	Goods classified chiefly by material
7	Machinery and transport equipment
8	Miscellaneous manufactured articles
9	Not classified elsewhere in the SITC

Graph 4: Merchandise trade balance

(Bln US$ by MDG Regions in 2015)

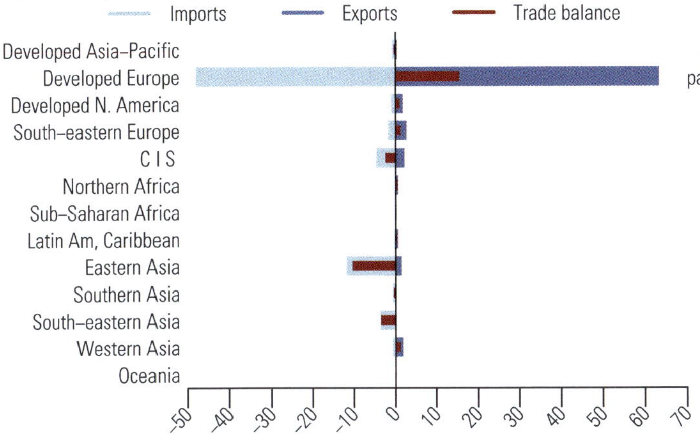

Graph 5: Partner concentration of merchandise trade

(Cumulative share by ranked partners in 2015)

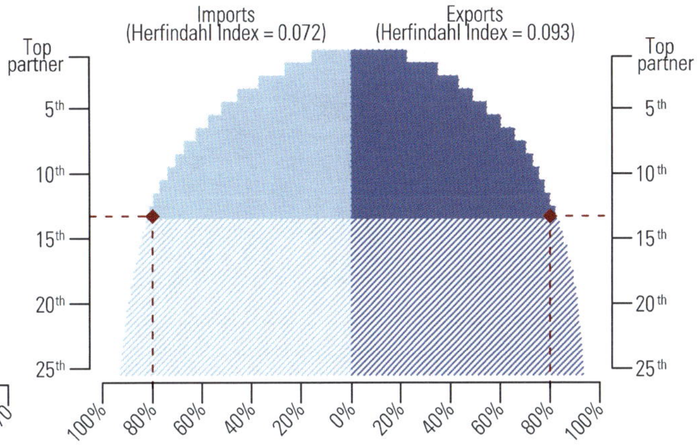

Graph 6: Imports of services by EBOPS category

(% share in 2014)

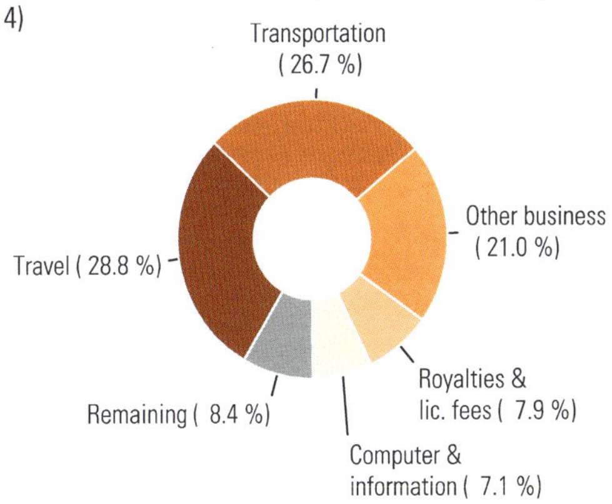

Imports Profile:

"Machinery and transport equipment" (SITC section 7), "Goods classified chiefly by material" (SITC section 6) and "Miscellaneous manufactured articles" (SITC section 8) were the largest commodity groups for imports in 2015, representing respectively 47.3, 15.0 and 12.6 percent of imported goods (see table 3). From 2013 to 2015, the largest import commodity was "Parts and accessories of the motor vehicles of headings 87.01 to 87.05" (HS code 8708) (see table 4). The top three partners for merchandise imports were Germany, the Czech Republic and Rest of Europe nes, accounting for respectively 15.7, 10.9 and 9.0 percent of total imports. "Travel" (EBOPS code 236) accounted for the largest share of imports of services in 2014 at 2.5 bln US$, followed by "Transportation" (EBOPS code 205) at 2.3 bln US$ and "Other business services" (EBOPS code 268) at 1.8 bln US$ (see graph 6).

Table 4: Top 10 import commodities 2013 to 2015

HS code	4-digit heading of Harmonized System 2012	Value (million US$) 2013	2014	2015	Unit value 2013	2014	2015	Unit	SITC code
	All Commodities	81295.1	81354.2	73147.0					
8708	Parts and accessories of the motor vehicles of headings 87.01 to 87.05	7306.2	7384.1	7410.6	*3.7*	*3.6*	*3.9*	US$/kg	784
8517	Electrical apparatus for line telephony or line telegraphy	4876.9	4994.7	4884.9					764
2709	Petroleum oils and oils obtained from bituminous minerals, crude	4529.0	3885.8	2440.7	0.8	0.7	*0.7*	US$/kg	333
2711	Petroleum gases and other gaseous hydrocarbons	3473.6	2354.9	1772.5	*0.6*	0.5	*0.9*	US$/kg	343
8703	Motor cars and other motor vehicles principally designed for the transport	1601.8	2077.7	2080.4	*5.7*	5.1	2.9	thsd US$/unit	781
8529	Parts suitable for use with the apparatus of headings 85.25 to 85.28	1747.5	1791.6	1569.8	*34.5*	*35.4*	*32.1*	US$/kg	764
9013	Liquid crystal devices	1880.3	1738.2	1481.3					871
3004	Medicaments (excluding goods of heading 30.02, 30.05 or 30.06)	1642.3	1604.9	1385.4	*90.3*	*103.2*	*82.8*	US$/kg	542
8471	Automatic data processing machines and units thereof	1468.2	1503.4	1270.1	*135.0*	126.6	124.8	US$/unit	752
2710	Petroleum oils, other than crude	1781.1	1403.3	962.4	*1.3*	*1.0*	0.8	US$/kg	334

Slovenia

Goods Imports: CIF, by origin	Goods Exports: FOB, by last known destination	Trade System: Special

Overview:

In 2015, the value of merchandise exports of Slovenia decreased substantially by 12.8 percent to reach 26.6 bln US$, while its merchandise imports decreased substantially by 14.3 percent to reach 25.8 bln US$ (see graph 1, table 2 and table 3). The merchandise trade balance recorded a relatively small surplus of 852.1 mln US$ (see graph 1). The largest merchandise trade balance was with MDG Eastern Asia at -2.0 bln US$ (see graph 4). Merchandise exports in Slovenia were diversified amongst partners; imports were also diversified. The top 16 partners accounted for 80 percent or more of exports and 18 partners accounted for 80 percent or more of imports (see graph 5). In 2014, the value of exports of services of Slovenia increased slightly by 4.8 percent, reaching 7.1 bln US$, while its imports of services increased moderately by 7.5 percent and reached 4.9 bln US$ (see graph 2). There was a moderate trade in services surplus of 2.3 bln US$.

Graph 1: Total merchandise trade, by value

(Bln US$ by year)

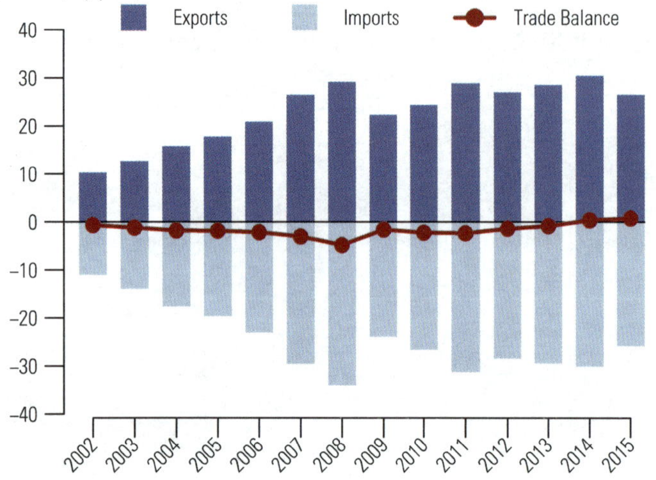

Graph 2: Total services trade, by value

(Bln US$ by year)

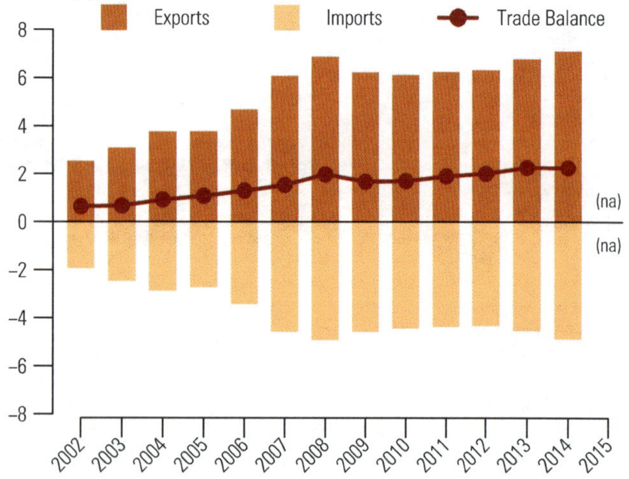

Exports Profile:

"Machinery and transport equipment" (SITC section 7), "Goods classified chiefly by material" (SITC section 6) and "Chemicals" (SITC section 5) were the largest commodity groups for exports in 2015, representing respectively 37.4, 21.0 and 17.3 percent of exported goods (see table 2). From 2013 to 2015, the largest export commodity was "Medicaments (excluding goods of heading 30.02, 30.05 or 30.06)" (HS code 3004) (see table 1). The top three destinations for merchandise exports were Germany, Italy and Austria, accounting for respectively 20.3, 11.6 and 8.6 percent of total exports. "Travel" (EBOPS code 236) accounted for the largest share of exports of services in 2014 at 2.7 bln US$, followed by "Transportation" (EBOPS code 205) at 2.0 bln US$ and "Other business services" (EBOPS code 268) at 1.0 bln US$ (see graph 3).

Graph 3: Exports of services by EBOPS category

(% share in 2014)

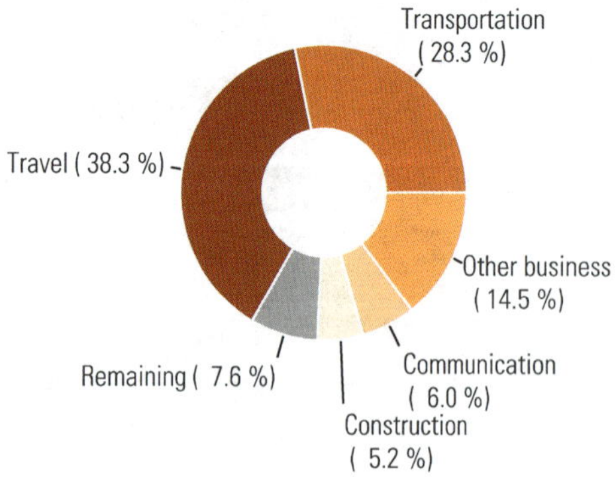

Table 1: Top 10 export commodities 2013 to 2015

HS code	4-digit heading of Harmonized System 2012	Value (million US$)			Unit value				SITC code
		2013	2014	2015	2013	2014	2015	Unit	
	All Commodities	28628.7	30522.1	26616.0					
3004	Medicaments (excluding goods of heading 30.02, 30.05 or 30.06)	2723.1	2873.7	2410.0	94.4	90.7	73.2	US$/kg	542
8703	Motor cars and other motor vehicles principally designed for the transport	2064.6	2610.5	2373.1	11.5	12.3	7.2	thsd US$/unit	781
2710	Petroleum oils, other than crude	1165.1	1187.0	802.6	1.1	1.0	0.6	US$/kg	334
8708	Parts and accessories of the motor vehicles of headings 87.01 to 87.05	778.5	851.1	860.4	7.4	7.3	6.9	US$/kg	784
2716	Electrical energy	677.9	545.5	439.1	58.2	51.9	44.5	US$/MWh	351
8512	Electrical lighting or signalling equipment	446.2	491.9	481.0					778
8516	Electric instantaneous or storage water heaters and immersion heaters	486.1	412.3	340.9					775
4011	New pneumatic tyres, of rubber	421.1	414.5	354.2	53.3	47.0	39.1	US$/unit	625
9401	Seats (other than those of heading 94.02)	401.0	409.4	329.6					821
8503	Parts suitable for use principally with the machines of heading 85.01	370.0	345.1	279.0	7.9	8.6	7.7	US$/kg	716

Services Imports and Exports: EBOPS 2002 categories

Table 2: Merchandise exports by SITC

(Value in million US$, growth and shares in percentage)

SITC	2015	Avg. Growth rates 2011-2015	Avg. Growth rates 2014-2015	2015 share
Total	26616.0	-2.1	-12.8	100.0
0+1	1118.1	1.8	-7.6	4.2
2+4	1008.6	-3.2	-17.0	3.8
3	1414.3	-4.0	-24.5	5.3
5	4608.6	-0.9	-16.3	17.3
6	5585.3	-4.4	-12.5	21.0
7	9962.2	-1.6	-10.0	37.4
8	2809.1	-1.6	-10.6	10.6
9	109.7	12.1	-7.6	0.4

Table 3: Merchandise imports by SITC

(Value in million US$, growth and shares in percentage)

SITC	2015	Avg. Growth rates 2011-2015	Avg. Growth rates 2014-2015	2015 share
Total	25763.9	-4.7	-14.3	100.0
0+1	2146.3	-1.9	-11.0	8.3
2+4	1513.7	-6.8	-16.7	5.9
3	2665.3	-13.5	-31.3	10.3
5	3875.0	-2.0	-13.0	15.0
6	4873.2	-5.0	-11.8	18.9
7	8097.8	-2.2	-10.6	31.4
8	2495.9	-4.2	-11.2	9.7
9	96.7	-9.5	7.7	0.4

SITC Legend

SITC Code	Description
Total	All commodities
0+1	Food, animals + beverages, tobacco
2+4	Crude materials + anim. & veg. oils
3	Mineral fuels, lubricants
5	Chemicals
6	Goods classified chiefly by material
7	Machinery and transport equipment
8	Miscellaneous manufactured articles
9	Not classified elsewhere in the SITC

Graph 4: Merchandise trade balance

(Bln US$ by MDG Regions in 2015)

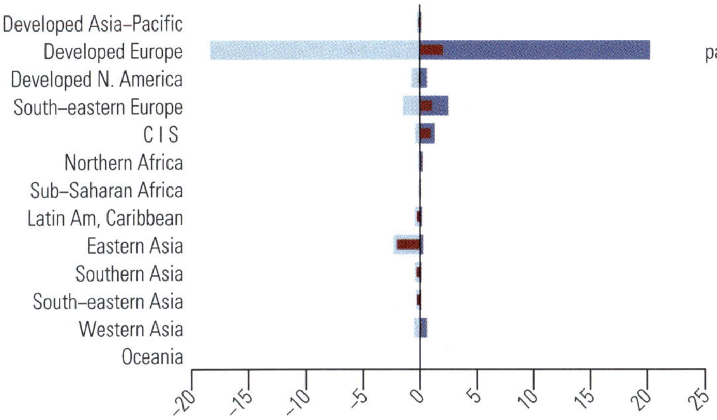

Graph 5: Partner concentration of merchandise trade

(Cumulative share by ranked partners in 2015)

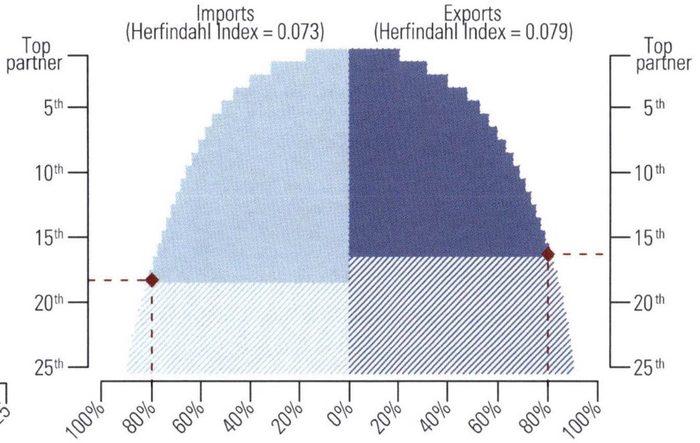

Graph 6: Imports of services by EBOPS category

(% share in 2014)

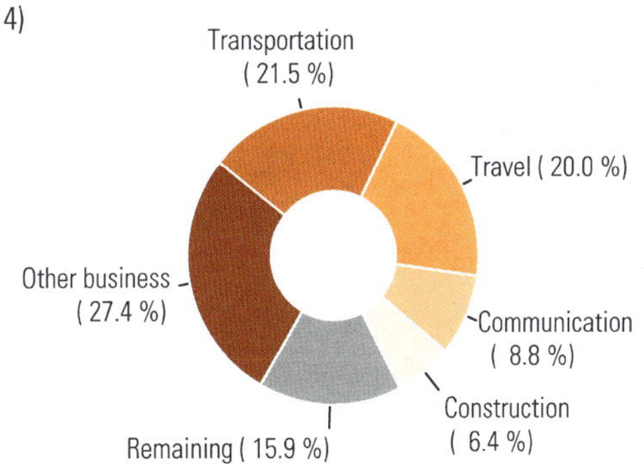

Imports Profile:

"Machinery and transport equipment" (SITC section 7), "Goods classified chiefly by material" (SITC section 6) and "Chemicals" (SITC section 5) were the largest commodity groups for imports in 2015, representing respectively 31.4, 18.9 and 15.0 percent of imported goods (see table 3). From 2013 to 2015, the largest import commodity was "Petroleum oils, other than crude" (HS code 2710) (see table 4). The top three partners for merchandise imports were Germany, Italy and Austria, accounting for respectively 16.9, 15.0 and 8.6 percent of total imports. "Other business services" (EBOPS code 268) accounted for the largest share of imports of services in 2014 at 1.3 bln US$, followed by "Transportation" (EBOPS code 205) at 1.0 bln US$ and "Travel" (EBOPS code 236) at 972.5 mln US$ (see graph 6).

Table 4: Top 10 import commodities 2013 to 2015

HS code	4-digit heading of Harmonized System 2012	Value (million US$) 2013	2014	2015	Unit value 2013	2014	2015	Unit	SITC code
	All Commodities	29375.4	30049.3	25763.9					
2710	Petroleum oils, other than crude	3220.0	2933.5	1787.8	1.0	0.9	0.5	US$/kg	334
8703	Motor cars and other motor vehicles principally designed for the transport	1533.3	1894.8	1540.3	15.0	15.8	11.6	thsd US$/unit	781
3004	Medicaments (excluding goods of heading 30.02, 30.05 or 30.06)	926.7	987.6	896.8	84.2	88.6	76.5	US$/kg	542
8708	Parts and accessories of the motor vehicles of headings 87.01 to 87.05	614.2	693.4	724.0	6.8	7.1	6.5	US$/kg	784
2711	Petroleum gases and other gaseous hydrocarbons	515.5	500.2	424.9	0.6	0.6	0.4	US$/kg	343
8517	Electrical apparatus for line telephony or line telegraphy	363.6	439.7	422.2					764
2716	Electrical energy	523.9	280.9	323.9	59.7	58.8	46.1	US$/MWh	351
8704	Motor vehicles for the transport of goods	293.2	337.9	345.5	23.4	23.6	6.7	thsd US$/unit	782
7601	Unwrought aluminium	287.7	317.6	264.2	2.3	2.3	2.1	US$/kg	684
7204	Ferrous waste and scrap; remelting scrap ingots of iron or steel	296.1	326.4	235.0	0.5	0.6	0.5	US$/kg	282

Solomon Islands

Goods Imports: CIF, by origin | **Goods Exports: FOB, by last known destination** | **Trade System: Special**

Overview:

In 2014, the value of merchandise exports of Solomon Islands decreased moderately by 6.3 percent to reach 458.5 mln US$, while its merchandise imports decreased substantially by 13.9 percent to reach 499.6 mln US$ (see graph 1, table 2 and table 3). The merchandise trade balance recorded a relatively small deficit of 41.1 mln US$ (see graph 1). The largest merchandise trade balance was with MDG Eastern Asia at 205.2 mln US$ (see graph 4). Merchandise exports in Solomon Islands were highly concentrated amongst partners; imports were moderately concentrated. The top 4 partners accounted for 80 percent or more of exports and 6 partners accounted for 80 percent or more of imports (see graph 5). In 2014, the value of exports of services of Solomon Islands decreased substantially by 11.0 percent, reaching 111.8 mln US$, while its imports of services decreased substantially by 10.6 percent and reached 210.4 mln US$ (see graph 2). There was a large trade in services deficit of 98.5 mln US$.

Graph 1: Total merchandise trade, by value

(Mln US$ by year)

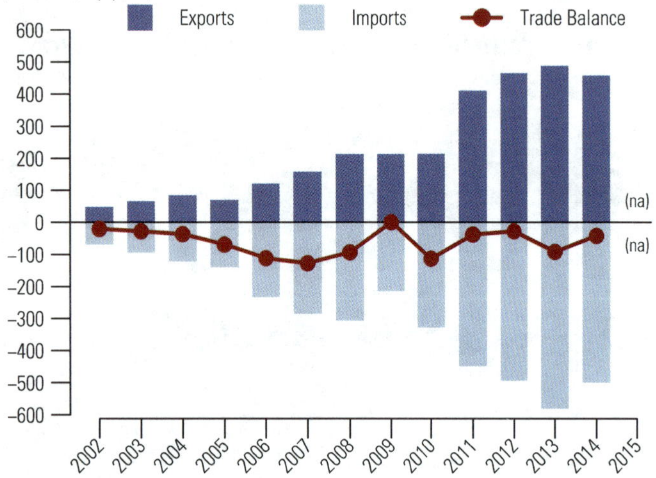

Graph 2: Total services trade, by value

(Mln US$ by year)

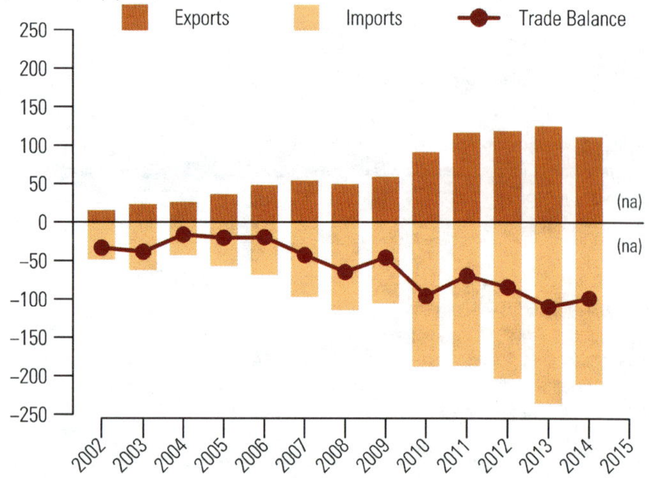

Exports Profile:

"Not classified elsewhere in the SITC" (SITC section 9), "Crude materials + anim. & veg. oils" (SITC section 2+4) and "Food, animals + beverages, tobacco" (SITC section 0+1) were the largest commodity groups for exports in 2014, representing respectively 84.8, 11.0 and 3.5 percent of exported goods (see table 2). From 2013 to 2014, the largest export commodity was "Commodities not elsewhere specified" (HS code 9999) (see table 1). The top three destinations for merchandise exports were China, Australia and the United Kingdom, accounting for respectively 46.9, 19.6 and 7.0 percent of total exports. "Travel" (EBOPS code 236) accounted for the largest share of exports of services in 2014 at 55.3 mln US$, followed by "Other business services" (EBOPS code 268) at 25.9 mln US$ and "Transportation" (EBOPS code 205) at 21.3 mln US$ (see graph 3).

Graph 3: Exports of services by EBOPS category

(% share in 2014)

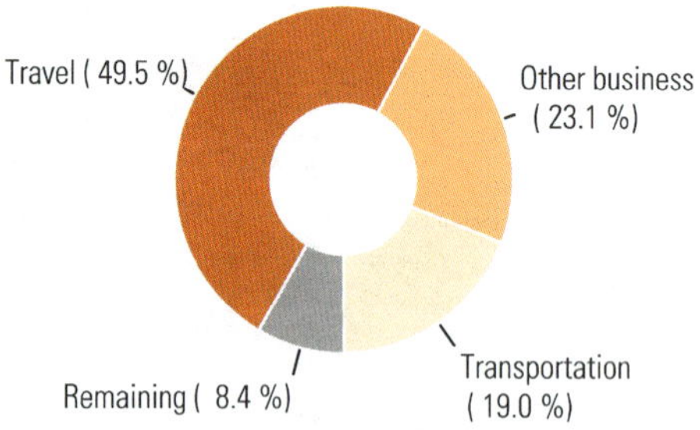

Table 1: Top 10 export commodities 2012 to 2014

HS code	4-digit heading of Harmonized System 1996	Value (million US$) 2012	2013	2014	Unit value 2012	2013	2014	Unit	SITC code
	All Commodities	466.3	489.2	458.5					
9999	Commodities not elsewhere specified	...	198.3	388.7					931
4403	Wood in the rough or roughly squared	195.2	234.4	...		117.4		US$/m^3	247
7108	Gold, unwrought, semi-manufactured, powder form	112.6	...	...					971
1511	Palm oil and its fractions, not chemically modified	37.7	26.4	25.4		*1.0*	*0.8*	US$/kg	422
1203	Copra	23.5	5.8	9.9		0.6		US$/kg	223
1801	Cocoa beans, whole or broken, raw or roasted	8.9	9.2	12.9		2.2	2.6	US$/kg	072
1513	Coconut, palm kernel, babassu oil, fractions, refined	8.4	5.4	10.3					422
0303	Fish, frozen, whole	22.9	...	...					034
0305	Fish,cured, smoked, fish meal for human consumption	21.6	...	...					035
4407	Wood sawn, chipped lengthwise, sliced or peeled	9.9	0.0	0.0		972.4	832.8	US$/m^3	248

Services Imports and Exports: EBOPS 2002 categories

Table 2: Merchandise exports by SITC

(Value in million US$, growth and shares in percentage)

SITC	2014	Avg. Growth rates 2010-2014	Avg. Growth rates 2013-2014	2014 share
Total	458.5	20.8	-6.3	100.0
0+1	16.1	-18.8	41.3	3.5
2+4	50.4	-25.9	-81.8	11.0
3	0.0	-8.3	-90.6	0.0
5	0.3	37.4	361.2	0.1
6	0.2	-14.9	128.9	0.0
7	2.7	-21.0	195.0	0.6
8	0.1	-41.3	-97.3	0.0
9	388.7	229.9	96.0	84.8

Table 3: Merchandise imports by SITC

(Value in million US$, growth and shares in percentage)

SITC	2014	Avg. Growth rates 2010-2014	Avg. Growth rates 2013-2014	2014 share
Total	499.6	11.1	-13.9	100.0
0+1	99.8	4.6	0.1	20.0
2+4	7.5	13.0	15.2	1.5
3	117.9	13.5	-31.9	23.6
5	7.7	-23.7	-27.3	1.5
6	18.7	-23.3	-8.1	3.7
7	41.4	-12.4	-25.0	8.3
8	17.5	-4.4	-17.9	3.5
9	189.0	404.4	-2.2	37.8

SITC Legend

SITC Code	Description
Total	All commodities
0+1	Food, animals + beverages, tobacco
2+4	Crude materials + anim. & veg. oils
3	Mineral fuels, lubricants
5	Chemicals
6	Goods classified chiefly by material
7	Machinery and transport equipment
8	Miscellaneous manufactured articles
9	Not classified elsewhere in the SITC

Graph 4: Merchandise trade balance

(Mln US$ by MDG Regions in 2014)

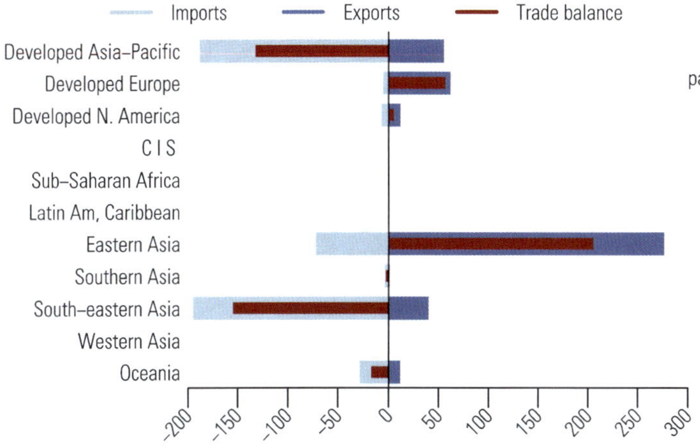

Graph 5: Partner concentration of merchandise trade

(Cumulative share by ranked partners in 2014)

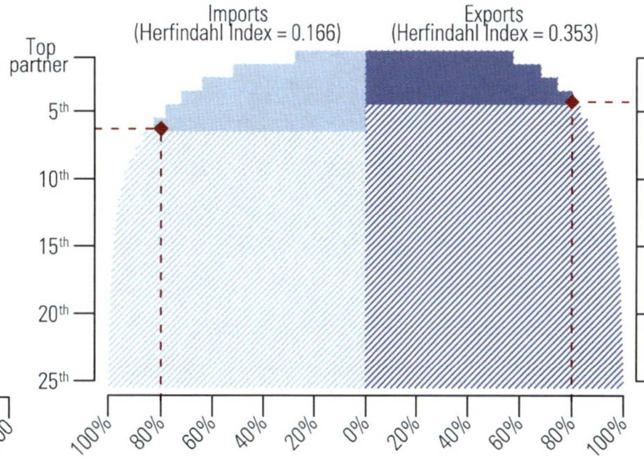

Graph 6: Imports of services by EBOPS category

(% share in 2014)

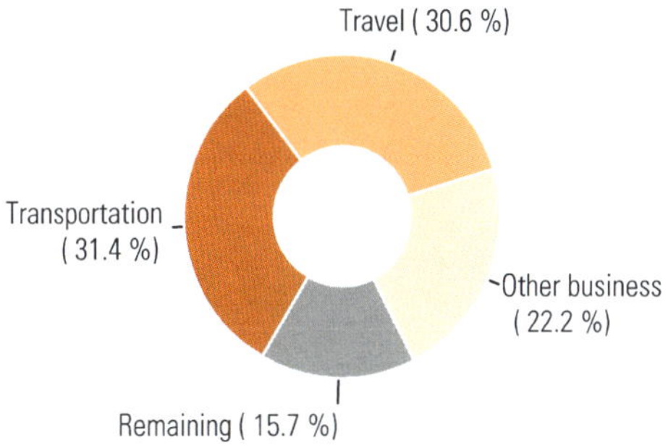

Imports Profile:

"Not classified elsewhere in the SITC" (SITC section 9), "Mineral fuels, lubricants" (SITC section 3) and "Food, animals + beverages, tobacco" (SITC section 0+1) were the largest commodity groups for imports in 2014, representing respectively 37.8, 23.6 and 20.0 percent of imported goods (see table 3). From 2012 to 2014, the largest import commodity was "Oils petroleum, bituminous, distillates, except crude" (HS code 2710) (see table 4). The top three partners for merchandise imports were Australia, Singapore and China, accounting for respectively 28.8, 28.0 and 9.5 percent of total imports. "Transportation" (EBOPS code 205) accounted for the largest share of imports of services in 2014 at 66.0 mln US$, followed by "Travel" (EBOPS code 236) at 64.4 mln US$ and "Other business services" (EBOPS code 268) at 46.7 mln US$ (see graph 6).

Table 4: Top 10 import commodities 2012 to 2014

HS code	4-digit heading of Harmonized System 1996	Value (million US$) 2012	Value (million US$) 2013	Value (million US$) 2014	Unit value 2012	Unit value 2013	Unit value 2014	Unit	SITC code
	All Commodities	493.4	580.2	499.6					
2710	Oils petroleum, bituminous, distillates, except crude	130.7	171.1	114.8		*1.3*	*0.9*	US$/kg	334
9999	Commodities not elsewhere specified	0.3	193.2	188.2					931
1006	Rice	41.3	42.1	43.2		5.3	*1.0*	US$/kg	042
1902	Pasta, couscous, etc	5.9	7.1	7.4		4.1	3.9	US$/kg	048
0207	Meat, edible offal of domestic poultry	4.3	6.1	6.7		4.0	3.6	US$/kg	012
1001	Wheat and meslin	4.0	5.5	6.7		0.4	0.5	US$/kg	041
4907	Documents of title (bonds etc), unused stamps etc	1.7	6.6	6.4					892
8517	Electric apparatus for line telephony, telegraphy	5.4	6.1	3.0					764
2202	Waters, non-alcoholic sweetened or flavoured beverages	3.4	4.0	4.2		2.7	*1.9*	US$/litre	111
8471	Automatic data processing machines (computers)	3.2	4.0	3.0			95.8	US$/unit	752

South Africa

Goods Imports: FOB, by origin **Goods Exports: FOB, by last known destination** **Trade System: General**

Overview:

In 2015, the value of merchandise exports of South Africa decreased substantially by 23.2 percent to reach 69.6 bln US$, while its merchandise imports decreased substantially by 20.3 percent to reach 79.6 bln US$ (see graph 1, table 2 and table 3). The merchandise trade balance recorded a relatively small deficit of 10.0 bln US$ (see graph 1). The largest merchandise trade balance was with MDG Sub-Saharan Africa at 11.0 bln US$ (see graph 4). Merchandise exports in South Africa were diversified amongst partners; imports were also diversified. The top 24 partners accounted for 80 percent or more of exports and 23 partners accounted for 80 percent or more of imports (see graph 5). In 2014, the value of exports of services of South Africa decreased slightly by 0.1 percent, reaching 16.8 bln US$, while its imports of services decreased moderately by 5.8 percent and reached 17.0 bln US$ (see graph 2). There was a relatively small trade in services deficit of 269.7 mln US$.

Graph 1: Total merchandise trade, by value

(Bln US$ by year)

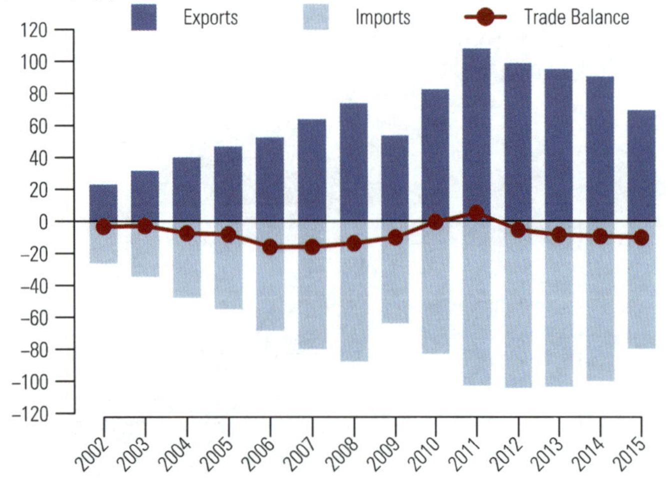

Graph 2: Total services trade, by value

(Bln US$ by year)

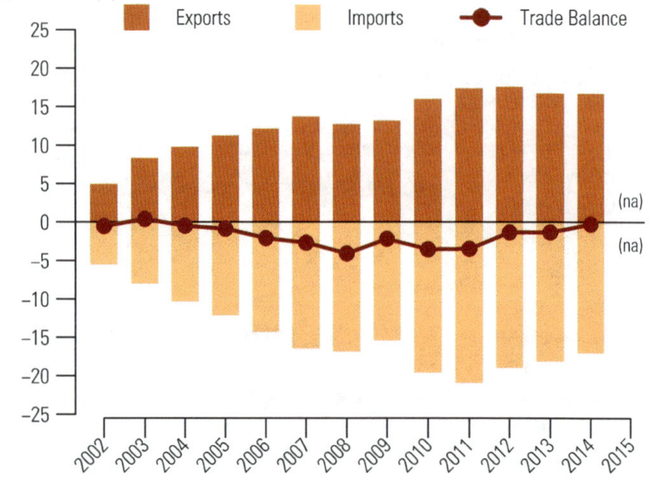

Exports Profile:

"Goods classified chiefly by material" (SITC section 6), "Machinery and transport equipment" (SITC section 7) and "Crude materials + anim. & veg. oils" (SITC section 2+4) were the largest commodity groups for exports in 2015, representing respectively 25.9, 22.4 and 13.8 percent of exported goods (see table 2). From 2013 to 2015, the largest export commodity was "Platinum, unwrought or in semi-manufactured forms, or in powder form" (HS code 7110) (see table 1). The top three destinations for merchandise exports were China, the United States and Areas nes, accounting for respectively 10.4, 7.3 and 6.0 percent of total exports. "Travel" (EBOPS code 236) accounted for the largest share of exports of services in 2014 at 9.4 bln US$, followed by "Transportation" (EBOPS code 205) at 3.0 bln US$ and "Other business services" (EBOPS code 268) at 2.0 bln US$ (see graph 3).

Graph 3: Exports of services by EBOPS category

(% share in 2014)

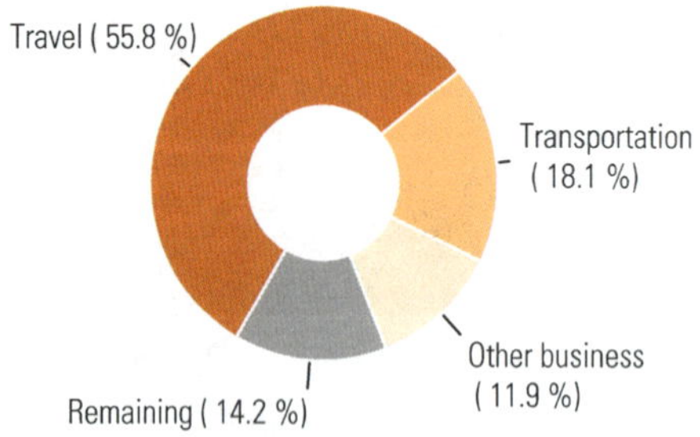

Table 1: Top 10 export commodities 2013 to 2015

HS code	4-digit heading of Harmonized System 2012	Value (million US$)			Unit value				SITC code
		2013	2014	2015	2013	2014	2015	Unit	
	All Commodities	95111.5	90612.1	69631.1					
7110	Platinum, unwrought or in semi-manufactured forms, or in powder form	8412.7	6504.4	6486.5	*32.2*	*29.3*	24.8	thsd US$/kg	681
2601	Iron ores and concentrates, including roasted iron pyrites	8458.4	6738.7	2652.2	*0.1*	0.1	0.1	US$/kg	281
2701	Coal; briquettes, ovoids and similar solid fuels manufactured from coal	5826.5	5192.9	4248.4	*0.1*	*0.1*	0.1	US$/kg	321
7108	Gold (including gold plated with platinum)	6614.0	4726.9	2005.3	44.6	40.3	36.8	thsd US$/kg	971
8703	Motor cars and other motor vehicles principally designed for the transport	3666.8	4372.0	4726.7	*14.7*	23.3	22.3	thsd US$/unit	781
7202	Ferro-alloys	3663.0	4099.3	2804.4					671
2710	Petroleum oils, other than crude	3206.4	3081.3	2793.7	*0.9*	*1.1*	*1.0*	US$/kg	334
8704	Motor vehicles for the transport of goods	2973.2	3024.5	2233.6		21.1	19.5	thsd US$/unit	782
7102	Diamonds, whether or not worked, but not mounted or set	2115.0	2423.3	1603.0					667
8421	Centrifuges, including centrifugal dryers	2089.4	1975.6	1361.1					743

Services Imports and Exports: EBOPS 2002 categories

Table 2: Merchandise exports by SITC

(Value in million US$, growth and shares in percentage)

SITC	2015	Avg. Growth rates 2011-2015	Avg. Growth rates 2014-2015	2015 share
Total	69631.1	-10.4	-23.2	100.0
0+1	7718.5	-2.7	-15.8	11.1
2+4	9607.4	-15.4	-37.2	13.8
3	8160.8	-7.9	-14.2	11.7
5	5563.5	-6.3	-21.0	8.0
6	18016.0	-11.1	-20.6	25.9
7	15598.0	-4.8	-16.6	22.4
8	2454.6	-7.6	-19.1	3.5
9	2512.4	-30.7	-51.6	3.6

Table 3: Merchandise imports by SITC

(Value in million US$, growth and shares in percentage)

SITC	2015	Avg. Growth rates 2011-2015	Avg. Growth rates 2014-2015	2015 share
Total	79590.9	-6.2	-20.3	100.0
0+1	4288.1	-7.4	-19.5	5.4
2+4	2067.2	-13.3	-24.6	2.6
3	13920.4	-10.0	-40.1	17.5
5	9261.7	-3.9	-14.6	11.6
6	8799.2	-4.6	-15.7	11.1
7	27303.9	-6.5	-15.8	34.3
8	7089.4	-5.0	-14.1	8.9
9	6861.2	3.0	3.8	8.6

SITC Legend

SITC Code	Description
Total	All commodities
0+1	Food, animals + beverages, tobacco
2+4	Crude materials + anim. & veg. oils
3	Mineral fuels, lubricants
5	Chemicals
6	Goods classified chiefly by material
7	Machinery and transport equipment
8	Miscellaneous manufactured articles
9	Not classified elsewhere in the SITC

Graph 4: Merchandise trade balance

(Bln US$ by MDG Regions in 2015)

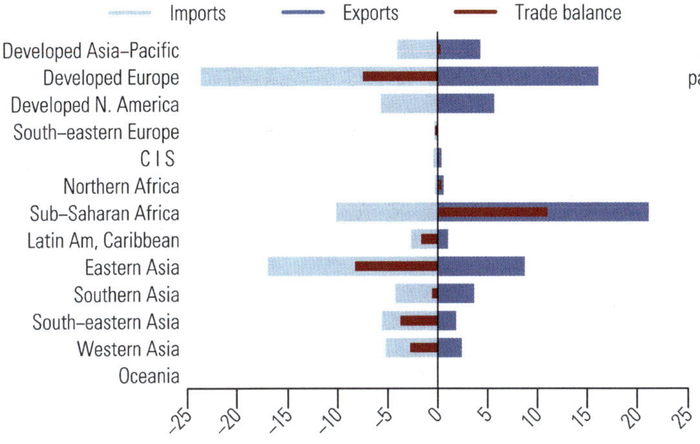

Graph 5: Partner concentration of merchandise trade

(Cumulative share by ranked partners in 2015)

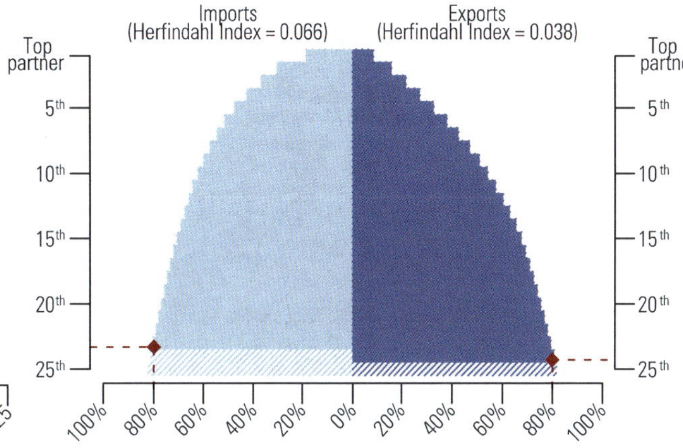

Graph 6: Imports of services by EBOPS category

(% share in 2014)

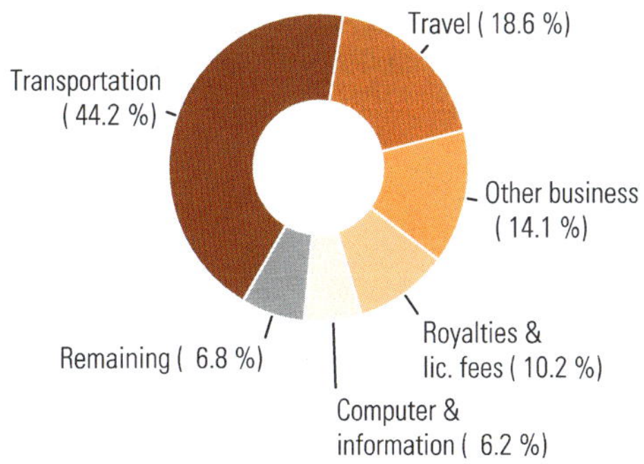

Imports Profile:

"Machinery and transport equipment" (SITC section 7), "Mineral fuels, lubricants" (SITC section 3) and "Chemicals" (SITC section 5) were the largest commodity groups for imports in 2015, representing respectively 34.3, 17.5 and 11.6 percent of imported goods (see table 3). From 2013 to 2015, the largest import commodity was "Petroleum oils and oils obtained from bituminous minerals, crude" (HS code 2709) (see table 4). The top three partners for merchandise imports were China, Germany and the United States, accounting for respectively 16.3, 10.6 and 6.5 percent of total imports. "Transportation" (EBOPS code 205) accounted for the largest share of imports of services in 2014 at 7.5 bln US$, followed by "Travel" (EBOPS code 236) at 3.2 bln US$ and "Other business services" (EBOPS code 268) at 2.4 bln US$ (see graph 6).

Table 4: Top 10 import commodities 2013 to 2015

HS code	4-digit heading of Harmonized System 2012	Value (million US$) 2013	2014	2015	Unit value 2013	2014	2015	Unit	SITC code
	All Commodities	103441.3	99892.7	79590.9					
2709	Petroleum oils and oils obtained from bituminous minerals, crude	14721.8	16212.1	8474.8	0.8	0.8	0.4	US$/kg	333
9999	Commodities not specified according to kind	6234.2	6607.9	6857.2					931
2710	Petroleum oils, other than crude	6433.1	5805.7	4263.0	*1.0*	*1.1*	*1.1*	US$/kg	334
8703	Motor cars and other motor vehicles principally designed for the transport	5494.3	4706.2	4037.7	*17.5*	14.8	13.2	thsd US$/unit	781
8517	Electrical apparatus for line telephony or line telegraphy	3404.3	3165.0	3126.9					764
8471	Automatic data processing machines and units thereof	2054.4	1978.9	1713.6		*156.0*	124.1	US$/unit	752
3004	Medicaments (excluding goods of heading 30.02, 30.05 or 30.06)	1812.0	1569.4	1433.9	*55.7*	*66.0*	52.4	US$/kg	542
8708	Parts and accessories of the motor vehicles of headings 87.01 to 87.05	1263.4	1300.3	1134.4	*9.1*	*8.8*	7.3	US$/kg	784
8704	Motor vehicles for the transport of goods	1241.0	1051.2	636.9		29.7	20.8	thsd US$/unit	782
8443	Printing machinery used for printing by means of the printing type, blocks	921.2	867.5	715.5					726

Spain

Goods Imports: CIF, by origin/consignment for intra-eu Goods Exports: FOB, by last known destination Trade System: Special

Overview:

In 2015, the value of merchandise exports of Spain decreased substantially by 12.7 percent to reach 278.1 bln US$, while its merchandise imports decreased substantially by 13.0 percent to reach 305.3 bln US$ (see graph 1, table 2 and table 3). The merchandise trade balance recorded a relatively small deficit of 27.1 bln US$ (see graph 1). The largest merchandise trade balance was with MDG Eastern Asia at -21.9 bln US$ (see graph 4). Merchandise exports in Spain were diversified amongst partners; imports were also diversified. The top 24 partners accounted for 80 percent or more of exports and 25 partners accounted for 80 percent or more of imports (see graph 5). In 2014, the value of exports of services of Spain increased moderately by 5.1 percent, reaching 132.9 bln US$, while its imports of services increased moderately by 8.4 percent and reached 68.5 bln US$ (see graph 2). There was a large trade in services surplus of 64.4 bln US$.

Graph 1: Total merchandise trade, by value

(Bln US$ by year)

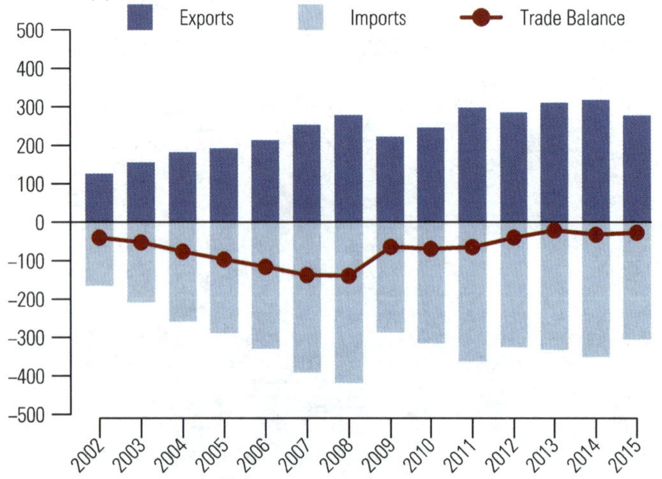

Graph 2: Total services trade, by value

(Bln US$ by year)

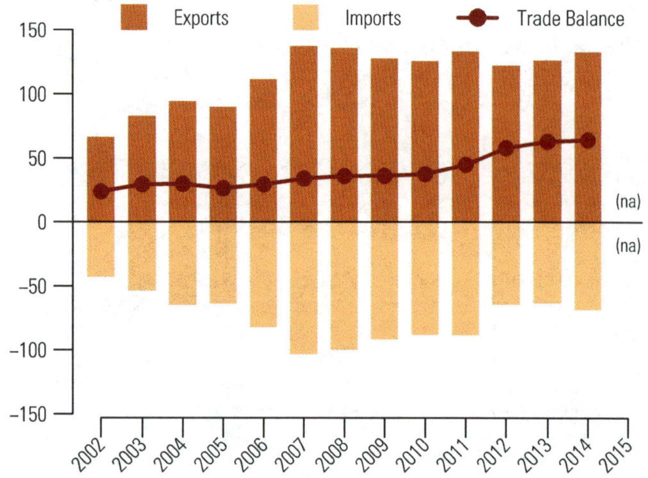

Exports Profile:

"Machinery and transport equipment" (SITC section 7), "Goods classified chiefly by material" (SITC section 6) and "Food, animals + beverages, tobacco" (SITC section 0+1) were the largest commodity groups for exports in 2015, representing respectively 33.9, 15.4 and 14.7 percent of exported goods (see table 2). From 2013 to 2015, the largest export commodity was "Motor cars and other motor vehicles principally designed for the transport" (HS code 8703) (see table 1). The top three destinations for merchandise exports were France, Germany and Portugal, accounting for respectively 15.7, 10.4 and 7.4 percent of total exports. "Travel" (EBOPS code 236) accounted for the largest share of exports of services in 2014 at 65.1 bln US$, followed by "Other business services" (EBOPS code 268) at 22.9 bln US$ and "Transportation" (EBOPS code 205) at 16.7 bln US$ (see graph 3).

Graph 3: Exports of services by EBOPS category

(% share in 2014)

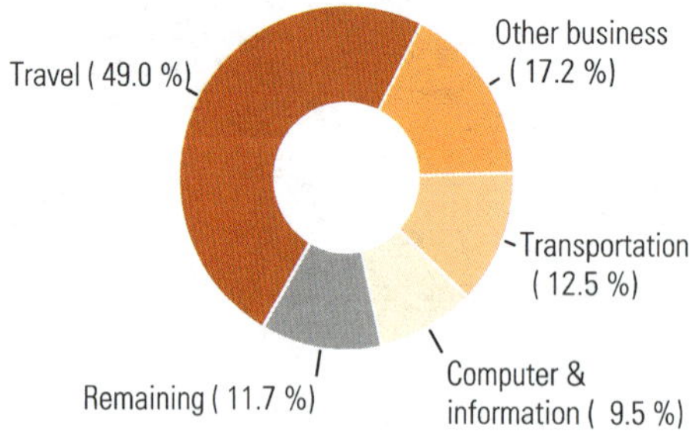

Table 1: Top 10 export commodities 2013 to 2015

HS code	4-digit heading of Harmonized System 2012	Value (million US$) 2013	2014	2015	Unit value 2013	2014	2015	Unit	SITC code
	All Commodities	310963.6	318649.3	278122.0					
8703	Motor cars and other motor vehicles principally designed for the transport	29175.6	31932.0	33131.2	13.5	*16.2*	*15.2*	thsd US$/unit	781
2710	Petroleum oils, other than crude	16541.9	14186.1	9528.9	0.9	0.8	0.5	US$/kg	334
9999	Commodities not specified according to kind	13109.6	12566.0	7842.7					931
8708	Parts and accessories of the motor vehicles of headings 87.01 to 87.05	10909.7	10712.3	9597.0	6.6	6.2	5.6	US$/kg	784
3004	Medicaments (excluding goods of heading 30.02, 30.05 or 30.06)	9555.2	8945.6	8208.3	51.3	49.1	37.3	US$/kg	542
8704	Motor vehicles for the transport of goods	5289.5	6113.7	4343.6	16.1	*20.2*		thsd US$/unit	782
0805	Citrus fruit, fresh or dried	3848.9	3820.3	3601.2	1.0	1.0	0.9	US$/kg	057
2204	Wine of fresh grapes, including fortified wines	3430.0	3401.3	2961.7			*1.2*	US$/litre	112
0203	Meat of swine, fresh, chilled or frozen	3170.6	3382.4	2998.2	3.2	3.1	2.4	US$/kg	012
1509	Olive oil and its fractions	2590.1	3621.1	2922.1	3.7	3.2	3.9	US$/kg	421

Services Imports and Exports: EBOPS 2002 categories

Table 2: Merchandise exports by SITC
(Value in million US$, growth and shares in percentage)

SITC	2015	Avg. Growth rates 2011-2015	Avg. Growth rates 2014-2015	2015 share
Total	278 122.0	-1.7	-12.7	100.0
0+1	40 856.1	1.6	-7.9	14.7
2+4	10 574.4	-3.9	-19.2	3.8
3	13 880.3	-11.0	-39.6	5.0
5	37 454.5	-0.7	-12.2	13.5
6	42 751.5	-4.2	-13.6	15.4
7	94 397.6	-1.0	-7.1	33.9
8	29 113.7	4.2	-4.5	10.5
9	9 094.0	-8.5	-34.7	3.3

Table 3: Merchandise imports by SITC
(Value in million US$, growth and shares in percentage)

SITC	2015	Avg. Growth rates 2011-2015	Avg. Growth rates 2014-2015	2015 share
Total	305 266.0	-4.2	-13.0	100.0
0+1	29 930.3	-3.0	-9.6	9.8
2+4	15 437.7	-6.5	-14.1	5.1
3	42 815.4	-13.8	-41.7	14.0
5	45 138.5	-2.1	-8.1	14.8
6	33 025.5	-4.9	-10.4	10.8
7	94 809.1	-0.3	-1.4	31.1
8	43 014.8	0.1	-0.9	14.1
9	1 094.6	-20.2	15.2	0.4

SITC Legend

SITC Code	Description
Total	All commodities
0+1	Food, animals + beverages, tobacco
2+4	Crude materials + anim. & veg. oils
3	Mineral fuels, lubricants
5	Chemicals
6	Goods classified chiefly by material
7	Machinery and transport equipment
8	Miscellaneous manufactured articles
9	Not classified elsewhere in the SITC

Graph 4: Merchandise trade balance
(Bln US$ by MDG Regions in 2015)

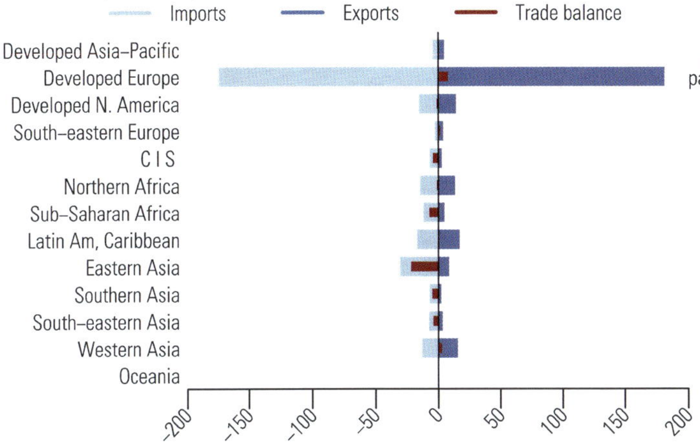

Graph 5: Partner concentration of merchandise trade
(Cumulative share by ranked partners in 2015)

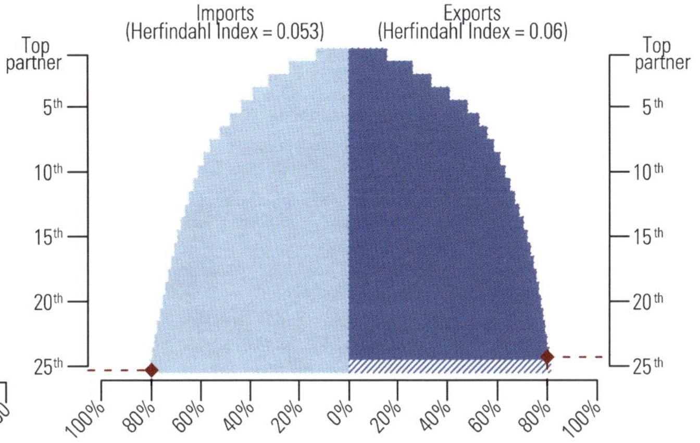

Graph 6: Imports of services by EBOPS category
(% share in 2014)

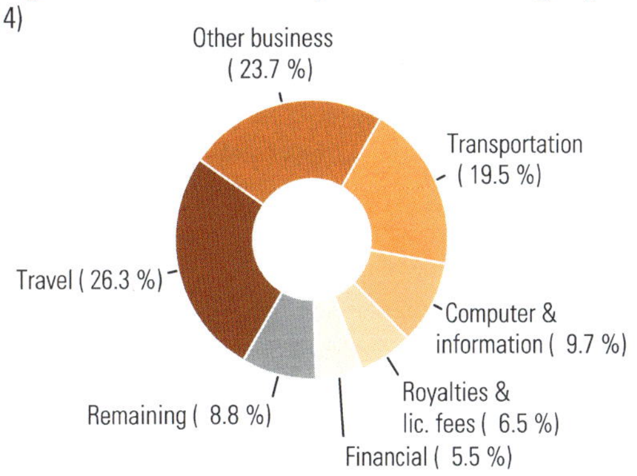

Imports Profile:

"Machinery and transport equipment" (SITC section 7), "Chemicals" (SITC section 5) and "Miscellaneous manufactured articles" (SITC section 8) were the largest commodity groups for imports in 2015, representing respectively 31.1, 14.8 and 14.1 percent of imported goods (see table 3). From 2013 to 2015, the largest import commodity was "Petroleum oils and oils obtained from bituminous minerals, crude" (HS code 2709) (see table 4). The top three partners for merchandise imports were Germany, France and China, accounting for respectively 12.1, 10.9 and 7.7 percent of total imports. "Travel" (EBOPS code 236) accounted for the largest share of imports of services in 2014 at 18.0 bln US$, followed by "Other business services" (EBOPS code 268) at 16.2 bln US$ and "Transportation" (EBOPS code 205) at 13.3 bln US$ (see graph 6).

Table 4: Top 10 import commodities 2013 to 2015

HS code	4-digit heading of Harmonized System 2012	Value (million US$) 2013	2014	2015	Unit value 2013	2014	2015	Unit	SITC code
	All Commodities	332 266.8	350 977.8	305 266.0					
2709	Petroleum oils and oils obtained from bituminous minerals, crude	45 308.1	44 262.0	24 769.2	0.8	0.7	0.4	US$/kg	333
8708	Parts and accessories of the motor vehicles of headings 87.01 to 87.05	17 275.3	19 697.4	17 150.7	5.9	8.8	7.4	US$/kg	784
8703	Motor cars and other motor vehicles principally designed for the transport	11 325.3	14 966.0	16 241.1	14.2	*5.3*	*19.0*	thsd US$/unit	781
2711	Petroleum gases and other gaseous hydrocarbons	14 268.5	14 081.2	8 674.0	0.5	0.5	0.4	US$/kg	343
3004	Medicaments (excluding goods of heading 30.02, 30.05 or 30.06)	11 153.6	11 445.3	11 165.2	90.3	91.2	74.7	US$/kg	542
2710	Petroleum oils, other than crude	13 948.4	12 481.5	6 971.4	0.8	0.7	0.4	US$/kg	334
8517	Electrical apparatus for line telephony or line telegraphy	5 320.9	5 752.2	5 616.9					764
8471	Automatic data processing machines and units thereof	3 669.3	3 699.9	3 255.4	127.5	*130.0*		US$/unit	752
2603	Copper ores and concentrates	3 076.7	3 245.8	2 593.7	2.0	1.8	1.5	US$/kg	283
6204	Women's or girls'suits, ensembles, jackets, blazers, dresses, skirts	2 524.1	2 784.2	2 919.7	8.9	*14.7*		US$/unit	842

Sri Lanka

Goods Imports: CIF, by origin	Goods Exports: FOB, by last known destination	Trade System: General

Overview:

In 2015, the value of merchandise exports of Sri Lanka decreased moderately by 7.6 percent to reach 10.4 bln US$, while its merchandise imports decreased slightly by 1.4 percent to reach 19.0 bln US$ (see graph 1, table 2 and table 3). The merchandise trade balance recorded a moderate deficit of 8.5 bln US$ (see graph 1). The largest merchandise trade balance was with MDG Eastern Asia at -4.3 bln US$ (see graph 4). Merchandise exports in Sri Lanka were diversified amongst partners; imports were also diversified. The top 21 partners accounted for 80 percent or more of exports and 14 partners accounted for 80 percent or more of imports (see graph 5). In 2014, the value of exports of services of Sri Lanka increased substantially by 19.6 percent, reaching 5.6 bln US$, while its imports of services increased moderately by 6.3 percent and reached 3.7 bln US$ (see graph 2). There was a moderate trade in services surplus of 1.9 bln US$.

Graph 1: Total merchandise trade, by value

(Bln US$ by year)

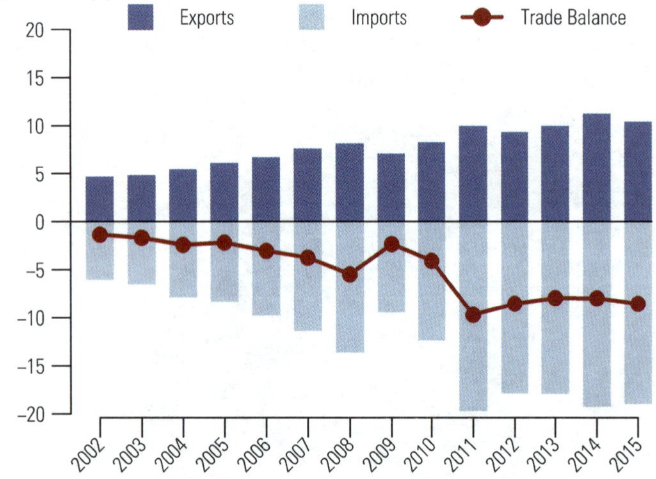

Graph 2: Total services trade, by value

(Bln US$ by year)

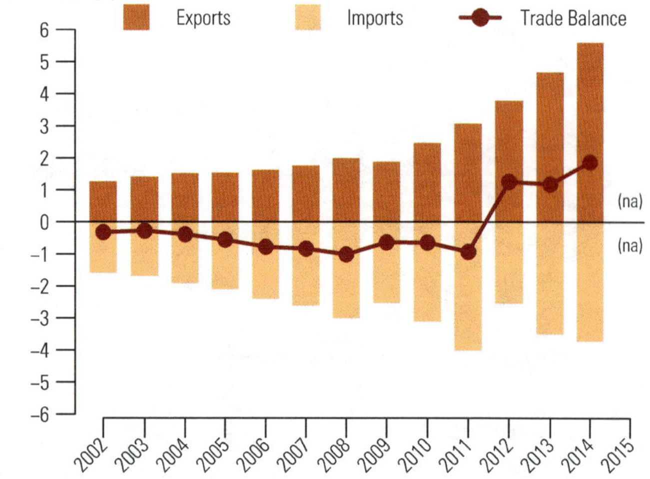

Exports Profile:

"Miscellaneous manufactured articles" (SITC section 8), "Food, animals + beverages, tobacco" (SITC section 0+1) and "Goods classified chiefly by material" (SITC section 6) were the largest commodity groups for exports in 2015, representing respectively 49.7, 23.9 and 12.6 percent of exported goods (see table 2). From 2013 to 2015, the largest export commodity was "Tea, whether or not flavoured" (HS code 0902) (see table 1). The top three destinations for merchandise exports were the United States, the United Kingdom and India, accounting for respectively 25.3, 10.2 and 6.3 percent of total exports. "Travel" (EBOPS code 236) accounted for the largest share of exports of services in 2014 at 2.4 bln US$, followed by "Transportation" (EBOPS code 205) at 1.9 bln US$ and "Computer and information services" (EBOPS code 262) at 627.9 mln US$ (see graph 3).

Graph 3: Exports of services by EBOPS category

(% share in 2014)

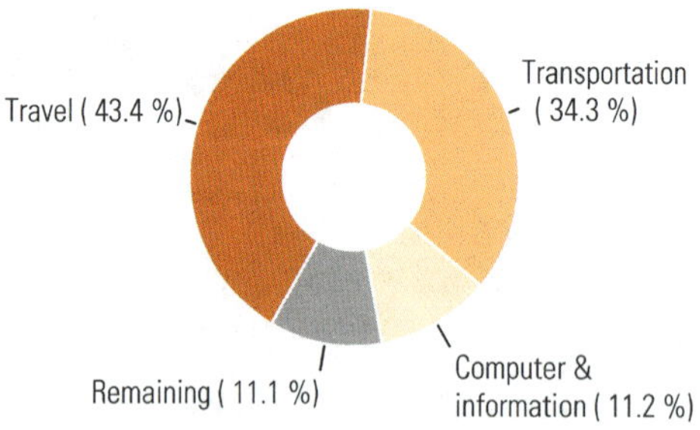

Table 1: Top 10 export commodities 2013 to 2015

HS code	4-digit heading of Harmonized System 2012	Value (million US$) 2013	2014	2015	Unit value 2013	2014	2015	Unit	SITC code
	All Commodities	10004.9	11295.5	10439.7					
0902	Tea, whether or not flavoured	1528.5	1609.3	1321.9	4.3	4.9	4.3	US$/kg	074
6108	Women's or girls'slips, petticoats, briefs, panties, knitted or crocheted	512.2	539.7	562.6		1.6	1.6	US$/unit	844
6204	Women's or girls'suits, ensembles, jackets, blazers, dresses, skirts	550.0	552.8	509.3		8.0	7.9	US$/unit	842
6212	Brassieres, girdles, corsets, braces, suspenders, garters	489.2	527.6	554.5	83.1	53.8	48.4	US$/kg	845
6109	T-shirts, singlets and other vests, knitted or crocheted	403.0	497.2	447.6	6.2	4.0	4.1	US$/unit	845
6104	Women's or girls'suits, ensembles, jackets, blazers, dresses, skirts	430.3	449.7	436.1		5.5	6.2	US$/unit	844
6203	Men's or boys'suits, ensembles, jackets, blazers, trousers	400.9	434.2	384.4		8.9	8.8	US$/unit	841
4012	Retreaded or used pneumatic tyres of rubber	347.8	356.6	301.6					625
6116	Gloves, mittens and mitts, knitted or crocheted	222.7	232.9	225.3	18.8	20.6	21.8	US$/kg	846
7102	Diamonds, whether or not worked, but not mounted or set	313.3	197.0	133.9					667

Services Imports and Exports: EBOPS 2002 categories

Table 2: Merchandise exports by SITC

(Value in million US$, growth and shares in percentage)

SITC	2015	Avg. Growth rates 2011-2015	Avg. Growth rates 2014-2015	2015 share
Total	10439.7	1.1	-7.6	100.0
0+1	2491.4	-0.7	-12.2	23.9
2+4	417.9	-2.0	4.2	4.0
3	184.5	43.0	-37.5	1.8
5	167.8	4.7	-1.4	1.6
6	1320.0	-4.1	-15.4	12.6
7	666.9	5.9	6.3	6.4
8	5191.1	2.4	-3.4	49.7
9	0.0	11.7	-100.0	0.0

Table 3: Merchandise imports by SITC

(Value in million US$, growth and shares in percentage)

SITC	2015	Avg. Growth rates 2011-2015	Avg. Growth rates 2014-2015	2015 share
Total	18967.2	-0.9	-1.4	100.0
0+1	2290.6	-0.1	-2.1	12.1
2+4	701.7	2.4	18.0	3.7
3	2652.9	-9.7	-39.7	14.0
5	2193.6	2.9	8.5	11.6
6	4931.5	0.6	0.1	26.0
7	5150.6	2.5	26.8	27.2
8	998.8	8.5	13.0	5.3
9	47.6	-47.1	128.2	0.3

SITC Legend

SITC Code	Description
Total	All commodities
0+1	Food, animals + beverages, tobacco
2+4	Crude materials + anim. & veg. oils
3	Mineral fuels, lubricants
5	Chemicals
6	Goods classified chiefly by material
7	Machinery and transport equipment
8	Miscellaneous manufactured articles
9	Not classified elsewhere in the SITC

Graph 4: Merchandise trade balance

(Bln US$ by MDG Regions in 2015)

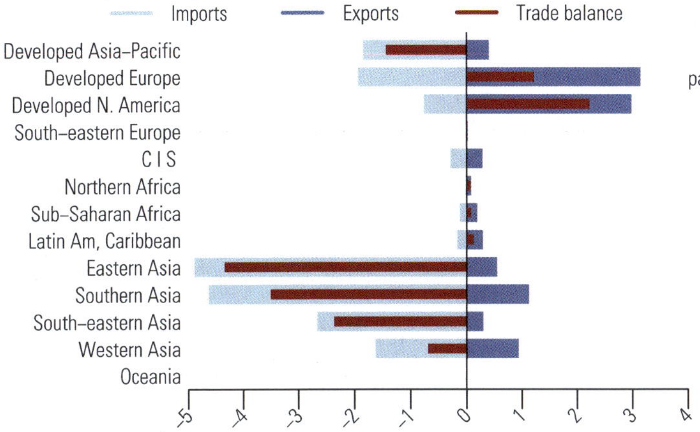

Graph 5: Partner concentration of merchandise trade

(Cumulative share by ranked partners in 2015)

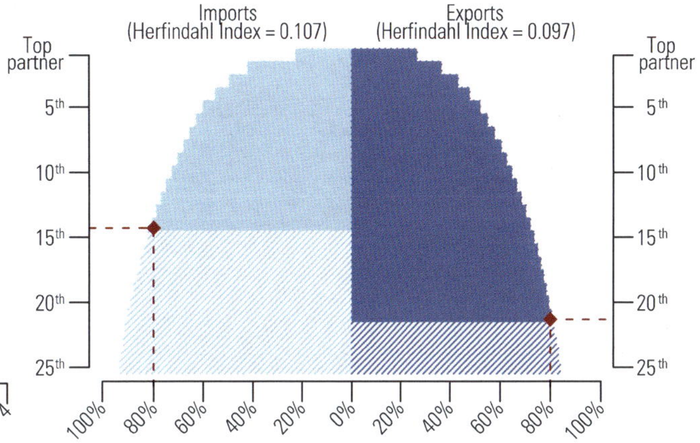

Graph 6: Imports of services by EBOPS category

(% share in 2014)

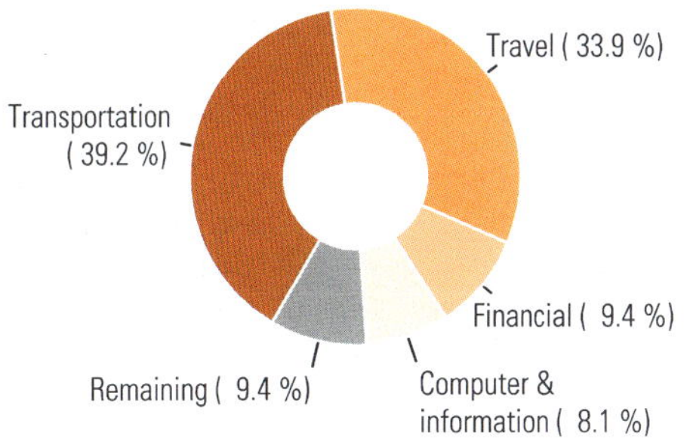

Imports Profile:

"Machinery and transport equipment" (SITC section 7), "Goods classified chiefly by material" (SITC section 6) and "Mineral fuels, lubricants" (SITC section 3) were the largest commodity groups for imports in 2015, representing respectively 27.2, 26.0 and 14.0 percent of imported goods (see table 3). From 2013 to 2015, the largest import commodity was "Petroleum oils, other than crude" (HS code 2710) (see table 4). The top three partners for merchandise imports were India, China and the United Arab Emirates, accounting for respectively 20.3, 18.0 and 7.2 percent of total imports. "Transportation" (EBOPS code 205) accounted for the largest share of imports of services in 2014 at 1.5 bln US$, followed by "Travel" (EBOPS code 236) at 1.3 bln US$ and "Financial services" (EBOPS code 260) at 349.6 mln US$ (see graph 6).

Table 4: Top 10 import commodities 2013 to 2015

HS code	4-digit heading of Harmonized System 2012	Value (million US$) 2013	2014	2015	Unit value 2013	2014	2015	Unit	SITC code
	All Commodities	17930.8	19244.5	18967.2					
2710	Petroleum oils, other than crude	2396.3	2592.0	1509.3		0.9	0.5	US$/kg	334
2709	Petroleum oils and oils obtained from bituminous minerals, crude	1344.2	1337.7	754.4		0.8	0.4	US$/kg	333
8703	Motor cars and other motor vehicles principally designed for the transport	593.1	800.7	1286.3	*12.7*	6.5	5.5	thsd US$/unit	781
6006	Other knitted or crocheted fabrics	499.8	566.6	550.3	*10.5*	9.0	8.6	US$/kg	655
2523	Portland cement, aluminous cement, slag cement	520.7	511.7	486.7		0.1	0.1	US$/kg	661
1001	Wheat and meslin	324.2	370.9	330.6	*0.3*	0.3	0.3	US$/kg	041
3004	Medicaments (excluding goods of heading 30.02, 30.05 or 30.06)	294.2	295.9	356.3		16.6	19.1	US$/kg	542
8517	Electrical apparatus for line telephony or line telegraphy	287.9	267.4	386.0					764
0402	Milk and cream, concentrated or containing added sugar	277.2	324.7	234.0	*3.7*	*4.8*	2.9	US$/kg	022
1701	Cane or beet sugar and chemically pure sucrose, in solid form	281.2	247.7	243.4	*0.8*	0.5	0.4	US$/kg	061

State of Palestine

Goods Imports: CIF, by origin	Goods Exports: FOB, by last known destination	Trade System: General

Overview:

In 2014, the value of merchandise exports of the State of Palestine increased slightly by 4.8 percent to reach 943.7 mln US$, while its merchandise imports increased substantially by 10.1 percent to reach 5.7 bln US$ (see graph 1, table 2 and table 3). The merchandise trade balance recorded a large deficit of 4.7 bln US$ (see graph 1). The largest merchandise trade balance was with MDG Western Asia at -3.6 bln US$ (see graph 4). Merchandise exports in the State of Palestine were highly concentrated amongst partners; imports were also highly concentrated. The top 1 partner accounted for 80 percent or more of exports and 3 partners accounted for 80 percent or more of imports (see graph 5). In 2013, the value of exports of services of the State of Palestine increased slightly by 0.2 percent, reaching 938.1 mln US$, while its imports of services decreased substantially by 17.5 percent and reached 987.6 mln US$ (see graph 2). There was a relatively small trade in services deficit of 49.5 mln US$.

Graph 1: Total merchandise trade, by value

(Bln US$ by year)

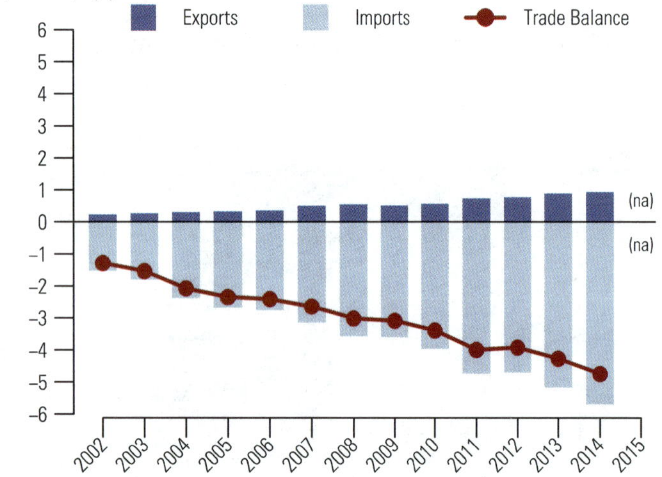

Graph 2: Total services trade, by value

(Bln US$ by year)

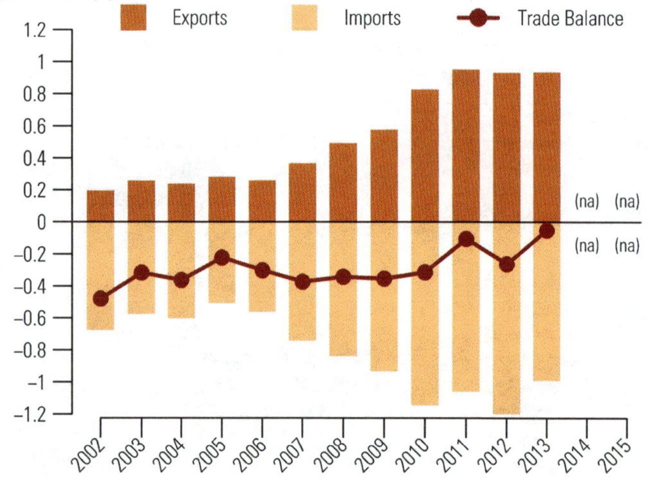

Exports Profile:

"Goods classified chiefly by material" (SITC section 6), "Miscellaneous manufactured articles" (SITC section 8) and "Food, animals + beverages, tobacco" (SITC section 0+1) were the largest commodity groups for exports in 2014, representing respectively 34.8, 23.8 and 20.4 percent of exported goods (see table 2). From 2012 to 2014, the largest export commodity was "Worked monumental or building stone (except slate) and articles thereof" (HS code 6802) (see table 1). The top three destinations for merchandise exports were Israel, Jordan and the United Arab Emirates, accounting for respectively 84.4, 6.9 and 1.4 percent of total exports. "Travel" (EBOPS code 236) accounted for the largest share of exports of services in 2013 at 788.5 mln US$, followed by "Construction services" (EBOPS code 249) at 57.7 mln US$ (see graph 3).

Graph 3: Exports of services by EBOPS category

(% share in 2013)

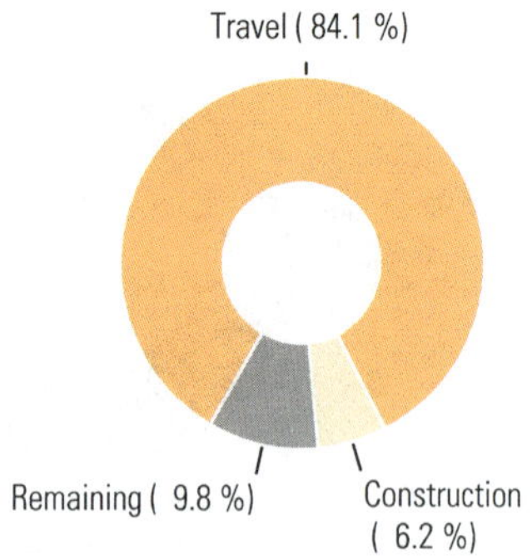

Table 1: Top 10 export commodities 2012 to 2014

HS code	4-digit heading of Harmonized System 2007	Value (million US$)			Unit value				SITC code
		2012	2013	2014	2012	2013	2014	Unit	
	All Commodities	782.4	900.6	943.7					
6802	Worked monumental or building stone (except slate) and articles thereof	124.0	131.8	176.3	*0.8*	*0.8*	*0.7*	US$/kg	661
7204	Ferrous waste and scrap; remelting scrap ingots of iron or steel	49.9	41.8	36.4	*0.4*	*0.4*	*0.3*	US$/kg	282
9403	Other furniture and parts thereof	30.6	40.7	49.0					821
3923	Articles for the conveyance or packing of goods, of plastics	32.3	40.1	44.8	*3.8*	*3.6*	*3.6*	US$/kg	893
2402	Cigars, cheroots, cigarillos and cigarettes	28.8	35.4	36.6		*14.4*	*14.7*	US$/kg	122
9404	Mattress supports; articles of bedding and similar furnishing	17.2	20.0	31.0					821
1211	Plants and parts of plants (including seeds and fruits)	8.1	52.4	3.4	*4.4*	*4.1*	*4.3*	US$/kg	292
9401	Seats (other than those of heading 94.02)	15.8	21.3	21.7					821
1509	Olive oil and its fractions	23.0	8.8	24.7	*4.2*	*4.0*	*4.5*	US$/kg	421
6404	Footwear with outer soles of rubber, plastics, leather	5.4	6.9	38.4					851

State of Palestine

Services Imports and Exports: EBOPS 2002 categories

Table 2: Merchandise exports by SITC

(Value in million US$, growth and shares in percentage)

SITC	2014	Avg. Growth rates 2010-2014	Avg. Growth rates 2013-2014	2014 share
Total	943.7	13.2	4.8	100.0
0+1	192.2	16.6	3.7	20.4
2+4	111.4	6.5	-27.0	11.8
3	2.2	9.5	2.3	0.2
5	46.9	0.5	-5.4	5.0
6	328.8	14.7	17.4	34.8
7	37.6	4.3	-6.3	4.0
8	224.7	18.7	17.7	23.8

Table 3: Merchandise imports by SITC

(Value in million US$, growth and shares in percentage)

SITC	2014	Avg. Growth rates 2010-2014	Avg. Growth rates 2013-2014	2014 share
Total	5683.2	9.5	10.1	100.0
0+1	1322.2	11.3	6.2	23.3
2+4	113.3	7.7	20.7	2.0
3	1868.9	10.8	16.0	32.9
5	491.0	10.8	9.1	8.6
6	889.3	6.7	-0.5	15.6
7	706.6	6.8	12.1	12.4
8	291.9	8.4	21.5	5.1
9	0.0	-81.7	-71.5	0.0

SITC Legend

SITC Code	Description
Total	All commodities
0+1	Food, animals + beverages, tobacco
2+4	Crude materials + anim. & veg. oils
3	Mineral fuels, lubricants
5	Chemicals
6	Goods classified chiefly by material
7	Machinery and transport equipment
8	Miscellaneous manufactured articles
9	Not classified elsewhere in the SITC

Graph 4: Merchandise trade balance

(Bln US$ by MDG Regions in 2014)

Graph 5: Partner concentration of merchandise trade

(Cumulative share by ranked partners in 2014)

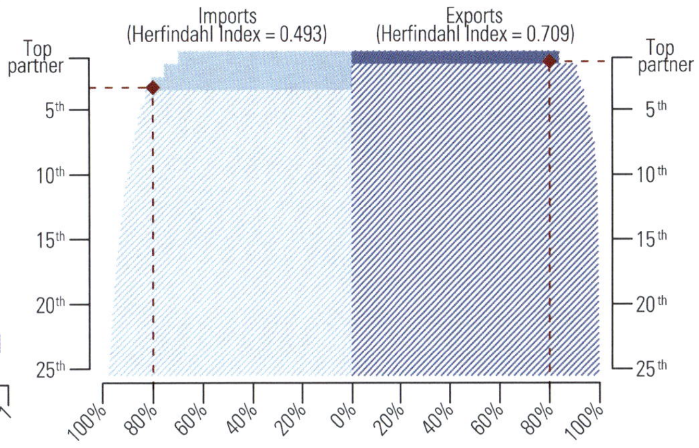

Graph 6: Imports of services by EBOPS category

(% share in 2013)

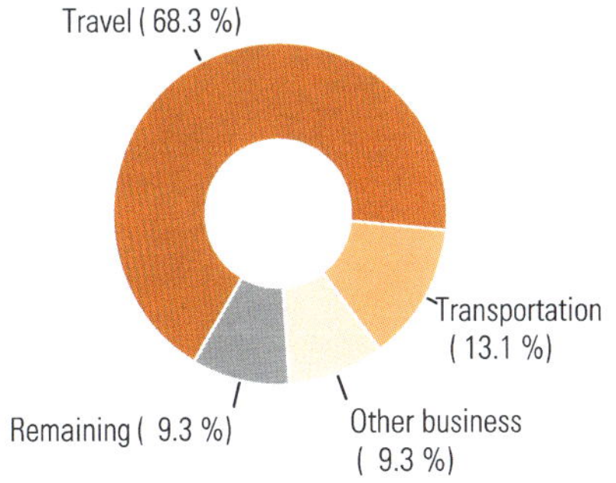

Imports Profile:

"Mineral fuels, lubricants" (SITC section 3), "Food, animals + beverages, tobacco" (SITC section 0+1) and "Goods classified chiefly by material" (SITC section 6) were the largest commodity groups for imports in 2014, representing respectively 32.9, 23.3 and 15.6 percent of imported goods (see table 3). From 2012 to 2014, the largest import commodity was "Petroleum oils, other than crude" (HS code 2710) (see table 4). The top three partners for merchandise imports were Israel, Turkey and China, accounting for respectively 70.8, 5.5 and 4.6 percent of total imports. "Travel" (EBOPS code 236) accounted for the largest share of imports of services in 2013 at 674.2 mln US$, followed by "Transportation" (EBOPS code 205) at 129.3 mln US$ and "Other business services" (EBOPS code 268) at 91.9 mln US$ (see graph 6).

Table 4: Top 10 import commodities 2012 to 2014

HS code	4-digit heading of Harmonized System 2007	Value (million US$) 2012	Value (million US$) 2013	Value (million US$) 2014	Unit value 2012	Unit value 2013	Unit value 2014	Unit	SITC code
	All Commodities	4697.4	5163.9	5683.2					
2710	Petroleum oils, other than crude	805.7	874.7	1009.3					334
2716	Electrical energy	464.0	504.6	625.7	*70.2*	*66.1*	*60.6*	US$/MWh	351
2711	Petroleum gases and other gaseous hydrocarbons	155.0	202.3	215.4	*0.5*		*0.8*	US$/kg	343
2523	Portland cement, aluminous cement, slag cement	161.4	134.6	158.7					661
2309	Preparations of a kind used in animal feeding	86.8	92.5	159.8	*1.7*	*1.6*	*1.7*	US$/kg	081
8703	Motor cars and other motor vehicles principally designed for the transport	102.4	96.2	118.4	*15.0*	*13.4*	*13.5*	thsd US$/unit	781
3004	Medicaments (excluding goods of heading 30.02, 30.05 or 30.06)	83.7	96.6	93.1					542
0102	Live bovine animals	77.0	72.0	73.7	*1.0*	*1.1*	*1.2*	thsd US$/unit	001
1101	Wheat or meslin flour	50.6	72.1	84.0	*0.6*	*0.6*	*0.6*	US$/kg	046
2202	Waters with added sugar	59.7	72.7	72.7	*1.2*	*1.2*	*1.2*	US$/litre	111

Sudan

Goods Imports: CIF, by origin **Goods Exports: FOB, by last known destination** **Trade System: General**

Overview:

In 2012, the value of merchandise exports of the Sudan decreased substantially by 62.3 percent to reach 3.4 bln US$, while its merchandise imports decreased substantially by 31.1 percent to reach 6.6 bln US$ (see graph 1, table 2 and table 3). The merchandise trade balance recorded a large deficit of 3.2 bln US$ (see graph 1). The largest merchandise trade balance was with MDG Eastern Asia at -1.2 bln US$ (see graph 4). Merchandise exports in the Sudan were highly concentrated amongst partners; imports were diversified. The top 3 partners accounted for 80 percent or more of exports and 19 partners accounted for 80 percent or more of imports (see graph 5). In 2014, the value of exports of services of the Sudan increased substantially by 15.8 percent, reaching 1.5 bln US$, while its imports of services increased slightly by 1.7 percent and reached 2.1 bln US$ (see graph 2). There was a moderate trade in services deficit of 606.9 mln US$. See footnote*.

Graph 1: Total merchandise trade, by value

(Bln US$ by year)

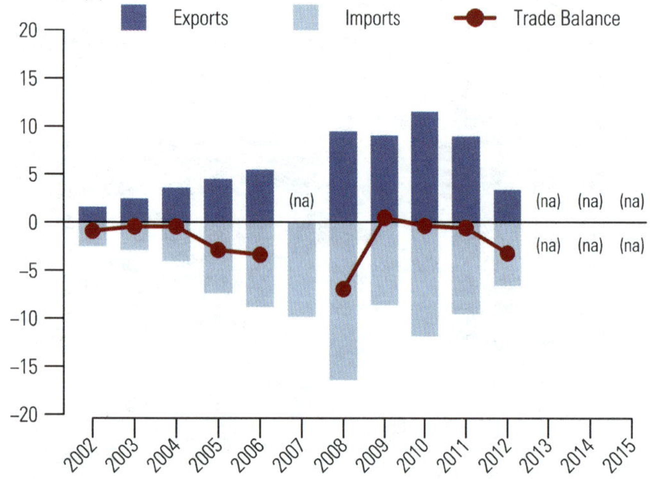

Graph 2: Total services trade, by value

(Bln US$ by year)

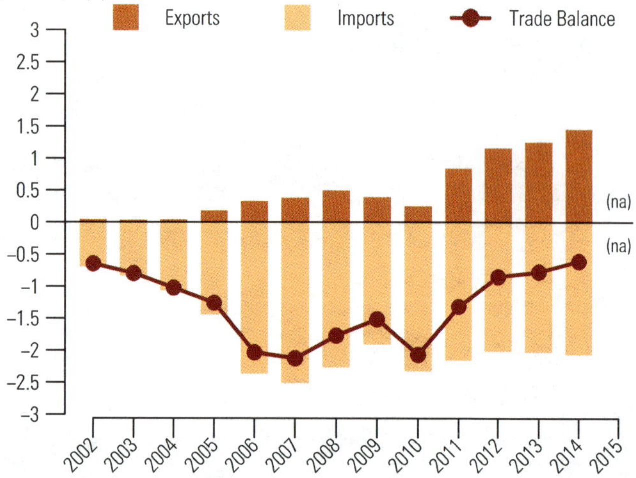

Exports Profile:

"Not classified elsewhere in the SITC" (SITC section 9), "Food, animals + beverages, tobacco" (SITC section 0+1) and "Crude materials + anim. & veg. oils" (SITC section 2+4) were the largest commodity groups for exports in 2012, representing respectively 64.1, 15.3 and 9.3 percent of exported goods (see table 2). From 2010 to 2012, the largest export commodity was "Petroleum oils and oils obtained from bituminous minerals, crude" (HS code 2709) (see table 1). The top three destinations for merchandise exports were China, the United Arab Emirates and Areas nes, accounting for respectively 62.0, 17.0 and 5.0 percent of total exports. "Travel" (EBOPS code 236) accounted for the largest share of exports of services in 2014 at 967.1 mln US$, followed by "Transportation" (EBOPS code 205) at 305.0 mln US$ and "Other business services" (EBOPS code 268) at 121.9 mln US$ (see graph 3).

Graph 3: Exports of services by EBOPS category

(% share in 2014)

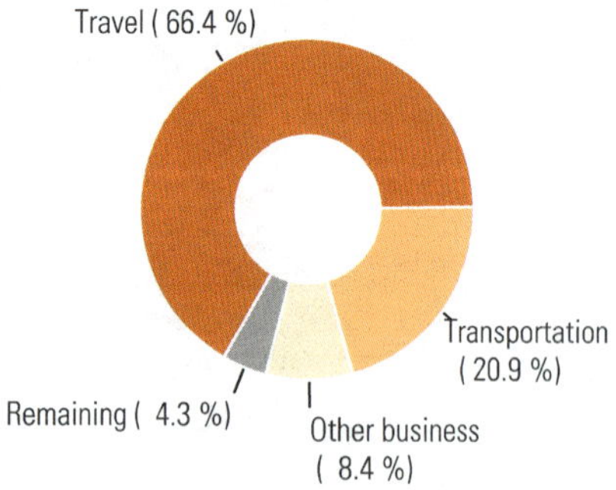

Table 1: Top 10 export commodities 2010 to 2012

HS code	4-digit heading of Harmonized System 2007	Value (million US$) 2010	2011	2012	Unit value 2010	2011	2012	Unit	SITC code
	All Commodities	11 529.3	8 981.7	3 383.9					
2709	Petroleum oils and oils obtained from bituminous minerals, crude	9 683.5	7 200.6	145.2	0.9	1.6	*0.5*	US$/kg	333
7108	Gold (including gold plated with platinum)	1 160.3	827.9	2 167.4	39.1	61.8	*49.6*	thsd US$/kg	971
0104	Live sheep and goats	130.6	257.6	284.1	228.1			US$/unit	001
1207	Other oil seeds and oleaginous fruits, whether or not broken	199.8	193.6	191.9	1.1	1.0	1.0	US$/kg	222
2710	Petroleum oils, other than crude	98.6	205.6	0.1	0.5	1.0	0.2	US$/kg	334
1301	Lac; natural gums, resins, gum-resins and oleoresins (for example, balsams)	67.8	69.8	65.4	1.3	1.4		US$/kg	292
2707	Oils and other products of high temperature coal tar	...	0.1	110.8			*1.2*	US$/kg	335
0102	Live bovine animals	2.1	4.1	85.8					001
5201	Cotton, not carded or combed	39.5	26.0	21.1	1.6	3.7	6.5	US$/kg	263
0204	Meat of sheep or goats, fresh, chilled or frozen	29.6	18.0	27.8	6.7	3.9	*6.0*	US$/kg	012

*Data up to 2011 refer to former Sudan (including South Sudan) and data beginning 2012 is attributed to Sudan without South Sudan.

Services Imports and Exports: EBOPS 2002 categories

Table 2: Merchandise exports by SITC

(Value in million US$, growth and shares in percentage)

SITC	2012	Avg. Growth rates 2008-2012	Avg. Growth rates 2011-2012	2012 share
Total	3383.9	-22.7	-62.3	100.0
0+1	519.1	42.4	41.4	15.3
2+4	314.4	-4.1	-6.2	9.3
3	256.1	-58.9	-96.5	7.6
5	78.5	190.9	653.0	2.3
6	36.0	6.7	24.4	1.1
7	5.9	-35.1	27.3	0.2
8	4.5	10.4	504.4	0.1
9	2169.3	409.4	161.9	64.1

Table 3: Merchandise imports by SITC

(Value in million US$, growth and shares in percentage)

SITC	2012	Avg. Growth rates 2008-2012	Avg. Growth rates 2011-2012	2012 share
Total	6580.6	-20.4	-31.1	100.0
0+1	940.7	-5.7	-40.9	14.3
2+4	269.0	35.0	-46.2	4.1
3	563.4	150.5	-40.4	8.6
5	797.6	19.2	-34.9	12.1
6	1152.5	-3.9	-21.1	17.5
7	1873.6	-32.0	-39.7	28.5
8	622.5	-1.2	-9.4	9.5
9	361.4	-45.0	1226.2	5.5

SITC Legend

SITC Code	Description
Total	All commodities
0+1	Food, animals + beverages, tobacco
2+4	Crude materials + anim. & veg. oils
3	Mineral fuels, lubricants
5	Chemicals
6	Goods classified chiefly by material
7	Machinery and transport equipment
8	Miscellaneous manufactured articles
9	Not classified elsewhere in the SITC

Graph 4: Merchandise trade balance

(Bln US$ by MDG Regions in 2012)

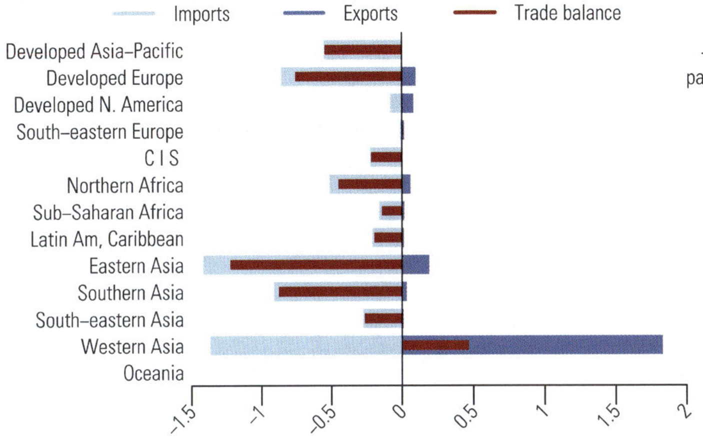

Graph 5: Partner concentration of merchandise trade

(Cumulative share by ranked partners in 2012)

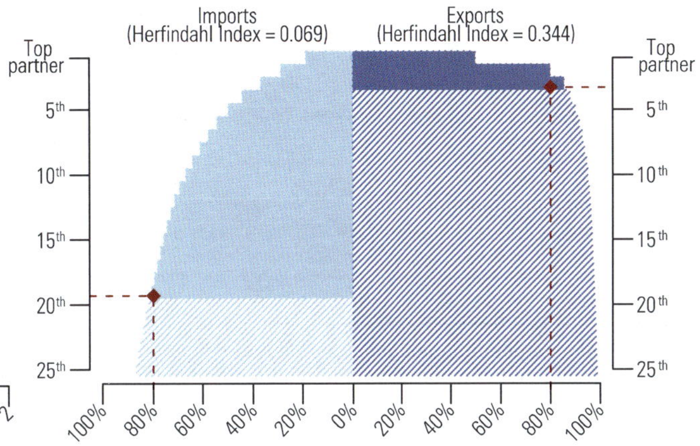

Graph 6: Imports of services by EBOPS category

(% share in 2014)

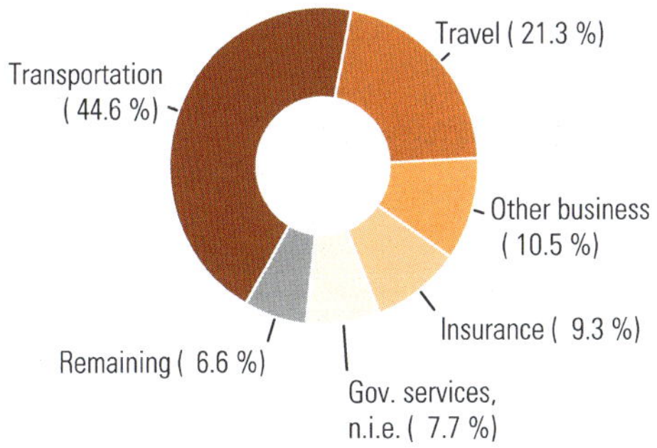

Imports Profile:

"Machinery and transport equipment" (SITC section 7), "Goods classified chiefly by material" (SITC section 6) and "Food, animals + beverages, tobacco" (SITC section 0+1) were the largest commodity groups for imports in 2012, representing respectively 28.5, 17.5 and 14.3 percent of imported goods (see table 3). From 2010 to 2012, the largest import commodity was "Petroleum oils, other than crude" (HS code 2710) (see table 4). The top three partners for merchandise imports were China, the United Arab Emirates and Saudi Arabia, accounting for respectively 19.2, 9.2 and 7.1 percent of total imports. "Transportation" (EBOPS code 205) accounted for the largest share of imports of services in 2014 at 921.1 mln US$, followed by "Travel" (EBOPS code 236) at 438.7 mln US$ and "Other business services" (EBOPS code 268) at 217.0 mln US$ (see graph 6).

Table 4: Top 10 import commodities 2010 to 2012

HS code	4-digit heading of Harmonized System 2007	Value (million US$) 2010	Value (million US$) 2011	Value (million US$) 2012	Unit value 2010	Unit value 2011	Unit value 2012	Unit	SITC code
	All Commodities	11874.8	9546.3	6580.6					
2710	Petroleum oils, other than crude	697.4	821.7	378.9	1.2	1.1	1.0	US$/kg	334
1001	Wheat and meslin	1290.1	580.1	0.0	1.0	0.4	0.3	US$/kg	041
1701	Cane or beet sugar and chemically pure sucrose, in solid form	388.4	409.3	443.6	0.5	0.9	0.8	US$/kg	061
8703	Motor cars and other motor vehicles principally designed for the transport	371.3	308.6	197.5			*9.6*	thsd US$/unit	781
8704	Motor vehicles for the transport of goods	393.7	331.6	121.8	*2.0*	*2.3*		thsd US$/unit	782
8517	Electrical apparatus for line telephony or line telegraphy	244.6	228.0	166.6					764
8708	Parts and accessories of the motor vehicles of headings 87.01 to 87.05	365.9	162.4	95.7	9.9	4.3	2.4	US$/kg	784
3003	Medicaments (excluding goods of heading 30.02, 30.05 or 30.06)	239.6	157.6	177.1	15.1	9.6	52.6	US$/kg	542
1513	Coconut (copra), palm kernel or babassu oil	509.6	7.2	2.8		0.9	1.1	US$/kg	422
2714	Bitumen and asphalt, natural	10.5	323.9	171.0	0.4	5.9	1.0	US$/kg	278

Suriname

Goods Imports: CIF, by origin | **Goods Exports: FOB, by last known destination** | **Trade System: General**

Overview:

In 2014, the value of merchandise exports of Suriname decreased substantially by 13.0 percent to reach 1.9 bln US$, while its merchandise imports decreased substantially by 20.9 percent to reach 1.8 bln US$ (see graph 1, table 2 and table 3). The merchandise trade balance recorded a relatively small surplus of 90.9 mln US$ (see graph 1). The largest merchandise trade balance was with MDG Western Asia at 413.8 mln US$ (see graph 4). Merchandise exports in Suriname were diversified amongst partners; imports were also diversified. The top 6 partners accounted for 80 percent or more of exports and 10 partners accounted for 80 percent or more of imports (see graph 5). In 2014, the value of exports of services of Suriname increased substantially by 18.0 percent, reaching 210.7 mln US$, while its imports of services increased substantially by 36.6 percent and reached 739.9 mln US$ (see graph 2). There was a large trade in services deficit of 529.2 mln US$.

Graph 1: Total merchandise trade, by value

(Bln US$ by year)

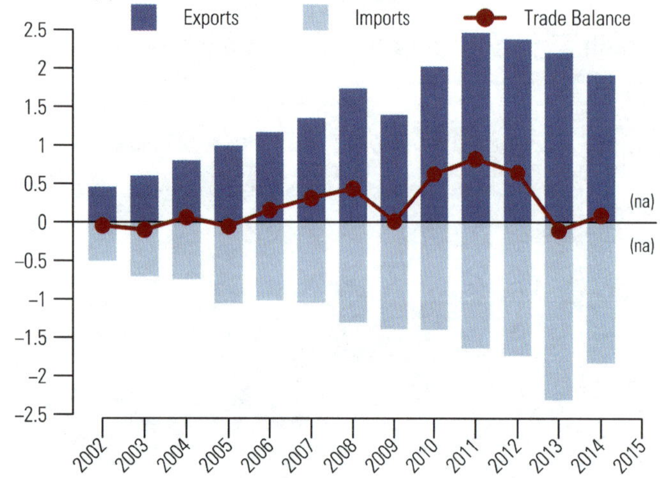

Graph 2: Total services trade, by value

(Mln US$ by year)

Exports Profile:

"Not classified elsewhere in the SITC" (SITC section 9), "Mineral fuels, lubricants" (SITC section 3) and "Food, animals + beverages, tobacco" (SITC section 0+1) were the largest commodity groups for exports in 2014, representing respectively 78.6, 10.5 and 5.2 percent of exported goods (see table 2). From 2012 to 2014, the largest export commodity was "Commodities not specified according to kind" (HS code 9999) (see table 1). The top three destinations for merchandise exports were the United Arab Emirates, Switzerland and the United States, accounting for respectively 30.3, 19.8 and 14.7 percent of total exports. "Travel" (EBOPS code 236) accounted for the largest share of exports of services in 2014 at 95.2 mln US$, followed by "Other business services" (EBOPS code 268) at 53.1 mln US$ and "Transportation" (EBOPS code 205) at 37.5 mln US$ (see graph 3).

Graph 3: Exports of services by EBOPS category

(% share in 2014)

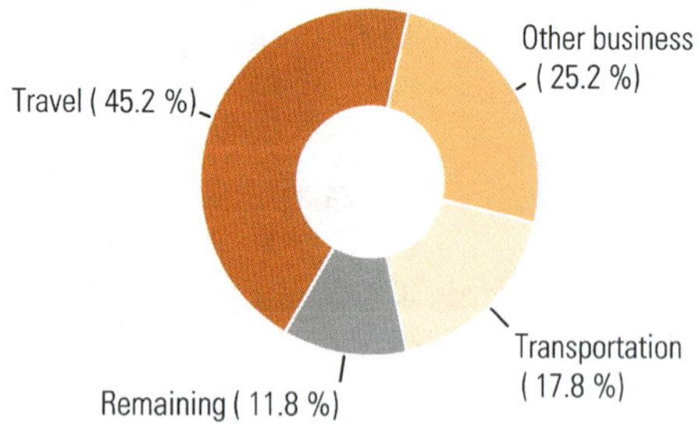

Table 1: Top 10 export commodities 2012 to 2014

HS code	4-digit heading of Harmonized System 2007	Value (million US$) 2012	2013	2014	Unit value 2012	2013	2014	Unit	SITC code
	All Commodities	2380.5	2204.4	1917.7					
9999	Commodities not specified according to kind	2058.9	1857.7	1508.0					931
2710	Petroleum oils, other than crude	128.6	183.5	199.8	0.7	0.7	0.6	US$/kg	334
1006	Rice	68.2	39.6	51.3	0.9	0.5	0.5	US$/kg	042
4403	Wood in the rough, whether or not stripped of bark or sapwood	13.1	12.5	18.3					247
2208	Alcohol of a strength by volume of less than 80 % vol	9.5	14.2	15.0	*5.4*	*6.2*	*6.0*	US$/litre	112
2402	Cigars, cheroots, cigarillos and cigarettes	5.5	7.4	11.3	4.6	3.5	4.8	US$/kg	122
2202	Waters with added sugar	12.1	5.5	6.3	*0.8*	*0.5*	*0.6*	US$/litre	111
7204	Ferrous waste and scrap; remelting scrap ingots of iron or steel	6.2	4.7	3.1	0.1	0.1	0.1	US$/kg	282
8431	Parts suitable for use principally with the machinery of headings 84.25	7.5	2.1	2.6	20.2	7.3	10.5	US$/kg	723
4409	Wood (including strips and friezes for parquet flooring, not assembled)	2.6	4.0	5.5		0.2	0.2	US$/kg	248

Services Imports and Exports: EBOPS 2002 categories

Table 2: Merchandise exports by SITC

(Value in million US$, growth and shares in percentage)

SITC	2014	Avg. Growth rates 2010-2014	2013-2014	2014 share
Total	1 917.7	-1.4	-13.0	100.0
0+1	100.6	19.9	33.2	5.2
2+4	38.6	27.0	32.8	2.0
3	200.5	-6.6	8.4	10.5
5	6.1	13.6	-23.5	0.3
6	8.3	12.6	22.1	0.4
7	29.8	8.7	7.5	1.6
8	25.9	30.0	75.1	1.4
9	1 508.0	-2.4	-18.8	78.6

Table 3: Merchandise imports by SITC

(Value in million US$, growth and shares in percentage)

SITC	2014	Avg. Growth rates 2010-2014	2013-2014	2014 share
Total	1 826.7	6.9	-20.9	100.0
0+1	231.4	4.5	-4.2	12.7
2+4	27.3	-7.2	4.5	1.5
3	383.6	9.8	-23.5	21.0
5	201.8	5.6	-2.5	11.0
6	262.4	4.5	-13.2	14.4
7	587.3	10.7	-31.8	32.2
8	121.8	-0.1	-22.0	6.7
9	11.1	13.2	-17.6	0.6

SITC Legend

SITC Code	Description
Total	All commodities
0+1	Food, animals + beverages, tobacco
2+4	Crude materials + anim. & veg. oils
3	Mineral fuels, lubricants
5	Chemicals
6	Goods classified chiefly by material
7	Machinery and transport equipment
8	Miscellaneous manufactured articles
9	Not classified elsewhere in the SITC

Graph 4: Merchandise trade balance

(Mln US$ by MDG Regions in 2014)

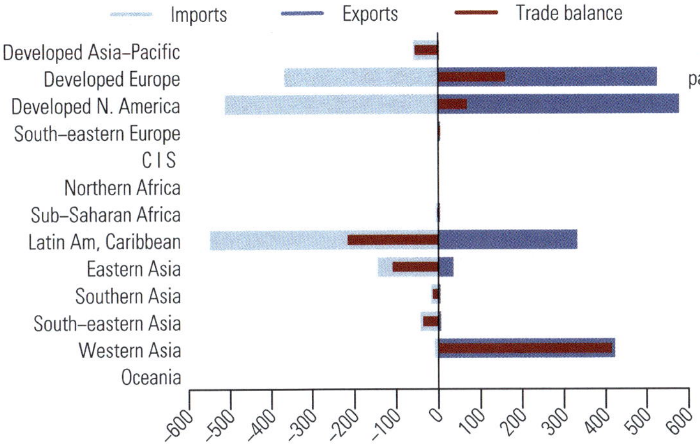

Graph 5: Partner concentration of merchandise trade

(Cumulative share by ranked partners in 2014)

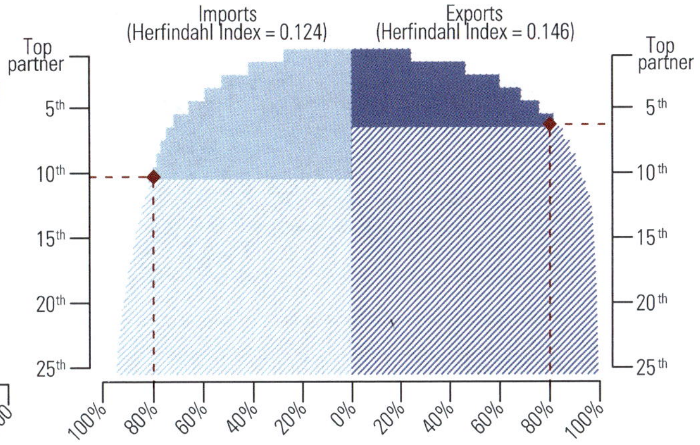

Graph 6: Imports of services by EBOPS category

(% share in 2014)

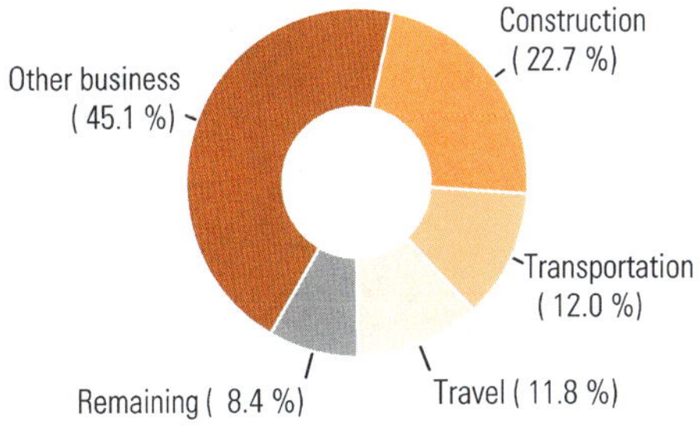

Imports Profile:

"Machinery and transport equipment" (SITC section 7), "Mineral fuels, lubricants" (SITC section 3) and "Goods classified chiefly by material" (SITC section 6) were the largest commodity groups for imports in 2014, representing respectively 32.2, 21.0 and 14.4 percent of imported goods (see table 3). From 2012 to 2014, the largest import commodity was "Petroleum oils, other than crude" (HS code 2710) (see table 4). The top three partners for merchandise imports were the United States, Trinidad and Tobago and the Netherlands, accounting for respectively 24.3, 15.6 and 15.3 percent of total imports. "Other business services" (EBOPS code 268) accounted for the largest share of imports of services in 2014 at 333.6 mln US$, followed by "Construction services" (EBOPS code 249) at 167.7 mln US$ and "Transportation" (EBOPS code 205) at 89.0 mln US$ (see graph 6).

Table 4: Top 10 import commodities 2012 to 2014

HS code	4-digit heading of Harmonized System 2007	Value (million US$) 2012	2013	2014	Unit value 2012	2013	2014	Unit	SITC code
	All Commodities	1 732.8	2 308.5	1 826.7					
2710	Petroleum oils, other than crude	261.9	481.6	375.1	0.3	0.9	0.8	US$/kg	334
8704	Motor vehicles for the transport of goods	58.0	72.4	70.2					782
8429	Self-propelled bulldozers, angledozers, graders, levellers, scrapers	71.6	59.2	69.2					723
8419	Machinery, plant or laboratory equipment	4.8	164.9	7.5					741
8703	Motor cars and other motor vehicles principally designed for the transport	64.0	54.7	52.5	*15.1*	*15.5*	*15.3*	thsd US$/unit	781
2815	Sodium hydroxide (caustic soda)	47.7	34.2	27.6	0.2	0.3	0.3	US$/kg	522
8517	Electrical apparatus for line telephony or line telegraphy	19.4	25.0	38.5					764
2523	Portland cement, aluminous cement, slag cement	26.8	27.6	24.4	0.1	0.1	0.1	US$/kg	661
8413	Pumps for liquids, whether or not fitted with a measuring device	19.9	32.8	18.1					742
0207	Meat and edible offal, of the poultry of heading 01.05	24.4	22.2	22.7	1.4	1.1	1.2	US$/kg	012

Sweden

Goods Imports: CIF, by origin/consignment for intra-eu **Goods Exports: FOB, by last known destination** **Trade System: Special**

Overview:

In 2015, the value of merchandise exports of Sweden decreased substantially by 14.8 percent to reach 140.1 bln US$, while its merchandise imports decreased substantially by 14.9 percent to reach 138.0 bln US$ (see graph 1, table 2 and table 3). The merchandise trade balance recorded a relatively small surplus of 2.1 bln US$ (see graph 1). The largest merchandise trade balance was with MDG Developed Europe at -13.2 bln US$ (see graph 4). Merchandise exports in Sweden were diversified amongst partners; imports were also diversified. The top 19 partners accounted for 80 percent or more of exports and 14 partners accounted for 80 percent or more of imports (see graph 5). In 2014, the value of exports of services of Sweden increased slightly by 4.4 percent, reaching 84.7 bln US$, while its imports of services increased moderately by 8.8 percent and reached 64.7 bln US$ (see graph 2). There was a moderate trade in services surplus of 20.0 bln US$.

Graph 1: Total merchandise trade, by value

(Bln US$ by year)

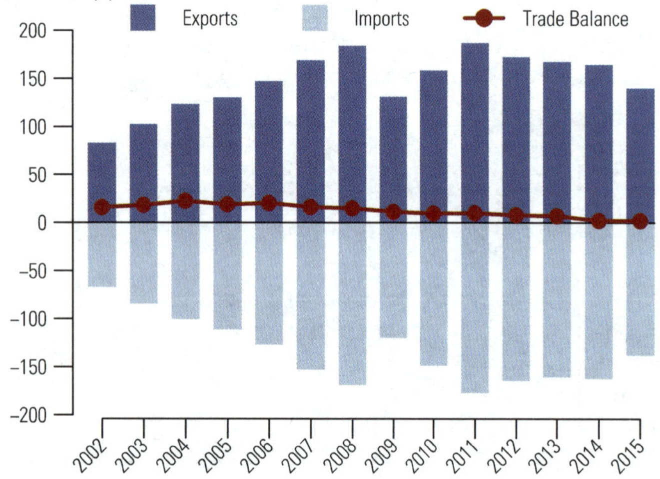

Graph 2: Total services trade, by value

(Bln US$ by year)

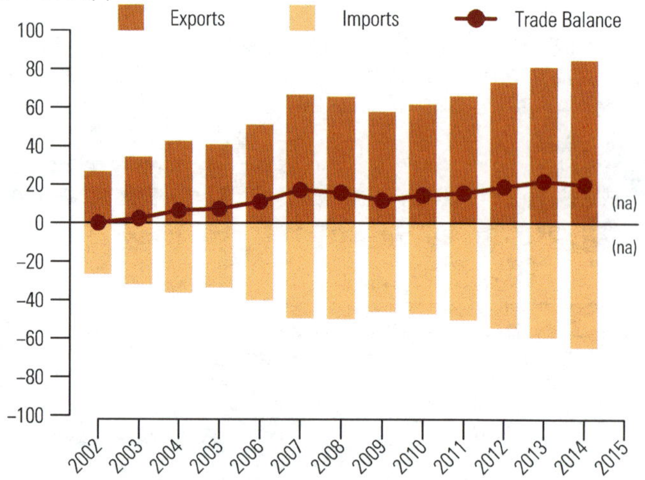

Exports Profile:

"Machinery and transport equipment" (SITC section 7), "Goods classified chiefly by material" (SITC section 6) and "Chemicals" (SITC section 5) were the largest commodity groups for exports in 2015, representing respectively 38.1, 17.6 and 12.3 percent of exported goods (see table 2). From 2013 to 2015, the largest export commodity was "Petroleum oils, other than crude" (HS code 2710) (see table 1). The top three destinations for merchandise exports were Norway, Germany and Finland, accounting for respectively 10.3, 9.8 and 6.9 percent of total exports. "Other business services" (EBOPS code 268) accounted for the largest share of exports of services in 2014 at 31.0 bln US$, followed by "Computer and information services" (EBOPS code 262) at 14.1 bln US$ and "Travel" (EBOPS code 236) at 12.7 bln US$ (see graph 3).

Graph 3: Exports of services by EBOPS category

(% share in 2014)

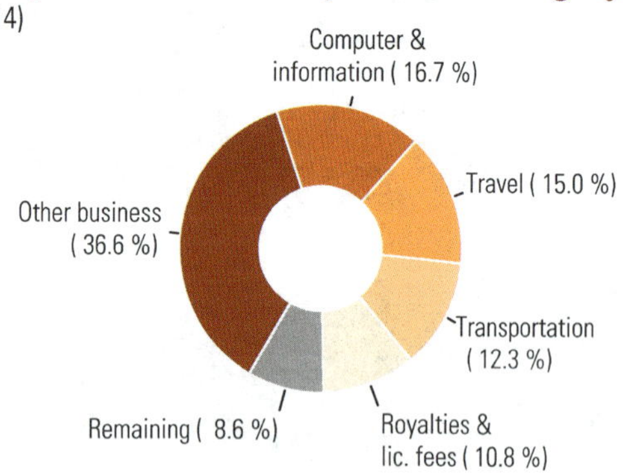

Table 1: Top 10 export commodities 2013 to 2015

HS code	4-digit heading of Harmonized System 2012	Value (million US$) 2013	2014	2015	Unit value 2013	2014	2015	Unit	SITC code
	All Commodities	167 494.7	164 413.8	140 089.8					
2710	Petroleum oils, other than crude	10 836.5	10 981.8	7 196.8	*0.9*	*0.8*	*0.5*	US$/kg	334
9999	Commodities not specified according to kind	8 226.0	6 935.1	5 844.6					931
8517	Electrical apparatus for line telephony or line telegraphy	6 381.7	6 695.7	5 815.4					764
3004	Medicaments (excluding goods of heading 30.02, 30.05 or 30.06)	6 297.6	6 353.9	5 969.4	*130.6*			US$/kg	542
8703	Motor cars and other motor vehicles principally designed for the transport	5 204.8	4 926.5	6 286.8	26.3	25.1	27.6	thsd US$/unit	781
8708	Parts and accessories of the motor vehicles of headings 87.01 to 87.05	5 597.0	5 276.4	4 483.2	*9.3*	*9.4*	*7.7*	US$/kg	784
4407	Wood sawn or chipped lengthwise, sliced or peeled	3 288.5	3 513.0	2 922.4	*285.6*	*289.3*	*230.4*	US$/m³	248
4810	Paper and paperboard, coated on one or both sides with kaolin	3 312.8	3 193.7	2 714.7	*1.1*	*1.0*	*0.9*	US$/kg	641
0302	Fish, fresh or chilled, excluding fish fillets	2 608.2	2 919.3	2 777.2					034
2601	Iron ores and concentrates, including roasted iron pyrites	2 942.3	2 792.3	1 567.6	*0.1*	*0.1*	*0.1*	US$/kg	281

Services Imports and Exports: EBOPS 2002 categories

Table 2: Merchandise exports by SITC

(Value in million US$, growth and shares in percentage)

SITC	2015	Avg. Growth rates 2011-2015	Avg. Growth rates 2014-2015	2015 share
Total	140 089.8	-7.0	-14.8	100.0
0+1	8 497.5	1.8	-12.3	6.1
2+4	8 973.6	-8.2	-22.6	6.4
3	8 640.8	-10.8	-35.1	6.2
5	17 195.8	-2.3	-8.3	12.3
6	24 658.6	-8.9	-16.6	17.6
7	53 376.0	-7.3	-11.0	38.1
8	12 256.5	-5.6	-12.0	8.7
9	6 490.9	-10.9	-14.8	4.6

Table 3: Merchandise imports by SITC

(Value in million US$, growth and shares in percentage)

SITC	2015	Avg. Growth rates 2011-2015	Avg. Growth rates 2014-2015	2015 share
Total	137 986.7	-6.0	-14.9	100.0
0+1	14 171.5	0.1	-12.7	10.3
2+4	4 285.4	-10.2	-19.9	3.1
3	13 422.0	-14.4	-38.9	9.7
5	15 097.9	-5.5	-17.0	10.9
6	16 635.5	-8.9	-16.1	12.1
7	51 046.5	-5.4	-10.3	37.0
8	16 153.1	-3.5	-11.0	11.7
9	7 174.9	5.2	27.3	5.2

SITC Legend

SITC Code	Description
Total	All commodities
0+1	Food, animals + beverages, tobacco
2+4	Crude materials + anim. & veg. oils
3	Mineral fuels, lubricants
5	Chemicals
6	Goods classified chiefly by material
7	Machinery and transport equipment
8	Miscellaneous manufactured articles
9	Not classified elsewhere in the SITC

Graph 4: Merchandise trade balance

(Bln US$ by MDG Regions in 2015)

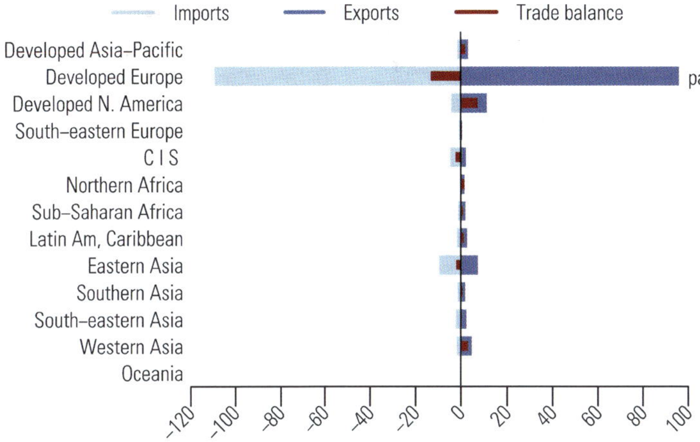

Graph 5: Partner concentration of merchandise trade

(Cumulative share by ranked partners in 2015)

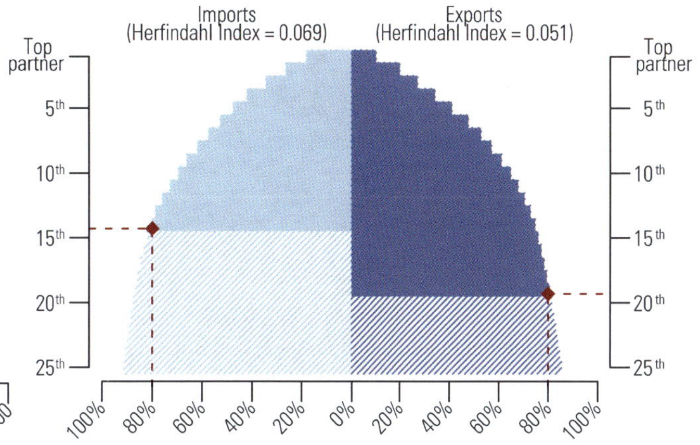

Graph 6: Imports of services by EBOPS category

(% share in 2014)

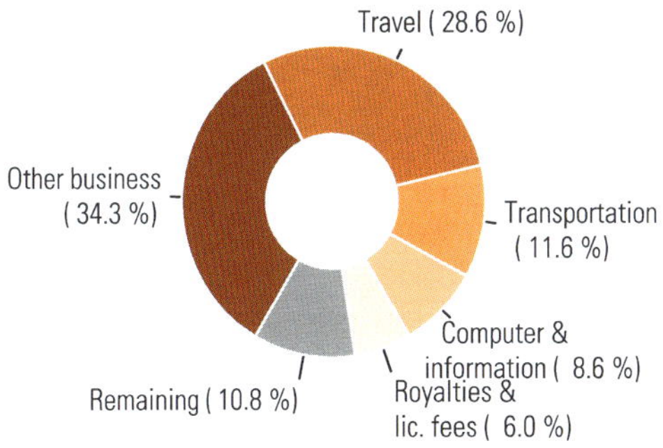

Imports Profile:

"Machinery and transport equipment" (SITC section 7), "Goods classified chiefly by material" (SITC section 6) and "Miscellaneous manufactured articles" (SITC section 8) were the largest commodity groups for imports in 2015, representing respectively 37.0, 12.1 and 11.7 percent of imported goods (see table 3). From 2013 to 2015, the largest import commodity was "Petroleum oils and oils obtained from bituminous minerals, crude" (HS code 2709) (see table 4). The top three partners for merchandise imports were Germany, Norway and the Netherlands, accounting for respectively 17.6, 8.4 and 7.9 percent of total imports. "Other business services" (EBOPS code 268) accounted for the largest share of imports of services in 2014 at 22.2 bln US$, followed by "Travel" (EBOPS code 236) at 18.5 bln US$ and "Transportation" (EBOPS code 205) at 7.5 bln US$ (see graph 6).

Table 4: Top 10 import commodities 2013 to 2015

HS code	4-digit heading of Harmonized System 2012	Value (million US$) 2013	2014	2015	Unit value 2013	2014	2015	Unit	SITC code
	All Commodities	160 588.8	162 220.7	137 986.7					
2709	Petroleum oils and oils obtained from bituminous minerals, crude	12 751.8	12 170.7	7 212.3	0.8	0.7	0.4	US$/kg	333
8703	Motor cars and other motor vehicles principally designed for the transport	7 364.9	8 014.1	7 651.4	22.2	20.5	19.2	thsd US$/unit	781
2710	Petroleum oils, other than crude	7 701.9	7 464.7	4 907.4	1.0	0.9	0.6	US$/kg	334
8517	Electrical apparatus for line telephony or line telegraphy	6 286.7	6 764.4	6 290.9					764
9999	Commodities not specified according to kind	5 819.3	5 583.8	7 132.3					931
8708	Parts and accessories of the motor vehicles of headings 87.01 to 87.05	5 065.0	5 206.4	5 141.1	8.0	8.8	7.8	US$/kg	784
8471	Automatic data processing machines and units thereof	4 039.4	4 003.5	3 046.5	258.1	247.1	213.4	US$/unit	752
3004	Medicaments (excluding goods of heading 30.02, 30.05 or 30.06)	3 163.7	3 024.5	2 487.2	82.9			US$/kg	542
0302	Fish, fresh or chilled, excluding fish fillets	2 766.6	3 005.0	2 828.9					034
8528	Reception apparatus for television	1 404.1	1 464.5	1 161.8	337.6	322.6	275.1	US$/unit	761

Switzerland-Liechtenstein

Goods Imports: CIF, by origin | **Goods Exports: FOB, by last known destination** | **Trade System: Special**

Overview:

In 2015, the value of merchandise exports of Switzerland decreased moderately by 6.2 percent to reach 292.0 bln US$, while its merchandise imports decreased moderately by 8.0 percent to reach 253.2 bln US$ (see graph 1, table 2 and table 3). The merchandise trade balance recorded a relatively small surplus of 38.8 bln US$ (see graph 1). The largest merchandise trade balance was with MDG Developed Europe at -36.6 bln US$ (see graph 4). Merchandise exports in Switzerland were diversified amongst partners; imports were also diversified. The top 16 partners accounted for 80 percent or more of exports and 16 partners accounted for 80 percent or more of imports (see graph 5). In 2013, the value of exports of services of Switzerland increased moderately by 5.0 percent, reaching 95.4 bln US$, while its imports of services increased substantially by 13.0 percent and reached 53.0 bln US$ (see graph 2). There was a moderate trade in services surplus of 42.4 bln US$.

Graph 1: Total merchandise trade, by value

(Bln US$ by year)

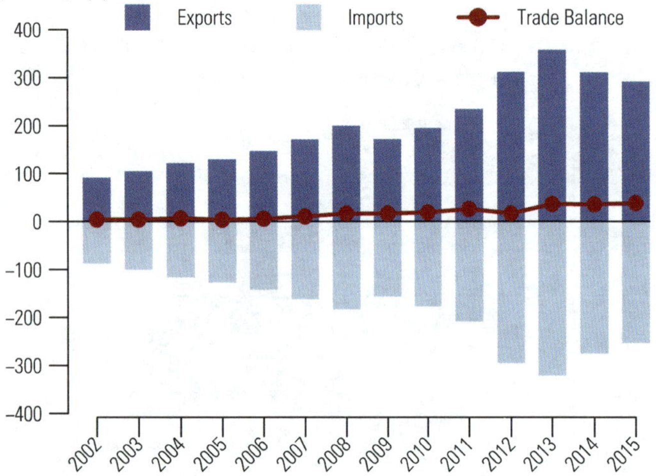

Graph 2: Total services trade, by value

(Bln US$ by year)

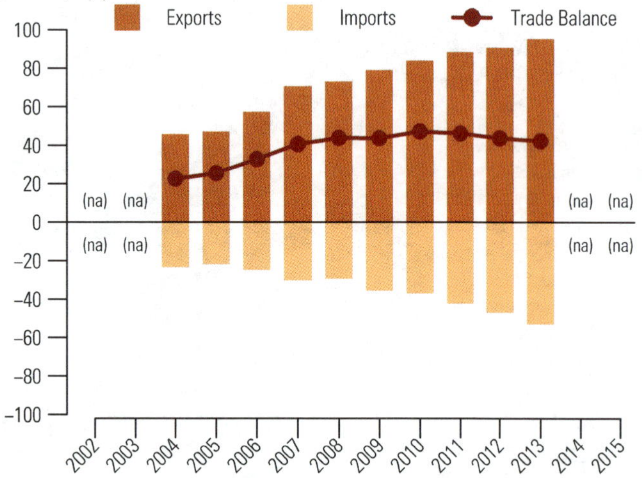

Exports Profile:

"Chemicals" (SITC section 5), "Not classified elsewhere in the SITC" (SITC section 9) and "Miscellaneous manufactured articles" (SITC section 8) were the largest commodity groups for exports in 2015, representing respectively 30.1, 26.1 and 19.4 percent of exported goods (see table 2). From 2013 to 2015, the largest export commodity was "Gold (including gold plated with platinum)" (HS code 7108) (see table 1). The top three destinations for merchandise exports were Germany, China, Hong Kong SAR and the United States, accounting for respectively 13.9, 10.5 and 9.3 percent of total exports. "Other business services" (EBOPS code 268) accounted for the largest share of exports of services in 2013 at 24.7 bln US$, followed by "Financial services" (EBOPS code 260) at 16.7 bln US$ and "Travel" (EBOPS code 236) at 16.5 bln US$ (see graph 3).

Graph 3: Exports of services by EBOPS category

(% share in 2013)

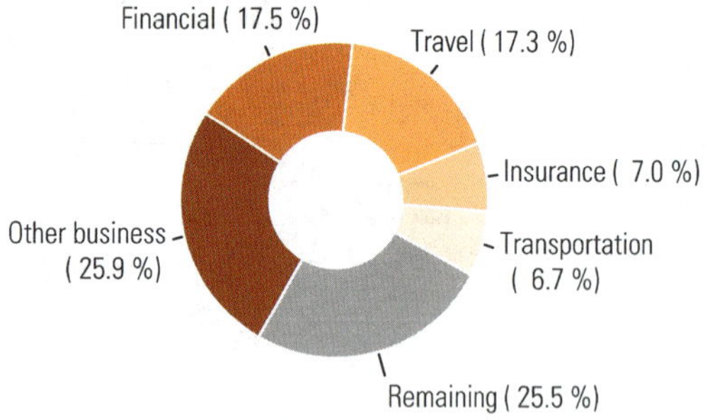

Table 1: Top 10 export commodities 2013 to 2015

HS code	4-digit heading of Harmonized System 2012	Value (million US$)			Unit value				SITC code
		2013	2014	2015	2013	2014	2015	Unit	
	All Commodities	357 905.2	311 145.9	291 959.2					
7108	Gold (including gold plated with platinum)	130 173.0	74 088.3	72 446.6	*45.6*	*40.6*	*37.6*	thsd US$/kg	971
3004	Medicaments (excluding goods of heading 30.02, 30.05 or 30.06)	32 337.9	35 466.5	34 544.4	*337.7*	*359.8*	*356.6*	US$/kg	542
3002	Human blood; animal blood prepared for therapeutic uses	23 907.5	25 897.9	24 943.3	*3.8*	*3.9*	*3.5*	thsd US$/kg	541
9102	Wrist-watches, pocket-watches and other watches, of base metal	13 843.6	14 259.1	13 212.5	499.7	505.7	476.2	US$/unit	885
7113	Articles of jewellery and parts thereof, of precious metal	9 024.4	10 789.1	11 057.1	*159.4*	*206.0*	*239.5*	thsd US$/kg	897
9101	Wrist-watches, pocket-watches and other watches, precious metal	8 441.0	8 697.7	8 015.1	15.2	15.8	16.3	thsd US$/unit	885
9021	Orthopaedic appliances, including crutches, surgical belts and trusses	6 302.9	6 411.6	6 237.5					899
2933	Heterocyclic compounds with nitrogen hetero-atom(s) only	5 676.0	6 377.9	6 670.1		*341.9*		US$/kg	515
9999	Commodities not specified according to kind	4 026.7	4 106.4	3 617.0					931
9018	Instruments and appliances used in medical, surgical, dental or veterinary	3 059.9	3 205.2	3 086.9					872

Services Imports and Exports: EBOPS 2002 categories

Table 2: Merchandise exports by SITC

(Value in million US$, growth and shares in percentage)

SITC	2015	Avg. Growth rates 2011-2015	Avg. Growth rates 2014-2015	2015 share
Total	291 959.2	5.6	-6.2	100.0
0+1	8 711.4	0.4	-7.3	3.0
2+4	1 580.3	-10.7	-22.7	0.5
3	2 771.9	-21.5	-20.0	0.9
5	88 014.6	1.3	-4.9	30.1
6	16 802.1	-6.7	-15.1	5.8
7	41 124.6	-4.2	-8.7	14.1
8	56 742.5	0.8	-6.2	19.4
9	76 211.9	80.9	-2.8	26.1

Table 3: Merchandise imports by SITC

(Value in million US$, growth and shares in percentage)

SITC	2015	Avg. Growth rates 2011-2015	Avg. Growth rates 2014-2015	2015 share
Total	253 152.5	5.0	-8.0	100.0
0+1	10 827.1	-1.4	-8.3	4.3
2+4	2 526.1	-5.8	-13.9	1.0
3	8 922.8	-15.7	-32.8	3.5
5	42 211.2	-0.9	-13.5	16.7
6	25 025.9	-5.8	-15.4	9.9
7	49 118.0	-2.7	-6.4	19.4
8	42 674.0	0.3	-3.1	16.9
9	71 847.5	114.4	-0.4	28.4

SITC Legend

SITC Code	Description
Total	All commodities
0+1	Food, animals + beverages, tobacco
2+4	Crude materials + anim. & veg. oils
3	Mineral fuels, lubricants
5	Chemicals
6	Goods classified chiefly by material
7	Machinery and transport equipment
8	Miscellaneous manufactured articles
9	Not classified elsewhere in the SITC

Graph 4: Merchandise trade balance

(Bln US$ by MDG Regions in 2015)

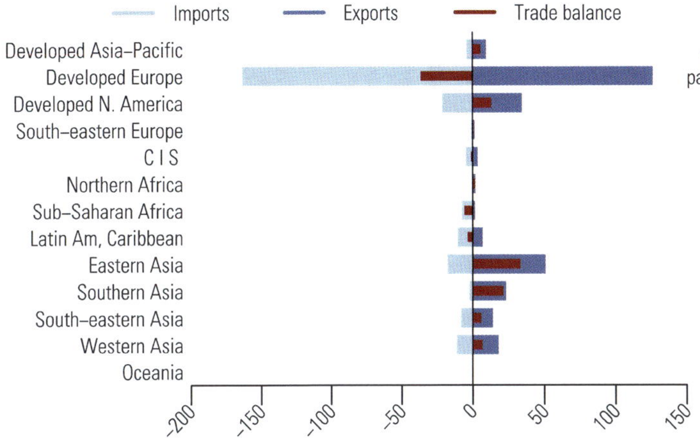

Graph 5: Partner concentration of merchandise trade

(Cumulative share by ranked partners in 2015)

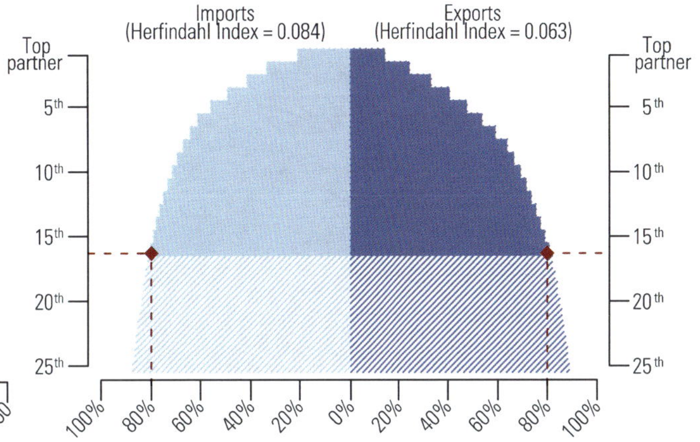

Graph 6: Imports of services by EBOPS category

(% share in 2013)

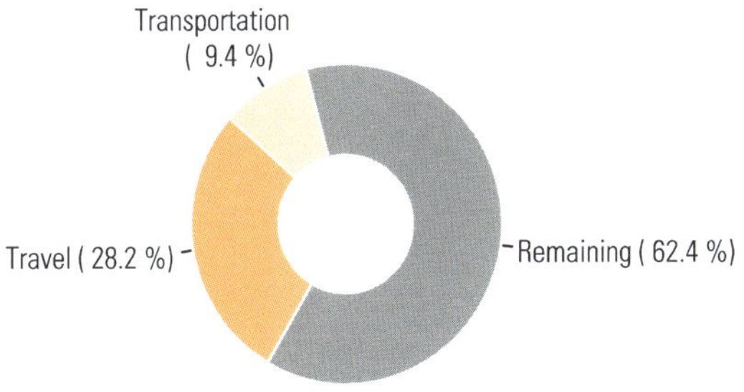

Imports Profile:

"Not classified elsewhere in the SITC" (SITC section 9), "Machinery and transport equipment" (SITC section 7) and "Miscellaneous manufactured articles" (SITC section 8) were the largest commodity groups for imports in 2015, representing respectively 28.4, 19.4 and 16.9 percent of imported goods (see table 3). From 2013 to 2015, the largest import commodity was "Gold (including gold plated with platinum)" (HS code 7108) (see table 4). The top three partners for merchandise imports were Germany, the United Kingdom and Italy, accounting for respectively 20.2, 16.0 and 7.9 percent of total imports. "Travel" (EBOPS code 236) accounted for the largest share of imports of services in 2013 at 15.0 bln US$, followed by "Transportation" (EBOPS code 205) at 5.0 bln US$ (see graph 6).

Table 4: Top 10 import commodities 2013 to 2015

HS code	4-digit heading of Harmonized System 2012	Value (million US$) 2013	Value (million US$) 2014	Value (million US$) 2015	Unit value 2013	Unit value 2014	Unit value 2015	Unit	SITC code
	All Commodities	321 050.5	275 054.0	253 152.5					
7108	Gold (including gold plated with platinum)	118 891.0	71 349.3	70 738.4	*38.5*	*31.8*	*28.1*	thsd US$/kg	971
3004	Medicaments (excluding goods of heading 30.02, 30.05 or 30.06)	15 363.7	15 838.9	14 058.2	*250.3*	*248.1*	*232.4*	US$/kg	542
8703	Motor cars and other motor vehicles principally designed for the transport	10 184.2	10 499.8	10 508.2	*29.7*	*31.1*	*28.1*	thsd US$/unit	781
7113	Articles of jewellery and parts thereof, of precious metal	8 806.5	9 429.9	9 907.8	*65.9*	*75.3*	*84.3*	thsd US$/kg	897
3002	Human blood; animal blood prepared for therapeutic uses	6 237.4	7 158.1	7 161.8	*846.2*	*935.8*	*853.8*	US$/kg	541
2933	Heterocyclic compounds with nitrogen hetero-atom(s) only	6 724.1	6 914.7	5 737.1		*188.3*		US$/kg	515
2710	Petroleum oils, other than crude	7 156.5	5 591.1	4 436.6		*0.9*	*0.6*	US$/kg	334
8471	Automatic data processing machines and units thereof	3 413.4	3 405.7	3 141.5	331.9	*326.4*	*343.1*	US$/unit	752
8517	Electrical apparatus for line telephony or line telegraphy	3 174.6	3 176.3	3 205.0					764
2709	Petroleum oils and oils obtained from bituminous minerals, crude	4 099.6	3 867.0	1 240.3	0.8	0.8	0.4	US$/kg	333

Source: UN Comtrade

Thailand

Goods Imports: CIF, by origin | **Goods Exports: FOB, by last known destination** | **Trade System: Special**

Overview:

In 2015, the value of merchandise exports of Thailand decreased moderately by 7.3 percent to reach 210.9 bln US$, while its merchandise imports decreased substantially by 11.4 percent to reach 202.0 bln US$ (see graph 1, table 2 and table 3). The merchandise trade balance recorded a relatively small surplus of 8.9 bln US$ (see graph 1). The largest merchandise trade balance was with MDG Eastern Asia at -14.5 bln US$ (see graph 4). Merchandise exports in Thailand were diversified amongst partners; imports were also diversified. The top 20 partners accounted for 80 percent or more of exports and 16 partners accounted for 80 percent or more of imports (see graph 5). In 2014, the value of exports of services of Thailand decreased moderately by 5.6 percent, reaching 55.3 bln US$, while its imports of services decreased slightly by 3.1 percent and reached 53.2 bln US$ (see graph 2). There was a relatively small trade in services surplus of 2.1 bln US$.

Graph 1: Total merchandise trade, by value

(Bln US$ by year)

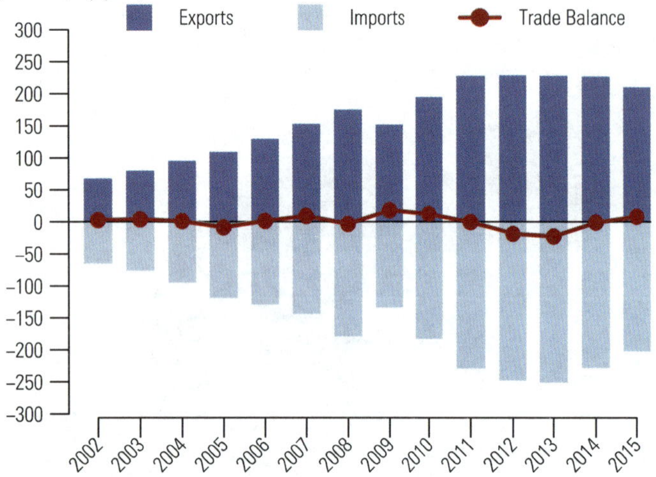

Graph 2: Total services trade, by value

(Bln US$ by year)

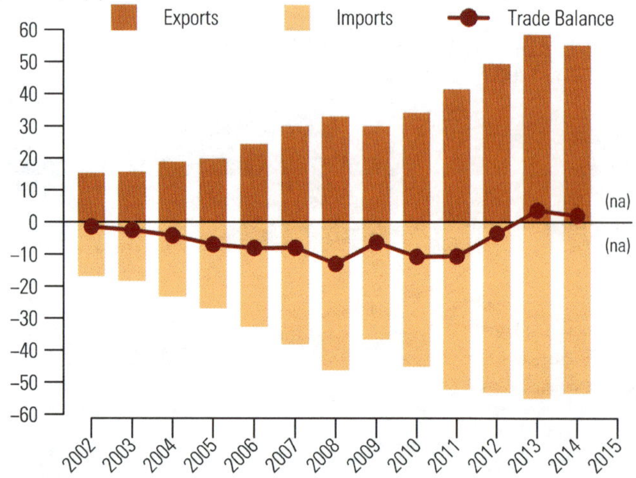

Exports Profile:

"Machinery and transport equipment" (SITC section 7), "Food, animals + beverages, tobacco" (SITC section 0+1) and "Goods classified chiefly by material" (SITC section 6) were the largest commodity groups for exports in 2015, representing respectively 44.9, 13.4 and 12.6 percent of exported goods (see table 2). From 2013 to 2015, the largest export commodity was "Automatic data processing machines and units thereof" (HS code 8471) (see table 1). The top three destinations for merchandise exports were China, the United States and Japan, accounting for respectively 11.3, 10.6 and 9.6 percent of total exports. "Travel" (EBOPS code 236) accounted for the largest share of exports of services in 2014 at 38.4 bln US$, followed by "Other business services" (EBOPS code 268) at 9.2 bln US$ and "Transportation" (EBOPS code 205) at 5.7 bln US$ (see graph 3).

Graph 3: Exports of services by EBOPS category

(% share in 2014)

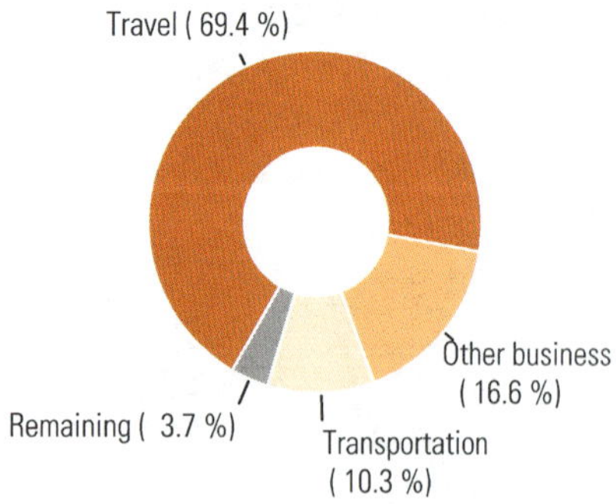

Table 1: Top 10 export commodities 2013 to 2015

HS code	4-digit heading of Harmonized System 2012	Value (million US$) 2013	2014	2015	Unit value 2013	2014	2015	Unit	SITC code
	All Commodities	228527.4	227572.8	210883.4					
8471	Automatic data processing machines and units thereof	12182.0	12115.7	11413.3			*49.4*	US$/unit	752
8704	Motor vehicles for the transport of goods	10590.5	10347.3	8160.1					782
2710	Petroleum oils, other than crude	11472.6	9811.1	6809.9					334
8703	Motor cars and other motor vehicles principally designed for the transport	6625.3	6524.5	9393.6	*14.1*	*13.8*	*1.9*	thsd US$/unit	781
8542	Electronic integrated circuits	7214.2	7502.6	7610.6					776
8708	Parts and accessories of the motor vehicles of headings 87.01 to 87.05	6352.0	6789.5	6729.7	*8.6*	*8.5*	*8.3*	US$/kg	784
4001	Natural rubber, balata, gutta-percha, guayule, chicle	8233.5	6021.5	4976.7	*2.4*	*1.8*	*1.4*	US$/kg	231
1006	Rice	4420.4	5438.8	4544.0	*0.7*	*0.5*	*0.5*	US$/kg	042
8415	Air conditioning machines, comprising a motor-driven fan	4506.8	4609.8	4525.9					741
3901	Polymers of ethylene, in primary forms	3686.6	4200.8	3403.1	*1.6*	*1.6*	*1.3*	US$/kg	571

Services Imports and Exports: EBOPS 2002 categories

Table 2: Merchandise exports by SITC

(Value in million US$, growth and shares in percentage)

SITC	2015	Avg. Growth rates 2011-2015	Avg. Growth rates 2014-2015	2015 share
Total	210 883.4	-2.0	-7.3	100.0
0+1	28 176.3	-2.1	-6.8	13.4
2+4	9 337.4	-15.4	-13.7	4.4
3	8 293.7	-10.4	-30.8	3.9
5	20 444.5	-2.7	-17.3	9.7
6	26 557.8	-2.0	-7.4	12.6
7	94 586.9	2.5	-3.4	44.9
8	19 700.7	-4.5	-3.6	9.3
9	3 786.0	-10.6	34.3	1.8

Table 3: Merchandise imports by SITC

(Value in million US$, growth and shares in percentage)

SITC	2015	Avg. Growth rates 2011-2015	Avg. Growth rates 2014-2015	2015 share
Total	202 019.4	-3.0	-11.4	100.0
0+1	11 140.2	4.8	0.7	5.5
2+4	5 851.9	-7.0	-10.8	2.9
3	30 181.5	-8.7	-37.2	14.9
5	21 684.8	-2.3	-7.5	10.7
6	34 578.0	-3.1	-8.3	17.1
7	76 282.1	0.5	-4.3	37.8
8	15 095.7	2.1	2.3	7.5
9	7 205.2	-18.7	9.0	3.6

SITC Legend

SITC Code	Description
Total	All commodities
0+1	Food, animals + beverages, tobacco
2+4	Crude materials + anim. & veg. oils
3	Mineral fuels, lubricants
5	Chemicals
6	Goods classified chiefly by material
7	Machinery and transport equipment
8	Miscellaneous manufactured articles
9	Not classified elsewhere in the SITC

Graph 4: Merchandise trade balance

(Bln US$ by MDG Regions in 2015)

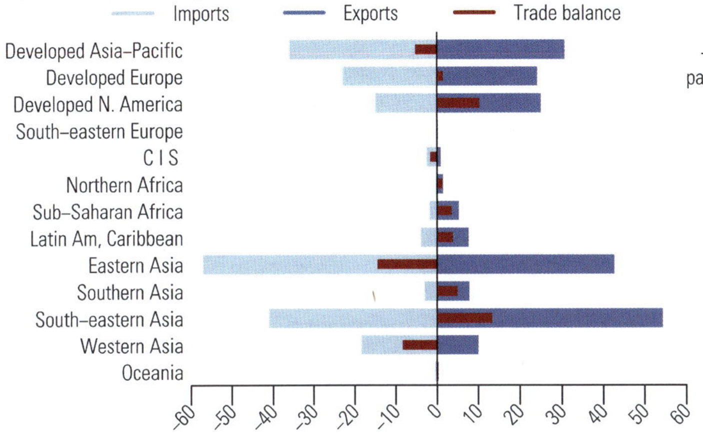

Graph 5: Partner concentration of merchandise trade

(Cumulative share by ranked partners in 2015)

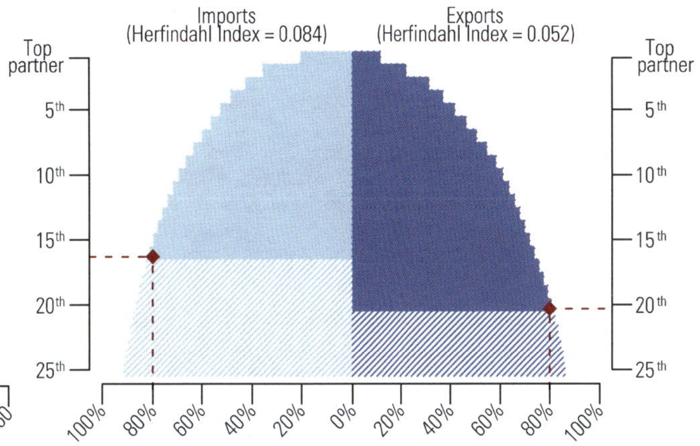

Graph 6: Imports of services by EBOPS category

(% share in 2014)

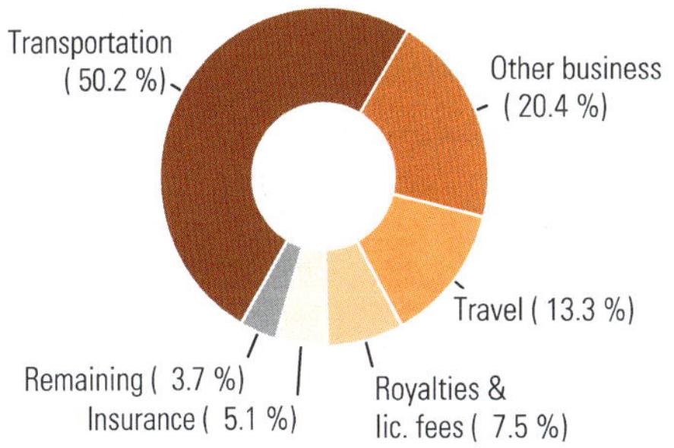

Imports Profile:

"Machinery and transport equipment" (SITC section 7), "Goods classified chiefly by material" (SITC section 6) and "Mineral fuels, lubricants" (SITC section 3) were the largest commodity groups for imports in 2015, representing respectively 37.8, 17.1 and 14.9 percent of imported goods (see table 3). From 2013 to 2015, the largest import commodity was "Petroleum oils and oils obtained from bituminous minerals, crude" (HS code 2709) (see table 4). The top three partners for merchandise imports were China, Japan and the United States, accounting for respectively 17.2, 15.9 and 6.4 percent of total imports. "Transportation" (EBOPS code 205) accounted for the largest share of imports of services in 2014 at 26.7 bln US$, followed by "Other business services" (EBOPS code 268) at 10.8 bln US$ and "Travel" (EBOPS code 236) at 7.1 bln US$ (see graph 6).

Table 4: Top 10 import commodities 2013 to 2015

HS code	4-digit heading of Harmonized System 2012	Value (million US$) 2013	2014	2015	Unit value 2013	2014	2015	Unit	SITC code
	All Commodities	250 708.2	227 931.5	202 019.4					
2709	Petroleum oils and oils obtained from bituminous minerals, crude	38 916.9	33 216.5	19 452.1	*0.9*	*0.8*	*0.4*	US$/kg	333
7108	Gold (including gold plated with platinum)	14 981.2	6 612.5	7 204.1	*44.2*	*39.9*	*35.9*	thsd US$/kg	971
8542	Electronic integrated circuits	9 206.2	9 680.8	9 356.3					776
2711	Petroleum gases and other gaseous hydrocarbons	6 890.7	6 585.9	5 370.3	*0.6*	*0.5*	*0.4*	US$/kg	343
8708	Parts and accessories of the motor vehicles of headings 87.01 to 87.05	7 877.0	5 313.0	5 300.4	*10.7*	*10.3*	*9.3*	US$/kg	784
8517	Electrical apparatus for line telephony or line telegraphy	4 794.0	5 454.3	6 108.7					764
2710	Petroleum oils, other than crude	3 676.2	5 573.1	2 983.5					334
8471	Automatic data processing machines and units thereof	3 888.1	3 560.7	3 425.3					752
8802	Other aircraft (for example, helicopters, aeroplanes); spacecraft	4 417.5	3 009.6	3 086.7	24.4	0.6	4.9	mln US$/unit	792
8473	Parts and accessories for use with machines of heading 84.69 to 84.72	3 146.5	3 004.3	2 690.6		*53.8*		US$/kg	759

Source: UN Comtrade

The former Yugoslav Republic of Macedonia

Goods Imports: CIF, by origin **Goods Exports: FOB, by last known destination** **Trade System: Special**

Overview:

In 2015, the value of merchandise exports of The former Yugoslav Republic of Macedonia increased substantially by 20.6 percent to reach 4.5 bln US$, while its merchandise imports increased substantially by 16.7 percent to reach 6.4 bln US$ (see graph 1, table 2 and table 3). The merchandise trade balance recorded a moderate deficit of 1.9 bln US$ (see graph 1). The largest merchandise trade balance was with MDG Developed Europe at -353.8 mln US$ (see graph 4). Merchandise exports in The former Yugoslav Republic of Macedonia were moderately concentrated amongst partners; imports were diversified. The top 11 partners accounted for 80 percent or more of exports and 18 partners accounted for 80 percent or more of imports (see graph 5). In 2013, the value of exports of services of The former Yugoslav Republic of Macedonia increased substantially by 11.4 percent, reaching 1.2 bln US$, while its imports of services increased moderately by 7.7 percent and reached 1.1 bln US$ (see graph 2). There was a relatively small trade in services surplus of 106.2 mln US$.

Graph 1: Total merchandise trade, by value

(Bln US$ by year)

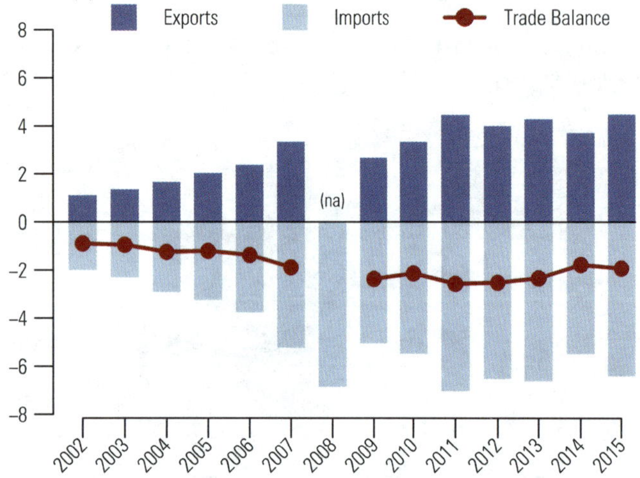

Graph 2: Total services trade, by value

(Bln US$ by year)

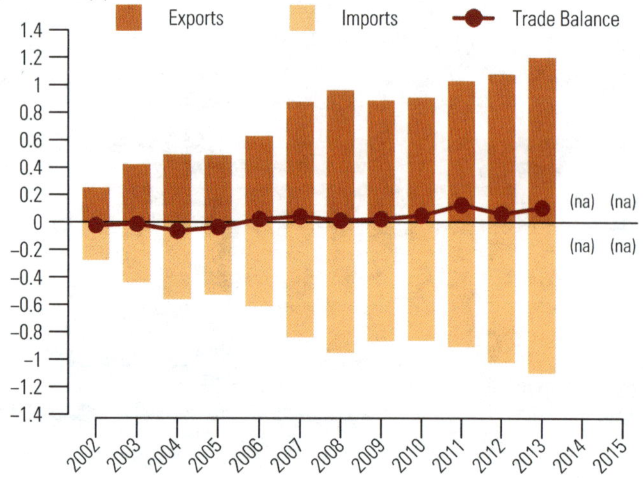

Exports Profile:

"Machinery and transport equipment" (SITC section 7), "Chemicals" (SITC section 5) and "Goods classified chiefly by material" (SITC section 6) were the largest commodity groups for exports in 2015, representing respectively 24.7, 22.8 and 17.8 percent of exported goods (see table 2). From 2013 to 2015, the largest export commodity was "Reaction initiators, reaction accelerators and catalytic preparations" (HS code 3815) (see table 1). The top three destinations for merchandise exports were Germany, Serbia and Bulgaria, accounting for respectively 40.5, 10.5 and 6.7 percent of total exports. "Transportation" (EBOPS code 205) accounted for the largest share of exports of services in 2013 at 376.5 mln US$, followed by "Travel" (EBOPS code 236) at 277.2 mln US$ and "Other business services" (EBOPS code 268) at 255.1 mln US$ (see graph 3).

Graph 3: Exports of services by EBOPS category

(% share in 2013)

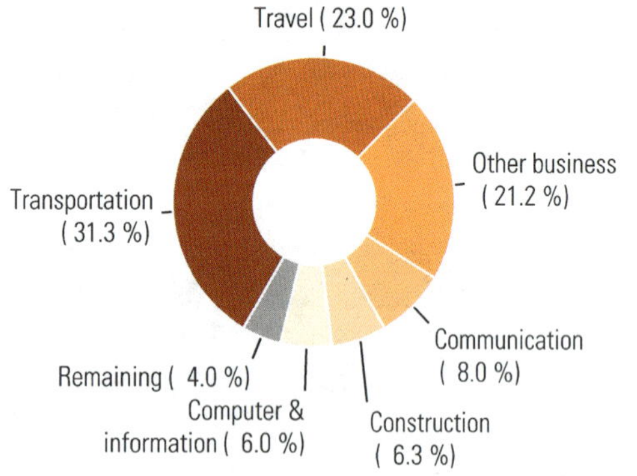

Table 1: Top 10 export commodities 2013 to 2015

HS code	4-digit heading of Harmonized System 2012	Value (million US$) 2013	2014	2015	Unit value 2013	2014	2015	Unit	SITC code
	All Commodities	4 298.8	3 723.0	4 489.9					
3815	Reaction initiators, reaction accelerators and catalytic preparations	638.3	649.9	856.7	140.7	89.1	93.4	US$/kg	598
8421	Centrifuges, including centrifugal dryers	267.7	320.9	474.3					743
7202	Ferro-alloys	438.9	288.2	300.4					671
8544	Insulated (including enamelled or anodised) wire, cable	62.3	201.0	274.6	10.3	15.7	15.1	US$/kg	773
6204	Women's or girls'suits, ensembles, jackets, blazers, dresses, skirts	157.7	113.2	108.6	17.9	13.1	15.1	US$/unit	842
2401	Unmanufactured tobacco; tobacco refuse	153.2	95.7	95.9	5.9	4.0	4.2	US$/kg	121
6203	Men's or boys'suits, ensembles, jackets, blazers, trousers	99.7	102.6	104.2	26.4	22.5	24.3	US$/unit	841
7210	Flat-rolled products of iron or non-alloy steel	123.1	76.9	85.2	1.2	0.8	0.7	US$/kg	674
7208	Flat-rolled products of iron or non-alloy steel	100.1	92.9	83.2	0.7	0.5	0.5	US$/kg	673
6205	Men's or boys'shirts	92.6	68.5	76.8	13.8	9.9	11.4	US$/unit	841

Services Imports and Exports: EBOPS 2002 categories

Table 2: Merchandise exports by SITC

(Value in million US$, growth and shares in percentage)

SITC	2015	Avg. Growth rates 2011-2015	Avg. Growth rates 2014-2015	2015 share
Total	4489.9	0.1	20.6	100.0
0+1	499.5	-4.8	8.3	11.1
2+4	237.5	-6.2	12.6	5.3
3	52.6	-39.4	-20.0	1.2
5	1021.8	8.1	28.4	22.8
6	798.7	-10.3	11.0	17.8
7	1108.4	33.1	40.7	24.7
8	770.2	-2.0	13.5	17.2
9	1.3	-18.1	-60.7	0.0

Table 3: Merchandise imports by SITC

(Value in million US$, growth and shares in percentage)

SITC	2015	Avg. Growth rates 2011-2015	Avg. Growth rates 2014-2015	2015 share
Total	6399.8	-2.3	16.7	100.0
0+1	677.8	-2.2	18.8	10.6
2+4	266.7	-11.8	11.8	4.2
3	696.0	-16.6	-11.6	10.9
5	760.8	-2.1	22.8	11.9
6	2273.9	3.7	21.2	35.5
7	1296.2	2.3	25.4	20.3
8	423.5	0.1	20.4	6.6
9	5.0	-14.4	-36.3	0.1

SITC Legend

SITC Code	Description
Total	All commodities
0+1	Food, animals + beverages, tobacco
2+4	Crude materials + anim. & veg. oils
3	Mineral fuels, lubricants
5	Chemicals
6	Goods classified chiefly by material
7	Machinery and transport equipment
8	Miscellaneous manufactured articles
9	Not classified elsewhere in the SITC

Graph 4: Merchandise trade balance

(Bln US$ by MDG Regions in 2015)

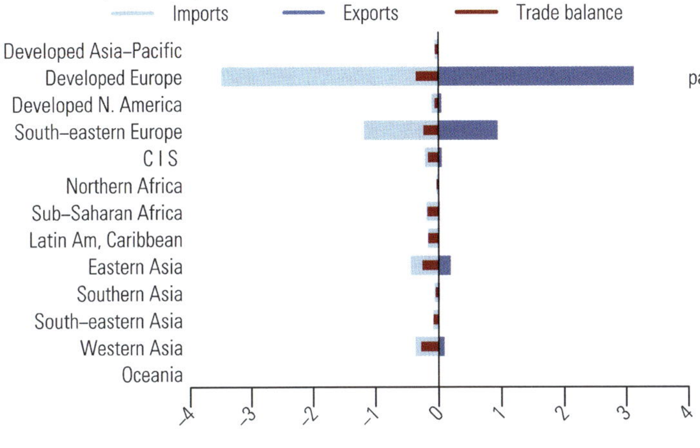

Graph 5: Partner concentration of merchandise trade

(Cumulative share by ranked partners in 2015)

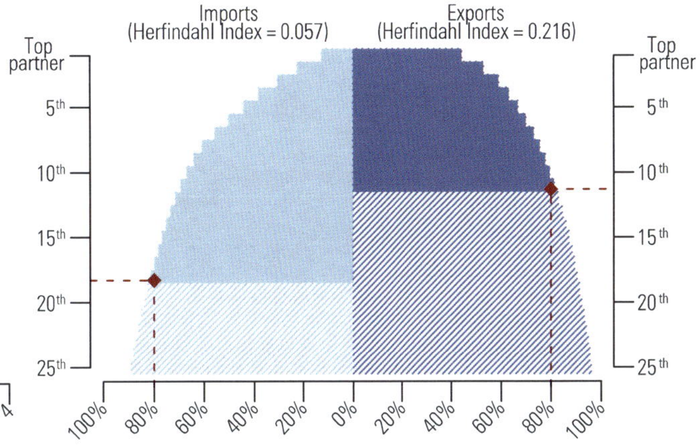

Graph 6: Imports of services by EBOPS category

(% share in 2013)

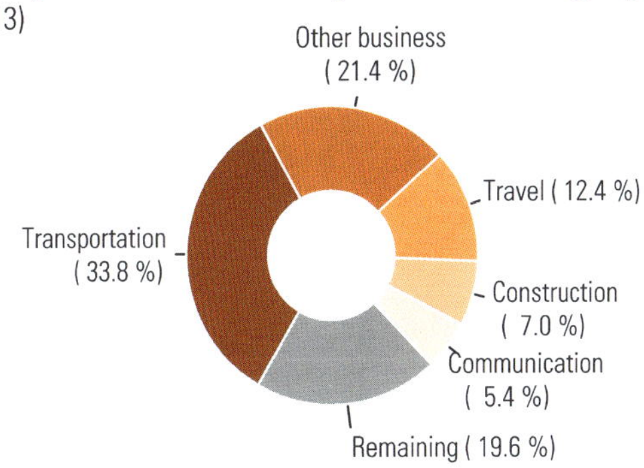

Imports Profile:

"Goods classified chiefly by material" (SITC section 6), "Machinery and transport equipment" (SITC section 7) and "Chemicals" (SITC section 5) were the largest commodity groups for imports in 2015, representing respectively 35.5, 20.3 and 11.9 percent of imported goods (see table 3). From 2013 to 2015, the largest import commodity was "Platinum, unwrought or in semi-manufactured forms, or in powder form" (HS code 7110) (see table 4). The top three partners for merchandise imports were Germany, the United Kingdom and Greece, accounting for respectively 11.4, 10.9 and 9.2 percent of total imports. "Transportation" (EBOPS code 205) accounted for the largest share of imports of services in 2013 at 371.0 mln US$, followed by "Other business services" (EBOPS code 268) at 234.4 mln US$ and "Travel" (EBOPS code 236) at 136.5 mln US$ (see graph 6).

Table 4: Top 10 import commodities 2013 to 2015

HS code	4-digit heading of Harmonized System 2012	Value (million US$) 2013	Value (million US$) 2014	Value (million US$) 2015	Unit value 2013	Unit value 2014	Unit value 2015	Unit	SITC code
	All Commodities	6619.6	5484.9	6399.8					
7110	Platinum, unwrought or in semi-manufactured forms, or in powder form	522.6	629.6	738.9	*38.9*	*29.7*	31.4	thsd US$/kg	681
2710	Petroleum oils, other than crude	664.5	505.4	438.8		*0.7*	*0.5*	US$/kg	334
2716	Electrical energy	171.2	140.7	133.3	67.0			US$/MWh	351
7208	Flat-rolled products of iron or non-alloy steel	170.4	112.3	146.0	0.6	*0.4*	0.4	US$/kg	673
8703	Motor cars and other motor vehicles principally designed for the transport	136.7	105.3	130.3	4.2	3.2	4.7	thsd US$/unit	781
3004	Medicaments (excluding goods of heading 30.02, 30.05 or 30.06)	127.7	103.1	108.6	*36.1*	*28.6*	*26.9*	US$/kg	542
6909	Ceramic wares for laboratory, chemical or other technical uses	65.0	91.3	170.0	*26.4*		*22.1*	US$/kg	663
2711	Petroleum gases and other gaseous hydrocarbons	110.2	86.0	83.0	*0.7*	*0.5*	*0.5*	US$/kg	343
2604	Nickel ores and concentrates	100.0	76.8	88.9	0.1	0.1	0.1	US$/kg	284
8517	Electrical apparatus for line telephony or line telegraphy	84.1	75.7	87.2					764

Togo

Goods Imports: CIF, by origin **Goods Exports: FOB, by last known destination** **Trade System: Special**

Overview:

In 2015, the value of merchandise exports of Togo decreased substantially by 16.4 percent to reach 671.9 mln US$, while its merchandise imports decreased slightly by 1.2 percent to reach 1.7 bln US$ (see graph 1, table 2 and table 3). The merchandise trade balance recorded a large deficit of 1.1 bln US$ (see graph 1). The largest merchandise trade balance was with MDG Developed Europe at -526.7 mln US$ (see graph 4). Merchandise exports in Togo were diversified amongst partners; imports were also diversified. The top 14 partners accounted for 80 percent or more of exports and 21 partners accounted for 80 percent or more of imports (see graph 5). In 2013, the value of exports of services of Togo increased substantially by 13.9 percent, reaching 487.4 mln US$, while its imports of services increased moderately by 5.3 percent and reached 463.4 mln US$ (see graph 2). There was a relatively small trade in services surplus of 24.1 mln US$.

Graph 1: Total merchandise trade, by value

(Bln US$ by year)

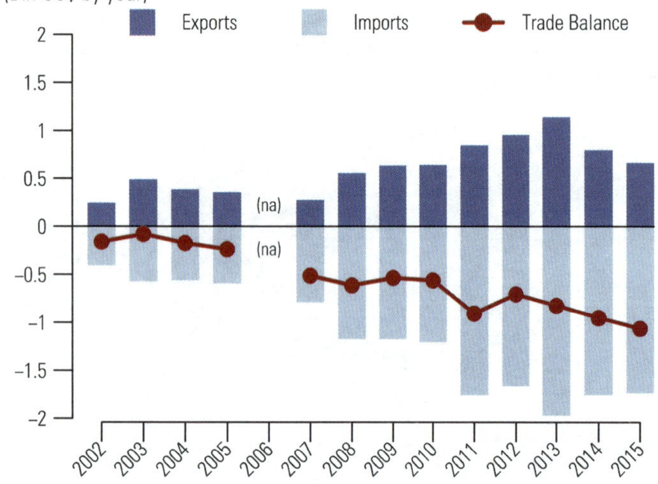

Graph 2: Total services trade, by value

(Mln US$ by year)

Exports Profile:

"Crude materials + anim. & veg. oils" (SITC section 2+4), "Miscellaneous manufactured articles" (SITC section 8) and "Goods classified chiefly by material" (SITC section 6) were the largest commodity groups for exports in 2015, representing respectively 30.6, 17.7 and 14.7 percent of exported goods (see table 2). From 2013 to 2015, the largest export commodity was "Natural calcium phosphates" (HS code 2510) (see table 1). The top three destinations for merchandise exports were Burkina Faso, Benin and the Niger, accounting for respectively 14.5, 11.8 and 10.7 percent of total exports. "Transportation" (EBOPS code 205) accounted for the largest share of exports of services in 2013 at 232.1 mln US$, followed by "Travel" (EBOPS code 236) at 125.4 mln US$ and "Government services, n.i.e." (EBOPS code 291) at 49.0 mln US$ (see graph 3).

Graph 3: Exports of services by EBOPS category

(% share in 2013)

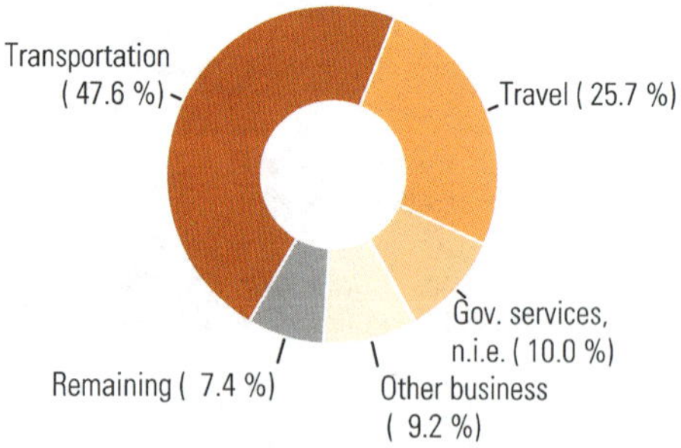

Table 1: Top 10 export commodities 2013 to 2015

HS code	4-digit heading of Harmonized System 2007	Value (million US$) 2013	2014	2015	Unit value 2013	2014	2015	Unit	SITC code
	All Commodities	1 146.5	803.8	671.9					
2510	Natural calcium phosphates	137.9	132.3	100.2	0.1	0.1	0.1	US$/kg	272
2523	Portland cement, aluminous cement, slag cement	165.5	98.1	49.3	0.1	0.1	0.1	US$/kg	661
3923	Articles for the conveyance or packing of goods, of plastics	52.5	63.8	66.1	2.0	1.9	1.7	US$/kg	893
5201	Cotton, not carded or combed	59.9	57.9	59.4	1.8	1.8	1.4	US$/kg	263
3304	Beauty or make-up preparations	44.3	39.3	43.3	3.1	3.6	3.5	US$/kg	553
7108	Gold (including gold plated with platinum)	43.4	42.0	26.5					971
1511	Palm oil and its fractions	43.2	17.5	27.2	0.9	0.6	0.5	US$/kg	422
8905	Light-vessels, fire-floats, dredgers, floating cranes and other vessels	76.5	4.6	3.7					793
6704	Wigs, false beards, eyebrows and eyelashes, switches and the like	24.9	28.0	22.8	5.8	5.5	3.8	US$/kg	899
0402	Milk and cream, concentrated or containing added sugar	18.9	30.5	23.7	1.3	1.5	1.0	US$/kg	022

Services Imports and Exports: EBOPS 2002 categories

Table 2: Merchandise exports by SITC

(Value in million US$, growth and shares in percentage)

SITC	2015	Avg. Growth rates 2011-2015	Avg. Growth rates 2014-2015	2015 share
Total	671.9	-5.8	-16.4	100.0
0+1	85.3	-6.7	-26.3	12.7
2+4	205.6	3.9	-10.2	30.6
3	9.7	-24.7	-19.2	1.4
5	84.6	-5.6	22.4	12.6
6	98.8	-22.5	-40.1	14.7
7	42.7	12.7	-6.6	6.4
8	118.7	6.3	-5.2	17.7
9	26.5	-5.6	-36.8	3.9

Table 3: Merchandise imports by SITC

(Value in million US$, growth and shares in percentage)

SITC	2015	Avg. Growth rates 2011-2015	Avg. Growth rates 2014-2015	2015 share
Total	1732.1	-0.3	-1.2	100.0
0+1	215.8	1.1	-4.2	12.5
2+4	73.1	-2.3	46.7	4.2
3	245.7	-4.3	-24.1	14.2
5	323.5	4.5	19.8	18.7
6	368.4	1.1	-0.8	21.3
7	415.1	-2.9	-1.8	24.0
8	90.5	1.4	0.1	5.2

SITC Legend

SITC Code	Description
Total	All commodities
0+1	Food, animals + beverages, tobacco
2+4	Crude materials + anim. & veg. oils
3	Mineral fuels, lubricants
5	Chemicals
6	Goods classified chiefly by material
7	Machinery and transport equipment
8	Miscellaneous manufactured articles
9	Not classified elsewhere in the SITC

Graph 4: Merchandise trade balance

(Mln US$ by MDG Regions in 2015)

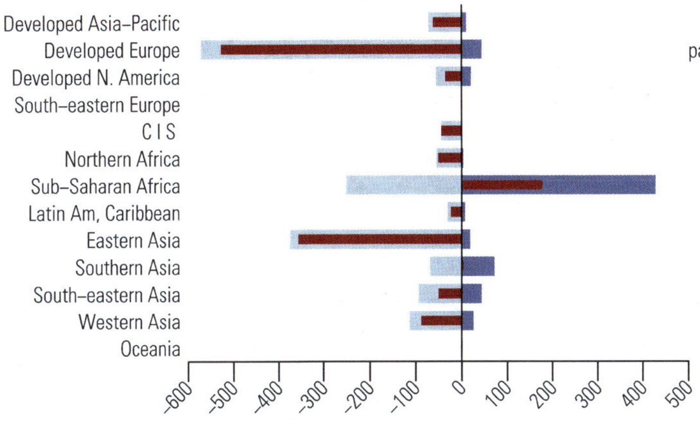

Graph 5: Partner concentration of merchandise trade

(Cumulative share by ranked partners in 2015)

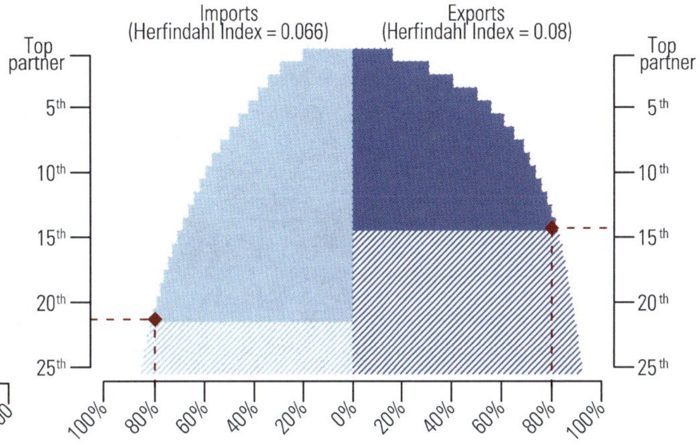

Graph 6: Imports of services by EBOPS category

(% share in 2013)

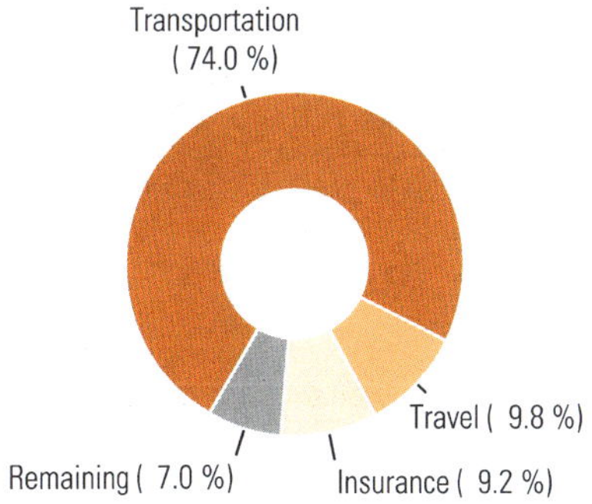

Imports Profile:

"Machinery and transport equipment" (SITC section 7), "Goods classified chiefly by material" (SITC section 6) and "Chemicals" (SITC section 5) were the largest commodity groups for imports in 2015, representing respectively 24.0, 21.3 and 18.7 percent of imported goods (see table 3). From 2013 to 2015, the largest import commodity was "Petroleum oils, other than crude" (HS code 2710) (see table 4). The top three partners for merchandise imports were China, France and the Netherlands, accounting for respectively 17.8, 8.8 and 4.9 percent of total imports. "Transportation" (EBOPS code 205) accounted for the largest share of imports of services in 2013 at 342.9 mln US$, followed by "Travel" (EBOPS code 236) at 45.2 mln US$ and "Insurance services" (EBOPS code 253) at 42.7 mln US$ (see graph 6).

Table 4: Top 10 import commodities 2013 to 2015

HS code	4-digit heading of Harmonized System 2007	Value (million US$) 2013	2014	2015	Unit value 2013	2014	2015	Unit	SITC code
	All Commodities	1967.3	1753.2	1732.1					
2710	Petroleum oils, other than crude	341.0	265.0	188.2	1.0	0.9	0.6	US$/kg	334
3004	Medicaments (excluding goods of heading 30.02, 30.05 or 30.06)	80.7	66.8	89.5	21.5	13.9	17.6	US$/kg	542
2523	Portland cement, aluminous cement, slag cement	86.4	80.3	39.4	0.1	0.1	0.1	US$/kg	661
3901	Polymers of ethylene, in primary forms	63.4	60.7	63.5	1.7	1.6	1.4	US$/kg	571
8703	Motor cars and other motor vehicles principally designed for the transport	35.8	49.5	47.7	*22.5*	*23.5*	*24.6*	thsd US$/unit	781
5208	Woven fabrics of cotton, containing 85 % or more by weight of cotton	40.1	42.1	32.7	1.4	1.4	1.3	US$/kg	652
8704	Motor vehicles for the transport of goods	36.3	42.0	25.0					782
8429	Self-propelled bulldozers, angledozers, graders, levellers, scrapers	26.3	39.7	24.1	*64.7*		*67.6*	thsd US$/unit	723
0303	Fish, frozen, excluding fish fillets and other fish meat of heading 03.04	28.4	26.8	34.7	0.6	0.6	0.6	US$/kg	034
5404	Synthetic monofilament of 67 decitex or more	27.5	27.6	30.0	5.8	5.8	6.5	US$/kg	651

Tonga

Goods Imports: CIF, by origin **Goods Exports: FOB, by last known destination** **Trade System: General**

Overview:

In 2014, the value of merchandise exports of Tonga increased substantially by 10.5 percent to reach 18.9 mln US$, while its merchandise imports increased substantially by 10.2 percent to reach 218.2 mln US$ (see graph 1, table 2 and table 3). The merchandise trade balance recorded a large deficit of 199.3 mln US$ (see graph 1). The largest merchandise trade balance was with MDG Developed Asia-Pacific at -83.6 mln US$ (see graph 4).Merchandise exports in Tonga were diversified amongst partners; imports were also diversified. The top 5 partners accounted for 80 percent or more of exports and 6 partners accounted for 80 percent or more of imports (see graph 5). In 2012, the value of exports of services of Tonga increased substantially by 26.5 percent, reaching 81.6 mln US$, while its imports of services increased substantially by 13.9 percent and reached 76.4 mln US$ (see graph 2). There was a relatively small trade in services surplus of 5.2 mln US$.

Graph 1: Total merchandise trade, by value

(Mln US$ by year)

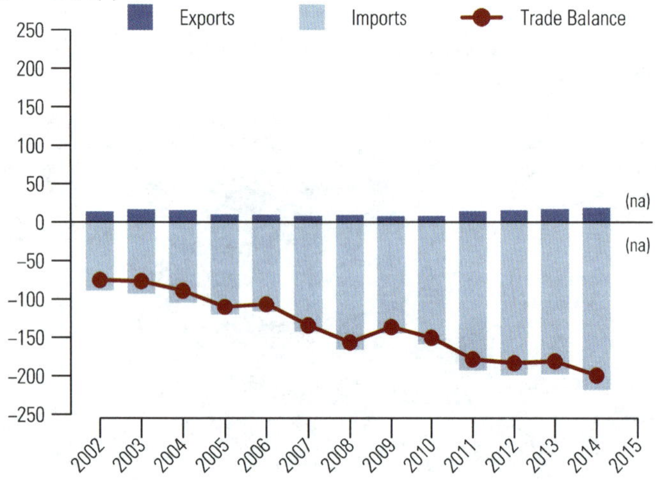

Graph 2: Total services trade, by value

(Mln US$ by year)

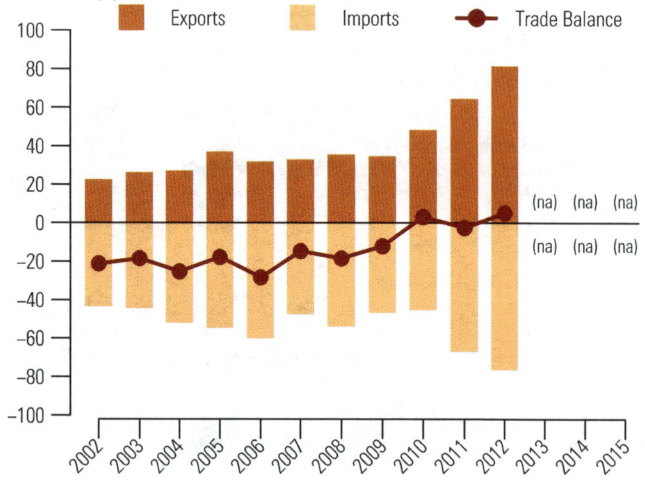

Exports Profile:

"Food, animals + beverages, tobacco" (SITC section 0+1), "Mineral fuels, lubricants" (SITC section 3) and "Crude materials + anim. & veg. oils" (SITC section 2+4) were the largest commodity groups for exports in 2014, representing respectively 68.7, 15.5 and 6.1 percent of exported goods (see table 2). From 2012 to 2014, the largest export commodity was "Fish, fresh or chilled, excluding fish fillets" (HS code 0302) (see table 1). The top three destinations for merchandise exports were New Zealand, the United States and China, Hong Kong SAR, accounting for respectively 24.4, 12.2 and 12.2 percent of total exports. "Travel" (EBOPS code 236) accounted for the largest share of exports of services in 2012 at 44.0 mln US$, followed by "Government services, n.i.e." (EBOPS code 291) at 11.4 mln US$ and "Transportation" (EBOPS code 205) at 11.4 mln US$ (see graph 3).

Graph 3: Exports of services by EBOPS category

(% share in 2012)

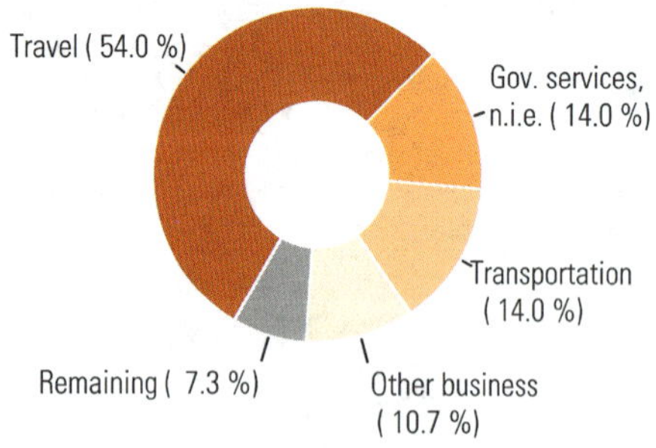

Table 1: Top 10 export commodities 2012 to 2014

HS code	4-digit heading of Harmonized System 2007	Value (million US$) 2012	2013	2014	Unit value 2012	2013	2014	Unit	SITC code
	All Commodities	15.6	17.1	18.9					
0302	Fish, fresh or chilled, excluding fish fillets	2.1	2.0	2.9	7.6	9.9	5.3	US$/kg	034
0714	Manioc, arrowroot, sweet potatoes and similar roots	1.7	2.5	2.7	1.0	0.7	0.6	US$/kg	054
0307	Molluscs, whether in shell or not	2.1	0.8	3.1	*15.7*	11.4	5.9	US$/kg	036
2710	Petroleum oils, other than crude	0.0	3.0	2.9			*1.1*	US$/kg	334
0709	Other vegetables, fresh or chilled	1.5	1.6	1.1	0.4	0.6	0.6	US$/kg	054
1212	Locust beans, seaweeds and other algae	1.9	1.0	1.4	4.1	5.1	7.9	US$/kg	292
0801	Coconuts, Brazil nuts and cashew nuts, fresh or dried	0.6	0.8	0.7					057
0303	Fish, frozen, excluding fish fillets and other fish meat of heading 03.04	0.4	0.6	0.3	1.1	2.1	1.0	US$/kg	034
1211	Plants and parts of plants (including seeds and fruits)	0.1	0.5	0.6	*6.3*	11.4	13.5	US$/kg	292
4907	Unused postage, revenue or similar stamps of current or new issue	1.1	0.0	0.0					892

Services Imports and Exports: EBOPS 2002 categories

Table 2: Merchandise exports by SITC
(Value in million US$, growth and shares in percentage)

SITC	2014	Avg. Growth rates 2010-2014	2013-2014	2014 share
Total	18.9	23.0	10.5	100.0
0+1	13.0	15.4	31.2	68.7
2+4	1.2	41.5	-12.5	6.1
3	2.9	...	-3.8	15.5
5	0.3	-3.4	-10.5	1.7
6	0.1	42.4	72.3	0.7
7	0.6	306.5	-47.3	3.1
8	0.7	31.3	-42.6	3.7
9	0.1	38.1	13.2	0.5

Table 3: Merchandise imports by SITC
(Value in million US$, growth and shares in percentage)

SITC	2014	Avg. Growth rates 2010-2014	2013-2014	2014 share
Total	218.2	8.3	10.2	100.0
0+1	58.6	6.4	1.4	26.9
2+4	5.9	6.8	27.1	2.7
3	46.5	6.5	5.6	21.3
5	9.8	7.2	4.2	4.5
6	23.1	2.5	20.0	10.6
7	55.5	15.7	37.3	25.5
8	15.6	6.7	7.1	7.1
9	3.2	33.7	-59.9	1.5

SITC Legend

SITC Code	Description
Total	All commodities
0+1	Food, animals + beverages, tobacco
2+4	Crude materials + anim. & veg. oils
3	Mineral fuels, lubricants
5	Chemicals
6	Goods classified chiefly by material
7	Machinery and transport equipment
8	Miscellaneous manufactured articles
9	Not classified elsewhere in the SITC

Graph 4: Merchandise trade balance
(Mln US$ by MDG Regions in 2014)

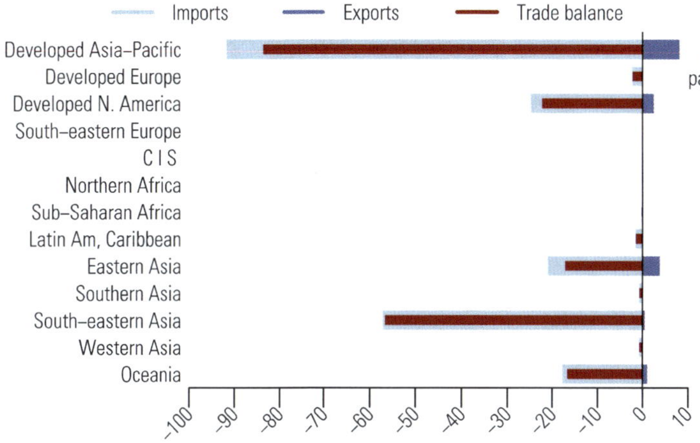

Graph 5: Partner concentration of merchandise trade
(Cumulative share by ranked partners in 2014)

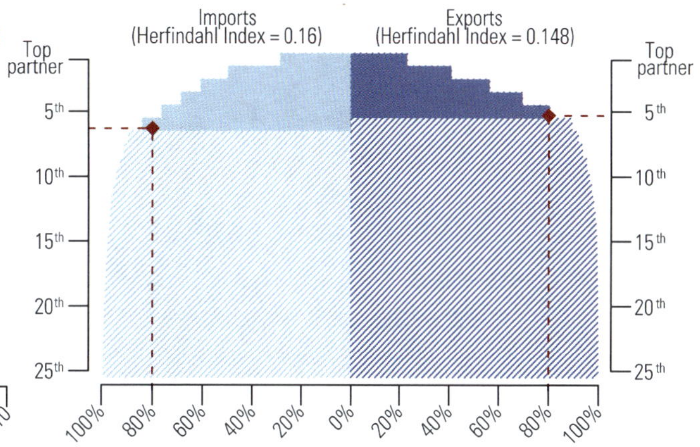

Graph 6: Imports of services by EBOPS category
(% share in 2012)

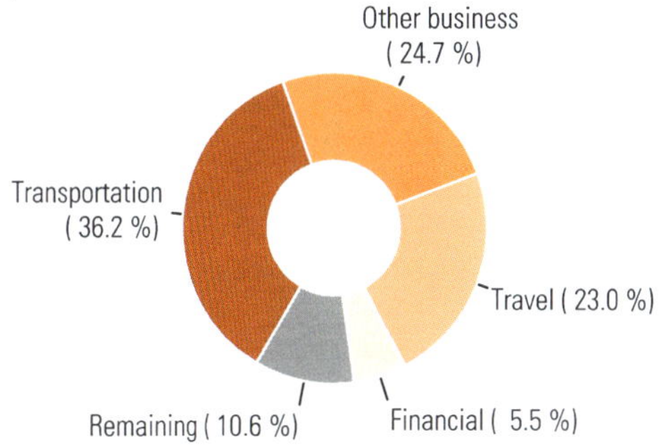

Imports Profile:

"Food, animals + beverages, tobacco" (SITC section 0+1), "Machinery and transport equipment" (SITC section 7) and "Mineral fuels, lubricants" (SITC section 3) were the largest commodity groups for imports in 2014, representing respectively 26.9, 25.5 and 21.3 percent of imported goods (see table 3). From 2012 to 2014, the largest import commodity was "Petroleum oils, other than crude" (HS code 2710) (see table 4). The top three partners for merchandise imports were New Zealand, Singapore and the United States, accounting for respectively 29.0, 23.3 and 11.7 percent of total imports. "Transportation" (EBOPS code 205) accounted for the largest share of imports of services in 2012 at 27.7 mln US$, followed by "Other business services" (EBOPS code 268) at 18.9 mln US$ and "Travel" (EBOPS code 236) at 17.6 mln US$ (see graph 6).

Table 4: Top 10 import commodities 2012 to 2014

HS code	4-digit heading of Harmonized System 2007	Value (million US$) 2012	2013	2014	Unit value 2012	2013	2014	Unit	SITC code
	All Commodities	199.2	198.0	218.2					
2710	Petroleum oils, other than crude	44.6	41.6	44.2			*1.1*	US$/kg	334
0207	Meat and edible offal, of the poultry of heading 01.05	12.4	11.8	12.5	1.6	1.5	1.4	US$/kg	012
8517	Electrical apparatus for line telephony or line telegraphy	2.6	9.5	6.2					764
8703	Motor cars and other motor vehicles principally designed for the transport	5.1	5.3	6.3	5.1			thsd US$/unit	781
8541	Diodes, transistors and similar semiconductor devices	0.0	0.2	11.3					776
1602	Other prepared or preserved meat, meat offal or blood	3.7	4.1	3.6	5.6	4.7	5.0	US$/kg	017
9999	Commodities not specified according to kind	0.1	7.9	3.2					931
1101	Wheat or meslin flour	3.8	3.6	3.3	0.7	0.6	0.5	US$/kg	046
0204	Meat of sheep or goats, fresh, chilled or frozen	4.0	3.4	2.8	4.3	4.3	4.2	US$/kg	012
2202	Waters with added sugar	2.8	3.1	2.7	0.8	0.7	0.7	US$/litre	111

Goods Imports: CIF, by origin | **Goods Exports: FOB, by last known destination** | **Trade System: General**

Overview:

In 2013, the value of merchandise exports of Tunisia increased slightly by 0.3 percent to reach 17.1 bln US$, while its merchandise imports decreased slightly by 0.8 percent to reach 24.3 bln US$ (see graph 1, table 2 and table 3). The merchandise trade balance recorded a moderate deficit of 7.2 bln US$ (see graph 1). The largest merchandise trade balance was with MDG Eastern Asia at -1.8 bln US$ (see graph 4). Merchandise exports in Tunisia were diversified amongst partners; imports were also diversified. The top 10 partners accounted for 80 percent or more of exports and 18 partners accounted for 80 percent or more of imports (see graph 5). In 2014, the value of exports of services of Tunisia decreased slightly by 1.5 percent, reaching 5.0 bln US$, while its imports of services increased slightly by 3.0 percent and reached 3.5 bln US$ (see graph 2). There was a moderate trade in services surplus of 1.4 bln US$.

Graph 1: Total merchandise trade, by value

(Bln US$ by year)

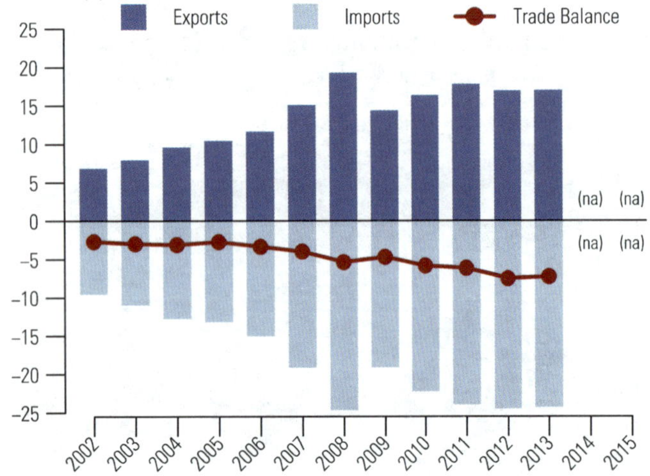

Graph 2: Total services trade, by value

(Bln US$ by year)

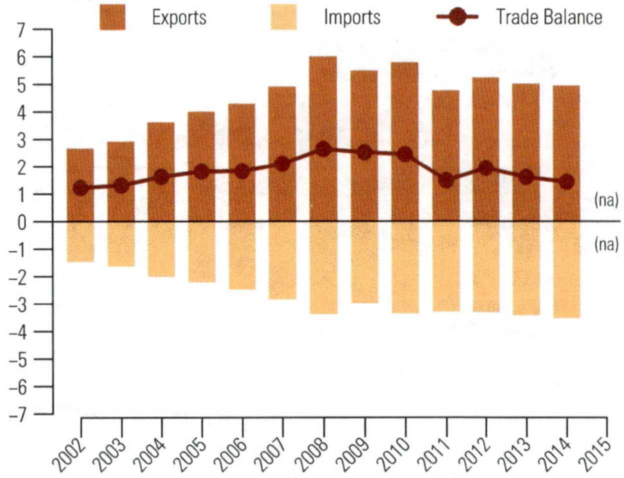

Exports Profile:

"Machinery and transport equipment" (SITC section 7), "Miscellaneous manufactured articles" (SITC section 8) and "Mineral fuels, lubricants" (SITC section 3) were the largest commodity groups for exports in 2013, representing respectively 31.3, 24.6 and 15.2 percent of exported goods (see table 2). From 2011 to 2013, the largest export commodity was "Petroleum oils and oils obtained from bituminous minerals, crude" (HS code 2709) (see table 1). The top three destinations for merchandise exports were France, Italy and Germany, accounting for respectively 28.1, 19.7 and 8.8 percent of total exports. "Travel" (EBOPS code 236) accounted for the largest share of exports of services in 2014 at 2.4 bln US$, followed by "Transportation" (EBOPS code 205) at 1.2 bln US$ and "Construction services" (EBOPS code 249) at 377.3 mln US$ (see graph 3).

Graph 3: Exports of services by EBOPS category

(% share in 2014)

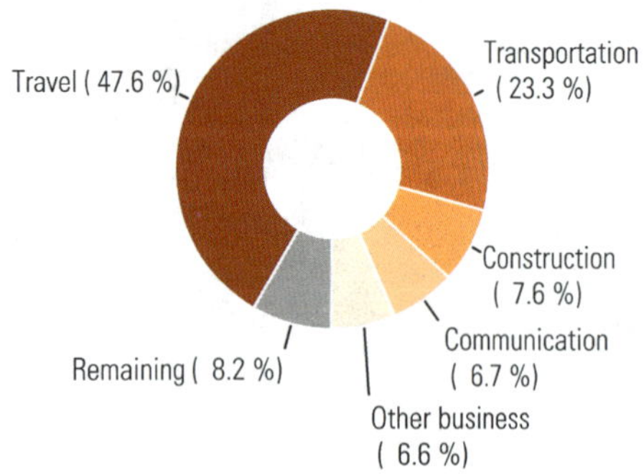

Table 1: Top 10 export commodities 2011 to 2013

HS code	4-digit heading of Harmonized System 2007	Value (million US$) 2011	2012	2013	Unit value 2011	2012	2013	Unit	SITC code
	All Commodities	17 847.0	17 007.4	17 060.5					
2709	Petroleum oils and oils obtained from bituminous minerals, crude	2 288.9	1 875.9	1 748.1	0.8	0.8	0.8	US$/kg	333
8544	Insulated (including enamelled or anodised) wire, cable	1 751.6	1 633.7	1 678.2	14.5	14.2	14.7	US$/kg	773
6203	Men's or boys' suits, ensembles, jackets, blazers, trousers	753.7	614.6	676.2	19.8	3.3	20.1	US$/unit	841
2710	Petroleum oils, other than crude	288.4	948.8	802.9	0.9	0.9	0.8	US$/kg	334
6211	Track suits, ski suits and swimwear; other garments	678.4	625.5	634.3					845
8528	Reception apparatus for television	572.3	492.6	487.0	101.4	89.0	99.9	US$/unit	761
8536	Electrical apparatus for switching or protecting electrical circuits	414.3	368.6	440.6	28.0	26.2	28.8	US$/kg	772
1509	Olive oil and its fractions	286.1	375.2	504.6	2.9	2.4	3.3	US$/kg	421
6109	T-shirts, singlets and other vests, knitted or crocheted	406.1	324.6	316.4	6.5		5.9	US$/unit	845
3105	Mineral or chemical fertilisers	237.3	331.5	378.4	0.6	0.6	0.5	US$/kg	562

Services Imports and Exports: EBOPS 2002 categories

Table 2: Merchandise exports by SITC

(Value in million US$, growth and shares in percentage)

SITC	2013	Avg. Growth rates 2009-2013	Avg. Growth rates 2012-2013	2013 share
Total	17 060.5	4.2	0.3	100.0
0+1	1 035.5	5.5	6.7	6.1
2+4	861.8	5.4	-3.2	5.1
3	2 595.5	7.1	-9.1	15.2
5	1 505.1	-0.3	2.0	8.8
6	1 512.1	0.6	3.7	8.9
7	5 348.1	10.2	3.1	31.3
8	4 200.9	-0.7	2.3	24.6
9	1.4	-17.6	-97.8	0.0

Table 3: Merchandise imports by SITC

(Value in million US$, growth and shares in percentage)

SITC	2013	Avg. Growth rates 2009-2013	Avg. Growth rates 2012-2013	2013 share
Total	24 266.4	6.2	-0.8	100.0
0+1	1 965.5	11.5	19.6	8.1
2+4	1 287.1	7.8	-5.1	5.3
3	4 318.4	18.7	1.4	17.8
5	2 859.7	8.5	6.0	11.8
6	4 628.3	1.7	1.1	19.1
7	7 416.0	2.9	-5.0	30.6
8	1 783.5	1.4	6.3	7.3
9	7.8	4.5	-98.3	0.0

SITC Legend

SITC Code	Description
Total	All commodities
0+1	Food, animals + beverages, tobacco
2+4	Crude materials + anim. & veg. oils
3	Mineral fuels, lubricants
5	Chemicals
6	Goods classified chiefly by material
7	Machinery and transport equipment
8	Miscellaneous manufactured articles
9	Not classified elsewhere in the SITC

Graph 4: Merchandise trade balance

(Bln US$ by MDG Regions in 2013)

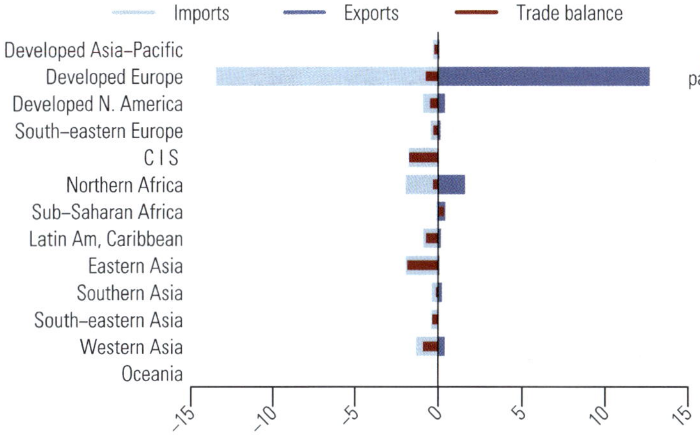

Graph 5: Partner concentration of merchandise trade

(Cumulative share by ranked partners in 2013)

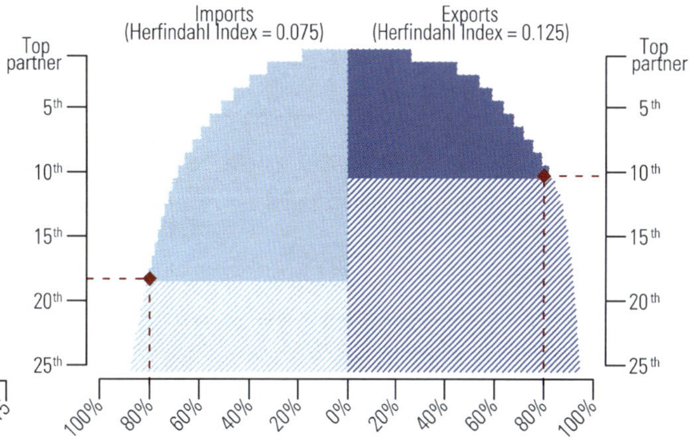

Graph 6: Imports of services by EBOPS category

(% share in 2014)

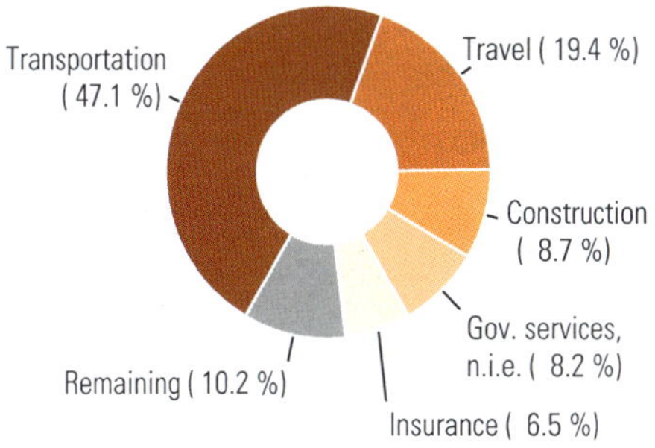

Imports Profile:

"Machinery and transport equipment" (SITC section 7), "Goods classified chiefly by material" (SITC section 6) and "Mineral fuels, lubricants" (SITC section 3) were the largest commodity groups for imports in 2013, representing respectively 30.6, 19.1 and 17.8 percent of imported goods (see table 3). From 2011 to 2013, the largest import commodity was "Petroleum oils, other than crude" (HS code 2710) (see table 4). The top three partners for merchandise imports were France, Italy and Germany, accounting for respectively 17.7, 14.8 and 7.1 percent of total imports. "Transportation" (EBOPS code 205) accounted for the largest share of imports of services in 2014 at 1.7 bln US$, followed by "Travel" (EBOPS code 236) at 680.0 mln US$ and "Construction services" (EBOPS code 249) at 306.0 mln US$ (see graph 6).

Table 4: Top 10 import commodities 2011 to 2013

HS code	4-digit heading of Harmonized System 2007	Value (million US$) 2011	2012	2013	Unit value 2011	2012	2013	Unit	SITC code
	All Commodities	23 952.1	24 470.6	24 266.4					
2710	Petroleum oils, other than crude	2 342.0	2 007.7	1 916.9	0.9	1.0	0.9	US$/kg	334
2711	Petroleum gases and other gaseous hydrocarbons	810.7	1 251.8	1 312.0	0.6	0.6	0.6	US$/kg	343
8703	Motor cars and other motor vehicles principally designed for the transport	622.6	801.5	820.0	14.3	14.1	13.8	thsd US$/unit	781
2709	Petroleum oils and oils obtained from bituminous minerals, crude	274.0	859.5	957.2	0.9	0.9	0.8	US$/kg	333
1001	Wheat and meslin	553.0	281.6	508.9	0.4	0.3	0.3	US$/kg	041
5209	Woven fabrics of cotton, containing 85 % or more by weight of cotton	506.8	380.4	376.6	14.4	13.0	12.9	US$/kg	652
8704	Motor vehicles for the transport of goods	347.2	466.7	441.8	18.8	20.5	19.3	thsd US$/unit	782
8536	Electrical apparatus for switching or protecting electrical circuits	445.2	381.5	404.1	28.6	25.6	25.9	US$/kg	772
7408	Copper wire	447.7	363.4	338.6	9.1	8.0	7.8	US$/kg	682
8544	Insulated (including enamelled or anodised) wire, cable	401.5	340.6	366.5	14.8	13.8	14.7	US$/kg	773

Source: UN Comtrade

Goods Imports: CIF, by origin	Goods Exports: FOB, by last known destination	Trade System: Special

Overview:

In 2015, the value of merchandise exports of Turkey decreased moderately by 8.7 percent to reach 143.9 bln US$, while its merchandise imports decreased substantially by 14.4 percent to reach 207.2 bln US$ (see graph 1, table 2 and table 3). The merchandise trade balance recorded a moderate deficit of 63.4 bln US$ (see graph 1). The largest merchandise trade balance was with MDG Eastern Asia at -30.5 bln US$ (see graph 4). Merchandise exports in Turkey were diversified amongst partners; imports were also diversified. The top 31 partners accounted for 80 percent or more of exports and 24 partners accounted for 80 percent or more of imports (see graph 5). In 2014, the value of exports of services of Turkey increased moderately by 7.3 percent, reaching 50.4 bln US$, while its imports of services increased slightly by 4.3 percent and reached 25.1 bln US$ (see graph 2). There was a large trade in services surplus of 25.4 bln US$.

Graph 1: Total merchandise trade, by value

(Bln US$ by year)

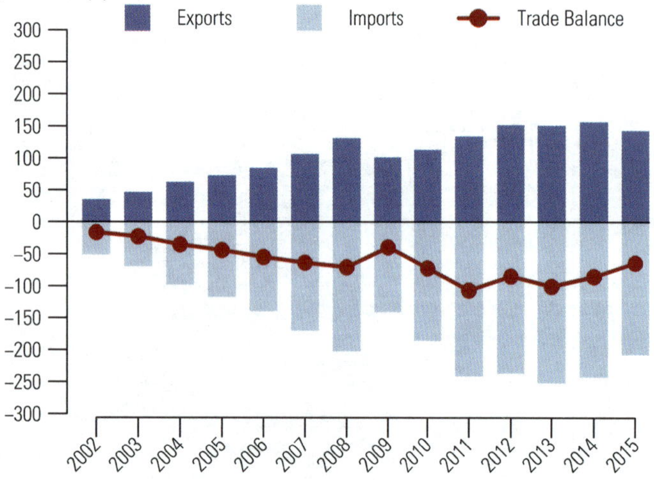

Graph 2: Total services trade, by value

(Bln US$ by year)

Exports Profile:

"Machinery and transport equipment" (SITC section 7), "Goods classified chiefly by material" (SITC section 6) and "Miscellaneous manufactured articles" (SITC section 8) were the largest commodity groups for exports in 2015, representing respectively 27.3, 24.7 and 18.7 percent of exported goods (see table 2). From 2013 to 2015, the largest export commodity was "Motor cars and other motor vehicles principally designed for the transport" (HS code 8703) (see table 1). The top three destinations for merchandise exports were Germany, Iraq and the United Kingdom, accounting for respectively 9.3, 6.9 and 6.5 percent of total exports. "Travel" (EBOPS code 236) accounted for the largest share of exports of services in 2012 at 26.3 bln US$, followed by "Transportation" (EBOPS code 205) at 12.8 bln US$ (see graph 3).

Graph 3: Exports of services by EBOPS category

(% share in 2012)

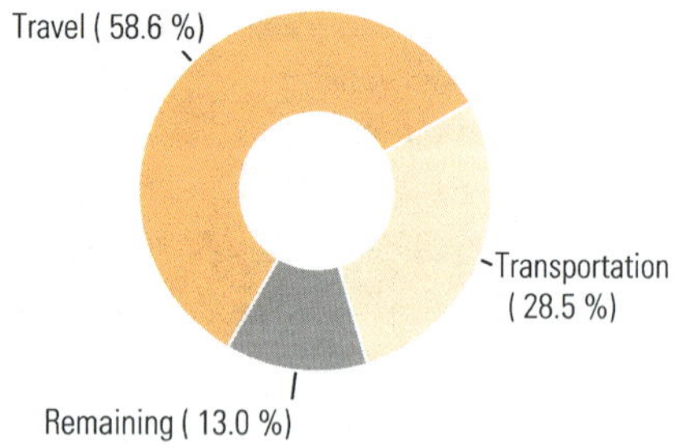

Table 1: Top 10 export commodities 2013 to 2015

HS code	4-digit heading of Harmonized System 2012	Value (million US$) 2013	2014	2015	Unit value 2013	2014	2015	Unit	SITC code
	All Commodities	151 802.6	157 610.2	143 850.4					
8703	Motor cars and other motor vehicles principally designed for the transport	6 856.5	7 256.0	6 899.8	12.4	11.8	10.3	thsd US$/unit	781
2710	Petroleum oils, other than crude	5 963.3	5 480.0	3 966.5	0.9	0.8	0.5	US$/kg	334
7108	Gold (including gold plated with platinum)	3 349.0	3 211.9	7 381.1	46.5	41.2	38.3	thsd US$/kg	971
7214	Other bars and rods of iron or non-alloy steel	4 849.1	4 341.1	3 077.9	0.6	0.6	0.4	US$/kg	676
8704	Motor vehicles for the transport of goods	3 850.7	4 138.9	4 248.9	14.8	15.1	12.8	thsd US$/unit	782
8708	Parts and accessories of the motor vehicles of headings 87.01 to 87.05	3 905.2	4 133.6	3 803.5	5.1	4.9	4.4	US$/kg	784
7113	Articles of jewellery and parts thereof, of precious metal	3 411.3	4 347.6	3 756.6	18.7	17.8	15.4	thsd US$/kg	897
6109	T-shirts, singlets and other vests, knitted or crocheted	3 276.0	3 566.4	2 979.6	4.3	4.2	3.8	US$/unit	845
6204	Women's or girls'suits, ensembles, jackets, blazers, dresses, skirts	2 283.1	2 417.5	2 195.4	13.7	13.3	11.2	US$/unit	842
8544	Insulated (including enamelled or anodised) wire, cable	2 499.7	2 421.3	1 947.1	6.2	5.8	5.0	US$/kg	773

Services Imports and Exports: EBOPS 2002 categories

Table 2: Merchandise exports by SITC

(Value in million US$, growth and shares in percentage)

SITC	2015	Avg. Growth rates 2011-2015	2014-2015	2015 share
Total	143 850.4	1.6	-8.7	100.0
0+1	15 569.6	4.2	-5.9	10.8
2+4	4 570.9	-0.6	-18.3	3.2
3	4 298.4	-9.5	-27.0	3.0
5	8 268.4	3.9	-9.7	5.7
6	35 537.6	-3.1	-15.9	24.7
7	39 253.5	1.2	-8.1	27.3
8	26 865.9	4.9	-9.5	18.7
9	9 486.1	27.5	63.9	6.6

Table 3: Merchandise imports by SITC

(Value in million US$, growth and shares in percentage)

SITC	2015	Avg. Growth rates 2011-2015	2014-2015	2015 share
Total	207 206.5	-3.7	-14.4	100.0
0+1	7 268.0	-0.6	-6.4	3.5
2+4	14 493.0	-9.6	-24.4	7.0
3	14 415.8	-7.5	-28.4	7.0
5	28 678.1	-1.7	-12.5	13.8
6	34 594.4	-2.6	-10.0	16.7
7	65 425.7	-0.6	-0.6	31.6
8	13 839.5	-0.4	-10.2	6.7
9	28 492.0	-9.1	-33.2	13.8

SITC Legend

SITC Code	Description
Total	All commodities
0+1	Food, animals + beverages, tobacco
2+4	Crude materials + anim. & veg. oils
3	Mineral fuels, lubricants
5	Chemicals
6	Goods classified chiefly by material
7	Machinery and transport equipment
8	Miscellaneous manufactured articles
9	Not classified elsewhere in the SITC

Graph 4: Merchandise trade balance

(Bln US$ by MDG Regions in 2015)

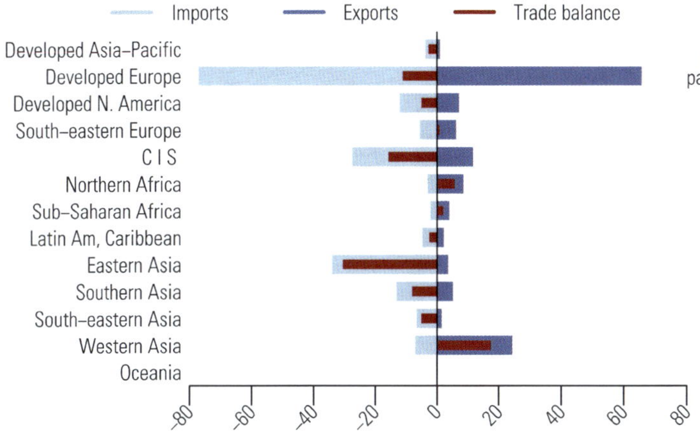

Graph 5: Partner concentration of merchandise trade

(Cumulative share by ranked partners in 2015)

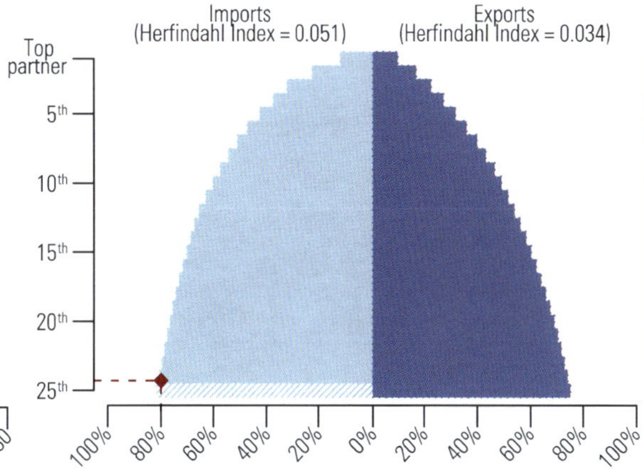

Graph 6: Imports of services by EBOPS category

(% share in 2012)

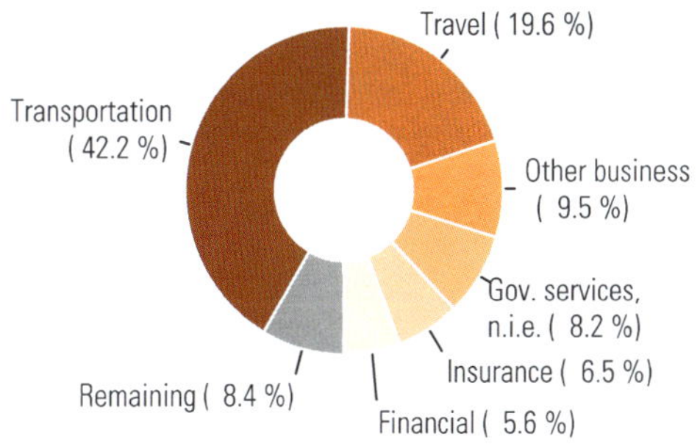

Imports Profile:

"Machinery and transport equipment" (SITC section 7), "Goods classified chiefly by material" (SITC section 6) and "Chemicals" (SITC section 5) were the largest commodity groups for imports in 2015, representing respectively 31.6, 16.7 and 13.8 percent of imported goods (see table 3). From 2013 to 2015, the largest import commodity was "Commodities not specified according to kind" (HS code 9999) (see table 4). The top three partners for merchandise imports were China, the Russian Federation and Germany, accounting for respectively 10.6, 10.1 and 9.7 percent of total imports. "Transportation" (EBOPS code 205) accounted for the largest share of imports of services in 2012 at 9.1 bln US$, followed by "Travel" (EBOPS code 236) at 4.2 bln US$ and "Other business services" (EBOPS code 268) at 2.0 bln US$ (see graph 6).

Table 4: Top 10 import commodities 2013 to 2015

HS code	4-digit heading of Harmonized System 2012	Value (million US$) 2013	2014	2015	Unit value 2013	2014	2015	Unit	SITC code
	All Commodities	251 661.3	242 177.1	207 206.5					
9999	Commodities not specified according to kind	36 542.2	35 565.4	25 065.9					931
2710	Petroleum oils, other than crude	15 439.0	15 369.4	9 023.7	1.0	0.9	0.5	US$/kg	334
8703	Motor cars and other motor vehicles principally designed for the transport	9 130.1	7 721.0	9 227.4	16.2	16.7	15.2	thsd US$/unit	781
7108	Gold (including gold plated with platinum)	15 127.2	7 106.9	3 425.9	43.2	37.0	32.8	thsd US$/kg	971
7204	Ferrous waste and scrap; remelting scrap ingots of iron or steel	7 511.2	7 150.5	4 288.1	0.4	0.4	0.3	US$/kg	282
8708	Parts and accessories of the motor vehicles of headings 87.01 to 87.05	4 894.1	4 950.8	4 966.0	10.0	10.1	8.8	US$/kg	784
8517	Electrical apparatus for line telephony or line telegraphy	3 950.7	4 420.1	4 674.8					764
3902	Polymers of propylene or of other olefins, in primary forms	2 973.6	3 314.3	2 649.7	1.7	1.7	1.4	US$/kg	575
3004	Medicaments (excluding goods of heading 30.02, 30.05 or 30.06)	2 822.9	2 875.2	2 642.6	77.0	76.5	63.0	US$/kg	542
8802	Other aircraft (for example, helicopters, aeroplanes); spacecraft	1 960.4	2 676.7	3 442.4	5.3	12.3	26.7	mln US$/unit	792

Turks and Caicos Islands

Goods Imports: CIF, by origin | **Goods Exports: FOB, by last known destination** | **Trade System: General**

Overview:

In 2012, the value of merchandise exports of the Turks and Caicos Islands increased substantially by 38.6 percent to reach 11.8 mln US$, while its merchandise imports increased slightly by 3.2 percent to reach 268.5 mln US$ (see graph 1, table 2 and table 3). The merchandise trade balance recorded a large deficit of 256.7 mln US$ (see graph 1). The largest merchandise trade balance was with MDG Developed North America at -191.5 mln US$ (see graph 4). Merchandise exports in the Turks and Caicos Islands were highly concentrated amongst partners; imports were also highly concentrated. The top 1 partner accounted for 80 percent or more of exports and 2 partners accounted for 80 percent or more of imports (see graph 5). No trade in services data is available.

Graph 1: Total merchandise trade, by value

(Mln US$ by year)

Graph 2: No Data Available

Exports Profile:

"Miscellaneous manufactured articles" (SITC section 8), "Food, animals + beverages, tobacco" (SITC section 0+1) and "Machinery and transport equipment" (SITC section 7) were the largest commodity groups for exports in 2012, representing respectively 65.7, 15.9 and 11.6 percent of exported goods (see table 2). From 2010 to 2012, the largest export commodity was "Unused postage, revenue or similar stamps of current or new issue" (HS code 4907) (see table 1). The top three destinations for merchandise exports were the United States, Areas nes and Haiti, accounting for respectively 83.3, 16.7 and 0.0 percent of total exports. Services data by detailed EBOPS category is not available for exports.

Graph 3: No Data Available

Table 1: Top 10 export commodities 2010 to 2012

HS code	4-digit heading of Harmonized System 2007	Value (million US$) 2010	2011	2012	Unit value 2010	2011	2012	Unit	SITC code
	All Commodities	...	8.5	11.8					
4907	Unused postage, revenue or similar stamps of current or new issue	...	4.9	7.3		3.5	6.2	thsd US$/kg	892
0306	Crustaceans, whether in shell or not	...	1.0	1.1		13.1	12.2	US$/kg	036
0307	Molluscs, whether in shell or not	...	0.2	0.8		4.7	4.2	US$/kg	036
9999	Commodities not specified according to kind	...	0.3	0.3					931
8429	Self-propelled bulldozers, angledozers, graders, levellers, scrapers	...	0.4	0.0		38.0	6.0	thsd US$/unit	723
8704	Motor vehicles for the transport of goods	...	0.1	0.2		41.8	5.5	thsd US$/unit	782
8502	Electric generating sets and rotary converters	...	0.1	0.2		30.8	122.5	thsd US$/unit	716
8903	Yachts and other vessels for pleasure or sports; rowing boats and canoes	...	0.2	0.1		97.2	37.5	thsd US$/unit	793
7113	Articles of jewellery and parts thereof, of precious metal	...	...	0.3			2.8	thsd US$/kg	897
8702	Motor vehicles for the transport of ten or more persons, including the driver	...	0.1	0.1		7.1	2.4	thsd US$/unit	783

Services Imports and Exports: EBOPS 2002 categories

Table 2: Merchandise exports by SITC

(Value in million US$, growth and shares in percentage)

SITC	2012	Avg. Growth rates 2008-2012	Avg. Growth rates 2011-2012	2012 share
Total	11.8	-16.9	38.6	100.0
0+1	1.9	-20.2	48.8	15.9
2+4	0.2	-0.6	31.0	1.8
3	0.0	-77.4	-33.3	0.0
5	0.0	-48.8	314.6	0.1
6	0.3	-29.2	13.5	2.8
7	1.4	-44.5	-2.6	11.6
8	7.8	79.8	53.1	65.7
9	0.3	-45.2	-23.3	2.1

Table 3: Merchandise imports by SITC

(Value in million US$, growth and shares in percentage)

SITC	2012	Avg. Growth rates 2008-2012	Avg. Growth rates 2011-2012	2012 share
Total	268.5	-17.9	3.2	100.0
0+1	66.9	-4.7	1.2	24.9
2+4	5.0	-28.6	-19.4	1.8
3	75.9	1.5	1.1	28.3
5	13.4	-22.1	-8.5	5.0
6	26.0	-30.9	-5.0	9.7
7	41.1	-26.9	24.7	15.3
8	36.8	-23.6	7.0	13.7
9	3.6	-33.2	-0.5	1.3

SITC Legend

SITC Code	Description
Total	All commodities
0+1	Food, animals + beverages, tobacco
2+4	Crude materials + anim. & veg. oils
3	Mineral fuels, lubricants
5	Chemicals
6	Goods classified chiefly by material
7	Machinery and transport equipment
8	Miscellaneous manufactured articles
9	Not classified elsewhere in the SITC

Graph 4: Merchandise trade balance

(Mln US$ by MDG Regions in 2012)

Graph 5: Partner concentration of merchandise trade

(Cumulative share by ranked partners in 2012)

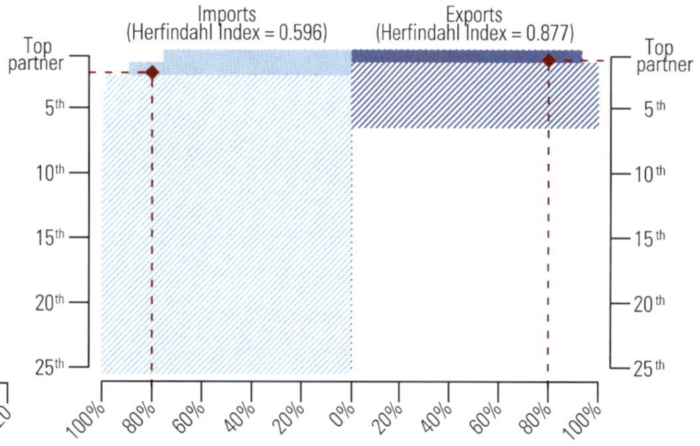

Graph 6: No Data Available

Imports Profile:

"Mineral fuels, lubricants" (SITC section 3), "Food, animals + beverages, tobacco" (SITC section 0+1) and "Machinery and transport equipment" (SITC section 7) were the largest commodity groups for imports in 2012, representing respectively 28.3, 24.9 and 15.3 percent of imported goods (see table 3). From 2010 to 2012, the largest import commodity was "Petroleum oils, other than crude" (HS code 2710) (see table 4). The top three partners for merchandise imports were the United States, the Bahamas and Areas nes, accounting for respectively 77.6, 13.9 and 7.0 percent of total imports. Services data by detailed EBOPS category is not available for imports.

Table 4: Top 10 import commodities 2010 to 2012

HS code	4-digit heading of Harmonized System 2007	Value (million US$) 2010	2011	2012	Unit value 2010	2011	2012	Unit	SITC code
	All Commodities	...	260.2	268.5					
2710	Petroleum oils, other than crude	...	72.2	73.5		0.6	0.7	US$/kg	334
8703	Motor cars and other motor vehicles principally designed for the transport	...	4.8	7.8		10.4	8.5	thsd US$/unit	781
7113	Articles of jewellery and parts thereof, of precious metal	...	5.7	5.8		855.3	899.1	US$/kg	897
0207	Meat and edible offal, of the poultry of heading 01.05	...	3.8	4.5		0.9	1.1	US$/kg	012
9403	Other furniture and parts thereof	...	3.7	4.1					821
2208	Alcohol of a strength by volume of less than 80 % vol	...	4.2	3.2		12.3	8.3	US$/litre	112
2009	Fruit juices (including grape must) and vegetable juices	...	3.7	3.6		*0.5*	0.6	US$/kg	059
9999	Commodities not specified according to kind	...	3.6	3.6					931
2203	Beer made from malt	...	3.8	2.8		1.9	1.3	US$/litre	112
1905	Bread, pastry, cakes, biscuits and other bakers' wares	...	3.0	3.3		0.9	1.1	US$/kg	048

Uganda

Goods Imports: CIF, by origin | **Goods Exports: FOB, by last known destination** | **Trade System: General**

Overview:

In 2014, the value of merchandise exports of Uganda decreased moderately by 6.1 percent to reach 2.3 bln US$, while its merchandise imports increased slightly by 4.4 percent to reach 6.1 bln US$ (see graph 1, table 2 and table 3). The merchandise trade balance recorded a large deficit of 3.8 bln US$ (see graph 1). The largest merchandise trade balance was with MDG Southern Asia at -1.6 bln US$ (see graph 4). Merchandise exports in Uganda were diversified amongst partners; imports were also diversified. The top 14 partners accounted for 80 percent or more of exports and 15 partners accounted for 80 percent or more of imports (see graph 5). In 2014, the value of exports of services of Uganda decreased moderately by 7.5 percent, reaching 2.0 bln US$, while its imports of services increased slightly by 2.2 percent and reached 2.7 bln US$ (see graph 2). There was a moderate trade in services deficit of 723.3 mln US$.

Graph 1: Total merchandise trade, by value

(Bln US$ by year)

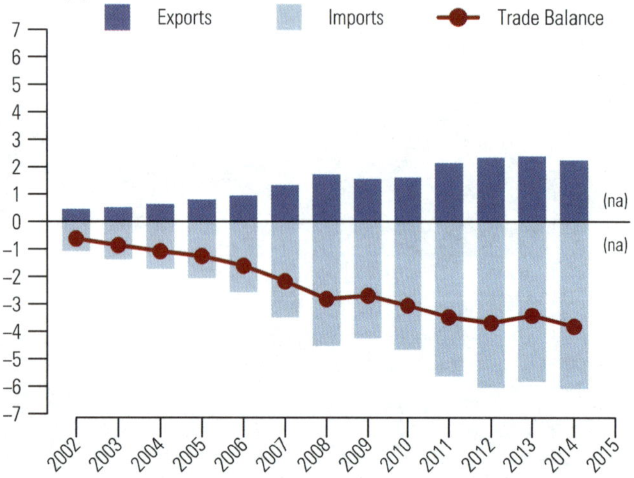

Graph 2: Total services trade, by value

(Bln US$ by year)

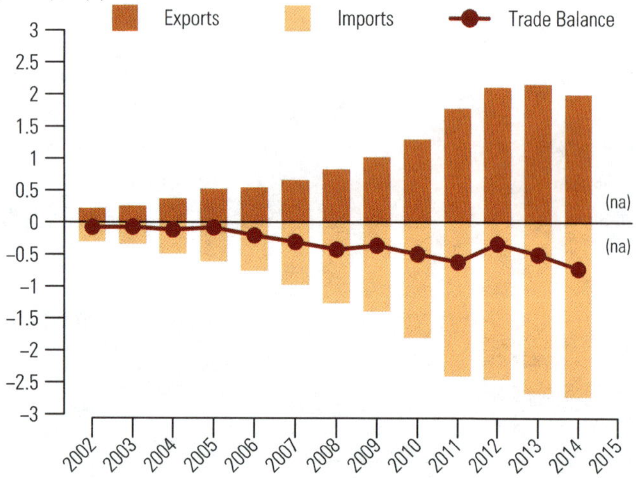

Exports Profile:

"Food, animals + beverages, tobacco" (SITC section 0+1), "Goods classified chiefly by material" (SITC section 6) and "Crude materials + anim. & veg. oils" (SITC section 2+4) were the largest commodity groups for exports in 2014, representing respectively 48.6, 15.4 and 11.9 percent of exported goods (see table 2). From 2012 to 2014, the largest export commodity was "Coffee, whether or not roasted or decaffeinated" (HS code 0901) (see table 1). The top three destinations for merchandise exports were Kenya, the Sudan and Democratic Republic of the Congo, accounting for respectively 12.3, 10.7 and 9.8 percent of total exports. "Travel" (EBOPS code 236) accounted for the largest share of exports of services in 2014 at 791.6 mln US$, followed by "Other business services" (EBOPS code 268) at 508.9 mln US$ and "Construction services" (EBOPS code 249) at 221.3 mln US$ (see graph 3).

Graph 3: Exports of services by EBOPS category

(% share in 2014)

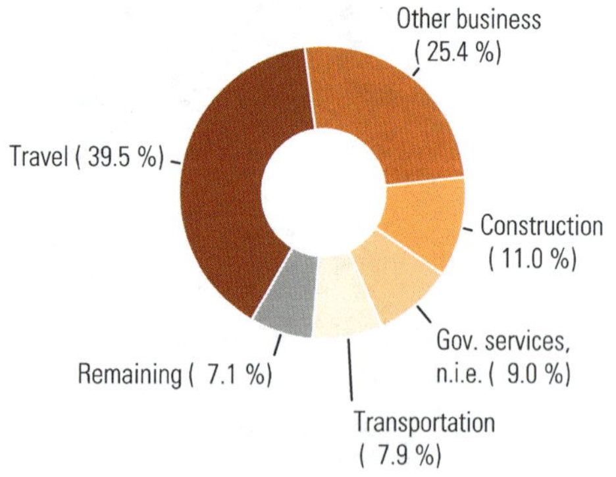

Table 1: Top 10 export commodities 2012 to 2014

HS code	4-digit heading of Harmonized System 2012	Value (million US$) 2012	2013	2014	Unit value 2012	2013	2014	Unit	SITC code
	All Commodities	2 357.5	2 407.7	2 262.0					
0901	Coffee, whether or not roasted or decaffeinated	372.2	425.4	410.1	2.2	1.8	1.9	US$/kg	071
2710	Petroleum oils, other than crude	138.3	135.3	149.0		*1.1*	*1.1*	US$/kg	334
2523	Portland cement, aluminous cement, slag cement	107.2	103.0	89.1	0.2	0.2	0.2	US$/kg	661
0304	Fish fillets and other fish meat (whether or not minced)	50.0	104.6	98.0	4.9	5.6	6.1	US$/kg	034
0902	Tea, whether or not flavoured	73.9	85.6	84.7	1.3	1.4	1.4	US$/kg	074
2401	Unmanufactured tobacco; tobacco refuse	58.3	115.0	61.9	3.3	3.5	2.6	US$/kg	121
1701	Cane or beet sugar and chemically pure sucrose, in solid form	76.4	79.8	64.6	0.8	0.7	0.6	US$/kg	061
8517	Electrical apparatus for line telephony or line telegraphy	148.0	49.3	8.2					764
9999	Commodities not specified according to kind	119.4	31.9	37.5					931
0602	Other live plants (including their roots), cuttings and slips; mushroom spawn	52.4	54.5	56.4					292

Services Imports and Exports: EBOPS 2002 categories

Table 2: Merchandise exports by SITC

(Value in million US$, growth and shares in percentage)

SITC	2014	Avg. Growth rates 2010-2014	Avg. Growth rates 2013-2014	2014 share
Total	2 262.0	8.7	-6.1	100.0
0+1	1 098.4	7.6	-8.7	48.6
2+4	269.9	13.3	11.6	11.9
3	184.0	20.2	19.7	8.1
5	94.9	15.5	-1.4	4.2
6	349.4	11.8	-6.3	15.4
7	157.5	-5.5	-32.3	7.0
8	70.1	13.6	-3.9	3.1
9	37.7	4.9	7.6	1.7

Table 3: Merchandise imports by SITC

(Value in million US$, growth and shares in percentage)

SITC	2014	Avg. Growth rates 2010-2014	Avg. Growth rates 2013-2014	2014 share
Total	6 073.5	6.8	4.4	100.0
0+1	551.7	9.7	30.3	9.1
2+4	421.7	10.4	18.3	6.9
3	1 440.6	11.5	7.5	23.7
5	936.1	13.0	2.0	15.4
6	886.7	3.6	4.0	14.6
7	1 460.9	0.9	3.8	24.1
8	374.0	4.6	-10.0	6.2
9	1.8	23.2	-98.3	0.0

SITC Legend

SITC Code	Description
Total	All commodities
0+1	Food, animals + beverages, tobacco
2+4	Crude materials + anim. & veg. oils
3	Mineral fuels, lubricants
5	Chemicals
6	Goods classified chiefly by material
7	Machinery and transport equipment
8	Miscellaneous manufactured articles
9	Not classified elsewhere in the SITC

Graph 4: Merchandise trade balance

(Bln US$ by MDG Regions in 2014)

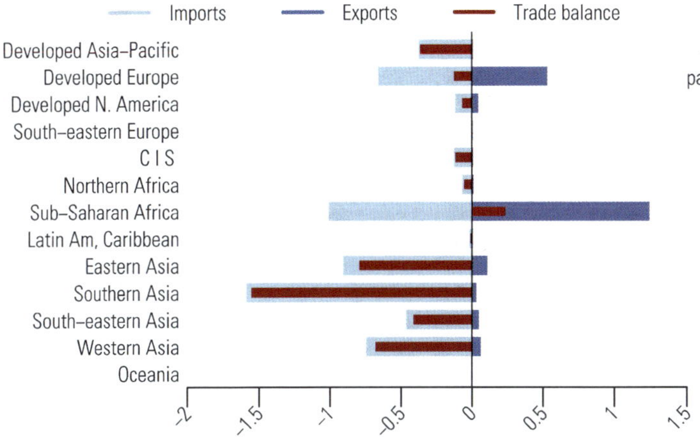

Graph 5: Partner concentration of merchandise trade

(Cumulative share by ranked partners in 2014)

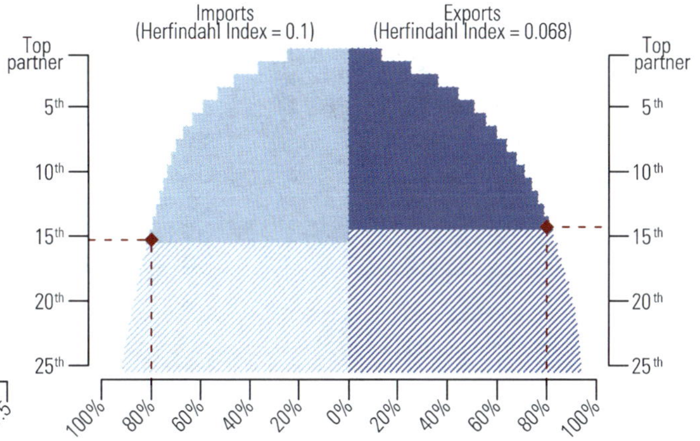

Graph 6: Imports of services by EBOPS category

(% share in 2014)

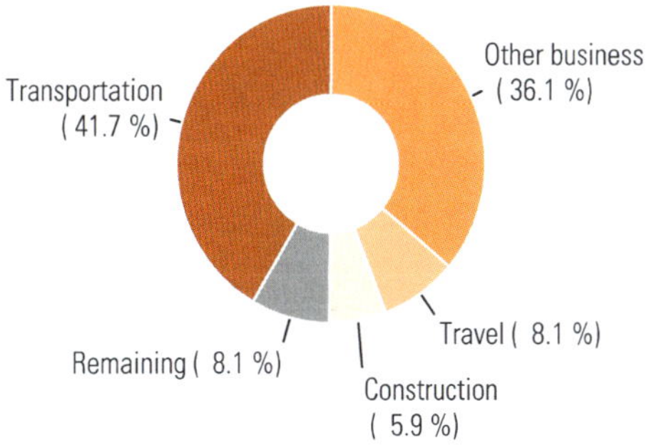

Imports Profile:

"Machinery and transport equipment" (SITC section 7), "Mineral fuels, lubricants" (SITC section 3) and "Chemicals" (SITC section 5) were the largest commodity groups for imports in 2014, representing respectively 24.1, 23.7 and 15.4 percent of imported goods (see table 3). From 2012 to 2014, the largest import commodity was "Petroleum oils, other than crude" (HS code 2710) (see table 4). The top three partners for merchandise imports were India, China and Kenya, accounting for respectively 24.1, 11.4 and 9.7 percent of total imports. "Transportation" (EBOPS code 205) accounted for the largest share of imports of services in 2014 at 1.1 bln US$, followed by "Other business services" (EBOPS code 268) at 984.4 mln US$ and "Travel" (EBOPS code 236) at 221.5 mln US$ (see graph 6).

Table 4: Top 10 import commodities 2012 to 2014

HS code	4-digit heading of Harmonized System 2012	Value (million US$) 2012	2013	2014	Unit value 2012	2013	2014	Unit	SITC code
	All Commodities	6 044.1	5 817.5	6 073.5					
2710	Petroleum oils, other than crude	1 309.0	1 281.1	1 392.0		1.0	1.0	US$/kg	334
3004	Medicaments (excluding goods of heading 30.02, 30.05 or 30.06)	203.2	290.8	297.7	13.7	19.2	17.8	US$/kg	542
1511	Palm oil and its fractions	229.5	209.9	247.7	1.1	0.9	0.9	US$/kg	422
8703	Motor cars and other motor vehicles principally designed for the transport	213.4	209.0	220.9	5.3	5.2	5.8	thsd US$/unit	781
8517	Electrical apparatus for line telephony or line telegraphy	249.4	165.9	100.1					764
8704	Motor vehicles for the transport of goods	144.8	112.4	134.5	11.7	11.1	*12.2*	thsd US$/unit	782
1701	Cane or beet sugar and chemically pure sucrose, in solid form	130.5	127.9	87.8	0.8	0.7	0.6	US$/kg	061
9999	Commodities not specified according to kind	235.4	104.5	1.8					931
2523	Portland cement, aluminous cement, slag cement	106.6	84.8	96.5	0.1	0.1	0.1	US$/kg	661
1001	Wheat and meslin	16.5	61.7	165.4	0.4	0.3	0.3	US$/kg	041

Ukraine

Goods Imports: CIF, by origin **Goods Exports: FOB, by last known destination** **Trade System: General**

Overview:

In 2014, the value of merchandise exports of Ukraine decreased substantially by 14.9 percent to reach 53.9 bln US$, while its merchandise imports decreased substantially by 29.4 percent to reach 54.4 bln US$ (see graph 1, table 2 and table 3). The merchandise trade balance recorded a relatively small deficit of 468.1 mln US$ (see graph 1). The largest merchandise trade balance was with MDG Western Asia at 5.4 bln US$ (see graph 4). Merchandise exports in Ukraine were diversified amongst partners; imports were also diversified. The top 27 partners accounted for 80 percent or more of exports and 18 partners accounted for 80 percent or more of imports (see graph 5). In 2014, the value of exports of services of Ukraine decreased substantially by 18.7 percent, reaching 9.9 bln US$, while its imports of services decreased substantially by 15.9 percent and reached 6.2 bln US$ (see graph 2). There was a moderate trade in services surplus of 3.7 bln US$.

Graph 1: Total merchandise trade, by value

(Bln US$ by year)

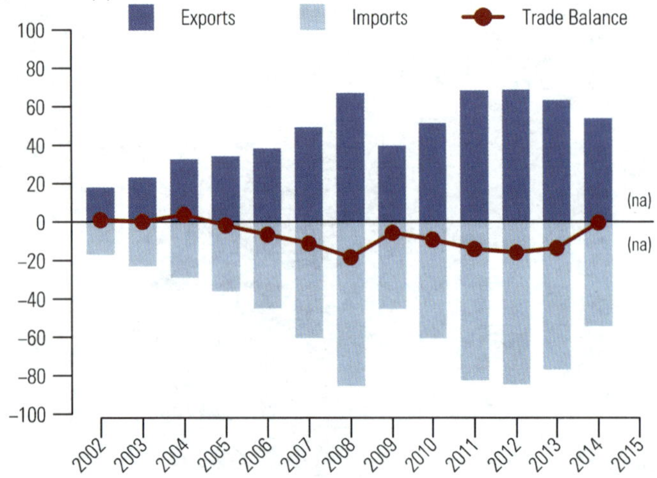

Graph 2: Total services trade, by value

(Bln US$ by year)

Exports Profile:

"Goods classified chiefly by material" (SITC section 6), "Crude materials + anim. & veg. oils" (SITC section 2+4) and "Food, animals + beverages, tobacco" (SITC section 0+1) were the largest commodity groups for exports in 2014, representing respectively 32.0, 20.8 and 20.6 percent of exported goods (see table 2). From 2012 to 2014, the largest export commodity was "Semi-finished products of iron or non-alloy steel" (HS code 7207) (see table 1). The top three destinations for merchandise exports were the Russian Federation, Turkey and Egypt, accounting for respectively 22.9, 5.9 and 4.6 percent of total exports. "Transportation" (EBOPS code 205) accounted for the largest share of exports of services in 2014 at 6.1 bln US$, followed by "Computer and information services" (EBOPS code 262) at 1.3 bln US$ and "Other business services" (EBOPS code 268) at 1.3 bln US$ (see graph 3).

Graph 3: Exports of services by EBOPS category

(% share in 2014)

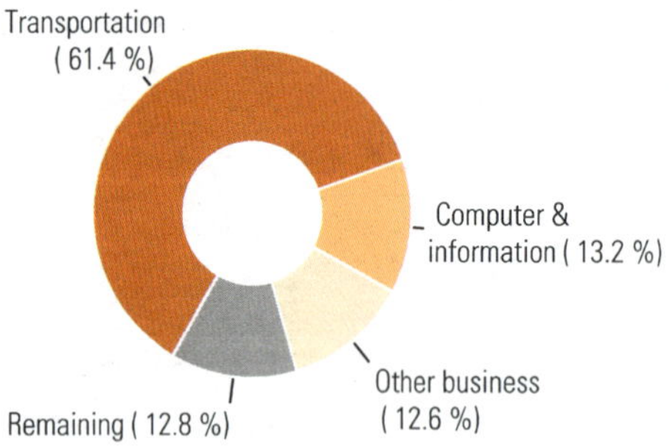

Table 1: Top 10 export commodities 2012 to 2014

HS code	4-digit heading of Harmonized System 2007	Value (million US$) 2012	2013	2014	Unit value 2012	2013	2014	Unit	SITC code
	All Commodities	68694.5	63320.5	53913.3					
7207	Semi-finished products of iron or non-alloy steel	5423.1	5254.8	4342.1	0.5	0.5	0.5	US$/kg	672
1005	Maize (corn)	3893.0	3833.3	3350.7	0.2	0.2	0.2	US$/kg	044
1512	Sunflower-seed, safflower or cotton-seed oil	3934.0	3281.3	3554.3	1.1	1.0	0.8	US$/kg	421
2601	Iron ores and concentrates, including roasted iron pyrites	3131.7	3739.1	3315.4	0.1	0.1	0.1	US$/kg	281
7208	Flat-rolled products of iron or non-alloy steel	2971.8	2763.0	2533.0	0.6	0.5	0.5	US$/kg	673
1001	Wheat and meslin	2330.5	1891.5	2290.8	0.3	0.2	0.2	US$/kg	041
8606	Railway or tramway goods vans and wagons, not self-propelled	2908.4	1330.9	234.4	*71.1*	*64.4*	*46.9*	thsd US$/unit	791
7214	Other bars and rods of iron or non-alloy steel	1605.2	1519.9	1322.4	0.6	0.6	0.5	US$/kg	676
3102	Mineral or chemical fertilisers, nitrogenous	1690.0	1133.5	646.1	0.3	0.3	0.3	US$/kg	562
8544	Insulated (including enamelled or anodised) wire, cable	945.8	1081.6	1170.2	15.2	17.8	18.2	US$/kg	773

Services Imports and Exports: EBOPS 2002 categories

Table 2: Merchandise exports by SITC

(Value in million US$, growth and shares in percentage)

SITC	2014	Avg. Growth rates 2010-2014	Avg. Growth rates 2013-2014	2014 share
Total	53 913.3	1.2	-14.9	100.0
0+1	11 122.2	15.3	-3.3	20.6
2+4	11 220.4	9.2	-3.0	20.8
3	2 012.7	-13.9	-29.8	3.7
5	2 824.4	-4.7	-30.8	5.2
6	17 251.7	-2.5	-14.1	32.0
7	7 095.5	-5.5	-30.9	13.2
8	2 110.3	4.2	-8.8	3.9
9	276.2	-6.8	-56.9	0.5

Table 3: Merchandise imports by SITC

(Value in million US$, growth and shares in percentage)

SITC	2014	Avg. Growth rates 2010-2014	Avg. Growth rates 2013-2014	2014 share
Total	54 381.4	-2.7	-29.4	100.0
0+1	5 309.5	1.2	-26.5	9.8
2+4	2 049.1	-5.9	-20.8	3.8
3	15 116.4	-6.3	-28.8	27.8
5	9 081.2	1.3	-18.7	16.7
6	7 674.7	-3.2	-27.4	14.1
7	11 314.2	-1.2	-38.5	20.8
8	3 247.3	-2.8	-33.0	6.0
9	589.2	-0.5	-37.7	1.1

SITC Legend

SITC Code	Description
Total	All commodities
0+1	Food, animals + beverages, tobacco
2+4	Crude materials + anim. & veg. oils
3	Mineral fuels, lubricants
5	Chemicals
6	Goods classified chiefly by material
7	Machinery and transport equipment
8	Miscellaneous manufactured articles
9	Not classified elsewhere in the SITC

Graph 4: Merchandise trade balance

(Bln US$ by MDG Regions in 2014)

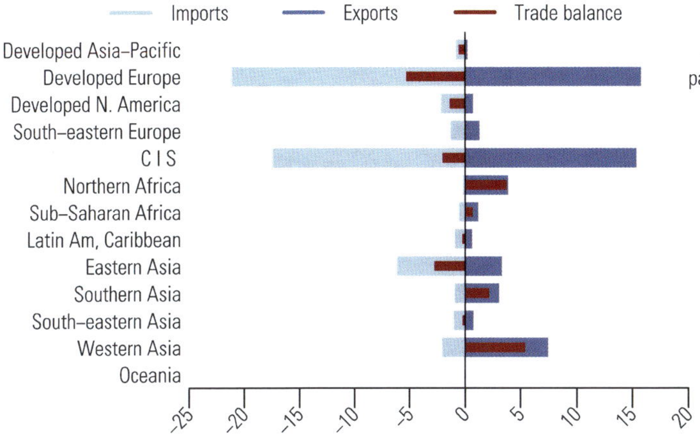

Graph 5: Partner concentration of merchandise trade

(Cumulative share by ranked partners in 2014)

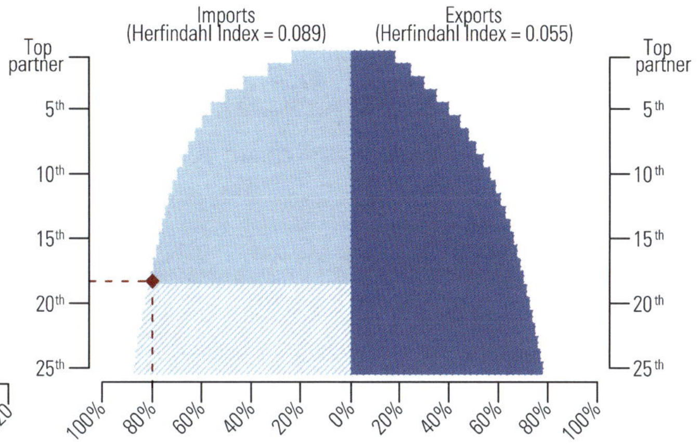

Graph 6: Imports of services by EBOPS category

(% share in 2014)

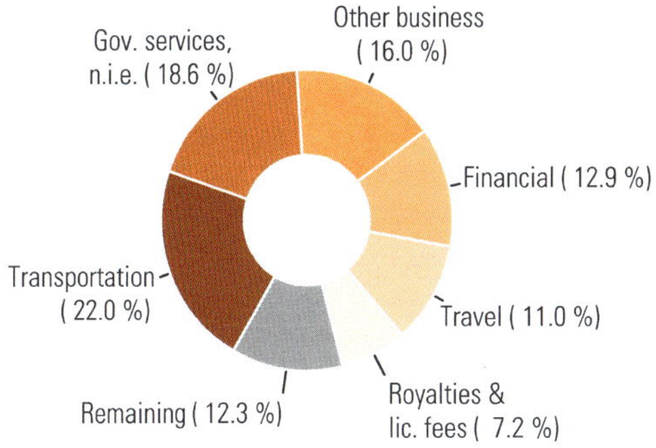

Imports Profile:

"Mineral fuels, lubricants" (SITC section 3), "Machinery and transport equipment" (SITC section 7) and "Chemicals" (SITC section 5) were the largest commodity groups for imports in 2014, representing respectively 27.8, 20.8 and 16.7 percent of imported goods (see table 3). From 2012 to 2014, the largest import commodity was "Petroleum gases and other gaseous hydrocarbons" (HS code 2711) (see table 4). The top three partners for merchandise imports were the Russian Federation, China and Germany, accounting for respectively 29.3, 9.8 and 8.8 percent of total imports. "Transportation" (EBOPS code 205) accounted for the largest share of imports of services in 2014 at 1.4 bln US$, followed by "Government services, n.i.e." (EBOPS code 291) at 1.2 bln US$ and "Other business services" (EBOPS code 268) at 993.9 mln US$ (see graph 6).

Table 4: Top 10 import commodities 2012 to 2014

HS code	4-digit heading of Harmonized System 2007	Value (million US$) 2012	2013	2014	Unit value 2012	2013	2014	Unit	SITC code
	All Commodities	84 656.7	76 986.0	54 381.4					
2711	Petroleum gases and other gaseous hydrocarbons	14 289.0	11 822.0	6 018.3	0.6	0.6	0.4	US$/kg	343
2710	Petroleum oils, other than crude	7 606.7	6 418.3	6 685.2	1.0	1.0	0.9	US$/kg	334
3004	Medicaments (excluding goods of heading 30.02, 30.05 or 30.06)	2 881.2	2 597.9	2 091.8	81.6	91.1	87.2	US$/kg	542
8703	Motor cars and other motor vehicles principally designed for the transport	3 247.1	2 995.5	1 209.9	15.8	17.3	19.3	thsd US$/unit	781
2701	Coal; briquettes, ovoids and similar solid fuels manufactured from coal	2 637.0	1 980.9	1 768.7	0.2	0.1	0.1	US$/kg	321
8517	Electrical apparatus for line telephony or line telegraphy	740.0	810.7	654.6					764
3808	Insecticides, rodenticides, fungicides, herbicides	754.6	769.5	608.4	8.3	9.0	8.2	US$/kg	591
2709	Petroleum oils and oils obtained from bituminous minerals, crude	1 235.9	630.3	146.5	0.8	0.8	0.8	US$/kg	333
8704	Motor vehicles for the transport of goods	846.6	755.1	359.6	5.8	6.0	4.4	thsd US$/unit	782
8401	Nuclear reactors; fuel elements (cartridges), non-irradiated	623.5	619.7	652.5	1.6	1.5	1.6	thsd US$/kg	718

United Arab Emirates

Goods Imports: CIF, by origin | **Goods Exports: FOB, by last known destination** | **Trade System: Special**

Overview:

In 2014, the value of merchandise exports of the United Arab Emirates increased slightly by 0.2 percent to reach 380.3 bln US$, while its merchandise imports increased slightly by 1.2 percent to reach 298.6 bln US$ (see graph 1, table 2 and table 3). The merchandise trade balance recorded a moderate surplus of 81.7 bln US$ (see graph 1). The largest merchandise trade balance was with MDG Developed Europe at -39.9 bln US$ (see graph 4). Merchandise exports in the United Arab Emirates were moderately concentrated amongst partners; imports were diversified. The top 12 partners accounted for 80 percent or more of exports and 23 partners accounted for 80 percent or more of imports (see graph 5). In 2013, the value of exports of services of the United Arab Emirates increased substantially by 14.3 percent, reaching 17.2 bln US$, while its imports of services increased substantially by 11.1 percent and reached 71.0 bln US$ (see graph 2). There was a large trade in services deficit of 53.8 bln US$.

Graph 1: Total merchandise trade, by value

(Bln US$ by year)

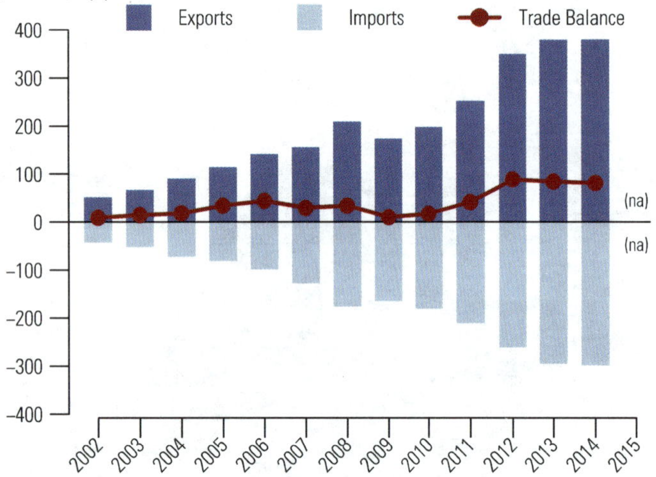

Graph 2: Total services trade, by value

(Bln US$ by year)

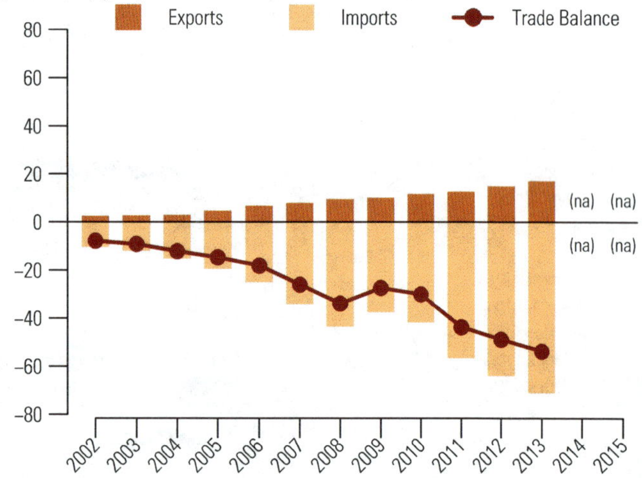

Exports Profile:

"Not classified elsewhere in the SITC" (SITC section 9), "Mineral fuels, lubricants" (SITC section 3) and "Machinery and transport equipment" (SITC section 7) were the largest commodity groups for exports in 2014, representing respectively 32.5, 28.4 and 18.5 percent of exported goods (see table 2). From 2012 to 2014, the largest export commodity was "Commodities not specified according to kind" (HS code 9999) (see table 1). The top three destinations for merchandise exports were Areas nes, Other Asia nes and India, accounting for respectively 27.9, 26.4 and 5.0 percent of total exports. "Travel" (EBOPS code 236) accounted for the largest share of exports of services in 2013 at 11.6 bln US$, followed by "Transportation" (EBOPS code 205) at 4.8 bln US$ (see graph 3).

Graph 3: Exports of services by EBOPS category

(% share in 2013)

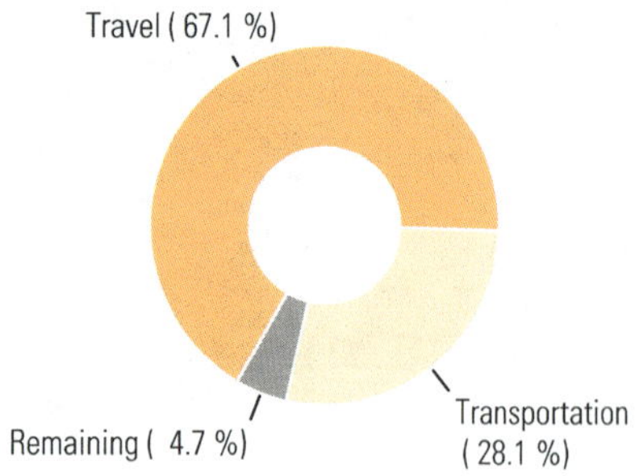

Table 1: Top 10 export commodities 2012 to 2014

HS code	4-digit heading of Harmonized System 2012	Value (million US$) 2012	2013	2014	Unit value 2012	2013	2014	Unit	SITC code
	All Commodities	350 123.0	379 488.8	380 339.6					
9999	Commodities not specified according to kind	79 116.9	91 660.3	111 131.5					931
2709	Petroleum oils and oils obtained from bituminous minerals, crude	96 590.2	87 299.3	72 072.1	0.7	0.6	0.6	US$/kg	333
2710	Petroleum oils, other than crude	13 760.9	30 494.6	27 400.2	*1.1*	*1.1*	*1.1*	US$/kg	334
7108	Gold (including gold plated with platinum)	33 751.9	23 121.7	12 332.3	51.7	44.3	38.5	thsd US$/kg	971
8517	Electrical apparatus for line telephony or line telegraphy	14 875.7	22 195.3	21 773.9					764
7102	Diamonds, whether or not worked, but not mounted or set	12 452.2	15 149.9	14 286.5					667
7113	Articles of jewellery and parts thereof, of precious metal	11 669.5	9 242.0	11 806.2	*27.8*	*16.1*		thsd US$/kg	897
2711	Petroleum gases and other gaseous hydrocarbons	7 728.8	8 513.1	8 380.7	*0.6*	*0.6*	*0.6*	US$/kg	343
8703	Motor cars and other motor vehicles principally designed for the transport	5 650.5	6 567.8	9 944.4	*18.7*	*18.0*	*17.1*	thsd US$/unit	781
8471	Automatic data processing machines and units thereof	5 608.0	5 889.6	6 207.4					752

Services Imports and Exports: EBOPS 2002 categories

Table 2: Merchandise exports by SITC

(Value in million US$, growth and shares in percentage)

SITC	2014	Avg. Growth rates 2010-2014	Avg. Growth rates 2013-2014	2014 share
Total	380339.6	17.7	0.2	100.0
0+1	9675.9	21.2	14.3	2.5
2+4	3269.8	23.3	9.1	0.9
3	108108.5	9.9	-14.6	28.4
5	9454.4	30.4	9.0	2.5
6	33363.0	10.1	-0.8	8.8
7	70386.3	36.8	8.2	18.5
8	22551.7	31.2	17.1	5.9
9	123530.1	17.6	7.6	32.5

Table 3: Merchandise imports by SITC

(Value in million US$, growth and shares in percentage)

SITC	2014	Avg. Growth rates 2010-2014	Avg. Growth rates 2013-2014	2014 share
Total	298611.3	13.4	1.2	100.0
0+1	19178.0	16.5	14.8	6.4
2+4	6505.0	20.0	2.9	2.2
3	9004.9	45.2	9.9	3.0
5	18969.2	22.5	9.3	6.4
6	43440.8	8.2	-2.4	14.5
7	109661.9	27.2	10.9	36.7
8	33527.0	19.9	10.6	11.2
9	58324.6	-3.4	-19.8	19.5

SITC Legend

SITC Code	Description
Total	All commodities
0+1	Food, animals + beverages, tobacco
2+4	Crude materials + anim. & veg. oils
3	Mineral fuels, lubricants
5	Chemicals
6	Goods classified chiefly by material
7	Machinery and transport equipment
8	Miscellaneous manufactured articles
9	Not classified elsewhere in the SITC

Graph 4: Merchandise trade balance

(Bln US$ by MDG Regions in 2014)

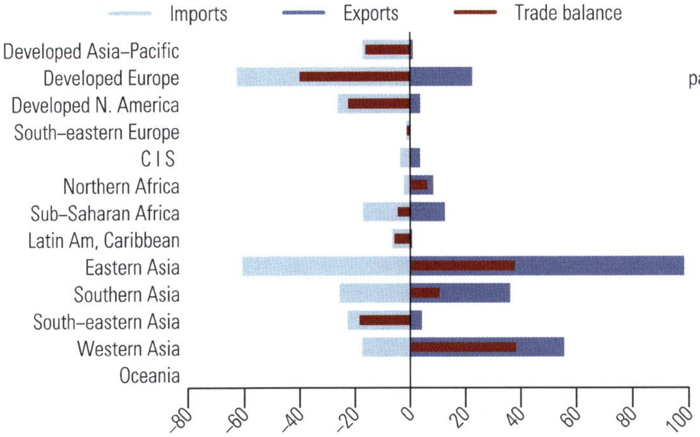

Graph 5: Partner concentration of merchandise trade

(Cumulative share by ranked partners in 2014)

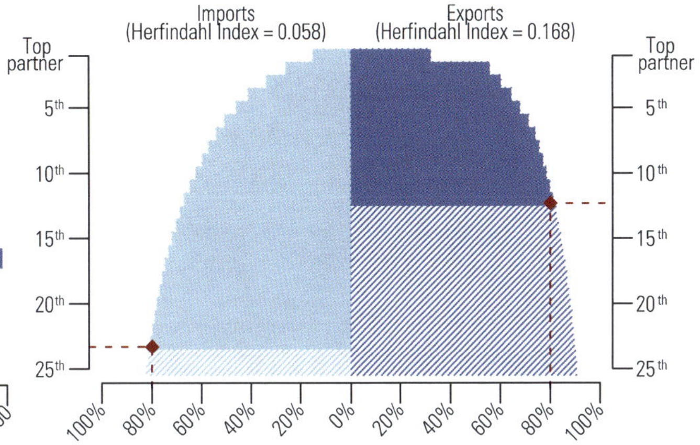

Graph 6: Imports of services by EBOPS category

(% share in 2013)

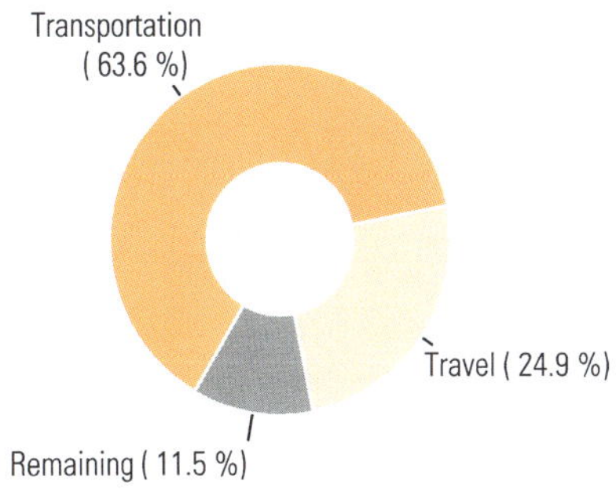

Imports Profile:

"Machinery and transport equipment" (SITC section 7), "Not classified elsewhere in the SITC" (SITC section 9) and "Goods classified chiefly by material" (SITC section 6) were the largest commodity groups for imports in 2014, representing respectively 36.7, 19.5 and 14.5 percent of imported goods (see table 3). From 2012 to 2014, the largest import commodity was "Gold (including gold plated with platinum)" (HS code 7108) (see table 4). The top three partners for merchandise imports were China, Areas nes and the United States, accounting for respectively 13.3, 9.1 and 8.5 percent of total imports. "Transportation" (EBOPS code 205) accounted for the largest share of imports of services in 2013 at 45.2 bln US$, followed by "Travel" (EBOPS code 236) at 17.7 bln US$ (see graph 6).

Table 4: Top 10 import commodities 2012 to 2014

HS code	4-digit heading of Harmonized System 2012	Value (million US$) 2012	2013	2014	Unit value 2012	2013	2014	Unit	SITC code
	All Commodities	261022.9	294966.9	298611.3					
7108	Gold (including gold plated with platinum)	41233.7	40902.2	29746.4	45.2	10.3		thsd US$/kg	971
9999	Commodities not specified according to kind	13333.4	31719.7	28546.1					931
8517	Electrical apparatus for line telephony or line telegraphy	13794.1	21257.3	25020.3					764
8703	Motor cars and other motor vehicles principally designed for the transport	12590.2	15034.4	15965.0	*23.5*	*23.7*	*24.5*	thsd US$/unit	781
7102	Diamonds, whether or not worked, but not mounted or set	12639.2	14479.1	12785.6					667
7113	Articles of jewellery and parts thereof, of precious metal	9127.8	9267.5	9804.6	34.4	*13.0*	*10.5*	thsd US$/kg	897
8471	Automatic data processing machines and units thereof	7121.9	7491.3	8573.9					752
2710	Petroleum oils, other than crude	7160.2	6969.9	7636.3	0.9	0.8	0.8	US$/kg	334
8802	Other aircraft (for example, helicopters, aeroplanes); spacecraft	6397.4	5148.7	5832.9					792
8411	Turbo-jets, turbo-propellers and other gas turbines	4284.7	4902.3	4891.9					714

Source: UN Comtrade

United Kingdom

Goods Imports: CIF, by origin/consignment for intra-eu **Goods Exports: FOB, by last known destination** **Trade System: General**

Overview:

In 2015, the value of merchandise exports of the United Kingdom decreased moderately by 8.8 percent to reach 465.9 bln US$, while its merchandise imports decreased moderately by 9.4 percent to reach 629.2 bln US$ (see graph 1, table 2 and table 3). The United Kingdom was the sixth largest trader in the World in 2015. The merchandise trade balance recorded a moderate deficit of 163.3 bln US$ (see graph 1). The largest merchandise trade balance was with MDG Developed Europe at -132.9 bln US$ (see graph 4). Merchandise exports in the United Kingdom were diversified amongst partners; imports were also diversified. The top 20 partners accounted for 80 percent or more of exports and 19 partners accounted for 80 percent or more of imports (see graph 5). In 2014, the value of exports of services of the United Kingdom increased moderately by 6.8 percent, reaching 363.4 bln US$, while its imports of services increased slightly by 2.9 percent and reached 215.3 bln US$ (see graph 2). There was a moderate trade in services surplus of 148.1 bln US$.

Graph 1: Total merchandise trade, by value

(Bln US$ by year)

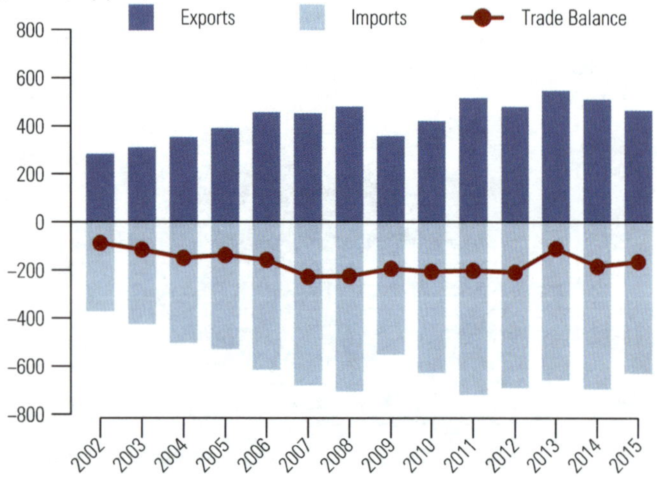

Graph 2: Total services trade, by value

(Bln US$ by year)

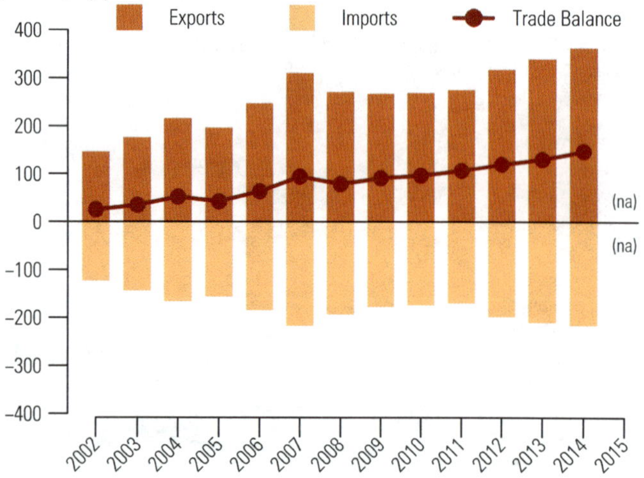

Exports Profile:

"Machinery and transport equipment" (SITC section 7), "Chemicals" (SITC section 5) and "Miscellaneous manufactured articles" (SITC section 8) were the largest commodity groups for exports in 2015, representing respectively 35.2, 16.4 and 13.6 percent of exported goods (see table 2). From 2013 to 2015, the largest export commodity was "Gold (including gold plated with platinum)" (HS code 7108) (see table 1). The top three destinations for merchandise exports were the United States, Germany and Switzerland, accounting for respectively 12.9, 9.6 and 9.2 percent of total exports. "Other business services" (EBOPS code 268) accounted for the largest share of exports of services in 2014 at 95.3 bln US$, followed by "Financial services" (EBOPS code 260) at 81.1 bln US$ and "Travel" (EBOPS code 236) at 46.7 bln US$ (see graph 3).

Graph 3: Exports of services by EBOPS category

(% share in 2014)

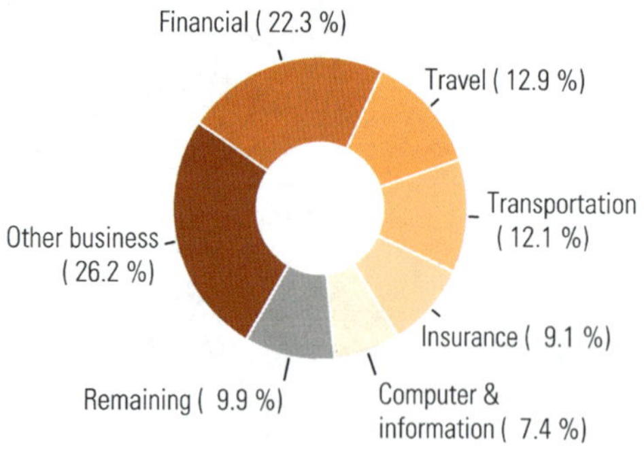

Table 1: Top 10 export commodities 2013 to 2015

HS code	4-digit heading of Harmonized System 2012	Value (million US$) 2013	2014	2015	Unit value 2013	2014	2015	Unit	SITC code
	All Commodities	548041.9	511145.4	465921.6					
7108	Gold (including gold plated with platinum)	79120.8	37575.2	38537.2	45.4	*39.8*	36.1	thsd US$/kg	971
8703	Motor cars and other motor vehicles principally designed for the transport	38228.3	42365.4	38949.7	25.1	*29.6*	*26.5*	thsd US$/unit	781
2709	Petroleum oils and oils obtained from bituminous minerals, crude	29793.9	28857.4	16055.3	0.8	0.8	0.4	US$/kg	333
3004	Medicaments (excluding goods of heading 30.02, 30.05 or 30.06)	20885.9	23430.1	24222.8	*111.7*	*129.6*		US$/kg	542
8411	Turbo-jets, turbo-propellers and other gas turbines	22130.9	21434.2	19570.3					714
9999	Commodities not specified according to kind	31381.6	13568.5	13566.7					931
2710	Petroleum oils, other than crude	25963.0	20186.7	11473.9	*0.9*	*0.8*	*0.5*	US$/kg	334
8803	Parts of goods of heading 88.01 or 88.02	...	13340.2	14674.1		*380.8*	*490.8*	US$/kg	792
3002	Human blood; animal blood prepared for therapeutic uses	7191.2	8093.5	9524.3	*342.9*	*343.2*	*387.8*	US$/kg	541
2208	Alcohol of a strength by volume of less than 80 % vol	8447.9	8352.2	7469.4	*19.5*	*19.6*	*17.9*	US$/litre	112

Services Imports and Exports: EBOPS 2002 categories

Table 2: Merchandise exports by SITC

(Value in million US$, growth and shares in percentage)

SITC	2015	Avg. Growth rates 2011-2015	Avg. Growth rates 2014-2015	2015 share
Total	465 921.6	-2.6	-8.8	100.0
0+1	27 962.2	-1.2	-10.1	6.0
2+4	8 730.6	-10.8	-19.6	1.9
3	32 608.0	-15.9	-40.7	7.0
5	76 305.8	-1.1	0.7	16.4
6	40 747.4	-7.5	-13.2	8.7
7	163 884.2	2.4	-7.2	35.2
8	63 352.9	3.9	0.6	13.6
9	52 330.6	-6.9	0.7	11.2

Table 3: Merchandise imports by SITC

(Value in million US$, growth and shares in percentage)

SITC	2015	Avg. Growth rates 2011-2015	Avg. Growth rates 2014-2015	2015 share
Total	629 228.9	-3.2	-9.4	100.0
0+1	59 084.6	-0.8	-7.2	9.4
2+4	15 535.9	-6.7	-16.2	2.5
3	50 921.6	-13.6	-37.1	8.1
5	75 311.9	-0.7	-6.9	12.0
6	65 668.4	-6.9	-10.5	10.4
7	231 510.8	2.2	-3.9	36.8
8	103 027.9	0.1	-2.5	16.4
9	28 167.7	-18.6	-7.2	4.5

SITC Legend

SITC Code	Description
Total	All commodities
0+1	Food, animals + beverages, tobacco
2+4	Crude materials + anim. & veg. oils
3	Mineral fuels, lubricants
5	Chemicals
6	Goods classified chiefly by material
7	Machinery and transport equipment
8	Miscellaneous manufactured articles
9	Not classified elsewhere in the SITC

Graph 4: Merchandise trade balance

(Bln US$ by MDG Regions in 2015)

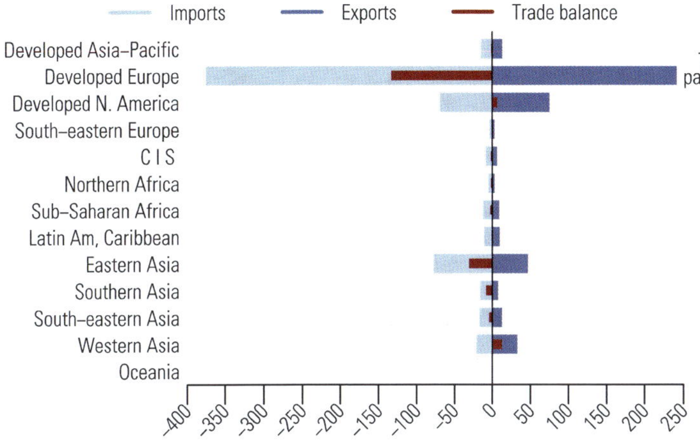

Graph 5: Partner concentration of merchandise trade

(Cumulative share by ranked partners in 2015)

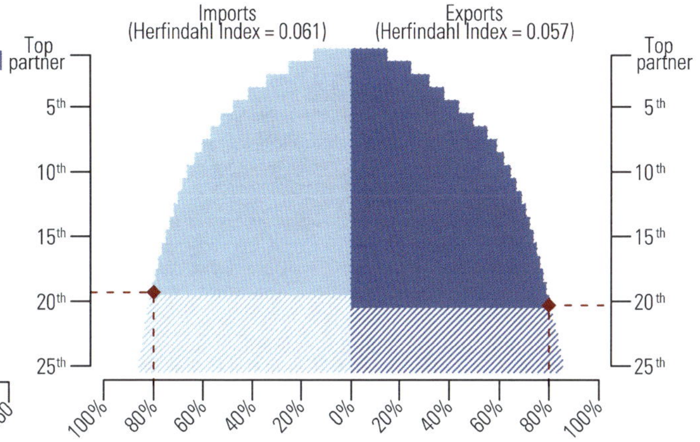

Graph 6: Imports of services by EBOPS category

(% share in 2014)

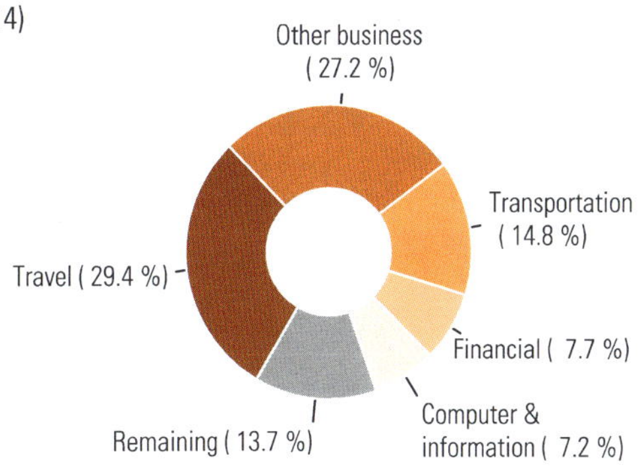

Imports Profile:

"Machinery and transport equipment" (SITC section 7), "Miscellaneous manufactured articles" (SITC section 8) and "Chemicals" (SITC section 5) were the largest commodity groups for imports in 2015, representing respectively 36.8, 16.4 and 12.0 percent of imported goods (see table 3). From 2013 to 2015, the largest import commodity was "Motor cars and other motor vehicles principally designed for the transport" (HS code 8703) (see table 4). The top three partners for merchandise imports were Germany, China and the United States, accounting for respectively 14.3, 9.3 and 8.6 percent of total imports. "Travel" (EBOPS code 236) accounted for the largest share of imports of services in 2014 at 63.3 bln US$, followed by "Other business services" (EBOPS code 268) at 58.5 bln US$ and "Transportation" (EBOPS code 205) at 31.9 bln US$ (see graph 6).

Table 4: Top 10 import commodities 2013 to 2015

HS code	4-digit heading of Harmonized System 2012	Value (million US$) 2013	2014	2015	Unit value 2013	2014	2015	Unit	SITC code
	All Commodities	657 222.5	694 344.3	629 228.9					
8703	Motor cars and other motor vehicles principally designed for the transport	38 762.8	46 331.0	48 691.5	*18.0*	19.6	*19.0*	thsd US$/unit	781
2709	Petroleum oils and oils obtained from bituminous minerals, crude	40 092.0	36 064.6	18 422.3	0.8	0.8	0.4	US$/kg	333
2710	Petroleum oils, other than crude	27 621.7	25 805.5	18 109.3	*1.0*	0.9	0.5	US$/kg	334
3004	Medicaments (excluding goods of heading 30.02, 30.05 or 30.06)	17 619.4	21 267.4	20 911.5	*103.3*	*109.8*		US$/kg	542
7108	Gold (including gold plated with platinum)	15 197.5	20 296.2	18 708.8	44.7	40.8	37.9	thsd US$/kg	971
8517	Electrical apparatus for line telephony or line telegraphy	17 507.7	16 651.6	17 460.3					764
8411	Turbo-jets, turbo-propellers and other gas turbines	16 393.3	16 276.7	15 736.2					714
8708	Parts and accessories of the motor vehicles of headings 87.01 to 87.05	15 388.3	16 584.0	15 531.3	*9.6*	*10.4*	*9.3*	US$/kg	784
9999	Commodities not specified according to kind	25 962.9	9 489.2	9 001.4					931
8471	Automatic data processing machines and units thereof	14 406.8	14 925.8	13 442.9	152.8	171.1	174.6	US$/unit	752

United Republic of Tanzania

Goods Imports: CIF, by origin | **Goods Exports: FOB, by last known destination** | **Trade System: General**

Overview:

In 2014, the value of merchandise exports of the United Republic of Tanzania increased substantially by 29.3 percent to reach 5.7 bln US$, while its merchandise imports increased slightly by 1.3 percent to reach 12.7 bln US$ (see graph 1, table 2 and table 3). The merchandise trade balance recorded a large deficit of 7.0 bln US$ (see graph 1). The largest merchandise trade balance was with MDG Developed Europe at -1.8 bln US$ (see graph 4). Merchandise exports in the United Republic of Tanzania were diversified amongst partners; imports were also diversified. The top 12 partners accounted for 80 percent or more of exports and 13 partners accounted for 80 percent or more of imports (see graph 5). In 2014, the value of exports of services of the United Republic of Tanzania increased substantially by 12.4 percent, reaching 3.4 bln US$, while its imports of services increased moderately by 6.9 percent and reached 2.7 bln US$ (see graph 2). There was a moderate trade in services surplus of 723.5 mln US$.

Graph 1: Total merchandise trade, by value

(Bln US$ by year)

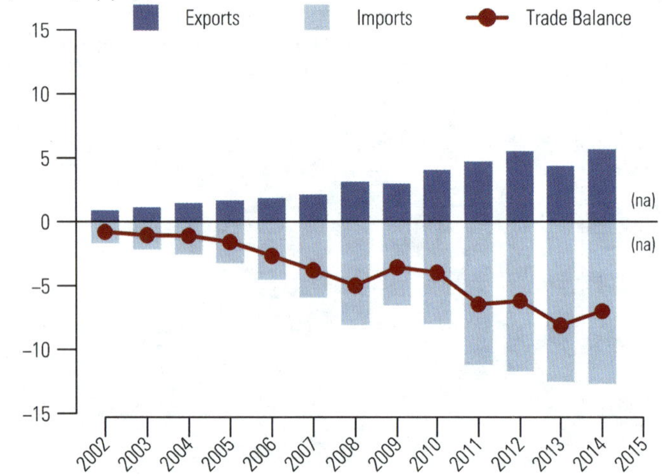

Graph 2: Total services trade, by value

(Bln US$ by year)

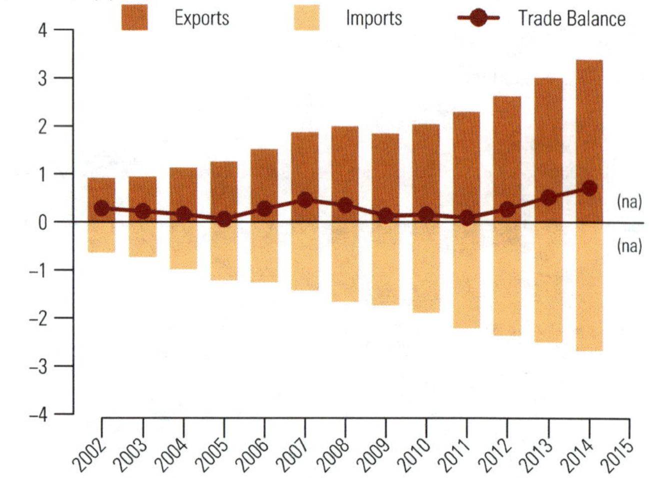

Exports Profile:

"Food, animals + beverages, tobacco" (SITC section 0+1), "Crude materials + anim. & veg. oils" (SITC section 2+4) and "Not classified elsewhere in the SITC" (SITC section 9) were the largest commodity groups for exports in 2014, representing respectively 33.5, 26.8 and 23.2 percent of exported goods (see table 2). From 2012 to 2014, the largest export commodity was "Gold (including gold plated with platinum)" (HS code 7108) (see table 1). The top three destinations for merchandise exports were India, South Africa and China, accounting for respectively 15.9, 15.6 and 9.7 percent of total exports. "Travel" (EBOPS code 236) accounted for the largest share of exports of services in 2014 at 2.0 bln US$, followed by "Transportation" (EBOPS code 205) at 892.6 mln US$ and "Other business services" (EBOPS code 268) at 352.5 mln US$ (see graph 3).

Graph 3: Exports of services by EBOPS category

(% share in 2014)

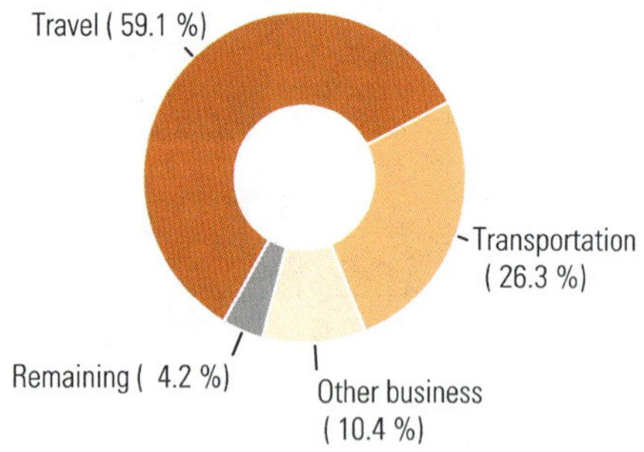

Table 1: Top 10 export commodities 2012 to 2014

HS code	4-digit heading of Harmonized System 2007	Value (million US$) 2012	2013	2014	Unit value 2012	2013	2014	Unit	SITC code
	All Commodities	5547.2	4412.5	5704.7					
7108	Gold (including gold plated with platinum)	1863.3	1549.6	1322.0	5.8	11.1		thsd US$/kg	971
2616	Precious metal ores and concentrates	421.3	301.6	566.5	10.0	7.8	7.1	US$/kg	289
0801	Coconuts, Brazil nuts and cashew nuts, fresh or dried	163.1	189.5	394.2	1.2	1.2	2.0	US$/kg	057
1207	Other oil seeds and oleaginous fruits, whether or not broken	94.4	140.4	337.8	1.1	1.3	2.5	US$/kg	222
2603	Copper ores and concentrates	324.3	90.9	145.6	8.7	7.0		US$/kg	283
2401	Unmanufactured tobacco; tobacco refuse	188.4	97.0	193.2	1.8	1.4	2.5	US$/kg	121
0901	Coffee, whether or not roasted or decaffeinated	187.7	163.1	123.6	3.5	2.6	2.6	US$/kg	071
0713	Dried leguminous vegetables, shelled, whether or not skinned or split	101.0	86.0	177.7	0.6	0.5	0.8	US$/kg	054
0304	Fish fillets and other fish meat (whether or not minced)	99.7	113.8	149.2	5.4	5.2	6.2	US$/kg	034
5201	Cotton, not carded or combed	126.4	86.6	38.7	1.4	1.3	1.1	US$/kg	263

Services Imports and Exports: EBOPS 2002 categories

Table 2: Merchandise exports by SITC
(Value in million US$, growth and shares in percentage)

SITC	2014	Avg. Growth rates 2010-2014	Avg. Growth rates 2013-2014	2014 share
Total	5704.7	8.9	29.3	100.0
0+1	1911.5	22.8	71.5	33.5
2+4	1529.2	3.7	86.1	26.8
3	95.5	5.5	-3.9	1.7
5	142.1	-5.2	57.3	2.5
6	405.1	3.6	5.0	7.1
7	156.9	-3.3	-35.8	2.8
8	142.3	3.2	37.9	2.5
9	1322.0	7.9	-14.9	23.2

Table 3: Merchandise imports by SITC
(Value in million US$, growth and shares in percentage)

SITC	2014	Avg. Growth rates 2010-2014	Avg. Growth rates 2013-2014	2014 share
Total	12691.1	12.2	1.3	100.0
0+1	750.8	6.7	0.4	5.9
2+4	627.5	19.3	68.3	4.9
3	3559.1	12.6	-26.6	28.0
5	1839.7	15.1	31.4	14.5
6	1876.1	13.0	0.9	14.8
7	3422.7	9.5	22.3	27.0
8	614.2	17.0	26.5	4.8
9	1.0	-33.2	-91.4	0.0

SITC Legend

SITC Code	Description
Total	All commodities
0+1	Food, animals + beverages, tobacco
2+4	Crude materials + anim. & veg. oils
3	Mineral fuels, lubricants
5	Chemicals
6	Goods classified chiefly by material
7	Machinery and transport equipment
8	Miscellaneous manufactured articles
9	Not classified elsewhere in the SITC

Graph 4: Merchandise trade balance
(Bln US$ by MDG Regions in 2014)

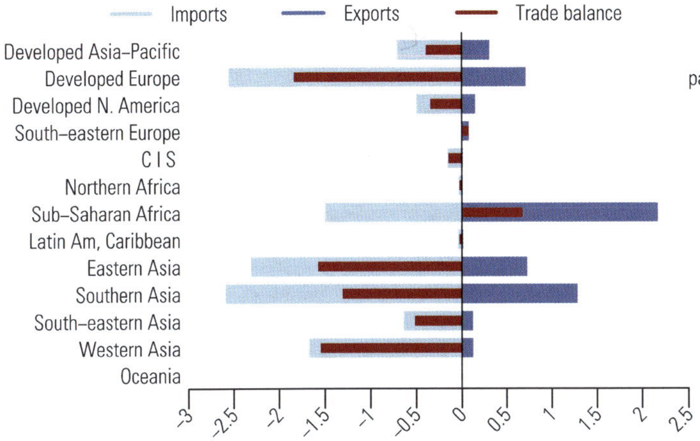

Graph 5: Partner concentration of merchandise trade
(Cumulative share by ranked partners in 2014)

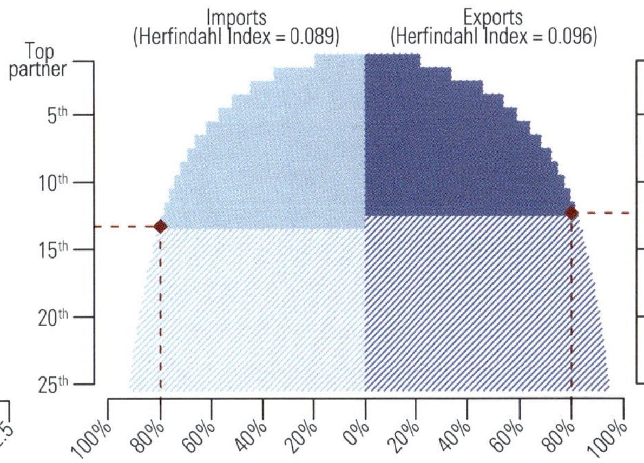

Graph 6: Imports of services by EBOPS category
(% share in 2014)

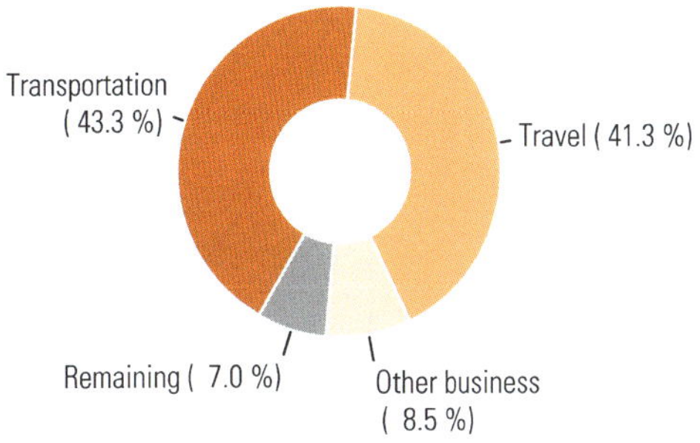

Imports Profile:

"Mineral fuels, lubricants" (SITC section 3), "Machinery and transport equipment" (SITC section 7) and "Goods classified chiefly by material" (SITC section 6) were the largest commodity groups for imports in 2014, representing respectively 28.0, 27.0 and 14.8 percent of imported goods (see table 3). From 2012 to 2014, the largest import commodity was "Petroleum oils, other than crude" (HS code 2710) (see table 4). The top three partners for merchandise imports were India, China and Switzerland, accounting for respectively 15.3, 13.0 and 11.1 percent of total imports. "Transportation" (EBOPS code 205) accounted for the largest share of imports of services in 2014 at 1.2 bln US$, followed by "Travel" (EBOPS code 236) at 1.1 bln US$ and "Other business services" (EBOPS code 268) at 226.0 mln US$ (see graph 6).

Table 4: Top 10 import commodities 2012 to 2014

HS code	4-digit heading of Harmonized System 2007	Value (million US$) 2012	Value (million US$) 2013	Value (million US$) 2014	Unit value 2012	Unit value 2013	Unit value 2014	Unit	SITC code
	All Commodities	11715.6	12525.4	12691.1					
2710	Petroleum oils, other than crude	3636.5	4665.4	3407.5	1.1	1.0	0.9	US$/kg	334
8703	Motor cars and other motor vehicles principally designed for the transport	302.4	311.4	327.1	*21.5*	*20.3*	*19.3*	thsd US$/unit	781
1001	Wheat and meslin	244.1	307.1	319.3	0.4	0.4	0.4	US$/kg	041
1511	Palm oil and its fractions	247.7	192.7	367.6	1.0	0.8	0.9	US$/kg	422
8704	Motor vehicles for the transport of goods	252.7	264.5	234.1					782
7208	Flat-rolled products of iron or non-alloy steel	214.2	237.1	189.2	0.8	0.7	0.6	US$/kg	673
3004	Medicaments (excluding goods of heading 30.02, 30.05 or 30.06)	132.6	163.7	337.7	10.3	13.0	13.5	US$/kg	542
8701	Tractors (other than tractors of heading 87.09)	226.2	193.5	199.9					722
8431	Parts suitable for use principally with the machinery of headings 84.25	240.0	141.4	139.1	0.6	16.5	13.7	US$/kg	723
4011	New pneumatic tyres, of rubber	166.8	163.8	147.7					625

Source: UN Comtrade

United States of America, including Puerto Rico and U.S.V.I.

Goods Imports: CIF, by origin | **Goods Exports: FOB, by last known destination** | **Trade System: General**

Overview:

In 2015, the value of merchandise exports of the United States decreased moderately by 7.2 percent to reach 1503.9 bln US$, while its merchandise imports decreased slightly by 4.3 percent to reach 2306.8 bln US$ (see graph 1, table 2 and table 3). Despite being overtaken by China in 2007 as the largest exporter of merchandise, the United States is still the world's largest importer. The merchandise trade balance recorded a moderate deficit of 803.0 bln US$ (see graph 1). The largest merchandise trade balance was with MDG Eastern Asia at -402.6 bln US$ (see graph 4). Merchandise exports in the United States were diversified amongst partners; imports were also diversified. The top 21 partners accounted for 80 percent or more of exports and 16 partners accounted for 80 percent or more of imports (see graph 5). In 2014, the value of exports of services of the United States increased slightly by 2.8 percent, reaching 688.2 bln US$, while its imports of services increased slightly by 3.0 percent and reached 470.0 bln US$ (see graph 2). There was a moderate trade in services surplus of 218.2 bln US$. In recent years, the United States has been the world's largest exporter and importer of services, with the United Kingdom being second for exports and China being second for imports of services both in 2013 and 2014.

Graph 1: Total merchandise trade, by value

(Bln US$ by year)

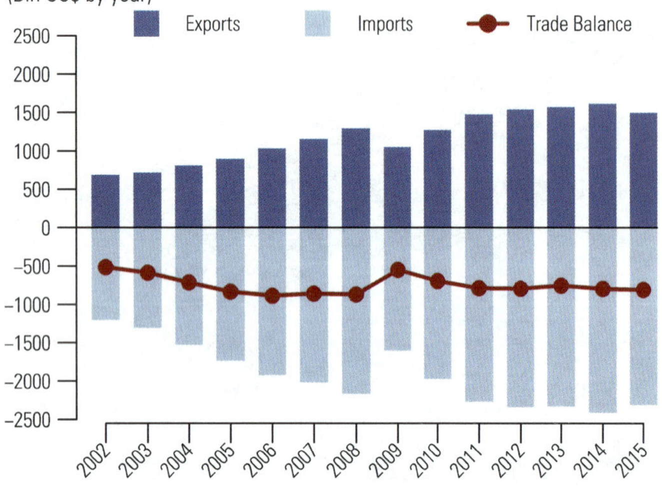

Graph 2: Total services trade, by value

(Bln US$ by year)

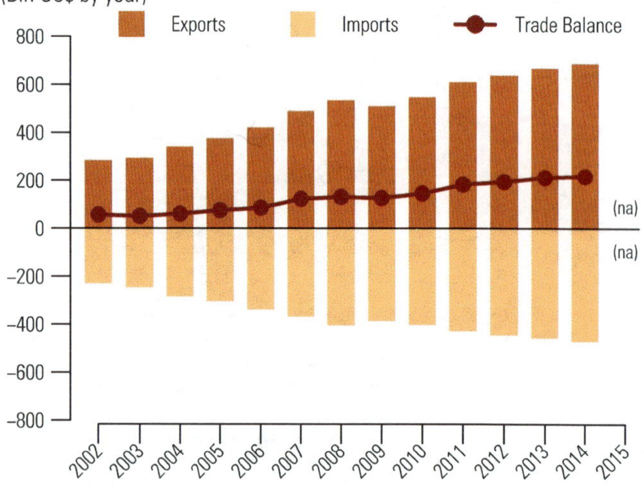

Exports Profile:

"Machinery and transport equipment" (SITC section 7), "Chemicals" (SITC section 5) and "Not classified elsewhere in the SITC" (SITC section 9) were the largest commodity groups for exports in 2015, representing respectively 35.0, 13.7 and 12.2 percent of exported goods (see table 2). From 2013 to 2015, the largest export commodity was "Commodities not specified according to kind" (HS code 9999) (see table 1). The top three destinations for merchandise exports were Canada, Mexico and China, accounting for respectively 19.0, 14.9 and 7.7 percent of total exports. "Travel" (EBOPS code 236) accounted for the largest share of exports of services in 2014 at 177.2 bln US$, followed by "Royalties and license fees" (EBOPS code 266) at 130.4 bln US$ and "Other business services" (EBOPS code 268) at 126.7 bln US$ (see graph 3).

Graph 3: Exports of services by EBOPS category

(% share in 2014)

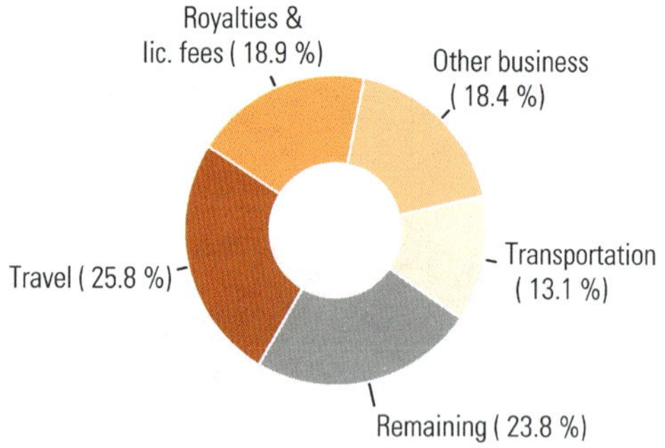

Table 1: Top 10 export commodities 2013 to 2015

HS code	4-digit heading of Harmonized System 2012	Value (billion US$) 2013	2014	2015	Unit value 2013	2014	2015	Unit	SITC code
	All Commodities	1 577.6	1 619.7	1 503.9					
9999	Commodities not specified according to kind	147.1	156.3	161.8					931
2710	Petroleum oils, other than crude	112.0	110.0	74.7	0.9		0.5	US$/kg	334
8703	Motor cars and other motor vehicles principally designed for the transport	57.3	61.7	55.3	20.3	*21.9*	21.8	thsd US$/unit	781
8708	Parts and accessories of the motor vehicles of headings 87.01 to 87.05	43.1	42.7	43.9	*11.0*	*10.8*	*10.9*	US$/kg	784
8542	Electronic integrated circuits	34.5	34.5	33.5					776
8517	Electrical apparatus for line telephony or line telegraphy	31.3	33.8	34.8					764
8471	Automatic data processing machines and units thereof	26.6	26.8	25.0	275.5		275.1	US$/unit	752
9018	Instruments and appliances used in medical, surgical, dental or veterinary	25.3	26.3	26.0					872
7108	Gold (including gold plated with platinum)	31.9	21.0	19.3	*45.2*		*37.4*	thsd US$/kg	971
3004	Medicaments (excluding goods of heading 30.02, 30.05 or 30.06)	23.1	24.4	24.6	186.5	216.4	236.8	US$/kg	542

Services Imports and Exports: EBOPS 2002 categories

Table 2: Merchandise exports by SITC

(Value in million US$, growth and shares in percentage)

SITC	2015	Avg. Growth rates 2011-2015	Avg. Growth rates 2014-2015	2015 share
Total	1 503 870.4	0.4	-7.2	100.0
0+1	109 145.9	0.3	-8.9	7.3
2+4	76 334.8	-5.7	-15.4	5.1
3	106 008.2	-5.0	-31.8	7.0
5	206 459.2	-0.1	-2.5	13.7
6	137 729.1	-0.4	-8.5	9.2
7	526 393.3	1.2	-4.7	35.0
8	159 067.4	2.6	-1.4	10.6
9	182 732.6	4.4	2.4	12.2

Table 3: Merchandise imports by SITC

(Value in million US$, growth and shares in percentage)

SITC	2015	Avg. Growth rates 2011-2015	Avg. Growth rates 2014-2015	2015 share
Total	2 306 822.2	0.5	-4.3	100.0
0+1	127 251.2	4.6	2.2	5.5
2+4	39 747.9	-2.6	-11.6	1.7
3	200 938.1	-18.8	-43.9	8.7
5	220 388.9	2.2	4.1	9.6
6	255 465.5	1.6	-3.8	11.1
7	987 201.6	5.0	3.2	42.8
8	383 587.4	4.6	6.2	16.6
9	92 241.6	4.6	4.0	4.0

SITC Legend

SITC Code	Description
Total	All commodities
0+1	Food, animals + beverages, tobacco
2+4	Crude materials + anim. & veg. oils
3	Mineral fuels, lubricants
5	Chemicals
6	Goods classified chiefly by material
7	Machinery and transport equipment
8	Miscellaneous manufactured articles
9	Not classified elsewhere in the SITC

Graph 4: Merchandise trade balance

(Bln US$ by MDG Regions in 2015)

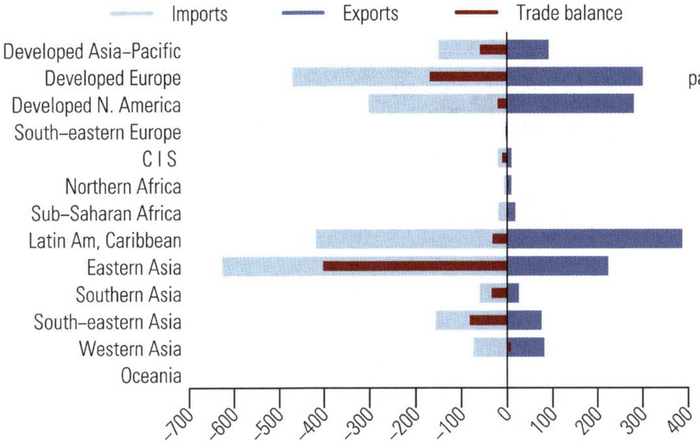

Graph 5: Partner concentration of merchandise trade

(Cumulative share by ranked partners in 2015)

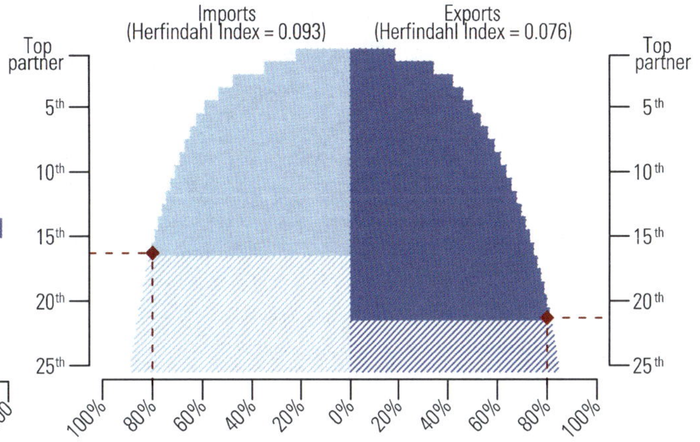

Graph 6: Imports of services by EBOPS category

(% share in 2014)

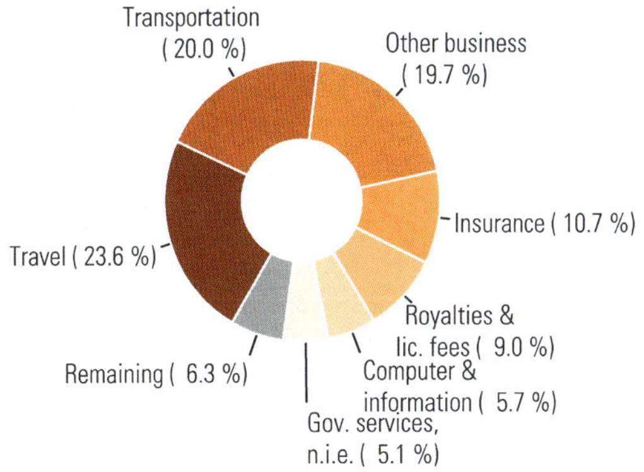

Imports Profile:

"Machinery and transport equipment" (SITC section 7), "Miscellaneous manufactured articles" (SITC section 8) and "Goods classified chiefly by material" (SITC section 6) were the largest commodity groups for imports in 2015, representing respectively 42.8, 16.6 and 11.1 percent of imported goods (see table 3). From 2013 to 2015, the largest import commodity was "Petroleum oils and oils obtained from bituminous minerals, crude" (HS code 2709) (see table 4). The top three partners for merchandise imports were China, Canada and Mexico, accounting for respectively 20.6, 14.1 and 12.5 percent of total imports. "Travel" (EBOPS code 236) accounted for the largest share of imports of services in 2014 at 110.8 bln US$, followed by "Transportation" (EBOPS code 205) at 94.2 bln US$ and "Other business services" (EBOPS code 268) at 92.5 bln US$ (see graph 6).

Table 4: Top 10 import commodities 2013 to 2015

HS code	4-digit heading of Harmonized System 2012	Value (billion US$) 2013	Value (billion US$) 2014	Value (billion US$) 2015	Unit value 2013	Unit value 2014	Unit value 2015	Unit	SITC code
	All Commodities	2 326.6	2 410.9	2 306.8					
2709	Petroleum oils and oils obtained from bituminous minerals, crude	279.5	253.2	132.6	0.7	*0.8*	0.4	US$/kg	333
8703	Motor cars and other motor vehicles principally designed for the transport	155.5	156.4	169.1	22.5	*22.4*	22.1	thsd US$/unit	781
8517	Electrical apparatus for line telephony or line telegraphy	89.8	96.1	102.4					764
8471	Automatic data processing machines and units thereof	83.1	82.1	81.4	141.3		166.6	US$/unit	752
9999	Commodities not specified according to kind	70.9	74.1	80.7					931
2710	Petroleum oils, other than crude	88.8	79.1	51.4	0.8		0.5	US$/kg	334
8708	Parts and accessories of the motor vehicles of headings 87.01 to 87.05	58.8	63.7	66.5	*11.4*	*11.6*	*11.9*	US$/kg	784
3004	Medicaments (excluding goods of heading 30.02, 30.05 or 30.06)	47.2	55.2	64.4	198.4	205.9	232.5	US$/kg	542
8542	Electronic integrated circuits	29.4	29.7	28.8					776
8528	Reception apparatus for television	27.4	27.3	26.9	201.2		196.2	US$/unit	761

Source: UN Comtrade

Uruguay

Goods Imports: CIF, by origin | **Goods Exports: FOB, by last known destination** | **Trade System: Special**

Overview:

In 2014, the value of merchandise exports of Uruguay increased slightly by 1.1 percent to reach 9.2 bln US$, while its merchandise imports decreased moderately by 7.6 percent to reach 10.8 bln US$ (see graph 1, table 2 and table 3). The merchandise trade balance recorded a relatively small deficit of 1.6 bln US$ (see graph 1). The largest merchandise trade balance was with MDG Latin America and the Caribbean at -1.1 bln US$ (see graph 4). Merchandise exports in Uruguay were diversified amongst partners; imports were also diversified. The top 14 partners accounted for 80 percent or more of exports and 12 partners accounted for 80 percent or more of imports (see graph 5). In 2014, the value of exports of services of Uruguay increased slightly by 1.8 percent, reaching 3.3 bln US$, while its imports of services decreased slightly by 4.9 percent and reached 3.2 bln US$ (see graph 2). There was a relatively small trade in services surplus of 143.3 mln US$.

Graph 1: Total merchandise trade, by value

(Bln US$ by year)

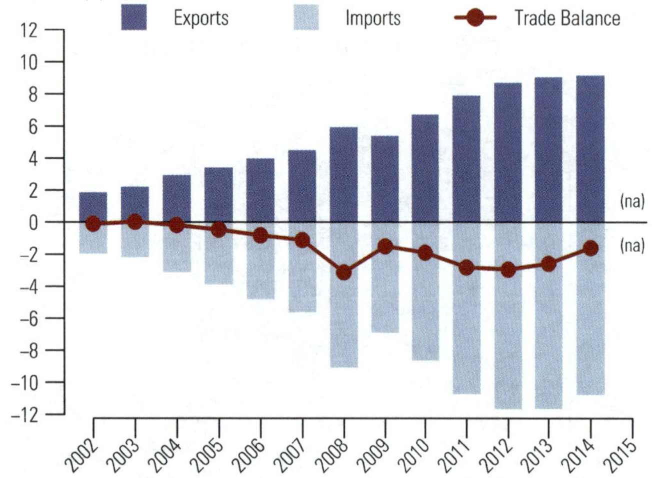

Graph 2: Total services trade, by value

(Bln US$ by year)

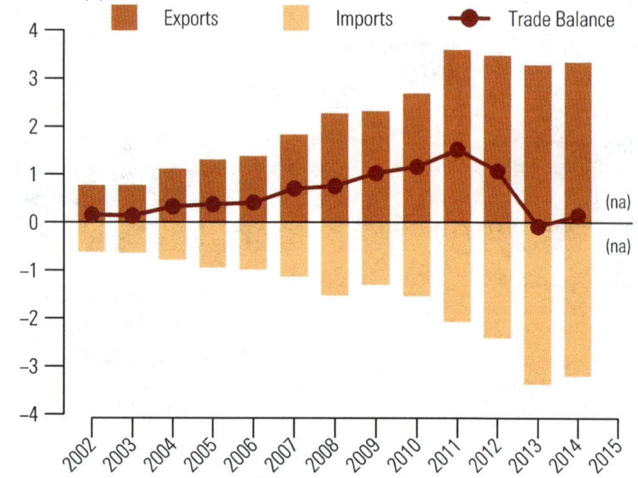

Exports Profile:

"Food, animals + beverages, tobacco" (SITC section 0+1), "Crude materials + anim. & veg. oils" (SITC section 2+4) and "Goods classified chiefly by material" (SITC section 6) were the largest commodity groups for exports in 2014, representing respectively 46.5, 28.7 and 8.6 percent of exported goods (see table 2). From 2012 to 2014, the largest export commodity was "Soya beans, whether or not broken" (HS code 1201) (see table 1). The top three destinations for merchandise exports were Brazil, Free zones and China, accounting for respectively 18.6, 16.7 and 12.3 percent of total exports. "Travel" (EBOPS code 236) accounted for the largest share of exports of services in 2014 at 1.8 bln US$, followed by "Transportation" (EBOPS code 205) at 643.6 mln US$ and "Other business services" (EBOPS code 268) at 436.7 mln US$ (see graph 3).

Graph 3: Exports of services by EBOPS category

(% share in 2014)

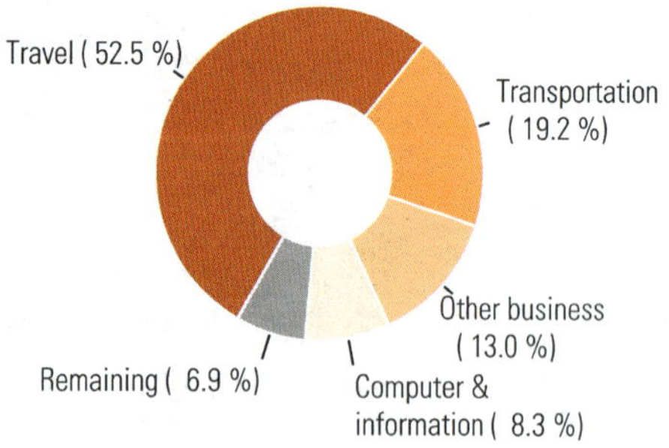

Table 1: Top 10 export commodities 2012 to 2014

HS code	4-digit heading of Harmonized System 2012	Value (million US$) 2012	2013	2014	Unit value 2012	2013	2014	Unit	SITC code
	All Commodities	8709.2	9065.8	9165.7					
1201	Soya beans, whether or not broken	1379.7	1874.5	1620.8	0.5	0.5	0.5	US$/kg	222
0202	Meat of bovine animals, frozen	1017.6	939.7	1037.2	4.9	4.8	5.1	US$/kg	011
1006	Rice	560.1	508.0	513.1	0.5	0.6	0.6	US$/kg	042
0402	Milk and cream, concentrated or containing added sugar	333.9	458.8	381.8	3.6	4.4	4.8	US$/kg	022
0201	Meat of bovine animals, fresh or chilled	384.7	361.0	401.8	8.7	9.0	10.1	US$/kg	011
4403	Wood in the rough, whether or not stripped of bark or sapwood	269.6	298.2	439.3					247
1001	Wheat and meslin	379.2	282.8	329.3	0.3	0.3	0.3	US$/kg	041
0406	Cheese and curd	264.3	251.5	241.4	5.6	5.6	5.4	US$/kg	024
1107	Malt, whether or not roasted	204.7	208.5	186.6	0.7	0.7	0.6	US$/kg	048
3923	Articles for the conveyance or packing of goods, of plastics	202.4	191.1	175.0	2.4	2.4	2.2	US$/kg	893

Services Imports and Exports: EBOPS 2002 categories

Table 2: Merchandise exports by SITC

(Value in million US$, growth and shares in percentage)

SITC	2014	Avg. Growth rates 2010-2014	Avg. Growth rates 2013-2014	2014 share
Total	9165.7	8.1	1.1	100.0
0+1	4264.7	6.1	5.1	46.5
2+4	2629.0	15.5	-4.5	28.7
3	101.9	-16.4	128.4	1.1
5	569.2	8.0	-0.3	6.2
6	784.4	6.7	5.2	8.6
7	387.0	9.0	-3.9	4.2
8	359.7	3.8	-9.8	3.9
9	69.9	-0.2	-25.0	0.8

Table 3: Merchandise imports by SITC

(Value in million US$, growth and shares in percentage)

SITC	2014	Avg. Growth rates 2010-2014	Avg. Growth rates 2013-2014	2014 share
Total	10762.3	5.7	-7.6	100.0
0+1	1067.1	9.7	-10.1	9.9
2+4	351.1	0.4	-17.8	3.3
3	1749.1	0.7	-18.4	16.3
5	1787.0	4.4	-12.1	16.6
6	1151.9	4.6	-9.0	10.7
7	3637.0	8.1	2.7	33.8
8	1019.2	9.4	-2.3	9.5

SITC Legend

SITC Code	Description
Total	All commodities
0+1	Food, animals + beverages, tobacco
2+4	Crude materials + anim. & veg. oils
3	Mineral fuels, lubricants
5	Chemicals
6	Goods classified chiefly by material
7	Machinery and transport equipment
8	Miscellaneous manufactured articles
9	Not classified elsewhere in the SITC

Graph 4: Merchandise trade balance

(Bln US$ by MDG Regions in 2014)

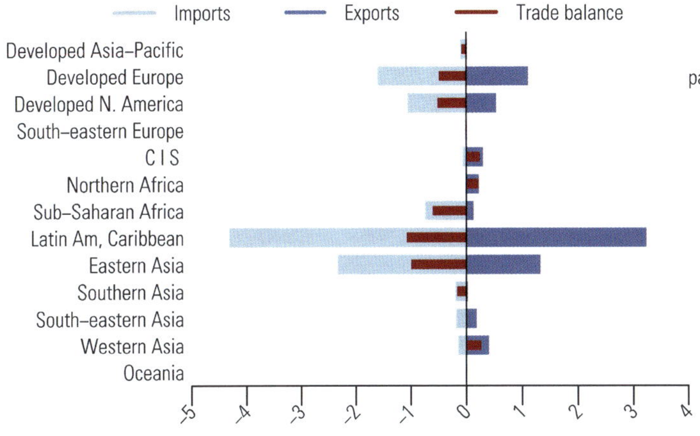

Graph 5: Partner concentration of merchandise trade

(Cumulative share by ranked partners in 2014)

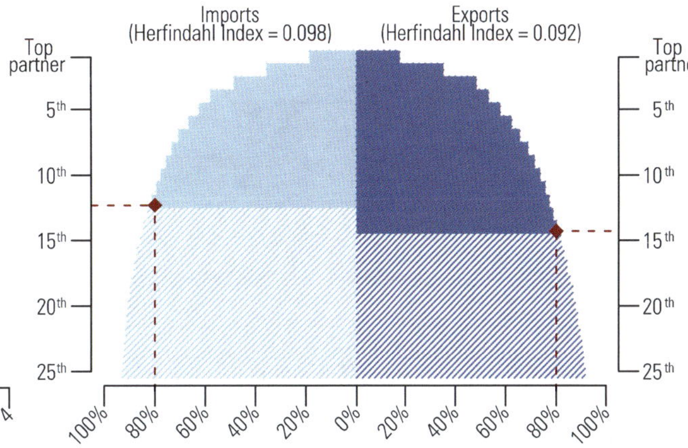

Graph 6: Imports of services by EBOPS category

(% share in 2014)

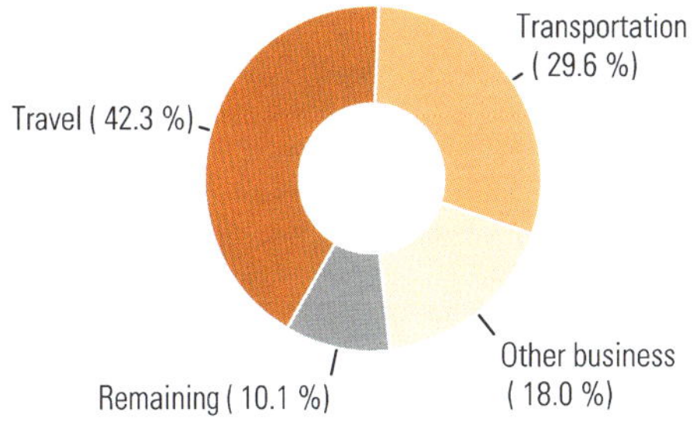

Imports Profile:

"Machinery and transport equipment" (SITC section 7), "Chemicals" (SITC section 5) and "Mineral fuels, lubricants" (SITC section 3) were the largest commodity groups for imports in 2014, representing respectively 33.8, 16.6 and 16.3 percent of imported goods (see table 3). From 2012 to 2014, the largest import commodity was "Petroleum oils and oils obtained from bituminous minerals, crude" (HS code 2709) (see table 4). The top three partners for merchandise imports were Brazil, China and Argentina, accounting for respectively 16.9, 16.5 and 14.0 percent of total imports. "Travel" (EBOPS code 236) accounted for the largest share of imports of services in 2014 at 1.4 bln US$, followed by "Transportation" (EBOPS code 205) at 946.7 mln US$ and "Other business services" (EBOPS code 268) at 577.6 mln US$ (see graph 6).

Table 4: Top 10 import commodities 2012 to 2014

HS code	4-digit heading of Harmonized System 2012	Value (million US$) 2012	Value (million US$) 2013	Value (million US$) 2014	Unit value 2012	Unit value 2013	Unit value 2014	Unit	SITC code
	All Commodities	11652.1	11642.4	10762.3					
2709	Petroleum oils and oils obtained from bituminous minerals, crude	1685.1	1564.1	1341.0	0.8	0.8	0.7	US$/kg	333
2710	Petroleum oils, other than crude	1172.1	494.8	354.5	1.0	1.0	1.0	US$/kg	334
8703	Motor cars and other motor vehicles principally designed for the transport	405.3	414.7	387.4	9.5	9.4	9.5	thsd US$/unit	781
8517	Electrical apparatus for line telephony or line telegraphy	244.2	298.2	381.5					764
8704	Motor vehicles for the transport of goods	253.6	280.3	222.6	15.0	15.4	15.8	thsd US$/unit	782
3808	Insecticides, rodenticides, fungicides, herbicides	189.5	222.7	213.5	5.0	5.8	5.4	US$/kg	591
8708	Parts and accessories of the motor vehicles of headings 87.01 to 87.05	144.9	256.6	200.5	8.1	8.0	7.2	US$/kg	784
8471	Automatic data processing machines and units thereof	161.7	172.2	137.1	92.9	84.1	90.1	US$/unit	752
3907	Polyacetals, other polyethers and epoxide resins, in primary forms	164.2	160.6	134.3	1.6	1.6	1.4	US$/kg	574
8502	Electric generating sets and rotary converters	12.0	136.0	278.7		4.8	*33.5*	thsd US$/unit	716

Vanuatu

Goods Imports: CIF, by origin | **Goods Exports: FOB, by last known destination** | **Trade System: General**

Overview:

In 2011, the value of merchandise exports of Vanuatu increased substantially by 37.6 percent to reach 63.5 mln US$, while its merchandise imports increased slightly by 1.7 percent to reach 280.6 mln US$ (see graph 1, table 2 and table 3). The merchandise trade balance recorded a large deficit of 217.1 mln US$ (see graph 1). The largest merchandise trade balance was with MDG Developed Asia-Pacific at -108.4 mln US$ (see graph 4). Merchandise exports in Vanuatu were diversified amongst partners; imports were moderately concentrated. The top 7 partners accounted for 80 percent or more of exports and 7 partners accounted for 80 percent or more of imports (see graph 5). In 2013, the value of exports of services of Vanuatu increased substantially by 10.3 percent, reaching 331.5 mln US$, while its imports of services decreased slightly by 0.3 percent and reached 145.5 mln US$ (see graph 2). There was a large trade in services surplus of 185.9 mln US$.

Graph 1: Total merchandise trade, by value

(Mln US$ by year)

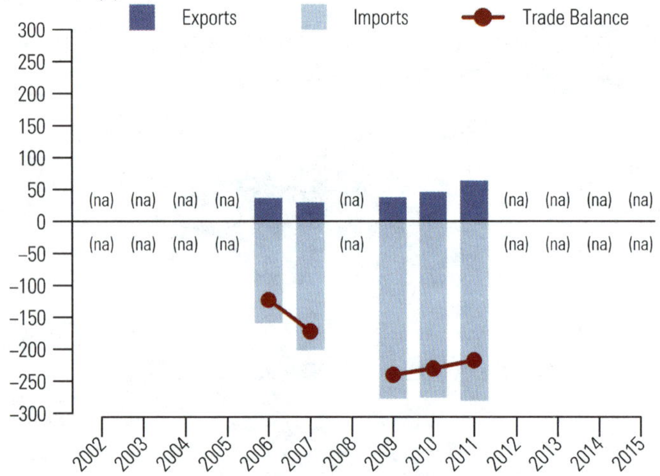

Graph 2: Total services trade, by value

(Mln US$ by year)

Exports Profile:

"Crude materials + anim. & veg. oils" (SITC section 2+4), "Food, animals + beverages, tobacco" (SITC section 0+1) and "Chemicals" (SITC section 5) were the largest commodity groups for exports in 2011, representing respectively 49.4, 40.3 and 5.4 percent of exported goods (see table 2). From 2009 to 2011, the largest export commodity was "Coconut (copra), palm kernel or babassu oil" (HS code 1513) (see table 1). The top three destinations for merchandise exports were the Philippines, Australia and Malaysia, accounting for respectively 14.8, 10.0 and 10.0 percent of total exports. "Travel" (EBOPS code 236) accounted for the largest share of exports of services in 2013 at 265.9 mln US$, followed by "Transportation" (EBOPS code 205) at 33.5 mln US$ (see graph 3).

Graph 3: Exports of services by EBOPS category

(% share in 2013)

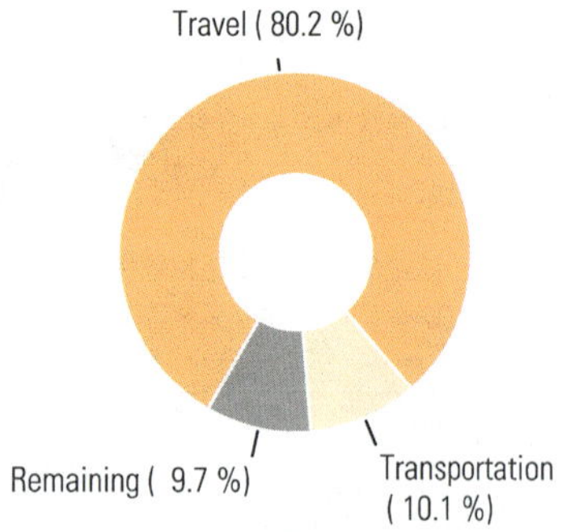

Table 1: Top 10 export commodities 2009 to 2011

HS code	4-digit heading of Harmonized System 2002	Value (million US$) 2009	2010	2011	Unit value 2009	2010	2011	Unit	SITC code
	All Commodities	37.7	46.2	63.5					
1513	Coconut (copra), palm kernel or babassu oil	2.5	9.3	16.8	*1.4*	*0.9*	*1.1*	US$/kg	422
1203	Copra	5.3	6.0	11.3	0.4	0.5	0.8	US$/kg	223
1212	Locust beans, seaweeds and other algae	6.0	5.3	7.4	12.3	10.5	10.9	US$/kg	292
0202	Meat of bovine animals, frozen	3.3	4.6	5.1	4.1	4.5	4.9	US$/kg	011
1801	Cocoa beans, whole or broken, raw or roasted	3.2	4.0	2.6	2.2	2.6	2.4	US$/kg	072
0301	Live fish	1.4	3.3	1.8	13.9	14.0	8.5	US$/kg	034
0302	Fish, fresh or chilled, excluding fish fillets	1.9	0.9	2.3	4.1	2.5	2.6	US$/kg	034
9999	Commodities not specified according to kind	1.2	1.5	1.3					931
2203	Beer made from malt	0.9	1.1	1.1	0.6	0.7	0.6	US$/litre	112
3205	Colour lakes; preparations	...	0.4	2.7			0.0	thsd US$/kg	531

Source: UN Comtrade

Services Imports and Exports: EBOPS 2002 categories

Table 2: Merchandise exports by SITC

(Value in million US$, growth and shares in percentage)

SITC	2011	Avg. Growth rates 2007-2011	Avg. Growth rates 2010-2011	2011 share
Total	63.5	20.7	37.6	100.0
0+1	25.6	30.8	16.5	40.3
2+4	31.4	32.1	78.3	49.4
3	0.0	-25.0	-57.5	0.1
5	3.4	81.1	61.8	5.4
6	0.3	-13.3	-13.3	0.5
7	1.0	4.7	-38.9	1.6
8	0.5	-10.6	-42.5	0.8
9	1.3	-37.5	-14.8	2.0

Table 3: Merchandise imports by SITC

(Value in million US$, growth and shares in percentage)

SITC	2011	Avg. Growth rates 2007-2011	Avg. Growth rates 2010-2011	2011 share
Total	280.6	8.6	1.7	100.0
0+1	68.7	13.8	9.8	24.5
2+4	5.0	3.7	-5.5	1.8
3	51.1	8.8	37.3	18.2
5	29.6	21.2	0.5	10.5
6	36.8	3.5	-3.5	13.1
7	53.1	1.8	-22.5	18.9
8	28.7	10.6	5.5	10.2
9	7.7	8.4	-0.1	2.7

SITC Legend

SITC Code	Description
Total	All commodities
0+1	Food, animals + beverages, tobacco
2+4	Crude materials + anim. & veg. oils
3	Mineral fuels, lubricants
5	Chemicals
6	Goods classified chiefly by material
7	Machinery and transport equipment
8	Miscellaneous manufactured articles
9	Not classified elsewhere in the SITC

Graph 4: Merchandise trade balance

(Mln US$ by MDG Regions in 2011)

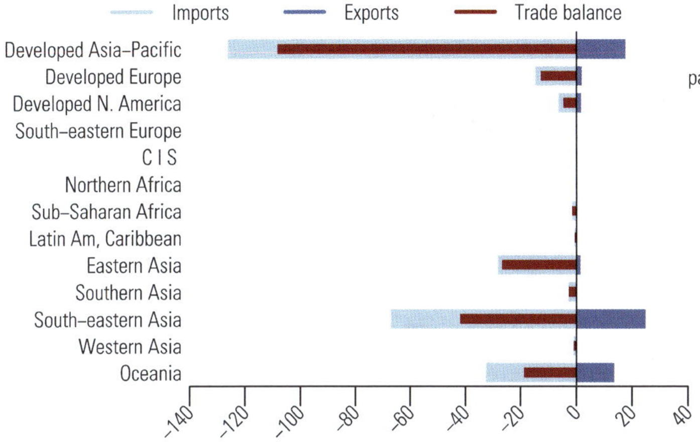

Graph 5: Partner concentration of merchandise trade

(Cumulative share by ranked partners in 2011)

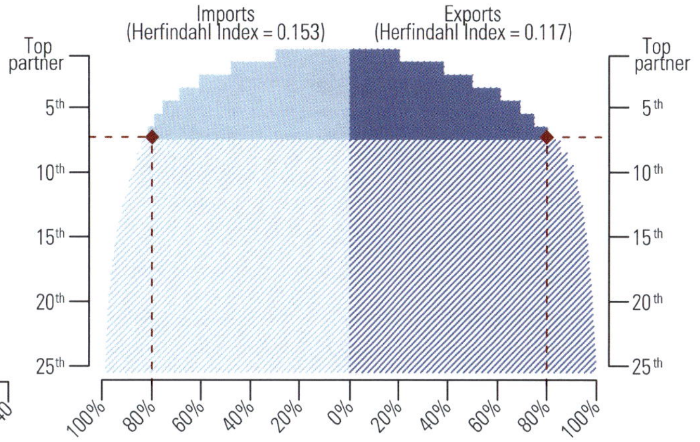

Graph 6: Imports of services by EBOPS category

(% share in 2013)

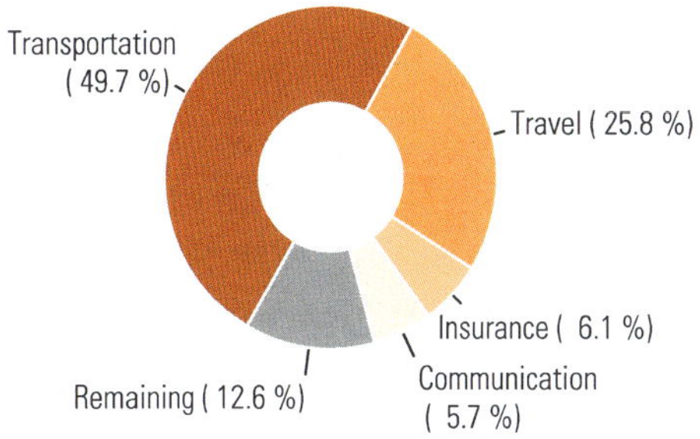

Imports Profile:

"Food, animals + beverages, tobacco" (SITC section 0+1), "Machinery and transport equipment" (SITC section 7) and "Mineral fuels, lubricants" (SITC section 3) were the largest commodity groups for imports in 2011, representing respectively 24.5, 18.9 and 18.2 percent of imported goods (see table 3). From 2009 to 2011, the largest import commodity was "Petroleum oils, other than crude" (HS code 2710) (see table 4). The top three partners for merchandise imports were Australia, Singapore and New Zealand, accounting for respectively 30.0, 13.7 and 13.3 percent of total imports. "Transportation" (EBOPS code 205) accounted for the largest share of imports of services in 2013 at 72.4 mln US$, followed by "Travel" (EBOPS code 236) at 37.6 mln US$ and "Insurance services" (EBOPS code 253) at 8.9 mln US$ (see graph 6).

Table 4: Top 10 import commodities 2009 to 2011

HS code	4-digit heading of Harmonized System 2002	Value (million US$) 2009	Value (million US$) 2010	Value (million US$) 2011	Unit value 2009	Unit value 2010	Unit value 2011	Unit	SITC code
	All Commodities	277.5	276.0	280.6					
2710	Petroleum oils, other than crude	32.6	34.3	48.2	0.8	1.0	1.2	US$/kg	334
3004	Medicaments (excluding goods of heading 30.02, 30.05 or 30.06)	15.5	15.3	15.5	100.0	113.9	*13.3*	US$/kg	542
1006	Rice	12.3	11.6	10.8	1.0	0.9	0.9	US$/kg	042
9999	Commodities not specified according to kind	7.5	7.7	7.7					931
8703	Motor cars and other motor vehicles principally designed for the transport	3.9	11.1	7.0	9.1	16.8	11.4	thsd US$/unit	781
8704	Motor vehicles for the transport of goods	11.9	3.9	3.2	*17.6*	16.8	16.6	thsd US$/unit	782
2523	Portland cement, aluminous cement, slag cement	4.4	5.1	4.3	0.2	0.3	0.4	US$/kg	661
1905	Bread, pastry, cakes, biscuits and other bakers' wares	3.1	4.5	5.5	2.0	2.2	2.0	US$/kg	048
0207	Meat and edible offal, of the poultry of heading 01.05	2.9	4.2	5.2	2.1	2.4	2.7	US$/kg	012
1101	Wheat or meslin flour	2.9	3.6	4.4	0.6	0.7	0.9	US$/kg	046

Venezuela (Bolivarian Republic of)

Goods Imports: CIF, by origin | **Goods Exports: FOB, by last known destination** | **Trade System: General**

Overview:

In 2013, the value of merchandise exports of the Bolivarian Republic of Venezuela decreased moderately by 7.4 percent to reach 88.0 bln US$, while its merchandise imports decreased substantially by 23.9 percent to reach 45.0 bln US$ (see graph 1, table 2 and table 3). The merchandise trade balance recorded a large surplus of 43.0 bln US$ (see graph 1). The largest merchandise trade balance was with MDG Eastern Asia at 19.8 bln US$ (see graph 4). Merchandise exports in the Bolivarian Republic of Venezuela were highly concentrated amongst partners; imports were diversified. The top 3 partners accounted for 80 percent or more of exports and 14 partners accounted for 80 percent or more of imports (see graph 5). In 2013, the value of exports of services of the Bolivarian Republic of Venezuela decreased slightly by 0.4 percent, reaching 2.2 bln US$, while its imports of services increased moderately by 9.1 percent and reached 19.9 bln US$ (see graph 2). There was a large trade in services deficit of 17.7 bln US$. See footnote*.

Graph 1: Total merchandise trade, by value

(Bln US$ by year)

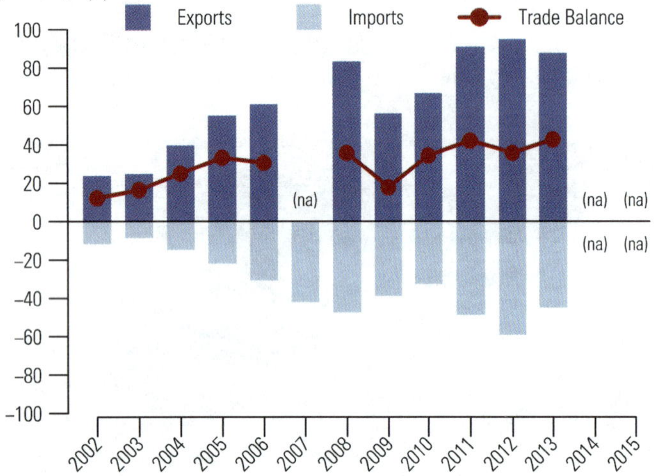

Graph 2: Total services trade, by value

(Bln US$ by year)

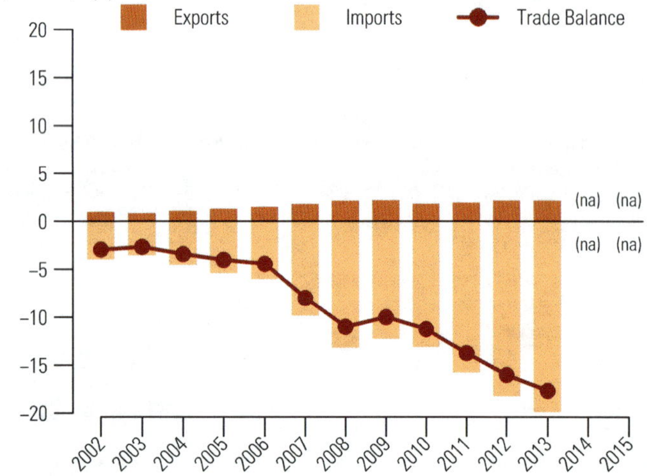

Exports Profile:

"Mineral fuels, lubricants" (SITC section 3), "Chemicals" (SITC section 5) and "Goods classified chiefly by material" (SITC section 6) were the largest commodity groups for exports in 2013, representing respectively 97.7, 1.1 and 0.6 percent of exported goods (see table 2). From 2011 to 2013, the largest export commodity was "Petroleum oils, crude" (HS code 2709) (see table 1). The top three destinations for merchandise exports were LAIA nes, North and Central America, Caribbean nes and Areas nes, accounting for respectively 24.4, 23.9 and 22.9 percent of total exports. "Travel" (EBOPS code 236) accounted for the largest share of exports of services in 2013 at 858.0 mln US$, followed by "Transportation" (EBOPS code 205) at 667.0 mln US$ and "Government services, n.i.e." (EBOPS code 291) at 367.0 mln US$ (see graph 3).

Graph 3: Exports of services by EBOPS category

(% share in 2013)

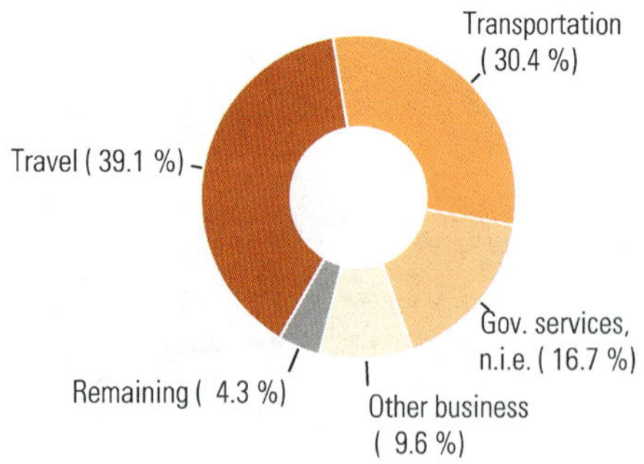

Table 1: Top 10 export commodities 2011 to 2013

HS code	4-digit heading of Harmonized System 2002	Value (million US$) 2011	2012	2013	Unit value 2011	2012	2013	Unit	SITC code
	All Commodities	91094.2	95034.9	87961.2					
2709	Petroleum oils, crude	60913.2	68912.5	74850.6	0.8	0.8	0.8	US$/kg	333
2710	Petroleum oils, other than crude	...	24656.5	11010.4		*1.1*		US$/kg	334
9999	Commodities not specified according to kind	27217.8	...	17.0					931
2905	Acyclic alcohols and their derivatives	53.1	401.1	597.4	0.5			US$/kg	512
7203	Ferrous products obtained by direct reduction of iron ore	447.6	304.5	204.5	0.2	0.2	0.2	US$/kg	671
2601	Iron ores and concentrates	567.3	...	262.3	0.1		0.1	US$/kg	281
3102	Mineral or chemical fertilisers, nitrogenous	128.3	250.6	152.8	0.4	0.4	0.3	US$/kg	562
7208	Flat-rolled products of iron or non-alloy steel	292.7	...	43.3	0.7		0.6	US$/kg	673
2814	Ammonia, anhydrous or in aqueous solution	73.0	131.6	83.3	0.5	0.5	0.4	US$/kg	522
7601	Unwrought aluminium	146.3	90.3	28.1	1.6	2.0	2.0	US$/kg	684

*Major export partners were defined as regions only and resulted in high partner concentration for exports in graph 5.

Services Imports and Exports: EBOPS 2002 categories

Table 2: Merchandise exports by SITC

(Value in million US$, growth and shares in percentage)

SITC	2013	Avg. Growth rates 2009-2013	Avg. Growth rates 2012-2013	2013 share
Total	87 961.2	11.7	-7.4	100.0
0+1	29.0	-18.6	5711.9	0.0
2+4	299.9	2.8	766.6	0.3
3	85 918.6	12.2	-8.2	97.7
5	998.1	37.1	20.5	1.1
6	488.1	-23.8	-0.9	0.6
7	171.8	-7.6	64.2	0.2
8	38.7	-7.1	1078.6	0.0
9	17.0	...	...	0.0

Table 3: Merchandise imports by SITC

(Value in million US$, growth and shares in percentage)

SITC	2013	Avg. Growth rates 2009-2013	Avg. Growth rates 2012-2013	2013 share
Total	44 951.8	3.8	-23.9	100.0
0+1	7 368.9	6.4	-12.8	16.4
2+4	1 386.6	5.9	-29.2	3.1
3	373.6	-28.7	-34.5	0.8
5	8 550.6	6.6	-20.5	19.0
6	6 739.7	4.1	-18.4	15.0
7	13 003.2	-0.6	-36.7	28.9
8	3 889.9	-2.4	-35.0	8.7
9	3 639.4	72.2	43.1	8.1

SITC Legend

SITC Code	Description
Total	All commodities
0+1	Food, animals + beverages, tobacco
2+4	Crude materials + anim. & veg. oils
3	Mineral fuels, lubricants
5	Chemicals
6	Goods classified chiefly by material
7	Machinery and transport equipment
8	Miscellaneous manufactured articles
9	Not classified elsewhere in the SITC

Graph 4: Merchandise trade balance

(Bln US$ by MDG Regions in 2013)

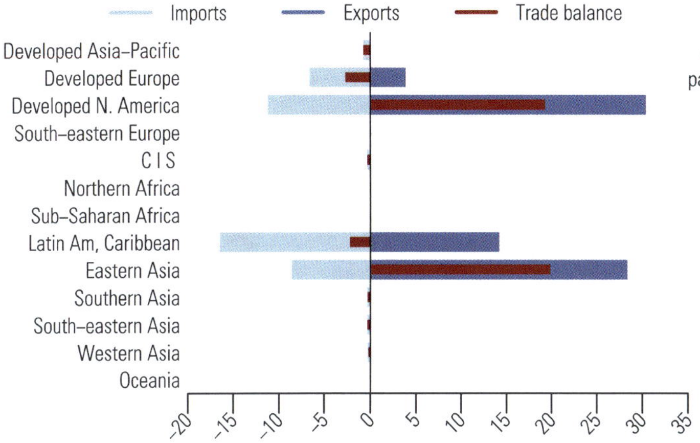

Graph 5: Partner concentration of merchandise trade

(Cumulative share by ranked partners in 2013)

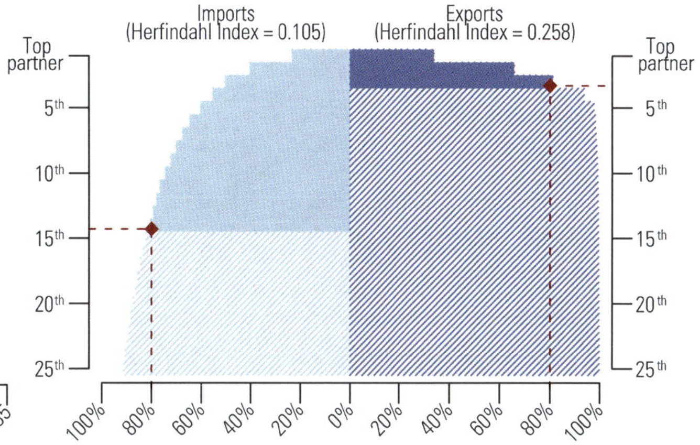

Graph 6: Imports of services by EBOPS category

(% share in 2013)

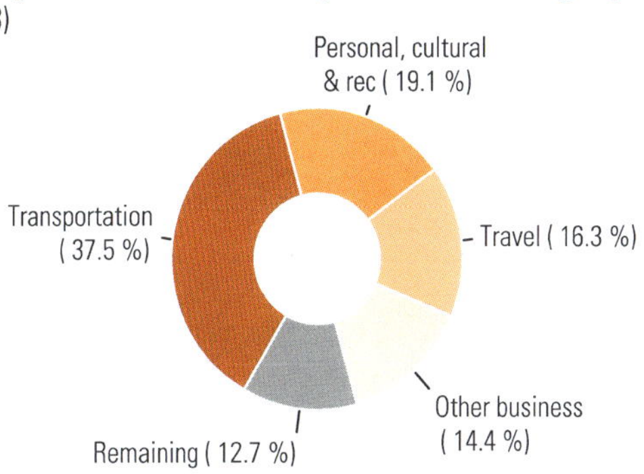

Imports Profile:

"Machinery and transport equipment" (SITC section 7), "Chemicals" (SITC section 5) and "Food, animals + beverages, tobacco" (SITC section 0+1) were the largest commodity groups for imports in 2013, representing respectively 28.9, 19.0 and 16.4 percent of imported goods (see table 3). From 2011 to 2013, the largest import commodity was "Commodities not specified according to kind" (HS code 9999) (see table 4). The top three partners for merchandise imports were the United States, China and Brazil, accounting for respectively 25.0, 15.9 and 9.4 percent of total imports. "Transportation" (EBOPS code 205) accounted for the largest share of imports of services in 2013 at 7.4 bln US$, followed by "Personal, cultural, and recreational services" (EBOPS code 287) at 3.8 bln US$ and "Travel" (EBOPS code 236) at 3.2 bln US$ (see graph 6).

Table 4: Top 10 import commodities 2011 to 2013

HS code	4-digit heading of Harmonized System 2002	Value (million US$) 2011	2012	2013	Unit value 2011	2012	2013	Unit	SITC code
	All Commodities	48 725.7	59 073.2	44 951.8					
9999	Commodities not specified according to kind	2 148.8	2 542.5	3 638.8					931
3004	Medicaments (excluding goods of heading 30.02, 30.05 or 30.06)	2 309.7	2 800.9	2 566.3	*49.0*	*55.7*	51.0	US$/kg	542
8525	Transmission apparatus for radio-telephony, radio-broadcasting	1 010.7	999.0	724.2					764
9018	Instruments and appliances used in medical, surgical, dental or veterinary	1 040.0	852.2	486.2					872
0102	Live bovine animals	603.2	1 118.8	633.9	*925.0*	*960.4*	*971.4*	US$/unit	001
0402	Milk and cream, concentrated or containing added sugar	682.8	869.4	729.5	4.2	4.1	4.0	US$/kg	022
0202	Meat of bovine animals, frozen	602.0	776.8	865.4	5.8	5.7	5.7	US$/kg	011
7304	Tubes, pipes and hollow profiles, seamless, of iron (other than cast iron)	489.1	663.5	918.8	*2.2*	*2.3*	3.0	US$/kg	679
2304	Oil-cake and other solid residues	592.7	618.7	747.2	0.5	0.6	0.7	US$/kg	081
8471	Automatic data processing machines and units thereof	624.4	728.3	480.3					752

Viet Nam

Goods Imports: CIF, by origin | **Goods Exports: FOB, by last known destination** | **Trade System: General**

Overview:

In 2014, the value of merchandise exports of Viet Nam increased substantially by 13.8 percent to reach 150.2 bln US$, while its merchandise imports increased substantially by 12.0 percent to reach 147.8 bln US$ (see graph 1, table 2 and table 3). The merchandise trade balance recorded a relatively small surplus of 2.4 bln US$ (see graph 1). The largest merchandise trade balance was with MDG Eastern Asia at -47.8 bln US$ (see graph 4). Merchandise exports in Viet Nam were diversified amongst partners; imports were also diversified. The top 20 partners accounted for 80 percent or more of exports and 10 partners accounted for 80 percent or more of imports (see graph 5). In 2014, the value of exports of services of Viet Nam increased slightly by 2.4 percent, reaching 11.0 bln US$, while its imports of services increased slightly by 4.9 percent and reached 14.5 bln US$ (see graph 2). There was a moderate trade in services deficit of 3.5 bln US$.

Graph 1: Total merchandise trade, by value

(Bln US$ by year)

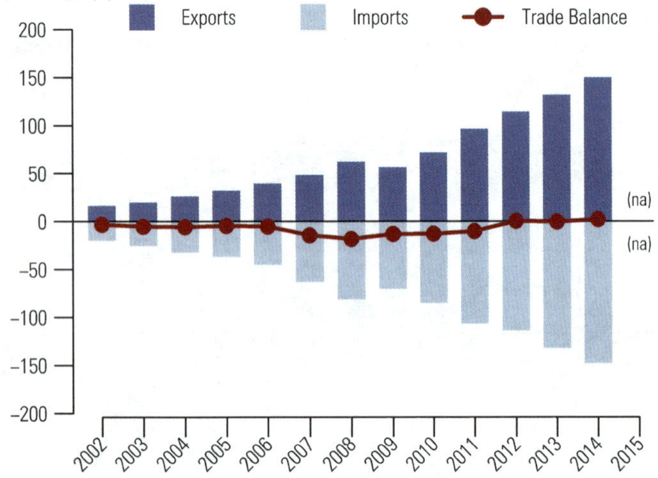

Graph 2: Total services trade, by value

(Bln US$ by year)

Exports Profile:

"Machinery and transport equipment" (SITC section 7), "Miscellaneous manufactured articles" (SITC section 8) and "Food, animals + beverages, tobacco" (SITC section 0+1) were the largest commodity groups for exports in 2014, representing respectively 32.4, 29.8 and 14.6 percent of exported goods (see table 2). From 2012 to 2014, the largest export commodity was "Electrical apparatus for line telephony or line telegraphy" (HS code 8517) (see table 1). The top three destinations for merchandise exports were the United States, Japan and China, accounting for respectively 18.2, 10.4 and 10.3 percent of total exports. "Travel" (EBOPS code 236) accounted for the largest share of exports of services in 2014 at 7.3 bln US$, followed by "Transportation" (EBOPS code 205) at 2.3 bln US$ (see graph 3).

Graph 3: Exports of services by EBOPS category

(% share in 2014)

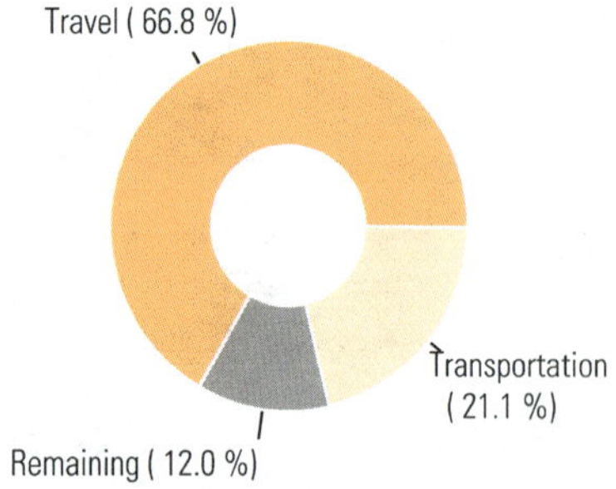

Table 1: Top 10 export commodities 2012 to 2014

HS code	4-digit heading of Harmonized System 2012	Value (million US$) 2012	2013	2014	Unit value 2012	2013	2014	Unit	SITC code
	All Commodities	114529.2	132032.9	150217.1					
8517	Electrical apparatus for line telephony or line telegraphy	13157.0	21853.0	24392.8					764
2709	Petroleum oils and oils obtained from bituminous minerals, crude	8398.0	7375.4	7224.2	0.9	0.9	0.8	US$/kg	333
6403	Footwear with outer soles of rubber, plastics, leather	3245.1	3639.2	4290.8		*32.7*		US$/pair	851
1006	Rice	3677.9	2926.3	2936.9		*0.4*	*0.5*	US$/kg	042
0901	Coffee, whether or not roasted or decaffeinated	3545.3	2551.4	3311.4	*2.1*	2.0	*2.0*	US$/kg	071
9403	Other furniture and parts thereof	2655.1	2961.8	3430.5					821
8471	Automatic data processing machines and units thereof	1491.4	3412.8	3811.9					752
6404	Footwear with outer soles of rubber, plastics, leather	2152.9	2865.1	3667.1					851
8544	Insulated (including enamelled or anodised) wire, cable	2159.3	2516.0	2719.1					773
6204	Women's or girls'suits, ensembles, jackets, blazers, dresses, skirts	2118.4	2440.9	2766.8					842

Services Imports and Exports: EBOPS 2002 categories

Table 2: Merchandise exports by SITC

(Value in million US$, growth and shares in percentage)

SITC	2014	Avg. Growth rates 2010-2014	Avg. Growth rates 2013-2014	2014 share
Total	150217.1	20.1	13.8	100.0
0+1	21965.8	12.5	16.9	14.6
2+4	4394.8	6.6	-12.0	2.9
3	9238.3	3.7	-4.6	6.1
5	4218.3	22.5	10.2	2.8
6	16414.5	18.2	19.1	10.9
7	48624.1	43.5	13.0	32.4
8	44799.9	15.8	20.1	29.8
9	561.4	5.0	-7.3	0.4

Table 3: Merchandise imports by SITC

(Value in million US$, growth and shares in percentage)

SITC	2014	Avg. Growth rates 2010-2014	Avg. Growth rates 2013-2014	2014 share
Total	147839.0	14.9	12.0	100.0
0+1	10975.9	14.1	16.7	7.4
2+4	8895.0	14.5	15.7	6.0
3	10355.7	6.2	2.3	7.0
5	19690.5	12.1	8.3	13.3
6	34567.9	11.5	15.3	23.4
7	55013.9	22.1	11.3	37.2
8	7479.3	15.7	15.5	5.1
9	860.9	-8.9	11.1	0.6

SITC Legend

SITC Code	Description
Total	All commodities
0+1	Food, animals + beverages, tobacco
2+4	Crude materials + anim. & veg. oils
3	Mineral fuels, lubricants
5	Chemicals
6	Goods classified chiefly by material
7	Machinery and transport equipment
8	Miscellaneous manufactured articles
9	Not classified elsewhere in the SITC

Graph 4: Merchandise trade balance

(Bln US$ by MDG Regions in 2014)

Graph 5: Partner concentration of merchandise trade

(Cumulative share by ranked partners in 2014)

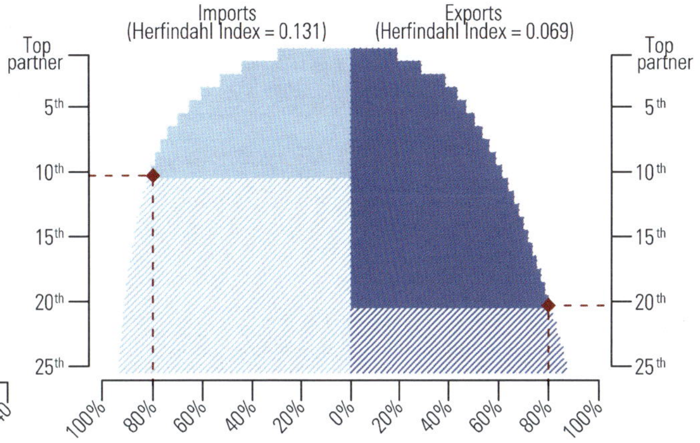

Graph 6: Imports of services by EBOPS category

(% share in 2014)

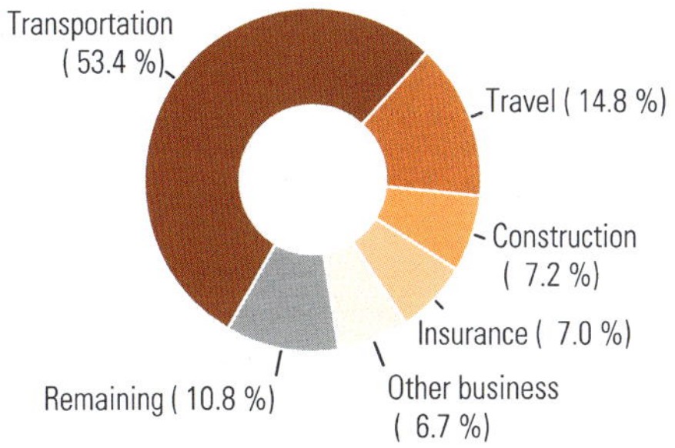

Imports Profile:

"Machinery and transport equipment" (SITC section 7), "Goods classified chiefly by material" (SITC section 6) and "Chemicals" (SITC section 5) were the largest commodity groups for imports in 2014, representing respectively 37.2, 23.4 and 13.3 percent of imported goods (see table 3). From 2012 to 2014, the largest import commodity was "Electronic integrated circuits" (HS code 8542) (see table 4). The top three partners for merchandise imports were China, the Republic of Korea and Japan, accounting for respectively 27.8, 14.7 and 9.1 percent of total imports. "Transportation" (EBOPS code 205) accounted for the largest share of imports of services in 2014 at 7.7 bln US$, followed by "Travel" (EBOPS code 236) at 2.1 bln US$ and "Construction services" (EBOPS code 249) at 1.1 bln US$ (see graph 6).

Table 4: Top 10 import commodities 2012 to 2014

HS code	4-digit heading of Harmonized System 2012	Value (million US$) 2012	2013	2014	Unit value 2012	2013	2014	Unit	SITC code
	All Commodities	113780.4	132032.5	147839.0					
8542	Electronic integrated circuits	7313.5	10152.8	10295.2					776
2710	Petroleum oils, other than crude	9356.3	7392.7	8028.9					334
8517	Electrical apparatus for line telephony or line telegraphy	5314.1	8559.3	9376.3					764
7208	Flat-rolled products of iron or non-alloy steel	2341.3	2607.7	2163.1	0.6	*0.6*	*0.6*	US$/kg	673
3004	Medicaments (excluding goods of heading 30.02, 30.05 or 30.06)	1642.8	1725.4	1870.1					542
3901	Polymers of ethylene, in primary forms	1394.2	1674.5	1934.4	1.5	*1.6*	1.7	US$/kg	571
6006	Other knitted or crocheted fabrics	1307.6	1675.2	1924.0		*9.5*	*10.0*	US$/kg	655
2304	Oil-cake and other solid residues	1269.8	1743.3	1859.8		*0.6*	*0.6*	US$/kg	081
8534	Printed circuits	1096.9	1454.2	1455.3					772
7204	Ferrous waste and scrap; remelting scrap ingots of iron or steel	1415.4	1247.1	1241.6	0.4	0.4	*0.4*	US$/kg	282

Yemen

Goods Imports: CIF, by origin | **Goods Exports: FOB, by last known destination** | **Trade System: Special**

Overview:

In 2014, the value of merchandise exports of Yemen decreased substantially by 66.1 percent to reach 2.4 bln US$, while its merchandise imports decreased moderately by 9.3 percent to reach 12.0 bln US$ (see graph 1, table 2 and table 3). The merchandise trade balance recorded a large deficit of 9.6 bln US$ (see graph 1). The largest merchandise trade balance was with MDG Western Asia at -1.7 bln US$ (see graph 4). Merchandise exports in Yemen were moderately concentrated amongst partners; imports were diversified. The top 6 partners accounted for 80 percent or more of exports and 18 partners accounted for 80 percent or more of imports (see graph 5). In 2014, the value of exports of services of Yemen decreased slightly by 1.1 percent, reaching 1.7 bln US$, while its imports of services increased substantially by 11.4 percent and reached 2.5 bln US$ (see graph 2). There was a moderate trade in services deficit of 825.4 mln US$.

Graph 1: Total merchandise trade, by value

(Bln US$ by year)

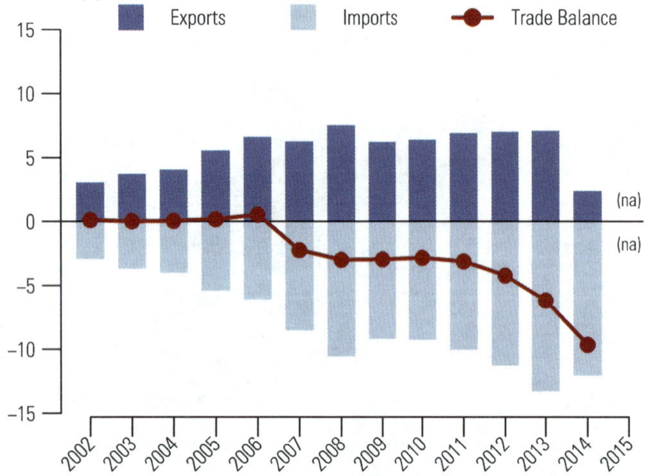

Graph 2: Total services trade, by value

(Bln US$ by year)

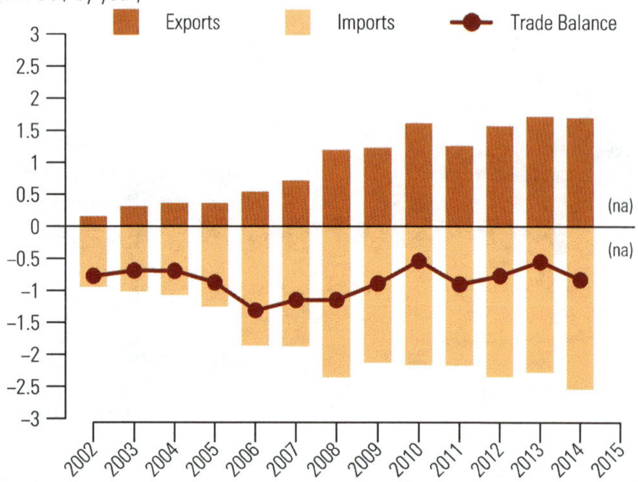

Exports Profile:

"Mineral fuels, lubricants" (SITC section 3), "Food, animals + beverages, tobacco" (SITC section 0+1) and "Machinery and transport equipment" (SITC section 7) were the largest commodity groups for exports in 2014, representing respectively 55.8, 19.2 and 17.5 percent of exported goods (see table 2). From 2012 to 2014, the largest export commodity was "Petroleum oils and oils obtained from bituminous minerals, crude" (HS code 2709) (see table 1). The top three destinations for merchandise exports were China, Thailand and India, accounting for respectively 33.0, 18.5 and 8.2 percent of total exports. "Travel" (EBOPS code 236) accounted for the largest share of exports of services in 2014 at 1.0 bln US$, followed by "Transportation" (EBOPS code 205) at 258.1 mln US$ and "Communications services" (EBOPS code 245) at 219.0 mln US$ (see graph 3).

Graph 3: Exports of services by EBOPS category

(% share in 2014)

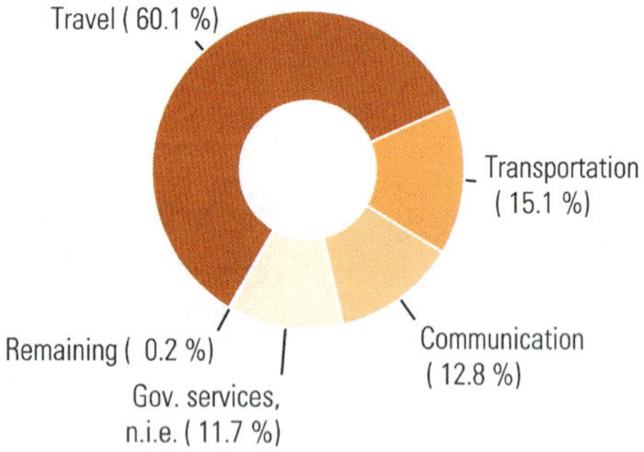

Table 1: Top 10 export commodities 2012 to 2014

HS code	4-digit heading of Harmonized System 2012	Value (million US$) 2012	2013	2014	Unit value 2012	2013	2014	Unit	SITC code
	All Commodities	7062.1	7129.8	2416.9					
2709	Petroleum oils and oils obtained from bituminous minerals, crude	5335.2	3248.7	1271.5	0.8	0.8	*0.8*	US$/kg	333
2711	Petroleum gases and other gaseous hydrocarbons	555.5	2053.7	68.8	0.2	0.3	*0.6*	US$/kg	343
2707	Oils and other products of high temperature coal tar	184.2	642.3	0.0	1.0	0.9	*0.9*	US$/kg	335
9999	Commodities not specified according to kind	1.5	483.6	0.2					931
0302	Fish, fresh or chilled, excluding fish fillets	101.1	121.3	114.1	1.9	2.0		US$/kg	034
2710	Petroleum oils, other than crude	250.5	20.8	8.8	0.8	0.6	*1.0*	US$/kg	334
8703	Motor cars and other motor vehicles principally designed for the transport	5.6	...	215.9	35.0			thsd US$/unit	781
0307	Molluscs, whether in shell or not	49.2	41.7	38.0	3.4	2.4	*4.2*	US$/kg	036
8708	Parts and accessories of the motor vehicles of headings 87.01 to 87.05	44.3	11.3	51.3	14.4	11.4	*17.6*	US$/kg	784
8803	Parts of goods of heading 88.01 or 88.02	6.7	27.8	67.2	750.4	632.4	961.6	US$/kg	792

Services Imports and Exports: EBOPS 2002 categories

Table 2: Merchandise exports by SITC

(Value in million US$, growth and shares in percentage)

SITC	2014	Avg. Growth rates 2010-2014	Avg. Growth rates 2013-2014	2014 share
Total	2 416.9	-21.7	-66.1	100.0
0+1	465.0	0.6	7.3	19.2
2+4	41.1	6.1	-19.8	1.7
3	1 349.1	-30.2	-77.4	55.8
5	40.6	1.9	4.0	1.7
6	72.2	7.2	72.3	3.0
7	424.1	30.7	367.2	17.5
8	7.6	-17.8	-28.6	0.3
9	17.3	-12.4	-96.5	0.7

Table 3: Merchandise imports by SITC

(Value in million US$, growth and shares in percentage)

SITC	2014	Avg. Growth rates 2010-2014	Avg. Growth rates 2013-2014	2014 share
Total	12 041.6	6.8	-9.3	100.0
0+1	4 404.4	15.0	24.4	36.6
2+4	557.9	7.4	44.0	4.6
3	259.0	-39.6	27.5	2.2
5	1 122.3	12.3	16.8	9.3
6	2 083.1	12.4	45.0	17.3
7	2 608.7	6.6	24.4	21.7
8	808.4	25.4	87.6	6.7
9	197.8	68.8	-95.3	1.6

SITC Legend

SITC Code	Description
Total	All commodities
0+1	Food, animals + beverages, tobacco
2+4	Crude materials + anim. & veg. oils
3	Mineral fuels, lubricants
5	Chemicals
6	Goods classified chiefly by material
7	Machinery and transport equipment
8	Miscellaneous manufactured articles
9	Not classified elsewhere in the SITC

Graph 4: Merchandise trade balance

(Bln US$ by MDG Regions in 2014)

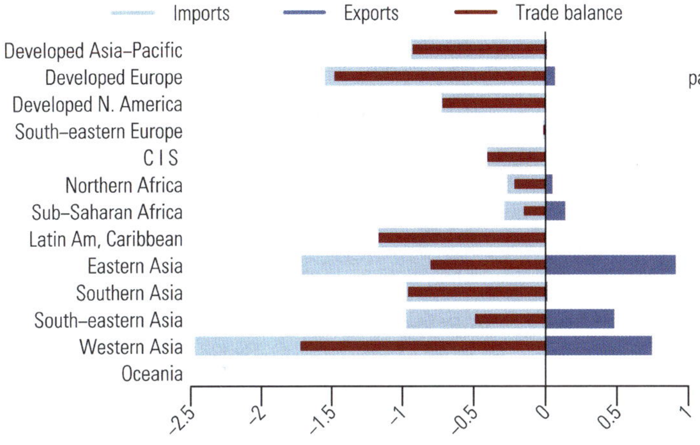

Graph 5: Partner concentration of merchandise trade

(Cumulative share by ranked partners in 2014)

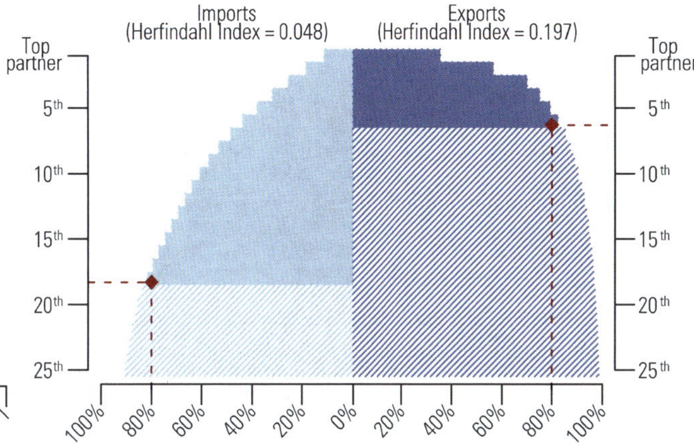

Graph 6: Imports of services by EBOPS category

(% share in 2014)

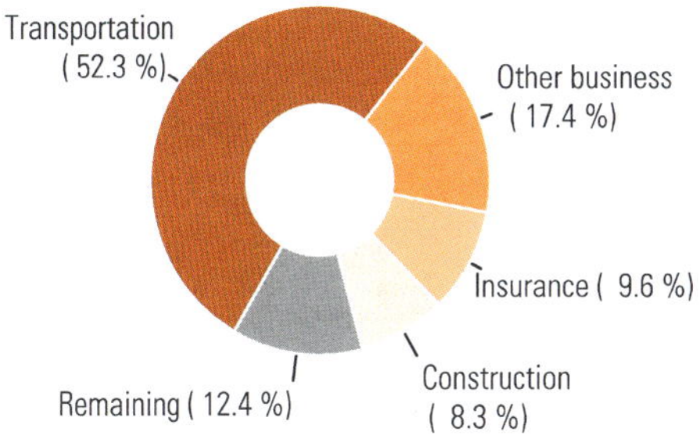

Imports Profile:

"Food, animals + beverages, tobacco" (SITC section 0+1), "Machinery and transport equipment" (SITC section 7) and "Goods classified chiefly by material" (SITC section 6) were the largest commodity groups for imports in 2014, representing respectively 36.6, 21.7 and 17.3 percent of imported goods (see table 3). From 2012 to 2014, the largest import commodity was "Commodities not specified according to kind" (HS code 9999) (see table 4). The top three partners for merchandise imports were the United Arab Emirates, China and Saudi Arabia, accounting for respectively 10.7, 8.8 and 6.3 percent of total imports. "Transportation" (EBOPS code 205) accounted for the largest share of imports of services in 2014 at 1.3 bln US$, followed by "Other business services" (EBOPS code 268) at 440.3 mln US$ and "Insurance services" (EBOPS code 253) at 243.9 mln US$ (see graph 6).

Table 4: Top 10 import commodities 2012 to 2014

HS code	4-digit heading of Harmonized System 2012	Value (million US$) 2012	2013	2014	Unit value 2012	2013	2014	Unit	SITC code
	All Commodities	11 259.6	13 272.9	12 041.6					
9999	Commodities not specified according to kind	354.7	4 173.4	0.1					931
2710	Petroleum oils, other than crude	3 024.2	138.6	195.7	1.0	1.7	1.5	US$/kg	334
1001	Wheat and meslin	983.8	1 048.4	1 060.3	0.3	0.3	0.3	US$/kg	041
8703	Motor cars and other motor vehicles principally designed for the transport	516.9	523.8	711.2	10.9	8.4	8.5	thsd US$/unit	781
1701	Cane or beet sugar and chemically pure sucrose, in solid form	444.7	342.1	583.8	0.7	0.6	0.5	US$/kg	061
1006	Rice	346.3	363.1	384.4	0.8	0.8	0.9	US$/kg	042
3004	Medicaments (excluding goods of heading 30.02, 30.05 or 30.06)	287.2	330.9	341.8	17.5			US$/kg	542
0402	Milk and cream, concentrated or containing added sugar	221.6	222.4	286.0	3.5	3.9	4.6	US$/kg	022
7214	Other bars and rods of iron or non-alloy steel	165.1	178.5	366.0	0.6	0.6	0.6	US$/kg	676
1511	Palm oil and its fractions	190.7	211.3	296.0	1.1	1.0	0.9	US$/kg	422

Zambia

Goods Imports: CIF, by origin | **Goods Exports: FOB, by last known destination** | **Trade System: General**

Overview:

In 2014, the value of merchandise exports of Zambia decreased moderately by 8.6 percent to reach 9.7 bln US$, while its merchandise imports decreased moderately by 6.1 percent to reach 9.5 bln US$ (see graph 1, table 2 and table 3). The merchandise trade balance recorded a relatively small surplus of 148.9 mln US$ (see graph 1). The largest merchandise trade balance was with MDG Developed Europe at 3.7 bln US$ (see graph 4). Merchandise exports in Zambia were highly concentrated amongst partners; imports were diversified. The top 5 partners accounted for 80 percent or more of exports and 10 partners accounted for 80 percent or more of imports (see graph 5). In 2014, the value of exports of services of Zambia increased substantially by 12.2 percent, reaching 850.9 mln US$, while its imports of services decreased moderately by 9.6 percent and reached 1.6 bln US$ (see graph 2). There was a large trade in services deficit of 778.9 mln US$.

Graph 1: Total merchandise trade, by value

(Bln US$ by year)

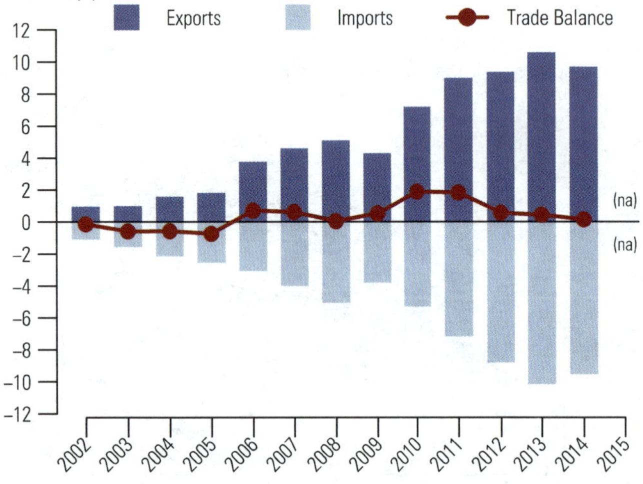

Graph 2: Total services trade, by value

(Bln US$ by year)

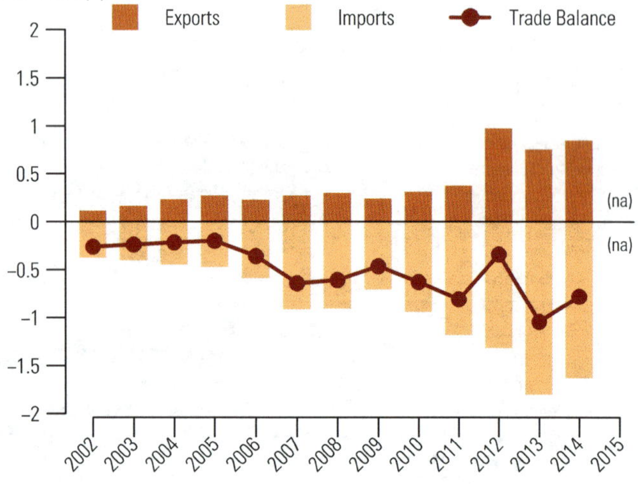

Exports Profile:

"Goods classified chiefly by material" (SITC section 6), "Food, animals + beverages, tobacco" (SITC section 0+1) and "Chemicals" (SITC section 5) were the largest commodity groups for exports in 2014, representing respectively 79.3, 6.6 and 4.0 percent of exported goods (see table 2). From 2012 to 2014, the largest export commodity was "Refined copper and copper alloys, unwrought" (HS code 7403) (see table 1). The top three destinations for merchandise exports were Switzerland, China and Democratic Republic of the Congo, accounting for respectively 41.2, 19.7 and 9.1 percent of total exports. "Travel" (EBOPS code 236) accounted for the largest share of exports of services in 2014 at 641.5 mln US$, followed by "Insurance services" (EBOPS code 253) at 79.5 mln US$ and "Transportation" (EBOPS code 205) at 61.1 mln US$ (see graph 3).

Graph 3: Exports of services by EBOPS category

(% share in 2014)

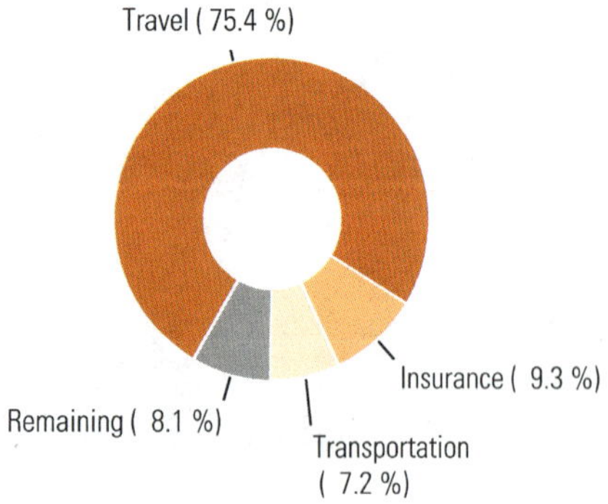

Table 1: Top 10 export commodities 2012 to 2014

HS code	4-digit heading of Harmonized System 2012	Value (million US$)			Unit value				SITC code
		2012	2013	2014	2012	2013	2014	Unit	
	All Commodities	9364.7	10594.1	9687.9					
7403	Refined copper and copper alloys, unwrought	5936.2	6607.4	7104.5	7.4	7.1	7.5	US$/kg	682
1005	Maize (corn)	414.2	154.8	65.4	0.6	0.9	0.7	US$/kg	044
2807	Sulphuric acid; oleum	76.4	254.0	217.7	0.2	0.7	0.5	US$/kg	522
2401	Unmanufactured tobacco; tobacco refuse	156.7	180.3	143.1	4.1	4.3	*4.5*	US$/kg	121
8105	Cobalt mattes and other intermediate products of cobalt metallurgy	214.5	132.5	122.7	13.0	24.2	24.9	US$/kg	689
7108	Gold (including gold plated with platinum)	138.5	162.9	117.7		43.3	41.9	thsd US$/kg	971
1701	Cane or beet sugar and chemically pure sucrose, in solid form	123.5	122.0	132.4	0.6	0.6	0.6	US$/kg	061
7409	Copper plates, sheets and strip, of a thickness exceeding 0.15 mm	276.0	79.0	10.7	9.6	7.9	*8.0*	US$/kg	682
7408	Copper wire	150.3	127.7	84.5	10.1	9.7	*7.6*	US$/kg	682
2523	Portland cement, aluminous cement, slag cement	65.8	209.8	68.5	0.2	0.8	*0.3*	US$/kg	661

Services Imports and Exports: EBOPS 2002 categories

Table 2: Merchandise exports by SITC

(Value in million US$, growth and shares in percentage)

SITC	2014	Avg. Growth rates 2010-2014	Avg. Growth rates 2013-2014	2014 share
Total	9687.9	7.7	-8.6	100.0
0+1	637.4	11.8	-38.7	6.6
2+4	354.8	-13.1	-22.9	3.7
3	106.5	30.7	-46.4	1.1
5	391.7	29.8	-39.3	4.0
6	7686.0	7.5	2.1	79.3
7	307.0	22.4	-27.9	3.2
8	74.1	31.8	-22.6	0.8
9	130.5	16.3	-35.6	1.3

Table 3: Merchandise imports by SITC

(Value in million US$, growth and shares in percentage)

SITC	2014	Avg. Growth rates 2010-2014	Avg. Growth rates 2013-2014	2014 share
Total	9539.0	15.7	-6.1	100.0
0+1	361.7	21.5	7.0	3.8
2+4	1763.1	15.8	-2.7	18.5
3	1337.8	21.3	24.2	14.0
5	1292.1	8.7	-18.0	13.5
6	1372.4	12.1	-10.2	14.4
7	3026.2	18.6	-9.9	31.7
8	374.6	15.8	-17.5	3.9
9	11.1	-16.2	-36.2	0.1

SITC Legend

SITC Code	Description
Total	All commodities
0+1	Food, animals + beverages, tobacco
2+4	Crude materials + anim. & veg. oils
3	Mineral fuels, lubricants
5	Chemicals
6	Goods classified chiefly by material
7	Machinery and transport equipment
8	Miscellaneous manufactured articles
9	Not classified elsewhere in the SITC

Graph 4: Merchandise trade balance

(Bln US$ by MDG Regions in 2014)

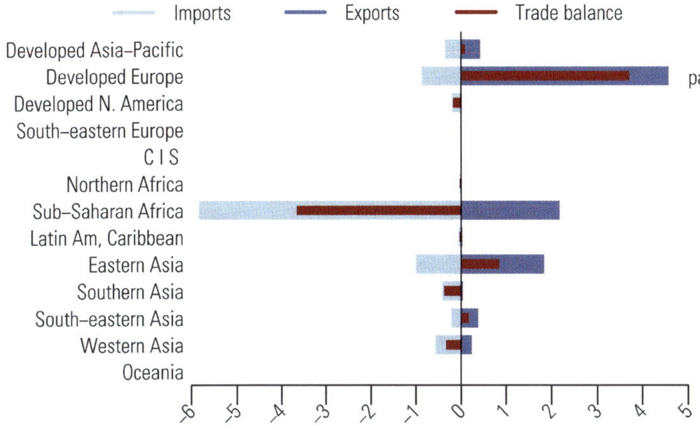

Graph 5: Partner concentration of merchandise trade

(Cumulative share by ranked partners in 2014)

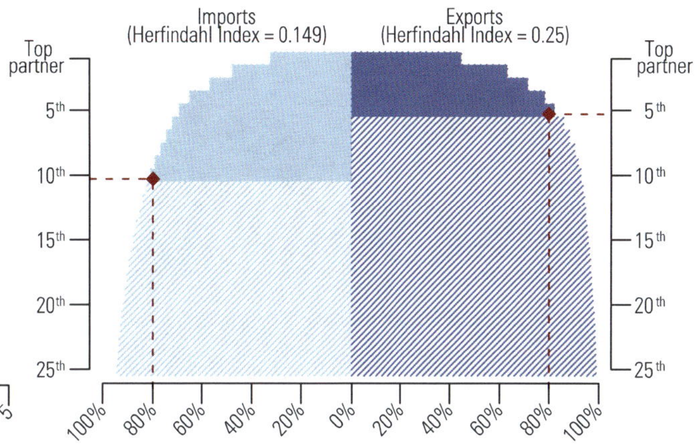

Graph 6: Imports of services by EBOPS category

(% share in 2014)

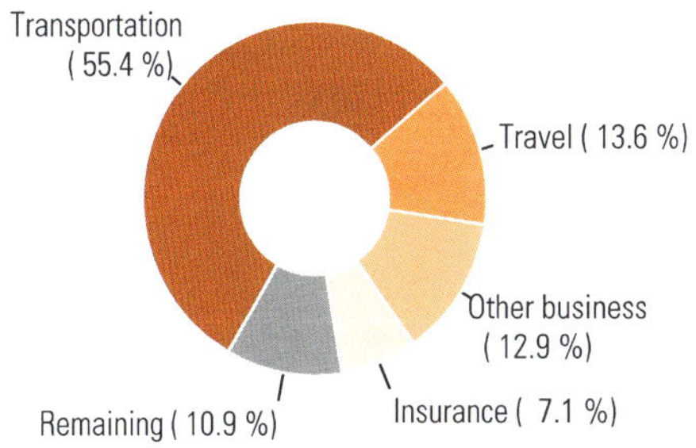

Imports Profile:

"Machinery and transport equipment" (SITC section 7), "Crude materials + anim. & veg. oils" (SITC section 2+4) and "Goods classified chiefly by material" (SITC section 6) were the largest commodity groups for imports in 2014, representing respectively 31.7, 18.5 and 14.4 percent of imported goods (see table 3). From 2012 to 2014, the largest import commodity was "Copper ores and concentrates" (HS code 2603) (see table 4). The top three partners for merchandise imports were South Africa, Democratic Republic of the Congo and China, accounting for respectively 32.1, 16.0 and 9.4 percent of total imports. "Transportation" (EBOPS code 205) accounted for the largest share of imports of services in 2014 at 902.8 mln US$, followed by "Travel" (EBOPS code 236) at 222.2 mln US$ and "Other business services" (EBOPS code 268) at 210.3 mln US$ (see graph 6).

Table 4: Top 10 import commodities 2012 to 2014

HS code	4-digit heading of Harmonized System 2012	Value (million US$) 2012	2013	2014	Unit value 2012	2013	2014	Unit	SITC code
	All Commodities	8805.2	10161.8	9539.0					
2603	Copper ores and concentrates	847.1	1389.4	1220.2	3.3	2.9	4.3	US$/kg	283
2710	Petroleum oils, other than crude	315.3	919.7	1075.8	1.5	0.9	1.6	US$/kg	334
8704	Motor vehicles for the transport of goods	366.8	341.0	348.1					782
2709	Petroleum oils and oils obtained from bituminous minerals, crude	543.9	89.1	179.5	0.8		0.7	US$/kg	333
7308	Structures (excluding prefabricated buildings of heading 94.06)	130.7	325.2	316.2	3.3	2.8	*2.9*	US$/kg	691
8429	Self-propelled bulldozers, angledozers, graders, levellers, scrapers	219.5	252.4	228.0					723
8474	Machinery for sorting, screening, separating, washing, crushing, grinding	140.5	295.5	208.7					728
8703	Motor cars and other motor vehicles principally designed for the transport	186.7	238.6	213.1	*18.5*	*17.4*	*17.5*	thsd US$/unit	781
3102	Mineral or chemical fertilisers, nitrogenous	158.5	254.3	203.5	0.7	0.7	*0.6*	US$/kg	562
2605	Cobalt ores and concentrates	190.5	167.4	203.4	2.5	2.7	2.4	US$/kg	287

Zimbabwe

Goods Imports: CIF, by origin | **Goods Exports: FOB, by last known destination** | **Trade System: General**

Overview:

In 2015, the value of merchandise exports of Zimbabwe decreased substantially by 11.7 percent to reach 2.7 bln US$, while its merchandise imports decreased moderately by 5.9 percent to reach 6.0 bln US$ (see graph 1, table 2 and table 3). The merchandise trade balance recorded a large deficit of 3.3 bln US$ (see graph 1). The largest merchandise trade balance was with MDG South-eastern Asia at -1.4 bln US$ (see graph 4). Merchandise exports in Zimbabwe were highly concentrated amongst partners; imports were moderately concentrated. The top 2 partners accounted for 80 percent or more of exports and 7 partners accounted for 80 percent or more of imports (see graph 5). In 2013, the value of exports of services of Zimbabwe increased substantially by 13.7 percent, reaching 439.9 mln US$, while its imports of services increased substantially by 20.4 percent and reached 1.2 bln US$ (see graph 2). There was a large trade in services deficit of 724.9 mln US$.

Graph 1: Total merchandise trade, by value

(Bln US$ by year)

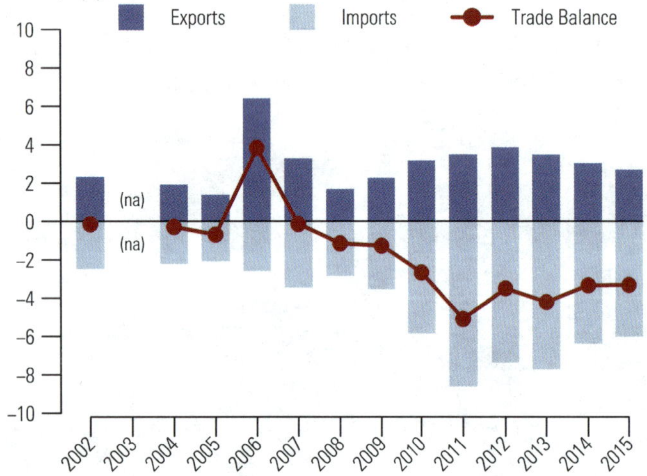

Graph 2: Total services trade, by value

(Bln US$ by year)

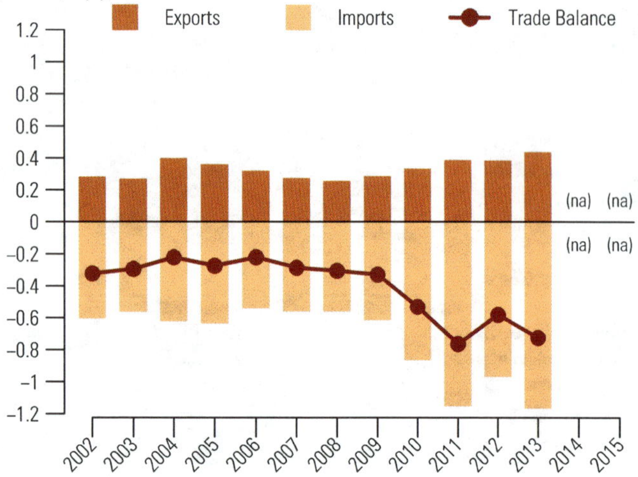

Exports Profile:

"Food, animals + beverages, tobacco" (SITC section 0+1), "Not classified elsewhere in the SITC" (SITC section 9) and "Crude materials + anim. & veg. oils" (SITC section 2+4) were the largest commodity groups for exports in 2015, representing respectively 40.0, 23.4 and 20.6 percent of exported goods (see table 2). From 2013 to 2015, the largest export commodity was "Unmanufactured tobacco; tobacco refuse" (HS code 2401) (see table 1). The top three destinations for merchandise exports were South Africa, Mozambique and the United Arab Emirates, accounting for respectively 71.0, 14.6 and 5.1 percent of total exports. "Travel" (EBOPS code 236) accounted for the largest share of exports of services in 2013 at 198.4 mln US$, followed by "Transportation" (EBOPS code 205) at 164.4 mln US$ and "Government services, n.i.e." (EBOPS code 291) at 41.3 mln US$ (see graph 3).

Graph 3: Exports of services by EBOPS category

(% share in 2013)

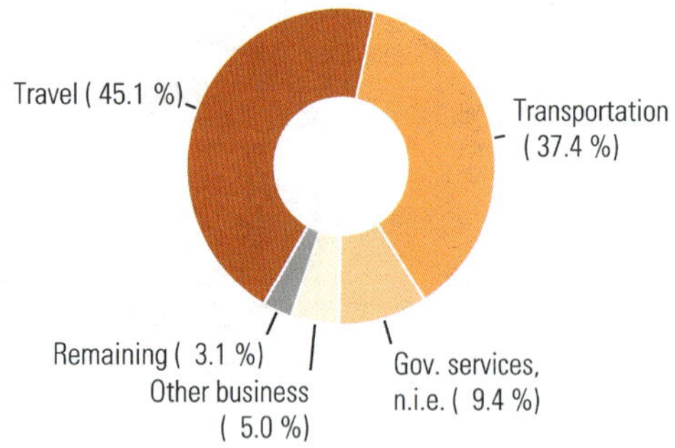

Table 1: Top 10 export commodities 2013 to 2015

HS code	4-digit heading of Harmonized System 2012	Value (million US$) 2013	2014	2015	Unit value 2013	2014	2015	Unit	SITC code
	All Commodities	3 507.3	3 063.7	2 704.1					
2401	Unmanufactured tobacco; tobacco refuse	869.9	807.6	865.0	5.9	5.7	5.8	US$/kg	121
7108	Gold (including gold plated with platinum)	502.5	532.9	630.6		40.5	36.6	thsd US$/kg	971
2604	Nickel ores and concentrates	326.7	354.4	218.4	2.1	1.9	1.3	US$/kg	284
7102	Diamonds, whether or not worked, but not mounted or set	326.6	233.6	179.1					667
7202	Ferro-alloys	148.4	271.4	158.8					671
7501	Nickel mattes, nickel oxide sinters and other intermediate products	411.2	4.1	22.2	55.8	50.5	50.8	US$/kg	284
1701	Cane or beet sugar and chemically pure sucrose, in solid form	90.6	150.3	99.8	0.6	0.6	0.5	US$/kg	061
7110	Platinum, unwrought or in semi-manufactured forms, or in powder form	140.2	136.9	35.5					681
5201	Cotton, not carded or combed	97.2	66.2	48.4	1.7	1.7	1.4	US$/kg	263
2516	Granite, porphyry, basalt, sandstone and other stone	16.9	24.1	31.6	0.2	0.2	0.2	US$/kg	273

Services Imports and Exports: EBOPS 2002 categories

Table 2: Merchandise exports by SITC

(Value in million US$, growth and shares in percentage)

SITC	2015	Avg. Growth rates 2011-2015	Avg. Growth rates 2014-2015	2015 share
Total	2704.1	-6.3	-11.7	100.0
0+1	1082.3	6.8	0.3	40.0
2+4	555.8	-21.9	-4.0	20.6
3	41.5	9.0	195.2	1.5
5	21.9	-4.9	6.3	0.8
6	293.6	-3.9	-60.5	10.9
7	36.5	-6.9	-28.7	1.3
8	40.4	-44.7	-7.5	1.5
9	632.0	19.7	18.5	23.4

Table 3: Merchandise imports by SITC

(Value in million US$, growth and shares in percentage)

SITC	2015	Avg. Growth rates 2011-2015	Avg. Growth rates 2014-2015	2015 share
Total	6002.2	-8.6	-5.9	100.0
0+1	844.4	-5.9	-0.5	14.1
2+4	200.6	-15.9	-16.4	3.3
3	1583.6	6.0	1.1	26.4
5	945.2	-23.3	-14.6	15.7
6	680.5	-2.7	-3.9	11.3
7	1411.4	-9.1	-5.3	23.5
8	293.4	3.1	-21.1	4.9
9	43.2	-0.3	-7.4	0.7

SITC Legend

SITC Code	Description
Total	All commodities
0+1	Food, animals + beverages, tobacco
2+4	Crude materials + anim. & veg. oils
3	Mineral fuels, lubricants
5	Chemicals
6	Goods classified chiefly by material
7	Machinery and transport equipment
8	Miscellaneous manufactured articles
9	Not classified elsewhere in the SITC

Graph 4: Merchandise trade balance

(Bln US$ by MDG Regions in 2015)

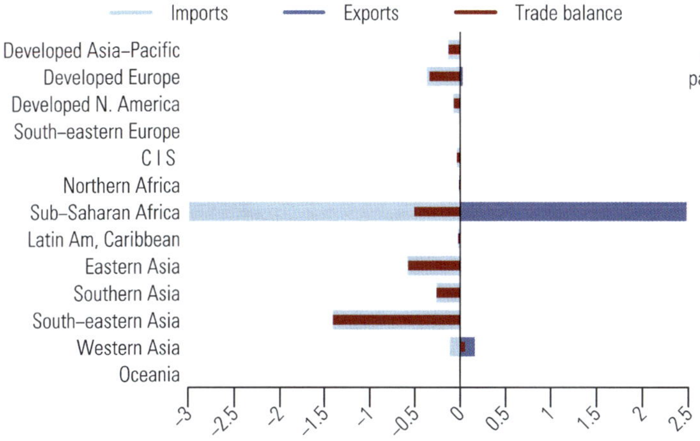

Graph 5: Partner concentration of merchandise trade

(Cumulative share by ranked partners in 2015)

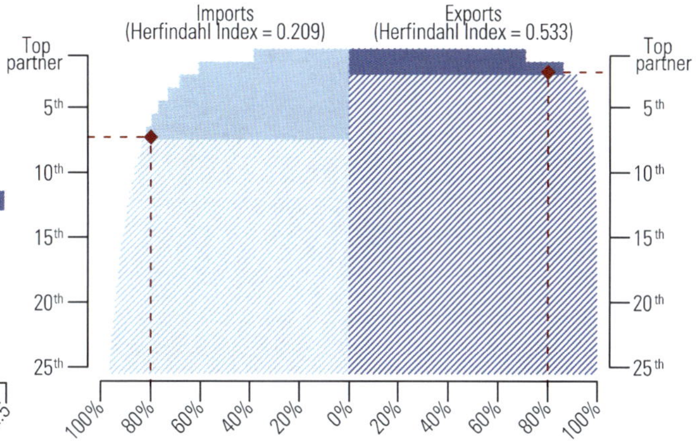

Graph 6: Imports of services by EBOPS category

(% share in 2013)

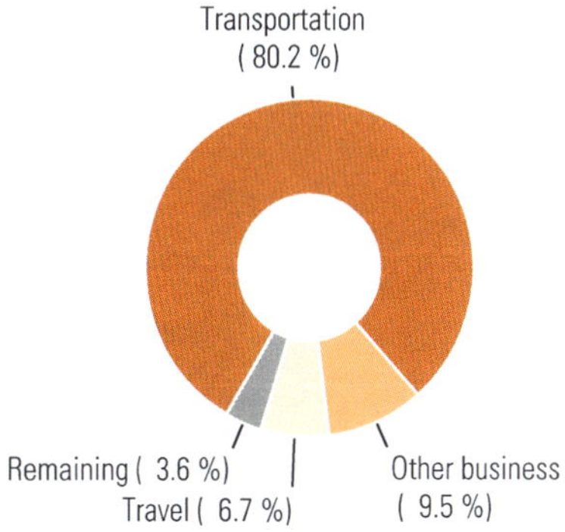

Imports Profile:

"Mineral fuels, lubricants" (SITC section 3), "Machinery and transport equipment" (SITC section 7) and "Chemicals" (SITC section 5) were the largest commodity groups for imports in 2015, representing respectively 26.4, 23.5 and 15.7 percent of imported goods (see table 3). From 2013 to 2015, the largest import commodity was "Petroleum oils, other than crude" (HS code 2710) (see table 4). The top three partners for merchandise imports were South Africa, Singapore and the United Kingdom, accounting for respectively 43.3, 12.8 and 8.6 percent of total imports. "Transportation" (EBOPS code 205) accounted for the largest share of imports of services in 2013 at 933.8 mln US$, followed by "Other business services" (EBOPS code 268) at 110.7 mln US$ and "Travel" (EBOPS code 236) at 78.4 mln US$ (see graph 6).

Table 4: Top 10 import commodities 2013 to 2015

HS code	4-digit heading of Harmonized System 2012	Value (million US$) 2013	2014	2015	Unit value 2013	2014	2015	Unit	SITC code
	All Commodities	7704.2	6379.8	6002.2					
2710	Petroleum oils, other than crude	1511.8	1478.9	1518.6	1.2	1.2	1.3	US$/kg	334
3105	Mineral or chemical fertilisers	979.4	89.3	82.4	7.0	0.6	0.6	US$/kg	562
8704	Motor vehicles for the transport of goods	269.2	174.8	171.7	*6.6*	*2.0*	*1.6*	thsd US$/unit	782
8703	Motor cars and other motor vehicles principally designed for the transport	257.7	197.0	152.0	3.0			thsd US$/unit	781
3004	Medicaments (excluding goods of heading 30.02, 30.05 or 30.06)	165.5	203.8	176.8	*20.8*	46.8	41.2	US$/kg	542
8517	Electrical apparatus for line telephony or line telegraphy	154.3	135.8	161.0					764
1005	Maize (corn)	108.7	114.6	174.3	0.4	0.4	0.3	US$/kg	044
1006	Rice	106.5	115.1	126.9	0.7	0.7	0.6	US$/kg	042
3102	Mineral or chemical fertilisers, nitrogenous	80.3	160.8	62.6	0.6	0.8	0.5	US$/kg	562
1001	Wheat and meslin	81.1	92.0	100.0	0.5	0.5	0.4	US$/kg	041

Goods Imports: CIF, by origin | **Goods Exports: FOB, by last known destination** | **Trade System: Special**

Overview:

In 2014, the value of merchandise exports of the EU decreased slightly by 2.4 percent to reach 2339.7 bln US$, while its merchandise imports decreased slightly by 0.1 percent to reach 2281.3 bln US$ (see graph 1, table 2 and table 3). The merchandise trade balance recorded a relatively small surplus of 58.4 bln US$ (see graph 1). The largest merchandise trade balance was with MDG Eastern Asia at -153.7 bln US$ (see graph 4). Merchandise exports in the EU were diversified amongst partners; imports were also diversified. The top 25 partners accounted for 80 percent or more of exports and 23 partners accounted for 80 percent or more of imports (see graph 5). In 2014, the value of exports of services of the EU increased moderately by 6.7 percent, reaching 955.3 bln US$, while its imports of services increased substantially by 11.2 percent and reached 774.0 bln US$ (see graph 2). There was a moderate trade in services surplus of 181.3 bln US$. See footnote*.

Graph 1: Total merchandise trade, by value

(Bln US$ by year)

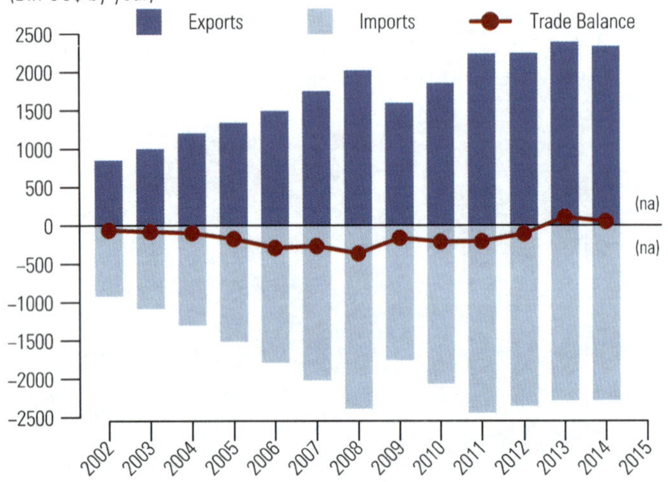

Graph 2: Total services trade, by value

(Bln US$ by year)

Exports Profile:

"Machinery and transport equipment" (SITC section 7), "Chemicals" (SITC section 5) and "Goods classified chiefly by material" (SITC section 6) were the largest commodity groups for exports in 2014, representing respectively 40.2, 15.5 and 11.2 percent of exported goods (see table 2). From 2012 to 2014, the largest export commodity was "Motor cars and other motor vehicles principally designed for the transport" (HS code 8703) (see table 1). The top three destinations for merchandise exports were the United States, China and Switzerland, accounting for respectively 16.7, 8.6 and 8.4 percent of total exports. "Other business services" (EBOPS code 268) accounted for the largest share of exports of services in 2014 at 265.6 bln US$, followed by "Transportation" (EBOPS code 205) at 184.7 bln US$ and "Travel" (EBOPS code 236) at 144.3 bln US$ (see graph 3).

Graph 3: Exports of services by EBOPS category

(% share in 2014)

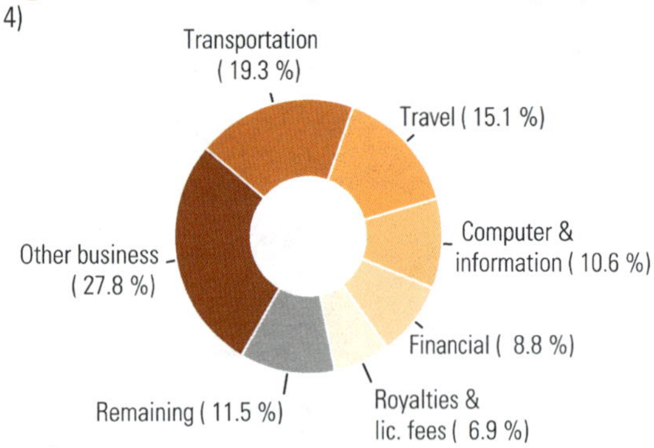

Table 1: Top 10 export commodities 2012 to 2014

HS code	4-digit heading of Harmonized System 2012	Value (billion US$) 2012	2013	2014	Unit value 2012	2013	2014	Unit	SITC code
	All Commodities	2 251.6	2 396.2	2 339.7					
8703	Motor cars and other motor vehicles principally designed for the transport	138.9	148.7	152.9	*23.8*	*24.4*	27.6	thsd US$/unit	781
9999	Commodities not specified according to kind	143.5	147.4	143.2					931
2710	Petroleum oils, other than crude	130.3	130.0	115.2	*0.9*	*0.9*	*0.8*	US$/kg	334
3004	Medicaments (excluding goods of heading 30.02, 30.05 or 30.06)	95.7	100.2	104.0	*126.5*	*127.1*	*126.4*	US$/kg	542
8802	Other aircraft (for example, helicopters, aeroplanes); spacecraft	52.0	57.9	55.6	*14.0*	*0.4*	*12.3*	mln US$/unit	792
7108	Gold (including gold plated with platinum)	23.9	90.5	46.4	*46.6*	*44.5*	*38.9*	thsd US$/kg	971
8708	Parts and accessories of the motor vehicles of headings 87.01 to 87.05	48.5	52.2	52.4	*10.8*	*11.3*	*11.8*	US$/kg	784
8411	Turbo-jets, turbo-propellers and other gas turbines	38.9	41.9	42.2					714
3002	Human blood; animal blood prepared for therapeutic uses	29.3	30.3	35.2	*711.1*	*667.2*	*682.3*	US$/kg	541
8517	Electrical apparatus for line telephony or line telegraphy	31.1	28.3	26.4					764

*Data beginning 2002 reporting EU-28. Trade in services reporting EU-15 for 2000-2002; EU-25 for 2003; EU-27 for 2004-2009; and EU-28 for 2010-2014.

Services Imports and Exports: EBOPS 2002 categories

Table 2: Merchandise exports by SITC

(Value in million US$, growth and shares in percentage)

SITC	2014	Avg. Growth rates 2010-2014	Avg. Growth rates 2013-2014	2014 share
Total	2 339 708.9	5.9	-2.4	100.0
0+1	143 006.6	9.2	3.0	6.1
2+4	56 520.4	3.6	-4.8	2.4
3	134 819.0	7.7	-11.0	5.8
5	363 482.6	4.8	1.8	15.5
6	262 404.0	4.0	-0.9	11.2
7	940 589.6	5.6	-0.4	40.2
8	248 158.8	8.0	3.2	10.6
9	190 728.0	7.2	-20.5	8.2

Table 3: Merchandise imports by SITC

(Value in million US$, growth and shares in percentage)

SITC	2014	Avg. Growth rates 2010-2014	Avg. Growth rates 2013-2014	2014 share
Total	2 281 341.9	2.5	-0.1	100.0
0+1	130 573.7	5.1	5.5	5.7
2+4	96 895.4	0.9	-3.9	4.2
3	558 051.4	3.9	-10.6	24.5
5	215 914.5	4.8	4.2	9.5
6	229 934.7	2.8	4.9	10.1
7	603 312.2	0.6	4.0	26.4
8	312 454.6	3.5	8.6	13.7
9	134 205.4	-1.0	-4.3	5.9

SITC Legend

SITC Code	Description
Total	All commodities
0+1	Food, animals + beverages, tobacco
2+4	Crude materials + anim. & veg. oils
3	Mineral fuels, lubricants
5	Chemicals
6	Goods classified chiefly by material
7	Machinery and transport equipment
8	Miscellaneous manufactured articles
9	Not classified elsewhere in the SITC

Graph 4: Merchandise trade balance

(Bln US$ by MDG Regions in 2014)

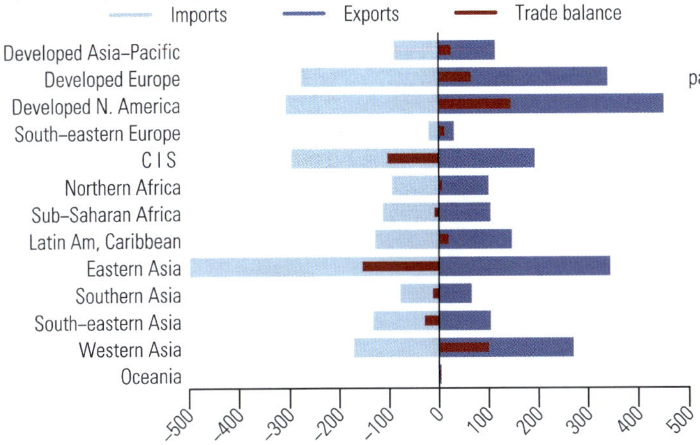

Graph 5: Partner concentration of merchandise trade

(Cumulative share by ranked partners in 2014)

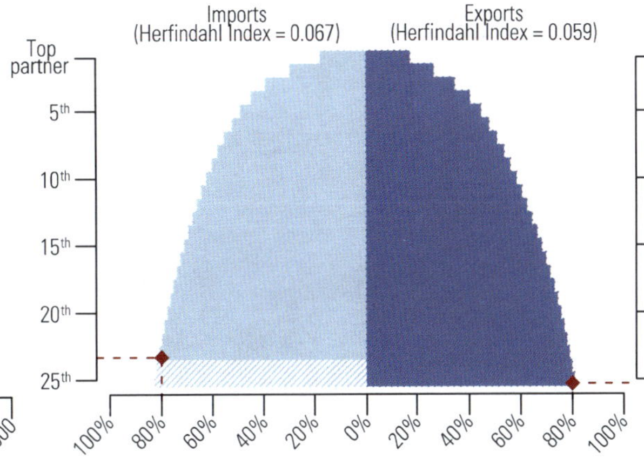

Graph 6: Imports of services by EBOPS category

(% share in 2014)

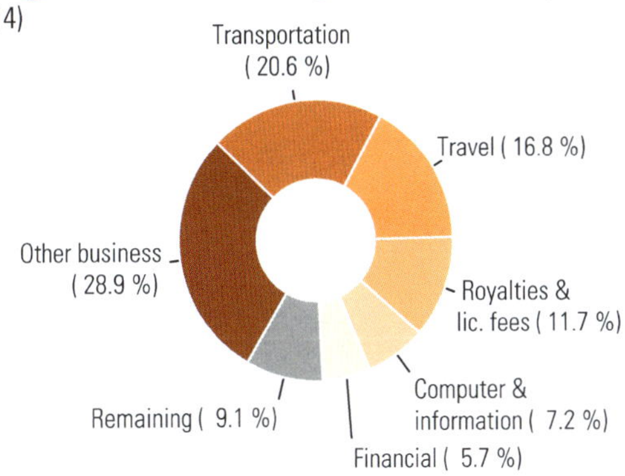

Imports Profile:

"Machinery and transport equipment" (SITC section 7), "Mineral fuels, lubricants" (SITC section 3) and "Miscellaneous manufactured articles" (SITC section 8) were the largest commodity groups for imports in 2014, representing respectively 26.4, 24.5 and 13.7 percent of imported goods (see table 3). From 2012 to 2014, the largest import commodity was "Petroleum oils and oils obtained from bituminous minerals, crude" (HS code 2709) (see table 4). The top three partners for merchandise imports were China, the United States and the Russian Federation, accounting for respectively 16.6, 11.5 and 11.2 percent of total imports. "Other business services" (EBOPS code 268) accounted for the largest share of imports of services in 2014 at 224.0 bln US$, followed by "Transportation" (EBOPS code 205) at 159.4 bln US$ and "Travel" (EBOPS code 236) at 130.1 bln US$ (see graph 6).

Table 4: Top 10 import commodities 2012 to 2014

HS code	4-digit heading of Harmonized System 2012	Value (billion US$) 2012	2013	2014	Unit value 2012	2013	2014	Unit	SITC code
	All Commodities	2 354.2	2 283.8	2 281.3					
2709	Petroleum oils and oils obtained from bituminous minerals, crude	436.9	401.7	359.5	*0.8*	*0.8*	*0.7*	US$/kg	333
9999	Commodities not specified according to kind	118.4	115.5	105.1					931
2710	Petroleum oils, other than crude	105.1	112.8	101.9	*0.9*	*0.9*	*0.8*	US$/kg	334
2711	Petroleum gases and other gaseous hydrocarbons	85.1	82.3	70.2	*0.6*	*0.6*	*0.5*	US$/kg	343
8517	Electrical apparatus for line telephony or line telegraphy	61.1	65.6	65.6					764
8471	Automatic data processing machines and units thereof	57.1	58.2	59.1	*133.0*	*132.6*	*108.6*	US$/unit	752
3004	Medicaments (excluding goods of heading 30.02, 30.05 or 30.06)	39.3	38.8	41.9	*247.6*	*234.0*	*243.4*	US$/kg	542
7108	Gold (including gold plated with platinum)	62.8	23.9	28.0	*51.1*	*41.1*	39.9	thsd US$/kg	971
8411	Turbo-jets, turbo-propellers and other gas turbines	32.8	34.1	34.8					714
8703	Motor cars and other motor vehicles principally designed for the transport	31.5	31.6	33.1	*14.7*	*14.5*	*14.6*	thsd US$/unit	781

Country Trade Profiles
Profils de pays de commerce

General notes:

For further information on Sources, Method of Estimation, Currency Conversion, Period, Country Nomenclature and Country Grouping of this table, as well as for a brief table description, please see the Introduction.

Remarque générale:

Pour plus d'information en ce qui concerne les sources, la méthode d'estimation, taux d'exchange, période, nomenclature des pays et groupement de pays, ainsi que pour une brève description de ce tableau, veuillez voir l'introduction.